THE BIOGRAPHICAL HISTORY OF BASEBALL

Donald Dewey
and
Nicholas Acocella

TRIUMPH
BOOKS
CHICAGO

Library of Congress Cataloging-in-Publication Data

Dewey, Donald, 1940–
  The biographical history of baseball / Donald Dewey, Nicholas Acocella.
    p. cm.
  ISBN 1-57243-470-8 (hard)
    1. Baseball players—United States—Biography—Dictionaries. 2. Baseball—United States—History. I. Acocella, Nick. II. Title.

GV865.A1 D45 2002
796.357'092'2—dc21
[B]

2002020035

This book is available in quantity at special discounts for your group or organization. For further information, contact:
Triumph Books
601 South LaSalle Street
Suite 500
Chicago, Illinois, 60605
(312) 939-3330
Fax (312) 663-3557

Printed in the United States of America
ISBN 1-57243-470-8
Front cover photo courtesy of Bettman Archive. Back cover photos courtesy of the National Baseball Hall of Fame and Museum, Cooperstown, N.Y.
Interior design by Carol Hansen
Photo insert design by Patricia Frey

FOR
GEORGE SHEA
AND
CAROLINE ACOCELLA

Contents

Foreword

by Jerome Holtzman

Official Historian for Major League Baseball

If you have been looking for a centerpiece for your baseball library, the search is over. This newly revised and extended edition of *The Biographical History of Baseball* is the answer. It is not the usual lengthy textbook treatment of how and where the game began, loaded with stats and standings, but a tapestry of biographical studies of the men and the few women who made significant contributions.

Better yet, instead of the usual chronological order beginning with the 1869 Cincinnati Reds, the biographies are an easier read and assembled in alphabetical order—from Hank Aaron to George Zoeter-man, who has been lost in the fog of time. The White Sox signed Zoeterman in 1947 in violation of the "spirit" of the high school rule and were suspended from the American League for one week, until they paid the $500 fine.

Virtually all of the Hall of Fame players, managers, and executives are accounted for. One would expect brief and cursory biographies, run-of-the-mill stuff, but the authors had the wisdom to lengthen them according to their relative importance. Also, and this is crucial, their subjects are exposed as never before. You won't find any pap here.

Introduction

On June 12, 1939, a dual ceremony was held in Cooperstown, New York. The more conspicuous one celebrated the opening of the National Baseball Hall of Fame and Museum. The second—implicit in the first—formalized major league baseball's move to enshrine itself as the national pastime and to charge an admission price for its past as well as its present.

In the six decades since that afternoon in Cooperstown, the history of baseball has lagged behind only the sport itself as a growth industry. Books, magazines, television documentaries, computer bulletin boards, newsletters, and academic treatises have charted the careers of all the Cincinnati milkmen who happened to drop by a ballpark and pitch a no-hitter in an 1882 exhibition game, while statistical research societies have furnished all the numbers necessary for demonstrating how many of those wunderkinder were really better than Cy Young (give or take 500 victories). The more expansive school of historians has produced mountains of evidence that major league baseball, while not always aware of it, had a revolutionary impact on racism, management-labor strife, the Nazi threat, and other evils plaguing American society as a whole. A third concentration of writings in recent years has identified baseball with the securities of the nuclear family and the sublimations of the detonated psyche—a force for the continuity of sons relating to fathers and potential rooftop snipers redirecting their furies at umpires. othat kind might be congratulatory.

It is not the intention of *The Biographical History of Baseball* to slap together another congratulatory tour of baseball's names and numbers. Although one of this book's assumptions is that the game has indeed served as a pastime for countless millions over 15 decades or more, and as such merits a cogent record of its development, *The Biographical History* does not accept that 19th-century trivia has become 20th-century significance merely for being recalled or that the journeymen players of the 1920s have turned into venerable all-stars simply for no longer being forgotten. We are not interested in electing people to the Hall of Fame or even in reducing the number of those already on the premises. What we *are* interested in is singling out those who, on and off the diamond, have been most responsible for developing baseball—primarily in athletic and business ways, but also in its larger cultural impact as a mass entertainment and in its smaller personal imprint as an arena for the imaginative, traumatic, and even tragic. The individuals listed in *The Biographical History* have, in the view of the authors, done the most for consolidating the legitimacy, respect, and criticism that the Hall of Fame and other repositories of baseball's chronicles and legacies have attracted over the years.

The Biographical History is not a Who's Who. There has been no attempt to include every distinguished player and front-office executive in the annals of the game. The criterion for choosing entries has been one, and only one: for better or worse, has the subject influenced the game, the popularity of the game, or the image of the game? Has baseball become richer or poorer as a sport, a business, or an entertainment because of his or her involvement in it? Did he or she leave a game that was different from the one entered?

The subjects covered by *The Biographical History* have been drawn mostly from the development of the National and American leagues. But since the history of the sport has hardly been exhausted by those two circuits, other entries owe their inclusion to their influence on a proto–major league (the National Association), the three 19th-century leagues (the American Association, the Union Association, and the Players League) recognized as having been major, the one defunct 20th-century circuit (the Federal League) accorded the same status, the more begrudgingly acknowledged Negro leagues, the minor leagues, and some foreign circuits. The individuals cited within these areas fall into the following—and sometimes overlapping—groups.

Hall of Famers. Admittedly, election to Cooperstown has allowed several figures to slip under the rope of restrictions against capable but otherwise uninspiring contributors to the sport. This has been particularly obvious with regard to players (e.g., Ted Lyons and Herb Pennock) who owe their election to the one-time preponderance of big city sportswriters among voters and to officials who owe their enshrinement to the sport's penchant for consecrating every aspect of the founding of the National League (e.g., Morgan Bulkeley) or its tendency to commemorate fealty over an extended period (e.g., Ford Frick). At the very least, however, the inclusion of all those who have received plaques at the Hall of Fame reflects Major League Baseball's own estimation of its standards, priorities, and achievements. Beyond that, naturally, are the numerous players, officials, and others who have been indisputably seminal in their athletic or organizational accomplishments.

The Protagonists. Those who have been at the center of the game's defining dramatic moments.

The Innovators. In everything from playing regulations and playing gear to administrative and broadcasting structures, changes in the sport have been the result of an individual's insight, resolve, or, in some instances, misfortune.

The Record Holders. More markedly than in other professional sports, baseball has always prized primacies, superiorities, and durabilities as part of its competitiveness. In some cases (e.g., Roger Maris and Hank Aaron), changes in the record holder have occasioned more than a bigger number as a standard.

The Character Actors. Baseball has always been replete with thieves, hustlers, clowns, and buffoons whose antics have provided the color for a franchise, a season, or even an era.

The Suits and the Scouts. Not all front-office functionaries have been defined by their ability to blend into the background.

The Fans and the Media. Baseball has never been a tree falling in an empty forest. The central contention of *The Biographical History* is that we would be watching an entirely different game today—if we were watching it at all—were it not for the impact of the people discussed in this book. Credit them or blame them. History, too, has always been a partisan sport.

A

HANK AARON (Hall of Fame, 1982)

Aaron ultimately prevailed over the racist lunatics who threatened him during his pursuit of Babe Ruth's career home run record, but he has had a much more difficult time erasing the impression that his feat was a sequel to Ruth's achievement rather than an improvement upon it. Baseball's vested interest in promoting its all-time icon has also served to reduce Aaron to a one-dimensional slugger, obscuring not only his all-around skills as a player but also his significant role as the farm director of the Braves for many years. This is why Willie Mays and other contemporaries have continued to insist into the new century that the righthand-hitting outfielder with a drawerful of lifetime offensive records and a plaque in Cooperstown has remained the game's most underrated figure.

Aaron started out with the Milwaukee version of the Braves in 1954 after Bobby Thomson's broken ankle opened up a starting spot in the outfield. Over the next 23 years he batted .305, forging major league career records not only with his 755 homers, but also with his 2,297 RBIs, 6,856 total bases, 1,477 extra-base hits, and 15 years of scoring 100 runs, 15 seasons with 30 or more home runs, and 20 campaigns with at least 20. He averaged higher than .300 14 times, won hitting titles in 1956 and 1959, led National League batters in home runs and RBIs four times each, drove in 100 runs 11 times, had the most doubles four times, reached 200 hits three times, and had at least 40 home runs in eight years. His 3,771 lifetime hits trails only Pete Rose and Ty Cobb. For all that, Aaron won merely one MVP award—in 1957 for leading the Braves to a pennant by pacing the NL

in home runs (44), RBIs (132), and runs (118), batting .322, and slugging a round .600. It was also the first of three straight years that he won a Gold Glove as the league's premier defensive right fielder.

Although he eventually lost his franchise in fielding awards to Roberto Clemente, the Gold Gloves suggested Aaron's defensive qualities. Before tearing up a leg, he was also a superior baserunner with a full complement of Negro league abilities at forcing infielders to hurry throws and outfielders to make them to the wrong base. Aaron had only three opportunities to show off his talents under postseason pressures, but he made the most of them. In the 1957 World Series against the Yankees, he clouted three home runs and batted .393. In another meeting with the Yankees the following year, he batted .333. And against the Mets in the first NLCS in 1969, he homered in each of the three games. Especially during the feel-good years in Milwaukee, Aaron seldom called attention to anything but his playing. With the Braves move to Atlanta in 1966, however, the Alabama native began responding to inevitable questions about playing in the South by denouncing baseball's continuing aversion to hiring blacks as managers or general managers. After years of pooh-poohing reassurances that the situation was much better than it had been, he himself demonstrated it wasn't by attracting death threats for encroaching upon the "white man's record" in 1973. As bad as the poisonous scrawls and anonymous telephone calls were the ostensibly intelligent, objective discussions held on radio and television about whether the Ruth record *should* be broken. The climate was thick enough with hatred for the Atlanta Police Department to assign Aaron a bodyguard. To complicate matters further, he ended the 1973 season with only 713 homers—one shy of Ruth—so police surveillance had to be continued over the winter. With the Braves scheduled to open the 1974 season in Cincinnati, Aaron came under additional pressures when Atlanta owner William Bartholomay made it clear he wanted the outfielder benched for the contests at Riverfront Stadium so the Ruth record could be broken at home for attendance purposes. This brought a storm of criticism from traditionalists and prompted Commissioner Bowie Kuhn to intervene with an order to have Aaron in the lineup for the opener against the Reds. The slugger responded by tying the record with his 714th home run in his first swing in the first inning, but that was it. Bartholomay got his wish when 53,775 poured into Fulton County Stadium on the cold and miserable night of April 8, 1974 and saw Al Downing of the Dodgers surrender number 715.

Only a few months after surpassing Ruth, Aaron got another lesson in baseball's race relations when Braves general manager Eddie Robinson ridiculed his candidacy as a successor to the fired Eddie Mathews as manager; Robinson also broke with franchise tradition by giving Clyde King a multiyear contract, just in case Aaron got the idea that he would be a fallback choice in the immediate future. The King appointment effectively ended the outfielder's ties to the Braves as a player; he agreed to return to Milwaukee, to the American League Brewers, after the season. Clearly on his last legs, he generated mild interest as a gate attraction in 1975 but made it clear prior to the start of the 1976 campaign that it was going to be his last. As it developed, his career as an active player ended sourly. On the final day of the season he singled in his last plate appearance and was then removed by manager Alex Grammas for pinch-runner Jim Gantner. Gantner eventually scored with a run that would have enabled Aaron to break a tie with Ruth for second place in that category behind Cobb. Chagrined by Aaron's anger at having been lifted for Gantner, Grammas explained he had only wanted to give him one last chance to run off the field to a standing ovation.

After his retirement Aaron served for a number of years as farm director of the Braves. Those who didn't write him off as merely an emblematic presence altogether were hard put to credit him with the development of several prospects who directly or indirectly led to the revival of the franchise in the 1990s. On several occasions he also gave interviews putting his own name forward as a candidate for baseball commissioner; he never received a serious response.

By his own admission Aaron has never been able to separate his satisfaction at retiring as baseball's greatest home run-hitter from the hatred he and his family endured over the months leading up to the drive off Downing. Not only has he kept the ball that broke the record, but also some 500 letters warning him off belting number 714.

CAL ABRAMS

Abrams became the shame of Brooklyn when he was thrown out at the plate in the ninth inning of the final game of the 1950 season with what would have been a run forcing a special playoff between the Dodgers and the Phillies for the pennant. Over the years, the bang-bang play on Richie Ashburn's throw to home after Duke Snider's single has been alternately attributed to Abrams's small lead off second and third base coach Milt Stock's rashness in sending him to home plate. In fact, the outfielder had little choice trying to score since Pee Wee Reese, the runner behind him, was dashing up his back to get to third base.

JOHN ADAM

Adam was honored by the Professional Baseball Athletic Trainers Society after the 2001 season for making his training staff on the Brewers the best in the major leagues. He received the award a few weeks after being fired by Milwaukee for not dealing adequately with the team's injuries.

BABE ADAMS

Adams had as flashy a rookie year for the Pirates in 1909 as he had a messy end with the same club 17 years later. After a debut season that saw him win 12 games and post an ERA of 1.11, the righthander stunned Detroit in the World Series by throwing three complete-game victories for a Pittsburgh championship. Until 1926 he remained a mainstay of the team's staff, winning 20 games twice. In that final year, however, he became innocently involved in a bitter me-or-him showdown between coach Fred Clarke and outfielder Max Carey. The nub of the controversy was a Carey-led mutiny against Clarke's presence on the bench after the coach had compared his effectiveness to that of the team batboy. Although a majority of the team refused to back Carey and another outfielder, Carson Bigbee, in the revolt, and Adams himself voted to keep Clarke on the premises, the coach wouldn't leave well enough alone, insisting that owner Barney Dreyfuss get rid of all those opposed to him. Mainly because Adams was on record for saying "managers should manage and nobody else should interfere," the owner agreed with Clarke that the pitcher had also been part of the uprising. The upshot was that two of the A(dams) B(igbee) C(arey) Mutineers, as the Pittsburgh press branded them, were released, while Carey was sold to the Dodgers. The three players protested to National League president John Heydler, but Heydler, while absolving the trio of insubordination, also upheld an owner's right to get rid of any player he wanted to. Adams, 44 and near the end of his pitching effectiveness, didn't attempt to catch on with another team.

DANIEL ADAMS

Among the candidates for the honorific title of Father of Baseball is Adams, a medical doctor and president of the Knickerbocker club from 1847 until 1862. As the head of the country's oldest baseball team, he was given the gavel at an 1857 convention of clubs, and in that role established nine innings (rather than 21 runs) as the duration of a game. After that first meeting seeded the National Association of Base Ball Players in 1858, Adams chaired the rules committee, and in his three years in the position set the distance between the bases at 90 feet and from the pitcher's box to home at 45 feet.

Adams had begun playing an early version of baseball in 1839 for exercise and amusement. He had a hand in making the Knickerbockers balls and bats, and claimed to have been the first to move into the shortstop position—less to improve infield defense than to make it easier to relay the relatively light balls of the day from the outfield.

FRANKLIN P. ADAMS

Writing for New York's *Evening Mail,* Adams published one of baseball's most famous verses in 1910 under the title of "Baseball's Sad Lexicon." The work's popularity was key to the election of Cubs infielders Joe Tinker, Johnny Evers, and Frank Chance to the Hall of Fame; in fact, not one of the trio ever led the National League in double plays for his position. Adams's verse goes:

"There are the saddest of possible words—
    Tinker to Evers to Chance.
Trio of bear Cubs and fleeter than birds
    Tinker to Evers to Chance.
Thoughtlessly pricking our gonfalon bubble,
Making a Giant hit into a double,
Words that are weighty with nothing but trouble—
    Tinker to Evers to Chance."

JOE ADCOCK

Although not on a level with Hall of Fame teammates Hank Aaron and Eddie Mathews, Adcock accomplished a number of prodigious slugging feats while playing for the Braves in the 1950s. His 336 career blasts included four in one game against the Dodgers, the first ball ever hit completely over the left field grandstand of Ebbets Field, and the first ball ever hit to the left-center field bleachers of the Polo Grounds (an officially estimated distance of 465 feet). In the July 31, 1954 game in which he hit Brooklyn pitchers for four home runs, he also clouted a double, setting a total bases record.

Adcock, a righthanded first baseman, also hit the "non-homer" that ended Harvey Haddix's 12-inning perfect game on May 26, 1959; when he ran past Aaron on the bases in what he later admitted was a "daze," the hit was scored a double. As a pinch-hitter in his 17-year career with the Reds, Braves, Indians, and Angels, he established the best career ratio for home runs, hitting a four-bagger every 12.75 times he came off the bench.

BOB ADDY

An outfielder for Chicago in 1876, Addy is credited with being the first player to slide into a base. He apparently pioneered the technique while playing for the Forest City Club of Rockford, Illinois in the 1860s. A bit of an eccentric, Addy was forever contriving schemes he considered more worthy of his talents than conventional baseball; among them was an effort to popularize ice baseball in a Chicago skating rink he owned.

TOMMIE AGEE

There have been many great catches made by outfielders in World Series games, but Agee has been the only one to make two in the same contest. Diving grabs of drives up the alley by Baltimore's Elrod Hendricks and Paul Blair in the third game of the 1969 World Series saved the Miracle Mets in two crucial situations, helping pave the way to New York's eventual championship. Although usually slotted in the leadoff spot for his speed, Agee also had five straight years of more than 100 strikeouts, including a high of 156 in 1970. Only Bobby Bonds had a worse strikeout ratio among leadoff men.

DANNY AINGE

Long before Deion Sanders was holding up the Braves for contract concessions that would allow him to play professional football, Ainge was lavished with the same rights by the Blue Jays so he could pursue basketball. In 1979 the high school star made it clear he preferred the court to the diamond, but Toronto was so insistent that it drew up a pact practically fitting baseball around the National Basketball Association schedule. After three partial seasons and a .220 batting average, Ainge dumped the major leagues for his first love.

EDDIE AINSMITH

Ainsmith's 15-year (1910–24) career as a backup catcher for the Senators and several other teams assumed secondary importance in 1918, when he appealed against being drafted into the military during World War I on the grounds that he was engaged in a patriotic endeavor since baseball was the national pastime. The appeal, engendered by Washington's Clark Griffith, prompted a ruling from Secretary of War Newton D. Baker that baseball was an inessential amusement, with all its players and personnel subject to the draft. Prior to the Ainsmith case players had been able to appeal their call-ups on a case-by-case basis. Earlier the same year Yankees pitcher Happy Finneran had successfully argued that his 10 years of professional baseball had left him unequipped for seeking another job after getting out of the service and that he had to play to maintain his standing. At the heart of both the Ainsmith and Finneran cases was baseball's refusal to ask for a special exemption as an essential public entertainment—as various branches of show business had. The ownership stance of asking the War Department to rule on a player-by-player basis aided Finneran but ultimately worked against Ainsmith and those called up after him.

DALE ALEXANDER

By being traded from the Tigers to the Red Sox during the 1932 season, Alexander became the first major leaguer to win a batting crown while splitting time between two teams. His overall average of .367 could not have come as a surprise to Detroit, since he had batted .343, .326, and .325 in his earlier seasons with the club and had also driven in more than 130 runs in two of the three years. Pressed to explain the exchange for outfielder Roy Johnson, manager Bucky Harris said that he couldn't stand watching Alexander's ineptitude around first base. As it developed, Boston had little to crow about. In 1933 team physician Doc Woods decided to treat an Alexander leg injury with an innovative heat lamp treatment during a game but then got so caught up in a home team rally that he forgot about his patient. By the time he got back inside the clubhouse, Alexander had third-degree leg burns that later degenerated into gangrene. That was the end of his career.

GROVER CLEVELAND ALEXANDER (Hall of Fame, 1938)

There weren't many things that Alexander didn't accomplish during his 20-year (1911–30) career—and not many that he wasn't forced to do afterward because of his physical ailments and his alcoholism. If the righthander had one statistical shortcoming, it was his failure to snatch the 374th victory that would have broken his tie with Christy Mathewson as the National League's all-time winner.

Alexander's biggest numbers include: six years of leading the NL in wins, five in ERA, six in complete games, six in strikeouts, seven years in shutouts (including a record-setting 16 in 1916), nine years of at least 20 wins (including three seasons in a row of more than 30, in which he also set the pace in ERA and strikeouts to take the pitching Triple Crown). Between 1915 and 1917 he rolled up 94 victories, while his ERAs between 1915 and 1920 were 1.22, 1.55, 1.83, 1.73, 1.72, and 1.91. Most astonishing, he achieved these numbers while pitching all but three of his seasons in hitter-friendly Baker Bowl and Wrigley Field.

As smooth as his accomplishments often appeared between the lines, Alexander had a full quota of off-the-field demons. Even before joining the Phillies, he had to battle attacks of double vision to win 29 games for a minor league Syracuse team. Toward the end of the 1917 season he made the mistake of informing Philadelphia's money-grubbing owner William Baker that he was about to be drafted and was promptly sold to the Cubs. An accident while in military uniform rendered him deaf in one ear and prone to epileptic seizures—both conditions strengthening his dependence on the bottle. For a few years Alexander kept all his disabilities at bay, winning two ERA crowns and posting two 20-win seasons for the Cubs, but by 1926 he was reeling off the field more frequently than he was reeling off victories on it. Waived to the Cardinals, he had enough left not only to provide key victories down the stretch for a St. Louis pennant, but also to hurl two complete-game wins in the World Series against the Yankees and then make a dramatic relief appearance in the seventh inning of the final game to strike out Tony Lazzeri with the bases loaded.

Alexander staggered through yet another year to compile 21 wins, but from that point on his waning effectiveness and the rising impatience of his employers before his drunkenness were synonymous. Even Baker's gate-inspired notion of bringing him back to Philadelphia in 1930 went for naught when he was belted around in three starts and six relief appearances. The club finally suspended him for showing up once too often under the influence. This last failure became even more poignant when research in the 1950s credited Mathewson with a 373rd win, creating the deadlock neither pitcher knew existed while they were active.

Alexander's post-major league life wasn't much better. At one point he grew a beard to join the House of David team; for another period he worked in a Times Square flea circus. None of these details emerged in *The Winning Season,* a 1952 Hollywood movie with Ronald Reagan portraying the hurler.

DICK ALLEN

Allen was among the more conspicuous players who inhaled the social protest atmosphere of the 1960s–1970s but who exhaled it in ways calculated to have him perceived merely as a reckless egotist. By both accident and design, he exposed a small army of hypocrites and toadies in the baseball establishment.

The righthand-hitting slugger began his 15-year (1963–77) career with Philadelphia, winning Rookie of the Year honors in 1964 for batting .318 with 201 hits, 29 homers, 91 RBIs, 38 doubles, and a league-leading 13 triples and 125 runs. He contributed all that offense while playing third base for the first time in organized ball—an effort that didn't spare him catcalls from Philadelphia fans for also leading the NL with 41 errors. In 1965 his relations with the hometown fans got even worse when his offensive production dipped somewhat, he paced the National League for the second year in a row in strikeouts, and he began issuing his ever-more-frequent pronouncements on the state of baseball. The atmosphere got particularly heated after an early July game when he and backup outfielder Frank Thomas traded blows during batting practice over alleged racial remarks, Thomas came off the bench in the ensuing game to hit a key pinch-hit home run, and then returned to the clubhouse to be told he was being released because of his conflict with the franchise's young star. Philadelphia fans became so abusive—even throwing garbage at him—that Allen wore his batting helmet in the field.

Over the next few years, he continued as the team's major run producer and major headline while the Phillies began sinking to the lower depths of the standings. Most of his observations were along the lines of his "Baseball is a form of slavery. Once you step out of bounds, that's it, they'll do everything possible to destroy your soul." At the same time he developed the habit of skipping exhibition games and missing team planes with feeble excuses. In June 1969 there was a showdown of sorts when manager Bob Skinner fined the slugger for not showing up for a game against the Mets. When owner Bob Carpenter first hesitated to collect the money, then rescinded the fine on the grounds that there had only been some kind of "misunderstanding," Skinner quit and the fans went even wilder. The reaction became so hostile that Allen requested a trade. When he was accommodated after the season, it was in the deal that helped change the economic structure of the game—the swap with the Cardinals that Curt Flood refused to accept.

Allen played only one season in St. Louis, but that was long enough to show his power (34 home runs) was not compromised even by the distant fences of Busch Stadium. With the Dodgers the following year, he and manager Walter Alston provided season-long proof of how oil did not mix with water. But, in retrospect, even their tense relations were only a warmup for his next three years in a White Sox uniform.

On the field Allen swung his way to American League MVP honors in 1972 by batting .308 while piling up league-leading numbers in homers (37) and RBIs (113). He took the trophy after playing tag with the White Sox right up to spring training, releasing announcements periodically that he was getting tired of being traded and was considering retirement. What ultimately talked him into reporting for his MVP season was the biggest contract ever awarded to a sports figure in Chicago. When his field performance attracted more than one million fans through the turnstiles of Comiskey Park for the first time in seven years, he received the biggest pact in the major leagues, while general manager Stu Holcomb and manager Chuck Tanner told anyone who would listen that the slugger was the franchise player. That didn't sit too well with righthander Stan Bahnsen, who had been offered only a modest raise after winning 21 games, and several other White Sox players who saw their salaries slashed. To make matters worse, Tanner and Holcomb went out of their way during 1973 spring training to keep a roster spot open for Allen's brother Hank, an outfielder of no particular talent. Hank Allen lasted only a handful of at bats into the season, but any relief in the clubhouse over that development dissipated in June when the franchise player, with 16 home runs already in the record books, fractured his fibula in a collision at first base and was sidelined for the rest of the year.

Allen's third and final year with Chicago was the most eventful of all. Although he came back in perfect health and began bashing the ball from Opening Day, he evinced gradually decreasing interest in the club's .500 fortunes as the season wore on. Whenever his hitting put the White Sox ahead in a game, however marginally, he persuaded the cooperative Tanner to yank him for the last couple of innings to he could avoid having to talk to sportswriters after the contest. Then, in early September, he called a club meeting and announced his retirement, effective immediately. Tanner's reply was to say only that Allen was "the greatest player I ever saw." He kept to that reaction even after the season, when the slugger said he had had another change of heart and would return the following year. The Chicago front office thought otherwise, trading him to the Braves for $5,000 and second-string catcher Jim Essian. Obscured during all the late-season melodramatics was that even after walking away from the White Sox with three weeks

to go, he ended up as the AL home-run king for the second time.

Informed that he had been dealt to Atlanta, Allen announced that he would never play for a team in the South, forcing the Braves to trade him back to his original home in Philadelphia. With the Phillies the second time he contributed enough clutch performances from part-time first-base duty to help the team to an Eastern Division win in 1976. But he boycotted the clubhouse celebrations for the clinching in protest against manager Danny Ozark's decision to leave veteran second baseman Tony Taylor off the postseason roster. Although Mike Schmidt and other players also remonstrated against Taylor's exclusion, it was Allen who paid for it by being released shortly after making his only appearance in postseason play. He ended his career as a platoon first baseman with Oakland in 1977.

Allen, who lost much of his baseball earnings on breeding and betting on horses, provided one of the more memorable quotes on artificial turf when he once declared: "If horses can't eat it, I don't want to play on it." He also earned a baseball footnote on April 12, 1965 by hitting the first indoor home run in a regular-season game, his two-run blast defeating Houston in the newly opened Astrodome.

JOHNNY ALLEN

Allen was a model "rabbit ears" whose transparent sensitivity to heckling underminded his mound effectiveness. It didn't help that he fueled his temper with liberal doses of alcohol. After one loss with the Indians in the 1930s, the righthander trashed a hotel lobby before dousing the desk clerk with the contents of a fire extinguisher; he responded to another defeat by thrashing his third baseman for having made a decisive error. Incidents of the kind were a mere prelude, however, to a game against Boston on June 7, 1938, when Allen stalked from the hill to the dugout rather than obey plate umpire Bill Mc-Gowan's order that he cut off the sleeve of his tattered uniform. While the fans in Fenway Park grew ugly, he sat stubbornly on the bench ignoring pleas from pilot Ossie Vitt and his teammates to snip off the offending sleeve before the game was forfeited to Boston. Finally, Vitt fined him $250 for leaving the mound without permission and told him he was out of the game. Allen promptly told Vitt to go to hell and announced his retirement. A couple of days later Cleveland owner Alva Bradley made the gesture of buying the controversial uniform from Allen for the $250 levied by Vitt and had it put on display in the department store he owned in Ohio. Although the owner's move calmed Allen temporarily, it also underlined the chaotic relations between Vitt and his employers; the latter situation would degenerate a few years later into the revolt of the so-called Crybaby Indians.

LEE ALLEN

As the historian of the Baseball Hall of Fame in the 1960s, Allen indefatigably pursued old ballplayers, tracking down the whereabouts of the living and uncovering the ultimate fates of the deceased in small towns across the country. A one-time Cincinnati sportswriter and then a public relations director for the Reds, he also wrote some highly regarded baseball histories.

MEL ALLEN

The Voice of the Yankees, Allen parlayed a relaxed Alabama drawl and an unabashed rooting interest into a popularity rivaling that of the New York players whose on-field activities he described on radio and television between 1938 and 1964. While his orotund style irritated almost as many people as his "homer" approach, to Yankees fans he was an indispensable link connecting several successive Bronx dynasties. As a result, his signature lines—introducing broadcasts with "Hi there, everybody"; following the flight of "Ballantine Blasts" with "Going . . . going . . . gone"; and punctuating everything but the most mundane field incidents with "How about that!"—became part of the New York vernacular. In addition, the sobriquets he popularized for almost every Yankees regular—from Old Reliable for Tommy Henrich, to the clunky Commerce Comet for Mickey Mantle—were efforts to impart some of his personal flair to a team that seemed to many a pennant machine. (Conversely, Red Barber was for much of the same period lending his sober approach to the often less than sober rival Dodgers.)

Allen's one-man-show approach annoyed several partners, including Jim Woods and Curt Gowdy, shortening their careers in the Yankee Stadium booth. He also showed hostility toward sharing play-by-play with what he considered unqualified former players (e.g., Joe Garagiola, Phil Rizzuto), and this won him no popularity contests in the Yankees front office. Allen's absence from the booth during the 1964 World Series and his subsequent dismissal in December have been attributed variously to sponsor Ballantine's irritation at a perceived aloofness, the Yankees front office's desire to project a new image, and the annoyance on both their parts at Allen's undisguised on-the-air consumption of the product he hyped and after-hours taste for harder stuff. Coming on the heels of the firing of Yogi Berra as Yankees manager, the dismissal was a public relations disaster, and accelerated the mid-century end of the Yankees dynasty.

In 1978 Allen and one-time partner Barber were the first recipients of the Ford C. Frick award and a place in the broadcasters' corner of the Hall of Fame.

ARTHUR ALLYN, JR.

When Allyn bought the White Sox in 1961, it marked the end of the Comiskey family's involvement in the franchise. And nobody was more surprised than the Comiskey heirs.

Head of the Artnell conglomerate of oil and clothing companies, Allyn purchased the majority interest in the franchise held by his father, Arthur Allyn, Sr.; Bill Veeck; and Hank Greenberg. But the acquisition did not deter Chuck Comiskey from selling his 46 percent interest in the team to Chicago insurance executive William Bartholomay as part of a grand scheme in which Bartholomay would also buy out Allyn to assume total control and give the organization presidency back to the family that had been running the White Sox since the founding of the American League in 1901. Unfortunately for Comiskey, Allyn rejected the Bartholomay offer; moreover, aware that their 46 percent would make for only a loud but ineffective minority, Bartholomay and his associates then sold their holdings to Allyn.

Allyn wasn't so fortunate in actually running the franchise for most of the 1960s. Although the club played .500 ball more often than not during the decade, it was a dull squad that attracted fewer and fewer spectators every year. The low point was reached on Opening Day in 1968, when a mere 7,756 fans showed up in the immediate wake of the assassination of Martin Luther King, Jr. Claiming that the black neighborhood around Comiskey Park was discouraging white fans, Allyn kept badgering the city for the construction of a new downtown stadium.

When his appeals continued to fall on deaf ears, he announced that the White Sox had agreed to play 10 home games in 1968 in Milwaukee's County Stadium—ostensibly to give the AL an incentive for including Milwaukee in its planned 1969 expansion but mainly to find ammunition if he sought to sell the team to a Wisconsin group. The games in Milwaukee accounted for a third of Chicago's home attendance in 1968, spurring Wisconsin lobbyists headed by Bud Selig into making an outright $13 million offer for the club. In the meantime, Texas millionaire Lamar Hunt made another approach with a similar offer and with the declared intention of moving the franchise to Dallas. But before Allyn could decide between the tenders, the league told him it would never approve any transfer out of the Chicago market. He finally opted to sell 50 percent of his Artnell stock to his younger brother John and retire to Florida.

JOHN ALLYN

Allyn took over the White Sox from his brother Arthur in 1970 just in time to preside over the worst team (106 losses) in organization history. Things improved only minimally after that.

On the plus side Allyn brought in Northwestern University athletic director Stu Holcomb to head baseball operations, Harry Caray as the team announcer, and Dick Allen as the most highly paid player to wear a uniform up to that time; on the minus side he brought in Holcomb, Caray, and Allen. Within a couple of years the owner was having to mediate ongoing intrigues among Holcomb, personnel director Rollie Hemond, and manager Chuck Tanner, finally getting rid of Holcomb and Hemond. As for Caray, his initial popularity and role in bringing fans back to Comiskey Park was soon counterbalanced by repeated snipes at the team and individual players, leading Allyn to accuse him of discouraging atendance. Meanwhile, Allen was alternately winning league honors and taking off when the mood hit him.

By the middle of the decade Allyn was pleading poverty before both the Internal Revenue Service and his brother Arthur, who had to go to court to claim $500,000 that he still had coming from selling the franchise. The situation grew so critical that catcher Ed Herrmann was sold to the Yankees because Chicago couldn't pay him his salary and outfielder Buddy Bradford was dealt to the Cardinals to meet the payroll. When Allyn went to the AL for help, he was greeted with an elaborate plan that would have forced him to sell the franchise to a Seattle group that included comedian Danny Kaye and that would have left Chicago open for one of Charlie Finley's periodically broached invasions, this time from Oakland. Allyn said no, deciding instead to close a 15-year circle by selling the club back to Bill Veeck, from whom his brother Arthur had originally bought the White Sox in 1961. Allyn retained a 25 percent interest in the second Veeck ownership.

ROBERTO ALOMAR

Offensively and defensively, in speed and in spittle, Alomar was the second baseman of the 1990s. A career .300 batter with enough power to be slotted third in lineups, he also topped 30 stolen bases seven times and monopolized Gold Glove awards for his position in successive stints for the Blue Jays, Orioles, and Indians. His ability to star for three different franchises epitomized the era of the high-priced free agent.

Alomar's diamond feats were overshadowed for some time by a September 27, 1996 field argument that culminated in the infielder's spitting in the face of umpire John Hirschbeck. The ugly confrontation, uncharacteristic of the normally mild-mannered Alomar, triggered a near-crisis in relations among Major League Baseball, the players union, and the umpires union over the appropriate punishment for the assault. Alomar was eventually suspended for five games at the start of the 1997 season—a slap on the wrist that incensed umpires and helped fuel subsequent frictions with the commissioner's office. Although fans around the country booed Alomar for years after the episode, they never hesitated to give him enough votes as the AL's starting second baseman for annual All-Star Games.

Originally with the Padres, Alomar was dealt to the Blue Jays with Joe Carter for Fred McGriff and Tony Fernandez in 1990. During the 2001 winter meetings the suddenly cost-conscious Indians traded him back to the National League in an eight-player swap with the Mets.

FELIPE ALOU

The oldest of the three Alou brothers, Felipe had the most power, topping the 20-homer and 30-double marks four times each. With the Braves in 1966, he led the National League in both hits and runs scored; two years later he once again led NL batters in safeties. His 17-year (1958–74) career, which began with the Giants, ended with three plate appearances in 1974 with the Brewers—enabling him to join Hank Aaron and Phil Roof as the only players to appear for both of Milwaukee's big league franchises in the second half of the 20th century. While with San Francisco on September 10, 1963, Alou and his brothers Matty and Jesus wrote a footnote to baseball history by making all three outs in an inning, against the Mets. Five days later they appeared together in the only all-sibling outfield. Alou managed the Expos from 1992 to 2001, keeping the club respectable and even better while the front office dealt away one star after another. Among those he managed in Montreal were his son Moises and nephew Mel Rojas.

Matty, the middle brother, won a National League batting crown in 1966 with a .342 average while a member of the Pirates after batting .231 the year before. The lefty-hitting outfielder attributed the difference to batting coach Harry Walker's insistence he choke up on the bat. Alou kept the lesson in mind for the rest of his career, reaching the .330 mark in three additional years and averaging .307 for 15 big league seasons. The 111-point improvement to the batting title is the biggest by a regular from one season to the next.

Jesus, the youngest of the Alous, lacked Felipe's extra-base punch and Matty's consistency but still managed to hit .280 over 15 seasons with four clubs. His most memorable game came on July 10, 1964, when, as a member of the Giants, he collected six hits off an equal number of Chicago pitchers. When the righty-hitting outfielder picked up his 1,000th hit, it not only made the Alous the only triumvirate of brothers to reach that mark but also assured them of first place in combined career hits for three or more siblings. Against the Alous' 5,094 safeties, for instance, the three DiMaggios managed only 4,853 and the five Delahantys a mere 4,217.

WALTER ALSTON (Hall of Fame, 1983)

Working off 23 one-year managerial contracts between 1954 and 1976, Alston was an integral part of the Dodgers gradual shift in identity from Brooklyn's blue-collar franchise that seemed to generate its glories and crises spontaneously to the buttoned-down-collar Los Angeles organization that seemed to have a wired-up producer behind even its most volatile events. His image as a loyal, quiet, but intestinally strong tactician worked as a tempering influence both on those who wanted to believe that the Dodgers would always be the Dodgers whether on the East Coast or West Coast and those who were only too quick to accuse the franchise of going Hollywood.

Not that Alston always appreciated his role. From the day his appointment was announced in Brooklyn, and greeted by headlines of WALTER WHO?, to his final campaign in California, when he acted baffled by innovations like free agency, he was seldom allowed to forget he wasn't the most exciting figure to grace a dugout. Team owner Walter O'Malley, for instance, made a habit of flanking him with such coaches as Leo Durocher, Charlie Dressen, and Bobby Bragan for "creative tension." With Durocher, at least, the tension became a little too creative in the mid-1960s, prompting Alston to ream his coach on the bench in front of the team for second-guessing him. A typical O'Malley solution was to fire Durocher but also to bounce Alston's righthand man Joe Becker as a warning that a one-year contract was still a one-year contract. During Alston's tenure the Dodgers won seven pennants and three World Series (including the only one won by Brooklyn, in 1955).

NICK ALTROCK

More noted as one of baseball's first professional clowns, Altrock had two 20-win seasons for the early-century White Sox. The southpaw posted 23 victories and an ERA of 1.88 in 1905, then came back the following year to help Chicago to a pennant with 20 more wins. Although his arm went the following year, he had a friendship with Clark Griffith to thank for being picked up by the Senators in 1909. Altrock set a dubious record of sorts by appearing on the Washington roster 10 times between 1912 and 1933, never once in that time getting into more than five games and usually listed only so he could make the questionable claim of being a five-decade player. His main value to the Senators, usually in partnership with Al Schacht, was in a pantomime act before games and between ends of doubleheaders. The original Sunshine Boys, Altrock and Schacht got into an argument early in their careers and went through their routine for years without talking to one another on or off the field.

SANDY AMOROS

Left fielder Amoros's startling one-handed catch of an opposite-field drive by Yogi Berra in the seventh game of the 1955 World Series squashed a late-inning rally by the Yankees and helped ensure the only world championship won by the Brooklyn Dodgers. Amoros made the grab after being put into the game for defensive purposes. Following his retirement, the Cuban outfielder became a symbol of the impoverished state many former major leaguers were reduced to because of inadequate pension and medical plans. His plight helped energize players in better financial circumstances to organize the Baseball Assistance Team.

BRADY ANDERSON

Anderson created the biggest power anomaly since the 19th century when he belted 50 home runs for the Orioles in 1996. In a 14-year career that began in 1988 he has otherwise never hit more than 24, topping even 20 only on two other occasions. Twelve of the blasts led off games—a big league record. The lefthand-hitting outfielder also stole 53 bases for Baltimore in 1992, making him the only American Leaguer to attain the half-century mark in a season for the two categories.

WILL ANDERSON

Anderson was the composer of "Tessie," a Broadway tune from the 1903 musical *The Silver Slipper* that became the unofficial anthem of Boston baseball fans in both the American and National leagues. Both Braves and Red Sox rooters chorused it during successful World Series triumphs between 1903 and 1918, then stopped. Since neither Boston franchise won another title after that, the Tessie Curse has explained a great deal of life to Massachusetts fans not in thrall to stories about the Curse of the Bambino.

SPARKY ANDERSON (Hall of Fame, 2000)

The only manager to win world championships for teams in both leagues, Anderson was never quite convincing as either the latter-day Casey Stengel or the successful Gene Mauch that media pundits alternately represented him as over the years. While he was not always at ease with the English language and was occasionally given to elaborate chess games with opposing pilots, his 25 years of steering Cincinnati and Detroit were more conspicuous for his Dodger-trained belief that Opening Day rosters should be changed as little as possible and for his view of starters as relievers who just happened to be on the mound at the beginning of games.

One of a handful of major leaguers who played regularly for one season (with the 1959 Phillies) but never appeared in a single game before or afterward, Anderson called the shots for the Big Red Machine between 1970 and 1978, winning five division titles, four pennants, and two World Series. Most of his field decisions with the heavy-hitting team involved knowing when to go to the bullpen because of so-so starters; his frequent trips to the hill earned him the sobriquet of Captain Hook. For the most part he remained aloof from his star players' recurrent salary battles, generally winning their loyalty by consulting a circle of clubhouse veterans (Joe Morgan, Johnny Bench, Tony Perez, and Pete Rose) whenever some issue threatened club cohesion. If he had one notable failure in team relations, it was his inability to prevent the disastrous trade of Perez to the Expos following the 1976 season. When he himself was cut loose from the club after the 1978 season by newly installed general manager Dick Wagner, even the mayor of Cincinnati joined the outcry by charging that the Reds front office had "gone bananas." At the time Anderson's winning percentage of .596 was second only to Joe McCarthy's.

Moving over to the Tigers during the 1979 season, Anderson found another club without deep pitching and accustomed to banging its way to victory. For his first decade at the helm, he kept the team above .500, winning a world championship in 1984 and an Eastern Division title in 1987; that gave him a record (later tied by Bobby Cox) for winning the most pennant playoff series (five). He frequently pointed to the 1987 win as his most satisfying achievement in baseball because of the aging and modest talents on the team. With such stars as Kirk Gibson and Lance Parrish leaving as free agents, however, the Tigers soon disintegrated, exhausting Anderson in the process. In 1989 he suffered a breakdown caused as much by family problems as by the strain of managing a team that would lose 103 games. Sent home for three weeks, he returned with a relatively casual attitude, rarely missing an opportunity to tell interviewers he could no longer manage "25 hours a day." With the added incentive of owning a small interest in the team, he hung on until 1995 before retiring for good.

In the name of boosting the self-confidence of prospects, Anderson was embarrassed more than once by spring training evaluations of rookies (e.g., Chris Pittaro, Rico Brogna, Torey Lovullo, and Ricky Peters) as sure bets for the Hall of Fame. He stubbed his toe again in unloading Howard Johnson on the Mets in 1984 behind the view that the third baseman couldn't hit and didn't have the fortitude to last as a major leaguer. His penchant for extravagant assertions probably reached its low point following the 1976 World Series, when he called the Reds the greatest team in the history of the National League, mocking suggestions that Yankees catcher Thurman Munson could be compared to Bench.

MIKE ANDREWS

A second baseman for Oakland in the 1973 World Series, Andrews made two 12th-inning errors that enabled the Mets to win the second game. When owner Charlie Finley attempted to have him declared physically unfit for the rest of the Series and to replace him with Manny Trillo, Athletics manager Dick Williams announced that, win or lose, he intended quitting as soon as the season was over. Even though Commissioner Bowie Kuhn turned thumbs down to Finley's ploy, the Oakland players showed their resentment of the owner by having the infielder's number sewn on their uniforms for the rest of the Series.

JOAQUIN ANDUJAR

Andujar saw vague conspiracies against him everywhere, but the one time he pointed a finger produced one of the nastiest incidents in postseason play. A journeyman for most of his 13-year (1976–88) career, the righthander turned into a 20-game winner in 1984 and 1985 after Cardinals manager Whitey Herzog started pitching him on three days rest; tiring toward the end of the latter season, he was ineffective in the League Championship Series against the Dodgers and was reduced to mopping up in the final Series game, with the Royals holding a commanding lead. Walking the first batter he faced and yielding a hit to the next, the Dominican decided to blame his—and the Cardinals—fate on home plate umpire Don Denkinger for a blown call that had given Kansas City a win the previous day. Denkinger tossed both the pitcher and Herzog but not before the former threw a tantrum on the mound.

Herzog later blasted Andujar, and was quick to deal him to the Athletics in the offseason.

PETER ANGELOS

A Baltimore attorney who specialized in defending labor unions and pursuing workers disability claims, Angelos headed the consortium that purchased the Orioles in 1993 for $173 million. His high-profile partners included novelist Tom Clancy, movie director Barry Levinson, sportscaster Jim McKay, and tennis player Pam Shriver. Described by some as a second Steinbrenner and by others as the second coming of Charlie Finley, Angelos refused to sign the September 1994 owners' declaration that formally ended the season after the players strike. According to the longtime defender of workers rights, the document's charges that the players had not bargained seriously were "counterproductive." On the other hand, he has also come under fire for listening too much in formulating Orioles policy to his young sons John and Lou, whose only previous connection with baseball was as managers of a rotisserie league team. The influence of the Angelos offspring prompted the departure of such veteran baseball ball men as Davey Johnson, Frank Robinson, Rollie Hemond, and Doug Melvin in the 1990s, while the owner himself seemed to identify experience only with the out-of-touch Syd Thrift, usually to be seen nodding to Angelos during Baltimore games. After years as a power in the American League East, the precipitously aging Orioles became a distant also-ran at the turn of the millennium.

CAP ANSON (Hall of Fame, 1939)

Anson was to 19th-century field managers what Al Spalding was to club owners of the same era: coldly efficient, militarily strict, and highly successful. The fates of the pair were intertwined for the first decade-and-a-half of the National League's existence; only when the pitcher-turned-magnate withdrew from active involvement in the affairs of the Chicago club after the 1891 season, in fact, did the first baseman-manager's fortunes begin to decline.

Anson's jump from the National Association Philadelphia Athletics to Chicago paralleled Spalding's from the Boston Red Stockings in the events leading up to the founding of the National League in 1876. A righthanded batter, he won four batting championships, was the first major leaguer to record 3,000 hits (in comparatively short seasons), and finished with a lifetime average of .333. Anson was also durable, serving as a regular for all 22 of his National League seasons (in addition to five in the NA). He is the oldest major leaguer to hit a grand slam, knocking in four runs with one clout in July 1894 at age 42, and the second-oldest—at age 45—to hit a home run at all, connecting for two on October 3, 1897, the last day of his career.

After succeeding Spalding as manager in 1879, Anson won five pennants, compiled a .636 won-lost percentage during the 1880s, and was among the first to use more than one pitcher, employ the hit-and-run, and formalize spring training routines. A ferocious disciplinarian, he barred even Spalding from the clubhouse when he thought it necessary, and enforced his rules with fists. A temperance enthusiast, he administered a no-drinking pledge to the entire team in the owner's office in 1886. He also knew a little about promotion, often dressing his players in outfits ranging from Native American garb to formal wear and parading them through the streets of National League cities in open carriages to irritate local fans and stimulate them to buy tickets. The extent of the public's identification of Anson with the franchise was measurable by its nickname changes—from the traditional White Stockings to Colts, when he launched a youth movement in 1886, then to Orphans after he left the team in 1897.

Anson's troubles with the team trace to the arrival of James Hart as president in 1892. He disliked Hart so much that he had refused to contribute toward the purchase of diamond cuff links Spalding had given the then-travel secretary for handling arrangements on an international goodwill tour after the 1888 season. It didn't help that the team had twice as many losing seasons as winning ones after Hart took over from Spalding. Fired after the 1897 season, Anson indignantly refused Hart's offer to hold a benefit game for him. Out of organized baseball after a three-week stint as Giants manager in 1898, he dabbled in the formation of abortive new leagues (the New American Association, of which he was briefly president in 1900, and the United States League in 1914); politics (he was elected city clerk of Chicago in 1905 but left office two years later under a cloud of financial scandal); and writing (his autobiography denouncing players who had sabotaged him and owners who had betrayed him).

Especially after his political career ended, Anson fell on hard times, but he still refused NL president John Tener's offer of a pension with the same scorn he had shown toward Hart's charity game.

Anson's literary endeavor confirmed the racism he had manifested in the 1880s in refusing to let his team take the field against clubs that included black players Fleet Walker and George Stovey. Among other things, his memoir referred to Clarence Duval, the mascot and clown who was part of the 1888–89 world tour, as a "chocolate-covered coon" and a "no-account nigger."

LUIS APARICIO (Hall of Fame, 1984)

Aparicio's 18-year (1956–73) major league career has generated more than one misconception. It is not true, for example, that the righthand-hitting shortstop, who had most of his glory years with the White Sox, was the ideal leadoff man; on the contrary, he batted more than .280 only once, drew more than 53 walks only once, and had an overall on-base average of only .313. On the other hand, he was no mere spear-carrier in the revival of the running game in the late 1950s and early 1960s; years before Maury Wills appeared on the scene, the Venezuelan speedster broke all existing records by leading the American League in stolen bases in his first nine big league seasons. And although he ended up with fewer career steals than Wills, he also had a better success rate (79 percent to 74 percent).

In the field, Aparicio was the Ozzie Smith of his day, establishing career marks for assists and double plays along the way to nine Gold Gloves. Some of that achievement was due to his hardiness, since he played in at least 100 games in every one of his 18 seasons. Another part of it was due to his longtime Chicago partner, second baseman Nellie Fox, the other half of Aparicio's double-play mark. As key members of the 1959 Go-Go Sox, Aparicio and Fox regularly fashioned the wins of their pennant-bound club with little more than a single and stolen base by the shortstop, a ground ball to the right side by the second baseman, a sacrifice fly, and then nine innings of vacuum-cleaning defense. Aparicio provided some of the same leadership with the world champion 1966 Orioles. Ironically, however, he also literally fell down on the job with the Red Sox in 1972, when, carrying a decisive run in late September, he fell in the third-base coach's box to kill a rally and doom Boston to a second-place, half-game finish behind Detroit.

LUKE APPLING (Hall of Fame, 1964)

Before Ernie Banks came along, Appling was Chicago's most exasperated player—toiling for 20 years (between 1930 and 1950) as the shortstop for the White Sox without getting closer to the World Series than a couple of third-place finishes. As Comiskey Park's only consistent offensive light for two decades, however, he compiled a .310 batting average, going over the .300 mark 15 times. In 1936 the righthanded slap hitter reached a peak of .388, winning the batting title in a duel with Cleveland's Earl Averill by going four-for-four on the final day of the season; Appling took another title in 1943. Although he never hit more than eight home runs in a season, his .388 mark in 1936 sent 128 runners across the plate.

To the chagrin of the Comiskeys and other American League owners, Appling was as proficient at fouling off balls as he was at dropping them out of the reach of opposition fielders. He once retaliated against Washington owner Clark Griffith's refusal to cough up passes for a group of friends by fouling off an estimated 16 straight pitches into the grandstand at Griffith Stadium. On another occasion, Detroit hurler Dizzy Trout became so incensed at having more than a dozen deliveries wasted that he fired his glove at Appling in the batter's box. The infielder was so raw defensively when he came up that manager Lew Fonseca pressed the front office to deal him away. Mainly because the club didn't have a feasible alternative, he remained where he was, going on to lead the AL in assists seven years in a row and maintaining enough range that, in 1949 at age 42, he became the oldest starting shortstop in baseball history.

Appling's nickname of Old Aches and Pains derived in part from hypochondria and in part from rooming for many years with the White Sox trainer; in fact, a broken leg in 1938 was his only serious big league injury.

As a follow-up to the bizarre 1964 trade between Detroit and Cleveland of managers Jimmy Dykes and Joe Gordon, Appling and Jo-Jo White were also swapped in the first recorded exchange of coaches. Playing in the Cracker Jack All-Star Game of Old Timers at Washington's Robert F. Kennedy Stadium in 1984, Appling belted a 275-foot home run into the left field seats off Warren Spahn, thereby equaling or topping his long-ball production for 11 of his 20 seasons in a Chicago uniform. When he hit the ball, Appling was 77 years old.

BUZZ ARLETT

Selected the premier minor league player of all time by the Society for American Baseball Research, Arlett's atrocious fielding limited his big league career to only one season. In 19 years in the high minors between 1918 and 1937, the switch-hitter batted .341 and clouted 432 homers. (Having begun as a pitcher with the Pacific Coast League Oakland Oaks, he also won 108 games in his first five seasons.) While with the International League Baltimore Orioles in 1932, he twice knocked four home runs in a game.

Finally given a berth in the majors with the Phillies in 1931, Arlett hit .313 with 18 homers. But manager Burt Shotton kept looking for a place to hide his leaden glove by moving him from the outfield to first base to a pinch-hitting role before finally giving up and letting him drift back to the minors.

HAROLD ARLIN

On August 5, 1921 Arlin became baseball's first play-by-play man when Pittsburgh radio station KDKA carried his broadcast of an 8–5 Pirates win over the Phillies. The announcer completed the assignment from a Forbes Field box seat.

LIZZIE ARLINGTON

Taught to pitch by Boston hurler Jack Stivetts, Arlington became the first woman to appear for a professional team, in 1898. She was hired for exhibitions in several Atlantic League cities by Ed Barrow, then president of the minor circuit. Born as Lizzie Stroud, she chose what she considered a less humdrum name for her efforts to boost attendance during the doldrums of the Spanish-American War.

BOB ASBJORNSON

A backup catcher for the 1932 Reds, Asbjornson was given a day in his honor by fellow natives of Concord, Massachusetts, during a team trip to Boston. After receiving a hefty check in pregame ceremonies, he celebrated by hitting his only major league home run. After the game he discovered that the check had not been signed. When he brought it to the restaurant where he was due to be honored with more festivities, he discovered that no one had showed up.

EDDIE ASHENBACH

A minor league manager and the Cincinnati scout widely credited with having been the first to recommend the signing of Christy Mathewson, Ashenbach not only lived baseball day and night, but he lost his mind to it. Felled by a stroke at the age of 40 in 1911, he whiled away his final days suffering from the hallucination he was at a ball game, continually erupting in cheers for the home team and yelling out instructions to his invisible players. Reporting Ashenbach's death, one paper commented: "The mind that invented so many witty sayings and amused so many . . . began to weaken. It was a blank when the end came in an asylum in Cincinnati."

RICHIE ASHBURN (Hall of Fame, 1995)

Because he lacked the power of contemporaries such as Willie Mays and Duke Snider, Ashburn rarely received his due as one of the preeminent center fielders of the 1950s; a similar neglect stymied his election for years to the Hall of Fame. A career .308 hitter who occupied the leadoff spot for the Phillies from 1948 to 1959, the lefty swinger won NL batting titles in 1955 and 1958, led the league by collecting 200 hits in three seasons, and paced the circuit twice in triples and four times in walks. His career 1,198 bases on balls and 2,574 hits fed a 15-year on-base percentage of .397. Defensively, Ashburn established the outfield records for most years (nine) with 400 or more putouts and most years (four) with 500 or more. But his single most important fielding play was an assist—in the final game of the 1950 season, when he snatched a single by Brooklyn's Snider and threw out Cal Abrams at the plate to cut down a run that would have forced a pennant playoff the following day; instead, the throw put Philadelphia in position to take the flag with Dick Sisler's three-run home run in the 10th inning.

EMMETT ASHFORD

Ashford was the first black to umpire in the major leagues. Hired by the American League in 1966 after extensive minor league service, he lasted five seasons, just long enough to qualify for a pen-

sion. Theatrical in the performance of his duties and equally showy in his attire, Ashford nonetheless kept to himself off the field, rarely socializing with fellow arbiters.

PAUL ASSENMACHER

Though preceded by Oakland's Rick Honeycutt, nobody epitomized the situational reliever needed for only one or two batters more than Assenmacher. In a 14-year big league career, the southpaw appeared in 884 games, but compiled only 855 $^2/_3$ innings. Between 1992 and 1999, for the Cubs, Yankees, and Indians, Assenmacher ripped off nine straight years of fewer innings than games pitched.

DAVE AUGUSTINE

Augustine never homered in 29 major league at bats, but he came legendarily close on September 20, 1973. Facing the Mets in the top of the 13th inning, the Pittsburgh outfielder hit what appeared to be a tie-breaking round-tripper, only to have the ball bounce on top of the Shea Stadium fence and back into left fielder Cleon Jones's glove. Jones and third baseman Wayne Garrett relayed the ball home to catch runner Richie Zisk to end the inning. When New York won the game and went on to win the division, Augustine's non-home run was pointed to as the turning point for the club.

GENE AUTRY

Autry stumbled into the ownership of the Angels in 1960 and never regained his feet. At the same time his image as the genial singing cowboy of Hollywood and "Rudolph the Red-Nosed Reindeer" fame succeeded in shifting all of the blame for the club's failure to reach a World Series on a parade of inept front office people and overrated players. In fact, before being forced by age to surrender practical boardroom control of the franchise to his second wife, Jackie, at the beginning of the 1990s, Autry was behind a series of chaotic management decisions that alternated between overpaying aging free agents and rushing untried rookies into the lineup. Little of this responsibility was reflected in the annual *mea culpas* by managers and players that they had once again failed to win a pennant for the beloved cowboy.

Autry took over the expansion Angels through a broadcast contract he had signed with a consortium headed by Hank Greenberg, the originally projected owner of the new American League team. When other owners rejected the bid of the Greenberg group (mainly because it included the flamboyant Bill Veeck), Autry and partner Bob Reynolds were talked into moving in for $2.5 million. After playing a year in Los Angeles's Wrigley Field, the expansion owners had to pay exorbitant rents to Walter O'Malley for another four seasons at Dodger Stadium. The fleecing was typical of the relations between the two owners: on the one hand, O'Malley had needed the help of Autry's broadcasting network in the 1950s to swing voters behind the referendum giving him Chavez Ravine and Autry had O'Malley's fear of Veeck to thank for getting the Angels in the first place; on the other hand, O'Malley took Dodgers games off Autry's stations as soon as he had won the referendum and made sure the cowboy paid for as much toilet paper in the Dodger Stadium johns as he had to, no matter the vast disparity in the number of fans attending the games of the two California clubs.

Reflecting both his Hollywood career and a need to outheadline the market rival Dodgers, Autry was usually open to players with marquee value, even if their activities off the field (for instance, Bo Belinsky) outstripped their talents between the lines. Decisions of the kind (often fueled by heavy drinking) led to managers and general managers coming and going, with each new administration promising a reversal of the previous one's policies and the long-sought World Series victory for Autry. That reversal never came, and Autry sold 25 percent of the club to the Disney Corporation in May 1995 along with an option to buy the remaining interest when he died. Disney took over as sole owner when Autry succumbed in October 1998 at the age of 91.

EARL AVERILL (Hall of Fame, 1975)

Averill took one of the quieter walks into Cooperstown after a 13-year career in which he batted .318 with 238 home runs. One reason for the right-handed outfielder's low profile was that he spent most of his major league service with the also-ran Cleveland clubs of the 1930s. Another was that, aside from setting the pace in hits and triples in 1936, he never led the American League in any significant offensive category. On the other hand, he was in double figures in home runs in every one of his 10 full seasons with the Indians. On April 16, 1929 Averill also became the first AL player to homer in his first big league at bat. His most conspicuous foray into controversy occurred during the 1935 season, when he went up against the majority of his teammates in seeking support for unpopular manager Walter Johnson. Fans stirred up by reports of Johnson's dictatorial ways let loose with a couple of bottles against the outfielder for his loyalty to the pilot, and he was booed regularly until Johnson was replaced.

JOE AZCUE

Catcher Azcue is the last major leaguer to sit out an entire season in protest over a contract offer. After working for a construction firm during the 1971 season, he settled his differences with the Angels and came back in 1972 for the final campaign of his 11-year career.

B

CARLOS BAERGA

On April 8, 1993 Cleveland second baseman Baerga became the only player to hit home runs from both sides of the plate in the same inning.

JEFF BAGWELL

Bagwell was the most gifted player ever acquired through a September "pennant insurance" trade. A minor league third baseman in the Red Sox chain, he was swapped to Houston on August 31, 1990 in return for reliever Larry Andersen. While Andersen appeared in only 15 games for Boston before moving on the following year to San Diego, Bagwell became the most potent hitter in the history of the Astros, collecting (among other things) Rookie of the Year (1991), MVP (1994), and Gold Glove (1994) awards. What made his debut season more astonishing was that, faced with the choice of going back to the minors or learning how to play first base on the very last weekend of spring training, he adapted to the latter position with minimal impact on his offensive concentration. But even with his 11-year average of .303 and more than 30 home runs and 100 RBIs a season, Bagwell's repeated batting woes in the postseason also became emblematic of Houston's chronic inability to advance as far as the World Series.

BILL BAILEY

Bailey is one of only two pitchers to endure 10 consecutive losing seasons in the major leagues. After winning four and losing one for the Browns in his rookie season of 1907, he never again got above .500 for the Baltimore Terrapins and Chicago Whales

of the Federal League, the Tigers, or the Cardinals. The southpaw's lifetime record was 38–76. The hurler who matched this feat was Ron Kline, in the 1950s and 1960s.

HAROLD BAINES

On May 9, 1984 Baines ended the longest game in major league history when he clouted a home run against Milwaukee in the 25th inning. The game, which began May 8 and went to a 17-inning, 6–6 tie before being suspended for resumption the next day, lasted eight hours and six minutes. A lefty-hitting outfielder who held most of Chicago's power records prior to Carlton Fisk, Baines was at the center of a controversial trade in 1989 in which he was packed off to Texas for outfielder Sammy Sosa, infielder Scott Fletcher, and pitcher Wilson Alvarez. White Sox owner Jerry Reinsdorf was so skeptical of the deal worked out by general manager Larry Himes that he embarrassed his own front office executive when the Rangers came to Comiskey Park later in the season by staging ceremonies for the retirement of Baines's number.

FRANK BAKER (Hall of Fame, 1955)

The deadball era's ultimate slugger, Baker led the American League in home runs in four consecutive seasons (1911–14) without ever compiling more than a dozen in one year; the lefty-swinging third baseman earned the nickname of Home Run for round-trippers he clouted to win the second game and to tie the third game of the 1911 World Series for the Athletics. Part of the $100,000 infield that helped Connie Mack win four pennants between 1910 and 1914,

Baker batted .307 in a 13-year career while leading the AL in RBIs twice and triples once. Following the 1914 season he flirted with the Federal League in an effort to get Mack to match the money the upstart circuit was promising; rebuffed, he sat out the 1915 season at his Maryland farm. Sold to the Yankees, Baker spent four seasons in New York before retiring again, to nurse his terminally ill wife, then returned again for the 1921 and 1922 seasons before calling it quits for a third and final time.

WILLIAM BAKER

A former New York City police commissioner, Baker ran the Phillies between 1913 and 1930—ran them right into the ground. As habitually hungry for quick cash as he was addicted to collecting every negative item ever printed about one of his players for use in contract negotiations, he reduced the franchise to such straits that the club became known as the Phoolish Phillies. Toward the end of his reign bookmakers refused to take bets on the team unless they were wagers on their margin of defeat. The cigar box that became known as Baker Bowl was allowed to degenerate to the point that foul balls striking the stadium beams released showers of rust on the stands below; fortunately for Baker and the organization's lawyers, there were seldom fans sitting in the lower stands to instigate lawsuits. As for the occasional star players who wore a Philadelphia uniform, they were viewed as valuable only for what money they would bring in sales to other clubs. In one of Baker's more notorious moves, he ordered that a screen be added to Baker Bowl's short right field porch so that future Hall of Famer Chuck Klein would not be able to break Babe Ruth's home run record and hold him up for a substantial raise. Not content with selling off his players, he enlisted some sportswriter cronies to spread rumors that he had been forced into some deals because those departing had been acting "suspiciously" on the field. A suggestion in 1921 that traded outfielder Irish Meusel and fired manager Bill Donovan had been on the take finally forced Commissioner Kenesaw Landis to conduct an investigation and, after finding no grounds for suspecting anything illegal, to blast Baker publicly for inspiring the gossip. Baker died of a heart attack in December 1930 just as other league owners, tired of paltry receipts from Philadelphia, were about to force him to sell the club.

LADY BALDWIN

Baldwin, who got his nickname because he neither smoked, swore, nor swilled, was less than delicate with opponents in 1886, when, as a Detroit Wolverine, he set the National League season record of 42 victories by a lefthander. His dazzling fastball was attributable to his hop-skip-and-jump delivery, similar to that of a cricket bowler. With new rules limiting hurlers to one step from a fixed position in 1887, he dropped to 13 victories and thereafter never again won in double figures.

NEAL BALL

Cleveland shortstop Ball made the first officially recognized unassisted triple play, against the Red Sox, on July 19, 1909. As a member of the Yankees the previous year; he had committed 81 errors for a fielding percentage of .897, the worst figures in the majors in 1908.

PHIL BALL

A manufacturer of cold-storage units, Ball was among the first baseball owners to bring a personal fortune to the game; he also brought with him a penchant for litigation. A minor league player until he lost the use of his left hand in a knife fight, Ball became one of the beneficiaries of the Federal League war when, following the 1915 season, he swallowed a $182,000 loss, folded the St. Louis Terriers along with the rest of the FL, and bought the Browns for another $250,000. His wealth, lavished on the franchise over the next 18 years, provided the luxury of remaining essentially a fan with a very expensive hobby. After a nail-biting victory in May 1922, for example, he remonstrated with traveling secretary Willis Johnson for bothering him with "unimportant details" like the $12,000 visitors share of the gate.

In 1917 Ball lost his general manager, Branch Rickey, to the rival Cardinals in St. Louis but not before getting an injunction compelling Rickey to honor his five-year contract by serving one additional day. With his next operations chief, Ball was a victim of his own generosity when Bob Quinn used a bonus after a second-place finish in 1922 to invest in a part-ownership of the Red Sox. While the owner stayed, for the most part, out of personnel matters, he released one player for having breakfast in bed, because "I don't have time to eat breakfast in bed; he shouldn't either." On another occasion, Ball came to regret a remark that Doc Lavan and Del Pratt had deliberately lost a 1917 game against the White Sox, when the double-play combination sued him for $50,000. Matters were settled only through the intervention of American League president Ban Johnson and the subsequent trade of both players; 10 years later, when Swede Risberg and other Black Sox were tossing around allegations about games thrown during the 1917 season, Ball went so far as to deny his earlier suspicions.

It was for Commissioner Kenesaw Landis that Ball reserved his most irascible moments. Animosity between the two dated to Landis's inattention, as a federal judge, to a lawsuit filed by the Federal League against the two older circuits, and was so intense that the owner refused to sign the judge's appointment as baseball commissioner, leaving Quinn to represent the Browns in the matter. The enmity was still there in 1930, two years before Ball's death, when he became the only owner ever to question Landis's powers in court. The occasion for the suit was the right of the Browns to keep outfielder Fred Bennett in the minor leagues, but the underlying issue was Ball's right to run his business as he saw fit. The challenge was abandoned when it became clear that it might lead to the overturning of baseball's antitrust exemption.

DAVE BANCROFT (Hall of Fame, 1971)

Bancroft was dubbed Beauty for his shortstop play, but he was also a beautiful example of the way the Giants put a good face on their practical control of the Braves for many years. After three sparkling years in the Polo Grounds defensively and offensively (.318, .321, and .304), the man described by John McGraw as "the best shortstop in baseball" was dealt to Boston so he could manage the New England club. According to McGraw, the gift was made in the interests of "helping Matty"—the ailing Christy Mathewson, who had been installed as Boston president; what he did not say was that Bancroft's departure also gained the Giants outfielder Billy Southworth; made room for Travis Jackson at the Polo Grounds; and, not least, assured more dubious trades between the two clubs for a few more years. Bancroft went on to additional good years in the field and at the plate but found himself without the players necessary to raise the Braves above the nether regions. He concluded his 16-year (1915–30) career with a .279 average.

FRANK BANCROFT

Bancroft, who spent 43 years as a manager and executive with major and minor league teams, introduced baseball to Latin America when he led the International League Worcester club on a tour of Cuba in 1879. When the same Brown Stockings entered the National League the following year, Bancroft assumed the reins of the first of his record seven major league teams. While managing Providence in 1883, he conducted the first spring training for a big league club, taking the Grays to Washington, D.C. On September 18, 1893, as business manager of Cincinnati, a post he held for 29 years, he persuaded groundskeeper Louis Rapp and Rosie Smith to be the principals in the first wedding ceremony performed at home plate. Bancroft also convinced baseball officialdom that Cincinnati, in tribute to the pre-NL Red Stockings, should have exclusive rights to play the first game of each season—a practice generally observed until the mid-1990s when cable TV contracts imposed other priorities.

SAM BANKHEAD

Bankhead was the first black to manage in organized baseball, piloting Farnham in the Class C Provincial League to a seventh-place finish in 1951. Manager of the Negro league Homestead Grays the two previous seasons, he also played shortstop for the club. Bankhead's brother Dan was the first black pitcher in the major leagues, debuting for the Dodgers in 1947 and shuttling back and forth between Brooklyn and the minors for a few years.

ERNIE BANKS (Hall of Fame, 1977)

Banks's most noted frustration—the record for most games (2,528) without appearing in a World Series—was shared in more than one way by the city of Chicago: He is also the only one to have made 2,000 appearances for a single team without a World Series.

Arriving with Gene Baker in 1953 as the first black players on the Cubs, Banks never again managed the .314 he hit in a handful of at bats that year but started instead to demolish most of the franchise's power records. In 13 seasons he hit at least 20 homers, topping the 40 mark five times, and he drove in 100 runs eight times. In 1958 and 1959 he won back-to-back MVP awards despite the fact that Chicago finished in fifth place both years. After doing most of his damage as a shortstop for nine years, he took his slower reflexes over to first base for the remainder of his career. Not quite the hitter he had been while turning the double play in the middle of the infield, he still managed three more years of 100-plus RBIs.

Banks was already 38 in 1969, when the Cubs got their first real taste of a flag race, and he performed ably enough to drive in 101 runs. But he was also a key illustration for criticisms that Leo Durocher's insistence on playing regulars every day ended up costing the club the division title to the Miracle Mets. Durocher's defense was that Banks, in particular, continually came to him asking for rest but then turned around to complain to reporters whenever the manager acceded to his requests.

On May 8, 1973 Whitey Lockman, Durocher's successor, turned the reins over to Banks after being kicked out of a game; it is the first recorded instance of an African American managing even temporarily in the big leagues.

Periodic fan polls have voted Banks the greatest player in Cubs history for his 512 home runs and 1,636 RBIs. But however popular he was for his "Let's play two" attitude, Mr. Cub also found himself on the outs for a while with the Chicago *Tribune* ownership that succeeded the Wrigley family, because of the organization's desire for less of an association with its losing years.

RED BARBER

Barber made baseball a game for the imagination as much as for the diamond. Brought to Cincinnati by Larry MacPhail in 1934, he was vital to disproving accepted wisdom that broadcasting games would devastate attendance. More than delivering basic radio play-by-play, he used his down-home twang and dry humor to underline the game's dramatic values and to personalize players who had remained little more than tin heroes or lifeless statistics in the sportswriting of the era. The consequences were twofold: an empathy by listeners who were able to project themselves into his detailed descriptions of field action and a more human identification by the audience with the players involved in the action.

When MacPhail moved to Brooklyn in 1938, Barber went with him, immediately establishing the depth of his appeal by having even the crustiest fans of the East accept such folksy phrases as "the rhubarb patch" (a field argument), "the catbird seat" (an ad-

vantageous situation), and "tearin' up the pea patch" (scoring runs in a batch). So sure was MacPhail of the Barber weapon that he unilaterally broke an accord with the Giants and Yankees not to air home games. While in Brooklyn, Barber also called the plays for the first televised game (August 26, 1939) and the first game televised in color (August 10, 1951). He also conducted the first televised player interview, getting Cincinnati pitcher Bucky Walters to demonstrate how he gripped various pitches.

Because of Barber's southern background, Branch Rickey used him as an early sounding board for gauging reaction to the decision of breaking the color barrier with Jackie Robinson. He had a much less confidential relationship with the Walter O'Malley regime that succeeded Rickey and left the Dodgers after O'Malley threw him a take-it-or-leave-it offer for taking on extra broadcasting duties in the 1953 World Series. For 12 years he worked in the Yankees broadcasting booth, but that relationship also came to a brusque end when, on the last day of the 1966 season, he told the cameraman to pan the empty seats of Yankee Stadium to underline a point that bad teams did not draw fans.

SAM BARKLEY

An infielder of modest talents, Barkley's efforts to escape from Chris Von der Ahe's St. Louis Brown Stockings in 1885 brought about the firing of American Association president Denny McKnight and the defection of the Pittsburgh Alleghenys to the National League. The trouble started when Von der Ahe agreed to trade Barkley to both Baltimore and Pittsburgh, and the second baseman signed contracts with both teams. The AA then stepped in to fine the infielder (but not Von der Ahe) and suspend him for the 1886 season on charges of "dishonorable conduct." When league president and Pittsburgh stockholder McKnight rejected the recommendation and Barkley ran to a lawyer, the AA called another meeting, this time intending to censor its chief executive and discipline the player. McKnight foiled the plan by not informing Barkley of the second meeting and, pleading illness, failing to show up himself. The outcome was an out-of-court settlement that included a heftier fine, but no suspension, for Barkley; compensation in the form of an equally mediocre player for the Orioles; and a pink slip for president McKnight. Within the year the Alleghenys jumped to the NL.

AL BARLICK (Hall of Fame, 1989)

Barlick's resonant strike calls over a 32-year (1940–71) umpiring career in the National League were about the most conspicuous thing about him on the field; otherwise, he was known for his unobtrusive handling of games. In 1970 he barked a particularly loud strike to the league office when he led a walkout of umpires prior to that season's championship series between Pittsburgh and Cincinnati. When the arbiters returned to action in time for the second game of the playoffs, they had new four-year accords calling for increased pay for postseason and All-Star Game assignments. When he retired after the 1971 season, Barlick's seven All-Star appearances were a record.

ERNEST BARNARD

Barnard was baseball's first enthusiast for articulated working agreements between major league clubs and minor league organizations. As Cleveland vice-president in 1910, a full decade before Branch Rickey turned the system into a science, he convinced owner Charles Somers to conclude pacts with minor-level clubs in New Orleans, Toledo, Portland (Oregon), Waterbury (Connecticut), and Ironton (Ohio). Somers eventually had to pull out of the agreements and then out of the Indians altogether because of financial problems. Barnard himself remained in the hierarchy of the franchise as either vice-president or president until 1927, but never again had access to Somers's kind of capital to return to his idea.

Barnard was also elected American League president in 1928, after the death of Ban Johnson, and served in that office until his own death in 1931.

DON BARNES

Barnes's 10 years as principal owner of the Browns included the worst of times and the best of times; in between, only a world war prevented him from abandoning St. Louis and introducing major league baseball to the West Coast.

When the executors of the Phil Ball estate offered a $25,000 bounty in 1936 for anyone who came up with a buyer for the franchise, Branch Rickey, the rival Cardinals operations chief, proposed Barnes. The president of American Investment Company of Illinois, he teamed with longtime Browns employee Bill DeWitt to head a syndicate that took over the club for $325,000. Within three years the never-very-successful franchise reached its nadir, finishing the 1939 season with a 43–111 record, a staggering $64\frac{1}{2}$ games behind the pennant-winning Yankees. Finances were so desperate by the end of the decade that keeping the outfield grass trim became the responsibility of a goat.

When other American League clubs expressed concern in 1940 that they couldn't recoup their travel and hotel expenses for trips to St. Louis, AL president Will Harridge suggested they "go a little socialistic for their own good," each of them selling one of their players to the Browns for $7,500. In this way Barnes picked up an aging Eldon Auker, whose 16 wins made him the staff ace, and outfielder Walt Judnich, whose .303 average and 24 homers provided the club's only offensive threat. Not only did the organization go on the dole, but individual players, strapped by paltry salaries, received off-season unemployment compensation of $15 a week. By the end of the 1941 season Barnes was forced to strip the franchise bare, abandoning five farm clubs and firing all team scouts; this in turn dropped the value of club stock to 40 percent of his original purchase price. The AL had to intervene with a $25,000 loan to meet operating expenses.

In early December 1941 Barnes orchestrated a shift of the franchise to Los Angeles for the 1942 season. Cubs owner Phil Wrigley agreed to surrender not only his territorial rights to the California city but also his minor league park there. Anticipating improved road attendance, other AL owners gleefully agreed to the move. Barnes had a schedule drawn up including Los Angeles and priced the cost of air transportation to the West Coast for all teams. Cardinals owner Sam Breadon didn't have to be asked twice to put up some cash to speed the Browns on their way, since that meant he would have St. Louis to himself. All that was missing was official ratification of the move at the annual AL meeting, on December 8. The bombing of Pearl Harbor the day before exploded the transfer plan along with a lot of other things.

Stuck in St. Louis, Barnes sold controlling interest in the club to Richard Muckerman, head of the St. Louis Fuel and Ice Company, for $300,000, reducing himself to a minority partner. He nevertheless remained as club president long enough to be titular head of the team when it won its only pennant, in 1944.

ROSS BARNES

The National League's first superstar, Barnes was also the first player to sue his team. After leading the National League with a .404 average in 1876, he dropped to .272 in 1877 after the banning of his specialty, the fair-foul hit (a ball driven into fair territory just in front of home plate and spinning into foul ground out of the reach of defensemen). More devastating, however, was a muscular disorder that kept Barnes out of all but 22 of Chicago's 59 games. When club owner William Hulbert refused to pay his erstwhile star $1,000 of his $2,500 salary for the year, Barnes brought suit. A Chicago court ruled for Hulbert, saying no employer was obligated to pay for undelivered services.

CLYDE BARNHART

Pittsburgh third baseman Barnhart is the only major leaguer to hit safely in three games in one day. He accomplished it against Cincinnati on October 2, 1920, in the last major league tripleheader.

GEORGE BARR

Barr was a National League umpire who, in 1943, made the mistake of calling a balk against the frequently hysterical Johnny Allen. Before the Brooklyn hurler could be pulled off him, Barr had almost choked from the way Allen was wrapping his tie around his throat. Largely because of the attack, ties were soon afterward dropped from umpiring garb.

Barr also opened the first umpiring school, in 1935.

JIM BARR

Pitching for the Giants in 1972, Barr retired 41 consecutive batters over two games for a major league record; neither game was a no-hitter. The righthander was otherwise known for his questionable taste in personal antagonists. As a member of the Angels in 1979, he got into a brawl with liquored-up broadcaster Don Drysdale after the one-time Dodgers star had accused him of dogging it during California's ALCS loss to Baltimore. Back with the Giants in 1983, he reacted to being lifted from a game by flipping the ball to manager Frank Robinson and starting off the mound; Robinson grabbed him by the shirt and lifted him back to the hill with some words about mound decorum.

Despite early indications he would be the anchor of the San Francisco staff for the 1970s, Barr never won more than 15 games in a season and ended with a 101–112 record.

ED BARROW (Hall of Fame, 1953)

As Boston manager in 1918, Barrow converted Babe Ruth from the ace of his pitching staff to the most significant weapon in his offensive arsenal; as general manager of the Yankees, he reaped the full benefit of his move. After a successful career in the minors as a manager, owner, and league president (during which he discovered Honus Wagner), as well as a less successful season-and-a-half as pilot of the Tigers, Barrow managed the Red Sox to a pennant in 1918, with Ruth's slugging leading the way. Ambivalent about what he had wrought, he put himself on record first as fearing a lynching if he converted the best lefthander in baseball to an outfielder, then as arguing that Ruth should have batted .400 instead of swatting all those four-base blasts.

With the sale of Ruth to New York in 1920, Barrow realized that there was little in Boston's future but debts followed by more player sales; deciding he would rather be on the buying than the selling end, he moved into the top job in the New York front office before the 1921 season. Within two months, he had dipped back into the Boston well for future Hall of Fame righthander Waite Hoyt, catcher Wally Schang, shortstop Everett Scott, and pitchers Joe Bush and Sam Jones; he would return to the same source several times over the next year for third baseman Joe Dugan, righty George Pipgras, and Hall of Fame southpaw Herb Pennock. The immediate dividends were three straight pennants and dominance of the American League for a decade.

When the supply of Boston players dried up, Barrow brought in George Weiss in 1932 to head a farm system to be modeled on Branch Rickey's minor league chain for the Cardinals. Expensive as the system was, it led to the next great Yankees era, in which the club won seven pennants between 1936 and 1943. Overall under Barrow's direction, the Yankees won 14 pennants and 10 World Series in 25 years. (There might have been yet another pennant but for Barrow's unwillingness in 1940 to tarnish the Yankees image by admitting the team needed the services of rookie Ernie Bonham. Finally promoted from the minors in August, the righthander put together a 9–3 record, but New York finished third, only two games behind first-place Detroit.)

As lavish as he was with owner Jacob Ruppert's money in developing and acquiring talent, Barrow was equally stingy in doling it out to the same players. Basing his negotiating strategy on a conviction that underpaid players hungered more for a World Series check, he would sit in a tattered sweater and offer take-it-or-leave-it deals. He drummed shortstop Leo Durocher not only off the Yankees but out of the AL for daring to ask for a raise in 1929. He even insisted that Joe DiMaggio take a cut in salary out of wartime patriotism after having hit in 56 consecutive games in 1941.

As humorless and unimaginative as he was penurious, Barrow opposed virtually every innovation (except the farm system) that came along, spurning night ball and promotions as unnecessary for a winning club. This attitude made the arrival of champion promoter Larry MacPhail as his new boss in 1945 all the more galling. Kicked upstairs from the club presidency, a position he had held since the death of Ruppert in 1939, to a hollow chairman-of-the-board position, Barrow endured the ignominy of a title without authority or responsibility for only two years, refusing for the duration even to enter the newly and flashily renovated Yankees offices in midtown Manhattan.

DICK BARTELL

Dubbed Rowdy Richard for his belligerence with opponents and umpires, Bartell earned goat's horns in the 1940 World Series for a hesitation that approximated the more famous delayed relay by Boston's Johnny Pesky six years later. With the Tigers ahead, 1–0, and Cincinnati's Frank McCormick on second base in the seventh inning of the seventh game, the shortstop took a throw from right field and held the ball. Unable to hear over the roaring home crowd, he failed to respond to cries of "Throw! Throw! Throw!" from his own bench and similarly frantic screams of "Run! Run! Run!" from the Cincinnati dugout; this enabled McCormick, who had held up around third base, to score the tying run. The Reds went on to win the game and the Series.

WILLIAM BARTHOLOMAY

An Illinois insurance company executive, Bartholomay managed to convert a series of initial miscalculations into profits for himself and associates for some three decades. His first apparent misadventure was in allying himself with Chuck Comiskey in the early 1960s in a labyrinthine scheme for assuming control of the White Sox; when the scheme didn't work, he jettisoned Comiskey and sold his minority interest in the franchise for a substantial gain. In 1962 he headed the syndicate that purchased the Milwaukee Braves from Lou Perini and that, three years later, announced its intention of moving the franchise to Atlanta. This prompted a lawsuit headed by auto dealer Bud Selig that forced the Braves to spend a disastrous lame-duck season in Wisconsin and Bartholomay and his partners to spend rivers of money to fight the case in court. But in finally getting to Georgia in 1966, he found even more local appreciation for his club because of the delay over the court battle and was quick to make up for his lost 1965 revenues with the team's new television market.

Bartholomay could still chuckle 10 years later, by which time the novelty of Atlanta baseball had long since worn off. In 1976 he sold out to Ted Turner, who not only made up for the Braves slow years in the early 1970s, but who also asked Bartholomay to stay with the organization—first as president, then as chairman of the board. The insurance man was still in place for the Time-Warner purchasers of Turner's holdings at the start of the new millennium.

MONTY BASGALL

Basgall was Branch Rickey's test to himself that he could unload anybody on Pittsburgh owner John Galbreath. Something of a laughing stock for his atrocious deals with Rickey in the 1940s, Galbreath told the Brooklyn executive they could no longer do business together. Rickey's response was to bet a new $200 suit that he could sell a player to the Pirates for at least $50,000 within a year. Several months later Galbreath paid exactly $50,001 for Basgall, a second baseman in the Dodgers chain. The infielder batted .215 in parts of three seasons for Pittsburgh. Rickey won the suit and never tired of telling people where it had come from.

JIM BAUMER

Baumer made the mistake of making his major league debut at Yankee Stadium. Called up by the White Sox at the end of the 1949 season amid fanfare that he would be Chicago's shortstop of the future, he took the field in the bottom of the first inning, threw some warm-up tosses over to the first baseman, then took in the New York crowd, fainted, and had to be carried off the field. Although he got a sufficient grip on himself to play in a handful of games before the end of the year, he wrote another footnote when he disappeared into the minors for the entire decade of the 1950s, not reappearing in the majors again until 1961, with Cincinnati.

BUZZIE BAVASI

Walter O'Malley's righthand man for much of his 30-year front office career, Bavasi was accused more than once of sharing the Dodgers owner's sensitivity.

As Dodgers general manager in Brooklyn and then Los Angeles, Bavasi thought nothing of selling off or even trying to farm out team veterans while informing the press before the affected players or of building up one player in contract talks at the expense of talking down another. Another reported ploy was to leave players alone in his office with a phony contract on his desk so that visitors would think offers to them had been higher than those to teammates. It was precisely to overcome such tactics that Sandy Koufax and Don Drysdale approached Bavasi as a tandem prior to the 1966 season, warning him that they intended sharing information on their individual pact negotiations. For most of his reign with the Dodgers, he relied on the organization's farm system for new blood, rarely entering into major trades except for a fourth starter and implementing O'Malley's disdain for free agents.

In 1969 Bavasi left the Dodgers to take over the expansion Padres. Although fulfilling expectations by hiring a succession of managers with a Dodgers pedigree, he was also clearly apprehensive about stirring up charges of collusion between the two southern California teams, so went out of his way to avoid deals with Los Angeles. In the first decade of their existence, the Padres made only one trade with the Dodgers—a minor 1969 exchange of reliever Al McBean for shortstop Tommy Dean. But not even this display of discretion ever completely muted suspicions in some quarters that O'Malley had let Bavasi take on the San Diego job so the competing franchise would fail and the Dodgers would be able to solidify their hold on the southern California market.

In the latter part of the 1970s Bavasi was hired by Angels owner Gene Autry to staunch the franchise's financial bleeding. The appointment so irritated general manager Harry Dalton that he quit to go off to the Brewers, leaving Bavasi with responsibility for the club's baseball operations. It wasn't long before he too, in the chaotic style typifying the California franchise, began offering inflated free agent contracts to second-line players; to that extent, anyway, he had traveled a great distance from O'Malley.

Bavasi's sons Peter and Bill followed him into baseball's executive suites.

DON BAYLOR

Baylor holds the career mark for getting hit by a pitch, working his way to first base the hard way 267 times. A righthanded slugger who played for half a dozen teams between 1970 and 1988, he became the first designated hitter to win an MVP award, in 1979, when he sparked the Angels to a Western Division title by batting .296, belting 36 home runs, and leading the league in both RBIs (139) and runs (120). In later years, he gained a reputation as a clubhouse leader who provided the extra push needed for winning teams; Boston, Minnesota, and Oakland all won pennants during his brief stays with them.

After a couple of years of being passed over as a managerial choice (in at least one case for racial reasons), Baylor was given the reins of the first-year expansion Colorado Rockies in 1993. His skills as a hitting tutor became evident in the transformation of Andres Galarraga into the National League batting champion. Although he got Colorado into the playoffs in its third year of existence, he was gone after the 1998 season for not being able to repeat that success. He took over the Cubs in 2000.

GENE BEARDEN

Rookie Bearden was an unexpected hero of the Indians last world championship. Despite his league-leading 2.43 ERA, it came as a surprise when manager Lou Boudreau chose him over Bob Feller and Bob Lemon to pitch the one-game showdown playoff for the 1948 flag against the Red Sox. In the event, the southpaw notched his 20th victory of the season with a five-hit, 8–3 effort sparked by two homers from player-pilot Boudreau. In the ensuing World Series against the Braves, the knuckleballer hurled a complete-game shutout in the third game and earned a save in the sixth game. In six other major league seasons Bearden was never better than a .500 pitcher for Cleveland and four other American League teams, ending his career with a 45–38 record.

GEORGE BECHTEL

Bechtel was practically the Louisville Fifth. In 1876 the outfielder was suspended by the Grays after teammate Jim Devlin accused him of wiring him a $500 offer to throw a game. Cited for drunkenness rather than dishonesty, he was blackballed despite an anonymous letter claiming Bechtel's name had been forged on the telegram. At the conclusion of the 1877 season, the National League made his suspension permanent—along with those of Devlin and three other Grays whose involvement in a game-fixing scandal won them the designation of the Louisville Four.

Bechtel and Bill Craver (another of the Louisville Four) were part of the first recorded player sale, moving from the National Association Philadelphia Centennials to the Athletics of the same city, in 1875.

BOOM BOOM BECK

Beck was a journeyman who went back and forth between the majors and minors between 1924 and 1945, squeezing in 12 years of big league service. The reasons for all his wanderings were implicit in the nickname fastened on him by teammates—the first boom suggesting the whack of a bat against one of his pitches, the second one the sound of the ball caroming off an outfield wall. Beck entered Dodgers lore in 1934, when, steamed at being removed from a game, he fired the ball at the right field wall at Philadelphia's Baker Bowl. A distracted and hungover Hack Wilson instantly charged after the ball, grabbed it, and shot it back to the infield on the assumption it was another hit by an opposition batter.

ERV BECK

In the Opening Day game against Chicago on April 24, 1901, Indians second baseman Beck doubled for the American League's first extra-base hit. He also clouted the league's first home run, the next day.

JAKE BECKLEY (Hall of Fame, 1971)

Beckley's last appreciable record fell in 1994, when Eddie Murray surpassed him for most games played at first base. But for a 20-year span from 1888 to 1907 he was one of the National League's principal offensive threats, reaching the .300 plateau 13 times and closing with a .308 average. Doing most of his damage for the Pirates and Reds, the lefty swinger also knocked in 100 runs four times and scored 100

runs in each of five seasons. A member of the Pittsburgh entry in the 1890 Players League, Beckley batted .324 and led the Brotherhood rebels in triples. When Pittsburgh traded him to the Giants in 1897, the deal cost owner William Kerr mass defections in attendance and set into motion the maneuverings that would bring Barney Dreyfuss from Louisville into the Pittsburgh front office.

Beckley's career came close to being short-circuited three years before his retirement when Jack Taylor, his drinking companion on the Cardinals, fell under a cloud for throwing exhibition games in 1903. Dreyfuss lobbied for banning both players, but St. Louis owner Stanley Robison resisted the move, knowing how severely such a purge would damage his club.

BO BELINSKY

No big leaguer received more publicity for doing less on a diamond than Belinsky. By the time he had wound up an eight-year career that included lengthy stays in the minors and on the disabled list, he had won a mere 28 games, only once managing more victories than losses. When he joined the Angels in 1962, however, his reputation as a womanizer, pool hustler, and all-around *bon vivant* was just what the market-minded Angels needed in their rivalry with the Dodgers. When the southpaw reeled off five quick victories, one of them a no-hitter against Baltimore, the media fastened on to him as a symbol of the "new ballplayer." Particularly avid for his company was aging Hearst columnist Walter Winchell, who saw the pitcher as an access to the starlets and actresses he wanted to bed down. With Winchell and every other gossip columnist worth his dirt chronicling his adventures, Belinsky did the town with the likes of Iran's Queen Soraya, and actresses Connie Stevens, Tina Louise, and Ann-Margret. The lengthiest relationship was with actress Mamie Van Doren, whose regular appearances at Dodger Stadium in low-cut outfits allowed the Angels to out-Hollywood the Dodgers.

Belinsky's chief antagonist during all the fun was manager Bill Rigney, who objected not only to his gradually poorer performances on the mound but also to his influence on such teammates as Dean Chance. With backing from general manager Fred Haney, Rigney thought he had solved his problem in July 1962 by completing a trade with Kansas City for reliever Dan Osinski for "a player to be named later." Athletics manager Hank Bauer, who wanted no part of the player to be named later, let Belinsky know that he was Kansas City-bound, prompting a brouhaha in the American League office. In the end, AL president Joe Cronin had to accept Belinsky's contention that there was a whiff of the unethical about a player performing for one team while aware that he was headed for another, and ordered the Angels to send Ted Bowsfield to the Athletics instead.

Rigney tried again in 1963. After a relentless series of fines against Belinsky and Chance, the manager persuaded the front office that Belinsky's 1–7 record had earned him a demotion to the minors. When Belinsky realized that California's chief farm club was in Hawaii, he not only didn't object, he even refused a recall to the parent club in August because he was having so much fun on the islands. The air finally went out of the balloon during the 1964 season, when a punch-up with Los Angeles *Times* sportswriter Braven Dyer turned the media against the pitcher. Together with arm and drinking problems, the brawl greased his slide from the Angels; he ended up drifting from one National League team to another before finally retiring in 1971. Friends said after his death in the fall of 2001 that he had found Jesus Christ in his later years.

BUDDY BELL

In 18 years spanning 2,405 games, third baseman Bell never appeared in postseason play—the record for unfulfilled expectations in the era of divisional play. Bell labored for the Indians, Rangers, Reds, and Astros from 1972 to 1989.

COOL PAPA BELL (Hall of Fame, 1972)

While there is a wealth of apocrypha about Bell's swiftness, there is also enough documentation to strengthen the claim the outfielder was the fastest man ever to play at a professional level.

In 20 Negro league seasons Bell played for three of the greatest teams ever assembled—the St. Louis Stars (1922–31), the Pittsburgh Crawfords (1933–36), and the Homestead Grays (1943–46). With Bell as their center fielder, the clubs combined for 11 championships. Given his nickname by Stars manager Bill Gatewood after he had calmly struck out Oscar Charleston in a clutch situation, Bell moved from the pitching mound to the outfield in 1924 and aver-

aged better than .300 16 times, reaching the .380 mark on more than one occasion. The switch-hitter also spent one season (1937) in the Dominican Republic and four more (1938–41) in Mexico, where he won a Triple Crown in 1940 for his .437 average, 12 homers, and 79 RBIs. In addition, he played winter ball in Cuba, Mexico, and California for 21 years. Even his Negro leagues career average of about .340 was eclipsed by a .391 mark in exhibition games against big league players.

One tall tale about Bell's running, made famous by Satchel Paige, is that he once got a hit up the middle but was declared out when his batted ball struck him as he slid into second. It was also Paige who cracked that Bell could throw the light switch and be in bed before the room was dark. (This actually happened but only because of an electrical short in the wiring of the hotel where the pair was staying.) The fish stories aside, Bell once stole 175 bases in 200 games. There are also numerous eyewitness accounts of his going from first to third on a sacrifice fly, beating out two-hoppers to the infield, and stealing two bases on one pitch. The most astonishing of Bell's feats occurred in an exhibition game against big league players when he scored from first base on a sacrifice bunt, so shocking Red Sox catcher Roy Partee and Indians pitcher Bob Lemon that they became proselytizers of his myth; Bell was already several years past 40 at the time.

Lured to the Dominican Republic in 1937 by Paige, Bell and other Negro league stars were kept under armed guard in a compound in San Pedro de Macoris, where they were told that dictator Rafael Trujillo would be assassinated unless their team won the pennant; the club did, beating out Santiago on the final day of the season.

Bell's last four seasons were spent as a playing manager for minor black teams—the Detroit Senators and Kansas City Stars. In 1951 he refused Bill Veeck's offer to join the St. Louis Browns because he was 48 years old.

GEORGE BELL

Bell has been the most successful Rule V pickup by a team committed to keeping a drafted minor league player on its big league roster for an entire season. Purchased by the Blue Jays from the Phillies farm system prior to the 1981 season, the slugger went on to have eight seasons with at least 20 home runs and four with a minimum of 100 RBIs. In 1987, the righthand-hitting outfielder took MVP honors in the American League by batting .308 with 47 homers and a league-best 134 RBIs.

For most of his 12-year (1981, 1983–93) career with Toronto and other clubs, Bell stirred controversy about his defensive limitations, especially in 1988, when Blue Jays manager Jimy Williams indicated that untried rookies Rob Ducey and Sil Campusano were preferable in the field to the previous season's MVP. Although both rookies failed and Bell was eventually shifted back to left field from his initial role as a designated hitter, his resentment of Williams carried through the season and helped make the Toronto clubhouse the most fractious in the major leagues. While with the White Sox in 1993, Bell and Bo Jackson got into such a public sulk about who should be the DH in the American League Championship Series against Toronto that neither player was offered a new contract with the White Sox following the season. Bell had gotten to the White Sox after the 1991 season in what turned out to be the most one-sided trade in the history of Chicago baseball: In exchange for him the Cubs received Sammy Sosa.

ESTEBAN BELLAN

Bellan was the first Latino to play at any level of organized ball in North America, appearing for Troy and New York in the proto-major league National Association in the early 1870s. The infielder was also one of the fathers of Cuban baseball in the 19th century.

ALBERT BELLE

Belle's off-field boorishness, and the media's delight in it, obscured one of the great power careers. Before a degenerative hip forced his retirement in 2001, the outfielder's 12-year career with the Indians, White Sox, and Orioles included eight seasons in a row with 30 home runs and 100 RBIs; leading or tying for the best (in 1995) in slugging, doubles, home runs, total bases, RBIs, and runs scored; and becoming the first player (also in 1995) ever to swat 50 home runs and 50 doubles in the same year. When it came to MVP votes, however, Belle was left at the door because of a demeanor as The Ugly Free Agent—one who got into brawls with heckling fans, who pushed reporters out of his way, and who

set up a website to proclaim his gifts to anyone who knew how to type www. While with the White Sox in 1998, he was also involved in a gambling scandal, trading testimony against sports bookmakers in exchange for immunity from prosecution. Although the affair garnered none of the publicity of the Pete Rose turmoils, it contributed to Chicago's indifference when Belle, citing an unprecedented contract clause enabling him to declare free agency if he didn't remain among the top three salaried players in baseball, walked off at the end of the year. His clashes with fans, owners, and the media notwithstanding, Belle had relatively few problems in the clubhouse. Cleveland teammates riled him deliberately (usually through some canard involving the media) so he would take the field in a boil against opponents.

Belle's hip ailment was costly to more than the Orioles: while Baltimore was able to make up most of its losses with insurance, the insurance companies soon afterward began multiplying rates for covering baseball players.

JOHNNY BENCH (Hall of Fame, 1989)

Often cited as the greatest all-around catcher in National League history, Bench was a vital offensive and defensive cog in the Big Red Machine of the 1970s. Although more attention was paid to his hitting, his work behind the plate and with pitchers might have been even more significant, not least because of the mostly lackluster mound corps that Cincinnati had in the period.

Never one to hide his light under a bushel, Bench joined Cincinnati at the end of 1967 and saw enough to predict that he would be the NL Rookie of the Year in 1968. He was right—becoming the first player at his position to cop rookie honors. It was also the first of 10 straight seasons in which he would win a Gold Glove. With a bat his best years were 1970 and 1972, when he was named the league's Most Valuable Player. In 1970 he led the circuit in both home runs (45) and RBIs (148), then did it again in 1972 with 40 homers and 125 RBIs. The righthanded slugger won a third RBI crown in 1974, and all told topped the 100 mark six times. His 389 career home runs include 327 in the lineup as a catcher—the most ever by an NL receiver.

One of Bench's most conspicuous moments came in the 1976 World Series against the Yankees, in which he collected six hits over the first three games, then clouted two homers in the finale for a sweep. In the first game he threw out New York's Mickey Rivers attempting to steal and never had another Yankees base runner test his arm. The performance indirectly caused a mini-controversy when Reds manager Sparky Anderson asserted that New York's Thurman Munson didn't belong in the same ballpark as Bench, the Yankees fired back, and then old Dodger Duke Snider chimed in with an opinion that Bench would have been only a backup to Roy Campanella.

Bench lingered in Cincinnati longer and more awkwardly than other members of the Big Red Machine. Declaring that he no longer wanted to catch, he persuaded manager John McNamara to allow him to end his career as a third baseman. The result in 1982 was not only a club-leading 19 errors, but also a marked lack of range that had pitchers moaning about having the 14-time All-Star behind them rather than in front of them. He called it quits after the 1983 season. Reflecting conflicting personalities from their days with the Big Red Machine, Bench has always defended the exclusion of Pete Rose from the Hall of Fame.

CHIEF BENDER (Hall of Fame, 1953)

The first Native American elected to the Hall of Fame, Bender was a mainstay of the Athletics rotation between 1903 and 1914, when he recorded the vast majority of his 212 career victories and led the American League in won-lost percentage three times. His jump to the Federal League Baltimore Terrapins in 1915 is sometimes said to have convinced Connie Mack that his four-time (in five years) champions had become too expensive and obstreperous, leading to one of the franchise's periodic dismantlings. The righthander played out the string with the Phillies in 1916 and 1917, making a one-inning cameo appearance with the White Sox in 1925. An effective reliever as well as starter, Bender tallied six of his 21 wins in 1913 (one of only two 20-win seasons) out of the bullpen; he also led the AL in saves with 13 that year. A half Chippewa, he tolerated the use of his nickname but, calling himself Charley, never used it himself.

CHARLIE BENNETT

A popular catcher with the National League Detroit Wolverines in the 1880s, Bennett lost his legs in January 1894 attempting to jump on a moving train in Wellsville, Kansas. When Detroit joined the Western League two years later, the home park was named Bennett Field in his honor. The Tigers used the field through their first 11 American League seasons.

EDDIE BENNETT

Born with a malformed spine, Bennett was the only man to wear the uniform of three different pennant-winning teams in three consecutive years. First adopted as a batboy-mascot by Happy Felsch of the 1919 White Sox, who thought rubbing Bennett's misshapen back would bring good luck, he filled a similar role for the 1920 Dodgers and 1921 Yankees. He stayed with New York through the 1920s, eventually becoming a full-time cheerleader while subordinates did the bat carrying.

FRED BENNETT

When Bennett successfully appealed to Commissioner Kenesaw Landis in 1930 that the Browns had buried him in their farm system after only a brief stint with the big club, the verdict affected more than the outfielder's future. For Bennett it meant free agency and an additional major league season; for the rest of baseball it meant the validation of farm systems. In deciding the suit brought by St. Louis owner Phil Ball, a federal trial judge ratified the commissioner's broad authority to liberate individual players but upheld the essential legality of minor league networks. Realizing that further pursuit of his point might jeopardize baseball's antitrust exemption, Ball dropped the matter.

ROBERT RUSSELL BENNETT

Bennett composed the most elaborate music ever inspired by baseball. His 1941 *Symphony in D for the Dodgers* consisted of four movements—*Allegro con brio* ("Brooklyn Wins"), *Andante lamentosa* ("Brooklyn Loses"), *Scherzo* ("Larry MacPhail tries to give Cleveland the Brooklyn Bridge for Bob Feller"), and *Finale* ("The Giants Come to Town").

ALLEN BENSON

A bearded pitcher from the House of David team, Benson was signed by Washington in 1934 as a quickie gate attraction. After getting pounded by Detroit, he asked for another start and for the right to shave off his beard. Senators owner Clark Griffith agreed to the start but insisted the beard made Benson "special." The righthander was banged around again, this time by the lowly Browns, and retired with a mark of 0–1 and an ERA of 12.10.

The House of David was a Michigan-based religious sect that spawned baseball teams for fundraising purposes at the beginning of the century. By Benson's time it had fragmented into rival groups that sponsored teams at semipro levels, though with a common identity of extremely long beards and shoulder-length hair.

RUBE BENTON

A fringe character caught up in the 1919 World Series scandal, Benton had either his imagination or his bad memory to thank for a one-year suspension. The southpaw's troubles began in the summer of 1920, when he accused Buck Herzog and Hal Chase of having asked him to throw a 1919 game to the Reds that he was scheduled to start for the Giants; Herzog retaliated by producing signed affidavits from several players declaring that Benton had boasted of winning $1,500 from the 1919 World Series because of his prior knowledge of the Black Sox fix. Summoned before the grand jury looking into the tainted Series, the pitcher admitted having won money in 1919, but insisted that it was only $20 and that his bets had been placed on the basis of nothing more than the general rumors going around. Once off the witness stand, he reiterated his charges against Herzog, adding the particular that he had been approached in a Chicago bar and that one of the bartenders on the premises had heard every word.

For his part, National League president John Heydler wanted the heavy-drinking Benton to go back to the mound for the Giants and let matters die. But with the hurler periodically returning to his accusations against Herzog, Heydler finally had to agree in 1921 to go to Chicago with him to find the bartender. Once in the Windy City, however, Benton claimed he was disoriented by the interim replacement of saloons by speakeasies and couldn't remember exactly where Herzog had approached him. An infuriated Heydler passed the word to NL owners that Benton would not be welcome on any league roster in 1922.

There matters stood until 1923, when Cincinnati owner Garry Herrmann decided that Benton's big 1922 season with St. Paul of the American Associa-

tion entitled him to another major league chance. But when Herrmann went to Heydler, the NL executive insisted Benton remained "morally undesirable." Deciding that Heydler had lost his objectivity because of the wild-goose chase to Chicago, Herrmann then went to Commissioner Kenesaw Landis. Landis not only reinstated Benton but also took the opportunity to blast Heydler, Herzog, and various sportswriters for having slandered the pitcher's character. Benton won 14 games for the Reds in 1923.

JOHNNY BERARDINO

Berardino was the first player to rattle an owner by insisting that an agent handle negotiations for his services. In November 1947 the Browns infielder was traded to the Senators for second baseman Gerry Priddy but refused to go unless Washington owner Clark Griffith negotiated a new contract for the following season. When Griffith scorned the idea of having to deal with an agent, Berardino announced his retirement and intention of trying to make it as an actor. Commissioner Happy Chandler stepped in to dissolve the trade, prompting Berardino to announce his unretirement. Three weeks later he agreed to a trade to the Indians when Cleveland owner Bill Veeck promised him not only regular playing time but also an introduction to a Hollywood producer. Never one to avoid a good publicity gimmick, Veeck also had his new infielder's face insured against accidents on the field. Retiring after the 1952 season, Berardino went to Hollywood, where he dropped the second "r" in his name and eventually began a 30-year stretch as Dr. Steve Hardy on the daytime soap opera *General Hospital*.

MOE BERG

Berg has enjoyed a reputation as the most accomplished—and the most shadowy—backup catcher in the game's history. Few of the receiver's achievements came in the batter's box. It was, in fact, Berg whom Mike Gonzalez was describing when he coined the phrase "Good field, no hit" while scouting the eventual .243 career hitter for the Cardinals in the early 1920s.

After coming up with the Dodgers in 1923 as a slick infielder, Berg spent two seasons (1926–27) with the White Sox as a utility man, then found a niche as a second-string backstop, filling that role until 1939 with the Indians, Senators, and Red Sox as well as the White Sox; in only one of his 15 big league seasons did he appear in more than 100 games. Along the way, he picked up degrees from Princeton University and Columbia Law School, and studied philology at the Sorbonne; however, his linguistic skills, which inspired Chicago teammate Ted Lyons's observation that "he can speak 12 languages, but he can't hit in any of them," did not involve proficiency in Sanskrit, as he once alleged, or in a dozen tongues.

The mystery surrounding Berg involved his self-proclaimed exploits as a U.S. spy both during and after his baseball career. His most noted supposed escapade while still active was to take home movies of Tokyo from the roof of a hospital building during a 1934 barnstorming tour of Japan that, he claimed, were later used to plan the 1942 air raids led by General Jimmy Doolittle. Secretive about his avocation, he nevertheless frequented foreign embassy social functions and unhesitatingly introduced teammates to President Franklin D. Roosevelt.

His baseball career ended, Berg worked for the OSS during World War II, tracking the whereabouts of German scientists. The information he gathered may or may not have enabled U.S. forces to capture Werner Heisenberg, head of the Nazi atomic bomb effort, and several other noted nuclear physicists, in 1945. Berg rarely spoke of his wartime experiences until the late 1960s when, out of financial necessity, he agreed to write a book. The project collapsed when, at a first meeting, the young editor assigned to the project glowingly praised the prospective author's movies on the mistaken assumption that he was about to sign a contract with Moe of The Three Stooges.

BILL BERGEN

Counting all players who had at least 1,000 plate appearances, Bergen was the worst hitter in baseball history. In 11 seasons for the Reds and Dodgers from 1901 to 1911, the catcher averaged only .170 in 3,028 official at bats. The fact that he was a first-string receiver for most of his career suggests what a defensive wizard he was.

MARTY BERGEN

Bergen provided baseball with one of its more chilling stories at the close of the 19th century. A member of the Braves and brother of Bill Bergen, he got into the habit of jumping the team for days at a time because, he said, his family needed him. All his

coming and going divided the club between those who warned the front office that he should be treated with kid gloves and those who resented what they perceived as favored treatment. With the sudden death of the catcher's son in 1898, however, teammates overcame their rancor and united behind him, reminding him daily that he was vital to the club's success. The sympathy boomeranged when Bergen said the players reminded him too much of his son in their love for him and he resumed his periodic returns to his farm. By the end of the 1899 season the clubhouse was united in the opposite way, warning owner Arthur Soden they would not come back to Boston the following year if Bergen were still on the team. Their threat became academic on January 19, 1900, when Bergen used a razor and an ax to kill his wife, three-year-old son, six-year-old daughter, and himself. Outfielder Billy Hamilton was the sole Braves representative at the funeral.

YOGI BERRA (Hall of Fame, 1972)

As a player, Berra carried a public image as a lovable, cuddly figure with a propensity for malapropisms along with one of the most potent clutch bats in the American League; as a manager, he tended to show the crustier side of his personality, although this did not prevent him from winning a pennant with a New York club in each league.

Over a 19-year playing career (all but four games of it with the Yankees), Berra batted .285 with 358 home runs. The winner of three Most Valuable Player awards (1951, 1954, and 1955), the lefty-swinging catcher reached the 20-homer mark 11 times (10 of them consecutive from 1949 and 1958); topped 100 RBIs five times; and holds records for appearing in the most World Series (14) and the most Series games (75), as well as for collecting the most Series hits (71). A notorious bad-ball hitter who once whacked a one-bounce delivery from Early Wynn for a double, Berra nonetheless connected often enough to keep his yearly strikeout totals between 12 and 38, and to lead an otherwise potent Yankees offense in RBIs every year from 1949 to 1955. He was particularly productive in late-inning situations, to the point that he was often walked in extra innings even though he represented the potential winning run.

A defensive liability when he first joined the club in 1946, Berra was often used in the outfield as well as behind the plate until manager Casey Stengel hired Hall of Fame receiver Bill Dickey to tutor the young catcher. The mentor succeeded to the extent that his pupil eventually became regarded as the best backstop in the league at pouncing on bunts and calling a game. The most enduring image of the catcher is, in fact, of him with his limbs wrapped around Don Larsen, after having called the pitches in the righthander's 1956 World Series perfect game.

The short, squat figure in that picture squared perfectly with the author of innumerable Yogiisms. Among the most widely quoted are: "It ain't over till it's over"; "It gets late early out here"; "Nobody goes there anymore; it's too crowded"; "It's déjà vu all over again"; "The other teams could make trouble for us if they win"; "We made too many wrong mistakes"; "Why buys good luggage? You only use it when you travel"; "They were as close as Damon and Runyan"; and "You can observe a lot by watching." Although the unwitting witticisms endeared Berra to Yankees fans and others, the warm popular image was the creation of broadcasters Phil Rizzuto (an ex-teammate) and Joe Garagiola (a boyhood friend from St. Louis). Actually, the man who retired in 1963 and took over as the Yankees pilot the following year was a successful and somewhat grumpy New Jersey businessman with more baseball sense than his image allowed. Hired primarily to offset the widespread popularity of Stengel, who had signed on with the Mets after his firing by the Yankees, Berra made the 1964 season memorable for his altercation with infielder Phil Linz over a harmonica; his sourness that had both players and reporters complaining constantly to general manager Ralph Houk; an unexpected pennant; and an equally unexpected (but long-planned) firing in favor of Johnny Keane, whose Cardinals had just defeated the Yankees in the World Series.

Joining Stengel's coaching staff in 1965, Berra served under four managers in Shea Stadium before succeeding Gil Hodges as pilot in 1972. Nominally in charge during the "You gotta believe" Mets pennant drive the following year, the manager lost points in the front office for allowing players a much freer rein in making on-field decisions than chairman M. Donald Grant thought wise. Grant fired Berra in August 1975 on the grounds that he had lost control of the club. Reemerging in 1984 to pilot the Yankees a second time, Berra brought a mediocre club home

third and accepted owner George Steinbrenner's accolades and promises that he would have all of 1985 to bring another pennant to the Bronx; instead, he was replaced 17 games into the season by Billy Martin in his fourth tour of duty. Vowing he would not step foot in Yankee Stadium again until Steinbrenner was no longer in charge, Berra packed his bags and didn't return until the owner apologized in 1998. Since throwing out the first ball at Opening Day in 1999, and especially since the deaths of Mickey Mantle and Joe DiMaggio, Berra has been the franchise's chief link back to New York's mid-century dynasty.

BILL BEVENS

Prior to Don Larsen's perfect game in 1956, Bevens came closer than anyone to pitching a World Series no-hitter. With only one out to go against the Dodgers in the fourth game of the 1947 Series, however, the Yankees righthander yielded a double to pinch-hitter Cookie Lavagetto that scored two runners and saddled Bevens with a 2–1 loss. It was the last game Bevens pitched in the major leagues.

HUGO BEZDEK

Bezdek was the most improbably successful manager in National League history. When he was drafted for the job by the 1917 Pirates after Honus Wagner had a change of heart about piloting the cellar club after only five games, he was the organization's business manager; before that, he had been a star football player and wrestler in college, then football coach at the University of Oregon. If his charges were waiting for his inexperience to show up, they weren't disappointed when he signaled for such plays as having runners on both second and third try to score on a suicide squeeze. But Bezdek got those glitches out of his system during the final months of the season, then returned to lead the Pirates over .500 in both 1918 and 1919. But just when Pittsburgh players and sportswriters were warming to the unlikely manager, he quit baseball to coach the Penn State football team. Bezdek never went back to the major leagues, though he did end up taking three different college teams to the Rose Bowl and coaching the NFL Cleveland Rams.

LOU BIERBAUER

A second baseman with solid if unglamorous credentials over 13 major league seasons, Bierbauer has been remembered mostly for his role in the naming of a franchise; less well known is that the episode resulted in the demise of an entire major league. Having jumped the American Association Athletics for the Brooklyn Players League club in 1890, the infielder's contract should have reverted to Philadelphia when the PL collapsed after one season. But when new Philadelphia owner J. Earl Wagner neglected to include the names of Bierbauer and outfielder Harry Stovey on the list of those he claimed as spoils of the war, the pair went over to the National League, the former with Pittsburgh and the latter with Boston. Pittsburgh president J. Palmer O'Neill soon became "J. Pirate O'Neill" in the newspapers, and his club has been called after his less-than-flattering nickname ever since. More significant, the AA withdrew from the National Agreement over the piracy, precipitating a new trade war in which it was completely overmatched; the circuit lasted only one more season.

IVAN BIGLER

Bigler's single appearance in a major league game, as a pinch-runner for the 1917 St. Louis Browns, developed into a decades-long saga of arcane research. Listed in early editions of Hy Turkin and S. C. Thompson's *The Official Encyclopedia of Baseball*, his name was later thought to be a typographically erroneous rendering of Hall of Famer George Sisler's. But more recent investigation has established that Bigler actually did have the briefest of cups of coffee.

W. E. BILHEIMER

A St. Louis insurance executive, Bilheimer conceived the first Knothole Gang while a member of the local syndicate headed by James Jones that purchased the Cardinals in 1916. His scheme, advanced as an antidote for juvenile delinquency, allowed investors to reserve one bleacher seat for a young fan with every $50 of stock purchased. Adopted several years later as a pet project of general manager Branch Rickey, the program proved a valuable tool in building several generations of Cardinals fans. Rickey later brought the idea with him to Brooklyn.

STEVE BILKO

The only thing as popular as the arrival of major league baseball in California was Bilko. A bulky first baseman as noted for his gargantuan whiffs as for his occasional titanic blasts, he gained an enormous following among minor league fans in the Los Angeles area in the early 1950s. Both the Dodgers in 1958 and the Angels in 1961 made sure he was aboard for their inaugural California seasons.

JACK BILLINGHAM

Billingham was as close as the Big Red Machine had to a pitching ace for more than one season in the 1970s. Although he never won 20 games, he came close in both 1973 and 1974, with 19 victories. At 0.36 for seven games in 1972, 1975, and 1976, the righthander also holds the mark for the best World Series ERA over at least 25 innings. On Opening Day in 1974, Billingham gave up Hank Aaron's record-tying 714th home run.

MAX BISHOP

Known as Camera Eye for his mental picture of the strike zone, Bishop's skill at waiting out pitchers for walks boosted a lifetime .271 batting average to a .423 on-base percentage, the largest gap between the two statistics for players with at least 4,000 at bats. The second baseman and leadoff batter for the Athletics from the early 1920s to the early 1930s, he collected 100 hits and 100 walks in seven seasons, with more bases on balls than safeties in five of those years; he also set a major league record by walking eight times in a doubleheader on May 21, 1930.

EWELL BLACKWELL

Although he finished his career only four games over .500 (82–78), Blackwell generated more dread among National League batters than any other righthander in the late 1940s and 1950s. Labeled The Whip for a treacherous sidearm, buggy-whip delivery, he totally dominated the league for Cincinnati in 1947, at one point winning 16 games in a row on his way to leading NL hurlers in victories, strikeouts, and complete games. More astonishing, he came within two outs of duplicating teammate Johnny Vander Meer's 1938 feat of pitching successive no-hitters—holding the Braves hitless on June 18 and then getting one out in the ninth inning against the Dodgers on June 22 before Eddie Stanky managed a single. Although he had a couple of other good seasons of 17 and 16 victories for bad Reds teams, he was eventually undone by a kidney operation, an appendectomy, and an arm injury.

CLIFF BLANKENSHIP

Blankenship, a backup catcher for the 1907 Senators, had a drastic impact on the future of the franchise by breaking his finger. Unable to play, he was told to go to Kansas and Idaho to scout a couple of prospects. In Wichita he signed outfielder Clyde Milan; in Weiser he inked Walter Johnson.

ELMER BLASCO

An advertising and sales manager for Rawlings Sporting Goods, Blasco was the engine behind the Gold Glove awards, first conferred in 1957. His promotional idea was cosponsored by *The Sporting News,* which initially entrusted the choice of annual all-defensive teams to a panel of journalists. Since 1965, the voting has been restricted to major league managers and coaches.

Like all awards, the Gold Gloves have come in for substantial criticism. One common plaint is that the balloting managers and coaches have been lazy about their selections, more often than not choosing players based on past reputation rather than present performance. The most indefensible choice attributed to this habit occurred in 1999, when Rafael Palmiero of the Rangers was given the AL nod for fielding at first base in spite of having only played 28 games there during the season.

STEVE BLASS

Blass suffered as mysterious an end to a dominating career as anybody in major league history. After anchoring the Pittsburgh staff for several years, including leading the National League in winning percentage in 1968 (.750, 18–6) and recording 19 victories in 1972, the righthander showed up at spring training in 1973 completely unable to throw strikes. While his ERA blew up from 2.49 to 9.85, he was sent through a gauntlet of doctors, psychiatrists, hypnotists, and minor league pitching coaches for an explanation—all to no avail. Theories ran the gamut from some deep disturbance at watching teammate Bob Moose wild-pitch home the pennant-winning run for Cincinnati in 1972 to a profound trauma over the off-season death of Roberto Clemente. Whatever the cause, Blass was out of baseball after a final major league appearance in 1974.

RON BLOMBERG

When he came to bat for the Yankees in Boston's Fenway Park on Opening Day of 1973, the lefty-swinging Blomberg became baseball's first designated hitter. Otherwise a first baseman, Blomberg hit .293 in eight seasons, all but one of them with the Yankees.

VIDA BLUE

The least of Blue's accomplishments over a roller-coaster 17-year career between 1969 and 1986 were his battles with Charlie Finley, his reliance on a president of the United States for contract-negotiation advice, and his prison term for dealing drugs. Still, these episodes ultimately overshadowed the southpaw's 209 victories, three 20-win seasons, and 301 strikeouts in 1971.

Blue became a household name in 1971 when, pitching for Oakland, he took both MVP and Cy Young honors in the American League for a record of 24–8 and a league-leading 1.82 ERA. Having already spun a no-hitter in his rookie year of 1970, the lefty's performance was the biggest media event of the year—translated into a *Time* cover, several television commercials, and increased attendance whenever he was due to take the mound. Aware that part of the hurler's appeal was his unusual name, Finley pressed publicly and relentlessly to gild the lily by having him drop the Vida in favor of True, but Blue refused, in the process winning even more publicity. What he didn't reject, on the other hand, was an off-season observation by President Richard Nixon that he was the most underpaid player in the game. Blue promptly hired an agent to have Nixon's case made to Finley. This led to a spring training holdout in 1972, an eventual compromise agreement—and a disastrous season in which the unprepared hurler went only 6–10 and was booed constantly by the same fans who hadn't been able to get enough of him the year before. His main consolation for the year was in nailing down Oakland's pennant win over Detroit with four innings of brilliant relief in the American League Championship Series.

Blue rebounded in 1973 for another 20-win season and settled in as the ace of the Athletics staff for the next few years. Then, in 1976, with Finley unloading all his high-priced stars, he was sold to the Yankees for $1.5 million. Commissioner Bowie Kuhn put a hold on the deal (and another sale of pitcher Rollie Fingers and outfielder Joe Rudi to Boston), however, and for two weeks it remained in limbo until the transaction was canceled "in the best interests of baseball." The delay proved pivotal when

Oakland ended up losing the division title to Kansas City by only 2 1/2 games. Once again in 1977 Finley sought to sell the pitcher, this time for $1.75 million to Cincinnati, and once again Kuhn stepped in to say no, arguing that the Reds were already too dominant in the National League. Finally, before the 1978 season, Blue was sent packing to the Giants. The deal, which also brought the owner $300,000, set a major league record in its exchange of one player for seven—pitchers Dave Heaverlo, Alan Wirth, John Henry Johnson, and Phil Huffman, catcher Gary Alexander, shortstop Mario Guerrero, and outfielder Gary Thomasson.

Blue spent four seasons with the Giants before returning to the AL, with the Royals in 1982. What initially appeared to be only a deal for a pitcher who had seen his best days turned into a full-fledged scandal in 1983, when he was revealed as the main source of drugs for teammates Jerry Martin, Willie Wilson, and Willie Mays Aikens. It also turned out that Blue was the principal source of information to the police about club users, bringing him as many cold shoulders from players around the league as indignation from the Kansas City front office, which promptly released him. When Kuhn once again stepped into the fray to impose one-year suspensions on the four players, an arbitration panel allowed the order to stand only against Blue, as the pusher; all four players, however, ended up doing three-month jail terms after original felony charges had been dropped to misdemeanors. After his forced sidelining in 1984, the southpaw persuaded the Giants that he was undergoing rehabilitation, and returned to San Francisco for a final two seasons.

BERT BLYLEVEN

Blyleven set the gopher record for a season in 1986, when, as a member of the Twins, he yielded 50 home runs. The righthander nevertheless managed to win 17 games. His negative mark was helped by having to pitch in the Metrodome, as well as by his league-leading 271 innings. During his 22-year career (between 1970 and 1992) for the Twins and several other clubs, Blyleven compiled a 287–250 record, also joining the handful of pitchers to register 3,000 strikeouts (3,701). In 1977 he was a key figure in baseball's last four-club trade, involving the Rangers, Braves, Mets, and Pirates.

WADE BOGGS

Boggs gained as much attention for his near-fanatical rituals and a long-running adulterous affair as for his lifetime .328 average over 18 seasons (1982–99). The winner of five batting crowns (1983, 1985–88) while with the Red Sox, the lefty swinger is the only player in major league history to collect 200 or more hits in seven consecutive seasons (1983–89). Although often criticized as a one-dimensional spray hitter, he also collected 100 walks four times; scored 100 runs seven times; and, moving from his customary leadoff spot to third in the batting order for a good part of the 1987 season, responded with 24 homers. Among his more impressive accomplishments was reaching base 340 times in two different seasons; among the three players who had previously crashed that barrier, only Babe Ruth and Williams did so more than once.

Complementing an almost mechanical swing was an array of rituals Boggs credited with his success: eating chicken before every game, running wind sprints at precisely 7:17 P.M. every evening, drawing a Hebrew letter in the dirt every time he stepped into the batter's box, etc. The 1988 revelation that he had been involved in an extramarital affair for some years with Margo Adams added a human dimension to his image, but it was hardly a welcome addition, especially after Adams, who traveled with the Red Sox on the road, revealed the escapades of some other members of the team in a palimony suit. The predictable clubhouse tussles and calls for getting rid of the third baseman ended when he won his fifth batting crown. But after slipping to a .259 average in 1992, he was allowed to depart as a free agent to the Yankees, where he collected four more .300 seasons.

In the 1996 World Series Boggs drew a 10th-inning bases-loaded walk to put the Yankees ahead in the fourth game, and the New Yorkers went on to win the Series and give him his only world championship ring. After one more season in the Bronx, he signed with Tampa Bay, for whom he collected his 3,000th hit on August 7, 1999. He is the only member of the 3,000-hit club to reach that plateau with a home run—the blast coming off Cleveland's Chris Haney. He retired at the end of the 1999 season with 3,010 hits.

TOMMY BOND

An early curveballer, Bond is the only pitcher to win 40 or more games in three consecutive seasons, in the process becoming the major leagues' first 100-

game winner and pitching Boston to National League pennants in 1877 and 1878. The righthander might have reached the century mark even sooner, except that while with Hartford in 1876, he accused manager Bob Ferguson of throwing games. That brought him a suspension for the final third of the season from club president Morgan Bulkeley, who sided with the pilot.

BARRY BONDS

Because of a succession of contracts he signed with the Giants ($43.75 million for six years prior to the 1993 season, $11.75 million for two years in 1998, and $20 million for one year in 2001), Bonds's on-field talents and contributions to winning clubs will never be described as invaluable. But at the beginning of the new century he had achieved enough to be considered an accredited member of a super-Hall of Fame.

For starters, Bonds in 2001 had the greatest offensive year by any player in baseball history: 73 home runs to shatter Mark McGwire's single-season record, an .863 slugging percentage that eclipsed Babe Ruth's .847 mark in 1920, 177 walks for breaking another Ruth record dating to 1923, and 107 extra-base hits for tying Chuck Klein's 1930 National League effort. In addition, his .515 on-base percentage was the highest in the National League since John McGraw's .547 all the way back in 1899. What it all added up to for the lefty-swinging left fielder—who also had a career-high 137 RBIs with a .328 batting average—was an unprecedented fourth MVP trophy, to go along with those he took in 1990, 1992, and 1993.

Entering his 17th big league season in 2002, Bonds ranked sixth on the all-time home run list (567), sixth in walks (1,724), and seventh in slugging (.585). He also had a record 355 intentional passes, 484 stolen bases, and had matched his father Bobby's mark of five 30–30 seasons. It has been all but an afterthought that he has also been the league's best defensive left fielder (if with a weak arm) practically since joining Pittsburgh in the 1980s.

For all his diamond feats, Bonds has been dogged throughout his major league career by his failure in the postseason and by a personality that has resisted the kind of public embrace extended to lesser players. Although he was a vital cog in three straight Division wins by the Pirates between 1990 and 1992

and by the Giants in 1997 and 2000, he has been completely stymied in postseason play—hitting merely .207 in Division Series and an even more dismal .191 in the LCS. His projection as an aloof, sometimes surly, multimillionaire with an ability to hit lots of baseballs to distant climes rebounded against him during the 2001 season, when his pursuit of McGwire's record attracted nowhere near the media interest that McGwire's own chase of the Roger Maris record in 1998 had; in fact, even as Bonds eclipsed the three-year-old mark, the media sometimes seemed more interested in talking about its own relative lack of interest. Otherwise, the outfielder's incredible season on the field shared print with stories about his isolated locker in the Giants clubhouse, his mutually cold relations with teammates, and strains that had developed with manager Dusty Baker and his godfather Willie Mays. When he sought to come across as a warmer and fuzzier Bonds toward the end of the season, his effort was written off as an attempt to influence the free agent contract he would be seeking during the winter. In fact, mainly because of his age, he ultimately accepted arbitration to remain with San Francisco.

BOBBY BONDS

The father of Barry Bonds was a player of enormous parts who managed only a decent whole. In a 14-year career that extended from 1968 to 1981, the righthand-hitting outfielder was the only major leaguer, aside from his son, to combine power and speed to record five different seasons with at least 30 home runs and 30 stolen bases. At the same time, however, he struck out enough to take both first and second places for whiffs in a season, fanning 189 times in 1970 and 187 times in 1969. He also struck out at least 120 times in eight other years. Making Bonds's situation even more anomalous was the fact that, strikeouts notwithstanding, a parade of managers insisted, because of his speed, on using him as a leadoff hitter; this resulted in six different seasons of his scoring at least 100 runs, but, despite his slugging, only two seasons of 100 RBIs.

Bonds entered the major leagues with the Giants, becoming the first major leaguer since Bill Duggleby in 1898 to hit a grand slam home run in his maiden game. After San Francisco despaired of its promotion of him as the second coming of Willie Mays, Bonds was dealt to the Yankees after the 1974 season in a controversial trade for Bobby Murcer that did neither of the sluggers much good. From that point on, Bonds was considered a power solution for several teams (Angels, White Sox, Rangers, Indians) that needed a year or less before deciding that his strikeout rate was too high a price to pay for his round-trippers and stolen bases; his travels and his power enabled him to set a record by hitting 30 or more homers in a season with five different clubs. It didn't help his case, either, that his raw numbers had made him one of the higher-paid players of the 1970s. He closed out his career with two painful years with the Cardinals and Cubs, during which it became obvious that leg injuries and his mid-30s had robbed him of his speed.

ZEKE BONURA

Bonura was a slugging first baseman for the Senators in the 1930s whose defense usually had fans and teammates covering their eyes. One of his patented plays was to wave off pitchers on ground balls and lose the race to the first-base bag. His most ardent fan was Vice President John Nance Garner, who spent every free moment at Griffith Stadium and who insisted that Bonura come over for a hug and a handshake every time the slugger crossed home plate after a home run.

BRET BOONE

When he made his debut with the Mariners in 1992, second baseman Boone, grandson of infielder Ray Boone and son of catcher Bob Boone, became baseball's first third-generation major leaguer.

IKE BOONE

Boone was the greatest minor league hitter of all time, compiling an average of .370 in a career that spanned 1920 to 1937. A conspicuous liability in the field for his slowness afoot, the lefty-swinging outfielder failed to stick in the big leagues despite a .319 average in all or parts of eight scattered seasons with four clubs. His best major league marks were back-to-back .333 and .330 averages as a regular in 1924 and 1925 for the Red Sox; his best minor league year was 1929, when he hit .407 in 198 games in the Pacific Coast League.

SCOTT BORAS

Next to obeisant owners, nobody has been more responsible for skyrocketing player salaries than agent Boras. A one-time minor league infielder for the Cardinals, he found it far more lucrative to represent high school and college players drafted by the majors. His first big negotiating success came in 1991, when he got the Yankees to pay $1.5 million for pitcher Brien Taylor (who hurt his arm and never reached the big leagues). A few years later he exploited loopholes to get unprecedented pacts for teenagers Travis Lee and Matt White, inevitably drawing descriptions as a Svengali cruelly exposing his clients to the disfavor of grandstands and the disgruntlement of veteran teammates. But another client, righthander Kevin Brown, had little problem playing Trilby after the 1998 season, signing with the Dodgers for $105 million, the first nine-figure pact in the game's history. Boras went that 250 percent better following the 2000 season, when he secured a mind-boggling agreement with the Rangers paying shortstop Alex Rodriguez $252 million.

JOE BORDEN

Calling himself Josephus the Phenomenal, Borden, while a member of the Philadelphia White Stockings, pitched the only no-hitter in the five-year history of the National Association, on July 28, 1875. The following year, on April 22, he won the National League's first game for Boston (a 6–5 victory in Philadelphia), then pitched the National League's first no-hitter, against Cincinnati, on May 23. The righthander is still not officially credited with this last feat, however, because official scorer O. P. Caylor idiosyncratically recorded walks as hits, and Borden allowed two bases on balls that day. Despite these highlights, Borden had only an 11–12 record when Boston president Nathaniel Apollonio released him, and, in a ploy to get out from under the pitcher's $2,000-per-year contract, insisted he work as a groundskeeper. The ex-pitcher took up his new duties until the owner offered a generous buyout, which Borden accepted, leaving baseball at age 22.

HANK BOROWY

Nobody is more responsible for the last appearance of the Cubs in a World Series than Borowy. A righthander for the Yankees, he had won 10 games by mid-July in 1945 when owner Larry MacPhail suddenly put him on waivers for reasons never satisfactorily explained. Chicago put in a claim, purchased him for $97,000, and then rode his 11–2 record the rest of the way to the National League flag.

Not only did Borowy become the third 20th-century pitcher (after Patsy Flaherty and Joe McGinnity) to win 20 games in a season split between two major leagues, but his 2.13 ERA was also the best in the NL. Most speculation around the deal has traced it to MacPhail's emergency need of cash.

BABE BORTON

Borton, who came to the Yankees as part of the 1913 deal that dumped Hal Chase on the White Sox, failed to live up to the standards established by his fellow first baseman. First, Borton was nowhere near the hitter Chase was, batting only .130 before being sent to the minors. Second, when Borton was blacklisted for crooked play, it wasn't from the major leagues, as in the case of Chase, but from the Pacific Coast League, in a 1921 scandal that involved five of the circuit's eight teams. If there was any closing of the circle, it was in the fact that Chase too was implicated in the PCL game fixing.

GENE BOSSARD

Bossard was the most illustrious member of the first family of groundskeeping while employed by the White Sox between 1941 and 1983. Bill Veeck, for one, praised him for helping Chicago snatch a few extra wins every season. In 1967, for example, the area around home plate became known as Camp Swampy when Bossard dug up and watered the dirt as an aid to Chicago sinkerballers. Conversely, he used clay and gasoline to harden soil if the opposition happened to be starting a sinker specialist. Other tricks included lowering or raising the bullpen mounds of adversaries to disturb their rhythm when they entered a game; keeping the grass long in front of slow-footed Chicago infielders; and adding more paint to the foul lines to tilt balls back into fair territory when the home team had gifted bunters.

Bossard's father, Emil, had held the same position with the Indians in the 1930s; Gene's son Roger succeeded him with Chicago in 1983; and other members of the family—Harold (with Cleveland in the 1960s), Marshall (also with Cleveland, in the 1970s), and Brian (with the Padres in the 1980s)—were similarly employed.

JIM BOTTOMLEY (Hall of Fame, 1974)

Bottomley was the first player to come through Branch Rickey's farm system—and almost the cause

of its demise. Promoted to the Cardinals in 1922, the lefthand-hitting first baseman was told by Syracuse owner Ernest Landgraf to stay put until Rickey reached that city. What Landgraf didn't say was that despite his commitment to develop Bottomley for St. Louis as part of a deal in which the Cardinals owned half of the Syracuse franchise, he had had second thoughts and had threatened Rickey with putting the power hitter up for auction unless he received more money. With the validity of his farm system idea at stake, the St. Louis general manager got into an all-night bargaining and screaming session with Landgraf, at the end of which the Cardinals had to buy the other half of the minor league club to assure the delivery of Bottomley. It was a situation that Rickey and St. Louis president Sam Breadon didn't allow to happen again, from then on insisting on total control or other contractual safeguards with the minor league teams in the franchise chain.

As for Bottomley, he had a 16-year career during which he averaged .310 and played a key role in four St. Louis pennants. Among his biggest years were 1925, when he batted .367 and led the National League in hits and doubles; 1926, when he led the way in doubles and RBIs; and 1928, when he took MVP honors for averaging .325 and setting the pace in triples, home runs, and RBIs. In that season he also became the only player in major league history to swat 40 doubles, 20 triples, and 40 homers. Over his first nine seasons he never hit fewer than 31 doubles, and for another string of six years he drove in at least 100 runs. In 1924 Bottomley established a single-game mark of 12 RBIs—a record tied by St. Louis outfielder Mark Whiten in 1993.

LOU BOUDREAU (Hall of Fame, 1970)

Boudreau was so popular in Cleveland that he turned the quintessential populist Bill Veeck into the Grinch Who Stole Baseball. And that was *before* the righthand-hitting shortstop and manager led the Indians to one of its only two world championships, in 1948.

After a couple of brief stints with the club at the end of the 1930s, Boudreau took over shortstop in 1940, batting .295 and driving in 101 runs in his first full season. In the years that followed, he won a batting crown (1944), led the American League in doubles (1941, 1944, and 1947), and collected an MVP trophy (in 1948 for a .355 average with 18 home runs and 106 RBIs). In the field he teamed with Roy Mack and then Joe Gordon to give the AL its steadiest double-play combination.

Boudreau the player was also Boudreau the manager as of 1942 and for most of the rest of his 15-year playing career, and that was where the trouble with Veeck began. Taking over the Cleveland franchise from John Sherwin and Alva Bradley in 1946, Veeck made little secret of his desire to replace Boudreau as pilot in favor of somebody (Casey Stengel was the most often-mentioned name) who would provide more colorful daily quotes to the press. When the shortstop made it clear, however, that he would find it difficult to play for the Indians under another dugout boss, Veeck held his fire, since he had no intention of trading away his star player. But then, at the end of the 1947 season, the Browns stepped forward with a tempting offer for Boudreau that would have included slugging shortstop Vern Stephens. As soon as Cleveland newspapers got wind of the proposal, Boudreau supporters organized protest demonstrations and circulated petitions demanding Veeck leave town instead of their hero. Veeck ran all over Cleveland, going from bar to restaurant to bar, to admit as personally as he could that he had been harboring impure thoughts while simultaneously denying that the St. Louis trade had been his idea. The upshot was that Boudreau was given an extension on his contract as player-manager, with Veeck grabbing the consolation prize of assigning his own coaches to the club.

In 1948 Boudreau paid back his fan support by leading Cleveland to its first pennant since 1920, dramatizing his own contribution by clouting two home runs in a special playoff game against Boston. The icing on the cake was a World Series victory against the Braves.

The years that followed were nowhere near as gratifying. Moving over to the Red Sox in the early 1950s as a manager with only a handful of at bats left in him, Boudreau discovered a city slow to forget that he had defeated both Boston teams in 1948. He only made his situation worse by announcing before the 1952 season that no one then on the club, including local demigod Ted Williams, would be untouchable if the right deal came along. In 1955 he took over the Athletics in their first transplanted year in Kansas City, and was a largely negligible presence over the next couple of years as the franchise

shipped its best players to the Yankees in one suspicious trade after another.

Boudreau's last opportunity to wear a uniform was in 1960, when he was asked to come out of the broadcasting booth to take over the Cubs. Despite not being able to lift the team out of the cellar, he demanded a two-year contract from Phil Wrigley at the end of the season and was turned down. While Boudreau returned to broadcasting Chicago games, Wrigley replaced him with his rotating managers scheme involving a handful of coaches.

JIM BOUTON

Bouton's early 1970s best-seller *Ball Four* scandalized both the baseball establishment and stiff-necked players by naming names in a diaristic narrative of the righthander's experiences with the 1969 Seattle Pilots and Houston Astros and recollections of his years with the Yankees. Although most of the uproar over the book was because of its casual depiction of the sex-obsessed lives of major leaguers, it also unnerved front office executives with its specific instances of settling rosters through racial quotas and of management hypocrisy in contract negotiations. Helped to the best seller list by Commissioner Bowie Kuhn's clumsy attempts to have Bouton apologize for it, the book generated still more hypocrisy when it was attacked by Mickey Mantle and Billy Martin for "betraying" player confidences; while maintaining their public contempt of Bouton even decades later, Mantle and Martin didn't decline the help of ghostwriters to write their own (boastful) versions of major league womanizing and carousing. The attack from Mantle, in particular, was seen as a key reason for the Yankees failure to invite Bouton back for annual Old Timers Day festivities. Only in the late 1990s, after the Hall of Fame outfielder had denied ever supporting the ostracism, did the pitcher join other veterans for the yearly nostalgia show.

Before becoming identified with his writing, Bouton had distinguished himself as a 21-game and 18-game winner for the pennant-winning Yankees in 1963 and 1964, respectively. Following his stint with Houston, he turned to sportscasting for several years, then tried to make a comeback as a knuckle-baller with the 1978 Braves. Although the effort was buoyed by Ted Turner's cable superstation, it ended after one victory in five games.

BOB BOWMAN

Bowman threw one of the most resounding bean-balls in baseball history when he decked Joe Medwick of the Dodgers in 1940. The St. Louis right-hander uncorked the pitch in Medwick's very first plate appearance against his former Cardinals team-mates, less than a week after he had been purchased by Brooklyn for a whopping $135,000. It also followed an angry exchange between the players before the game, making it clear that there had been nothing accidental about the delivery. Aside from precipitating an ugly brawl between the teams, the beanball knocked out Medwick and made him a relatively more tentative hitter for the rest of his career. More than that, it caused enraged Brooklyn president Larry MacPhail to demand that the district attorney's office open an investigation into what he called Beanball, Inc.—the suspicion that all National League pitchers were deliberately throwing at Dodgers hitters. As ludicrous as the charge might have sounded, it touched the right publicity nerve in the wake of the Murder, Inc. investigation, to the point that Burton Turkus, the prosecutor who had nailed Lepke Buchalter and his criminal associates, did indeed call in several Brooklyn and St. Louis officials for questioning. Still another consequence of the Bowman pitch was that it prompted MacPhail to order prototypes of batting helmets (actually, bands around the rim of uniform caps) for his players.

CLETE BOYER

Brooks Robinson had little on Boyer as a defensive third baseman, and there were years that he showed he was no automatic out at the plate, either. But Boyer's distinctions go beyond what he accomplished on the field. For one thing, he was one of seven brothers—the most in history—to have played in organized baseball; pitcher Cloyd and third baseman Ken also made the majors, while Wayne, Lynn, Ron, and Len had to be satisfied with the minors. When Clete joined the Athletics in 1955, he also became a symbol of the Yankees grip on the Kansas City franchise. Impressed by the infielder but not at all interested in carrying him on its roster for two years as a bonus baby, New York reached an under-the-table agreement to have the Athletics warehouse him while he was gaining experience, then grabbed him in a 1957 trade. Near the end of his career, with the 1971 Braves, Boyer got into a contract dispute

with general manager Paul Richards, was released, and found himself able to latch on only with Hawaii in the Pacific Coast League. From there he became the first professional American player ever traded to the Japanese leagues.

ALVA BRADLEY

Bradley was Cleveland's longest-running owner, heading the organization through its all-but-invisible period of 1928 to 1946. Only once in that span did the Indians get within single digits behind the American League pennant winner, and that was in 1940, when the club folded in the last week of the season against the Tigers. Although he and his brother Chuck owned considerable prime real estate in the center of Cleveland and made even more money from the profitable retail operations they installed on it, Bradley never spent a nickel when a penny would do. For years he refused to give the title of general manager to baseball operations chief Cy Slapnicka as an economy move, and he was inspired as much by thrift as intuition in giving the managing job to shortstop Lou Boudreau in 1942. But by the mid-1940s Bradley's penny-pinching had precipitated an organizational mess; typical of the team's foresight was that five members of the board of directors were widows who had little of their late husbands' interest in the Indians or in baseball. When the franchise's largest stockholder, John Sherwin, insisted on selling out to Bill Veeck, Bradley had little choice but to follow suit.

LAURIE BRADY

A one-time belly dancer and nightclub owner, Brady was on the payroll of the 1976 Oakland A's as an astrologer. She came to the attention of club owner Charles Finley initially by accurately predicting the team's five consecutive division titles between 1971 and 1975. Under Finley's orders, she sent daily charts throughout the 1976 campaign to A's pilot Chuck Tanner on the lunar dispositions of each and every one of his players—evaluations that went directly into Tanner's wastepaper basket. When Oakland finished second to Kansas City, Brady was fired.

BOBBY BRAGAN

A Branch Rickey protégé, Bragan had a stormy career as both player and manager. To Rickey's stated disappointment, he was one of the handful of Brooklyn players who refused to play with Jackie Robinson when the Dodgers announced their intention of breaking the color line in 1947. Although the Alabama-born infielder later said he regretted his stand, some of the same racist charges were in the air during his stint as manager of the Braves in the 1960s. As a tactician, Bragan was a study in unorthodoxy, at one point in Pittsburgh putting lead-footed sluggers one-two-three in the lineup because "they're the only ones who know how to hit, so they'll get up more this way." He became the center of an even longer controversy in Cleveland, where local legend attributed him with putting a hex on the team in retaliation for being fired during the 1958 season. Although Bragan himself always said the hex story was the fruit of a disc jockey's imagination, it gained sufficient currency (and promotion appeal) for the Indians to bring in a witch during the 1986 season to take the alleged spell off the team. The Cleveland firing also gave rise to one of baseball's more famous quotes, when Bragan related how general manager Frank Lane called him into his office and declared: "Bobby, I don't know how we're going to get along without you, but starting tomorrow, we're going to try."

RALPH BRANCA

Branca threw the most infamous pitch in National League history on October 3, 1951, when his one-strike delivery to Bobby Thomson in the ninth inning of the third game of a playoff duel was belted for a three-run homer and a pennant victory for the Giants over the Dodgers. The Brooklyn righthander had been summoned from the bullpen to face Thomson after New York had put the tying runs on base against faltering starter Don Newcombe. In the decades since the blast Branca and Thomson have made countless public appearances together to commemorate what many consider baseball's single most thrilling moment. Fifty years after the fact, in 2001, they got as close to old passions as could have been imagined following disclosures by then-Giants catcher Sal Yvars that New York had been stealing opposition signs all season. Thomson denied he had been tipped off to Branca's pitch.

If Branca's presence on the mound cost the Dodgers a pennant in 1951, his absence from the hill cost the club another flag, in 1946. Furious that the pitcher had given him a hard time in contract negotiations, club boss Branch Rickey insisted that he be used only for mop-up duties for the first five months of the 1946 campaign. Only when Brooklyn was in dire need of another starter, in September, did Rickey cancel the order, permitting Branca to hurl a couple of shutouts over the final weeks of the season. When the Dodgers finished in a tie with the Cardinals, the pitcher was given a playoff game start but didn't fare any better against St. Louis than he did against New York five years later; in fact, Branca holds the probably unassailable record of three losses (one in 1946 and two in 1951) in rare non-League Championship Series playoffs.

SAM BREADON

One of Branch Rickey's more neglected accomplishments was making Breadon seem like the junior partner in their running of the Cardinals in the 1920s and 1930s. In fact, the one-time automobile salesman held sway over the franchise as its boss of bosses for 27 years, most of the time preferring to think of Rickey as an overpaid employee rather than as a minority shareholder. It was his money that financed Rickey's ambitious farm system, his temper that exploded when the farm system almost ruined the organization, and his long-simmering resentment that he wasn't perceived as the boss that led to Rickey's departure for the Dodgers in the early 1940s.

Breadon got involved with the Cardinals initially to keep an eye on his money, which had been disappearing down a rathole during the "civic ownership" phase of the organization in the late 1910s under James Jones. Soon after taking over as team president in January 1920, he scored a financial and public relations coup by arguing that League Park had become dangerously decrepit and getting the city behind him in a campaign to have the Cardinals share the Browns-owned Sportsman's Park. When Browns owner Phil Ball rejected the idea of sharing quarters with what was then St. Louis's second team, Breadon took out newspaper ads urging readers to bring dirt to a quarry that he had leased to contribute to the construction of a new stadium. Terrified by the prospect of such a public demonstration, City Hall increased its pressure on Ball until he accepted the Cardinals as tenants. To put a ribbon on his victory, Breadon then turned around and sold the ramshackle League Park to the St. Louis Board of Education for $200,000 and some adjoining lots to other city agencies for $75,000. It was this money that seeded Rickey's farm system.

Breadon's baseball imagination encompassed more than his readiness to accept Rickey's ideas about building up a minor league chain of teams. It was Breadon, for instance, who began the practice of scheduling Sunday doubleheaders, in the conviction that people sought more than merely two hours of entertainment on their day off. He also lobbied for years for night baseball, first running into the wall of NL owners who thought the idea frivolous, then coming up against Ball, who was hardly ready to install lights in Sportsman's Park on the proposal of an unwanted tenant. It was in the context of such ongoing enmity between the two owners that Breadon always delighted in relating how Ball had enlarged Sportsman's Park in anticipation of big crowds for watching the Browns in the 1926 World Series, then gagged before the sight of the extra seating serving Cardinals fans instead.

The Cardinals first taste of postseason action, in 1926, was not without problems for Breadon. Most of all, there was his personal dislike for manager-second baseman Rogers Hornsby, who was never reluctant to use his star status as a lever for more money. When Hornsby rejected a one-year contract for 1927, Breadon took on the entire city by trading him to the Giants for Frankie Frisch. Not only did Frisch's aggressive play and another pennant in 1928 win over fans irate at Hornsby's departure, but the experience also persuaded Breadon that it would never be quite as difficult again to get rid of a manager, even after a winning season. This attitude was reflected over the years that followed in his abrupt derricking of the likes of Bill McKechnie, Gabby Street, Billy Southworth, and Ray Blades.

Despite presiding over clubs in the late 1920s and early 1930s that usually either won pennants or finished near the top, Breadon was so convinced that the Depression was going to linger and that the St. Louis market was going to become more prohibitive for two major league teams that he entered into negotiations for the sale of the club with Oklahoma oil millionaire Lew Wentz after the 1934 season. When those talks foundered on Wentz's refusal to accept his estimates on the value of the Cardinals farm system, Breadon turned his energies to moving the franchise to Detroit. The obstacle there turned out to be threats by the Tigers that any such move would

rekindle the early-century war between the leagues. In the end, the St. Louis owner fell back on the tried and true formula of building up his cash reserves by selling off star players—a tactic that in the case of the Cardinals was far less destructive than with other teams because of the prospects that kept arriving through the farm system.

In 1938 the Breadon-Rickey relationship started to unravel in the wake of Commissioner Kenesaw Landis's decision to release 74 St. Louis farmhands. In what was to be known as the Cedar Rapids Case, Landis defended his move by charging that Rickey had entered into "secret understandings" with minor league officials in violation of rules covering competitive opportunity. Although Landis never quite got around to making a formal presentation of the charges, Breadon resisted Rickey's urgings to file suit against the commissioner and refused to insist on the club's right to retain the services of the 74 players, the most noted of whom were outfielder Pete Reiser and infielder Skeeter Webb. To intimates, he claimed to have been embarrassed by the scandal and accused Rickey of endangering the very survival of the organization. For the next couple of years Breadon thought nothing of publicly contradicting Rickey statements to the press. The final tear came in 1942, when he told Rickey of his intention of assigning sponsorship rights for radio coverage of the Cardinals to the Hyde Park beer company. When the abstemious general manager protested, Breadon reminded him who was the owner. Rickey got the message and tendered his resignation in October.

Operating without Rickey didn't seem to faze Breadon. If anything, he appeared bent on being more royal than the king, completing countless trades that inevitably included some money for his pocket. The biggest setback over the final years of his reign came with the 1946 defection of several Cardinals, including prize southpaw Max Lanier, to the Mexican League organized by multimillionaire Jorge Pasquel. In defiance of the ban on the jumpers proclaimed by Commissioner Happy Chandler, Breadon went to Mexico to negotiate with Pasquel for the return of his players. It proved to be a fairly academic exercise, since the Mexican had never really had any long-range plans for his league, but the trip aggravated Chandler, precipitating a lot of shouting behind executive doors. Breadon finally had enough of it all in 1947, selling out to lawyer Fred Saigh.

TED BREITENSTEIN

With catcher Heinie Peitz, Breitenstein formed the so-called Pretzel Battery for the Cardinals in the 1890s. The southpaw also pitched a no-hitter in his first major league start, for the American Association Browns on the last day of the 1891 season. In September 1894, he was fined $100 by St. Louis president Chris Von der Ahe for refusing to relieve in the second game of a doubleheader after having pitched 43 innings in nine days, including a complete game in the first half of the twin bill.

ROGER BRESNAHAN (Hall of Fame, 1945)

A temperamental clone of his mentor John Mc-Graw, Bresnahan brawled and battled his way through a 17-year career, almost all of it in the earliest years of the 20th century. It was as much for his innovations in playing equipment as for his .279 lifetime average and the speed that made him one of the few catchers used in the leadoff spot that he earned a plaque in Cooperstown.

After a hospital stay necessitated by a beaning in 1901, Bresnahan took to wearing a protective helmet that was little more than a leather football helmet sliced in half; this "pneumatic head protector" failed to catch on. More successful were the receiver's efforts with shin guards. Surprised to discover in a collision at the plate that Philadelphia's Red Dooin wore papier-mâché protectors under his uniform, Bresnahan improved on the idea by sporting cricket leg pads on Opening Day of the 1907 season; while his inspiration met with initial scorn, less elaborate models were standard equipment within two years. The following year, he added padding to the inside rim of his catcher's mask to cushion the force of foul tips.

Traded by the Giants to the Cardinals in 1909, Bresnahan managed the club to financial if not artistic success—so much so that owner Helene Britton presented him with a lucrative five-year contract in 1911. A year later, however, Britton fired him as pilot and traded his player contract to the Cubs because of money shorts; the manager's cause was not helped by charges he had not fielded his best team in a key game against the Giants to give McGraw an edge in the pennant race against the Cubs and Pirates and by a subsequent four-letter-word defense of his innocence to the owner. It would be several years before he collected, in an out-of-court settlement, the $20,000 owed him.

Known as the Duke of Tralee, especially in New York, where an Irish connection never hurt a player's popularity, Bresnahan was actually born in Toledo.

GEORGE BRETT (Hall of Fame, 1998)

From the day he took over third base as a regular in 1974 to his retirement after the 1993 season, Brett was the franchise player for the Royals. A lefthanded swinger with significant extra-base power, he posted a career average of .305, reaching the 3,000-hit level in 1992 and finishing his career with 3,154. Among other offensive achievements was winning batting titles in 1976, 1980, and 1990—making him the only big leaguer to pick up a Silver Bat in three different decades. In 1980 he took MVP honors by leading Kansas City to a pennant with a .390 average; it was the highest mark in the big leagues since Ted Williams had hit .406 in 1941. Always more than a singles hitter, Brett led the American League in doubles twice, in triples three times, and in slugging average three times. In eight seasons he hit more than 20 home runs, and he topped the 100-RBI and 100-run marks four times each.

Franchise player or not, Brett had his uncomfortable moments in a Kansas City uniform. At the end of the 1974 season, he broke down in tears when he heard that manager Jack McKeon had fired his hitting mentor, Charlie Lau. In 1978 he mainly sounded bitter when Whitey Herzog, who had rehired Lau after succeeding McKeon, did the same thing. Despite his own solid hitting, including three home runs in the third game of the 1978 American League Championship Series, Brett admitted to being devastated by Kansas City's three straight losses to the Yankees in the playoffs between 1976 and 1978. When the club did finally make it past New York to the 1980 World Series against Philadelphia, he became the butt of nationwide jokes for a well-publicized case of hemorrhoids. Although he tried to make light of his ailment during the Series, his humor was in short supply the following season, when reporters kept referring to the condition. In one episode, he swung a crutch at a photographer who thought he was being cute about everything; in another, his slow recovery from an off-season operation to correct the problem caused him to break up a dugout toilet; in a third incident, he shoved a woman reporter.

On July 24, 1983 Brett was the protagonist of one of baseball's most farcical moments. In a game at

Yankee Stadium he hit what appeared to be a two-run home run off Goose Gossage with two out in the ninth inning to give the Royals a 5–4 lead. But then umpire Joe Brinkman agreed with New York manager Billy Martin's protest that pine tar had been applied to more of Brett's bat than was legal, nullified the home run, called him out for the violation, and declared the Yankees the winner of the game. After an enraged Brett was pulled away from Brinkman, Kansas City filed an official protest with the league office and won the argument when AL president Lee MacPhail decided that the pine tar regulation was too vague. A series of legal countermoves by the Yankees followed, but when these efforts to reverse the MacPhail decision failed, the teams took the field again in August to resume play from the moment of Brett's homer. With only 1,245 people in the stands to watch four outs and New York pitcher Ron Guidry pressed into service as a center fielder, Kansas City finally sealed its 5–4 win, but only after New York appealed—futilely—that Brett had missed each bag in circling the bases.

WALTER BRIGGS

After staying in Frank Navin's shadow for some 17 years as a partner in the Tigers, Briggs spent an equal amount of time as the franchise's most visible executive. Taking over baseball operations after Navin's death in 1935, the former auto body builder presided over a Detroit pennant in 1940 and a world championship in 1945 but otherwise had to content himself with runner-up clubs that usually featured a lot of hitting and little pitching. On the other hand, he left himself open for more than one run-in with the commissioner's office, other owners, and fans.

Briggs's biggest crisis occurred in 1940, when Commissioner Kenesaw Landis cut loose 91 Detroit farmhands on the grounds that their careers had been stymied by a lot of devious paperwork. Although general manager Jack Zeller took the rap for the violations, Briggs's refusal to fire or even criticize his lieutenant strongly suggested that he wasn't taken completely by surprise by Landis's charges. In 1941 the Detroit owner aroused the irritation of other owners by signing Dick Wakefield as baseball's first bonus baby; in language similar to later attacks on Ted Turner and George Steinbrenner for throwing big money at free agents, the owners fretted that the $52,000 and car given to Wakefield would set a

dangerous precedent for other high school and college players targeted by major league teams. In 1946 Briggs provoked fan protests when he put slugger Hank Greenberg on waivers and managed to get him out of the AL to the Pirates. The move followed Greenberg's announced ambition to take over as Detroit general manager and the owner's insistence that the first baseman wasn't ready for such a position. There was little doubt that the old-boy network was at work in allowing Greenberg to pass through the league without any claims being made on him.

By the time Briggs died in 1952, he had formalized his distance from Navin in the most conspicuous way possible—rebaptizing Navin Field as Briggs Stadium.

GUS BRITTAIN

Brittain's major league career consisted of one game as a catcher and two appearances as a pinch-hitter for the Reds in 1937. As far as manager Charlie Dressen was concerned, however, his offensive and defensive skills were beside the point, since his principal job on the team was to start brawls that Dressen deemed necessary for animating the team. Although Brittain held up his end of the bargain by jumping out of the dugout to precipitate several melees, Cincinnati still finished in the cellar.

HELENE BRITTON

Britton became the first woman to run a big league franchise when she inherited the Cardinals from her uncle Stanley Robison in 1911. After years of fighting off other owners who wanted her out of their exclusive male circle and of entrusting day-to-day operations to others, she took over the team presidency herself in 1916.

Britton's ownership got off to a deceptive start in 1911, when unprecedented figures allowed her to liquidate organization debts and even show a profit. She was so gratified by the showing she gave manager Roger Bresnahan a new five-year contract, with promises of 10 percent of the team's profits for its duration. She soon regretted her largesse. Aside from the fact that St. Louis played itself out of the 1912 race within the first month of the season, she began sinking financially again under legal fees piling up over who was the legal executor of the Robison estate. Bresnahan was no source of solace, either: first he came under charges that he had thrown some games to the Giants to allow his mentor John Mc-Graw to beat the Cubs and the Pirates for the pennant, then he defended himself in Britton's home with a tirade she considered uncouth and offensive to her station. When she replaced Bresnahan with Miller Huggins, the ousted manager began another legal wrangle for the money still due him on his five-year pact.

Suffragette Britton correctly calculated that attracting more women to Cardinals games would bring in more men as well, and she achieved her goal by increasing the frequency of Ladies Days and by hiring a crooner to perform between innings. Although hard-pressed herself, she even passed along part of her profits to the players when, in 1914, they delivered on her proposal to reward a third-place finish with 20-percent bonuses.

Britton's husband Schuyler did little as team president but follow her instructions and build a reputation as a kept man who liked to drink and womanize. When he returned home one night in a drunken state and smashed up the house, she initiated divorce proceedings and succeeded him at his franchise post. She personally handled the club's only deal in 1916—the sale of pitcher Slim Sallee to the Giants for some urgently needed cash. Her heart no longer in the job, however, she summoned Huggins and organization attorney James Jones after the season, telling them she wanted to sell and giving them both a headstart at coming up with the purchase money. Jones proved to be the winner of the competition when he put together a coalition of dozens of businessmen in St. Louis for meeting the $375,000 asking price. It would take a number of years and threatened lawsuits before Britton was able to collect all the money owed to her from so many disparate sources.

JOHNNY BROACA

Broaca predicted his own major league success, then walked away from it for a career in the ring. Playing for Yale in the early 1930s, the righthander told coach Joe Wood, a former Red Sox hurler, that he would take the mound only once a week because he was saving his arm for the major leagues. Inserted into the Yankees rotation in 1934, he won 39 games over three seasons. But with a starting assignment in the 1936 World Series imminent, he announced his retirement to become a boxer, predicting he would

one day fight Joe Louis for the heavyweight championship. While he did make two baseball comebacks (with New York in 1937 and Cleveland in 1939), he never won a professional fight.

LOU BROCK (Hall of Fame, 1985)

Brock's 3,023 career hits, .293 average, and National League-record 938 steals over 19 seasons (1961–79) assured him a place in the Hall of Fame, but he was anything but a traditional leadoff hitter. For one thing, the lefty-swinging outfielder struck out more than 100 times in nine seasons, and his lifetime total of 1,730 whiffs was only 27 fewer than another leadoff man, record-whiffer Bobby Bonds. For another, Brock's .344 on-base average was 13 points lower than Bonds's .356 and a full 53 points below Richie Ashburn's. To a considerable degree, in fact, Brock's value at the top of the Cardinals lineups in the 1960s and 1970s had to be underwritten by two of the best second-place hitters in baseball history—Curt Flood and Ted Sizemore.

Joining the Cubs in the early 1960s, Brock gained attention initially not so much for his speed as for his power, especially on June 17, 1962, when he became the only lefthanded batter to clout a ball into the right field side of the center field bleachers in the Polo Grounds, an estimated 488 feet from home plate. Even after being traded to the Cardinals for Ernie Broglio in one of baseball's worst deals two years later, he remained indifferent enough to the vast dimensions of Busch Stadium to reach double figures in home runs on seven occasions. It was Brock's running game that became his signature, however. In 1966 he swiped 74 bases to lead the league for the first of eight times; in 1974 he rolled up 118 steals, setting a new major league theft mark (later eclipsed by Rickey Henderson). He was even more devastating to opposition batteries in postseason play. In the 1967 World Series against the Red Sox, he stole a record seven bases while batting .414 with 12 hits; a year later, in the Series against the Tigers, he swiped another seven while increasing his average to .464 with 13 hits. Aside from tying Eddie Collins for most stolen bases (14) in World Series play, he also holds the record for the highest World Series batting average (.391) among players with at least 20 games.

Despite his contributions to the Cardinals for almost two decades, Brock was publicly embarrassed by general manager John Claiborne before the 1979 season when he was told he had only the month of April to show he wasn't washed up. Even though he was no longer a speed demon, he responded with a .304 average that allowed him to retire with dignity at the end of the year.

JIM BROSNAN

Brosnan's journal of Cincinnati's 1961 pennant-winning season, published as *The Long Season,* annoyed the baseball establishment for its less-than-reverential tone. Reds owner Bill DeWitt, for one, forbade the righthanded reliever from any further writing, on the basis of ambiguous contract clauses warning against conduct detrimental to baseball. Brosnan had the same problem with the White Sox after being dealt to the American League after the 1963 season, but by then he had foreseen the end of his pitching career and continued work on a second book, *Pennant Race,* in spite of front office warnings. Lost amid all the humorlessness of DeWitt and his colleagues was that Brosnan had been a key factor in the 1961 pennant by winning 10 games and saving 16 others.

DAN BROUTHERS (Hall of Fame, 1945)

Brouthers, who played for 11 teams in 18 seasons in the 19th century plus a brief return engagement in 1904, has the highest batting average (.349) of any first baseman in the history of the game and the fourth highest among all players. The lefty's five batting crowns were won for four different teams—the Buffalo Bisons in 1882 and 1883; the National League and American Association Boston clubs in 1889 and 1891, respectively; and the Dodgers in 1892. He also led the NL in slugging in his first six full seasons, and added a seventh title in the AA in 1891.

BOBBY BROWN

A platoon third baseman with severe defensive limitations in the late 1940s and early 1950s, Brown spent as much time in the Army and in medical school as he did with the Yankees. Retiring in 1954 to practice medicine, he became a successful cardiac surgeon but then left his practice to accept an appointment as American League president in 1984. In that role he was largely a bystander to the owner collusion, drug scandals, labor strife, and debates over television revenues and the future of the game

that marked his tenure; he also stood by as AL owners spent his decade in office eroding the powers of the league presidency.

JOE L. BROWN

The son of movie actor Joe E. Brown, Brown oversaw the revival of the Pittsburgh franchise in the late 1950s, remaining head of the team's baseball operations through its glory years in the 1970s. His most important moves as general manager were to be on the scene to succeed Branch Rickey when the latter's four-star farm club prospects began filtering into Pittsburgh in the late 1950s and to hire Danny Murtaugh as manager four different times. Brown came back for a second stint in the 1980s, mainly to shake high salaries out of the roster so the Galbreath family would find it easier to sell the franchise.

THREE FINGER BROWN (Hall of Fame, 1949)

Brown was the National League's Ed Walsh in forging most of the senior circuit's ERA records. Among other things, he established the standard for one-season stinginess in 1906 by yielding merely 1.04 runs per nine innings; his 14-year (1903–16) ERA of 2.06 has been bettered only by Walsh and Addie Joss among all big league hurlers. The dominating hill force of the champion Cubs teams in the first decade of the century, the righthander gained his nickname from two childhood accidents on his Indiana farm. In the first mishap, he caught his index finger in a corn shredder and had to have it amputated above the knuckle; a couple of weeks later, he broke his third and fourth fingers, and they never grew straight. At the height of his popularity with Chicago the corn shredder was the centerpiece of a tourist attraction in his hometown.

For six straight years from 1906 and 1911 Brown registered 20 wins, gaining a career-high 29 victories in 1908. In that year of Fred Merkle's boner, he kept Chicago in the running against the Giants by winning both ends of a doubleheader the day before the New York first baseman failed to touch second base and set off baseball's biggest stretch-run controversy. In the makeup game necessitated by Merkle's misadventure Brown relieved starter Jack Pfiester in the first inning without bothering to warm up, going on to blank the Giants the rest of the way for a 4–2 Cubs pennant. Coming in from the bullpen was nothing exotic for him: While racking up his 20 or more wins between 1908 and 1911, he also paced the NL in saves in each of the four campaigns.

Two years later, however, Brown, his skills eroded, fell victim to one of Cubs owner Charles Murphy's periodic economy moves and was sold to a minor league team, engendering widespread sentiment that 10-year veterans should at least be afforded the courtesy of an unconditional release in such circumstances. Largely because of Brown, the Players Fraternity made this one of its key bargaining issues with major league owners. The hurler resurfaced with the Reds and later in the Federal League in 1914 and 1915. On his last legs in 1916, Brown took to the mound for the Cubs against the equally aged Christy Mathewson for one final face-off. Mathewson, then with the Reds, recorded the last of his 373 victories in a messy 10–7 affair.

PETE BROWNING

Despite his preeminence among American Association hitters, Browning's most enduring baseball legacy has more to do with the manufacture of his bats than with what he accomplished with them. Convinced that each of his bats contained just so many hits, he nurtured and named them. When one of his favorites splintered during the 1884 season, the Louisville outfielder accepted an offer by woodworker Bud Hillerich to fashion a new one specifically tailored to his taste. Other players were so impressed with the first so-called Louisville Slugger that the company, eventually called Hillerich & Bradsby, was launched on its way to becoming the largest producer of baseball lumber.

Browning, whose .349 lifetime average and three batting titles (1882 and 1885 in the AA, 1890 in the Players League) have never sufficiently impressed Hall of Fame electors, was as incapable of handling fly balls and liquor as he was adept at hitting fastballs. His defensive deficiencies and his reluctance to slide may have made him a one-dimensional player, but coupled with his endless and boisterous monologues in saloons around the league about his bats, his eyes, and his hitting accomplishments, they also made him the AA's biggest drawing card.

Afflicted with a chronic mastoid infection that left him deaf, he may have turned to drink as a painkiller. A decade after his retirement, inadequate medical treatment led to brain damage misdiagnosed as insanity, and Browning was committed to an insane asylum.

JOHN T. BRUSH

Brush, who owned three National League franchises between 1889 and 1912, was predisposed toward schemes. As president of the Indianapolis Hoosiers in 1889, he persuaded the NL to accept a classification plan ranking players from A to E not on their on-field ability, but on their personal habits; salaries were to be doled out accordingly—$2,500 for A-level players, $2,250 for Bs, $2,000 for Cs, $1,750 for Ds, and $1,500 for Es. Only the intervention of Players Brotherhood leader John Montgomery Ward averted a strike over the plan, but it was also a major reason why the players decided to form their own league in 1890. As part of the NL's effort to shore up the hard-hit Giants during the Players League war, Brush reduced his Indianapolis franchise to minor league status and transferred its entire roster to New York before the season; then, with the Giants situation deteriorating daily, he forgave part of the payment in exchange for a minority interest in the club. His reward was control of the NL's franchise in Cincinnati.

In Cincinnati Brush soon fell to feuding with *Commercial-Gazette* sportswriter Ban Johnson. Johnson's criticism of the club became so irksome that Brush used his influence as owner of the Western League's Indianapolis club to have the sportswriter appointed president of the minor league in 1894, thereby getting him out from under foot (and also setting in motion the formation of the American League). But the relationship between the two didn't improve with Johnson's career change. Brush made a shambles of the WL by shuttling players between Indianapolis and Cincinnati, to the point that the two clubs became known disparagingly as Cincinnapolis-Indianatti. Johnson and the rest of the circuit fought equally hard to limit the effects of Brush's dual ownership, which was effectively the earliest example of a farm system.

It was also as Cincinnati owner that, in 1898, Brush pushed through his so-called plan "For the Suppression of Obscene, Indecent, and Vulgar Language Upon the Ball Field." While its principal tenet—suspension and possible expulsion for players charged with violations—was never enforced, the scheme left a legacy in attendant decisions to enforce it by employing two arbiters for every game and to pay for the increased umpiring staff by expanding to a 154-game schedule.

Brush's reputation for deviousness was never more evident than in the events that brought John

McGraw and then himself to the Giants in 1902. When New York majority stockholder Andrew Freedman lost his appetite for the business, Brush, still a junior partner, began increasing his Manhattan presence. It was to Brush that Baltimore executive John J. Mahon turned over the slightly more than 50 percent of the AL Orioles stock he had collected with McGraw's contrivance in the wake of the manager's sudden July departure from Baltimore and reemergence in New York. The situation of an NL owner exercising effective control over an AL franchise got even stickier when two Baltimore players were transferred to Cincinnati and six more to New York. The substance of the plot became much less murky in September when Brush sold the Reds and, with McGraw acting as intermediary, bought controlling interest in the Giants from Freedman.

The New York owner and manager remained the last holdouts against an accommodation with Johnson's American League, even refusing to allow the Giants to meet the Red Sox in the 1904 World Series. For the final eight years of his reign Brush, suffering from locomotor ataxia, a degenerative disease of the nervous system often brought on by syphilis, left most club operations to McGraw.

STEVE BRYE

A mere .258 hitter in nine seasons, Brye had his most memorable moment in the major leagues when he was accused of helping to throw a batting race. On the final day of the 1976 season, the Minnesota outfielder misjudged a fly ball by Kansas City's George Brett that fell safely over his head and rolled to the wall for an inside-the-park homer. The hit turned out to be the difference in the batting race between Brett and Royals teammate Hal McRae. After the game a seething McRae accused Twins manager Gene Mauch of having ordered Brye, normally a good fielder, to give an edge to Brett for racial reasons. Both Mauch and Brye initially denied any deliberate partiality, but the outfielder later admitted that most players around the league wanted to see Brett win the title—not because McRae was black, he said, but because he was a mere designated hitter.

BILL BUCKNER

First baseman Buckner had an outstanding 22-year (1969–90) career, primarily with the Dodgers and Cubs, that included one batting championship and recorded him as one of very few players to have 200-hit seasons in both leagues. But on October 25, 1986 he ransomed those accomplishments away in the minds of most Boston fans by booting the Mookie Wilson grounder that enabled the Mets to climax an incredible come-from-behind victory against the Red Sox in the 10th inning of the sixth game of the 1986 World Series. In fact, Buckner had played the entire Series in hightops to protect his bad ankles, and for some months had been replaced defensively by Dave Stapleton when Boston had a lead. The closest manager John McNamara ever came to providing a reason why he left the hobbled veteran on the field for the fateful 10th inning was one off-the-cuff comment that he had wanted him on the field when the Red Sox clinched the championship.

Buckner was released by Boston early in 1987. He stuck around with the Angels and Royals for another couple of seasons, then closed out his career back at Fenway Park. If there had been any hope of time healing the scars from 1986, it ended when he had to move his family from Massachusetts in 1993 because of constant harassment from Red Sox fans.

DOC BUCKNER

Buckner was one of several black trainers that early-century teams used as masseurs and sought to hide from the public. Employed by the White Sox, he had to be concealed on segregated trains and in whites-only hotels after players insisted that they needed his ministrations on the road as well as at home. Hotel managers knew not to say anything if they wanted to keep the Chicago account.

BOB BUHL

Buhl has several claims to being the worst-hitting pitcher in the history of the game. His most famous mark was the all-time futility of going 0-for-70 in 1962 while splitting his time between the Braves and Cubs. That was no statistical fluke, however, for in nine of his 15 major league seasons he couldn't reach the .100 mark, only on one occasion did he get as high as .200 (when he batted a mere 25 times in an injury-plagued season), and his lifetime average was .089. When he was on the mound, on the other hand, the righthander fashioned back-to-back 18-win seasons for Milwaukee in 1956 and 1957, also posting the National League's top winning percentage in the latter year.

MORGAN BULKELEY (Hall of Fame, 1937)

The owner of the Hartford franchise in 1876, Bulkeley became the National League's first president when his club's name was drawn first out of a hat in the original selection of league directors; more than six decades later, he was awarded a plaque in Cooperstown merely to balance the selection of Ban Johnson, the American League's founding president. Bulkeley was also the first club owner to move his team from one city to another, a step taken only after repeated denials that such a move was imminent. Despite inducements such as season tickets (another first) and prohibitions on the local press against printing scores until a game was over, crowds in Hartford were sparse; when they proved even more sparse in Brooklyn in 1877, Bulkeley dropped out of the league. Subsequently, he concentrated on building the Aetna Insurance Company that his father had founded and on a political career in which he rose from Hartford mayor to Connecticut governor to U.S. senator.

JIM BUNNING (Hall of Fame, 1996)

Bunning was the mound equivalent of Frank Robinson from the mid-1950s to the early 1970s, at least insofar as excelling in both the American and National leagues; his considerable accomplishments took more time, however, to impress Hall of Fame electors than they did Kentucky voters. The right-hander was the first pitcher since Cy Young to win 100 games in each league, the first since the same Young to strike out 1,000 batters in each league, and only the third (behind Young and Tom Hughes) to fashion a no-hitter in each circuit. Pitching for the Tigers, he held the Red Sox hitless on July 20, 1958; for the Phillies, he went one better, hurling a perfect game against the Mets on June 21, 1964. Bunning represented a Kentucky district in the U.S. House of Representatives from 1987 to 1999, when he advanced to a seat in the Senate.

GLENN BURKE

A backup outfielder for the Dodgers and Athletics in the 1970s, Burke was the first major league player to admit he was gay. The Dodgers, seeking to cover up his homosexuality, offered to pay for his honeymoon if he got married. Oakland manager Billy Martin was more direct in his disapproval, insisting "I don't want fags playing for me." Burke was discouraged enough by baseball's homophobia to quit the game midway through the 1979 season. Before leaving, he contributed to on-the-field rituals by giving the first high five. On October 2, 1977 he was the on deck batter when Dusty Baker of the Dodgers clouted his 30th homer—giving Los Angeles an unprecedented four players to reach that plateau; according to the outfielder, he instinctively raised his hands to the sky and Baker reciprocated with a high-five slap. After years of illness and misery, Burke died of AIDS in 1995.

The second player to admit he was gay was Billy Bean, an outfielder for the Tigers and Padres in the late 1980s and early 1990s.

KITTY BURKE

If St. Louis manager Frankie Frisch had had his way, Burke would have been the first woman to bat in a major league game. On July 31, 1935 the Cardinals played their first night contest, against Cincinnati at Crosley Field. Because of the overflow crowd drawn to the novelty, hundreds of fans had to be accommodated behind ropes on the playing field. With the Cardinals leading, 2–1, in the eighth inning, nightclub singer Burke suddenly ducked under the rope, grabbed the bat away from Reds slugger Babe Herman, and went up to the plate against Paul Dean. As a lark, Dean underhanded the ball to Burke, who promptly swung and grounded out. Never one to ignore a possible edge, Frisch screamed that Burke's ground ball should count as an out. He lost the argument and later the game.

MIKE BURKE

Burke brought the first hint of flair to the Yankees front office in almost a quarter-century when he assumed the club presidency in September 1966, but his stylishness was wasted on a franchise grown moribund under the previous owners and unable to rebound under a new regime unwilling to invest in the future. Worse, when he was finally about to assume an ownership position himself, he found himself with a senior partner whose flamboyance outdid his own.

A CBS vice president, Burke succeeded Dan Topping as chief executive of the New York club when its sale to the broadcasting giant became final. He immediately found himself between the rock of a talent vacuum left behind by Topping and partner

Del Webb (who had stopped investing money in the team after they had decided to sell several years earlier) and the hard place of demands for immediate results by CBS chairman William Paley and company president Frank Stanton (who thought they had bought the premier franchise in baseball). Faced with an attitude that relegated the franchise to a mere line item in the budget of a megacorporation, he presided over the liquidation of a dynasty—trading Roger Maris to the Cardinals in December 1966 and watching as Whitey Ford retired in 1967 and Mickey Mantle followed him in 1968. He endured the situation for more than six years, until ordered by Paley either to buy the club himself or unload it on someone else. His solution was to form a partnership with Cleveland millionaire George Steinbrenner, who arrived behind a vow that he would stick to his shipbuilding business and let professionals run the team. Burke was quickly disabused of any belief he was viewed as one of those professionals when Steinbrenner lured Gabe Paul away from the Indians to run the franchise.

Burke's greatest legacy was keeping the club in the Bronx by negotiating the renovation of Yankee Stadium with New York City mayor John V. Lindsay. The project, which started as a $24 million facelift and ended as a $120 million boondoggle, forced a two-year exile for the Yankees at the Mets home at Shea Stadium, but averted a potential permanent move by the club to the New Jersey Meadowlands.

JESSE BURKETT (Hall of Fame, 1946)

Burkett is one of four players (along with Ed Delahanty, Ty Cobb, and Rogers Hornsby) to hit higher than .400 in two consecutive seasons (for the Cleveland Spiders in 1895 and 1896); he also added a third batting title (for the Cardinals in 1901), while topping 200 hits in six different seasons. But the lefty outfielder irritated teammates and opponents alike with a disposition that won him the nickname of The Crab. References to his physical resemblance to Cleveland teammate and distant cousin Jack Glasscock, especially taunts about being the shortstop's son, annoyed him twice over. His carping while a coach with the 1921 Giants so angered team members that they excluded him from a share of World Series money; manager John McGraw had to pay Burkett an equivalent amount out of his own pocket.

JOHNNY BURNETT

Playing for Cleveland on July 10, 1932, Burnett smashed two doubles and seven singles in an 18-inning contest against the Athletics. The nine hits are the most by a player in a major league game of any length. Burnett was a lefty-swinging shortstop who averaged .284 in nine major league seasons.

WATCH BURNHAM

Burnham was appointed manager of the Indianapolis Hoosiers in 1887 solely because he had discovered that a National League franchise was available to the city. Within a month of Opening Day, he almost caused a rebellion among players by fining every one of them $5 for refusing to practice in uniforms dampened by a leaky roof. Worried about the reaction of club president Louis Newberger, the out-of-his-depth pilot forged a contrite letter from team captain Jack Glasscock. Newberger saw through the forgery and fired him, but Burnham restored himself to favor by signing Larry Corcoran, once the ace of the Chicago pitching staff. The players' attitude failed to improve in Burnham's second tour, and after they learned the reason for his temporary departure, they directed their antagonism toward the president as well. With the possibility of an open revolt looming, Burnham was canned a second time. His managerial record was 6–22.

ELLIS BURKS

An outfielder who otherwise never rose to the superstardom predicted for him, Burks matched none other than Hank Aaron in 1996, when, while playing for Colorado, he became only the second player to stroke 200 hits, clout 40 home runs, and steal 30 bases.

TOM BURNS

Burns collected two doubles and a home run for the Chicago White Stockings in an 18-run seventh inning against Detroit on September 6, 1883. The shortstop's contribution to the eventual 26–6 rout was the single best individual offensive inning in baseball history.

GUSSIE BUSCH

Busch used his 36 years (1953–89) as owner of the Cardinals not only to run his own franchise's affairs but also to have his beer products associated with just about every club in the National and American leagues. Prior to the organization of civic groups in the 1980s intent on breaking the identification of beer with baseball, his biggest frustration had been his failure to get the Cardinals playing facility renamed Budweiser Park.

Busch took over St. Louis with the help of NL owners determined to get rid of Fred Saigh before he made a deal to transfer the franchise to Milwaukee. One of Busch's first moves was to purchase the Browns-owned Sportsman's Park and, failing at the Budweiser idea because of league sensitivities that it would have been too crass, to rename it Busch Stadium. His direct involvement in baseball matters was reflected in a chaos of managers and general managers for most of the 1950s and the early part of the 1960s, with little to show for it until 1964 except two second-place finishes. On the other hand, he had consistently more financial room for maneuvering than his predecessor, not only because of his beer company but also because the Cardinals were the only baseball team in town following the transfer of the Browns to Baltimore in 1954.

Busch's first significant crisis came in 1960, when first baseman Bill White protested the exclusion of black players from a public function held near the team's spring training camp in Florida. When a black newspaper in St. Louis got wind of the incident, it called for a nationwide boycott of Anheuser-Busch products as a means of getting the organization to apply pressure to Florida's segregationist policies in hotels and other public enterprises. With his dealers around the country warning of dire consequences, Busch gave St. Petersburg officials an ultimatum to provide integrated accommodations or face the loss of the team. That was enough for a local businessman to buy two of the best motels in the city and make them available to the Cardinals. Although the concession riled Florida racists, it also proved critical to clubhouse unity for the year, especially when such white stars as Stan Musial and Ken Boyer gave up their beachfront homes to move into the integrated hotels. The nucleus of the 1960 club would still be in place when the Cardinals returned to the World Series in 1964.

Busch invited other trouble after the 1962 season by bringing in the aged Branch Rickey as a special adviser. That led to two seasons of front office intrigues involving Rickey; vice president Dick Meyer; general manager Bing Devine; and the latter's successor, Bob Howsam; what only Devine appeared to perceive before his forced resignation was that Busch was playing the executives off against one another so he could have the final say on the issue of the moment.

In 1966 Busch moved the team into the current facility known as Busch Stadium—a cookie-cutter industrial park with an artificial surface. Under the terms of his agreement with the Civic Center Redevelopment Corporation, which supervised the construction of the stadium and floated a bond issue to develop surrounding land, Busch ceded parking and concession stand revenues in return for a 25 percent interest in the group. Once free agency hit the baseball world in the mid-1970s, however, he began griping that the franchise wasn't realizing enough of a profit from the facility, and made two offers to buy it outright. Rebuffed both times, he upped the ante in 1981 to threats of selling the club if he couldn't get his own way. When reports began circulating that he had opened negotiations with a Missouri-based oil company for a sale, Civic Center caved in, selling him the stadium for an estimated (and cheap) $53 million. The high-handedness brought the club reams of bad publicity, but it remained the only baseball team in town.

Once Busch brought in Whitey Herzog as manager and general manager in 1980, he meddled less in the team's baseball affairs. Herzog ingratiated himself both on and off the field—in the former instance by winning a world championship and three pennants in the 1980s, in the latter by doing it mainly through shrewd trades instead of waving millions at free agents. But what not even Herzog could head off were the increasing incidences of Cardinals players (Lonnie Smith, David Green) admitting themselves to clinics for drinking problems, and the burgeoning movement for creating alcohol-free zones in ballparks and for reducing the beer advertising that had become as ubiquitous as the major league logo. On one level, Busch's response was publicity campaigns emphasizing the historic roots of beer and the need to be "responsible" in its consumption; on another, he continued to play up the link between his industry and the sport, not least in his regular stunt of driving an old beer wagon around Busch Stadium before games and in having the organist play the "King of Beers" theme song instead of "Take Me Out to the Ball Game" during the seventh-inning stretch.

Busch died on September 29, 1989, at age 90; he was succeeded by his son August Busch III. The younger Busch sold the team to a syndicate headed by Frederick Hauser and Bill DeWitt, Jr., for $150 million in December 1995.

GEORGE W. BUSH

The future President of the United States fronted for a syndicate that bought the Texas Rangers from Eddie Chiles for $46 million in April 1989 and spent the next five years advancing his future political career.

Bush's group won out over two other prospective buyers: a Florida group that wanted to move the team to Tampa but that couldn't overcome the objections of minority partner Edward Gaylord, who had the right of first refusal to Giles's stock, and Gaylord himself, who couldn't get approval from other American League owners. The impasse was overcome only when commissioner Peter Ueberroth solicited an offer from Bush and Dallas investment banker Rusty Rose.

The Rose-Bush syndicate's major accomplishment was building The Ballpark at Arlington, but Bush demonstrated less interest in running the club than in traveling around Texas to give speeches. At the time he justified his activities by describing his job as "selling tickets," but the exposure hardly hurt when he ran for governor of the state in 1994. When he announced his candidacy for governor, Bush sold his share in the club for $10 million, which brought him an impressive return on his original $605,000 investment and criticism for having profited excessively from the public funds that went into building the team's state-of-the-art facility. Asked to defend his business acumen during his first campaign, he admitted baseball officialdom's most transparent accounting secret when he told the Houston *Post* that the club's stated financial losses were "for book purposes only, not for cash purposes. Cash flow-wise the Rangers are doing very well."

JOE BUSH

Bush was one of the Yankees acquisitions from the Red Sox in the early 1920s who formed the nucleus of the first New York dynasty—and one of the few the club came to regret. A slightly better than .500 pitcher in his first 10 seasons, the righthander led the American League in won-lost percentage in 1922, his first year in New York, picking up 26 wins

while setting the major league record for most victories without a shutout. He then proceeded to undo all his good work during the season by blowing a 2–0 lead in the eighth inning of the first game of the World Series against the Giants and then blowing up at manager Miller Huggins for ordering him to walk Ross Youngs to get to George Kelly in the eighth inning of the fifth game. The pitcher's tirade was so loud that both patrons and sportswriters could hear the four-letter words, leaving him with little defense against accusations that he grooved the next pitch to Kelly, who converted the gift into a Series-winning two-run single. Bush's relationship with Huggins never recovered, and the pitcher was dealt to the Browns in 1925, starting what became a five-team odyssey over his final four seasons. He retired with a 194–183 record.

CHARLES BYRNE

The founder of the franchise that became the Brooklyn Dodgers, Byrne not only created the club, he also moved it from league to league until he found its permanent home in the National League. With the financial backing of Rhode Island casino operator Ferdinand Abell, he placed a Brooklyn entry in the minor Interstate League in 1883; switched to the major American Association the following year; and, in 1888, bought respectability by purchasing the entire New York Metropolitans club to get first baseman Dave Orr and outfielder Paul Radford and by then handing over $18,500 to the St. Louis Browns for pitchers Bob Caruthers and Dave Foutz and catcher Doc Bushong. The moves paid off in a pennant the following season, but the race exacerbated the already none-too-friendly relationship between Byrne and Browns owner Chris Von der Ahe. In spite of the player transactions completed between them, they disagreed on everything from league policy to the St. Louis president's level of intelligence. Their differences erupted at a winter meeting at which both owners controlled four votes for the election of a new AA president. Byrne broke the tie by withdrawing from the AA altogether and signing on with the NL, where his team won another pennant the following year.

TOMMY BYRNE

In 1949 Byrne walked 179 batters in 196 innings, the worst ratio of bases on balls to innings pitched in major league history. The other side of the story is that the Yankees southpaw gave up only 5.74 hits per nine innings (the eighth-lowest total in history) and ended the year with a 15–7 record. Overall, Byrne averaged almost seven walks for every nine innings he pitched in his 13-year career (between 1943 and 1957), yet he won 85 and lost only 69 games for the four AL teams for which he pitched.

Byrne was also responsible for the so-called Kimono Ball, which he developed while on a tour of Japan in 1955. The delivery, made from behind the back and over the head, baffled the only batter— Pee Wee Reese of the Dodgers in an exhibition game during spring training in 1956—ever to face it, and was declared illegal on the spot by umpire Larry Napp.

C

FRANCISCO CABRERA

First baseman-catcher Cabrera vindicated the importance of the 25th man in the seventh game of the 1992 National League playoffs when, with Pittsburgh one out away from the pennant, he came off the Atlanta bench to single in the tying and flag-winning runs for the Braves. It marked the first time a League Championship Series ended with a home team coming from behind in its final at bat. Cabrera had spent most of the 1992 season shuttling between Atlanta and the club's chief farm club in Richmond.

GEORGE CAHILL

The first night baseball game, a 16–16 tie played on September 2, 1880 at Nantasket Beach between employees of the Jordan Marsh and R.H. White department stores, was a commercial for the one-year-old electric light staged by the Northern Electric Light Company of Boston. It remained for Cahill to produce the first night game in a major league stadium. On June 18, 1909, using a portable lighting system of his own invention, he illuminated Cincinnati's League Park sufficiently for two local amateur teams to play a game before 3,000 people. The demonstration impressed Reds president Garry Herrmann, but it would be another 30 years before Cincinnati general manager Larry MacPhail would install lights at the same site (although in a different stadium) and receive permission to play the first major league game after sundown.

LES CAIN

Cain won the only legal judgment requiring a baseball team to compensate a player for the rest of his life. In 1973 the Michigan Bureau of Workmen's Compensation upheld the Detroit southpaw's claim that manager Billy Martin had ruined his career by forcing him to pitch with a sore arm; the Tigers were ordered to pay him $111 a week for life. The two sides later agreed on a single lump-sum payment.

RAY CALDWELL

Caldwell was one of the numerous early-20th century pitchers who sacrificed his talent for a drink. Still hopeful that he could wring a successful season from the righthander, Cleveland manager Tris Speaker proposed a bizarre bargain during spring training of 1920: If Caldwell stayed away from liquor otherwise, he could drink himself into oblivion every night following a starting assignment. The alternative would have been his immediate release. Caldwell accepted Speaker's terms and had his only 20-win season. The following year he lapsed back into his earlier form and was released. On July 10, 1917, while with the Yankees, Caldwell threw a record $9\,^2/_3$ hitless innings in relief to defeat the Browns in a 17-inning contest.

HELEN CALLAGHAN

Callaghan was not the biggest star in the All-American Girls' Professional Baseball League, formed during World War II by Cubs owner Phil Wrigley, but she was a major reason why the initiative was remembered years later. Her older son Kelly Candaele coproduced a 1987 television documentary on the league that directly inspired the Hollywood film *A League of Their Own*. Her younger son Casey Candaele rarely played a major league game for the Expos or Astros in the 1980s and 1990s without an announcer pointing out that the utility infielder-outfielder had learned the basics of the game not from his father but from his mother.

JOHNNY CALLISON

Callison provided the power in the most bizarre rally in baseball annals. On April 22, 1959 the lefty-swinging White Sox outfielder singled in the course of an 11-run uprising against Kansas City. That was the only hit in a seventh inning that otherwise consisted of 10 walks, a hit batsman, and three Athletics errors. Chicago won the game, 20–6.

JOE CAMBRIA

Cambria was the pioneering scout who signed the Cuban and other Latin players who figured prominently on the Washington Senators roster in the 1940s and 1950s. He made his first trip to Havana in the mid-1930s after Senators owner Clark Griffith had pinpointed the Caribbean as a potential source of gifted (and cheap) prospects; Griffith had been optimistic about Latin players since managing a couple of them in Cincinnati some years before. It was largely because of Cambria's discovery of talents such as pitchers Connie Marrero, Pedro Ramos, and Camilo Pascual that other clubs, notably Brooklyn and Pittsburgh, also devoted more attention to Latin America.

DOLF CAMILLI

Camilli was a typical example of the solid players the Phillies auctioned off for almost 30 years in the desperate quest by three successive ownerships for quick cash. Dealt to the Dodgers for $45,000 after the 1937 season, the lefthand-hitting first baseman turned in four 100-RBI seasons for Brooklyn, including a 1941 pennant contribution of leading the league in both RBIs and home runs. Although normally soft-spoken, Camilli was as tried as most of his teammates by the antics of Brooklyn general manager Larry MacPhail and on one occasion concluded a clubhouse contract talk with his employer by lifting him by his tie several feet off the floor. He also took the rivalry between the Dodgers and Giants extremely seriously, preferring to retire after the 1943 season rather than accept a trade to the Giants.

WILLIAM CAMMEYER

Cammeyer's introduction of the first enclosed ballpark, in 1862, paved the way for baseball to de-velop into a modern multimillion-dollar enterprise. By surrounding the Union Grounds in Brooklyn with a six-foot fence, the entrepreneur was able not only to charge admission but also to keep nonpayers from viewing his product. Union Grounds opened on May 15, 1862, with "The Star-Spangled Banner" being played at a ball game for the first time; within two years teams were being paid a percentage of the gate, sounding the death knell for amateurism. Cammeyer later owned the New York Mutuals, a team plagued by allegations of gambling scandals throughout the life of the National Association and into the first year of the National League. While one of the founding tenets of the NL in 1876 was the extirpation of gambling, the Mutuals were expelled, after only one season, not for crookedness but for failure to complete their schedule. Seeking to cut his losses, Cammeyer refused to send his team on its last western trip, even after receiving a guarantee of $400 for the final five games in Chicago and St. Louis.

RICK CAMP

A righthander with the Braves in the 1980s, Camp was at the center of baseball's most bizarre extra-inning game. In a 1985 night contest against the Mets that began on July 4 but ran well past midnight, the lifetime .074 hitter was forced to go to bat in the bottom of the 18th inning because Atlanta had run out of pinch-hitters; he promptly hit his only major league home run—a three-run shot that tied the game. After the Mets came back with six runs in the top of the 19th, the Braves responded with still another rally, pushing across two runs and putting two other runners on—once again for Camp. This time, however, he fanned, ending the game after six hours and 51 minutes, including a couple of rain delays. Despite the fact that it was 3:55 A.M. when Camp went down, the Atlanta management decided to go ahead with a planned fireworks demonstration to celebrate the holiday—provoking scores of protests from nearby residents.

ROY CAMPANELLA (Hall of Fame, 1969)

Campanella became the last important piece of The Boys of Summer when he went behind the plate for the Dodgers in 1948; he also became a melancholy symbol of those teams in more than 30 years of public appearances in the wheelchair to which he had been confined following a devastating 1958 auto accident. Defensively, he has been considered the standard not only for his era but, along with Johnny Bench, for the history of the National League. Offensively, the righthanded slugger whacked 242 home runs in only 10 seasons; these included a high of 41 in 1953. Together with his handling of pitchers and clubhouse cheerleading role, his defensive and offensive talents netted him MVP trophies in 1951, 1953, and 1955.

Already 27 when he completed the journey from the Negro leagues through the Dodgers farm system to Ebbets Field, Campanella was bedeviled throughout his career by hand and leg injuries, accounting for precipitous drops in his production between MVP seasons. His most significant injury might have been the muscle pull he suffered on the last day of the 1951 season, sidelining him for the playoffs against the Giants that New York won on Bobby Thomson's home run. Carl Erskine, who was warming up in the bullpen along with Ralph Branca at the time, has always said he was not brought into the game not because of the pitch he bounced in the dirt just before manager Charlie Dressen called for Branca but because Campanella, who often assured him that he would stop the righthander's low-breaking curve, was not behind the plate to prevent a similar pitch from becoming a wild pitch.

Although he never played for the California version of the Dodgers, Campanella triggered the biggest crowd in major league history when 93,103 fans showed up at Los Angeles Coliseum for an exhibition game on May 7, 1959, to pay him tribute. Reduced to paraplegia by his car accident, he nevertheless coached a couple of decades of Dodgers catchers, including Steve Yeager and Mike Scioscia.

Prior to joining the Dodgers in Brooklyn, Campanella earned a footnote as the first black to manage in organized baseball when, during a 1946 game as a member of Nashua in the Class B New England League, pilot Walter Alston turned the team over to him after being kicked out. He managed the squad to a 7–5 win.

BERT CAMPANERIS

Campaneris was the sparkplug of the brawling Oakland teams in the early 1970s. A nimble defensive shortstop, he paced the American League in stolen bases six times, reaching a career-high 62 thefts in 1968, when he also led the league in hits.

Campaneris was at the center of one of the ugliest incidents in League Championship Series play in 1972, when he responded to a suspected brushback by Detroit's Lerrin LaGrow by firing his bat at the hurler. Despite recommendations to the contrary, he was allowed to play in that year's World Series, serving a one-week suspension only at the beginning of the following season.

As a member of the Kansas City version of the Athletics on September 8, 1965, Campaneris, who had always boasted of his versatility, was encouraged by owner Charlie Finley to play a different position every inning in a game against the Angels as a gate attraction. He was smart enough to leave his catching stint to the ninth inning, since he had to be removed from the game with a damaged shoulder after a collision at home plate.

AL CAMPANIS

The last of the old executive guard that moved from Brooklyn to Los Angeles with the Dodgers, general manager Campanis sent the franchise—and major league owners in general—spinning when he unwittingly revealed the persisting depths of the sport's racism during a 1987 network television show. Interviewed on the ABC public affairs program *Nightline* on the occasion of the 40th anniversary of Jackie Robinson's debut in the major leagues, Campanis spewed forth one stereotype after another about the mental and physical abilities of black players, declaring among other things that they "may not have the necessities" to be managers or general managers. Faced with a storm of nationwide criticism the following day, both team president Peter O'Malley and his general manager issued apologies, but when that proved insufficient, Campanis was fired. Over ensuing months the Dodgers and every other major league franchise came under intense scrutiny for their minority hiring policies. Depending on the organization, there were meaningful or less meaningful hirings, but the overall impact of the *Nightline* interview was to point up the hypocrisy of baseball's commemoration of Robinson. Campanis had been a last-minute substitute on the television program for Robinson teammate Don Newcombe.

COUNT CAMPAU

A 21-year minor leaguer who spent only parts of three seasons in the majors, Campau is the only player ever to lead two leagues in home runs in the same season. When the minor International League folded on July 10, 1890, the outfielder's three homers was tops in that circuit; picked up by the St. Louis Browns for the rest of the season, Campau slugged nine more four-baggers to lead the major league American Association as well.

BILL CAMPBELL

Campbell was the first reentry-draft free agent to be signed after the Messersmith-McNally decision cleared the way for free agency. Represented by agent LaRue Harcourt, the righthanded reliever got a four-year, $1 million pact from the Red Sox in November 1976; he had made $23,000 from the Twins the previous year. Although he turned in a career-high and league-high 31 saves for Boston in 1977, Campbell was soon afterward beset by arm miseries and never again broke into double figures in saves.

BUCK CANEL

The Argentine-born Canel pioneered Spanish-language broadcasts of major league baseball throughout the Western Hemisphere in the 1930s. In addition to delivering the play-by-play on decades of World Series games, he worked for some years with the Yankees.

ROBERT CANNON

A Milwaukee judge, Cannon was the "legal adviser" to the players prior to the selection of Marvin Miller as executive director of the Players Association. Recommended for the post by the owners, he was effectively a shill for their interests and was never without a word of caution to the players lest they act as ingrates in pressing any of their modest demands. In 1965 Cannon saw little contradiction in sharing his counsel with the players while advancing his own candidacy for baseball commissioner.

JOSÉ CANSECO

The first 40–40 player, Canseco spent the first nine years of his career daring his antics to undermine his on-the-field abilities. With Oakland between 1986 and 1991 he clouted at least 31 home runs five times, including league-leading figures of 42 in 1988 and 44 in 1991; it was also in 1988 that he stole 40 bases. As a member of the Athletics, the righthand-hitting outfielder also drove in 100 runs five times. Along with that production, however, went a cocky

personality that delighted in his numerous run-ins with traffic cops for late-night, high-speed joy rides; enjoyed the press and fan reaction to his assignations with the likes of rock star Madonna; and liked to put an adventurous face on brawls with his equally volatile wife, Esther.

Tiring of Canseco's perceived disruption of the team, Oakland traded him to Texas in the heat of a division race in 1992, even though all three players received in return (Ruben Sierra, Bobby Witt, and Jeff Russell) were in the walk year of their pacts. More disaster awaited with the Rangers in 1993, when Canseco, already suffering from arm twinges, persuaded manager Kevin Kennedy to allow him to pitch in a game; the result was a rotator cuff injury that sidelined him for all but 60 games, cost Texas a shot at the division title, and confined the slugger almost exclusively to designated hitting duties. Along with that went a divorce from Esther.

In succeeding years Canseco went from one team to another—Red Sox, back to the Athletics, Blue Jays, Devil Rays, Yankees, White Sox—as a home run-or-nothing DH, far from the glory years in Oakland when he and Mark McGwire had been dubbed the Bash Brothers. The highlight of his wanderings was with Toronto in 1998, when he drilled 46 home runs and drove in 107 runs; the lowlight was with an independent Newark team in 2001, from where he battled back to sign with Chicago. Entering the 2002 season, Canseco had collected 462 homers.

PAT CARAWAY

Caraway was a southpaw for the White Sox who won a relatively unexceptional 10 games in 1930. In one of his victories, however, he struck out Cleveland shortstop Joe Sewell twice. Sewell, the holder of every major league record for putting the bat on the ball, fanned only one other time the entire season.

HARRY CARAY

The original Holy Cow play-by-play sportscaster, Caray managed to shill for four clubs and countless sponsors over five decades without letting listeners forget that his chief product was himself. Starting with the Cardinals in 1945, his often tart evaluations of home team players and their (mutual) employers led him into a series of scrapes with humorless front offices—always with the rationale that he was "just a normal fan with a microphone." After pointing out once too often in 1969 that St. Louis was not what it had been, he was sent packing, ending up with Charlie Finley's Athletics for a year. When Finley had enough of the broadcaster's on-air cracks, the Oakland owner traded his contract to the White Sox for that of the more obeisant Bob Elson. It was the start of something loud.

For his first few years in Chicago Caray was a responsible as anyone for attracting the fans who showed up at Comiskey Park to watch generally mediocre clubs. By the middle of the 1970s, however, his jabs at several White Sox players, most notably home-run slugger Bill Melton, had created so much trouble in the clubhouse that owner John Allyn announced his intention of making changes in the broadcasting booth in 1976. But then Allyn had more urgent problems with his cash flow, and ended up having to sell out to Bill Veeck. Veeck, who had never particularly liked Caray's bluster, held off on a decision about rehiring him for several weeks, but then finally yielded to a threat by the announcer's station to hire him or look for another radio outlet. It was during their edgy years together that Veeck came up with the idea of having Caray punctuate the seventh-inning stretch with a ballpark singalong of "Take Me Out to the Ballgame."

Caray moved over to Wrigley Field in 1982 after the new White Sox ownership of Jerry Reinsdorf and Eddie Einhorn began crowding out his air time with their newly launched cable television operation. With the Cubs he carried on all his trademarks—the seventh-inning off-key crooning, his barbs at what he considered overpaid players when they failed in the clutch or made an error, and his flaunting of himself as the "typical fan." A stroke in 1987 forced him to miss his first game ever, to sit out the first six weeks of the season, and to curtail the afterhours carousing that earned him the nickname The Mayor of Rush Street. Following his death of heart problems in 1998, the Cubs decided to continue with the seventh-inning singalong with special game guests. Caray's son Skip has been an announcer for the Braves for some years and his grandson Chip has replaced him in the Chicago booth.

BERNIE CARBO

Carbo hit one of the most dramatic home runs in World Series history in 1975, when he came off the bench for Boston in the eighth inning of the sixth game and delivered a three-run shot against Rawley Eastwick of Cincinnati. The blast, his second pinch-homer of the Series, set the stage for the 12-inning marathon that would end with the more noted Carlton Fisk drive into the Fenway Park screen. Carbo's reputation otherwise was as a member of the Boston band in the 1970s that went out of its way to taunt managers Darrell Johnson and Don Zimmer. The outfielder was something of a later-day Dusty Rhodes in his apparent obliviousness to game situations when he was sent up to pinch-hit. On one occasion, after hitting a pinch-grand slam home run off a southpaw, the lefty swinger admitted he hadn't realized the bases were loaded or even noticed with what arm the pitcher had thrown.

ROD CAREW (Hall of Fame, 1991)

The American League's most proficient batsman for most of his 19-year career from 1967 and 1985, Carew hit .328 for the Twins and Angels. With a crouched, open stance that would influence hitting coaches as much as players, the lefty-swinging second baseman-first baseman collected 3,053 hits and seven batting titles, including a 1977 average of .388 that threatened the .400 mark until well into September. One of the greatest bunters in baseball history, he was also, in his younger years, a nimble base stealer; in 1969 he stole home seven times and would have tied Ty Cobb's major league record of eight but for a bowled-over umpire who failed to see that he had eluded a tag at the plate.

Carew left Minnesota after the 1978 season in one of the most protracted negotiations ever conducted. He might not have left at all if owner Calvin Griffith hadn't gotten drunk one night and boasted before a booster group that his franchise player had been a "damn fool" for accepting a two-year pact in 1977 that paid him the relatively low sum of $170,000 a year. Incensed by both Griffith's smugness and the feeling that the Minnesota owner had acted intolerably toward his Jewish agent, Carew demanded a five-year, $3.5 million contract at the next bargaining round, pointing out that he had approval rights on any deal Griffith might try to make rather than see him just walk off as a free agent. When San Francisco came forth with an offer, Carew said he didn't want to play in the National League. California was next, and it offered the player satisfactory money but failed to satisfy Griffith with players. The

Yankees were next, and Griffith was agreeable to the players, but Carew said he had no intention of playing for George Steinbrenner. Only after intervention by Commissioner Bowie Kuhn did Griffith go back to the Angels and Carew end up in Anaheim.

Although he himself averaged only about 50 strikeouts a year during his playing days, Carew the batting coach was mortified when his 2001 Milwaukee Brewers set the all-time record for team strikeouts. He resigned his post as soon as the season was over.

MAX CAREY (Hall of Fame, 1961)

Carey's 10 stolen base titles is second only to Rickey Henderson's 12 for the most in a career. A switch-hitting outfielder who spent most of his 20 years (1910–29) in the majors with the Pirates, he swiped at least 30 bases 14 times, retiring with 738 thefts. Carey also used his speed to pace National League hitters in triples twice and aggravated pitchers as well by drawing the most walks in the league twice. A lifetime .285 hitter, he batted over .300 in six full seasons, including a career high of .343 in Pittsburgh's world championship year of 1925. He also sparked the club in that season's World Series against Washington by getting 11 hits and batting .458.

A year later, however, Carey became *persona non grata* with owner Barney Dreyfuss after he attempted to stir up a team revolt against coach Fred Clarke; at issue were Clarke's sarcastic cracks about the outfielder's sudden offensive falloff and his urgings that Carey be benched. Packed off to the Dodgers in a mid-season trade, Carey played out the string for a couple more years, then was appointed Brooklyn manager in 1932. With the same crustiness he had brought to his play, he talked the Dodgers front office into a couple of deals—the acquisition of the bloated and perpetually hungover Hack Wilson, the trading off of Ernie Lombardi and Babe Herman—that haunted the franchise for the rest of the decade. He was eventually replaced by Casey Stengel when general manager Bob Quinn decided that the club needed a pilot less hostile to the New York press.

STEVE CARLTON (Hall of Fame, 1994)

The first pitcher to win four Cy Young awards, Carlton was the game's dominant southpaw for a good part of his 24-year (1965–88) career, to the point that there were no doubts as to who was meant by references to Lefty. Because of a mid-career de-

cision to stop talking to the media and his practice of strengthening his hands and forearms by twisting them into buckets of rice, he was relentlessly portrayed as an oddball. That was half-true: He *was* an eccentric, but not because he refused to talk to the press or did strengthening exercises.

Carlton came up with the Cardinals in 1965, but it wasn't until he developed a slider during a team trip to Japan in 1968 that he suggested the pitcher he was to become. While on his way to a 17-win season in 1969, he tied the National League record for strikeouts in one game by fanning 19 in a losing effort against the Mets. In 1971 he recorded 20 victories for the first of six times. Unfortunately for St. Louis, the other five times weren't in a Cardinals uniform. Because of a contract dispute that involved less than $10,000, trade-frenzied general manager Bing Devine dispatched him to the Phillies in exchange for Rick Wise prior to the 1972 season.

It was in Philadelphia that Carlton attacked the record book, starting with a league-leading 27 wins in 1972 that accounted for a stunning 45 percent of the club's victories. He also struck out 310 batters during the year—the first of five times that he would pace the NL in that category—and completed pitching's Triple Crown by posting a 1.97 ERA. His other 20-win seasons were in 1976 (best NL winning percentage), 1977, 1980, and 1982; the Cy Young trophies were collected for these last three years and 1972. His worst year in a Philadelphia uniform was 1973, when too much offseason banqueting after his triumphant 1972 campaign left him out of shape and contributed to 20 losses. It was mainly due to that experience that Carlton became a conditioning zealot, practicing isometrics and kung fu regularly as well as following his rice-bucket ritual. Aside from going 24–9 during the season in 1980, he beat the Royals twice during the World Series to secure the only world championship won by the Phillies.

In the mid-1980s Carlton and Nolan Ryan jockeyed past each other almost weekly in first surpassing Walter Johnson's all-time strikeout record and in then claiming the primacy for their own. But while Ryan was getting another wind that would enable him to leave everyone in his wake, the Phillies lefthander gradually ran out of gas. In 1986 he was released by Philadelphia, setting off an embarrassing three-year odyssey through the Giants, White Sox, Indians, and Twins. His overall 22–46 mark during this period, with accompanying ERAs rarely below five runs per nine innings, took some of the juice out of his career numbers, leaving him with an overall record of 329–244 (.574), with a 3.22 ERA. On the other hand, he ended up with the most strikeouts (4,000) by an NL pitcher and the most (4,136) by a lefthander in either league.

Carlton lived as a recluse after leaving baseball, and interviewers descending on him after his election to Cooperstown elicited observations along the lines of the conspiracy theories publicized by Lyndon LaRouche. At one time or another, he has accused the federal government, Moscow, and a cabal of Jewish-Swiss bankers of plotting to "keep humanity down." His long-time battery mate Tim McCarver has observed that Carlton has "a problem about being human."

BOB CARPENTER

Carpenter's takeover of the Phillies during World War II would have been a cause of grief in most franchises, but coming after decades of rum ownership by William Baker, Gerry Nugent, and William Cox, it seemed like a relief. The club was actually purchased by Carpenter's father, Robert, Sr., a multimillionaire member of the DuPont family who made it clear from the start that his main interest in the purchase was to find something for his son to do. One thing the younger Carpenter did in sitting in the club president's chair was to hire Red Sox farm director Herb Pennock to oversee baseball operations. The positive result was that Pennock was free to develop a Philadelphia farm system that eventually bore fruit with the Whiz Kids pennant of 1950; the negative result was that Carpenter grew increasingly resentful of the praise heaped on Pennock, so that when the veteran baseball man died of a stroke in 1948, he decided to handle the club's day-to-day affairs directly. Among the other things he handled were keeping the Phillies the most lily-white team in the National League: It wasn't until 1957, 10 years after Jackie Robinson's arrival on the major league scene, that the club had its first black player in backup infielder John Kennedy and not until 1960 that it had its first black regular in second baseman Tony Taylor.

Because of Philadelphia's 1950 pennant Carpenter could not be dissuaded for years that he was only a middle reliever or a backup catcher away from taking another flag. He was abetted in his illusion by

a series of front office aides, most notably Roy Hamey, who were markedly timid traders. Until Johnny Callison in 1959, not a single star player was imported, while veterans such as Richie Ashburn and Del Ennis were allowed to show their age before being exchanged for second-liners. That the franchise didn't begin to flounder as it had in the Baker-Nugent-Cox days was primarily due to the 1954 transfer of the Athletics to Kansas City, leaving the Philadelphia market entirely to the Phillies.

After a decade of mostly nondescript managers, Carpenter brought in John Quinn as general manager, and he in turn hired Gene Mauch as field boss. With Dick Allen emerging as the first four-star prospect from the club's farm system in years, Mauch appeared on the way to securing Carpenter another pennant in 1964 but then directed one of the biggest stretch collapses in baseball history, enabling the Cardinals to pick up the marbles. Carpenter never again came so close.

RULY CARPENTER

The National League has Carpenter's zeal for fishing to thank for not having adopted the designated hitter rule. In 1979 the Phillies owner took off with his rod and reel on the eve of a league meeting scheduled to discuss duplicating the American League's DH rule. Although junior partner Bill Giles had been told to vote in favor of a DH proposal because of the presence of gimping slugger Greg Luzinski on the roster, he himself was opposed to the ninth batter and tried to reach Carpenter to pose his arguments again before the vote. When he was told the owner was out on a boat, Giles returned to the meeting and abstained, leaving the pro-DH forces one vote short. The DH question was never again raised at a league meeting.

Carpenter took over the Phillies in 1973 from his father Bob Carpenter. It was a contradictory eight-year reign, especially where signing free agents was concerned. In 1978, for instance, he was so intent on signing Pete Rose that he agreed to the star's demand that he receive the highest salary of any player in professional sports; at the time, that meant bettering the contract of David Thompson of the NBA Denver Nuggets. To get the money he claimed the organization didn't have, Carpenter entered into an agreement with local television station WPHL to guarantee $600,000 of Rose's annual payment. In the wake of the 1981 players strike, on the other hand, the owner professed himself as disgusted with ownership concessions, asserting that he no longer "recognized the game I grew up with" and predicting that the walkout would be the "final nail" in the coffin of the national pastime. Shortly afterward, he sold out to Giles and the Taft Broadcasting Company for $30 million.

GARY CARTER

Carter gave smiling a bad name. Although recognized as the National League's best all-around catcher since the heyday of Johnny Bench, Carter was the constant target of snipings from teammates about his readiness to light up for the television cameras; originally nicknamed The Kid when he took over behind the plate for Montreal in the late 1970s, he was also known pejoratively as The Kodak Kid. Despite the criticism Carter was one of the dominating sluggers in the NL through the 1980s, winding up with 324 home runs and 1,225 RBIs. He was particularly effective in clutch situations, batting over .400 for the Expos in both the 1981 divisional playoff with the Phillies and the subsequent League Championship Series with the Dodgers. As a member of the Mets in 1986, he turned the World Series against the Red Sox around by clubbing two home runs in the third game after Boston had taken the first two contests. More memorably, it was Carter who started New York's astonishing sixth-game comeback in the 10th inning after the first two batters had made out; his two-strike single led to the three runs that were climaxed by Bill Buckner's error at first base on Mookie Wilson's grounder.

JOE CARTER

Carter had to create World Series history in 1993 before he gained overdue attention as baseball's most consistent slugger in the late 1980s and early 1990s. The righthand-hitting Toronto outfielder seized center stage with a three-run home run in the bottom of the ninth inning of the sixth game that gave the Blue Jays their second consecutive world championship; the blast, off Philadelphia southpaw Mitch Williams, marked the first time that a World Series ended with a come-from-behind sudden-death home run. Carter's 33 homers and 121 RBIs during the 1993 regular season represented the fifth time in seven years that he topped the 30-level in round-trippers and the seventh time in eight seasons that he

knocked across more than 100 runs. Between 1986 and 1994 his annual slugging averaged 30 homers and 110 RBIs, far and away the best in the major leagues.

ALEXANDER CARTWRIGHT (Hall of Fame, 1938)

Cartwright became one of the putative parents of baseball when he wrote its first rule book in 1846 for the benefit of the Knickerbocker Base Ball Club that he and his friends had formed. The bank clerk's role in the development of the sport came to light in 1936, when his descendant Bruce Cartwright objected to published reports of the Abner Doubleday myth on the centenary of the alleged invention of the game. Although most of the Knickerbockers refinements followed Cartwright's departure from the club, he can be credited with such innovations as settling on the four-base, diamond configuration of the field and the elimination of "soaking" (the practice of making a putout by hitting a batter or runner with the ball while he is between bases). For decades it was supposed that Cartwright umpired the first real baseball game—a 23–1 victory by the New York Baseball Club over the Knickerbockers at Hoboken's Elysian Fields on June 19, 1846. If earlier matches have since come to light, they haven't affected his pioneering role in formalizing the increasingly popular sports pastime.

As a baseball missionary, Cartwright's legacy is even more secure. Traveling overland to the California Gold Rush in 1849, he organized games along the way (among mountain men and Native Americans as well as traveling companions) and on the West Coast. Moving on to Hawaii in 1852, he introduced baseball on the islands before it had become a rage even in Philadelphia.

RICO CARTY

Carty was the first star player to reach the majors from the Dominican mill town of San Pedro de Macoris. An injury-prone slugger, he spent 15 seasons moving from team to team, enjoying his best year in 1970, when he won the National League batting title as a member of the Braves. Although San Pedro de Macoris has gained a special reputation for incubating slick-fielding shortstops, it has also produced, in addition to Carty, such notable sluggers as Sammy Sosa, George Bell, and Pedro Guerrero. The town's baseball roots go back to an invasion by Cuban all-stars at the turn of the century.

GEORGE CASE

Speedster Case was the last major leaguer to promote cigarettes in full uniform, and the first to appear in a big league promotion by Bill Veeck. The right-hand-hitting outfielder batted .282 for the Senators and (for one year) the Indians between 1937 and 1947 and led the American League in stolen bases six times. It was because of the perceived inconsistency between Case's baserunning prowess and his nicotine habit that AL president Will Harridge, responding to protests from fans, canceled a series of magazine advertisements for Camels scheduled to appear early in the 1940 season; Case later made his endorsement in street clothes.

While with the Indians in 1946, Case raced Olympic track star Jesse Owens in an exhibition arranged soon after Veeck assumed control of the club; it was the only match race the outfielder ever lost.

DAN CASEY

An unlikely prototype for the hero of Ernest L. Thayer's "Casey at the Bat," lefty Casey never let his lifetime .164 batting average deter him from claiming that honor. His main proof, aside from his surname, was that in the late 1880s he had pitched for the Phillies, whose Huntington Avenue Grounds was in an area once known as Mudville. Casey cited as Thayer's source the events of a game against the Giants, but the date he gave turned out to be an off-day for the Phillies. As late as March 3, 1938, Casey, then in his mid-70s, appeared on Gabriel Heatter's radio program *We the People* to press his claim to literary immortality.

HUGH CASEY

Reliever Casey threw the pitch that made Mickey Owen a goat in the 1941 World Series; he is also the only major leaguer to throw punches at Ernest Hemingway. The righthander's sparring match with the novelist took place at Hemingway's Havana home while the Dodgers were in the Cuban city for spring training in 1942. Invited over with several other members of the team for a few drinks, Casey drank enough to make him susceptible to a Hemingway challenge to put on boxing gloves. When the Dodgers pitcher beat him, the ego-sore novelist proposed a duel with pistols or swords. It failed to materialize.

Owen's passed ball on a third strike to the Yankees Tommy Henrich in the ninth inning of the fourth game of the 1941 Series, which led to a comeback victory for New York, may or may not have come on a spitball. But Casey got revenge of a sort. Six years later he became the only hurler to win a Series game by throwing merely one pitch; coming into the fourth game of the 1947 Series in the ninth inning with the bases loaded and one out, he got the same Henrich to bounce into a double play and then went back to the bench to watch Cookie Lavagetto ruin Bill Bevens's no-hitter with a two-out double for a 3–2 Brooklyn victory.

Casey compiled a 75–42 record, mostly for Brooklyn, in his nine-year career on both sides of World War II. In 1951 he committed suicide following his failure to patch up his marriage after years of heavy drinking and womanizing.

NORM CASH

Cash demonstrated the wonders of illegally hollowed-out bats in 1961, when he clouted 41 home runs, drove home 132 runs, and paced the American League in both batting (.361) and hits (193). The lefty-swinging first baseman also combined with Detroit teammate Rocky Colavito in knocking in 272 runs—two more than Roger Maris and Mickey Mantle managed as they were clouting 115 home runs. Although he had a couple of other seasons with conspicuous long-ball numbers, Cash never again hit as high as .290 over his 17-year (1958–74) career, never again had 100 RBIs, and never again had more than 168 safeties in a season. He later confirmed what opposition managers had been charging throughout the 1961 campaign—that he had hollowed out and reinforced his lumber.

PHIL CAVARRETTA

Despite a playing career that included a batting championship and an MVP trophy (both in 1945), Cavarretta cemented his place in Cubs lore mainly for being too honest. After two-and-a-half seasons of managing dreary Chicago clubs, he was asked by owner Phil Wrigley in spring training of 1954 to assess the team's chances for the coming season. When Cavarretta replied that the Cubs didn't look much better than they had the previous year, he was summarily fired for being "defeatist."

Brought up to the majors when he was still in his teens, Cavarretta was the only player who could claim to have been on a major league roster at the same time as both Babe Ruth and Hank Aaron.

O. P. CAYLOR

As sports editor of the Cincinnati *Enquirer,* Caylor straddled the line between observing and participating in the city's baseball affairs for two decades. Whatever journalistic objectivity he might have claimed before disappeared with the expulsion of the Reds from the National League in 1880; from that point on he pursued a vendetta against the circuit and its founder-president, William Hulbert. As he had hoped, an 1881 journey to St. Louis with a makeshift Cincinnati team for a series of games with the local Brown Stockings led directly to the formation of the American Association the following year. A cofounder of the league, Caylor also managed the AA version of the Reds for two seasons (1885–86) and represented the loop in peace talks with the NL. It wasn't until 1887 that his dual role caught up to him: Although the manager and a minority stockholder in the AA's New York Metropolitans in 1887, he was refused admission to the league's annual meeting because he was also a journalist.

Caylor's permanent transfer to New York in 1890, as editor of the New York *Sporting Times,* was calculated to set up a weekly organ in support of the owners during the Players League war and to counter the influence of Francis Richter's *Sporting Life,* which endorsed the player position. From this pulpit he denounced the Brotherhood defectors as spoiled, greedy ingrates. Two years later, however, he turned his pen against the owners when every club released its personnel on the last day of the season and agreed not to sign each other's players only to avoid paying each man the two additional weeks salary their contracts stipulated.

BETTY CAYWOOD

Caywood was the first woman to be a regular part of an on-air baseball broadcasting team. Hired by Kansas City owner Charlie Finley on a dare in the late 1960s, she did mostly color commentary on events in the grandstands and dugouts.

CESAR CEDEÑO

Cedeño never lived up to predictions of a Hall of Fame production on the field but he had few equals during his 17-year (1970–86) career for ending up on a police blotter. Between the lines the outfielder sprang out of the box with Houston with two seasons of leading the league in doubles, two consecutive .320 years, another campaign when he clouted 26 homers and batted in 102 runs, and six consecutive marks of at least 50 stolen bases. Even when he was nearing the end of the trail, with the 1985 Cardinals, he proved to be the difference for a division title by replacing an injured Jack Clark in September and batting .434 in 28 games. But the righthand-hitting Cedeño, whom Leo Durocher had habitually compared to Willie Mays (first positively, then negatively), rarely let an off-season go by without ending up in a courtroom. In 1974 he was convicted in his native Dominican Republic of the involuntary manslaughter of his girlfriend; he got out of that scrape by paying a fine of a mere $100. In 1985 he attacked a heckler in the stands of the Astrodome; although charges weren't pressed, he was fined $5,000 by the Astros. In 1985 he paid out another $7,400 for drunk driving and property damage. In 1988 he was arrested for attacking another girlfriend, trying to take their child, and assaulting a number of policemen called to the scene by the woman.

ORLANDO CEPEDA (Hall of Fame, 1999)

Cepeda's 17-year (1958–74) career had to weather incessant reevaluation because of a tug-of-war over his Hall of Fame credentials. San Francisco's first grandstand hero when the Giants moved to California in 1958, the righthand-hitting first baseman clouted 379 home runs and drove in 1,365 runs while compiling a .297 average. Included in the numbers were league-leading totals in home runs in 1961 and in RBIs in 1961 and 1968, a Rookie of the Year award in 1958, and an MVP trophy in 1967 for his crucial role in a pennant win by the Cardinals.

Cepeda's troubles with keepers of the flame started after his career was over, when he did prison time in his native Puerto Rico for drug dealing. Although his rehabilitation and community work eclipsed that episode, moralists among Cooperstown voters continued to deny him his place among the sport's superstars. The situation got even stickier in 1993 when the Giants front office launched an unprecedented Oscar-like campaign to get him elected. As in a similar case with Phil Rizzuto, he only gained admission after some long-time friends joined the Veterans Committee.

Cepeda's father Pedro was known as the Babe Ruth of the Caribbean.

RON CEY

In was because of Cey's beaning by Goose Gossage of the Yankees during the 1981 World Series that the major leagues passed a regulation requiring batters to wear helmets with double earflaps. A righthanded batter known as The Penguin for his hot streaks in the colder months, third baseman Cey was part of the two most famous quartets in Los Angeles Dodgers baseball: the first foursome to hit 30 home runs in a year (in 1977, with Steve Garvey, Reggie Smith, and Dusty Baker) and the longest-running intact infield (1973–81, with Garvey, Davey Lopes, and Bill Russell).

HENRY CHADWICK (Hall of Fame, 1938)

The English-born Chadwick is the only writer in the Hall of Fame proper, having earned his berth for a half-century of refining and proselytizing for the game.

A rounders player as a boy, Chadwick was the cricket reporter for *The New York Times* when he was converted to baseball in 1856. From initial nonpaying pieces he published in the *Times,* his output grew to include thousands of articles in newspapers and magazines as well as various annual summaries of the game, including those in the *Spalding Guide,* which he edited from 1881 until his death in 1908. Chadwick reinforced this body of work with service on the rules committee of every major amateur association and several professional leagues in his effort to convert baseball into a "manly" and "scientific" pursuit worthy of being called "a national sport for America." Among his accomplishments were the collecting of historical (and quasi-historical) tales about the earliest days of the game; the development of a set of rules that attempted to blend the proper proportions of offense and pitching; the refinement of the box score into something very similar to what appears in newspapers today; the creation of a scoring system that has survived with very few changes; and the fostering of the mystique of statistics that still surrounds baseball.

Chadwick had the title Father of Baseball applied to him even in his lifetime, but a $600 pension awarded to him by the National League for his long service on the Rules Committee so irritated Andrew Freedman that the Giants owner accused him of greed; Chadwick kept the pension, shunned the Polo Grounds, and recommended for the rest of Freedman's reign that others follow his lead. Like most fathers, he could also be cranky when the hobby horses he chose to ride were not everyone's idea of an ideal mount. As early as the 1860s, he complained that the ball was too lively. He advocated the addition of a 10th player, a right shortstop, arguing that "there is not a reasonable objection that can be made against it." He lamented the founding of the National League as "a sad blunder." He proposed that NL owners lower prices, not to spare the financially beleaguered fan but to generate less revenue as an excuse for lowering the salaries of players, whom he deemed overpaid and pampered. He complained that the emphasis on swinging for home runs was ruining the game—this in the 1890s. He castigated the influence of gambling and its potential for corruption so often and for so long that Harry Wright, for one, felt that he was alarming the public without cause. Chadwick declared the Players League a "terrorist" organization that forced players to join through high-pressure tactics. And he winked at Al Spalding's creation of the Doubleday creation myth, which he knew to be patently untrue.

Around the turn of the century Father Baseball had become the object of so much derision in major league clubhouses that his annual pennant prognostications came to be regarded among players as the kiss of death for the teams he slated first.

CHRIS CHAMBLISS

Chambliss hit 185 regular-season home runs, but none of them came close to the drama of his one postseason clout. The first baseman's solo blast, in the bottom of the ninth inning of the fifth game of the 1976 League Championship Series off Kansas City's Mark Littell, broke a 6–6 tie, gave the Yankees their first pennant in a dozen years and created such havoc on the field that he couldn't touch home plate; he later had to reemerge from the clubhouse under police protection to make his game-ending run official. The lefty swinger spent 17 seasons (1971 to 1988) with the Indians and Braves in addition to the Yankees, batting .279 and leading his league in an offensive category only once—pinch-hits in his final full season, 1986.

AARON CHAMPION

A Cincinnati civic booster and president of the local Red Stockings in 1869, the aptly named Champion decided to hire Harry Wright as club manager and to field the first openly all-professional team. Wright's recruits went on to a legendary consecutive-game winning streak of 56 (or up to 130, depending upon whose research is used) games. The streak ended on June 14, 1870, after which Champion wired back to Cincinnati: "Atlantics 8; Cincinnati 7. The finest game ever played. Our boys did nobly, but fortune was against them. Eleven innings played. Though beaten, not disgraced." What the wire failed to reveal was that he and Wright had insisted on continuing a nine-inning, 5–5 tie and that the Brooklyn club had rallied for three runs in the home half of the 11th after Cincinnati had taken a two-run lead in the top of the inning. The Red Stockings disbanded soon afterward when sponsors could no longer afford the high salaries their players' success could command; so strapped was the club at the end that its ballpark had to be dismantled and the lumber sold to stave off creditors. Nevertheless, the Red Stockings play-for-pay-openly experiment encouraged similar moves by other clubs and led directly to the formation of the National Association, the first professional league, in 1871.

FRANK CHANCE (Hall of Fame, 1946)

Chance is less indebted than Johnny Evers or Joe Tinker to Franklin Adams for his election to the Hall of Fame. A lifetime .296 hitter, he was that rare species of a first baseman who could steal bases with consistency, leading the National League in that category with career highs of 67 in 1903 and 57 in 1906; nor was he averse to taking a walk or, as almost proved fatal, getting hit by a pitch to reach first base. As the Cubs playing manager from 1905 to 1912, Chance rolled up two world championships, four pennants, and two second-place finishes. Nowhere near as cantankerous as Evers or Tinker, at least in his early years, he often took public stands on behalf of his players against the Cubs ownership, ultimately losing his job for his efforts. Some of his charges weren't being sardonic when they referred to him as The Peerless Leader.

Throughout his stay in Chicago Chance relied on strong pitching and "little ball" tactics for winning. In common with other managers of the period, he had charge of his own deals, and his pickups of outfielder Jimmy Sheckard from the Dodgers and third baseman Harry Steinfeldt from the Reds proved crucial to his club's success. His main problem in the Windy City, however, was owner Charles Murphy, who sought any excuse to cut back on salaries and who battled his first baseman-manager almost annually over contract concessions. The crisis point in their relations came after the 1911 season, when Chance was revealed as having developed a blood clot in his head from having taken too many fastballs in the skull. With his chief antagonist apparently out of the way in an intensive care unit, Murphy took to the newspapers to denounce several Cubs veterans as drunkards and threaten their release. To the owner's chagrin, Chance got up out of his hospital bed to portray the alcoholism allegations as mere pretexts for cutting salaries. Although the press was won over to the manager's side, it didn't come as a shock when Murphy notified Chance the following year that he was through as the dugout boss.

When the Yankees waved a $40,000 contract in front of Chance, Murphy, who still had the right to his services as a player, blocked the way. What ensued was a round-robin of negotiations among Murphy, Cincinnati owner Garry Herrmann, New York co-owner Frank Farrell, and the presidents of both leagues before they could all agree that Tinker would be dealt to Cincinnati, the Reds would withdraw a claim they had made on Chance (mainly as leverage for acquiring Tinker), and The Peerless Leader would be released so he could take over the Yankees.

New York had wanted Chance mainly to offset the popularity of John McGraw in the city, but he proved to match the Giants manager only in an authoritarianism that had risen sharply after a hearing loss caused by all the beanings. It didn't help either that the Yankees were drifting around at the bottom of the standings or that Hal Chase, a former club manager, was still on the premises. When Chase wasn't mocking Chance's starched-collar ways, he was ridiculing his whiney voice (the result of his deafness) or complaining about the manager's attempts to continue playing first base while shoving the so-called Prince of the position over to second. The friction ended with Chance accusing Chase of laying down during games and trading him to the White Sox for a pair of bench-warmers. The trade stuck in the craw of New York owners Farrell and

Bill Devery, and lingered as the cause of a shoving match between the pilot and Devery the following year. Chance was soon gone from the premises, being replaced by 23-year-old Roger Peckinpaugh.

Chance had one more year in a uniform, as manager of the cellar-dwelling 1923 Red Sox, before retiring with a .593 winning percentage, the sixth highest in history.

HAPPY CHANDLER (Hall of Fame, 1982)

Chandler was never quite the pliable creature that major league owners expected him to be when they elected him to succeed Judge Kenesaw Landis as commissioner in 1945, but he wasn't the revolutionary that he painted himself as, either. At his best, he made the right enemies; at his worst, he tried to pass off their manipulations as part of some master plan of his own.

Chandler was given baseball's top administrative post in April 1945, after he had impressed several owners, and particularly Larry MacPhail of the Yankees, with his defense of the sport's interests as a member of the U.S. Senate from Kentucky; he had been especially vocal in opposing moves to shut down the game as an inessential activity during World War II. The owners had even more reason to be satisfied in 1946, when Chandler ignored protests by Philadelphia first baseman Tony Lupien that his trade by the Phillies to a minor league club violated National Defense Act statutes protecting the jobs of military veterans; worked feverishly behind the scenes to thwart attempts by Robert Murphy's American Baseball Guild to unionize members of the Pirates; and blacklisted the major leaguers who had jumped to play in Jorge Pasquel's Mexican League. Although Chandler made a gesture of fining Cardinals owner Sam Breadon $5,000 for trying to negotiate separately with Pasquel, he later admitted giving the money back to the St. Louis executive "because I had made my point."

It was with New York teams, however, that Chandler had his stormiest moments. Most conspicuously, there was Brooklyn president Branch Rickey's breaking of the color line in 1946 by signing Jackie Robinson. Rickey himself always voiced appreciation of Chandler's stand on the issue, which amounted more to noninterference than to support. In the Kentuckian's own eyes, however, that merited him at least as much recognition as Rickey for brav-

ing the antagonism of the other 15 big league owners of the day. He never tired of pointing out how he had told reporters in 1946 that "if a black can make it in Okinawa and Guadalcanal, hell, he can make it in baseball"—if usually omitting the detail that he said it to newsmen for black dailies. In this as in other situations, Chandler showed more wiliness than depth of conviction—a stance that reflected his political reputation at home and that he would later seek to parlay into the Democratic Party's presidential nomination.

If he was only a minor player in the Robinson story, Chandler was very much the protagonist of the 1947 suspension of Dodgers pilot Leo Durocher. The suspension followed a tangle of scandals linking Durocher to everything from underworld gambling activities to adultery. The announcement that the manager had to sit out the 1947 season inflamed a New York press that had always viewed Chandler as a boastful hillbilly who had usurped the commissioner's job from Ford Frick, the National League president who had started his career as a reporter. One typical comment was that "Chandler has found Durocher guilty of running a red light, so gave him the chair." Even years later the harshness of the Chandler sentence for what was never a specifically cited violation prompted theories that Durocher was merely the fall guy for Rickey. One school of thought, for instance, said that Chandler had been carrying out the orders of the anti-integration owners in depriving Robinson of the dugout support he would have gotten in his rookie season from Durocher. Others discerned the hand of Dodgers attorney Walter O'Malley, who had been making moves to force out Rickey and for whom the Durocher suspension might prove useful ammunition. But in view of Chandler's own ambitions and his admitted irritation at being unfavorably compared to his predecessor Landis, it would not have been beyond him to create—in order to immediately clean up—his own Black Sox scandal.

By 1951 it wasn't only the New York press that wanted Chandler out. The Braves were infuriated with him because he had declared infielder Jack Lohrke a free agent after some irregularities in his demotion to the minors, and the Cardinals were no happier after he rejected a request to let St. Louis play its Sunday games at night during the summer because of the city's sweltering temperatures. But

Chandler's chief nemesis was Yankees co-owner Del Webb, whose gambling interests in Las Vegas and connections to the mob there and elsewhere sparked an official investigation by the commissioner's office. Unfortunately, the man entrusted with the probe, Walter Mulbry, tipped off Webb, leaving the inquiry dead before it started. Under the impression that he still had enough owners in his camp in 1951, Chandler asked for an extension on his six-year contract, due to run out in 1952. He was stunned when the Yankees, Braves, and Cardinals mustered enough opposition to deny him a necessary three-quarters majority. Informed he was going to be succeeded by Frick, Chandler commented: "Well, the owners had a vacancy and I guess they decided to keep it."

SPUD CHANDLER

Toiling for the Yankees from 1937 to 1947, Chandler was the only pitcher besides Babe Ruth to post winning marks every season for a career lasting at least 10 years. His record of 109–43 also represents the highest winning percentage (.717) for pitchers with a minimum of 100 wins. Despite such prestigious numbers, the righthander managed to lead the New York staff in victories only twice.

BEN CHAPMAN

A solid outfielder for the Yankees and other clubs in the 1930s, Chapman left his deepest impression on baseball as the bigoted Phillies manager whose racist invective against Jackie Robinson in 1947 did more to unite the Dodgers than Branch Rickey's relentless sermons on brotherhood. Aside from objecting to Robinson on general racist principles, Chapman had special fits whenever someone referred to the Brooklyn star's running ability, since he himself had led the American League in steals four times.

Chapman's viciousness against Robinson erupted during the first 1947 Brooklyn trip to Philadelphia; his game-long diatribes through a weekend series were encouraged by Phillies owner Bob Carpenter and general manager Herb Pennock, who sat behind their dugout without comment during the Dodgers visit. Off the field the manager was also given to such pearls as telling members of the Brooklyn party that they would soon have a team of "24 niggers and one dago [Carl Furillo]." But less than a year after all his raving, Chapman found himself in the embarrassing position of having to ask Robinson for a favor to save his job. Because of regular hammering from syndicated Hearst columnist Walter Winchell for his racist outbursts, he asked that the Brooklyn star be photographed with him in a handshake to show that he wasn't as nasty as the newspaperman was telling the country. Robinson acceded to the request and Chapman got his picture, but by then Carpenter and Pennock had decided they were better off with a lower-profile manager and fired him anyway.

As a player, Chapman batted .302 over 15 seasons. In 1937 he was traded by the Yankees to the Senators for Jake Powell, the outfielder who preceded him by some years in embarrassing baseball officialdom for his racist posture.

FRED CHAPMAN

Chapman became the youngest player ever to appear in a major league contest when, four months shy of 15, he was summoned from Reading and given the ball for the American Association Philadelphia club on July 22, 1887. With Cleveland ahead, 6–4, in the bottom of the fifth inning, a substitute umpire named Mitchell called Athletics batter Henry Larkin out for interfering with the catcher on an attempted steal of home. When the Spiders objected too strenuously that it was the runner who should have been called out, Mitchell declared the game a forfeit. Chapman was denied the victory, however, and never appeared in another big league contest.

RAY CHAPMAN

Chapman gained tragic singularity on August 16, 1920, when a Carl Mays fastball made him the only beaning fatality in big league history. The Indians shortstop lingered 24 hours before succumbing to a fractured skull. In the wake of the accident, numerous lunatics threatened to get even with Mays the next time the New York righthander arrived in Cleveland. The danger was overcome in good part because Chapman's replacement, Joe Sewell, sparked the club to a successful pennant run down the final weeks of the season.

Chapman had been a fixture in the Cleveland lineup since 1913, enjoying his best season in 1917, when he hit .302 with 52 stolen bases.

JOE CHARBONEAU

The cocky Charboneau was baseball's ultimate one-year wonder. After taking Rookie of the Year honors for a .289 average and 23 home runs with the Indians in 1980, the righthand-hitting outfielder played only 70 more major league games (averaging .211 with six homers) before curveballs and back problems forced his retirement. True to character, he responded to being farmed out in 1981 by refusing to find an apartment in Charleston, West Virginia, insisting on sleeping at the minor league stadium because of his confidence that he would soon be called back to Cleveland. After a few weeks he went apartment-hunting.

OSCAR CHARLESTON (Hall of Fame, 1976)

No less an authority than John McGraw thought Charleston the greatest player in the Negro leagues. Compared to Ty Cobb for his aggressiveness both on and off the field, to Babe Ruth for his power hitting and fan appeal, and (at least early in his career) to Tris Speaker for his defensive skills from a short center field, the lefty swinger is credited with a batting average in the .350s over his 27-year (1915–41) career with the Indianapolis ABCs, Harrisburg Giants, Homestead Grays, Pittsburgh Crawfords, and other clubs. He topped the .400 mark in several seasons and led his league in homers six times.

Charleston also had something in common with his admirer McGraw: brawling. At various junctures he mixed it up with an umpire, a Dominican agent trying to recruit players from his team, a Ku Klux Klansman, and several Cuban soldiers (during one of his nine stints of winter ball in the country). Moving to first base later in his career, he became a playing pilot for several teams, including the famed Crawfords for the better part of the 1930s. He was felled by a fatal heart attack soon after leading the Indianapolis Clowns to a Negro American League title in 1954.

MIKE CHARTAK

Chartak helped demonstrate that scoundrels don't always wait for patriotism to be their last resort. In 1942 the first baseman-outfielder was about to be sold by the Yankees to the Browns for $14,000 when Washington owner Clark Griffith remonstrated with New York that the prospect would benefit baseball and the nation as a whole if he were showcased instead in the wartime capital. The Yankees bought the argument, even selling Chartak to Griffith for a lower price of $12,000. The Washington boss promptly turned around and resold him to the Browns for the original $14,000.

HAL CHASE

Chase was simultaneously baseball's most notorious crook and its most unjustly maligned player. Charming and charismatic, he also had a reputation for petty theft, for cheating at cards, and for an incessant womanizing that cost him two marriages. When he didn't like a manager, he didn't hesitate to show him up on the field, in the clubhouse, or in meetings with club executives. For all that, attempts to link his every untoward move on or off the field with gamblers, especially early in his 15-year (1905–19) career, have been based more on image than on reality—an image that baseball officials had motives of their own for propagating.

Dubbed Prince Hal for his defensive prowess and his flamboyant indulging in New York's night life, Chase was the premier first baseman of the deadball era. When allowing his performance to match his abilities, he exhibited a previously unseen flair at charging bunts even to the third-base side, throwing to third for force-outs, and turning the first-to-shortstop-to-first double play. At the plate, the righthand-hitting (but lefthand-throwing) Chase batted .291, posting the highest average in the National League in 1916 and pacing the Federal League in homers in 1915.

Signed by the New York Highlanders (later the Yankees) in 1905, Chase had his first run-in with management in September 1908 when, angry at not being appointed manager, he bolted the club in favor of the outlaw California League. Allowed to return after paying a nominal $200 fine, he was welcomed back by teammates who presented him with a silver loving cup. If manager George Stallings was also relieved to get his best hitter back for the 1909 season, he was much less happy about it the following year, when he accused Chase of undermining his authority by "laying down"—a generic expression about lack of effort that some historians have erroneously identified exclusively with game fixing. Stallings picked on the wrong player: Because the Yankees had no intention of getting rid of their chief box-office draw and because American League president Ban Johnson despised Stallings, it was the manager himself who got the thumb—replaced by none other than Chase. That lasted only through the 1911 campaign, by which time there was general agreement that Chase had too many groundballs, poker hands, and women to pick up to be distracted by managing.

With the arrival of Frank Chance as manager in 1913, Chase began counting down the days to the end of his first stay in New York. Frictions started in spring training with the aging Chance's decision to try to play first base for another year, forcing the lefthand-throwing Chase to move to second. Injuries to both ended that experiment, but by then Chase had become something of a clubhouse clown for mimicking the hard-of-hearing Chance behind his back. When Chance found out about the mocking, he wasted little time in unloading his first baseman on the White Sox in a June 1 swap for bench-warmers Rollie Zeider and Babe Bolton. The trade had more than one repercussion. For one thing, it led to punches between Chance and Yankees co-owner Bill Devery, making inevitable another managerial change in 1914. More central to Chase fables, it triggered retroactive accusations that he had been throwing games for gambling purposes while with New York. Six decades after the events, sportswriter Fred Lieb was writing that just before the deal with Chicago, Chance had told him and Heywood Broun that Chase was throwing games, that Lieb's editor had talked him out of writing about it, and that Broun had touched on it only glancingly. But Chance never made any such accusation and there was never any mention of it in print by Broun, glancing or otherwise.

Chase stayed with Chicago barely long enough to claim reciprocity for the standard clause in contracts that gave owners the right to release a player with 10 days notice. Chase being Chase, though, he signed with the Federal League Buffalo Blues only five days after leaving the White Sox and made his FL debut the next day. Afterwards he hid out in Canadian a hotel room for three days to evade an injunction sought by Chicago owner Charlie Comiskey and arrived for his home game in Buffalo dressed in drag. When he finally was served with the court papers, he found a judge who refused to make the injunction permanent, ruling that the reserve clause was "despotism" and "quasi-peonage."

After the collapse of the Federal League, Chase landed with the Reds in 1916, quickly establishing himself as the best player on the team—and the National League batting champion. Despite ongoing clubhouse chatter about his honesty, it wasn't until August 1918 that Reds manager Christy Mathewson announced that he was suspicious of the frequency with which his usually sure-handed first baseman was making marginally errant tosses on plays in which the pitcher had to cover first. The reason for Mathewson's delay in making his accusation was that nobody, least of all Reds owner Garry Herrmann with his German background, wanted a baseball scandal while the country was fighting Germany in World War I and while baseball was trying to secure draft-exempt status for its players. One reason the accusation came at all was a July 25 game in which Chase and second baseman Lee Magee collaborated in losing far too conspicuously. Another was that Mathewson learned around this time that Chase had been cheating in their regular bridge games.

Suspended for the rest of 1918, Chase was acquitted at a winter hearing before NL president John Heydler despite testimony by several Cincinnati teammates that he had approached them about collaborating in his schemes. The exculpatory evidence included the fact that Chase had hit a home run to win one of the games that he was accused of throwing and that the chief witness against him, pitcher Jimmy Ring, couldn't keep his story straight. It hardly helped that the prime mover of the charges, Mathewson, was in France with the American Expeditionary Forces.

Chase found himself traded to the Giants in 1919 even though New York manager John McGraw had been called to testify against him at the Heydler hearing. While the standard telling of the story has it that McGraw became suspicious of the way Chase and third baseman Heinie Zimmerman were playing toward the end of the season, the facts are that, while Zimmerman was suspended for throwing games and Chase was present at approaches made to players, the injured first baseman was never suspended, but remained with the club through the rest of the season and beyond to a postseason exhibition tour. McGraw subsequently perjured himself during the Black Sox scandal trial with the claim that he sent both players contracts so laughable, he knew they would have to reject them. While he might have done so with Zimmerman, the pact received by Chase for 1920 called for only a modest $1,000 cut from his 1919 contract—inevitable given his age (37) and injury-plagued 1919 season. And even that had been only an initial offer subject to subsequent talks with the negotiation-savvy Chase.

Chase's role in the 1919 World Series fix has been obscured by his escape from punishment and exaggerated by those with reason to shift the blame onto him. His name was a constant refrain at the 1920 grand jury hearings that indicted the Chicago Eight, both inside the courtroom and especially in post-session press conferences at which McGraw and Heydler lost no opportunity to blame Chase for as much of the conspiracy as they could. Giants pitcher Rube Benton chimed in with preposterous testimony that the Prince had pocketed $40,000 betting on Cincinnati in the 1919 World Series. (At the prevailing odds, Chase would have had to bet about $36,000—a ridiculous sum for someone making $7,000 a year—to win anything like that.) In fact, Chase was on a barnstorming tour with the Giants through New England and Canada while the conspiracy was being hatched. That he knew of the plot is certain from the number of long-distance phone calls he made while on the trip; that he masterminded the entire plot or was even a major figure in it, as the prevailing wisdom has had it, is absurd.

Arrested in California to force his return to Chicago to stand trial with the other defendants, Chase was released on a technicality, then immediately forgotten by the same prosecutors who had been so ardent to tie him into the conspiracy a short time before. For his part, Commissioner Kenesaw Landis never included him among the players outlawed over the 1919 Series. Years later, Landis responded to a letter from Chase inquiring about his status by officially informing him that there were no charges against him. By then, however, the first baseman had long been *persona non grata* with all 16 major league teams. Playing for (and owning part of) the San Jose team in the independent Mission League in 1920, he found time to become implicated in a gambling ring that involved five of the eight clubs in the Pacific Coast League. He later drifted through several outlaw leagues in Arizona mining towns before moving back to California, where he died in 1947.

TOM CHENEY

On September 12, 1962 Cheney set the record for the most strikeouts in a game of any length—striking out 21 Orioles in 16 innings for Washington. He won only 18 other games in an eight-year career.

JACK CHESBRO (Hall of Fame, 1946)

Chesbro holds the modern record for most victories in a season—41 for the 1904 Highlanders. But with his team within percentage points of first place on the last day of the season, an errant spitball in the ninth inning against Boston cost him number 42 and New York the pennant. Overall, the righthander won only 198 games (and lost 132) in an 11-year (1899–1909) career, almost exclusively with Pittsburgh and New York; he did, however, have five 20-win seasons. Chesbro is also the only pitcher to lead both the National and American leagues in won-lost percentage, pacing NL hurlers with percentages of .677 (21–10) in 1901 and .824 (28–6) in 1902 and topping the AL with .774 (41–12) in his best-of-times-worst-of-times 1904 campaign. The New Yorkers had entered the final day of that season needing a doubleheader sweep of the Red Sox to move into first place, but with two out, a runner on third, and the score tied, 2–2, in the opening contest, catcher Red Kleinow could not grab a 1–2 pitch against Freddy Parent, enabling Boston to go ahead for good. Chesbro's wife campaigned for years to have the official scorer's call changed to a passed ball against Kleinow.

HILDA CHESTER

The raspy-voiced Chester was the most raucous of the Dodgers fans who cheered on the team at Ebbets Field in the 1940s and 1950s. After she suffered the first of two heart attacks and was forbidden by doctors to keep yelling, she turned up in the bleachers with a frying pan and iron ladle, banging away from the first pitch to the last out. Dodgers players later presented her with a cowbell, which became her most lasting signature. Chester was so enamored of Leo Durocher that she perjured herself during a trial over the Brooklyn manager's assault on a fan, claiming to the judge that the victim "called me a cocksucker and Leo came to my defense."

Although she could have sat anywhere in the park she desired, Chester generally preferred the center field bleachers so she could be closer to her favorite players, Dixie Walker and Pete Reiser. On one celebrated occasion she yelled for Reiser to pick up a note she dropped on the field and take it to Durocher. On his way to the dugout Reiser paused to say hello to Dodgers boss Larry MacPhail, sitting along the first-base line, then handed the note to Durocher.

The manager read it, then ordered Hugh Casey to get up in the bullpen. Although starter Whitlow Wyatt had been sailing along up to that point, Durocher brought in Casey, who was promptly knocked around. After the game a furious Durocher warned Reiser never to hand him another note from MacPhail during a game. The note had said, "GET CASEY UP, WYATT'S LOSING IT." That made Chester the only bleacher fan ever to change pitchers.

STEVE CHILCOTT

Chilcott came to epitomize the perils of the annual amateur draft after he was chosen by the Mets in 1966. The number one choice in the nation, the catcher never rose above the low minor leagues, in part thanks to an arm injury. By choosing Chilcott first, the Mets enabled the Athletics to draft future Hall of Famer Reggie Jackson.

Two years later the Mets fared only marginally better by choosing shortstop Tim Foli with their number one pick. The Yankees went fourth and chose Thurman Munson.

EDDIE CHILES

As owner of the Rangers for most of the 1980s, oil millionaire Chiles saw that as little of his money as possible was spent on the team. Already 70 when he bought out Brad Corbett in January 1980 and with a reputation for America first bluster, he made it clear that he considered free agents the next worst thing to Communists, so allowed his front office to do little more than make endless deals involving second-stringers. By the middle of the decade, with his own fortune dwindling with the price of crude oil, he made the first of several attempts to reach an accord with Edward Gaylord of Gaylord Broadcasting as a buyer or majority partner—forays that were instantly thwarted by other American League owners who didn't want the media giant turning Texas into another national superstation entry. Chiles next sought to sell out to a New York-based syndicate, but that deal foundered on the refusal of the prospective buyers to guarantee that the Rangers would not be moved. But in 1988, after declaring his oil company bankrupt, he was less bothered by the commitment to remain in Texas, announcing that he intended selling his majority interest to a group that was very definite about shifting the club to Tampa. Minority owner Gaylord managed to hold up the sale—winning some points with the public, but still failing to overcome league resistance to his occupying the franchise's biggest executive chair. With Chiles clearly over one of his emptying barrels, Commissioner Peter Ueberroth moved in to broker a sale to a consortium headed by George W. Bush, son of the President of the United States. Chiles complained loudly that Ueberroth was trying to run his business and threatened to go back to the Tampa group and start a court fight, but ultimately agreed to sell out.

Chiles's most memorable contribution to front office idiocy was the introduction of formalized goal-setting to baseball. The management tactic calls on a supervisor (i.e., the manager) to set down in writing the expected output of each worker (i.e., player) over several weeks, then have each worker do the same for himself. The prospect of each player's predicting how many home runs he would hit and how many runs he would score in a given 21 days amused everyone for a time, but the experiment ended when manager Don Zimmer threw the mandated index cards in the garbage during a team meeting.

HARRY CHITI

Catcher Chiti became part of Mets lore in 1962 when he was obtained from the Tigers in exchange for "a player to be named later"; a few weeks later, he was sent back to Detroit as that player. Chiti was actually only one of several players effectively traded for himself; among the others have been first baseman Vic Power, catcher Brad Gulden, and pitchers Hoyt Wilhelm and Willis Hudlin.

NESTOR CHYLAK (Hall of Fame, 1999)

An American League umpire for 25 years (1954–79) and then the league's assistant supervisor for arbiters, Chylak combined the authoritarian manner of Bill Klem with a sense of humor his National League counterpart never possessed. Among his more noted observations about his profession was that "An umpire must be perfect on the first day of the season and then get better every day." A Players Association poll conducted in the 1970s named Chylak and Ron Luciano as the only AL arbiters meriting the rating of Excellent.

EDDIE CICOTTE

It was Cicotte's testimony before a Chicago grand jury in late September 1920 that officially confirmed months-long rumors about the Black Sox scandal. The ace of the Chicago pitching staff at the time, the righthander admitted having received $10,000 to throw the first game of the 1919 World Series against Cincinnati. His testimony followed published accusations the day before by professional gambler and former major leaguer Bill Maharg that the pitcher had been the first to indicate that several White Sox players were open to bribes because of their resentment against miserly Chicago owner Charles Comiskey. Along with the other members of the so-called Chicago Eight, Cicotte was acquitted at a 1921 conspiracy trial but was immediately banned from baseball anyway by Commissioner Kenesaw Landis.

Prior to his involvement in the fix, Cicotte had been among the American League's premier hurlers. In 1917 he had paced Chicago to another pennant with a league-leading 28 wins, then repeated the trick in 1919 with 29 victories. Amid the swirling reports of an investigation in 1920, he won another 21 games. In the World Series against Cincinnati, however, it was his performance more than that of his co-conspirators that prompted suspicions of something shady going on. In the opening game he was battered around for five runs in the fourth inning of a losing effort; in the fourth game Cincinnati's only runs in a 2–0 victory came during a rally in which Cicotte made two errors and deliberately cut off a perfect throw home by Joe Jackson that appeared likely to nail a Cincinnati baserunner.

BILL CISSELL

Some of Chicago's more superstitious fans have been prone to attribute the misfortunes of the White Sox over the years to the Cissell Curse. Cissell was an infielder who arrived at Comiskey Park in 1928 with predictions of being another Eddie Collins, but who developed a drinking problem that reminded people more of Tom Collins. For a couple of years after his nine-year career ended, he worked as a laborer in the ballpark, solidifying the legend of a haunting presence. Cissell died of malnutrition at age 45.

JOHN CLAPP

Having jumped from the National Association Philadelphia Athletics during the 1875 season because the club refused to rescind a $200 fine, Clapp took advantage of the formation of the National League the following year to hold the first silent auc-

tion for a player's services; the winners, for $3,000, were the St. Louis Brown Stockings. Despite his refusal of a $5,000 bribe by Chicago bookmakers to throw games in 1881, the catcher was blacklisted for the 1882 season for dissolute behavior. As a manager, Clapp was in charge when three National League franchises—Indianapolis in 1878, Buffalo in 1879, and the Giants in 1883—played their first games; he was not hired for a second season by any of them.

FRED CLARKE (Hall of Fame, 1945)

Clark played his entire 21-year (between 1894 and 1915) career for Barney Dreyfuss, going from Louisville to Pittsburgh when the owner moved into the executive offices of the Pirates after the 1899 season. It was an alliance that was solidified through an almost equally long 19 years as a player-manager and that helped Clarke save face during a player revolt.

The lefty-hitting outfielder broke in with the Colonels on June 30, 1894, collecting a debut-record five hits (four singles and a triple). Over the next five years in Louisville he dipped as low as .307 only once, averaging as high as .390 in 1897. A line-drive hitter who led the National League in doubles, triples, and RBIs once each, he could also run the bases, as attested to by his 509 career steals. It was, in fact, Clarke rather than teammates Honus Wagner and Rube Waddell who was considered the greatest gain for the Pirates when Dreyfuss folded the Louisville franchise in 1899 after "trading" his stars to Pittsburgh so they would be on hand when he took up half-ownership of the club in the new century. Another part of the deal with incumbent Pittsburgh owner William Kerr called for Clarke to continue the double role of outfielder-manager he had been playing for the Colonels since 1897. Not that the pilot had a long honeymoon with Dreyfuss, however: A hard-nose who was accustomed to defending himself on the field with his fists and who expected similar aggressiveness from his players, he was scolded regularly by the puritanical owner for abusive language and other actions regarded as detrimental to the decorum Dreyfuss insisted on for the franchise. If the personality differences between the men didn't lead to a definitive clash, it was largely because Clarke was the most successful manager in the league in the first decade of the 20th century, steering the Pirates to three pennants and four second-place finishes.

Clarke's longest stint with the club ended after the 1915 season, when it became clear that his retirement from playing (during which he compiled a .312 average) had also sapped him of enthusiasm for managing. He reappeared on the scene in 1925 as a Dreyfuss ploy for lighting a fire under manager Bill McKechnie; variously described as a minority shareholder, an organization vice-president, an assistant manager, and a coach, he was a source of tension from Opening Day, all the more so when Dreyfuss began pointing to his return to uniform as a major reason why the Pirates were driving toward a pennant. Player resentment ran so high against Dreyfuss's "spy," as he was labeled, that a majority of the club took the owner at his word that Clarke was an executive and voted not to give him a World Series share along with the other coaches. When McKechnie got wind of the snub, he talked the players into at least voting $1,000 for his unwanted shadow; Clarke trumped that move by returning the check after Pittsburgh had defeated Washington in the World Series.

The pot boiled over in 1926. Knowing that outfielder Max Carey had been one of the strongest opponents of giving him any postseason money, Clarke was hard-pressed to contain himself when Carey started the season in a slump; while urging McKechnie to bench the outfielder, he also suggested to a Pittsburgh newsman that the batboy would be of more help to the club in the lineup. Carey's response was to circulate a petition for Clarke's removal. Although the initiative failed, Clarke would not let it pass, demanding that Dreyfuss get rid of what the local newspapers began calling the ABC Mutineers (for pitcher Babe Adams, outfielder Carson Bigbee, and Carey). Although Dreyfuss knew that he was on slippery ground, especially where Adams's involvement was concerned, he accented what he termed Clarke's "historical significance" to the franchise, acquiescing in dealing Carey to the Dodgers and releasing Adams and Bigbee. When the owner also fired McKechnie for not containing the crisis, it appeared that Clarke would be back as manager. But then Dreyfuss, apparently less enthralled by historical contributions, also pressured Clarke into returning to retirement.

NIG CLARKE

On June 15, 1902 Clarke hit eight home runs for Corsicana in a Texas League game against Texarcana; in nine major league seasons the catcher managed only six long balls. Clarke also gets a footnote in the history of catching equipment: Although no one knew it at the time, he wore soccer guards under his uniform pants while playing for Cleveland in 1905; it would be two years before Roger Bresnahan openly wore shin guards for the Giants.

JOHN CLARKSON (Hall of Fame, 1963)

Clarkson's 53 victories for Chicago in 1885 is second only to Charlie Radbourne's 60 the year before for most wins in a season. Four years later with Boston, however, the righthander was unable to produce the additional victory that would have won the National League pennant, losing to below-.500 Pittsburgh in the first flag race decided in a season finale. Had he managed his 50th win, Boston would have had one more victory than the Giants, and, despite a lower won-lost percentage, been declared the champions; as it turned out, the two clubs had the same number of wins (83), but Boston, with two more losses (45 to 43), finished second. The situation compelled NL owners to change the rule granting first place to the team with the most wins (with a tie broken in favor of the team with the fewest losses) to one rewarding the team with the highest winning percentage.

Chicago's sale of Clarkson to Boston in 1888, one year after batterymate King Kelly had been shipped East for an identical $10,000, was among the major sources of player dissatisfaction that led to the formation of the Players League in 1890.

JIMMY CLAXTON

Claxton is one of several claimants to the title of being the first (secret) black to play in organized ball in the 20th century. A southpaw pitcher, he joined the Oakland Oaks of the Pacific Coast League in May 1916 after identifying himself as an Indian. Although quickly dropped after team officials discovered that he was in fact only part-Indian, Claxton was an Oak long enough to become part of a series of Zeenut baseball cards, the biggest name in the business before the Topps company. That made him the first black player on a baseball card.

ROGER CLEMENS

Clemens is the only pitcher to win six Cy Young Awards. Opponents in both leagues would give him an equal number of Don Drysdale Awards for headhunting.

Clemens spent his first 13 major league seasons with Boston, earning wide acceptance as the all-time Red Sox franchise pitcher for his three 20-win seasons (two of them good for league-leading totals in both victories and won-lost percentage). His first three Cy Young seasons came in 1986, 1987, and 1991; his 1986 mark of 24-4 and 2.48 ERA additionally netted him an MVP prize. The righthander also led the American League in shutouts five times, in ERA four times, and in strikeouts three times. His most dramatic achievement for Boston was racking up two nine-inning games in which he recorded an unprecedented 20 whiffs; the first came against the Mariners on April 29, 1986 and the second a decade later on September 18, 1996 against the Tigers.

Despite his strikeout effort against Detroit, Clemens endured four rocky seasons in a row with the Red Sox and was allowed to walk away as a free agent after the 1996 campaign. While that was bad enough for the pitcher's faithful, general manager Dan Duquette made it worse by suggesting he was through as a quality starter, this in turn bringing bitter responses not only from Clemens but from other Red Sox veterans. Signing with Toronto, the hurler not only resumed his winning ways, but posted back-to-back Triple Crown years of leading the AL in wins, strikeouts, and ERA. They were good enough for his fourth and fifth Cy Young trophies.

Traded to the Yankees before the 1999 season, Clemens didn't find quite the reception he might have expected in New York, in good part because his acquisition had cost popular southpaw David Wells. His pitching also appeared more tentative—winning 14 in his first year in pinstripes but with an ERA of 4.60 and completing only two of 62 starts in two seasons. What was much less questionable was his reputation for throwing at heads—a practice the Yankees themselves had been the first to denounce when he had been with the Blue Jays but that they learned to shrug at coming from a teammate. The worst personal confrontations came with Mike Piazza of the Mets. After years of being battered by the slugging catcher, Clemens beaned him during a 2000 interleague game. The incident raised temperatures between the New York teams, but also seemed to stiffen Clemens on the mound against protests from both the media and fans. In that year's World Series he made matters worse by flinging the handle

of a splintered bat in Piazza's direction, raising serious questions about his mental state on the mound.

Clemens returned to his Cy Young form in 2001. He started the season 20-1—the best out-of-the-gate mark in history—before finishing 20-3 with a 3.51 ERA for his sixth award despite becoming the only pitcher ever to win 20 games without a complete game. His career totals after 17 seasons stood at 280-145 and 3,717 strikeouts (third place behind Nolan Ryan and Steve Carlton). In his three New York years he had also pitched the first one-hit complete game in League Championship Series play (against Seattle in 2000) and won all three of his World Series decisions.

ROBERTO CLEMENTE (Hall of Fame, 1973)

Except for batting average, few of Clemente's offensive numbers were as impressive as those of contemporaries Hank Aaron and Willie Mays, but there was hardly a player of the 1960s who did not regard him as the decade's third greatest outfielder. A righthanded swinger who spent his entire 18-year (1955–72) career with the Pirates, he won batting titles in 1961, 1964, 1965, and 1967; had at least 200 hits four times; had seven seasons of double figures in doubles, triples, and home runs; drove in 100 runs twice; and scored 100 runs three times. Along with his steady bat (a lifetime average of .317) went a defensive skill that gained him 12 consecutive Gold Gloves and earned him a reputation as the league's best right field arm for most of his career. As Pittsburgh's franchise player for many years, he rose from its cellar subsistence in the 1950s, to its 1960 championship against the Yankees, to more years of humdrum performances, back to the top of the league in the early 1970s. In both the 1960 World Series and in the 1971 postseason duel (against the Orioles) he had at least one hit in every one of the seven games; his clutch home runs in the sixth and seventh games of the 1971 Series, in which he hit .414 overall, netted him the MVP nod.

Clemente had a hide-and-seek start and a tragic end to his major league career. Originally signed by the Brooklyn Dodgers, he found his way to Ebbets Field blocked by Carl Furillo. Because he had been signed for more than $4,000, however, he was vulnerable to draft rules applying to minor leaguers in the 1950s, and, despite Brooklyn attempts to hide him by allowing him to play for top farm club Montreal as seldom as possible, was drafted by former Dodgers boss Branch Rickey.

In his final game of the 1972 season Clemente collected his 3,000th hit. On New Year's Eve that year he was killed in a plane crash while carrying food and medical supplies to Nicaraguan earthquake victims. Because of the circumstances of his death, the Hall of Fame waived the usual five-year waiting period for candidates and elected him right away; he was the first player from Latin America to be admitted to Cooperstown. An almost mythical figure in his native Puerto Rico, Clemente has had streets, ballparks, and buildings named after him in San Juan and other cities. The U.S. Postal Service made him the subject of a stamp, and several Puerto Rican players have requested uniform number 21 in his honor. Although often depicted during his career as a hypochondriac given to grousing through the 100-plus games he played in every one of his 18 seasons, Clemente did in fact continually suffer from an arthritic spine caused by an automobile accident.

JACK CLEMENTS

Clements was the first known major league catcher to wear a chest protector—a piece of equipment he used as a rookie with the Union Association Philadelphia Keystones in 1884. His innovation did not catch on until Roger Bresnahan of the Giants began using a similar device after the turn of the century. Clements stayed around for a 17-year career, most of it spent with the Phillies, as the longest-running lefthanded catcher.

DAVID CLYDE

The country's top draft pick in 1973, the 18-year-old Clyde was rushed to the mound by the Rangers after being signed to help create interest in a sagging team. When 36,000 fans showed up to watch him struggle through five innings to a debut victory on June 27, Texas owner Bob Short insisted the southpaw be kept in the rotation the rest of the year. In fact, Clyde's starts ended up accounting for one third of the club's home attendance. But they also proved destructive to his development and self-confidence, and he ended up with a career record of 18–33.

TY COBB (Hall of Fame, 1936)

The only contradictions in Cobb were those brought to him by others. For himself, he was a virulent character who made little distinction between attacking baseballs, teammates, opponents, fans, or blacks who had never heard of the game's greatest hitter for average (.367). That he found unexpected allies in some of his worst moments was mainly a testament to his significance between the lines and the desire of others to profit from it.

Perhaps the most daunting of all the statistics attached to Cobb is that over the past 60 years only 13 times has a player batted higher in a single season than he averaged over his entire 24-year (1905–28) career. Between 1907 and 1915 the lefthand-hitting outfielder won nine straight batting titles, then added another three later on (although revisionist historians have challenged two of these crowns). Not counting his maiden year for Detroit, when he had only 150 at bats, he never hit below .316, and three times topped .400. He also left his mark on every other offensive category, leading the American League in doubles three times, in triples four times, in steals six times, and in slugging average eight times. Although he broke into double figures in home runs only twice, he even managed to lead the AL in that category when his nine round-trippers in 1909 were high. Not that he couldn't hit the ball out of the park when he wanted. In a celebrated incident in 1925 the already 39-year-old Cobb, who had been fuming for years about the attention showered on Babe Ruth's slugging feats, told newsmen that he could have hit 30 to 40 home runs a year if he had so desired. When one of those present noted that his odd batting stance (he left several inches between his hands on the lumber) made that improbable, he went out and clouted three balls over the fence in a game to prove his point.

Cobb's hold on baseball's statistical imagination extended over generations to Lou Brock's surge over his 892 stolen bases, Pete Rose's conquest of his 4,191 hits, and Rickey Henderson's overtaking his 2,245 runs scored. Still standing, however, is his primacy in stealing home (50 times); nor has Rickey Henderson or anybody else duplicated his feat of stealing second, third, and home in the same inning on four occasions. As much as Rose, he attributed a sacred importance to numbers, even if it occasionally meant taking a back seat. During the 1926 season, for instance, the manager-outfielder took himself out of the lineup in June because his .392 average at the time was lower than that of three other Tigers outfielders—Heinie Manush, Harry Heilmann, and Fats Fothergill—who were all over the .400 mark. All four players eventually hit slumps, but he stayed on the bench as long as he was hitting less than they were.

Then there was the other Cobb. The overture to what was baseball's ugliest great career was struck up in the summer of 1905, a few weeks before he joined the Tigers, when the Georgian's mother was arrested for the fatal shooting of his father. Police connected the killing to the woman's alleged infidelities, but a trial ruled otherwise, finding that the mother had mistaken the father for a burglar and fired in good faith. Even without the shooting on his mind, Cobb admitted years later, he had gone to Detroit in a decidedly edgy mood—first because he hadn't received any money from his sale by a Sally League club in Augusta, secondly because, as a southern Protestant, he fully expected trouble from a club dominated by northern Irish Catholics.

The first of the many Tigers to view Cobb's edginess as arrogance was left fielder Marty McIntyre, who showed his feelings for his freshman teammate by giving opposition catchers clear shots at throwing him out on attempted steals and by feinting after fly balls that would end up dropping and making center fielder Cobb look bad. After one such maneuver by McIntyre, pitcher Ed Siever attacked Cobb in a hotel lobby, accusing him of blowing a win for the hurler; Cobb's response was to knock down Siever and to keep kicking him in the head until he was dragged away by teammates. The outfielder's isolation was so complete after that incident that he not only had to eat most of his meals alone but started packing a gun in case some of his teammates ganged up on him. By the middle of the 1906 season the strain became too much for him, and he had to spend a month in a Detroit sanitarium for a nervous collapse.

Cobb's reputation as a racist has, if anything, been understated. In one 1907 episode he got into an argument with a black groundskeeper about the condition of the club's spring training field in Augusta and ended up choking the man's wife when she sought to intervene. In 1909 he slapped a black elevator operator in Cleveland for being "insolent," precipitating a brawl with knives and a security guard's billyclub. Although Detroit owner Frank Navin talked the hotel out of a civil suit, the Cleveland prosecutor pressed an assault charge, making it necessary for Cobb to miss Ohio games against the Indians for some time. In 1914 Cobb attacked a Detroit butcher for report-

edly insulting his wife, then used the butt of his gun against a black shop assistant. The word "nigger" was not merely his single frame of reference for blacks but also his handiest pejorative in his ongoing sniping at Ruth. In June 1924 the two superstars ignited a riot in Detroit when their mutual taunting led to a punchup at home plate while a couple of hundred fans started smashing up grandstand seats.

Long before the Ruth episode Navin had been tempted more than once to trade his star because of the chaos around him. In 1907 he went so far as to give his tentative agreement to Cleveland for a swap involving outfielder Elmer flick, but the deal came to nothing when the Indians had second thoughts about importing the Georgia Peach's personality with his bat. On another occasion Washington manager Clark Griffith boasted to intimates that he was near a trade for Cobb, but that too came to nothing. Navin had another reason to be lured by offers: Cobb's annual truculence at contract negotiations. It was after one such round of balky talks in 1908 that the outfielder explained his position to reporters as: "It isn't a question of principle with me. I want the money." Together with his diamond accomplishments, it was a stance that rarely failed to achieve its objectives. (As determined about money as he was about base hits, he later made a fortune by buying considerable stock in Coca-Cola for $1.18 a share.)

As Cobb continued to pile up batting championships and victims from his spikes-first slides into bases, players around the league and fans went after him as bitterly as some of his teammates. On the final day of the 1910 season St. Louis manager Jack O'Connor was so resolved to stop him from winning another hitting crown that he ordered his third baseman to play deep during a doubleheader so that Cleveland's Nap Lajoie could beat out enough bunts to capture the title; O'Connor was banned from baseball for the ploy. In 1912 a New York fan named Claude Luecker taunted Cobb for seven innings, until the outfielder charged into the stands and began punching and kicking him. After Hilltop Park police pulled him away, narrowly avoiding another riot, Cobb justified his assault by saying that Luecker had called him "a half-nigger." Informed that Luecker had lost four of his fingers in a printing press accident, he shrugged that he didn't care if the fan "has no feet."

What followed was one of several episodes in which the outfielder found unexpected solidarity.

When AL President Ban Johnson suspended Cobb for the attack on Luecker, the Tigers players sent a telegram to the league office warning that they would not take the field for a May 18th game against the Athletics if the ban were not revoked. When it wasn't, the players went through with their threat, forcing Navin and manager Hughie Jennings to scour Philadelphia for amateurs who could replace the major leaguers, thereby saving the owner a $1,000 fine. The amateurs were trampled by the Athletics, 24–2, and Johnson rushed to Philadelphia to warn his players they would all be blacklisted if they didn't play their next scheduled game against Washington. Even with that threat hanging over them, the Tigers refused, not changing their minds until Cobb himself met with them and urged them to take the field. Because of his peace-making efforts, he was given only a retroactive suspension and a $50 fine, while the other players were assessed $100 each. Those who explained their solidarity said either that nobody should be penalized for reacting to the insult of being called a "half-nigger" or that no club should be forced to play without its best player. The incident otherwise had little impact on Cobb's relations with his teammates.

Cobb's siege mentality while playing in the North had the converse effect of making him even more popular in his native Georgia, where reports of his violent encounters only confirmed him as a Southern David against the Yankees Goliath. That attitude proved beneficial to him prior to the 1913 season when Navin refused to grant him a $2,000 raise. The owner changed his mind when Georgia Senator Hoke Smith threatened to open an investigation into baseball's skirting of trust regulations. It was also Smith and influential Georgians like him who repeatedly threw business opportunities (e.g., the Coca-Cola stock) Cobb's way. They made him even more of a hero in 1918, after he barely escaped with his life from an accident with poison gas in a military testing laboratory in France; the same mishap caused serious lung problems for pitcher Christy Mathewson for the rest of his short life.

After the 1920 season Navin stunned Cobb and everybody else by naming him as manager. Like many other great hitters turned into dugout bosses, he knew what he could do, recognized similar talents in other budding or proven hitters, grew impatient when less talented position players couldn't

emulate him, and had barely a clue about pitching. It was during his managerial reign, for instance, that the club was quick to trade off Howard Ehmke (who won 39 games in his first two years elsewhere) and send Carl Hubbell back to the minors with a shake of the head; on the other hand, he spotted Charlie Gehringer during a tryout, talked the club into signing him, and shepherded the future Hall of Fame second baseman through his fledgling years. As for the team as a whole, he managed five .500 seasons in six tries but was in serious contention only once. It was to remain a thorn in his career that he never played on or managed a world champion.

In November 1926 Navin sprang another surprise with the announcement that Cobb was resigning as manager and retiring as a player. It emerged shortly afterward that both Cobb and Cleveland manager Tris Speaker had been forced out amid allegations by former Detroit hurler Dutch Leonard that the three of them plus Indians outfielder Joe Wood had conspired to fix a September 1919 game to assure the Tigers of a third-place finish behind the White Sox and Indians. As evidence of his charges, Leonard sent two letters—one written by Cobb, the other by Wood—to AL president Johnson after the 1926 season. Over Johnson's insistence that the two resignations had closed the affair, Commissioner Kenesaw Landis intervened to conduct his own investigation. After traveling to California to interrogate Leonard, and despite the explicit indication in the Wood letters that Cobb had wagered on the 1919 game and an implication that the more serious allegation was also true, Landis ruled that the charges were unfounded, attributing them to Leonard's resentment that he had been released by Cobb in 1925 and denied a tryout with Cleveland by Speaker. While the verdict led to a showdown between Landis and Johnson over the extent of a commissioner's authority, Cobb let it be known that he was entertaining suing Leonard and Johnson over what he termed "absolute slander"; he also insinuated that the whole affair had been sparked by Navin as a ploy for breaking his multiyear contract. He dropped any idea of suing around the same time that Landis emerged even stronger from his confrontation with Johnson. Landis, who had used far skimpier evidence to blacklist less renowned players accused of game fixing, then persuaded both Cobb and Speaker to reject the several offers they had received from National League clubs

THE BIOGRAPHICAL HISTORY OF BASEBALL

and to stay in the junior circuit. Cobb signed with the Athletics, Speaker with the Senators.

Landis's suspect clearing of Cobb has been ascribed to his reluctance to undermine the reputations of baseball's luminaries. It was an attitude shared by others in 1936, when Cobb received the highest number of votes in the very first balloting for the Hall of Fame. Then, if not always in subsequent years, diamond ability was the only criterion for election to Cooperstown.

MICKEY COCHRANE (Hall of Fame, 1947)

Although he never led the American League in any offensive category and topped 20 home runs and 100 RBIs only once, Cochrane is considered by many as the chief obstacle to Mike Piazza as the greatest-hitting catcher of all time. In a 13-year (1925–37) career with the Athletics and Tigers, the lefty swinger compiled a .320 average, with a personal high of .357 in 1930; he also clouted 30 or more doubles for seven consecutive years (1929–35).

Sold in 1934 for $100,000 in one of Connie Mack's periodic offloadings of stars, Cochrane took over the managerial reins as well as the backstop chores for Detroit, leading the club to pennants in his first two seasons and a world championship in his second year. His playing career ended abruptly on May 25, 1937, when Yankees righthander Bump Hadley fractured his skull with a a fastball, leaving him unconscious for 10 days. He returned to manage at the end of the season, but showed little taste for just being the dugout boss and didn't survive another full season.

ANDY COHEN

Cohen was one of several victims of the frantic quest by New York teams to find a Jewish player to appeal to Jewish fans. To make matters worse, he succeeded Rogers Hornsby as the Giants second baseman in 1928. As if that weren't enough, he stroked game-winning hits a couple of times in April, leading anti-Hornsby contingents in the press to post daily comparisons of his efforts at the Polo Grounds and the Hall of Famer's in Boston. Even the habitually sour Hornsby was moved to ask the Giants and the New York press to let up on Cohen. The infielder held down his starting job for only two years. He batted an acceptable .274 and .294, but with little clout and without much defensive range.

ROCKY COLAVITO

Colavito's trade by the Indians to the Tigers after the 1959 season initiated a Cleveland version of the Curse of the Bambino. One of the most popular players in Indians history, the righthanded slugger overcame the cavernous dimensions of Municipal Stadium to become the first hometown player to reach the 40-mark in homers more than once, leading the American League with 41 in 1958 and following up with 42 more in 1959. On June 10, 1959 the outfielder also became the last AL player to stroke four homers in a game. Despite these feats, Colavito was shipped to Detroit after the season for batting champion Harvey Kuenn. General manager Frank Lane justified the move to outraged Clevelanders by claiming the Indians needed consistency more than power at the plate, but the deal appeared triggered mostly by front office apprehensions that Colavito's statistics and popularity would give him too much leverage in contract negotiations. For the next 35 years Cleveland never rose higher than third.

Colavito clubbed 139 homers in four years with the Tigers, turning in his best season (.290, 45 homers, 140 RBIs) in 1961. After the 1963 season he was shipped to Kansas City along with $50,000 for slap-hitting second baseman Jerry Lumpe in a deal even less fathomable than the Kuenn trade. Reacquired by the Indians in 1965, he still had enough clout left in his bat to lead the AL in RBIs. But two years later he ran afoul of general manager Gabe Paul with accusations that the front office boss was forcing manager Joe Adcock to platoon him with Leon Wagner and found himself forced out of Cleveland a second time (destination, Chicago). Playing out the string, Colavito bounced from the White Sox to the Dodgers to the Yankees over the next season-and-a-half before calling it quits with a .266 average and 374 round-trippers.

It was with the Yankees, who had passed over the Bronx native 15 years earlier, that Colavito ended not only his slugging career but also a two-game mound avocation. In three innings with Cleveland in 1958 and $2\,^2/_3$ more with New York a decade later, the shotgun-armed right fielder compiled a 0.00 ERA; grabbing the win in his second appearance, he became the last position player to record a major league victory.

NATE COLBERT

Slugging first baseman Colbert was as close as San Diego got to a franchise player over the first several years of its existence, averaging 30 home runs a season between 1969 and 1973. Indicative of the club's problems, however, he hit the 100-RBI mark only once. Even more telling, in 1972 his 111 RBIs represented 22.75 percent of the Padres runs—a major league record. Colbert's most conspicuous day on the field was August 1, 1972, when he clouted five home runs and drove in 13 runs in a double-header against the Braves.

GORDY COLEMAN

Coleman, the Reds regular first baseman for a good part of the 1960s, was even more effective coming off the bench. His 40 hits in 120 at bats (.333) represents the best average for pinch-hitters with at least 100 plate appearances.

JERRY COLEMAN

As a Yankees second baseman between 1949 and 1957, Coleman had several moments in the sun. For one, he knocked a bases-loaded single in the eighth inning of the last game of the 1949 season to beat Boston out of a pennant; for another, he drove in the only run in the first game of the 1950 World Series against the Phillies, then singled home the winning run in the bottom of the ninth of the third game.

As San Diego's longtime broadcaster, Coleman has often sounded as though he needed introductions to players in the league less than five years. His relations with phrasemaking have been equally—if more humorously—distant. Sample Coleman-isms over the years include:

"Those amateur umpires are certainly flexing their fangs today."

"There's a fly ball to deep center field. Winfield is going back, back. . . . His head hits the wall. It's rolling toward second base."

"Rich Folkers is throwing up in the bullpen."

"Somehow Pendleton managed to catch that. . . . Yes, with his hands."

"Grubb goes back, back, he's under the warning track."

"He slides into second base with a stand-up double."

"You have to wonder what Lasorda's thinking about. I wonder if Lasorda is wondering what he's thinking about."

"George Hendrick simply lost that sunblown pop-up."

"Benedict may not be hurt as much as he really is."

"And Kansas City is at Chicago tonight, or is that Chicago at Kansas City? Well, no matter, Kansas City leads in the eighth, 4 to 4."

"Enos Cabell started out here with the Astros. And before that he was with the Orioles."

JOHN COLEMAN

Righthander Coleman holds the unapproachable records of yielding 772 hits and losing 48 games in one season, both as a rookie with the dismal Phillies in their inaugural season of 1883; somehow, he also managed to win 12 games that season. Two years later, on May 10, 1885, he did something else not to be seen again on a major league diamond: Called on to fill in for an injured right fielder in the sixth inning, Coleman, not scheduled to be in the lineup that day, played the rest of the game in street clothes.

His lifetime record in six seasons was 23–72.

VINCE COLEMAN

When he came up with the Cardinals in 1985, Coleman gave every indication of waiting for Rickey Henderson to shoot his wad before he climbed up to claim all the big league stolen base records. After three disastrous years with the Mets in the early 1990s, however, the switch-hitting outfielder was hard put to find a team that wanted him as its leadoff hitter.

In his first six seasons with St. Louis Coleman paced the National League in steals, shattering previous rookie records with 100 thefts, then following that up with 107 and 109. Between September 18, 1988 and July 26, 1989 he established another mark for consecutive swipes when he filched 50 bases in 50 attempts. But although Coleman's running figured prominently in 1985 and 1987 St. Louis pennants, he was pursued by charges from manager Whitey Herzog that he ran too often merely for adding to his numbers and didn't have half the baserunning smarts of such teammates as Ozzie Smith and Willie McGee. A similar attitude was partly behind the decision of subsequent manager Joe Torre and general manager Dal Maxvill to let the speedster go on his way as a free agent after the 1990 season.

Coleman signed with the Mets for the 1991 season, initiating a marriage made in Hell. For one thing, he spent more time on the disabled list than on the field over his three years with the club, attaining a high of 38 steals in 1993. For another, he alienated more than New York's baseball traditionalists with a lack of sophistication that extended on one occasion even to wondering aloud who Jackie Robinson had been. In 1992 he was implicated with Dwight Gooden and Darryl Boston in the alleged rape of a woman near the Mets spring training camp in Florida; although no charges were pressed in the affair, the episode hung more heavily over the unpopular Coleman than over his teammates. What turned out to be his last act for the Mets occurred in June 1993, when, following a game against the Dodgers, he hurled a firecracker at some fans in the Dodger Stadium parking lot. He was suspended for the rest of the season, agreed to a plea-bargained reduction of felony assault charges to a misdemeanor, and was sued by the family of a young girl injured by the explosive. After trying to get rid of him for some time, the Mets finally traded him to Kansas City after the season. He played out the string with Seattle, Cincinnati, and Detroit.

As though he didn't have enough trouble in New York, Coleman drew another barrage of ridicule for his complaint to one reporter that Shea Stadium's natural grass "might keep me out of the Hall of Fame."

EDDIE COLLINS (Hall of Fame, 1939)

The longest running act among American League players, Collins batted .333 over 25 years of service for the Athletics and White Sox from 1906 to 1930. Because of Ty Cobb's presence in the league at the same time, the lefty-hitting second baseman never won a batting title, but he bested the Detroit star regularly as a base thief and figured in just as many of the game's signal events in the first decades of the 20th century.

When he first came up to the Athletics, Collins used the alias of Eddie Sullivan because he was still a student at Columbia University and in violation of intercollegiate rules covering student athletes. Manager Connie Mack wasted little time in moving him from the role of a backup player to second base, where he became the keystone of the so-called $100,000 infield that also included first baseman Stuffy McInnis, shortstop Jack Barry, and third baseman Frank Baker. Between 1910 and 1914, while Philadelphia won four pennants and three world championships,

he never batted below .324 and won the first of four steals titles by swiping 81 bases in 1910. He also paced the AL in runs scored three consecutive years. But following the Athletics loss to the Miracle Braves in 1914, Mack began breaking up the team, and one of the first to go was Collins—sold to the White Sox for $50,000.

Even before he suited up with Chicago, Collins became a source of friction in the clubhouse because, while owner Charles Comiskey was routinely slashing the salaries of some of his veterans, he had given Mack the $50,000 and then agreed to a five-year $75,000 contract with a $15,000 signing bonus for the infielder. Some of the resentment was put on hold when Collins steadied the White Sox infield to return it to contender status and then provided field leadership for a pennant win in 1917. A highlight of the four-games-to-two victory over the Giants in the World Series came when New York third baseman Heinie Zimmerman found himself in a one-sided rundown with Collins in the final game and ended up futilely chasing the runner across the plate.

By 1919 Collins's privileged contract situation had made him a minority in a clubhouse seething over Comiskey's miserly ways. While teammates such as Joe Jackson limited themselves to periodic complaints that they weren't making as much as the second baseman, others, like shortstop Swede Risberg, expressed their contempt by refusing even to throw the ball to him during infield warmups. For his part, Collins didn't bother to disguise his satisfaction when the 1919 World Series scandal coughed up the names of most of the players who had been giving him a rough time. (What he might have been less sanguine about was that two of the Eight Men Out, Jackson and third baseman Buck Weaver, significantly outhit him in the tainted games against the Reds.)

With the White Sox devastated by the bans imposed by Commissioner Kenesaw Landis over the 1919 scandal, Comiskey came to rely on Collins even more over the first part of the 1920s, even appointing him as a playing manager in 1925. After two years of lifting the team back up to the .500 level from the cellar, he returned to Philadelphia for a few years as a backup infielder before finally calling it quits. Aside from his offensive contributions over the years, he ended up with most career fielding records for a second baseman, including the highest number of games (2,650), assists (7,630), and chances (14,591).

From 1932 to his death in 1951, Collins headed Boston's baseball operations for Tom Yawkey; although his long tenure as Red Sox general manager covered such important purchases as Jimmie Foxx from the Athletics and Ted Williams from the minor leagues, it also encompassed the period when the franchise didn't want to hear about black players. More often than not, in fact, it fell to Collins to put a good public face on the ostensibly benevolent Yawkey's resistance to integration. Among those he turned away after a Fenway Park tryout held to appease an aroused City Hall in the mid-1940s was Jackie Robinson.

JIMMY COLLINS (Hall of Fame, 1945)

Collins did as much as anybody to give legitimacy to the American League at the dawn of the century. After starring in Boston for the Braves at third base for several years in the 1890s, he jumped at an offer to become playing manager of the newly created Red Sox in 1901, taking with him outfielders Buck Freeman and Chick Stahl. In the club's inaugural season Collins not only steered the team to a second-place finish but had his players performing excitingly enough to outdraw the Braves two-to-one. In 1903 he guided Boston to its first pennant and then called the shots in the first World Series, defeating Pittsburgh five games to three in a best-of-nine confrontation. Although John McGraw refused to meet a second Red Sox pennant winner in a World Series the following year, the publicity around his stand ultimately redounded to the reputation of Collins and his charges.

As a player, the righthand-hitting Collins had five .300 seasons, led the National League in home runs in 1898, drove in 100 runs twice, and scored that many four times. As a manager, he was a law unto himself, barring even his employers from the clubhouse if he thought they were infringing upon his authority.

EARLE COMBS (Hall of Fame, 1970)

The center fielder and leadoff batter for the Murderers Row Yankees of the 1920s, Combs batted .325 over 12 seasons (1924–35). Playing in the shadow of the likes of Babe Ruth and Lou Gehrig, the lefthanded hitter had his best season in 1927, when he hit .356 and led the American League in hits and (for the first of three seasons) triples. It was in the bottom of the ninth inning in the fourth World

Series game against the Pirates that year that Combs had his most dramatic diamond moment: With the bases loaded and two out, his feints and fakes toward the plate from third base so unnerved Pittsburgh pitcher Johnny Miljus that the righthander uncorked a wild pitch to allow the game- and Series-ending run to score. Always plagued by injuries, Combs effectively ended his career in 1934 when he crashed into the center field wall in St. Louis's Sportsman's Park and fractured his skull.

CHARLIE COMISKEY (Hall of Fame, 1939)

As a manager, Comiskey provided a buffer between his players and an erratic, often penurious owner; as an even more tightfisted owner himself, he had no such intermediary. The result was baseball's most sensational scandal and the historical judgment that a good deal of the blame for the 1919 World Series fix rests in the Chicago owner's lap.

As a player, Comiskey popularized playing off the first-base bag, a technique he picked up from manager Ted Sullivan with the independent Dubuque Rabbits in 1879. He later became the first manager to win four consecutive pennants, for the American Association St. Louis Browns between 1885 and 1888. A .267 righthanded hitter in 13 major league seasons, Comiskey ranks third among all big league managers in winning percentage (.608), having endured only one losing season (his last) in a 12-year career with the Chicago Pirates of the Players League and the Cincinnati Reds, in addition to the Browns. With the Browns, he spent as much time correcting the public utterances of the notoriously baseball-ignorant owner Chris Von der Ahe as he did making out lineup cards, and even more time trying to talk Von der Ahe out of levying inappropriate fines and completing damaging player transactions.

Comiskey served as a catalyst in getting Cincinnati owner John T. Brush to recommend local sportswriter Ban Johnson for the presidency of the Western League. Joining Johnson after the 1894 season as owner of the Sioux City club, he played a key role in the newly rechristened American League's assault on the National League's monopoly, especially after moving his franchise into Chicago in 1900. Acceding to Cubs owner Charles Murphy's request that the new team not explicitly identify itself with Chicago, Comiskey retaliated by nicknaming the club the White Stockings, the original name of the NL team.

In winning the AL's first major league pennant a year later, Comiskey's White Sox outdrew the Cubs by about 150,000, but a rift developed between the owner and the league president in August, when Johnson expelled shortstop Frank Shugart. The episode was merely the first of a series of confrontations between the two most powerful figures in the AL. As in the Shugart incident, they patched up their differences after the suspensions of Chicago outfielder Ducky Holmes in 1905 and of playing manager Fielder Jones in the middle of a tight pennant race in 1907. But that was not the case in 1919, when Johnson resolved a dispute between the White Sox and the Yankees over the contract of pitcher Jack Quinn in favor of the New Yorkers. Thereafter, Comiskey was Johnson's sworn enemy, and played a significant role the following year as part of the ownership group that humbled the league executive in a quarrel over whether the Red Sox could trade pitcher Carl Mays to the Yankees while he was under suspension. The animosity between the pair reached a point where, when a humbled Johnson retired in 1927, Comiskey refused even to sign the pro forma resolution thanking him for his contributions to the league.

Comiskey showed himself reluctant to share with his players the profits from Chicago pennants in 1906 and 1917, as well as from the club's generally successful first two decades. His 1919 pennant winners were woefully underpaid, some of them getting only half of what comparable players on other teams received; this made them ripe for the plucking by the gambling fraternity. The owner suspected skullduggery as early as the first game of the World Series against Cincinnati and knew conclusively, from at least two sources, of the actions of the Black Sox within weeks of the Series; he even withheld their World Series checks for a time. His subsequent public statement on the fix, issued in September 1920 during the grand jury investigation of the affair, was both an admission of his earlier knowledge and, in his offer of a $10,000 reward for anyone coming forth with information about the scandal, a sham.

The owner's purpose in suppressing information was to protect his investment in the offending players, all of whom except Chick Gandil he resigned for the 1920 season for uncharacteristically large salary increases. His complicity in the pilferage of the players' confessions from the district attorney's office made a conviction improbable, and his sole contribution to the 1921 jury trial of seven Black Sox was to explode in righteous denial before the allegation that he had jumped his contract with the Browns to join the PL in 1890—which, in fact, he had.

The effect of the Black Sox scandal on Comiskey's career was to make him appear a martyr for suffering 11 more seasons without fielding a club that rose higher than fifth. When he died in 1931, there was some sentiment to rename one of the streets bordering Comiskey Park, which he had opened to much fanfare in 1910, Comiskey Road; local newspaper wags suggested a better name might have been Seventh Place.

CHUCK COMISKEY

Comiskey represents baseball's most pathetic boardroom tale. The grandson of the first owner of the White Sox, he waited 20 years to get his hands on the franchise that had been willed to him twice; then, suddenly impatient, he outsmarted himself for good. In one way or another, his father, mother, and sister all contributed to the failure of his ambition.

Comiskey's problems began in 1940, when his father Lou, the son of Charlie Comiskey, died of a heart attack. Under the terms of his father's will, the White Sox franchise was left in trust to Chuck, then in his early teens, until he reached 35. But because of ambiguities in other parts of the document, Lou's widow, Grace, had to go to court to take control of the team from the Chicago bank her husband had named as executor for fear that there wouldn't be any club for anyone to inherit. Grace ended up staying in charge until 1956, with Chuck's older sister Dorothy taking over as organization treasurer.

After finishing college, Comiskey served a two-year stint with one of Chicago's minor league affiliates; then, in the late 1940s, he moved into Comiskey Park as a vice-president. His first significant move was to urge his mother to hire Frank Lane as general manager; shortly afterward, he clashed with Grace by backing Lane's demand that Jack Onslow by fired as manager and be replaced by Paul Richards. Grace eventually relented, and for a couple of years Comiskey wasn't hesitant about telling everyone that the rise of the White Sox in the standings was due to his insistence on hiring Lane and Richards. Unfortunately for him, neither the local press nor his mother bestowed praise for the club's turnaround much beyond Lane and Richards—a point borne home when Grace refused her son's demand for a substantial raise. Infuriated by his mother's stand as well as by a passing disclosure that Lane had an attendance bonus, Comiskey resigned from his administrative position—a posture he maintained for six months. For the next two years he worked at peaceful coexistence with Lane despite his own resentment over the attendance bonus and the general manager's fury that Chuck had told Chicago papers about the incentive clause.

After Grace Comiskey found enough reasons to get rid of Lane in 1955, she divided day-to-day operations in the organization between Chuck and her son-in-law, Dorothy's husband Johnny Rigney; she also made it clear that Dorothy had the ultimate say in corporate matters. That was how the situation remained when Grace died in 1956. Ignoring her son's expectations of finally succeeding her as president, Grace awarded Dorothy enough stock to give her practical control, with a second chunk going to Chuck (still in his early 30s) and a third block being put in trust for him until the 35 years originally stipulated by Lou. But Comiskey was tired of waiting for his majority control, so over the next 18 months he and Dorothy dragged each other from courtroom to courtroom over everything from the validity of Grace's will to rival contentions about who had taken too much silverware from their late mother's house. Dorothy cracked first, but not in the way Chuck had anticipated: Instead of offering her brother the shares he didn't already have, she went looking for an outside buyer.

The farce went on for three years. At one point both brother and sister sought to overturn a motion initially offered by Dorothy herself; at another point an Illinois judge blasted both Comiskeys for attempting to turn the state's judicial system into a rumpus room; in 1957 and 1958 the White Sox had no formal president at all. Finally, in 1959, Bill Veeck took over Dorothy's share of the franchise.

Since he still had his significant minority holding, Chuck Comiskey remained on the premises, buoyed by the hope that Veeck's reputation for diving into things that he couldn't handle would ultimately leave him with the power he had been promised since 1940. He appeared vindicated in 1960 when Veeck disclosed that his health would no longer permit him to operate the White Sox and that the club was up for sale. Aware that Arthur Allyn, Jr., the son of one of Veeck's partners, had the inside track on the majority holdings, Comiskey got too clever by half. First, he sold his 46 percent interest in the franchise to a group headed by Chicago insurance executive William Bartholomay. The agreement between the sides was that, with the Comiskey shares accounted for, the Bartholomay syndicate would draw enough heavy investors to overwhelm Allyn with an offer to buy a majority interest right back, making a profit for the Bartholomay people and finally securing the president's chair for Charlie Comiskey's grandson. (The deal also formally severed the Comiskey name from the White Sox.) The scheme lasted only until Allyn said no; moreover, once he did, it was Bartholomay who ended up selling his 46 percent to Allyn. That gave Allyn the absolute control that Chuck had been promised by both his father and mother.

DAVE CONCEPCION

At the shortstop for the Big Red Machine in the 1970s, Concepcion was the first player to realize the new defensive possibilities artificial turf offered by deliberately bouncing long throws to first base.

DAVID CONE

Cone has jammed several reputations into his career since being traded by the Royals to the Mets in 1987: hot head, hired gun in the free agency era, comeback kid, and articulate media schmoozer. He has also been alone as a genuine star for both New York teams.

Cone's best year at Shea Stadium was 1988, when he went 20–3 (2.22), fanning 200 batters for the first of six times. But the righthander's success was dogged by explosions of temper. During one game in Cincinnati he became so enraged by a safe call at first base that he forgot to call time while he raved at the umpire, allowing not just one, but two, runners to cross the plate. The 1988 NLCS against Los Angeles also showed him at his worst and best. In a column for a New York newspaper the would-be sportswriter attacked the depth of the Dodgers bullpen, and was promptly tattooed by an aroused Los Angeles lineup in the second game. After several days of Dodgers hectoring and New York press criticism, however, he came back to hurl a masterful sixth-game win.

Cone's womanizing also got him into trouble in the Mets years. On the last day of the 1991 season he was informed that Philadelphia police were investigating a rape charge against him; Cone took the mound at Veterans Stadium, tied the then-NL mark for strikeouts in a game by whiffing 19, then came off the field to hear that no charges were being pressed. The following spring, in the midst of a number of scandals involving Mets players at their Florida training camp, he was accused by two women of masturbating before them in the bathroom of the New York bullpen. This episode also evaporated behind questions about why the women had invited themselves to the john in the first place.

Cone was traded to the Blue Jays as pennant insurance in August 1992; the exchange prevented him from leading the NL in strikeouts for the third consecutive year. He then signed on as a free agent with his original club Kansas City, where in 1994 he won the Cy Young Award (16–5, 2.94) despite neither leading the league in any statistical category nor playing for a first-place club. He then made two more roundtrips—first back to Toronto for the first part of 1995, then back to New York, only this time to Yankee Stadium instead of Shea Stadium. He proved to be a mainstay of the rotation that dominated the league for the rest of the decade despite a shoulder aneurysm in 1996 that threatened his life as much as his career; in his first appearance after the surgery he threw seven innings of no-hit ball before being removed because of a prearranged pitch count. In 1998 he won 20 games for the second time.

Cone's last height for the Yankees was a July 17, 1999 perfect game against Montreal. From that point on he was unable to complete anything—a streak that was still alive at the end of the 2001 season. When the Yankees gave up on him at the end of 2000, Cone disappointed expectations that he would retire, instead joining the Red Sox. Although he could squeeze only 136 innings out of 25 games, he managed to win nine times and have one of the better seasons among Boston's starters.

Cone's reputation as a hired gun has been exaggerated, at least as a calculation of his own. He has generally been the one moved by clubs, and when he has had an option about a destination, he has more often that not gone back to a former city.

TONY CONIGLIARO

The Red Sox Impossible Dream of 1967 turned into a nightmare for Conigliaro. With Boston bat-

tling Detroit, Minnesota, and Chicago down to the wire in a torrid pennant race, the outfielder, who had busted 104 home runs in almost four seasons and who was working on a .287 average with 20 long balls, took a fastball in the cheek from California's Jack Hamilton on August 18 and was put out on the sidelines for a year-and-a-half. The good news was that he was able to return in 1969 to hit another 20 homers, following that up with 36 more in 1970. The bad news was that the righty slugger's eyesight had been permanently damaged.

The Red Sox, keeping Conigliaro's degenerative condition secret, exacted a cynical revenge by peddling him to the Angels—the source of his problems. He lasted little more than a few months before retiring as much for the psychological effects of his injury as for his deteriorating vision. After an attempted comeback with the Red Sox in 1975, he quit for good with a .264 lifetime average and 166 homers, but his life went from bad to worse when he suffered a debilitating heart attack in 1982. He died eight years later, at age 45.

JOCKO CONLAN (Hall of Fame, 1974)

Conlan is the only ex-player to become a Hall of Fame umpire. He began his arbiting career in 1935, when, as a reserve outfielder for the White Sox, he filled in for Red Ormsby, who had succumbed to heat prostration during a game in St. Louis. Bringing his trademark polka-dot bow tie back to the big leagues in 1941, Conlan remained in the National League for 24 years, becoming as noted for his frequent run-ins with the likes of Frankie Frisch, Jackie Robinson, and Leo Durocher as for his ability to call balls and strikes. Even in retirement he would claim that the only two baseball people he didn't like were Robinson and Durocher, because the pair used foul language on the field. Conlan's most notable habit was using his left hand for all hand signs.

GENE CONLEY

While others have played two sports professionally, Conley has been the only one to do so with championship teams in both sports. Over 11 summers in the 1950s and early 1960s the righthander won 91 and lost 96 pitching for the Braves (in both Boston and Milwaukee), Phillies, and Red Sox; with Milwaukee in 1957, he appeared (ineffectively) in the team's World Series victory over the Yankees.

Over seven winters between 1952 and 1964 the six-foot, eight-inch Conley also played for the National Basketball Association Boston Celtics; during his hoop career, the Celtics won six NBA championships.

TOM CONNOLLY (Hall of Fame, 1953)

Connolly began an American League-record 31-year career as an umpire after two-and-a-half seasons with the National League. He officiated at both the first AL game in 1901 and the first World Series, between the Red Sox and Pirates in 1903. From the beginning of his AL tenure Connolly provided the strong anti-rowdyism approach sought by league founder Ban Johnson, ejecting 10 players in the circuit's first season. His most noted confrontation came with Orioles pitcher Joe McGinnity, who spat in his face and was suspended by Johnson as a result. After retiring in 1931, Connolly became umpire-in-chief for the circuit, a position he held for 23 years.

ROGER CONNOR (Hall of Fame, 1976)

The foremost home-run hitter of the 19th century, Connor is best remembered for hitting the first major league grand slam, on September 10, 1881; he did it while playing for Troy in a home game that took place across the Hudson River, in Albany. Another of his memorable clouts, while he was with the Giants, cleared the right field wall at the first Polo Grounds, at 110th Street and Fifth Avenue, so impressing a group of stockholders in attendance that they collected $500 and bought the first baseman a watch from Tiffany's. Although the lefty swinger led his league in homers only once (in the Players League in 1890), he ended his 18-year career with 138 four-baggers, the major league standard until Babe Ruth switched from pitching to the outfield.

CHUCK CONNORS

A first baseman for the Dodgers and Cubs in the early 1950s, Connors was the most successful of the major leaguers who established a second career in show business. Aside from his popular television series *The Rifleman,* he appeared in scores of motion pictures, most notably as the heavy in *The Big Country* with Gregory Peck.

STANTON COOK

As president of the Cubs in 1992, Cook lit the fuse that exploded Commissioner Fay Vincent out of his chair. When Vincent announced a National League realignment plan for 1993 that would have moved Chicago and St. Louis to the Western Division and dropped Atlanta and expansion Florida into the Eastern Division, Cook went to court to block the proposed change. His main bone of contention—aside from what he saw as Vincent's strongarm tactics—was that a shift to the Western Division would have inconvenienced eastern viewers of the club's WGN superstation, forcing them to watch more games at later Mountain and Pacific starting times and thereby threatening lower ratings and less advertising. The court issued a restraining order that effectively killed the Vincent plan and added another enemy against the commissioner in the ensuing pressures for him to step down.

JACK COOMBS

Coombs was a pretty good (158–110 in 14 seasons) pitcher and a very good one for two seasons; in World Series play, however, he was perfect. One of a succession of college-trained hurlers recruited by Connie Mack for the Athletics in the first decade of the 20th century, the righthander's 31–9 record in 1910 included a record 13 shutouts. The following year, he paced American League pitchers again with 28 wins, though this time with only a single blanking. In three World Series—1910 and 1911 for Philadelphia and 1916 for the Dodgers—he won five games, the most by any pitcher without a loss.

MORT COOPER

Few pitchers in baseball history have stuck it to opposing batters as graphically as Cooper. In his glory years of 1942, 1943, and 1944, when he compiled 65 wins, the Cardinals righthander went to the mound wearing the number of the victory he expected to record that day. In case batters missed the significance of the number, Mort's batterymate, brother Walker Cooper, tossed in reminders during the game.

BRAD CORBETT

Corbett's ownership of the Rangers in the 1970s prompted volumes of quotes about his incompetence—many coming from other owners and front office officials. He was "a Charlie Finley without the imagination," "a George Steinbrenner with a drinking problem." Or: "Giving Corbett a baseball team is like giving a three-year-old a handful of ra-

THE BIOGRAPHICAL HISTORY OF BASEBALL

zors," and "Corbett thinks the Texas franchise is a toy that he can play with or throw in a closet at will." An industrial parts manufacturer, Corbett invited the criticisms by working out trades behind the backs of his general manager and manager; by appointing rivals with the powers of a general manager so he could resolve the inevitable (and regular) conflicts; by agreeing to long-term contracts for players who irritated the manager, subsequently firing the manager and releasing the players; and by staggering through the press box denouncing the players on the field as "dogs." In one particularly notorious incident in 1978 he insisted that he would personally handle the final phase of a major trade between the Rangers and the Yankees after a briefing from his front office people. The swap, which cost Texas prospect Dave Righetti for worn-out bullpen ace Sparky Lyle, might have been more justifiable if the Rangers had also succeeded in obtaining second baseman Damaso Garcia, as had been projected. When the Yankees instead palmed off shortstop Domingo Ramos on him, Corbett told his astonished aides that he didn't see the difference between one Latin infielder and another. He was finally forced to sell out by other team investors in January 1980.

JACK CORBETT

The owner of the El Paso Texans of the Class C Arizona-Texas League, Corbett sued organized baseball when he was denied permission to sign banned players returning from Jorge Pasquel's Mexican League in 1946. His suit, for $300,000 in damages, was later combined with that of Yankees farmhand George Earl Toolson and resulted in a U.S. Supreme Court decision upholding baseball's antitrust exemption and right to police itself.

LARRY CORCORAN

The ace of the White Stockings staff in the early 1880s, Corcoran's dalliance with the Union Association in 1884 was cut short when Chicago president Al Spalding interpreted the pitcher's earlier request for an advance on a new contract as a legally binding commitment, effectively expanding the scope of the reserve clause. In his first five seasons (1880–84) Corcoran won 170 games, became the first pitcher to hurl three no-hitters, and led the White Stockings to three consecutive pennants.

PAT CORRALES

A backup catcher to Johnny Bench of the Big Red Machine and on three other National League teams in the 1960s and early 1970s, Corrales batted a mere .216; it was, however, as a manager that he suffered his worst baseball indignity. When he was fired by the Phillies on July 18, 1983, he became the only pilot axed while his team was in first place (with a 43–42 record). Philadelphia went on to win the NL pennant under Paul Owens.

FRANK CORRIDON

Although Bobby Mathews had thrown a spitball as early as the 1860s, it was Corridon's rediscovery of the wet pitch that led to its greatest popularity. The righthander developed the pitch in collaboration with Providence teammate George Hildebrand in 1902. Moving later that season from the International League to the Pacific Coast League, he taught it to Sacramento teammate Elmer Stricklett. It was Stricklett who taught it to future Hall of Famers Jack Chesbro and Ed Walsh.

STAN COVELESKI (Hall of Fame, 1969)

Coveleski was one of the more consistent American League pitchers during his 14-year (between 1912 and 1928) career, posting 20-win seasons four years in a row for Cleveland, then moving over to the Senators and winning another 20 in Washington's 1925 pennant-winning year. As both an Indian (1923) and a Senator (1925), he also led the AL in ERA. The righthander's most brilliant efforts came in the 1920 World Series against the Dodgers, when he allowed only two runs in three complete-game victories.

Coveleski's older brother Harry had three consecutive 20-win years, for the Tigers between 1914 and 1916. No other pair of brothers has had eight 20-victory seasons.

BOBBY COX

Working in the shadows of such managerial "geniuses" as Tommy Lasorda, Jim Leyland, and Tony LaRussa, Cox has in fact been the most successful pilot in the National League since the days of John McGraw. After an initial mediocre stint with the Braves in the late 1970s and then moving to Toronto to develop the Blue Jays into a contender, he returned to Atlanta as general manager in 1986. After watching in vain for four years for the club to improve, he went back down to the dugout in 1990 to endure one last losing season before turning around the franchise. From 1991 to 2001 the one-time Yankees infielder led the way to 10 straight division titles—the first three in the NL West, the last seven in the NL East. The divisional title run has been the longest in major professional sports (baseball, football, basketball, hockey, soccer) in the United States or Europe. Even considering the smaller number of teams involved in a division (as opposed to an entire league), the first-place finishes stand comparison to McGraw's ability to keep the Giants out of the second division during his tenure with New York.

The reverse side of Cox's regular season success has been Atlanta's fate, once in the postseason, to win only one world championship (1995). One reason for this has been such a heavy reliance by Cox on his starting rotation (specifically Greg Maddux, Tom Glavine, and John Smoltz) over the years that he hasn't been as attentive to generally less-than-glorious offenses. In short playoff series this has translated into having his own mound stars going up against those of the opposition; i.e., risking their neutralization while exposing Atlanta's offensive shortcomings.

WILLIAM COX

Following William Baker and Gerry Nugent, Cox was the third owner of the Phillies during a lurid 26-year period that saw the team get into the first division only once. A millionaire lumber magnate, he was practically handed the franchise by other league owners on the recommendation of National League president Ford Frick to put an end to Nugent's ramshackle way of operating. Cox was enthusiastic but little else. At spring training in 1943, he showed how hands-on an owner could be by insisting on taking regular turns at pitching, fielding, and hitting, thereby earning the mockery of his players and tensions with manager Bucky Harris. Harris wasn't too much happier about the owner's normal post-midnight calls suggesting better ways to manage. Another early source of trouble was an ex-coach for the Hungarian Olympic team whom Cox insisted was necessary for getting the players into better shape. The coach turned out to be ahead of his time in decreeing that he didn't want players chewing tobacco, recommending instead that they partake of the orange slices he laid out on the bench for every game. Unfortunately, once the game started, the coach had little interest in

the proceedings, and when Harris caught him asleep on the bench, the manager had the excuse he had been seeking to get Cox to fire him.

Given such incidents, sportswriters covering the team were hardly surprised when Cox fired Harris midway into the season. What they hadn't been prepared for, however, was a revolt by the players and threats to sit out a game against the Cardinals unless Harris were reinstated. It required an appeal by the ousted manager before the players agreed to take the field. The incident might have ended right there if the exhausted Harris hadn't decided that he needed a drink with a couple of sportswriters before returning home. Between one raised elbow and other, he let slip that Cox was so naive about the skills of the team that he frequently bet on games. That nugget got back to Commissioner Kenesaw Landis, before whom Cox acknowledged that he had made "some small sentimental bets" without realizing that he had violated baseball's rules. When Landis told the owner to come back for another meeting with a lawyer, Cox read the writing on the wall and put the club up for sale; he was later formally blacklisted. Along with Horace Fogel, also of the Phillies, he is one of the only two major league owners to be banned from the game for life.

Before fading into the sunset, Cox had also solicited suggestions for renaming the Phillies as a symbol of the organization's break with its sorry past. Mrs. John L. Lucas got her proposal of Blue Jays accepted. Aside from a briefly used uniform patch, what this mainly brought was a letter from students at Johns Hopkins University asking the team not to use the school's nickname because it would "disgrace and dishonor" the collegiate Blue Jays.

ROGER CRAIG

Craig had practically four different identities after beginning his career with the 1955 Dodgers. For both the Brooklyn and Los Angeles versions of the franchise, he was a tightrope-walking righthander who seemed to have a full count on every batter but who ultimately contributed significantly to three pennants. With the expansion Mets in 1962 and 1963, he lost a combined 46 games; in 1963 alone, he lost 18 in a row at one stretch, during which the team was shut out eight times. As a pitching coach with the Padres, Astros, and Tigers in the 1970s and 1980s, he was considered something of an alchemist in getting career performances out of journeymen, all the more so when be began teaching the split-finger fastball to his charges. Finally, as manager of the Giants between 1985 and 1992, Craig was credited with ending years of clubhouse rifts on the team by getting behind rookies Will Clark, Robby Thompson, and Jose Uribe and driving them to a division title in 1987 and a pennant two years later. While with the Tigers under Sparky Anderson between 1980 and 1984, Craig also popularized the trend of having coaches call pitches from the dugout. Between this habit and a proclivity for pitchouts, his presence on the bench usually signified games as long as the ones he had once pitched for the Dodgers.

DOC CRAMER

Although he batted .296 over a 20-year (between 1929 and 1948) career, Cramer has the American League mark for most at bats in a season without a homer. With the Red Sox in 1938, the lefty-hitting outfielder went to the plate a league-leading 658 times without reaching the seats. He had 37 career blasts.

DOC CRANDALL

Although others had been tried in the role before, Crandall was baseball's first successful reliever. After a year as a starter for the Giants in 1908, manager John McGraw used the righthander primarily out of the bullpen for the next five seasons. In 1913 he became the first hurler to make at least 30 relief appearances. Crandall was nicknamed Doc by Damon Runyon because he was "first aid to the injured . . . the physician of the pitching emergency."

GAVVY CRAVATH

Cravath may have been baseball's most successful opposite-field power hitter. An outfielder for the Phillies in the years just prior to Babe Ruth's emergence as a slugger, the righthanded hitter took aim at the friendly right field distance of Baker Bowl (officially 280 feet down the line, but suspected of being much less) to the tune of six National League home-run titles between 1913 and 1919. Indicative of the era's power standards, he broke the 20-home-run mark only once and won another title with a mere eight round-trippers. On the other hand, Cravath was a genuine clutch hitter, driving in 100 runs three times, leading the league in hits once, and setting the pace in slugging average twice.

BILL CRAVER

The only one of the so-called Louisville Four never specifically accused, let alone convicted, of selling games, Craver was blackballed for refusing to allow club officials to read his private telegrams, general misconduct, and "suspicious play." Evidence against the shortstop and field captain, given in a closed-door inquiry, consisted primarily of accusations by second baseman Joe Gerhardt and first baseman Juice Latham that he had deliberately rattled them into making errors; Gerhardt, however, recanted the next day, explaining that he and Latham had simply wanted to get rid of the irascible assistant manager.

Craver certainly carried a lot of baggage. In 1869, playing behind the plate for the Troy Haymakers, he protested an umpire's call so furiously that the entire team walked off the field in the sixth inning after the Cincinnati Red Stockings had tied the score at 17-all; the protest was a prearranged scene to spare club owner John Morrissey the reported $17,000 he had bet on the Haymakers, and the tie turned out to be the single blemish in Cincinnati's legendary consecutive-game winning streak. In 1870 Craver was suspended by the Chicago White Stockings and then banned for life by the amateur National Association of Base Ball Players for insubordination and gambling. In 1874, while with the proto-major league National Association Philadelphia White Stockings, he was implicated in the attempted bribe of an umpire. It therefore came as no surprise when the Brooklyn *Eagle* included him in its 1875 all-star "starting lineup of rogues." (That year he also became part, along with George Bechtel, of the first cash transaction for a player contract, moving from the Philadelphia Centennials to the Philadelphia Athletics after the former team folded.)

Nevertheless, at least in the Louisville affair, there is no definitive evidence that Craver played any part in the fixes attributed to his teammates. He himself always denied the allegations, while admitting he did have a taste for late-hour gambling and drinking. After his forced retirement, he became a Troy policeman.

SAM CRAWFORD (Hall of Fame, 1957)

The only player to lead both leagues in home runs and triples, Crawford also had an important role in assuring that there were two leagues to be led. It was in fact only when Cincinnati owner Garry Herrmann withdrew his objections to the lefty-hitting outfielder's defection from the Reds to the Tigers after the 1902 season that the National and American leagues hammered out their mutual coexistence agreement. What Herrmann lost was a career .309 batter who had paced the NL with 16 home runs in 1901 and 22 triples in 1902; what Detroit gained was the AL home run leader in 1908 (with a mere seven round-trippers) and baseball's all-time triples king (with 309) who topped that category in six seasons. Crawford also led the AL in RBIs three times, reaching the 100-mark in six seasons. In addition, he scored the most runs in the junior circuit in 1907 and belted the most doubles in 1909. The one asterisk to his extra-base power was in the fact that 50 of the speedy outfielder's 97 home runs were inside-the-park tears around the bases.

While with the Tigers, Crawford was a member in good standing of the anti-Ty Cobb faction and had more than one scuffle with the Georgia Peach before calling it quits in 1917. Asked once to explain the antagonism to Cobb, he replied: "He's still fighting the Civil War and he sees us as just damn Yankees." For all that, Crawford was also one of the leaders of the team revolt against the suspension of Cobb in 1912 for hitting a fan.

GEORGE CREAMER

Second baseman Creamer was the fourth of five managers with the feckless 1884 Pittsburgh Alleghenys of the American Association. Lasting only eight games, he established a major league mark for managerial futility by losing all of them. Player Creamer didn't help manager Creamer's cause: He batted only .183.

JOSEPH CREAMER

A wealthy physician who also worked for the Giants, Creamer was barred from baseball after the 1908 season behind accusations that he sought to bribe umpire Bill Klem. According to Klem, the doctor approached him before the winner-take-all makeup contest between New York and Chicago necessitated by the Merkle Boner and offered $3,000 if the arbiter would "call close plays the Giants way." Creamer always denied the allegations. The official inquiry into his reputed approach to Klem was entrusted to Giants owner John T. Brush. The incident was just one of many linking John McGraw's club to bribes or attempted bribes at the beginning of the century.

JIM CREIGHTON

Baseball's first superstar, Creighton died in October 1862 at age 21, four days after rupturing his bladder while hitting a home run for the Excelsior club of Brooklyn. Though nominally an amateur, he became the first paid player by surreptitiously accepting money from the Excelsiors in 1860. A phenom at bat, Creighton went through the entire 1862 season making only four outs. As an outfielder, he started the first recorded triple play; with runners on second and third in a game against the Baltimore Excelsiors on July 22, 1860, he caught a long fly ball, threw to third for the second out, and watched as the relay to second retired the side. But it was as a pitcher that Creighton revolutionized the game, first by employing (illegally) a snap wrist action to add speed to the required underhand delivery of the day and then by learning to change speeds to fool hitters.

Creighton is buried in Brooklyn's Greenwood Cemetery beneath an ornate stone monument featuring sculpted paraphernalia of the game, including a pair of crossed bats, a scorebook, a base, and a cap; the leitmotiv is topped by the carved word "Excelsior" and, above that, a granite baseball.

JOE CRONIN (Hall of Fame, 1956)

Cronin wore just about every uniform and suit there was to wear in baseball, but the only threads he sported with particular distinction were those of a player. A righthand-hitting shortstop with extra-base power, he made his first mark with the Senators in 1929 after a couple of unimpressive trials with the Pirates. With Washington he drove in 100 runs five years in a row, led the American League in doubles and triples once each, and batted as high as .346. Before he ended his big league career in 1945 with Boston, he would rack up 100 RBIs three more times and build a lifetime .301 average.

From 1933, however, Cronin's hitting and wide-ranging defensive play had to share the spotlight with his managing. His biggest success as a pilot came in his maiden year, when he led the Senators to a franchise-high 99 victories to finish ahead of the Yankees by a surprising seven games. The following season, injuries and clashes with star players Goose

Goslin and Alvin Crowder sent Washington skidding down toward the bottom of the league. The campaign became even more of a nightmare when Cronin had to endure constant grandstand catcalls following an announcement that he planned to marry the niece of owner Clark Griffith in the fall. Griffith heard the jeering, too, and with the help of a $250,000 offer from Boston, decided that his player-manager would be under too much pressure to return the team to the top of the standings; the result was an October 1934 trade with the Red Sox that brought Washington shortstop Lyn Lary with the quarter-million dollars.

For his first 11 years at the helm of Boston, Cronin managed four second-place finishes but nothing better despite the presence on the roster of such fellow future Hall of Famers as Ted Williams, Jimmie Foxx, and Bobby Doerr. His own stubbornness about remaining at shortstop in the face of a perceptible slowing down also led the club to sell hot minor league prospect Pee Wee Reese to the Dodgers. In 1946 he finally returned to the World Series but saw that accomplishment shorted in the seventh game, when Enos Slaughter scored on Johnny Pesky's delayed relay to give the Cardinals the world championship. A year later, with the retirement of Eddie Collins, owner Tom Yawkey announced Cronin's promotion to general manager.

As the head of Boston's baseball operations from 1948 to 1959, Cronin was behind the decision to bring in another shortstop-manager, Lou Boudreau, to take over the dugout, but neither that move nor a regular series of second-line trades could get the Red Sox any higher than third in the 1950s. It was also during this period that the franchise became identified as the most reluctant in baseball to sign a black player; it was not until 1959 that Pumpsie Green broke the color line at Fenway Park, and that just happened to coincide with Cronin's election as president of the AL.

As the league's chief official between 1959 and 1973, Cronin presided over the franchise shifts of the Senators to Minnesota, the Athletics to Oakland, the Pilots to Milwaukee, and the second 20th-century Washington team to Texas. In some of these financial maneuvers he had more than the customary passive role of a league president. At the league meeting that approved Washington's move to Minnesota, for instance, he rejected an attempt by Baltimore to reverse its initially positive vote on the grounds that it hadn't understood the significance of the ballot; if the Baltimore appeal had been accepted, Cronin's brother-in-law Calvin Griffith would have been blocked from transferring to the Twin Cities. After a couple of years of encouraging Kansas City owner Charlie Finley to explore the possibilities of moving the Athletics to California, Cronin had to act fast when the actual league vote approving a transfer to Oakland brought down the wrath of Missouri politicians. Disabused of the idea that Kansas City would accept some vague commitment for another major league team sometime in the future, he railroaded through a promise that the league would include the market in a 1969 expansion—a vow carried out with the creation of the Royals. But it was also Cronin who had the league rush to near-havoc in accepting the bid by William Daley and Dewey Coriano for setting up the Pilots as the second new team in 1969.

FRANK CROSETTI

As a shortstop (1932–46), player-coach (1947–48), and coach (1949–68) for the Yankees, Crosetti picked up more World Series checks (23) than anyone else in the history of baseball. As a player, the righthanded hitter retired with a .245 average and eight league-leading totals in being hit by a pitch; as a coach, his grim visage became a fixture in the third-base coaching box. Severe and humorless, Crosetti was so irritated by the antics of Max Patkin that he clobbered the baseball clown one day. That incident wasn't Crosetti's first on-field assault; in the 1942 World Series he shoved umpire Bill Summers and was suspended for the first 30 days of the 1943 season.

POWEL CROSLEY

Crosley, who made his fortune in everything from broadcasting to manufacturing radios and automobiles, was talked into taking over Cincinnati in 1934 by Larry MacPhail, who wanted to get out from under the financial restrictions placed on him by the trust company into whose portfolio the franchise had fallen. His radio operation proved critical to MacPhail's pioneering use of Red Barber to air Reds games. In 1936, however, a simmering dispute between the pair exploded when MacPhail slugged Crosley during an organization meeting; two days later, the general manager was out. At the height of the Red scare in the 1950s, Crosley changed the team's nickname to Redlegs lest some dim segment of the American public conclude that the occupants of Crosley Field endorsed Communism. In the late 1950s he seriously pursued the idea of moving the club to New York to fill the gap left by the defecting Dodgers and Giants; he was ultimately dissuaded by a congressional investigation then delving into baseball's exemption from antitrust statutes and fears that another franchise transfer might suggest that major league teams were more interested in money than market loyalty.

LAVE CROSS

Cross is the only player to play for four different teams in the same city: Between 1889 and 1907 he wore the uniforms of the American Association Athletics, the National League Phillies, the Players League Quakers, and the American League Athletics—all of Philadelphia.

TONY CUCCINELLO

Cuccinello was a casualty of the end of World War II. Two days before the end of the 1945 season, he was released by the White Sox and told he would not be invited back because of the younger players expected to be released from the military. At the time, the third baseman had been locked in a duel with George Stirnweiss of the Yankees for the batting title. The .309-hitting New York second baseman ended up taking the crown by .00009 points, the smallest margin in baseball history.

CANDY CUMMINGS (Hall of Fame, 1939)

The most commonly accepted progenitor of the curveball, Cummings claimed to have received the inspiration for what was the first trick pitch as a teenager chucking clam shells in his native Massachusetts. The righthander first used the delivery in competition in 1866. After five seasons in the National Association, he made his National League debut with Hartford in 1876, pitching a shutout against St. Louis in which 24 of the 27 outs were pop-ups—21 of them to the catcher and another three to Cummings himself. Later that season, on September 9, he won both ends of the first major league doubleheader, besting Cincinnati by scores of 14–4 in the morning and 8–4 in the late afternoon. Joining the same Reds the following season, he quit with a mid-season record of 5–14 following some abusive newspaper accounts of his diminished abilities.

Although Cummings owes his place in Cooperstown largely to Henry Chadwick's verification of his claim to have thrown the first curve, the historian also maintained from time to time that an unnamed Syracuse pitcher had beaten Cummings to the pitch by at least a decade. After retirement, Cummings served as the first figurehead president of the proto-minor league International Association.

NED CUTHBERT

Outfielder Cuthbert has been credited with being the first to steal a base, executing a theft of third against the astonished Brooklyn Atlantics while playing for the Philadelphia Keystones in 1865. The reason he gave for his innovation: there was nothing in the rules forbidding it.

KIKI CUYLER (Hall of Fame, 1968)

Of all the great outfields the Pirates have boasted over their history, the greatest of all should have been the 1927 array of Cuyler and the two Waner brothers. A .321 hitter over his 18 big league seasons (1921–38), the righty swinger topped the .300 mark 10 times, had at least 200 hits on three occasions, and in one season or another paced the National League in doubles, triples, runs scored (twice), and stolen bases (four times); for good measure, he also drove in 100 runs three times. But just as Lloyd Waner was joining his brother Paul on the Pittsburgh picket line, Cuyler got into a spat with manager Donie Bush that mushroomed into one of the worst deals ever completed by the Pirates.

The trouble started when Bush, in an attempt to shake the Pirates out of an early-season slump, moved Cuyler from third to second in the lineup. Cuyler protested, claiming that he wasn't a good hit-and-run man and was better suited to driving in runs from the third hole; he backed up his argument by going hitless in a few games. Deciding his authority was being questioned, Bush kept the lineup the way he wanted it, then fined Cuyler $25 for failing to slide to break up a double play in a game. This precipitated shouting matches on the bench and stirred up both the press and the fans against Bush for being bullheaded. When owner Barney Dreyfuss backed up Bush, Cuyler was benched for the rest of the year and for the 1927 World Series against the Yankees.

It came as a shock to nobody when Cuyler was shipped off to the Cubs after the season. His revenge was to pick up his career where it had left off, playing a major role in Chicago's 1929 and 1932 pennants. The Pirates didn't really fare that badly, either: Between 1927 and 1930 they used three different outfielders in place of Cuyler, all of whom batted well over .300.

D

JAY DAHL

Dahl was the pitcher in the all-rookie starting line-up Houston fielded against the Mets on September 27, 1963. He lasted only three innings in a 10–3 thrashing and never appeared in another major league game. Two years later, at age 19, he was killed in a car crash; no major leaguer or ex-major leaguer has ever died at a younger age. The other starters in the contest were Rusty Staub (1B), Joe Morgan (2B), Glenn Vaughan (3B), Sonny Jackson (SS), Brock Davis (OF), Aaron Pointer (OF), and Jimmy Wynn (OF).

STEVE DAHL

Dahl was a Chicago disc jockey who, on July 12, 1979, helped create one of the most chaotic scenes ever played out in a major league ballpark. With the backing of Mike Veeck, son of White Sox owner Bill Veeck, he presided over a Disco Demolition promotion that invited fans to bring their passé disco records to Comiskey Park for destruction between games of a doubleheader against the Tigers. No sooner had a pile of recordings been blown up than thousands of fans, some of whom had spent the first game firing vinyl through the stands, streamed onto the field, drinking beer, ripping up the turf, and improvising their own fires. After futile attempts by the senior Veeck to restore order, the police and fire departments had to be summoned. In the middle of the melee, which made it impossible to complete the doubleheader, Dahl himself simply stole away from the stadium. American League president Lee Mac-Phail awarded the second game of the twin bill to Detroit by forfeit.

HUGH DAILY

Despite losing his left hand in a gun accident as a youth, Daily was the first pitcher to notch back-to-back one-hitters. In the first of them, on July 7, 1884, he also fanned 19 batters and lost a 20th when, under the rules at the time, catcher Ed Crane dropped a third strike and the batter reached first base. To compensate for his missing hand, the pitcher used an adjustable wrist pad fastened at his elbow to absorb the impact of batted or thrown balls.

STEVE DALKOWSKI

Dalkowski was the most anticipated prospect in baseball history. As a Baltimore farmhand at Kingsport of the Class D Appalachian League in 1957, he was clocked regularly at more than 100 miles an hour while averaging almost two strikeouts an inning. But the other side of the coin was that he walked 129 batters over the same 62 innings in which he fanned 121, leading to a record of 1–8 and an ERA of 8.13. He never pitched in the majors despite widespread predictions in and out of the Orioles organization that he would make people forget Walter Johnson.

ABNER DALRYMPLE

The left fielder for the Chicago White Stockings in the 1880s, Dalrymple kept an extra ball inside his uniform for use in emergencies. He stole a home run from Boston's Ezra Sutton on a hazy day in 1880 by backing up against the fence and pulling the concealed ball out of his shirt as the game ball soared out of the park; the umpire, unable to see because of the fog, called Sutton out. Dalrymple won a batting crown while with Milwaukee in 1878, but recent research gave Paul Hines a higher average and the title.

CLAY DALRYMPLE

Catcher Dalrymple has been the only major leaguer to challenge a 19th-century rule intended to discourage ambidextrous pitching. On July 17, 1969, while with the Orioles, he took up his normal position behind the plate with a mitt on his left hand and a fielder's glove in his back pocket. Questioned by umpire John Rice, he explained that he intended using the fielder's glove for plays at the plate to take advantage of its greater flexibility. Citing the rule limiting players to one glove at a time, Rice ordered Dalrymple to toss his spare back into the dugout.

TOM DALY

Daly hit the first pinch-hit home run in the major leagues when he came off the bench to bat for ailing Dodgers left fielder Hub Collins in the ninth inning of a game in Boston on May 14, 1892; the utility man's heroics tied the game for Brooklyn. Collins died a week later of typhoid fever.

RAY DANDRIDGE (Hall of Fame, 1987)

Dandridge was a bowlegged third baseman who spent the better part of the 1930s setting the standard at his position in the Negro leagues, then almost all of the 1940s as a star of Jorge Pasquel's Mexican League. He introduced the gimmick, later made famous by Dodgers third baseman Billy Cox, of holding the ball just long enough to allow batters trying to leg out a hit to arrive a split second after his throw. The righthanded slap hitter is credited with batting averages in the .310s in the United States and the .340s in Mexico, but below .300 in Cuban winter ball.

In 1939 Dandridge jumped the Newark Eagles to play with the Vargas club in Caracas, then moved on to Vera Cruz, Mexico, batting higher than .300 in both places and helping both teams win pennants. He almost completed the hat trick, topping .300 again for the Cienfuegos entry that finished a half-game out of first place in the Cuban winter league. His stay in Mexico was interrupted in 1944 when Eagles owner Abe Manley had his draft exemption revoked to force him back to the United States. Two years later, with white North American stars receiving large amounts to play in the Mexican League, Dandridge forced a $10,000 bonus from Pasquel.

In 1947 Bill Veeck tried to lure Dandridge north of the border to play for the Indians, but he refused to leave Mexico without a signing bonus. Signed by the Giants at age 35, he was sent to their Triple-A farm club in Minneapolis, where he batted .362, .311, .324, and .292 in four seasons, taking Rookie of the Year honors in 1949 and an MVP award in 1950 for his role in the Millers American Association championship; many claimed that New York's refusal to promote him in 1950 cost the team a pennant. His primary function in 1951 was to prepare a young Willie Mays for his entry into the big leagues.

Dandridge is a member of the Mexican Baseball Hall of Fame as well as a Cooperstown honoree.

JOSEPH DANZANSKY

Danzansky's antics to keep one team in Washington and benighted efforts to attract another one there showed how easy it was to paralyze the major leagues. The owner of a chain of grocery stores and the president of the Washington Board of Trade, he stepped out on the stage in 1971, when he offered Bob Short $8.4 million for the Senators. When the offer was judged too modest and the team appeared headed for Texas, Commissioner Bowie Kuhn and other American League owners urged the businessman to come up with more money so the nation's capital wouldn't lose its second club of the century. Aware that Kuhn and the owners were fearful that a move to Texas would encourage another congressional look into baseball's antitrust exemption, Danzansky played them along for months, periodically reporting new investment sources and getting them to apply more pressure on Short. Finally, however, Short ran out of patience and challenged everybody concerned for concrete evidence of the additional money. When Danzansky produced nothing to back up his boasting, Kuhn and the AL had no choice but to endorse the transfer of the Senators to Texas.

The episode was still in everybody's mind two years later when Danzansky entered into an agreement with San Diego owner C. Arnholt Smith to bring the Padres to Washington in time for the 1974 season. To demonstrate his commitment, he gave Smith a $100,000 deposit on a projected $12 million while waiting for National League owners to approve the sale. Not only didn't the owners give their approval because of opposition to abandoning the Southern California market, but they also initiated an eight-month circus of seeking, interviewing, and rejecting prospective buyers who would keep the club in San Diego. In the meantime, Danzansky became the only outsider in baseball history to approve or veto trades, since his deposit money had bought from Smith the right to have the final say on all exchanges. Ever optimistic that he would be bringing the team to Washington in 1974, for instance, he turned thumbs down to a deal that would have sent Clay Kirby to St. Louis because the pitcher was from the capital and therefore a potential gate attraction. On the other hand, he permitted the Padres to sell pitcher Fred Norman to the Reds and infielder Dave Campbell to the Cardinals behind Smith's pleas that the club needed ready cash.

As the saga dragged on, Smith, becoming increasingly anxious about the threat of a federal indictment citing him for $23 million in unpaid taxes, decided to ignore his commitment to Danzansky and work out another arrangement with Marjorie Everett, main stockholder in the Hollywood Park racetrack. This prompted a lawsuit from Danzansky and trembling from NL owners; for the record, the latter said they were opposed to Everett's racetrack connections, but what they were mainly worried about was awakening congressmen again if Washington were denied a franchise in such a fashion. The upshot was that the owners vetoed the Everett bid and, turning full circle, indicated that they were ready to abandon San Diego and endorse Smith's original agreement. But then Danzansky popped up to announce that, together with the abuse he had suffered from both Smith and the league, the rising interest rates since he had first made his offer made it impractical for him to pursue any team ownership. He had his deposit refunded, and shortly afterward the Padres were sold to Ray Kroc.

ALVIN DARK

With the possible exception of Billy Sunday, no major leaguer mixed baseball and fundamentalist religion as extravagantly as Dark. Although the blend wasn't always evident during his 14-year career as a ferociously competitive shortstop for the Braves, Giants, and several other clubs, it was the glaring trademark of his stints as manager of the Giants, Kansas City Athletics, Indians, Oakland Athletics, and Padres. Even when he wasn't calling down heavenly vengeance on one of his employers, as he did with Charlie Finley, he was getting into other troubles with racist attitudes toward his players.

As a player, Dark became baseball's second Rookie of the Year (after Jackie Robinson) in 1948 by spearheading the Braves pennant that season. Two years later he and double play partner Eddie Stanky were traded to the Giants, where they proved to be the heart of New York's miracle 1951 win climaxed by Bobby Thomson's playoff home run. Again in 1954, Dark was a big reason for the Giants pennant, not least for the deft bat-handling that made him the best hit-and-run swinger of the period.

After wandering around the National League for a few years, Dark got his first managerial job in 1961 with the transplanted Giants in San Francisco. In 1962 he led the team to a pennant, squeezed out of the Dodgers in a postseason playoff. But then in 1964 he came close to causing baseball's first 20th-century racial strike when he accused San Francisco's black and Latin players of lacking the "mental alertness" of their white teammates and having "no pride" in their jobs. The remarks prompted most of the team's blacks and Latins to threaten an indefinite boycott until Dark was replaced. The situation was resolved only when Willie Mays, the manager's teammate in the Polo Grounds in the 1950s, interceded. Dark was fired at the end of the season—mostly because of the racial incident, but also because the front office dreaded the fallout from disclosures that the Bible-quoting pilot had been carrying on an adulterous affair with an airline hostess.

With the Kansas City version of the A's in 1967, Dark became enmeshed in another player revolt—this one aimed against team owner Finley. Although Dark had no part in a petition protesting Finley's niggardly ways, he was fired for not heading off the trouble; afterward, he called the uprising "one of the most courageous things I've ever seen in baseball." His next stop was in Cleveland in 1968, where he doubled as general manager. Mainly because of the players he had inherited, he steered the Indians to a rare first-division finish, but then found himself constantly outwitted by other general managers, leading to one transaction fiasco after another.

In 1974 Dark returned to Finley—and to an Oakland clubhouse where revolt was an everyday occurrence. The players so despised him for replacing Dick Williams, who had stood up to Finley, that Sal Bando, for one, openly declared that he "couldn't manage a meat market." Dark had enough wits, however, to turn a blind eye to the daily brawls that afflicted the Oakland clubhouse and produced two division wins and a pennant. He also won some respect for his own run-ins with Finley over the owner's determination to pare the organization to the bone. In September 1975 he sealed his fate by telling a congregation of fundamentalists: "To God, Charlie Finley is just a very little, bitty thing. If he doesn't accept Jesus Christ as his personal savior, he's going to hell." Finley waited only until Oakland had lost to Boston in the American League Championship Series before announcing that Dark was being replaced because he was "too busy with church activities."

Although anxious to get back to the National League, Dark turned down an offer from the Cardinals on the grounds that his religious principles wouldn't permit him to work for a team owned by a beer company. Instead, he took over the Padres 48 games into the 1977 season. As soon as he told the San Diego players that they were prohibited from drinking beer anywhere in his presence, they, too, rose up in arms; he also quickly alienated his pitching and hitting coaches by assuming most of their duties. Because he preferred viewing Dark as a loner up against the odds, owner Ray Kroc insisted that he be retained for the following season. But when tensions resumed even in spring training, Kroc got the message and replaced him with Roger Craig.

JAKE DAUBERT

Nobody was better than Daubert in the pre-agent era at getting an owner over a barrel during contract talks. As a member of the Dodgers, he won the National League batting title in both 1913 and 1914, each time serving notice on owner Charlie Ebbets that he would take his first baseman's mitt over to the Federal League if his salary demands were not met. They were. At the end of the 1918 season, which had been abbreviated because of World War I, Daubert read his contract meticulously enough to conclude that baseball ownership's ploy of prorating wages on the basis of the shortened schedule violated the pact, and asked for the full sum. When Ebbets took to the press to denounce him as "unpatriotic, selfish, and greedy," Daubert filed suit against the team. Panicky owners in both leagues pressured Ebbets to reach an out-of-court settlement lest a verdict come down against all of them. Ebbets sought

to save face by trading the first baseman to the Reds before the start of the 1919 season, but ended up sitting in the stands watching him play in that year's World Series. After batting .281 for Cincinnati in 1924, Daubert died at age 40 of complications from an appendectomy.

HELEN DAUVRAY

A noted actress and the wife of future Hall of Famer John Montgomery Ward, Dauvray convinced Detroit owner Frederick Stearns and St. Louis boss Chris Von der Ahe to have a silver cup designed by Tiffany's, name it after her, and award it to the first team to win three postseason championship series between the National League and American Association pennant winners. Dauvray, Ward, and the trophy, the last accompanied by a round-the-clock hired guard, took in the entire 15-game, 10-city 1887 Detroit-St. Louis series, often attracting more attention than the two teams. Her union with the Giants shortstop, an early version of the Joe DiMaggio-Marilyn Monroe match, created a media sensation. Although it lasted longer than the marriage, the cup was retired when cooperation between the two leagues ended in 1891. Although no team won the required three series, each of the four yearly victors—the Detroit Wolverines in 1887, Ward's Giants in 1888 and 1889, and Brooklyn in 1890—was a National League club.

BOB DAVIDS

Davids was the founder of the Society for American Baseball Research (SABR). A career civil servant with the Defense Department, Atomic Energy Commission, and Energy Department, he started the publication *Baseball Briefs* early in 1971, then in August of that year founded SABR at a meeting of 16 baseball historians and researchers at Cooperstown. The Hall of Fame later named its reading room after him.

DONALD DAVIDSON

The four-foot-tall Davidson came close to aborting midget Eddie Gaedel's distinction in baseball. While serving as the batboy for the Red Sox in 1938, he was told by manager Joe Cronin to hit for Moe Berg. Umpire Bill Summers didn't share Cronin's sense of humor, however, and demanded that Berg take his turn. Davidson divided his batboy chores between the Red Sox and Braves. He ended up remaining with the Braves through their transfers to Milwaukee and Atlanta, moving up the ladder from team mascot to public relations director to traveling secretary.

MORDECAI DAVIDSON

Taking over ownership of the Louisville Colonels in 1888, Davidson launched a two-year tyranny that culminated in the first major league player walkout, in June 1889. The owner traveled with the club to maintain discipline, levied $100 fines for errors as well as rules infractions, left players on the road penniless, kept up a running attack on the team in the press, and changed managers capriciously (even serving two brief terms in the dugout himself). The strike, led by Pete Browning and Guy Hecker, lasted two days and ended only when the American Association confiscated the franchise and returned more than half of the fines Davidson had collected.

GEORGE DAVIS (Hall of Fame, 1998)

After batting over .300 for nine consecutive seasons and leading the National League with 136 RBIs in 1897, shortstop Davis jumped from the Giants to Chicago in the rival American League in 1902. It was the start of something messy. Hardly excited by owner Charlie Comiskey's salary scale, he retreated to New York the following year—only to be ordered right back to Chicago after four games in line with the peace treaty between the leagues. Davis refused to report and sat out the rest of the schedule while his attorney, John Montgomery Ward, fought the decision and New York owner John T. Brush cheered them both on. Davis, Ward, and Brush all lost, but not before the suit had threatened the agreement between the leagues and not without seeding a lifelong enmity between AL president Ban Johnson and the attorney. As for Davis, he played the last six years of his 20-year (1890–1909) career as a Comiskey employee. He never hit again as well as he had for the Giants, but he overcame injuries in the 1906 World Series to drive in six runs over the last three games to lead the Hitless Wonder White Sox over the powerhouse Cubs.

MARK DAVIS

Davis has been the Cy Young Award's most anomalous recipient. A lefthanded reliever for the Padres in 1989, he took the honor for leading the National League with 44 saves. That effort followed a brilliant second half in 1988 during which he compiled most of his 28 rescues on the season. But aside from that patch of bullpen dominance, he was not only bad, he was atrocious. Minus his 1988 and 1989 campaigns, for instance, Davis had only 26 saves with an ERA well over five for his 15 big league seasons between 1980 and 1997.

SHERRY DAVIS

Davis became the first woman to work as a field announcer when she was hired by the Giants for Candlestick Park in 1993.

TOMMY DAVIS

Davis was the best hitter ever caught in baseball's revolving doors. Although a couple of other major leaguers have been traded more often, none can claim the two batting championships (1962 and 1963 for Los Angeles) and RBI title (1962) that the right-hand-hitting outfielder captured before changing uniforms 12 times. Following the Dodgers, he moved to the Mets, White Sox, Pilots, Astros, A's (twice), Cubs (twice), Orioles, Angels, and Royals. Some of the trades were in the interests of having Davis's bat on a pennant contender in September; others were motivated by the bad leg that slowed him up on the field.

JOHN B. DAY

Day's career as a baseball mogul began as a result of a chance meeting with Jim Mutrie, who, after watching him pitch (badly) for a New Jersey club he had organized, offered to help put together a winning team. Together they founded the New York Metropolitans; leased the original Polo Grounds, at 110th Street and Fifth Avenue, from James Gordon Bennett; fielded a team in the first professional game ever played in Manhattan (on September 29, 1880); and ran one of the best and most profitable minor league teams in the country for two years.

In 1882 Day flirted with the fledgling American Association but finally decided against sacrificing the certainty of exhibition games with National League teams for the uncertainty of membership in a rival circuit. Invited to join both warring organizations the following year, he avoided making a choice by entering the Metropolitans in the AA and forming an entirely new team for the NL. The new club, eventually known as the Giants, was made up in large part of players from the ousted Troy franchise. From the beginning the older Mets were decidedly the lesser asset, relegated to the less desirable of the back-to-back fields at the Polo Grounds (or, worse, to Metropolitan Park, where the contents of the city dump underneath seeped upward). Dual ownership proved lucrative for Day but an irritant to the rest of the AA, especially when manager Mutrie began leaking the proceedings of Association meetings to his boss. The irritation turned to pain when Day, deciding that all his stars should be consolidated on the team that could charge double the AA's 25-cent admission fee, transferred third baseman Dude Esterbrook and pitcher Tim Keefe from his pennant-winning Mets to the Giants after the 1884 season, then sold the Mets altogether.

Day had been a stalwart in the Union Association war of 1884, when he was the first to suggest blacklisting players who jumped their contracts; the Players League war six years later was another matter. Well liked by his players, he was blind to the possibility of even a strike by the Players Brotherhood, let alone the wholesale defection of virtually his entire roster to a new, employee-dominated circuit. He had, after all, just won two successive pennants and completed construction on a new version of the Polo Grounds, at the foot of Coogan's Bluff in northern Manhattan. In late 1889, when star shortstop and Brotherhood organizer John Montgomery Ward offered him a job with the PL for the following season, he still didn't see the handwriting on the wall. The script became clear to him only after the loss of court battles to prevent both Ward and catcher Buck Ewing from appearing for the PL. By midseason Day was in such desperate straits that other teams had to pump money into the franchise during the season lest it fold and leave the NL with no New York presence.

Outsmarted by his players before the war, Day was also outmaneuvered in its aftermath by Edward Talcott, the PL Giants financial backer, who ended up with a larger chunk of stock than Day after a merger of the two teams. The new senior partner flexed his muscles early, insisting that the Giants play the 1891 season in Brotherhood Park, next door to Day's stadium, and that it become the third Polo Grounds. When Talcott then teamed with John T. Brush, one of the midseason angels, it spelled the

end for both Mutrie (after the 1891 season) and Day himself (a year later). In 1899 the former owner, bankrupt and in failing health, returned to manage the club for Andrew Freedman in a pathetic publicity stunt. An appointment as the NL's supervisor of umpires in 1900 was, in reality, an act of charity by former associates and didn't last all that long anyway. Day then disappeared until 1923, when he was discovered paralyzed in a Bowery room, unable to care for himself or his dying wife. The Giants held an exhibition game for his benefit, but he died a ward of the state a short time later.

LEON DAY (Hall of Fame, 1995)

An all-around athlete who played every position except catcher and a hitter good enough to bat as high as .469 in 1946, Day was the Negro National League's premier pitcher in the late 1930s and 1940s and the pioneer of the no-windup delivery. The righthander spent his best seasons, both before and after World War II, with the Newark Eagles. His main weapon was a blazing fastball that helped him strike out a NNL-record 18 batters in a game in 1942 and pitch a no-hitter on Opening Day in 1946 (after having spent two years in the military). His most noted effort, however, was a five-hit victory over Satchel Paige and the Kansas City Monarchs in the 1942 Negro World Series after being added to the roster of the Homestead Grays in the middle of the Series. He also pitched in Puerto Rico, Mexico, Cuba, and Venezuela. Day was so dominant while in Venezuela that the league broke up for lack of adequate competition.

Plagued by a sore arm late in his career, Day nonetheless signed with Toronto of the International League in 1951; in his minor league debut season, he went 1–1 with a 1.58 ERA and 20 strikeouts in 40 innings. The following year he pitched for Scranton in the Red Sox organization, winning 13 and losing nine with a 3.41 ERA.

DIZZY DEAN (Hall of Fame, 1953)

Dean so dominated the National League for five years that not even a career-abbreviating injury and a relatively meager 150 wins could prevent his election to Cooperstown. The Cardinals righthander spun off 102 victories between 1933 and 1936; the 30 he won in 1934 marked the last time a NL hurler reached that plateau. He also paced the league four consecutive years (1932–35) in strikeouts. On the other hand, Dean was never unhittable, even in his best years: He got below three runs per nine innings only once while he was winning big and led the NL in hits yielded even as he was winning 28 games in 1935.

On his way to what looked like another big season in 1937, Dean had his toe broken by an Earl Averill line drive in the All-Star Game; he came back to the team too fast after the injury and, altering his motion to compensate for his discomfort, developed a sore arm. Prior to the 1938 campaign the Cardinals traded him to the Cubs for three players and $185,000. Although he pitched well in Chicago's drive to a pennant, he never again won in double figures. His last appearance on the mound came in 1947 for the Browns, after he had already been a broadcaster for six years; he pitched four scoreless innings in what was essentially a stunt appearance.

Dean's mangling of the English language as a broadcaster rivaled his earlier fame as a pitcher. When he didn't have runners "sludding" into bases, he was getting off such observations as: "Don't fail to miss tomorrow's game" (a broadcasting promo); "He's standing confidentially at the plate"; and "The players have returned to their respectable bases." As a player, he was able to laugh as much as his teammates when a headline announced the results of his examination for a possible concussion as: DEAN'S HEAD EXAMINED, X-RAYS REVEAL NOTHING. Asked on one occasion to explain his success, he told a newsman: "The Good Lord was good to me. He gave me a strong body, a good right arm, and a weak mind." In 1952 Dan Dailey starred as the pitcher in the Hollywood film *The Pride of St. Louis*.

Dean's brother Paul won 19 games for the Cardinals in both 1934 and 1935.

PAT DEASLEY

Catcher Deasley talked St. Louis Browns owner Chris Von der Ahe into signing him to a contract without a reserve clause for the 1884 season. Assuming that made him a free agent the following year, he was informed by the American Association that nobody would sign him because the 1884 contract had been a fraud. Having asserted the right to reserve a player even without a specific reserve clause, Von der Ahe then released the receiver. Deasley eventually signed with the Giants.

EDWARD DeBARTOLO

The multimillionaire owner of shopping malls, banks, race tracks, hotels, and the National Hockey League's Pittsburgh Penguins, DeBartolo was stymied three times in the 1980s in attempts to buy an American League team because of his alleged underworld associations. After making a fruitless pass at the Mariners in early 1980, he worked out a $20 million deal with Bill Veeck to take over the White Sox later the same year. But over the next several months AL owners raised one objection after another, pretending not to notice DeBartolo's formal concessions to each and every point. When the owners began leaking hints of the businessman's reputed gangster connections, Italian-American lobbying groups got into the act by accusing the league of ethnic prejudice. After the White Sox were awarded to Jerry Reinsdorf and Eddie Einhorn, DeBartolo turned his attention to the Indians, openly declaring that he intended moving the franchise to New Orleans. AL owners who had previously shown little opposition to such an idea immediately took up the cause of Cleveland fans, using it as a stick to discourage DeBartolo from pursuing the matter further.

DAVE DeBUSSCHERE

More than one athlete has tried to play two professional sports simultaneously, but DeBusschere also attempted to manage in the bargain. A righthander for the White Sox in 1962 and 1963, he spent the off-season playing for the National Basketball Association's Detroit Pistons. Still regarded as a top prospect, he was farmed out to Indianapolis in 1964, where he posted the first of two successive 15-win seasons. But when the Pistons also made him a player-coach at age 24, the six-foot, six-inch DeBusschere began wilting under the pressure and eventually chose to concentrate exclusively on basketball. His baseball record in the majors was 3–4; as a hoop star he ended up in the Hall of Fame.

HARRY DECKER

A backup catcher for the Phillies in 1890, Decker spent some of his bench time designing the forerunner of the modern catching mitt. The first player to use what was called the Decker Safety Catching Mitt was New York receiver Buck Ewing.

ROB DEER

Deer made even Gorman Thomas and Dave King-man look like contact hitters. In 10 major league seasons (1984–93) with the Giants, Brewers, and Tigers, the righthand-hitting outfielder struck out 1,379 times in 3,831 at bats—for a strikeout average of .360. (Runner-up Thomas whiffed 1,339 times in 4,677 appearances, an average of .286 percent.) In 1991 Deer also became the first player to hit 25 home runs without batting .200: He hit a mere .179.

ED DELAHANTY (Hall of Fame, 1945)

The only player to win batting titles in both the National and American leagues, Delahanty was the most accomplished of a record five brothers to reach the majors. A righthand-hitting outfielder, he put together a lifetime .346 average and three .400 marks during his 16 big league seasons (1888–1903), primarily with the Phillies. On July 13, 1896 he became the second player to hit four home runs in a game.

After claiming a batting crown with Philadelphia in 1899, Delahanty won another in his first season with Washington, in 1902. Despite this, he jumped back to the Giants the following spring, only to be reassigned to the Senators when the NL and AL worked out their peace treaty before the 1903 season. Suspended in June for excessive drinking, he left the Senators in Detroit, scuffled with a conductor, was thrown off the train, and was killed—in what has never been firmly established as either an accident, a suicide, or a homicide—when he went over the International Bridge and into the Niagara River. The suicide speculation was abetted by a sizable insurance policy he had taken out with his daughter as beneficiary shortly before his death.

VIC DELMORE

Umpiring balls and strikes for a Cubs-Cardinals game on June 30, 1959, Delmore precipitated the greatest field chaos since the Merkle Boner of 1908. The trouble started when Stan Musial drew a walk in the fourth inning and Chicago catcher Sammy Taylor argued that the final pitch had ticked the St. Louis slugger's bat for a foul ball. Taylor became so embroiled in making his point that he neglected to retrieve the ball after it had glanced off him, and Delmore was so preoccupied with rebutting the receiver that he forgot about declaring the ball still in play. The first to realize what was going on were

Musial, who immediately rounded first base and headed for second, and Cubs third baseman Alvin Dark, who ran for the ball. Before Dark could get to it, however, a batboy picked it up and tossed it to Wrigley Field field announcer Pat Pieper, who, along with his other duties, took care of the bag where the discarded balls were kept. When he saw Dark charging at him, Pieper instantly dropped the ball so that the infielder could retrieve it and fire down to second.

In the meantime, the still oblivious Delmore handed another ball to Taylor with an order to end his arguing. Taylor barely got his hand on it before pitcher Bob Anderson grabbed it away again and fired to second to get Musial. Although the Dark ball and the Anderson ball arrived practically simultaneously, Musial saw only the latter, which sailed wildly into center field; he promptly started for third, only to be tagged out by Chicago shortstop Ernie Banks, who caught the Dark throw. After a protracted argument Musial was called out—erroneously because the ball was in fact dead as soon as the batboy had touched it and irrelevantly because, after a protest, the Cardinals won the game anyway. As for the four-year veteran Delmore, the fiasco weighed heavily in a league decision at the end of the year not to rehire him.

BUCKY DENT

Dent's three-run home run off Boston's Mike Torrez in the seventh inning of the winner-take-all playoff game in 1978 provided the Yankees with a pennant-winning margin. Only his fifth homer of the season, the blow made him an instant darling of both female Yankees fans and Madison Avenue. When all the glory had settled, however, the shortstop had little to show for it except a fur coat commercial that irritated animal rights activists, a trade to Texas for another New York cover boy, Lee Mazzilli, and a stormy 89-game stint in 1989 and 1990 as one of George Steinbrenner's revolving-door managers.

JIM DERRINGTON

Derrington became the youngest pitcher to start a 20th-century big league game when, at age 16 years and 10 months, he took the hill for the 1956 White Sox. Although he ended up the losing pitcher, he also singled to set the record for the youngest American League player to get a hit. After a few appearances the following year, Derrington was demoted to the minors, never to return—washed up before his 18th birthday.

BILL DEVERY

A former New York City police chief, Devery had political connections that were reason enough for American League president Ban Johnson to ignore his reputation as a grafter and accept him as co-owner of the New York Highlanders (later the Yankees) in 1903. At first, the man described as the most corrupt police commissioner in the history of New York City played silent partner to gambling kingpin Frank Farrell, preferring to concentrate on building a real-estate fortune with the payoff money he had accepted as a cop and bagman for Tammany Hall. But after 1908 he became more active in the club's operations, siding with Hal Chase in his feud with manager Frank Chance to the point of engaging in a shoving match with the pilot after he traded the first baseman to the White Sox. By then he had also been in the habit of sitting behind the New York dugout and loudly second-guessing the moves of his own managers.

In 1915 Devery and Farrell, unable to build a winning team, sold out to Jacob Ruppert and Cap Huston for a 250 percent profit on their original investment.

BING DEVINE

Devine is the Players Association's best argument against contentions that free agency has been responsible for undermining player loyalty to a team. Although other general managers (Branch Rickey, Frank Lane, Jack McKeon, etc.) have had greater reputations for being trigger-happy traders, the king of the hill was in fact Devine. Between 1969 and 1979, for instance, he completed or blueprinted no fewer than 193 deals (an average of 16 a year) for the Cardinals—and that counts transactions only at the major league level. In 1967, while running the Mets, he kept the door revolving so frantically between trades and call-ups that 27 pitchers and 27 position players ended up wearing the New York uniform at one time or another during the season. Fittingly, it was Devine who brokered the clash between big league baseball and Curt Flood's challenge to the reserve clause. During an initial stint with the Cardinals in the late 1950s, he obtained Flood from the Reds in one of the franchise's best deals. In 1969,

following his return to St. Louis from New York, he sought to send the outfielder to the Phillies in a headline-making swap involving, among others, Dick Allen and Tim McCarver. When Flood refused to report to Philadelphia, the stage was set for the years-long drama that would end in free agency and arbitration rights for players.

JIM DEVLIN

Winner of 65 games in the National League's first two seasons, Devlin was one of the infamous Louisville Four expelled from baseball for throwing games in 1877. With the Grays comfortably in first place by $5\frac{1}{2}$ games in mid-August, the righthander, who pitched every inning on the schedule (the only time that has been done), lost 13 of his last 20 outings; Boston meanwhile surged to the pennant by winning 20 of its last 21. A postseason investigation, prompted by anonymous tips from gamblers, uncovered a tangle of conspiracies, recriminations, and doublecrosses.

Devlin admitted accepting, at left fielder George Hall's instigation, two $100 bribes to lose an exhibition game in Indianapolis and then a contest with the Cincinnati Reds, who were laboring under the threat of a suspension that would discount all their games from official standing. He also admitted lying to Hall about the amounts involved and to giving the outfielder only $25 of the gamblers' money. But that was as far as he went, dismissing accusations about other suspicious performances against the Hartfords of Brooklyn and Boston and pointing out that even the Cincinnati game would not count in the standings. Nor did Devlin implicate the other two Louisville Four—Bill Craver and Al Nichols. As for why he had suddenly become so ineffective, he blamed it on a combination of hand boils that made it impossible for him to grip his sinker and a general lack of team hitting.

Devlin's explanations fell on deaf ears, and all four of the named players were suspended indefinitely on October 30, 1877. After the NL made the suspension permanent as its winter meeting, he made repeated appeals for reinstatement to Philadelphia manager Harry Wright, Chicago stockholder Al Spalding, and NL president William Hulbert. All he got for his trouble were a $50 handout from Hulbert (or so Spalding claimed), the proceeds from a benefit game (about $1,000) just before he died in 1883, and a league resolution promising not only never to commute the sentences of the quartet, but also never even to hear further arguments on the case.

THOMAS DEVYR

Devyr was the central figure in baseball's first gambling scandal. Bribed by teammates Ed Duffy and William Wansley to throw an 1865 game against the underdog Brooklyn Eckfords, the shortstop temporarily escaped punishment when the New York Mutuals, run by the notorious Boss Tweed, managed to persuade the judiciary committee of the National Association of Amateur Baseball Players to drop the charges against him. On the other hand, Duffy and Wansley were banned, and when the case was reopened in 1869, so was Devyr. All three were reinstated by the full association the following year.

BILL DEWITT

DeWitt conducted a running fire sale of the Browns in the late 1940s and early 1950s. Given a chance later on to run clubs that didn't have to auction off players to pay the utility bill, he made one of the most meaningless, then one of the worst, trades in baseball history.

A Robert Hedges protégé, DeWitt started with the Browns as a teenage vendor, then moved with Branch Rickey to the Cardinals. In 1936 he joined a group assembled by Don Barnes to purchase the Browns from the estate of Phil Ball. Handling baseball operations while Barnes ran the financial side of the franchise, DeWitt presided over the dismal teams of the late 1930s; built the Browns only pennant-winning team (1944), largely with the money provided by new partner Richard Muckerman; probably cost the club a second pennant, the next year, by insisting that one-armed outfielder Pete Gray stay in the lineup; and executed orders from a disgusted Muckerman to recoup losses after second-division finishes in 1946 and 1947. What followed—between January 1947 and January 1949—were 20 deals, 16 of which brought cash to the revenue-starved club.

The carnage was interrupted only long enough for DeWitt and his brother Charley to buy Muckerman's almost 57 percent of the franchise behind claims that interests in Baltimore, Milwaukee, Los Angeles, and Dallas had offered more than the ostensible price tag of $1 million paid by the DeWitts. In reality the sale was mainly a reward for the deals DeWitt had engineered to recoup Muckerman's losses and amounted to junk bond corporate raid: a three-step process of borrowing heavily to make the deal, selling off the most valuable assets one at a time, then selling the shell of the structure. To assume control of the club, the DeWitts put up only $75,000 of their own money, borrowed $300,000 from the American League (on condition that they keep the team in St. Louis), and let Muckerman hold notes on another $650,000. In an effort to retire some of the debt, DeWitt continued selling players, receiving cash in 10 of 11 major transactions between March 1949 and June 1951. The only difference between this and his earlier binge was that now it was his own head that had to be kept above water. Together with the sale of the Browns Toledo farm club to Detroit, the player sales netted more than $500,000. Finally, DeWitt sold the team to Bill Veeck in July 1951.

DeWitt resurfaced as president of the Tigers in October 1959. On the plus side of his 11 months in the job were swaps with Cleveland's Frank Lane for first baseman Norm Cash (for Steve Demeter) and outfielder Rocky Colavito (for Harvey Kuenn); even more memorable, if only for its ineffectiveness, was the swap of managers Joe Gordon and Jimmy Dykes he worked out in August 1960, also with Lane.

Moving on to the presidency of the Reds in November 1960, DeWitt inherited from Gabe Paul the team that would win the NL pennant in 1961, adding only an infield anchor in Don Blasingame three weeks into the season. In 1962 he purchased the club from the estate of Powel Crosley. His six years as Cincinnati owner were memorable mostly for guaranteeing that the club would be even better than it was by trading Frank Robinson to the Orioles in December 1965 for journeyman pitchers Milt Pappas and Jack Baldschun. His rationale for the deal, one of the worst in baseball history, was that the slugger was "an old 30." DeWitt sold the Reds to a group headed by Francis Dale and brothers William and James Williams in January 1968.

BILL DICKEY (Hall of Fame, 1954)

One of the best catchers in American League history, Dickey's bat and defensive skills were major components of the Murderers Row New York lineups of the 1930s, while his teaching skills contributed to Yankees championship teams well into the 1960s. In his 17-year (1928–43, 1946) career, all of it with the Bronx club, the lefty swinger batted .313, topping .300 11 times, with a career high .362 in 1936 (the highest ever by a catcher who appeared behind the plate in at least 100 games). Between 1936 and 1939 Dickey reached the seats 20 times and drove in more than 100 runs each year. He also established a major league record (later tied by Johnny Bench) for catching at least 100 games in 13 consecutive seasons, and earned a reputation as the best handler of pitchers of his time.

Ordinarily mild-mannered, Dickey received an extraordinary suspension for an on-field fracas on July 6, 1932. After breaking Washington outfielder Carl Reynolds's jaw following a home plate crash on a squeeze play, the receiver was slapped with a $1,000 fine and a suspension for the duration of the Washington outfielder's stay on the disabled list— an eventual 30 days.

In August 1940 Dickey became embroiled in a legal battle with the New York *Daily News* and sportswriter Jimmy Powers, who demonstrated his lack of medical knowledge by writing a column blaming the Yankees fifth-place status and the poor performance by several noted players on "a mass polio epidemic" spread by Lou Gehrig, Dickey's best friend who was actually suffering from the non-communicable amytrophic lateral sclerosis; the columnist singled out Dickey, who would bat a career-low .247 for the year. After Gehrig sued for $1 million, Dickey led other players in following suit. The controversy and the legal actions ended in late September, when Powers apologized under a three-and-a-half column headline that offered "our apologies to Lou Gehrig and the Yankees."

Dickey succeeded Joe McCarthy as Yankees manager in May 1946 but quit in September when New York president Larry MacPhail hired Bucky Harris as a transparent manager-in-waiting. He returned to the Yankees as a coach in 1949, his primary duty to work with Yogi Berra on his catching skills. As Berra later put it, "Dickey learned me all his experiences." He did the same for Elston Howard in the mid-1950s before retiring.

MURRY DICKSON

Dickson provided the smoking gun that enabled the Internal Revenue Service to jail Cardinals owner Fred Saigh for tax evasion in the early 1950s. After several years of solid work for St. Louis, the right-hander was sold to the Pirates in January 1949 for an announced $125,000. According to IRS investigators, however, the money never found its way to the Cardinals, ending up instead in Saigh's private (and undeclared) account.

Dickson had an 18-year career between 1939 and 1959 that left him just short of a four-decade pitcher. For the Cardinals he led the National League in winning percentage in 1946, while managing the even tougher feat in 1951 of winning 20 games for the seventh-place Pirates. Between 1946 and 1954 he never started fewer than 40 times.

MARTIN DIHIGO (Hall of Fame, 1977)

Dihigo is the only player elected to halls of fame in three countries—his native Cuba, Mexico, and the United States. The most versatile and the most traveled of the Negro leaguers elected to Cooperstown, he was a star at every position on the diamond—so much so that, in the 1980s, he was voted by former teammates and opponents as the greatest second baseman of all time, while also receiving votes at third base and the outfield. A 15-year (1923–36, 1945) veteran of the North American black leagues, Dihigo also played in Mexico from 1937 to 1944 and from 1946 into the early 1950s. In addition, he played winter ball in his native Cuba for 24 years (1922–29, 1931–46), as well as in Puerto Rico and the Dominican Republic.

In North America the righthanded Dihigo was primarily a position player; in Latin America, a pitcher. A consistent .300 hitter with considerable power north of the border, he topped the .400 mark several times in Cuba. As a pitcher, he won 115 games in Mexico (including the Mexican League's first no-hitter) and 119 in Cuba. He also managed several entries on both sides of the border.

A supporter of Cuban leaders Fidel Castro and Che Guevara, Dihigo was appointed minister of sport after the 1959 revolution and charged with converting baseball into an amateur sport in the country.

WALTER J. DILBECK

Spurned in an effort to purchase the Kansas City Athletics from Charlie Finley for $10 million and inspired by a Pentagon-sponsored trip to Vietnam, Dilbeck set out to take on the "monarchical monopolists" of organized baseball and bring the essence of American culture to the rest of the world by founding the so-called Global League. Ignoring his lack of financing, he began a three-year shell game in 1966, changing the venue of putative franchises in the United States, Latin America, and Japan on whim; saying he would not raid the major leagues, then changing his mind and approaching, among others, future Hall of Famers Don Drysdale and Roberto Clemente with fabulous offers; he also claimed backing from Howard Hughes and the Hughes Sports Network.

Dilbeck's main accomplishments were to entice former commissioner Happy Chandler to fill a similar post for the Global League; to sign future Cooperstown residents Johnny Mize and Enos Slaughter as a manager and coach, respectively; and to involve retired umpires Jocko Conlan and Bill McKinley. The venture collapsed only three weeks after play began in May 1969. Paychecks bounced for teams representing both Japanese and North American cities (but playing in Caracas, Venezuela), and players were thrown out of hotels. Mize, Slaughter, and two full rosters were stranded in the Dominican Republic in the middle of a revolution. Dilbeck's later misadventures included serving time in a federal prison for income tax evasion.

POP DILLON

Of all ballpark inaugurals, none had the drama of the first game at Detroit's Bennett Park on April 25, 1901, when Dillon doubled home the winning run to cap a 10-run bottom of the ninth and give the Tigers a 14–13 comeback victory in their American League premier. Otherwise, the lefthand-hitting first baseman had an undistinguished five-season career, batting .252 for four clubs.

JOE DiMAGGIO (Hall of Fame, 1955)

DiMaggio spent 13 years (1936–42, 1946–51) with the Yankees, establishing himself as not only the greatest all-around player of his time but also as the enduring symbol of his era. As player, he drew almost no criticism from any quarter—fans, reporters, teammates, and opponents admired his wide stance and picture-perfect swing, his gracefulness afield, and his apparently unemotional approach to the game. As a symbol, he entered literature as a personification of perfection for novelist Ernest Hemingway's fisherman in *The Old Man and the Sea*, popular culture as a metaphor for the good old days through Paul Simon and Art Garfunkel's lyric of

"Where have you gone, Joe DiMaggio?" from their song "Mrs. Robinson"; and show business as the husband of Marilyn Monroe. Through it all he kept his eye on what he thought being Joe DiMaggio meant as intently as he ever did on a Bob Feller fastball and stayed equally focused on the hoarding of the material wealth his fame brought.

With San Francisco of the Pacific Coast League in 1933, DiMaggio hit in 61 consecutive games, attracting a swarm of major league scouts until he damaged a knee getting out of a cab. Only the Yankees persevered after the injury, watching in gleeful expectation as he racked up a .398 average with 34 homers and 154 RBIs in his final minor league campaign, in 1935. Brought up to New York the following year, the righthand-hitting outfielder went on to win two batting championships (1939 and 1940) and to pace the American League in home runs, RBIs, and slugging twice each. Along the way, he picked up three MVP trophies (1939, 1941, and 1947) and concluded his career with a .325 average and 361 home runs while striking out a mere 369 times. Appearing in 10 World Series, DiMaggio batted .271; in the 1947 Series against the Dodgers he let his emotions show through for one of the few times on the diamond by kicking the dirt as he rounded second base after Brooklyn's Al Gionfriddo made a spectacular catch to rob him of extra bases. His most memorable diamond achievement was his 56-game hitting streak in 1941, a record made all the more impressive by the fact that after it was halted (only because of two sterling plays by Cleveland third baseman Ken Keltner on July 17), he batted safely in 17 more consecutive games.

Hobbled by injuries late in his career, DiMaggio had a knack for returning from the disabled list with flair. On June 28, 1949, for example, after missing the first 10 weeks of the campaign, he returned to spark a three-game sweep of the Red Sox, with four home runs and nine RBIs. On the other hand, suffering from viral pneumonia, he took himself out of the pennant-winning game in the ninth inning against the Red Sox on the final day of the season after letting a Bobby Doerr drive go over his head for a triple.

His consistency and slugging aside, what made DiMaggio so admired among peers as much as the public was the seeming effortlessness of his classic swing and the equal ease with which he covered center field. Without flash or flourish, he used a knowledge of opposing batters and an ability to get a more than ordinary jump to arrive almost instinctively under fly balls. His most fabled defensive play came when he tracked down a Hank Greenberg blast in 1939 behind the monuments in Yankee Stadium's center field, 460 feet from the plate; ironically, the play also marked one of his rare mistakes in the field, since he failed to realize that his spectacular catch was only the second out and neglected to make a throw back to the infield.

DiMaggio's relations with Yankees brass varied with the occupants of the front office. He fought with Ed Barrow over money, holding out in 1938 until advised by prizefight manager Joe Gould to settle, then protesting again when Barrow used the limping excuse of World War II to try to cut his salary after the feats of 1941. In 1947 he intervened with teammates on the verge of an insurrection against Larry MacPhail for fining players unwilling to attend promotional events and for insisting that the team travel on a decrepit C-54 transport plane. He largely ignored general manager George Weiss and dealt directly with co-owner Dan Topping, who in 1949 made him the first $100,000 major leaguer.

Under manager Joe McCarthy DiMaggio flourished as just the kind of reticent, all-business performer McCarthy relished, but the arrival of Casey Stengel in 1949 proved less happy. While parroting the veneration everyone heaped on the center fielder late in his career, Stengel pulled several embarrassing moves during the 1950 season, dropping the aging star from his accustomed cleanup spot to fifth on one occasion and penciling him in at first base on another—neither time discussing the switch with him beforehand. Perhaps the most plangent moment involving the two was when the pilot sent Cliff Mapes out to replace DiMaggio in the field in the middle of an inning of a spring training game; DiMaggio waved Mapes back to the dugout, then took himself out of the game after the end of the inning.

The Yankee Clipper's relationship with the fans was largely one-sided. As the successor to the gregarious Babe Ruth as the darling of New York, he disappointed with his shyness, taking meals in his room and generally remaining aloof. A host of New York celebrities, especially restaurateur Toots Shor, protected him from the public in exchange for their own access to the diamond star. New York sportswriters also contributed to the DiMaggio myth, de-picting his reticence as synonymous with class and as an extension of his on-field behavior.

With his injuries finally catching up to him, DiMaggio refused a fourth six-figure contract and retired after the 1951 season because he could no longer live up to his own expectations. In the early years of his retirement he mellowed somewhat, seeming more comfortable with his fame. His union with Monroe, the celebrity marriage of the period, ended in divorce, but their continuing intimacy until her death and his devotion to her after it enhanced rather than tarnished his image. Not even performing in television commercials—for a coffee company and a New York bank—could taint the dignity he had affected as a player. Also remaining was the old unwillingness to look ridiculous, leading him, after a time, to refuse to take part in Old-Timer games. And the self-assurance never left either: Told that old rival Ted Williams had called him the greatest player he had seen, DiMaggio accurately, if ungraciously, responded with an observation that Williams was the greatest lefthanded hitter he had ever seen.

It was only after DiMaggio's death in 1999 that the seamier details emerged: a slush fund that New York underworld figures set up for him while he was still an active player, the bag of cash hidden in his San Francisco home that he rushed to salvage in the wake of the 1989 earthquake (all the while allowing police and fire personnel to believe that he was anxious to reach his sister, who lived in the house), and the autographed memorabilia he doled out in chunks small enough to keep their purchase prices high. There were even suggestions that his well-publicized hostility to Monroe's Hollywood crowd was based on embarrassment that Frank Sinatra, in particular, had discovered that he had physically abused the actress during their marriage.

DiMaggio's brothers Dom and Vince also had substantial major league careers, the former as the leadoff batter and center fielder on the Red Sox in the 1940s and early 1950s and the latter as a freeswinging outfielder with several National League clubs in the late 1930s and 1940s.

BILL DINNEEN

Dinneen was the only major leaguer both to pitch and umpire a no-hitter. In fact, in his 29 seasons (1909–37) as an American League arbiter, he called balls and strikes for six such masterpieces. His own came against the White Sox on September 27, 1905, while he was pitching for the Red Sox. The right-hander compiled a 170–177 record in 12 big league seasons (1898–1909) with four clubs. Dinneen was also the pitching star in Boston's 1903 world championship, winning three games against the Pirates in the first World Series.

BILL DOAK

In 1920, Doak, then a pitcher with the Cardinals, used the first glove with a preformed pocket and reinforced webbing.

LARRY DOBY (Hall of Fame, 1998)

Aside from all the other obstacles he had to negotiate as the American League's first black player in July 1947, Doby had to overcome a widespread impression that he was just one more of Cleveland owner Bill Veeck's box-office ploys.

The second baseman (alongside shortstop Monte Irvin) for the Newark Eagles, Doby was hitting .414 in 1947 before Veeck selected him to integrate the AL. After an unspectacular start as an infielder over the final weeks of his maiden season, Doby began making his case in 1948 by moving to the outfield and batting .301 to help the Indians to a world championship. Over the next eight seasons the lefty slugger never hit fewer than 20 home runs, twice paced the AL in the long ball category, and led in RBIs once as well. Unlike Jackie Robinson, who had broken the color barrier in the National League on Opening Day in 1947, Doby made no pledge about turning the other cheek, so that opposing teams got the message early on that he would retaliate promptly against brushback pitches and deliberate spikings. He ended his 13-year career, with the White Sox and Tigers as well as the Indians, with a .283 average and 253 homers.

It was also Veeck who, as owner of the White Sox in 1978, named Doby as the AL's second black manager after Frank Robinson. He lasted little more than a half-season after replacing Bob Lemon.

BOBBY DOERR (Hall of Fame, 1986)

Except for his first two seasons, in 1937 and 1938, Doerr played his entire 14-year career with the Red Sox in the shadow of Ted Williams. Williams himself, however, always pointed to the second baseman as the indispensable Boston player of

the 1940s. The righthanded hitter's most conspicuous offensive numbers were his six seasons of more than 100 runs batted in and his 13 straight years of between 21 and 37 doubles. Because of back problems, Doerr was one of few major league stars to play through most of World War II. He was also the only second baseman with as long a major league tenure never to have played even a single game at another position.

MIKE DONLIN

Whatever was right and wrong with the extravagant characters who played under John McGraw was right and wrong with Donlin. In a 12-year (between 1899 and 1914) career interrupted more than once by forays into jail and show business, the left-hand-hitting outfielder vacillated between suggesting a Hall of Fame ability on the diamond and undermining the suggestion with off-field drunkenness and violence.

Donlin came into the majors originally with the Cardinals, for whom he hit .323 in half a season and where he met McGraw. In 1901 he jumped after his mentor to the American League's new franchise in Baltimore, where he hit .340. On the eve of the 1902 season, however, he was smitten with actress Mamie Fields and followed her and her boy friend down a Baltimore street. When the boy friend suggested he get lost, Donlin smacked him, then also clouted the actress for trying to intervene. Two days later he was arrested in Washington, thrown out of the AL, and sentenced to several months in prison for assault. He was released in time to play a handful of games that year for the Reds, who had been persuaded by McGraw that he was worth the risk. He was, too, going on to lead the club in 1903 with a .351 average.

Over the first half of the 1904 season Donlin was even better, keeping neck-and-neck with Honus Wagner for the batting race by averaging .356. By then, however, he had so alienated Reds owner Garry Herrmann with his nightly escapades that he was put on waivers as a prelude to an arranged deal with the Browns. Instead, McGraw claimed him for the Giants. In 1905 Donlin batted another lusty .356, collected 216 hits, and led the National League with 124 runs scored. The only thing that remained the same over ensuing years was the .300 average.

In 1906 Donlin was arrested again, this time for brandishing a gun at a train porter while drunk. Although he spent only a night in jail, McGraw suspended him for the incident and his general alcoholic behavior for the beginning of the season. When he did get back in the lineup, the outfielder was moving along at a .314 clip when a broken leg put an end to his year. He spent his recuperation time falling in love with both vaudeville star Mabel Hite and show business. When McGraw wouldn't give in to his deliberately outrageous contract demands, Donlin took the 1907 season off to tour the vaudeville circuit with his new wife Hite. He came back to the Giants in 1908 (to hit another .334) but then once again staged a holdout lasting the next two seasons; as a consolation, he and Hite became more popular than ever on the stage.

In 1911 Donlin tried again with baseball, and though he started off at .333 over the first couple of weeks of the season, McGraw got tired of him and peddled him to Boston. With the Braves he hit .315; the following year it was .316, this time with the Pirates. Pittsburgh owner Barney Dreyfuss was just about to follow the lead of Donlin's previous employers by unloading him when Hite died of cancer, sending the outfielder into disabling depression and alcoholism. He was fished back by McGraw for a final shot in 1914 as a pinch-hitter, but his skills were gone.

Donlin still had his show business career, however, and he ended up appearing in or producing a score of Hollywood silents over the next two decades; among those appearing in them was McGraw. The outfielder was known as Turkey Mike for his habitual strut; or, in the words of his favorite manager; "He was born on Memorial Day and he hasn't stopped parading since."

RED DOOIN

After the Black Sox scandal became public in 1920, Dooin revealed that he and several Phillies teammates had been offered bribes to throw late-season games to the Giants in 1908. The catcher embellished his role in the episode with a lurid tale of having been kidnapped by gamblers and escaping to rejoin the team in time to beat New York in the second-last game of the season, creating a tie with the Cubs and forcing a replay of the Merkle Boner game. Dooin also stands out for his initial reluctance to claim credit for his major innovation, papier-mâché shin guards, which he wore under his uniform for two years for

fear they would provoke cracks about his manhood; he owned up to them only after Roger Bresnahan had begun wearing sturdier models openly. Also a pioneer in the effort to ban the spitball, Dooin blamed its unsanitary nature for Philadelphia pitcher Ad Brennan's tuberculosis in 1912. To emphasize his vigilance in defense of the public health, he once doused a game ball with disinfectant.

TAD DORGAN

Cartoonist Dorgan commemorated Harry M. Stevens's introduction of frankfurters at the Polo Grounds in 1901 with a sketch that included the first known use of the term "hot dog."

HERM DOSCHER

After an uneventful three-year career as a third baseman that ended with the Cleveland Forest Citys in 1882, Doscher agreed to do some scouting for the team during the off-season; at about the same time he signed to manage Detroit for 1883. When, on Cleveland's time, he began conscripting for the Wolverines not only the players he had been sent out to scout but also some former teammates, his Forest Citys employers had him blacklisted for double-dealing. The banishment lasted three years, until Doscher pulled some strings to have himself reinstated as an umpire.

Doscher was also the older generation in the first father-son combination to play in the major leagues; his son Jack pitched for three National League teams from 1903 to 1908, compiling a record of 2–11.

ABNER DOUBLEDAY

Born in Ballston Spa, 65 miles northeast of Cooperstown, and reared in Auburn, 85 miles northwest of there, Doubleday could not have been in the village with which his name has been linked in baseball lore when he was supposed to have devised the rules of the game because he was then a first-year student at West Point and ineligible for leave. Nor did the eventual Gettysburg hero make even passing mention of the sport in his extensive memoirs. His relationship to baseball has always rested solely on the recollections of octogenarian Abner Graves, collected by a 1907 commission established by sporting goods manufacturer Al Spalding for the purpose of proving that the game was a pure American invention. Asked once about Doubleday's place in baseball history, Branch Rickey noted that the future major-general gave the command to fire the first shot by the Union at Fort Sumter in 1861, adding: "The only thing Doubleday started was the Civil War."

LARRY DOUGHTY

Doughty was that rare baseball executive who was fired for publicly admitted incompetence. After serving as Pittsburgh general manager between 1989 and 1991, he was bounced by president Mark Sauer for what were referred to as "too many mistakes." Among Doughty's gaffes were neglecting the draft status of top organization prospect Wes Chamberlain, forcing his trade to the Phillies for bench-warmer Carmelo Martinez; prematurely identifying another prospect, outfielder Moises Alou, as a "player to be named later," necessitating his early departure for Montreal; spending more money than he had been budgeted for journeyman righthander Bob Walk while allowing first baseman Sid Bream, one of manager Jim Leyland's favorite players, to walk off as a free agent; and alienating Bobby Bonilla with several cracks before the slugger declared for free agency.

PHIL DOUGLAS

Douglas took one too many tongue lashings from Giants manager John McGraw in 1922, so got even by getting himself banned from the major leagues. Smarting over one of the pilot's regular tirades near the end of August, the righthander fortified himself with alcohol, then wrote a letter to St. Louis outfielder Les Mann suggesting that he was ready "to go fishing" for the rest of the season if the Cardinals came up with enough money to make it worth it. At the time New York and St. Louis were running neck-and-neck in the race for the National League pennant. By the time Douglas sobered up, Mann had passed the letter along to Cardinals manager Branch Rickey, who in turn sent it to Commissioner Kenesaw Landis. As soon as he conceded his authorship, Douglas was outlawed from the game. The ban came less than a year after he had led the Giants to a world championship over the Yankees with two World Series victories.

GEORGE DOVEY

Dovey and his brother John took over Boston's National League franchise in 1907; during their tenure, the club was known as the Doves. George died of a lung collapse in 1909, and a year later John sold the club to William Russell. The 1909 team was the worst in the 76-year-history of the Braves franchise in Boston, compiling 108 losses.

BRIAN DOYLE

Doyle lasted only four seasons (1978–81) in the major leagues and batted only .161, but in the 1978 World Series he might as well have been Willie Keeler. Replacing the injured Willie Randolph, the second baseman had the ultimate moment in the sun, hitting .438, scoring four runs, and driving in two more as the Yankees defeated the Dodgers in six games.

JOE DOYLE

Despite being the first American Leaguer (and the first 20th-century pitcher in either league) to notch shutouts in his first two appearances (on August 25 and 30, 1906), Doyle was fated never to live up to that beginning. The righthander finished his rookie season with a 2–1 record; never won more than 11 games in any of his five years with the Yankees and (briefly) the Reds; and, even though seven of his career 22 victories were shutouts, retired with a won-lost percentage of .512. His nickname of Slow Joe referred to the pace of his deliberations on the mound.

LARRY DOYLE

Doyle's 1911 exclamation of "Goddamn! It's great to be young and a New York Giant!" served as an emblem of the arrogance and enthusiasm of John McGraw's early-century clubs. In that year's World Series the second baseman tallied the winning run of the fifth game when he tagged up from third on a fly ball in the home half of the 10th inning; his slide, however, carried him around not only Athletics catcher Jack Lapp but home plate as well. Umpire Bill Klem kept his own counsel until all the Philadelphia players had left the field before calling a Giants victory; Philadelphia closed out the Series the next day, anyway. The lefthanded batter closed his career in 1920 after spending all but one-and-a-half seasons with New York. He won a batting crown in 1915 and finished with a lifetime average of .290.

MOE DRABOWSKY

Although he also had his moments on the mound in a 17-year career from 1956 to 1972, Drabowsky earned greater fame as a pioneering bullpen prankster. His specialty was the use of the bullpen phone to order food from establishments or to call long distance to find out the weather in Tokyo or Paris. His visits to Fenway Park allowed him to tinker with the hand-operated scoreboard so that unwitting broadcasters were prone to telling their listeners long before interleague play had begun how the Mets were doing against the Tigers or the Astros against the Indians. The righthander's greatest moment of pitching glory came as an Oriole in the 1966 World Series, when he entered the first game in the third inning and fanned 11 Dodgers the rest of the way, including six in a row at one point.

Born in Poland, Drabowsky returned home in 1987 to assist in the creation of the first Polish Olympic baseball team.

DAVE DRAVECKY

Dravecky put in eight seasons with the Padres and Giants in the 1980s, only to have his career end in a horrifying moment. Operated on for a cancerous growth on his pitching arm in 1988, the southpaw made a dramatic comeback the following season with a one-hit, seven-inning stint against the Reds on August 10. But in his next start, against the Expos five days later, he was working on a three-hitter in the sixth inning when he delivered a pitch that fractured his humerus with a crack that resounded throughout Olympic Stadium. Following the discovery of another tumor in November, Dravecky retired with a 64–57 record. The arm was later amputated.

CHARLIE DRESSEN

After a modest eight-year career as a third baseman for the Reds and Giants, Dressen hit his stride as one of the most knowledgeable managers and coaches in the game, with a special talent for stealing signs. He also initiated long yo-yo relationships with his frequent employer Larry MacPhail and his on-and-off crony Leo Durocher.

As manager of MacPhail's Reds in the mid-1930s, Dressen was particularly adept at instigating on-the-field brawls to cover the mediocrity of his players. When MacPhail was fired, he was out the door soon afterward for mouthing off to a host of Cincinnati sportswriters that his boss had gotten a raw deal. In the early 1940s, as a coach for the Dodgers under MacPhail, he abetted manager Durocher in the all-night drinking bouts and poker games that the team president and pilot considered essential to Brooklyn's success. On numerous occasions it was also Dressen's task to talk MacPhail out of his drunken firings of Durocher and to persuade Durocher to go back. But when Branch Rickey replaced MacPhail, Jolly Cholly (as sportswriters took to calling him) became the fall guy for Durocher, first being told that he was being fired for being a bad influence on the players, then being offered a new contract at a considerably lower wage.

Dressen swallowed his pride and stayed with Rickey's Dodgers until MacPhail purchased the Yankees after World War II, then once again got caught between his perennial boss and the stormy manager. What ended up as an investigation into the gambling associates of both men was actually sparked by MacPhail's poaching of Dressen for a coaching job in the Bronx. After a tortuous investigation, Commissioner Happy Chandler found Dressen guilty of violating a contract with Rickey that stipulated that he could leave the Dodgers only for a managing post; he was suspended for 30 days before being allowed to take the coaching job with the Yankees. Appropriately enough, MacPhail sold out his interests in the Yankees not long afterward.

The next phase of Dressen's career began in 1951, when Walter O'Malley appointed him manager of The Boys of Summer Dodgers, at least in part because the new Brooklyn owner knew that the choice would irritate his predecessor Rickey. Jackie Robinson and Pee Wee Reese, among others, called him the best manager they ever played for, and Dressen agreed. Known as a man incapable of forming a sentence without the word "I" in it, he added to baseball's compendium of famous quotations one day when, with Brooklyn on the short end of a 9–0 score early in a game, he told his charges, "Just hold them there, and I'll think of something." What he couldn't think of, however, was a way to stop the unprecedented Giants drive against Brooklyn in 1951 that was climaxed by Bobby Thomson's ninth-inning home run in the final game of the playoffs. If other Dodgers were stunned by the defeat, Dressen was apoplectic before the fact that he had lost to a club managed by Durocher. After Dressen had led the team to a pennant the following year, he tried to use his success as leverage for obtaining more than a one-year contract. When his wife also wrote to O'Malley singing her husband's praises and demanding a longer pact, Jolly Cholly was replaced by Walter Alston.

Dressen went on to manage the Senators, Braves, and Tigers, and even rejoined the Dodgers in Los Angeles briefly as a coach under Alston.

CUTTER DREUERY

Although several pitchers had previously thrown a knuckleball using the upper joints of three fingers, career minor leaguer Dreuery was the first known practitioner of the fingertip pitch of more recent vintage. Already retired and working as a plumber, he taught the technique to Ed Rommel in 1920. Rommel, who had been sent to the minors for lacking an out pitch other than the recently banned spitball, went on to a 13-year career as a mainstay of the Philadelphia pitching staff.

BARNEY DREYFUSS

Starting off as a bookkeeper for a distillery, Dreyfuss worked himself up to the longest-running executive act in the National League, maintaining personal control of the Pirates for more than three decades. He believed so ardently in his image as a benevolent, decorous man that he left himself open for an embarrassing confrontation with John McGraw that haunted him to his grave and was so dedicated to his abstemious principles that he turned away future Hall of Famers because they indulged in the wrong habits. Given his longevity in NL ruling circles, the surprising thing about Dreyfuss was not that he used his standing to fill key league and team positions but that he didn't do it more often. He was a Walter O'Malley without the cigars.

Dreyfuss bought his way into Pittsburgh from his position as owner of the NL Louisville Colonels, a franchise eliminated in the league's cutback from 12 to eight clubs after the 1899 season. As part of the deal with incumbent Pittsburgh owner William Kerr, he took over 50 percent of the team after engineering a mass movement of Louisville players to the Steel City. Because the Kentucky franchise was still formally in existence at the time of the transaction, the move of such future Hall of Famers as Honus Wagner, Fred Clarke, and Rube Waddell amounted to the most one-sided trade in baseball history; it became even more so a couple of weeks later when another Cooperstown resident, pitcher Jack Chesbro, who had been sent to the Colonels to put a semblance of reason on the exchange, returned to the Pirates with the dissolution of Louisville. Mainly thanks to the players acquired in the dubious deal, Pittsburgh won pennants four times and finished second another four times in the first decade of the 20th century. But because Kerr could not tolerate the idea that it was Dreyfuss who had brought success to the organization, he went through a series of boardroom and courtroom maneuvers aimed at getting rid of his new partner. This resulted in nothing more than an even more untenable position, from which Kerr was forced to sell his half of the club to Dreyfuss.

Like other NL owners, Dreyfuss had some bad moments when Ban Johnson began recruiting for the new American League in 1901. Although he didn't lose as many players (Chesbro was the key casualty) as other NL teams, he had to deal with the far more threatening possibility that Johnson would move his Detroit franchise to Pittsburgh to challenge the Pirates for fans. To head off that development, he pressed successfully during the 1903 peace negotiations between the leagues for a commitment by Johnson to stay out of Pittsburgh. A few months later, however, the same Dreyfuss went farther than any other NL owner in legitimizing the new circuit when he endorsed public calls for his pennant-winning club to meet AL champion Boston in what was the first World Series. Although Pittsburgh lost the best-of-nine meetings, the owner professed himself so proud of the players that he added his personal profits to their pool so that they ended up with more money than the winning Red Sox. He was so committed to the World Series idea that the following year, when New York owner John T. Brush and manager McGraw refused to dignify the existence of the AL with another World Series against Boston, he set up an interleague series between the Pirates and their corresponding fourth-place finisher in the AL, the Indians.

The World Series wasn't the only issue that divided Dreyfuss and McGraw. In a 1905 incident that climaxed years of sniping by the New York manager, McGraw spotted the executive sitting behind the Pittsburgh dugout before a game against the Giants and challenged him to bet $10,000 on the outcome. When Dreyfuss ignored the taunt, he withdrew the challenge with some equally sarcastic crack about how the owner always welshed on his bets. Dreyfuss was so outraged by the attack on his character that he insisted that NL president Harry Pulliam suspend McGraw. Instead of letting the matter slide, Pulliam, a former Pittsburgh employee, did indeed announce a 15-day suspension and a fine of $150. In his turn at rage, McGraw accused Pulliam of being a toady for Dreyfuss and refused to go along with either the suspension or the fine. With the league's honor called into question, NL owners met, issuing a plague-on-all-your-houses verdict that included rapping Dreyfuss for misbehavior. The owner acknowledged years later that he would never get over the insinuation that he had indeed trafficked in some way with gamblers. In an even more righteous vein, he insisted he never regretted failing to sign Tris Speaker and Walter Johnson when he had a chance; Speaker's handicap was that he was a smoker, Johnson's that he had been brought to Dreyfuss's attention by a cigar salesman.

Managers came and went under Dreyfuss's ownership, but almost every one of them was portrayed as "resigning" rather than getting the ax, in line with the owner's proto-Dodgers philosophy that all his employees constituted a "family"; by the same token, many of them were fished back a couple of years later as coaches or scouts. Through the teens and the 20s, Dreyfuss presided over several club uprisings against pilots, inevitably coming down on the side of the managers until he could dispense with them as easily as he had gotten rid of offending players; the most serious of the brouhahas involved outfielder Max Carey and coach Fred Clarke in the mid-1920s. The one crisis he could not weather, on the other hand, was the death of his son Samuel at age 36 in 1931. For months afterward Dreyfuss went around in a daze, to the point that NL president John Heydler urged him to appoint somebody to take over the franchise on a daily basis. Leery of outsiders, he chose his son-in-law Bill Benswanger, an insurance company executive. Although Benswanger agreed to step in only temporarily, he found himself with a new profession when Dreyfuss contracted pneumonia after a glandular operation in January 1932 and, after a one-month battle, died. Benswanger ran the team until 1946, when he sold it to a consortium headed by banker Frank McKinney, realtor John Galbreath, and entertainer Bing Crosby.

DAN DRIESSEN

In the 1976 World Series against the Yankees, Driessen, a first baseman-third baseman for the Reds, became the first designated hitter for a National League team.

WALT DROPO

Dropo's 12 consecutive hits for the Tigers in 1952 both tied and bettered the major league mark set by Pinky Higgins with the 1938 Red Sox: Although both players officially went 12-for-12 in their streaks, Higgins also had two walks in the middle of this skein. Dropo, a righthand-hitting first baseman, also stands as a model victim of the sophomore jinx. With the Red Sox in 1950, he was named American League Rookie of the Year for a .322 average, 34 home runs, 101 runs scored, and a league-leading 144 runs batted in. A year later he was down to .239 with merely 11 home runs, 37 runs scored, and 57 RBIs. In a 13-year career spent wandering through several teams, Dropo reached the 20-mark in home runs in only one other season.

DON DRYSDALE (Hall of Fame, 1984)

The righthanded half, along with southpaw Sandy Koufax, of one of the most daunting pitching tandems of all time, Drysdale was a fixture in the Dodgers rotation for most of his 14-year (1956–69) career. The six-foot, five-inch righthander was something of a Ewell Blackwell raised another notch—a whipping-motion intimidator who relished his modern National League record of 154 hit batsmen and who kept hitters tentative enough to lead the NL in strikeouts three times and top the 200-level six times His best year was 1962, when he paced the NL with 25 wins and 232 strikeouts—good enough for a Cy Young Award. Six years later he hurled 58 $^2/_3$ consecutive scoreless innings—a record later eclipsed by another Dodgers righthander, Orel Hershiser.

Prior to the 1966 season Drysdale and Koufax directed their joint act against the Los Angeles front office after they suspected that general manager Buzzie Bavasi was playing them off against one another during contract negotiations. As soon as they made clear their intention of keeping one another fully informed of offers, the pitchers were called in for settlements. It turned out to be something of a bittersweet victory: Koufax had only one more season left in his arthritic left arm, while Drysdale's record after the negotiations was 45–48. When he retired after the 1969 season with a lifetime mark of 209–166 (and a 2.95 ERA), Drysdale broke the last link of Dodgers players who had started out in Ebbets Field. Playing his entire career for Walter Alston, he also holds the record for the longest tenure under one manager.

Drysdale was one of the best-hitting pitchers in baseball. In two different years he tied Don Newcombe's NL record of seven home runs, ending with 29 altogether. His post-playing days saw him announcing for several clubs, including the Angels, White Sox, and Dodgers. While broadcasting for California in 1976, he teamed up with manager Dick Williams in an ill-advised attempt to get owner Gene Autry to fire general manager Harry Dalton and give the job to him; the foray mainly led to Williams's ouster as pilot.

CLISE DUDLEY

As a righthanded pitcher, Dudley compiled an unimpressive 17–33 record in his five-year (1929–33) career with three National League teams; as a hitter he was just as bad, batting .185. But in his April 27, 1929 debut with the Dodgers, he became the first player to knock the first major league pitch thrown to him for a home run.

HUGH DUFFY (Hall of Fame, 1945)

One of Boston's Heavenly Twins with fellow outfielder Tommy McCarthy in the 1890s, Duffy's hitting reached the ethereal in 1894, when he followed up a league-leading .363 average in 1893 with an all-time-best .440 and led the National League in home runs, hits, and doubles. (While no asterisk mars his Cooperstown plaque, Duffy's average came in a year when National League batsmen took full advantage of the new pitching distance of 60 feet, six inches, and collectively established another still unbroken record by hitting .310.) After another spectacular .353 in 1895, pitchers began to readjust, and Duffy's (and the rest of the NL's) hitting dropped back closer to earth for the remainder of his 17-year career.

On August 7, 1901, while manager of the Brewers, Duffy punched out umpire Al Mannassau over a ninth-inning call that cost Milwaukee a loss. He escaped the lifetime banishment handed out by American League president Ban Johnson for similar offenses mainly because the entire franchise was playing out the string before being transferred to St. Louis. Duffy went on to a long career as a hitting instructor for the Red Sox; his most famous pupil was Ted Williams.

JOE DUGAN

When the Red Sox sold Dugan to the Yankees for $40,000 on July 23, 1922, New York filled its hole at third base with a .287 hitter and went on to win the pennant by a game over the Browns. The protests from St. Louis, whose National League fans had also been victimized by the Boston Braves July trade of pitcher Hugh McQuillan to the Giants, compelled Commissioner Kenesaw Landis to prohibit interleague transactions after June 15 unless every other team in the league declined the players involved. This waiver rule remained in force for some 60 years.

BILL DUGGLEBY

A lifetime 93–104 pitcher at the turn of the century, Duggleby entered the record books when he became the first player to hit a grand slam home run in his first major league at bat, for the Phillies on April 21, 1898.

FRED DUNLAP

The premier player of the Union Association in 1884, Dunlap ignored the reserve clause in his contract with the National League Cleveland Blues and signed for a then-record $3,400 with the new league's St. Louis club. The second baseman led the UA in practically everything—batting (.412), hits, home runs, slugging, and on-base average. After the collapse of the one-year UA, Dunlap was readmitted to the NL's St. Louis franchise only after paying a $500 fine.

JACK DUNN

A pitcher good enough to win 23 games for the Dodgers in 1899 before switching to the infield for the Phillies, Orioles, and Giants after the turn of the century, Dunn went on to become a grandly successful minor league club operator. After managing Baltimore in the International League for three seasons, he bought the Orioles franchise from Ned Hanlon in 1910 and began developing and selling players to the major leagues.

The 1914–15 Federal League war gave Dunn a role in two of the most significant events in baseball history: the start of Babe Ruth's major league career and the sport's exemption from antitrust legislation. Although the Orioles president had struck a deal with the FL's Baltimore Terrapins that left his roster intact, a local appetite for the Fed team forced Dunn into temporary exile in Richmond, Virginia. Strapped for funds, he held a fire sale of his best players, including pitcher Ruth (who went to the Red Sox for a mere $2,500 after Connie Mack has passed on him for lack of money). After the Feds faltered, Terrapins president Carroll W. Rasin sought to work out a deal with Dunn, by either selling him the FL franchise or buying the IL franchise and hiring him as manager. Dunn settled for buying Rasin's ballpark and sat on the sidelines while the Terrapins engaged major league baseball in a court battle that did not end until 1922, when the U.S. Supreme Court declared baseball to be outside the reach of antitrust laws.

Dunn rebuilt the Orioles to win seven consecutive IL pennants between 1919 and 1925, and resumed an earlier lucrative relationship with Mack, shipping him such major figures on Philadelphia's 1929–31 pennant winners as pitchers Lefty Grove, George Earnshaw, and Rube Walberg, and infielders Joe Boley and Max Bishop. The sale of Grove alone brought more than $100,000, and endless complaints from the southpaw that he had to take a cut in pay to get to the majors. Dunn lost his enthusiasm for the game when his son died in 1921, however, and never again set foot in the team's clubhouse.

DAN DUQUETTE

Duquette's run as Boston general manager had become so poisonous by the end of the 2001 season that few remembered the sleight of hand he pulled after taking on the job in 1995 to propel the Red Sox into the playoffs. In his first season he made so many deals to cover up gaping offensive and pitching holes that 50 players came and went at Fenway Park. He was only slightly less frenetic in patching together the teams that made it to the postseason in 1998 and 1999. Beyond that, though, and despite a franchise tradition of one executive clown after another, Duquette merited disastrous comparison to Dick Walsh of the Angels as the single most unpopular general manager in recent American League history. His first misstep was in allowing Roger Clemens to walk away as a free agent in 1996 on the argument that the future Hall of Famer was washed up; since then, Clemens has won three Cy Young awards. Although he later (in 1998) filled the pitching ace role with a free agent signing of his own in Pedro Martinez, he found no replacement for first baseman Mo Vaughn, Fenway's most popular player since Carl Yastrzemski who was told to take a walk after the 1998 campaign.

While Clemens and Vaughn took every opportunity to say something about his (lack of) baseball acumen, Duquette dedicated himself to a roster of Martinez, shortstop Nomar Garciaparra, several left-hand-swinging designated hitters, and pitchers either coming off arm operations or off scales they had just broken with their heft. The final ingredients were added in 2000 when noncommunicative manager Jimy Williams, pitching guru and backroom politician Joe Kerrigan, and periodically raving center fielder Carl Everett indulged their specialties while Duquette went around saying everything was fine. Against all expectations, the three of them were still on the scene in 2001—at least until September, when Duquette fired Williams, said Kerrigan was too inexperienced for the job, got turned down by Felipe Alou, then declared that Kerrigan had suddenly acquired the experience.

RYNE DUREN

Yankees manager Casey Stengel said of Duren, "He takes a drink or 10, comes in with them Coke bottles, throws one on the screen, and scares the shit out of 'em." Whether it was the drinks, the poor eyesight, natural wildness, or cunning design, the hard-throwing righthander's trademark warm-up toss on the screen behind home plate certainly kept American League batters edgy.

Coming out of the bullpen for New York, Duren saved a league-leading 20 games in 1958 and followed up with 14 more in 1959, striking out a combined 183 batters and yielding only 89 hits in $152^{1}/_{3}$ innings. The rest of his 10-year career, with six teams in addition to the Yankees, was marked by plenty of strikeouts, even more drinks, and not much else. In retirement Duren battled through his alcoholism to head up treatment programs in his native Wisconsin.

LEO DUROCHER (Hall of Fame, 1994)

For more than four decades as a player, manager, and coach, Durocher was a boiling advertisement for the sly, the crass, the pugnacious, and the hypocritical. From Babe Ruth to Judge Roy Hofheinz, he played everything from the stooge to the standup guy to the sneerer, earning a footnote to every major development in the sport along the way and usually more than that. He won big and lost big, but most of all he won and lost loudly. Even his sobriquets were numerous—tabbed the All-American Out for his weak offensive play, C-note for an incessant need of cash to subsidize a high-stepping private life, and The Lip for his relentless hectoring of umpires and opposition players.

Durocher first came to the big leagues with the Yankees in 1925 for a single at bat, not returning for good until three years later. A righthand-hitting shortstop (he experimented briefly with switch-hitting), he won the open admiration of manager Miller Huggins for his defensive play and, even more, for a brashness that sometimes led him to call time in a crucial situation just so he could walk toward the batter's box to yell an insult at an opposing hitter that was guaranteed to upset him. Although he came to rely on Babe Ruth for protecting him during melees sparked by some of his insolent gestures, he had an uneasy relationship with the slugger—epitomized by Ruth's insistence on calling him the All-American Out. His relationship with club president Ed Barrow was even worse, and when he rejected a take-it-or-leave-it contract proposal after the 1929 season, he was summarily sent off to Cincinnati. It was while with the Reds between 1930 and the middle of the 1933 season that Durocher's regular visits to team owner Sidney Weil for $100 loans or advances on his salary gained him the nickname of C-note. It was also during this period that his habitually unpaid bills with restaurants and haberdashers started him on career-long visits to the commissioner's office, with Kenesaw Landis on at least one occasion offering to help him pay off a debt.

In the middle of the 1933 season Durocher was traded to the Cardinals for pitcher Paul Derringer—a deal that put him together with Branch Rickey for the first time. For the next four-plus seasons he was the regular shortstop for the snarling and flamboyant Gas House Gang, even enjoying some unanticipated hitting success by driving in 70 runs two years in a row. Durocher attributed at least part of his improved play to the austerity budget that he was put on by Rickey: For his first couple of years in a Cardinals uniform he received no more than $50 a week, with the rest of his salary being paid directly by the club officials to creditors. His relations with manager Frankie Frisch, on the other hand, had little of the filial about them, and by the end of the 1937 season Frisch was issuing me-or-him ultimatums to

Rickey. Durocher was packed off to the Dodgers amid reports that he was only the vanguard for Rickey himself moving to Brooklyn. Instead, the St. Louis executive stayed where he was, recommending instead that the top baseball job at Ebbets Field be given to Larry MacPhail.

If some Durocher baseball relationships were stormy, the one with MacPhail was a hurricane. Trouble arose almost immediately in 1938 after MacPhail signed Ruth as a coach and batting practice attraction, and the retired slugger got it into his head that he was being groomed as Burleigh Grimes's successor as Brooklyn manager. Throughout the season the equally ambitious Durocher taunted both Grimes and Ruth about their baseball smarts, while MacPhail waited until he had his usual drinks in him before ranting that he would never turn the club over to an umpire-baiter such as his loud-mouthed shortstop. But it was indeed Durocher who was named to the helm for 1939, with Grimes being paid off, Ruth quitting in disgust, and MacPhail not remembering his previous declarations. As playing manager, Durocher brought enough electricity to the team to restore Ebbets Field fans as a 26th player. In one typical instance of the new enthusiasm, fans took up a collection to pay a $25 fine that he had incurred for slugging Giants first baseman Zeke Bonura. The intention (called off only with the 11th-hour intervention of National League President Ford Frick) was to change the money into pennies, then throw the coins onto the field and have league officials crawl around to retrieve them.

By Durocher's estimate he was fired by MacPhail dozens of times during their five-year stay together in Brooklyn—usually after the executive had uncorked a bottle. In the event, however, it was MacPhail who quit the Dodgers first, resigning after the 1942 season (before he was pushed) to join the military. In his place came Rickey, who kept Durocher on the job despite some severe strains. In 1943, for instance, the pilot provoked a team revolt over an unwarranted suspension of pitcher Bobo Newsom and subsequent lies to the press about the incident. In 1945 he maintained Rickey's support despite criminal charges of having teamed up with an Ebbets Field guard for beating up a heckling fan under the stands. More generally, there was the puritanical owner's distaste for Durocher's card playing, pool shooting, and womanizing. When the manager wasn't taking road trips with a Copacabana nightclub dancer, there were actress Nanette Fabray, Kay William (the future Mrs. Clark Gable), or other women from New York's nightlife. What emerged clearly only in 1947 was that Rickey had turned a blind eye to his pilot's doings because of an overriding belief that he was the dugout boss best equipped for carrying out his plan for integrating baseball—a confidence more than borne out during spring training that year when Durocher stopped cold a protest by Dodgers players against playing with Jackie Robinson. (In fact, he had even urged Rickey to promote Robinson from Montreal in 1946 when the team had been head-to-head with the Cardinals in the pennant race.)

But not even the frictions caused by racial integration were Durocher's biggest problem in 1947. Less than a week before the opening of the season, he was suspended for a year by Commissioner Happy Chandler for what was termed an "accumulation of unpleasant incidents . . . detrimental to baseball." The problems stemmed from three areas. The first was a series of charges and countercharges involving alleged offers from MacPhail (resurfaced as owner of the Yankees) for Durocher to leave the Dodgers to manage in the Bronx and the poaching of Brooklyn coaches by the former Ebbets Field executive. The second centered around Durocher's association with George Raft and professional gamblers close to the actor. The third involved Durocher's romance with actress Laraine Day, who was still legally married to someone else. The Raft and Day controversies became daily fodder for newspaper columnists, especially the priggish Westbrook Pegler. When Day and Durocher sought to end all the gossip about the adultery by flying off to Mexico to get her a quickie divorce and then returning to Texas to get married, Pegler did his part in whipping up Catholic organizations to withdraw from official promotions connected with the Dodgers. (The Catholic crusade, led by a couple of priests named Vincent Powell and Edward Lodge Curran, appeared to have as much to do with Rickey as with Durocher. For some time part-owner Walter O'Malley, who had more Brooklyn Catholic connections than the bishop, had been giving Rickey the rope named Durocher so he could hang himself and be forced to sell out his Dodgers interests.) Although Chandler never publicly linked the romance with Day to the MacPhail and Raft stories, he made it clear that his suspension decision was based on elusive moral considerations more than on any solid evidence of specific wrong-doing.

Durocher did not react to the suspension well, especially after his one-year replacement Burt Shotton steered the Robinson Dodgers to a pennant; returning in 1948, he took every opportunity to note that the flag winners had been "his" players. With the Robinson experiment successfully launched, Rickey began nudging him out the door in June. The pilot refused to take the hint, however, until he managed the NL All-Star team—a right given to him by Shotton's pennant win the previous year. When Rickey told him Horace Stoneham was looking for a manager, Durocher made the most controversial leap between the Dodgers and Giants since Wilbert Robinson had gone in the opposite direction 30 years before. The pilot he was replacing in the Polo Grounds—Mel Ott—had been the target of the most famous of Durocherisms in 1946. As recorded by sportswriter Frank Graham, the exact quote was: "Do you know a nicer guy than Mel Ott? Or any of the Giants? Why they're the nicest guys in the world. And where are they? In last place!" The observation was subsequently telescoped into the maxim that "nice guys finish last."

As with the Dodgers, with whom he won a pennant in 1941, Durocher needed three years with the Giants to field what he boasted of as "his kind" of team. The last important piece of his 1951 winners was Willie Mays, whose initial failures at the plate elicited Durocher's most conspicuous success as a psychologist, when he reassured the outfielder that they would stay in the lineup "even if you go 0-for-the-rest-the-season." The relationship with Mays was also notable for representing one of the few instances in which Durocher showed a talent for piloting younger players. The 1951 campaign ended with Bobby Thomson's playoff home run against the Dodgers, climaxing the most dramatic comeback to a pennant in baseball history.

Durocher had more success with the Giants—in 1954, when he captured his only World Series as a manager in a four-game sweep of the favored Indians. Otherwise, his seven years at the Polo Grounds were characterized by the most acrimonious chapter in the Dodgers-Giants rivalry, with field fights regularly following Robinson's taunts of Durocher's sex life with the much younger Day or New York righthander Sal Maglie's shaving of Brooklyn chins. He resigned his post near the end of the 1955 season amid increasing conflicts with owner Stoneham.

Durocher went to work for NBC as a sportscaster for a few years but had several opportunities to return to the dugout. In the late 1950s negotiations over money stopped him from going to Cleveland. In 1960 he was called in by Stoneham to appraise the work of his successor Bill Rigney, with the understanding that his report on the club would merely be a prelude to returning to the helm; instead, after filing a tentative criticism of Rigney's relations with star Mays, he was left out in the cold in favor of Alvin Dark. Only a couple of months later he lost out to Rigney as the first pilot of the expansion Angels, largely because of his reputation for dealing most effectively with veteran teams. In 1964 he came the closest of all, when he reached a midseason agreement to take over the Cardinals, only to have incumbent manager Johnny Keane pull off a stunning pennant win. Instead, Durocher spent the first half of the 1960s as a Dodgers coach under Walter Alston. That stint ended when, after more than one scene with Alston on the bench during the 1964 season about game strategy, he boasted to several reporters that he would have prevented the club's flop into sixth place; at that point even owner O'Malley conceded that he had wrought too much of his so-called "creative tension" by flanking Alston with Durocher, firing the coach.

Durocher got his next managerial chance with the Cubs in 1966, ending owner Phil Wrigley's College of Coaches experiment. At the press conference announcing his assumption of the job, he contributed his second most famous Durocherism when he assured reporters that Chicago was "not an eighth-place team," as it had been in 1965; he was proved correct when the Cubs slipped to tenth in the first season under his command. But far more embarrassing for the man who had pulled off the Miracle at Coogan's Bluff in 1951 was the 1969 campaign, when the Cubs held first place for 155 days during the season but still ended up finishing eight games behind the Miracle Mets. Durocher came in for heavy criticism for the debacle—for getting rid of popular center fielder Adolfo Phillips without having an adequate backup; for playing his veterans into a bone-deep weariness; for keeping NL umpires in a state of agitation against the team through his incessant baiting; and even for leaving the team at two different junctures to attend to private business matters.

Worse followed. By 1971 Durocher had so alienated his players with personal attacks, dugout hectoring, and what many viewed as antiquated tactics ("stick it in his ear!" cries to his pitchers and other beanball provocations from the Ebbets Field-Polo Ground days) that relations between the sides were at best an armed truce. Whenever the Players Association sought to apprise the Cubs of the latest developments on the labor-management front, Durocher first sought to prevent the meetings, then did his best to undercut the credibility of the union and Marvin Miller. While all this was going on, a gaggle of Chicago Republicans, with the help of the daily *Tribune,* sought to get at a Democratic-appointed investigator-brother of Durocher's third wife by inventing links between him and a local mobster. This brought Commissioner Bowie Kuhn running—and then running away again when Mrs. Durocher made it clear that she would sue him if he played the *Tribune's* games by suspending her husband. But although also supported through his travails by Cubs owner Wrigley, Durocher finally stepped down in July 1972.

Durocher's last dugout stint was just as dreary. With merely a month to go in the 1972 schedule and the Astros having a genuine shot at the Western Division title, owner Roy Hofheinz fired Harry Walker for somebody he described as "able to whip the horses down the final stretch." Durocher did the whipping as expected, but Houston players, resentful of Walker's ouster, barely managed a .500 record and finished 10$\frac{1}{2}$ games behind the Reds. The following year player contempt for his methods was so obvious that, together with an intestinal ailment, it prompted him to resign before the season was over. As one of Durocher's last loyalists, Wrigley asked him back as pilot in 1975, but he held out for a general managership with Maury Wills coming along as the pilot and was turned down.

Durocher's overall record for 24 years of managing was 2008–1709 (.540), with three pennants and one world championship. If nice guys always finish last, he didn't always finish first, either.

JIMMY DYKES

Dykes established a mark for futility by managing for 21 years (between 1934 and 1961) without ever bringing a team home in first place; in stints with the White Sox, Athletics, Orioles, Reds, Tigers, and Indians, he never finished higher than third. For 22 years (1918–39) Dykes played all over the infield for the Athletics and White Sox, batting .280 overall with a personal best of .327 in 1929. His career both on the field and in the dugout was eclipsed, however, by an antic trade engineered by Frank Lane of the Indians and Bill DeWitt of the Tigers. The midseason deal sent Dykes from Detroit to Cleveland for Joe Gordon in baseball's only swap of non-playing managers.

LEN DYKSTRA

To the delight of New York fans in the 1980s and Philadelphia fans in the 1990s, Dykstra carried on the Pete Rose tradition of the leadoff man as somebody who abhorred a clean uniform. To the chagrin of the baseball establishment, he also built his reputation as one of the National League's most versatile offensive players while almost matching Rose for off-field controversies and surpassing everyone for on-field exhibitions of how to get rid of chewing tobacco.

The brash, lefthand-hitting outfielder came up to the NL with the Mets in 1985, and in the middle of his first game told the manager-first baseman Rose of the Reds that he intended to play for him someday. In 1986 Dykstra won over Shea Stadium for teaming with second-place hitter Wally Backman as ideal table-setters for the team that took few prisoners in its march to a world championship. He contributed conspicuously to the National League Championship Series win over Houston by clouting a game-winning homer in the ninth inning of the third game and sparking a comeback rally with a triple in the ninth inning of the sixth game; he belted two more home runs in the World Series against the Red Sox. But home runs also turned out to be a bone of contention between Dykstra and New York manager Davey Johnson, who pleaded futilely for two years with the outfielder to cut down on his swing and who then approved his trade to the Phillies in 1989.

Although the exchange of Dykstra and reliever Roger McDowell for infielder-outfielder Juan Samuel turned out to be one of the best trades in Philadelphia history, it was so only after the Phillies had tried unsuccessfully to deal him back to New York and after a rib accident had persuaded the speedster that he could be more effective swinging half as hard. The result in 1990 was a league-leading 192 hits and a .325 batting average. He was even more productive in 1993 when he batted .305, leading the NL in hits (194), walks (129), and runs scored (143), while setting an all-time major league mark for plate appearances (773). In that year's World Series against Toronto he belted four home runs and drove in eight runs.

Dykstra's impact on Philadelphia was also felt in 1991 and 1992, when his presence in the lineup produced twice as many team victories as was the case when he was sidelined. Unfortunately, he appeared in a mere 63 games in 1991 following an auto accident in which he and catcher Darren Daulton almost lost their lives while driving under the influence; in 1992 he broke his collarbone twice during the season on dives in the field, limiting him to 85 games. Aside from the drunken driving episode, Dykstra attracted league office attention for being involved in a high-stakes poker game and for allegedly abusing a U.S. Senator in a restaurant. What unnerved officials almost as much was his addiction to chewing tobacco and his casual (and casually televised) disposal of globs of plug on the diamond, on his shoes, or on his uniform shirt. Protests over his chewing helped hasten the ban on smoking and chewing tobacco imposed on minor league players in 1993.

A spine condition forced Dykstra to the sidelines in 1996, but though he never played another game, he refused to retire officially until two years later.

E

JOSEPH EASTMAN

Eastman was the head of the World War II Office of Defense Transportation who lent his name to baseball's Landis-Eastman Line. The line, accepted by Commissioner Kenesaw Landis, was drawn through the Ohio and Potomac rivers as the western and southernmost boundaries, respectively, for locating wartime spring training sites for every team except the Cardinals and Browns. The government order was aimed at saving fuel and decongesting railway lines. The biggest losers were the Dodgers, who had to shift their spring camp from Havana to frigid Bear Mountain in upstate New York, and the Cubs, who had to give up owner Phil Wrigley's private California island for freezing in French Lick, Indiana.

CHARLIE EBBETS

Ebbets was both a sower and reaper of Brooklyn baseball lore. An Horatio Alger who worked his way up from scorecard vendor to owner and president of the Dodgers, he also combined a miserliness and an extravagance that several times threatened to return him to his grandstand hawking. Not the least of his contradictory feats was having his death prove fatal to more people than to himself.

Taking over as president of the Brooklyn franchise following the death of Charles Byrne in 1898, Ebbets didn't need the national edginess caused by the Spanish-American War to deter fans from watching the team; the club's miserable play had accomplished that without having to remember the *Maine*. In the interests of both attracting more fans and shoring up his own shaky financial footing, he entered into an 1899 agreement with Baltimore's Har-

ry Von der Horst that would change the face of baseball for decades to come. In an era in which conflict of interest was a concept foreign to the sport, the pair devised an interdependent relationship between the clubs that brought to Brooklyn such star names as Ned Hanlon, Dan McGann, Hughie Jennings, Willie Keeler, and Joe Kelley. While retaining his title as president of the Orioles, Hanlon also became manager of Brooklyn and delivered in a big way in 1899 by riding his fellow-Baltimore transplants to a National League pennant. The victory came as a mixed blessing to Ebbets, who chafed under the idea that, as club president, he was making only a fraction of what Hanlon, his nominal underling, was taking in salary. The resentment festered until 1902, when, with the help of $30,000 from Brooklyn furniture dealer Henry Medicus, Ebbets was able to buy out Von der Horst and his other partners and take complete control. His first order of business was to call a board meeting at which he more than doubled his own salary as president and shaved Hanlon's to less than his own. Mainly because he didn't have other job offers, Hanlon rejected the unsubtle invitation to leave, remaining in Brooklyn for another three years of agitating the owner-president.

Between 1903 and 1914 Ebbets presided over the worst teams in franchise history, at least in the beginning of the period because of the defection of Keeler and other key players to the newly formed American League. Endangering the organization even more were the attempts by New York Giants owner Andrew Freedman to get Brooklyn out of the league so he could have the metropolitan market to himself; among other maneuvers, Freedman used his City Hall connections to make sure that Brooklyn's Washington Park wasn't a site for one of the scores of new subway stations being planned for the outer boroughs. Ebbets's main strategy for staying afloat was thinking up what he termed "free entertainments" that would skirt the league's ban on paid admissions to Sunday games. In April 1904, for example, he announced no charge for a contest between Brooklyn and Boston; the only requirement was that fans had to buy scorecards—which just happened to be color-coded according to prices that corresponded to those for the seating in boxes, grandstands, and bleachers the rest of the week. The income from such Sunday games more than made up for the sparse attendance on other days.

Ebbets's most lasting contribution to the franchise came in a January 1912 announcement that he had been secretly buying up land in a Prospect Park area known as Pigtown where he intended to build a new ballpark. By the time Ebbets Field opened on April 5, 1913, however, he had had to weather more money problems by selling half-interest in the franchise to contractors Edward and Stephen McKeever for finding the finances to complete the project. Even Opening Day was less than glorious when he belatedly realized that the stadium had only one rotunda entrance and was ripe for tragedy with 24,000 people jamming the area at the same time; he had to spend more money cutting additional accesses into the street walls.

Like other owners, Ebbets sought to stave off the threat posed by the Federal League in 1914 by offering his players multiyear contracts that would dissuade them from jumping; also like other owners, he sought to make up for that expense by slashing salaries across the board after the Feds went out of business and most of the pacts expired a year later. In Brooklyn's case the result was a player revolt that died only when star outfielder Zack Wheat agreed to a new deal on the eve of the 1917 season. The cutback tactic seemed all the more sour because it came after manager Wilbert Robinson had led the club to its first pennant in 16 years in 1916. Robinson won another flag in 1920. In between the field successes Ebbets's major accomplishment was finally forcing the repeal of blue laws in New York against playing on Sunday.

The 1920 pennant did nothing for Ebbets's growing reputation as New York's chief penny-pincher

and his worsening relations with the local press because of it. A typical lashing came from a New York *Herald* columnist covering the 1922 season opener who asserted that "President Ebbets was in the parade but dropped a dime just before the band signaled the start of the procession, and the parade passed on while he was searching for it." When the owner remonstrated against such a caricature, the columnist came back the following day to declare: "I was in error when I wrote that Squire Ebbets held up the Opening Day parade by searching for a dime that had dropped. The president of the Brooklyn club has informed me that the amount involved was 15 cents." Caricature or not, it was an image that not only followed Ebbets into his grave, but that also was affixed to the franchise as a whole for the next 15 years.

Ebbets died at the age of 65 on the eve of the 1925 season. After a pomp-filled funeral that included driving the hearse around Ebbets Field prior to a game and then to the former site of Washington Park, he was buried at Greenwood Cemetery before hundreds of mourners who had to stand around in a cold rain while the gravediggers expanded the hole for the unexpectedly large coffin. One of the mourners was Edward McKeever, Ebbets's successor as club president; because of an influenza that he picked up at the cemetery, McKeever also died 11 days later, setting the stage for the era of Brooklyn's Daffiness Boys.

DENNIS ECKERSLEY

A starter for his first 12 seasons (1975–86) with the Indians, Red Sox, and Cubs, Eckersley enjoyed even greater success afterward as the ace of the Oakland bullpen. The transition from starter to reliever corresponded with even more dramatic changes in the righthander's private life.

Starting out with Cleveland, Eckersley's solid status on the mound included a no-hitter against California on May 30, 1977. The following year, however, he was traded to the Red Sox, in part to ease the tensions caused when his wife left him for teammate Rick Manning. In Boston he threw himself into the bachelor's life; over his first five seasons he compiled an 77–50 record, but with his partying degenerating into alcoholism, he then slumped to 74–78 over the next seven years. After playing a key role in the Cubs 1984 East Division win, injuries and continued drinking made him expendable, and Chicago sent him to Oakland in 1987. What the Cubs did not benefit from was an offseason six-week stay in a Rhode Island clinic that dried him out.

Once with the Athletics, Eckersley was not only sober, but a reliever. Under the tutelage of pitching coach Dave Duncan he racked up between 33 and 51 saves every year between 1988 and 1993. In 1990 he saved 48 with an 0.61 ERA, permitting merely 45 baserunners in 73 $^1/_3$ innings; in 1992 he reached a career-high 51 saves (1.91) to take both the MVP and Cy Young prizes in the American League. With trademark flowing locks and a heavy mustache making him one of the sport's most recognizable faces, he also rewrote control ratios—between 1989 and 1990, for instance, walking only seven while striking out 128. With one melodramatic exception he was equally notable in the off-season. In the 1988 ALCS against Boston he saved all four victories of the Oakland sweep; in 1989 he saved three more in the five-game LCS win over Toronto and picked up another in the World Series sweep of the Giants; in 1990 he closed out the Red Sox twice. As he was the first to admit, however, he will probably be most remembered in postseason history for the home run he surrendered to the gimping Kirk Gibson of the Dodgers in the ninth inning of the first game of the 1988 World Series.

When pitching coach Duncan and manager Tony LaRussa moved from Oakland to St. Louis in 1996, Eckersley wasn't far behind them, and added another 66 saves over two years before finally winding down with Boston in 1998. At the end of his 24-year career he had 197 wins and 390 saves—in a league of his own for the combination.

WILLIAM ECKERT

Even for the shallow waters of a baseball commissioner, Eckert was out of his depth. A retired Air Force lieutenant-general with no knowledge of the sport, he was recommended for the post initially in 1965 by General Curtis LeMay, the sword-rattling SAC commander who had been the first choice of major league owners. When his appointment was announced, a sportswriter (whose identity has changed depending on the telling) was heard to crack: "They went and got the Unknown Soldier."

In one sense, Eckert was not such a strange choice since the owners had been looking for a military man to head the commissioner's office since 1951, when the election of Ford Frick had come af-

ter failed forays after other generals. He also brought to the post a reputation as an able administrator who knew how to defer to the powers-that-be. In the event, however, he wasn't even much good at the paperwork, and teams had to detach some of their own front office people to help him get through the day. Worse, Eckert stepped on the wrong toes in April 1968, when he supported the decision of Rusty Staub, Bob Aspromonte, Roberto Clemente, and Maury Wills not to play in a spring training game scheduled in the immediate wake of the assassination of Martin Luther King. The owners made sure he didn't repeat that mistake after the assassination of Robert Kennedy later in the year. Eckert was fired in December 1968 amid signs of a coming strike by players.

DAVE EGAN

Egan was a columnist for the Boston *Record* who so dedicated himself to making life miserable for Ted Williams that the Red Sox star rarely referred to him as anything but "that old drunken bastard." A pompous writer who liked to call himself The Colonel and affected the style of a rural philosopher, Egan blasted Williams for everything from not shaking hands enthusiastically enough with teammates after home runs to winning "cheap publicity" by reporting to the Marines for active duty during the Korean War. One of his other hobby horses in the 1950s was tearing into Boston for holding on to Williams rather than making room in left field for Faye Throneberry, a Red Sox farm prospect and brother of Marv. When pressed once on the fact that he kept up his screed despite never going to Fenway Park, Egan claimed that his absence from the ballpark enabled him to be more objective. It was also the *Record* columnist who, after Braves manager Casey Stengel was hit by a taxi in 1943, nominated the driver as "the man who did the most for Boston baseball" that year for sidelining the manager of the cellar-dwelling club.

DAVE EGGLER

The center fielder for Philadelphia in the first National League game on April 22, 1876, Eggler converted a fly ball into the first double play when he threw a runner out at the plate on the play.

HOWARD EHMKE

Ehmke was a washed-up, seven-game winner when Athletics manager Connie Mack chose him over aces Lefty Grove and George Earnshaw to start the opening game of the 1929 World Series against the Cubs; the move resulted in a 3–1 victory and 13 strikeouts, for a new World Series record. The choice of Ehmke was no whim on Mack's part; he had counted on the righthander's sidearm delivery foiling Chicago's heavily righthand-hitting lineup and had sent him to scout the eventual National League pennant winners toward the end of the season. Ehmke ended his 15-year career, after only one more season, with a 166–166 record.

DAVE EILAND

Eiland is the only pitcher who both yielded a home run to his first major league batter and clouted a four-bagger of his own when he got into the batter's box for the first time. As a member of the Yankees in 1988, the righthander was given a rude welcoming by Paul Molitor of the Brewers; as a member of the Padres in 1992, he tagged Bob Ojeda of the Dodgers for a homer in his first plate appearance.

JIM EISENREICH

Eisenreich's once-trumpeted talents almost foundered altogether on the dangerous ignorance of the Minnesota front office. Hailed by Twins owner Calvin Griffith as a coming superstar in 1982, the lefthand-hitting rookie outfielder got no farther than a few weeks into the season when a facial tic and breathing difficulties forced him to the bench in a game against Milwaukee. The same symptoms plus involuntary vocalizations brought jeers from Fenway Park fans in another game, compelling Eisenreich to withdraw once again. For the next three years he spent most of his time on the disabled list for what was generally viewed as agoraphobia. When the Twins discovered in 1984 that he had been taking medication for Tourette's Syndrome, they gave him an ultimatum to be treated for agoraphobia or return to the minors; instead, Eisenreich announced his retirement. After a couple of years of being treated for Tourette's, Eisenreich found Minnesota unwilling to bring him back but willing to sell his contract to Kansas City for the insulting sum of $1. With the Royals he worked his way back to a status as one of the best platoon players in the league, contributing significantly to pennant wins by the Phillies in 1993 and Marlins in 1997. He retired in 1998 with a .290 average for his 15 seasons.

KID ELBERFELD

When American League president Ban Johnson maneuvered shortstop Elberfeld to the Highlanders in 1903, he almost exploded the recently concluded peace between the National and American leagues; he definitely exploded the 1904 World Series.

A .271 hitter for six clubs between 1898 and 1914, Elberfeld was claimed by the Giants after the 1902 season, but then permitted to go back to his team of origin in Detroit as part of the inter-league accord. At least as far as Giants owner John T. Brush and manager John McGraw were concerned, the understanding was for the hot-tempered infielder known as The Tabasco Kid to remain with the Tigers. But when AL president Ban Johnson decided that Elberfeld was exactly the kind of player his new franchise in New York needed to compete with the Giants for fans, he wasted little time shepherding a deal with the Highlanders. Brush and McGraw got nowhere with attempts at obtaining an injunction against the move and their protests of a betrayal, but they did get back at Johnson the following year when they refused to pit their pennant-winning team against the Red Sox in the second World Series.

As the Giants had feared, the positive thing about Elberfeld's macho persona was that he was good box office. Regular tales of him pouring whiskey on his cuts and gashes between innings gave New York's AL fans at least a semblance of the roughhouse appeal of McGraw's Giants. On the other hand, that same persona included a temper that turned even his rooters against him at times. In August 1905, for instance, he assaulted arbiter Jack McCarthy from behind, then landed two more shots when McCarthy tried to defend himself. Teammates and police had to escort him from the field before Chicago fans came down from the stands to help McCarthy, and Johnson suspended him indefinitely. The following September, Elberfeld became so furious that a Philadelphia runner had been called safe at third that he began chasing umpire Silk O'Loughlin around the field. To his astonishment, his own fans—bored with his regular eruptions and impatient to get on with the game—started booing him. The mood turned so ugly that police once again had to escort him off the field.

Teammates didn't fare much better than umpires with Elberfeld. He and third baseman Wid Conroy, for example, developed such a volatile contempt for each other that manager Clark Griffith found it easier to accede to Conroy's request for a shift to the outfield than abet a violent spectacle from the two infielders going after the same pop fly. Another non-favorite of the shortstop was Hal Chase, whose popularity in New York had come to eclipse his own.

Griffith had other problems with Elberfeld, as well. In 1907 a prolonged slump at bat and in the field generated criticism from both the press and fans. An initial funk at the hostility toward him erupted into defiance during the first game of a July 26 doubleheader when the shortstop ever so slowly retrieved a ball after making an error and insolently admired it. Owner Frank Farrell responded by slapping him with another of his several suspensions. In spring training the next year, Griffith, exasperated because Elberfeld had missed 164 games over the previous four seasons due to leg and other injuries, suggested he wear a shin guard while playing the infield. Despite the heckling of opposing players, Elberfeld went along for a few weeks. But then in early May Bob Ganley of the Senators slid into him, destroying the shin guard and the rest of his playing season. That was bad news for Griffith on two counts: it cost him a shortstop and gave the idled infielder a lot of time to share his thoughts with Farrell about how badly the club was being managed.

A year after being suspended for his less than sterling effort on the field, Elberfeld was named to succeed the resigning Griffith.

As a pilot, Elberfeld was most (transparently) known for his pet tactic of having the Highlanders pass along hit-and-run signs to one another through the N (for No) and Y (for Yes) on their uniforms. According to several players, the grazings of the team logo were about as subtle as shouted commands and accounted for the constant thwarting of New York rallies. Elberfeld was fired after compiling a record of 27–71 and contributing mightily to a franchise-mark 103 losses.

LEE ELIA

As manager of the Cubs in 1983, Elia had one of the more original views of the then-boiling controversy over whether Wrigley Field should be equipped with lights. Infuriated that his humpty-dumpty club was the constant target of catcalls at home, he told reporters in August that Chicago fans were "gar-bage" and that "while 85 percent of the country is out working (during the day), the other 15 percent come here to boo my players." The owner of the Cubs, the circulation-reliant Chicago *Tribune,* decided that wasn't the best reason for switching to night baseball and showed Elia the door.

HOD ELLER

The anchor of the 1919 Cincinnati pitching staff, Eller was approached by gamblers before that season's World Series to see if he would be interested in $5,000 for throwing his scheduled start against Chicago in the eighth game. Although the righthander reported the bid to manager Pat Moran (adding the detail that he had threatened to punch out the gambler's lights), his disclosures that both teams had been at least initial prey for gamblers were lost in all the subsequent publicity attending the investigation of the Black Sox.

DOCK ELLIS

By his own account, Ellis was under the influence of LSD when he no-hit the Padres for the Pirates on June 12, 1970, and could remember nothing about the game when he saw a videotape some time later. For the righthander the no-hitter was the centerpiece of a stormy career that saw him sprayed with Mace by a stadium security guard on one occasion when he refused to show his identification and that pitted him relentlessly—and publicly—against (rigid) managers and (cheap) owners. While still with the Pirates in 1971, Ellis fumed over the admitted dread his teammates experienced whenever they had to face Cincinnati's Big Red Machine, finally taking matters into his own hands the next time he pitched against the Reds by hitting the first three batters to face him; walking the cleanup hitter on four high, inside fastballs; and then decking the fifth batter. At that point manager Danny Murtaugh removed him from the game but conceded at the end of the season that Ellis's demonstration had indeed worked to make the Cincinnati players edgier against the Pirates and to instill more confidence in the Pittsburgh clubhouse.

KEVIN ELSTER

Although he never batted in more than 55 runs in any other of his 13 major league seasons between 1986 and 2001, the righty-swinging shortstop accomplished the all-but-impossible for the Rangers in 1996 by collecting 92 of his 99 RBIs from the ninth spot in the batting order.

ELEANOR ENGLE

Engle's aspirations to play professional baseball were squelched in June 1952 when George Trautman, the president of the National Association, the governing body of the minor leagues, decreed that women could not be signed to baseball contracts. The stenographer and would-be shortstop had been signed by Dr. Jay Smith, president of the Harrisburg club of the Class B Interstate League; Engle's career ended after taking infield practice just once.

CARL ERSKINE

Known to some of the Brooklyn faithful as Oisk, Erskine was the most popular pitcher on The Boys of Summer Dodgers. An overhand curveball specialist, the righthander no-hit the Cubs in 1952, then had his best season in 1953, when he won 20. On the way to Ebbets Field one day in 1956, Erskine read an article quoting Giants scout Tom Sheehan as saying that he was washed up because of recurring arm ailments. That afternoon the admittedly depressed Erskine pitched another no-hitter, against New York. As soon as the last out was recorded, Jackie Robinson, who had played the game with mysterious padding in his pants, pulled out the newspaper containing the scout's quotes and shoved it at Sheehan, declaring, "Stick this up your ass."

BILLY EVANS (Hall of Fame, 1973)

In 1906 Evans, at age 22, became the youngest umpire in major league history. Before retiring 21 years later, he made a mark for his often bloody experiences on the field and for helping to bring about four-man umpiring crews.

Evans was one of the few umpires ever suspended by American League president Ban Johnson. The penalty came for a confrontation with Tigers outfielder Davy Jones in June 1912, even though the planned fight between the two never materialized. On another occasion he did fight Ty Cobb, receiving a thorough thrashing while trying to insist that the brawl be conducted according to Marquis of Queensbury rules. In 1918 the official was knocked unconscious by a bottle thrown from a grandstand.

During the 1909 World Series between Pittsburgh and Detroit, Evans, who was umpiring the game with Bill Klem, momentarily lost sight of a drive hit by Dot Miller of the Pirates down the right field line. He calmly went out to the grandstand, polled the fans sitting there about where the ball had gone, and gave Miller a double based on their reply. The forever-irritated Johnson censured him after the game for depending on fans for a call, but bowed before the argument that a survey wouldn't have been necessary if there had been umpires on the foul lines to begin with. The following day the World Series had its first four-man umpiring crew.

After retiring as an umpire, Evans worked as the general manager for both Cleveland and Detroit.

DARRELL EVANS

Evans hit the quietest 414 home runs in baseball history. It was, in fact, only toward the end of his 21-year career as a lefthand-hitting third baseman and first baseman that he underscored his power skills by becoming the first player to hit at least 40 homers in a season in both leagues and then, in 1987, by becoming the first 40-year-old to wallop at least 30. Prior to these feats for the Tigers, Evans's chief claims to fame had been as one of the only trio of teammates (with Hank Aaron and Davey Johnson) to hit 40 homers in the same season and as the only major leaguer on record to claim having witnessed a UFO landing.

JOHNNY EVERS (Hall of Fame, 1946)

Evers earned his nickname of The Crab much more than he did his place in Cooperstown. The chief beneficiary of the Franklin P. Adams poem that celebrated the supposed defensive superiority of the Cubs infield at the dawn of the 20th century, the left-hand-swinging second baseman left a long trail of irritated teammates, adversaries, front office executives, and umpires in his wake over an 18-year (between 1902 and 1929) playing career and aborted attempts at managing. On the other hand, and despite the paeans of the Adams work, he never once led National League second baseman in double plays or fielding average and paced his contemporaries in assists on only one occasion; he also made the most errors for a NL second baseman twice.

Like the Dick Bartells and Billy Martins of later eras, Evers was the sort of hustling infielder who was appreciated as a goad during winning seasons and detested as an obsessive when the victories didn't come so readily. The former situation prevailed between 1906 and 1911, when Frank Chance's Cubs finished either first or second. Offensively, he was a slap hitter who reached the .300 mark twice, including a totally uncharacteristic .341 in 1912; his lifetime average was .270. He saved some of his best performances for the World Series, contributing significantly to two Chicago world championships in 1907 and 1908 by batting .350 each time and by topping that with a .438 mark for the Miracle Braves of 1914. It was also Evers who sent the league spinning in 1908 by noticing that the Giants Fred Merkle had not touched second base on what appeared to be the winning base hit in a late September game at the Polo Grounds and called for the ball to record a forceout; his sharpness ultimately necessitated a makeup game in which the Cubs defeated the Giants for the pennant.

Personal relations were never Evers's forte, and, as in the case of Ty Cobb, his alienation from teammates ended up costing him physically. In 1905 his cantankerous infield partner Joe Tinker stopped talking to him because of a banal mixup over an appointment to cab together to the ballpark; the second baseman and the shortstop didn't speak to each other for 33 years. Manager-first baseman Chance tinkered with the idea of moving Evers to the outfield just so he would not have to listen to his constant chattering and hectoring during games. On the eve of the 1911 season Evers suffered a nervous breakdown, causing him to miss most of the year. Matters didn't improve when he was named as Chance's successor as manager in 1913. Tinker, still brooding about the taxi he had missed eight years earlier, declared himself unable to play under his infield partner and had to be accommodated with a trade to Cincinnati. The players who stayed behind tangled with Evers in one row after another, some of them on the playing field. In one incident, Al Bridwell slugged him in the middle of an argument over how to play opposition hitters. In another, outfielder Tommy Leach ran all the way in from his position to the mound to take on the manager for what he had concluded had been ridicule of his defensive play.

Evers was fired as manager at the end of the 1913 season, but he didn't go alone. When he heard that Chicago president Charles Murphy was working on trading him to the Braves, he threatened to defect to the newly formed Federal League. That was enough for NL president John Tener to call Murphy in on the carpet to lace into him for risking the loss of one of the league's stars to the Feds; together with previous administrative imbroglios, the incident was enough to force out Murphy as organization head. As for Evers, he ended up being traded to Boston anyway, and his field leadership proved invaluable to the club's 1914 world championship. Within a couple of years, however, Braves players were pressing for the removal of their frequently snarling teammate, and he was sent off to the Phillies, where he effectively ended his playing career in 1917.

In 1921 William Veeck brought Evers back for a second managing tour with the Cubs, but it ended more quickly than even his initial stint after familiar run-ins with players; one of them, five-time 20-game winner Hippo Vaughn, was so demoralized by his clashes with Evers that he quit baseball in the middle of the season. Evers returned to uniform for the White Sox in 1924, when he was one of owner Charles Comiskey's stopgap managerial solutions for reassembling the franchise splattered by the 1919 World Series scandal. In a final appearance for the Braves in 1929 he made an error on his only chance in the field and didn't come to bat.

Asked once what he thought of NL umpiring, Evers replied: "My favorite umpire is a dead one."

BUCK EWING (Hall of Fame, 1939)

Considered by many contemporaries the greatest star of the 19th century, Ewing became a focal point of the National League's battle against the Players League in 1890 when, despite his status as baseball's highest-paid player, he led the Giants in a mass defection to the New York entry in the new league. Federal Judge William P. Wallace rebuffed Giants owner John B. Day's request for a federal court injunction to prevent Ewing from appearing for the identically named PL Giants, ruling that the reserve clause in the catcher's contract gave the club nothing more than the "prior and exclusive" right to make an offer for the following season. The singling out of Ewing probably saved his reputation among fellow players, since he had earlier expressed sympathy for Day's situation and had met with the owner secretly to discuss the possibility of declaring his intention to return to the NL after the inevitable demise of the PL; Ewing later claimed that he had been spying for the Brotherhood.

In 18 big league seasons (1880–97) the righthand-batting receiver batted .307. He was a sufficiently swift base runner to be used regularly in the leadoff spot and slugger enough to top the NL in homers in 1883. It was, however, as a catcher, possibly the first to go into a full crouch behind the plate, that he outshone his contemporaries. Especially adept at throwing out runners, he was also something of a psychologist, using compliments and flattery to win over umpires both in his playing days and as a manager.

F

RED FABER (Hall of Fame, 1964)

Faber's 20-year career (1914–33) was a little too synonymous with the White Sox. A favorite of owner Charlie Comiskey, the righthander had four 20-win seasons by 1922, in the process also taking two American League ERA titles. But for the next decade he posted a record of 103–113, never once getting his ERA under 3.41 and prompting more than one manager to complain that he was in charge of "24 players plus Faber." The pitcher's most visible moment of glory came in the 1917 World Series against the Giants, when he won three games to nail down a world championship. In the second game of the same Series, however, Faber pulled one of the biggest gaffes in postseason play when he sought to steal third base with teammate Buck Weaver already standing on the bag.

Before he had ever taken the mound for Chicago, Faber had been "loaned" to the Giants during an offseason 1913–1914 world barnstorming trip by the New Yorkers and the White Sox. He was belted around by his future teammates in the tour's concluding game in England before King George V.

ELROY FACE

Face was almost too successful for his own good with the 1959 Pirates. Because he compiled his 18–1 record as a reliever, critics have been quick to note he blew numerous games for starters, yielding a batting average of .318 in the process. His reputation as a fireman hasn't been helped, either, by the record 21 homers he gave up over his career in extra innings. On the other hand, the righthander was a major force in Pittsburgh's 1960 world championship by winning 10 and saving 24 during the regular season, then compiling another three saves in the World Series against the Yankees. In addition, Face led the National League in saves in both 1961 and 1962.

PAUL FAGAN

Heir to a California banking fortune and part owner of the San Francisco Seals, Fagan launched an all-out assault in 1946 to have the Pacific Coast League acknowledged as a third major league. His chief tactics were to dissuade other PCL owners from selling their players to the National and American leagues and to pay members of the Seals more than they would have made in the majors. The strategy worked only insofar as the San Francisco team ran roughshod over the PCL while the league as a whole broke all-time attendance records because of fan support for Fagan's scheme. Other owners, however, continued to make deals with major league clubs, insisting that they didn't have Fagan's funds for increasing player salaries or for getting into a lengthy war with the NL and AL. Conceding the failure of his plan, Fagan himself returned to selling players to the big leagues after the 1946 season. First baseman Ferris Fain, among others, protested when told he had been dealt to the Athletics, noting his promotion to the AL was going to cost him money.

FRANK FARRELL

Farrell was the owner of a posh casino on West 33rd Street in New York City that was the place to go for the city's elite in the 1890s, especially after he hired Stanford White to redecorate the interior for

$100,000. American League president Ban Johnson was more impressed, however, by Farrell's willingness to hand over $25,000 of his profits as a binder on a New York franchise in 1903. Taking over the AL spot vacated by Baltimore, Farrell and partner Bill Devery, a former New York City police chief, built Hilltop Park and put the Highlanders (later the Yankees) in business.

Farrell's gambling establishment was the finest of its era, decorated with paintings, velvet carpets, Persian rugs, and a $20,000 bronze door found in the wine cellar of a Venetian palace and installed at the rear of the casino's entrance hall as much as a security device as for its ornamental value. His ballclub was less imposing, managing three second-place finishes and only one other as high as fourth in 13 seasons. Farrell's major contribution to the club was thawing relations between the Yankees and the rival Giants by inviting the National Leaguers to become temporary tenants in Hilltop Park after a fire destroyed the Polo Grounds in 1911; two years later, the Giants returned the favor, inviting the Yankees to leave their deteriorating rock pile in Washington Heights and share the luxury of a rebuilt Polo Grounds.

Much of Farrell's tenure as an owner was spent wrangling with his first baseman Hal Chase, a succession of managers that included Clark Griffith, George Stallings, and Frank Chance, and AL president Johnson's attempts to exploit the crisis of the moment to gain greater leverage over the franchise. Although he succeeded in his original intention of gaining "respectability" by owning the team, he was exhausted enough by 1915 to sell out to Jacob Ruppert.

CHARLIE FAUST

Faust was baseball's most legendary good luck omen. Presenting himself to John McGraw before an early-season game in St. Louis in 1911, he told the New York manager the Giants would win the pennant if he were allowed to pitch. Although he showed nothing during drills as a pitcher, batter, or fielder, McGraw kept him around for a few days, during which New York went on a winning run. With the players dubbing him Victory, he stuck around for most of the year, right into the World Series.

After the season Faust took to the vaudeville circuit to explain how his presence had helped ensure a New York pennant. During both the 1912 and 1913 seasons, he was called to New York during losing streaks, and on both occasions the club immediately started winning. By 1913, however, McGraw had begun entertaining doubts about what he had wrought, and he devoted more than one locker room talk to assuring the players that they were capable of winning on their own. When the speeches fell on deaf ears, he made up his mind to tell Faust anyway that his services would not be required in 1914. But Faust disappeared before McGraw could get to him, not resurfacing until months later, in an Oregon mental institution. He died in 1915 in a Washington State asylum. As for the Giants in 1914, they finished 10 games behind Boston.

The record books indicate that McGraw allowed Faust to take the mound in two games at the end of the 1911 season, when the pennant had already been clinched. He yielded a run in two innings in what was a burlesque performance by everybody, including the opposition Braves and Dodgers, except Faust himself.

CHUB FEENEY

Feeney served as president of the National League during the critical 1970–86 period when relations between players and owners were radically redefined by the introduction of free agency and arbitration, when the drug crisis descended on Pittsburgh and St. Louis (among other teams), and when the Pirates and Padres underwent traumatic ownership changes as a last resort against moving. For all that, most obituaries following his death in January 1994 could say little about him except that he had been opposed to introducing the designated hitter to the NL.

A nephew of Horace Stoneham, Feeney worked for the Giants with various titles from 1946 to his election as league president. In 1968 he was proposed by several NL owners as the next commissioner, but when a deadlock ensued between him and Michael Burke of the Yankees, Bowie Kuhn was elected as a compromise candidate. After stepping down as NL president for Bart Giamatti in 1986, Feeney was given a similar title with the deteriorating San Diego franchise. His refusal to sign free agents and various run-ins with players, the press, the fans, and even the club's own broadcasters prompted the regular appearance of SCRUB CHUB banners at Jack Murphy stadium. Spotting one of them during Fan Appreciation Night in 1988, Feeney gave the bearers the finger, leading to his dismissal shortly thereafter.

KATY FEENEY

The daughter of Chub, Feeney's title of Vice President of Club Relations and Scheduling makes her the highest-ranking woman in major league baseball. She succeeded Phyllis Collins as vice president of the National League and maintained the title when the league offices were all but eliminated at the turn of the century.

DONALD FEHR

Fehr succeeded Ken Moffett in the top post of the Players Association in December 1985 just as the basic agreement between owners and players was about to expire. The union's former general counsel weathered that introductory storm, fending off the owners' demands (for limitations on salary arbitration and, for the first time, a salary cap) by leading a two-day walkout in the spring and finally agreeing to add a year to the length of service a player had to accumulate before being eligible for arbitration. Fehr also managed to steer through other controversies, including several ownership collusion conspiracies against free agents (by emerging victorious from three arbitration hearings), Commissioner Peter Ueberroth's insistence on universal drug testing in 1985 (by countering with his own insistence that drug testing was an item to be negotiated), the expiration of the basic agreement in 1990 (by waiting out a spring training lockout to win an expansion of eligibility for salary arbitration), and the switch to a three-division format in each league in 1994 (by agreeing to the move only after winning concessions on the number of postseason games in whose revenue the players would share). As the pointman for the players in the 1994 strike, on the other hand, he became a figure of growing exasperation before the refusal of the owners to discuss anything but an imposed salary cap wearing the disguise of a payroll tax on club budgets.

For several years after the 1994 job action, Fehr appeared to buy into ownership claims that the dispute had alienated fans almost fatally and that only the trumpeted heroics of Cal Ripken, Jr. and then Mark McGwire and Sammy Sosa restored the game to previous popularity levels. But his regular vows that the players would do everything possible to avoid repeating "another 1994" faced a reality test after the 2001 season when Commissioner Bud Selig unfurled his contraction plan for disposing of

two franchises without first consulting with the Players Association. Among other things, the Selig maneuver postponed negotiations on a new basic agreement—a pact Fehr and his aides had been cautiously optimistic about for some time.

BOB FELLER (Hall of Fame, 1962)

Feller's brilliant pitching career for 18 seasons between 1936 and 1956 was sandwiched between some brazen illegalities and a personal venality that would never qualify the righthander as Mr. Charm.

On the mound, the Cleveland hurler left most of his contemporaries in the dust with six league-leading 20-win seasons and seven strikeout titles. His most dominating year was 1946, when he won 26, had an ERA of 2.18, threw 10 shutouts, and struck out a modern record 348 batters in 371$\frac{1}{3}$ innings. Individual-game performances were equally striking. In his rookie year of 1936, while still in high school, he struck out 17 Athletics in one contest. That outing followed an exhibition game appearance in which, facing major league batters for the first time, he fanned eight Cardinals in three innings. On the last day of the 1938 season, he struck out 18 Tigers to set the then record for the modern era. On April 16, 1940, he celebrated Opening Day by no-hitting Chicago (and thereby making the White Sox the answer to the trivia question of what club had all its players end a game with exactly the same batting average they had going into it). Before he was through, Feller would hurl two more no-hitters, to go along with 12 one-hitters. On the other hand, he would always admit to frustration at never winning a World Series contest; his 0–2 record in postseason play included a 1–0 loss to the Braves in the first game of the 1948 Series.

Feller's fastball and curve aroused awe in opposition hitters. They also prompted some widely circulated newsreels in the 1940s both demonstrating his velocity and providing graphic evidence that balls did indeed curve. Aside from his talent, the Indians pitcher was an obvious candidate for such promotional pieces because of the added popularity he had gained by enlisting in the Navy with the eruption of World War II and winning eight citations during a four-year stint as a gun crew chief. For all that, his career with Cleveland was almost stillborn because of the transparent paperwork dodges general manager Cy Slapnicka resorted to in rushing the teenager to the major leagues in violation of baseball's age and schooling rules. When the owner of a minor league team in Des Moines filed a formal complaint against Slapnicka's tactics, arguing that he should have had first rights to Feller, Commissioner Kenesaw Landis, who had been very much aware of the Cleveland irregularities, reluctantly interceded to decide whether the pitcher should be declared a free agent. Landis's decision to leave him where he was stemmed from two considerations: Feller and his father both stated a preference for the Indians, and the two other main contenders for his services were the Yankees and Tigers—teams the commissioner regarded as already too talented for the good of competition in the American League. The Des Moines club owner received a sop indemnity of $7,500.

Although one of baseball's more articulate players for his era, Feller also had a long suit in crankiness against what he perceived as underappreciation of his talent or overappreciation of the skills of others. Nowhere was this clearer than in his constant criticisms of the significance of Jackie Robinson's breaking the color barrier in 1947. When he wasn't claiming that Robinson was at bottom "a no-hit-good-glove" player, he was trying to make the case that his own mound heroics were more important to the development of the game than racial integration. What he did not say was that Robinson usually treated him as a batting practice pitcher during post-season games between major league and Negro league all-star squads and that he himself lost substantial money when integration made the barnstorming tours a thing of the past. Feller has never been averse, either, to picking up as much money as he could from autographs. In one particularly tawdry scene at Cooperstown in 1993, he arrived too late for a signing, but then stood on the sidewalk with an aide, hawking his signature to any passerby who had the money to pay for it.

HAPPY FELSCH

Felsch was one of the eight hapless White Sox players outlawed from baseball for involvement in the 1919 World Series game rigging. A righthand-hitting outfielder, he played all six of his major league years with Chicago, batting .293. Like many of the other ostracized players, he was enjoying a particularly good season in 1920 (career highs in batting, home runs, doubles, triples, and RBIs) when

grand jury testimony by teammates Eddie Cicotte and Joe Jackson in late September led to his suspension for the remainder of the campaign.

The outfielder was one of the four Black Sox who confessed—in his case to accepting $5,000 but not to any direct action that led to the loss of the Series. In 1923 Felsch sued White Sox owner Charlie Comiskey for conspiring to deprive him of a living but failed to collect any damages; two years later, he collected a little more than $1,100 in an out-of-court settlement of a breach of contract suit.

TERRY FELTON

Felton is the most unsuccessful pitcher in baseball history. A righthander for the Twins, he went 0–3 in 1980 and 0–13 in 1982—the 16 losses adding up to the most by any pitcher without a victory.

BOB FERGUSON

Between 1864 and 1891 Ferguson served at one time or another as player, league president, manager, front office official, and umpire. As a player he became the first recorded switch hitter, when, playing for the Atlantics of Brooklyn on June 14, 1870, he moved across the plate to bat lefthanded for the first time in his career to avoid the wide range and sure hands of Cincinnati Red Stockings shortstop George Wright; his single in the plate appearance drove in the tying run, and he himself later scored the winning run in the game that broke the Red Stockings legendary two-year winning streak. He also earned the sobriquet of Death to Flying Things for his sure-handedness as an infielder.

The manager-third baseman of the Atlantics in the National Association between 1872 and 1874, Ferguson was euchred into accepting the NA presidency by New York Mutuals owner Bill Cammeyer, fulfilling Cammeyer's expectations by neglecting his club to run the league and thus allowing the Mutuals to take over as the chief club in New York City. As a player, he ended up with a .271 average in a nine-year career in the National League and American Association. He was usually less acceptable in a series of managerial assignments in the late 1870s and 1880s. Most notable was his experience in Philadelphia in 1883, where his authoritarian ways provoked such hostility among Phillies players that he was removed from field command after only 17 games; he did, however, continue with the club in the unique position of second baseman-business manager. An even greater clash was averted the following year when several members of the Giants, who had endured Ferguson's temperamental fits while with Troy, refused to play for him, causing New York owner John Day to cancel his contract even before Opening Day.

As an umpire in later years, Ferguson once settled a dispute by breaking a player's arm with a bat.

RICK FERRELL (Hall of Fame, 1984)

Ferrell is usually the catcher on the all-time team of Hall of Famers who don't belong in Cooperstown. A Veterans Committee pick, he played through much of his 18-year (between 1927 and 1947) career deep in the shadows of Bill Dickey and Mickey Cochrane, rarely belonging to a first-division team. Usually cited for his defensive brilliance, he was actually only a notch above such contemporary American League journeymen as Luke Sewell, but made fewer enemies. Ferrell reached his offensive peak with the Red Sox in the mid-1930s after being obtained from the Browns in Tom Yawkey's first deal for Boston; in 1935 he batted .301, following that up with a .312 mark the following season. Mainly because of his brother Wes Ferrell's tantrums on the mound and in the clubhouse, he was traded with his sibling to Washington in 1937 in a swap that became known as the Harmony Deal for its anticipated impact on Boston.

WES FERRELL

Almost as many questions might be raised as to why Ferrell isn't in the Hall of Fame as to why his brother Rick is. After a couple of cups of coffee with the Indians in 1927 and 1928, the righthander returned for good in 1929 and promptly became the only 20th-century pitcher to post 20 wins in his first four seasons. Topping the 20-victory mark again in 1935 and 1936 for the Red Sox, he became the only eligible hurler without a Cooperstown plaque to post six 20-win seasons in the 20th century. (In fact, 28 pitchers enshrined in Cooperstown have failed to record as many 20-win seasons.)

Ferrell was equally dangerous with a bat in his hands. He holds both the season (9) and career (37) records for home runs by a pitcher and had five seasons of at least 24 RBIs in his limited plate appearances. In 1933, when Cleveland outfielder Joe Vos-

mik was sidelined with injuries, Ferrell replaced him for 13 games, hitting .300 over the span. Ferrell's major problem with Hall of Fame voters has been his quick decline after his sixth 20-win season. For the last few years of his 15-year career, he pitched for mostly humpty-dumpty teams and was batted around with regularity.

MARK FIDRYCH

Fidrych was as much of a shooting star as baseball has had. A nonroster player with the Tigers in 1976, the righthander didn't get into a game until five weeks into the season, but from there he went on to fascinate the country with both his mound skills (19 wins, a 2.34 ERA, Rookie of the Year award) and idiosyncrasies. He talked to the ball, got down on his hands and knees to landscape the pitching hill, refused to pitch with a ball that had been knocked for a base hit, and ran over to shake the hands of his infielders after difficult plays. After some initial resentment that he might have been showing them up, even opposition hitters recognized that there was nothing false or calculated in the enthusiasm of the hurler who soon enough became known as The Bird. Fidrych also contributed critically to the Detroit coffers: In his 29 starts at home and on the road, he drew 901,239 fans, with his 18 home starts accounting for 605,677 clicks of the turnstile (i.e., more than 40 percent of the franchise's Tiger Stadium attendance total). The phenomenon ended in the spring of 1977, when the pitcher tore up his right knee. After some signs in May that he had recovered from the injury, he developed tendinitis, shelving him for the rest of the season. He won only 10 more games after his rookie season and called it quits in 1980.

CECIL FIELDER

The overweight Fielder looked so little like a major league player after hitting only 31 home runs in four years of bouncing up and down from the minors that the Blue Jays sold him to the Hanshin franchise of the Japanese Central League in 1989. When he returned to the States with the Tigers in 1990, he became the first American Leaguer to top the 50-homer mark (51) since Roger Maris in 1961. Adding to the embarrassment in the Toronto front office, the righthand-hitting first baseman led the AL in four-baggers a second consecutive year in 1991, and paced AL hitters in RBIs for three consecutive years (1990–92), something no other player had accomplished since Babe Ruth's last season in Boston and first two in New York.

ROLLIE FINGERS (Hall of Fame, 1992)

Although Hoyt Wilhelm beat him to the Hall of Fame by seven years, Fingers confirmed the new prestige of the relief pitcher in another, equally significant way—no sooner had he entered Cooperstown than his record for most saves (341) was eclipsed by first Jeff Reardon and then Lee Smith. The right-hander was also the last of baseball's dominant relievers who went to the bullpen after failing in a big way as a starter.

Fingers made the first mark of his 17-year (1968–82, 1984–85) career as a member of the Athletics. When self-admitted nerves allowed him to finish only four of 35 starts over his first few years, he was assigned to the bullpen for good, teaming with south-paw Darold Knowles to give Oakland fearsome late-inning relief during its glory years in the early 1970s. Mainly because he had to share the club's save opportunities, however, he never recorded more than 24 rescues for the A's. In 1976 owner Charlie Finley sold him and outfielder Joe Rudi to the Red Sox for $1 million apiece, but the deal was nullified by Commissioner Bowie Kuhn, who didn't like the image of Finley's fire sale of Oakland stars as a tactic against free agency. Signing with the Padres in 1977 as a free agent, Fingers racked up 72 saves in his first two years but then began experiencing the arm miseries that would crop up at increasingly frequent intervals for the rest of his career.

In 1980 Fingers became a prime exhibit of the trading reputations of Jack McKeon and Whitey Herzog, when first he was swapped to the Cardinals in an 11-player exchange and then, five days later, redirected to the Brewers in another seven-man transaction. During the strike-shortened 1981 season he picked up an American League-leading 28 saves and six victories to go with a 1.04 ERA to earn both MVP and Cy Young honors. In 1982 he collected another 29 saves, but was forced to the sidelines with tendinitis at the end of the year; his absence in Milwaukee's subsequent World Series duel with the Cardinals was regarded as the difference in the seven-game St. Louis win. After missing all of the 1983 season with his arm problem, he came back in 1984

to notch another 23 saves for the Brewers by early July, but then had to go to the sidelines for good because of a herniated disc.

While with Oakland, Fingers was among those who responded most eagerly to Finley's offer of money for team members who grew mustaches; for the rest of his career, his wispy handlebar mustache became a trademark.

CHARLIE FINLEY

Blowhard, innovator, tyrant, and miser, Finley's two decade (1961–80) run as owner of the Kansas City and Oakland versions of the Athletics marked one of the most erratic administrations in baseball history. By the time he stepped aside, it was difficult to say whether he was more hated by players, other owners, the baseball commissioner, the fans of two cities, or U.S. congressmen. What was beyond doubt was that the Indiana insurance executive had filled his own pockets while his enemies were taking turns to get at him.

In the 1950s and early 1960s there was hardly a franchise in either league with money shorts that didn't attract a Finley purchase offer. He finally realized his ambition when he forked over $2 million to the widow of Arnold Johnson after the 1960 season to take over Kansas City, which up to that point had been a laughing stock franchise used by the Yankees as little more than a farm team. In his first public act as owner, Finley staged the burning of an old bus to point up his claim that the era of the Yankees Shuttle was over; in his typical style, he then promptly turned around and traded the Athletics best pitcher, Bud Daley, to the Bronx. For Finley contradictions of the kind were irrelevant; having little appreciable major league talent on the field to boast of, he kept up dog-and-pony shows to attract fans. Among other things, he dressed his players in flamboyant kelly green and gold uniforms, introduced livestock to Municipal Stadium in promotions aimed at farmers, had his team enter the ballpark on a mule train (and set aside one of the animals as a mascot named Charlie O), sodded an area behind the outfield fences for grazing sheep, installed a mechanical rabbit behind home plate that popped up from the ground to give balls to umpires, and insisted that his players autograph all balls so that fans catching fouls and home runs would have "personalized" souvenirs.

But when Finley wasn't making Kansas City

laugh, he was making it cringe. No sooner had he taken over than he ordered his staff to end the popular practice of personally delivering season tickets; he had so alienated fans with such moves that the atmosphere was ripe for a campaign to buy tickets to "save the A's"—precisely the climate that the owner had sought for extorting better lease terms for Municipal Stadium and, then, for trying to persuade the American League that he needed a bigger market than Kansas City for survival. Throughout the early 1960s he was rumored to be on the verge of moving the team to Dallas, Atlanta, and Oakland. More concrete was a 1964 announcement that he had signed a conditional two-year lease on Louisville's Fairgrounds Stadium and formally petitioned the AL for a move to Kentucky. Aggravated by the relentless campaigns to go elsewhere and anywhere, the other league owners rejected the bid by a nine-to-one margin and ordered Finley to conclude a new pact with Municipal Stadium or face expulsion from the circuit. The Athletics owner responded by first signing a new four-year lease for the stadium with the city and then suing to reclaim rights to an older contract that contained a critical escape clause. Having muddied the waters sufficiently with that tactic, he then announced that he was putting the franchise up for sale. With Denver and San Diego descending with offers and the stadium-lease suit threatening to expose a lot of dirty laundry, AL president Joe Cronin was empowered by the other owners to promise Finley that a way would be found for moving the franchise out of Kansas City within three years; with that, the owner withdrew his lawsuit and took the club off the market.

Finley's last years in Kansas City were also marked by a revolt by players over what was seen as a gratuitous fine against pitcher Lew Krausse. Before the tensions subsided, manager Alvin Dark was fired for not disassociating himself from the player uprising, slugger Ken Harrelson was given his outright release for being one of the leaders of the rebellion, and Finley himself was hauled before the National Labor Relations Board to answer charges of having harassed his players. Kansas City fans were still enjoying the almost-daily revelations of some new Finley caper when the AL dropped the other shoe confirming that the club would be shifted to Oakland for the 1968 season. Eleventh-hour negotiations to commit an expansion club to Kansas

City in 1969 did not spare Finley an avalanche of attacks from Missouri politicians at all levels; among the most vocal was Senator Stuart Symington, who called him "one of the most disreputable characters ever to enter the American sports scene."

The major difference between Finley in Kansas City and Finley in Oakland was that he had good teams in California. Otherwise, it was the same pregame promotions of milking cows and chasing greased pigs, familiar tensions with star players over contracts, and meticulously timed complaints about how the franchise couldn't survive where it was located. The early 1970s were also Finley at his most creative where the playing and business of the game was concerned, although other owners were not always quick to accept his ideas. What they accepted was his call in 1973 for the use of a designated hitter to beef up offense; what they rejected was his promotion of an orange ball, again in the interests of giving batters an edge; what they left up to him was his use of a designated runner (Herb Washington)—an experiment that crashed after little more than one season. If the other league owners made one big mistake with Finley during the 1970s, however, it was in laughing off his proposal, following the Messersmith-McNally decision in 1975, that teams should routinely declare all their players free agents at the end of every year; according to Players Association director Marvin Miller, that in fact would have been the only sensible response by the owners to the abrogation of the reserve clause, but it was thwarted by a combination of automatic hostility to a Charlie Finley idea and simple lack of imagination.

Finley began his transfer tune in Oakland even as the club was tearing up the American League and individual players were tearing up one another in the clubhouse. He himself professed indifference to the often-savage scenes between the players and to their united contempt for him, pointing to three straight world championships as an acceptable tradeoff; on the other hand, he wasn't so indifferent to what he viewed as modest attendance figures for the best AL team of its time. After initial hints that he was thinking of moving still again, this time to Toronto or Seattle, he let his trial balloon deflate for a couple of years. But then in 1974, with his popularity at an all-time low because of his crude attempt to have infielder Mike Andrews disabled during the 1973 World Series after making a couple of errors and the subsequent resignation of manager Dick Williams, he began a series of on-and-off romances with potential franchise purchasers from Toronto and Denver. He also returned to his Kansas City tactics of slashing costs, firing employees, and cutting back on ticket plans and promotions to help make his case to the league that he was in need of a bailout. When that produced no immediate results, he went on national television during the 1974 World Series between the Athletics and Dodgers to complain that Oakland couldn't support the club.

It got worse. After the 1974 season pitching ace Catfish Hunter walked off as a free agent because Finley had neglected to fulfill a contract stipulation. In 1975, he failed in a headlined attempt to get rid of Commissioner Bowie Kuhn. In 1976, with the implications of the Messersmith-McNally decision sinking in, he began gutting his championship club before his stars made good on threats to walk away from him into free agency. When Kuhn intervened to thwart proposed sales of pitcher Vida Blue to the Yankees and outfielder Joe Rudi and reliever Rollie Fingers to the Red Sox for a combined $3.5 million, a furious Finley branded him "the village idiot" and sued to have the deals go through; he lost the suit. By 1977 some of his own players were demanding that the league take over team operations. Bay Area fans stayed away from the Coliseum to such an extent that the facility became known as the Mausoleum; even when Finley resorted to a half-price scheme for Monday-to-Thursday games, annual attendance dipped below the half-million level. The rights to broadcast coverage of A's games were given to a college radio station. The Coliseum scoreboard went untended, and amenities from concession stands to rest rooms were the worst in the major leagues since the dark ages of Ebbets Field in the 1930s.

Finley, however, kept making money. With a page torn from Branch Rickey's book, he completed only deals that brought him significant cash. If all this proved embarrassing to Kuhn and other AL owners, they could do little abut it because of the building militancy of Oakland authorities against allowing the club out of its commitment to the Coliseum. Several times in the late 1970s the Coliseum issue thwarted what otherwise appeared done deals to move the club to Denver, to shift it to New Orleans, or to have different groups buy out Finley and keep the team in Oakland. Even Giants owner Bob Lurie

agreed at one point to contribute cash and several home dates to the Coliseum if it meant returning the Bay Area exclusively to San Francisco. But if none of the prospective arrangements worked out individually, they collectively began wearing down even Finley. Finally, on August 23, 1980, in failing health and admitting that he couldn't keep battling the league, the city of Oakland, and the Coliseum, he announced the sale of the franchise for $12.7 million to Levi-Strauss Company head Walter Haas, his son Wally, and his son-in-law Roy Eisenhardt. In bidding goodbye to Finley, AL president Lee MacPhail managed to keep a straight face in hailing him for "the new ideas" he had brought to the game.

HAL FINNEY

Finney ended his five-year career as a backup catcher for the Pirates in 1936 on the worst possible note. By going to the plate 35 times without a hit, he set the record for most at bats by a position player going hitless for an entire season.

BILL FISCHER

Pitching for Kansas City in 1962, Fischer went a record-breaking $84\frac{1}{3}$ innings without issuing a walk before Bubba Morton of the Tigers ruined the streak. It was just as well that the righthander had his control, since he was belted around otherwise and closed the season with a 4–12 record.

RAY FISHER

Fisher was banned from baseball by Commissioner Kenesaw Landis in June 1921 without benefit of formal charges, a hearing, or even a letter of explanation. His crime was that he had refused to sign a one-year contract with the Reds in favor of taking a coaching job with the University of Michigan. When the Fisher file was unearthed three decades later in the commissioner's office; it was found to contain various letters from Cincinnati officials claiming that the pitcher had refused a substantial salary increase, had negotiated with Michigan without permission, had applied for reinstatement, and had signed with an outlaw club while his case was being considered—all lies. The fact was, Landis had simply caved in to the vindictiveness of Cincinnati owner Garry Herrmann, contenting himself with sending the righthanded hurler a terse telegram informing him of his fate. Only with the discovery of the fallacious file did some teams find the nerve to hire Fisher after 38 years of college coaching. In 1960 he worked as a spring training instructor for the Braves, then later on in the same role for the Tigers. He was formally reinstated only in 1980 by Commissioner Bowie Kuhn.

CARLTON FISK (Hall of Fame, 2000)

Fisk gained his standing as one of baseball's greatest catchers at the same methodical pace that he ran games. It wasn't until the conclusion of his 24-year (1969, 1971–93) career that his numerous records for longevity together with his power feats put him in proper context. One reason for the belated acknowledgement was that the righthanded slugger had only two bust-out seasons, almost a decade apart. Even then he remained primarily identified with the Red Sox, although he actually ended up playing more years (13 to 11) with the White Sox, for whom he also established various franchise long-ball marks.

Statistically, Fisk's most significant records are those for the most games (2,226) and most home runs (351) by a major league receiver. Other longevity marks include most seasons (24) most putouts (11,369) and most chances (12,417) by an American League catcher. Overall, he averaged .269 with 376 home runs and 1,330 RBIs. His single best offensive years were for Boston in 1977, when he hit .315 with 26 home runs and 102 RBIs, and 1985 for Chicago, when he clouted a career-high 37 round-trippers and knocked in 107 runs. Defensively, Fisk's greatest asset was his game calling, a vital ingredient of which was making sure that pitchers didn't rush their deliveries. To offset this danger, he developed a habit of rising from his crouch with practically every pitch before returning the ball to the mound—a time-consuming process that was pointed to in the 1980s as the main reason why White Sox games lasted substantially longer than those of other teams.

With both the Red Sox and the White Sox, Fisk had extremely high and equally low moments. One low point in Boston was in 1975, when he was singled out as a leader of the club faction bent on getting rid of manager Darrell Johnson. In that same year's World Series against the Reds, however, he entered postseason lore by "waving" a 12th-inning shot down the left field line fair for a home run to give the Red Sox a sixth-game win. In 1976 Fisk

and teammates Fred Lynn and Rick Burleson became involved in bitter, months-long contract renewal negotiations that attracted all the more attention because the three players were represented by agent Jerry Kapstein. Although Kapstein ultimately won substantial raises for the trio in the first significant player-management duel since free agency, the victory came only after the city's pro-management sportswriters had roasted the players, going so far as to accuse them and their representative of being partly responsible for the death of long-time Red Sox owner Tom Yawkey. The three contracts came back to haunt the franchise again with their expiration in 1980. While Burleson was quickly dealt off to the Angels, Fisk and Lynn again became entangled in protracted bargaining—a process that apparently so distracted general manager Haywood Sullivan that he failed to observe a mailing date for contract submissions, effectively making the two stars free agents. Fisk seized the opportunity to sign with the White Sox.

Fisk's first bad moments in Chicago came in 1985, when the loud, change-for-the-sake-of-change general manager Ken Harrelson decided to move him to left field to open up the catching spot for prospects Joel Skinner and Ron Karkovice. The experiment lasted only a few weeks into the season, when the embarrassed Fisk, backed by the team's pitching corps, returned behind the plate. His return wasn't so fast a few years later, however, when newly arrived manager Gene Lamont also thought Karkovice should do the brunt of the catching. Well into his 40s and hobbled for some time by injuries, Fisk continued to insist he should be the club's starting catcher—or if not that, at least treated with the respect due to somebody who had been so for many years. The sullenness on both sides eventually involved owner Jerry Reinsdorf, who was less subtle than Lamont about declaring Fisk a relic. Only a few days after the veteran had broken Bob Boone's record for the most games played by a catcher, Reinsdorf personally ordered Fisk's release.

ED FITZGERALD

Fitzgerald was the most recent player to make two separate appearances in a game. With the agreement of Cubs manager Phil Cavarretta, the Pirates catcher, who had already been used earlier as a pinch-hitter, was permitted to go behind the plate in a late 1952 contest because of injuries to Pittsburgh's other receivers.

MAX FLACK

Outfielder Flack was one of the handful of players who began their major league careers in the Federal League; in moving from the Chicago Whales to the Cubs after the 1915 season, he came into the National League as a tandem with Wrigley Field. In 1922 he gained another footnote to baseball history when, between games of a Cubs-Cardinals doubleheader, he was traded for outfielder Cliff Heathcote—the only deal ever made between games of a twin bill. Both players appeared in both games.

JOHN FLAHERTY

On April 12, 1992 Flaherty made his debut for the Red Sox in the first game of a doubleheader against the Indians. His batterymate, Matt Young, pitched eight hitless innings but ended up losing the game, 2–1. Although rule changes had recently barred such efforts from being considered no-hitters, Flaherty was the first catcher to break in by helping to hold opposition batters hitless for what amounted to a complete game.

JOE FLANNER

The editor of *The Sporting News,* Flanner epitomized the cozy relationship between the Baseball Bible and major league owners by drawing up the February 1903 peace treaty between the National and American leagues. A lawyer as well as a journalist, he even set the agreement into type in the newspaper's St. Louis office for forwarding to all interested parties. Not a single word of the Flanner document was changed before ratification by the leagues.

DANIEL FLETCHER

Fletcher tried to turn a 1910 postseason barnstorming tour of major leaguers into a third major league. He got his foot in the door only because the National and American leagues had vetoed the original promoter of the exhibitions, Tex Rickard; Rickard's sin was that he had only recently organized the heavyweight bout in which the black Jack Johnson had taken the title from Jim Jeffries. But no sooner had Fletcher taken over from the "dubious element" (Rickard) than he announced that the contracts he had secured from such all-stars as Walter Johnson,

Christy Mathewson, and Ty Cobb contained far-reaching commitments for the seeding of a new circuit. The established leagues quickly changed their minds about the tour, ordering players to return advances paid to them by Fletcher. The promoter himself kept several of the players on the hook by telling them the advances were theirs to keep one way or another, then spent most of the fall showing up at hotels where league meetings were held in the hope of adding to his roster. In the end, hotel managers were alerted to kick him out of lobbies if they expected big league clubs to continue patronizing their establishments. Fletcher finally had to disappear one step ahead of debt collectors.

Fletcher's League, as the aborted initiative became known, still proved profitable to several of the players, including Mathewson and Cobb: NL and AL orders or not, they never returned the money advanced to them.

ELBIE FLETCHER

A first baseman for Boston and Pittsburgh in the 1930s and 1940s, Fletcher's entrée to the National League in 1934 came about because he won a newspaper contest to select the Boston high school player most likely to make it to the big leagues. The lefty won the prize—a trip to spring training with the Braves—as much because every member of his extensive family voted for him as for his diamond skills.

On September 21, 1938 Fletcher's ordinarily superior defensive skills failed him epically when he called for a pop-up behind the mound and then watched the ball get carried into the distant left field stands of Braves Field. It was only at that point that umpires acceded to game-long requests that the contest be suspended because of a hurricane that was ripping through New England and that would end up taking 600 lives.

ELMER FLICK (Hall of Fame, 1963)

Flick was once considered good enough by the American League to risk continued war with the National League, then considered good enough by the Tigers for a proposal of a straight-up trade for Ty Cobb. A lefthand-hitting outfielder who had few peers with a glove, Flick, along with Nap Lajoie and Bill Bernhard, jumped to the AL Athletics from the Phillies during the interleague hostilities at the dawn of the 20th century. When a Pennsylvania court enjoined them against playing in the state for the junior circuit, AL president Ban Johnson persuaded Connie Mack to deal them to Cleveland, for whom they could at least play all scheduled games except those in Philadelphia and remain in the league.

Flick's best years with the Indians were 1905, when he led the league in hitting and slugging average, and 1906, when his .311 mark included leading the AL in doubles, steals, and runs scored. In 1908 the Tigers were so concerned about the club rifts caused by Cobb that they offered him to Cleveland for Flick one-for-one. Indians owner Charles Somers said no and had reason to regret it twice over—for Cobb's assault on the record books and for injuries that had Flick out of the league by 1910. The outfielder ended up batting .313 in 13 seasons.

CURT FLOOD

Flood was as crucial to the economic rights of players as Jackie Robinson was to the breaking of the color barrier; unlike Robinson, however, he didn't benefit personally from his pioneering challenge.

A key part of the Cardinals teams that won three pennants in the 1960s, Flood refused to accept a trade to the Phillies in October 1969, saying he was getting tired of being treated like a commodity and declaring war on the reserve clause in court. With the backing of the Players Association and with former U.S. Supreme Court Justice Arthur Goldberg arguing on his behalf, the outfielder pursued the case known as *Flood v. Kuhn* (Commissioner Bowie Kuhn) from January 1970 to June 1972 at district, circuit, and Supreme Court levels, gaining supporting testimony from (among others) Robinson, former owner and Hall of Famer Hank Greenberg, frequent owner Bill Veeck, and retired pitcher Jim Brosnan. On June 6, 1972 the Supreme Court came down against Flood by a margin of 5–3 with one abstention. But the language upholding baseball's exemption from anti-trust statutes (the situation was described as "anomalous" and "aberrational" among other things) was so riddled with ludicrous contradiction and rationalization that it merely invited closer looks at the sport's status, setting the stage for the 1975 Messersmith-McNally rulings and the advent of free agency. The painful equivocation of the Supreme Court decision also reinforced suspicions that Flood would have been vindicated much more directly if Goldberg, distracted for much of the suit

by his gubernatorial campaign in New York, had put more energy and eloquence into his brief.

As he had known before getting into the suit, Flood's big league career effectively ended with his legal action. The one exception was a short stint with Bob Short's Senators in 1971 while the case was still pending, and that prompted a series of tortuous documents by all concerned attesting that his wearing a Washington uniform did not mean either that the commissioner recognized the player's right to reject the deal with Philadelphia or that the player accepted a subsequent exchange between the Senators and Phillies for his services. It all became academic after 35 at bats, when Flood jumped the team.

Between 1958 and 1969 the righthanded hitter averaged better than .300 six times, topping the 200-hit mark twice and serving as the ideal cover batsman for steals king Lou Brock. Defensively, he was considered on a par with Willie Mays for the first part of the 1960s, and maybe better when the Giants star lost a step toward the middle of the decade. For all that, he is remembered equally by some Cardinals diehards for misjudging a fly ball in the seventh inning of the seventh game of the 1968 World Series; what was scored a two-run triple off the bat of Detroit's Jim Northrup decided the world championship.

Aside from the principle involved in the 1969 trade, Flood always made it clear that he didn't appreciate learning about it third-hand from a newsman after 12 years in a St. Louis uniform and that he was especially annoyed at having been sent to Philadelphia, a city he had always viewed as racist.

HORACE FOGEL

Fogel was a Philadelphia sportswriter who, unfortunately for the cities of Indianapolis, New York, and Philadelphia, got to fulfill his dreams of being a manager and then a president of a big league club. Although he was merely inept as the pilot of Indianapolis's 1887 entry in the National League, he came close to aborting a Hall of Fame career when, as manager of the Giants in 1902, he tried to convert Christy Mathewson into a first baseman. Even when he was officially fired 41 games into the season, he still hopped back into the dugout from time to time to call the plays—and to get a closer look at his successor Heinie Smith's rival inspiration that Mathewson belonged at shortstop instead of first.

After being cast aside with the arrival of John Mc-

Graw in New York, Fogel returned to his notebook until resurfacing in 1909 as the front man for a business consortium taking over the Phillies. His first insight in his new position was that the club shouldn't be called the Phillies (or the Quakers, as they had also been known) but rather the Live Wires. To promote this cause, he sold or gave away thousands of watch fobs that featured the figure of an eagle carrying sparking wires. Mainly thanks to the pitching of Grover Cleveland Alexander, Fogel's Phillies (as fans adamantly continued to call them) weren't the worst team in the league; Fogel himself, however, had doubts about what was the best team. After one too many drunken accusations that the Giants had beaten the Cubs in 1912 mainly because Cardinals manager Roger Bresnahan had not fielded his best nine against his former Giants teammates and because league umpires were pro-New York, he was summoned to a league meeting to back up his charges. When he couldn't, he was banished for having "undermined the integrity of the game."

LEW FONSECA

Fonseca pioneered the use of film for detecting flaws in the swings of hitters and deliveries of pitchers. A batting champion for the 1929 Indians, the righty-hitting infielder initially got interested in the medium while playing a small part in the 1927 Joe E. Brown comedy *Slide, Kelly, Slide*. He was able to put his ideas into practice while managing the White Sox between 1932 and 1934. Fonseca later expanded his activities into providing an annual film review of American League highlights and a summary of World Series and All-Star Games for the armed forces during World War II. When the National League joined the program in 1946, he was appointed head of major league baseball's motion picture division—a position he held until the formation of the Major League Baseball Promotion Corporation in 1968.

BARRY FOOTE

Foote's greatest claim to fame after 10 major league seasons (1973–82) was that he was the highest-paid manager in minor league history. In 1984 he took over the Class A Fort Lauderdale club in the Yankees organization while working off an annual salary of more than $400,000 obtained a couple of years earlier when George Steinbrenner gave him a multiyear pact as a backup catcher.

RUSS FORD

The most successful early practitioner of the Emery Ball, Ford is the only pitcher besides Hall of Famers Christy Mathewson and Grover Cleveland Alexander to win 20 games and strike out 200 batters as a rookie. The righthander followed his 1910 season (26–2, 209 strikeouts) for the Yankees with a 22–11 effort, then slipped to an AL-leading 21 losses in 1912. He later had a third 20-win season, with the Federal League Buffalo Blues in 1914, and ended his career a year later with an overall 99–71 mark.

WHITEY FORD (Hall of Fame, 1974)

Ford was a very good pitcher who became a great one simply by being allowed to pitch in a four-man rotation instead of every fifth day. In 16 seasons, all of them with the Yankees, the lefthander won 236 games and compiled a .690 winning percentage—the third-highest ever and the best among 20th-century pitchers with 200 or more victories.

After a 9–1 rookie record in 1950 and two years in the Army, Ford quickly became the ace of the New York staff under manager Casey Stengel. Until 1960 the southpaw paced American League hurlers in victories and winning percentage once each and in ERA and shutouts twice apiece, but a 20-game season eluded him mostly because Stengel insisted that he was too small to pitch more than once every five days; in addition, the pilot often held him back from his regular turn for a big game in a subsequent series. The Yankees front office actually contemplated trading Ford to the Tigers for Al Kaline after a subpar 16–10 record in 1959, when a pulled tendon in his left arm was misdiagnosed as neuritis; a similar result in 1960 (12–9) did little to dispel a conclusion that his career—at least with the Yankees—was just about over.

After Ralph Houk replaced Stengel, however, Ford worked every four days, posting records of 25–4 in 1961 and 24–7 in 1963 to lead the AL in victories in both seasons but also developing a reputation as a seven-inning pitcher. While the perception had some validity (especially in 1961, when Luis Arroyo recorded 15 of his 29 saves in relief of Ford), it is also true that he topped AL hurlers in innings pitched for the only two times in his career in his two 20-win seasons.

Catcher Elston Howard dubbed Ford The Chairman of the Board for his uncanny ability to direct his fielders, but the pitcher and playmate Mickey Mantle called each other Slick for Stengel's reference to them as "a couple of whiskey slicks." While he was often a prominent part of late-night team carousing, Ford more often than not stayed in two nights before his scheduled starts and often convinced Mantle to stay in as well, thereby probably preventing the slugger from damaging himself even more than he did.

Especially in his later years on the mound, Ford became a master at doctoring the ball. Aside from developing a spitter, he came up with a scuffball with the help of a ring until umpire Hank Soar ordered him to remove the offending jewelry during a game; from that point on, it was Howard who provided the slash with a sharpened rivet on his shin guard. In addition, Ford learned how to throw a mud-ball from the Braves Warren Spahn and Lew Burdette during the 1957 World Series. His mudder led to a rule preventing pitchers from reaching for the resin bag while holding a ball in a bare hand, a trick the lefthander had used to rub a moistened ball in the dirt.

Ford holds the World Series records for both most victories (10) and most losses (8), a result of having pitched for 11 pennant winners in his 16-year career.

BILL FOSTER (Hall of Fame, 1996)

A half-brother of Rube, Foster was the Negro leagues' greatest lefthanded pitcher. The mainstay of the Chicago American Giants staff for more than a decade, he was a big part of the club's pennants in various leagues in 1926, 1927, 1932, and 1933—the final pennant coming in the inaugural season of the second Negro National League. In the 1926 playoffs against the first-half winner Kansas City Monarchs he pitched and won both ends of a doubleheader to clinch the pennant, then followed that up in the Negro World Series against the Bacharach Giants with two complete games (including a shutout), a relief appearance in a third contest, two wins, and a 1.27 ERA. In the following year's Series, the southpaw hurled two more complete games, relieved twice, and picked up two more victories. After managing the Giants in 1930, Foster jumped to the Homestead Grays in 1931 but, after beating the Kansas City Monarchs in a September contest, switched teams for the remainder of the season. After retiring he

coached at Alcorn State College until shortly before his death in 1978.

RUBE FOSTER (Hall of Fame, 1981)

Foster wore four hats—as a winning lefthander, a highly successful manager, the owner of the Chicago Black Giants, and the founder of the original Negro National League. As a southpaw, he was good enough to tutor Christy Mathewson in the screwball and to earn his own nickname by beating Rube Waddell of the Athletics in 1902; the victory over Waddell was one of 51 he won that year. In 1903 Foster posted a 54–1 record for the Cuban X-Giants, then beat the Philadelphia Giants four times in a postseason championship. The following year the lefthander jumped to the Philadelphia club and led them to the first of three consecutive championships by beating the X-Giants two out of three in the playoffs.

Beginning his managerial career with the Leland Giants in 1907, Foster piloted the team to records of 110–10 (in 1907) and 128–6 (in 1910) before forming the Black Giants in 1911. His partner in the venture was John Schorling, a Chicago saloonkeeper and a son-in-law of White Sox owner Charlie Comiskey; the connection enabled the new team to play its home games in Comiskey Park. So dominant were the Black Giants that, for more than a decade, they won almost every national black championship.

In the winter of 1919 Foster organized the original Negro National League, the first viable black professional league. As president and secretary of the circuit until 1926, he ruled autocratically, taking five percent of the gate from every game in lieu of a salary; as manager of the Black Giants, he ruled it on the field as well, winning the championship in the first three seasons.

BUD FOWLER

Second baseman Fowler became the first black to be paid for playing baseball when he signed with an otherwise all-white New Castle, Pennsylvania, team in 1872. Fowler played for dozens of teams, several of them part of white organized baseball, in a career that lasted until past the turn of the century. His birth in 1857 to migrant workers in Cooperstown, New York is the only known 19th-century connection between baseball and that village.

DICK FOWLER

Righthander Fowler won one game for the 1945 Athletics—a no-hitter over the Browns. He is the only pitcher to have accomplished this economical feat.

NELLIE FOX (Hall of Fame, 1997)

Fox was one of the slowest players on the Go-Go Sox of the 1950s and also the heart of the team. A lifetime .288 hitter, the lefty-swinging second baseman used one of the last of the slim-handled, wide-barreled bottle bats to win MVP honors in driving Chicago to a pennant in 1959. Four times during his 19-year (1947–65) career, he paced the American League in hits, also reaching the .300 mark six times. The quintessential contact hitter, 2,261 of his 2,663 safeties were one-basers, and he never struck out more than 18 times in a season. Defensively, he teamed with Luis Aparicio to forge the best middle infield in the AL in the 1950s and early 1960s. Fox's trade from the Athletics to the White Sox in 1949 for catcher Joe Tipton was the biggest steal in Chicago franchise history; the deal came about because Chicago manager Jack Onslow had traded punches with Tipton and demanded his removal.

JIMMIE FOXX (Hall of Fame, 1951)

Foxx was the righthanded complement to Babe Ruth and Lou Gehrig as the most potent American League sluggers of the 1920s and 1930s. In fact, he tied the two Yankees greats for the major league record of 100 or more RBIs in 13 seasons and also established a record of his own by clouting at least 30 homers in 12 consecutive years. A lifetime .325 hitter in 20 seasons with the Athletics, Red Sox, and several other clubs, Foxx knocked 534 home runs, drove in 1,922 runs, and compiled a .609 slugging percentage. He won a Triple Crown while with the Athletics in 1933; led the AL in batting one other season, for Boston in 1938; topped the AL in home runs in three additional seasons; and led in RBIs two more years. He also paced AL hitters in slugging five times, posting three season figures over the .700 mark. His 58 home runs in 1932 were as close as anyone came to Ruth's 60 until Roger Maris, and Foxx might have passed the 60-mark himself but for a wrist injury in August. Among his prodigious blasts were the first ever hit over the left field second tier at Comiskey Park (and clear across West 34th

Place) and one that broke a seat in the distant Yankee Stadium left field third deck.

Coming to the Athletics as a 17-year-old rookie receiver in 1925, Foxx backed up Mickey Cochrane and tried his hand at third base before manager Connie Mack installed him at first in 1929, in time for the first of three consecutive pennants. (Foxx hit .344 in the three World Series.) By 1935, however, Mack had sold off most of his stars to deal with one of his periodic cash shortages; when Mack asked Foxx to take a $6,000 pay cut for the 1936 season, the slugger uncharacteristically exploded, and Mack honored his request for a trade by selling him to Boston for $150,000 in December 1935. Aside from his own productive seasons at Fenway Park, he was on the scene to tutor the young Ted Williams in 1939.

As prodigious a drinker and spender as he was a hitter, Foxx choked to death on a piece of meat while dining with his brother in July 1967.

PAUL FOYTACK

On July 31, 1963 Angels righthander Foytack endured the embarrassment of surrendering four consecutive home runs. The blasts were hit by Woodie Held, Pedro Ramos, Tito Francona, and Larry Brown of Cleveland.

JOHN FRANCO

Franco entered the 2002 season with more saves (422) than any other lefthander in baseball history, second only to Lee Smith overall. Despite this, he has never inspired effusive confidence from hometown Mets fans, who have by and large treated his 11 years in a New York uniform as having to provide a roof for Cousin Johnny Who Eats Too Much. In an era that has prized late-inning *mano a mano* duels with fireball closers, at least part of the Shea Stadium attitude has traced to Franco's success with fadeaway sliders that make the batter look stupid more than the pitcher heroic. For all that, he has pitched longer for the Mets than anyone in franchise history but Jerry Koosman—a veteran status that has made him one of the rare hurlers (and only reliever) to be named team captain.

Franco's impressive bullpen numbers are not confined to trailing only Smith in the career saves category. Among active closers, for example, he has blown merely 36 games since taking over as the ace of Cincinnati's bullpen in 1986; as a point of comparison, Mariano Rivera, the Yankees closer since only 1997, had 34 blown saves going into the 2002 season. Moreover, with the exception of Tom Henke, Franco's 2.75 ERA is significantly lower than that of all relievers with a 10-year career; this includes not only Smith, but also such fabled bullpen aces as Bruce Sutter and Dennis Eckersley (counting only relief efforts).

TITO FRANCONA

Baseball's capricious rules for batting titlists claimed Francona as a victim in 1959, when the Cleveland outfielder averaged .363. Although that was 10 points higher than runner-up Harvey Kuenn, Francona was denied the crown because he fell one short of the required 400 official at bats. In other years, the lefty swinger would have been able to take advantage of regulations requiring only 100 games, a formula combining at bats with walks and hit batsmen into plate appearances, or artificially added plate appearances for reaching the minimum. In his 15-year career for a number of teams, Francona attained .300 in only two other seasons, closing out with a .272 mark.

HARRY FRAZEE

For more than 70 years Frazee has been the 26th player for the Red Sox—the one who erases all the successes of his teammates and makes sure Boston never wins another world championship. Worse, he has done everything possible to guarantee that New York teams win what Boston should have, whether it be his actual sale of Babe Ruth to the Bronx in December 1919 or his haunting presence over Bill Buckner in Flushing in October in 1986. In short, the Boston owner from 1917 to 1923 has been baseball's biggest ghost story.

A New York theatrical producer, Frazee bought the Red Sox from Joseph Lannin with more paper than cash, in the first transfer of an American League franchise completed without the complicity of founding president Ban Johnson. But within only months of taking over the club, Frazee had to hide behind no-comment replies to rumors that he had put the franchise back on the block merely to pay off what he owed Lannin. Unfortunately for future generations, however, Boston won the pennant and the World Series in 1918, making Frazee think he could make a go of it. That illusion lasted only several months when losses from the Broadway plays he was producing persuaded him to sell off such noted players as Ernie Shore, Duffy Lewis, Dutch Leonard, and Carl Mays. Even the fact that Shore, Lewis, and Mays went to the Yankees served as a mere prelude in Boston agitation to the sale of Ruth for $100,000 plus a $300,000 mortgage on Fenway Park. Frazee's immediate defense of the deal was that not even Ruth's burgeoning slugging after a few years of being a dominating pitcher had prevented the Red Sox from finishing sixth in 1919; what he didn't say was that the money received from New York went right back to Broadway to keep *No! No! Nanette* on the boards. And, as it turned out, the sale of Ruth was hardly the last transaction between the Yankees and Red Sox.

With the critical assistance of Ed Barrow, who in 1920 went from being Boston manager to New York general manager, Frazee sent the likes of Waite Hoyt, Herb Pennock, Everett Scott, Wally Schang, and George Pipgras south at the beginning of the decade. Even more revealing of the incestuous relationship between the teams, in October 1922 the Yankees acknowledged that one of the conditions of their "loan" in the Ruth transaction was that they should be "consulted" before Frazee completed any deal with another club. This came to light when Colonel Jake Ruppert protested a Boston-Detroit exchange that had brought pitcher Howard Ehmke to Fenway Park. Informed that New York had also been interested in Ehmke, Frazee's abject response was to claim that he had already cashed a Detroit check sent along with the pitcher, so he couldn't do Ruppert's bidding by canceling the deal.

Shortly after the Ehmke embarrassment, Frazee made a bigger mistake that ended up costing him the franchise. Anxious to cash another check, from Toronto of the International League for Frank O'Rourke, the owner forgot to secure waivers from the Phillies before shipping the outfielder to Canada. When Philadelphia protested, AL president Johnson, with whom Frazee had been at loggerheads since an abortive effort to install former U.S. President William Howard Taft as commissioner of baseball in 1918, used it to round up other alienated AL owners and force the producer to sell out to a consortium headed by Bob Quinn. It was with the advent of the Quinn ownership that Frazee became more of a spiritual than material director of the Red Sox misfortunes.

Hank Aaron (pg. 1) clouts his 714th career home run on April 4, 1974, in Cincinnati. *Photo reprinted courtesy of the Atlanta Braves.*

Sparky Anderson (pg. 10) is the only manager to win world championships for teams in both the American and National leagues. *Photo reprinted courtesy of the Cincinnati Reds.*

George Brett (pg. 41) was the Kansas City Royals' franchise player for two decades. *Photo reprinted courtesy of the Kansas City Royals.*

A favorite promotional stunt of Gussie Busch (pg. 48), longtime owner of the St. Louis Cardinals and the Anheuser-Busch company, was to drive around the stadium named after him in an old beer wagon. *Photo reprinted courtesy of the St. Louis Cardinals.*

The greatest all-around player of his time, Joe DiMaggio (pg. 102) transcended baseball to become a cultural icon. *Photo reprinted courtesy of the authors' personal collection.*

The untimely death of Roberto Clemente (pg. 72) made him a legend in his native Puerto Rico. *Photo reprinted courtesy of the Pittsburgh Pirates.*

ROY CAMPANELLA
catcher BROOKLYN DODGERS

Roy Campanella (pg. 53) was the last player to join the group of Dodgers who would come to be known as the "Boys of Summer." *Photo reprinted courtesy of the authors' private collection.*

Sam Crawford (pg. 86) is the all-time leader in triples. *Photo reprinted courtesy of the authors' private collection.*

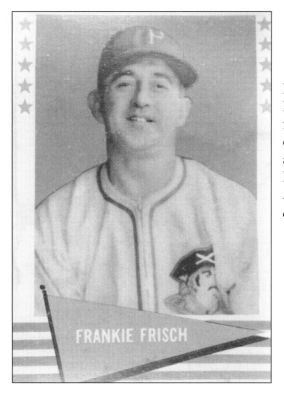

FRANKIE FRISCH

Frankie Frisch (pg. 141) managed the Pirates to a surprising second-place finish in 1944 but is better known as one of the greatest second basemen of all time and the pilot of the "Gas House Gang" Cardinals in the 1930s. *Photo reprinted courtesy of the authors' private collection.*

"Shoeless" Joe Jackson (pg. 207) was the only one of the infamous "Black Sox" who was of Hall of Fame caliber. *Photo reprinted courtesy of the authors' private collection.*

JOE JACKSON
RIGHT FIELD
CHICAGO "WHITE SOX" A. L.

The "G-Men"—Goose Goslin (pg. 159), Hank Greenberg (pg. 164), and Charlie Gehringer (pg. 151)—were the heart of the Detroit Tigers offense from 1934 to 1936. *Photo reprinted courtesy of the National Baseball Hall of Fame and Library, Cooperstown, N.Y.*

Joe Morgan (pg. 294) won consecutive Most Valuable Player awards with Cincinnati's "Big Red Machine" in 1975 and 1976. *Photo reprinted courtesy of the Cincinnati Reds.*

Hall of Fame third baseman George Kell (pg. 223) had the kind of numbers that are usually associated with players who just miss election to Cooperstown. *Photo reprinted courtesy of the authors' private collection.*

GEORGE FRAZIER

Frazier is the only pitcher to lose three games in a World Series. The reliever did it in the Yankees losing effort to the Dodgers in 1981; his ERA for the three games was 17.18. Curiously, the righthander did not feel the sting of owner George Steinbrenner until the following year when, toward the end of an August 3, 1982 doubleheader against the White Sox, Steinbrenner had Yankee Stadium public address announcer Bob Sheppard, the embarrassment apparent in his voice, offer each of the 34,000 fans present a free ticket to any future home game for having endured a 1–0 loss followed by a 14–2 drubbing. Frazier, the final victim in the nightcap, sat on the mound, his head hung in humiliation.

ANDREW FREEDMAN

Even in a business noted for crooks, incompetents, misers, and paranoids, Freedman, who controlled the New York Giants from 1895 until 1903, stood out on all counts. A real estate lawyer and bagman for Tammany Hall's Boss Croker, he characteristically accumulated Giants stock for what amounted to an unfriendly takeover not in his own name but in that of James Bailey—without bothering to inform the future circus impresario. Taking over the organization in January 1895, he immediately canceled all free passes and demanded that the Brooklyn franchise pull out of the league and leave the entire New York market to him; when Brooklyn owner Charles Byrne simply laughed, Freedman got his cronies on the City Council to make sure that none of the new subway lines planned for the city would go anywhere near Brooklyn's Washington Park.

The first conspicuous critic of Freedman's methods was Sam Crane of the New York *Commercial Advertiser*. When Crane accused the owner of trying to destroy the franchise, Freedman responded by voiding his press credentials and then alerting his ticket sellers not to allow him in the park even with a paid admission. When other New York writers came to Crane's defense, they were also put on his blacklist. Particular targets included the New York *Sun*, against which Freedman filed 25 unsuccessful lawsuits in five years, and *The New York Times*, whose beat writer the owner slugged for suggesting that he was the source of the franchise's problems. Freedman even engaged in a feud with venerable sportswriter Henry Chadwick, who ended up boycotting the Polo Grounds and urging his readers to do the same.

If anything, Freedman's relations with his managers and players were even worse than with the press. He employed 12 different managers—two of them twice each in eight years—but couldn't lift the team above seventh place more than once. Among the pilots who came and went with dizzying rapidity were Harvey Watkins, an actor and errand boy for Bailey; John B. Day, a former Giants owner who was down on his luck; Fred Hoey, a Tammany hanger-on who had no discernible baseball credentials; Horace Fogel, who tried to convert Christy Mathewson to a first baseman; Heinie Smith, who thought the future Hall of Fame righthander would make a better shortstop than first baseman; and John McGraw, who would survive Freedman with the franchise by three decades. He alienated ace pitcher Amos Rusie over a $200 fine for a trumped-up charge, causing a rift that included a year-long sitdown by the righthander. He overplayed an ugly anti-Semitic remark by former Giant Ducky Holmes into a firestorm that saw the National League suspend Holmes, players around the league threaten a boycott of Giants games, and a judge order the Baltimore outfielder's reinstatement.

Freedman's genius for making trouble reached its apex with his presentation in 1901 of a scheme, actually concocted by Cincinnati owner John T. Brush, to syndicalize the NL by pooling all players and reassigning them to teams each season. The proposed trust called for the Giants to hold 30 percent of the stock; Boston, St. Louis, and Cincinnati to retain 12 percent each; and Philadelphia, Chicago, Pittsburgh, and Brooklyn to accept 10 to six percent each. The issue came down to a choice for NL president at the December 1901 league meeting, with Freedman and the three 12 percenters favoring incumbent Nick Young, and the four projected minority stockholders advancing the candidacy of Al Spalding. The comic opera affair ended with the election of compromise candidate Harry Pulliam, the demise of the syndicate baseball scheme, and the end of the NL's patience with Freedman, who had been tolerated only because his Tammany connections had kept Ban Johnson's American League from entering the New York market. With the election of reform mayor Seth Low in 1901, however, Freedman's usefulness to other owners frayed at the edges. Although still in titular control of the franchise, he was a mere by-stander to Brush's machinations to collapse the AL Baltimore franchise in the middle of the 1902 season and bring its manager, McGraw, and several of its stars to the Polo Grounds. Brush finally took over formal control of the Giants from Freedman in 1903.

M. C. FREY

A diminutive Swedish physician hired by the Reds in 1898, Frey was the first team doctor. Although he knew virtually nothing about baseball, Frey's reliance on massage to cure most ills proved popular with the players; despite his popularity, he quit after two years to become a jockey.

FORD FRICK (Hall of Fame, 1970)

Frick's chief claim to being in the Hall of Fame was that, as National League president in the 1930s, he was a prominent supporter of establishing the Cooperstown museum to help mark baseball's 1939 chimerical centennial. As both league president and later commissioner, on the other hand, he was rarely more than a mascot for major league owners. On one of the rare occasions that he did assert himself, he played a major part in averting a strike by Cardinals players who were reluctant to take the field for the first time against Jackie Robinson. On another, however, the results were less edifying when he insisted in 1961 that the record books would carry an asterisk if Roger Maris succeeded in surpassing Babe Ruth's mark of 60 home runs in a season.

Frick worked himself up to the game's biggest titles after working as a reporter and an NL public relations officer. He took over the NL office in 1934, remaining there until his election as commissioner in 1951. His presidency was largely subordinated to the sway of Commissioner Kenesaw Landis—a relationship he reversed when he himself moved into the commissioner's office, ruling again and again that issues brought to him were the prerogative of one of the leagues. His most significant moment as NL chief came when he had St. Louis owner Sam Breadon read a statement to the Cardinals players before their first 1947 game with Brooklyn that threatened "If you do strike, you will be suspended from the league." His other major move as a league official came in 1943, when he arranged the sale of the Phillies to lumber magnate William Cox; Cox was later blacklisted by Landis for placing bets on his own team.

Frick won the first of two seven-year elections as commissioner after big league owners had to concede failure in their attempts to find a military man for the post; his chief supporter as a compromise candidate was Brooklyn owner Walter O'Malley. It was hardly a coincidence that O'Malley reigned during Frick's tenure as the first among equals within ownership circles. The closest the two men had to a public disagreement was in 1958 over the ground rules for the left field fence of the Los Angeles Coliseum, Frick insisting that a second fence be erected behind a planned one only 250 feet away from the batter's box and that any balls dropping between the two would be declared ground-rule doubles; he lost that argument to the Dodgers boss with the discovery of some arcane California earthquake regulation. On the other hand, he was a passive spectator to O'Malley's move to Los Angeles from Brooklyn, as well as to other transfers by the Giants, Braves, Athletics, Browns, and Senators.

In 1961 Frick used the excuse of the recently introduced 162-game schedule to announce midway through the season that anyone surpassing the Ruth record after a 154th game, the number under the old schedule, would have an asterisk next to his name; at the same time, he declined to apply the same criterion to other records affected by the extra contests. What he also failed to mention was that he had been a relatively close associate of Ruth's and had even ghostwritten the slugger's autobiography. In some measure because of the asterisk ruling, only 23,154 were in attendance when Maris hit his 61st home run at Yankee Stadium in the 162nd game of the year. Commissioner Bowie Kuhn later deleted the asterisk.

It was also during Frick's tenure as commissioner that the Hall of Fame established a standing Veterans Committee for electing players and officials no longer eligible for voting by sportswriters. It was the Veterans Committee that elected him to Cooperstown in 1970. Later on, the Hall of Fame named its special honors for broadcasting personnel the Ford C. Frick Award.

BOB FRIEND

Friend's 16-year (1951–66) record of 197–230 makes him the only major league hurler to have lost more than 200 games without winning at least 200. The righthander broke in with the dreary Pirates of the early 1950s and earned his status as the staff ace by leading the National League in ERA in 1955 for his last-place club. With Pittsburgh on the rise by 1958, Friend also topped the league with his 22 wins. In tirelessness he ranked second in the league only to Robin Roberts, breaking a five-year streak by the Phillies righthander for the most innings pitched by topping the NL in that category in both 1956 and 1957.

DAN FRIEND

A southpaw by trade, Friend played left field for the Cubs for two-thirds of an inning against the Giants on August 30, 1897, and cost his team the game without ever touching the ball. With New York leading, 7–5, in the top of the ninth inning, Chicago manager Cap Anson was ejected from the game for arguing with home plate umpire Bob Emslie about the twilight playing conditions. The Cubs went on to score five runs and take the lead, but in the bottom of the ninth the regular left fielder had to go to first base to replace Anson, with Friend recruited for the outfield. The only problem was that he had already showered and dressed, so he took his position wearing a bathrobe over his street clothes and with only his uniform hat in place. New York manager Bill Joyce raved so long to Emslie about the rule violation that the umpire finally realized that it had become too dark to continue, declaring the game over and reverting the score to the 7–5 Giants lead.

FRANKIE FRISCH (Hall of Fame, 1947)

One of John McGraw's balkier disciples, Frisch was a speeding arrogance in 19 years (1919–37) of playing and 16 years of managing (between 1933 and 1951) who always seemed to invite deflating. He never had any trouble finding someone to do the job.

A switch-hitting second baseman known as The Fordham Flash for captaining the baseball, football, and basketball teams at the Bronx university, Frisch took a couple of years to get his feet wet with the Giants before bursting through with a .341 mark and a league-leading 49 steals in 1923. It was the first of 11 straight seasons in which he batted .300 and the first of three times that he would pace the National League in thefts. His other significant numbers include reaching 200 hits three times, cracking 30 doubles eight times, scoring 100 runs seven times, and driving in 100 three times. A defensive whiz at second base, setting the season record for the most as-

sists (641) in 1927. The combination of superior hitting and fielding left him only a couple of votes short of an MVP trophy in 1927 but netted him the award four years later.

Frisch's son-father relationship with McGraw made for stormy times on the Giants in the 1920s. In 1924 the infielder was implicated in an attempted bribe of Philadelphia shortstop Heinie Sand, but he was ultimately exonerated in good part because of his manager's intervention with Commissioner Kenesaw Landis. McGraw wasn't so understanding otherwise, however, and Frisch's bearing as a younger alter ego acted only to make him the pilot's favorite whipping boy when New York stumbled on the field. In August 1926 he finally broke under McGraw's hectoring and jumped the team for several days. After the season, McGraw traded him to the Cardinals in a stunning swap for Rogers Hornsby, deliberately throwing in journeyman pitcher Jimmy Ring so Frisch didn't entertain the thought he was worth Hornsby straight up.

For the next 10 years Frisch was the field brain of the St. Louis club that evolved into the Gas House Gang in the 1930s. He was so determined to show up McGraw in 1927 that his dazzling hitting (.337), running (a league-leading 48 steals), and fielding were described by some teammates even decades later as the single greatest season they had ever seen a player enjoy. Another result of the performance was that it took Cardinals owner Sam Breadon off the hook with St. Louis fans who had vehemently protested the departure of Hornsby. For the first part of 1933 the fans appeared to have their cake and be able to eat it too when Hornsby returned amid rumors that he was about to begin a second tour of duty as manager. Instead, Breadon announced in July that Hornsby was being released, incumbent manager Gabby Street was being fired, and Frisch would take over as player-manager.

Although the Gas House Gang was the most colorful NL team of the 1930s, it actually won its only pennant and world championship in 1934. Frisch's contributions to the effort were another .300 season and a masterly manipulation of a pitching staff that, beyond the Dean brothers, was decidedly mediocre. In the seventh game of the World Series against the Tigers, he cracked a bases-loaded double in the third inning that climaxed a seven-run outburst and put Detroit so far into the hole that disgruntled Tigers fans started pelting outfielder Joe Medwick with fruit, causing a near-riot. Over the next few years, while unable to steer the club any higher than second, Frisch himself was a series of mini-riots over the predilection of such charges as Dizzy Dean and Pepper Martin for sticking a pin in his ever-ready gruffness; rare was the week that he wasn't the target of a water balloon or that he wasn't threatening to trade one of the team cutups. But what also became clear from the incidents, especially from Martin's continued stay on the club, was that he maintained slightly more room between egotism and pompousness than his mentor McGraw ever had.

After retiring as a player in 1937 with a .316 average, Frisch showed less interest in managing and was replaced shortly afterward by Mike Gonzalez. He reemerged as manager of the Pirates in 1940 for what turned out to be a seven-year stint, most of it during the war years when organizations rarely blamed managers or wanted to hire new ones for the 4F teams on the field. Frisch's best moment in Pittsburgh came in 1944, when he guided the club to an unexpected second-place finish. On the other hand, his tenure was marked by constant personality clashes with the team's best players (Arky Vaughan, Vince DiMaggio, Bob Elliott) that both sent him into deep brooding and prompted him to press for stupid trades. Team morale was considered so bad by 1946 that Robert Murphy, head of the American Baseball Guild, picked the Pirates as an ideal testing ground for his attempts to unionize major leaguers. Murphy didn't succeed but not because of any player solidarity with Frisch.

Frisch's last uniform was that of the Chicago Cubs, whom he managed from the middle of 1949 to the middle of 1951. After some initial boasting that he and general manager Charlie Grimm were going to turn around the second-division franchise with some key trades, they made the mistake of getting into locked rooms with Brooklyn's Branch Rickey and Boston's Lou Perini, achieving nothing but giving away the Wrigley family's money for players who had mostly reached their level at Triple A. It was another trade in which he was not involved directly, however, that ended Frisch's tenure with the Cubs: After Wid Matthews announced the June 1951 deal that dispatched local favorite Andy Pafko to Brooklyn, the manager was overheard agreeing with most Chicago fans that the general manager

had been swindled by the Dodgers. He was fired shortly afterward.

Frisch had a sportscasting career linked to the televising of Giants games for awhile in the 1950s. It was from that forum that he became popularly identified with his signature moan of "Ooooh, those bases on balls!"

A dominant force on the Veterans Committee from 1967 until his death in 1973, Frisch was instrumental in giving Hall of Fame plaques to former teammates Dave Bancroft, Ross Youngs, and George Kelly (with the Giants) and Jesse Haines and Chick Hafey (with the Cardinals).

EMIL FUCHS

Fuchs was the most colorful of the early-century Boston Braves owners who got their hands on the franchise because of John McGraw and who then showed their gratitude by agreeing to just about any trade the Giants manager proposed. A former judge and assistant attorney general for New York State (and, before that, a lawyer who numbered among his clients gambling kingpin Arnold Rothstein), he differed from such predecessors as George Washington Grant in actually living in Boston (rather than New York) and going out of his way to win over a New England press hostile to the years-long manipulations of the franchise from Manhattan. But most of the rest of his tenure as owner in the 1920s and early 1930s was marked by one fiasco after another, not least his stint at manager of the team in 1929.

While sitting on the bench, the Judge, as he preferred to be called, would make such moves as yanking a righthanded hitter in favor of a lefty even when the opposition had a southpaw on the mound; questioned about a decision of the kind, his usual reply was that he hadn't noticed who had been pitching. He didn't think too much of the squeeze play, either, lecturing his players that it wasn't "an honorable way" of scoring a run. National League umpires usually dreaded working Braves games because of another Fuchs habit: recounting long-winded stories to his charges in the middle of crucial game situations, the tales preventing batters from going up to the plate and adding an average half-hour to Boston games. In the end, however, it was the Judge as owner rather than the Judge as manager that led to his demise.

Sinking under debt, Fuchs announced during the

1934 winter meetings that he intended converting Braves Field into a dog racing track and moving the Braves into Fenway Park. Unfortunately, he had failed to mention this to Red Sox owner Tom Yawkey, who promptly rejected any idea of sharing Boston's American League park. When it emerged subsequently that the dog track idea had been pressed on Fuchs by Braves Field stockholders bent on evicting the baseball team because it was a losing financial proposition, the National League had to step in to mediate the crisis; one key consequence was that Fuchs was given six months to resolve his money problems or sell the club. The coup de grâce came when the Judge hired Babe Ruth—in his eyes as a gate attraction, but in the Bambino's as the club's imminent manager. When Ruth discovered that he had no chance of taking over the reins of the club, he lashed out bitterly at Fuchs and soon afterward announced his retirement. The controversy was the last straw for the league, which gratefully accepted the Judge's resignation as team president in July.

PAUL FUGIT

Fugit was at the center of the last baseball scandal involving collusion with gamblers to throw games. The first baseman-manager of the Houma club in the Class D Evangeline League in 1946, Fugit hit .327 with 23 homers and 130 RBIs and piloted the team to a championship. He also became involved in a conspiracy with Louisiana gamblers and teammates Bill Thomas, Leonard Pecou, and Alvin Kaiser, as well as Don Vettorel of the Abbeville team to fix playoff games; all five were expelled from organized baseball. Although the incident occurred in the low minors, it sensitized the baseball establishment to the dangers of association with gamblers and, breaking as it did in December 1946, contributed to the harshness of Brooklyn manager Leo Durocher's one-year suspension for such associations the following spring.

DAVE FULTZ

A .271 outfielder for four teams between 1898 and 1905, Fultz attempted to make a larger mark by organizing the Base Ball Players Fraternity in 1912. Backed at the beginning of the venture by a majority of players on 13 teams, the New York University Law School graduate confronted the National Commission with the decidedly modest goal of assuring that both owners and players lived up to the terms of contracts; even at its most radical, the Players Fraternity never staked out a position more extreme than a request for a five-year limit on each player's reserve clause. The Commission, composed of the two league presidents and Reds owner Garry Herrmann, vacillated between ignoring the Fraternity and expressing a willingness to meet with its representatives as long as they were not accompanied by Fultz, whom they termed an outsider and an agitator. That approach lasted until November 1913, when about 500 major and minor league players threatened not to sign their contracts for the 1914 season unless the Commission acted on their grievances; their victory—on such minor points as agreement to provide each player with a copy of his contract and written notification of the details behind trades and releases—had more to do with the impending threat posed by the Federal League than with any negotiating skill on Fultz's part.

The peace was only temporary, however, unraveling as soon as the Fraternity president refused to condemn the Feds. Fultz and the players involved emerged as victors in claims brought by pitcher Casey Hageman and first baseman Clarence Kraft, but the first came only after a protracted legal battle and the second only when the owners declined to test the players' will to participate in a strike called by Fultz. In later years the Fraternity concentrated on improving conditions for minor leaguers. It was, in fact, in response to the rejection of demands made on their behalf in 1916 that Fultz made a fatal error—calling, for the second time, upon the organization's by then 1,215 members to strike. At first several hundred major leaguers, most notably Tris Speaker, were prepared to walk out in solidarity with the minor leaguers. Then, realizing that with the demise of the Feds they were risking permanent unemployment, enough of them signed contracts for the 1917 season to force Fultz to cancel the action. Although the Fraternity was to last on paper for another year, its effectiveness ended when Fultz released the strike's supporters from their pledges.

CARL FURILLO

Furillo was the quintessential blue-collar player of the Boys of Summer Dodgers. Despite falling merely one hit short of a career .300 average for 15 seasons, winning a batting title, shining as a clutch hitter, and possessing the best right field arm among his contemporaries, he seldom received the respect accorded his numerous Hall of Fame teammates. Part of the trouble stemmed from a tight-lipped personality that furnished neither the anger nor the geniality that made other Brooklyn players of the 1950s good copy. Another problem was the almost annual lull the righthand-hitting outfielder fell into between early June and mid-July, when All-Star Game voters were prone to selecting players on the basis of recent heroics. Aside from this regular slump, however, Furillo was, with Jackie Robinson, the Brooklyn player most likely to curl an opposing pitcher's hairs by stepping into the batter's box with the game on the line.

Furillo's special cachet in the eyes of Brooklyn fans was his ferocious play against the Giants. This was never more apparent than on September 6, 1953, when, after being struck on the wrist by a Ruben Gomez fastball and jeered at by New York manager Leo Durocher, he charged into the Giants bench. With umpire Babe Pinelli shouting "Get him, Carl, get him!" Furillo swung at everybody around him. He emerged from the melee with a broken hand that sidelined him for the rest of the year—but that also allowed him to sit on a league-leading average that was not surpassed.

To a great extent, Furillo's defensive play, and especially his mastery of the right field scoreboard in Ebbets Field, overshadowed his offensive skills. It was not unusual for him to throw out hitters at first base or to turn apparent singles into forceouts by getting the ball to second before a runner could advance 90 feet. His throwing darts earned him the nickname of The Reading Rifle, while his reading of line drives earned him the gratitude of Brooklyn clothier Abe Stark, whose right field advertisement promised a new suit of clothes to any batter hitting the sign.

Furillo's 15 years with the Dodgers were framed at both ends by unhappy episodes. Along with Dixie Walker and Bobby Bragan, he was one of the chief resisters to the presence of Robinson on the club in 1947. Branch Rickey talked Furillo out of his posture, spreading the impression that the outfielder was an ignorant dupe of the other two players. In 1960 Los Angeles general manager Buzzie Bavasi demanded that the veteran accept a minor league demotion for what were termed "temporary roster problems." Furillo not only said no, but following his outright release from the team, he gave testimony before a congressional committee on the reserve clause and sued the Dodgers for breach of contract. Although he won the suit, he was effectively blackballed from baseball. This was borne home in 1962, when not even the newly created Mets, hungry for any player with an Ebbets Field background, could find room for him.

G

EDDIE GAEDEL

Gaedel was the star of Bill Veeck's most famous production. On August 19, 1951, between games of a doubleheader, the St. Louis owner celebrated the American League's 50th birthday with an oversized birthday cake out of which popped the three-foot, seven-inch Gaedel wearing a Browns uniform with the number $1/8$. The festivities were mere prelude to what followed, however, as Gaedel, armed with a toy bat and threatened by Veeck with a violent end if he used it, marched to the plate as a pinch-hitter for leadoff batter Frank Saucier in the first inning of the second game. Assured by manager Zack Taylor that the midget had signed a valid contract, umpire Ed Hurley let Gaedel keep his appointment with baseball immortality—a base on balls issued by Detroit's Bob Cain, whose laughter as much as Gaedel's one-and-a-half-inch strike zone contributed to his wildness.

Veeck and Gaedel teamed together for several other stunts over the next decade. In 1960 Gaedel and three other midgets, all dressed as Martians, helicoptered onto the infield at Comiskey Park for a meeting with Luis Aparicio and Nellie Fox, then notified the crowd that they had arrived to assist the dimunitive double play combination in their struggle against earthlings. The final Veeck stunt involving Gaedel was the employment of midget vendors on Opening Day of 1961 in Comiskey in response to fans who had complained that hot dog and peanut salesmen blocked their view of the game. Gaedel died the following June; the only baseball figure in attendance at his funeral was Cain.

JAMES GAFFNEY

Gaffney was the most ambitious of the New York-based owners who ran the Braves in the first part of the 20th century. A former policeman who had built up a fortune as a contractor through his use of Tammany Hall contacts, he was brought into the Boston franchise by John Montgomery Ward, the former Giant who needed some conspicuous financial backing for his grand plans for overhauling the team. Gaffney ended up doing most of the overhauling himself when Ward belatedly realized that other owners were not ready to deal with the player-lawyer who had bested so many of them in courtrooms over contract disputes.

Gaffney's first innovation was renaming the club he had invested in; inspired by the nickname used by Tammany Hall politicians, he ended years of switches from Beaneaters to Nationals and from Doves to Rustlers by calling the team the Braves and redesigning uniforms so that they bore the profile of a Native American warrior. His second most significant contribution was in ordering construction of a new ballpark after Boston had been playing for almost four decades in dilapidated South End Grounds. He had ideas about what the new Braves Field should look like, too: Convinced that fans were more entertained by seeing runners scoot around the bases than by watching balls disappear into outfield seats, he insisted that the park be spacious enough to encourage inside-the-park home runs. The result was a field that measured 420 feet down each foul line and 550 feet to dead center. It would not be until 1925, 10 years after the opening of the facility, that a Boston player would be able to reach the left field seats even in batting practice; some weeks after outfielder Bernie Neis managed that feat, New York catcher Frank Snyder walloped the first official home run into the area.

As for teams that played within such grand confines, Gaffney quickly tired of Ward's inability to complete deals with other National League clubs and forced him out of the organization. Although nominally taking charge himself, he brought in George Stallings as manager and chief negotiator, giving the veteran baseball man a free hand to clean house with the cellar-dwelling team. The result in 1914 was the Miracle Braves world championship. But with the club not quite able to repeat in 1915 and faced with too many due notes over the construction of Braves Field, Gaffney decided to get out while the getting was good. A terse announcement in January of 1916 said only that he had sold the franchise to a consortium of bankers and politicians for a price "considerably higher" than the $187,000 he had produced at Ward's urging.

JOHN GAHERIN

Appointed in 1967 as the first head of the Player Relations Committee, Gaherin made his mark by warning the owners that the reserve clause would not hold up against free agency demands and by arguing for a negotiated settlement on the issue. The former labor negotiator for the newspaper and airline industries was fired early in 1977 after reaching an accord on the details of free agency with the Players Association in the wake of the Messersmith-McNally case. Accused of having given away the store, he was essentially canned for failing to prevent what he had predicted would happen unless his bosses changed their approach.

ANDRES GALARRAGA

When Galarraga won the 1993 National League batting title as a member of the Rockies, it marked the first time that a player on a new expansion club led the way in any significant hitting category. The first baseman's .370 average was also the highest posted by a righthanded hitter since Joe DiMaggio's .381 in 1939. In his two previous seasons the injury-afflicted and strikeout-prone Galarraga had batted only .243 and .219. In 1996 and 1997 he led the NL in RBIs (with 150 and 140, respectively), also topping the league in homers (with 47) in 1996. De-spite predictions his production would decline without the friendly Denver atmosphere, he moved on to Atlanta as a free agent in 1998 and proceeded to belt 44 home runs and drive home another 121. That made him the first player ever to post back-to-back 40-homer seasons for different clubs. Galarraga sat out the 1999 campaign while receiving chemotherapy for non-Hodgkin's lymphoma in his back, but then rebounded in 2000 with another 100-RBI year for the Braves. The Big Cat, as he has been called for his defensive agility around first base, appeared to wear down with the Rangers in 2001, but was then dealt to the Giants and came back still again for a solid second half.

DANIEL GALBREATH

Galbreath took over as president of the Pirates from his father John just as the club was pulling up stakes after 61 years at Forbes Field and moving into Three Rivers Stadium. It proved a symbolic co-incidence insofar as the stadium came to dominate his ownership.

John Galbreath, a Columbus realtor and horse breeder, had been in Pittsburgh's executive suites since 1946, when he joined Indianapolis banker Frank McKinney and entertainer Bing Crosby in purchasing the franchise from Barney Dreyfuss's widow. After buying out McKinney in July 1950, he entrusted the club's baseball affairs, first, to Branch Rickey and, then, to Joe L. Brown. With only one pennant to show for all that time, however, Daniel arrived on the scene with a decidedly less passive approach. The good news was that Pittsburgh won East Division titles in 1970, 1971, 1972, 1974, and 1975, as well as a world championship in 1971; the bad news was that the new president was far from satisfied with merely one World Series appearance and pressured Brown to resign. Making his nerves even more frayed was the severe economic weather that hung over Pittsburgh most of the 1970s, sharply reducing attendance.

In 1981 Galbreath decided to make Three Rivers Stadium the focus of his exasperation and demanded that the city renegotiate its rental terms; among other things, he wanted City Hall to foot the bill for repairs, maintenance, and new access roads, claiming this was the only way for the franchise to reverse a reported $6 million in losses and prevent it from having to be sold or transferred to another city. As soon as the latter threat was aired, New Orleans Superdome general manager Cliff Wallace sought to lure the club to Louisiana—a bid that prompted the City of Pittsburgh to file a preventive suit.

Galbreath kept up the pressure over the next couple of years, winning nominal concessions here and there but never disavowing completely persistent rumors of the club's imminent move out of Pittsburgh. In 1983 he tried another revenue path by taking on Warner Communications as a 48-percent partner, but after only a few months of reports that the media giant's involvement was a prelude to some pay-per-view scheme for covering Pirates games, both sides abruptly announced that they wanted out from one another. Finally, in 1986, Galbreath sold the franchise to a local public-private consortium headed by Mayor Richard Caliguiri.

DENNY GALEHOUSE

Galehouse contributed so mightily to Boston baseball lore that Red Sox fans presented him with the new first name of Why—as in Why Galehouse? The question was asked in 1948 after manager Joe McCarthy ignored his rested aces Mel Parnell and Ellis Kinder in favor of the journeyman righthander for the winner-take-all playoff game that year against Cleveland. Galehouse was quickly battered around, giving the Indians the pennant. McCarthy always justified his pitching selection by noting that earlier in the season Galehouse had relieved Parnell in the first inning of a game against Cleveland and surrendered only two hits in an eight-inning-plus victory. What the manager didn't say was that his playoff pick had also been shellacked in two subsequent regular-season efforts against the Indians.

JIM GALLAGHER

Sportswriter Gallagher was hired as the Cubs general manager in 1941 after boasting that he could do better than the club's incumbent front office people. He spent most of the next 15 years making bad trades, skirmishing with perceived rivals within the organization, and being bounced up and down the franchise hierarchy. During his first few years as head of baseball operations, he also assured the hostility of the Chicago press toward the club by refusing to announce player transactions and even having beat writers informed of daily lineups through the field announcer just prior to the start of games. His

reasoning was that local newspapers had attacked the franchise unfairly, so he owed them little cooperation. Most of the players Gallagher was talked out of by other general managers ended up on the Dodgers; prominent among them were future Hall of Famers Billy Herman and Eddie Stanky. Not that this won him gratitude from Brooklyn president Branch Rickey, who once described the official as "nothing more than a glorified office boy."

Even Gallagher has his moments, though. The first was in persuading owner Phil Wrigley that Chicago needed a farm system if it expected to compete in the National League. Although the minor league chain never achieved the productivity of the Brooklyn and St. Louis systems, it at least made the club less reliant on short-range deals. Gallagher was also nimble enough not to look a gift horse in the mouth when the Yankees offered him Hank Borowy in 1945—a move that was decisive in the team's last pennant. His own best deal was acquiring outfielders Hank Sauer and Frankie Baumholtz from the Reds in 1949.

During World War II Gallagher offered a proposal that won the enmity of players and owners for diametrically opposed reasons. Arguing that the war would not only pare major league talent to the bone but would also leave a scarcity of good players after the hostilities because of expected casualties, he dusted off an early-century scheme for pooling those who remained among big league clubs. According to Gallagher, such a syndication plan should eventually lead to a rewriting of baseball contracts, including the elimination of the reserve clause. While players objected to the prospect of losing their contractual rights, owners blasted the idea as a threat to franchise integrity. For St. Louis owner Sam Breadon, for instance, the Gallagher proposal was "unthinkable, unworkable . . . an offspring of socialism that has no place in baseball."

PUD GALVIN (Hall of Fame, 1965)

As troublesome as he was effective in a 14-year career, primarily with the National League Buffalo Bisons and Pittsburgh clubs in three different leagues, Galvin was the first 300-game winner. A holdout in 1880, the righthander hid in a California outlaw league until Buffalo sent someone to retrieve him. Three years later he agreed to jump to the American Association's Pittsburgh Alleghenys but reneged under threats of legal action. Back with the Bisons and not in a pretty mood, he almost bolted again when he decided the team's new blue uniforms made him look fat. Between 1890 and 1892 Galvin faced Tim Keefe in the first four meetings of 300-game winners and the last such contests until Phil Niekro and Don Sutton opposed each other in 1986. Galvin ended with 361 victories.

CHICK GANDIL

If any of the Black Sox players can be said to be responsible for the scandal surrounding the 1919 World Series, it was Gandil. It was the first baseman who planned the fix as early as August, who initiated contacts with gamblers three weeks before the Series, and who kept the plot moving in the face of various double crosses and defections. Since he had already retired, he was also the only one of the Chicago Eight not devastated by Commissioner Kenesaw Landis's 1920 ban of the implicated White Sox players.

Prior to his involvement in the scandal, Gandil had been a .277 hitter for Chicago, Washington, and Cleveland. In 1927 he resurfaced briefly to support charges by Swede Risberg, another of the outlawed White Sox players, that Ty Cobb's Tigers had thrown back-to-back doubleheaders to Chicago in 1917. The charges were dismissed by Landis but prompted a series of new regulations covering gambling in baseball.

RON GANT

Gant incurred the most expensive broken leg in baseball history in 1994 when the injury cost him $4 million. The outfielder was disabled by a motorcycle accident shortly after signing a one-year $5-million pact with the Braves. Despite the fact that Gant had provided most of the righthanded power for three Atlanta division winners between 1991 and 1993, the team decided to cut its losses by paying him a required $900,000 before a March 15 spring training deadline and release him as a free agent.

JIM GANTNER

A .274-hitting second baseman with the Brewers from 1976 to 1992, Gantner was a latter-day Yogi Berra—but without the notoriety. Among his mala-props was the observation that "The most important thing for a infielder is to be up on the palms of your feet." On another occasion he sought to point out that an opposing player had impeded the progress of a runner by telling an umpire: "That's construction! That's construction!" Another time he told teammates he would be spending the winter "fishing up in those Canadian proverbs."

JOE GARAGIOLA

Garagiola was one of the first players to turn a mediocre playing career (1946–54) into the fodder for a successful sportscasting one. Especially after the publication of his best-selling *Baseball Is a Funny Game,* he became identified with the foibles of playing with such bad teams as the Pirates and the Cubs of the 1950s. Garagiola wasn't quite so comic, however, when he was one of the more conspicuous rednecks on the Cardinals teams of the late 1940s who never missed the opportunity to spike Jackie Robinson or taunt the Brooklyn infielder from the bench; in the 1970s, he also testified on the side of the owners against Curt Flood's challenge to the reserve clause. In recent years he has been a visible spokesman for the BAT assistance program for needy former major leaguers and for anti-tobacco-chewing groups.

DANNY GARDELLA

For the first couple of years of his brief career in 1944 and 1945, Gardella mainly entertained sportswriters with his efforts to play the outfield and his New York Giants teammates with an endless series of practical gags. He was in fact such an inept defensive player that one wit thought it informative to add the word "unassisted" to a recording of his putouts; he was so committed to getting a laugh that he once spent a week portraying himself to a roommate as a would-be suicide, then one morning threw open the window of their 20th-floor hotel room and hid out on the ledge while raising blood-curdling screams of a suicide plunging to his death. But that Gardella ended in 1946, when he became one of the first major leaguers to accept cash from the Pasquel brothers and jump to Mexico.

Like the other jumpers, Gardella was banned for five years by Commissioner Happy Chandler; unlike them, he didn't accept the ban and, after returning to the U.S., filed a $300,000 suit in terms guaranteed to question baseball's exemption from antitrust laws. Although the basis for his suit was found invalid in a first go-round in July 1948, an appeals tribunal not only upheld his claim about the illegality of the Chandler blacklist, but also issued a blistering indictment of organized baseball that effectively reversed the 1922 Supreme Court verdict that declared the sport didn't engage in interstate commerce; a principal point of the ruling was that the radio and television coverage of games alone constituted an adequate definition of interstate commerce.

With a U.S. Supreme Court hearing on the Gardella suit imminent and fearing too many headlines of any kind until the final verdict, Chandler was persuaded by the leagues to drop his ban and announce an "amnesty" for players he suddenly regarded as "basically good boys." The ploy worked: Gardella settled out of court for $60,000. His own hopes of returning to the majors, however, were quickly scotched: He managed only one further at bat—for the 1950 Cardinals.

BRUCE GARDNER

An All-American pitcher for the University of Southern California in 1960, Gardner recorded a 40–5 record and struck out 280 batters in his three-year (1958–60) college career. Marked for stardom, he was signed by the Dodgers, but after going 20–4 for Reno of the Class C California League in 1961, the lefthander languished in the minors until 1964 when an arm injury ended his career. Seven years later Gardner blew his brains out on the mound of USC's Bovard Field after leaving a suicide note for coach Rod Dedeaux that blasted the school's athletic program and the expectations it created in its amateur athletes.

WAYNE GARLAND

Garland received the first career-long contract after the coming of free agency, signing a $2.5 million, 10-year pact with Cleveland in 1976. When he told his mother the news, she replied: "You're not worth it." Many in Cleveland agreed with her when the righthander, who had won 20 for Baltimore the year before, managed only 13 victories and then suffered a rotator cuff injury. His overall record was 55–66.

STEVE GARVEY

The first-base anchor for the long-running Dodgers infield (with Davey Lopes, Bill Russell, and Ron Cey) in the 1970s, Garvey managed the difficult trick of having one public image overwhelm appreciable diamond skills, then having a second one totally contradict the first. As a player for Los Angeles, he was second only to manager Tommy Lasorda as a relentless flack for the "bleeding Dodger blue" way of playing baseball, honoring one's parents, and saluting the flag. Constantly portrayed as Mr. Clean, he had to labor for years to persuade cynical observers that he was in fact a durable performer (he still holds the National League record of 1,207 consecutive games played); a great clutch hitter; and, despite not having an arm, the savior of the club's infield through regular acrobatic leaps for the errant tosses of Lopes, Russell, and Cey. The cynical observers included some of his own teammates, who referred to him as "Senator" for his political ambitions and with whom he got into more than one clubhouse scuffle over what was perceived as press favoritism for his willingness to accommodate reporters. On the other hand, he clashed with Lasorda after the 1977 World Series for showing sportsmanship in applauding Reggie Jackson on the field as the Yankees slugger was rounding first base after hitting his third home run in the final game of the postseason competition.

Typical of Garvey's ability to inspire public enthusiasm was his election as a write-in candidate to the starting lineup of the All-Star Game in 1974, the first time a player was chosen without having his name on the ballot; equally typical of his ability to take advantage of the spotlight was his MVP performance in the contest. In 1978 he became the first player to earn Most Valuable Player honors in two All-Star Games. Moving on to San Diego as a free agent in 1983, Garvey was again in the limelight when he led the Padres to a come-from-behind victory over the Cubs in the following year's League Championship Series. But then, after his first, supposedly storybook marriage dissolved to national headlines, there came disclosures that Mr. Clean had spent his off-field hours impregnating two women while pressing a third one to walk down the aisle with him. This prompted Southern California bumper stickers declaring: STEVE GARVEY IS NOT *MY* PADRE.

ELMER GEDEON

An outfielder who had a handful of at bats for the Senators in 1939, Gedeon was one of only two major leaguers killed in action during World War II. A member of the United States Air Corps, he was shot down over France in April 1944. The only other fatality during the war was Harry O'Neill, who died during the fighting at Iwo Jima. O'Neill had gone behind the plate as a late-inning defensive replacement in a single game for the Athletics in 1939.

JOE GEDEON

A light-hitting second baseman for three teams between 1913 and 1920, Gedeon became the Ninth Man Out in the 1919 Black Sox scandal when Commissioner Kenesaw Landis banished him from baseball for "guilty knowledge" of the affair. Initial accounts said his chief crime was betting on the Reds at the urging of Chicago shortstop Swede Risberg and sitting in on discussions of the plot with gamblers. His defenders pointed to his blacklisting as a perfect illustration of Landis's capriciousness since others (such as Johnny Rawlings of the Phillies and Ivy Olsen of the Dodgers) had also profited from their knowledge of the fix without being banished. But in fact his involvement was much deeper.

Abe Attell, the former lightweight boxing champion who was at the center of the conspiracy, named Gedeon as nothing less than an organizer of the plot for traveling from one city to another to line up gamblers who could contribute to the payoff money for the Black Sox; in particular, the infielder served as an intermediary between the players and St. Louis blouse maker Carl Zork and East St. Louis theater manager Harry Redmon. He also approached Charles Comiskey immediately after the Series professing a willingness to confess all in order to collect the $20,000 reward the White Sox owner had offered for information about the rigging. (Comiskey claimed his story was not conclusive enough to deserve the money.) With a grant of immunity in his pocket in 1920, Gedeon stood ready to tell his story to the grand jury investigating the Series, but was never called to testify.

LOU GEHRIG (Hall of Fame, 1939)

For all his accomplishments, Gehrig is still the most underrated player in big league history. He is almost always thought of as The Iron Horse, whose consecutive-game streak was ended by a disease later named after him, when not being remembered as "the guy who hit all those homers the year Babe Ruth hit 60." In fact, the lefthanded first baseman retired with a prodigious batting record that could have been obscured only by the abruptness of its end and overshadowed only by the even more prodigious feats (partly made possible by having Gehrig bat behind him in the order) and outsized personality of his teammate and sometime rival. After Ruth's departure in 1934, Gehrig had to share the spotlight with, first, the anticipation surrounding the impending arrival of Joe DiMaggio from the Pacific Coast League, and then, from 1936 on, with the center fielder's actual presence. John McGraw and Mickey Cochrane also stole some of Gehrig's thunder—one on Gehrig's greatest day, the other in his greatest season.

In his 17-year (1923–39) all-Yankees career, Gehrig hit .340 (to Ruth's .342), slugged .632 (third on the all-time list behind Ruth and Ted Williams), drove in 1,995 runs (third behind Hank Aaron and Ruth), and knocked 493 homers. He reached the 30-mark in home runs 10 times but failed to hit more than Ruth until 1934, the outfielder's last season with New York; in 1931 he was relegated to a tie (with Ruth) for the league lead when a baserunning lapse by shortstop Lyn Lary negated one four-bagger. Gehrig topped .700 in slugging average three times, leading the American League in that category twice but losing out with such totals as .765 in 1927 and .721 in 1930 (to the Bambino's .772 and .732, respectively). For 12 consecutive seasons Gehrig's batting average topped .300, and he parlayed his lone batting championship, in 1934, into a Triple Crown—a distinction never gained by Ruth and ignored by sportswriters, who selected Detroit's Cochrane as the AL's Most Valuable Player. The first baseman did win two MVP trophies (in 1927 and 1936) to Ruth's one, but the 1927 award came only because Ruth had already taken the honors in 1923 and the rules of the day precluded anyone from repeating. Appearing in seven World Series, Gehrig was, if anything, even better than in regular-season play, ending up in the top 10 in every significant offensive category.

Among Gehrig's feats that neither Ruth nor anyone else ever matched are: 13 straight years with both 100 runs scored and 100 RBIs, 200 hits and 100 walks in the same season seven times, a record 23 grand slams, and the best one-season ratio of homers (49) to strikeouts (31) of any player with 40 or more round-trippers (in 1934); he also holds an AL season record for his 184 RBIs in 1931. On June 3, 1932 Gehrig became the first American Leaguer to hit four homers in a game, following them in his fifth at bat with his longest shot of the day—caught by Al Simmons in the farthest reaches of center field at Philadelphia's Shibe Park. Coincidentally, McGraw, who had once dismissed the schoolboy Gehrig as not of major league caliber, retired the same day after 30 years as Giants manager, stealing all the sports headlines.

Throughout the 1920s Gehrig and Ruth, despite the glaring differences in their personalities, had both a social and a business relationship, hunting and playing bridge together in the off-season. A rift developed between them when Gehrig declined Ruth's suggestion that they both hold out for more money in 1929; the split intensified into a feud when Gehrig's mother made it clear that Ruth and his wife failed to measure up to her lofty standards of child rearing. The two men did not speak for several years, until a long-retired Ruth, in a moment captured in one of the most memorable photographs in sports history, impetuously threw his arms around an already dying Gehrig during ceremonies held between games of the July 4, 1939 doubleheader to honor the Yankees captain.

The Gehrig myth about his on-field performance involves almost exclusively the consecutive game streak that began when he pinch-hit for shortstop Pee Wee Wanninger on June 1, 1925 and that didn't end until he removed himself from the lineup on May 2, 1929. In between, he played in 2,130 consecutive games, but not all of them at first base and not for nine innings in all of them. The streak at first base ended at 885 games on the final day of the 1930 season, when he played in the outfield. After another game as an outfielder in 1933, he preserved the streak, despite an attack of lumbago, by appearing in the lineup as the shortstop and leadoff batter in a 1934 road contest only long enough to come to the plate once before taking an unaccustomed place on the bench; Gehrig being Gehrig, he singled to begin the game.

The rest of the legend involves Gehrig's sudden affliction with the rare and invariably fatal amyotrophic lateral sclerosis in 1939. Weak throughout spring training that year, he ended his streak after pitcher Johnny Murphy congratulated him after a routine first-to-pitcher play; he learned his fate at the Mayo Clinic several weeks later. The Hall of Fame waived its customary five-year waiting period and gave him entry immediately. On July 4, Lou Gehrig Day, in a moment depicted in the Hollywood film *Pride of the Yankees* starring Gary Cooper, he became the first player to be honored by having his number (4) retired. He also delivered an emotional speech, ending with "All in all, I can say on this day that I consider myself the luckiest man on the face of the earth. I may have been given a bad break, but I have an awful lot to be grateful for." He died less than two years later, just weeks shy of his 38th birthday.

CHARLIE GEHRINGER (Hall of Fame, 1949)

If Ty Cobb had ever had an alter ego, it would have been his protégé Gehringer, dubbed The Mechanical Man for the unassuming way that he ripped apart American League pitching for 19 years (1924–42) while saying practically nothing to anybody. The convergence of his diamond skills and personality was never more on display than near the end of the second baseman's career, when Detroit sponsored a Charlie Gehringer Day at which the lefthanded hitter was presented with a set of righthanded golf clubs. In the ensuing game he hit the first pitch thrown to him for a home run, banged out three other safeties, then won the contest by stealing home. Years later he admitted he had learned to play golf righthanded so as not to embarrass his well-wishers.

Gehringer came under Cobb's wing in 1924, when the then-manager of the Tigers warned the prospect to ignore advice that he change his batting stance. Cobb was still in the dugout when the infielder won the second base job with what turned out to be a mild offensive performance. From that point on, however, Gehringer compiled a career .320 average by hitting over .300 13 times (including a league-leading .371 in 1937), banging out 200 hits seven times, clouting 30 or more doubles 10 times, ending up in double figures for triples seven times, scoring 100 runs 12 times, and knocking in 100 runs seven times. Defensively, he paced the AL in fielding average six times, in putouts three times, and in assists a record seven times. His best years were 1929, when he led the league in eight offensive and defensive categories while batting .339, and 1937, when he took MVP honors for his batting crown, 209 hits, 40 doubles, 96 RBIs, and 133 runs scored.

In the 1930s Gehringer was lumped together with Hank Greenberg and Goose Goslin as Detroit's G-Men—a takeoff on the enormous publicity being given at the time to the FBI's battles with notorious criminals. But he never quite lost his greater reputation as The Mechanical Man, especially after he averaged the same .320 in his three World Series appearances in 1934, 1935, and 1940 that he compiled in regular-season performances. His 10-for-20 in six All-Star Games represents the highest average for any player with at least that number of at bats.

In the early 1950s Gehringer served briefly as Detroit's general manager.

PHIL GEIER

When Phillies owner John Rogers balked at the asking price of $1,500 for outfielder prospect Geier, the owner of the Fall River club in the New England League offered to add an infielder to the package. Geier went on to hit .249 in a five-year major league career; throw-in Nap Lajoie went on to the Hall of Fame.

BERNICE GERA

Gera was the first woman to umpire a professional baseball game—and quit immediately afterward. The Queens housewife officiated at one contest in the Class A New York-Penn League on June 24, 1972, after fighting through the New York courts for the right to practice her profession. As for why she quit so quickly, Gera placed the blame less on an ugly midgame confrontation with Auburn manager Nolan Campbell than on the hostility of the league and other umpires and on anonymous threats she had received in the weeks leading up to her debut swan song.

DICK GERNERT

When the Red Sox traded first baseman Gernert to the Cubs in 1959 in return for Dave Hillman and Jim Marshall, it marked the first modern interleague trade that didn't require waivers.

CESAR GERONIMO

Geronimo's Gold Glove work in center field for the Big Red Machine in the 1970s was not matched by his hitting, leading to several dubious records. In the 1975 League Championship Series against Pittsburgh, he struck out seven times in a row—contributing significantly to his other playoff mark of going 30 straight at bats without a hit. Somewhat more incidentally, he was Bob Gibson's 3,000th strikeout victim on July 17, 1974, then happened to be in the batting box again when Nolan Ryan chalked up number 3,000 on July 4, 1980.

BART GIAMATTI

The seventh commissioner of baseball, Giamatti found himself embroiled in the Pete Rose scandal for every one of his 154 days in office in 1989. By his own claims, on the other hand, he never spent a minute on the established collusion of National League owners against free agents while serving as president of the loop between 1986 and 1989.

A professor of Renaissance studies and an unabashed Red Sox fan, Giamatti first came to the attention of baseball owners with his nonscholarly, often mawkish, writings on baseball and through his truculence with unions while serving as president of Yale. Named NL chief in December 1986, he took office just as baseball owners were agreeing not to go after one another's eligible free agents as a ploy against further player salary increases. Asked once if such collusion didn't amount to an attack on the integrity of the game since it restrained clubs from putting the best available players on the field, he said only that he had never heard a whisper of any such conspiracy among the owners.

By contrast, Giamatti heard plenty about Rose. Already in 1988, as NL president, he suspended the Cincinnati manager for 30 days for pushing umpire Dave Pallone during an argument at Riverfront Stadium. Even as he was being sworn in as Peter Ueberroth's successor at commissioner on April 1, 1989, he was aware of stories that Rose's known addiction to gambling had included wagers on baseball games—a violation that at best carried an automatic one-year suspension, but that, if involving Reds games, could entail lifetime banishment. An investigation conducted for Giamatti by Washington lawyer John M. Dowd dragged on interminably, with media reporters uncovering more sordid details almost daily. Giamatti finally presented the all-time-hit leader with the charges against him on May 11. If the purpose of the delay had been preparation to avoid litigation, the commissioner was sorely disappointed because Rose immediately filed suit to bar him from passing judgment on the grounds that he had already made up his mind. The impasse was resolved on August 24 when the two released a joint statement in which the manager accepted permanent banishment and abandoned his legal redress. For his part, Giamatti stipulated that he "will not make any formal findings or determinations on any matter including without limitation the allegation that Peter Edward Rose bet on any major league baseball games." That on the record, he immediately turned around at the press conference that followed and informally accused Rose of betting on major league contests—including Reds games. Eight days later, the heavy-smoking Giamatti was felled by a fatal heart attack.

TED GIANNOULAS

Dressed as the San Diego Chicken, Giannoulas was the first of the grandstand mascots that became a staple of big league franchises in the 1970s. After some years of entertaining fans by cavorting atop dugouts and along outfield fences at Jack Murphy Stadium, he got into a squabble with the Padres over the patent rights on his costumed character and had to take it elsewhere in the majors and in the minors without reference to San Diego.

In his first performance, on Opening Day 1974, Giannoulas became frightened at the outbursts of new Padres owner Ray Kroc, who not only apologized to the fans for the poor quality of the team but also screamed for the apprehension of a streaker; his concern was that the founder of McDonald's "would think I was representing Kentucky Fried Chicken or something."

BOB GIBSON (Hall of Fame, 1981)

Gibson was a byword for competitiveness in his 17-year career with the Cardinals in the 1960s and 1970s. The asthmatic righthander won 251 games (with an ERA of 2.91) in anchoring otherwise unstable St. Louis mound staffs, along the way becoming the first pitcher since Walter Johnson to strike out 3,000 batters. Gibson's grit was never more in evidence than in 1967, when he was sidelined for two months with a broken leg but then came off the disabled list to pitch three complete-game victories against the Red Sox in the World Series. In 1968 he was the Pitcher of the Year in the Year of the Pitcher

when he racked up 22 victories with a record-breaking 1.12 ERA; while assuring himself both the MVP and Cy Young awards for that effort, he also fanned 17 Tigers in the opening game of the World Series to set another record. Although his 35 strikeouts against Detroit established yet another World Series mark, he ended up on the losing end of a classic mound duel with Mickey Lolich in the deciding seventh game.

Even with his mound heroics, and conspicuous talents as a hitter and fielder (nine straight Gold Gloves between 1965 and 1973), Gibson generated almost as many tales for his fierce aggressiveness. In one spring training game against the Mets in the early 1970s, for instance, he and the equally competitive Tom Seaver startled players on both teams by hitting one another in a mutual declaration of war for the coming season. Intolerant of mound conferences, Gibson also chased receiver Tim McCarver away on one occasion, telling him to "get behind the plate. The only thing you know about pitching is how hard it is to hit." Before joining St. Louis, Gibson played for the Harlem Globetrotters for a year.

JOSH GIBSON (Hall of Fame, 1972)

Gibson has been called the black Babe Ruth, but so impressive was his ability to hit for average as well as for tape-measure distances that, Ruth's own accomplishments in these areas notwithstanding, he was regarded by some as the greatest hitter of all.

The righthand-hitting catcher was credited with more than 900 home runs and a lifetime batting average higher than .350 in a career running from 1930 to 1946. Included in the homer total were nine league-leading figures in North America, 44 in only 450 at bats in the Mexican League, and 13 in a mere 123 at bats one winter in Puerto Rico; his lifetime average was built on several seasons when he topped the .400 mark, and two (1938 and 1939) in which he not only hit higher than .400 but also posted slugging averages in excess of 1.000. His round-trippers were rarely of the dime-store variety. Among other things, he hit the longest verified shot in Yankee Stadium—a blast that struck two feet from the top of the wall behind the center field bleachers, some 580 feet from home plate. An eye-witness account by infielder Jack Marshall of the Chicago American Giants had him knocking another ball over the third deck next to the left field bullpen in 1934 for the only drive ever hit completely out of Yankee Stadium. His blasts were measured regularly at more than 500 feet.

Gibson teamed with Satchel Paige on the Pittsburgh Crawfords for parts of the 1936 and 1937 seasons to form the most popular battery in black baseball history, but it was with the Homestead Grays that he earned his greatest fame. Missing only two of the Grays nine straight Negro National League pennant-winning teams between 1937 and 1945 (he played in Venezuela and Mexico in 1940 and in Mexico in 1941), he attracted the attention of at least two major league owners—Pittsburgh's Bill Benswanger and Washington's Clark Griffith. Benswanger actually offered Gibson and first baseman Buck Leonard tryouts in 1939, but then, depending upon who is telling the story, either thought better of the consequences of trying to integrate the Pirates or was talked out of the move by Grays owner Cum Posey. It was also Posey who years later forced Gibson to abandon the Mexican League by slapping him with a $10,000 lawsuit and claiming title to his house, even though he always claimed that his star slugger lacked the color to make his relatively high salary worthwhile.

Gibson's health began to deteriorate after he returned to he United States. In 1943 a brain tumor left him in a coma for 10 days and with recurring headaches afterward. He turned to drink to kill the pain, while continuing to play. He was felled by a fatal stroke in January 1947, just after his 35th birthday and just before Jackie Robinson made his debut with the Dodgers.

KIRK GIBSON

Gibson hit the most Hollywoodian home run in World Series history as a member of Los Angeles in 1988, when he hobbled up to home plate with a severe leg injury in the bottom of the ninth inning of the first game and, with two strikes on him, belted a two-run blast to defeat Oakland's Dennis Eckersley. It was his only appearance in the Series, won by the Dodgers in five games. The club reached postseason play primarily because of Gibson's MVP season. The lefthanded swinging outfielder had signed with the Dodgers from Detroit that year after an arbitrator's ruling that he had been a victim of collusion among owners against free agents two years earlier.

WARREN GILES (Hall of Fame, 1979)

As National League president from 1951 and 1969, Giles usually played Tweedledum to Commissioner Ford Frick's Tweedledee in rubberstamping whatever Walter O'Malley or others wanted. Among other events that he presided over in relative silence were the franchise shifts of the Dodgers and Giants to California, relocations by the Braves from Boston and then from Milwaukee, and the 1962 NL expansion to include the Astros and Mets. In one of his rare public frothings, on the other hand, he lashed into his American League counterpart Joe Cronin in the late 1960s for breaking an agreement that committed both circuits to holding off on further expansion until the early 1970s. Cronin's decision to bring the timetable forward to 1969—made under heavy political pressure from Kansas City and Missouri politicians—disrupted an O'Malley schedule for expanding the leagues simultaneously, and the NL too was forced to push things ahead to 1969 to accommodate the Expos and Padres.

Prior to pushing paper in the league office, Giles had served as general manager and then president of the Reds. As Larry MacPhail's successor in Cincinnati in 1936, he was the one who put the final touches on the teams that won pennants in 1939 and 1940 and the world championship in the latter year. His most inspired moves as the head of Cincinnati's baseball operations in the prewar years included hiring Bill McKechnie as manager, obtaining third baseman-turned-pitcher Bucky Walters from the Phillies, and shortening the distances to the outfield walls of Crosley Field; the effect of the last change was still being felt in the 1950s with the home run production of the first version of The Big Red Machine. During the war, when Giles saw his power show menaced by the significantly less resilient balata ball, he threatened to use his own balls at Reds home games unless Commissioner Kenesaw Landis and the Spalding company did something about the horsehided rock in use; it was largely because of the threat that the balata ball was phased out even before the end of the war.

FLOYD GIEBELL

Giebell was promoted from the minors by Detroit at the end of the 1940 season and immediately thrown into a pennant-vital game against Cleveland ace Bob Feller on September 27. The rookie righthander defeated the Indians, 2–0, to clinch the flag for the Tigers. Detroit pilot Del Baker defended the move by saying he didn't want to "waste" one of his veteran pitchers against Feller with two games still left on the schedule. As for Giebell, it was his third and last major league victory.

WARREN GILL

First baseman Gill's single year of major league service, for the Pirates in 1908, was enough to help set the stage for the most controversial gaffe in baseball history. In a September 4 game against the Cubs, he was on first base in the 10th inning of a scoreless contest when Owen Wilson singled in the winning run from third. Gill, however, went no more than 40 feet toward second before turning around and running into the dugout to celebrate with his teammates. Chicago second baseman Johnny Evers called for the ball with the intention of recording a forceout at second base, but umpire Hank O'Day had also run off the field. Chicago protested unsuccessfully that Gill's failure to touch second and Evers's force erased the winning run. Later that month the same Evers and O'Day were key costars of an identical play that became known as Merkle's Boner and that forced an unprecedented makeup game between Chicago and New York for the National League pennant.

JAMES A. GILMORE

The reason the Federal League was able to transform itself from a struggling minor league into a threat to the National and American leagues was the work of Gilmore. Elected president of the FL in 1914 as part of the strategy to gain major status, the millionaire coal dealer persuaded Charles Weeghman to take over a majority interest in the Chicago Whales from him, then brought in such other money men as Philip Ball of St. Louis and Robert B. Ward of Brooklyn to back clubs. He later persuaded oil magnate Harry Sinclair to join the initiative as something of an all-purpose angel.

With his first season under his belt in 1914, Gilmore proposed that the pennant-winning Indianapolis Hoosiers play a true world's championship against the winner of the Braves-Athletics World Series; he received no printable reply. In 1915 he issued another futile challenge to the NL and AL to commit the pennant-winning Phillies and Red Sox

to a round-robin tournament with the Whales. That became academic when the Feds folded their tents before a third season. Under terms of a settlement with the two older circuits.

Weeghman was allowed to purchase the Cubs, Ball to buy the Browns, and Sinclair to sell off individual players for a tidy profit. Once outside the game, Gilmore decided that "there is no room for three major leagues. The reserve clause, to which I objected, is vitally important to clean promotion of the sport."

AL GIONFRIDDO

Gionfriddo's initial claim to fame was as the outfielder who brought Branch Rickey $100,000 of Pittsburgh's money as part of the Brooklyn executive's dumping of five players for him and the cash in May 1947. But in that year's World Series with the Yankees he speared a drive by Joe DiMaggio that assured him a permanent place in postseason highlight films, not least because it triggered one of the Yankee Clipper's rare shows of exasperation on the field. Gionfriddo was cut by the Dodgers prior to the 1948 season.

JACK GLASSCOCK

Glasscock jumped leagues three times and figured prominently in an effort to form a fourth circuit during his 17-year (1879–95) career. Two-thirds of the way through the 1884 season he and two others left the National League Cleveland Forest Citys for Cincinnati of the upstart Union Association, the righthand-hitting shortstop declaring: "I have played long enough for glory, now it is a matter of dollars and cents." A lifetime .290 hitter, his defection was a major boost for the Unions. After the 1889 campaign he agreed to leave the NL once again for the Players League, but then double-jumped back to the fold before the start of play. In 1894 Glasscock was active in trying to secure backing for a Cleveland franchise in the abortive effort to revive the American Association.

Glassock was known as Pebbly Jack for his constant landscaping of the shortstop position, including a habit of tossing away pebbles whether or not they were actually in his hand.

TOM GLAVINE

Despite five 20-win seasons, Glavine's reputation as a clutch performer would not seem borne out by some numbers; in fact, the Atlanta southpaw and teammate Greg Maddux have the most defeats in postseason play (13). On the other hand, his overall Division Series, League Championship Series, and World Series mark of 12–13 in 32 starts between 1991 and 2001 includes 23 games in which he did not yield more than two earned runs.

KID GLEASON

The 1919 World Series scandal was something of a payback for Gleason, who came across as a markedly ineffectual Chicago manager after a 22-year (1888–1908, 1912) career as an all-time snarling personality. Aside from the fact that he admitted having largely turned a blind eye to clubhouse tensions throughout the season, he was even painted by some as an unwitting abettor of the Series fix by urging his players to spend their day off on the eve of the postseason meeting with Cincinnati at a race track. Although claims of the kind died of their own absurdity, they still marked quite a distance from the days when Gleason had been more known for spiking, rabbit-punching, or just beating up opponents. Originally a righthanded pitcher with the Phillies, he won 62 games between 1890 and 1891. When he developed a sore arm later on in his career, he was converted to a lefty-swinging second baseman more known for defense than offense. Returning to Philadelphia as in infielder in 1903, Gleason was named team captain and showed how seriously he took the honor by displaying a leather strap and knuckle-duster in his locker.

JOHN GOCHNAUER

The reason Gochnauer lasted two full seasons as Cleveland's shortstop could not have been his ability with either a bat or a glove. In 1902 and 1903 he put together back-to-back .185 batting averages, the absolute nadir over two consecutive years for a player with 400 at bats. In 1903 he also made 98 errors, the most by any major league player since the end of the 19th century.

FRED GOLDSMITH

Despite four 20-plus victory seasons with Chicago in the 1880s, Goldsmith was more noteworthy for demonstrating that a baseball could be made to curve. Responding to a challenge from writer Henry Chadwick on August 16, 1870, the righthander set up two posts separated by 20 feet between the pitch-

er's box and home plate, then proceeded to throw several pitches that sailed to the right of the first one but to the left of the second. The convinced Chadwick hailed Goldsmith as the inventor of the curveball, at least until he heard of the earlier claims of Candy Cummings.

Goldsmith originally credited Yale pitcher Charles Avery with teaching him the pitch, but then began believing his press clippings and changed his story. He never got over the official recognition given to Cummings. When he died in 1939, he was found holding a 69-year-old newspaper describing his encounter with Chadwick.

LEFTY GOMEZ (Hall of Fame, 1972)

Gomez was a standout on the staid Bronx Bombers Yankees of the 1930s as much for his zany wit as for his mound performance. He collected 189 wins in 14 big league seasons (1930–43), all but one game of his career for the New Yorkers. The southpaw had two seasons (1934 and 1937) in which he took the pitching Triple Crown, leading the American League in victories, ERA, and strikeouts. He also topped 20 wins two other times, paced AL hurlers in strikeouts in one additional season, and placed first in shutouts on three occasions. Gomez's six World Series wins are the most by any pitcher without a loss. A notoriously bad hitter (.147 lifetime average), he nevertheless drove across the first run of All-Star competition in the 1993 contest and knocked in the winning run in the final game of the 1937 World Series against the Giants.

Most of Gomez's barbs were self-deprecatory; many involved nemesis Jimmie Foxx, to whom he once refused to pitch, explaining to catcher Bill Dickey, "Maybe he'll just get tired of waiting and leave." Dubbed Goofy by writer Bob Considine, Gomez once stopped a World Series game against the Giants to watch an airplane pass overhead. On another occasion he foiled a perfect double play by taking a ball hit back to him with a runner on first and firing it at second baseman Tony Lazzeri, who was several feet from the bag, instead of to shortstop Frank Crosetti, who was covering; he told the startled Lazzeri: "I was just reading in the paper the other day what a smart fellow you were, and I was curious to see what you would do in a spot like that." His most quoted line was that "the secret of my success was clean living and a fast outfield." But perhaps his best was his response to Yankees owner Jacob Ruppert's attempt to slash his salary from $20,000 to $7,500 after a 12–15 record in 1935: "You keep the salary, I'll take the cut."

PRESTON GOMEZ

When he took over the Padres in 1969, the Cuban Gomez became the first Latin American to be signed to a regular managerial contract. With both San Diego and later Houston, he infuriated his bosses by yanking pitchers who had completed eight no-hit innings; he defended the removal of Clay Kirby in 1970 and Don Wilson in 1974 by noting that both had been trailing at the time because of a combination of walks and errors. More interested in the box office cachet of a no-hitter for a cellar team than in a relatively meaningless victory, the general managers of both the Padres and Astros used Gomez's win-at-all-costs attitude as a final excuse for firing him.

Gomez's other obsession was defending against stolen signs; to this end he had separate signs worked out with every one of his players.

RUBEN GOMEZ

Although he had a couple of good seasons as a starting pitcher for the Giants in the 1950s, Gomez gained more notoriety as one of manager Leo Durocher's beanball specialists and as a not especially valiant brawler. Known as *El Divino Loco* (The Divine Crazy) in his native Puerto Rico, he once plunked Dodgers outfielder Carl Furillo with a pitch, prompting the Brooklyn star to charge into the Giants bench; went after Pittsburgh manager Danny Murtaugh with a bat; and slugged it out with teammate Willie Mays. Gomez's most memorable moment on the diamond, however, occurred in 1955, when he hit Milwaukee first baseman Joe Adcock with a pitch, tried to stop Adcock's charge to the mound by firing a second ball at him, then fled more than 500 feet to the clubhouse in center field with the muscular Braves slugger in pursuit. Once in the clubhouse, Gomez grabbed an ice pick and sought to return to the field after Adcock, but he was knocked to the floor and disarmed by teammates.

In one of his calmer moments Gomez sparked a revolt by black and Latin players on the Giants for road accommodations equal to those of white teammates. He had his most notable day on the mound at Seals Stadium on April 15, 1958, when he started

the first major league game in California, going on to blank the Dodgers for the Giants, 8–0.

JUAN GONZALEZ

Nobody has synthesized the advantages and disadvantages of being a top-dollar free agent better than Gonzalez, for whom MVP has come to mean Most Vagabond Player. Despite winning recognition twice as the American League's most significant offensive force, he changed uniforms every year from 1999 to 2002.

The righthand-hitting outfielder spent the first 11 years (1989–99) of his career with the Rangers, where he tore apart franchise power records. In both 1992 and 1993 he led the AL in home runs, two of five times he topped the 40-mark. The club's biggest run producer and main reason for its arrival in the postseason in 1996, 1998, and 1999, he also racked up more than 100 RBIs seven times. In 1996 and 1998 he took home MVP honors. After a 1999 campaign of 39–128–.326 the odyssey started. Because the Rangers didn't see themselves meeting Gonzalez's expected free agent contract demands after the 2000 season, they anticipated matters by swapping him to the Tigers in a nine-player deal. Gonzalez hated the Tigers, hated their brand new pitcher-friendly Comerica Field, and hated a multiyear contract they offered to him—sentiments returned by Detroit fans for his injury-plagued, relatively unproductive year. It wasn't the best of circumstances for entering the free agent market, so Gonzalez agreed to a one-year-with-second-year-option pact with the Indians to get back on top of the heap before making a longer commitment. On the bright side he blossomed for Cleveland's Central Division title winner, taking the AL RBI crown for the second time; on the dim side he once again found himself priced out of a budget-cutting franchise, so had to hit the trail once more. After weeks of a campaign that came close to turning into a plebiscite among Mets fans and members of the team, he snubbed New York to return to Texas for the 2002 season.

LUIS GONZALEZ

A solid outfielder with modest power numbers for his first nine seasons, Gonzalez blossomed in the desert air to hit 57 home runs over his first two years (1999 and 2000) with Arizona. He also drove in more than 100 runs in both seasons after a previous high of 79, hit better than .300 for the first two times, and led the National League in hits in 1999. But all that was a mere prelude to 2001, when he clouted another 57 homers and knocked in a career high 142 runs to go along with a third straight .300 season. The lefty swinger capped his year by singling in the bottom of the ninth inning of the seventh game of the World Series against the Yankees to drive home the winning run and make the Diamondbacks the quickest expansion team to claim a world championship.

DWIGHT GOODEN

If a Hall of Fame career were gold dust, Gooden would be the conclusion of *The Treasure of the Sierra Madre*. Thanks to drug and alcohol addictions, the one-time New York whirlwind left as his most conspicuous legacy the popularization of K corners around major league stadiums.

Gooden burst onto the scene with the Mets in 1984 with a 17–9 (2.60) mark that netted him Rookie of the Year honors; his rookie-record 276 strikeouts earned him the sobriquet of Dr. K and the K corner in Shea Stadium. He was even better in 1985, becoming the youngest pitcher (he was 21) to win a Cy Young Award and the youngest to win 20 games (24–4, 1.53); for the second straight year he also led the National League in strikeouts, this time with 268. He was so dominating during the season that Las Vegas bookmakers refused to accept bets on the Mets when he was the scheduled starter.

From that point on Gooden began disappointing the gods. In 1986 he again fanned 200 but declined to 17 wins for a team that won 108. In 1987 he missed the first two months undergoing drug abuse therapy. Even his good years (18 wins in 1988, 19 in 1990) seemed haunted by his spectacular 1985 performance, prompting Hall of Famer Bob Gibson to note that not even Gooden himself would ever be that good again. In 1991 he suffered a rotator cuff injury that sidelined him a good part of the season. The following year he was named as one of three Mets who raped a woman hanging around the team in spring training; the charges were shelved after numerous lurid headlines. In 1993 and 1994 he lost more time to injuries; in 1994 as well, he was suspended for 60 days for having failed the drug tests he had been obligated to submit to since 1987, then failed a couple of more while ostensibly under-

going treatment during his suspension. The Mets made no attempt to hold on to him when his contract expired.

After sitting out the 1995 season, Gooden reappeared with the Yankees as a George Steinbrenner reclamation project. He won 11 games, including a May 14 no-hitter against the heavy-hitting Mariners but left the Yankees after the 1996 season.

His last three years were spent bouncing around from the Indians to the Astros to the Devil Rays and back to the Yankees again for a combined 17 wins—the same number he had won in his rookie season on the mound.

GLADYS GOODING

Organist Gooding was the answer to a hoary New York riddle about the only person to have played for the Dodgers, the hockey Rangers, and the basketball Knicks. Hired by Larry MacPhail in 1942 after he had noticed her impact on Madison Square Garden spectators, she got into trouble almost immediately when she set Ebbets Field fans roaring by playing "Three Blind Mice" at the appearance of the umpires. The tune was especially aimed at umpire Bill Stewart, who worked as a hockey referee in the off-season and who had angered Rangers fans with some questionable calls the previous winter. After Stewart protested to the National League office, Gooding had to stick to more innocuous melodies.

BILLY GOODMAN

Goodman is the only player since the turn of the 20th century to win a batting title while serving as a utility man. The lefty swinger hit .354 for the Red Sox in 1950 while playing 45 games in the outfield, 27 at third base, 21 at first base, five at second base, and one at shortstop. The only other player to lead offensively while wandering around defensively was King Kelly in 1884 and 1886.

MARV GOODWIN

Although he didn't know it, Goodwin was at the center of one of the more ghoulish squabbles between teams over a player transaction. In September 1925 the Cardinals sold the righthander to the Reds on the condition that he stick with Cincinnati for at least 30 days into the following season before the deal became final. Although he lost a couple of games for the Reds in the waning days of 1925, the team reiterated its intention of having him on the roster in spring training. But on October 22 Goodwin, a flying instructor, became the first player to be killed in an air crash when his plane went down near Houston during a practice flight. Branch Rickey didn't let that deter him from demanding the Reds make full payment of money and promised players for the pitcher. For its part, Cincinnati noted that since Goodwin hadn't lasted the stipulated 30 days into the 1926 season, the deal had been voided. Commissioner Kenesaw Landis finally had to step in and rule that the Cardinals were not entitled to anything in exchange for the dead hurler.

GLEN GORBUS

Gorbus was a modest outfielder for the Reds and Phillies who hung on as long as he did because of his exceptional throwing arm. Responding to a challenge in 1957, he fired a ball an estimated 445 feet, 10 inches out of Connie Mack Stadium. There is no recorded instance of anyone hurling a baseball farther.

JOSEPH W. GORDON

The first figurehead president of the New York Highlanders in 1903, Gordon indirectly contributed to the club's nickname because of the association of his own surname with the elite British military regiment known as the Gordon Highlanders. He was selected for his baseball position by American League president Ban Johnson who had the image fidgets about the franchise's chief owners—professional gambler Frank Farrell and grafter Bill Devery. Gordon's résumé included a stint as the city's Deputy Inspector of Buildings, marital ties to Tammany Hall, and past investments in the New York Giants. He lasted at his position only until 1907, when Farrell decided to stop apologizing for his gambling associations and to run the club more visibly. As for the name Highlanders, inspired even before Gordon by the Manhattan terrain where Hilltop Park had been laid out, it ceded the ground gradually to Yankees.

GEORGE GORE

A .306 hitter in 14 seasons, mostly with Chicago and New York, Gore won a National League batting championship in 1880. But it is for his inestimable patience at the plate that he should be remembered. In 1886, when the Chicago outfielder became the first to crack the century mark in walks, each of his

102 free passes required seven balls under the rules in effect at the time.

GOOSE GOSLIN (Hall of Fame, 1968)

It says something for the richness of Goslin's career that his reputation as one of Detroit's G-Men was only the final phase of his 18 big league seasons. Brought to the big leagues by Washington in 1921, the lefty-swinging outfielder batted .300 over each of his first full seven seasons, reaching a high (and a hitting title) in 1928 with .379. Unlike many of the other Senators in the period, he hit with power, achieving double figures in doubles, triples, and home runs for five straight years, later doing it another three times before calling it quits. In five consecutive seasons between 1924 and 1928 he drove in 100 runs, including an American League-high of 129 in 1924. Although initially gifted with a strong throwing arm, Goslin reduced his value to the club dramatically during spring training in 1928 when he got into a shotput contest with some high school athletes. The following morning, he was unable to raise his arm, and he never completely regained the zip on his throws.

Mainly because of incidents such as that with the shotput, Goslin drew constant criticism for his work habits from newly installed manager Walter Johnson, prompting a 1930 trade to the Browns. With St. Louis he showed that only the gigantic dimensions of Griffith Stadium had prevented him from being even more of a power hitter than he had been, racking up another three years of 100-plus RBIs with significantly more home runs. Washington traded to get him back in 1933, whereupon he joined Ossie Bluege as the only Senators to appear in all three of the franchise's World Series (1924, 1925, 1933). Dealt off to the Tigers in 1934, Goslin played in two more fall classics, joining with Charlie Gehringer and Hank Greenberg as Detroit's G-Men. He had three more 100-RBI seasons with the Tigers; his last big year was 1936, when he averaged .315 with 24 home runs, 125 RBIs, and 122 runs scored. After a third, brief stint with Washington, in 1938, he retired with a .316 average.

GOOSE GOSSAGE

Gossage lasted longer in the major leagues than his fastball did. A dominating righthanded reliever in the late 1970s and early 1980s, especially with the Yankees, he was still wandering from one team to another until 1994, even taking his glowering, mustached visage to Japan for a year.

Gossage's first big year was with the White Sox in 1975, when he led the American League with 26 saves. He matched that number with the Pirates in 1977, then returned to the AL as a free agent with the Yankees in 1978, topping the 30-mark twice. He became so indispensable to the New York bullpen that the team just about counted itself out of the division race in 1979 when he tore a thumb ligament in an early-season shower room tussle with teammate Cliff Johnson.

Signing on with the Padres as a free agent in 1984, Gossage played a critical role in the team's pennant win with 10 victories and 25 saves (2.90), then returned to close out another 26 wins the following year. But then his never-cordial relations with ownership hit the skids over an edict banning beer drinking in the clubhouse after games. Noting that Jack Murphy Stadium was plastered with Budweiser signs and billboards, he blasted the order as "hypocritical," then went on to accuse owner Joan Kroc, the head of McDonald's fast food chain, of "poisoning the world with her hamburgers." He was suspended until he agreed to make a humiliating apology claiming that he and his family were regular customers at McDonald's.

Gossage ended his 22-year career in 1994 after a few years of working as a middle reliever.

HANK GOWDY

Catcher Gowdy played for 17 years for the Giants and Braves between 1910 and 1930, but his on-field career was identified with a single foul ball hit in the 12th inning of the seventh game of the 1924 World Series. Circling under the pop hit by Washington's Muddy Ruel, he tripped over his own mask and never got to the ball. With a second life, Ruel then doubled and later scored the world championship run for the Senators.

Off the field, Gowdy was a World War I volunteer who embarrassed the efforts of baseball officialdom to get players exempt from military service.

HARRY GRABINER

Grabiner rose from a Comiskey Park peanut vendor to the linchpin of the White Sox organization. His diary of the year 1920, lost until a Bill Veeck

nephew found it in the bowels of old Comiskey Park and Veeck used it as the basis of a chapter of his book *The Hustler's Handbook* in 1965, contained details of the 1919 Black Sox scandal, the ensuing cover-up, and the role played by Grabiner's boss Charlie Comiskey. The journal has been missing since Veeck told family members of his intention of sending it to the Hall of Fame after using it for his book. Cooperstown claims never to have received it, while Grabiner family survivors say they have never seen it.

According to the Grabiner diary (as related by Veeck), Joe Jackson showed him $5,000 in cash immediately after the Series and told him where he got it. The executive's advice was for the outfielder to go home and wait to hear from Comiskey; he never did. The diary also named Grover Cleveland Alexander, Rabbit Maranville, and Bill Killefer as among "27 players" active in the period implicated in game fixes that were never publicized. Other notations referred to compromised games, series, and even World Series aside from that played in 1919.

Twenty years after the Black Sox scandal, while the Comiskey heirs battled each other in courtrooms over control of the team, Grabiner worked off an unprecedented 10-year contract behind various front office titles to make sure there was a club still to be had. In 1945 he sought to persuade Grace Comiskey to sell the franchise to him and Bill Veeck; when she said no, he ended his association with the organization, becoming a key member of the Veeck group that purchased Cleveland shortly afterward. The executive's death shortly after the Indians had won the 1948 World Series contributed to the decision by Veeck to sell the franchise.

MOONLIGHT GRAHAM

A late-inning outfield replacement for the 1905 Giants in an 11–1 thrashing of the Dodgers, Graham's name was omitted from early editions of *The Baseball Encyclopedia* probably because he neither came to bat nor handled a chance in the field. The oversight was corrected after Graham appeared as a character in W. P. Kinsella's novel *Shoeless Joe*.

JACK GRANEY

A .250-hitting outfielder with Cleveland between 1908 to 1922, Graney was the first player to go from the diamond to the broadcasting booth after his retirement. He ended up doing play-by-play of Indians games for 32 years.

CHARLIE GRANT

A black second baseman with the Columbia Giants of Chicago, Grant so impressed John McGraw with his skills during spring training in 1901 that the Baltimore manager tried to bring him into the American League. Concocting a bizarre tale that Grant was actually a half-Cherokee named Chief Tokahoma, McGraw almost got away with his scheme until White Sox owner Charlie Comiskey pointed out that "the Cherokee of McGraw is really Grant, the crack Negro second baseman, fixed up with war paint and feathers," and threatened "to get a Chinaman of my acquaintance to put him on third" if McGraw persisted.

EDDIE GRANT

A third baseman for the Giants, Grant was the only big leaguer killed in action during World War I. A Polo Grounds monument in his honor stood in center field until the stadium was demolished in 1964. He is commemorated in New York today by the Edward L. Grant Highway—situated (oddly) just north of Yankee Stadium in the Bronx.

GEORGE WASHINGTON GRANT

Grant was one of several early-century owners of the Braves whose links to John McGraw helped reduce the Boston franchise to something of a major league farm club for the Giants. When he bought the team from a consortium headed by Percy Haughton after the 1918 season, the one-time film distributor and Wall Street speculator did so through McGraw's mediation efforts; at the same time he was partnered with the New York manager in a bid to buy a Havana racetrack and had both a Manhattan office and a Polo Grounds box adjoining those of Giants owner Charles Stoneham. Within months of taking over the Braves, Grant endorsed several deals with the Giants that benefited the latter much more than the former. When the Boston press turned on him over both the propriety of the exchanges and his refusal to move from New York to Massachusetts, he claimed the team had needed the cash it had received along with some mediocre players and that he himself didn't have the money to afford two residences. The low point of Grant's ownership came

in 1921, when it was revealed that Boston manager Fred Mitchell had been liberally handing out fines against the smallest infraction of club rules and that the penalties just so happened to cover most of Boston's traveling expenses. Grant finally sold out—at a substantial profit to another McGraw crony, Emil Fuchs.

M. DONALD GRANT

The board chairman of the Mets over most of the club's first two decades in the 1960s and 1970s, Grant became a byword for executive interference and was linked to all of the franchise's worst public relations moments in the period. His unpopularity reached such a level at one point that bodyguards had to be assigned to him for fear of a lunatic fan attack. Even his singularity as the only member of the Giants board of directors to vote against the transfer of the franchise from New York to San Francisco in 1957 was ultimately interpreted as merely a no-lose tactic aimed at winning local plaudits.

As the principal adviser to original Mets owner Joan Payson, Grant was largely responsible for installing George Weiss as the team's first baseball operations chief—if only because he was averse to bringing in Branch Rickey and his power demands. Grant stayed pretty much in the background until Weiss's departure in 1967, then insisted on two hirings—of manager Gil Hodges and of general manager Johnny Murphy—that would profit the team on one level and set the stage for relentless infighting on another. Shortly after the Hodges-Murphy tandem led the Mets to their 1969 world championship, the general manager died of a heart attack, and Grant, seething over the way he had been kept away from baseball decision-making for three years, installed the reluctant Bob Scheffing as his successor. One consequence of the change was a tightened control of the clubhouse by Hodges against both Grant and Scheffing. With most of the press already lined up on the side of the popular manager, the chairman and the general manager didn't need another incident to lower their media image, but they created one anyway when, following the debacle trade of Nolan Ryan to the Angels in exchange for Jim Fregosi, Grant accused New York *Daily News* sportswriter Jack Lang of having "forced" the club into the deal.

With Yogi Berra replacing the deceased Hodges

in 1972, Grant became even more embroiled in the club's daily affairs. Although the team would eventually win the National League pennant in 1973, its play was so desultory as late as August that one paper conducted a poll on who should be fired first—Grant, Scheffing, or Berra. In good part because he had negotiated the Ryan-Fregosi trade, Scheffing was the dubious winner, with Berra a close second. In 1975 Grant dragged outfielder Cleon Jones before New York reporters to apologize for having been arrested in Florida on charges of having had sexual relations with a woman in a van. Jones proved even more useful to Grant a couple of months later when his refusal to take the field in the late innings of a game was the excuse the executive had been seeking for some time to fire Berra.

After Payson's death in 1975, Grant gained even more boardroom power. While formal control of the team passed to Payson's widower Charles, his lack of interest in baseball prompted him to give the reins to his daughter Linda de Roulet. With Grant as her Richelieu, de Roulet invoked one austerity measure after another, not least a decision to ignore free agents. Grant's hard line on player salaries also led to the trading of Rusty Staub and an attempt to peddle franchise star Tom Seaver to the Dodgers in exchange for Don Sutton. De Roulet prevented the latter move when she was overwhelmed with calls and letters from Mets fans, but she could do nothing in 1977 when an anti-Seaver drive fueled by Grant and *Daily News* sportswriter Dick Young led the righthander to demand a trade to Cincinnati. In the wake of what was called locally the Midnight Massacre, Grant was bombarded by threats on his life and accepted a bodyguard for the rest of the 1977 season.

The end of the trail came in 1978, when de Roulet made a surprise announcement that she was replacing Grant as the organization chairman. It emerged subsequently that the move had been inspired by Charles Payson, who might not have liked baseball but who had always distrusted Grant's influence on his wife and daughter. Grant went out fuming that he had never been appreciated by the Paysons, the players, the press, or the fans.

ABNER GRAVES

One of hundreds of respondents to the plea of a commission established by Al Spalding in 1905 to settle the controversy over the origins of baseball, Graves recounted a tale of how his boyhood chum Abner Doubleday had reconfigured town ball for a prep school contest in Cooperstown, New York in 1839, in the process not only inventing a new game but explicitly christening it "Base Ball." Dismissing the initial protests of historian and commission member Henry Chadwick, Spalding, ever anxious to deny that baseball had evolved from the British game of rounders, jumped at this "proof" that the game's beginnings were "free from the trammels of English traditions, customs, and conventionalities," no less so because Doubleday had been a noted Civil War general. It was, however, precisely the beginnings of the general's military career that gave the lie to Graves's 68-year-old recollections, since Doubleday, a West Point plebe in 1839, was not allowed to leave the citadel at the very time Graves had him in Cooperstown drawing a diagram of the first baseball field. Spalding didn't allow this inconvenient fact deter him, though: In December 1907 he had former National League president Abraham Mills, a wartime associate of Doubleday's and a pallbearer at his funeral in 1893, draft the commission report endorsing the myth of the game's spontaneous domestic creation.

While no one any longer subscribes to the Spalding fable, the Hall of Fame still has a dilapidated old ball that was found in a trunk by Graves's son and that was once claimed to have been used by Doubleday. Graves ended his days in a mental institution where he was confined after shooting his wife to death.

PETE GRAY

Gray was a one-armed outfielder for the 1945 Browns who aroused more resentment than admiration from his teammates. A subject of nationwide publicity and War Department propaganda for a successful minor league season in 1944, he was purchased by St. Louis for $20,000 behind adamant denials that the club was only looking for some freak attraction to outdraw the Cardinals in the city. Although Gray played well enough in spring training to make the team and drew praise in the clubhouse for dealing with his handicap, the tune changed when he batted a powerless .218 and when his relative nimbleness in taking off his glove and making throws still provided a second more of incentive for opposition runners to take an extra base. As the season wore on, several Browns pointed to the opposition baserunning as a major reason St. Louis was hard pressed to repeat as American League pennant winners. Manager Luke Sewell also made it clear that he didn't appreciate the front office suggestions that he play Gray more than he had intended. The player most affected by those starts, Mike Kreevich, created enough turmoil in the clubhouse to be waived to Washington in the middle of the season. None of this did anything for Gray's already spiky personality, and he was generally represented as surly and uncooperative. He drove in only 13 runs in 234 at bats, and was farmed out to Toledo the following year. Years later Sewell echoed the contentions that Gray's starts had cost St. Louis another pennant (the club finished in third place, six games behind Detroit) and insisted that, good spring training or not, he had not been up to the major leagues.

RAY GREBEY

Succeeding John Gaherin as head of major league baseball's Player Relations Committee early in 1977, Grebey latched on to the issue of free agent compensation as a means of bringing down the Players Association, thereby putting him in a position to succeed Bowie Kuhn as commissioner. The former General Electric union buster was undone by his own strategy, though. Wrongly assuring the owners that they had won the right to compensation during 1980 negotiations, he misgauged the players' determination to preserve free agency; by holding out for direct compensation to the club losing a free agent from the roster of the team signing him, he made the 1981 players walkout all but inevitable. Grebey was replaced by Lee MacPhail as chief negotiator for the owners during the strike and was fired altogether in April 1984.

DALLAS GREEN

Green's outspokenness as a manager and front office official not only obliterated his eight years as a mediocre pitcher for several teams in the 1960s but also cost the teams he headed some quality players. As a pilot, he called the shots for the only World Series victory ever recorded by the Phillies, in 1980. Despite his carefully-tended reputation as a booming back-slapper and ass-kicker, however, he took a back seat at a crucial moment in that year's pennant

drive to general manager Jim Owens, who lashed into the team at a clubhouse meeting for worrying about individual statistics and griping to every newsman available. His own bluster was more in evidence when he took over the Yankees in 1989, fired off some sarcastic cracks about the interference of George Steinbrenner, and was promptly fired with the owner's verdict that Green had been "one of the biggest mistakes I ever made."

In 1993 Green resurfaced as pilot of the Mets with the mandate of rebuilding the deteriorated club with young players. His biggest success initially was threatening to farm out infield prospect Jeff Kent, who responded with a notable slugging performance over the second half of the season. His biggest failures were in badmouthing lefthander Pete Schourek and outfielder Jeromy Burnitz to the point that they lost confidence and had to be dealt away. He was bounced in August 1996 after declaring that two of the club's headlined prospects, pitchers Jason Isringhausen and Paul Wilson, "don't belong in the big leagues."

Between managerial stints Green made a decidedly more enduring impression as head of baseball operations for the Cubs in the early 1980s. With his knowledge of the Phillies his main asset, he completed a series of trades with Philadelphia that brought such veterans as Keith Moreland, Dick Ruthven, Gary Mathews, Bob Dernier, and Larry Bowa to Wrigley Field; moreover, the deal that imported Bowa (in exchange for Ivan De Jesus) also brought franchise infielder Ryne Sandberg. All of the ex-Phillies played key roles in Chicago's 1984 East Division title—the first time the franchise had experienced postseason play since 1945. But for Windy City traditionalists there was a significant tradeoff for his tenure in his incessant campaigning for the installation of lights in Wrigley Field. Mainly because of this issue, Green was never a candidate for Man of the Year in Chicago, and few tears were shed when he was forced to resign his post after the 1987 season. The first night game at Wrigley was played the following August.

PUMPSIE GREEN

In 1959 infielder Green became the first black player on the Red Sox, the last major league team to drop the color barrier. He joined the team just as Joe Cronin, the Boston general manager who had held the Yawkey franchise line against blacks, was elected to the presidency of the American League.

HANK GREENBERG (Hall of Fame, 1956)

For most of his 13-year career in the 1930s and 1940s Greenberg was presumed to be carrying the Jewish people on his back whenever he strode to the plate for the Tigers. That he ranked below only Jimmie Foxx as his era's greatest righthanded American League slugger has suggested to some that he might have been second to nobody if he had merely had to worry about opposing pitchers. He himself said that he came up against more open anti-Semitism in his later days as an executive than he ever encountered on the diamond.

After failing in tryouts with the Giants (despite manager John McGraw's incessant search for a Jewish star) and the Senators, Greenberg made his first big impression on the AL in 1934, when he batted .339 while clouting 26 home runs, driving in 139 runs, and belting a league-leading 63 doubles. It was also toward the end of the 1934 campaign that his Jewishness became an issue for the sports pages when he admitted consulting a rabbi about whether or not he should get into uniform for Rosh Hashanah and Yom Kippur in late September. Mindful of the tense pennant race underway between the Tigers and the Yankees, the rabbi compromised by declaring that Greenberg should play on the happy occasion of Rosh Hashanah but dedicate himself to prayer on Yom Kippur. The first baseman acquiesced, with his 10th-inning home run deciding the contest played on the Jewish New Year.

In 1935 Greenberg won the first of two MVP awards by averaging .328 with AL-leading numbers in both home runs (36) and RBIs (170). A broken wrist, however, all but sidelined him for that year's World Series against the Cubs and, when it was re-broken at the beginning of the following season, he ended up missing most of 1936. The following year he came back with a vengeance, emerging as the biggest G of the so-called G Men (along with Charlie Gehringer and Goose Goslin) with 40 homers, 49 doubles, 137 runs scored, and an astonishing 183 RBIs. In 1938 he led the league in homers for the second of four seasons by whacking 58.

Despite his team-leading slugging, Greenberg was never particularly close to Walter Briggs, and was given an abrupt ultimatum by the Detroit owner after the 1939 campaign to move to the outfield to make room at first base for defensively inadequate receiver Rudy York or expose himself to a $10,000 pay cut. Greenberg went to left field, where he put together another MVP season (he led the AL in home runs, RBIs, doubles, and slugging average), but most of his friends were critical of him for acting too much like a good soldier before the Briggs ultimatum. They could make the same complaint more literally in May 1941, when the newly converted outfielder was the first ALer drafted into the U.S. Army. He remained in khaki all the way through the 1945 season, again making it clear that he regarded himself as a role model not only for big league players but for Jews more generally. When he did return to the Tigers, he dispelled speculation that his skills could not survive such a long layoff by homering in his first at bat and by leading a sweaty flag battle down the stretch against Washington; he personally nailed down matters on the final day of the season by clouting a grand slam home run.

After still another season of pacing the AL in homers and RBIs in 1946, the 35-year-old Greenberg applied for the job of Detroit general manager left open by the resignation of George Trautman. Briggs not only turned him down as unqualified, but with the obvious connivance of other AL owners, managed to get him waived out of the league to the Pirates. Speculation at the time attributed the owner with fears that Greenberg would call his in-laws (the department store Gimbels) in an attempt to take over the Tigers franchise altogether. In his final season as a player, the righty swinger belted 25 homers, partly because of a shortened left field fence at Forbes Field that created a handy target that became known as Greenberg Gardens; he also exerted a significant tutorial role on Pittsburgh prospect Ralph Kiner. His lifetime numbers totaled out at 331 home runs, 1,276 RBIs, a batting average of .313, and a slugging percentage of .605.

In 1949 Greenberg joined the Cleveland front office under owner Bill Veeck, and was in position after the season to join with insurance executive Ellis Ryan in purchasing the franchise. For several years he had to do little but add extra pieces to the winning clubs that were based on a Hall of Fame starting rotation of Bob Lemon, Bob Feller, and Early Wynn. By the mid-1960s, however, he was under fire for allowing the Cleveland farm system to go to seed and for adding little beyond washed up veterans (Kiner, Sal Maglie, Billy Cox). His chief response was to blame city newspapers for turning a still-respectable club into a mockery in the eyes of fans. If that didn't bring enough heat, he turned even previously sympathetic sportswriters against him during the 1957 season when he urged the organization's board of directors to move the franchise to Los Angeles before the Dodgers got there. Instead, the board voted to sell out to Cleveland banking and railroad magnate William Daley, leaving Greenberg with little alternative but to follow suit. Before going, he leveled one final charge at Cleveland fans and the press for being unable to support a big league team.

In 1959 Greenberg was back with Veeck as the key figures in a consortium taking over the majority interest in the White Sox. It wasn't too long, however, before Comiskey Park was mainly serving as an office for Greenberg and Veeck to lay plans for winning ownership rights to the expansion California franchise due to begin operations in 1961. They were so confident of being awarded the new club that they signed a tentative agreement to broadcast the Angels games over Gene Autry's KMPC and unloaded their interest in the White Sox to Arthur Allyn, Jr. But then reality raised its head in the form of Dodgers owner Walter O'Malley and several AL owners, who made it clear that the Greenberg offer would be studied seriously only if Veeck were cut out. When Greenberg wouldn't throw over his partner, the California franchise was awarded to Autry.

Greenberg was among those testifying on Curt Flood's behalf when the outfielder challenged the reserve clause in court in the early 1970s.

GUS GREENLEE

The owner of the Pittsburgh Crawfords and the driving force behind the founding of the second Negro National League in 1933, Crawford built one of the great black teams around Satchel Paige and Josh Gibson in the 1930s. He also ran a string of boxers, including lightheavyweight champion John Henry Lewis; the Crawford Cabaret, the place to go for any kind of action in Pittsburgh in the 1930s; and one of the city's biggest numbers operations. While serving as NNL president, Greenlee built Greenlee Field, the only black-owned park in the league. He dropped out of the circuit in 1936 after losing Paige and Gibson and taking a huge hit on a heavily played number.

BOB GREENWOOD

Greenwood was denied a win in his first major league start for the Phillies, even though Philadelphia won the game and no teammate appeared on the mound. On July 18, 1954, with the righthander holding an 8–1 lead over the Cardinals in the top of the fifth inning of a game interrupted several times by rain, St. Louis manager Eddie Stanky decided to stall. With darkness only minutes away and the rules of the day prohibiting turning on the lights in the middle of a contest, Stanky changed pitchers twice; when a call went out for the third reliever, however, umpire Babe Pinelli forfeited the game to Philadelphia. The Phillies received a victory, but because the game had not lasted the regulation five innings, none of the players received credit for their performances. Later in the season Greenwood recorded his first—and only—major league win.

KEN GRIFFEY, JR.

On August 31, 1990 Griffey became the first major leaguer to get a hit in the same inning as his father. The ultimate baseball generational promotion saw Ken, Jr. and Ken, Sr., both lefthand-hitting outfielders for the Mariners, each single and score. Prior to their joint offensive performance, the Griffeys had been the only father-son combination to play together on the same club; a year before, they had been the only two generations active simultaneously in the major leagues. Griffey, Sr. retired after the 1991 season with a lifetime average of .296.

Griffey, Jr. was hailed by most as the best player in the American League in the 1990s. In 1993 he collected 45 home runs and drove in 109 runs while maintaining his five-season average above .300. Among the homers were those he banged out in eight consecutive games between July 20 and 28 to tie a major league mark previously reached by Dale Long and Don Mattingly. He went on to lead the AL in home runs four times (with 56 in both 1997 and 1998) and in RBIs once (never falling below 134 from 1996 to 1999). In addition to his lively bat, he was considered the best defensive center fielder in the AL, with a particular penchant for spiking walls to gain the leverage for spectacular catches.

With free agency looming, Griffey forced Seattle

to trade him to his hometown of Cincinnati after the 1999 season. Although he clouted 40 homers and drove in 118 runs in his National League debut, he was slowed considerably by leg injuries and went through the season having to deal with astronomical expectations that he would lead an otherwise medio- cre club to the playoffs. It didn't help that his sign- ing aroused speculation that his father, the Reds hit- ting coach, would imminently be named manager in place of the sitting Jack McKeon. As it turned out, Bob Boone was given the managerial job, and Grif- fey had to endure an even tougher year in 2001, los- ing the first half of the campaign to his persisting leg problems. He entered the 2002 season at 32 years of age and with 460 home runs, leading Hank Aaron to predict that he would be the one to pass the career home run mark held by the Hall of Famer.

MIKE GRIFFIN

Lefty-swinging outfielder Griffin was the first player to hit a home run in his initial major league at bat when he connected for the American Associa- tion's Baltimore Orioles in the first inning on Open- ing Day (April 16) in 1887. Within minutes outfield- er George Tebeau duplicated the feat, while playing for Cincinnati of the same league.

CALVIN GRIFFITH

Mocked even by his fellow owners as a Nean- derthal, Griffith said as much as anybody about the organizational mentality of the major leagues in the second half of the 20th century by surviving for close to three decades as the head of the Washington Senators-Minnesota Twins. As in the case of Marge Schott, his crassness was frequently only an over- sized mirror that his colleagues preferred not to look into to avoid seeing someone familiar. For better or worse, he was also one of the last owners who thought about nothing but baseball.

Griffith was born Calvin Griffith Robertson but switched his second and third names when he was taken in by his uncle Clark Griffith; because he was already too old when he filed the request, he was nev- er formally adopted by Clark but was otherwise al- ways treated as a son. From 1942 he took an active role in the affairs of the Senators, usually, but not always, doing as his uncle demanded. One notable exception occurred in 1953, when Calvin decided that Clark wasn't thinking clearly in supporting the

move of the St. Louis Browns to Baltimore, since that would present Washington with a rival for its market. When Clark found out that Calvin had been speaking against the proposal at league meet- ings, he insisted on dragging his 84-year-old bones to the final vote to guarantee that promises made to the prospective Baltimore owners were carried out. Clark died soon after, leaving behind a will that gave Calvin practical control of the franchise, since his 26 percent interest was backed by another 26 percent from his rubber-stamping sister Thel- ma Haynes.

The team Calvin inherited was the one that was first in war, first in peace, and last in the American League—and the one that served as an appropriate fantasy victor for the musical *Damn Yankees*. With no talent to speak of on the field and few coins in the till, Calvin became a natural target of lobbying groups from Louisville, Houston, Los Angeles, and San Francisco—all bent on either buying the team from him or inducing him to move from Washing- ton. When the District of Columbia intervened to of- fer a new ballpark, he objected that the proposed site would have been in a black neighborhood and would, in any case, have left him without the rental money and concessions income from Redskins games at Griffith Stadium that had been keeping the franchise afloat. He stuck to that position against warnings from other AL owners that a move out of Washing- ton would expose the major leagues to another in- vestigation of the sport's exemption from antitrust statutes by congressmen irritated at losing a local team. In the end, the league had to accept Griffith's dried-up treasury as a reality and the feasibility of an offer made by the Minneapolis-St. Paul lobby; to put off any congressional consequences, a new Washing- ton team was created as part of an expansion from eight to 10 teams.

Minnesotans welcomed Griffith as a hero, espe- cially when the team climbed to second place in its second season. The players thought differently, most of all during bitter annual contract negotiations. In one particularly embarrassing instance, manager Sam Mele was practically forced to grovel before accepting a salary cut to return the following year. It was the same Mele who led the club to its first pen- nant in 1965, but, little more than a year later, he was gone. In 1969 Griffith and Billy Martin kept saying how much they loved each other, while all the time the owner was collecting evidence about the manager's night crawlings in order to get rid of him without alienating fans. Never one to understate a labor-management crisis, Griffith termed a 1970 strike by umpires "a disgrace to humanity" and savaged his fellow owners as "appeasers" for giving up too quickly on a 1972 players walkout. His hardline attitude was reflected in the fact that Twins players were involved in a number of significant contract firsts in the 1970s: Dick Woodson the first to benefit from binding arbitration, Jim Kaat and Jim Perry the first American Leaguers to insist on their five-and-10 trading rights, and Bill Campbell the first regular free agent signee. It was Kaat who once described Griffith as "throwing quarters around like manhole covers;" lost to the ages, however, is the identity of the player who claimed that "swimming was invented the day Calvin came across his first toll booth."

Because of his aversion to free agents, Griffith allowed such stars as Rod Carew and Lyman Bostock to get away, and had trouble holding onto more than one manager who complained of not being able to send a competitive team out on the field. As cool as the fans and the press had turned for these reasons, the atmosphere dropped to freezing after a reporter published excerpts of a speech a drunken Griffith gave to a Lions Club affair in Waseca, Minnesota, on the evening of September 28, 1978. Amid a flood of racial invective, he said he was glad to have left Washington because the city had too many blacks who were more interested in wrestling than baseball; stunned that a black player like Carew had been stupid enough to accept the last pact he had given him; and annoyed that catcher Butch Wynegar had spent his spring training chasing his wife around the bedroom instead of settling for one-night stands that would have allowed him to concentrate more on baseball. Carew, who had already been enraged by what he had seen as Griffith's anti-Semitic attitude toward his Jewish agent, got his revenge by forcing the club to trade him into a lucrative contract with the Angels; Minnesota fans got their revenge by staying away from Metropolitan Stadium and wearing TRADE CALVIN buttons.

By the late 1970s even a good Twins team and a popular Griffith would have had a problem luring fans into the dangerously deteriorated Metropolitan Stadium. Although the facility had served a diplomatic purpose by being in Bloomington, a suburb

that was neither Minneapolis nor St. Paul, it became obvious even to the owner that he had to move. After once again contemplating a transfer to another state altogether, he swallowed his traditionalist baseball pride by accepting arguments for the construction of the indoor Metrodome in downtown Minneapolis. The biggest argument of all was financial; since the Twins relied more heavily than other teams on fans traveling from distant places, the dome was a guarantee they wouldn't be coming only to see snow piled up on the infield. With the help of an escape clause that allowed him to leave the state if the franchise did not prove profitable over a three-year period, Griffith presided with a smile over the inauguration of the dome in 1982. But what not even the Metrodome's roof could cover was the worst club in franchise history, making Minnesota the only team in the majors unable to draw a million fans that year.

Over the next year or so Griffith evinced decidedly mixed emotions about the fact that the sparse attendance was going to allow him to exercise the escape clause. In the end, he decided to sell out to a consortium headed by banker Carl Pohlad. Much of the fight had gone out of him after years of strife with his son Clark. His total absorption in baseball had previously cost him his marriage, ostensibly because his wife had never gotten over being separated from the social and cultural whirl of Washington. As he once told *Sports Illustrated:* "I like to look at magazines, read a few stories, read the captions. I don't like to socialize too much. You run into people who aren't athletic-minded. They're bookworms or symphony patrons, and that's all they want to talk about."

CLARK GRIFFITH (Hall of Fame, 1946)

Although associated primarily with the Washington franchise during his 64-year career as player, manager, and owner, Griffith could claim an identification with he American League as a whole. As much as Ban Johnson and Charlie Comiskey, he was responsible for the very existence of the junior circuit in his unmatched recruitment of National League stars. If he often came off as a poor cousin to Johnson and Comiskey, it wasn't for lack of desire to match their influence; during both world wars he could even relish their gratitude for his indispensable role in seeing to it that baseball continued being played at all.

Griffith's numbers as a pitcher for the Cubs, White Sox, and several other teams at the turn of the 20th century would have been sufficient in themselves to gain him consideration for Cooperstown. Between 1894 and 1899 the righthander turned in 20 victories every season, also pacing the NL with an ERA of 1.88 in 1898. Between his debut for the American Association's St. Louis franchise in 1891 and a final token appearance for the Senators in 1914, he put together a record of 237–146. Although he never again matched the mastery of his Cubs years, he came through with a seventh 20-win season for the White Sox in 1901. By then, however, Griffith was already paying attention to more than his personal wins and losses. As a representative of the Ball Players Protective Association the year before, he had gotten to work persuading some of his Cubs teammates to jump the NL after the season. As a reward for his efforts, he was named the first playing-manager of Chicago's AL franchise; he repaid that confidence immediately not only by collecting 24 wins and steering the White Sox to the best record in the fledgling major league, but also by creating enough excitement on the diamond to outdraw the Cubs by 150,000.

When Johnson needed a familiar name at the helm for the inaugural season of his AL entry in New York in 1903, he persuaded White Sox owner Comiskey there might not be any league at all unless Griffith took over the club that was to become the Yankees. Griffith was again successful insofar as he helped consolidate the New York franchise, even leading the team to a couple of second-place finishes in his five-year tenure; on the other hand, he was gradually worn down by intrigues among club executives, especially when they began seeping down into the clubhouse, and finally quit early into the 1908 season. After an unsuccessful bid to latch on as manager of the Senators, he accepted the pilot's post with the Reds. Throughout his three-year return to the NL, however, Griffith never let Cincinnati owner Garry Herrmann or Washington owner Thomas Noyes forget that he would be available as soon as the Senators needed a new dugout boss. His biggest profit from piloting the Reds was the presence on the 1911 roster of Cubans Armando Marsans and Rafael Almeida; decades later, he would point out their abilities as the reason why he signed so many Latins during his reign in Washington (in reality, it was one of three reasons).

On October 27, 1911 Griffith finally realized his hopes by signing on as manager of the Senators; moreover, the 10 percent interest he bought in the franchise instantly made him its single biggest investor. Predictions that he would have personality problems with Noyes became academic when the Washington owner died suddenly in the middle of the 1912 season and was replaced as club president by Ben Minor. Although as obstinate as Noyes on financial matters, Minor had few of his predecessor's airs about being a baseball genius, leaving Griffith even more of a free hand. He didn't waste any time waving it around. Convinced that the Senators needed only one more heavy hitter to rise from their already surprising second-place slot to the top of the AL, he cornered Detroit owner Frank Navin during the 1913 season and handed him a personal check for $100,000 for the services of Ty Cobb. When Navin voiced skepticism that Griffith could back up the paper, the Washington manager admitted that he couldn't but promised that he would be able to within two weeks if the Tigers would sit on his proposal for that long. Griffith then went to work on hostile shareholders, outlining a plan by which he would place 100,000 tickets on sale for $1 apiece to raise the money needed for the purchase of Cobb. The outcome was still in doubt among the investors when Navin returned the check, saying that he had decided to hold on to his star. The Senators had to hold on for second place.

During World War I (and again during World War II), Griffith proved invaluable to both leagues in persuading the U.S. Government not to eliminate baseball as a nonessential activity. In 1918, after league president Johnson had failed in an effort to gain deferments from military service for players (and in the process sharpened the antagonism of federal bureaucrats toward the big leagues), he worked out a deal with Secretary of War Newton Baker under which the players would perform pregame drills (with bats instead of rifles) in exchange for remaining exempt from the draft until Labor Day. The Washington manager also spearheaded a fundraising drive to buy bats and balls for servicemen in Europe. But none of this tap dancing on behalf of baseball as a whole endeared him any more to Senators stockholders who were still waiting to celebrate their first pennant. By 1919 boardroom grumbling had turned to open calls for his replacement as manager. Griffith's response was to round up capital from the Metropolitan National Bank and from Philadelphia grain exporter William Richardson and to take over as both majority owner and president; the deal allowed him to speak for Richardson's holdings as well as his own.

Once he could no longer be taken for an employee, Griffith began brushing in the master strokes of a 35-year franchise rule. Soon after the 1920 campaign he stepped down as manager in favor of George McBride; from McBride to the arrival of Charlie Dressen in 1955, the club would be piloted only by those who had or were still playing for it. In 1924 with Bucky Harris and then in 1933 with Joe Cronin, he went to younger infielders as skippers for teams he regarded as only some enthusiasm and an odd arm or two away from the pennant; Harris won the franchise's first two pennants in 1924 and 1925, Cronin its last in 1933. Both managers also saw the downside of Griffith's zealous patronage when he insisted on squiring them around the nation's capital. In Harris's case it led to a marriage with the daughter of a U.S. senator, charges from sportswriters and his own players that he had become too stuck up because of his new circles, and a fast ride to the Tigers; in Cronin's case it led to marriage with Griffith's niece Mildred, taunts from the locker room and the stands that he was marrying into the family only to hold onto his job, and an even more celebrated deal with the Red Sox for $225,000 of Tom Yawkey's money. Although Griffith was quick to stress that he had sold Cronin mainly because he didn't want the shortstop at the mercy of nepotism accusations, that didn't bother him where numerous other members of his family were concerned, especially as of the 1940s. By then he had his nephew Calvin acting as his right arm, Calvin's sister Thelma working in the front office, and Calvin's brothers Sherry, Billy, and Jimmy all nearing executive positions. Retired Washington pitcher Joe Haynes, Thelma's husband, would also have a vice presidency later on.

If a Yankees Hater's Club had existed in the 1930s, Griffith would have been president. Part of his resentment stemmed from the frequently vicious field fights that broke out between the teams; another, undoubtedly more important part had to do with New York's regular perch atop the AL standings between the wars. In a farcical attempt to get back at the

Bronx franchise he had been so instrumental in establishing, he sprang a surprise resolution at the AL winter meetings in 1940 that prohibited a previous year's pennant winner from making trades with other clubs. Although there was enough of an anti-Yankees majority to get the resolution approved, it turned out to be a vain exercise twice over: first, because New York had been depending for years on its own farm system more than on trades for building flag winners; second, because Detroit ended up winning the pennant in 1940. The Griffith resolution was overturned as soon as that year's World Series was completed.

During World War II the Washington owner again proved to be an effective diplomat in turning away congressional calls for stopping baseball as an nonessential activity. Far more established in the capital's political circles than he had been during World War I, Griffith wasn't above discussing some of his own players with draft officials at power lunches; at the very least, it struck some other big league owners as curious that Washington players weren't receiving greetings from Uncle Sam as regularly as members of other teams. The war also increased the importance of Griffith's Latin card; since Cubans, in particular, remained exempt from the draft registration until 1944, they appeared in appreciably growing numbers at Washington's spring training camps during the war. Aside from his experience with Marsans and Almeida at Cincinnati and the draft board issue, Griffith zeroed in on the Latins because they could be signed cheaply.

The 1940s also saw Griffith outsmarting himself on several occasions. Prior to the 1945 season, for instance, he was so skeptical of the club's chances to contend seriously that he scheduled a slew of September doubleheaders at Griffith Stadium in order to free up Sunday dates for the NFL Redskins, from whom he exacted considerable rental and concession revenues; in the event, Washington lost out to Detroit by merely a game-and-a-half, mainly because its pitching staff was worn thin by all the doubleheaders. In 1949 he learned that he had taken too much for granted with the stock of the Philadelphian Richardson; when the grain merchant's heirs sold their 40 percent stake in the franchise to a wheeler-dealer named John Jachym, Griffith needed to use every ounce of clout he had in Washington to round up the votes to beat back the only serious threat to his rule he ever encountered.

With his nephew Calvin taking over most of his tasks, beating off the Jachym power play turned out to be Griffith's last significant act. Until his death in 1955 at the age of 85, The Old Fox, as he was known, became increasingly obsessed with his own Horatio Alger story, asking every visitor to his office to name others who had started out as players and ended up as owners (only the tactless would have submitted Comiskey or Connie Mack as an answer). Asked on one occasion whom he most admired in America, Griffith replied: "The Lone Ranger has been my guiding star—the sort of man I want to be."

HAL GRIGGS

A less-than-mediocre righthander who won only six games while losing 26 in a four-year career with the Senators, Griggs, just called up from Chattanooga, managed to get Ted Williams to ground out to second in his first at bat on September 24, 1957, after the Boston slugger had reached base safely in a record 16 straight plate appearances. In his next at bat Williams homered off him to provide the winning margin in a 2–1 game.

BURLEIGH GRIMES (Hall of Fame, 1964)

Grimes was the last of the legal spitballers, and there weren't many of his contemporaries who could think of any other compliment to throw his way. Known as Old Stubblebeard for his perpetual bad mood, the righthander compiled five 20-win seasons in his 19-year (1916–34) travels through most of the National League. Four of his biggest campaigns came for the Dodgers in the 1920s after Brooklyn scout Larry Sutton had recommended he be obtained from the Pirates despite a grim 3–16 record in 1917. With the exception of his 23–11 contribution to the Dodgers pennant of 1920, Grimes's best efforts at Ebbets Field were generally for second-division clubs. His single biggest year was in 1928, during a second tour with Pittsburgh, when he won a league-leading 25 for a club that finished fourth. On the other hand, when he wasn't a staff ace, as with the Cardinals in 1930 and 1931, Grimes provided enough mound insurance to get his club into postseason play. His most conspicuous moment in a World Series was in 1931, when he won the seventh game for St. Louis over the Athletics.

A master of the brushback as much as of the spitter, Grimes took particular delight in decking Frankie Frisch. On one occasion, after Frisch had accidentally spiked him on a close play at first base and immediately apologized, Grimes waited for the Cardinals second baseman to get up again, and promptly beaned him. When the apoplectic Frisch protested that he had been sincere in his earlier apology, Grimes said he knew that but that Frisch had neglected to smile.

Old Stubblebeard's dourness was on full display when he replaced Casey Stengel as manager of the Dodgers in 1937, and used his first meeting with the press to complain that he was making less money than his idled predecessor. Grimes worsened an already bad situation in 1938 when he ridiculed the idea that Babe Ruth, hired as a coach by general manager Larry MacPhail, could ever succeed him as manager. When Ruth, who had been deceived into such ambitions by MacPhail, decided he would get a jump on his plans by first reactivating himself as a player, Grimes won the ex-slugger's hostility for good when he insulted his mental and physical capabilities.

For many years after getting out of a uniform, Grimes held sway over the Veterans Committee of the Hall of Fame, where he gained a reputation for forging votes on his pet likes and dislikes.

RAY GRIMES

Grimes had his lumbago to thank for not receiving more attention for one of baseball's more productive streaks. As a member of the 1922 Cubs, the righthand-hitting first baseman drove home at least one run in 17 consecutive games. He achieved the major league mark through two absences from the lineup because of a bad back. It was an ailment that would eventually abbreviate a more than promising career: Over six seasons Grimes compiled a .329 average, including a high of .354 in 1922.

CHARLIE GRIMM

Through 20 years of playing between 1916 and 1936 and 19 seasons of managing between 1932 and 1960, Grimm was a constant answer but only a short-term solution. In 1920 the deft fielder and lifetime .290 batter appeared to resolve a decades-long quest by the Pirates for a solid first baseman. But although his tenure with Pittsburgh included a career year in 1923 of .345 with 99 RBIs, his afterhours antics with shortstop Rabbit Maranville persuaded humorless owner Barney Dreyfuss to trade both of the them to the Cubs. The benefit to Grimm was that Chicago became home for the rest of his playing career and that he starred in two World Series for the club in 1929 and 1932, hitting an overall .364. Even better, he took over as pilot of the latter pennant-winning team in midseason after Rogers Hornsby had been ditched. But the managing job also marked the beginning of a yo-yo relationship with the Cubs for the best part of the next 30 years.

Grimm's first nemesis was Chicago president William Walker, an ex-fish merchant who acted like one in regular screaming matches with his manager over what had or had not been done; Walker regularly capped his rages by firing Grimm, then changing his mind after calming down. In spite of Walker's proclivity for terrible trades, Grimm came up with another pennant-winner in 1935, to a large extent because of his decision to step aside and hand first base over to 19-year-old rookie Phil Cavarretta. When Walker was replaced by Phil Wrigley, the manager's problem became yes-men who surrounded the owner and who always had a second-guess about some field strategy. In 1938 Grimm had enough and submitted his resignation; Wrigley was so grateful that he didn't have to pull the trigger first that he gave the outgoing pilot a job as team broadcaster. Grimm stayed in the broadcast booth through 1941, when he became partners with Bill Veeck in the Milwaukee American Association franchise and managed the club as well. In 1945 he was back at the helm of the Cubs when they made their last World Series appearance.

After World War II the team declined precipitously, especially because of lack of hitting. It was in this context that Grimm became involved in one of baseball's more noted tales. After receiving a telegram from a scout that read "Spotted a pitcher who stopped a good team cold for nine innings; only one foul fly hit out of the infield," the manager purportedly wired back: "Forget the pitcher. Send the guy who hit the foul fly. We need hitters." By 1949, however, Wrigley had decided that the club's real problem was that Grimm and general manager Jim Gallagher had the wrong jobs, so while kicking Gallagher off to a less meaningful post, he brought in Frankie Frisch as the pilot and put Grimm in charge of baseball operations. The next six months were even more of a fiasco with Grimm and Frisch making terrible

deals and Gallagher jeering at them from the sidelines. Once again Grimm had enough of the franchise's politics and resigned. After a couple of years of managing the Braves chief farm club in Milwaukee, he succeeded Tommy Holmes as manager of Boston.

No sooner had Grimm arrived in Boston than the franchise moved to his former stomping ground in Milwaukee; only in retrospect did owner Lou Perini admit that he had brought Grimm to Boston largely to acquaint him with the players he would be piloting in the city where he had gained substantial popularity. With the likes of Hank Aaron and Eddie Mathews in his lineup, Grimm moved Milwaukee into a contender's status over the next three years. But then in 1956 Perini decided he wasn't quite forceful enough and replaced him with Fred Haney. Asked to take over the Cubs for a third time in 1960, Grimm lasted little more than a month; behind an official explanation that his health wouldn't permit the daily rigors of piloting, he was traded back up to the broadcasting booth in exchange for Lou Boudreau. For those who had followed his career, it hardly came as a surprise that Grimm was named as one of the revolving managers in Wrigley's College of Coaches the following year. In fact, he never actually revolved back into the dugout.

HEINIE GROH

Groh helped breed generations of singles hitters with a specially designed bottle bat whose thick barrel and thin handle met without tapering. A defensive whiz at third base for Cincinnati between 1914 and 1921, he was the model contact hitter, batting below .280 only once in that span and attaining the .300-mark four times.

LEFTY GROVE (Hall of Fame, 1947)

Grove had two careers—and a different personality during each of them. With the Athletics from 1925 to 1933, he was a flamethrowing hothead; traded to the Red Sox in 1934, he became a finesse pitcher with a more subdued demeanor to match.

While he labored for Connie Mack in Philadelphia, Grove was the best pitcher in baseball and had the numbers to prove it: seven consecutive 20-win seasons, including 31 in 1931 and three other American League-leading totals; pacing the league in strikeouts in his first seven seasons; and back-to-back pitching Triple Crowns, topping AL hurlers in wins, strikeouts, and ERA in 1930 and 1931. The southpaw's most infamous tirade came on August 23, 1931 after an error by substitute outfielder Jimmy Moore had cost him a 17th consecutive victory with a 1–0 loss. In the clubhouse after the game Moore hid as the volatile Grove tore apart everything in sight, beginning with his own uniform and working his way up to several lockers, all the while damning the culprit who cost him a new AL record. The frightened outfielder emerged only when he realized that the target of the pitcher's wrath wasn't him but regular left fielder Al Simmons, who had missed the game because of an infected ankle that necessitated the playing of Moore.

In his first season in Fenway Park in 1934, Grove's arm went mysteriously dead, his record dropped to 8–8, his ERA exploded to 6.50, and his temper tantrums dwarfed the fits he had thrown in Shibe Park. But switching from fireballer to a change-of-speeds craftsman, he became canny enough to notch one more 20-win season and to top AL hurlers in ERA four more times; combined with the five ERA crowns he had won while with Philadelphia, this gave him a major league-record nine ERA season-lows. At the same time, the man who had once trashed clubhouses around the league with regularity mellowed to the point that even a protracted quest for this 300th victory failed to ruffle him. Winning only 14 games in his final two seasons, Grove notched his 300th and last victory on July 25, 1941, stumbling home against the Indians by a score of 10–6.

RON GUIDRY

Guidry is best remembered for his career year of 1978, when he helped the Yankees to a stunning come-from-behind pennant win; if New York manager Billy Martin had had his way, however, the lefthander would have performed his heroics elsewhere. Convinced that the five-foot, 11-inch, 160-pound Guidry wasn't big enough to be a winner in the majors, Martin had the Yankees front office shop him around throughout 1977 and into spring training of 1978 to, among others, the Cardinals (for Pete Vuckovich) and the Blue Jays (for Bill Singer). When there were no takers, Guidry went on to establish a record .893 winning percentage (25–3) for pitchers with 20 or more wins, lead the American

League with a 1.74 ERA, and tie Babe Ruth's AL record of nine shutouts by a southpaw. The left-hander also topped the 20-win mark on two other occasions, paced AL hurlers in ERA in one other season, and led all major league pitchers with 168 victories between 1977 and 1986.

Guidry was the first pitcher to be greeted by fans rising and clapping with every two-strike count; the custom began at Yankee Stadium on June 17, 1978, when 33,000-plus rooters roared through his 18-strikeout performance against the Angels.

TONY GWYNN

Gwynn worked hard to gain his status as San Diego's all-time franchise player. Aside from compiling a .338 average over 20 seasons (1982–2001) and winning eight batting titles to tie Honus Wagner for the most in the National League, the lefty-hitting outfielder had to close his ears to the crashing of the organization around him on two occasions and pretend bafflement at being the source of season-long clubhouse conflict a third time.

A slap hitter who also gradually turned himself into one of the National League's best defensive right fielders, Gwynn won batting titles in 1984, 1987–89, and 1994–97; he also paced the league in hits in seven seasons (in five of them with totals over 200), and scored more runs than anyone else in 1986. His .394 mark in the shortened 1994 season was the highest in the NL since Bill Terry's .401 in 1930 and the highest in either league since Ted Williams's .406 in 1941. He recorded his 3,000th hit on August 5, 1999.

While the Joan Kroc ownership deteriorated in the late 1980s, Gwynn remained the franchise's prize jewel, and went to the press on more than one occasion to blunt the possibility of being traded off. He showed the same attitude in 1993 when the Tom Werner ownership began holding a fire sale on such stars as Gary Sheffield and Fred McGriff—eliciting admiration in San Diego for sticking with the franchise in miserable circumstances, but drawing equal suspicion outside southern California that he had grown too comfortable with his local popularity and preferred being a big fish in a small pond to playing with a contending club as just one of the cast.

In 1990 Gwynn was also at the center of months-long tensions with Jack Clark over the slugger's charges that he worried about his own hitting more than team victories. Although Clark received some backing in his allegations from Garry Templeton and other Padres, it was all the accusers who were wearing different uniforms a year later, while Gwynn went to work on another .300 season. Gwynn attributed much of his batting success to his almost manic study of the videotaping of his plate appearances.

H

STAN HACK

Third baseman Hack was a perennial favorite with Cubs fans, as much for his good looks and sunny disposition as for his .301 average over 16 seasons. In 1935 vendors in the Wrigley Field bleachers did a vigorous trade in "Smile with Stan" mirrors, which the faithful used to reflect the sun in opposing batters' eyes.

HARVEY HADDIX

On May 26, 1959 Haddix pitched The Game. In baseball's single greatest mound performance, the Pittsburgh southpaw retired 36 consecutive batters through 12 innings, only to lose everything, 1–0, in the 13th on third baseman Don Hoak's error, a sacrifice by Eddie Mathews, an intentional pass to Hank Aaron, and a shot by Joe Adcock into the left field stands (scored as a double when he passed Aaron on the bases). After the shattering defeat, Haddix was asked by a reporter in the Pirates clubhouse if that had been his best game in the major leagues.

It was also Haddix who, as a reliever, was credited with the victory in the final game of the 1960 World Series against the Yankees decided by Bill Mazeroski's home run.

CHICK HAFEY (Hall of Fame, 1971)

An early product of Branch Rickey's farm system, Hafey also later became a prime example of the St. Louis executive's trading philosophy. A righthanded hitter with some clout, the outfielder batted .317 over 13 seasons between 1924 and 1937. In 1927 he paced the National League in slugging average, then four years later led the circuit in batting with a .349 mark. But so sooner had Hafey won the hitting title than he was traded to Cincinnati. It was a classic Rickey transaction: bringing the executive a lot of cash for a player who had held out two years in a row and illustrating his view that it was better to deal off a player at his crest or slightly past it (especially if he was afflicted with an often debilitating sinus problem and questionable eyesight, as was Hafey). Although Hafey went on to three more .300 seasons with the Reds, two of those years saw him plagued by shoulder injuries that limited his appearances. As for Rickey, he had the consolation prize of Joe Medwick as his new left fielder.

CASEY HAGEMAN

Hageman's case against the Red Sox in 1913 was the first to gain the backing of the Players Fraternity. Demoted to the minors with promises that he would be recalled again shortly and would continue receiving his major league salary in the interim, the righthander appealed first to the Boston club and then to the National Commission when he was subsequently dropped to an even lower minor league and his paycheck slashed. When neither Red Sox president Jimmy McAleer nor National Commission chairman Garry Herrmann would recognize his claim, Hageman went to union president Dave Fultz, who brought suit in New York State Supreme Court. The case took five years to resolve, by which time the Red Sox were being run by the perpetually strapped Harry Frazee, who refused to pay the court's judgment of $2,348 until threatened with a contempt citation.

JESSE HAINES (Hall of Fame, 1970)

Although he won 20 games three times for the Cardinals in the 1920s, Haines was almost as known for providing three footnotes to that franchise's history. One occurred in the seventh game of the 1926 World Series against the Yankees, when a bleeding blister forced his removal in the seventh inning, bringing on Grover Cleveland Alexander to strike out Tony Lazzeri with the bases loaded. Haines was also an implicit testament to the effectiveness of Branch Rickey's farm system, since his acquisition from the Kansas City club of the American Association after the 1919 season marked the last time for 25 years that the Cardinals were compelled to make an outright purchase of a prospect. Lastly, the right-hander's 18 years of service for the team between 1920 and 1937 was the longest by any pitcher in organization history and second only to Stan Musial among all players. Haines hung on with the club as long as he did partly because he was able to develop a knuckleball that prolonged his career but mainly because he was given a second role as an unofficial pitching coach; in fact, after his third 20-win season, in 1928, he never again won more than 13 games in a year and reached double figures only three times over his final nine campaigns.

ODELL HALE

Cleveland third baseman Hale recorded the most painful assist ever to start a triple play. With the bases loaded in the ninth inning of the first game of a September 7, 1935 doubleheader, Boston's Joe Cronin smashed the ball off Hale's head—directly into the hands of shortstop Bill Knickerbocker, who got the second out by tossing it to second baseman Roy Hughes, who relayed it to first baseman Hal Trosky to retire the side.

DICK HALL

In a 19-year career covering the 1950s and 1960s, Hall uncorked only a single wild pitch. His control was all the more remarkable in that he played his first couple of years for Pittsburgh primarily as an outfielder before becoming a bullpen ace for the Orioles.

GEORGE HALL

The first man to lead the National League in home runs (with five in 1876), Hall was at the center of the Louisville Crooks scandal a year later. When he con-

fessed to club vice president Charles E. Chase in late October, the conspiracy (or rather conspiracies, since there were actually two separate illicit partnerships) unraveled, ending several months of rumor and speculation.

Placing the blame on utility man Al Nichols, Hall admitted he had cooperated in exhibition losses to teams in Lowell, Massachusetts (on August 30) and Pittsburgh (on September 3), while denying he had been party to throwing any NL games. In a separate deal with pitcher Jim Devlin, the outfielder told Chase, he contributed to losses to the NL Cincinnati Reds (September 6) and the minor league Indianapolis Blues (September 24); but since Cincinnati was about to be suspended and its games not to be counted in the standings, he argued, that contest had also amounted to an exhibition game. Hall initially fingered Devlin as the instigator of the Cincinnati-Indianapolis fixes, but then admitted he had been the one to approach the hurler with the scheme. He was banned for life by the league, along with Devlin, Nichols, and shortstop Bill Craver.

BILLY HAMILTON (Hall of Fame, 1961)

No one will ever know how many times Hamilton stole a base, because until 1898 a runner received credit for a steal if he advanced more bases than the batter advancing him. But however many of the 914 stolen bases recorded next to his name in a 14-year (1888–1901) career were earned by going from first to third on a single, Hamilton's .344 average and daring head-first slides, mostly for the Phillies and Braves, place him in the first rank of leadoff hitters and base runners. The lefthand-hitting outfielder crossed home plate more times in one season (198 in 1894, in the Phillies 132-game schedule) than anyone else, and also averaged the most runs scored per game (1.06) in a career.

NED HANLON (Hall of Fame, 1996)

It was as much Hanlon's instinct for timely trades and genius for inside baseball as the fiery execution of his players that made the Baltimore Orioles a dominant force in the National League between 1894 and 1898. A fine defensive center fielder in the 1880s, Hanlon took over a feeble Baltimore club in 1892 after having managed Pittsburgh entries in the NL and the Players League. He first move was to get rid of potential trouble by trading his predecessor, center fielder George Van Haltren, to the Reds for outfielder Joe Kelley; the following year he added shortstop Hughie Jennings; first baseman Dan Brouthers; and Willie Keeler, whom the manager converted from an infielder to an outfielder. Joining third baseman John McGraw and catcher Wilbert Robinson, the six future Hall of Famers formed the nucleus of the 1894 team, all of whose regulars batted over .300 and drove in more than 90 runs in the first of three consecutive pennant-winning seasons.

Hanlon's moves sometimes even took on the uncanny. Typical was the sequence that began with switching Kid Gleason, a 15-game-winner on the mound in 1894, to second base. After Gleason hit .309 in 1895, Hanlon traded him to the Giants for Jack Doyle, who batted .339 and .354 the next two seasons. In 1898 he shipped Doyle and second baseman Heinie Reitz to Washington for first baseman Dan McGann, who enjoyed his only 100-RBI year; second baseman Gene DeMontreville, who hit 25 points higher than Reitz; and righthander Doc McJames, who led the club with 27 victories in his only 20-win season.

While the Orioles never had pitching to match their everyday lineup, Hanlon was among the first to recognize that the new 60-foot, six-inch distance between the mound and home plate that was adopted in 1893, would mean wearier arms sooner. To counter this, he instituted a three-man rotation that kept changing as pitchers wore out, held out, or were thrown out of the league. Perhaps his most spectacular feat was winning the 1894 pennant while juggling a mound corps that eventually numbered an unprecedented 10 pitchers.

Hanlon was the progenitor of the clever and aggressive (and often illegal and brutal) style that characterized the Orioles. Outfielders hitting the cutoff man, pitchers covering first base on grounders to their left, runners taking the extra base, and McGraw and Keeler executing the hit-and-run became staples. Realizing that the new pitching distance also gave bunters and base runners an advantage, Hanlon had Orioles runners scampering around the basepaths on sacrifices, squeeze plays, and stolen bases. He encouraged cutting across the inside edge of the infield on the way from first to third and bumping opponents on the basepaths. Nor did he discourage the vituperation and brawling that played such a large role in intimidating opponents, cheerfully reimburs-

ing players for their repeated fines out of the handsome profits he realized from his 20 percent interest in the club.

In 1899 Hanlon moved his managerial skills—and most of his players—to Brooklyn while retaining the presidency of the Orioles as part of a new syndicate that controlled both clubs. A year later, when the NL cut its roster from 12 teams to eight, he clashed with Brooklyn president Charlie Ebbets, arguing for keeping the Baltimore franchise and abandoning Brooklyn. The collaboration lasted through 1905, but the outcome was evident as early as 1902, when after pennant wins in 1899 and 1900, Ebbets used his newly acquired controlling interest in the club to raise his own salary from $4,000 a year to $10,000 and to slash Hanlon's from $12,000 to $7,500.

CARROLL HARDY

Although he never drove in more than 36 runs in a season and ended an eight-year (between 1958 and 1967) career with a .225 batting average, outfielder Hardy was called upon at various times to pinch-hit for Ted Williams, Roger Maris, and Carl Yastrzemski.

BUBBLES HARGRAVE

Aside from Ernie Lombardi, Hargrave is the only full-time receiver to win a batting crown. The right-handed hitter did it in 1926 with a .353 mark—one of seven times in his 12-year career between 1913 and 1930 that he reached .300.

JACK HARPER

Harper incurred the wrath of Cubs manager Frank Chance and was driven out of baseball for it. After winning 23 games twice (for the Cardinals in 1901 and the Reds in 1904), the righthander beaned Chance early in the 1906 season. Vowing vengeance, the pilot traded pitcher Chick Fraser to Cincinnati to get Harper on his own club, slashed his salary from $4,500 to $1,500, then used him in exactly one game before releasing him at the end of the season. Harper appealed his treatment to the National Commission to no avail and, disgusted, left the major leagues with a 80–64 record.

TOMMY HARPER

Harper had his moments as a speedy outfielder, but none was as provocative as his departure from the Red Sox as a coach. In 1970, while with the Brewers, he showed uncharacteristic power, banging 31 homers while stealing 38 bases, to become the first American League player to reach the 30-mark in both categories since Ken Williams of the Browns in 1922. He also led the AL in thefts twice and the National League in runs once in his 15-year (1962–76) career with eight teams.

After serving as a Boston coach for five seasons, Harper called attention to the lingering indifference of the franchise toward racial matters by suing the team in 1985 over its membership in a segregated Florida golf club where Red Sox brass and coaches (Harper excluded) would gather during spring training. The action was later dropped but only on conditions never revealed; to this day, both Harper and the Red Sox officials involved have declined to reveal details of the accord.

KEN HARRELSON

Both on and off the field outfielder Harrelson was considered baseball's chief fashion plate in the mid-1960s. On the field, he was the first player to wear batting gloves during a game, for the Kansas City Athletics in 1964; off the field, he helped popularize the period's craze for Nehru jackets. He was eventually cut loose by Kansas City after leading a player rebellion and calling owner Charlie Finley "a menace to baseball." Finley was so infuriated with Harrelson that he didn't even expose him to waivers but merely dropped him into free agent status. The slugger then made his own deal with the Red Sox and enjoyed a couple of good years in Fenway Park before going on to broadcasting and (short-lived) front office positions. With both the Red Sox and White Sox, his on-air comments have helped grease the skids for managers—not always to the surprise of his employer.

WILL HARRIDGE (Hall of Fame, 1972)

As president of the American League from 1931 to 1958, Harridge was the ultimate careerist. In 1911 he attracted the attention of AL founder Ban Johnson while employed as a clerk for the Wabash Railroad assigned to the league office in Chicago to handle arrangements for team transportation. After accepting Johnson's offer to become his private secretary, Harridge rose to league secretary upon Johnson's resignation in 1927, then succeeded Ernest Barnard in the top job in 1931. Lukewarm about night baseball

and other innovations of his time, Harridge's most memorable decision was to negate midget Eddie Gaedel's appearance as a pinch-hitter for the Browns in 1951 by erasing his name from official American League statistics. Since baseball was between commissioners at the time, St. Louis owner Bill Veeck had no place to go to appeal the decision. Gaedel's appearance was subsequently restored to the record book, but forever after the midget accused Harridge of ruining his baseball career.

BOB HARRIS

The violation of Harris's returning-GI rights by the Athletics in 1946 exemplified organized baseball's disregard for any law but its own and of its cozy relationship with the federal officials who made such disregard possible. A mediocre five-year big league righthander, Harris returned from World War II only to be cut by Philadelphia in spring training of 1946. Some months later he arranged a meeting with Connie Mack for receiving the 1946 salary that was due him under the law guaranteeing returning veterans their jobs. The U.S. attorney, who should have been siding with Harris, informed him at the meeting of what a great man Mack was and how much he meant to baseball, inducing the pitcher to accept a settlement for about two-thirds of what was due him. The federal prosecutor even prevailed upon Harris to pose with a beaming Mack for a photograph.

BUCKY HARRIS (Hall of Fame, 1975)

Harris's presence in Cooperstown stems in part from his rookie managing success with the Senators in the mid-1920s and in part from his sheer availability as a pilot for another 28 seasons. In fact, he won only one more pennant after his 1924–25 successes with Washington, with his overall record a decidedly modest 2,157–2,218 (.493).

As a player, Harris was a solid second baseman for the Senators through most of the 1920s. His most conspicuous moment with a bat in his hand came in the final game of the 1924 World Series against the Giants, when he banged a clutch two-run single in the eighth inning that tied up the contest and set the stage for Earl McNeely's pebble hit over the head of New York third baseman Freddie Lindstrom in the 12th inning. Washington's comeback world championship climaxed a year that began with the 27-year-old Harris being appointed manager and having to weather months of media and fan disapproval as Griffith's Folly. The following year Harris led the Senators to another pennant but had to put up with criticism even from American League president Ban Johnson when the club faltered in the World Series against Pittsburgh. For the next few seasons he was a constant target of Griffith Stadium boobirds, not only because of the team's drift downward but also because of press reports that his marriage to the daughter of a U.S. senator had made him snobbish and distant from his players. In 1929 he was scuttled in favor of Walter Johnson—the first of several occasions when he would lose a managing job to a high-profile diamond personality.

Harris immediately moved to the Tigers as a playing manager; it was the start of another trend in which, despite the lack of success of the teams under his command, he ran off a string of 20 straight years without having to join the unemployment line. As the Tigers pilot, he presided over four of the grimmest years in franchise history, announcing his own resignation when he learned that the organization was considering replacing him with Babe Ruth. In 1934 Harris got in another year, as the dugout leader of the Red Sox—this time being shown the door for Joe Cronin. The trade-off was that he got to succeed Cronin with a second, eight-year stint with Washington. There were no 1924 miracles this time, however, and Harris managed only one first-division finish, finally resigning in 1942. For a change of pace, he then went over to the National League, to the Phillies, lasting only a single season because of constant conflicts with owner William Cox. The climax to this brief tenure came when he agreed to talk Phillies players out of a sitdown strike over his firing led by pitcher Schoolboy Rowe, then lingered at a bar with some sportswriters, disclosing between drinks that Cox had been betting on Philadelphia games. The revelation eventually led to the blacklisting of the executive.

After sitting on the sidelines for a couple of years, Harris returned to controversy in September 1946, when Yankees owner Larry MacPhail hired him for an unspecified front office job. The appointment so angered acting manager Bill Dickey that he quit, and the way was open for Harris to go back to the dugout. In 1947 he steered New York to a world championship, but not without cost to his nerves because of constant interference from loose cannon MacPhail. At one point in the season the pilot and Joe DiMaggio had to talk the team out of an insurrection against the owner; after the World Series victory against the Dodgers, it was Harris himself who threw MacPhail out of the clubhouse for upbraiding outfielder Johnny Lindell for having left the sixth game with a cracked rib. Although it might have seemed like an improvement at the time, MacPhail's departure from the organization and the arrival of George Weiss as general manager turned out to be worse for Harris. Despite keeping the Yankees in the 1948 pennant race down to the next-to-last day of the season, he was fired. Once again his players protested; once again he was pushed aside for a colorful name (Casey Stengel); and once again he wasn't out of work very long.

Back with the Senators for the third time, in 1950, Harris squeezed out the last two .500 seasons the franchise would ever have but accomplished little else. After five years, he was out the door again—his replacement this time being Charlie Dressen. Harris being Harris, he immediately latched on to another managing position, this time with a return engagement with the Tigers. Although he made up for his first stint with Detroit by keeping the club above .500 for two seasons, he finished fifth both times, making another change inevitable. The one difference, in what turned out to be his last dugout assignment, was that he was finally succeeded by someone with less box office cachet than he had: Jack Tighe.

GREG HARRIS

Harris capped off a 15-year journeyman career (1981–95) with nine teams by becoming the first pitcher since Icebox Chamberlain in 1888 to throw with both arms in a major league game. Using a specially designed six-finger glove, he faced two Cincinnati batters from his normal right side and two as a southpaw in a scoreless ninth inning of a 9–7 Montreal loss on September 28, 1995.

JOE HARRIS

Harris's one moment of diamond glory wasn't really all that glorious, either. On September 1, 1906 the Red Sox righthander dueled Philadelphia's Jack Coombs for 24 innings, thereby dividing the record for most innings pitched in an American League game. Unfortunately for Harris, he ended up a 4–1 loser; even worse, he finished the year at 2–21 and his three-year career at 3–30.

LENNY HARRIS

On the final weekend of the 2001 season the lefty-swinging Harris singled for his 151st career pinch-hit, eclipsing the record previously held by Manny Mota. The utility infielder-outfielder for the Mets had plenty of opportunity to set the new mark, since his 95 at bats off the bench in the course of the season also established another pinch-hitting record.

JACK HARSHMAN

A power-hitting first baseman in the minor leagues, Harshman was used almost exclusively as a pitcher in the majors. His power didn't vanish, however, as evidenced by the fact that 21 of his 76 hits (primarily for the White Sox in the 1950s) were home runs—by far baseball's highest ratio of homers to safeties.

JOHN HART

As Cleveland general manager in 1992, Hart came up with management's most ambitious swerve around arbitration by signing 12 young Indians to long-term contracts. That disqualified them from salary arbitration for the duration. Among those inking the agreements were Carlos Baerga, Albert Belle, and Sandy Alomar. Even though Baerga and Belle were traded in 1996, Hart's strategy of building around young players paid off in six consecutive first-place finishes in the American League Central Division. Along the way, however, he drew criticism for concentrating too much on offense at the expense of pitching and gained a reputation as a merciless finger-pointer when he fired manager Mike Hargrove after the team blew a two-games-to-none lead over Boston in the 1996 American League Division Series.

With budgetary restrictions looming over Cleveland, Hart left the Indians after the 2001 season to take a similar position with the Rangers.

FRED HARTMAN

Hartman achieved a measure of immortality by driving in the first two American League runs. The RBIs came when the White Sox third baseman singled with the bases loaded in the bottom of the first inning of the AL's inaugural game, on April 24, 1901, off Cleveland righthander Bill Hoffer; otherwise, the righthanded hitter batted .278 in a six-year (between 1894 and 1902) big league career with four clubs.

GABBY HARTNETT (Hall of Fame, 1955)

The National League's best all-around catcher in the first half of the 20th century, Hartnett matched his American League contemporaries Bill Dickey and Mickey Cochrane in the curious fact that, for all his hitting ability, he never once led in any significant offensive category. On the other hand, his 19 years (1922–40) with the Cubs and a final season with the Giants (1941) added up to a .297 average, 236 home runs, and 1,179 RBIs. His stellar years included 1930, when he batted .339 with 37 homers and 122 RBIs; and 1935, when he took MVP honors for swatting .344. Hartnett also hit the most famous home run in Chicago history when, on September 28, 1938, his twilight "homer in the gloamin' " in the ninth inning against Pittsburgh's Mace Brown enabled the Cubs to take a half-game lead over the Pirates that the team never relinquished. At the time he was also the manager of the club.

Defensively, Hartnett had few equals—leading the NL in putouts four times, assists six times, and fielding average six times. The one asterisk to his defensive brilliance was in 1929, when what was diagnosed as a "dead arm" forced manager Joe McCarthy to sideline him in favor of Zach Taylor for all but pinch-hitting duties and a single game behind the plate. While doctors could offer no reason for the ailment, Hartnett's mother insisted that it was only a psychosomatic problem related to this wife's pregnancy; as soon as the Hartnett child was born during the off-season, the catcher had no more difficulty throwing.

Hartnett created a flap in 1931 when he was photographed leaning over the railing in front of a Wrigley Field box seat to sign an autograph for Al Capone's son and to chat with the Chicago mobster, then under indictment for income tax evasion. The public relations implication of the picture so distressed Commissioner Kenesaw Landis that he reprimanded Hartnett and so disturbed National League president John Heydler that he rushed through a rule forbidding players from socializing with fans before a game.

SCOTT HATTEBERG

As a part-time catcher for the Red Sox between 1995 and 2001, Hatteberg racked up the worst percentage of throwing out would-be base stealers (10 of 109) since such records have been kept. Following the 2001 season, he was signed by the Athletics—to play first base.

On August 6, 2001 Hatteberg also gained attention in a game against Texas for being the first player to hit into a triple play and then swat a grand slam home run in his next plate appearance two innings later.

CLINT HARTUNG

Pitcher-outfielder Hartung has become synonymous with baseball's skeptical use of the term "phenom." When he joined the Giants in 1947, he was hailed by publicists as a combination Christy Mathewson-Babe Ruth; over six seasons of moving back and forth between the mound and the outfield, however, he managed a record of only 29–29 (with a 5.02 ERA), while hitting merely 14 home runs to go with a .238 average. Even Hartung's most noted diamond moment, in the 1951 playoffs against the Dodgers, was not due entirely to his baseball talent. After Don Mueller broke his ankle sliding into third base on the play immediately before Bobby Thomson's pennant-winning homer, manager Leo Durocher called in Hartung to take over as a pinch-runner. Durocher later admitted that he had chosen the Hondo Hurricane over a couple of faster runners because of his fears that Brooklyn pitcher Don Newcombe would come after him for his game-long baiting, and he wanted the strapping Hartung between him and the Dodgers righthander.

ERNIE HARWELL

Harwell is the only baseball broadcaster ever traded for a player. He got his start as a major league announcer in 1948, when Brooklyn's Branch Rickey traded catcher Cliff Dapper to the minor league Atlanta Crackers to obtain his services as a complement to Red Barber and Connie Desmond. He later became the voice of the Tigers for several decades.

JOHN HASKELL

Umpire Haskell was American League president Ban Johnson's chief enforcer in his battle against field violence in the circuit's 1901 inaugural season; that was also his only year of big league service. After a series of run-ins with John McGraw that resulted in a suspension for the Baltimore manager and a forfeited game for the club, Haskell turned up the heat. On August 5 he ejected Orioles first baseman

Burt Hart for throwing his glove at him and slugging him after being called out trying to stretch a double into a triple; Johnson Hart suspended the rookie for life. White Sox shortstop Frank Shugart suffered the same fate after punching out Haskell and initiating a riot that required the intervention of police during an August 21 contest.

RON HASSEY

Although never known as a particularly deft defensive player, Hassey is the only catcher in history to have called the signals for two perfect games. As a member of the Cleveland Indians on May 15, 1981, he handled Len Barker's masterpiece against Toronto. On July 28, 1991, while winding down his career with Montreal, he was behind the plate for Dennis Martinez's immaculate no-hitter against the Dodgers.

PERCY HAUGHTON

A onetime Harvard football coach, Haughton took over as president of the Braves in 1912 and announced that he intended to stop the foul language used by players on the field. In a clubhouse talk to the team he suggested that whenever a player was tempted to use a four-letter word to decry a strikeout or some other frustration, he think instead of the children in the stands and substitute the shout "Good!" The experiment in decorum lasted only until first baseman Sherry Magee had a ball bounce over his head into right field and began screaming "Good! Good!" Boston's tempestuous manager George Stallings had to be restrained by players on the bench from running onto the field to throttle Magee. Haughton decided to let the matter slide.

BILL HAWKE

Only a .508 pitcher in a three-year career with the Cardinals and Orioles, Hawke holds the distinction of having pitched the first no-hitter from the current mound distance of 60 feet, six inches. After his 5–0 victory over Washington on August 16, 1893, no pitcher would hold an opponent hitless for nine innings until more than four years later, the longest hiatus between no-hitters in major league history.

ANDY HAWKINS

Nobody ever gave up more runs without yielding a hit in a regulation effort than Hawkins. Pitching for the Yankees against the White Sox on July 1,

1990, the righthander carried a no-hitter into the bottom of the eighth inning, when his defense suddenly sabotaged him to allow Chicago to score four runs. Because the White Sox didn't have to bat again in the ninth, Hawkins was credited with an eight-inning no-hitter and saddled with a 4–0 loss.

PINK HAWLEY

An erratic righthander, Hawley hit a major league record 210 batters in only 10 seasons (1892–1901) with five clubs. By contrast, it took runnerup Walter Johnson 21 years to plunk 205 hitters.

BOB HAZLE

Few players blew onto the scene as loudly as Hazle did with the 1957 Braves. The lefthand-hitting outfielder, dubbed Hurricane by teammates, batted .403 in 41 games after being promoted from the minors in July, and was considered the savior of Milwaukee's drive to the pennant. Only a handful of games into the 1958 season, however, he was packed off the Tigers and was soon out of the majors altogether.

Hazle picked up his nickname from the devastating 1954 storm dubbed Hurricane Hazel.

RICHIE HEBNER

Hebner holds the National League record for appearing in the most League Championship Series: eight. He also holds the mark for being on the most losing LCS teams: seven. The lefthand-hitting third baseman had a lot to do with not making it eight-for-eight by cracking key home runs for Pittsburgh in the final two games of the 1971 postseason series against San Francisco. Five of Hebner's appearances were with the Pirates (1970–72, 1974–75), two with the Phillies (1977–78), and one with the Cubs (1984). A .276 hitter over 18 major league seasons, he was the butt of endless jokes throughout his career for his off-season job as a grave digger. The humor had more of an edge to it during his one season with the Mets, in 1979, when he spent most of the campaign berating the club, Shea Stadium, and New Yorkers in general—and got as good as the gave from the grandstands.

GUY HECKER

Hecker is the only one who has ever led his league in both pitching wins and batting average. Playing

for Louisville of the American Association for all but one of his nine major league seasons, the righthander topped AA pitchers with 52 victories in 1884; two years later his .341 average was the league-best. In the second game of an August 15, 1884 doubleheader, Hecker became the only player to score seven runs in a game and the first of only two pitchers to hit three home runs in a single contest. (Jim Tobin of the Boston Braves tied the latter mark on May 13, 1942.)

Hecker's effectiveness on the mound disappeared in 1887, when he strained his arm trying to adjust to a new rule limiting hurlers to one forward step in delivering the ball; he had always employed what was, in effect, a running start.

ROBERT HEDGES

Hedges had a long-range impact on the development of the major leagues when, as president of the Browns early in the 20th century, he explored a prototypical version of the farm system. His chief aide at the time was Branch Rickey. Although he never exploited the system beyond moving a handful of players back and forth between the majors and the minors, behind what were described as "gentlemen's agreements," his manipulations remained with Rickey as a means of building up a franchise.

A Cincinnati-based carriage manufacturer, Hedges rescued American League President Ban Johnson after one of the circuit's original teams, the Milwaukee Brewers, proved to be a financial disaster in 1901. With the club transplanted to St. Louis, Hedges turned it into a steady money-maker despite the fact that the Browns never reached a World Series under his 13-year ownership. In 1905 he made Sportsman's Park the first concrete, double-decked stadium in either league. Hedges was as close to a mentor as Rickey ever had in the big leagues.

JIM HEGAN

Hegan was regarded as the defensive standard behind the plate in the American League for most of his 17-year (1941–42, 1946–60) career. Thanks to spending most of his time with the Indians, he handled more 20-game-winning seasons by pitchers (19) than any other catcher in major league history.

HARRY HEILMANN (Hall of Fame, 1952)

Heilmann took a few years to get used to American League pitching, but then became one of the most potent offensive players in the game. The righthand-hitting outfielder, who spent all but the final two of his 17 big league seasons (between 1914 and 1932) with the Tigers, batted a career high of .403 in 1923—an average since eclipsed in the junior circuit only by Ted Williams's .406 in 1941. That was also one of four seasons in which he won the AL batting race. His batting crowns came in the odd-numbered years of 1921, 1923, 1925, and 1927, and his other three titles were also assaults on .400—coming in at .394, .393, and .398. He recorded four 200-hit seasons, eight with at least 40 doubles and 100 RBIs, and four with 100 runs. Heilmann batted .342 overall.

TODD HELTON

Helton's accomplishments got lost in the fanfare over Barry Bonds's record-breaking year. In 2001 the lefty-swinging first baseman for Colorado became the first player since Lou Gehrig to accumulate 400 total bases twice and the first ever to bang out more than 100 extra base hits in back-to-back seasons.

SOLLY HEMUS

Hemus was to Eddie Stanky as Stanky had been to Leo Durocher. As both a middle infielder for St. Louis and Philadelphia in the 1950s and manager of the Cardinals from 1959 to 1961, he sought to make up in provocative tactics and brawling what he lacked in natural talent. In his first year as St. Louis pilot, he was tossed from games eight times and made it clear that he judged some of his players by their aggressiveness toward umpires as much as toward adversaries. Initially entertaining to fans, Hemus alienated a good part of Missouri when he announced in 1960 that he intended benching local icon Stan Musial and give more playing time to young prospects. The outcry was so great, including threats to boycott home games, that he had to relent on his plan, for the most part sitting Musial down only for road games.

DAVE HENDERSON

Henderson had more dramatic RBIs in two 1986 games than most players have in a career. With two strikes on him and two outs in the ninth inning of the fifth game of the League Championship Series, the righthand-hitting Boston outfielder reached California's Donnie Moore for a two-run homer that gave the Red Sox a one-run lead and saved them from pennant elimination. After California tied the game in the bottom of the inning, he came back to hit a sacrifice fly in the 11th inning that put his team ahead for good and started a three-game comeback victory for the flag. The home run off Moore was Henderson's first hit of the playoffs; he had also helped the Angels to a lead earlier in the game by accidentally tapping a Bobby Grich drive over the wall for a home run.

In the ensuing World Series against the Mets, Henderson outhit everyone on both teams by getting 10 safeties in 15 at bats; his most important blow was a home run in the top of the 10th inning of the sixth game that appeared to seal a Boston championship. It went for naught, however, when the Mets staged their own startling comeback in the bottom of the inning to pull out the contest and head for their seventh-game victory two days later.

RICKEY HENDERSON

Baseball's all-time leadoff man, Henderson has suffered from stereotypes about black players as much as anyone in recent decades. Mainly because of his on-field arrogance and round-the-clock self-absorption, he has had his every poor performance put down to a caricatured laziness or racial bitterness. In fact, the righthand-hitting outfielder has erased Ty Cobb's (in two instances) and Babe Ruth's (in one) names from the record book to become the all-time leader in stolen bases (1,395), runs scored (2,248), and walks (2,141). He has also made a perfect set with Cobb and Pete Rose in going out of his way to stick it to the opposition (as in patented snap catches) and in complaining constantly about teammates having more lucrative contracts than he has. Perceptions of Henderson the Dog have survived despite the adamant denials of two of his managers, Billy Martin and Tony LaRussa, not the most likely candidates for shielding an alleged jaker.

Henderson began his demolition of the record book when he joined Oakland in 1979 and swiped 33 bases in only 89 games. He led the American League in thefts for the next seven seasons, topping the century mark three times and establishing an all-time one-season record in 1982 with 130. Before slowing down in the early 1990s, he took four more stolen base titles, while also pacing the league three times in walks, once in hits, and five times in runs scored. At the same time, he was boasting unusual power for a hitter usually slotted in the leadoff spot, turning in three seasons of 20-plus home runs; entering the 2002 season, he had a firm grip on the mark for leading off a game with a four-bagger by having done it 79 times. Henderson's best regular-season performance came in 1990, when he took MVP honors for batting .325 with 28 homers and 65 steals. He was never more devastating, however, than during the 1989 ALCS for Oakland against the Blue Jays, when he reached base 14 of 23 times; his performance included six hits, seven walks, one hit-by-pitch, five RBIs, eight runs scored, and eight stolen bases.

Henderson was traded by Oakland to the Yankees in 1985. In his first season in the Bronx he scored a league-leading 146 runs in 143 games, the best ratio since 1939. Despite some good seasons in New York, he failed to spur the club into postseason play and became the target of more than one derisive headline for hamstring pulls. In 1989 he was traded back to the Athletics just in time for two pennants. It was during this stint with Oakland, on May 1, 1991, that he swiped his 939th base to pass Lou Brock, an event he commemorated by pulling the base from the ground and brandishing it triumphantly over his head.

Toward the end of the 1993 season Henderson was swapped to the Blue Jays for pennant insurance; although Toronto won its second straight world championship, it did so without any significant contribution from Henderson, and he returned to Oakland for a third time as a free agent. After two seasons in Oakland, he moved (as a free agent) to the Padres, who traded him to the Angels in midseason 1997. Again a free agent, he signed for a fourth tour with the A's for 1998, when he added a record 12th stolen base title (as the oldest player, at 39, to lead a league in thefts) and a record 13th season with 50. He also led the league in walks a fourth time. Signing with the Mets in 1999, he batted .315 toward the team's wild card finish but soured manager Bobby Valentine and Shea Stadium fans by retiring to the clubhouse for a card game with Bobby Bonilla after being removed from the sixth game of the NLCS. But even that wasn't enough for the club's management to part with so productive a player, so he lasted in New York until the following May, when he went into a home run trot on a ball that ended up hitting the left field wall. That was enough for the Mets, and he was released, finishing out the year with the Mariners.

After going through spring training in 2001 with no takers for his complicated services, Henderson finally hooked up for his second tour with the Padres in a year that would see him reach milestones had had never denied aiming for—the runs scored primacy over Cobb, the walks mark over Ruth, and his 3,000th hit (on the final day of the season). He celebrated the runs record by sliding into home plate on a home run

The most storied example of Henderson's self-absorption and obliviousness to his surroundings occurred when he joined Seattle in 2000. Inquiring about why John Olerud wore a helmet in the field, he was told the first baseman had had an operation to remove an aneurysm on his brain while in college and the helmet was a precaution against injury. Henderson, clearly unaware that Olerud had been his teammate in both Toronto and New York, observed that he had known a guy on the Mets with the same problem.

BOB HENDLEY

Hendley's most noted big league moment was a losing effort. As a member of the Cubs on September 9, 1965, the southpaw pitched a one-hitter against the Dodgers but lost, 1–0, because mound opponent Sandy Koufax was in the meantime fashioning a perfect game. Aside from Koufax, Hendley's greatest nemesis was Frank Howard, who over one span clouted five successive home runs off the lefty, made out a couple of times, then hit a sixth blast.

CLAUDE HENDRIX

Hendrix won 144 games for the Pirates, Chicago Whales (of the Federal League), and Cubs between 1911 and 1920, but he made a far bigger mark for being replaced by Grover Cleveland Alexander as the Cubs starting pitcher on August 31, 1920. The righthander was scratched by club president William Veeck after several phone calls and telegrams warning that he had been paid off to drop the game to the Phillies. The story sparked Cook County District Attorney MacClay Hoyne into summoning a special grand jury for an investigation—a probe that was eventually expanded to include allegations and rumors about the 1919 World Series. Hendrix, a three-time 20-game winner, got lost in the frying of larger fish, was released over the winter, and never appeared in another major league game.

TOMMY HENRICH

Henrich had his own initiative—and a critical assist from Commissioner Kenesaw Landis—to thank for his 11-year (1937–42, 1946–50) career with the Yankees. Convinced that he was being illegally hidden in the minor leagues by Cleveland general manager Cy Slapnicka, the outfielder reported the infraction to Landis, who took one look at his bush league record and another at the Indians manipulation of his contract and declared him a free agent. With the Yankees winning an eight-team auction for his services, Henrich went on to bat .282 and to lead the American League in triples twice and in runs scored once. The lefty swinger had his most memorable diamond moments in World Series play against the Dodgers: In 1941 he was at the plate when Mickey Owen let a third strike get away from him and reached first to begin a fourth-game winning rally; in 1947 he drove in the winning run in three of the four New York victories; and in 1949 he ended a scoreless duel between Allie Reynolds and Don Newcombe with a ninth-inning, sudden-death home run in the first game.

JOHN HENRY

If syndication baseball was dead in the 21st century, you couldn't prove it by Henry. When the commodities dealer's bid for the Red Sox was accepted in December 2001, he was not only the majority owner of the Marlins but also had a one-percent interest in the Yankees. Asked how he had been allowed to retain his interest in New York throughout his ownership in Florida, the official answer was that Yankees owner George Steinbrenner had "not gotten around to" dealing with the apparent conflict. In fact, neither Steinbrenner nor Commissioner Bud Selig had gotten around to dealing with it in more than three years, since Henry had bought out Wayne Huizenga.

Henry's involvement in the Red Sox purchase was part of an elaborate chess game laid out by Selig in 2001. His role called for him to then sell the Marlins to Expos owner Jeffrey Loria, leaving the way open for Montreal to be administered by the league for a year before being contracted or moved to the Washington, D.C. area.

BABE HERMAN

It was somewhat typical of Herman's career that stories about his most famous field moment—the 1926 game against the Braves in which he "doubled into a double play"—usually omit the particular that the hit also won the contest for the Dodgers.

A lefthand-hitting first baseman-outfielder, he was in fact one of the best hitters in the National League in the late 1920s and early 1930s, averaging .324 over 13 seasons. Especially for the two-year span of 1929–30, he ranked statistically with Bill Terry and Lefty O'Doul as the hardest outs in both leagues—turning in batting marks of .381 and .393, respectively, the latter second to Terry's .401.

Even though he led the league in errors at different positions in successive years (first base in 1927, the outfield in 1928), a good part of Herman's public image as a goof falling over his feet or being hit on the head by fly balls was inaccurate, especially in the nostalgic misconception that he symbolized the Daffiness Boys—a term that originally referred not to the Brooklyn players on the field, but to the bungling and quarrelsome executives who ran the club. The distinction was never more clear than in 1932, when the front office, irritated by Herman's threats to sit out the season if his contract demands were not met, swapped both him and future Hall of Fame catcher Ernie Lombardi to Cincinnati; more than any other single transaction, that move doomed the Dodgers to the nether regions of the league for the rest of the decade. When he was 42 and out of baseball for eight years, Herman was brought back to Ebbets Field as a wartime gate attraction in 1945. In what some saw as a deliberate crowd-pleasing move, he singled in his first at bat—and then promptly tripped over first base.

BILLY HERMAN (Hall of Fame, 1975)

Herman had a way of making both his presence and his absence noticed. It was a tendency that announced itself with his very first at bat for the Cubs, on August 29, 1931, when, facing Si Johnson of the Reds, he hit a foul in front of the plate that bounced back to knock him out and force his removal from the field on a stretcher. For the rest of the decade, however, the righthand-hitting second baseman captured attention for his key offense and defense on three Chicago pennant winners. The span included seven full seasons of .300 or better, with his best numbers coming in 1935, when he batted .341, scored 113 runs, and led the National League in both hits (227) and doubles (57). In 1941 his absence was noticed over the first weeks of the season in Brooklyn, which badly needed a second baseman to make a pennant run, and then in Chicago, where newly installed general manager Jim Gallagher was talked into a one-sided deal with the Dodgers. In Ebbets Field Herman sparked the Dodgers to the expected pennant with a .291 mark but then came up practically absent again when a rib injury sidelined him for most of Brooklyn's loss to the Yankees in the World Series.

Herman's tenure with the Dodgers came to an end in 1946, when he charged an all-night party to team president Branch Rickey. Dealt to the Braves, he contributed field leadership and a .306 mark to Boston's first finish in the first division in 12 years. In 1947 Braves owner Lou Perini held an auction on his services, finally surrendering him to the Pirates, who wanted him as a playing manager. When Herman arrived in Pittsburgh, the first words out of his mouth were that the Pirates had paid too much for him—an accurate observation since he was at the end of the line as an infielder, he couldn't pilot the club even to .400 ball, and the player given away for him, Bob Elliott, went on to win the MVP trophy and lead the Braves to a pennant.

ENZO HERNANDEZ

A shortstop for the Padres in the 1970s, Hernandez holds the record for the worst clutch hitting in a season. In 549 official at bats in 1971 he drove in merely 12 runs.

GUILLERMO HERNANDEZ

Hernandez provided one of the biggest and quickest payoffs for a trade when he won both the American League MVP and Cy Young Award for the Tigers in 1984; Detroit had obtained the southpaw reliever from the Phillies in exchange for catcher John Wockenfuss and outfielder Glenn Wilson only a month before the start of the season. Hernandez, who had posted merely 35 saves over seven preceding seasons, notched 32 for the Tigers to go along with nine wins and a league-leading 80 appearances. The screwballer also picked up a save in the League Championship Series against Kansas City and two against San Diego in the World Series to nail down a Detroit championship.

For much of his career Hernandez was known as Willie, but then insisted on being addressed by his name at birth.

KEITH HERNANDEZ

If not everyone has been ready to call Hernandez the best defensive first baseman, nobody has been confident about naming someone better. He was the heart of the 1980s Mets teams *after* he had won National League MVP honors, and his fielding brilliance was contained not only in his own range and catlike instincts but also in his attendant ability to hide the mediocrity of fellow infielders by covering much of their territory and pulling down their errant throws. Off the field Hernandez's leadership was more of a sometime thing, especially in two periods years apart when he was linked to drugs and when he was mainly consumed by his own injuries. With the exception of Jackie Robinson and Roberto Clemente, however, nobody inspired more contemporaries to wear a uniform number in his honor; among those to adopt his No. 17 have been Mark Grace and onetime Mets teammates David Cone, Ron Darling, Bob Ojeda, and Darryl Strawberry.

Hernandez spent the first nine and a half years of his 17-year (1974–90) career with the Cardinals. In 1979 the lefthanded swinger shared MVP honors (the only such tie) with Willie Stargell of the Pirates for leading the National League in batting (.344), on-base percentage (.421), doubles (48), and runs scored (116), while also banging out 210 hits and driving in 105 runs. He never again reached any of those category numbers, but he did have six more .300 seasons to contribute to a career .296 average. Despite being considered one of the bulwarks of the young St. Louis team that won the world championship in 1982, he was abruptly traded to New York the following year in exchange for pitchers Neil Allen and Rick Ownbey. In his initial explanation of the mystifying deal, Cardinals manager Whitey Herzog claimed that he had gotten tired of Hernandez's habit of doing crossword puzzles in the clubhouse; it wasn't until 1985 that real light was shed on the transaction, when the first baseman was called to testify in the Pittsburgh drug trials and he admitted that he had been a cocaine user. The degree of his popularity at Shea Stadium by that point was demonstrated when fans gave him a standing ovation in his first game after the testimony—a reaction that infuriated media moralists.

While in New York, Hernandez's off-the-record quotes to reporters about the latest dramas engulfing the team became enough of an open secret that almost as many people called him "a team source" as others referred to him as "Mex." If many of the nonattributed observations were self-serving, they were equally effective in sending wake-up calls to dragging teammates, not least slugger Strawberry. More important, Hernandez could back them up with his continued deftness in the field and strong clutch hitting—indispensable ingredients for the Mets rise to the world championship in 1986. His biggest hit of all came in the sixth inning of the seventh World Series game against Boston when, with the bases loaded and the Red Sox ahead, 3–0, he singled in two runs and set in motion the rally to a victory.

The ensuing years were not as glorious. Although the Mets won a second Eastern Division title in 1988, Hernandez himself was bogged down with hamstring problems. In 1989 he traded punches with Strawberry at spring training after needling the outfielder about his hangovers and field performance. At this point the same reporters who had been hanging on his every (anonymous) word for years began referring to him as The Dark Prince for his critical assessments of the team they were only too keen to publish, if still without attribution. Hernandez finished his career under contract to Cleveland, but rarely appeared in an Indians uniform; thanks to lingering leg problems, he played in merely 43 games through a two-year pact.

While it was recognized as an official statistic, Hernandez compiled the most career game-winning RBIs (129) and the most in a single season (24 in 1985).

GARRY HERRMANN

Herrmann's 25-year reign (1902–27) as boss of the Reds demonstrated that outlandishness and pliability could coexist. A man with a taste for checked suits and pinky rings, he was known so some as The Walking Delicatessen for his habit of going everywhere with a supply of sausages that he would gobble down, whatever the setting. He was no stranger to taverns, either, and continually boasted of his ability to outdrink all comers. But behind the cartoon character was an owner whose partners included a Cincinnati political thug (George Cox) who got his way by threatening municipal or physical reprisals against anyone opposed to franchise desires and who delighted in humiliating Herrmann with public declarations that "When I whistle, you dogs come out of your holes."

The Cincinnati official was the prime mover in the National League's acceptance of the American

League as an equal in 1903, surrendering his claim to future Hall of Fame outfielder Sam Crawford to effect the peace, and was considered reliable enough by his colleagues to be given the crucial swing vote on the three-man National Commission (the other members were the presidents of the two leagues) that dictated policy for all of organized baseball before Kenesaw Landis was chosen commissioner in 1920. Herrmann was, however, frequently criticized by his NL colleagues for siding too often with AL president Ban Johnson in squabbles involving both circuits. On the other hand, he was innovative enough to advocate interleague play as early as 1912. The scheme called for a reduction of the regular schedule to 112 games followed by 64 games, eight each against each team in the other league. The catch that doomed the idea was that the interleague games would replace the World Series, whose big payoffs for participating teams had begun to irritate the owners of also-ran clubs.

Herrmann the clown and Herrmann the lawmaker came together in one incident when he cast the deciding vote obligating a San Francisco minor league team to pay for second baseman Eddie Colligan even though the infielder had been secretly hospitalized with a broken leg at the time of the sale. When San Francisco owner J. Cal Ewing protested the decision, Herrmann replied that Ewing should have informed himself of Colligan's condition before accepting the deal. A few weeks later the Cincinnati president received five barrels of sauerkraut COD from Ewing, only to discover after paying for it that it was completely rancid. When Herrmann protested to Ewing, the San Francisco owner blithely pointed out that Herrmann should have informed himself of the sauerkraut's condition before paying for it.

Herrmann had a particularly bad World War I. Working in a city seething with anti-German hatred, he had to perform a precarious balancing act between vaunting himself as a German-American patriot and pressuring Washington for military draft exemptions for major leaguers. A 1918 War Department order decreeing baseball an inessential activity saved him from a public pratfall. He took enough of them on other matters, anyway, not least around game-fixing scandals involving Reds first baseman Hal Chase. By the time he lost authority as a National Commission member to Landis, he had been considered little more than a chair-filler for some time.

WILLARD HERSHBERGER

Hershberger has probably been the most noted of the numerous suicides that have afflicted the Cincinnati franchise over the years. A reserve catcher for the team in 1940, he severed his jugular vein with a razor in a Boston hotel room during a road trip. It emerged subsequently that the despondent Hershberger had alluded to his intentions in a conversation with manager Bill McKechnie but that the pilot had regarded the threat as only a passing glumness. Some Reds players attributed the suicide to the receiver's shock over having called for a pitch against Harry Danning of the Giants a few days earlier that had ended up as a grand slam home run, costing Cincinnati a key game; for his part, McKechnie never revealed the details of his talk with the catcher. The lack of a suicide note has tantalized newspaper reporters for more than six decades, prompting some bizarre theories that Hershberger might even have been murdered.

Among other Cincinnati players to take their own lives were Cannonball Crane (chloral acid, 1896), Danny Mahoney (carbolic acid, 1911), Pea Ridge Day (gunshot, 1934), and Benny Frey (exhaust fumes, 1937).

OREL HERSHISER

Hershiser set a major league record of 59 consecutive scoreless innings for the Dodgers by preventing any opponent from crossing the plate between August 30 and September 28, 1988. He took Cy Young honors that year for his 23–8 record and National League–leading eight shutouts.

BUCK HERZOG

John McGraw could never get enough of Herzog—except when he was around. A second baseman with more defensive than offensive abilities. he was traded away by McGraw's Giants three times—once in managerial pique, once as a test of power between the pilot and the New York ownership, and once amid suspicions of World Series chicanery. The first deal, to the Braves in 1910, came after McGraw decided that Herzog's constant questioning of strategic moves indicated managerial ambitions best served in Boston. Braves manager Fred Tenney felt the same cramps, so he swapped the infielder back to New York the following year. Then, during the 1913–14 off-season, McGraw, who had always made his own

trades, was informed after the fact that newly installed president Harry Hempstead had sent Herzog to the Reds. This prompted a McGraw ultimatum to Hempstead either to leave the baseball to him or replace him; Hempstead backed down.

The Cincinnati transaction allowed Herzog to realize his managerial ambitions but little else. When the Reds finally got tired of his stewardship over cellar-dwelling clubs, they sent him back to the Giants once again—this time in the so-called Hall of Fame Trade of 1916 in which New York surrendered Cooperstown residents Christy Mathewson, Edd Roush, and Bill McKechnie. Back in the Polo Grounds, Herzog held down second base without much comment until the 1917 World Series against the White Sox. When Chicago won the postseason contest after some dubious New York fielding at key junctures, McGraw let some intimates know that he suspected Herzog of having played out of position deliberately. Although charges were never brought against him, he once again hit the trail after the World Series, going back to Boston.

Herzog's name popped up again in connection with game-fixing in 1920, when lefthander Rube Benton testified before the Chicago grand jury investigating the 1919 World Series that the infielder had offered him "some easy money" to drop a September 1919 game between the Giants and the Cubs. Herzog produced affidavits from other players alleging that Benton had fabricated the tale to cover the fact that he had profited from the Black Sox Series fix, but that didn't save him from an enraged fan who stabbed him for being the fixer Benton had charged. Whatever the truth of the matter, the Cubs released the second baseman in January 1921, although National League president John Heydler exonerated him and Cubs president William Veeck gave him a letter stipulating that the release had nothing to do with Benton's accusations. Herzog parlayed these declarations into a managing job in the minor leagues.

WHITEY HERZOG

Herzog achieved enough to rival Gene Mauch as baseball's brightest dugout mind in the closing decades of the 20th century—and also enough to stand comparison to Earl Weaver for crustiness and gratuitousness.

A backup outfielder of no distinction for several American League clubs in the 1950s and 1960s. Herzog made his first impression as a strategist as player development chief for the Mets, for whom he groomed the team's formidable pitching staffs in the late 1960s. Annoyed that he was never given a shot as manager or general manager of the club, he moved on to Texas, where, as pilot in 1973, his first pronouncement was that the Rangers were "one of the worst teams" he had ever seen. Things went downhill from there, and after a season-long battle with owner Bob Short over the forced feeding of 18-year-old southpaw David Clyde as a major leaguer, he was replaced in September by Billy Martin. He reappeared with Kansas City midway through the 1975 season, a prelude to the three consecutive division titles he would win while managing the Royals. All three times, however, his clubs fell to the Yankees in the League Championship Series—losses that Herzog did not suffer easily. After the 1977 playoffs, for instance, he blamed the defeat at least partly on slugging first baseman John Mayberry, hinting broadly that the player had been on drugs and demanding he be dispatched elsewhere. Following the 1978 series, he risked the disaffection of star players George Brett and Hal McRae by firing Charlie Lau, blaming the hitting coach for making the offense too homogenized. When he could manage only a second-place Western Division finish the following year, he was fired.

In 1980 Herzog took over the Cardinals early in the season and so impressed owner Gussie Busch by keeping the club over .500 until August despite no front-line pitching that he was asked to leave the dugout before the end of the year for a bigger policy role, as general manager. In this capacity he engineered several major swaps to import the likes of relief ace Bruce Sutter. Once Herzog had completed his transactions, he left the front office paperwork in the hands of Joe McDonald and returned to the dugout in 1981 for what would be a nine-and-a-half year run; in that time he won three pennants (1982, 1985, and 1987) and a world championship (1982). Another postseason appearance was denied the club by the bizarre split-season formula employed in 1981 following the players strike: Although the Cardinals ended up with the best overall East Division record, they finished a game-and-a-half behind the Phillies over the first half and a half-game behind the Expos over the second half.

Herzog's St. Louis teams were heavy on switch-hitting speedsters who could exploit to the full, offensively as well as defensively, the artificial turf at Busch Stadium. When he no longer had an ace reliever like Sutter, he pioneered the bullpen-by-committee system. His tactical agility earned him the sobriquet The White Rat, but it was a nickname that returned to haunt him in his last years with the club, when impatience with underachieving players was often interchangeable with surliness. He had several major clashes with players—most serendipitously when his fury at an obscene on-field gesture by shortstop Garry Templeton prompted a swap for Ozzie Smith, most disastrously when he rushed Keith Hernandez off to the Mets. During his reign the Cardinals were also beset by an inordinate number of drug or drinking casualties (Hernandez, Lonnie Smith, and David Green) and sore-armed pitchers (Ken Dayley, Jeff Lahti, Danny Cox, Greg Mathews, and Joe Magrane). When the aged Busch assured him that he had a lifetime contract with the organization despite such problems, Herzog's barbed reply was, "Whose lifetime—mine or yours?" By the end of the decade he was complaining, "I can't get these guys to play for me"; shortly afterward, he resigned.

JOHN HEYDLER

Heydler's main claim to fame while serving as National League president between 1918 and 1934 was in exonerating Hal Chase of charges that the first baseman had been throwing games and then trying to make up for it, even to the point of stretching the truth. Otherwise, he was largely an appendage to both NL owners and Commissioner Kenesaw Landis. Once Landis took office in 1920, in fact, league owners routinely went over his head to the commissioner if they didn't like the first answer. This was particularly clear in the early 1920s in the case of pitcher Rube Benton, whom Heydler wanted kept out of the game for his involvement in the 1919 Black Sox scandal; determined to have the hurler on his staff, Cincinnati owner Garry Herrmann not only won Benton's reinstatement from Landis but also had the commissioner publicly scold the league official for trying to block the move. Heydler was also mostly a conspicuous silence during the deterioration of the Brooklyn and Philadelphia franchises in the 1920s and the ongoing dubiousness of Giants manager John McGraw's selection of various owners for the Boston Braves. In the late 1920s, in an attempt to counter the publicity won by the American League because of Babe Ruth's slugging feats, he proposed the adoption of a designated hitter rule but failed to win over enough NL owners to the innovation.

Heydler's obsession with Chase started in the fall of 1918, after Cincinnati manager Christy Mathewson had accused his first baseman of throwing games. By the time Heydler convened a hearing on the case in January 1919, chief witness Mathewson was in France recuperating from a gas attack and not available for testimony. For more than a year afterward Heydler welcomed any other game-fixing scandal (e.g., the Lee Magee case) as an opportunity to get back to Chase. Although he knew better, he went to the extreme of congratulating McGraw's (perjured) testimony during the Black Sox trial that the first baseman had been effectively outlawed by being sent a ludicrously low contract offer for the 1920 season.

Heydler's most significant decision affecting onfield play came in response to the rabbit-ball year of 1930, when the NL established records for batting (.304), slugging (.448), and ERA (4.98). The American League, facing a similar glut of offense, voted to raise the stitching on its balls to the advantage of curveball pitchers, but Heydler went further by adding a thicker cover. The result was a decline in the league's overall batting average to the .270s.

Prior to sitting behind a desk, Heydler had been an umpire. He quit in 1898 in outrage over the verbal and physical abuse heaped on arbiters by the Baltimore Orioles and also because of his difficulties with Giants owner Andrew Freedman. Later, as a typesetter for the Washington *Star,* he took to compiling statistics and caught the attention of Pittsburgh owner Barney Dreyfuss, who recommended him as a secretary to NL president Harry Pulliam. He succeeded Pulliam on an interim basis when the league official committed suicide in 1909, served as secretary-treasurer under Thomas Lynch and John Tener, then was elected to the job after Tener's resignation in 1918.

Heydler's departure was less quiet than his arrival. In 1934, with the Giants blowing a pennant by losing six of their last seven games, he hired detectives to monitor a season-ending Cardinals-Reds series as a precaution against the possibility of accusations of wrongdoing. When the story broke in the press after St. Louis had won the World Series, Car-

dinals owner Sam Breadon took umbrage at what he regarded as an aspersion on his team's pennant and wrote the league president suggesting that senility had gotten the better of him. Heydler, already in poor health, called a special league meeting and resigned on December 14, 1934.

KIRBY HIGBE

Higbe was the only major league pitcher who owed some of his success to pinochle. Obtained by the Dodgers for the 1941 season after a couple of humdrum years with the Cubs and Phillies, he impressed manager Leo Durocher as being more interested in cards and liquor than in pitching. Himself no stranger to a card table, Durocher played a season-long pinochle game with the righthander, offering to cancel 200 points of his continuous lead whenever Higbe pitched Brooklyn to a victory. By the time Higbe had erased his deficit with Durocher, he had led the National League with 22 wins and helped the Dodgers to a pennant.

PINKY HIGGINS

In 1938 Red Sox third baseman Higgins established the big league mark for most consecutive hits, with 12; the streak, later tied by Walt Dropo, included two walks. A righthanded hitter, Higgins had a 14-year career between 1930 and 1946 for the Athletics, Red Sox, and Tigers, over which he averaged .292 as a batter. As Boston's manager from 1955 to 1962, he was all too comfortable with the pervasive franchise racism, once telling Boston beat writer Clif Keane that he was "nothing but a fucking nigger-lover" for the opinion that a young Minnie Minoso was the best all-around player in the league.

DICK HIGHAM

Higham is the only umpire ever expelled from baseball for corruption. On June 24, 1882 he faced a special National League meeting to consider charges that he had conspired with gamblers to fix games. When a handwriting expert hired by Detroit Wolverines president W. C. Thompson showed that Higham had penned incriminating letters, the umpire tendered his resignation. He later became a bookie and reappeared publicly only in 1889 as the victim of a Kansas City crowd that beat him for spreading malicious rumors about a bartender's wife.

PAUL HINES

A superstar of the National League's first decade, Hines may or may not have made the first unassisted triple play (and the only one by an outfielder) and won the first Triple Crown. Playing for the Providence Grays on May 8, 1878, he made an impressive shoestring catch in short left-center field, then tagged third to retire, according to the rules of the day, the two runners, both of whom had already rounded that base; the confusion about the accomplishment arises from his subsequent throw to second base, which, while necessary to complete a triple killing under modern rules, was a superfluous gesture at the time. Also from 1878, the center fielder's .358 average, four homers, and 50 RBIs are now recognized as league-leading figures, though Hines himself got to wear only two of the crowns because of contemporary statistics showing Abner Dalrymple of Milwaukee as the batting champion.

Unlike Babe Ruth's putative called shot in the 1932 World Series, Hines's prediction of a home run in a game in Boston attracted considerable press attention; before the game, he had marked the round-tripper next to his name in the fifth-inning column on the official scorer's sheet, then made good on his prediction. With less fanfare the outfielder raced Cap Anson to become the first major leaguer to stroke 1,000 hits; ending the 1884 season with 1,027 as against his former teammate's 1,026. Hines has also been credited with being the first to wear sunglasses in the field, a practice he began in 1882.

CHARLES E. HINTON

Professor Hinton unveiled his invention, the first pitching machine, in the Princeton University gymnasium on December 15, 1896.

JOHN HIRSCHBECK

Largely because of the sympathetic attention he had received from being spat upon by Roberto Alomar in 1996, Hirschbeck emerged as the most prominent rebel against Richie Phillips's suicidal strategy in 1999 to have umpires offer a mass resignation to force new contract talks with the American and National leagues. He was eventually elected president of the World Umpires Association, the group that replaced Phillips's Major League Umpires Association with Major League Baseball's blessings.

DON HOAK

An infielder for the Dodgers, Reds, and Pirates among others in the 1950s and 1960s, third baseman Hoak's reputation as a hothead often slighted his baseball smarts. On April 21, 1957, while with Cincinnati, he even prompted a change in baseball's interference rules when, as the lead runner on second, he deliberately grabbed a potential double-play ball headed for the shortstop so while he would be declared out, the twin killing could be avoided. Although it was the third time that season the Reds had pulled the play, Hoak's cavalier toss of the ball to Milwaukee's shortstop Johnny Logan underscored the loophole. The National and American leagues subsequently ruled that both the runner and the batter are out in such cases of willful interference.

BUTCH HOBSON

Hobson's .899 fielding average for Boston in 1978 represented the first time since 1916 that a major league regular couldn't maintain a defensive average of .900. Suffering from severe elbow problems, the slugging third baseman had to traverse half the infield to make even routine throws to first; the situation became so dire that he begged manager Don Zimmer to take him out of the lineup because of the damage he was doing to the team. The right-hand-hitting Hobson lasted eight seasons (1975–82) with the Red Sox, Angels, and Yankees.

GIL HODGES

As both a player for the Boys of Summer Dodgers and the manager of the Miracle Mets, Hodges was the guest of honor at a New York admiration feast for much of his career. But his popular image of a silent, forbearing Mr. Stalwart also obscured his ranking among the greatest mid-century sluggers and his tactical deviousness as a pilot.

Hodges's move from catcher to first base midway through the 1948 season (to make room in the Brooklyn lineup for Roy Campanella) corresponded with the power outburst that would give him 370 home runs over an 18-year career. Using the barometers of hits, home runs, runs batted in, runs scored, stolen bases, and batting average, the righthanded slugger was among the top five major leaguers in offensive production in the 1950s (the others were Stan Musial, Duke Snider, Richie Ashburn, and Mickey Mantle).

Among other things, he drove in more than 100 runs in seven consecutive seasons and hit at least 25 homers eight times. Four of the round-trippers came in a single game, against the Braves on August 21, 1950, marking the first time that anybody had accomplished that feat at night.

With the possible exception of Pee Wee Reese, Hodges was the most popular of the mid-20th century Dodgers, not least because he was one of the team's few year-round Brooklyn residents. Much of the borough went into mourning when he went hitless in 21 at bats in the 1952 World Series against the Yankees and started the 1953 season by going only 14-for-75. Then, in June 1953, a priest named Herbert Raymond cemented the first baseman's place in Brooklyn lore by telling his parishioners: "It's too warm this morning for a sermon. Go home, keep the Commandments, and say a prayer for Gil Hodges." Within days Hodges erupted for a season that eventually produced 31 home runs, 122 runs batted in, and a .302 average. In 1955 he even avenged his miserable 1952 World Series by driving in both runs in the 2–0 win by Johnny Podres in the seventh game of the Series that brought Brooklyn its one and only world championship.

A natural candidate for the 1962 expansion Mets, Hodges kept things symmetrical by hitting the franchise's first home run, on April 11, but otherwise contributed little but nostalgia for New York's NL fans. The following year he was traded to the Senators for outfielder Jimmy Piersall and immediately announced his retirement to take over as Washington manager. Because he had still been technically active for the swap, Hodges narrowly missed gaining another baseball footnote when, in 1967, he was shipped back to Shea Stadium to manage the Mets in exchange for Bill Denehy and $150,000; no other retired player has come as close to being traded for active major leaguers twice in order to manage.

In New York Hodges inherited the nucleus of the Miracle Mets—not least ace righthander Tom Seaver. From the point of view of the standings, his influence on the team in 1968 seemed minimal; it even appeared perilously strenuous when he suffered a heart attack after the season. The following year, however, he offered numerous reminders that, his altar boy image notwithstanding, he had played under such masters of the devious as Leo Durocher and Charlie Dressen. What became the most noted of all his juiced-up tactics was the Shoe Polish Gambit: Like Dressen, he always kept a couple of balls in the dugout smeared with shoe polish just in case there was ever an opportunity to argue that a New York hitter had been struck by a pitch. In the fifth game of the 1969 World Series against Baltimore, just such an opportunity arose with Cleon Jones at bat, and gullible umpires sent the outfielder to first base in what proved to be the turning point of New York's conclusive victory. It was also Jones who, on July 30 of the same year, had helped demonstrate Hodges's no-nonsense command of the team. After the outfielder had gone after a couple of balls with little energy, the pilot called time and walked ever so slowly out to left field where, against a deathlike silence from the Shea Stadium stands, he ordered Jones to accompany him back to the dugout. Many of the Mets players said later that the episode was crucial to the team's victory.

With the death of general manager Johnny Murphy after the 1969 season, Hodges began to act almost as concerned with keeping intrusive board chairman M. Donald Grant and new general manager Bob Scheffing out of the clubhouse as he was about keeping the team above .500. That not too much was made of this by the press attested to his popularity with the local media and his players. Hodges was felled by a second, fatal heart attack on April 2, 1973 while playing golf during a spring training break.

RUSS HODGES

Hodges was responsible for baseball's single most memorable broadcasting moment after Bobby Thomson's home run in the 1951 New York-Brooklyn playoff. His hysterical call of "THE GIANTS WIN THE PENNANT! THE GIANTS WIN THE PENNANT! THE GIANTS WIN THE PENNANT!" was preserved only because a Dodgers fan recorded it off the radio.

ART HOELSKOETTER

In four seasons with the Cardinals Hoelskoetter set the standard for versatility. Between 1905 and 1908 he appeared in 78 games as a second baseman, 77 as a third baseman, 49 behind the plate, 28 at first base, 20 in the outfield, 16 at shortstop, and 15 on the mound; he ended his career with a .236 batting average and a 1–5 won-lost record.

JEROLD HOFFBERGER

Hoffberger spent his 15 years as Baltimore owner alienating just about everyone who was not part of the Orioles front office. The head of the National Brewing Company that had sponsored the club's games since 1962, his major contribution to the winning teams of the late 1960s and 1970s was the expansion of the club's farm system. On the other hand, his paternalistic approach led to continuing the organization's policy of releasing, trading, or leaving unprotected in expansion drafts every Orioles player representative from 1960 and 1968, when Brooks Robinson assumed the post.

In the events leading to the spring training strike of 1972, Hoffberger clashed repeatedly with Players Association chief Marvin Miller, who accused him of trying to compel players to desert the union. Whatever the truth of that specific allegation, Hoffberger was not quite the "hard-line reactionary" that Miller claimed; in fact, he supported an increase in pension benefits, the main issue in the 1972 stoppage, and disagreed vocally with the tactics of Ray Grebey, head of the owners' Player Relations Committee. After the 1972 strike Hoffberger boycotted owners meetings, not abandoning his stance until 1976, and then only to join forces with George Steinbrenner of the Yankees and Charlie Finley of the A's in an effort to oust Commissioner Bowie Kuhn.

When Baltimore failed to sell out its home games in the 1974 American League Championship Series, Hoffberger contemplated selling out but ran up against Kuhn's politically motivated fixation on putting a team in Washington. Committed to keeping the club in Baltimore, he wouldn't even consider Kuhn's suggestion of a stadium between the two cities or another commissioner-inspired resolution at the December 1976 major league meetings calling on the Orioles to play "a suitable number of games" in the national capital. Hoffberger finally sold out to Washington attorney Edward Bennett Williams, the owner of the football Washington Redskins. The sale was contingent on Williams's promise to keep the Orioles in Baltimore.

TREVOR HOFFMAN

Hoffman is the only closer to chalk up five seasons of 40 or more saves. The Padres righthander also holds the record for single-season conversions, providing the backbone for San Diego's pennant win in 1998 by gaining 53 saves in 54 opportunities.

ROY HOFHEINZ

Hofheinz promoted indoor baseball by building the Astrodome; that was about as positive as it got with the judge.

Hofheinz bought into the Houston team in 1962 on the coattails of Robert E. Smith, then considered the richest man in Texas. Over the next couple of years he hocked everything he owned to buy out Smith in a series of bitter boardroom confrontations. But even before then his reputation as a penny-wise, pound-foolish blowhard had undone the organization's first important hire, of Gabe Paul as head of baseball operations; Paul, who had resigned as general manager of the Reds to take the post with Houston, backed out as soon as he was informed of Hofheinz's 11th-hour involvement with Smith. Paul's successor Paul Richards fared only minimally better, lasting through the 1965 season but with constant squabbling with the owner as the price. Even years later, Richards could reject a reporter's suggestion that Hofheinz was his own worst enemy by declaring, "Not while I'm alive he isn't."

Hofheinz was calling the shots when the Colt .45s changed into the Astros upon moving into the Astrodome in 1965. Major league baseball's first indoor facility, it was trumpeted by publicists as the Eighth Wonder of the World and by Hofheinz himself as a cash cow for its potential to draw spectators for concerts, circuses, and conventions as well as for baseball games. Among the judge's inspirations for the plant was to introduce particularly long dugouts so he could sell more seats at higher prices with the come-on that they were directly behind the players. When players complained about losing fly balls in the dome's 4,500 plastic skylights, he ordered the skylights painted over, this in turn reducing the day lighting by 40 percent, killing the natural grass, and necessitating the first use of artificial turf, in 1966.

The painting over of the skylights was one of the few times that Hofheinz could be accused of listening to his players. With general manager Spec Richardson acting as his enforcer, he insisted on an All-American-Boy image for the team, imposing a strict dress code and curfews and fuming whenever a member of the club didn't take the opportunity of a media interview to say how devoted he was to the harmony of the organization. To help along his "family" atmosphere, Hofheinz refused to pay players by check, instead depositing their salaries in a local bank in which he had a significant holding. As he proudly pointed out to any-one who asked about the policy, the maneuver en-abled the bank to hold on to the money a little longer and got the Houston players used to thinking about his institution when it came to money matters.

All of Hofheinz's financial deviousness and con-cern with image came together in an embarrassing explosion in 1975, when it was revealed that he could not meet $38 million in debts to franchise creditors. In a desperate move to stave off bankruptcy, he agreed to share power with creditor representatives on a three-man committee. There he found himself in a minority when the other two board members vot-ed to oust Richardson. After a brief period of hanging on as a minority voice, Hofheinz sold the franchise to the creditors (the General Electric Credit Corporation and the Ford Motor Credit Corporation).

BILL HOLBERT

The original good-field, no-hit catcher, Holbert came to bat a record 2,342 times in a 12-year career starting in 1876 without hitting a home run. He also had the most at bats in a season without an extra base hit, slapping 50 singles in 244 official appear-ances for the National League franchises in Troy and Syracuse in 1879.

BOBO HOLLOMAN

Holloman pitched baseball's most costly no-hit-ter. A bulbous righthander for the 1953 Browns, he was about to be farmed out after some disastrous re-lief efforts when he convinced owner Bill Veeck to give him a start. The first result was a May 6 no-hit-ter over the Athletics that made Holloman the only 20th-century hurler to fashion such a gem in his ini-tial starting assignment. The second result was that, having to hold on to the only gate attraction he had for the miserable Browns, Veeck had to exercise a $25,000 option on the pitcher. The third result was that, because of the money committed to Holloman, St. Louis was unable to put together the $31,500 earmarked for purchasing minor league shortstop Ernie Banks. The icing on the cake was that the no-hitter itself came on a night that was so cold and rainy that Veeck announced before the start of the game that the 2,473 fans in attendance would be able to use their rain checks for another game as a reward for their hardiness. As for Holloman, his effort against the Athletics was his only complete game, and he closed out his single major league season with a rec-ord of 3–7 and an ERA of 5.23.

DUCKY HOLMES

Outfielder Holmes precipitated baseball's worst anti-Semitic episode. On July 25, 1898, while playing for the Baltimore Orioles against his former club, the Giants, he responded to a Polo Grounds heckler by shouting, "I glad I don't have to work for no Sheeny anymore." Incensed at the reference to his Jewish background, New York owner Andrew Freedman charged onto the field accompanied by security guards to remove Holmes from the park. The other Orioles responded by forming a bat-wielding circle around their teammate as the increasingly hostile crowd urged the guards to use their truncheons, while Freedman demanded that umpire Thomas Lynch eject Holmes from the game. Instead, Lynch declared the game a forfeit to Baltimore and escaped to the visiting team's clubhouse.

Over the next few days National League presi-dent Nick Young fined the Giants $1,000 for delib-erately provoking a forfeit and suspended Holmes for the rest of the season, players around the league threatened to strike unless the suspension were lift-ed, and a Maryland judge granted an injunction bar-ring the suspension. As for Freedman, he protested every game in which Holmes appeared for the rest of the year but to no avail. The incident did nothing to raise consciousnesses in the media; typical was the reaction of *Sporting Life,* which declared itself aghast that Holmes should have been disciplined for "the trifling offense of insulting the Hebrew race."

OLIVER WENDELL HOLMES

Holmes wrote the U.S. Supreme Court's 1922 unanimous decision exempting baseball from feder-al antitrust legislation and establishing organized ball's right to regulate its own affairs. The suit, *Fed-eral Baseball Club of Baltimore v. National League,* accused the major leagues and the Federal League magnates who had capitulated to them of seeking to institute a monopoly and requested $900,000 in dam-ages. The Baltimore interests pursued their cause through the federal courts for almost seven years, until May 29, 1922, when Holmes issued his often misunderstood decision.

In point of fact, Holmes drew no distinction be-tween sports and business, as is commonly assumed.

The less quotable distinction he did make was between personal effort (what have come to be called service industries, including lawyers and doctors as well as performing artists) and trade or commerce (businesses that make, sell, or transport goods). In those limited and antiquated terms, baseball was held not to be commerce, nor subject to antitrust laws, nor liable to federal restraint in its business practices. Almost as an aside, Holmes also upheld the necessity of the reserve clause, even though baseball's counsel, mindful of the many legal losses on the issue, had not made it an essential part of their argument. Curiously, a year later, the jurist went through a tortuous distinction to rule that vaudeville *was* interstate commerce and, as such, subject to the same federal laws from which he had exempted baseball.

TOMMY HOLMES

Holmes had a career year in 1945—for both himself and for the 20th-century Boston version of the Braves franchise. By batting .352 and leading the National League in hits (224), doubles (47), home runs (28), and slugging average (.577), the lefthand-hitting outfielder exposed the organization's perennial problems in offense by setting almost all of its major season records. In striking out merely nine times, he also became the only major leaguer to win a home-run title while simultaneously proving to be the most difficult player in the league to fan.

JEROME HOLTZMAN

Chicago *Sun-Times* sportswriter Holtzman won the gratitude of relievers in both leagues for his successful campaign in the 1960s to have baseball formally acknowledge saves as an official pitching category.

RICK HONEYCUTT

Honeycutt has a late-season trade to thank for an ERA title. In August 1983 the Rangers swapped the southpaw to the Dodgers while he topped the American League with a 2.42 mark. In nine appearances with Los Angeles he was battered around to the tune of a 5.77 ERA, but since that wasn't transferable to the AL, he remained the junior circuit's stingiest hurler of the year.

HARRY HOOPER (Hall of Fame, 1971)

Hooper's .281 lifetime average and sterling right field play helped the Red Sox to four pennants in the 1910s, but his greatest contribution to baseball was his role in converting Babe Ruth from a pitcher to an outfielder. He also played a major part in a threatened player strike during the 1918 World Series against the Cubs.

A lefthanded leadoff batter for most of his 17-year (1909–25) career with the Red Sox and White Sox, Hooper possessed a reputation for defensive brilliance, especially after a bare-handed catch to rob Larry Doyle of the Giants of a home run in the final game of the 1912 World Series. He is also the only player ever to lead off both ends of a doubleheader with a home run, a feat he accomplished on Memorial Day 1913 in a season in which he had only four round-trippers.

In spring training in 1918 Hooper approached new manager Ed Barrow with a suggestion that Ruth was more valuable in the lineup every day than on the mound once every four days. Rebuffed at first on the ground that the fans would murder any pilot who tried to convert the best lefthanded pitcher in baseball, he kept at Barrow with arguments about the drawing power of Ruth's bat that finally had the desired effect on the manager, who was also a part-owner of the club. Ruth got his first assignment as a position player, at first base, on May 6 before being moved to the outfield shortly afterward. Hooper's further role in the switch was to move to center field himself to help the new left fielder learn his position.

Upset by the low wartime attendance at the first four games of the 1918 World Series, teammates asked Hooper to head a delegation of Boston and Chicago players to confront the ruling National Commission with an ultimatum to increase the players' share of the proceeds or risk a strike. But with American League president Ban Johnson reeling from a liquid lunch and spewing truisms about the players' patriotic obligation in the war year to continue the Series, Cincinnati owner Garry Herrmann delivering speeches about how much he had contributed to baseball, and National League president John Heydler saying nothing, Hooper and his associates realized they were getting nowhere, concluded they wouldn't get much farther with reporters or fans, and retreated.

Hooper, who is credited with patenting the sliding catch, owes his election to Cooperstown to a concerted campaign by his sons and friends in the late 1960s.

LOLLY HOPKINS

Hopkins was called Megaphone Lolly for her use of the instrument to inform everyone what she thought players were doing right and umpires were doing wrong during her regular trips to both Fenway Park and Braves Field in the 1930s and 1940s. "A positive fan" who cheered visitors as well as local heroes, the Rhode Island resident was rewarded with season passes by both Boston clubs.

BOB HORNER

Horner's nine years with the Braves from 1978 to 1986 were weighty in all senses of the word. The third baseman went directly from Arizona State University to 1978 National League Rookie of the Year honors by belting 23 home runs. He followed that up with three seasons of at least 30 home runs, and on July 6, 1986 joined the handful of players to tag four round-trippers in a game. On the other hand, Horner was in continual conflict with Atlanta owner Ted Turner over his own bulging waistline and contract demands, worsening his position with a series of sidelining injuries.

The first clash with Turner took place after Horner's rookie season, when he claimed that his six-figure signing bonus was part of his salary and that any negotiations for 1979 should begin from there; an arbitrator decided in the third baseman's favor in June 1979 but declined to grant his request of free agency. The worst clash between the two occurred in 1980, when the owner decided that he wasn't getting his money's worth because of Horner's excess poundage and demanded that he be sent to the minors to play himself back into shape. The order provoked tensions with both Braves general manager John Mullin, who argued that even an overweight Horner was one of the best hitters in the league, and with the Players Association, which filed a grievance for "improper disciplinary action." Horner sat out for a few days, then went on to finish second in the league in homers. By the mid-1980s, however, hand and wrist injuries had finished 1978's number one draft pick.

ROGERS HORNSBY (Hall of Fame, 1942)

The career hitting gap between Ty Cobb's .367 and Hornsby's .358 was nine points; the personality difference between the two greatest average hitters was between the ugly and the obnoxious. The most potent righthanded batter ever to wear a National League uniform, The Rajah also had few equals, as either player or manager, in crassness and manic self-absorption. Even his one admitted vulnerability—gambling at the track—became a lever for ridiculing teammates, demeaning charges, and blackmailing franchises.

Hornsby's numbers were beyond debate. Although his seven batting titles were one less than Honus Wagner's and Tony Gwynn's, his six straight between 1920 and 1925 for the Cardinals included three years of better than .400 and one season (1924) of an all-time post–19th-century high of .424. In both 1922 and 1925 he won the Triple Crown. He was the class of the field in safeties four times, in doubles four times, in triples twice, in homers twice, in runs scored five times, in RBIs four times, in walks three times, and in slugging average nine times. He attained 200 hits seven times, 40 doubles seven times, 20 home runs seven times, 100 runs six times, and 100 RBIs five times. Perhaps most startling, his composite average between 1921 and 1925 was .402. Hornsby's overall on-base average of .434 was a point higher than Cobb's, while his slugging average of .577 was 65 points higher than that of the Detroit star. He won MVP awards for St. Louis in 1925 and for Chicago in 1929.

With the numbers went enough abrasiveness and turmoil to keep both his teams and the league offices busy for a major part of his career. The first big ruckus came in 1923, when the second baseman decided that Branch Rickey might have had his virtues as a general manager but was far too much a theorist to serve as a dugout boss as well. For the next season-and-a-half the two most visible members of the Cardinals franchise were constantly at one another, with Rickey's main rejoinder being ornately expressed suspicions that his hitting star wasn't always as injured as he often claimed and that he was merely trying to earn some extra time at the track. With the club still dithering in the middle of the league standings, however, owner Sam Breadon came down on Hornsby's side on May 30, 1925, firing Rickey as manager. Although he maintained his various front office titles, Rickey insisted on selling all his stock in the franchise, and found a ready buyer in Hornsby, who managed to find the money with the help of a Breadon note to the bank.

In his first full year as manager, in 1926, Hornsby

brought the Cardinals their first pennant and then a World Series victory over the Yankees. But even as St. Louis was celebrating, Breadon was adding up his grievances against the city's new hero. To begin with, there was the owner's personal distaste when, on the eve of the postseason meeting with the Yankees, Hornsby's mother died; the manager responded by saying he would skip the funeral to stay with the club in the World Series. If that left Breadon shaking his head, he had already had some practice a few weeks earlier, when Hornsby had refused to allow the club to play an exhibition game arranged by the owner on the grounds that full attention should be paid to the pennant race. Worst of all for Breadon was Hornsby's rejection of a one-year contract to return as playing manager in 1927, demanding instead a multiyear pact at a figure significantly higher than the proffered $50,000. Weighing personal dislike and financial grievances, Breadon took on the entire city of St. Louis by trading his star to the Giants for Frankie Frisch and Jimmy Ring. Even when the crank phone calls and editorial blasts died down, the issue was kept alive by Hornsby's refusal to sell the stock he had purchased from Rickey unless he came out of the deal with a substantial profit. Because of a league rule against a player performing for one club while owning a piece of another, NL president John Heydler had to put together a deal under which his office, the Giants, and the Cardinals all threw money into a pot so that Hornsby came away with a $66,000 profit.

As a Giant in 1927, Hornsby got into Rickey-like clashes with John McGraw, but that didn't prevent McGraw from turning the team over to him when he was away for business or health reasons. In gratitude, Hornsby spent much of his time on the bench lecturing players on how McGraw did things the wrong way. With several prominent players complaining to owner Charles Stoneham that they wouldn't play for Hornsby even as a fill-in pilot, even a .361 average for the year didn't stop him from being traded again, this time to the Braves for the rock-bottom price of catcher Shanty Hogan and outfielder Jimmy Welsh. With Boston in 1928, he batted another league-leading .387 and needed only a few weeks to persuade owner Emil Fuchs that he was a better manager than incumbent Jack Slattery, whom he referred to as "that dumb collegiate coach." It took about the same amount of time for the other Braves players to begin petitioning Fuchs to get rid of the infielder; among other things, they accused Hornsby of attacking them on the bench for ruining his RBI opportunities with weak hitting or inept baserunning. Fuchs was so relieved to have a gate attraction on his cellar dwellers that he responded to the protests by giving Hornsby a new six-year contract even before the end of the season.

But Hornsby himself saw little future with the Braves and, six-year contract or not, persuaded Fuchs to trade him to the Cubs for a boatload of young prospects who would do the club more good in the long run. Fuchs also got $200,000 out of the deal. The script wasn't too different in Chicago. First, Hornsby led the team to a pennant in 1929. Then, after replacing Joe McCarthy as pilot in 1930, he so ridiculed the heavy-drinking Hack Wilson that the slugger stopped hitting and was soon packed off to the Cardinals. His glee at once again being in charge of a dugout even led him to make an uncharacteristic (and soon broken) promise in writing to Commissioner Kenesaw Landis that "I do not in the future intend to have anything to do with gamblers, bookmakers, horse races, or bets, etc."

Within two years, however, when it had become clear that Hornsby's knowledge of pitching extended only to the fact that he could hit it, even the press began calling for his ouster. If owner William Wrigley didn't go along, it was in considerable part because his manager owed the club tens of thousands of dollars advanced to him to cover track losses. Only with Wrigley's death in January 1932 did his successor, his son Phil, decide that the IOUs weren't reason enough to hold on to a bad pilot, and he switched to Charlie Grimm in July. No sooner was Hornsby out the door than the team discovered that, aside from getting regular advances on his salary, he had been borrowing from his players for years; the money was eventually paid back by the club rerouting the wages it still owed him. Knowing they didn't have to worry about irritating their debtor, the players voted not to give Hornsby a penny of their 1932 World Series share. The Rajah promptly filed a protest with Commissioner Kenesaw Landis, who ruled that the players were free to vote as they wanted.

With his playing career all but behind him, Hornsby signed with the Cardinals again in 1933, as a pinch-hitter. Rumors that he would be named manager were dispelled when he was released halfway through the season. He was immediately signed to manage the Browns by owner Phil Ball, who relished the prospect of outdrawing the Cardinals with one of the latter's emblematic stars. Ball was wrong several times over: Shortly after reaching the agreement with Hornsby, Ball died; the executors of his estate knew nothing about baseball and were easily cowed into doing whatever the manager wanted; and one too many second-division finishes doomed the Browns in 1935 to a major league-record-low home attendance of 80,922. Things didn't get much better the following year except for the presence of a new ownership less willing to be bullied by Hornsby. Put on notice that his gambling habit would no longer be tolerated, he vowed to comply, unaware that he was being shadowed by Pinkerton detectives whenever he placed a bet. He was fired during the 1937 season.

For the next 15 years Hornsby managed in the minors, continuing to patronize whatever track was handy, lashing out at his players for being less entertaining than his sure things, and telling any small-town reporter who would listen that he never strained his eyes by going to the movies or reading a book. It was also in the minors that he was first recorded as taking a shower with one of his losing pitchers and urinating on him to show his displeasure. That he returned to the major leagues in 1952 was due to Browns owner Bill Veeck's willingness to try anything to annoy the Cardinals. But though he had the same intentions as Ball 20 years earlier, Veeck remained alive, and long enough to realize he didn't want Captain Bligh managing his team. Ironically, the owner came under more attack than Hornsby when the firing was announced in June because of suspicions that Veeck had merely been ridiculing the old man. The impression was solidified when the players presented Veeck with a two-foot loving cup for liberating them from the manager.

Hornsby had one more managerial stint left in him. No sooner had he been fired by the Browns than Powel Crosley decided that the NL's greatest hitter of all time was exactly what Cincinnati needed. Hornsby lasted through the 1953 season, when he was fired for all the usual reasons, including his shower specialty. But he had the next-to-last laugh: Because he was still operating on Veeck's contract as well, his release at the end of the year meant that he collected 1954 salaries from two clubs he was no longer managing. But all that money, too, had been lost at the track by the time he was working as a coach for the Cubs in 1958 and 1959. His last connection with baseball was as a batting coach for the expansion Mets in 1962.

For someone whose big league career was identified with humorlessness, Hornsby had an atypical beginning, getting his first baseball job with the Boston Bloomer Girls team that barnstormed through Texas with several male ringers who played in drag.

TONY HORTON

Horton's fragile self-esteem left him unprepared for the harsh give-and-take of salary negotiations in the pre-agent era. After a solid year with Cleveland (27 home runs and 93 RBIs) in 1969, he demanded a salary hike from $30,000 to $100,000. Alvin Dark, who had spent the season as manager telling the first baseman how invaluable he was to the club, changed gears in his second role as general manager to downplay the slugger's significance. After protracted talks, Horton finally agreed to a figure closer to Dark's proposal but never overcame the criticism of his abilities raised during the bargaining. He moped through a good part of the 1970 season, then revealed how troubled he was when he ran out to his position after the final out of a game, compelling Dark to lead him back off the field. Horton was diagnosed as having suffered a nervous breakdown, never played another major league game, and was even ordered by his psychiatrist to stop watching televised games. Dark called the episode the saddest of his career and pointed to it as a reason why clubs should always have separate managers and general managers.

PETE HOTALING

Primarily an outfielder during his nine-year major league career with six teams, Hotaling was the first professional catcher to wear a mask. He adopted it in 1877 as a member of the independent Syracuse Stars.

CHARLIE HOUGH

Aside from its sheer length (25 years from 1970 to 1994), Hough's pitching career was noteworthy for reversing the usual transition from a starter to a reliever. In fact, it wasn't until the righthanded knuckleballer's 14th season, with the Rangers in 1982, that he became a fixture in a starting rotation rather than a bullpen specialist. It was because of Hough's butterfly pitch that Gino Petralli of Texas broke all American League passed-ball records in 1987—including most for a season (35 in only 63 games), a game (six, on August 30) and an inning (four, on August 22).

RALPH HOUK

Houk is the only major league manager to win a World Series in each of his first two years as a pilot. He added a third consecutive pennant for the Yankees in 1963, but then got kicked upstairs, where he presided over the deterioration of the franchise. In subsequent managerial assignments—including a reprise with the Yankees and stints with the Tigers and Red Sox—he was unable to duplicate his early success. Through it all, he achieved the distinction of never having been fired.

The former third-string catcher (who played in only 91 games in eight seasons with the Yankees) was tabbed to succeed Casey Stengel at the New York helm in 1961 because of fears that some other club would snatch him away from the organization and benefit from the training course he had been undergoing as bullpen catcher, minor league manager, and big league coach at the Yankees expense. Undoing the Stengel legacy of strict rules, extensive platooning, and irregular starting assignments for pitchers, Houk installed a regular lineup and a stable rotation, winning not only his trio of pennants but also the appreciation of his players. It didn't hurt that the 1961 team he inherited featured Roger Maris's 61 home runs and the then-record 240 by a club.

Houk's promotion to general manager in 1964 was a failure: As a front office figure, he was able to make little use of his ability to motivate players; instead, he spent too much time indulging the gripes of those same players about his successor Yogi Berra. Deciding well before the season was over that Berra had lost control of the team, he settled on Cardinals pilot Johnny Keane as a successor and concluded a secret agreement with the NLer. The plan hit a snag when both teams pulled themselves together to win pennants, presenting the general manager with the anomalous situation of having his team pitted in the World Series against one piloted by its next field chief. After the St. Louis victory, Berra was dumped as planned, while Houk went into a song and dance to deny that he even knew Keane had quit the Cardinals; it took only a couple of weeks for the

official announcement of the switch. His credibility already impaired by the treatment of Berra, Houk reached his public relations low by firing popular television broadcaster Mel Allen later in the year.

Soon after the takeover of the franchise by CBS in 1966, Houk stepped down from the front office for another tour in the dugout. His most notable achievement in almost seven seasons this time around was to bring a young and relatively untalented team into second place in 1970. The arrival of George Steinbrenner in late 1972 altered the franchise chemistry once again, and the new combination of elements would have produced an explosion had Houk not resigned after only one season. So tense was Houk working for Steinbrenner that he told players he had to get out or punch out his employer. Nobody doubted the possibilities in his rage, especially after he charged the mound in a game that year to snatch the cap off the head of Gaylord Perry's in search of the foreign substance he was certain the Cleveland righthander was applying to the ball.

After five seasons (1974–78) in Detroit directing the breakup of a once successful but now aging team in favor of a young and not very good one, he spent two years as a consultant to the Tigers. Bored from too much golf, he went back to the dugout, this time with the Red Sox. Saddled with a front office so inept that it lost stars Carlton Fisk and Fred Lynn by neglecting to mail them their contracts on time, he was able to do no better than a tie for second place in the second half of the strike-induced split season of 1981. In spite of his reputation as a pitcher's manager, in fact, he was unable to bring any hurler up to even 15 wins in his four seasons at Fenway Park.

FRANK HOWARD

Between May 12 and May 18 in 1968, Washington outfielder Howard joined baseball's all-time sluggers by swatting 10 home runs in 20 at bats. The performance keynoted his years with the Senators, when his titanic shots were about the only reasons fans had to watch the team. Upon retirement the six-foot, seven-inch Howard became a manager and hitting coach whose on-bench lectures seemed to inspire rookies and drive veterans off the deep end. Mainly because many of his managers perceived him as having too much influence over younger players, he seldom lasted as a batting instructor on any team for more than a couple of years.

STEVE HOWE

Howe holds baseball's unofficial record for the most times (seven) suspended by a club or league. In the case of the southpaw reliever, the violations centered around his use of cocaine since arriving with the Dodgers in 1980 as a Rookie of the Year closer. The repeated second chances—opportunities not made available to others—raised questions about the sport's drug policies, not least in relation to the race of the player involved and the financial clout of the organization for which he played.

Despite two rehabilitation stints in 1983, Howe was suspended in June (for reporting late for a game) and September (for missing a team flight). Then, after testing positive three times in November, Commissioner Bowie Kuhn disqualified him for the entire 1984 season to protect the "image of baseball." After receiving treatment yet again, he returned to the Dodgers in 1985, but after falling back into his old habits, was suspended, released, then picked up by the Twins. After Minnesota also discerned evidence of continued drug use, he was cut loose again, ending up with the California League San Jose Bees (Class A), where he was suspended twice from organized ball in general, once for an incident with police. In 1987 Texas general manager Tom Grieve worked out a deal with Commissioner Peter Ueberroth under which Howe would pitch for the Rangers top farm club in Oklahoma City but not be promoted to Arlington without the express approval of the commissioner. No sooner was the ink dry on the accord than Grieve promoted the reliever to Texas, incurring a fine of $250,000. Worse, Howe once again admitted a relapse, and was again suspended from baseball.

The lefthander returned still again, with the Yankees in 1991. Midway through the following season, he was cited by authorities in his Montana hometown for possession and dealing. Without waiting for a Montana court to hand down a verdict, Commissioner Fay Vincent banned the hurler as an incurable recidivist. When the Players Association responded to a formal complaint by Howe by taking testimony from Yankees officials, Vincent decided his authority was being usurped and warned New York general manager Gene Michael and another club executive to adhere to his line or start thinking about other employment. The upshot was that Howe pleaded *nolo contendere* in Montana, an arbitrator accepted the argument that the pitcher relied on cocaine for help in combating the attention deficit disorder from which he suffered, and the pitcher was reinstated for 1993 with a big contract.

Howe stayed with the Yankees until June 22, 1996, when he was released after nagging injuries and prolonged ineffectiveness. Two days later, he was arrested at New York's Kennedy Airport for carrying a loaded .357 Magnum in his luggage. A guilty plea got him three years probation and 150 hours of community service.

Aside from all the other aspects of Howe's curious longevity, there was also the diamond factor: After racking up 17 saves for the Dodgers in his maiden year, he reached double figures in bullpen rescues only three more times and never saved as many as 20 games in a season.

BOB HOWSAM

Howsam was the architect of the Big Red Machine in the 1970s. A Branch Rickey protégé, his most significant moves in putting together the Cincinnati powerhouse were hiring Sparky Anderson as manager in 1970 and acquiring Joe Morgan, Jack Billingham, and George Foster in 1971 trades with Houston and San Francisco.

Howsam went to the Reds after a baptism by fire as general manager of the Cardinals in the mid-1960s. Succeeding Bing Devine largely on the say-so of mentor Rickey, he fell into the middle of a power struggle orchestrated by St. Louis owner Gussie Busch and ending with Rickey's firing as a special adviser. After initially declaring his intention of quitting in solidarity with Rickey, Howsam remained long enough to work out a trade with the Yankees that brought Roger Maris to St. Louis—a key element in the club's 1967 and 1968 pennant wins.

Although generally hailed for building Cincinnati's wrecking crew in the 1970s, Howsam had his bad moments. One came when the organization's policy against signing free agents cost it the services of lefty Don Gullett after the 1976 season. Only a couple of weeks later, the executive invited criticism from prominent Reds players for trading first baseman Tony Perez to the Expos. Howsam was also attacked in some quarters for not carrying through on threats to sue Bowie Kuhn after the commissioner had nullified Cincinnati's $1.75-million purchase of Oakland southpaw Vida Blue on the grounds that, with Tom Seaver already on the Reds through a deal with the Mets, the acquisition of the lefty would have turned the National League pennant race into an embarrassment.

Howsam stepped down from his post after the 1978 season, saying he wanted to reduce his workload because of age. But when successor Dick Wagner made one unpopular move after another over the next few years, he was called out of retirement in 1983 to salvage what was salvageable while negotiations were completed for the sale of the franchise to Marge Schott. His most significant moves in what turned out to be a two-year stay were signing free agent Dave Parker and bringing back both Perez (as a free agent pinch-hitter) and Pete Rose (as manager).

DUMMY HOY

Left deaf at age three from meningitis and mute because of his deafness, Hoy's disabilities prompted the introduction of hand signals to indicate balls and strikes—not by umpires, as is often claimed, but by his team's coaches. Regarded as one of the game's best center fielders during his 14-year (between 1888 and 1902) career with six teams, Hoy became the first outfielder to throw three runners out at the plate in one game, on June 19, 1889. He called flanking outfielders off fly balls with a high-pitched squeak, and insisted that his teammates learn to sign so he could participate in their off-field activities.

WAITE HOYT (Hall of Fame, 1969)

Hoyt's career as a starting pitcher was ruined by relieving between starts, but he developed another one as a bullpen specialist. A schoolboy sensation from Brooklyn, the righthander had a one-game tryout with the Giants in 1918 and a two-year apprenticeship with the Red Sox in 1919 and 1920 before moving down the Boston pipeline to the Yankees. He had impressed New York for, among other things, a "perfect game" relief effort against it between the fourth and 13th innings on September 24, 1919.

With the Yankees Hoyt won 157 games in 10 (six of them pennant-winning) seasons. In 1927 he paced American League hurlers in wins (22) and winning percentage (.759), and added a 2.63 ERA, following that up with 23 victories in 1928. Overall he won 237 games in a 21-year (1918–38) career with seven teams. In six World Series with the Yankees he won six games and, in the 1921 Series against the Giants, he tied Christy Mathewson's record of 27 in-

nings without yielding an earned run (although he did give up two unearned runs, one of them resulting in a 1–0 defeat in the eighth and concluding game).

Used regularly between starts, Hoyt had as many as 16 relief appearances (in 1925), while never dropping below 25 starts; in 1928 he led the league in saves (8) in addition to his 23 wins. By 1929, though, the wear and tear had brought his record down to 10–9 and his ERA up to 4.24, after which he bounded from one team to another before landing with the Pirates in 1933. In Pittsburgh he learned to husband his arm and became a bullpen ace, fashioning an ERA under 3.00 over four full seasons and part of another.

Articulate and talented, Hoyt was an amateur painter and a professional singer, appearing in the latter capacity at the Palace Theater and elsewhere on the vaudeville circuit. He was also a Broadway dandy and, after ending his career in 1938, used his connections to do regular radio work on New York stations. Moving to Cincinnati in 1942, he began a 24-year stretch as Reds announcer, first on radio and later on television. In 1945 he disappeared for several days, initially claiming he had had an attack of amnesia, then announcing that he was suffering from alcoholism; when an outpouring of mail supported his continuing in the broadcast booth, Cincinnati had the anomalous situation of a publicly recovering alcoholic not only doing baseball broadcasts but also pitching the product of sponsor Burger Brewing Company. Hoyt's announcing trademarks were endless monologues on Babe Ruth and other former Yankees teammates, and an odd delivery of play-by-play in the past tense.

AL HRABOSKY

Hrabosky was the best act in the National League for several years in the 1970s and one of the worst acts in Atlanta in the 1980s. Especially in 1975 for the Cardinals, when he won 13 games and posted a league-leading 22 saves, the southpaw reliever known as The Mad Hungarian delighted the country with his Fu Manchu mustache and flowing hair, his perpetually infuriated looks, and his spastic switches from communing with the gods to pounding the rubber in a challenge to batters to get ready. That phase of the Hrabosky show ended in 1977, when the martinetish Vern Rapp took over as manager of St. Louis and demanded the pitcher shave. After going through a disastrous season in the mood of a shorn Samson, the lefthander moved on the Kansas City, where he had another brief moment of glory, with 20 saves (according to the pitcher, mainly because of the Gypsy Rose of Death ring he wore to ward off werewolves). Ignoring the fireman's clear decline from his heyday in St. Louis, Atlanta's Ted Turner agreed to a free agent contract that would pay him $170,000 annually for 30 years, the gimmick being an assurance that Hrabosky would have a place as a broadcaster on Turner's cable television network after his playing days were over. In fact, they were already over, with the reliever picking up a mere seven saves in three years. Hrabosky and Turner later agreed to a buyout of the pact.

CAL HUBBARD (Hall of Fame, 1976)

Hubbard is the only resident of Cooperstown who is also a member of the college and pro football halls of fame. His American League umpiring career lasted from 1936 to 1951 before being interrupted by a hunting accident that affected the sight in his left eye. For the next 15 years he served as a supervisor of the AL umpiring staff, returning to active duty sporadically between 1954 and 1962. On June 20, 1944 he became the first umpire to eject a pitcher (Nelson Potter of the Browns) for violating the rule prohibiting spitballs.

Hubbard earned his other Hall of Fame plaques as a tackle with Centenary and Geneva colleges and as a linebacker and end for the New York Giants and Green Bay Packers.

CARL HUBBELL (Hall of Fame, 1947)

Before a longtime organization star was referred to as a franchise player, he was known as a meal ticket, and nobody deserved the sobriquet more than Hubbell. A lefthanded screwballer, he spent his entire 16-year (1928–43) career with the Giants, at one point in the 1930s ripping off five consecutive 20-win seasons, leading the National League in ERA three times, in shutouts once, in strikeouts once, and even in saves once. On July 17, 1936 he won the first of a record-shattering 24 consecutive games over two seasons. Equally famous was his 1934 All-Star Game performance when he struck out Babe Ruth, Lou Gehrig, Jimmie Foxx, Al Simmons, and Joe Cronin in succession. His postseason efforts were slightly more checkered: Although boasting an overall record of 4–2 with a 1.97 ERA as the Giants ace in the 1933,

1936, and 1937 World Series, the southpaw managed it despite sharing the dubious record for yielding the most runs (seven) in an inning.

Hubbell was originally signed by the Tigers but was forbidden by Detroit manager Ty Cobb to use his screwball in a spring training tryout because it supposedly would hurt his arm. It was only after failing with the Tigers that he resumed throwing, in the Texas League, what Cobb had ridiculed as a "butterfly pitch"; it was there that he was spotted by Giants scout Dick Kinsella. Hubbell's association with the Giants lasted well beyond his playing days: After running the organization's farm system for decades, he remained on the payroll as a scout until the mid-1980s.

MILLER HUGGINS (Hall of Fame, 1964)

As manager of the Yankees throughout most of the Ruthian era, the dyspeptic Huggins was overshadowed by the outsized personality of his biggest star but came off the winner in their most celebrated showdown.

A second baseman for the Reds and Cardinals, Huggins led the National League in bases on balls four times and hit .265 in his 13-year (1904–16) career. Taking over as Cardinals pilot even before the end of his playing days, he was offered an opportunity to purchase the club after the 1916 season but found himself beaten to the punch when club attorney James Jones put together a coalition of St. Louis businessmen to buy out owner Helene Britton while the manager was off in his hometown of Cincinnati trying to raise the money for his own bid. After a 1917 season of seething over what he regarded as a fast shuffle by Britton and Jones, Huggins accepted an offer from New York owner Jacob Ruppert to take over the Yankees.

Huggins's New York career falls into three distinct chapters. A first, pre-Ruthian installment lasted three humdrum years. The second, from 1920 to 1925, brought three pennants, a World Series victory, and trouble with Ruth's off-field antics. The slugger's predilection for nightlife rubbed off on other players, most notably fellow outfielder Bob Meusel, causing constant friction not only between Ruth and Huggins but also involving co-owners Ruppert and Cap Huston. The 1922 season added clubhouse and dugout brawling to the list of Yankees activities, with Ruth and first baseman Wally Pipp going at it for a few rounds; pitcher Carl Mays and catcher Al De-

Vormer tangling; DeVormer switching sparring partners to fellow catcher Fred Hofman; and pitcher Waite Hoyt tussling with Huggins himself. Despite losing control of the team, Huggins managed to win the second of three consecutive pennants.

If 1922 was bad, 1925 was hell. The year began with the manager getting thrown into a Daytona, Florida jail for eight hours in a case of mistaken identity involving a hotel burglary. Then Ruth collapsed on the way home from spring training but continued his all-night sprees even while recuperating from surgery; the manager reached the end of his patience when the home run king twice ignored signs, first bunting when told to swing away, then swinging away when told to bunt. With a seventh-place finish imminent, he fined the slugger $5,000 and suspended him indefinitely for showing up late for an August 29 game in St. Louis. The confrontation concluded with Ruppert emerging from a closed-door meeting with Ruth to announce that "Huggins is in absolute command."

Despite their troubles Huggins actually liked Ruth, and he came down harder on Meusel, who, he felt, never played hard enough to live up to his potential. But his true animosity was reserved for pitchers Joe Bush and Mays. Huggins never forgave Bush for shouting at him during the final game of the 1922 World Series, then serving up a fat pitch to George Kelly, who knocked it for a Series-ending base hit; he also believed to his dying day that Mays had sold out the 1921 Series.

The final phase of Huggins's tenure witnessed an unchallenged managerial authority and a chastened (but hardly reformed) Ruth contributing to three additional pennants and two more world championships. In 1929, however, an overconfident team never got started, frustrating its manager, who was ill for much of the season. Huggins died of erysipelas on September 25 of that year; he was 50.

JIM HUGHEY

A righthander for five teams during the last decade of the 19th century, Hughey posted a career record of 29–80, giving him the worst winning percentage (.266) of any pitcher with at least 100 decisions. Part of his problem was that he pitched for the 1898 Browns and the 1899 Spiders—two of the worst teams ever—for whom he dropped a combined 54 games; his efforts in the latter year produced the last 30-game-losing season. Indicative of his plight, Hughey managed to complete 100 of his career 113 starts. He never pitched a shutout.

WAYNE HUIZENGA

Huizenga was a combination of Connie Mack in a bad mood and Gordon Gecko in a good one. Within weeks of his Marlins winning the 1997 world championship, the millionaire who had built his fortune from waste management and the Blockbuster Video chain was tearing the club apart, claiming (dubious) financial losses because of Miami's failure to build him a new stadium.

Few owners asserted themselves as quickly within baseball's ruling councils as Huizenga did after entering the National League. Immediately after the November 1992 expansion draft, he succeeded in blocking the all-but-done transfer of the Giants to St. Petersburg, thereby leaving his Miami-based franchise alone in Florida. He then secured exclusive rights for Blockbuster to handle video production for Major League Promotions and to distribute the sport's official line of videotapes. On the field it took him only five years to build his World Series winner—the fastest by any expansion team until then. But with Miami still rejecting his demands for a baseball-only domed facility at taxpayer expense, he barely waited for manager Jim Leyland to finish a victory lap around Joe Robbie Stadium before ordering a halving of the club's $54-million payroll. The bloodbath that ensued included getting rid of sluggers Moises Alou, Devon White, and Jeff Conine, starters Kevin Brown and Al Leiter, and closer Robb Nen. Gary Sheffield, Bobby Bonilla, and Charles Johnson followed early in the next year in a trade for Mike Piazza that was only a first step to also sending the Dodgers catcher on to the Mets. The result was a drop from a 92–70, wild card second-place finish to the bottom of the National League East with a 54–108 record.

After negotiating for several months with club president John Smiley, Huizenga realized he would have to go elsewhere for a sale, finally dealing the club to John Henry for $150 million on November 6, 1998. Most sports economists scoffed at his claims that he lost millions even during the 1997 pennant-winning season.

WILLIAM HULBERT

For its first six seasons the National League was virtually a one-man show, and that man was founder Hulbert.

Soon after the Chicago coal merchant and wholesale grocer became associated with the National Association White Stockings in 1874, he realized that his proto-major league was hopelessly flawed; a year later, after being selected club president, he staged a palace revolt. Incensed by the defection of shortstop Davy Force to the Philadelphia Athletics and the NA's subsequent approval of the transfer, Hulbert retaliated by signing not only Boston's Big Four (pitcher Al Spalding, second baseman Ross Barnes, first baseman Cal McVey, and catcher Deacon White), who were in the process of leading the Red Stockings to a runaway pennant, but also Philadelphia third baseman Cap Anson. Knowing he could be expelled for tampering with another club's players during the season, Hulbert solved the problem with a series of preemptive moves. After recruiting the NA's St. Louis franchise and two strong independent clubs from Cincinnati and Louisville as a western half league, he presented a take-it-or-leave-it plan to four selected eastern teams (Hartford, New York, and the aggrieved Boston and Philadelphia) in a locked-door meeting.

What they took was a monopolistic scheme to control the best players and markets by setting up an association of clubs rather than players (what all previous organizations had been). The new league limited membership with a franchise system that excluded cities with fewer than 75,000 people, granted member clubs exclusive rights to their territories, and required teams to complete a predetermined schedule. The league, for its part, was committed to being vigilant against the influence of gamblers, "hippodroming" (crooked play), and "revolving" (the offense Spalding and the others had committed); a blacklist was to be maintained to keep offending players out of the league.

Even though Morgan Bulkeley of Hartford became the first NL president, Hulbert was in control from the start. He expelled New York and Philadelphia for not completing their 1876 schedules, and, after assuming the league presidency himself in 1877, applied the same penalty to four Louisville players for throwing games. On the other hand, he applied the rules with something less than rigor when it suited his or the league's purposes. He hastened, for example, to reorganize the Cincinnati franchise early in 1877 after it had violated the same rule for which New York and Philadelphia had been terminated; he

didn't mind raiding the Reds for Charley Jones and other players for his own team, either.

During Hulbert's brief reign the NL prospered, at least in part because restrictions on player mobility kept salaries from escalating. But while imitation followed prosperity, the league founder was not around to help combat the 1882 challenge from the American Association. On April 22, less than two weeks before the rival circuit played its first game, he suffered a fatal heart attack.

RANDY HUNDLEY

Hundley pioneered the use of the hinged flipover mitt, which has given catchers more flexibility. Following his retirement in 1977 after 14 years with the Cubs and three other teams, he also popularized the fantasy camp vacations for never-were big leaguers.

KEN HUNT

Hunt effectively ended his promising career by swinging a bat in the on-deck circle. Following an impressive 1961 rookie season for the Angels when he clouted 25 home runs, the righthand-hitting outfielder stood flexing his back in the on-deck area in April 1962 when he suddenly snapped his collarbone. He never played a full schedule again.

RON HUNT

Hunt holds all the important National League records for being hit by pitches. A righty-swinging second baseman who liked to boast that "some people give their bodies to science, but I give mine to baseball," he was clipped 243 times over his 12-year (1963–74) career with the Mets, Dodgers, Giants, Expos, and Cardinals. In 1971 he set the season record for being plunked (50 times); that was also one of seven straight seasons when the lifetime .273 hitter paced all big leaguers in getting to first base the hard way.

Hunt's penchant for being hit enraged opposition managers throughout his career, especially after his own admission that he wore special protective pads under his uniform, but umpires seldom found him violating the letter of the rules.

CATFISH HUNTER (Hall of Fame, 1987)

His Hall of Fame pitching credentials notwithstanding, Hunter's most lasting contribution to baseball was a result of his not getting paid.

In a 15-year (1965–79) career with the Athletics (in both Kansas City and Oakland) and Yankees, the righthander won 224 games, fashioning five consecutive seasons over the 20-mark, leading the American League in victories twice, in winning percentage twice, and in ERA once. The ace for the Oakland dynasty of the early 1970s, he achieved initial prominence by pitching the first regular-season perfect game in 46 years, on May 5, 1968, against the Twins. His final 20-win season came in New York, in 1975, when he became the last pitcher to complete as many as 30 starts. Weakened by diabetes and with his arm worn out, Hunter later helped New York to three pennants and two world championships, pitching much of the time on little more than grit.

In 1973 Hunter agreed to a two-year contract calling for him to receive $100,000 a year, with half the amount payable directly by Oakland owner Charlie Finley into an annuity. When it was reported during the 1974 season that Finley had failed to make the annuity payment, the righthander refused to talk about it until after the World Series with Los Angeles; when the owner tried to hand the pitcher a check for the $50,000, he refused the payment. Immediately after the A's clinched the world championship, the Players Association claimed breach of contract and won free agency for Hunter after a hearing before arbitrator Peter Seitz. The hurler's liberation prompted a dual reaction from other owners: First, they were shocked that he had won his case; then they lined up to make him extravagant offers. He eventually signed with the Yankees for $3 million. Although the universal right to free agency did not come until the conclusion of the Messersmith-McNally case the following year, Hunter's victory plainly illustrated how much the players had to gain from the elimination of the reserve clause.

Hunter's nickname was provided by Finley, who loved the promotional value of nicknames in general and the sound of this one in particular. The owner had been a fan of George (Catfish) Metkovich, a journeyman first baseman-outfielder in the 1940s and 1950s.

HERB HUNTER

Hunter didn't have much of a career as an infielder for several teams in the late 1910s and early 1920s, but he was a living testament to how far Commissioner Kenesaw Landis would go when he decided not to like somebody. Hunter's attempts to organize a 1931 all-star tour of Japan were thwarted when Landis barred players from signing up. The reason? The commissioner accused Hunter of having let a team of Korean amateurs beat another all-star grouping of major leaguers during a 1922 tour of Asia. Landis ultimately permitted the 1931 junket but only after replacing Hunter as tour leader with his personal representative, sportswriter Fred Lieb.

TIM HURST

Umpire Hurst is best known for his paean to his profession: "The pay is good, it keeps you out in the fresh air and sunshine, and you can't beat the hours." He also liked the power of his position, even going so far as to violate the first rule of umpiring by changing a call. When infielder George Moriarty protested a called strike, claiming that the pitch had been farther off the plate than the previous one, a called ball, the arbiter agreed and made both pitches strikes. What Hurst seemed to like most about his job, however, were the opportunities it offered for physical violence. While in the National League, his most notable victim was a Cincinnati fireman knocked cold when Hurst, returning fire from the grandstand, tossed a beer stein into the crowd; the umpire was fined $100.

Taking a year off to manage the Cardinals in 1898, Hurst earned a reputation as a rabid baiter of his former colleagues. He continued his confrontational ways after moving back into blue, in the American League in 1905. In one game, after tailing Clark Griffith to the dugout, he coldcocked the New York manager. He was finally fired in August 1909 after spitting in the face of Philadelphia second baseman Eddie Collins and precipitating a riot. Hurst later became a boxing referee.

CAP HUSTON

Huston (full name Tillinghast L'Hommedieu Huston) was a half-owner of the Yankees for eight-and-a-half years but almost never got his way. A rumpled, hard-living Army Corps of Engineers captain and self-made millionaire, he made an odd couple with partner Jacob Ruppert, a polished socialite and honorary colonel on the staff of the New York governor. Brought together by Giants manager John McGraw to buy the Yankees, the two fell into conflict on almost every club matter from the beginning, when Huston (gauchely, in Ruppert's opinion) put up his half of the $460,000 purchase price in $100 bills.

The first major conflict between the partners was over the hiring of a new manager in October 1917. Ruppert wanted St. Louis pilot Miller Huggins; Huston preferred his drinking buddy Wilbert Robinson, who was piloting the Dodgers and whom Ruppert thought too old at 50 to handle the chore. The brewery magnate won, mostly because Huston was off in France at war, but the engineer never forgave his partner for the signing and spent the rest of their association trying to undermine the manager. While over in Europe, Huston also made sure to keep annoying Ruppert—and the rest of the baseball establishment—with regular letters to newspapers suggesting that the game be closed down and every able-bodied player shipped to the front lines.

Not surprising, Huston sided with Babe Ruth in his ongoing confrontations with Huggins—a preference made all the easier by their constant carousing together. After the Yankees lost a second consecutive World Series to the Giants in 1922, he lost his patience, declaring that "Huggins has managed the Yankees for the last time." The threat backfired when general manager Ed Barrow, despite his close friendship with Huston, sided with Ruppert in a decision to stay with Huggins. With little alternative, Huston negotiated a $1.5 million buyout from Ruppert in May 1923.

Huston's major contribution to the club came as a result of his friendship with theatrical producer Harry Frazee, whose constant need for cash as owner of the Red Sox Ruppert and Huston satisfied in return for such future Hall of Famers as Ruth, Waite Hoyt, and Herb Pennock.

I

PETE INCAVIGLIA

Incaviglia made his most enduring contribution to baseball when he refused to sign with the Expos after being selected in the amateur draft of 1985 unless the team guaranteed to trade him. When Montreal broke the stalemate by trading the slugging outfielder to the Rangers, worried owners saw nothing but trouble ahead from other draft choices who didn't like the teams that had picked them. The result was the Incaviglia Rule, which bars clubs from trading amateur draft selections until at least one year after signing them. In his rookie year for the Rangers, in 1986, Incaviglia established a first-year mark for strikeouts by fanning 185 times.

MONTE IRVIN (Hall of Fame, 1973)

But for Branch Rickey's refusal to offer compensation to the Newark Eagles for his services, Irvin might have beaten out Jackie Robinson for integrating the major leagues. Irvin had been the choice of many Negro leagues owners for that role, but three years in the Army during World War II had rusted his skills sufficiently to make Rickey balk at demands for $5,000 in exchange for his contract. As it turned out, Horace Stoneham of the Giants coughed up the $5,000; when Irvin asked for (and was refused) part of the payment, he became the first black player to receive a bad press for "greed."

As a shortstop and center fielder, the righthanded hitter won Negro National League batting titles in 1941 (.395) and 1946 (.404). He also led the Mexican League (.397) after jumping the Eagles in 1942 over a contract dispute. Playing for Vera Cruz, he also paced the circuit in homers (20) to win MVP honors even though he missed the first third of the season.

After debuting with the Giants in 1949, Irvin hit .312 with 24 home runs and a league-leading 121 RBIs in the miracle-pennant year of 1951 while also serving as mentor to rookie Willie Mays. In the ensuing World Series loss to the Yankees, Irvin hit .458 and stole home in the second game. But after breaking his ankle sliding into third base in a spring training game in April 1952, then reinjuring the leg the following year, he never was the same player. His overall average for seven seasons with the Giants and one with the Cubs was .293.

From 1968 to 1984 Irvin was a special assistant in the commissioner's office. He also served as chairman of the Hall of Fame's Special Committee on the Negro leagues after his own election to Cooperstown and shepherded the passage of Ray Dandridge, Martin Dihigo, Rube Foster, Judy Johnson, and John Henry Lloyd through that body.

ART IRWIN

In an effort to protect two broken fingers, Irwin, playing for the Providence Grays, invented the first fielder's mitt in 1885 by adding padding to a buckskin glove. The shortstop's most extraordinary double play became public only in 1931, when, after he had drowned while commuting between New York and Boston, it was learned that he had maintained two wives and two sets of children, one in each of the cities on the itinerary of his final boat ride.

J

BO JACKSON

Jackson's insistence on playing professional baseball and football simultaneously cost him stardom in both sports when he incurred a serious hip injury. Although he eventually returned to the diamond with an artificial hip, his drastically reduced speed erased predictions of being a dominant force in baseball, while making it impossible for him to reappear at all on the gridiron. The righthand-hitting Jackson joined the Royals in 1986 after winning college football's Heisman Trophy. The media attention focused on the outfielder created significant tension in the Kansas City clubhouse, especially after his assertion that he intended pursuing his football career with the Los Angeles Raiders as "a hobby." When he responded badly to teammates' criticism that he didn't take baseball seriously enough, he became a target of fan booing in Royals Stadium and did more striking out than hitting. By 1989, however, he had won over the fans with his power hitting and circus catches; in that year he clouted 32 home runs and drove home 105 runs; what's more, he was on the verge of an even bigger season until he separated his shoulder trying to make a diving catch in Yankee Stadium in July; before he was removed form the game, he had smacked three home runs in his only plate appearances. When he returned to the lineup in August, he belted the first pitch he saw from Seattle's Randy Johnson for his fourth consecutive home run. Jackson sustained his hip injury while playing for the Raiders in 1991. The Royals responded by releasing him on the eve of the season, insinuating that he would never be able to play again. But a short time later, Jackson signed with the White Sox. Although he was applauded na-

tionally for his grit, he offered a melancholy spectacle trying to run and ultimately decided to submit to a hip replacement. After missing the 1992 season, he returned to Chicago as a designated hitter in 1993, banging out 16 homers in part-time duty. During the League Championship Series against Toronto, both Jackson and alternate DH George Bell griped bitterly about who should be in the lineup; for his part, Jackson went hitless in 10 at bats, including six strikeouts. He played for the Angels in 1994.

JOE JACKSON

Although Jackson was never actually asked to "say it ain't so," he did try to tell White Sox owner Charlie Comiskey that it was so and was brushed off for his efforts. A year later, he became the most famous of the eight Chicago players banned for collusion in fixing the 1919 World Series against Cincinnati. The nearest thing to a consolation until his death 30 years later was knowing that Walter Johnson thought him "the greatest natural ballplayer I've ever seen," and that he was the best hitter outside the Hall of Fame.

The lefthand-hitting outfielder came up originally with Philadelphia in 1908, but had little more than 40 at bats over two seasons with Connie Mack. Convinced that the South Carolina-born Jackson was too uncomfortable in the eastern city, Mack dealt him to the Indians, where he began putting together his lifetime .356 average In his first full season, in 1911, he whaled American League pitching to the tune of .408, following that up with marks of .395 and .373 and pacing the league in one year or another in hits, doubles, triples, and slugging percentage. With the birth of the Federal League in 1914, Jackson received several offers to jump Cleveland but stayed where he was on the advice of his wife, who handled all his business affairs. At least from a financial point of view, it proved to be an error when Indians owner Charles Somers became so desperate for cash that he sold the outfielder to the White Sox and to the penurious policies of Comiskey. In a Chicago uniform, Jackson put together four more .300 seasons between 1916 and 1919, developing so much admiration for his offensive abilities among teammates and opponents that many of them, including Babe Ruth, acknowledged emulating his stance. Even in the tainted 1919 Series against the Reds, he was one of the hardest to read for any suspicious behavior because of his .375 average and a club-leading six RBIs. Shortly after the Series, however, Jackson and his wife wrote a letter to Comiskey confirming rumors of a fix and offering to provide details. But Comiskey, who was only too aware that any substantiation of the rumors would cost him the services of Jackson and other players of star quality, chose to ignore the letter. What he couldn't ignore was testimony from pitcher Ed Cicotte and Jackson before a grand jury on September 28, 1920, naming names and detailing particulars. It was allegedly after this appearance that Jackson was approached by a boy who pleaded with him to "say it ain't so, Joe." (It was also after this testimony that Jackson told reporters something that few historians have noted: that the tainted players had tried to throw the third game of the Series as well as the first two contests but that the pitching of Dickie Kerr thwarted their efforts.)

In his testimony, Jackson admitted receiving $5,000 from professional gamblers—the basis for his subsequent ostracism from the major leagues by Commissioner Kenesaw Landis despite an acquittal of the Chicago Eight in a jury trial. On the eve of that trial, Jackson's admission and other confessions disappeared from the county prosecutor's office amid strong indications that the theft had been organized by gambler Arnold Rothstein with the full cooperation of Comiskey. The confession stayed lost until 1924, when Jackson filed suit against Comiskey for $18,000 in back pay; as miracles would have it, the Chicago boss's attorney inexplicably produced the suddenly rediscovered documents to sustain his argument that Jackson had not lived up to the terms of a multiyear pact signed shortly before the 1919 season.

Before he was thrown out of the game in the final week of the 1920 season, Jackson had been enjoying one of his biggest years, averaging .382 with 218 hits; 42 doubles; a league-leading 20 triples; and, for the first time in his career, knocking in more than 100 runs. Such numbers have periodically marshaled supporters for his reinstatement; among the first was Yankees general manager Ed Barrow, who mistakenly believed Jackson had fallen on hard times financially, and most recently Ted Williams has led the call for Cooperstown to drop its moralistic objections and admit the outfielder as a *bona fide* Hall of Famer.

REGGIE JACKSON (Hall of Fame, 1993)

Jackson was Mr. October—and he wasn't too shabby in the other months of the season, either. On the other hand, the outfielder's braggadocio caused as much trouble with teammates as his bat did with opponents.

Although he managed to pass the .300 barrier only once in his 21-year (1967–87) career, Jackson clouted 563 home runs (eighth on the all-time list) and is the only player to hit as many as 100 homers with three different clubs (the Athletics, Yankees, and Angels). The lefthand-hitting slugger paced AL hitters in homers four times, slugging three times, runs scored twice, and RBIs only once. Among his best individual seasons were 1973 (when he took MVP honors for Oakland with a .293 average and league-leading totals in slugging, homers, runs, and RBIs) and 1980 (when he reached a career high of .300 and reached the seats 41 times for the Yankees). The downside of his offense was a record 2,597 strikeouts—a category in which he topped the 100 mark 18 times and led the American League five times.

Jackson, however, always seemed to save his best for the autumn; he had plenty of opportunity to shine in post season play, appearing for 11 division championships, six pennant winners, and five world championship teams. His World Series career batting average bested his regular-season mark by almost 100 points (.357 to .262), and in Series play he ranks in the top 10 in almost every significant offensive category, including first in slugging (.755). His most memorable slugging feat was his three consecutive home runs for the Yankees in the sixth game of the 1977 World Series on three consecutive pitches off three different Dodgers pitchers.

Jackson was one of the young players Charlie Finley took with him from Kansas City to the West

Coast, where the A's won five AL West titles in the 1970s. He was also among the most restive of the brawling Athletics, tangling with Finley over the size of a salary increase after a stellar 1969 season (47 homers and 118 RBIs), with Dick Williams over the manager's dictatorial style, and (physically) with teammate Billy North. As free agency approached in 1976, Finley shipped Jackson and Ken Holtzman to the Orioles for Don Baylor and Mike Torrez. From the start, it was clear that Baltimore would not meet Jackson's demands for a three-year, $675,000 contract, and even when he settled for a one-year, $200,000 pact, the rest of the team became so unsettled that several other key players followed him into the first free agent market after the season.

Jackson arrived in the Bronx with baggage aplenty. First, there were his claims that if he played in New York there would be a candy bar named after him: He may have wished no one had bothered when Yankees fans showered the field with free Reggie bars handed out on Opening Day of 1978. Then there was the resentment of teammates generated by the outfielder's statements about "the magnitude of me," a reaction that only got worse with the early-season publication of a magazine article in which he called himself "the straw that stirs the drink," disparaging any notion that Yankees captain Thurman Munson could fill such a role Jackson only exacerbated the situation by pointedly ignoring the extended hands of teammates after hitting a home run the night the article appeared. When Jackson casually played a bloop single into a double on national television in June, manager Billy Martin sent Paul Blair to replace him in right field in mid-inning. The ensuing dugout scene showed the outfielder screaming at Martin, and the manager trying to break out of a cordon of coaches to get at the outfielder.

In the 1977 World Series, Jackson hit .450 and set records with five home runs, 25 total bases, and 10 runs scored. But matters disintegrated further the following year. Amid griping to owner George Steinbrenner, slumping, and being relegated to a DH role, he was suspended for five days for defying orders to bunt in a July game against Kansas City, then some days later bunted when called on to swing away. The tension among the owner, manager, and slugger reached critical mass when Martin called Jackson a "born liar" and alluded to Steinbrenner's conviction for illegal campaign contributions. The cracks cost Martin his job.

Jackson himself departed form the Yankees in 1982 the way he had arrived, as a free agent. Steinbrenner admitted his mistake in letting him leave when the slugger led the AL (for the final time) in homers in his first season for California. After that, Jackson merely played out the string for four more years with the Angels and a final season with the Athletics.

TRAVIS JACKSON (Hall of Fame, 1982)

Jackson was so unassuming during his 15-year (1922–36) career with the Giants that even Ebbets Field fans usually didn't bother to boo him. The regular shortstop for the final phase of the John McGraw reign and most of Bill Terry's rule, Jackson squeezed six .300 seasons into his .291 lifetime mark. Defensively, Jackson began with an ouch, leading the league in errors in his first full season but then went on to pace NL shortstops in assists four times. When leg injuries began slowing him up, he was shifted over to third base. Jackson's biggest RBI year—1934, when he topped the 100 mark for the only time—was the season that Terry had inflamed Brooklyn fans by inquiring if the Dodgers were still in the league. When even Jackson was greeted by catcalls at Ebbets Field, the New York manager understood how ably the Brooklyn front office had twisted his words to stir up the local faithful.

BILL JAMES

James was a high school English teacher in Lawrence, Kansas when he began publishing *The Baseball Abstract* annually in 1977 and became the foremost sabermetrician. Perhaps the most popular of the statistical tools he developed was Runs Created, which strives to use statistical achievement in every offensive category to estimate how good a player is at generating runs for his club.

STUART JANNEY

Janney was the attorney for the directors of the Federal League Baltimore franchise in its protracted negotiations with the National and American leagues after the FL's collapse had left the Terrapins with what its owners considered an inadequate offer to liquidate. In those negotiations, Chicago White Sox owner Charlie Comiskey dismissed a Baltimore offer to purchase the St. Louis Cardinals for $250,000, calling the tender "the proper price for a minor league franchise" and referring to Baltimore as "a minor league city and not a hell of a good one at that." When Brooklyn owner Charlie Ebbets added, "You have too many colored population to begin with. They are a cheap population when it gets down to paying their money at the gate," there was no place left for Janney to go except to the courts. The case was eventually decided by the U.S. Supreme Court, with Justice Oliver Wendell Holmes writing a majority opinion in favor of organized baseball's claim of exemption from federal antitrust legislation.

BROTHER JASPER

Jasper, a member of the religious order of Christian Brothers, has been credited with originating the seventh-inning stretch. The coach of the Manhattan College baseball team in the 1880s, he insisted that players and spectators sit at games with the decorum appropriate for young men at a strict Catholic college. But on one occasion in 1882, just as Manhattan was coming to bat in the seventh inning, he instructed students in the grandstand to rise and stretch to alleviate their heat-induced discomfort. The practice became a habit at the college's games and was passed on to major league fans during the frequent exhibition games the college squad played with the Giants at the Polo Grounds.

LARRY JASTER

Southpaw Jaster won 11 games for the Cardinals in 1966, but five of those victories were shutouts over the Dodgers. The only other pitchers to administer as many whitewashes to one team in a season were Tom Hughes of the 1905 Senators, who mastered the Indians five times among his 17 victories, and Grover Cleveland Alexander of the 1916 Phillies, who dominated the Reds an equal number of times among his 33 wins.

JOEY JAY

When he joined the Braves in 1953, righthander Jay became the first major leaguer to come out of the organized Little League. It was a distinction he wore uneasily, and in later years he warned of the threats posed to children by overbearing parents and overly structured games for young people.

HAL JEFFCOAT

Jeffcoat was the last player to have separate appreciable careers at a major league level as a posi-

tion player and a pitcher. Between 1948 and 1953 he played in at least 80 games five times as an outfielder for the Cubs. Discouraged that his offense was falling off from highs of .279 in 1948 and .273 in 1951, he developed a knuckleball that allowed him to return to Chicago as a pitcher in 1954. Used mainly as a reliever by the Cubs and then by the Reds, he turned in a better-than-even 39–37 record over six years.

FERGUSON JENKINS (Hall of Fame, 1991)

Jenkins is the Ernie Banks of pitchers, his 284 victories in 19 big league seasons making him the winningest modern pitcher who never appeared in a postseason game. The righthander collected many more distinctions than that, however. Inserted into the rotation by the Cubs 1967 after a deal with Philadelphia, he won 20 games for six consecutive years—a feat that had been considered implausible because of hitter-friendly Wrigley Field. In 1971 he took Cy Young honors for leading the National League with 24 victories, while fanning 263 and walking only 37 batters. Three years later, with the Rangers, he paced American League hurlers with another 25 victories. A gifted hitter, he clouted six home runs in 1971.

Following his banner 1975 season with Texas, Jenkins turned in several more years of wins in the high teens, but his diamond performance was frequently overshadowed by his off-field antics and problems. With the Red Sox in 1976 and 1977, for instance, he gained more print for being one of the ringleaders (along with Bill Lee and Bernie Carbo) in the relentless taunting of manager Don Zimmer. Traded back to the Rangers in 1977 after Zimmer had accused him of falling asleep in the bullpen, he was stopped by a Canadian customs official in 1980 for carrying drugs, prompting a suspension by Commissioner Bowie Kuhn. Although the suspension was overruled by an arbitrator shortly afterward, the incident held up his election to Cooperstown for several years.

HUGHIE JENNINGS (Hall of Fame, 1945)

Jennings's animated and boisterous cheerleading, particularly his trademark "Eeh-yah" screech, were seen as positive components of team chemistry as long as things were going well; when they weren't, emphasis invariably shifted to his clubhouse sarcasm. The righthand-hitting infielder brought a meager .136 batting average from Louisville to the Baltimore Orioles in a mid-1893 trade for Voiceless Tim O'Rourke and *his* .363 average. But then Jennings learned to avoid stepping into the bucket by keeping his back against a batting cage while teammate John McGraw threw to him over a winter the pair spent as undergraduates at St. Bonaventure College. So effective was McGraw's tutelage that Jennings pushed his mentor over to third base and went on to establish a batting record for shortstops, with a .401 average in 1896. While barnstorming after spring training that same year, he showed his Orioles colors when he precipitated one of the ugliest incidents in that team's often unattractive history by starting a fight with a player with a member of the minor league franchise in Petersburg, Virginia. Pursued to their hotel by an irate mob of fans, the Baltimore players were whisked to the train station by police and cooler-headed locals but not before the hotel lobby had been utterly trashed.

Shipped from Baltimore to Brooklyn in 1899 as part of the maneuvers of the syndicate that owned both clubs, Jennings flirted with the backers of the abortive new American Association, the became secretary of the Protective Association of Professional Baseball Players. After the rest of the leadership of the proto-union had been co-opted, he had to be content with minor league managerial assignment until Detroit owner Frank Navin rescued him in 1907. Managing the Tigers meant trying to manage Ty Cobb, and Jennings's first reaction was not even to try offering the difficult outfielder to the Indians for holdout Elmer Flick. Turned down, the manager was forced to turn his attention to containing the furor over such incidents as Cobb's assault of a black groundskeeper and his wife, and to resolving his star's various feuds with other Detroit outfielders by repeatedly shifting him from one position to another to keep him as far away as possible from his foe of the moment. Jennings himself contributed to the turmoil by refusing to give up a whistle he began using in the third base coach's box when his voice gave out and getting slapped with a two-week suspension for his insistence. Despite all the commotion, there were three consecutive pennants (1907–09) to point to. Only when the club began its long slide out of contention did Jennings vent his sarcasm on the Tigers. After hanging on for more that a decade after his last flag, he packed it in for health reasons in 1920.

Always accident-prone, Jennings was almost killed three times: by a beanball in 1897; from a dive into an empty swimming pool at Cornell, where he studied law in the off-season; and in a winter automobile accident that took the life of his companion. Despite failing health, he took a job as a coach on the Giants in 1921 and filled in as manager for an even more ailing John McGraw in 1924, when the New Yorkers won their fourth consecutive pennant, and again in 1925, when they failed to repeat. He then suffered a nervous breakdown that kept him out of baseball for the final three years of his life.

DEREK JETER

Although lacking the power of Alex Rodriguez and Nomar Garciaparra, Jeter has been no less an offensive force at shortstop since taking over the position for the Yankees in the mid-1990s. The clutch in the New York vehicle that stormed through baseball at the turn of the millennium, he has had few equals as a postseason player, either at bat or in the field. His introduction to the majors in starring for four world championship clubs (1996, 1998–2000) in his first five full seasons has been topped only by Joe DiMaggio's four titles in four years (1936–39). On the other hand, his three 200-hit seasons are already one more than DiMaggio had in his 13-year career.

Jeter's spectacular handoff to catcher Jorge Posada on an errant relay throw in the third game of the 2001 playoffs to catch Oakland's charging Jeremy Giambi not only turned the series around in favor of the Yankees, but already stands as the Anti-Pesky Play in postseason lore.

MANNY JIMINEZ

Jiminez had his appointment with history canceled by fireworks. As a member of the Athletics on July 4, 1964, the lefty-swinging outfielder walloped three consecutive home runs. He didn't get a chance at a fourth because the game was called as a tie after the ninth inning because of a commitment to celebrate Independence Day with a fireworks display. Jiminez, who had only 26 homers in his seven-year career, was one of the first natives of the Dominican municipality of San Pedro de Macoris to reach the major leagues.

TOMMY JOHN

Nobody had a more unexpectedly long career than John. While with the Dodgers in July 1974 the southpaw snapped a ligament in his pitching elbow, apparently ending his playing days. But then orthopedic surgeon Frank Jobe reconstructed the elbow using a tendon from the right forearm. After John sat out the 1975 season, he went on to complete a 26-year career—the longest of any pitcher except Nolan Ryan. The Bionic Arm, as the hurler came to be called, ended up with 288 victories, those in his later years with the Yankees coming on sheer guile.

ALBERT JOHNSON

The financial backer of the Cleveland Players League club, Johnson spent the fall of 1890 meeting with National League owners over terms for the dissolution of the PL in a classic sellout of the players who had been his partners; as a freelance entrepreneur, he was also meeting with Cincinnati president Aaron Stern to complete a purchase of the Reds for the purpose of moving them into the PL. When the NL gave John T. Brush rights to its Cincinnati franchise and, at about the same time, the negotiations to abolish the PL succeeded, Johnson sought a buyout for his team without a league. Refusing to deal with Brush and rebuffed by the NL as a whole, he turned to the American Association. Awarded a franchise in that league, he promptly turned around and talked the NL into giving him $30,000 to deprive the AA of a foothold in the Cincinnati market. Johnson never got his money, though: Other PL investors he had brought into the Cincinnati deal questioned his right to sell, tying the transaction up in court until his death a decade later.

ALEX JOHNSON

Johnson was the first player to be put on the disabled list for emotional rather than physical reasons. The outfielder achieved the distinction in 1971, after two years of divisive incidents on the Angels that had several teammates attack him with fists, another draw a gun on him, and manager Lefty Phillips levy an astonishing 29 fines against him in less than half a season. Among other things, Johnson regularly abused sportswriters covering the team, poured coffee into the typewriter of Los Angeles *Herald-Examiner* writer Dick Miller, insisted on playing the outfield within the shadow of a light tower on a hot afternoon, fired a soda bottle at pitcher Clyde Wright, and had periodic punch-ups in the batting cage with teammates. Through it all, the righthand-hitting slugger

argued that it was baseball's "antiblack bias" that painted him as a bad guy—a contention that scored mostly with general manager Dick Walsh, who was nervous about the franchise's sorry record with blacks. When Walsh finally suspended the outfielder, however, Players Association director Marvin Miller argued successfully before an arbitration panel that Johnson was suffering from acute mental distress and should be disabled with full pay.

When he felt like it, Johnson posed an appreciable threat at the plate. After being traded by the Reds to the Angels in 1970, he collected 202 hits and won the American League batting title with a .329 average. Following the arbitration panel's ruling, he was dealt to the Indians.

ARNOLD JOHNSON

In purchasing the Athletics from the Mack family and transferring them from Philadelphia to Kansas City for the 1955 season, Johnson gave the Yankees in particular, and baseball owners in general, a lot to be thankful for. An executive of the Chicago-based Automatic Canteen company, he worked out deals so unsubtly with the Yankees during his ownership reign that Kansas City functioned as little more than a New York farm club on the major league level; between 1955 and 1960, for instance, the teams completed 16 trades involving some 60 players, with such talents as Roger Maris, Clete Boyer, Ralph Terry, and Ryne Duren ending up in the Bronx. None of this should have come as a surprise to the other owners since, before purchasing the Athletics, Johnson had been the landlord of both Yankee Stadium and the Kansas City ballpark used by New York's chief farm club. But if AL owners, especially, had reason to resent the constant player traffic between New York and Kansas City, they and their National League counterparts had only gratitude in their hearts after Johnson had his attorneys press the Internal Revenue Service for a definitive ruling on the status of players as organization property; it is thanks to the IRS's response to the Johnson query that major league franchises are able to depreciate the value of player contracts over a number of tax years. Johnson died of a heart attack during spring training in 1960.

BAN JOHNSON (Hall of Fame, 1937)

Johnson created and nurtured the American League until it was the equal of the National. At the same time, however, he thrived on making and getting even with enemies—a flaw that eventually brought him down.

In 1890 Johnson succeeded O. P. Caylor as sports editor of the Cincinnati *Commercial-Gazette* and immediately started a feud with John T. Brush that made the Reds owner amenable to suggestions for getting him out of the city. Through the contrivance of Cincinnati manager Charlie Comiskey, Brush recommended Johnson for the post of president of the minor Western League in 1894. When Johnson proved to be more of a nuisance as a league executive than he had been as commentator, Brush sought to unseat him, but Johnson survived the battle with sufficient authority to force Brush to sell the WL franchise he had in Indianapolis and that he was using a little too slickly to provide players for Cincinnati. Joined by Comiskey, who took over the Sioux City franchise in 1895, Johnson ran the most successful minor league in the nation for several years until deciding to go for the brass ring of major league status. Announcing a change in the circuit's name to the American League in 1900, he invaded several territories abandoned by the NL when it reduced its roster from 12 to eight teams after the 1899 season, and transferred Comiskey's club from St. Paul (where it had gone after Sioux City) to Chicago. While recognizing the threat to its monopoly, the NL fought back only ineffectually, doing little more than making noises about reviving the American Association and threatening to blacklist defecting players.

Johnson had it all his way. He set up a wartime strategy of holding 51 percent of each franchise's stock and the leases on their ballparks in the league's name. He lined up millionaires, most importantly coal industrialist Charles Somers, to finance his undertaking. He supported umpires against the spread of the rowdyism that infected the NL, and he threw players out of his league for violence. He raided NL clubs for such future Hall of Famers as John McGraw, Jimmy Collins, and Nap Lajoie. He engineered trades to circumvent legal rulings that went against the AL; the most famous such deal sent Lajoie and Elmer Flick from the Athletics to the Indians to get out from under an injunction against the pair appearing in Pennsylvania for anyone but the NL Phillies. His eight teams even outdrew the NL's in his second year of operation at a major league level.

By the end of the 1902 season, Johnson was synonymous with the AL, despite the embarrassing defection of McGraw, who became manager of the Giants and in the process trashed the AL Baltimore franchise. Johnson recouped his losses from this near-disaster by moving the Orioles to New York in a direct challenge to the Giants and raided the Pirates for, among others, pitchers Jack Chesbro and Jesse Tannehill to stock the new club. It was after this coup that Pittsburgh's Barney Dreyfuss led NL owners in suing for peace. Among other things, the settlement created the National Commission, consisting of the two league presidents and Cincinnati president Garry Herrmann, one of the prime movers in the NL's capitulation. With Herrmann more often than not voting with him, Johnson was the most powerful figure in baseball for more than a decade.

But it was also a series of votes on the National Commission that began to erode that power. In awarding George Sisler to the Browns instead of the Pirates in 1915, Johnson lost the support of Dreyfuss. In the Scott Perry case in 1918, Johnson irritated the rest of the NL when he refused to honor a commission vote awarding the pitcher to the Braves, then supported Connie Mack's courtroom efforts to keep the pitcher with the Athletics. That same year, what had over the years become a hot-and-cold relationship with Comiskey turned frigid when pitcher Jack Quinn was assigned to the Yankees in a dispute with the White Sox.

With new enemies snapping at his heels, Johnson won no new friends with his behavior in the face of a threatened strike during the 1918 World Series, showing up drunk at a meeting with a delegation of Red Sox and Cubs players. The following year, he lost the support of Boston's Harry Frazee, already incensed over the league president's singling out Fenway Park as a hotbed of gambling, and New York's Jacob Ruppert and Cap Huston when he refused to let the Red Sox trade Carl Mays to the Yankees while the pitcher was under suspension. That decision set off a sequence of events that included a court order restraining Johnson from interfering with Mays's transfer to New York; a demand by Detroit owner Frank Navin for Johnson to throw out Mays's nine wins for the Yankees and thereby award third place and the World Series money that went with it to the Tigers; and a bombardment of lawsuits by Ruppert and Huston alleging that the league president was trying to force them out of baseball and that he was guilty of a conflict of interest because he held stock in the Indians and really wanted Mays transferred to Cleveland.

The so-called Insurrectos—Comiskey, Frazee, and the New York duo—carried the day in a showdown league meeting in February 1920 that finally sanctioned the Mays-to-New York deal and imposed a review committee to pass on all but the most routine league affairs. The Loyal Five teams caved in again the following November when the Insurrectos joined the National League in insisting on the appointment of Federal Judge Kenesaw Landis as commissioner of baseball, holding out the threat of putting a rival team in Detroit and creating a 12-team NL unless the rest of the AL went along.

With little to do after the superimposition of Landis, Johnson took out after the Black Sox. Even though his legendary initial reaction on hearing of Comiskey's suspicions about some of his own players was, "That's the yelp of a beaten cur," Johnson took the inaction of Landis and the dropping of the first indictment against the Chicago Eight as an opportunity to win back some of his lost prestige and, not incidentally, embarrass Comiskey. Traveling 2,000 miles in two months, Johnson lined up enough evidence for the Cook County district attorney to bring another indictment. But Johnson's plans fell apart when a jury found the Black Sox not guilty on August 2, 1921, and Landis stole his thunder by banning them from baseball anyway. Infuriated by the commissioner's show-stealing, Johnson spent his last years in office picking fights with Landis. One confrontation occurred in December 1924 after the league president had called for a federal probe into the events leading up to the banning of Giants outfielder Jimmy O'Connell and coach Cozy Dolan and what he claimed as a whitewashing of other New York players involved. With Landis reminding them that they had pledged themselves not to contest any of his decisions in court, the AL owners publicly rejected their president's demand for an investigation. The end came two years later, in the wake of the Dutch Leonard-Ty Cobb-Tris Speaker affair, when Landis undid Johnson's quiet dismissal of the two future Hall of Famers behind accusations by the pitcher that they had bet on and fixed a game on September 25, 1919. After suffering a complete breakdown when the AL owners once again repudiated him in a January 1927 meeting, Johnson resigned the following July. He died on March 28 1931, of diabetes.

CLIFF JOHNSON

A well-traveled catcher in the 1970s and 1980s who was much better off with a bat in his hands, Johnson holds the record for career pinch-hit home runs with 20. More notoriously, he had a hand in costing two teams relief aces. In 1979, while a member of the Yankees, he got into a shower room tussle with bullpen ace Goose Gossage that left the pitcher with a torn thumb ligament and New York with little chance of winning a division flag. When he signed with the Rangers as a free agent in 1984, his previous team, the Blue Jays, secured as compensation Tom Henke, the righthander who would go on to be their Terminator for several seasons.

DAVEY JOHNSON

Despite his achievements as a Gold Glove second baseman for the Orioles in the late 1960s and early 1970s, Johnson has mainly been a disciple of the Earl Weaver school of Three-Run-Homers-Cure-Everything-and-Let's-Be-Arrogant-About-It-When-We-Get-One. As a player, some of his most illustrious moments involved the long ball. In 1972, playing for Atlanta, Johnson joined Hank Aaron and Darrell Evans as the only trio of teammates to hit 40 homers in a season, in the process tying Rogers Hornsby's season record for most home runs by a second baseman. In 1978, while winding down with the Phillies, Johnson became the first player to hit two pinch-hit grand slams in a season. He is also the answer to the trivia question about the name of the player who walked out of the on-deck circle to greet both Aaron and Sadaharu Oh as they crossed the plate with the home runs that put them ahead of Babe Ruth's 714 career blasts. As the manager of the Mets between 1984 and 1990, Johnson never hesitated to play the likes of Howard Johnson and Kevin Mitchell at shortstop in the interests of getting another slugger into the lineup, defense be damned.

It was also as the New York pilot that Johnson set the tone for what was perceived as the most arrogant National League club in years, especially after his preseason prediction in 1986 that the team would not only win the East Division but also "dominate" it. In fact, the Mets left the runner-up Phillies in the dust by an unprecedented $21\frac{1}{2}$ games. Dynastic forecasts notwithstanding, that year's world championship turned out to be one of a kind. By the time he was replaced early in the 1990 season, Johnson had been conveying for some time the image of a bruised loser in the battle of egos with general manager Frank Cashen. For all that, however, Johnson still left Shea Stadium with a .588 managerial winning percentage, and the curious lack of interest of other teams in hiring him raised suspicions that he was being blackballed for his readiness to talk back to his employers. When Johnson finally did get another job, in 1993, it was under the worst possible circumstances—replacing Cincinnati's popular Tony Perez, who had been fired after serving his purpose as a sop to critics of the organization's minority hiring policies. Johnson barely navigated through the rest of the season with a team in a state of near-mutiny over the treatment of Perez. Johnson came back to keep the Reds in first place in the shortened 1994 season and lead them into the playoffs as the Central Division titlist in 1995. But growing hostility from owner Marge Schott, especially over his lack of haste about marrying the woman he was living with, got him fired for Ray Knight after the postseason. In moving immediately over to Baltimore, he found the same combination of on-field success and off-field trouble. After leading the club to a wild card playoff berth in his maiden year, he guided it to an East Division title in 1997. But even though the Orioles were only the third American League team ever to remain in first place every day of the regular season, Johnson rarely had a week of peace with owner Peter Angelos; two of the steadier themes in their feuds were the owner's attentiveness to the advice of one of his sons, a rotisserie league fantasy freak, and the manager's less than adulatory treatment of icon Cal Ripken, Jr. The upshot was that Johnson had to collect his various manager-of-the-year trophies while on the unemployment line.

There was little of Johnson's old fire visible in running the Dodgers in 1999 and 2000. About all he had left before leaving the organization was his disdain for the front office suits he had always regarded as more obstacle than help in piloting a club. With the exception of slugger Gary Sheffield, there weren't too many players unhappy to see him go, either.

JUDY JOHNSON (Hall of Fame, 1975)

The best third baseman of the Negro leagues in the 1920s and 1930s, Johnson was known as the black Pie Traynor, but he hit for a higher average than the Pittsburgh Hall of Famer and his defensive play has been compared favorably to that of Brooks Robinson.

In a 16-year (1921–36) career with the Hilldale club of Darby, Homestead Grays, Darby Daisies, and Pittsburgh Crawfords, the righty-swinging Johnson was a regular .300 hitter, topping .400 in 1929. He also managed the Grays in 1930, discovering Josh Gibson along the way, and the Daisies in 1931–32. Johnson retired after Crawfords owner Gus Greenlee traded him and Gibson to the Grays after the 1936 season.

Connie Mack, an old admirer, hired Johnson as a scout in the late 1940s, but he switched to the Phillies after the post-Mack Philadelphia front office turned down his suggestions to sign Larry Doby, Minnie Minoso, and Hank Aaron. Johnson also worked for the Braves, whose center fielder Billy Bruton became his son-in-law.

KEN JOHNSON

Johnson is the only major league pitcher to lose a nine-inning no-hitter. Pitching for the Astros at home on April 23, 1964, the righthander was beaten by Cincinnati, 1–0, on a couple of errors and a sacrifice fly.

LOU JOHNSON

Johnson was already in his 30s after years of travels around the minor leagues when he blossomed into the Cinderella Man who animated consecutive pennants for the Dodgers in 1965 and 1966. A right-hand-hitting outfielder of modest defensive abilities, his clutch hitting down the stretch of both years made him a more popular figure with Los Angeles fans than some of the team's higher-priced stars. On September 9, 1965, Johnson was the only base runner in a duel between Sandy Koufax and Chicago's Bob Hendley. While Koufax was twirling a perfect game, Johnson walked and came around to score the game's only run on a steal and an error; later in the game, he had a bloop double off Hendley for the only hit of the contest.

RANDY JOHNSON

The most intimidating pitcher of his era, the six-foot, 10-inch Johnson entered the 2002 season with only Nolan Ryan standing in his way of prestigious strikeout marks. Even more than Ryan, his size, wildly flowing hair, and pockmarked, frowning countenance—all combined with fastballs in the high 90s and sliders not much slower—established him as a character in an ongoing baseball play. Nowhere was this demonstrated more aptly than during two show bizzy All-Star Games in the 1990s, with first John Kruk and then Larry Walker clowning out their fears of standing in as lefthanded hitters against the southpaw. In fact, no pitcher in recent memory has triggered as many disabling "minor injuries" and "illnesses" in opposition batters as Johnson. This has also been one of the reasons why he has given the appearance of being oddly vulnerable to usually light-hitting bench players: The scrubs have been pressed into service against him with regularity because of suddenly unavailable stars.

If Johnson didn't have the best year of his career in 2001 since coming up with the Expos in 1988, Ryan's reputation as the game's greatest strikeout pitcher will fall much sooner than later. His 21–6 (2.49) mark for the Diamondbacks included a 20-K effort against the Reds to tie Roger Clemens (twice) and Kerry Wood for whiffs in a nine-inning game; a 16-K relief outing against the Padres for a bullpen record; 10 or more strikeouts in a game 23 times for the third season; and an overall 372 strikeouts, the seventh time he led a league in that department and the fourth time he topped the 300-plateau. His average of 13.4 Ks per nine innings was the highest in baseball history, eclipsing Pedro Martinez's 13.2 ratio for the 1999 Red Sox. Those numbers were good enough for Johnson to match Martinez and Gaylord Perry as the only hurlers to win Cy Young awards in both leagues, but ended up being only spectacular prelude to three wins (one in relief) against the Yankees in Arizona's World Series championship. The lefthander known as The Big Unit earned another trophy when he and Curt Schilling were named co-MVPs of the Series.

Although it didn't seem so when he was part of a package to Seattle for Mark Langston in 1989, Johnson has probably been Montreal's biggest loss since the Expos began unloading talent at the end of the 20th century. After a couple of seasons with the Mariners when he walked too many batters for any manager's nerves, he began to zero in on his potential in 1992, with the first of four straight years of leading the AL in strikeouts; as of 1994, he also kept his bases on balls under 80. His best years with the Mariners were 1995, when he went 18–2, and, after being sidelined for most of the following year with a herniated disk, 1997, when he won 20 games for the first time (against only four losses). As would be the case in subsequent years with Ken Griffey, Jr. and

Alex Rodriguez, Johnson's very success made him expendable to the cost-conscious Mariners, who entertained few illusions about being able to meet his expected free agent demands at the end of the 1998 season. But instead of dealing him before the start of the campaign, the club hung on to him through the opening months of the season, making for an unhappy and ineffective Johnson and a gloomy clubhouse. In July Seattle finally traded him to the Astros for a package of pitchers Freddy Garcia and John Halama and infielder Carlos Guillen.

For Houston Johnson went 10–1 (1.28) for the rest of the season, clearing up any doubts that he could be as effective in the National League as he had been in the AL. But despite giving up only three runs in 14 innings he was bested twice by San Diego's Kevin Brown in the Division Series, eliminating the Astros. He then signed with the Diamondbacks as a free agent, where the Mets also beat him in the 1999 Division Series, helping him build a seven-game losing streak in the postseason before coming back against the Yankees. Realistically, Johnson's chances for eradicating more than some of Ryan's single-season records would seem slim. While entering his 15th campaign in 2002 with an edge over the Hall of Fame righthander in strikeouts (3,412–3,109) at such a point of major league service, he was also five years older than Ryan had been.

TIM JOHNSON

As a player, infielder Johnson had the dubious distinction of going seven seasons (1973–79) for the Brewers and Blue Jays without hitting a single homer in 1,269 at bats. As a manager for Toronto in 1998, he sought to strengthen his numbers by recounting to the team his Marine experiences in the Vietnam war. When it was revealed that he had never fought in the war, he was replaced in spring training in 1999 for having lost authority over the club.

WALTER JOHNSON (Hall of Fame, 1936)

Johnson has the most credible claim to the title of baseball's greatest pitcher. Although Cy Young won more games, Johnson's 416 victories (the most in the American League) over 21 seasons (1907–27) were for a team, the Senators, that lived in the second division and that didn't win a pennant until its ace was 37. Despite that kind of backing, the righthander won more than 30 games twice, had 10 consecutive years of 20 wins or more, and led the league in wins six times, in ERA five times, and in strikeouts 12 times. Until the 1980s, he had the major league mark with his 3,508 strikeouts, accomplishing them almost exclusively with a sidearm fastball. His single greatest performance came in 1913, when he went 36–7 with a 1.14 ERA, yielding six hits per nine innings and fanning 243 batters against a mere 38 walks. In that year he also hurled 11 of his major league-high 110 shutouts. Seven of his blankings occurred on Opening Day, for a record not likely to be broken. Another of Johnson's astounding numbers was ending up with a record of 38–27 in 1–0 games; all told, he lost 65 games in which Washington failed to score. It hardly came as a surprise when The Big Train, as he was known, joined Ty Cobb, Babe Ruth, Honus Wagner, and Christy Mathewson as one of the Five Immortals elected to Cooperstown in the first year of balloting.

Johnson made his first splash for Washington during a 1908 weekend series against the Yankees, when he hurled three shutouts in a four-game series. Despite catching on almost immediately as a fan favorite, he had one contract problem after another with Washington officials. Prior to the 1911 season, for instance, he walked out of spring training camp when club president Thomas Noyes refused to give him a salary equal to that of Ty Cobb ($9,000). When fans protested the possible loss of their mound star, Noyes used his newspaper connections to plant stories about how Johnson was headed for the Tigers. That only brought more vehement outcries, and the two sides eventually settled on a contract slightly less that Cobb's. During the 1914–15 off-season, there was an even bigger crisis when Noyes's successor as president, Ben Minor, told the pitcher that his "mere 28 wins" in 1914 did not entitle him to the same $12,000 he had received after winning his 36 games in 1913. Johnson was so furious that he promptly signed with the Federal League Chicago Whales. Without consulting Minor, manager and minority stockholder Clark Griffith traveled to Johnson's Kansas home and won the hurler back by promising to match the FL offer. In fact, Griffith had to get the money from White Sox owner Charlie Comiskey and then only through a heavy-handed warning to him that a Johnson FL presence in Chicago might ruin the White Sox.

By the early 1920s, Johnson appeared to have left his best diamond moments behind him, with not even his belated mastery of a curveball failing to prevent four years in a row without reaching the 20-win mark. But then in 1924, with the Senators smelling a pennant for the first time in their existence, he suddenly reverted to old form, winning 13 straight games down the stretch and winding up with league-leading numbers in both wins (23) and ERA (2.72). Although he had only a single win, and that in relief, in the World Series against the Giants, the lone victory turned out to be in the decisive seventh game, giving Washington a world championship. That wasn't his last World Series victory, either. In 1925 Johnson came back for still another 20-win season as the Senators won another pennant. When he wasn't driving the team on from the mound, he was ruining opposition clubs with his hitting: While always a competent batsman, he surprised even himself by setting an all-time-high batting average of .433 for pitchers, in 1925. The postseason duel with Pittsburgh brought both further glory and ugly disappointment. While Johnson won two games, including a shutout, he was also knocked around by the Pirates for nine runs and 15 hits in the finale. Worse, a furious Ban Johnson, president of the American League, sent a bitter telegram to Washington manager Bucky Harris criticizing the decision to leave the righthander in the entire game for what he called "sentimental reasons."

After retiring as a player, Johnson tried his hand at managing, with less than brilliant success. He piloted the Senators to two winning seasons in the early 1930s, but it took blazing finishes by the team to regain respectability after playing humdrum ball for most of these campaigns. Fired by Griffith for not showing enough animated leadership, he moved over to the helm of the Indians for three years, encountering hostility from a general manager (Billy Evans) who hadn't been told of his hiring, from players (Willie Kamm and Glenn Myatt) who objected to his high-handed ways, and finally from the fans. Especially after his release of Kamm and Myatt behind charges that they had sought to stir up a team plot against him, Johnson was booed whenever he stepped onto the field in Cleveland. At one point before being let go, he was so unpopular in Cleveland that extra police were assigned to the ballpark and beverages were dispensed in soft cups rather than bottles.

SMEEDERINO JOLLIANI

Smeederino Jolliani was the Italianized name of Smead Jolley, an outfielder for the White Sox and

Red Sox in the early 1930s who could have used the designated hitter rule. Disturbed that Boston's large Italian-American community didn't have an ethnic hero at Fenway Park, Johnny Garro, editor of the Italian-language daily *Notizia,* decided to invent one with the name change. What Boston's cheering Italian Americans got to see was a lefthanded slugger who averaged .305 over four major league seasons but who was so terrified of walls that he refused to chase fly balls anywhere near them. At Fenway he had an even greater nemesis in a left field incline that usually had him tripping over his feet even when running toward the infield after a drive. As Chicago had previously, Boston added up the runs that Jolley had driven in and, weighing them against the ones he had allowed, dropped him.

BUMPUS JONES

Jones is often depicted as a brash youngster who presented himself to Reds manager Charlie Comiskey on the last day of the 1892 season as a pitcher the equal of anyone on the Cincinnati staff, proceeded to throw a no-hitter in his major league debut, and proved his feat was a fluke by managing only a 1–4 record and a 10.19 ERA the following year. In fact, the righthander was a highly regarded prospect who had already won 27 minor league games before appearing in the Reds clubhouse; he faltered in 1893 because he was unable to adapt to the new pitching distance of 60 feet, six inches. What remains true from the familiar story is that Jones is the only pitcher to twirl a no-hitter in his first big league game.

CHARLEY JONES

An early slugger and good-time Charley, Jones managed to get involved in wrangles involving the two most powerful owners of the National League's first decade. In 1877, after league president William Hulbert had temporarily suspended the Cincinnati franchise, the outfielder signed with the Chicago White Stockings, owned by the same Hulbert, but only on the condition that the Reds remain out of the league for the rest of the year. After the righthanded power hitter had spent two games in a Chicago uniform, other league owners forced Hulbert to return his prize to the reconstituted Reds.

In 1880 Jones so exasperated Boston's Arthur Soden with his profligacy and demands for back pay that the owner suspended him, citing unsatisfactory performance and "conduct aggravating beyond the patience of most people." Jones, who was batting .300 with five home runs and who had led the NL with nine homers the year before, won a court judgment for the rest of his 1880 salary. Despite a second courtroom venture that resulted in a nasty, losing trial that made much of the outfielder's drinking, he remained on the blacklist until the American Association Reds allowed him to join the team in 1883. Three years later, Jones's wife ran into him with another woman on his arm and threw cayenne pepper in his eyes, temporarily blinding him and permanently damaging his eyesight.

CLEON JONES

Jones was the object of the two most humiliating incidents in Mets history. Although the righthand-hitting outfielder was on his way to a franchise-high .340 average at the time, he gained the attention of manager Gil Hodges for not hustling after an extra-base hit in the first game of a July 30, 1969, double-header. Hodges proceeded to walk all the way out to Jones's position in left field and order him back to the dugout with him—a move that was later hailed by other Mets as the turning point in the club's pennant-winning season. In May 1975 he was dragged before the media by board chairman M. Donald Grant to apologize for having been seized in a van by Florida police on charges of having sexual relations with a woman in public. Although initial "indecent exposure" charges were eventually dropped, Grant insisted on collecting a $2,000 fine from Jones for "betraying the image" of the team.

FIELDER JONES

Best known as the manager of the 1906 world champion Hitless Wonder White Sox, Jones also holds the distinction of having scored the first American League run when he was singled home from third by Fred Hartman in the bottom of the first inning of the AL inaugural game between Chicago and Cleveland on April 24, 1901. A lifetime .285 hitter for the Dodgers and White Sox in his 15 big league seasons between 1896 and 1915, the center fielder later managed the Federal League St. Louis Terriers and the Browns, whom he quit on June 15, 1918, after the team had blown a ninth-inning, six-run lead. He never returned to baseball.

NIPPY JONES

Jones's otherwise bland eight-year National League career was forgotten with his very last plate appearance. Pinch-hitting for the Braves in the fourth game in the 1957 World Series against the Yankees, the righthand-hitting first baseman jumped out of the way of a low fastball delivered by Tommy Byrne. When umpire Augie Donatelli called a ball, Jones and Milwaukee manager Fred Haney argued that he had been hit by the pitch and pointed out shoe polish smears on the ball. Donatelli awarded Jones first base; the Braves went on to rally, win the game, and eventually capture the Series.

MIKE JORDAN

An outfielder for the 1890 Pirates, Jordan is the only player to have had 100 major league at bats without reaching a .100 average. He managed merely 11 singles and a double in 125 official plate appearances for an .096 average.

ADDIE JOSS (Hall of Fame, 1978)

Joss was such an overwhelming performer for the Indians in the first decade of the century that the Hall of Fame waived its normal condition of at least 10 years of major league service for entry into Cooperstown. In his nine seasons (1902–10) with Cleveland, the righthander won 20 games four times, led the American League in ERA twice, and finished second to Ed Walsh for career ERA (1.89). Joss's single most memorable outing took place on October 2, 1908, when he hooked up against Walsh, defeating the Chicago righthander, 1–0, while fashioning a perfect game.

Stricken with meningitis, Joss grew progressively weaker during the 1910 season, and died in April 1911. Anticipating a refusal to their request to be allowed to attend his funeral in Toledo because it coincided with the Indians season opener in Detroit, the pitcher's teammates took off for the services without waiting for an answer. After overnight stories that the club was in open revolt, Cleveland owner Charles Somers stepped in to calm AL president Ban Johnson and the Tigers, and the opener was played the following day—as Joss's teammates had requested in the first place.

BILL JOYCE

A major league third baseman for eight seasons in the 1890s, Joyce was half responsible for the term Texas Leaguer. He made his contribution to the baseball lexicon in 1889, while still in the minor leagues. When he and outfielder Art Sunday, both recently transferred from Houston of the Texas League, opened their first game for the International League Toledo club with back-to-back bloop hits, teammates jeered at the alleged source of the cheap hits.

BILLY JURGES

An often brutal shortstop for the Cubs and Giants from 1931 to 1947, Jurges almost got more than he gave early in his career. On July 6, 1932, he received a visit from a dancer named Violet Valli in his room at Chicago's Carliss Hotel, but, when he spurned her advances, she produced a pistol and threatened suicide. Jurges intervened and received a bullet in the ribs and another in the hand for his trouble. (The episode was a source for a similar scene in Bernard Malamud's *The Natural*.) After recovering from his wounds in little more than two weeks, he got into earnest about a 17-year career that earned him equal amounts of applause for his deft defensive work and protests over his murderous, waist-high takeouts at second base. A retaliatory beanball against his tactics around second base almost ended Jurges's career in 1940, but he stuck around for another seven seasons before retiring with a .258 batting average. In 1959, as manager of the Red Sox, he presided over the integration of the last team to carry a black player when Pumpsie Green joined the club.

K

JIM KAAT

If Tommy John managed to hang on for 26 years thanks to his bionic arm, Kaat stretched his big league career to 25 seasons thanks to the quick pitch. A southpaw who was written off by several clubs in the 1970s and 1980s, he was the plague of concessionaires by forcing fans to keep their eyes on the mound whenever a batter was in the batting box. If this often led to unintentional toppers back to the pitcher, Kaat was ready with another of his talents—one that brought him a record 16 Gold Gloves.

Before becoming all guile, the lefthander was one of the dominant pitchers in the American League, compiling a circuit-leading 25 wins for the Twins in 1966, then going on to win 20 games in his only two full seasons with the White Sox, in 1974 and 1975. In three other seasons he won at least 17 games, closing out with 283 victories. Kaat went from Minnesota to Chicago in 1973 after joining teammate Jim Perry as the first American Leaguers to invoke their five-and-10 rights (five years with one club, 10 in the majors) to approve any transactions. It was a fitting climax to his years of contract wars with Twins owner Calvin Griffith, once described by Kaat as somebody who "threw quarters around like manhole covers."

AL KALINE (Hall of Fame, 1980)

Kaline was almost more curious for what he didn't accomplish than for what he did during his 22-year (1953–74) career for Detroit. Among other things, the righthand-hitting outfielder never led the American League in either home-runs or RBIs, never hit 30 homers in a season, managed 200 hits only once, won only one batting title, and was never awarded an MVP trophy. His career batting average fell three points short of .300, and his home-run total was one shy of 400. On the other hand, Kaline established himself as the Tigers franchise player of the 1950s and 1960s almost as soon as he made his big league debut. Only a few days after his high school graduation, he took the field in a game against Chicago and threw out base runners at second, third, and home in successive innings—a foretaste of the 10 Gold Gloves he would accumulate. In 1955, at age 20, he became the youngest player to win a batting title when he averaged .340. In 1959 he paced the AL in slugging average, and in 1961 in doubles. In 1968, after missing a good part of the season with a broken arm, Kaline was restored to the outfield for the World Series against the Cardinals, cracking 11 hits and driving home eight runs in the seven-game Detroit victory. Ending up with 3,007 hits, he was the first member of the 3,000-hit club who failed to bat .300 for a career.

JERRY KAPSTEIN

As the first prominent player agent in the wake of the Messersmith-McNally decision in 1975, Kapstein became Public Enemy Number One for the baseball establishment and its media allies. He was particularly vilified in Boston in 1976, when his attempts to obtain new contracts for soon-to-be free agents Carlton Fisk, Rick Burleson, and Fred Lynn coincided with the hospitalization of Red Sox owner Tom Yawkey. When Yawkey died shortly after voicing his bafflement at the money being asked for his three players, more than one newspaperman in Boston suggested that Kapstein's demands had been a contributory cause.

BENNY KAUFF

Kauff was the Ty Cobb of the Federal League, but never quite lived up to his own boast that he would "make Cobb look like a bush leaguer if I can play for the Giants." On the other hand, the fault was not entirely his own.

After a brief stint with the Yankees in 1912, the lefthand-hitting outfielder led the Federal League in hitting with a .370 average in 1914, also toping FL batters in hits, doubles, runs scored, and stolen bases. Transferred to the Feds' Brooklyn club as part of a deal that saw the Indiana franchise moved to New-ark, Kauff hit a three-run homer to win the first game of the 1915 season; then, feeling slighted by his own team over a money matter, he crossed the East River to ink a pact with John McGraw's Giants. When McGraw tried to use him in a game, however, Braves owner John Gaffney protested that the New York club had violated a prohibition against signing players already under contract to the FL. In the en-suing fracas, Boston manager George Stallings re-fused to let his team take the field, one umpire de-clared a forfeit of the game to New York, the other (after consulting with National League president John Tener) forfeited the contest to Boston, and the two teams played an "exhibition" game that Tener later validated as official after the fact. While Mc-Graw blasted Tener and American League chief Ban Johnson for double-crossing him after encourage-ments to go after Kauff, the outfielder took the ferry back to Brooklyn, where he went on to repeat as FL batting champion, this time with a .342 mark.

With the demise of the Feds after the 1915 sea-son, the Giants purchased Kauff in a more orthodox fashion. He went on to be a productive but hardly spectacular performer, reaching the 300 level twice (once in a part-time role) in five seasons. Although declining a $500 bribe from teammates Hal Chase and Heinie Zimmerman to throw a 1919 contest and reporting the incident to McGraw, Kauff fell afoul of both civil and baseball law when he was indicted in February 1920 for auto theft and for receiving stolen vehicles as part of a used-car business he op-erated with his brother. Without waiting for a trial Commissioner Kenesaw Landis banished him prior to the 1921 season on the grounds that his presence on a major league playing field would "burden pa-trons of the game with grave apprehension as to its integrity." Even after Kauff's acquittal, with both McGraw and Tener serving as character witnesses, Landis refused to lift the ban, claiming that the trial was "one of the worst miscarriages of justice that ever came under my observation."

EWING KAUFFMAN

The head of Marion Laboratories who gained the Royals expansion franchise in 1968, Kauffman served as the point man for major league owners in 1975 in their attempt to avoid going to arbitration over the free agent claims of pitchers Andy Messersmith and Dave McNally. In a motion filed with a Missouri court, Kauffman claimed that the attack on the re-serve clause integral to the Messersmith-McNally case fell beyond the purview of baseball's arbitra-tion panel. Kauffman also argued that part of the ba-sis of his investment in the Royals was the assump-tion that there would be no interruption of the reserve clause; failure to maintain it, he contended, jeopar-dized his investment unfairly. Both the arbitration panel and the Missouri court dismissed the claims.

Kauffman's tenure as Kansas City owner from 1968 to his death in 1993 was otherwise chiefly characterized by his seesawing business relationship with Memphis real-estate developer Avron Fogel-man. When Kauffman's pharmaceuticals company suffered setbacks in 1983, he surrendered 49 percent of his interest in the Royals to Fogelman for $10 million; Fogelman also threw in another $1 million for the first option on buying the club altogether be-fore 1991. A couple of years later, Kauffman picked up a little more money from the Tennessee business-man in exchange for making him a full 50–50 part-ner. But by 1990 it was Fogelman who needed cash after a downturn in the real-estate market; Kauffman obliged by advancing a $34 million loan secured by Fogelman's stock that effectively returned him to sole ownership.

Prior to his death, Kauffman entrusted the team to a coalition of local businessmen and civic leaders to assure its survival in Kansas City. It was partly in recognition of this gesture that Royals Stadium was rebaptized Kauffman Stadium as of the 1994 season.

JOHNNY KEANE

Each of Keane's two managerial assignments— with the Cardinals and Yankees in the 1960s—end-ed abruptly, less for his performance than because of front office machinations. After 31 years in the St.

Louis organization, he became dugout boss in mid-1961, kept the team above .500 for that half-season and the next three full ones, and won a National League pennant in 1964. When Keane's friend and sponsor general manager Bing Devine was fired in July 1964, he resolved to quit at the end of the season, and made arrangements with Yankees general manager Ralph Houk to succeed Yogi Berra at the helm of the New York club. When both the Cardinals and Yankees won their respective pennants, Keane was saved from complete embarrassment only because no one aside from the participants in the scheme knew he was going to take over the team his club beat in the World Series.

The circumstances of his hiring got Keane off on the wrong foot with the Yankees in 1965. His sanctimonious clubhouse lectures on proper behavior didn't improve matters. With player, press, and fans against him from the start, Keane's inflexibility and his secrecy (with Houk's complicity) about the extent of injuries to Elston Howard and Roger Maris merely hastened the inevitable. In 1965, for the first time in 40 years, the Yankees fell below .500, and Keane was fired after a slow start the following May.

DAVE KEEFE

Keefe's invention of the forkball was the result of a childhood accident that cost the future major leaguer the middle finger on his right hand. The pitch helped him, however, to only a 9–17 record between 1917 and 1922 for the Athletics and Indians.

TIM KEEFE (Hall of Fame, 1964)

Keefe's career spanned the last year of the 45-foot pitching distance (1880) and the first of the 60-foot, six-inch distance (1893); in between, from 50 feet, he was a workhorse with both the American Association Metropolitans and the National League Giants, winning more than 40 games once for each of the New York teams, and 30 or more in three other seasons. As a rookie, the righthander compiled the lowest ERA (0.86) for any pitcher with 100 innings pitched, but finished the season with a mediocre 6–6 record for Troy. He came to New York following the NL's abandonment of the Troy franchise, but whereas once and future teammates Buck Ewing, Roger Connor, and Mickey Welch all went directly to the Giants, Keefe was assigned by John B. Day, who owned both clubs, to the Metropolitans.

Keefe's most notable one-day accomplishment came on July 4, 1883, when he won both games of a doubleheader against Columbus, pitching a one-hitter in the morning and a two-hitter in the afternoon.

In 1885 Day decided to consolidate his stars on the more profitable Giants, so he released Keefe and third baseman Dude Esterbrook from their Metropolitan contracts, shipped them on a Bermuda cruise to wait out the required 10-day period, then inked them to pacts with the Giants. The fallout from this fast shuffle led to, among other things, an early effort to establish ground rules for interleague player transfers.

Keefe picked up 172 of his eighth-ranking 342 victories in a half decade with the Giants. His best season was probably 1888, when he won a record 19 consecutive games (matched by fellow Giant Rube Marquard in 1912); led the NL in wins, won-lost percentage, and strikeouts; added four more victories against the St. Louis Browns in a postseason championship series; and designed the team's "funeral uniforms," featuring black blouses with "New York" in large white letters stitched across the chest.

The pitcher served as secretary of the Players Brotherhood, despite tensions with organization president John Montgomery Ward, who had earlier married and separated from Keefe's sister-in-law. Keefe also formed a sporting goods company that manufactured the balls used in Players League games. After retirement, Keefe turned to umpiring but quit in the middle of his third season after being showered with bottles and having to leave the Polo Grounds under a police escort for calling several plays against the Giants.

WILLIE KEELER (Hall of Fame, 1939)

Often regarded as the quiet man on the rowdy Baltimore clubs of the 1890s, Keeler also earned a reputation as the greatest slap hitter of all time, compiling a .341 average in 19 seasons. A lefty-throwing third baseman with the Giants, he was moved to the outfield in Baltimore, collected 200 hits every year from 1894 to 1901, and won the first of back-to-back batting crowns in 1897 with a .422 average, the highest ever by a lefty swinger. In one stretch he poked base hits in 44 consecutive games, a major league record that stood until Joe DiMaggio reached 56 in 1941 and that, among National League hitters, has been matched only by Pete Rose, in 1978. This season record is marred, however, by complaints against the Baltimore official scorer for awarding Keeler hits on dropped fly balls and unmistakably wild throws by infielders. No defensive slouch either, the right fielder made a diving, barehanded catch in June 1898 before crashing into a barbed wire fence in Washington; John McGraw forever extolled the play as the greatest catch he had ever seen.

Only five feet, 4 $\frac{1}{2}$ inches and 140 pounds, Keeler was dubbed Wee Willie, but limited size didn't preclude typical Orioles behavior when he was pushed too far. Needled unrelentingly by the same McGraw about defensive lapses during the 1897 season, the little outfielder took on his antagonist in a naked brawl on the floor of the clubhouse and shower room as teammate Jack Doyle stood guard over the fracas to prevent interference and prove himself right in his prediction that McGraw would be the first to cry uncle.

If there was a flaw in Keeler's skills, it was a lack of power. Almost 86 percent of his hits were singles, and the difference between his lifetime batting (.341) and slugging (.415) averages is the smallest among all players who hit at least .310. His famous dictum about hitting, a response to a suggestion by Abe Yager of the Brooklyn *Eagle* that he write about his batting philosophy, expressed his talent precisely: "I have already written a treatise," he told the sports editor, "and it reads like this: 'Keep your eye clear and hit 'em where they ain't'; that's all.'"

GEORGE KELL (Hall of Fame, 1983)

Kell's numbers are usually found with players who have just missed election to Cooperstown. A .306 hitter in 15 years (1943–57) of major league service, the righthand-hitting third baseman concentrated his two greatest efforts into 1949 and 1950—in the former season winning the batting title with a .343 mark, and in the latter averaging .340 and pacing the American League in hits and doubles for the first of two straight seasons. In 1950, as well, he broke the 100 mark in RBIs and runs scored for the only time in his career. Kell's best performances were with the Tigers, who obtained him in a 1946 trade with the Athletics. He later played with several other American League teams.

CHARLIE KELLER

Given the nickname King Kong for his brawny body and bushy brows, Keller figured prominently in two dramatic World Series plays. In the fourth game of the 1939 Series against the Reds, the Yankees outfielder barreled into Cincinnati catcher Ernie Lombardi while scoring the second run driven home by a Joe DiMaggio single in the top of the 10th inning. With Lombardi lying semiconscious about three feet from the ball and the rest of the Reds slow to react, DiMaggio also circled the bases to score. It was also Keller who drove in the winning run in the fourth game of the 1941 Series against the Dodgers after Brooklyn catcher Mickey Owen let a Hugh Casey delivery get away from him on a third strike to Tommy Henrich. Keller played 13 seasons between 1939 and 1952, all but two of them for New York. He topped the 30-homer mark three times before retiring with a .286 batting average.

JOE KELLEY (Hall of Fame, 1971)

A .317 hitter in 17 seasons with Baltimore (in both the National and American leagues), Cincinnati, and three other NL teams, Kelley was the master of the Orioles ploy of planting spare baseballs in the deliberately high outfield grass and using them as opportune occasions arose. The left fielder's gambit was discovered in a game against St. Louis, after he scooped up what appeared to be a Tommy Dowd single and threw to third to nail a runner trying to advance from first, only to face a wrathful umpire when center fielder Steve Brodie chased down the actual hit and fired the game ball to second base; the game was forfeited to the Cardinals. Kelley became manager of the Reds in the aftermath of a plot by Cincinnati owner John T. Brush and New York Giants manager John McGraw to destroy the AL Orioles in 1902. One element of the intrigue had Baltimore stockholder John J. Mahon collecting a majority of club stock and handing it over to Brush, who moved Kelley, as player-manager, along with outfielder Cy Seymour, to the Reds, and six others to New York. Mahon was Kelley's father-in-law.

GEORGE KELLY (Hall of Fame, 1973)

Kelly's inclusion in Cooperstown owes as much to teammate Frankie Frisch's plumping for him as a member of the Veterans Committee as it does to his on-field accomplishments. Gifted with a strong arm but clumsy on his feet, the righthand-hitting first baseman batted .297 over 16 years (between 1915 and 1932), spent most prominently with John McGraw's Giants. His best years were 1921, when he led the

National League with 23 home runs and batted across 122 runs, and 1924, when he hit .324 with 21 home runs, and a league-leading 136 RBIs. Accused of complicity in an October 1924 bribery scandal that led to the banning of New York outfielder Jimmy O'Connell and coach Cozy Dolan, Kelly was exonerated along with other future Hall of Famers Frisch and Ross Youngs. Mainly because of his ungraceful fielding, Kelly was a prime target of New York sportswriters in his early years; later, however, he was portrayed by beat writers as the most approachable of McGraw's Giants.

KING KELLY (Hall of Fame, 1945)

The most frequently repeated of Kelly's escapades—that one day in the 1890s, he jumped off the bench, declared himself a replacement for teammate Charlie Ganzel, and caught a pop foul out of the catcher's reach to retire the side in a clutch situation—is almost certainly apocryphal. But almost everything else that had been said about Kelly is true:

- that he not merely won two batting crowns (in 1884 and 1886) but also played every position adequately, if not spectacularly, and shone both in the outfield and behind the plate;
- that he contributed pivotally to nine pennants (two of them in the same year) in 16 seasons;
- that he made staggering amounts of money, sometimes through bizarre subterfuges in his contract, and spent it equally lavishly;
- that he turned down an even more staggering sum;
- that his popularity in Chicago went unmatched until Ernie Banks, eight decades later;
- that his unrivaled hold on Boston fans gave him the power to make and break franchises by his inclusion on and withdrawal from their rosters.

With Chicago, Kelly gave manager Cap Anson fits, once claiming that he was taking a day off to sweat off some excess weight, only to be discovered at the local racetrack. On the other hand, he led the White Stockings to five flags, thrilled crowds with the Kelly Spread (an early version of the hook slide that inspired the popular tune "Slide, Kelly, Slide"), and incited admiration for his ingenuity in thinking up such tricks as throwing his catcher's mask in the first-base path to trip batters. In 1887 Chicago owner Al Spalding was still able to ignore all these contributions when Kelly made salary demands he considered excessive, selling him to Boston for a then-sensational $10,000.

Meeting the righthanded slugger's $5,000 contract demand proved less difficult for Boston's Arthur Soden; he simply gave his new acquisition the official major league maximum of $2,000, then slipped him another $3,000 under the table for the use of his picture. Three years later, Kelly supplied the Players League with instant box office appeal by jumping to the Boston Reds as player-manager and became the object of a National League scheme to wreck the PL by wooing him back. Approached by Spalding with a $10,000 bribe to defect from the union cause, he took a walk to consider the offer, then told his former boss, "I want the $10,000 bad enough, but I've thought the matter over, and I can't go back on the boys. And neither would you." In Spalding's version of the encounter, they shook hands, and Kelly accepted both the owner's congratulations and a $500 loan. The Reds went on to win the PL's only pennant.

With the end of the PL war in 1891, Kelly agreed to lend his cachet to the formation of an American Association franchise in Cincinnati. The Porkers lasted only 90 games, but Kelly made the brief experience interesting. Before games, he let a collection of veterans and rookies nobody else wanted pick the positions they wanted to play that day. On the field he led them in almost daily brawls. In the clubhouse he led them in regular postgame banquets. And on Sundays he led them directly from the ballfield to the local magistrate's court to be found not guilty of violating municipal blue laws prohibiting baseball on the Sabbath.

That adventure over in August, Kelly signed once again with the Reds, now part of the AA and locked in an attendance war against the Beaneaters. For four days, Boston fans poured into the AA club's Congress Street Grounds to see their returning hero, then went in equal numbers to the NL team's South End Grounds after Kelly succumbed to Soden's offer of a larger salary and a trip to Europe for him and his wife. Each team won its league's pennant, but Kelly won the fans for the NL entry.

After one more season (and one more pennant) in Boston and a final year with the Giants, Kelly, who had appeared in vaudeville from time to time, took to the stage full time. It was, in fact, on his way to a performance at Boston's Palace Theater that he succumbed to an attack of what was termed "typhoid-pneumonia" in 1894, several weeks shy of his 37th birthday. So reduced were his circumstances that NL owners raised $1,400 by subscription for his widow.

KEN KELTNER

Best known for making two fine stops in the game that ended Joe DiMaggio's 56-game hitting streak in 1941, Keltner also made history of a different sort by seeking, with the support of Cleveland president Alva Bradley, unemployment compensation after the 1939 season. His application was denied by Ohio authorities on the grounds that he was under a year-long contract. The righty-swinging third baseman played 13 years for the Indians between 1937 and 1950, compiling a .276 lifetime average.

BOB KENNEDY

Kennedy had the longest uninterrupted run as one of Phil Wrigley's rotating managers in the Chicago owner's College of Coaches scheme in the early 1960s; Kennedy was, in fact, the Cubs pilot in everything but title from 1963 to the beginning of 1965. Later he went on to manage the Athletics in their inaugural season in Oakland in 1968 and to hold down several front office jobs in the 1970s and 1980s.

Wrigley introduced the College of Coaches system in 1961 behind the argument that clubs required a change of managers during the season as much as starters needed relievers during games. What he didn't say was that he was exasperated by having had to make almost annual managerial changes and that it was cheaper to extend the duties of a coach than to hire a dugout boss. The coaches originally named to the managerial rotation were Rip Collins, Charlie Grimm, Rube Walker, El Tappe, Harry Craft, Bobby Adams, Gordie Holt, and Vedie Himsl. Only Tappe, Craft, and Himsl from that group actually called the shots for any perceptible period. Along with Kennedy, Lou Klein and Charlie Metro were later added to the system, and took over as pilots for stretches.

BRICKYARD KENNEDY

Kennedy was the model small-town boy at odds with the big city. A four-time 20-game winner for the Dodgers at the end of the 19th century, he could never quite get the hang of Brooklyn or Manhattan. In his most legendary escapade, he set out one morning from his Brooklyn home to pitch against the Giants in the Polo Grounds, got lost, and ended up on a train heading for the Midwest. Asked how he had made such a mistake, Kennedy shrugged and said that a policeman he had asked for directions "heard I was from Ohio and figured that was where I should be."

W. H. KENNETT

Kennett was president of the Cincinnati Reds in 1880, when the National League decided to purge its rank of clubs that put immediate profits above the principle of long-term respectability. The Reds, whose German immigrant fans enjoyed beer at the ballpark and saw no reason not to play on Sunday, had never been in compliance with the National League's prevailing moral attitudes. League officials looked the other way until the Worcester *Spy* launched an editorial attack on the club both for selling beer and for renting its park for amateur Sunday games. The conflict came to a head in October 1880 when, with only Kennett dissenting, the league announced that at its next meeting it would pass legislation expelling any team that violated the bans on beer and Sunday ball; the next item on the agenda was the immediate expulsion of the Reds for breaking a rule that had not yet been enacted.

DICKIE KERR

Kerr's two victories over Cincinnati in the 1919 World Series were one of the few positives for Chicago, but he still ended up sharing the fate of the players outlawed in the Black Sox scandal. After two subsequent seasons during which he posted a combined 40 wins, the southpaw demanded a $500 heftier raise than the team was about to grant and backed up his position by sitting out the 1922 season. During that year he appeared in a semipro game against some of the blacklisted White Sox players, and for Commissioner Kenesaw Landis that was grounds for banning him from the majors as well. Kerr got the ban rescinded in time for the 1925 season, but by then he had lost his effectiveness. Later, while managing at Daytona Beach, he had the foresight to change Stan Musial from a lefty pitcher with an injured shoulder into an outfielder.

BULL AND EDDIE KESSLER

The Kessler brothers set the standard for abusiveness among Philadelphia fans in the 1920s and 1930s by seating themselves on opposite sides of the infield and bellowing at each other about the inadequacies of both visiting and hometeam players. They reserved their worst attacks for native Philadelphian Jimmy Dykes, who became so distracted that Athletics owner-manager Connie Mack served up a bribe of season tickets for the brothers. When even that bit of uncharacteristic generosity failed, Mack took the Kesslers to court in an effort to get them off his infielder's back. In fact, only a trade to the White Sox in 1933 enabled Dykes to escape his antagonists, except, of course, when he returned to Shibe Park in a visitor's uniform.

HARMON KILLEBREW (Hall of Fame, 1984)

Killebrew was the most prolific righthanded power hitter in American League history, clouting 573 home runs in a 22-year career between 1954 and 1975. His ratio of one home run for every 14.22 at bats ranks behind only Mark McGwire (10.61), Babe Ruth (11.76), and Ralph Kiner (14.11). Originally brought up by the Senators as a third baseman, Killebrew spent most of his career with Washington and its successor franchise in Minnesota going to defensive positions (first base, the outfield) where his manager of the moment considered him least likely to hurt the team in the field. Through it all, he kept putting up numbers sufficient to lead the AL in homers six times, top the 40 level in round-trippers eight times, and deliver 100 RBIs nine times. In 1969 he took MVP honors for helping the Twins to a division title with his league-leading 49 homers and 140 runs batted in. He also led the league in walks four times and topped the 100 mark in that category seven times. Aside from his defensive limitations, Killebrew was very much a hit-or-miss offensive proposition—not only striking out more than 100 times in seven seasons and for never batting higher than .288 in a full year but also for the streakiness of his long-ball hitting. In both 1962 and 1963, for instance, he ended slumps of seven-weeks duration; he ended the dry spell in 1962 by belting 11 home runs in his final 11 games and in 1963 by knocking seven in his last six games. Annoyed that he wasn't given the Minnesota managerial job at the end of 1974, Killebrew signed for a final, woeful year with Kansas City, when he batted only .199. Seeking to capitalize on the slugger's return to the Twin Cities and to help his ailing attendance, Twins owner Calvin Griffith staged a Harmon Killebrew Night on the Royals first

visit, but only 2,946 fans showed up. Things didn't get much better for Killebrew after retirement. Following some unsuccessful efforts at broadcasting, he went bankrupt and had to rely on personal loans to get along. The slugger was initially recommended to Washington by Idaho Senator Herman Welker.

MATT KILROY

In his rookie season of 1886, Kilroy established an all-but-invulnerable record by striking out 513 batters for the American Association Baltimore Orioles. The next year, with the number of strikes for an out raised from three to four, his total dropped to 217, but he established a second major league record: 46 wins by a lefthanded pitcher.

RALPH KINER (Hall of Fame, 1975)

Kiner came as close as anyone to being a one-man team. Brought up by the Pirates in 1946, the righthand-hitting outfielder became the first National League rookie to lead the circuit in home runs in 40 years. In a career that spanned only 10 years, he bashed 369 home runs, including five straight seasons of at least 40, giving him third place behind Mark McGwire and Babe Ruth for career long-ball frequency. More remarkable, Kiner accomplished his power feats (including leading the league in homers in every one of his seven seasons in a Pittsburgh uniform) in lineups that sometimes seemed to have not even a second major league player. The situation became so marked in the early 1950s that many fans didn't bother showing up at Forbes Field until the second inning, assuming that the first three Pirates would be retired in the first inning and cleanup hitter Kiner would be leading off in the second frame; by the same token, his final at bat in the eighth inning usually signaled a mass exit. Given his lack of protection, it was hardly surprising that he received at least 100 walks seven years in a row; despite that, he still managed to drive in 100 runs five times. Kiner credited his early survival in Pittsburgh (he had a ferocious strikeout rate) to Hank Greenberg, who was acquired in 1947 precisely for tutoring the slugger in a better appreciation of the strike zone. Equally emphatically, Kiner has attributed the end of his career in the Steel City to organization president Branch Rickey. Among the other things Rickey didn't like about his ostensible franchise player were Kiner's visibility in Players Association causes and the frequency with which his name was linked in gossip columns to Elizabeth Taylor, Janet Leigh, and other actresses. On another level, Kiner irked the executive for winning over Pittsburgh fans with the generally one-dimensional skills that Rickey had always preached against in dispensing his views about ideal players. For his part, Kiner didn't hesitate to describe Rickey as a hypocrite and a liar for his devious negotiating tactics. The thorny relationship came to an end on June 4, 1953, when Rickey packaged the outfielder to the Cubs in a 10-player deal that also brought the Pirates $150,000. To enraged fans, Rickey reiterated what he had previously told Kiner: that the Pirates could finish last without him as easily as with him.

Once out of Pittsburgh, Kiner fell prey to various leg injuries and retired from the major leagues within three years. After serving as general manager of the Pacific Coast League franchise in San Diego for five years and being associated with several attempts to lure a big league club to California, he went into the broadcasting booth for the White Sox. In 1962 he became one of the original announcers for the Mets—a job he still had 40 years later. As a broadcaster, Kiner has frequently betrayed his Hollywood days in continually fumbling the names of even the most veteran players; throughout his seven-year stay with New York, for instance, Gary Carter seldom got through a game without being identified by Kiner as Gary Cooper. Kiner has also had trouble distinguishing third baseman Tim Wallach from Eli Wallach—to the point that the infielder's teammates also began calling him Eli.

SILVER KING

After averaging almost 30 wins a year in his first six full seasons, King lost his effectiveness when the pitcher's rubber was introduced in 1893. In his old delivery he had crossed from one side of the five-and-a-half-by-four-foot pitcher's box to the other; with his more restricted windup he managed only 24 victories in three more seasons. The righthander also lost an opportunity to pitch the only Players League no-hitter, on June 21, 1890, when Chicago manager Charlie Comiskey elected to have his Pirates bat first in a home game against Brooklyn. Because King surrendered a run on errors in the seventh, the visiting Wonders did not have to bat in the bottom of the ninth, so the hurler had to be satisfied with eight innings of no-hit pitching.

DAVE KINGMAN

Kingman bids fair to hold in perpetuity the mark for the most home runs by a player not in the Hall of Fame. In 16 years, the outfielder-first baseman clouted 442 balls out of the park—many of them titanic blasts that had public relations people scrambling after tape measures. The rest of Kingman had people scrambling to get away from him. Aside from being a worse-than-average fielder, he was the epitome of homer-or-nothing at the plate; his .204 batting average for the 1982 Mets was the lowest ever recorded for a home-run champion. His relations with the media were even worse than his consistency. In June 1986, for instance, he displayed his notion of humor by having a live rat delivered to a woman sportswriter for the Sacramento *Bee*. That episode brought a fine and a decision by the Athletics not to offer him another contract despite the fact that he led the club with 35 home runs. When no other team signed him as a free agent, it gave Kingman the consolation prize of various records (35 homers, 94 RBIs) for a final career year.

ANDREA KIRBY

Kirby has done as much as anybody to prevent baseball players from having an interesting thought escape from their mouths during media interviews. A former television reporter in New York, she has been hired by a number of clubs to instruct major leaguers in showing themselves to best effect before the cameras. What this has usually meant is even more guardedness from players and managers about criticizing opposition players or suggesting that a clubhouse is not an extension of paradise.

GEORGE KIRKSEY

A public relations flack by profession, Kirksey was the idea man behind the Houston Sports Association lobby that brought major league baseball to Texas. Among his inspirations was to call the team (initially) the Colt .45s to firm up a pending advertising deal with the Colt Firearms Company. His ventures into contract negotiations, however, were another story. With no other Houston executive available, he had to handle the bargaining in the early 1960s with top-rated prospect Rusty Staub. Kirksey managed to sign Staub—but at twice the figure the organization had agreed to, plus sign the outfielder's brother to a three-year pact, plus agree to a scouting job for

Staub's father. Kirksey was eventually squeezed out of his job with Houston after a number of years of being assigned to less and less meaningful positions.

CHUCK KLEIN (Hall of Fame, 1980)

Few players have depended on a ballpark as much as Klein relied on Baker Bowl. The Phillies most potent offensive star prior to the arrival of Mike Schmidt, the lefty-swinging outfielder spent the overwhelming majority of his 17 big league seasons (1928–44) taking aim at the friendly right field wall of the bandbox, making clear his disaffection during brief stints with the Cubs and Pirates. Between his rookie year and 1933, Klein racked up batting averages between .337 and .386. Within that period he also won a Triple Crown (in 1933, when he additionally paced the National League in doubles and slugging average), three other home run titles, another RBI title, scored the most runs in the league three consecutive years, and even stole more bases than anyone else once. When he was traded to the Cubs in 1934, on the other hand, Klein barely reached the 20 mark in home runs in his two seasons and had an RBI high of only 80. Reobtained by the Phillies during the 1936 season, he went back over the 100-RBI mark again.

Klein's power feats at Baker Bowl were a mixed blessing for cheapskate owner William Baker. Terrified that his star's slugging would make him intractable in contract negotiations, Baker had an extension placed atop the right-field wall in the early 1930s so that he wouldn't have to deal with somebody boasting Babe Ruth-like numbers. It was Baker's equally parsimonious successor Gerry Nugent who dealt the outfielder to Chicago in 1934 and to Pittsburgh in 1939 to pick up some quick cash. The tininess of Baker Bowl also helped Klein defensively, enabling him to set a never-approached modern record of 44 outfield assists in 1930. After hanging on as a would-be gate attraction in Philadelphia for a third stint, during World War II, he retired with an overall batting average of .320 and with exactly 300 home runs.

BILL KLEM (Hall of Fame, 1953)

Klem was to the no-nonsense umpire as Babe Ruth was to the slugging outfielder. For a record 37 years (1905–41), Klem held sway over National League games with an autocratic bearing and encyclopedic knowledge of the rules that brooked little dispute from players, coaches, or managers. One of his more noted tactics during an argument was to draw a line in the dirt with his shoe and warn his adversary of the moment not to cross it. He didn't leave much leeway to his colleagues, either, and for his first 16 years insisted on calling balls and strikes for every game; his acknowledged superiority behind the plate led other league arbiters to comply with his preference. On the rare occasion that he was questioned about one of his calls, he was content to reply, "I never called one wrong," only late in his career adding a tap to the left side of his chest and qualifying "from here." Klem's reputation for honesty was such that when he accused New York Giants trainer Joseph Creamer of trying to bribe him before the final game of the 1908 season, a league meeting called to investigate the charge was little more than a formality before the physician was banned from baseball for life. On the other hand, Klem was the first umpire fined for unbecoming behavior during a World Series, running afoul of Commissioner Kenesaw Landis for responding in kind to Washington outfielder Goose Goslin's four-letter-word outburst. Among other things, Klem popularized the inside chest protector and the over-the-shoulder stance for calling balls and strikes. His records include the most World Series games (108) and being the oldest umpire (at 68) to work a major league game. After retiring from the field, The Old Arbiter, as he took to calling himself in his later years, served as the NL's supervisor of umpires until his death in 1951. Two years later he became the first umpire elected to the Hall of Fame.

EDDIE KLEPP

Klepp was Jackie Robinson in reverse. A white pitcher, he was signed by the all-black Cleveland Buckeyes in 1946 in an effort to integrate the Negro leagues the same year Robinson was crashing through organized baseball's color barrier with Montreal in the International League. Klepp's experiences sound like a parody of Robinson's: Run off the field—and prohibited even from sitting in the Cleveland dugout—by racists during an exhibition game in Birmingham, he was forced to sit in the white section of the grandstand. Excluded from the team's road accommodations, Klepp was compelled to eat alone at whites-only restaurants and sleep in whites-only hotels. He appeared in only a handful of games for the Buckeyes.

JOHNNY KLING

Kling was the regular catcher on the formidable Cubs squads that dominated the National League in the first decade of the 20th century. Deciding to leave the team in 1909 to pursue a career as a professional pool shooter, he was blamed for Chicago's second-place finish. Kling sought to return to the club in 1910 but during his year off had played a few games against outlawed players. The National Commission bent its rules for him and reinstated the receiver after imposing a $700 fine. When he did rejoin the Cubs, Kling contributed to still another pennant but was the target of so much clubhouse resentment for his defection the year before that he was dealt to the Braves soon afterward.

TED KLUSZEWSKI

It was mainly because of Kluszewski's bulging biceps that Cincinnati thought it would be a good idea in the mid-1950s to go to sleeveless uniforms to gain a psychological edge on other teams. It worked to the extent that the 1956 team tied the National League record for most home runs in a season (221), but it didn't pay off in any pennants. Kluszewski himself was a somewhat contradictory slugger. Over his first five seasons, he hit a mere 74 home runs, not breaking out until 1953 with 40 round-trippers. In the power years that followed, he remained an unusually discriminating batter: While belting 49 home runs in 1954, he struck out only 35 times, following that up with a season of 47 homers and merely 40 strikeouts. On the other hand, the lefthanded first baseman's fielding was deceptive: Although he led the league five straight times in fielding percentage, much of the mark was due to a modest range that kept him away from errors of ambition.

MICKEY KLUTTS

Klutts may have been baseball's most aptly named player. In eight major league seasons from 1976 to 1983 he appeared in only 199 games, mainly because of 10 lengthy stays on the disabled list.

LON KNIGHT

The starting pitcher for home team Philadelphia on April 22, 1876, Knight threw the first pitch in major league history; he went on to lose the game, 6–5, to Boston. Aside from that inaugural season, when he won 10 games while losing 22, his entire major league career consisted of a handful of games in 1884 and 1885.

RAY KNIGHT

Knight was one of the National League's best performers under pressure during his 13-year (1974–88) career. Installed by Cincinnati at third base in 1979 to replace fan favorite Pete Rose, Knight responded by hitting .318 and playing a major role in the club's unexpected division win. With the Mets in 1986, the righthand-hitting third baseman had two of the most dramatic hits in franchise history. In the 10th inning of the sixth game of the 1986 World Series against the Red Sox, with two out and two strikes on him, he singled to reduce the New York deficit to a run and drove Kevin Mitchell around to third, from where he tallied on a Bob Stanley wild pitch; a few pitches later, Knight himself scored the winning run on Bill Buckner's error on the grounder hit by Mookie Wilson. In the seventh game, Knight hit a seventh-inning home run that put the Mets ahead to stay. After being voted MVP in the World Series, however, Knight turned down a New York contract and ended up playing out his days for a considerably lesser sum with the Orioles and Tigers.

DAROLD KNOWLES

Knowles is the only pitcher to appear in every game of a seven-game World Series. The southpaw reliever did it for the Athletics in 1973, picking up saves in both the first and last games and not yielding a single earned run in a combined $6\frac{1}{3}$ innings.

LEN KOENECKE

Koenecke occasioned one of Casey Stengel's rare admissions of sincere regret. An outfielder for the 1935 Dodgers, he began to try manager Stengel's patience with such lapses as wandering off first base on a mistaken assumption that a third out had been made and going to the wrong position in taking the field. On another occasion he got a hit-and-run sign, dribbled the ball in front of the plate, and stood arguing with the umpire that he had hit a foul while the catcher pounced on the ball and overthrew second base in an attempt to get the runner, the center fielder retrieved the errant toss to get the runner at third, and the third baseman fired back to the catcher to tag Koenecke for a double play. Exasperated by such incidents during a road trip, Stengel put Koenecke on a train back to Brooklyn from St. Louis ahead of the rest of the team. But Koenecke left the train in Detroit and chartered an airplane to Buffalo, where he had friends. While over Canadian territory, he tried to wrest control of the plane away from pilot William Mulqueeny, who picked up a fire extinguisher and bludgeoned Koenecke to death. Two separate hearings in Canadian courts absolved Mulqueeny of any crime and found that Koenecke had drunk heavily during his stopover in Detroit. The hearings also floated the suggestion that the player had actually been bent on suicide in his attempt to take over the plane. Whenever Stengel mentioned the incident for the rest of his life, he blamed himself for not having recognized the signs of Koenecke's severe mental disturbance.

MARK KOENIG

Koenig was the indirect cause of Babe Ruth's "called shot" in the 1932 World Series. Acquired by the Cubs from Detroit late in the season, the shortstop proved invaluable down the stretch with his nifty fielding and .353 average. Despite that, he was voted only a half share of the World Series pool by his teammates. When the Yankees began mocking the Cubs for their miserliness toward their own one-time teammate, tensions rose between the clubs, to the point that Ruth allegedly felt compelled to ridicule the National Leaguers by preannouncing a home run against Charlie Root in the third game. Root himself always denied that Ruth pointed to the center field bleachers before depositing a fastball there.

JIM KONSTANTY

Konstanty was the first National League pitcher celebrated as a reliever rather than as a failed starter who ended up being helpful from the bullpen. With the pennant-winning Phillies in 1950, he made 74 appearances out of the pen, winning 16 games and saving 22 others. Despite the fact that he hadn't started a game all year, he was handed the ball for the opening contest of the World Series against the Yankees; the righthander allowed only four hits but lost 1–0.

SANDY KOUFAX (Hall of Fame, 1972)

The most telling indication of Koufax's mastery of National League hitters in the 1960s was that he continually tipped his pitches and still couldn't be hit. One of the bonus babies of the 1950s who had to be carried on a major league roster for two seasons, the southpaw was no better than 36–40 after six years with the Dodgers. Even during his long orientation, however, he gave signs of what was to come by posting more strikeouts than innings pitched in three of those years, just missing the 200-K mark even when he managed only eight wins in 1960. The turning point of his career came when catcher Norm Sherry noticed during a workout that Koufax's motion momentarily blocked his view of home plate. This helped produce a transition season in 1961, when the lefthander won 18 games and led the NL in strikeouts with 269 but still got roughed up for a 3.52 ERA and continued to issue too many walks (96). Then, over the next five years, he turned into one of the most dominant pitchers baseball has ever seen.

In all five seasons, Koufax paced the league in ERA; in 1963, 1965, and 1966, he won the Cy Young Award for leading in wins and strikeouts; twice he had the best winning percentage; twice he led the way for complete games and innings pitched; and three times he hurled more shutouts than anybody else. His 111–34 record over the span also included four no-hitters—one of them, a perfect game against the Cubs in 1965. If there was any fly in the ointment, it was an arthritis in his pitching elbow that first became noticeable in 1964 and that prompted Dodgers physicians to go against the book the following year by advising the lefthander not to throw between starts. Then, in 1966, despite another glowing performance (27–9, 1.73), Koufax announced that the constant pain wasn't worth it and that, at age 31, he was retiring. If unwillingly, this gave him two final entries in the baseball record book: the best performance by a pitcher in a final season and, five years later, the distinction of being the youngest player ever elected to Cooperstown.

CLARENCE KRAFT

Kraft was a first baseman of no particular distinction whose demotion to the minor leagues almost provoked baseball's first general strike. The trouble started when he was farmed out by the Dodgers to Newark of the Class AA International League in 1914. The National Commission, however, supported a prior claim by Nashville of the Class A Southern Association, even though the ruling body had reached an agreement with the Players Fraternity not to force a player to perform at a level lower than the classification of the highest team that wanted him. American League president Ban Johnson justified the about-face with a contention that Nashville's claim predated the agreement and that it had never been made retroactive. Fraternity president Dave Fultz then called a strike of his 500 or so members for July 22, forcing Brooklyn owner Charlie Ebbets to capitulate and send Nashville a $2,500 check for allowing Kraft to stay in Newark. Kraft's entire major league career consisted of three games with the Braves later in the 1914 season.

LEW KRAUSSE

Krausse was the trigger for a team revolt against Kansas City owner Charlie Finley in 1967. The trouble started when Finley levied a $500 fine on the pitcher for alleged rowdyism on a team flight. Charging that Finley was merely seeking to save money on Krausse, Athletics players drafted a petition demanding that the owner put an end to his nickel-and-diming ways. The petition cost manager Alvin Dark his job and led to the release of slugger Ken Harrelson, one of the drafters of the document. When the Players Association demanded a meeting with Commissioner William Eckert, Finley sought to block the move, this in turn leading to the association's first complaint with the National Labor Relations Board that a baseball owner was trying to harass its members. Under the threat of the NLRB's intervention, Finley and the association reached a compromise on general matters but left it up to Krausse to pursue a hearing with Eckert on the fine. A few days before he was due to meet with the commissioner, however, the pitcher suddenly withdrew his appeal request. The decision followed a mysterious shooting incident at the hotel where Krausse and teammates were staying. A subsequent police report named only the hurler as having been questioned, saying that he had been cleared of any involvement. Signed as an 18-year-old phenom in 1961 for $125,000 by his father, a Kansas City scout, Krausse began his otherwise undistinguished career immediately thereafter with a three-hit shutout of the Angels; 30 years earlier, his father, who had the same name, had made his debut with a shutout for the Philadelphia Athletics.

PAUL KRICHELL

By at least one yardstick, Krichell was the most successful major league scout ever. A backup catcher of little note with the Browns in 1911 and 1912, he served as a Yankees scout from 1920 until his death in 1957. Among his discoveries were five eventual Hall of Famers: Lou Gehrig, Leo Durocher, Tony Lazzeri, Phil Rizzuto, and Whitey Ford. He is the only scout to have inked so many future Cooperstown residents.

JOAN KROC

As soon as she took over the Padres after her husband's death in January 1984, Kroc made it clear that she wanted to unload the team. It was a quest, however, that took her the rest of the decade, mainly because of her condition that potential buyers undertake a formal commitment not to move the club out of San Diego. The low point of her hunt was in March 1987, when she announced that she had reached a $60 million sale agreement with Mariners owner George Argyros. The announcement turned out to be extremely premature, since Argyros still had not found a buyer for his Seattle franchise, and National League owners came out in chorus against the American League operator. It emerged subsequently that Kroc had been so hasty because her son-in-law, team president Ballard Smith, was divorcing her daughter, and she wanted him out the door as quickly as possible. Although Kroc got rid of Smith, she needed another three years before finally concluding a sale, with a consortium headed by television producer Tom Werner in April 1990. Prior to the deal, she had shown how serious she was about keeping the club in San Diego by opening negotiations to sell it to the city; she was talked out of the move by NL owners horrified by the prospect of a municipal ownership.

RAY KROC

Kroc exemplified the millionaire businessman who got into baseball counting on having a serious pastime and who ended up passing the time counting. When he took over the Padres in January 1974, the McDonald's fast food pioneer was already in his 70s and mainly interested, in his own words, in "going into the locker room to kick one player in the fanny and pat another on the back." He found the kicking part more instinctive on the very first game played under his ownership when he grabbed the public address microphone and blasted the Padres for "some of the most stupid ballplaying I've ever seen." Although the club didn't improve too much under such hectoring, San Diego fans flocked to Jack Murphy Stadium in greater numbers in the hope that the owner would put on another performance. For a couple of years he tried to return the fan interest by joining Ted Turner and George Steinbrenner as a no-holds-barred pursuer of free agents, but the club was still unable to break the .500 mark. When he drew a $100,000 fine for tampering with free agents Joe Morgan and Graig Nettles prior to the 1980 season, he declared himself disgusted with the whole business and turned most of the club's operations over to his son-in-law Ballard Smith. Kroc died in January 1984, a little more than nine months before the Padres captured their first flag.

TONY KUBEK

Yankees shortstop Kubek was felled by one of the costliest pebbles in baseball history. In the eighth inning of the seventh game of the 1960 World Series, a double-play ball off the bat of Pittsburgh's Bill Virdon took a bad bounce and struck him in the throat. After Kubek was carried off the field, the Pirates rallied for five runs, setting the stage for New York to tie the game in the top of the ninth and for Bill Mazeroski to become a hero in the bottom of the frame.

Kubek, the American League Rookie of the Year in 1957, retired with a .266 average after the 1965 season at age 29 because of chronic back and neck problems. He later became an outspoken broadcaster, doing both network games and working in the booth for the Blue Jays and Yankees. Unlike others in the booth, he was particularly critical of owners, including his own employers.

BOWIE KUHN

Kuhn managed to survive more than 15 years as baseball's commissioner, the second-longest tenure after Kenesaw Landis, despite annoying just about everyone connected with the game either by his decisions, half-decisions, or indecision. Presiding over an era that saw attendance in major league parks triple, he dealt with crises either by sidestepping the issue or by placating both sides; when he did make firm decisions, they tended, at best, to reinforce the status quo and, at worst, attempt to restore the status quo ante.

The National League's attorney when he was boosted into the commissioner's chair by Los Angeles owner Walter O'Malley in February 1969, Kuhn was faced almost immediately with the refusal of Cardinals outfielder Curt Flood to accept a trade to the Phillies and found himself the defendant in Flood's suit to have the reserve clause overturned. A hard-liner on the issue, Kuhn ignored a long history of legal precedent against reserving players in perpetuity and fought the case to a successful conclusion in the U.S. Supreme Court.

Turning his attention in early 1971 to the creation of a Negro leagues wing in the Hall of Fame, Kuhn made enemies on both sides of the issue: with the purists by failing to see any reason to include players who had performed outside the major leagues and with the activists by ignoring that black players had been excluded through the racism of the day. Preoccupied by an obsession with returning baseball to Washington, D.C., after the second version of the Senators departed for Texas in 1972, he embarked on a series of misadventures that reached a climax when he tried to prevent the American League from expanding into Seattle and Toronto in 1977. His alternative—awarding new National league franchises to Toronto and Washington—was shot down by erstwhile patron O'Malley. The most visible result of Kuhn's fixation with Washington was the alienation of Baltimore owner Jerold Hoffberger.

With little time left over from these escapades, Kuhn played no part in the 13-day players strike of 1972. By his own choice, however, he was not so fortunate in the next labor-relations crisis. Realizing the futility of the owner-imposed 1976 lockout in spring training in the aftermath of the Messersmith-McNally arbitration decision on the reserve clause, he ordered the spring training camps opened on March 17, making no friends among his employers in the process. Learning his lesson, Kuhn stayed in the background during the 1981 players strike, largely at the request of Player Relations Committee negotiator Ray Grebey. That made Kuhn the target of sports commentators, most notably columnist Red Smith, who regularly delivered such barbs as "This strike wouldn't have happened if Bowie Kuhn were alive today."

Not content with irritating owners wholesale, Kuhn also struck out at individuals. He earned the enmity of Charlie Finley for his veto of the Oakland owner's attempt to place second baseman Mike Andrews on the disabled list for errors made in the 1973 World Series. Negating Finley's 1976 cash deals for Joe Rudi and Rollie Fingers to the Red Sox and Vida Blue to the Yankees (as well as a later sale of Blue to the Reds) for not passing "the best interest of baseball" clause in the Basic Agreement did nothing to restore the relationship. Atlanta boss Ted Turner drew a one-year suspension for tampering with Giants outfielder Gary Matthews, also in 1976. But Kuhn's most lingering battle was with George Steinbrenner of the Yankees. In November 1974, he suspended Steinbrenner for two years as baseball's punishment for a guilty plea in making illegal contributions to Richard Nixon's 1972 reelection campaign but lifted the suspension during the 1976 lockout; later there were intermittent fines for Steinbrenner's criticism of umpires and of staffers in the commissioner's office.

Kuhn's relations with some players weren't much smoother. Calling Jim Bouton to task for publishing *Ball Four* in 1970, the straitlaced commissioner questioned the credibility of the former pitcher's tales of player carousing; he helped make the book an instant best-seller not only by appearing to be censoring its content but also by (unsuccessfully) insisting that Bouton deny that they had ever talked about the book. In the same year, Kuhn suspended Detroit pitcher Denny McLain for two months for his involvement in a Michigan bookmaking operation, drawing fire for the halfway penalty. He made no such mistake in barring Hall of Famers Willie Mays and Mickey Mantle (in 1979 and 1983, respectively) from any involvement in baseball because of their employment by Atlantic City casinos; he made those proscriptions look even worse by grandfathering Steinbrenner and Pittsburgh boss Daniel Galbreath when, in 1980, he forbade baseball's owners from having any interest in racetracks or racehorses.

Kuhn's firmest position—and the cause of his most consistent defeats—was his insistence on mandatory drug testing for players, a proposition anathema to the Players Association. He was overruled in arbitration in all but one instance in which he suspended a player for drug use. The sole exception was the case of Vida Blue, who was convicted of dealing as well as personal use.

Kuhn was finally ousted not by AL owners, with whom he had had so much trouble over the years, but by the NL. The showdown came when he alienated Cardinals owner Gussie Busch in 1981 by refusing to intercede with the networks to get Budweiser beer, an Anheuser-Busch product, commercial time

on broadcasts of sporting events. In the final vote for another term in November 1982, Kuhn carried the AL, 11 teams to three, but failed to secure the necessary two-thirds vote of the NL, gathering only seven yes votes from the 12 clubs. After the vote, the aged Busch banged the table with his cane, announcing gleefully, "He should clean out his desk tomorrow." Kuhn, however, served out the rest of his term, until Peter Ueberroth was sworn in on October 1, 1984.

In the end, Kuhn offended as much by his stiff pomposity and last-minute wheedling as by anything he did. His lasting image is of a man in denial that anything had changed in baseball, or the world, even when he himself had been responsible for the changes. The most memorable illustration of his tendency was his sitting coatless and hatless, apparently oblivious to the freezing weather at Baltimore's Municipal Stadium, during the initial contest of the 1971 World Series—the first played under a new contract, negotiated by Kuhn, that allowed Series night games for the first time.

JOHN KULL

"The man with the million-dollar arm," according to Connie Mack, Kull nonetheless pitched only three innings for the Athletics, in 1909. But even that brief career was long enough to set an unmatched standard for perfection: As a pitcher (a win and no losses), a batter (a single in his lone at bat), and a fielder (an assist in his only chance), the righthander left baseball with three 1.000 marks.

EMIL KUSH

The Presence of Kush on the same Cubs staff as Bob Rush in the late 1940s prompted Wrigley Field fans to come up with a variation on the "Spahn, Sain and pray for rain" formula that helped the Boston Braves to a pennant in 1948. The less successful Chicago version was "Kush, Rush, and two days of slush." The righthander never won more than nine games in any of his six major league seasons.

BOB KUZAVA

Although Yankees second baseman Billy Martin drew all the headlines for his dash to snare Jackie Robinson's seventh game, seventh-inning pop-up in the 1952 World Series, it was southpaw Kuzava who retired the final eight Brooklyn batters in the seventh game to preserve a 4–2 New York victory. His appearance in the game, coming in with the bases loaded and one out in the seventh inning, was more than a little surprising, since Ebbets Field and the Dodgers predominantly righthanded lineup were supposedly lethal for lefties. Overall, Kuzava, who had also saved the final game of the 1951 Series, against the Giants, compiled a 49–44 record in 10 big league seasons with eight clubs.

L

CHET LAABS

Laabs's two home runs in the final contest of the 1944 season sealed the only pennant captured by the St. Louis Browns. Although the righthanded first baseman had enjoyed power moments earlier in his 11-year career (1937–47), the blasts off New York's Mel Queen were only his fourth and fifth of the year and brought his season RBI total up to a dismal 23.

CLEM LABINE

In addition to being the top reliever for The Boys of Summer Dodgers in the 1950s, Labine pitched two of the most important shutouts of the era. In 1951 he was a 10–0 winner over the Giants in the only playoff game won by Brooklyn before Bobby Thomson's Shot Heard 'Round the World. In the 1956 World Series he took the mound the day after Don Larsen's perfect game and blanked the Yankees, 1–0, over 10 innings. The righthander also had the odd statistic in 1955 of getting three hits in 31 plate appearances, with all three hits home runs.

BOB LACEY

A journeyman reliever in the 1970s and 1980s, Lacey might have been baseball's biggest sport. After surrendering a home run to Kansas City's Amos Otis on September 14, 1978, the Oakland righthander joined several Royals at home plate to greet the outfielder after his tour of the bases. "Nobody ever hit one of my changeups like that," he said, shaking hands with Otis "That's the way it's supposed to be."

JEAN LAFITTE

Lafitte, a descendant of New Orleans pirate Jean Lafitte, is the only pitcher to throw a no-hitter but never a shutout. As a member of the Federal League Brooklyn Tip-Tops on September 19, 1914, he kept Kansas City hitless but not runless in a 6–2 victory. In 37 wins over five seasons Lafitte never managed to go the distance without surrendering a run.

FIORELLO LaGUARDIA

In 1925 Congressman and future New York City mayor LaGuardia introduced federal legislation calling for a 90 percent tax on player sales unless the player received half of the purchase price. Wondering whether he was "up against the same kind of proposition as I am when I am fighting the steel trust, the railroad, or other interests," The Little Flower watched his bill die without so much as a floor debate.

NAP LAJOIE (Hall of Fame, 1937)

The American League's biggest star before Ty Cobb, Lajoie was the rare big leaguer to have even a team named after him. A lifetime .338 hitter in 21 big league seasons (1896–1916), the second baseman was a stinging line-drive hitter with a reputation for gracefulness afield. While compiling 3,242 hits, the righthanded infielder led his league in batting and RBIs three times, hits and slugging four times, doubles five times; and home runs and runs scored once each.

Lajoie began his career with the NL Phillies. After five successful seasons, he jumped to the new American League Philadelphia franchise, established an AL record with his .422 average (a record 75 points over runnerup Mike Donlin), and complete the 20th century's first Triple Crown by also topping AL batsmen in homers (14) and RBIs (125). When the upstart Athletics almost doubled the attendance of his Phillies, owner John Rogers got the Pennsylvania State Supreme Court to grant an injunction barring Lajoie from playing in the state for any team but the NLers. After only a single game in 1902 with the Athletics, Lajoie was shipped off to Cleveland in a ploy by AL president Ban Johnson to keep the drawing card in his own circuit.

The second baseman became such an instant favorite in his new city that a poll conducted by the Cleveland *Press* in 1903 made the Naps an easy winner in the search for a new club nickname; he was installed as manager two years later. Lajoie's biggest moment as a dugout boss came in 1908, when he led his namesakes to a second-place finish, a half-game behind the Tigers, in the closest pennant race in AL history. On the other hand, he became convinced that the pressures of managing were responsible for dropping his average below .300 for the first times in his career in 1907 and 1908, so he gave up the piloting task after the 1909 season. He responded in 1910 with a .384 average to challenge Cobb for the batting crown, and therein lay a 71-year tale.

Lajoie had a big assist in his battle with Cobb from Browns third baseman Red Corriden, who played deep enough to allow him to collect six bunt singles in a season-ending doubleheader. St. Louis was so transparent in its partisanship that manager Jack O'Connor was banned from baseball, but not even that was enough to give Lajoie the batting title. For its part, the Chalmers automobile company awarded its annual prize to both hitters. And there matters rested until 1981, when *Sporting News* researcher Paul MacFarlane discovered that one of Cobb's games had been counted twice and that the one-point margin in his favor should have been a deficit. Commissioner Bowie Kuhn refused to heed the call for awarding the title to Lajoie retroactively, however, for fear of opening a Pandora's box of revised statistics.

Athletics owner-manager Connie Mack brought Lajoie back in 1915 as part of a public relations push to deny he was breaking up his four-time pennant winners. But the 39-year-old had lost his defensive magic, tying the league record of five errors in a game, and batted only .280. After slipping to .246 the following year, he called it quits.

Lajoie and Cleveland teammate Harry Bay were featured in the first motion picture of a baseball game—a 1903 postseason exhibition between the Indians and Reds.

GROVER LAND

As a catcher for the Brooklyn Tip-Tops of the Federal League in 1915, Land turned baseball's only pool break into a home run. Because he was working the game alone, umpire Bill Brennan did his officiating from behind the pitcher, with a stack of baseballs on the mound behind him. Land succeeded in hitting a line drive into the pile, scattering balls all over the field. Because he had lost sight of the ball actually in play, the confused Brennan ruled an automatic home run, and then spent the next half-hour trying to convince the opposition Baltimore Terrapins of his wisdom.

KENESAW MOUNTAIN LANDIS (Hall of Fame, 1944)

Usually portrayed as baseball's Abraham Lincoln, Landis was actually closer to Lyndon Johnson in trying to make an instant positive impression on his electors, accomplishing that and then going on to rule with equal doses of whim and obstinacy. His major achievement as the first commissioner was to lift the odor of fixes from the sport in the wake of the 1919 World Series scandal. His most enduring public relations triumph was to project himself as a defender of helpless players and a foe of greedy owners. His most notable failure was to act as the very opposite of a great emancipator by thwarting attempts to integrate the big leagues during his 25-year (1920–44) reign.

Landis originally came to the attention of big league owners in 1915, when, as a federal judge in Chicago, he sat on a Federal League suit against the National and American leagues long enough to head off a legal test of the game's monopoly status. In 1920, following several scandals and disputes that bankrupted the credibility of baseball's ruling three-man National Commission, Cubs owner William Wrigley proposed Landis as commissioner. Although there was some skepticism about Wrigley's choice of a known Cubs fan for the new post, it disappeared rather quickly as the proportions of the Black Sox bribes became even more evident and disclosures of other fixes triggered calls for outside policing of the major leagues. Landis accepted the position only after receiving an ironclad assurance that the owners would never publicly criticize his decisions or penalties.

The judge's first rulings were geared to demonstrating that he was impartiality incarnate and that he was resolved to end gambling's encroachment on the game. Intervening in a dispute between the St. Louis teams over rights to first baseman Phil Todt, he came down in favor of the Browns despite the fact that owner Phil Ball had stood alone in refusing to sign the papers sanctioning his appointment as commissioner. His objectivity established, Landis's actions against players implicated in the Black Sox scandal were equally definitive—even at the cost of ignoring due process. As he saw it, the important thing was not the August 2, 1921 jury verdict that acquitted Chicago players of collusion in throwing games to Cincinnati in the 1919 World Series but the statements of various witnesses that there had indeed been a conspiracy. Thus, one day after the jury verdict, Landis banned the Chicago Eight with his own pronouncement that "No player who throws a ballgame, no player that undertakes to throw a ballgame, no player that sits in conference with a bunch of crooked players and gamblers where the ways and means of throwing a ballgame are discussed and does not promptly tell his club about it, will ever play baseball." He later added Browns infielder Joe Gedeon for "guilty knowledge" of the affair.

Landis maintained his hard-line approach in the face of several appeals for reinstatement from the affected players. Between 1921 and 1924 he also banned other big leaguers—some on the basis of little more than his own arrogance. Giants outfielder Benny Kauff, for example, was blacklisted after being indicted for auto theft; when he too was sent home by a jury, the judge refused to lift his order, claiming the verdict was just wrong. Pitcher Ray Fisher was ostracized for taking a job at the University of Michigan instead of accepting a contract from the Reds. White Sox hurler Dickie Kerr was declared *persona non grata* because he pitched against a couple of the exiled Black Sox in an exhibition game.

Landis loyalists have contended that the lack of bans after 1924 demonstrated his success in cleaning up the sport. But the fact is that, even before he took office, embarrassed owners had already begun quietly blacklisting suspect players and that he remained sensitive enough to an ongoing problem to

hire detectives to shadow players perhaps not all that responsive to his righteousness. The concentration of life sentences within his first four years reflected at least as much of a desire to project his office instantly as a higher forum than the league presidencies and an attempt to assure the public that he was not merely a new front for old habits. For sure, he showed little interest in expulsions decided at a league level—never explicitly endorsing them and in one case (that of pitcher Rube Benton) annulling it as soon as he received a direct appeal. The notion of a justice tempered by public relations also seemed borne out by scandals later in the 1920s that appeared to incriminate some players as badly as those in the 1919 affair but that produced no new outlaws (although they were serious enough to prompt a baseball penal code relating to gambling). Also striking, with the exception of Joe Jackson, none of the players banished by Landis was of Hall of Fame caliber, while, on the other hand, in 1924 and 1926, he was quick to exonerate such future Cooperstown residents as Ross Youngs, Frankie Frisch, George Kelly, Ty Cobb, and Tris Speaker of attempted bribery and game-fixing charges. Neither did the self-declared nemesis of professional gambling have much to say about the well-publicized racetrack habits of Rogers Hornsby and John McGraw, even though Hornsby's addiction weighed on several teams for which he played.

Landis's high-handedness inevitably produced clashes. He spent a considerable part of the 1920s doing battle with AL president Ban Johnson, who never got over the discarding of his fiefdom on the three-man National Commission and who took every opportunity to undermine the authority of the commissioner's office. Johnson was finally forced to withdraw from the scene after he couldn't find a majority of owners to back him in 1926 charges that Landis had covered up for Cobb and Speaker in a game-fixing investigation. Then, as on several occasions before and afterward, Landis retaliated against the attacks with a one-two punch of high dudgeon that anyone would dare question his integrity and sulky threats to resign if the owners didn't give him full and immediate support. Afraid of the reaction in the press if the judge walked off, the owners were always quick to cave in. It was an experience their successors would keep in mind when choosing future commissioners

Landis's reputation as a paternalistic defender of

players against greedy owners stemmed largely from his opposition to the minor league farm team concept pioneered by Branch Rickey of the Cardinals in the 1920s; the commissioner, who prided himself on being a David up against various Goliaths bent on ruining the healthy ambitions of modestly fixed Americans, branded the farm chains "a rape of small towns." In fact, his stance was not as radical as it might have been in subsequent eras for the simple reason that owners without the money and the imagination of the St. Louis organization didn't like the system either and were hardly disposed toward ganging up on him over the issue. He didn't have too much more to fear from the owners as a group when he went to bat for players who had been buried in the minors to the point of compromising their careers: If he angered the contract-holding team by ordering the player released, he equally pleased the clubs waiting to bid for the player's services. Even when he winked at regulations, as he did in allowing the Indians to hold on to Bob Feller in 1936 in the face of a number of glaring improprieties, he created front office allies as well as enemies—in that specific case, Cleveland and the other AL teams that saw the already talent-laden Yankees and Tigers ready to pounce on the righthander if he were declared a free agent. The end result was that only one owner, Ball of the Browns, ever went back on the assurances given to Landis that his decisions would never be appealed in a courtroom, and that challenge fell before a judge who sanctioned the powers ceded to the commissioner.

If Landis had a special irritant, it was Rickey—not only for the farm system question but for a sanctimoniousness that matched his own. The main character difference between the two was that Rickey was a genuine teetotaler who gave even his ruthless business smarts a rest on the Sabbath, while Landis never had to be asked twice after working hours to have a drink or recite the latest four-letter words that he had heard. Their biggest public explosion came in 1938, when Landis informed the Cardinals that he was granting free agent status to 74 of the organization's farm hands because Rickey had entered into "secret understandings" with minor league operators aimed at denying the players a competitive opportunity. Rickey immediately insisted that St. Louis owner Sam Breadon file a suit so that the issue might be aired in a courtroom. The threat was effective to the degree that Landis never got around to conveying

formal charges to the Cardinals; on the other hand, Breadon was so embarrassed by the accusation, and by his own awareness that something untoward had been going on, that he refused to even back Rickey in insisting on the franchise's rights to the 74 minor leaguers (among whom was future batting champion Pete Reiser). In 1940 Landis issued a similar dictum against the Tigers, granting free agency to 91 Detroit farm hands and ordering the franchise to come up with $47,000 in damages for another 15 players who had been buried in the minors. The Tigers emulated the Cardinals in not challenging the order.

As zealous as Landis seemed to be about the rights of minor leaguers, he was as ardent about keeping the major leagues a strictly white domain. One of his first diktats after assuming office was to eliminate postseason exhibition games between big league clubs and Negro leagues teams, permitting major leaguers to appear only in the guise of all-star squads. He always denied that his order sought to protect pennant-winning clubs from potential embarrassment at the hands of the black teams and went on insisting to his dying day that he knew of no formal regulation prohibiting blacks from signing with the big league clubs. What he omitted saying was that he lashed into both the Pirates and the Senators in the early 1940s for even exploring the possibility of inking a couple of black players and blocked an ownership bid by Bill Veeck for the Phillies after being informed that Veeck planned to break the color barrier. Only with Landis's death in 1944 did Rickey begin laying serious plans for desegregating the Dodgers.

A month after his death, Landis was elected to the Hall of Fame.

HOBIE LANDRITH

Landrith made two key contributions to the legend of the 1962 Mets. The first came when he was the expansion franchise's very first pick, and manager Casey Stengel explained the selection of the left-hand-batting receiver by saying, "If you don't have a catcher, you get a lot of passed balls." The second came midway through New York's inaugural season, when Landrith was traded to Baltimore for the most publicized Mets clown of all: Marv Throneberry.

TITO LANDRUM

Landrum hit baseball's most famous pawnshop home run when his 10th-inning blast in the fourth game of the 1983 American League Championship Series broke up a scoreless duel and enabled Baltimore to edge Chicago for the pennant. The outfielder had been dealt to the Orioles during the season by the Cardinals, and was reclaimed by St. Louis during spring training in 1984.

FRANK LANE

Lane earned his sobriquet of The Trader by completing 165 deals involving more than 400 major leaguers during a 12-year run as general manager of the White Sox, Cardinals, Indians, and Athletics. Although many of the transactions stemmed from little more than a desire to net a headline, the majority of them ending up improving Lane's club of the moment. His most conspicuous successes were with Chicago (1948–55), when he obtained southpaw Billy Pierce from the Tigers in 1948 in exchange for backup catcher Aaron Robinson and when he acquired second baseman Nellie Fox from the Athletics in 1949 for backstop Joe Tipton. While with the White Sox he also claimed to be one of the few executives to outwit Branch Rickey. As he usually told the story, he got Rickey to speculate in 1949 on what the Dodgers executive *might* ask for minor league shortstop Chico Carrasquel if he ever decided to trade him, waited a few days, then called back to say he accepted the asking price. Rickey's disclaimers that he had never actually offered Carrasquel—in the Lane version—got lost in a lot of doubletalk about honoring one's word, with the result that the shortstop went to Chicago for two minor leaguers. (Rickey loyalists claimed their hero knew what he was doing all along.)

As one of the architects of the Go-Go Sox of the 1950s, Lane alternately drew praise and jealousy from franchise scion Chuck Comiskey, leading to periodic run-ins with the family. One of his more important mistakes, at least in the eyes of the Comiskeys, was coming out publicly in support of a Bill Veeck plan that would allow a visiting club to share in the revenues from local television coverage of games. The breaking point in his relations with the owners took place near the end of the 1955 season, when Lane, infuriated by an umpiring decision that went against Chicago, confronted American League president Will Harridge at Comiskey Park and shouted obscenities about the caliber of the league's arbiters. When Harridge fined him $500 and Comiskey de-

nounced him for embarrassing the organization. Lane took the hint and resigned.

Moving to the Cardinals for the 1956 season, Lane lived up to his reputation by completing 26 transactions in less than two years. Although the swaps helped boost St. Louis to second place after three straight seasons of playing under .500, he resigned again before the continued dissatisfaction of owner Gussie Busch, saying he couldn't work for "an irrational organization." Back in the AL with the Indians, he completed some 60 swaps at a major league level between 1958 and 1960. If for different reasons, three of them stood out. In the first, in June 1958, he shipped young slugger Roger Maris, pitcher Dick Tomanek, and first baseman Preston Ward to Kansas City in exchange for shortstop Woodie Held and first baseman Vic Power. The deal was denounced throughout the AL because it left Maris with a club—the Athletics—that operated as a major league affiliate of the Yankees. Lane, who had rejected a couple of direct offers from the Yankees for the outfielder and whose dislike for New York was such that a 1950 purchase of backup catcher Gus Niarhos represented his only career deal with the Bronx, took the stance that he was not responsible for Kansas City's future decisions (which did indeed include sending Maris on to the Yankees). The fallout from trading fan favorite Rocky Colavito to the Tigers for Harvey Kuenn in 1960 was far worse. Lane's public justification for the transaction was that the Indians needed Kuenn's consistency at the plate more than Colavito's long ball, but that rationale faded before statistics showing that Colavito was superior to Kuenn in just about every offensive category (including on-base average) except batting average. The actual trigger for the swap was Lane's fears that Colavito's power numbers and appeal to the fans would make him intractable in salary negotiations. Then, in August 1960, he pulled off his most antic swap—sending manager Joe Gordon to Detroit for Tigers pilot Jimmy Dykes. He had little compunction about admitting that the trade had been worked out with Detroit's Bill DeWitt mainly for reviving interest in two decidedly also-ran teams.

Lane's last—and least successful—prominent position was as general manager of Charlie Finley's A's in 1961. He lasted only several months on a two-year contract, and ended up having to sue Finley to get the money due him.

BILL LANGE

A dazzling base runner with a .330 lifetime batting average, Lange's penchant for the high life of the Gay Nineties made him unpopular with Cubs manager Cap Anson but the darling of Chicago fans. His speed and defense in center field sparked fables of sensational catches that were still making the rounds decades after his retirement.

Typical of Lange's off-field behavior was his holdout in 1897 so he could attend fellow San Franciscan Jim Corbett's defense of his heavyweight boxing title against Bob Fitzsimmons in Carson City, Nevada. As chagrined as he was pleased when his contract demands were met almost immediately, he altered his tactics by leaking the story that he had sprained an ankle and would report to spring training as soon as he could—which turned out to be right after Corbett had been knocked out in the 14th round on March 17. In the ensuing season he led the NL in steals (73), while batting .340.

Considered by many as gifted a player as Ty Cobb, Lange quit baseball after the 1899 season at the age of 29 to marry into a family that wanted nothing to do with baseball players. The union ended in divorce, and after spending years in the insurance business, Lange did some scouting for Cincinnati and became an important baseball figure in the Bay Area.

MAX LANIER

Lanier's promising career stumbled over his decision to jump to Mexico in 1946. Because of his pivotal role in three St. Louis pennants between 1942 and 1944, when he posted 45 victories, the southpaw was considered the biggest coup in the major league raids by the Pasquel brothers. By his own admission, however, the pitcher went with the Pasquels because of fears that arm twinges he had kept secret from the Cardinals might end his big league career in any case. When Commissioner Happy Chandler imposed a five-year ban on the jumpers, Lanier tried to make ends meet upon his return from Mexico by organizing a barnstorming team of fellow defectors. He discovered the reach of Chandler's ban when even semipro and college teams declined to play his club. He eventually returned to the Cardinals for another three seasons but was no longer in peak form.

ERNEST LANIGAN

A nephew of the Spink brothers who founded *The Sporting News,* Lanigan was the first baseball encyclopedist. At various times a sportswriter, a minor league executive, and both historian and director of the Hall of Fame, he was the major proponent of including runs batted in as an offensive category. His most important contribution to the history of the game was the publication of *The Baseball Cyclopedia* in 1922. Lanigan was once quoted as confessing: "I really don't care much about baseball or looking at ball games. All my interest in baseball is in its statistics."

JOSEPH LANNIN

As owner of the Red Sox in 1914, Lannin took the lead in efforts to stymie the insurgent Federal League by bankrolling minor league clubs that shared markets with the Feds. The tactic paid off in another way when the real estate tycoon's good relations with Jack Dunn of Baltimore's International League Orioles enabled Boston to purchase Babe Ruth and Ernie Shore. Throughout his three-year tenure with the Red Sox, Lannin was accused of being too close to AL president Ban Johnson. It was Johnson who eased his way into the Boston hierarchy, who arranged for him to deal holdout outfielder Tris Speaker to the Indians, and who introduced him to New York theatrical producers Harry Frazee and Hugh Ward when Lannin announced that he wanted to sell the franchise.

GENE LARKIN

Dogged throughout his somewhat humdrum career by his reputation as the first Columbia University student to reach the majors since Lou Gehrig, Larkin finally had a moment under the moon in the seventh game of the 1991 World Series when his bases-loaded pinch-single in the bottom of the 10th inning gave Minnesota the championship over Atlanta. The hit ended a scoreless duel between the Twins Jack Morris and John Smoltz (for nine innings) and Mike Stanton of the Braves.

DON LARSEN

Larsen's perfect game against the Dodgers in the World Series on October 8, 1956 always bemused the righthander, who otherwise had a less than scintillating career (81–91) and who was never shy about his rambunctious off-field activities. On the same day that the Yankees righthander hurled his no-hitter, for instance, his estranged wife served him with a suit demanding back payment of court-ordered support. His last service to New York came in a December 1959 trade that saw him go to Kansas City in exchange for Roger Maris.

Larsen's career got a second wind when Casey Stengel taught him the no-windup delivery that had so baffled the New York manager when he was a young outfielder; Stengel had first encountered it at the hands of Patsy Flaherty, a mediocre southpaw on the Boston Braves. Bob Turley, who came to the Yankees from the Orioles along with Larsen in baseball's biggest (18-player) trade in 1954, was also helped by adopting the Flaherty style. Six years to the day after his perfect game, Larsen defeated the Yankees in relief for the Giants in the fourth game of the 1962 World Series.

LYN LARY

Lary is usually charged with sloppy baserunning for costing Lou Gehrig the exclusive 1931 home-run title. But while he did allow Gehrig to go by him on the bases after the first baseman had reached the Griffith Stadium bleachers in an April 26 game against Washington, the fault lay more with manager Joe McCarthy. The pilot's ambiguous signal to slow down convinced Lary that the ball, which had rebounded out of the stands and into the Washington center fielder's hands, had been caught. McCarthy, in a tacit admission of his mistake, removed himself from the coach's box for the rest of the season. The basepath mixup also cost New York the game.

TOMMY LASORDA (Hall of Fame, 1997)

As Dodgers manager from 1977 to 1996, Lasorda fused the organization's assumptions of total loyalty and Hollywood's assumptions of relentless self-promotion. Just as Casey Stengel was the darling of the print media, so Lasorda was television's paramour, showing up not just on sports shows but also on talk programs and variety hours to spout a well-rehearsed line of anecdotes, cracks, and homilies about the Dodger Way and the American Way. As for his managing abilities, they were considerable in many areas but also circumscribed by his excessive use of starting pitchers and by mood swings that ended up alienating many players he had been fond of embracing in front of cameras. For every player who

credited him with helping to shape or salvage a career, there was another who voiced relief at being able to get out from under his bluster. The Los Angeles franchise itself couldn't wait to send him to the sidelines after a disastrous stint as general manager at the end of the 1990s.

As a minor leaguer in the Dodgers system in the 1950s, Lasorda set a number of pitching records, including most victories (112) by an International League hurler; as a major leaguer, he lost his roster spot in Brooklyn to Sandy Koufax, had his trade to the St. Louis Browns canceled when American League owners forced out Bill Veeck, and lost his only four major league decisions, as a member of Kansas City in 1956. After coaching and managing in the Dodgers system for years, he was named to replace Walter Alston in 1976. Lasorda's record from 1977 to 1993 showed eight division titles, four pennants, and a pair of world championships. Until 1983, not even his success or 'round-the-clock promotion of the franchise moved the organization from its traditional stance of offering pilots only one-year contracts; but when the Yankees refused to deny reports that they were interested in signing Lasorda as a combination manager-general manager, Peter O'Malley finally coughed up a three-year pact.

In terms of personnel, Lasorda's biggest feat was nurturing lefthander Fernando Valenzuela in the early 1980s into the biggest gate attraction in the league. On the other hand, he presided over a clubhouse that almost annually exploded into rifts and fistfights among star players; among those who took him on either directly or through the media were Steve Garvey, Don Sutton, and Rick Sutcliffe. Lasorda also showed marked crudity in his public disparagement of slugger Pedro Guerrero, who was later revealed to be borderline retarded, and in responding to the 1994 release of Darryl Strawberry, chiding the drug-afflicted outfielder for not being as loyal as a dog who goes after a ball.

Lasorda was forced to give up managing after a 1996 heart attack. His two-year tenure as Los Angeles general manager was mainly intended to give the franchise a credible bridge after the O'Malleys sold out to Rupert Murdoch's News Corp., but the credibility barely survived some disastrous trades. He recovered from that debacle to find an even larger forum for his shtick as the coach of the winning U.S. Olympic baseball team in 2000.

ARLIE LATHAM

At one point or another in his 76 years in baseball the puckish Latham served in almost every capacity in the game, but he is best remembered for a pair of firsts—as clown and as coach. As the third baseman for the American Association St. Louis Browns from 1883 to 1889, he fashioned the first clown act on the diamond. But unlike his successors in the field, he had a strategic purpose in the acts he generally performed in the third-base coaching box: arousing fans to join him in hazing, camouflaging sign stealing, and irritating opponents. An accomplished acrobat, Latham often turned cartwheels over the last 20 feet on the way to first base after a hit, and once, while playing for Cincinnati, somersaulted over the head of dour Chicago manager Cap Anson. In 1889 he put these talents to professional use as a song-and-dance man in a Broadway vehicle called *Fashions*.

Latham's playing days effectively ended in 1895, but that didn't prevent Browns owner Chris Von der Ahe, a regular target of his lampoons, from bringing him back the following year to play eight games and manage three of them (all losses) as a publicity stunt. The infielder's skills had so eroded by then that "to do a Latham" had become an expression for an ineffective wave at a groundball.

In 1909 John McGraw made Latham baseball's first full-time coach. The hiring by the Giants manager was at least partly a reward for his perpetuation of the old Orioles myth. (Latham had once said of his new employer: "He eats gunpowder for breakfast and washes it down with warm blood.") But the move paid dividends when Latham tutored the club in stealing a record 347 bases on the way to the 1911 pennant. (He himself had been activated for a few games in 1909 and, at the age of 49, established the geriatric record for steals.)

Between 1912 and 1937 Latham lived in London where he organized baseball leagues and sought to teach both King George V and the Prince of Wales subtleties of the game. Back in the United States, he worked at both the Polo Grounds and Yankee Stadium until his death, at age 92, in 1952.

CHARLIE LAU

Lau provoked more passionate defenses and heated criticism than any other hitting coach. With his stress on balance and weight shifts and swinging through the ball, he was able to claim particular suc-

cess with George Brett, Hal McRae, and other members of the Kansas City Royals in the 1970s. Despite that baseball traditionalists have accused him and his chief disciple, Walt Hriniak, of ruining potential power hitters. They have also mocked the onetime catcher's own offensive abilities (a .255 lifetime average with a mere 16 home runs in 11 seasons) as a qualification for teaching others, asserting that his most successful students accomplished what they did in spite of him rather than because of him.

Facts suggest otherwise. In his only year as Baltimore's batting instructor, in 1969, Lau's team averaged .265 with 175 home runs; the previous year the club had hit .225 with 133 home runs. His 1970 charges in Oakland batted .249 with 171 homers; the year before the club had also hit .249, but with 23 fewer long balls. When he went to Kansas City in 1971, Lau helped lift the team average by six points in his first season. When he took over as the batting coach for the Yankees in 1979, homers rose by 25 over the previous year. Moving to the White Sox in 1982, he had a squad that clouted 60 more home runs than it had in 1981 (if partly because of the strike-shortened campaign). Overall, and notwithstanding his image as a tutor bent on having everyone hit singles to the opposite field, Lau had 27 of his charges blast at least 20 home runs in a season.

Lau's impact as a mentor was particularly evident in Kansas City, where players blasted both Jack McKeon and Whitey Herzog when the managers released him. In those instances, as with his other pilots elsewhere, he got caught up in clubhouse jealousies because of player insistence on seeking his advice about more than just how to swing a bat.

COOKIE LAVAGETTO

Lavagetto delivered the most dramatic pinch-hit in World Series history in 1947, when he reached the Yankees Bill Bevens for a two-out, two-run double in the bottom of the ninth inning of the fourth game. The blow by the Dodgers veteran prevented Bevens from completing the first World Series no-hitter and also gave Brooklyn a last-gasp 2–1 victory. It was third baseman Lavagetto's last hit in a 10-year big league career.

ANDY LAWSON

With an undercapitalized bank account and an inflated sense of his own importance, Lawson sought to challenge the monopoly of the National and American leagues with the formation of the first Continental League in December 1920. Announcing that play would begin on May 1 of the following year, the promoter moved around the country for several months issuing press statements at every stop about his successes, real and imaginary. The principles of his new circuit were ambitious. Franchises would represent states, not cities; ballparks would be built where old Federal League fields could not be acquired (he even offered to buy Fenway Park from perennially strapped Red Sox owner Harry Frazee); there would be no reserve clause; and as many players as possible would be assigned to clubs from home states. Players were to come from a variety of sources, including the ranks of those recently outlawed after the 1919 World Series. Even more revolutionary, Lawson planned to tap the Negro leagues, where, he estimated, there were at least a hundred players the equal of major leaguers. Lawson was last heard from saying he would have to push back the starting date for his league from May 1 to May 20.

JOHNNY LAZOR

Under rules then in force, Boston outfielder Lazor should have been awarded the 1945 American League batting title for his .310 average in 101 games. But then AL president Will Harridge stepped in to rule that since Lazor had played only 81 games of a necessary minimum of 100 in the field and the test as a pinch-hitter or pinch-runner, the title should go to New York's George Stirnweiss for his .309.

TONY LAZZERI (Hall of Fame, 1991)

Lazzeri is the only Hall of Famer who is most famous for striking out. The second baseman for the Murderers Row Yankees, he hit .292 in a 14-year (1926–39) career, almost all of it with New York. He reached the .300 mark five times, with a high of .354 in 1929; drove in 100 runs seven times; and reached double figures in homers 10 times. Lazzeri's most glaring moment centerstage came in the seventh inning of the seventh game of the 1926 World Series when, with the bases loaded and two out, the hungover Grover Cleveland Alexander struck him out in relief to preserve a 3–2 win for the Cardinals.

BILL LEE

Lee's 14-year (1969–82) career was cut short by a field fight, media humorlessness, and his own taste for staging one-man solidarity strikes for teammates. He ultimately became the victim of an informal major league blacklist.

Lee's best years were with the Red Sox between 1973 and 1975, when he won 17 games three times in a row. At the same time, the southpaw was attracting off-the-field attention as a rare counterculture symbol in the game for his dedication to yoga and for more than one hint that he had inhaled marijuana. It was in this context that teammate John Kennedy first dubbed him Spaceman—a sobriquet writers thereafter used as shorthand for explaining their wariness of the pitcher's often enigmatic remarks. For his part, Lee wasn't above using the media for what he thought of as serious baseball purposes. On one occasion he announced that he had thrown three spitballs to Detroit's Tony Taylor in order to goad American League president Joe Cronin into fining him as he had previously penalized Texas pitcher Jim Merritt for the offense; according to Lee, the fine levied on the sore-armed Merritt had to be challenged all the way up the Supreme Court. Another time he proclaimed his support of school busing in Boston for the avowed purpose of drawing the ire of redneck fans and columnists who might have otherwise continued to dun the Red Sox with reminders of the Babe Ruth Curse during a stretch race against the Yankees.

Lee's demeanor kept him at odds with such old school managers as Eddie Kasko, Darrell Johnson, and Don Zimmer, and he succeeded on the mound as often as he did only after they had tried to bury him as a mop-up reliever. He became a particular nemesis of Zimmer after he joined with pitchers Ferguson Jenkins, Rick Wise, and Jim Willoughby and outfielder Bernie Carbo in a group calling itself the Loyal Order of the Buffalo Heads; the group's main activity was mocking Zimmer's ineptitude with Boston's pitching staff. Lee earned himself an extra demerit with Zimmer for once describing the pilot as a "designated gerbil"—an association the veteran baseball man never shed. Lee's career started going downhill in May 1976, when Yankees third baseman Graig Nettles dumped him on his shoulder during a field fight. The resulting torn ligaments turned the southpaw into a junkballer—and gave Zimmer still further reason for trying to ignore him. Only when Fenway Park fans began applauding his every appearance on the bullpen mound did the pilot relent, bringing him back into meaningful situations.

Lee was peddled to the Expos in 1979, and only a few days after reporting got caught up in another series of sports headlines because of a crack that he was fond of sprinkling marijuana over his pancakes in the morning. On the hill he won 16 games for Montreal in his first year, but then succumbed to a series of injuries over the next couple of seasons. In 1982 he burned his bridges with the Expos by walking out briefly on the team because of the release of second baseman Rodney Scott. He had staged similar protests in Boston over the trading away of Carbo and pitcher Sonny Siebert.

In his autobiography *The Wrong Stuff,* Lee cited then-Padres manager Dick Williams and other baseball people as having told him he would never pitch in the big leagues again because of an unofficial blacklisting encouraged by the Expos. He also accused Montreal of doing the same thing to Scott by, among other ways, spreading a false rumor that the infielder was gay. In the book Lee admitted pitching one game for the Red Sox while under the influence of hashish.

MARK LEE

Lee didn't have much of a career with the Padres and Pirates in the 1970s and 1980s, but he had one of the more notable farewells to organized baseball. Toward the end of the 1982 season the righthander was told he was being released by the Portland Beavers of the Pacific Coast league but was also instructed to wait around should he be needed for that night's game. After indeed being called in from the bullpen in the ninth inning, he got the first batter on a pop, the second on strikes, then called manager Tom Trebelhorn out to the mound to announce that he was quitting then and there, with the strikeout as his swan song. On the way to the dugout he tossed his cap and jersey onto the field. "It was my way of saying," he explained later, "that organized baseball didn't quite control *all* of me."

RON LeFLORE

LeFlore is the only player to have led both leagues in stolen bases, accomplishing it with the 1978 Tigers and the 1980 Expos. The righthand-hitting outfielder reached the majors thanks to Billy Martin, who met him while LeFlore was serving time for armed robbery. Despite his great speed he lasted only nine years in the majors because of a combination of a ferocious strikeout rate, nagging injuries, and old-school managers who objected to his independent manner.

CHARLIE LEIBRANDT

Leibrandt's troubles in the 11th inning of the sixth game of a World Series devastated the Braves two years in a row. In 1991 the southpaw surrendered a home run to Minnesota's Kirby Puckett to keep the Twins alive and set up their world championship victory the following day. In 1992 he yielded a two-run double to Toronto's Dave Winfield that turned out to be the lock on a Blue Jays world championship.

BOB LEMON (Hall of Fame, 1976)

Lemon was Babe Ruth in reverse—a major league pitcher who reached the Hall of Fame after starting his American League career as a position player. A 26-year-old when he toed the mound for the first time in 1946, the righthander went on to post 20 wins seven times, closing out a 13-year career spent entirely with Cleveland with 207 wins. As a hitter, his 37 career home runs rank him second to Wes Ferrell's 38 for career long balls by a pitcher. On April 30, 1946 Lemon was the Indians center fielder in Bob Feller 1–0 no-hitter over the Yankees. Two years later he himself threw the first AL no-hitter at night, against the Tigers.

Following his retirement as a pitcher, Lemon managed the Royals, White Sox, and Yankees; with all three organizations, his fabled laid-back manner first earned him kudos for his patience and then cost him his job for lacking drive. In 1978, while piloting Chicago, Lemon was offered to the Yankees for Billy Martin by owner Bill Veeck in a straight-up trade of managers. Although rejected by New York, the deal triggered an outburst by Martin against George Steinbrenner that got him fired and opened up the Bronx job to the equally fired Lemon anyway. But after steering the Yankees to a flashy come-from-behind pennant and World Series win, Lemon was devastated by the death of his 26-year-old son in an auto accident, and acknowledged that he was relieved when he was replaced by the same Martin in one of Steinbrenner's musical chair rounds the next season. He came back for another stint of managing New York in 1981–82.

MARK LEMONGELLO

Lemongello was the most crazed loser baseball has ever seen. Among his other reactions to being driven from the mound were to bite his shoulder until it bled and to beat on his pitching hand. When he was removed from his last starting assignment for the Blue Jays in 1979, the righthander fired the ball at the head of manager Roy Hartsfield before marching into the clubhouse. Neither Lemongello nor his lifetime 22–38 record was ever seen in the majors again.

BUCK LEONARD (Hall of Fame, 1972)

Leonard was Josh Gibson's Lou Gehrig. A left-hand-hitting first baseman, he batted cleanup behind Gibson on the Homestead Grays, slugging line drives for both power and average while Gibson specialized in Ruthian blasts. The similarity to Gehrig didn't end there, either. Unlike most Negro league stars, Leonard spent virtually all of his career with one club, joining the Grays in 1934, staying through nine Negro National League pennants in a row (1937–45), and remaining until the demise of the franchise in 1950, two years after the collapse of the entire circuit. He was also a *bona fide* Iron Man, playing with all manner of injuries, including a broken hand in the black World Series of 1942 against the Kansas City Monarchs.

Like other Negro leaguers, Leonard played winter ball for leagues in Venezuela, Cuba, Puerto Rico, and Mexico. In 1952 he turned down a Bill Veeck offer to be a member of the St. Louis Browns, saying he was too old and "didn't want to embarrass anyone or hurt the chances of those who might follow." The following year, however, he got a taste of organized ball when he suited up for the Portsmouth club in the Class B Piedmont League, hitting .333 in 10 games. Two years later he had enough left to play 62 games for Durango in the Central Mexican League, batting .312 with 13 home runs; he was 48 years old at the time.

DUTCH LEONARD

Leonard was the key figure in baseball's most notorious coverup of a game-fixing scandal and what was definitely the Waterloo for American League president Ban Johnson. The scandal ended up overshadowing Leonard's career year of 1914, when, as a member of the Red Sox, he established the major league ERA mark of a mere 0.96 while compiling a 19–5 record.

In the autumn of 1926 the retired hurler wrote a letter to Johnson asserting that he, Ty Cobb, Tris Speaker, and Cleveland outfielder Joe Wood had conspired to fix the last game of the 1919 season as a means of assuring a third-place finish for Detroit behind the White Sox and the Indians. According to Leonard, Wood had also laid down bets for Cobb and Speaker on the September 25, 1919 contest. Johnson, never a fan of either future Hall of Famer, reportedly paid Leonard $20,000 for a couple of letters—one from Wood and the other from Cobb—that clearly implicated Cobb but nowhere mentioned Speaker. Within a month of one another Cobb and Speaker were forced out as manager of the Tigers and Indians, respectively, to the undisguised delight of Johnson. (Wood had been out of the game for several years and drew almost no fire in the controversy.) Just as the two outfielders started musing aloud about filing lawsuits against everyone involved, however, Commissioner Kenesaw Landis initiated his own investigation, beginning with a trip to California to interrogate Leonard. Despite the suggestiveness of the Wood letters, especially where Cobb was concerned, Landis decided the fix charges against *both* stars were unfounded and were due solely to Leonard's resentment that Cobb had released him in 1925 and that Speaker had declined to give him a tryout with Cleveland.

The commissioner's verdict was ridiculed by many, not least by Johnson. With his reputation at stake, Landis summoned a meeting of AL owners and asked them to choose between him and the league president. Even before the session was convened, however, the owners persuaded Johnson to take a sabbatical, put Detroit owner Frank Navin in charge of the league's day-to-day business, and publicly reiterated their confidence in the integrity of Landis. Johnson never regained his stature in league circles. Leonard always insisted that the American League owners had supported Landis because they were afraid of losing such stars as Cobb and Speaker to the National League. In fact, after being dissuaded by Landis from pursuing lawsuits against Leonard and Johnson, Cobb signed with the Athletics and Speaker with the Senators.

DUTCH LEONARD

In contrast to an earlier namesake involved in a Detroit-Cleveland game-fixing scandal, the knuckleballer Leonard of the 1944 Senators shrugged off a $10,000 bribe attempt to throw the final game of the season, defeating the Tigers and dooming them to finish a game behind the pennant-winning Browns. In 1945 Leonard, Roger Wolff, Mickey Haefner, and Johnny Niggeling comprised the only starting rotation in major league history made up exclusively of knuckleballers.

JEFFREY LEONARD

Few players have had as much of a talent for irritating the opposition as Leonard, who seemed to thrive on accusations of showboating. During the 1987 National League Championship Series against the Cardinals, the San Francisco outfielder raised his act to a *casus belli* when he gave the "dead arm" trot to each of his four home runs, holding his left arm stiffly at his side as he rounded the bases; his accompanying number of having his batting gloves flop from his back pockets so annoyed umpires that a rule was thereafter enforced against having the gloves dangle. Amid all the consternation Leonard became the first player in an LCS to get an MVP nod despite being on a losing team. The righthand-hitting slugger also had his own solution for dealing with catchers who sought to distract him in the batter's box: He made sure that receivers always saw the spot on his bat where he had carved the words "Fuck you."

On August 21, 1979 Leonard was the protagonist of baseball's most protracted final out. Facing New York's Pete Falcone as a member of the Astros, he hit what appeared to be a game-ending fly ball. But then the umpires ruled that New York shortstop Frank Taveras had called time before the pitch, so Leonard used a second chance to hit a single. But then that at bat was also nullified when the umpires realized that Mets first baseman Ed Kranepool, thinking the original fly ball had ended the game, had not taken his position in time for the hit. As Leonard was called back to the plate for a third try, the Astros announced they were playing the game under protest; immediately afterward, the outfielder again skied out. But after the game National League president Chub Feeney upheld the Houston protest, ordering Leonard back to first base with his single and a resumption from that point before a regularly scheduled contest the next day. Kevin Kobel finally ended matters by getting José Cruz on a grounder. The main victim of the fiasco was Falcone, who still had a 5–0 win but who lost his complete-game shutout.

BUDDY LeROUX

A real-estate wheeler-dealer and former Red Sox trainer, LeRoux entered into a partnership in 1977 with Boston scouting director Haywood Sullivan to purchase the franchise from the estate of Tom Yawkey. Nothing that followed over seven years was reminiscent of Yawkey's smooth 40-year control.

To begin with, LeRoux and Sullivan were so undercapitalized that they needed Yawkey's widow, Jean, not only to reject a higher offer from A-T-O, the parent of the Rawley Sporting Goods company, but also to add some of her own money to make their bid credible. A-T-O promptly sued Yawkey on the grounds that she couldn't serve simultaneously as a purchaser and the executor of her husband's estate, but the language of the will was sufficiently vague to allow the LeRoux-Sullivan offer to stand. For its part, however, the American League warned Le Roux and Sullivan not even to seek endorsement of the sale until they had obtained more solid financing. This the pair managed after many months by selling limited partnerships and by getting Yawkey to increase her financial presence in the new ownership.

No sooner had LeRoux and Sullivan settled into their now positions than they began going at one another. As the more visible head of baseball operations, Sullivan offered a better target, especially after a LeRoux confidant, Boston broadcaster Ken Harrelson, decided Bucky Dent's playoff home run in 1978 would never have happened if Don Zimmer hadn't been the manager and Sullivan the general manager. During the 1980–81 off-season bickering between the owners became so constant that it was viewed as the major reason for the club's failure to send stars Fred Lynn, Carlton Fisk, and Rick Burleson their proposed contracts on time, in effect making them free agents. It was in the wake of this snafu that one Boston sportswriter began referring to the organization's general partners as Dumwood Sullivan and Shoddy LeRoux.

The next act of the follies took place in June 1983, when LeRoux, claiming he had majority backing from the club's limited partners, staged a coup by bringing in an administrative team to Fenway Park and declaring himself in charge. For two days the franchise operated under parallel administrations; then Sullivan and Yawkey secured a restraining order to evict the usurpers. The Massachusetts Superior Court decided some weeks later that LeRoux's move was illegal but also rejected a motion by Sullivan and Yawkey that LeRoux and his fellow insurgents (representing about 42 percent of the stock) be forced to sell out. Not content with the ruling, LeRoux appealed it—only to regret his move a year later, when he was ordered to sell out.

W. R. LESTER

The sports editor of the Philadelphia *Record,* Lester proposed the plan setting the distance between the mound and home plate back from 50 feet to the 60 feet, six inches it has been for more than a century. He offered his proposal following the 1892 season, when owners began complaining that pitching had come to dominate the game and that the lack of high-scoring games would eventually drive away spectators. As it was conceived initially, the plan would have pushed the mound back to 65 feet within a general broadening of the infield to 93 feet between bases. But at a March 7, 1893 conference in New York the owners found this too radical a change, compromising on the 60 feet, six inches. In 1892 only 12 players of the 184 who had appeared in at least 15 games batted .300; with the pitcher moved back 10 feet, six inches, 65 players reached the magic circle a year later.

Lester himself batted .500 on two of his other proposals at the meeting. His call for the elimination of the flat bat was accepted, but the owners rejected his suggestion that all foul balls be charged as strikes. It wasn't until eight years later that the National League agreed to charge the first two fouls as strikes. The American League adopted the same rule in 1903.

DUTCH LEVSEN

On August 28, 1926 Indians righthander Levsen beat the Red Sox in both ends of a doubleheader, 6–1 and 5–1. He is the last major leaguer to hurl two complete-game victories on the same day. He didn't record a strikeout in either game.

DAVID LEVY

Levy effectively ended the petty practice by major league clubs of chasing after balls hit into the stands. In August 1934 the teenager suffered a fractured skull in an attack by Yankee Stadium ushers after he tried to dislodge a ball that Lou Gehrig had fouled into a screen. In 1937 a federal court awarded him $7,500 for the assault. Thereafter, front offices put out the word that patrons could keep any ball they could reach without interfering with a game.

ED LEVY

First baseman Levy joined the Yankees in 1942 amid a publicity circus aimed at drawing more Jewish fans to the Bronx. When he tried to tell team president Ed Barrow that Levy was his stepfather's name and that he had been raised as the very Irish Catholic Edward Clarence Whitner, the team executive shot back: "You may be Whitner to the rest of the world, but if you're going to play for the Yankees, you'll be Ed Levy." In less than 200 plate appearances over two seasons, Levy batted a mere .215, after which he was sent back to civilian life as Whitner.

DARREN LEWIS

Lewis holds title to the greatest fielding streak in baseball history. Before overrunning a single in late June 1994, the center fielder, then with San Francisco, had gone 392 consecutive games (938 chances, another record) without making an error. No other position player has come close to such a streak. Lewis's miscue was also the first in his major league career, going back to his debut with the Athletics in 1990. The streak was even more remarkable for the outfielder's aggressiveness and in light of the unpredictable winds of his home field of Candlestick Park.

DUFFY LEWIS

Lewis's mastery of Fenway Park's hilly left field between 1910 and 1917 inspired decades of sportswriter to refer to the terrain as Duffy's Incline. Deemed the defensive equal of long-time fielding companions Tris Speaker and Harry Hooper, Lewis also stroked .284 over 11 big league seasons. His most successful moments at bat came during the 1915 World Series against the Phillies, when he drove in the deciding runs of the third and fourth games, then belted an eighth-inning home run in the fifth game to tie the score and set up a Boston world championship. Lewis earned another historical footnote when he became the first player to pinch-hit for Babe Ruth, in 1914. The outfielder left Boston in December 1918 in one of owner Harry Frazee's desperate deals with the Yankees for quick cash.

TED LEWIS

Ordained minister Lewis justified jumping from the Boston Braves to the new Red Sox in 1901 by declaring the reserve clause illegal and immoral. The righthander stayed with his new club only one year, however, quitting baseball entirely at 29 with a 94–64 record to accept a position teaching English at Columbia University. From 1927 until his death in 1936, he served as president of the University of New Hampshire. His favorite relaxation in Durham was discussing poetry while playing catch with poet Robert Frost in the backyard of the university president's house.

JIM LEYLAND

Baseball's touchy-feely manager, Leyland had plenty to be sensitive about in having two franchises cut out from under him in the 1990s. Ultimately, he had little passion left but for walking out on a third club.

A career minor leaguer, Leyland took over a dismal Pirates team in 1986 and, through stops and starts, led it to division wins in 1990, 1991, and 1992. Aside from the so-called Killer Bees regulars of Bobby Bonilla, Barry Bonds, Wally Backman, Jay Bell, and Sid Bream, the club's trademark was the ever-suffering, ever-smoking Leyland, continually portrayed as a dugout genius ready to share a good cry with his loving players. Three straight playoff losses didn't discourage tears, nor did the front office decision by the Pirates to let key free agents (Bonilla and Bream, then Bonds and pitching ace Doug Drabek) walk away to other teams. Leyland stuck around for four more years anyway, making it clear that he felt a loyalty to the organization that had given him his first big league managerial post. But with still no improvement on the horizon and winning too many annual awards as the game's most wasted manager, he finally moved over to the Marlins in 1997.

The good news was that the Florida roster included numerous all-stars (Bonilla, Gary Sheffield, Moises Alou, Kevin Brown, Al Leiter) at or nearing their career peaks. The better news was that Leyland piloted the Wild Card club to a world title. The bad news was that, no sooner had he completed a tear-filled run around Miami's Joe Robbie Stadium to celebrate the World Series victory over Cleveland, than owner Wayne Huizenga began to unload his stars in wholesale lots. Dismayed as he obviously was by the abrupt breakup of his team, Leyland stayed on the job for 108 Florida losses in 1998 before moving to Colorado. But with the 1999 season only weeks old, he made it clear that, his new multiyear contract notwithstanding, he was thinking of withdrawing from baseball at the end of the campaign. Variously interpreted as a confession of exhaustion, deep depression, or simply a desire to become more of a homebody with a recently born child in Pittsburgh, his pronounced intention hung over the Rockies all season, ultimately prompting even Leyland supporters in the media to call on him to step down immediately in the name of club morale. But only when Colorado had stumbled to a finish 18 games under .500 did he formalize his resignation.

L'IL RASTUS

Rastus epitomized baseball's early 20th-century treatment of blacks. A teenager found sleeping in Bennett Park by Ty Cobb in July 1908, he was adopted by the notoriously racist outfielder as a good-luck charm for the Tigers. While Cobb himself was generally content to have Rastus around for self-confidence, other players refused to enter the batter's box without running their hands through the boy's hair. Throughout the summer of 1908 the players conspired in hiding Rastus on trains and under hotel room beds during road trips, convinced they couldn't win without him. By early September, however, the relationship between the club and its mascot had begun to founder. Aside from the fact that Detroit started losing even with their good-luck charm on hand, there were charges that Rastus had stolen equipment from the clubhouse and that he was endangering the "image" of the franchise by sneaking out of Cobb's room to parade his prestige before black bellhops. Told to hit the bricks, Rastus immediately offered his services to the Cubs, and was on the Chicago bench when the National Leaguers defeated the Tigers in the World Series. That was enough for Cobb to bring him back to Detroit in 1909, when the Tigers won another pennant. Cobb later brought Rastus home as a servant—an arrangement that lasted only a brief time before the teenager drifted off, never to be heard from again.

JOHNNY LINDELL

Lindell was a hard-drinking pitcher-turned-outfielder-turned-pitcher. The biggest hit of his 12-year career was an eighth-inning homer on the next-to-last day of the 1949 season to give the Yankees a 5–4 victory; the blast pulled the Yankees into a tie for first place and positioned them to win the first of Casey Stengel's pennants the day after. The right-handed Lindell also batted .500 in the 1947 World Series for New York but was blasted by owner Larry MacPhail for leaving the sixth game with a cracked rib; the attack, which led manager Bucky Harris to throw MacPhail out of the clubhouse celebration after the team had clinched the world championship, was one of a sequence of events that marked the owner's mental breakdown and departure from the club. Lindell's aggressiveness on the bases also led rule makers to reconsider what was permissible in breaking up a double play. A 1950 rule prohibiting bodily contact unless the fielder is in proximity to the base followed soon after a game in which he chased White Sox second baseman Nellie Fox into left field to deliver a bone-crushing block.

Lindell began his career as a hurler; despite a 2–1 record and a 3.76 ERA, he was converted to the outfield. A .273 lifetime hitter, he stayed with the Yankees into the 1950 season, when he was traded to the Cardinals. Released at the end of that year, he went to the Pacific Coast League, where he learned to throw a knuckleball. Accompanied by his personal catcher Mike Sandlock, he returned to the majors to compile a 6–17 record with the Pirates and Phillies in 1953 before concluding his career as a pinch-hitter.

FREDDIE LINDSTROM (Hall of Fame, 1976)

Lindstrom was one of several Giants in the first decades of the century destined to be associated with a critical mishap; unlike Fred Merkle and Fred Snodgrass, however, he was completely blameless. It was Lindstrom who, in the final game of the 1924 World Series against Washington, stood helplessly at third base as first Bucky Harris in the eighth inning and then Earl McNeely in the 12th inning hit bouncers that took pebble-aided hops into left field for what added up to a world championship for the Senators. Manager John McGraw and teammates were quick to absolve the third baseman of any responsibility.

From the time he broke into the majors in 1924 as an 18-year-old, the righthand-hitting Lindstrom showed little awe of the older future Hall of Famers around him. Still working on his own credentials as a career .311 hitter over 13 seasons, he was invari-

ably in the middle of the rifts that beset the club as McGraw's control waned in the late 1920s. He was so certain of his own managerial abilities that he went into a fury when McGraw passed him over as his successor in favor of Bill Terry; one of Terry's first acts as pilot, in December 1932, was dealing Lindstrom to Pittsburgh. In November of 1934, however, Terry decided to move up to the front office and sought to get Lindstrom back from the Pirates to replace him in the dugout. But by then the Pirates had completed a deal to send the third baseman to the Cubs, who refused to part with their new acquisition. Only 31 at the time, Lindstrom became so disgusted with a muffed fly ball by a Dodgers teammate in 1936 that he announced he couldn't play with clowns and retired.

Lindstrom's biggest years were for the Giants in 1928, when he averaged .358, and 1930, when he batted .379; he collected 231 hits both seasons.

PHIL LINZ

Linz's principal claim to fame was that he once tried to play "Mary Had a Little Lamb" on a harmonica. His foray into music occurred on the Yankees team bus on August 20, 1964, just after New York had lost a doubleheader to the White Sox. When an enraged manager Yogi Berra ordered Linz to "shove that thing up your ass," the infielder flipped the instrument in the general direction of the pilot, succeeding only in hitting teammate Joe Pepitone. For reasons never clear to the immediate participants, the episode was blown up as a turning point for New York's successful pennant drive. Most of the press took its cue from the team's prissy coach Frank Crosetti, who allowed as how the incident was the worst he had ever witnessed as a Yankee.

JOHN HENRY LLOYD (Hall of Fame, 1977)

An itinerant Negro leagues shortstop who was once called the greatest player of all time by Babe Ruth, Lloyd reminded more than one observer of Honus Wagner, not least for the way both scooped glovesful of infield dirt with each ground ball. For his part, Wagner once said he "felt honored that they would name such a great player after me."

Lloyd played for 12 teams in a 27-year career that began in 1905, because, as he put it, "Where the money was, that's where I played." The lefty swinger averaged in the .360s, topping .400 in several seasons. He also spent 12 winters playing in Cuba. It was there, in 1910, that he encountered the racist Ty Cobb, on a barnstorming tour with the Tigers. Outhitting the American League batting champion .500 (in 12 games) to .369 (in only five of the contests), the shortstop also nailed Cobb in three consecutive steal attempts. Lloyd's answer to Cobb's spikes-high slides—metal shin guards under his socks—caught the American League baserunning champion totally by surprise. In his later years Lloyd moved to first base, picked up the nickname Pop, and piloted several of the teams for which he played.

Ruth's assessment came in an interview with Graham McNamee, after specifically inquiring whether the broadcaster wanted him to restrict himself to the big leagues in answering a question about the identity of the best player in baseball.

BILLY LOES

Although good enough to be a member of the starting rotation for The Boys of Summer Dodgers, Loes gained more notoriety for a steady stream of quotes that marked him as one of the era's eccentrics. Asked on the eve of the 1952 World Series matching Brooklyn against New York who would win, the righthander said unhesitatingly that it would be the Yankees. In the same Series he justified his turning-point bobble of a ground ball by saying he had lost it in the sun. Questioned another time why, despite his talent, he never seemed to be able to win more than 14 games, his explanation was that "If you win 20, they expect you to do it every year."

Loes is also the answer to the trivia question about the identity of the only major leaguer who was on the field when four different players accomplished the rare feat of hitting four home runs in a game. He was a member of the Dodgers when Brooklyn's Gil Hodges did it in 1950 and Milwaukee's Joe Adcock did it in 1954, with Baltimore when Cleveland's Rocky Colavito did it in 1959, and with the Giants when teammate Willie Mays did it in 1961.

TOM LOFTUS

Loftus is the only man to have managed teams in four major leagues. His career included stops in the Union Association (1884) with Milwaukee; the American Association (1888) with Cleveland; the National League (1889–91, 1900–01) with Cleve-

land, Cincinnati, and Chicago; and the American League (1902–03) with Washington.

JACK LOHRKE

Even for normally superstitious ballplayers, Lohrke, a utility infielder for the Giants after World War II, was regarded as the charm of charms. He laid first claim to his nickname of Lucky in 1943, when he emerged unhurt from a troop train crash that killed three companions and gravely scalded dozens more. After getting through the D-Day landings and the Battle of the Bulge without a scratch, he returned to the United States for mustering out of the Army, boarding a military transport plane in New Jersey, only to be thrown off again for a late-arriving officer. The plane ended up crashing in Ohio, killing everybody on it. Back in baseball, Lohrke was playing with a minor league Spokane club when he was told he was being called up by San Diego in the Pacific Coast League. Receiving word of his advancement at a highway diner, he was given the choice of proceeding to the next train station on the team bus or making his own connections back to Spokane to get his things. Because he opted to leave his teammates right away, he wasn't on the bus when it plunged over a 500-foot embankment, killing nine and ending the baseball careers of all the survivors.

Lohrke's last season with the Giants was 1951, the year of Bobby Thomson's miracle playoff home run against the Dodgers.

MICKEY LOLICH

Lolich won 217 games in a 16-year career between 1963 and 1979, but none compared to his three victories for Detroit in the 1968 World Series against St. Louis. Aside from giving his club the world championship, the wins defused angry racial tensions in Detroit that had been building since the assassination of Martin Luther King, Jr., in April. Despite notching 47 victories over the 1971 and 1972 seasons the southpaw never won a Cy Young trophy.

ERNIE LOMBARDI (Hall of Fame, 1986)

Although he won two batting titles and averaged .306 in 17 seasons between 1931 and 1947, Lombardi's most impressive achievement might have been his eight career steals. The righthand-hitting catcher was considered so slow that infielders on the left side regularly played on the outfield grass with little anxiety about being able to get him at first on a bunt or a topper. By the same token, his 10 seasons of .300 or better were all the more creditable for including few cheap hits, since the defensive alignment against him also cut down on loopers over the infield.

Lombardi and Babe Herman were traded by the Dodgers to the Reds in 1932—one of the best swaps in Cincinnati history. After winning a batting crown in 1938 and helping the Reds to pennants in 1939 and 1940, he was traded to Boston in 1942, where he promptly won his second hitting title. That production helped make him the biggest name affected by the salary cap that was in force in the major leagues during World War II. Because Boston could not afford a raise that the organization itself admitted he was due, he was traded to the Giants, whose budget permitted the pay boost. (Under the wartime cap a player could not receive less than the lowest nor more than the highest salary paid by his team in 1942.)

HERMAN LONG

An acrobatic shortstop with five National League flag-winning Boston teams in the 1890s, Long made 1,096 errors at his regular spot (and 32 at other positions) in his 16-year career, the most miscues by any major leaguer.

DAVEY LOPES

In 2001 Lopes unwittingly demonstrated the growing comprehensiveness of baseball statistics, and in the process drove another spike into the they-don't-play-today-like-they-did-in-my-day mentality. As manager of the Brewers, he threatened retaliation against Rickey Henderson for stealing a base while the outfielder's Padres held a 12–5 lead over Milwaukee. Researchers immediately provided the information that Lopes himself, a league-leading stealer twice during his 16-year career between 1972 and 1987, had swiped bases eight times with his team ahead by seven runs or more. Confronted with the contradiction, he snapped at a reporter and refused further comment on the episode.

AL LOPEZ (Hall of Fame, 1977)

Lopez had most of the longevity records for catchers before the coming of Bob Boone and Carlton Fisk. A 19-year (1928, 1930–47) major leaguer for Brooklyn, Boston, Pittsburgh, and Cleveland, he was a defensive whiz with an unimposing bat (.261

lifetime). More than one manager cited him as a voice of sanity in the midst of dreary second-division seasons; in fact, only with the 1944 Pirates did Lopez play for a club that reached even second place. He turned his bench chats to good purpose during his own managerial career, ending up with a .581 mark in 17 years of piloting the Indians and White Sox in the 1950s and 1960s; unlike his playing days, he managed clubs to first- or second-place finishes 12 times. By guiding the Indians to a flag in 1954 and the White Sox to another one in 1959, Lopez interrupted what would otherwise have been 16 consecutive American League championships for the Yankees.

TOM LOVETT

Lovett became baseball's first season-long holdout in 1892, when he refused to accept a salary cut from Brooklyn. The righthander, who had won 53 games in the previous two seasons, took his stand in response to a National League-wide attack on player salaries after the dissolution of the Players League and the American Association. Lovett returned to the Dodgers in 1893 but was knocked around to the tune of a 6.56 ERA.

BILL LUCAS

Lucas was the first black to have a meaningful front office position. Employed by the Braves in the 1960s and 1970s, he worked his way up from farm director to director of player personnel and then acting general manager. At age 43, however, he died of a brain hemorrhage. Lucas was Hank Aaron's brother-in-law.

RED LUCAS

Lucas is the best pinch-hitting pitcher of all time. Although his 114 hits as a substitute batter has been surpassed by several players, none has been a pitcher; in addition, the lefty swinger held the overall pinch-hitting record for almost 30 years, until Smokey Burgess passed him in 1965. As a hurler, Lucas fashioned a 157–135 record in a 15-year career between 1923 and 1938, primarily with the Reds and Pirates.

WILLIAM V. LUCAS

As the chief backer of the 1884 Union Association, Lucas threatened the monopoly of the National League and the American Association. Founded on a fuzzy blend of sound business sense and principled opposition to the reserve clause and blacklisting, his league initially refused to ask players to violate contracts but was soon involved in a no-holds-barred war to get them to jump from the established circuits. The enterprise was doomed from the beginning by an inability to attract top players and keep franchises from dissolving, but Lucas hastened its destruction by spending most of the available money on his own St. Louis Maroons and by such Louis XIV-like declarations as "I am the Union Association. Whatever I do is all right." The Maroons ran roughshod over the rest of the UA, winning the pennant by 21 games and putting together the highest won-lost percentage (.832) in major league history.

The UA died after one year, with Lucas accepting an NL berth in1885 and publicly embracing the reserve rule. He ended up jobbed by both the Cleveland Blues, who sold him their franchise without turning over any players, and St. Louis Browns owner Chris Von der Ahe, who received reparations not only for the damage he had suffered in the UA war but also for allowing his territorial rights to be compromised. Von der Ahe then put the finishing touches on everything by winning four consecutive flags in the AA to drive Lucas out of business in St. Louis.

RON LUCIANO

Luciano was the most ostentatious example of a new breed of umpires in the 1970s who acted more interested in drawing attention to themselves than in perpetuating any ideal anonymity. His trademark gestures in calling an out—pumping his arm more times than necessary and making a shooting gesture with his fingers—so irritated Frank Robinson, among others, that in 1975 the Indians manager fined players for talking to him on the field. Luciano's chief nemesis was Baltimore pilot Earl Weaver; their mutual disdain and reciprocal showboating, dating to their days in the International League (Luciano once ran Weaver out of four consecutive minor league games), reached the point that the American League office wouldn't let Luciano work Orioles games. The 13-year veteran retired after the 1980 season to parlay his notoriety into careers as an author and sports commentator. When the spotlight began to fade, he became increasingly despondent, finally committing suicide in January 1995.

CHARLEY LUPICA

There have been fanatical baseball fans, and then there was Lupica. On May 31, 1949 the Cleveland druggist climbed up to a platform atop a 20-foot flagpole with the announcement that he would stay there until the Indians, then mired in seventh place, repeated their 1948 world championship. After some stabs at getting him down, Cleveland police decided he was harmless, while Indians owner Bill Veeck decided he was the best advertisement the team could have. Lupica remained on his flagpole perch 117 days, coming down only on September 25, when Veeck persuaded him that Cleveland's rise to the first division in fourth place was as good as it was going to get. The owner later presented the druggist with a new car in gratitude for the publicity he had generated around the country for the team.

TONY LUPIEN

Lupien challenged his trade to the minor leagues by the Phillies after World War II on the grounds that it violated the National Defense Act covering the reintegration of veterans into their jobs. Economic necessity forced him to settle out of court. The lefthanded first baseman later signed with the White Sox for the final one of his six major league seasons.

THOMAS J. LYNCH

Former umpire Lynch became National League president in 1910 as a compromise candidate to break a voting deadlock. He was sponsored by Giants owner John T. Brush on the grounds that his experience qualified him to perform the primary function of a league chief executive—supervising umpires. In fact, Lynch did irritatingly more, as far as the owners were concerned. Humorless and tactless, he annoyed them all when he levied a $500 fine on Brooklyn boss Charlie Ebbets for hiding a player in the minor leagues. After a 1913 decision to ban Phillies president Horace Fogel for claiming that the Giants had won the previous year's pennant with the collusion of umpires and Cardinals manager Roger Bresnahan, league owners decided his arrogance was becoming as important as the merits of the specific situations brought to his attention. Lynch survived another year, but was then ousted for Pennsylvania governor John Tener. What irked him as much as his removal were the disclosure that his successor would make $25,000 to his $9,000 and that the formal announcement of the change predicted Tener would add "dignity and prestige to the office." Lynch's parting shot was the hope that owners would "inject some of that same dignity expected of him into yourselves."

FRED LYNN

Two protracted contract squabbles and a trade thwarted predictions of a Hall of Fame career for Lynn. The lefty-swinging outfielder certainly got a big start on diamond glory with the Red Sox in 1975 when he became the first major leaguer to win Rookie of the Year and MVP honors in the same season. Four years later he won the batting title by averaging .333 while clouting 39 home runs and driving in 122 runs. In 1976, however, Lynn was one of three Red Sox players whose contract demands produced a Boston soap opera that ultimately prompted the removal of general manager Dick O'Connell. He signed on that occasion, but landed back in the same situation with the expiration of his pact in 1980, when front-office confusion about mailing him his contract on time put him in an advantageous position for approving any contemplated deals. When he finally okayed a trade to the Angels, he left behind a career average of .350 in Fenway Park and headed into another 10 seasons in which, through a combination of different surroundings and nagging injuries, he would never again attain .300.

Lynn triggered a change in waiver rules in 1980 when Detroit acquired him from Baltimore on the evening of August 31. Because he was unable to reach the city where his new team was playing before midnight, he was declared ineligible for any postseason play for which Detroit might qualify. The publicity over the incident—and especially over Tigers owner Tom Managhan's honesty in admitting the outfielder had been unable to join his new teammates until the calendar had been turned to September—pressured the major leagues into eliminating the Cinderella waiver condition.

Lynn is the only player to have hit a grand slam home run in an All-Star Game, tagging San Francisco southpaw Atlee Hammaker for a four-run four-bagger in the 1983 contest.

BILL LYONS

Lyons was signed to a baseball contract for his singing voice. In the years immediately prior to World War I pitcher Marty McHale assembled a foursome of Boston players, known as the Red Sox Quartette, that toured the vaudeville circuit in the off-season. When third baseman Larry Gardner decided that show business wasn't for him, Lyons was drafted as a replacement. Because the team considered the group good publicity in its market war with the Braves, the Red Sox gave Lyons a formal player contract so nobody would question the legitimacy of the quartet's name. Aside from Lyons and McHale (dubbed The Baseball Caruso), the group included first baseman Hugh Bradley and pitcher Buck O'Brien.

TED LYONS (Hall of Fame, 1955)

Like Red Faber, Lyons followed up some dominating years with the White Sox with far too many seasons of mediocre or worse pitching for the franchise; unlike Faber, he came up with a solution near the end of his career that gave him a second wind. The right-hander joined Chicago in 1923 amid owner Charlie Comiskey's frantic attempts to put together another rotation after the Black Sox scandal. In both 1925 and 1927 Lyons paced the American League with 20-win seasons, then reached the mark again in 1930. But for the rest of that decade he lost more than he won, and with earned-run averages that suggested it wasn't just the fault of the wretched clubs behind him. Then, in 1939, at the suggestion of manager Jimmy Dykes, he limited himself to pitching on Sundays, and turned in four straight season of winning ball, topping it off with the ERA crown in 1942. The experiment was successful not only artistically but financially as well, with "Sunday with Lyons" developing into one of Chicago's few gate attractions in the period. Lyons closed out his active playing career with a few appearances in 1946, toting up a record of 260–230; thanks to his weekly regimen, his ERA of 3.67, one of the highest in the Hall of Fame, wasn't still higher. As Lyons himself was forever telling sportswriters, he would have preferred taking off his uniform then and there, but Dykes's abrupt resignation after a contract squabble in 1946 led him to accept the managership of the club for an uninspired two-and-a-half years.

M

CONNIE MACK (Hall of Fame, 1937)

No other individual was so closely identified with a franchise as Mack was with the Philadelphia Athletics over 54 years of very high peaks and very low valleys. Through a half-century as manager and the organization's entire lifetime as at least part-owner, he won nine pennants, but also finished dead last 17 times as pilot (and 18 overall). A key organizer of the AL in 1901, Mack outlasted all his contemporaries. By the time he left the dugout after the 1950 season, shortly before his 89th birthday, he had become the venerable Grand Old Man of Baseball to some; to others, including members of his own family, he was little more than a senile object of derision.

A catcher with Washington and Pittsburgh in the National League and Buffalo of the Players League, Mack (born Cornelius McGillicuddy) averaged .246 between 1886 and 1896; his career as a first-string receiver ended in a home-plate collision with Boston's Herman Long in 1893. Named manager of the Pirates at the end of the 1894 season, he developed a trick of freezing baseballs to deaden them for use when opponents were at bat; it was also in Pittsburgh, in 1895, that he was ejected from a game for the only time in his 61 years as a major league player and pilot.

Following his dismissal by Pittsburgh in 1896, Mack threw in his lot with Ban Johnson's minor Western League, taking over its Milwaukee franchise in 1897. This left him well positioned when Johnson decided to challenge the NL in 1901. With the backing of Ben Shibe, a partner in the A. J. Reach Sporting Goods company and a big stockholder in the rival Phillies, he put together the new league's Phila-delphia franchise, built its first ballpark (Columbia Park), and came up with the team logo of a white elephant (which John McGraw predicted the Athletics would be). His biggest coup in the early going was signing future Hall of Famer Nap Lajoie away from the Phillies—a deal that was undone after only one season by a legal battle that necessitated trading the second baseman to Cleveland to get him out of the jurisdiction of Pennsylvania's courts. Despite losing Lajoie, Mack won the first of his nine pennants in 1902, following it with another in 1905.

From the start Mack showed a preference for college players, eventually scouting and developing dozens of them; in contrast, he rarely made trades involving front-line players, and when he did, they were almost always disasters. In different eras, he yielded Joe Jackson to Cleveland for Bris Lord, Charlie Jamieson to the same club for Braggo Roth, George Kell to the Tigers for Barney McCoskey, and Nellie Fox to the White Sox for Joe Tipton.

After opening Shibe Park, the first steel and concrete stadium, in 1909, Mack captured four pennants and three world championships between 1910 and 1914 with a team that featured the $100,000 Infield (Stuffy McInnis, Eddie Collins, Jack Barry, and Frank Baker). But he broke up the A's first dynasty for reasons more numerous than ever definitively confirmed: complacent players with large salary demands, fans made indifferent by to much success, a stunning upset loss to the Miracle Braves in the 1914 World Series, big-money overtures by the Federal League to some of the Philadelphia stars, and even the suggestion that the A's might not have lost the 1914 Series to Boston the square. In any case it was around this time that he promulgated his theory that a close second-place finish was better for business then a runaway pennant, since it kept patrons pouring through the turnstiles without having to raise player salaries drastically. After selling off his best players, Mack finished last every year from 1915 to 1921; the 1916 entry, which won only 36 games, was one of the worst teams of the 20th century. During these lean years Mack, sometimes known in the press as The Tall Tactician, became The Slim Schemer for his manipulative attempts to keep Scott Perry in the face of a National Commission ruling that the pitcher belonged to the Braves, and for his role in the owner collusion to release every player in the majors rather than pay them for the final few weeks of the war-shortened 1918 season.

Rebuilding in the 1920s, Mack assembled a second dynasty, which brought him two world championships, in 1929 and 1930, and a final pennant in 1931. This time, the Depression did him in. When a bank that had been providing financing for the club called in a $400,000 note, he began selling off players once again. Future Hall of Famers Al Simmons, Mickey Cochrane, Lefty Grove, and Jimmie Foxx, among others, went to pay off the debt, and the club went back to the basement, this time finishing last nine times and seventh twice between 1935 and 1946.

In 1946 the aging Mack made a miscalculation that would come back to haunt him. Like King Lear prematurely dividing his kingdom, he gave each of his three sons 10 percent of the club. Although there was worse to come, that was enough for his second wife to go into a public furor because this meant that her son Connie, Jr., ended up with only half of what the two sons from Mack's first marriage received; the couple even separated for a time over the perceived injustice. Meanwhile, trying to rebuild again after World War II, Mack relied heavily on coaches Simmons and Earle Brucker. He certainly needed somebody: Almost totally deaf and often napping on the bench; he was more and more given to mental wanderings, more than once calling on long-retired sluggers to grab a bat and pinch-hit. Players began to refer to him as The Old Man—but without the respect that had once been attached to the familiarity. The A's relative success in 1947—a fifth-place finish and the first record on the plus side of .500 since 1933—offered encouragement. But the following year Mack vented his frustration over only modest improvement by, among other things, publicly berating 37-year-old pitcher Nelson Potter and releasing him on the spot after the reliever blew a game in the ninth inning.

After the 1949 season trouble erupted in the boardroom, which, for the Athletics, meant the family room. In October Connie, Jr., and Shibe heirs Ben and Frank Macfarland engineered the release of coaches Simmons and Brucker in favor of former players Cochrane and Jimmy Dykes. The following May they completed their coup by moving eldest son Earle out as assistant manager, a post he had held since the late 1930s and from which he and everyone else assumed he would succeed his father. Dykes was inserted as assistant manager, with Cochrane becoming the club's first general manager. But the victory proved only temporary when Earle and his brother Roy turned around to buy out Connie, Jr., the Macfarlands, and several other Shibe heirs in August and assume control of almost 80 percent of the club's stock.

Mack retired on October 18, 1950. Publicly, the elder sons had insisted their father could stay on as long as he chose; privately, they had applied pressure on him to call it a career. For the next four years Mack remained a minority stockholder and he played only a supporting role in the comic opera that followed the 1954 season as Earle and Roy tried to sell the franchise, accepting and then rejecting offers from various groups and fighting with each other about which bid to accept. In fact, the only offer of substance came from Chicago vending machine and real-estate magnate Arnold Johnson, who made no effort to disguise his intention of moving the club to Kansas City. Mack's penultimate involvement in club affairs was a sentimental plea before an AL meeting in October that other owners reject Johnson's offer and sanction a rival bid from a Philadelphia-based group that lacked the backing to complete the deal. His request was not only ineffective, it was hypocritical since he himself had agreed to the Johnson proposal and its rejection would have landed him in a major legal wrangle. The final act took place in November, in Mack's Germantown home, where Johnson gave the ailing nonagenarian a check for $604,000 in exchange for his 302 shares in the club.

Mack holds the records for both most victories (3,731) and most losses (3,948) by a major league manager.

REDDY MACK

An otherwise forgotten second baseman, Mack revealed a gaping hole in baseball's rules when, after scoring a run in a July 9, 1887 American Association game, he lingered at home plate to prevent Brooklyn catcher Bob Clark from making a play on two additional Louisville runners who scored the apparent tying and winning runs. Umpire Wesley Curry disallowed both runs even though there was no specific rule allowing for interference by anyone but a base runner, which Mack had ceased to be as soon as he had crossed the plate. The rule book did not address the problem until 1904.

LARRY MacPHAIL (Hall of Fame, 1978)

With one conspicuous exception MacPhail was the main force behind baseball's most significant innovations in the 1930s and 1940s. As general manager of the Reds, chief operating officer of the Dodgers, and part owner and general manager of the Yankees, he introduced night baseball to the major leagues, secured the first contract for continuous radio coverage of games, pioneered television coverage, and devised such popular fan promotions as Old Timers Day. In addition, he was the first executive to fly his team regularly from city to city, the first to stress corporate seat purchases and season ticket plans as marketing devices, the first to institute a stadium club for patrons who wanted more than hot dogs, and the first to hire women as ushers. But for all his accomplishments MacPhail was also a ferocious opponent of baseball's single most important midcentury innovation: racial integration. This plus his general bluster, hot temper, and penchant for one cocktail too many created enough enemies to delay his election to the Hall of Fame until 30 years after his retirement and three years after his death.

MacPhail was already nearing his 40th birthday as an automobile dealer when Branch Rickey, a law school classmate form the University of Michigan, asked him to help turn around St. Louis's financially beset farm team in Columbus. MacPhail did it so well that he had Columbus outdrawing St. Louis in 1932; he did it so arrogantly, refusing to send Rickey second baseman Burgess Whitehead unless the Cardinals gave him back five players, that he was tossed out on his ear at the end of the 1933 season. Only months later, however, Rickey recommended him for the general manager's position with Cincin-

nati. One of MacPhail's first moves was to persuade automobile and radio manufacturer Powel Crosley to buy into the Reds so he would have the capital necessary for drastically overhauling an organization that had gone to seed.

Under MacPhail night baseball came to Cincinnati, and to the major leagues, on May 24, 1935. The main reason other owners offered only token resistance to the innovation was that they hadn't been making money on their road trips to the city for years and had little more to lose. MacPhail being MacPhail, he wasn't content just to advertise the contest against Philadelphia and then nod to a technician at the appointed second to switch on the lights. To begin with, there were military bands and elaborate fireworks displays culminating in configurations of the American flag and an enormous "C" with "REDS" in the middle. Then came a presentation of special guests, who included George Cahill, an inventor who had staged a demonstration of the possibilities of night baseball as far back as 1909, and George Wright, the last surviving member of the fabled Cincinnati Red Stockings of 1869–70. Finally, a signal went to Washington, where President Franklin Roosevelt gave the go-ahead to MacPhail to light up the stadium by turning a key in a special switch installed in the White House. The Reds put the finishing touches on the evening by defeating Philadelphia, 2–1, before 20,422 fans.

It was also MacPhail who introduced night baseball to New York City—with the Dodgers (June 15, 1938) and with the Yankees (May 28, 1946). As in Cincinnati, he made sure that Brooklyn's encounter with history occurred with as much fanfare as possible, hiring Olympic star Jesse Owens to race several Dodgers around Ebbets Field before the game; unlike Cincinnati, the Brooklyn game also improvised its own significance when Reds southpaw Johnny Vander Meer used the occasion to hurl his second consecutive no-hitter, a headline-making achievement that did more than Roosevelt had in 1935 to make the country aware of night baseball.

There was one ironic foot note to the innovation: Although he had lobbied tirelessly for night ball, MacPhail was dissatisfied with the scanty seven games other NL owners agreed to commit to the experiment in 1935. Because he didn't consider these enough to cover lighting expenses, he was the only member of the Cincinnati board to vote *against* his own proposal.

Next to night games, MacPhail's greatest impact on the game stemmed from his perception that the broadcast media could help rather than hinder stadium attendance. His vital ally in this belief was announcer Red Barber, whose play-by-play introduced the game to millions of people in the Ohio area, then later in New York. The two would also be responsible for the first baseball telecast. However profitable his innovations were, MacPhail never endeared himself to boardrooms. One problem was his insistence that revenues be put back into a team rather than divided among shareholders, while he himself enjoyed an appreciable salary and attendance bonus; another was a tendency to pursue this strategy with bluster and fists. It was, in fact, following a punch-up with Crosley at a September 1936 meeting that MacPhail left Cincinnati. Landing with the Dodgers in 1938, he generally kept to the script he had written with the Reds—night games, bringing in Barber, overhauling the ballpark right down to the ushers' uniforms, and completing a series of major trades aimed at returning the club to a contender's status. Just as the Reds players he had left behind brought Cincinnati its first pennant in 20 years, in 1939, the Dodgers got into the World Series for the first time in more than two decades in 1941.

Once again, however, MacPhail's road to success was littered with bodies. He angered the Giants and Yankees by unilaterally breaking an agreement not to broadcast any games in the city for at least five years. He held Babe Ruth up to public ridicule by hiring him behind some vague promise that the slugger might one day be named manager, while being interested only in the Bambino's draw as a batting-practice act. His love-hate relationship with Rickey was all love when he hired Branch Rickey, Jr., as his farm director and all hate when the younger Rickey began complaining to his father that it was a title without a meaningful job; all love when he purchased slugger Joe Medwick from Rickey's Cardinals and all hate when the outfielder was beaned in the very first meeting between the clubs; all love when he consented to "hide" Cardinals free agent Pete Reiser in the Dodgers farm system for a couple of years and all hate when he decided that Reiser was needed in Ebbets Field. With Brooklyn's owners it was the familiar tale of gratitude that the franchise had paid its debts and *seemed* to be registering a profit, but wonder at why every penny of the profits had to be channeled back into operating the team. Most of all, however,

MacPhail's tenure with the Dodgers was marked by his volcanic relationship with Leo Durocher.

By Durocher's estimate, MacPhail fired him as Brooklyn manager 27 times between 1939 and 1942, almost always as the end of a shouting match fueled by drinking. On the final day of the 1939 season, for instance, the executive lauded his pilot before a packed Ebbets Field for having brought the Dodgers back to the first division, then after the game told him he was gone for having started a rookie pitcher who had almost cost the team a third-place finish. Following Brooklyn's pennant win in 1941, MacPhail and Rickey rushed up to 125th Street to climb aboard the team train for a gala welcoming at Grand Central Station, unaware that Durocher had arranged for the team to bypass the station lest some of the players get off and wander into Harlem bars; this time, he fired Durocher in the middle of the victory party. After that year's World Series loss to New York, MacPhail sank low enough into his cups not only to fire his manager but also to propose a roster-for-roster swap with the St. Louis Browns. Apropos of such incidents (which always ended with MacPhail sobering up and forgetting about the firings), Durocher once declared of his employer: "There is not question in my mind that Larry was a genius. There is a line between genius and insanity, and in Larry's case it was sometimes so thin that you could see him drifting back and forth."

MacPhail and Durocher infused a swagger in the Dodgers players that made the club the most hated in the league. In one 1942 game Chicago pitchers knocked down 15 consecutive Brooklyn hitters. But after the team had blown a $10^1/_2$-game lead to the Cardinals that season, raising the temperature of stockholders already aggrieved they weren't receiving dividend payments, MacPhail resigned to enter the military. When he reemerged in January 1945, it was as part-owner of the Yankees.

While continuing the flamboyant promotions in the Bronx that had worked with Cincinnati and Brooklyn (e.g., Nylons Day for attracting women), MacPhail also set out to consolidate a corporate clientele through such measures as setting aside more season tickets and opening a stadium club for businessmen and their guests; it was, in fact, under the veteran showman's ownership that the Yankees paradoxically gained their image as a bloodless General Motors of the sport. In 1946 the installation of lights in Yankee Stadium helped the franchise break the two-million mark in attendance for the first time in baseball history. MacPhail's manner, however, continued to make enemies. Joe McCarthy and Bill Dickey both quit on him as managers. Joe DiMaggio and Charlie Keller were fined for not attending a team promotion. While MacPhail bragged about making the Yankees the first team to travel by air, the players protested his use of a rickety C-54 military transport that narrowly missed crashing a couple of times; after one of the near-misses DiMaggio and manager Bucky Harris had to head off a team insurrection. More trouble beckoned in 1947, when the owner became entangled in a mare's nest of charges about gambling associations and the poaching of coaches under contract to other teams—a scandal that also embroiled Durocher, Rickey, and Charlie Dressen and that ended up costing MacPhail a fine.

By the middle of the 1947 season MacPhail was approaching a nervous collapse even as New York was charging toward a world championship. He played out his last scene as a baseball executive at the club victory party, where he took swings at partner Dan Topping and general manager George Weiss. The next day he sold his interest in the team to Topping and Del Webb.

MacPhail's hostility to desegregating baseball was one part racism, one part a resentment that old foe Rickey had brought Jackie Robinson to the major leagues, and many parts financial calculations. To begin with, there was his corporate clientele marketing priorities and too few black executives to make the two compatible. Second, he had been making significant extra money by arranging and promoting offseason All-Star Games between major leaguers and stars from the Negro leagues. Third, he didn't mind sharing the opinion that black ballplayers equaled black fans equaled depreciated franchises. Fourth, there was his pursuit of radio (and eventually television) ad money and his apprehension that Madison Avenue would not be eager to go after a racially mixed audience. It was also to gall him no little that the final nod to Robinson's arrival came from Happy Chandler, the commissioner whom MacPhail had pressed on other owners soon after taking over the Yankees. As in the case of the first night game in Cincinnati, the executive whom Bill Veeck called "the brightest, most imaginative guy in our business" had ended up regretting his own inspiration.

LEE MACPHAIL (Hall of Fame, 1998)

Son of Larry MacPhail, Lee was known as "the man who says nothing" by both admirers and critics. Brought into the Yankees organization when his father owned the team in the 1940s, he worked his way up to farm director, then moved around as general manager for Baltimore, as special assistant to Commissioner William Eckert; back to the Yankees as general manager, and finally, in 1974, as American League president for a decade. In this last post his compliant behavior toward owners during confrontations with players over free agency and arbitration confirmed for many his talent for saying nothing. When his son, Minnesota general manager Andy MacPhail, helped guide the Twins to a championship in 1987, Lee showed little hesitation about admitting: "I have been in the game for 42 years and never won anything."

The MacPhails are the only father-son combination in the Hall of Fame.

GARRY MADDOX

Maddox was such a deft center fielder for the Giants and Phillies in the 1970s and 1980s that he inspired one of the game's more memorable quotes; as Mets broadcaster Ralph Kiner put it: "Two-thirds of the world is covered by water, the other one-third by Garry Maddox." Despite that reputation, it was Maddox's error in the ninth inning of the fourth game of the 1978 National League Championship Series that gave Los Angeles a pennant over the Phillies. Because of a severe rash he picked up while fighting in Vietnam, Maddox was allowed to wear a beard even when team policies prohibited facial hair.

GREG MADDUX

Baseball's most successful pitcher in the 1990s with 176 victories, Maddux is also the only hurler to win the Cy Young Award in four consecutive years. The righthander picked up the trophies for the Cubs in 1992 and for the Braves in 1993, 1994, and 1995. Although he won 20 games in both 1992 and 1993 and took three of his four ERA titles in 1993, 1995, and 1998, he was even more overpowering in the shortened 1994 campaign when he posted a 16–6 record. His 1.56 ERA was more than two-and-a-half runs below the National League—the greatest differential in major league history; almost as an afterthought, he set another ERA record spread by finishing 1.09 runs per nine innings ahead of the major league runnerup, Steve Ontiveros of Oakland. Perhaps Maddux's most impressive numbers, however, revolve around his pinpoint control. Entering the 2002 season, for instance, he held the career mark for the most strikeouts per walk, fanning 3.32 batters for every free pass. For all that, however, his lifetime 10–13 record in the postseason was also a mirror of Atlanta's frustrations in playoff and World Series games.

Maddux's knowledge of the game's arcana has been unrivalled among players since the retirement of Pete Rose. Just as Rose was able to spout out at a moment's notice the percentage of fly balls to groundouts produced by given hitters, the hurler has casually tossed off such calculations as how long a fly remains in the air and how the speed of this outfielder would have made it an out, and the speed of that one permitted it to fall for a hit. He has been able to back up his (subtly critical) observations about the intricacies of defense with 12 consecutive Gold Gloves.

BILL MADLOCK

Madlock won four batting titles in his 15-year (1973–87) career, but was equally noteworthy as a crucial hired gun for two division titles and a world championship. A righthanded spray hitter, the third baseman won his first two Silver Bats as a member of the Cubs in 1975 and 1976. The other two came as a Pirate in 1981 and 1983. Overall, he turned in nine years of .300 or better for a career mark of .305.

Madlock's first significant contribution to a winning club came in 1979, when he was obtained by Pittsburgh from San Francisco at the end of June; the deal, involving a number of players who had officially cleared waivers, just about put an end to the artificial June 15 trading deadline that had been in effect for a half-century. With the Pirates Madlock hit .328 for the rest of the year, following that up with a .375 mark in the team's victorious World Series with Baltimore. In 1985 he went from the Pirates to the Dodgers under similar circumstances, proceeding to bat .360 over the final part of the regular season and to whack three homers and drive in seven runs in the NLCS with the Cardinals. Again, in 1987, he was looked upon as division victory insurance—going from the Dodgers to the Tigers, for whom he clouted 14 home runs and drove in 50 runs in 326 at bats as Detroit's designated hitter.

Madlock's departures were not always regretted by his managers. In Pittsburgh his open criticisms of the organization and of manager Chuck Tanner were portrayed by front-office flacks as "poisonous" to the club's younger players. In Los Angeles he didn't win points from Tommy Lasorda for suggesting more than once that not every member of the team was as committed to bleeding Dodger blue as the manager claimed.

LEE MAGEE

Magee was the warmup act for the Black Sox scandal. A second baseman of some ability on both sides of the ball, he was anything but deft in trying to be one of the World War I era's numerous players for sale. Between his brain and his mouth he not only got himself thrown out of the major leagues, but also provided a final nail in the coffin of Hal Chase.

In 1918 Magee and Chase, then teammates on the Reds, approached a Boston gambler with a scheme for throwing the first game of a July doubleheader against the Braves. Each player put up a $500 check, accepting a promise of one-third of the gambler's winnings when Cincinnati lost. But despite Magee's own efforts in the contest (two crucial errors, dawdling on the basepaths), Cincinnati won, 4–2, with the infielder himself forced to score the decisive tally after reaching base on a bad-hop single. To make matters worse, he then stopped payment on his check. None of this did anything for his relations with Chase, on the one hand, or with teammates suspicious of his behavior, on the other, and it didn't come as much of a surprise when he was packed off to the Dodgers in 1919. But when Brooklyn visited Boston in June, the aggrieved gambler had Magee served with papers for non-payment of a debt. This prompted the Dodgers to unload him on the Cubs and NL president John Heydler to start sniffing around into the gambler's charges.

Heydler needn't have bothered because it was Magee himself who, in January 1920, confessed to Cubs owner William Veeck that he had been involved with Chase in the Boston shenanigans, insisting, however, that his bet to the gambler had been on the Reds, not against them. When Veeck responded by cutting him from the Cubs, Magee went to court to get the salary owed him under his contract with Chicago. Thanks to a parade of league officials, newspapermen, and former teammates who showed up as witnesses for the Cubs, he didn't have a chance. More to the point, the June 1920 trial emphasized the role played by Chase in everything, and offered final justification for the unofficial blacklisting of the first baseman. It was three months after the Magee trial that the grand jury began hearing testimony about the 1919 World Series.

GEORGE MAGERKURTH

Magerkurth had the shortest fuse of any umpire. In the very first game of his 19-year (1929–47) National League career, he tossed Giants manager John McGraw. But it was his encounters a decade and more later with the Dodgers, especially with manager Leo Durocher, that sealed his reputation. On one occasion he threw Durocher out of the same game twice, once for arguing a balk call on pitcher Hugh Casey and a second for charging back onto the field when the umpire chastised Casey for throwing at the next batter. Relations between Magerkurth and Brooklyn became so unpleasant that the parade celebrating the team's 1941 pennant included a coffin labeled "Magerkurth." After once fining Durocher $50 for spraying him in the face with saliva, he arrived at home plate at Ebbets Field to find a bag filled with five thousand pennies collected by fans. It was a small miracle that only one Dodgers fan ever jumped out of the stands to pummel him.

His history with the Dodgers notwithstanding, Magerkurth's most famous fight was with Giants shortstop Billy Jurges in 1939, during a dispute about whether a drive into the seats of the Polo Grounds had been fair or foul. While neither of them had anything to do with the play, the umpire flattened the shortstop with one punch after Jurges spat in his face. The results of the ensuing melee included fines for both combatants and a 10-day suspension for Magerkurth. A more lasting consequence of the encounter was the attachment of screens on the foul poles to make such calls easier.

SAL MAGLIE

The ace of the Giants in the early 1950s, Maglie was known as The Barber for his ability to shave corners with his curve and chins with his fastball. While the righthander had only one 20-win season, leading the league with 23 victories in New York's miracle pennant year of 1951, he had a reputation for winning the big game because of his success against the perennially contending Dodgers,. After several years of pitched battles against Brooklyn, he ended up as a Dodger himself in 1956, and his 13 victories were the difference in the club's pennant struggle with the Braves. In the final week of the season, with Milwaukee seeming to have an insurmountable lead, Maglie no-hit the Phillies, then three days later beat the Pirates. In the World Series that year against the Yankees he was the tough-luck loser to Don Larsen's perfect game, 2–0. Before winding up his career in 1958, he completed the New York hat trick by also pitching for the Yankees. Maglie's success with the Giants followed a suspension for being one of the players who jumped to the Mexican League in 1946.

BILLY MAHARG

Maharg's three claims to notoriety were all under an assumed name. First, he was one of the Philadelphia teenagers rounded up by the Tigers to play the Athletics on May 18, 1912, after the regular Detroit team had staged a walkout over the suspension of Ty Cobb. Second, he was the only one to reappear in the majors after that game—turning up with the Phillies for another single-game appearance, in 1916. Third, he became a critical whistle-blower in the 1919 Black Sox scandal, sharing details about the conspiracy with Jimmy Isaminger of the Philadelphia *North American* just as the games were being probed in Chicago. A gambler and occasional boxer, Maharg fancied spelling his real name—Graham—backward.

WALTER MALMQUIST

Playing for York of the Nebraska State League in 1913, Malmquist batted .477—the highest average in organized baseball since the founding of the National League in 1876. The outfielder never made it to the big leagues.

JIM MALONEY

Maloney is the only hurler to carry more than one no-hit game into extra innings. On June 14, 1965 the Cincinnati righthander stumbled through 10 innings against New York, walking a no-hitter record 10 batters, before Johnny Lewis led off the 11th with a home run to defeat him. A couple of months later, on August 19, he pitched a 10-inning no-hitter against the Cubs. Maloney, who had a career record of 134–84 before arm miseries forced his retirement, also no-hit the Astros, on April 30, 1969.

ABE AND EFFA MANLEY

A Camden numbers banker, Manley moved to New York after mobsters bombed his nightclub and set himself up as a real estate investor in Harlem. But then he met Effa at Yankee Stadium during a 1932 World Series game, and she convinced him to invest in the Negro leagues.

Purchasing the Brooklyn Eagles and Newark Dodgers, Manley consolidated them into the Newark Eagles in 1936, operating the club until his death 10 years later. Effa, a white woman who passed for a fair-skinned black, was the club's business manager and succeeded her husband as owner. Even before his death she had been partial to younger players, as much for the affairs she carried on with them as for any on-field talent, and often insisted that a current interest play on a day when her ladies club would be at the ballpark so she could show him off. One of her favorites was dandyish pitcher Terris McDuffie, but when she and the hurler had a knockdown lovers quarrel in a train station in 1938, Abe traded him to the New York Black Yankees for two bats and a pair of sliding pads. Effa was a ferocious negotiator and forced Bill Veeck to pay her for the release of Larry Doby so the Cleveland owner could integrate the American League in 1947. She sold the team the following year.

LES MANN

Mann had a creditable 16-year career as an outfielder wandering from one NL team to another, but he made a greater impression off the field. After playing regularly for the 1914 Miracle Braves, for example, he angered the league establishment by becoming a prize catch for the insurgent Federal League the following season. Then, as a key member of the 1918 pennant-winning Cubs, he was in the forefront of a rebellion by Chicago and Boston Red Sox players that threatened to interrupt the World Series unless owners of the two teams were more generous in sharing the gate receipts. In 1936 Mann was also responsible for organizing the first team of baseball players to perform in the Olympics. (Earlier baseball demonstrations had been given by track-and-field athletes.) Because the Olympics in question were those held in Nazi Berlin, the initiative was frowned upon by major league baseball, which wanted to avoid the hot debate whether the United States should be part of the Hitler extrava-

ganza. With funds raised from private investors and the General Mills cereal company, Mann led a group of collegians and members of the Penn Athletic Club to Germany for a split-squad contest. (The only participant to reach the major leagues later on was pitcher Bill Sayles.) Estimates varied on how many curious Germans packed Berlin Stadium to watch the game; the lowest reported figure was 90,000. In his own subsequent report to major league owners, Mann claimed that the attendance was 125,000, which would make it the largest crowd ever to see a baseball game. For years afterward, however, the former outfielder had to refute press charges that the amateur players had given the stadium the Nazi salute before playing ball.

FELIX MANTILLA

Mantilla was at opposite ends of the two most notorious errors of the 1959 season. On May 26 the Milwaukee shortstop led off the 13th inning of a game against Pittsburgh by hitting a grounder to Don Hoak that the Pirates third baseman threw away; the miscue ended Harvey Haddix's perfect game. In the 12th inning on the final day of the season, Mantilla himself fired wildly to first after grabbing a bounding ball hit by the Dodgers Carl Furillo; the misplay sent Gil Hodges home with the pennant run for Los Angeles in the second game of that year's special playoffs.

MICKEY MANTLE (Hall of Fame, 1974)

Named for Hall of Famer Mickey Cochrane and raised by his father to emulate his namesake, Mantle combined power and average as no other switch-hitter had previously; nevertheless, it took a decade of spectacular slugging feats for him to gain forgiveness for a host of perceived sins, not the least of which was being Joe DiMaggio's successor in center field at Yankee Stadium.

In an 18-year (1951–68) all-Yankees career, Mantle belted 536 home runs while averaging .298. His 10 seasons above .300 and four with at least 40 round-trippers included league-leading totals in home runs four times, in slugging on three occasions, in runs scored in six seasons, and in walks in five different years. He won the first of three MVP trophies in 1956 for his Triple Crown year of .353, 52 home runs, and 130 RBIs; he won the other awards in 1957 and 1963. Mantle holds records for the most homers by a switch-hitter and for the most round-trippers (18), runs scored, RBIs, and walks in World Series competition.

With an assist from club PR director Red Patterson, Mantle introduced the era of the tape-measure home run with a titanic blast off Chuck Stobbs on April 17, 1952; the ball was alleged by Patterson to have traveled 565 feet over the back wall of Washington's Griffith Stadium's left-field bleachers. Two later shots hit the filigree wrought-iron façade above the third deck in Yankee Stadium's right field; one, off Pedro Ramos of the Senators on May 30, 1956, struck 18 inches from the top of the façade and was as close as any big leaguer had come to hitting a ball out of the Bronx park; another, off the Athletics Bill Fischer on May 22, 1963, landed just below the earlier one but was still rising when it caromed.

Mantle was anything but a one-dimensional player. An excellent bunter, he was adept at dragging the ball lefthanded for a base hit; his speed also enabled him to reach double figures in steals in six consecutive seasons. He accomplished all this even though hobbled by a succession of injuries that left teammates and opponents wondering how he managed to suit up, let alone excel on the diamond. His most infamous injury was a torn knee he suffered stepping on an open drain in the Yankee Stadium outfield during the second game of the 1951 World Series. Perhaps his most statistically significant setback was an infection that resulted from a flu shot administered by a doctor recommended by broadcaster Mel Allen in early September 1961. With 53 homers at the time, he continued to play every day but hit only one more the rest of the season, while teammate Roger Maris went on to establish a new major league record with 61.

For all his accomplishments, Mantle was booed by the home fans throughout the 1950s. Every year there was a new reason for the catcalls. In his rookie season it was his slow start after an avalanche of favorable advance publicity and a temporary demotion to the minors. In 1952 it was because he had been moved from right to center to take over for a retired DiMaggio. In 1953 it was because he had failed a physical examination for the army. In 1954 it was because he lacked the panache of New York rival Willie Mays. Even after his Triple Crown year, the boobirds were over him for every strikeout (there were 1,710 of them in his career) and for temper tantrums that led him to smash dugout water coolers or whatever else was handy after a failure at the plate. Regular pronouncements by manager Casey Stengel that "every year he ought to lead the league in everything" didn't help matters.

Attitudes in both the press and the grandstand changed with the arrival of Maris, and especially during their 1961 race after Ruth's record when Maris became the public whipping boy. But by then Mantle had begun to slow down, the victim of too much late-night carousing as much as of the accumulated effects of his various injuries. The hard living was linked to a fear that he, too, would contract the hereditary Hodgkin's disease that killed his grandfather, father, and later a son, all before age 40. Even at 37, when he retired, Mantle was already cracking, "If I'd known I was going to last this long, I'd have taken better care of myself when I was younger." Despite the sentiment, Mantle did not enter a rehabilitation program until 1994, a year before his death.

MOXIE MANUEL

Every pitcher ever removed for a pinch-hitter should be grateful to Manuel. Taken out in the eighth inning of a game against the Yankees on June 14, 1908, he watched as his White Sox rallied to come from behind to win; afterward, American League president Ban Johnson established the precedent of awarding a victory to the hurler lifted in such circumstance rather than to his successor on the mound.

HEINIE MANUSH (Hall of Fame, 1964)

Manush never allowed being traded bother him. In his 17-year (1923–39) career the lefty-swinging outfielder won a hitting title with one team, led the American League in hits for a second one, and paced American Leaguers in both hits and triples while on a third. The lifetime .330 batter started out with the Tigers, with whom he captured the batting title in 1926 with a .378 mark. Following a clash with manager George Moriarty, he was dealt to the Browns for the 1928 season, matching that .378 high, banging out a league-best 241 safeties and 47 doubles; he wasn't so bad the following year, either, in averaging .355 with another 204 hits and another league-leading 45 doubles. Swapped to the Senators in the middle of the 1930 season because St. Louis wanted power hitter Goose Goslin, Manush found Griffith Stadium equally appealing, batting over .300 for five straight years, collecting two more 200-hit seasons, and staying in double figures in both doubles and triples. Before he was finished, he would also register two seasons of 100 RBIs and six years of at least 100 runs scored.

RABBIT MARANVILLE (Hall of Fame, 1954)

No one in Cooperstown invites as much of a "You had to be there" reaction as Maranville. A .258 batter over 23 years (1912–33, 1935) with five National League teams, the shortstop-second baseman had the range to top middle infielders in putouts six times, assists four times, double plays five times, and fielding average three times, but also had seasons of 74 and 65 errors—high even for miscues of ambition. What has never been debated about Maranville, on the other hand, was his flair (he patented the basket catch before Willie Mays) and his stature as a Hall of Fame practical joker. The list of his diamond antics includes going up to bat by crawling through the legs of the home plate umpire; sticking eyeglasses on umpires in the middle of arguments; and, on the pretext of administering first aid to a scratched arbiter, "discovering" one facial nick after another until he had completely covered his victim in iodine. His exploits off the field (usually fueled by alcohol) ran the gamut from walking on the ledges of highrise hotels and dangling teammates from upper windows to pursuing a stage career of singing, telling jokes, and demonstrating his catches at the belt buckle.

Maranville came up with the Braves and teamed with Johnny Evers to give the club the best middle infield defense in the league in its 1914 championship season. His next stop was Pittsburgh, where he even managed solid offensive years of .294 and .295, but also turned so unruly off the field that he caused one managerial firing and thought nothing of involving even prim owner Barney Dreyfuss in his gags. In 1925 Cubs president William Veeck decided the best solution for his antics was to make him the manager—an experiment that lasted only a few weeks when the infielder took his players out to celebrate every win as though it were a World Series victory, engaged in a headline-making fight with a Brooklyn cabdriver, emptied a spittoon on fellow train passengers, and made life hell for traveling secretary John Seys. In between subsequent travels to the Dodgers, Cardinals, and Braves (again), Maranville cured his alcoholism, so that when he returned to Boston,

his constant needling of owner-manager Emil Fuchs was at least a sober commentary. For all practical purposes, Maranville's career ended when he broke his leg in a collision at home plate in spring training of 1934, causing him to miss the entire season and retire after an ineffective comeback effort in 1935. So painful were the multiple fractures he suffered in the collision that he called on on-deck hitter Shanty Hogan to knock him out; the catcher accommodated him with a single punch.

FIRPO MARBERRY

Baseball's first great relief pitcher, Marberry led the American League in appearances six times and in saves five times in the 1920s and early 1930s while working for the Senators. The righthander was pushed into the bullpen role by the fact that Washington's starters of the period were all over 35 and prone to running out of gas. He owed a lot of his effectiveness to what became known locally as Marberry Time—the twilight hours in which the late innings of afternoon games were usually played in the capital. An unrepentant fastballer, Marberry played a key role in Washington pennants in 1924 and 1925, and then in Detroit's 1934 flag. For all his speed, however, he had relatively few strikeouts, breaking the 100-mark only once in his 14-year (1923–36) career.

Paradoxically, Marberry's record as a starting pitcher (94–52) was extraordinary. The pitcher, whose real name was Frederick, gained his nickname form his resemblance to the heavyweight fighter who once knocked Jack Dempsey out of the ring.

JUAN MARICHAL (Hall of Fame, 1983)

Marichal was the best righthander in baseball for most of the 1960s, turning in a record of 154–65 (.703) for the Giants between 1963 and 1969. Because of Bob Gibson and Sandy Koufax, however, he never won a Cy Young Award. His career mark of 243–142 (with 2.89 ERA) included six 20-win seasons and leading the National League in ERA (2.10) in 1969.

On August 22, 1965 Marichal was involved in one of the most violent brawls in diamond history after he attacked Dodgers catcher John Roseboro with his bat. The melee was ignited by the hurler's belief that Roseboro was returning the ball to Koufax by way of his ear in retaliation for some alleged knockdown pitches. When Marichal clubbed the receiver with his bat, a free-for-all ensued. Marichal was fined $1,750 and suspended for nine days. The suspension cost him two starts, and San Francisco ended up losing the pennant to Los Angeles by two games.

ROGER MARIS

When Hank Aaron was chasing Babe Ruth's career home run record, he had to deal with morons of an anonymous kind; when Maris was chasing Ruth's season home run mark, he at least knew the moron was sitting in the commissioner's office. If nothing else, Commissioner Ford Frick's insistence on asterisking the lefty-swinging outfielder's 61st home run in 1961 ultimately had the converse effect of pointing up the negligible difference in establishing major league marks established within the former 154-game schedule and the newer 162-game slate.

Maris took a controversial path to his 1961 celebrity as a member of the Yankees. Originally brought to the major leagues by the Indians in 1957, he was traded to the Athletics the following year by Frank Lane in a move widely predicted as the prelude to a second swap, to New York. Even usually somnolent American League president Will Harridge, already under fire for allowing Kansas City to operate as a major league farm club for the Yankees, was moved to caution the Athletics not to send the outfielder to the Bronx for at least 18 months. Kansas City owner Arnold Johnson obeyed and at one point was on the verge of dealing Maris to Pittsburgh for Bill Mazeroski, but then came to his senses and, only a few hours after the 18-month period had expired, did indeed send him to New York.

Maris's first year in pinstripes, in 1960, netted him the first of two consecutive MVP trophies for belting 39 home runs and pacing the league in both RBIs (112) and slugging (.581). But that performance was quickly forgotten in the circus atmosphere surrounding his 1961 effort. In pure numbers, he tagged 61 home runs and led the AL in both RBIs (142) and runs (132). What went less noticed (except by his teammates and adversaries) was that he also consolidated his standing as one of the game's best all-around players—fielding, throwing, and running as intelligently as athletically. Far more conspicuous was the media caravan that grew longer the closer Maris got to Ruth's fabled number and his growingly sullen reactions to being the center of national attention. Making everything worse were the Frick ruling

and the clear preference of Yankees rooters for Mickey Mantle (who ended up with 54 homers) to break the record before the outsider from Kansas City did. Maris became so frayed by the various pressures that he began losing his hair.

Maris finally broke the record with a blow into the right-field seats off Boston's Tracy Stallard in the last game of the season before a Yankee Stadium crowd of merely 23,154. The modest attendance was attributed to the slighted significance the asterisk had given the feat. When longtime New York fan Sal Durante sought to give Maris the ball he had caught in the stands, the star declined, insisting that Durante should get the $5,000 posted for the ball by a California restaurateur. He would say later that Durante's generosity meant more to him than the media pressures and all the catcalls from the pro-Ruth and pro-Mantle fans.

In 1967 Maris was dealt to the Cardinals, for whom he played a key role in back-to-back pennants before retiring. In the 1967 World Series against the Red Sox he batted .385 with seven RBIs.

RUBE MARQUARD (Hall of Fame, 1971)

On the mound, on the stage, and in team lore, Marquard was the most accomplished of John McGraw's starstruck Giants in the early part of the century. The fastballing southpaw had three successive 20-win seasons between 1911 and 1913, topping the National League in winning percentage and strikeouts in 1911 and in victories (26) in 1912. His 1912 numbers included a record 19 consecutive games; he was denied a 20th by scoring rules of the day that didn't recognize his right to a victory for being on the hill as a reliever when his team overcame a deficit to win. For all his achievements, however, Marquard remained very much the club's second pitcher behind Christy Mathewson.

Off the field Marquard was one of several Giants of the period whose name was as likely to pop up in show business columns as on the sports page. He toured the country with Blossom Seely, the reigning queen of vaudeville, later marrying her after being chased through several states by her estranged husband and process servers. Marquard also appeared in the Hollywood film *Nineteen Straight* with Maurice Costello.

After his three big years with New York, Marquard was waived to the Dodgers, where he contributed more sting to the city rivalry between the clubs. Although he never again won 20, his 13 victories and 1.58 ERA in 1916 played a big role in a Brooklyn pennant, and he came back the following season with 19 wins. Marquard's career mark was 201–177, with a 3.08 ERA.

MIKE MARSHALL

Marshall should have been one of the most influential pitchers of the 1970s, but his maverick behavior tended to estrange even those who were awed by his stamina on the mound and impressed by the fervor of his ideas off it. He has also spawned conflicting stories about his role in organizing the players' strikes of the 1970s.

A righthanded reliever who specialized in a screwball, Marshall initiated his 14-year (1967, 1969–81) career with the Tigers, moving on to eight other teams before he called it quits. In 1974 he became the first bullpen specialist to win the Cy Young Award, when his 15 victories, 21 saves, and record 106 appearances provided the backbone for a Los Angeles pennant. His appearances record topped his own National League mark of 92, set the year before for Montreal. He also set the standard of 90 games for the American League while with Minnesota in 1979.

Marshall attributed his durability to his personal theories on physical conditioning, acquired while gaining a doctorate in kinesiology. This left him constantly at odds with managers and pitching coaches, and was the main reason for his travels from team to team. What especially alarmed some of the older guard was his influence on young hurlers who only had to see his effectiveness to begin raising questions of their own about the tried and true methods of developing hurlers. But although Marshall was always glad to share his insights on conditioning, he also unnerved would-be disciples with a more general skepticism of the role of major leaguers in American society. One of his favorite themes was identifying himself as an educator rather than a ballplayer. He also had little use for the questions of sportswriters, once describing them as "useless at best." As for fans, he objected on principle to signing autographs, occasionally crossexamining an autograph seeker on the relevance of his quest to anything meaningful.

Teams that weren't put off by Marshall's ideas on conditioning and public relations were quick to jettison him because of his union activism. But although one of the Players Association's earliest advocates of militancy in dealing with owners, the pitcher has always been coy about the reasons why he cast the only negative vote on the 1976 free agency agreement. According to Association director Marvin Miller, Marshall was simply misguided in initially resisting any accord that didn't demand all-out free agency rather than permitting it only after six years of big league service. Another reading of the vote, however, is that it was a Marshall-Miller tactic for allowing the latter to pose to the owners as a moderate alternative to more radical views from within the Association. The most glaring case of Marshall's paying for his union militancy occurred in 1980, when he was cut by the Twins despite overcoming a bad start to yield only one run in 12 innings. The Players Association filed a grievance to obtain the full amount of salary still due on the reliever's contract, and Minnesota owner Calvin Griffith settled before the case went to the National Relations Board.

PAUL AND NANCY MARSHALL

The Marshalls were 1993 season ticketholders in San Diego who filed an unprecedented class-action suit against the Padres for trading away their best players. The basis of the action was a preseason form letter from club president Dick Freeman to ticketholders that promised San Diego would contend for years to come because of a nucleus of young stars who would not be dealt away. Soon afterward, the team began to pare its payroll by trading off such key players as Gary Sheffield, Tony Fernandez, and Darrin Jackson. The Marshalls' suit was settled out of court, with the Padres committed to liberalizing their refund policy and the plaintiffs withdrawing a demand that the franchise vow not to trade slugger Fred McGriff. Five days after the agreement was reached, the club unloaded McGriff on the Braves.

BILLY MARTIN

As both player and manager, Martin excelled under pressure—on the field. As soon as he was in a clubhouse or bar, however, he turned into a model study in self-destruction. Unfortunately for someone desperate to be thought of always as a Yankee, he found more than one accomplice in pursuing his bent.

A light-hitting second baseman for 11 seasons between 1950 and 1961, Martin saved his most memorable moments as a player for the World Series. His most conspicuous performances were a game-saving shoetop catch of a Jackie Robinson pop with the bases loaded in the seventh game of the 1952 World Series against the Dodgers and a record 12 hits, including an RBI single to drive in the Series-ending run, against the same Brooklyn club a year later. But weighing against him, at least in the eyes of New York general manager George Weiss, were his truculence on the field (Clint Courtney and Jimmy Piersall were notable sparring partners) and his late-night carousing off it (usually with Mickey Mantle and Whitey Ford in tow). Weiss found his excuse to unload him after a Martin birthday party at the Copacabana night club on May 16, 1957; although the infielder had nothing to do with a drunk who started bothering the celebrating party and outfielder Hank Bauer was the one to flatten the pest with a punch, the general manager ignored even manager Casey Stengel to trade him to Kansas City.

Out of New York, Martin bounced around for four-and-a-half more years, landing with six different clubs; he distinguished himself chiefly in this period by breaking the jaw of Cubs reliever Jim Brewer and bringing on a lawsuit that took nine years to settle. Remaining with the Minnesota organization after his retirement in 1961 (with a .257 career batting average), he got his first managerial shot in 1969 after a season-long barrage of mail and phone calls from fans calling for his promotion from the coaching lines. Despite a divisional title, his relationship with Calvin Griffith began to sour when the Twins owner became convinced that his frequent scenes with umpires were to gain personal headlines. It was destroyed for good when Martin worked over one of his own pitchers, Dave Boswell, after getting hit accidentally while trying to break up a barroom fight.

It was the same story in Detroit: Two successful years and another division title with a veteran club were followed by a series of petty altercations with general manager Jim Campbell. Martin was finally dismissed after admitting that he ordered Tigers pitchers to throw at Cleveland batters in retaliation for Gaylord Perry's spitballing. The next stop was Texas, where owner Brad Corbett declared he would have fired his own mother for him. He departed again a year-and-a-half later, after taking the young club from last to second and then taking the heat for Corbett's suddenly extravagant expectations. Then the curtain was raised on a years-long Yankees psycho-

drama with owner George Steinbrenner and outfielder Reggie Jackson.

Martin returned to Yankee Stadium as manager to complete a third-place finish in 1975, then took a relatively calm pennant in 1976. Despite this success, Steinbrenner and general manager Gabe Paul engineered a series of offseason deals that irritated the touchy manager, sending favorites Oscar Gamble and Dock Ellis elsewhere; displacing a third, Fred Stanley, with the acquisition of Bucky Dent; and saddling the manager with an unwanted Ken Holtzman. The straw that broke the camel's back, however, was signing the strutting free agent Jackson. The inevitable explosion took only a few months—already a period filled with players conspiring against Martin, Steinbrenner firing him at least five times, everyone resenting Jackson's incessant blather about "the magnitude of me" and celebration of himself as "the straw that stirs the drink," and Martin attacking the slugger's ego by dropping him from the cleanup spot and making him the designated hitter. After Jackson played a bloop single into a double in a nationally televised game on June 18, Martin sent Paul Blair out to right field to replace him in the middle of the inning. Viewers from coast to coast then watched the manager having to be held back from going after the near-hysterical outfielder in the dugout.

This turned out to be merely a prelude to events in 1978. Capping off a period during which Jackson both disobeyed a bunt sign and bunted when told not to and during which Steinbrenner was said to be discussing a trade of managers with the White Sox, an overwrought Martin allowed to reporters in late July as how "the two of them deserve each other—one's a born liar, the other's convicted." The reference to Steinbrenner's suspension for making illegal contributions to Richard Nixon's presidential campaign brought the axe down. But then only a few weeks later a packed house at Yankee Stadium on Old Timers Day was stunned by the announcement that successor Bob Lemon would be promoted to the front office in 1980, with Martin coming back as manager. With that timetable pushed up by six months, Martin was back in the Yankees dugout in June 1979, only to be taunted throughout the rest of the season by Steinbrenner with the necessity for good behavior. In October the manager got into a fistfight in a Minnesota hotel with a marshmallow salesman named Joseph Cooper and was fired a second time.

Martin's greatest managerial success came not with the Yankees but during a subsequent stint with Oakland; at the very least, the experience with the A's offered the most graphic evidence of his strength (an aggressive offense) and weakness (an inability to handle a pitching staff) as a dugout boss. Hired by Charlie Finley in 1980, he took over a team with young pitchers, a talented outfield, and a lusterless infield, taught it Billy Ball (emphasizing the hit-and-run, the suicide squeeze, double and even triple steals, and stealing home), and finished second. The downside was a propensity to overuse his starting pitchers, so much so that Rick Langford (28 wins), Mike Norris (22), and Matt Keough (20) became the only teammates to finish one-two-three in complete games.

Given the responsibility for personnel decisions in 1981 by the Haas family after it had bought out Finley, Martin used the same tactics to turn a first-place finish in the first half of the split season into a West Division win. The end of his enchanted period with the A's began in the middle of the 1982 season, when he once again started with the irrational scenes that always prefaced his departures. This time it was his demand for a five-year extension on his contract and an office-destroying tantrum after a defeat that somehow also ended up being about his pact. Club president Roy Eisenhardt could also point to his overuse of young starters Langford, Norris, Keough, Steve McCatty, and Brian Kingman—and their resulting sore arms—when he announced the end of Martin's stay in the Bay Area in October.

Martin eventually returned to manage the Yankees for all of 1983, most of 1985, and part of 1988 in what became an obsessive quest to please Steinbrenner sufficiently to be named to the post permanently. Rumors of his return for a sixth tour continued up to his death in an automobile accident on Christmas Day 1989. Most final analyses of his life cited alcoholism, an insatiable appetite for young women, and a need for dominance (sometimes physical, sometimes psychological) as contributing to his inability to handle success.

J. C. MARTIN

Martin's sole at bat in World Series play produced an explosive turning point victory for the 1969 Miracle Mets. Pinch-hitting in the bottom of the 10th inning of the fourth game with New York and Baltimore deadlocked at 1–1, the lefty-swinging catcher bunted down the first-base line with runners on first and second. Orioles pitcher Pete Richert fielded the bunt and fired to first, but the ball struck Martin's wrist and caromed into foul territory, allowing pinch-runner Rod Gaspar to score the winning run from second. Baltimore jumped all over home plate umpire Shag Crawford that Martin had run to first illegally within the baseline, but the protest was to no avail despite the apparent legitimacy of the complaint. The Mets clinched their championship the next day.

PEPPER MARTIN

Martin was the rambunctious heart of the 1930s Gas House Gang teams in St. Louis. A righthanded outfielder-third baseman, he hit .298 in 13 seasons between 1928 and 1944 with the Cardinals and double that in his ability to aggravate managers and general manager Branch Rickey with his penchant for doing anything for a laugh. On the field his forte was the kind of daring baserunning that enabled him to lead the National League in steals three times. Martin had his greatest offensive moments in two World Series: In 1931 against the Athletics, he went 12-for-24 with five stolen bases, a home run, and four doubles; in 1934 he helped defeat the Tigers by going 11-for-31.

Martin's notions of daring extended to never wearing an athletic supporter. His ideas of leisure included trapping snakes for a local zoo and racing cars; the latter pastime usually caused him to miss batting practice at home games, driving manager Frankie Frisch into regular spouts of fury until his third baseman took the field and showed no effects from his morning derring-do. A beaning inspired Rickey to call him The Wild Horse of the Osage, one of several tags dreamed up by the executive in the 1930s to give more box office color to his players.

BUCK MARTINEZ

Martinez suffered baseball's most productive career-throttling injury. On July 9, 1985 the Blue Jays catcher fractured his leg tagging Seattle's Phil Bradley on a play at the plate, then fired wildly over third in an effort to nail Gorman Thomas. With left fielder George Bell retrieving the ball and throwing home as Thomas rounded the bag, the prostrate receiver held his ground and completed an excruciating double play. Martinez attempted to come back in 1986 as a backup, but hit only .181 and hobbled into retirement at the end of the season.

DENNIS MARTINEZ

Martinez went from the bottom of a bottle with the Orioles in the early 1980s to the status of a national hero in his native Nicaragua, where he was tagged *El Presidente* for fighting his alcoholism and rebounding as one of the National League's top winners with the Expos in the late 1980s and 1990s. His biggest moment in Montreal came on July 28, 1991, when he twirled a perfect game against the Dodgers.

When Martinez ended his 23-year (1976–98) career, he retired with 245 victories, two more than Juan Marichal for the most by a Latin American pitcher.

EDGAR MARTINEZ

Martinez figures to be the litmus test on the Hall of Fame's receptivity to inducting a designated hitter. Originally a third baseman, a series of leg injuries cut down further his already compromised range in the early 1990s, since when he has served almost exclusively as Seattle's designated hitter. In that role he has won a second batting title, driven in 100 runs six times (including one league-leading total), topped the 50-doubles mark twice, and paced the AL in on-base percentage three times. His lifetime average of .319 entering the 2002 season, together with his years-long reputation among teammates and opponents as baseball's "most natural hitter," figure to prevail ultimately over old guard objections that even the most inept fielders of the Harmon Killebrew stripe are preferable to designated hitters in Cooperstown.

Martinez had one of the most dramatic hits in the history of postseason play in the fifth and deciding game of the 1995 Division Series. With Seattle down by a run and two outs in the bottom of the 11th inning, he clouted a two-run double off New York's Jack Mc-Dowell to move the Mariners into the League Championship Series for the first time. The blow not only accounted for his 12th hit and ninth and 10th runs batted in during the Series, but clinched the prospects for the franchise to get approval for a new stadium and remain in Seattle.

PEDRO MARTINEZ

The most deceptive of the dominating pitchers at the turn of the millennium, Martinez has had more difficulties with his employers and his body than with opposition hitters. Both problems came to the fore in 2001 when the Red Sox were slow to disable him with a bad arm because of an unwillingness to admit the team could not overcome the Yankees for the AL East Division title.

Martinez and his 95-mph fastball first raised eyebrows while with the Dodgers in 1993, when he won 10 games and averaged more than a strikeout an inning in a relief role. But convinced the 165-pound righthander would never have the stamina of his older brother Ramon to be a consistent winner, Los Angeles dealt him to Montreal after the season for second baseman Delino DeShields. At first Martinez's precocious reputation as a headhunter didn't desert him: His 23 starts in 1994, for example, produced 11 hit batsmen, 12 ejections, and three major field brawls. Even more illustrative of his habits (and of the assumption he would fall back on them whatever the situation), Reggie Sanders once charged him on the mound after being hit by a pitch in the eighth inning—even though the Cincinnati outfielder's right to first base broke up a perfect game. Under the tutelage of pitching coach Joe Kerrigan, however, Martinez brought his aim and his temper under control; adding a curveball and the best changeup in the league to his repertoire, he received his first Cy Young Award in 1997 for a 17–8 record, 305 strikeouts, and a league-leading 1.90 ERA. His reward was to be traded to Boston after the season for a couple of pitching prospects because of Montreal's inability to meet his expected free agent demands.

With the Red Sox, where Kerrigan had preceded him by a year, Martinez raised his game to another level. In 1999 he turned in one of the most blistering pitching performances in history when he ran away from the rest of the league with his record of 23–4, 313 strikeouts, and a 2.07 ERA. Not only was his ratio of 13.2 strikeouts per nine innings the best ever (until surpassed by Randy Johnson two years later), but his 313 strikeouts made for a record-burning ratio of 8.5–1 for his mere 37 walks. (In his third Cy Young season of 2000 he topped even this, striking out 284 and walking just 32, for a ratio of 8.89–1.) Also in 1999 the Dominican righthander took the mound in Fenway Park as the AL's starter in the All-Star Game, striking out his first four batters and five of the only six he faced. He provided still more drama in the Division Series against Cleveland, when, after being forced to leave the first game with a strained back muscle, he made an unexpected appearance from the bullpen in the fifth and decisive game, keeping the Indians hitless for six innings until Boston won. He strolled to his Cy Young Award, and would have also taken MVP honors over Ivan Rodriguez if two writers hadn't left him totally off their ballots with the rationalization that pitchers didn't deserve consideration. With or without the MVP acknowledgement he had become the AL's biggest box draw by the end of the year.

In both 1999 and 2000 Martinez lost time to arm miseries. In 2001 a diagnosis of a torn labrum ended any chance Boston had of catching the Yankees in the division race, but that didn't prevent general manager Dan Duquette and Kerrigan from sending the organization ace out to the hill for a couple of dangerous starts. Even Boston fans who couldn't get enough of the stylish righthander were disgusted by the abuse.

BOBBY MATHEWS

Although Frank Corridon (in 1902) is usually cited as the pioneer of the spitball, Mathews was known to have been loading up the ball as early as 1867, while still a teenager on the Lord Baltimore club. Four years later the righthander won the first professional league game when he shut out the National Association Cleveland Forest Citys for the Fort Wayne Kekiongas, 2–0. That would also be the lowest scoring game in the four-year history of the league that preceded the formation of the National League in 1876.

EDDIE MATHEWS (Hall of Fame, 1978)

Half of the greatest one-two home-run combination in the history of baseball, Mathews was destined to be eclipsed among third basemen in Cooperstown by Mike Schmidt as much as he was in Braves lineups by Hank Aaron. But his slugging marks and able glove make him the runner-up only to Schmidt as the major leagues' greatest all-time power-hitting third baseman; among other things, he shares with Schmidt the record for most consecutive seasons (nine) in the NL with at least 30 home runs.

Between 1954 and 1966 Mathews and Aaron teamed up for 863 home runs—more than the combination of Babe Ruth and Lou Gehrig as teammates. Mathews was the only Brave to play with the franchise in Boston, Milwaukee, and Atlanta. Despite that he had to find out through a beat writer that, after 15 years with the organization, he had been traded to the Astros for the 1967 season. When the Atlanta press chided the front office for such shabbiness, the club sent a letter of apology addressed to "Edward" Mathews. (His first name was Edwin.) He came back to manage the team at the end of 1972 but lasted only until midway through 1974.

CHRISTY MATHEWSON (Hall of Fame, 1936)

Mathewson was the only one of the National League's great early-20th century pitchers who would have received the *Good Housekeeping* Seal of Approval. In studied contrast to his tobacco-chewing contemporaries, he was a Bucknell student who had headed two college literary societies, sung for the campus choir, and attracted attention for his championship play in everything from football to checkers; as a member of John McGraw's rowdy Giants over the first 17 years of the century, he was publicized as such a model of clean living (he was rarely asked to pitch on Sunday because of a promise he had made to his fanatically religious mother) that he inspired fictional heroes for children and was considered personally responsible for attracting women and families to the Polo Grounds. While much of this was image making at its best (among other things, he was an obsessive gambler), Mathewson also happened to be good enough to post 373 wins, tying him with Grover Cleveland Alexander for the National League record, and to gain election to Cooperstown in 1936 as one of the Five Immortals.

Mathewson reached the Giants before McGraw did, and that was almost his undoing. In December 1900 he was traded by Cincinnati to New York for the over-the-hill Amos Rusie in what has been called the worst swap in baseball history; in fact, however, the deal was engineered by Reds owner John T. Brush shortly before his own departure for the Polo Grounds, so that, whatever else was involved, there was no Cincinnati miscalculation. Even though the righthander immediately produced the first of 13 20-win seasons for the Giants, that wasn't sufficient for Horace Fogel and Heinie Smith, the clowns who managed New York over the first half of the 1902 season and who vied with one another in seeking to convert the mound star to first base and shortstop. Only with McGraw's arrival at the end of the year did the experimenting come to an end.

Between 1903 and 1914 Mathewson's lowest victory total for a season was 22. Four times he topped the 30-mark, and five times he lapped the field in strikeouts. His single greatest year was 1908, when he led the league in wins (37), ERA (1.43), complete games (34), strikeouts (259), and shutouts (11). He was no less formidable in World Series games, employing his famous fadeaway (screwball) to record the most shutouts (four) and complete games (10) in Series history. His stellar moment in October competition came in 1905, when he shut out Connie Mack's Athletics three times in five days for a New York championship. His overall ERA in 11 World Series appearances was 1.15.

From the moment McGraw took over the Giants in 1902, he made it clear he had one set of rules for Mathewson and another set for the rest of his players. The negative side of this for the pitcher was that he was fined twice and three times as heavily as teammates if discovered at one of the endless crap games he promoted and that the manager had banned from the clubhouse ("Matty should have known better"); the positive side was that McGraw and his wife came to regard him as a son, even insisting that the Mathewsons share an apartment with them for an extended period. In the eyes of his teammates Mathewson was the ultimate stand-up guy—a perception that he confirmed in September 1908, when he stood alone on the planet in his insistence that Fred Merkle had touched second base before veering off into the dugout and into history for the game's most infamous bonehead play. His standing with opponents was such that Cubs manager Frank Chance saw nothing ludicrous in offering $50,000 for him even as Chicago and New York were clawing at one another down the stretch of the 1908 season: "Of course, I didn't expect McGraw to say yes," Chance said, "but what did it cost me to dream?"

When Mathewson finally *was* dealt in 1916, it was back to the Reds so that, his pitching career over, he could realize a managerial ambition. The transaction went into the books as the Hall of Fame Trade because it also exported future Cooperstown residents Edd Roush and Bill McKechnie to Cincinnati for infielder Buck Herzog. Mathewson appeared to be on the verge of building the club into respectability when, in 1918, he suddenly signed up for World War I military service. The move followed months of clubhouse turmoil around the ambiguous figure of Hal Chase and was announced at the same time that Mathewson suspended the first baseman for purportedly throwing games. An official hearing convened months later acquitted Chase of the accusations, in part because Mathewson, still in Europe recovering from a poisonous gas accident in a military chemical lab, was unavailable to testify. Upon his return to the U.S. he ended up coaching for McGraw's Giants, whose regular first baseman was none other than Chase.

During the 1919 World Series, which he was covering for *The New York Times,* Mathewson and Chicago sportswriter Hugh Fullerton took careful note of plays they regarded as suspicious by the White Sox; despite going through quite a few pencils, however, he didn't share any of his misgivings about the tainted Series with his readers.

McGraw had never made a secret of his desire to have Mathewson succeed him as New York manager, but that became impossible when his protégé was struck by progressively more serious pulmonary problems—generally attributed to a family history of tuberculosis aggravated by the gas attack. When McGraw helped him get the presidency of the Boston Braves, it was little more than a last hurrah before the TB entered a terminal stage. Mathewson died during the 1925 World Series, at age 47.

GARY MATTHEWS

Few free agents created as much trouble as Matthews did in 1976. No sooner had he been signed away from San Francisco by Ted Turner than Commissioner Bowie Kuhn smacked the Atlanta owner with a tampering charge, levying a $10,000 fine and stripping the Braves of their first-round amateur draft pick in January. When the dissatisfied Giants brought further tampering evidence to Kuhn, the commissioner increased his penalties to a one-year suspension of Turner and the loss of Atlanta's June draft selection. Turner responded by suing Kuhn, but fared only marginally better in the courtroom: regaining the draft picks, but still having to pay the fine and serve the suspension.

In New York, meanwhile, ace righthander Tom Seaver pointed to Atlanta's signing of Matthews as evidence the Mets were not serious about seeking free agent hitters. The criticism soon blew up to a regular war of words between the future Hall of Famer and franchise chairman M. Donald Grant, preparing the ground for Seaver's traumatic June 1977 trade to Cincinnati.

As for Matthews, the righthand-hitting outfielder averaged .283 with decidedly mild power numbers for the Braves in 1977.

DON MATTINGLY

Mattingly played more seasons (14) for the Yankees without appearing a World Series than anyone else in the franchise's history. He seemed particularly plagued in his final two seasons, when the 1994 labor disputes shortcircuited an East Division title for New York and Edgar Martinez's desperation double in 1995 gave the Mariners a Division Series win over the Yankees.

Mattingly won the American League batting championship in 1984 with a .343 mark, then followed that up with MVP honors in 1985 for batting .324 with 35 homers and league-leading numbers in both RBIs (145) and doubles (48). In 1987 the lefthand-hitting first baseman set records for hitting 10 home runs over eight consecutive games and for clouting six grand slam mers in the season. A back injury later robbed him of a good deal of his power. In his lone postseason appearance, against Seattle, he averaged .417 over five games.

GENE MAUCH

Mauch is either the smartest man never to win a pennant or the most expert at pulling defeat out of the jaws of victory. In 26 years of managing the Phillies, Expos, Twins, and Angels between 1960 and 1987, the onetime infielder piloted his clubs to merely two division titles. Worse, even the division victories (with California in 1982 and 1986) ultimately served to solidify his reputation for stumbling inches away from the finish line. In 1982 the Angels took the first two games of the ALCS from Milwaukee, then lost three in row; in 1986 the club had the Red Sox on the ropes in the ninth inning of the fifth game with one out to go, only to have Dave Henderson hit a home run and Boston rumble back for three consecutive wins.

Mauch first attracted the reputation of a loser with the 1964 Phillies, who were in first place by 6 1/2 games with 12 to go but lost 10 in a row, allowing the apparently dead Cardinals to sneak through for the flag. Blame for the collapse was laid to the pilot's insistence on using Jim Bunning and Chris Short on two days rest over the last two weeks of the season. With Minnesota in the mid-1970s he used his "little ball" tactics of the first-inning sacrifice, the stolen base, and the hit-and-run to pull the team up from the depths of the West Division but again presided over August and September skids. For all that, numerous players who have been on Mauch teams have singled him out as the most insightful manager they ever played for.

DAL MAXVILL

Slick-fielding Maxvill might as well have thrown away his bat in his 14-year career in the 1960s and 1970s. A career .217 hitter, the shortstop set several marks for offensive ineptitude. With the Cardinals in 1970, for example, his 89 total bases marked a major league low for players in at least 150 games. Two years earlier he had established the record for most at bats in a World Series (22) without getting a hit.

CHARLIE MAXWELL

Mainly because of his prowess against the Yankees, outfielder Maxwell gained a reputation in the 1950s as The Sunday Home Run Hitter. Although 40 of the Detroit slugger's 148 career home runs were indeed blasted on the seventh day, he also had 23 blows against New York, a staple weekend home attraction for the Tigers. Maxwell always attributed much of his reputation to a Sunday, May 3, 1959, doubleheader against the Yankees, when he reached the seats in his final at bat in the first game, then clouted three more homers in the nightcap.

CARL MAYS

Righthanded submariner Mays is most immediately associated with the only fatal beaning in major league history—that of Cleveland shortstop Ray Chapman. But he was also the booty in an internecine war that came close to wrecking the American League before the Yankees could fully claim his services, then made the club wish it hadn't bothered.

A two-time 20-game winner with the Red Sox by 1919, Mays stalked off the mound in Chicago after working only two innings of a July 13 game. Accepting the pitcher's claims of an injury and personal problems, Boston owner Harry Frazee saw no reason not to trade him to the pennant-contending Yankees shortly afterward. AL president Ban Johnson took exception, however, claiming he couldn't allow a player to be rewarded for the Comiskey Park tantrum. The ensuing fracas saw lawsuits flying back and forth, three club owners threatening to jump to National League, and the other five magnates caving in to their blackmail. With Johnson humbled and his power seriously compromised, Mays went on to win

26 games for New York in 1920 and another (league-leading) 27 the following year.

But in the 1921 World Series against the Giants, Mays aroused the suspicions of, among others, New York manager Miller Huggins and team co-owner Cap Huston by blowing a lead in the eighth inning of Game Four. After the game, sportswriter Fred Lieb carried a tale to Huston about an eyewitness who had seen May's wife signal him on the mound that a payoff had been made just prior to a three-run outburst that put the Giants in the lead. A subsequent investigation by Commissioner Kenesaw Landis turned up nothing, but Huggins never doubted the truth of the accusation and used the hurler infrequently over the next two years. (He made a pointed exception on July 17, 1923, when he left him on the mound to endure a 20-hit, 13-run drubbing by Cleveland.) Mays subsequently spent five years with the Reds, including one last 20-victory season, and one with the Giants.

Chapman's death occurred on August 16, 1920 at the Polo Grounds. The beaning brought numerous death threats to Mays from Indians fans, but there were no physical attacks on him. He himself showed little mental scarring, proving as effective on the hill after the tragedy as before it.

WILLIE MAYS (Hall of Fame, 1979)

When Leo Durocher observed that only the greatest players could hit, hit with power, run, field, and throw, he had Mays in mind. Although the outfielder shared the limelight during his 22-year career for the Giants and Mets (between 1951 and 1973) with a host of other superstars, few exceeded his accomplishments at any of the five and none performed as consistently at his level in all five. Moreover, he not only did it all, he did it with a flair and a style seldom matched.

Mays could hit: The righthanded slugger accumulated 3,283 safeties for a career average of .302 that included 10 seasons above .300 and one batting crown. He could hit with power: He finished his career with 660 home runs (third behind only Hank Aaron and Babe Ruth), including 17 seasons of more than 20 and two topping the 50 mark. Against the Braves on April 30, 1961 he joined the select group of players with four round-trippers in one game. He also posted six season slugging averages above .600, five of them league-leading totals. Mays could run:

He topped the league in stolen bases four consecutive years at the end of the 1950s; he and his godson Barry Bonds are the only players to compile more than 400 homers and more than 300 stolen bases. He could also hit in the clutch: He drove 1,903 runs across the plate (although he never led the league in RBIs) and clouted a record 22 extra-inning homers.

Mays could field. The best center fielder of his era, he covered the vast outfield spaces of the Polo Grounds as if they had been designed with him in mind and won 12 consecutive Gold Gloves beginning with the first such awards in 1957. Most fans point to his back-to-the-plate snare of Vic Wertz's 460-foot blast in the first game of the 1954 World Series against Cleveland as his greatest defensive play. Branch Rickey and other connoisseurs singled out one he made in Pittsburgh's Forbes Field when he caught up to a 400-foot hooking line drive off the bat of Rocky Bridges, and, with his back to the infield and the ball trailing down and to the right, reached out to nab it bare-handed at his knees. He could throw, too: As memorable as his catch off Wertz was, he also whirled and threw on a line to second baseman Davey Williams with enough force to drive himself to the ground and enough accuracy to hold Larry Doby, on second, to one base and to send Al Rosen scurrying back to first. Perhaps his greatest defensive play of all came against the Dodgers on August 15, 1951, just as the Giants were starting the stretch drive that would end with Bobby Thomson's miracle home run. With the score knotted in the eighth inning, the center fielder picked a Carl Furillo drive off his shoetops, spun in the air, and threw a 300-foot perfect strike to nail Billy Cox at the plate. Brooklyn manager Charlie Dressen, flabbergasted for once, could only say, "I'd like to see him do that again."

But the numbers and the eye-opening defensive plays tell only part of the story. Arriving in the major leagues four years after the breaking of the color line, Mays completed the revolution begun by Jackie Robinson. His flash and dash, so common in the Negro leagues, took big league fans by surprise. It wasn't just the belt-high basket catches or the cap flying off his head with every moderately hard run in the outfield or on the bases (a touch Mays later admitted he embellished by choosing headgear a size too small); it wasn't even that he could go from his exploits at the Polo Grounds to a stickball game in Harlem. The additional factor was that, in contrast to the businesslike demeanor of other stars of the 1940s and 1950s (and, in a different way, to the fierce intensity of Robinson), Mays was having fun of a kind communicable to fans. What he very much shared with Robinson, on the other hand, was his perception of baseball as a contact sport—a trait he displayed in his penchant for slowing down around third base to draw a throw, then crashing into the catcher.

The best player of his generation got off to a slow start, making a lone hit in his first 26 at bats after being asked to abandon his .477 batting average with New York's Triple-A farm club in Minneapolis to join the Giants in late May 1951. Although that hit was a homer off Warren Spahn, Durocher had to talk a despondent Mays out of appeals to be sent back to Minneapolis. He went on to take Rookie of the Year honors for his part in the Giants pennant drive that year, and an MVP Award in 1954 for his batting crown (.345), 41 homers, and 110 RBIs in the team's last pennant-winning year in New York.

The darling of New York fans, their collective Say Hey Kid, Mays had several unpleasant surprises when the franchise resettled in San Francisco after the 1957 season. First, there were racial incidents. The seller of the house he wanted to buy tried to back out of the deal at one point behind pressure from neighbors; then, when the sale was finally completed, a brick was tossed through the living room window. More lasting was the Bay Area preference for rookies Orlando Cepeda (in 1958) and Willie McCovey (in 1959), who carried none of the perceived taint of New York. It didn't help, either, that manager Bill Rigney predicted that Mays would top Babe Ruth's 60 home runs, bat .380, and drive in 150 runs, or that Mays himself talked too much about the good old days under mentor Durocher in the Polo Grounds. He might not have lived up to Rigney's predictions, but his career-high .347 average, NL-leading totals in runs scored and stolen bases, 29 homers, and 96 RBIs in 1958 hardly merited the boos that greeted him at Seals Stadium; at the end of the Giants first season on the West Coast fans voted Rookie of the Year Cepeda the team's Most Valuable Player.

The club's move to Candlestick Park in 1960 presented more problems. Hitting into the stadium's unpredictable winds proved frustrating; fielding was even more trying until the center fielder realized that, if he stood stark still after the ball had been hit, he could gauge the direction in which the wind would

take it. It wasn't until 1962 that San Franciscans warmed up to Mays. What it took was an eighth-inning homer on the last day of the season to pull the club into a tie for first, two round-trippers to win the first game of the playoffs against the Dodgers, and a line drive that tore reliever Ed Roebuck's glove off and keyed the game-winning rally in the third and final contest. Mays's prestige among teammates had, on the other hand, always been high, and he needed it all to quell an uprising over some racist remarks by manager Alvin Dark. His main argument to a seething clubhouse was that, whatever Dark's racial views, they had never prevented him from presenting a lineup with a majority of minority players.

In May 1972 Mays returned to New York in a trade with the Mets and received a hero's welcome, especially after homering against the Giants in his first Shea Stadium game in a Mets uniform. His skills diminished, he lasted just long enough to appear in the 1973 World Series against Oakland, first embarrassing himself by falling in pursuit of a line drive that sparked a second-game rally, then redeeming himself with a single to put New York back ahead.

In later years Mays came in for criticism from the Mets for not showing up often enough for his coaching duties, got into a demeaning squabble with the Giants over a mixup about giving his uniform to Cooperstown, and was barred from baseball activities by Commissioner Bowie Kuhn for his employment at Bally's Atlantic City casino. His public appearances frequently suggested a sour man who didn't feel quite appreciated enough for what he had accomplished. What remained constant was his philosophy about playing: "When they hit it, I catch it: When they throw it, I hit it."

BILL MAZEROSKI (Hall of Fame, 2001)

The best defensive second baseman of the 1950s and 1960s, Mazeroski gained even greater fame for the ninth-inning, seventh-game home run that gave Pittsburgh a World Series victory over the Yankees in 1960. That moment of glory was made possible only because Pittsburgh manager Danny Murtaugh succeeded in voiding a trade to send the infielder to Kansas City after the 1958 season for Roger Maris.

Admitted to Cooperstown for his fielding skills and only after a lengthy promotional campaign by supporters, Mazeroski holds records for most double plays by a second baseman in a single season

(161 in 1962) and over a career (1,706 from 1956 to 1972). The .260 hitter spent all 17 of his big league years with Pittsburgh.

JIMMY McALEER

A swift center fielder primarily with the National League Cleveland Spiders in the 1890s, McAleer became one of American League president Ban Johnson's chief lieutenants in his battle to gain respectability for the junior circuit. The bond was developed when Johnson persuaded him to take control of the AL's St. Louis franchise in 1902; as pilot of the Browns, he recruited, among others, Hall of Famers Jesse Burkett and Bobby Wallace from the rival Cardinals. After launching the Browns and serving a brief stint with the Washington Senators, McAleer used Johnson's secret financial support to form a partnership with former AL secretary Bob McRoy for the purchase of a half-interest in the Red Sox in December 1911; another silent partner was a banker who happened to be Boston manager Jake Stahl's father-in-law. Trouble erupted when McAleer insisted, over Stahl's objections, on starting rookie Buck O'Brien in Game Six of the 1912 World Series. Even thought the righthander lost, Boston's championship victory two days calmed tempers—temporarily.

The president and manager were back at it the following year over increasing clubhouse factionalism between the Protestant Masons and the Catholic Knights of Columbus on the team. Faced with a choice between his ally McAleer and the continued financial goodwill of Stahl's father-in-law, Johnson started dropping broad hints that it might be best for all involved if the manager moved up to the front office. McAleer retaliated by replacing Stahl, whom he had accused of encouraging the Masonic faction, with Irish-Catholic catcher Bill Carrigan. He won the battle but lost the war: While he was away on a postseason tour, Johnson arranged for the sale of his and McRoy's shares in the team to Joseph Lannin.

GEORGE McBRIDE

McBride holds the records for the lowest batting (.218) and slugging (.264) averages for players with at least 4,000 at bats. Despite such near-invisible numbers, the shortstop's defensive abilities kept him in the major leagues for 16 years between 1901 and 1920. One ball he didn't catch, however, cost him a managerial career. At the helm of Washington in 1921, McBride suffered partial facial paralysis after being struck by a batting-practice line drive; the injury led to a nervous breakdown, and he never returned as a dugout boss.

JACK McCARTHY

In the top of the first inning on April 24, 1901, while a member of the Indians, McCarthy bounced a ground ball off White Sox third baseman Fred Hartman for the first American League hit. While with the Cubs three years later, the outfielder, sliding across home plate, broke his ankle on a long-handled broom that the plate umpire had cast aside after wiping off the dish; the injury prompted both leagues to dispose of the domestic brooms in use until then and to replace them with the pocket whisk variety. A year after his accident, on April 26, 1905, McCarthy was sufficiently recovered to become the only player to begin three outfield-to-catcher double plays in the same game when he foiled three attempted sacrifice flies by the Pirates.

JOE McCARTHY (Hall of Fame, 1957)

McCarthy is the most successful manager in big league history, compiling a .615 winning percentage in 24 years of piloting between 1926 and 1950. Because he spent 16 of those years with a powerhouse Yankees lineup that won eight of his nine pennants, he was tagged by Jimmy Dykes as "a push-button manager." But the fact is, he never finished out of the first division during an earlier stint with the Cubs or a later one with the Red Sox, either; moreover, he handled a potentially explosive situation involving an envious Babe Ruth as ably as he ever outmaneuvered field opponents.

McCarthy was hired by the Cubs in 1926 despite never having played in the major leagues and never having managed above the American Association; the move drew fire from Grover Cleveland Alexander and other veterans. McCarthy persuaded team president William Veeck to ship Alexander off to the Cardinals, then demonstrated the value of his minor league experience by recommending that the club go after AA outfielders Hack Wilson and Riggs Stephenson. After two fourth-place finishes and a third-place season, the acquisition of Rogers Hornsby from the Braves put the club over the top by 10½ games in 1929.

His pennant win notwithstanding, there were recurrent rumblings throughout the 1930 season that

McCarthy was on his way out, mainly because of his testy reply to owner William Wrigley's criticism of Chicago's losing performance in the World Series against the Athletics; most reports had him going to the Braves as part of a secret codicil to the Hornsby deal. Instead, he ended up with the Yankees, where he introduced to the clubhouse the same coldly professional atmosphere that prevailed in the front office. Card playing was banned. There was a dress code. Players had to be clean shaven at all times. Nevertheless, he won over the Yankees players—all but Ruth, who had grown increasingly vocal about his desire to manage the Yankees and who had now been passed over for a National Leaguer who had never even played in the big leagues. McCarthy's approach to the slugger's frustration was to bide his time, reprimanding others for the same infractions he passed over in silence when Ruth was the culprit. The inevitable showdown came after the 1934 season, when the slugger demanded that owner Jacob Ruppert and general manager Ed Barrow fire McCarthy and install him in his place. By then, however, McCarthy had won his first world championship (in 1932) in the middle of a record streak of 308 games (between August 1931 and August 1933) without being shut out. McCarthy made the tactical gesture of offering to step aside, but it was hardly necessary: The Yankees brass not only rejected Ruth's demands, but showed him the door to the Boston Braves.

McCarthy's Yankees rolled to seven more pennants and six more world championships between 1936 and 1943. The honeymoon finally ended in January 1945, when the flamboyant Larry MacPhail bought a controlling interest in the franchise. The new owner's razzle-dazzle, not to mention his interference, made the club's fall to the depths of fourth place (and a "mere" 81 victories, McCarthy's lowest total) in 1945 intolerable for the manager, whose stomach ailments sent him home to upstate New York in May. MacPhail was able to talk him into returning, but the reconciliation lasted only until a few weeks into the 1946 season, when McCarthy, unable to cope with his employer's antics, a still-foundering team, and constant battles with lefthander Joe Page, quit for good.

After turning down Branch Rickey's offer to manage the Dodgers while Leo Durocher was serving a suspension in 1947, McCarthy turned up as pilot of the Red Sox in 1948. In Boston he brought the Red Sox into a first-place tie with Cleveland but lost the 1948 pennant when he started righthander Denny Galehouse instead of veteran Ellis Kinder in a do-or-die playoff game. The following year, he finished second to New York by a single game when his team failed to beat the Yankees in the last two games of the season. His final year-and-a-half with Boston was marked by impatience with rookies, testiness with veterans he felt were coddled by owner Tom Yawkey, a greater-than-ever suspicion of the press, and a tendency to rely too much on the whiskey bottle kept for him on the end of the bench by trainer Gus Froelich.

TOMMY McCARTHY (Hall of Fame, 1946)

McCarthy owes his Cooperstown standing to having been paired with teammate Hugh Duffy as Boston's Heavenly Twins in the 1890s; he certainly didn't get it through his 13-year (1884–96) average of .292 and fielding percentage of .887. The only future Hall of Famer to debut in the Union Association (with the Boston Reds), the righthand-hitting outfielder ended up playing mostly with the American Association St. Louis Browns and the National League Boston Beaneaters. His specialty play was trapping a pop fly to eliminate speedier runners from the basepaths. Another McCarthy habit—feigning possession of a ball by tipping it from one hand to the other as he ran toward the infield—is sometimes cited as the reason for the rule allowing a runner to tag up and advance as soon as a fly ball makes contact with the fielder; but while he practiced the deception, it wasn't until 1920 that a clean-catch stipulation for advancing the runner was struck from the rulebook.

TIM McCARVER

McCarver has not had to make jokes about his lousy catching career to further his standing as one of the sport's more articulate broadcasters. In a 21-year career (between 1959 and 1980) for the Cardinals, Phillies, Expos, and Red Sox, the lefthand-hitting receiver averaged .271 while developing a reputation as a canny game caller. His best offensive display came with St. Louis in 1964, when he contributed to a World Series win over the Yankees by going 11-for-23 (.478). In 1966 he was the rare catcher to lead a league in triples.

McCarver's major defensive liability was his arm—a deficiency that was minimized in his final years as the batterymate for Steve Carlton because of the southpaw's pickoff move. He was the first to admit that his playing career was extended years because of Carlton's insistence on throwing to him; their collaboration also gave rise to a crack that they would someday be "buried 60 feet, six inches away from one another."

The Carlton years in Philadelphia in the 1970s followed McCarver's teaming with Bob Gibson in St. Louis the previous decade. This teaming produced more than its share of Savage Bob stories, not least his warning on one occasion to his catcher to stop bothering him on the mound because "the only thing you know about pitching is how hard it is to hit."

As an announcer for the networks and in New York, McCarver has been praised for his astute insights while being criticized for a frequently pedantic tone. His remarks have led to more than one run-in with players and managers; in the late 1990s,for example, his contract was not renewed by the Mets after many years when Bobby Valentine indicated he didn't appreciate a second manager in the broadcasting booth. McCarver immediately moved over to the Yankees.

GEORGE McCONNELL

McConnell was an unwitting cause of increasing pressures for the outlawing of the spitball. While pitching for a minor league team in Buffalo, he was scouted by Cubs manager Frank Chance as a possible addition to the Chicago rotation. Although the righthander hurled a 2–0 shutout, Chance was so alarmed at the discovery that three Buffalo catchers had been hurt handling his serves and so repelled at the sight of fielders having to wipe off their hands whenever they touched the ball that he soon became an influential spokesman in major league executive circles for banning the pitch.

McConnell eventually wound up on the Cubs, but only after Chance was gone. In 1915, as a member of Chicago's entry in the Federal League, he employed his spitter to lead the circuit with his 25 wins.

BILL McCORRY

McCorry was a Yankees traveling secretary who cost the club the services of Willie Mays. Dispatched in 1949 to provide a second opinion on the 18-year-old outfielder who had received rave notices from regular scout Joe Press, McCorry reported back that the prospect couldn't hit a curveball. Chided years lat-

er by John Drebinger of *The New York Times* for his error, McCorry betrayed his conformity to the racism that pervaded the Yankees front office at the time: "I got no use for [Mays] or any of them," he declared. "I wouldn't arrange a berth on the train for any of them."

WILLIE McCOVEY (Hall of Fame, 1985)

Nobody ever hit a ball harder than McCovey, and nobody ever had a career so punctuated by other Hall of Famers. Called up by the Giants in July 1959, the lefthand-swinging first baseman debuted by rocking two triples and two singles in a game against Robin Roberts. After the game, McCovey attributed his success to the batting tips he had picked up in Phoenix from Ted Williams; after his career 22 years later, he had the same number of home runs (521) as Williams had. In between there were Rookie of the Year honors in 1959, an MVP trophy in 1969, three years of leading the National League in home runs and slugging average, and two years of setting the pace in RBIs. There was also the ultimate tribute from opposition pitchers in the record-making 45 intentional walks he received in 1969.

Despite his splashy rookie year McCovey was bounced around for a couple of seasons after that, including return trips to the minors, because of the presence at first base of Orlando Cepeda. Depending on the San Francisco strategy of the moment, the two were moved back and forth between first base and left field, until Cepeda was finally traded to the Cardinals in 1966. During their joint stay on the team, the two sluggers were also rivals for the affections of Giants fans—both of them viewed as native sons in a way that Willie Mays wasn't. McCovey's popularity was never more evident than on Opening Day in 1977, when, returning to the club after a few years with the Padres and Athletics, he was reduced to tears in the batting box by an endless ovation. At age 39, he responded by winning Comeback Player of the Year honors with 28 home runs.

CLYDE McCULLOUGH

In 1945 McCullough became the only major leaguer to miss an entire regular season but still appear in the World Series the same year. He achieved the distinction by being discharged from the Army just before his Cubs met the Tigers in the Series. The 15-year (between 1940 and 1956) catcher made out in his only appearance against Detroit.

WILLIE McGEE

McGee is the only player to be traded in midseason from one league to another and still win a batting crown. The switch-hitting outfielder did it in 1990, when an August swap sent him from the Cardinals to the Athletics. Although his overall mark for the season with the two teams was lower than that of National League runner-up Eddie Murray of the Dodgers, he was awarded the title because his .335 strictly as a Cardinal was higher. McGee also won the NL hitting race in 1985, a year in which he took MVP honors for playing a critical role in the Cardinals pennant win.

TIM McGINLEY

McGinley was the Boston catcher in the very first National League game, played against Philadelphia on April 22, 1876. He was the first major leaguer both to strike out and to score a run.

DAN McGINN

McGinn had only a 15–30 record as a reliever, but he had two of the most memorable hits in Montreal history. On April 8, 1969 he hit the expansion franchise's first home run (and the only one of his career), off Tom Seaver. A few days later, the southpaw pitcher singled across the winning run to give himself the victory in the first big league game played in Canada.

JOE McGINNITY (Hall of Fame, 1946)

There wasn't much that McGinnity didn't cram into his 10 years of big league service from 1899 to 1908. Among other things, the righthander was a prominent actor in the turn-of-the-century shenanigans involving two Baltimore and two New York franchises, won more games than Christy Mathewson even when the latter posted 30 victories, and starred in some of baseball's most notorious brawls.

McGinnity forged a career-long alliance with John McGraw as a member of the NL Orioles in 1899, when as a rookie, he led the circuit with 28 wins. He racked up the victories in a Baltimore uniform only because he had agreed to a McGraw request not to unveil his curve until April 15—the date by which Ned Hanlon had to choose the Orioles players he wanted to take with him to Brooklyn as part of a syndicate scheme that saw the same people running the two clubs. When the Baltimore franchise folded at the end of the year, McGinnity went over to Brooklyn anyway, where he again paced NL hurlers, with another 28 victories. Hanlon barely had time to savor that triumph when McGraw returned to Baltimore as manager of the city's American League franchise and McGinnity jumped back to his mentor, this time not leading the league but still throwing 26 victories. Then came the second boondoggle, when McGraw himself helped arrange the dissolution of the Orioles franchise by moving to the Giants in 1902, taking along McGinnity. Dividing his season between the teams and the leagues, the hurler posted 21 victories. Then he got into really high gear.

Between 1903 and 1906 McGinnity won 114 games for New York, racking up 31 in 1903 and 35 the following season; in the latter year he also paced the NL in both winning percentage (.814) and ERA (1.61). In 1903 and 1904 he combined with Mathewson for a staggering total of 129 wins, in each of the two years edging his fellow Hall of Famer in the victory column. Two more 20-win seasons followed, in 1905 and 1906. Having worked in an iron foundry, he was known as Iron Man even before becoming a mound workhorse who holds the post–19th-century NL season record for innings pitched (434 in 1903); in addition, he pitched both games of a doubleheader five times and hurled two complete-game victories on the same day three times—all six wins coming in the same month (August 1903). His overall career record was 246–142 (2.66).

McGinnity's success didn't come quietly. He was fined on numerous occasions for instigating field and grandstand brawls. NL president Harry Pulliam accused him of "attempting to make the ballpark a slaughterhouse," and not all that irrationally. At the peak of his career McGinnity had the frightening big league record of hitting one of every 19 batters he faced. His reputation was such that even when an explosion of violence wasn't his fault, he was still fingered as its catalyst; typical was a 1908 episode in Boston when the pitcher and McGraw went to the aid of a Braves fan being roughed up by security guards and, despite having most of the spectators on their side during an ensuing melee, were arrested for fomenting a riot. McGinnity, coaching at third base, was the first Giant to realize what the Cubs were up to after Fred Merkle failed to touch second base on September 23, 1908; he grabbed the ball before Chicago players could and fired it into the stands in what turned out to be a futile attempt to stave off the consequences of Merkle's Boner.

BILL McGOWAN (Hall of Fame, 1992)

McGowan was the Lou Gehrig of umpires. During his 30 years (1925–54) with the American League he put together a record streak of 2,541 consecutive games—a stretch of $16\frac{1}{2}$ seasons without an absence.

JOHN McGRAW (Hall of Fame, 1937)

McGraw and his Giants held sway over baseball for one-third of the 20th century with a dynastic consistency that only the Yankees ever matched on an organizational level and that nobody ever equaled individually. Between 1903 and 1931 Little Napoleon compiled 10 pennants, 11 second-place finishes, and six other first division showings. But over and above the statistics McGraw imbued the game with a personality—tough and often vicious, insightful and often innovative, enigmatic and often suspect—that defined the contours of the national pastime for generations. In the context of his earlier, electrifying playing career, of his run-ins with every luminary of the sport for more than four decades, and of his practical, administrative impact on more franchises than his own, even his managing of the Giants accounted for only a part of his significance.

For the first decade of his big league life, McGraw was a lefthand-hitting third baseman for Baltimore—initially with the American Association Orioles (1891), then with the National League franchise operating under the same nickname (1892–99). After breaking in with a couple of passable seasons, he came in to his own in 1893 with an average of .321, 101 walks, and 123 runs scored. That turned out to be his lowest batting mark for nine years, with a high of .391 (the best ever by a third baseman) in 1899. It was also the first of three times that he would draw 100 bases on balls and the first of five seasons that he would score 100 runs. (He led the NL in both categories in 1898 and 1899.) Thrown into the mix were two seasons of more than 70 steals. When he retired as an active player in 1906, he had a .334 average, again the highest by anyone at his position.

But as with his managing record, McGraw's numbers as a hitter were the least of it. As a disciple of manager Ned Hanlon, he embodied the Old Orioles style of play in all its legal and illegal aspects. In the first category he teamed up with Willie Keeler to perfect the hit-and-run play, mastered the Baltimore Chop, and elevated the squeeze play to an art; in the second category he seldom got closer than 10 feet to second base when going from first to third if an umpire had his back turned, grabbed the belts of runners when they were tagging up from third, and continually interfered with catchers on throws to nab would-be base stealers. More than any of his teammates with the exception of shortstop Hughie Jennings, McGraw was also identified with the intimidation tactics (honing spikes in full view of opponents) and incessant invective unleashed on adversaries and umpires characteristic of the Baltimore squad. If there was a brawl on the field, the Oriole nicknamed Muggsy was sure to be in the middle of it. The worst such melee took place in Boston on May 16, 1894, when fans became so caught up in a fistfight between McGraw and Tommy Tucker they didn't notice South End Grounds was burning down around them. On the other hand, McGraw also gave the lie to the legends that would grow up around the Orioles in later years about how they were too tough ever to allow physical problems to stop them from playing: In 1895 he played only 96 times after being felled by malaria, and in 1896 he appeared only 23 times because of a typhoid fever attack. Once questioned sardonically about these ailments, McGraw, who rivaled Jennings and Wilbert Robinson in telling tales of the supposedly invincible Baltimore clubs, shrugged: "I came back, didn't I?"

Under a syndication scheme worked out in 1899 between the Orioles and Dodgers, McGraw was left behind in Baltimore as player-manager while Hanlon took most of his best players off to Brooklyn. Hanlon fulfilled expectations by winning the pennant, but McGraw collected some unplanned consolation prizes. For one thing, he managed to hold on to righthander Joe McGinnity by persuading the rookie not to display his curve until it would be too late for him to be included in the Hanlon exodus; future Hall of Famer McGinnity ended up leading the league with 28 victories. If that wasn't enough to irk Hanlon, McGraw managed it by swinging a couple of deals on his own that allowed Baltimore to remain a respectable fourth, by continuing the kind of field set-tos that kept attention focused on his club, and, most annoying of all, by outdrawing the superior Dodgers on the road.

With the dissolution of the NL Orioles after 1899,

McGraw moved over to the Cardinals for a season but only after holding out for a contract without a reserve clause. Despite regular appeals by St. Louis that he stick around as playing manager, he held to his original intention of returning to Baltimore in 1901 to assume that double role for the new American League's franchise in the city. Along with Robinson, he also invested in the fledgling club. But troubled started brewing to a boil even before the opening of the season, when McGraw supporters, representatives of the old Hanlon Orioles, and city marshals clashed over the right of the new AL team to the park used by the defunct NL franchise. McGraw and his followers were ultimately evicted from the site, and a new facility had to be built. Two weeks into the season the manager ignited a year-long war with umpires, involving protracted field tantrums, fines, and suspensions. AL president Ban Johnson, who had promised his clubs would behave more decorously than those in the NL, held his fire only to avail himself of some of McGraw's contacts for planting a franchise in the New York market.

The truce with Johnson ended quickly in 1902. On Opening Day McGraw was thrown out for protesting a call. A few days later he punched a visiting Dodgers official for trying to lure outfielder Jimmy Sheckard to Brooklyn. At the end of April he got into a war of attrition with umpire Jack Sheridan, during which he was hit by a pitch in five successive at bats but not allowed to take first base. When he sat down at home to protest the fifth plunking, Sheridan kicked him out of the game. Ignoring the immediate circumstances around the ouster and agreeing that the umpire had reason for his hostility, Johnson earned McGraw's enmity for good by suspending him for five days. McGraw's revenge was thorough. In mid-June, he met secretly with Giants owner Andrew Freedman to plot his escape to the Polo Grounds—and to take the Orioles down with him. Step one saw him deliberately provoke an argument with umpire Tom Connally, prompting an indefinite suspension from Johnson. He then went to the Baltimore board of directors and suggested that, since he was so much trouble to everyone, he would cancel some $7,000 in chits from covering club traveling expenses if the team would tear up his contract. Step three was selling out his interest in the team and signing a four-year contract with the Giants. Step four was persuading Robinson and other minority shareholders to sell out to Joseph France, a front for Freedman; together with the stock purchased from McGraw, France ended up with a majority interest long enough (24 hours) for Freedman to gut the Orioles of McGinnity, Roger Bresnahan, McGraw himself, and others for the Giants, while also authorizing the dealing of Joe Kelley and Cy Seymour to the Reds. Before Johnson woke up to what was happening, his Baltimore franchise had been reduced to tatters.

Within 10 minutes of his first meeting with Freedman and the Giants at the Polo Grounds McGraw released nine players and announced the end of a plan by his immediate predecessors Horace Fogel and Heinie Smith to convert Christy Mathewson into an infielder. Although he didn't accomplish much in the standings for the remainder of the 1902 season, it was an informative enough period to permit him to guide the club from the cellar all the way to second place in 1903 and to take his first pennant in 1904. His success was the result of several ingredients whipped into an original whole: an eye for baseball talent and a freedom from front office restraints to go after it, his nerve-wracking Old Orioles style of play that kept opponents constantly on the defensive, a purposely tendered image of the Giants as couldn't-lose swaggerers (which made other teams press more against them), and constant umpire baiting aimed at getting the next call. Little Napoleon, as he had begun being called in Baltimore, was also a master psychologist, both in seeming to cater to the team's superstitions while tactfully turning them to the club's advantage and in concentrating most of his confidence-building on players who were being pilloried by fans or the press for perceived shortcomings. With regard to the superstitions he manipulated the bizarre saga of Victory Faust as the club's good luck charm between 1911 and 1913; for confidence building he could not have been a more staunch defender of Fred Merkle after the first baseman's infamous baserunning lapse in 1908 or of Fred Snodgrass after the outfielder's error in the 1912 World Series had given the Red Sox a world championship.

McGraw's reign at the Polo Grounds breaks down into two major periods. In the pre-World War I years he owed most of his achievements to pitching staffs that included eventual Cooperstown residents Mathewson, McGinnity, and Rube Marquard, as well as such solid starters as Red Ames and Jeff Tesreau; he also pioneered the frequent use of relievers, most notably Doc Crandall. Over the same period the only position player with superior credentials was catcher Bresnahan. With the coming of outfielder Ross Youngs in 1917, however, McGraw's squads took on a more offensive look, becoming identified with the likes of Frankie Frisch, George Kelly, Casey Stengel, Travis Jackson, Bill Terry, Freddie Lindstrom, Rogers Hornsby, Edd Roush, and Mel Ott. Common to both eras was the pugnacious personality the manager strove to give all his teams—not merely in the interests of intimidating opponents, but also of improving ticket sales. Typical was a decision to have special uniforms designed in 1906 that proclaimed the 1905 World Series victors over Philadelphia as WORLD CHAMPIONS. It was in these togs that the team traveled by horse and carriage from their hotels to visiting ballparks, infuriating the local population along the way. In the odd circumstance that crowds figured to be kept down by bad weather or by a host club out of the pennant race, McGraw would send telegrams from the team train requesting police protection upon arrival because of some "anonymous threats"; the sight of police reinforcements at the station was generally enough to stimulate ticket sales.

Field fights were incessant, and as often as not involved fans jumping down on the field to join in. McGraw personally was: blamed for inciting two Polo Grounds melees against umpires in 1907; arrested for fomenting a riot in Boston in 1908; arrested for joining umpire Cy Rigler in a 1911 brawl against some Cuban fans in a Havana bar; chased off a New Jersey field by fans wielding sticks and rocks after protesting a call in an exhibition game against a black team in 1912; beaten up by Philadelphia fans for assaulting pitcher Ad Brennan in 1913; fined for slugging umpire Bill Byron in Cincinnati in 1917; and accused of attacking Philadelphia pitcher George Smith in 1922. No one in the league had any doubts, either, that the manager's temperament was the catalyst for the regular series of Giants punchups he himself was not directly involved in.

If he wasn't mixing it up with opponents and umpires, McGraw was going after league owners. In one instance, he began shouting across the field at Brooklyn's Charlie Ebbets, who was sitting next to the Dodgers dugout; when Ebbets stood up and demanded to know whether McGraw had called him a "bastard," the manager replied, "No, I called you a

son of a bitch!" Although few owners were spared such scenes (again, largely in the interests of getting an opponent to press against his club), McGraw's favorite target was Barney Dreyfuss, the prim boss of the Pirates. The messiest clash between the two took place in 1905, when McGraw began orating about Dreyfuss's (fictitious) gambling debts and refusal to pay them, Dreyfuss insisted that NL president Harry Pulliam fine and suspend him for the slander, McGraw accused Pulliam of being a Dreyfuss puppet, and the other owners had to step in to deliver a plague-on-all-your-houses verdict. The incident forged an almost irrational animosity in McGraw toward Pulliam, to the point that he even snickered when the NL official committed suicide a few years later in the wake of another anti-Giants ruling over the Merkle Boner. As for Dreyfuss, he never bothered to hide his contempt for the Giants manager over more than a quarter-century, accusing him of everything from cultivating shady associates to attempting to pilfer Pittsburgh players by advising them to reject contract offers so they would become more attractive as trade commodities (among those named in this context was Pie Traynor, in 1924).

Dreyfuss was right when it came to McGraw's associates. One of his partners in a New York pool hall was professional gambler Arnold Rothstein, a principal figure in the Black Sox scandal. Rothstein was also close to Charles Stoneham, the bucket shop operator who bought the Giants in 1919 and advanced McGraw the money to buy a piece of the franchise. Both Stoneham and McGraw had interests in race tracks. Between the late teens and the mid-1920s, the Giants were also at the center of more game-fixing or bribery scandals than even the White Sox. Four different pennant races and World Series carried the stench of some hanky-panky or other, always with McGraw and his team implicated in one way or another. The 1919 club was a rogue's gallery of accused fixers and others who were later outlawed or investigated for one illegality or another. Through it all, though, McGraw remained the original Teflon Man. As a witness in the Black Sox probe he was even praised for driving Hal Chase out of baseball by offering him a ridiculously low contract; the only problem with that story was that it was a lie and that by asserting it under oath McGraw perjured himself. In 1924 Kenesaw Landis didn't even bother interviewing him about the bribe approach by young New York outfielder Jimmy O'Connell to Philadelphia infielder Heinie Sand. By the time one of the tendrils of that case got to a courtroom Landis made sure he was vacationing abroad and was unavailable for testimony.

Certainly, the commissioner was not about to forget that, when he wasn't paying attention to his own team, McGraw was helping to keep the sorely tested NL together by by arranging for one New York contact after another to take over the chronically failing Braves franchise in Boston. It was also McGraw who had brought together Jacob Ruppert and Tillinghast L'Hommedieu (Cap) Huston to purchase the Yankees in 1915. Aside from the gratitude of league officials, the manager's mediation efforts earned the Giants an unending supply of talented players from the Braves in one-sided trades (one of the reasons they were also failing) and annually increased rents from the Yankees as tenants of the Polo Grounds.

As innovative as he had been in such areas as making extensive use of relievers and hiring full-time coaches, McGraw never accepted the slugging baseball introduced by Babe Ruth, adding a new-versus-old theme to the 1921, 1922, and 1923 World Series between the Giants and the Yankees. He admitted savoring his wins in the first two Series as much as anything he had ever accomplished, just as he couldn't deny a particular sourness over the Yankees triumph in 1923. The Ruthian Yankees were eventually given the gate at the Polo Grounds and forced to build Yankee Stadium because of his embarrassment and irritation that his own team was being outdrawn by the home run-rich AL club.

After winning the last of his three world championships in 1922 and the last of his 10 pennants two years later, McGraw became increasingly distracted on the bench, and began turning over the club for long periods to the likes of Dave Bancroft, Stengel, and Hornsby. One special cause of distraction was a Florida land deal he had been inveigled into endorsing in the newspapers; when it turned out to be a scam, depriving investors of some $100,000, he spent years paying back as much of the money personally as he could even though he was never charged or even sued for being part of the hustle.

By the late 1920s McGraw had been sapped of energy by minor ailments and the deaths of his closest friends—Jennings, Mathewson, journalist Sam Crane, and Youngs. This made him even more alternately distant and authoritarian with players, fueling constant speculation that he was ready to step down. Instead, he hung on until June 3, 1932, when he called Terry into his office to offer him the job as his successor.

Less than two years after he retired, McGraw died of uremia in a New Rochelle hospital at the age of 61. His final record as a manager was 2,763–1,948 (.586). His most enduring eulogy was an observation by Connie Mack that "there has been only one manager and his name is John McGraw."

TUG McGRAW

McGraw's cry of "You gotta believe" became the rallying cry of the pennant-winning Mets in 1973. It also served as an example of the southpaw reliever's quick footwork, since it was initially uttered as a sarcastic crack to a late-season locker room pep talk by board chairman M. Donald Grant, whose baseball smarts were rarely recognized by anyone working for him. McGraw made the observation stand up by registering 25 saves during the year, most of them down the stretch drive and all of them followed by his trademark slapping of his glove against his thigh. The bullpen ace also had a lot to do with Philadelphia's world championship in 1980, returning from the disabled list in July and yielding only three earned runs over more than 52 innings for the rest of the year; he picked up two additional saves in the League Championship series against Houston, and two saves and a win in the World Series against Kansas City. The redheaded fireman was a feast for reporters with such observations as describing his fastball as a Peggy Lee—as in, "Is That All There Is?"

'NUF SAID McGREEVEY

The unofficial leader of the rabid Boston loyalists known as the Royal Rooters from the 1890s to the early 1910s, McGreevey's expertise in all questions touching upon baseball was universally acknowledged throughout the Hub City. The saloonkeeper's opinion, once expressed, halted further debate; it was "'Nuf said."

DEACON McGUIRE

McGuire is the only position player to appear in 26 major league seasons. The catcher, who hit .279 in a career that included stops with a record 12 teams, had his best years with the National League Washington Senators in the 1890s; it was with that team, in 1895, that he became the first receiver to set up behind the plate in every game. On July 27, 1907, as manager of the Boston Red Sox, he sent himself up to the plate and became the oldest player to hit a pinch-hit home run. Five years later, on May 18, 1912, while a coach for Detroit, he was activated during the one-day strike by the Tigers players over Ty Cobb's suspension; the 48 year old got a hit in two at bats and made two putouts and three assists. Pitcher Mike Morgan tied McGuire's record of playing for 12 teams.

BILL McGUNNIGLE

McGunnigle is the only manager to win two consecutive pennants in two different major leagues; he has the added distinction of getting fired immediately afterward. The pennants came for Brooklyn—in the American Association in 1889 and the National League in 1890. The firing came about when Brooklyn Players League backer George Chauncey acquired a share of the NL club in 1891 and convinced new partner Charles Byrne that John Montgomery Ward should also move in from the PL as pilot.

MARK McGWIRE

In spite of a succession of injuries that cost him considerable playing time and forced him into premature retirement after 16 seasons (1986–2001) with Oakland and St. Louis, McGwire was, from several points of view, the most prodigious home run hitter of all time. The righthand-hitting first baseman's most publicized feat came in 1998 for the Cardinals when he surpassed Roger Maris's season home run record of 61 and didn't stop until he had reached the once unthinkable total of 70. But when he retired, he also had the marks for most home runs by a first year player (49 with Oakland to win Rookie of the Year honors in 1987), hitting more than 20 homers in two leagues in the same season (34 with the A's and 24 with the Cardinals in 1997), the most four-baggers over two seasons (135 in 1998–99), and the lowest career ratio of at bats to home runs (10.61 to Babe Ruth's 11.76). He also shares records for belting 50 or more homers in four years, two in one inning, and five over two games twice. A career total of 583 round-trippers put him in fifth place on the all-time list.

It was as much the quality of McGwire's towering home runs as their quantity that won him media acclaim. For example, five of his 70 homers in 1998

traveled, by *The Sporting News*'s measurement, more than 500 feet and another 42 went more than 400 feet. He also won points during his pursuit of Maris's mark for a graciousness that belied his innate shyness and for enhancing the drama of the moment by having Maris's family on hand for the record-breaking clout. In the same vein, his mutual show of affection with Chicago's Sammy Sosa during their chase after the record became a subplot of the 1998 campaign, to the point that baseball officialdom trumpeted it as the sport's salvation after the 1994 labor troubles.

McGwire's main nemesis during his career were back and heel injuries that all but kept him on the sidelines in 1993 and 1994 and that remained a threat after he had been dealt by the Athletics to the Cardinals in July 1997. Another shadow over his accomplishments was his admission that, for the avowed purpose of heading off further time on the disabled list, he had been using the power supplement androstenedione—a steroid banned by several sports but technically legal in baseball. Embarrassed baseball officials, worried that the admission might taint his feel-good efforts for the game and not at all in the mood for journalistic investigations of pill-taking habits in the majors, breathed a sigh of relief when the media by and large left it at the slugger's decision to stop taking the supplement after the 1998 season.

When his body again sidelined him for conspicuous periods in 2000 and 2001, McGwire announced his retirement. He finished with a .263 average and only 785 singles among his 1,626 lifetime hits.

BILL McKECHNIE (Hall of Fame, 1962)

Following a modest 11-year career as a third baseman for several teams before 1920, McKechnie hit his stride as a National League managerial standby, accumulating 25 years of piloting during which he won four pennants and two world championships. Although depicted as a hard-nosed disciplinarian, he frequently found himself in untenable positions between his players and employers and, just as often, reacted with a marked passivity.

McKechnie got his first taste of managing while still playing with the 1915 Newark Peppers of the short-lived Federal League. After the league folded and he wound up his playing career with a few more years in the NL, he was hired by Pittsburgh owner

Barney Dreyfuss in 1922 with two specific mandates: to polish the skills of third-base prospect Pie Traynor and to reimpose discipline on a club that had become notorious for its antic ways. McKechnie succeeded with Traynor but had considerably less luck with Pittsburgh's two resident clowns—shortstop Rabbit Maranville and his roommate, hurler Chief Moses Yellowhorse. At one point he became so exasperated with their practical jokes that he insisted on rooming with them on the road; that led to folly when he returned to their shared hotel room one evening, found the two players sleeping off one of their regular drunks, and opened the drawer of a bureau to be smacked in the face with a couple of dozen terrified pigeons. Because he was satisfied with McKechnie otherwise, Dreyfuss's solution was to get rid of Maranville, Chief Yellowhorse, and a third prankster, Charlie Grimm, and flank the manager with Fred Clarke as something of a prefect of discipline.

In 1925 McKechnie led the Pirates to a world championship; on the other hand, he was helpless to stem the player resentment against Clarke, manifested at the end of the year when the team voted not to award him a World Series share. McKechnie managed to squeeze a compromise out of the players for awarding their ostensible coach a nominal sum, but Clarke rejected the gesture and went to war on the players the following year. The upshot was a player mutiny in 1926 that ended with outfielder Max Carey being traded, outfielder Carson Bigbee and pitcher Babe Adams being released, Clarke being pensioned off, and McKechnie being fired for not having shown enough authority during the crisis.

In 1928 McKechnie popped up in the Cardinals dugout. With a squad featuring such future Hall of Famers as Frankie Frisch, Chick Hafey, and Jim Bottomley, he won the pennant, but then got swept in the World Series by the Yankees. With the argument that the team hadn't been prepared adequately for taking on Murderers Row, St. Louis owner Sam Breadon returned McKechnie to the Rochester club he had managed a year earlier and hired Billy Southworth for the Cardinals. But in the middle of the 1929 campaign Southworth's martinet ways with a floundering club caused Breadon to have another change of heart, and he switched the St. Louis and Rochester pilots. For a couple of months McKechnie kept the club at .500, but then started taking time off to run for public office back in his hometown in

Pennsylvania. Knowing Breadon was furious at his part-time manager, the Braves asked for permission to talk to McKechnie about going to Boston the following year, and the Cardinals owner was only too glad to get rid of the future alderman.

McKechnie piloted the Braves for eight dreary years, during which the club got no higher than fourth place; in 1935 it set a franchise-low record of 38–115 (.241), finishing 61½ games out of first place. For a while he even served as club president while the organization tried to undo decades of mess caused by owners foisted on it by John McGraw of the Giants. Just before a new front office under Bob Quinn was about to fire him, McKechnie submitted his resignation to take over the Reds. For the first seven of his nine years in Cincinnati, he kept the club above .500, in the process winning a pennant in 1939 and beating Detroit for a world championship the following year.

McKechnie's versatility as a coach was such that Lou Boudreau credited him as a major influence on both pitcher Bob Lemon and outfielder Larry Doby on the pennant-winning Indians in 1948.

STEPHEN McKEEVER

McKeever was the daffiest of The Daffiness Boys. A Brooklyn contractor, he and his brother Edward gained half-ownership of the Dodgers in 1913 as the price for putting up the money to complete construction on Ebbets Field. A windy man, he liked to be referred to as The Judge—not for any juridical standing but because of his intimacy with the borough's Democratic Party bosses and his proprietorial air on social occasions.

McKeever never disguised his desire to run the Dodgers or his exasperation when one opportunity after another to do so was thwarted. In April 1925, for example, he and Edward had it out over who should succeed Charlie Ebbets even as the team president's body was still being waked. Although Edward got the best of that argument, his victory lasted literally only a few days because he contracted pneumonia at Ebbets's funeral and died shortly afterward. The Judge was already dusting off the president's chair when he was informed that Ebbets's heirs were throwing their support behind manager Wilbert Robinson as the new organization head. From then on The Judge let everyone know he had found an exception to his frequent boast that he had never met a man he didn't like. It was, in fact, because of the relentless conflict between McKeever and Robinson that sportswriters began referring to the team's front office as The Daffiness Boys. While the organization went to seed around them in the 1920s and early 1930s, McKeever sat in the club offices in downtown Brooklyn banging his cane on the desk with endless denunciations of the manager-president, while Robinson kept shaking his head from separate quarters at the St. George Hotel.

By the beginning of the 1930s the situation had become so desperate that National League president John Heydler named a brother-in-law of U.S. Supreme Court Chief Justice Charles Evans Hughes to referee brawls. Even when Robinson was forced out, there was little appreciable improvement in the organization, with creditors descending regularly and office phones repeatedly shut off for nonpayment of bills. McKeever's one consolation was that, at age 78 and with nobody else willing to take on the job, he finally claimed the presidency from a divided board of directors. What was never really clear to his aging mind through a good part of the 1930s was that the board considered him only a figurehead, maneuvering him at will. He died in 1938, shortly after Larry MacPhail arrived and began raising the franchise from the gutter.

JACK McKEON

Although dubbed Trader Jack for his readiness to complete ambitious deals, McKeon had equal experience managing for franchises that were falling down around his ears. Sometimes he himself got a jump on matters by causing havoc in the clubhouse.

McKeon's first managing stint was with the Royals in 1973, leading the team to a second-place finish in his maiden year but also precipitating a near-revolt in 1974 after he fired popular hitting coach Charlie Lau. Among others, George Brett, Steve Busby, and Fred Patek accused him of jealousy over Lau's regular tips (about pitching as much as hitting) to the players. With Oakland in the late 1970s, McKeon was in and out of the dugout while Charlie Finley dismantled the franchise by disposing of the club's remaining stars and allowing the Coliseum to fall into such disrepair that it was known as the Mausoleum. From there he moved to San Diego, where he had an oasis of success between two periods of chaos.

Taking over as general manager from the fired Bob Fontaine in 1979, McKeon gradually accumulated power as owner Ray Kroc distanced himself from the franchise and as organization president Ballard Smith fought a publicity war with Dave Winfield over resigning the outfielder as a free agent. By 1982 he had gained enough leverage to bring in Dick Williams as manager and to embark on a series of deals that would earn him his nickname and the Padres a 1984 pennant. Among the players acquired within a two-year period were Steve Garvey, Graig Nettles, and Goose Gossage—all with the pedigree of winners. But what generally went unnoticed as McKeon became The Trader was that all three of these key players had been signed as free agents, while his most conspicuous swap of the period—obtaining shortstop Garry Templeton from the Cardinals—cost San Diego Ozzie Smith.

McKeon's deals after the 1984 pennant earned similar results. A 1987 exchange with the Mets that exported outfielder Kevin McReynolds to New York brought potential slugger Kevin Mitchell but also a couple of mediocre minor league players who had better Shea Stadium notices than abilities; when Mitchell spent more time hanging out with toughs from his old neighborhood than delivering on the field, he was traded to the Giants, where he finally fulfilled his long-ball promise. McKeon's one consolation was that the deal with San Francisco brought one-year wonder—and Cy Young winner—Mark Davis.

In 1988 McKeon also had to tote up manager Larry Bowa as a failure, and went back to the dugout himself. For the next few seasons he wore two hats as owner Joan Kroc became more frantic about selling the club. When she finally succeeded in April 1990, the new ownership of television producer Tom Werner discovered that McKeon was about the only one in the organization who knew what was going on. Before Werner felt confident enough about holding the reins, McKeon talked him into giving a multiyear pact to Greg Riddoch as manager and confined himself to his front office duties. That lasted about a year, when he was ousted in favor of Joe McIlvaine.

In 1997 McKeon took over as manager of Cincinnati, enduring successive turmoils while the league tried to figure out what to do with owner Marge Schott and the media decided he was just warming the pilot's seat for Ken Griffey as part of the price for attracting Ken Griffey, Jr. to the Reds. He brought the team to a do-or-die playoff game against the Mets in 1999 (the Reds died) and kept them over .500 again in 2000 before being replaced—not by Griffey, but by Bob Boone.

AMERICUS McKIM

When McKim agreed to extend the major leagues west of St. Louis by forming a Kansas City club to succeed Altoona in the Union Association in 1884, he accepted the most humiliating terms ever imposed on a franchise: The team's games were to be included in their opponents' records, but the Unions, as the team was known, could not win the pennant no matter how many games they won. The owner's revenge was that he made a $7,000 profit at the end of the season, while UA angel Henry V. Lucas lost about $100,000.

DENNY McKNIGHT

A cofounder and the first president (1882–85) of the American Association, McKnight guided the always unstable league through turf wars with the National League (in 1882) and the Union Association (in 1884), only to be undone because of his association with the Pittsburgh club. The president of the Alleghenys until 1884 and a stockholder thereafter, he was accused of partisanship in a dispute over the rights to infielder Sam Barkley in 1885 and summarily fired from his league job. His ouster made a weak circuit even weaker, especially after the Alleghenys transferred to the National League in 1887 in protest over the AA's treatment of their former official.

DENNY McLAIN

McLain's off-field activities as a player and his involvement in a string of felonies after his retirement have cast long shadows over his status as the last 30-game winner. With one 20-game season already under his belt, the righthander became the cover boy of baseball in 1968, when he went 31–6 (with an ERA of 1.96) to lead the Tigers to a pennant and take both MVP and Cy Young honors. He led the league again in 1969 with 24 victories, sharing a second Cy Young prize with Baltimore lefty Mike Cuellar. But that was only part of the story.

McLain had already raised some eyebrows in 1967 when he claimed a mysterious foot injury down the stretch of a heated American League pennant race

involving four teams; at the time, he had been closing in on another 20-win season. In 1969, even as he closed in on his second Cy Young trophy, the hurler clashed often with Mayo Smith over the manager's role in getting pitching coach Johnny Sain fired; ultimately, McLain began showing his displeasure by missing workouts between starts and arriving at the park only shortly before games were due to start. The tension with Smith went on display nationally at that year's All-Star Game, when McLain, the scheduled AL starter, showed up late for the pregame hoopla in Washington, then left the capital altogether to return to Detroit for a dental appointment after rains had forced a one-day postponement of the contest. By the time he got back to Washington the next day, Smith had given the start to Mel Stottlemyre.

In 1970 McLain drew two suspensions from Commissioner Bowie Kuhn and a third from the Tigers, reducing his season to 14 games and a record of 3–5. Kuhn's first punishment came in February, when the pitcher was implicated in an investigation of a Michigan bookmaker who had profited from the Tigers loss to the Red Sox in 1967, the year that McLain had incurred his mysterious foot problem. When writers tried to question him about the investigation during spring training, he dumped ice water over them, causing the team to act. Kuhn's second suspension came at the end of the season, after the pitcher had been accused of waving a gun in a Chicago restaurant. That was enough for the Tigers, and he was traded to the Senators in October.

After leading the AL in losses in 1971, McLain hung on for another campaign with the Athletics and Braves before quitting with an overall record of 131–91. Things didn't go any more smoothly for him following his retirement. In 1984 he was convicted of a series of federal charges covering everything from racketeering and extortion to distributing cocaine, and given a lengthy prison term.

BILLY McLEAN

McLean has the strongest claim to being called the first professional umpire. A one-time prize fighter, his ability and fairness while officiating in the National Association led the National League to pay him $5 per game. He ended up calling games for both the NL and the American Association from 1876 to 1890. The Boston native regularly walked to assignments in Providence by setting out at 4:00 A.M.

JACK McMASTERS

A former conditioner for professional boxers, McMasters became baseball's first full-time trainer when he tended to the minor ailments of the American Association's Brooklyn Bridegrooms in 1887.

FRED McMULLIN

McMullin was a utility player for both the White Sox and the Black Sox. One of the eight players banned for involvement in the 1919 World Series fix, he joined the plot after overhearing a locker-room discussion between conspirators Chick Gandil and Swede Risberg, immediately demanding a piece of the action. Even though he came to the plate only twice in the Series (with one hit) and was the only defendant not reindicted after a mysterious loss of evidence caused the original charges to be thrown out of court, Commissioner Kenesaw Landis did not distinguish his actions from those of the other accused.

McMullin never appeared in more than 70 games in a six-year career, he had his most conspicuous moment on the diamond at Fenway Park in 1917, when he and Buck Weaver, later to be another of the Chicago Eight, slugged it out with gamblers who had invaded the field in an attempt to force a forfeit that would protect their bets. American League president Ban Johnson later praised him for defending the integrity of the game.

DAVE McNALLY

McNally joined the 1975 challenge that ended baseball's reserve clause and opened the way for free agency purely out of principle. He had already announced a decision to retire before seconding the Andy Messersmith action and stuck to it even with the promise of big money offered by a free agent market. Although the lefthander quit the game from Montreal after a 14-year (1962–75) career, he was otherwise totally identified with Baltimore, turning in four straight 20-win seasons between 1968 and 1971. His single best year was 1968, when he won 22, struck out 202, and etched an ERA of 1.95. In 1971 he paced the American League with his .808 (21–5) winning percentage.

As both pitcher and hitter, McNally also starred for the Orioles in the postseason. Not only did he win nine times in LCS and World Series duels, but he swatted homers off both New York's Jerry Koosman in 1969 and Cincinnati's Wayne Granger in 1970. The blast off Granger was the only grand slam hit by a pitcher in a World Series.

JOHN McNAMARA

McNamara's 18-year managing career between 1969 and 1991 ended up being dominated by the lingering question that has become part of the lore of Red Sox futility in postseason play: Where was Dave Stapleton in the sixth game of the 1986 World Series?

Debuting as a major league pilot with the Athletics in the last few weeks of the 1969 season, McNamara was around to watch the conclusion of Reggie Jackson's first big year, then in his first full season was ordered by owner Charlie Finley to bench the slugger because of a salary squabble. Unable to mediate the differences between the two, he was sent packing, accompanied by accusations that he was too nice. After three humdrum seasons and part of a fourth (1974–77) with the Padres, he was put in an unenviable position of succeeding Sparky Anderson with the Reds in 1979. He surprised everybody by winning a division title with aging veterans and untested rookies. In the strike-shortened 1981 season, however, he got his own surprise when the Reds NL-best overall record proved useless because the team finished second in both halves under a convoluted split-season format. He left in 1982 while the team headed for a franchise-worst season.

After two years with the Angels, McNamara moved on to his fateful assignment in Boston. His contribution to the franchise's postseason jinx came in the 10th inning of the sixth game when he left backup first baseman Stapleton on the bench. A hobbled Bill Buckner then let a dribbler off the bat Mookie Wilson go through his legs for the error that scored the winning run and provided the impetus for the Mets to clinch a championship in the seventh game. McNamara never explained the decision, which went against a practice he had been following for some time when Boston had a late-inning lead; instead, he defended Buckner and pointed the finger at Calvin Schiraldi, who gave up key hits in the final rally, and Bob Stanley, who sent home the tying run with a wild pitch.

GRAHAM McNAMEE

McNamee was baseball's first network play-by-play man. A singer by profession, he was originally hired by New York's WEAF to broadcast the 1923

World Series between the Giants and the Yankees. He began making his calls from coast to coast in 1926 with the National Broadcasting Company (NBC).

BID McPHEE (Hall of Fame, 2000)

Widely acclaimed as the 19th century's best second baseman, McPhee played 14 seasons before becoming, at the start of the 1896 season, the last player to capitulate to the fashion of wearing a glove. The result was a .978 fielding average—a record for second basemen that stood for almost 30 years. McPhee had played barehanded for three years after most other players adopted the new style in 1893; he sat out spring training that year because of a salary dispute with the Reds and declined to try learning something new when he rejoined the team in April.

To take advantage of McPhee's sure-handedness, the Reds kept their home infield grassless and hard, an advantage that netted the second baseman a fielding average 10 points higher at home than on the road. A lifetime .277 hitter over 18 seasons with the Reds in the American Association and National League, McPhee retired after the 1899 season holding almost every defensive record at second; they included 529 putouts in 1886 and 6,550 in his career—peaks yet to be topped.

GEORGE McQUILLAN

Pitching for the Phillies in 1907, McQuillan got off to the greatest start of any pitcher—yielding not a single run in his first 25 big league innings. The right-hander then came back the following season to win 23 games and to top the National League in ERA (1.60) in 1910. Otherwise, though, he usually found himself on the short end of low-scoring games. When he threw his last pitch after 10 years, his 2.38 ERA had been translated into the less-than-mediocre record of 85–89.

JOHN McSHERRY

On Opening Day in Cincinnati in 1996, overweight umpire McSherry died of a heart attack in Riverfront Stadium. His death prompted calls for better conditioned umpires and even panicked a couple of them into going on crash diets, but overall there was no visible difference in blue waistlines until some veterans were weeded out during the 1999–2000 umpire labor crisis.

CAL McVEY

McVey was one of the original Big Four (along with Al Spalding, Ross Barnes, and Deacon White) whose move from the Boston Red Stockings to the Chicago White Stockings after the 1875 season signaled the death of the National Association and the birth of the National League. As a member of the first all-professional Cincinnati Red Stockings, he was involved in what were probably the two most significant plays in that club's history. On August 27, 1869 he hit a foul tip that the Troy Haymakers argued was a third strike, then used the dispute as a pretext to storm off the field, preserving a 17–17 score so that gambling associates would not have to pay off on a possible Cincinnati victory; the tie was the only scratch in the Red Stockings fabled winning streak. On June 14, 1870, with the Red Stockings ahead by two runs in the 11th inning, a Brooklyn fan leaped on McVey's back as he stooped to pick up a drive in right field; the batter picked up a run-scoring triple, and the Atlantics went on to score two more runs and hand the Red Stockings their first loss.

JOE MEDWICK (Hall of Fame, 1968)

Medwick's fractious personality was almost as conspicuous as his offensive abilities in his heyday with the Gas House Cardinals in the 1930s. When he wasn't tattooing National League pitchers, he was going after his own hurlers for being criticized for staying in the batting cage too long or not running hard enough after a line drive. At one time or another he squared off against Dizzy and Paul Dean, Tex Carleton, Ed Heusser, and Bob Bowman; more often than not, the righthand-hitting outfielder's bat sealed over the brawls.

Medwick's greatest year was his Triple Crown season of 1937, when he batted .374 with 31 home runs and 154 RBIs; the offensive explosion—which also included pacing the league in slugging average, doubles, runs scored, hits, and at bats—marked the last time an NL player swept the major hitting categories. He also led the league in doubles and RBIs in both 1936 and 1938. In the 1934 World Series against Detroit, he aided a St. Louis victory with a .379 mark. But that became secondary to the chaos that ensued in the seventh game after the Cardinals had built a virtually insurmountable 9–0 lead before the Tigers home fans. Zeroing in on Medwick because of a hard slide earlier in the game into Detroit third baseman Marv Owen, the fans vented their frustration by pelting him with fruit and eggs. Commissioner Kenesaw Landis finally had to pull the outfielder to enable the game to be played to the end.

In more ways than one Medwick was a typical Branch Rickey creature. A gem of the St. Louis farm system, he was called up to the majors in 1932 after Rickey had disposed of another future Hall of Famer, Chick Hafey, in accordance with his theory that it was better to get rid of stars before they began to decline. Medwick himself fell before the same philosophy in 1940, when Rickey dealt him to the Dodgers. It was also the St. Louis executive who fabricated Medwick's nickname of Ducky, claiming that a (never-found) woman in the stands had been struck by his odd walk. The outfielder hated the nickname but could do little about it when Rickey's public relations ploy of making characters out of his players once again proved successful.

Only days after joining the Dodgers, Medwick was beaned by old Cardinals nemesis Bowman. Although he still had a few .300 years left in him, he never again flashed the power he had in St. Louis. He ended up with a .324 average for 17 big league years.

RUBE MELTON

Melton was in the middle of one of Larry MacPhail's more obvious finagles in 1940. Although touted for some time by Branch Rickey as a prized Cardinals prospect, he stayed in the minors because other clubs had grown gun-shy of the St. Louis executive's windy claims. When Brooklyn's MacPhail finally tried to purchase him, Rickey set the price at $30,000. MacPhail not only rejected the price as exorbitant, but made a passing remark that he would wait and acquire the righthander more cheaply. Soon afterward, Philadelphia's cash-desperate Gerry Nugent bought Melton for $7,500, then immediately turned around and sold him to the Dodgers for $15,000. A howling Rickey went to Commissioner Kenesaw Landis with charges that MacPhail and Nugent had conspired on the deal and that the Brooklyn president had even advanced Philadelphia the original $7,500. Saying he agreed with Rickey that "something was smelly," Landis canceled the deal between Philadelphia and Brooklyn, ordered the Phillies to keep Melton for at least two years, and censured both MacPhail and Nugent. After two seasons of a combined 10–25 record, the pitcher was sent on to Ebbets Field, where he only provided more evidence that Rickey had indeed once again outsmarted his rivals.

MARIO MENDOZA

It was bad enough that Mendoza batted only .215 in nine seasons as a shortstop for the Pirates, Mariners, and Rangers between 1974 and 1982, but then George Brett noticed it. According to the Kansas City star, the cutoff point in the Sunday paper listings of big league batting averages was "The Mendoza Line"; printing limitations usually fix the point around .200. After retiring as a player, Mendoza went to work in the minor leagues—as a hitting instructor.

FRED MERKLE

Merkle holds the patent on rookie disasters. The Giants first baseman gained baseball infamy on September 23, 1908, in the ninth inning of a deadlocked contest between New York and Chicago with first place at stake. With Moose McCormick on third with the winning run and himself on first after delivering a clutch single, Merkle failed to touch second base after Al Bridwell singled home what appeared to be the tie-breaker. When Cubs second baseman Johnny Evers saw him veer off the basepath and go running to celebrate with his teammates, he yelled for center fielder Solly Hofman to throw him the ball. New York coach Joe McGinnity, realizing what the Cubs were up to, braved a cluster of fans to retrieve the ball and fire it into the stands. A second ball was thrown onto the field, and Evers grabbed it and stepped on second to record the out. But when he appealed to Bob Emslie for the force-out call, the umpire claimed he hadn't been watching Merkle and passed the buck to colleague Hank O'Day. Even though he agreed with Evers, O'Day refused to say so because of the thousands of New York fans swamping the Polo Grounds field. Only later that evening, in a conversation with National League president Harry Pulliam, did the arbiter recommend the out call.

Pulliam sat on his verdict for days, even allowing the Cubs and Giants to play again. Only with the visitors out of town did he rule that the tie stood and that the clubs would have to meet in a makeup contest after the regular season if the game had an impact on the pennant race. As it turned out, the contest proved decisive when New York and Chicago finished in a dead heat. Chicago ended up winning the makeup game and claiming the pennant.

Merkle had his defenders, most of them pointing out that touching second base in such a situation had always been a very sometime thing. Manager John McGraw was particularly quick to deflect blame from the 19-year-old rookie, noting that his team had plenty of other opportunities over the last week of the season to claim the championship. Merkle received his most extravagant support from Christy Mathewson—the only one in the Polo Grounds that day to insist that he actually did touch second.

The September 23 game was the first one that Merkle started. For the rest of his 16-year career (which concluded with a .273 batting average) and later in retirement, he refused to grant interviews on the subject of his baserunning lapse.

SAM MERTES

Mertes was a .279 hitter in 10 years for several clubs at the turn of the 20th century, but he was a 1.000 hitter when it came to breaking up extra-inning no-hitters. He first did it on May 9, 1901, when his 10th-inning single spoiled a gorgeous afternoon for Cleveland's Earl Moore and started the White Sox toward a 4–2 victory. He repeated the trick as a member of the Giants on June 11, 1904, when another 10th-inning single was the first hit off Bob Wicker of the Cubs. Wicker hung on to win, 1–0, in 12 innings, anyway. Through the 2001 season there had been 11 no-hitters ruined in overtime.

ANDY MESSERSMITH

Messersmith's successful challenge to the reserve clause in 1975 signalled the beginning of the free agent era. The righthander assumed his unintended pioneering role after the 1974 season, when his league-leading 20 wins failed to gain him the contract he had sought with the Dodgers. When the club unilaterally renewed his existing pact, Messersmith, backed by the Players Association, resolved to play through the 1975 and then enjoin Los Angeles from automatically extending its option still another year. Joined in the action by Montreal southpaw Dave McNally, he was vindicated by arbitrator Peter Seitz, who destroyed the century-old reserve clause by ruling that clubs did not have the right to renew contracts perpetually through one-year options.

In the wake of the Seitz decision Dodgers owner Walter O'Malley attempted to put a good face on his legal defeat by claiming that he was still interested

in resigning Messersmith; at the same time, however, he was laying plans for blackballing players who took advantage of their free agent status. The scheme was undone when Atlanta's Ted Turner signed Messersmith.

In addition to the Dodgers and Braves, Messersmith pitched for the Angels and Yankees during his 12-year (1968–79) career. A basic fastball-curveball pitcher, he had a second 20-win season, for California in 1971. A stipulation in his contract with Atlanta was that he wear the number 17, making him a living billboard for Turner's TBS cable superstation.

GEORGE METKOVICH

Metkovich was a journeyman first baseman-outfielder in the 1940s and 1950s who never lived down an accident that ruined a tryout with Casey Stengel's Braves in 1940. At spring training that year, he spent an off-day fishing, caught a catfish, and as he stood on his catch to remove a hook, got speared in his foot by the fish's fin. Surgery to remove the fin cost him his chance with the Braves and led Stengel to proclaim, "We got a first baseman who gets attacked by a catfish!" Labeled as Catfish for the rest of his career, Metkovich wound down his playing days with the grim Pittsburgh clubs of the early 1950s, where he himself became known for the odd, ridiculous quote. One day, for example, after waving futilely at another in a long series of line drives whizzing by him, he shouted to the first base umpire for all to hear: "Don't just stand there! Get a glove and give me a hand!"

BING MILLER

Miller contributed the decisive blow the first time that a home team came from behind by more than a single run in the bottom of the ninth inning of a World Series finale. An outfielder with the Athletics in the late 1920s and early 1930s, he singled in the winning run in the decisive fifth game of the 1929 World Series. His shot off the Shibe Park wall to score Al Simmons, in the same inning as a two-run homer by Mule Haas to tie the score, gave Philadelphia a 3–2 victory and a world championship.

JOHN MILLER

Miller is the only player to have homered in his first and last major league plate appearances. The righthand-hitting outfielder did it for the 1966 Yankees and the 1969 Dodgers. They were his only home runs in 61 official at bats.

MARVIN MILLER

By taking advantage of the free agency and arbitration decisions that destroyed the reserve clause and revolutionized labor-management relations, Miller, more than any other individual, was responsible for the dizzying economic gains of players in the 1970s and 1980s. As executive director of the Players Association between 1966 and 1984, his astute organization of members also served as a model for major league umpires, while his negotiating successes with owners proved to be an indispensable premise for every recent development in the sport from the increasing role played by player agents to the billions of dollars reaped through television contracts and merchandising markets.

Miller took the Association job in 1966 after 16 years as a researcher, economist, and legal consultant for the United Steelworkers of America. Major league players, on the recommendation of a committee headed by Robin Roberts, voted him into office by a margin of 489–136 after years of entrusting their affairs to Robert Cannon, an ownership toady who had primarily been interested in one day becoming baseball commissioner. The vote came in the face of attempts by National League president Warren Giles and others to paint Miller as a labor goon and only after initial attempts even by Roberts and other player spokesmen to flank him with Richard Nixon as a general counsel. Indicative of the wars on the horizon, Miller made it clear from his first meetings with the players that he regarded the Association as a union in the fullest sense and not merely a professional guild with pension concerns. It was an attitude that was to amuse, scandalize, and finally terrify owners over the next two decades as their various ploys for dividing players fell apart.

Miller negotiated five major contracts with ownership representatives. The first, worked out in 1967, increased management contributions to the pension fund and raised the minimum salary of major leaguers from $7,000 to $10,000 but was chiefly significant for having the owners concede to demands for collective bargaining. A 1969 negotiation session was thornier, with little progress made on salary and pension issues until Miller threatened a strike at spring training camps. When the owners returned to the bargaining table, they recognized the Players Association as an official negotiating party in all matters except individual salaries and conceded the right of players to use agents in talks on contracts. Years later, Miller himself would admit to some reservations about the arrival of agents on the scene, warning players not to become employees of their own representatives and suggesting that four percent, not the customary 10 percent, was a fair fee for their services.

When the owners played hardball in 1972 over another basic agreement contract, Miller secured strike empowerment by a 633–10 margin, then shut down spring training camps for 13 days and kept the players out of nine regular season games until the owners got the message. Both sides ultimately claimed victory with a compromise on salary and health benefits, but Miller walked off with the biggest prize in getting an extension on the arbitration principle, allowing major leaguers with only two years of service to seek arbitration in wage disputes. Arbitration soon emerged as the players' most powerful weapon in dealings with management.

Prior to the 1975 Messersmith-McNally verdict, Miller attempted to work out an accord on the reserve clause that would have saved the owners some face. But they closed their ears to the advice of even their chief negotiator John Gaherin to seek some compromise, suffering total defeat when arbitrator Peter Seitz handed down the ruling ending the contractual peonage of major leaguers. They also laughed off the counsel of one of their own, Oakland's Charlie Finley, who proposed that the clubs go Seitz one better by declaring every player a free agent—an approach that, according to Miller, would have been a logical countermove. Instead, after some useless courtroom challenges and a brief lockout, the owners came back to the table in 1976 to work out a pact that enabled the players to declare for free agency after six years in the big leagues.

The 1976 agreement stuck in the craw of Commissioner Bowie Kuhn and several owners; they were especially irritated by the stipulations that provided for only amateur draft selections as compensation for clubs losing free agents. By 1981, with a stiff-necked Ray Grebey succeeding Gaherin as the owners' spokesman, compensation was being publicized as the principal problem between the Players Association and management. That was false on two counts: first, because it was a squabble primarily between the owners of small-market and large-market franchises concerning their respective resources for hanging on to or signing free agents; second, because Grebey and Kuhn, in particular, were bent on using compensation issues as a pretext for breaking the union. As with past ploys, it didn't work, but this time that became obvious only after the players staged a 50-day walkout during the 1981 season to defend their earlier bargaining gains. The consolation prize for the owners was the creation of a compensation pool of unprotected minor leaguers and major league veterans for a team that had lost a player to free agency. The consolation lasted no more than four years: In 1985, after some bad publicity stemming from the White Sox grab of Tom Seaver from the Mets, the owners themselves asked that the pool idea be abandoned in favor of a return to a compensation system involving amateur draft choices.

Miller retired as Players Association director in 1982. But he was asked back on an interim basis less than a year later when his successor, former federal mediator Ken Moffett, estranged the players with both his secretive style and what were perceived as giveback tactics. Only with the election of Donald Fehr in 1984 did Miller step down for good. What he left behind were the greatest financial gains by any American union for such a short period in the country's history. Between 1876 and 1976, for instance, major leaguers averaged slightly less than seven times the standard U.S. salary; by the early 1990s, following the Association negotiations in the era of free agency and arbitration, big leaguers were averaging 50 times more than other American workers.

STU MILLER

Miller was the first reliever to win Fireman of the Year honors in both leagues. A righthanded junkballer who threw slow, slower and even slower, he racked up the most saves for the Giants in 1961 and for the Orioles in 1963. His 2.47 ERA for San Francisco in 1958 was the lowest in the league.

Miller provided the most graphic demonstration of the atrocious playing conditions at Candlestick Park when, in the middle of a delivery during the 1961 All-Star Game, he was blown off the mound by a gust of wind. He ended up as the winner for the NL.

A. G. MILLS

The third president of the National League, Mills made his biggest impact on the game by defining the extent to which the NL would share its monopoly. Succeeding to the presidency in 1882, he inherited a league so unstable he refused to list the franchises on his letterhead. He settled a struggle with the American Association the next year by convincing its leaders that a trade war gave players an opportunity to extract higher salaries by playing one league off against the other. The so-called Harmony Conference he convoked for February 17, 1883 produced the first National Agreement specifying the governance of baseball.

With the peace shattered again after the formation of the Union Association in 1884, Mills led the battle by, among other things, expanding the reserve rule to include 11 members of each club (even though he admitted privately that the rule was "technically illegal") and endorsing the AA's expansion to 12 clubs to control the contracts as many players as possible. At first he favored wooing back defectors, but the passage of the Day Resolution in 1884 (calling for the permanent blacklisting of contract-jumpers) encouraged him to take the opposite position so dogmatically that he ended up blowing his position over it. When the victorious NL turned around and not only reinstated the players on the blacklist but also offered a franchise to Union Association angel Henry V. Lucas, the disillusioned Mills resigned.

RUPERT MILLS

Nobody was ever more adamant about signatories living up to a contract than Mills, a first baseman for Newark's entry in the Federal League. After both the team and the entire league dissolved after the 1915 season, he announced he had no intention of following the lead of other players in accepting buyouts for contracts extending into 1916. When he insisted on total payment for the second year of his contract, club owner Patrick Powers sought to ridicule him by demanding he do a seven-hour work session by himself every day through a nonexistent season. Mills did precisely that, showing up for 65 days at the club's erstwhile field for "practice." Only after he had collected at least that percentage of the $3,000 due him did he agree to join a minor league team. A .201 hitter in 1915, Mills never played another major league game.

MINNIE MINOSO

One of the most popular of all White Sox players, Minoso had his actual career with the team blurred by both faulty memory and quick-buck hustling. Although associated by many with the Go-Go Sox of the 1950s, for example, the righthanded outfielder was not part of the club that won the 1959 flag, having been traded to the Indians a year earlier. He actually did most of his running for the team earlier in the decade, leading the American League in steals in 1951, 1952, and 1953. During his first stint at Comiskey Park the Cuban native also paced the league in doubles once, triples three times, and being hit by pitched balls six times; he reached the .300 mark on eight occasions. Back with the White Sox a year after their pennant, he led the AL in hits and drove in 100 runs for the fourth time; he was then officially (and only officially) pushing 40. In the crowd-pleasing style that had marked his first tenure with Chicago, he clubbed two home runs in the 1960 season opener, allowing Bill Veeck to set off the $350,000 exploding scoreboard that the owner had installed during the offseason. It was the first use of such a promotional device in the big leagues.

Most of the rest of Minoso's career was marked by the same public relations ploys. After wandering around with the Cardinals and Senators for a couple of seasons, he returned to Chicago a third time in 1964, for what was supposedly his swan song. But in both 1976 and 1980 Veeck brought him out of retirement for some at bats as a designated hitter so he could claim to be a five-decade player. When Jerry Reinsdorf tried the same hype again in 1990, with Minoso at least 70, Commissioner Fay Vincent said no.

GREG MINTON

A workhorse reliever for the Giants in the late 1970s and 1980s, Minton went a record 269$\frac{1}{3}$ innings without yielding a home run. The streak was finally broken by John Stearns of the Mets in 1982.

PAUL MIRABELLA

Southpaw Mirabella was the only player to return to the major leagues in a serious way after playing in the Florida Senior League of retired big leaguers. His 44 appearances for the 1990 Brewers dramatized, for many, the dearth of available lefthanded pitchers. Another southpaw, Daniel Boone, appeared in a couple of games for Baltimore after the collapse of the Senior League in 1989–90.

BOBBY MITCHELL

Mitchell was the first lefthanded pitcher in the majors, debuting for Cincinnati in 1877. He lasted only four seasons and compiled a 20–23 record.

JACKIE MITCHELL

When righthander Mitchell was signed by the Southern Association Chattanooga Lookouts in 1931, she gained the highest rung climbed by a woman player in organized baseball—at least technically. Taught to pitch by Hall of Famer Dazzy Vance, the 17-year-old faced the Yankees in an exhibition game on April 2, proceeding to strike out both Babe Ruth and Lou Gehrig. Although sportswriters insisted the two sluggers had only been clowning around, several New York players denied that was the case, saying their only instructions had been not to hit back up the middle. A couple of days after the exhibition Commissioner Kenesaw Landis voided Mitchell's contract with Chattanooga, claiming baseball was too rough for women.

JOHNNY MIZE (Hall of Fame, 1981)

Mize was in the long tradition of Cardinals first basemen who didn't let their power affect their consistency. Over a 15-year career (between 1936 and 1953) that also included big moments with the Giants and Yankees, the lefty slugger led the league in home runs four times and, in 1939, won the batting title with a .349 average. Aside from the fact that he batted over .300 in his first nine big league seasons (leading to a career average of .312), Mize demonstrated his batting eye by striking out more than 50 times in only one season. Although his brawny frame won him the name of The Big Cat early in his career, he also had sufficient speed to lead the NL in triples in 1938. In the power category, he is the only player to have walloped three home runs in a game six times.

Like Ralph Kiner, the man with whom he had to share two of his home-run titles, Mize was no Branch Rickey fan. In 1935, prior to his first major league season, he was peddled to Cincinnati on a trial basis, but when Larry MacPhail discovered that the first baseman had a bad leg, was promptly returned to St. Louis general manager Rickey. After the 1941 season, in which Mize hit .317 and drove in 100 runs, Rickey dealt him to the Giants with the view that the slugger had seen his best days, but while with the New Yorkers in 1947 and 1948 he hit a combined 91 homers. In 1949 the Yankees purchased him from the Giants, mainly to head off the Red Sox from making a similar move. Over the next five years he played a key role in five Yankees championships, especially coming off the bench.

Asked once about his greatest disappointment in baseball, Mize admitted it was his failure to "out-Rickey Rickey." This stemmed from the fact that his original contract with the Cardinals had been signed by his father, who at the time had not been his legal guardian. In similar cases, players had been declared free agents.

KEN MOFFETT

The first thing Moffett did after being elected executive director of the Players Association in December 1982 was tell the player representatives who had given him the job—and who had waged a highly successful walkout in 1981—that "No one ever wins a strike." The next thing he did was go on vacation. At the post only three months, the formal federal mediator praised owners for what was in fact a terrible television deal; he also failed to realize that his publicized opinion might jeopardize a pending suit by the Association requesting a role in future negotiations with TV networks. Clearly on a roll, Moffett blundered still further by supporting a joint drug program with the commissioner's office that had long been a sore spot among members of the Association. His gaffes caught up with him after a member of his staff confiscated a harsh memo from predecessor Marvin Miller, who had been retained as a consultant to the group. Moffett was fired after only 11 months on the job, eventually being succeeded by chief counsel Don Fehr.

PAUL MOLITOR

For the first 13 of his 21 (1978–98) seasons, Molitor ended up playing regularly at every position except catcher and pitcher at one point or another. Aside from a natural versatility and hitting and running skills that compelled his presence somewhere in the lineup, his mobility was dictated by injuries that opened up his most recent position to the latest rookie promoted by Milwaukee. For his final eight seasons (six of them as a member of the Blue Jays and then Twins), he was a full-time designated hitter—an assignment that extended his career sufficiently for him to compile 3,319 hits (.306 average),

while also clouting 234 home runs and stealing 504 bases. He collected 200 hits four times (leading the American League in that category three times), scored 100 runs five times (three of them league-leading totals), hit higher than .300 12 times, reached double figures in homers 13 times (with a high of 22 for the Blue Jays in 1993), stole 20 bases in 13 seasons, and even drove in 100 runs twice. He also led the AL in doubles and triples once.

In the 1982 World Series Molitor became the first player to rap out five hits in a Fall Classic game. His next World Series appearance was in 1993, when, as a free agent acquisition for Toronto, he took Most Valuable Player honors. Molitor's 3,000th hit, for the Twins on September 16, 1996, was a triple, making him the only player to join the 3,000-hit club with a three-bagger.

RICK MONDAY

Monday was the first prospect to be picked in the inaugural free agent draft of college and high school players in 1965. Selected by Kansas City, the lefthand-swinging outfielder went on to a 19-year (1966–84) career that never quite fulfilled expectations of a premier slugger with Gold Glove defensive abilities. Although he did hit 241 home runs, he reached the 20-mark only three times and never drove in more than 77 runs; on the other hand, he fanned at least 100 times in eight seasons. Monday's stellar baseball moment came in the ninth inning of the finale of the 1981 NLCS, when his homer off Montreal's Steve Rogers gave Los Angeles the pennant.

ROBIN MONSKY

Monsky's sex discrimination suit against the Braves in 1986 was a result of her difficulties with manager Chuck Tanner, who objected to the media information director's practice of including unflattering statistics in the pregame fact sheets distributed to reporters. Barred from the clubhouse and from traveling with the team, Monsky charged in August of that year that the manager's underlying objection was to a woman holding a position of authority. Fired in January 1987, she settled with Atlanta out of court in June 1989.

DONNIE MOORE

The closer for the 1986 Angels, Moore served up a two-run home run to Boston's Dave Henderson in the ninth inning of the fifth game of the ALCS, setting up a comeback pennant win by the Red Sox. The righthander never recovered either from the blow or from his arm troubles preceding it, and repeated accusations of malingering leveled by California general manager Mike Port over the next couple of seasons only made a bad situation disastrous. On July 18, 1988 Moore shot his estranged wife (who recovered), then put a bullet in his own head. Friends said he had never stopped blaming himself for blowing California's pennant.

WILCY MOORE

Moore became a 32-year-old rookie with the Yankees in 1927 after New York general manager Ed Barrow bought him sight unseen after reading about his heroics in the Class B South Atlantic League in *The Sporting News*. Finishing 30–4 for Greenville in 1926, the righthander repaid the executive's confidence by winning 19 games (13 in relief) for the Yankees in 1927 and saving 13 more. Injuries plagued the rest of Moore's six-year career, and he retired with a 51–44 record. He also notched two wins and a save in three World Series appearances.

PAT MORAN

Moran became the first big league manager to win pennants with two different clubs, piloting Philadelphia to a flag in 1915 and leading Cincinnati to a world championship over the White Sox in the blighted 1919 World Series.

JOE MORGAN (Hall of Fame, 1990)

Of all Cincinnati's 1970s Big Red Machine stars, Morgan had the biggest reputation as a winner. Aside form his critical offensive and defensive roles on the Reds, the lefthand-hitting second baseman had a major impact on the Astros, Giants, and Phillies after joining them in the 1980s; in fact, it wasn't until his swan song with the Athletics in 1984 that his presence failed to improve the fortunes of a club.

Offensively, Morgan was a force in just about every significant category. His biggest years in 1975 and 1976—when he won consecutive MVP awards as a member of the Reds—saw him bat .327 and .320, tag 17 and 27 home runs, produce 94 and 111 RBIs, slug .508 and .576, steal 67 and 60 bases, and walk 132 and 114 times. He reached the 100-plateau in both walks and runs scored eight times, stole at least

40 bases nine years in a row, and finished in double figures in two-base hits over his last 16 seasons. In his eight seasons with the Big Red Machine between 1972 and 1979, his on-base average was .410. Morgan's 268 career home runs included the mark (266) for second basemen until he was passed by Ryne Sandberg. It was his single in the seventh game of the 1975 World Series that erased the practical significance of Carlton Fisk's dramatic home run the day before, sealing a world championship for the Reds. Defensively, he used the smallest piece of leather in baseball to win Gold Gloves every year between 1973 and 1977.

Moving back to the Astros, his original major league team, in 1980, a perceptibly slower Morgan still managed to spark Houston to its first postseason appointment; though the club went down to the Phillies in the League Championship Series, his 11th-inning triple in the third game produced a 1–0 victory. Playing for Frank Robinson with the Giants in 1981 and 1982, he helped lift the club from the nether regions of the West Division, but ultimately had to settle for a home run on the final day of the 1982 season to knock Los Angeles out of contention and hand the half-pennant to Atlanta. In spite of Robinson's energetic support, he failed to win a raise from San Francisco general manager Tom Haller after the season, making his trade to Philadelphia a foregone conclusion. Reunited with Big Red Machine teammates Pete Rose and Tony Perez, Morgan slugged 16 home runs (the majority of them down the stretch) to key a division win, and then an LCS victory, for the Wheeze Kids.

After his retirement in 1984 Morgan turned down a couple of managerial offers in favor of becoming a broadcaster. While knowledgable about the game, his observations have tended to skirt direct criticism of anyone and exposed a very fragile sense of humor. In 2001 he and fellow Hall of Famer Tom Seaver promoted a series of election reforms geared toward giving members a greater say in Cooperstown inductions.

MIKE MORGAN

From his debut in 1978 for Oakland to his first World Series appearance in 2001 for Arizona, Morgan donned 12 major league uniforms to tie Deacon McGuire for the most ever. His stopoffs along the way included the Blue Jays, Yankees, Mariners, Orioles, Dodgers, Cubs (twice), Cardinals, Reds, Twins, and Rangers. Rushed to the mound as a publicity ploy by the A's Charlie Finley only two weeks after graduating from high school, the righthander didn't have a winning season until 1991 with the Dodgers (14–10), following that up with a career-best 16–8 with the Cubs in 1992. Morgan's 21-year record of 139–185 includes 13 losing seasons. Baseball's all-time mound percentage losers with at least 100 decisions, Hugh Mulcahy and Rollie Naylor (both at .336), had only 12 losing years between them.

GEORGE MORIARTY

A light-hitting third baseman for the Yankees, Tigers, and others between 1903 and 1916, then later an American League umpire for 22 years, Moriarty made his biggest impression on the game during a two-year hiatus from his second career. Assuming Detroit's managerial reins from Ty Cobb in 1927, he decided his charges were insufficiently schooled in the art of stealing home—an expertise he had demonstrated 11 times during his own playing career. Not content with his instruction on the field (and continually astonished by the inability of the Tigers), he couldn't help displaying his technique to anyone who shared his wonder at the failing of modern players—including guests in hotel lobbies around the league where he soon became a nemesis for his habit of knocking over patrons, plants, and anything else in the way of his improvised classes.

During the 1945 World Series between the Cubs and Tigers, Moriarty gained headlines for taking on the Chicago bench and its relentless Jew-baiting of Detroit star Hank Greenberg. An embarrassed Commissioner Happy Chandler, however, ended up fining the umpire as well as several Cubs players for calling attention to anti-Semitism.

JACK MORRIS

Morris adapted an old school pitching mentality to new school baseball economics: While never afraid to give up runs if he had a comfortable lead, he didn't hesitate to preserve those leads from one uniform to another as a free agent paladin. His lifetime mark of 254–186 (3.90) is also likely to trigger substantial debate about his Hall of Fame credentials, particularly with regard to several pitchers who compiled better records but have remained outside Cooperstown.

With the Tigers for all but the last four years of his 18-year (1977–94) career, Morris was the most successful pitcher of the 1980s, winning 162 times. The decade included two of three 20-win seasons, a league-leading 232 strikeouts in 1982, a no-hitter against the White Sox on April 7, 1984, and two complete-game victories over the Padres in the 1984 World Series. By 1990, though, the righthander had had more than his fill of Detroit's prominent role in collusion against free agents, striking out for more fertile fields. Over the next four years he pitched for the Twins, Blue Jays, and Indians, making two things clear on every stop: He still had enough left to win, and his employer better have enough to keep him from going elsewhere. The Morris attitude was particularly striking after his exciting 10-inning, 1–0 win over the Braves for Minnesota in the seventh game of the 1991 World Series: The very next day, even as local headlines were proclaiming the accomplishment of the Minnesota native, he declared for free agency. He ended up going to Toronto, where he led the league in wins and played for a world champion in his third uniform.

Although viewed by many as an inevitable Hall of Famer, Morris's wins and ERA leave him behind five other eligible pitchers in both categories who have been denied election—Tommy John, Bert Blyleven, Jim Kaat, Jim McCormick, and Gus Weyhing. Except for his 1991 stint with the Twins, when he was at 3.43, his ERA over the last six years of his career was never lower than 4.04.

DICK MOSS

In November 1994 player agent Moss announced plans for the formation of a United Baseball League as an alternative to the National and American leagues. The initiative attracted significant attention because it was outlined during the impasse in player-owner negotiations that had caused an interruption of the 1994 season. Moss and partner Robert Mrazek pegged 1996 for the launching of the league. They said it would encompass eight (never-identified) cities, each of which would have a 15 percent holding in the local club and be entitled to 15 percent of the capital gains upon any franchise sale. The settlement of the major league labor dispute ended talk of the United Baseball League. Moss always denied his initiative had largely been aimed at pressuring the player-management accord.

LANNY MOSS

When Moss was appointed general manager of the Portland Mavericks of the Class A Northwest League in 1975, she became the first woman hired to run a club in organized ball.

JOHNNY MOSTIL

Mostil was a one-man Go-Go Sox in the 1920s, prompting grandstand chants of "Steal! Steal!" whenever he reached first base at Comiskey Park. The righthanded outfielder listened to the crowd enough to pace the American League in stolen bases twice while running up a 10-year batting average of .301. Defensively, he was fast enough to be the only big league center fielder ever to catch a fly ball in foul territory, a feat he accomplished in a spring training game.

Mostil almost put an end to his own career in 1927, when he attempted suicide with a razor and remained unconscious in a hospital for several days. The official line was that he had been depressed by a painful jaw condition, but it emerged subsequently that he had been having an affair with teammate Red Faber's wife and had been threatened by the pitcher. Mostil recovered from his self-inflicted wounds to play one more full season, but without his previous dash.

GEORGE MUIR

Muir was traveling secretary for the 1899 Cleveland Spiders, who set every major league record for futility: a 20–134 record, a .130 won-lost percentage, finishing 84 games out of first place, and an unfathomable 35 games out of 11th in the 12-team National League. At the end of the season the team presented Muir with a diamond locket inscribed to "the only person in the world who had the misfortune to watch us in all of our games."

HUGH MULCAHY

A member of the Phillies rotation in the second half of the 1930s, Mulcahy was known as Losing Pitcher Mulcahy even before his career mark of 45–89 left him with the worst percentage (.336) of any modern pitcher with at least 100 decisions. He also lived up to his name by becoming the first major leaguer drafted into the military for World War II.

TONY MULLANE

Known as The Count for his good looks and suavity, Mullane played pawn in one of the more sordid demonstrations of 19th-century owner chicanery. In 1884, after two 30-win seasons, the righthander, ignoring the reserve clause in his contract with the American Association St. Louis Browns, jumped to the Union Association Maroons in the city, but then backpedaled again when threatened with blacklisting. However, when Browns owner Chris Von der Ahe realized he would have to come close to matching the Maroons offer, he shuffled Mullane off to the Toledo Blue Stockings. This accomplished three things: It kept Mullane away from the Unions, it preserved the Browns salary structure, and it gave the small-market, expansion Blue Stockings a *bona fide* star. At the conclusion of the season, which saw the demise of both the UA and Toledo, Von der Ahe reclaimed the pitcher, paid him an advance on his 1885 salary, and whisked him off to a hotel room to wait out the mandated 10 days before a contract could be signed. But Mullane had plans of his own, escaping from the hotel and signing with the AA Cincinnati Reds. For that he was slapped with a fine and suspended a year.

One of very few pitchers known to have thrown with both arms, Mullane holds a major league record for surrendering 16 runs to Boston in the first inning on June 18, 1894. Despite such outings, he posted eight 20-win seasons.

WILLARD MULLIN

Mullin was a cartoonist for the New York *World-Telegram* who inspired two of the most noted nicknames for National League teams in the 1930s. In one cartoon he depicted a band of grubby Cardinals going across railroad tracks with clubs in their hand toward a gasworks. Although Leo Durocher was sometimes credited with dubbing his team The Gas House Gang, Durocher himself admitted he was inspired by the Mullin cartoon. A couple of years later the cartoonist came up with an Emmett Kelly-like tramp as a symbol of the Dodgers, leading the team to be known as the Bums. Mullin drew the figure as commentary on a franchise that had deteriorated to the point that even its office phones had been shut off for nonpayment of bills. The most famous version of the Bum character was published in the wake of Brooklyn's 1955 World Series victory, with the headline NOW WHO'S A BUM?

VAN LINGLE MUNGO

Mungo's melodious name wasn't backed by a lyrical personality. Regarded as the Brooklyn franchise's hope in the early 1930s, the righthander gradually succumbed to the bad luck and bad teams undermining most of his mound appearances and eventually became better known as a drinker and brawler. Mungo probably reached his low point at the start of the 1936 season when, after promising he would keep a leash on his temper, he yielded a run to the Giants in the first inning on Opening Day, got ejected in the second inning for arguing, came right back the next day to lose 1–0 on an error, then lost a third game on what should have been a pop fly to end the contest. Following the third fiasco, he announced he was tired of playing with amateurs and jumped the team. Manager Casey Stengel talked him back to Brooklyn, and he went on to win 18 games for the year; of course, he also lost 19.

THURMAN MUNSON

Munson was the heart of Yankees teams bad and good for 11 seasons (1969–79) until he was killed in an airplane crash on August 2, 1979. Rookie of the Year in 1970 for his .302 average, the righthand-hitting catcher posted four more .300 seasons. Three of them came between 1975 and 1977, when he also drove in 100 runs each year and took an MVP trophy in 1976. He was even better in October, topping his overall regular-season average of .292 by 65 points in 30 postseason contest, including an average of .373 in three World Series. Moody with reporters and fans but very much the team captain, Munson became a clubhouse rallying point against free agent acquisition Reggie Jackson in 1977, especially after the appearance of the outfielder's *Sport* magazine interview claiming to be "the straw that stirs the drink" and charging that Munson "can only stir it bad."

Yankees brass had attempted for years to talk Munson out of virtually commuting from Yankee Stadium to his home in Canton in a private plane. His fatal crash came as he was practicing takeoffs and landings.

MASANORI MURAKAMI

The first Japanese to play in the major leagues, Murakami had a 5–1 record in 53 relief appearances and a single start for the Giants in 1964 and 1965. He returned to Japan after the 1965 season as part of an agreement that ended a brief spat between the major leagues and Japanese baseball over his services. Back home, he had a largely lackluster career for the Nankai Hawks and heard more than one grandstand cry of "Yankee, Go Home!" when he pitched ineffectively.

RUPERT MURDOCH

What Ted Turner once dreamed of, his business archrival Murdoch had accomplished by the turn of the century in transforming his media clout into the most extensive holdings in major league baseball. Through the vehicle of his umbrella News Corporation and Fox television subsidiaries he could claim ownership of the Dodgers, regional rights to the cablecasting or broadcasting of the games of all but seven of the major league teams, an exclusive multi-year contract for televising all postseason matchups, and prerogatives for game-of-the-week telecasts. In practice, this meant that at least 23 owners had to consider their arrangements with the Australian magnate at league gatherings. If they sometimes came to conflicting conclusions on specific issues, it wasn't because they were ready to challenge Murdoch's long-term priority of making big league baseball another international spectacle he had the assets to develop according to his tested formula of the expedient, the sensational, and the relentlessly dispersive. Whether in the signing of free agents for the Dodgers at preemptive salaries (Sean Green, Kevin Brown) or interrupting games for split-screen remotes of home run hitters at bat in situations meaningless except for their personal statistics, it was a formula that reduced to gibberish the solemn pronouncements of Commissioner Bud Selig and other guardians of the game about needing to preserve the traditional purity of the game.

TIM MURNANE

Murnane was the first major leaguer to turn to sportswriting after his playing career was over. A professional first baseman before the founding of the National Association in 1871, he appeared in the first National League game on April 22, 1876, recording the first major league stolen base. As a journalist, Murnane rose to be sports editor of the Boston *Globe*.

CHARLES MURPHY

As Cubs president between 1906 and 1913, Murphy put the finishing touches on the club that won four pennants in five seasons and then applied the touches that finished most of the team's pivotal players. Acting as a front man for Cincinnati magnate Charles Taft, Murphy appointed first baseman Frank Chance as Chicago manager—the key to turning the runnerup Cubs into a flag winner. By 1911, however, he had tired of his regular contract battles with Chance and other Chicago stars and was looking for a way to get rid of them. He found it when he claimed to have collected reports of numerous episodes of Chicago players taking the field in drunken or hungover states; when Chance denounced the charges as merely a ploy to save money on salaries, he was on his way out the door.

Murphy replaced Chance in 1913 with Johnny Evers—a choice that led Joe Tinker to demand (and obtain) a trade. When he sought to get rid of Evers too, dealing him to the Braves at the end of the season, the second baseman threatened to jump to the Federal League. That brought National League president John Tener running with warnings that Murphy was helping the Feds stock themselves with NL stars. Murphy didn't resist pressures from Tener and league owners to unload his minority interest in the Cubs on Taft and depart the scene.

JOHNNY MURPHY

Murphy held the major league records for most victories in relief (73) and most saves (107) until the advent of the era of the closer in the 1960s. After a cup of coffee in 1932 and one season (1934) as a starter for the Yankees, the righthander became a bullpen specialist, and virtually a private caddy for ace southpaw Lefty Gomez. Murphy's best year was 1941, when he led the American League in both saves and relief wins, and recorded an uncharacteristically low (1.98) ERA. One of the very few quality players to retire during World War II, he returned to New York in 1946 after a two-year absence to win four games and save seven more. After a final season with the Red Sox, he retired with a 93–53 record. The general manager of the Mets in the late 1960s, Murphy died in January 1970, only months after the club's Miracle world championship.

LIZZIE MURPHY

On August 14, 1922 Murphy became the first woman to take the field against a major league team, when she played two innings at first base in an exhibition against the Red Sox. Her Fenway Park appearance came during an 18-year (1918–35) barnstorming career with amateur and semipro clubs.

MORGAN MURPHY

Murphy had a steady career as a backup receiver in the 1890s but a more short-lived one as a buzzer operator. Playing for the Phillies in 1898, he set up a wire leading form the third-base coaching box to the clubhouse where, after glimpsing an opposing catcher's signals, he buzzed a shock code to the coach; the coach then relayed the sign to Philadelphia batters. Murphy's device, encouraged by Philadelphia manager George Stallings, was decommissioned after Cincinnati coach Tommy Corcoran uncovered the wire and alerted the umpire.

ROBERT MURPHY

A former National Labor Relations Board lawyer, Murphy took it upon himself to organize the American Baseball Guild in 1946. Selecting blue-collar Pittsburgh as his battleground, he applied for permission to hold a vote among the Pirates for the purpose of forming his first local. When owner Bill Benswagner stalled, announcing on the June 5 deadline that he needed more time to study the proposition, militant players pushed for a strike. Murphy blinked, however, calculating that by compromising he would win both the public relations battles and a favorable hearing for an unfair labor practices case he had filed with the NLRB. With the strike deadline postponed two days, Benswanger exerted his influence with players in a clubhouse meeting; when the vote came, the Guild managed a majority but not the two-thirds necessary for a job action.

The strike threat over, owners retaliated by establishing a minimum salary, providing spring training expense money ("Murphy money," as it came to be known), and funding a pension program for the first time. With the Guild's issues co-opted, 12 players didn't even bother to show up for an August 20 referendum on whether to unionize the team, and those who did cast ballots voted overwhelmingly not to organize. A despondent Murphy said afterward: "The players have been offered an apple, but they could have had an orchard."

TOM MURPHY

Murphy was the first groundskeeper to tailor a playing field to the skills of the home team. Conspiring with Baltimore manager Ned Hanlon in the 1890s, he sculpted the baselines at Oriole Park to incline toward fair territory to keep bunted balls in play. He also packed the ground in front of home plate to a concrete hardness to increase the height of Baltimore chops and around the infield to provide better footing for the speedsters on the club.

EDDIE MURRAY

Murray's power feats gained only begrudging acceptance in the media because of his years-long coolness to the press. Unlike Steve Carlton and others, he made the situation even worse by influencing younger players to adopt a similar attitude towards sportswriters, winning for himself a reputation as clubhouse poison. Slighted by all the bitchery on both sides was the most productive career by any major league switch-hitter outside Mickey Mantle.

By the time he retired after a 21-year (1977–97) career with the Orioles (twice), Dodgers (twice), Mets, Indians, and Angels, the first baseman had established records for driving in 75 or more runs in 20 consecutive seasons and for homering from both sides of the plate in 11 games. Only Hank Aaron beat him in all three career categories of 504 home runs, 3,255 hits, and 1,917 runs batted in. Murray also hit 20 or more homers 16 times and is the only player other than Tris Speaker to rack up 20 doubles for 20 consecutive seasons. His 128 sacrifice flies are a major league best. And despite his many appearances as a designated hitter he also holds the marks for most games (2,413) and most assists (1,865) by a first baseman.

Murray spent the first 12 years of his career with the Orioles. In 1977, he was the first designated hitter to win Rookie of the Year honors, bashing 27 home runs and driving in 88 runs while averaging .283. He led the AL in RBIs and tied for the lead in homers in the strike-shortened 1981 season—the only time he would top the lists in either category. It was also in Baltimore that he compiled five of his six 100-RBI seasons. In the fifth and final game of the 1983 World Series he homered twice to put the finishing touches on a world championship for the club.

Murray's first stint with Baltimore ended under clouds of resentment in 1988 after owner Edward Bennett Williams refused to grant him a contract extension and the *Sun,* the city's only conspicuous newspaper, unleashed regular attacks on him for not sharing Williams's vision of what was fair and what wasn't; it was because of the *Sun's* constant snipings that the previously communicative slugger soured

on the media and its malleability where owners like Williams were concerned. Traded to the Dodgers, he continued to produce on the field, but also came up against media-happy Tommy Lasorda before and after games and was soon carrying his tag as a clubhouse pollutant. At the end of the 1991 season the Dodgers let Murray walk off to the Mets as a free agent. Over the next two years, while driving home a combined 193 runs, he was cited constantly as a bad influence on Bobby Bonilla and other New York players; it didn't help, either, that his once-superior defensive skills had degenerated to a pathetic degree. It came as no surprise when he was once again allowed to walk off as a free agent at the end of the 1993 season, this time signing with the Indians. It was while he was with Cleveland that Murray picked up his 3,000th hit, on June 30 1995. In his final two seasons he made return engagements with Baltimore and Los Angeles, sandwiched around a stint with California.

RAY MURRAY

Outfielder Sherry Magee's long outs with men on third were the reason Murray, his manager with the Phillies, championed passage of a sacrifice fly rule in 1908. Since then, the rule abating an official at bat when a run scores on a fly out has been reversed and reinstated several times.

IVAN MURRELL

An outfielder for the Padres, Astros, and Braves in the 1960s and 1970s, Murrell was about the worst pinch-hitter who ever came off a bench. His career numbers of 21–180 (.117) included seasons of 2-for-35, 3-for-33, and 5-for-36.

DANNY MURTAUGH

Murtaugh was the only manager who didn't need George Steinbrenner's whims to pilot the same club four times. Thanks to an umbilical relationship with general manager Joe L. Brown, Murtaugh was called on to take over the Pirates from 1957 to 1964, for part of 1967, in 1970 and 1971, and from 1973 to 1976. Each of his exits was triggered more by concerns for a chronic heart condition than by front office dissatisfaction. In his combined 15 years at the helm Murtaugh won world championships in 1960 and 1971 and East Division titles in 1970, 1974, and 1975. Unlike other dugout bosses, he went out of his way to play down his importance to winning, making a preseason ritual of telling his clubs, "If you keep it close in the eighth inning, I'll lose it every time, so make sure we have a big lead by then." What his humor concealed was an ability to get the best out of teams that varied widely in talent but that reflected a preference for lumber company sluggers.

As a player, Murtaugh had a nine-year career as a second baseman in the 1940s for the Phillies, Braves, and Pirates. His main distinction as a player was ending up with the most steals (only 18) in the National League in 1941 despite being promoted to the majors by Philadelphia with the season already half over.

STAN MUSIAL (Hall of Fame, 1969)

The most popular player ever to wear a Cardinals uniform, Musial went through 17 seasons of his (St. Louis-record) 22-year career between 1941 and 1963 before his average dipped below .310, then found the energy to bounce back for one more .330 effort. Not the least of his accomplishments was compiling a higher career mark (.331) than comparable National League titlist Honus Wagner (.328), and without compromising his overwhelmingly superior power numbers.

Dubbed Stan the Man by admiring Brooklyn fans, the lefty-swinging outfielder-first baseman amassed seven batting crowns, eight years of leading the league in doubles, five years in triples, six years in base hits, and six years in slugging. He knocked in 100 runs 10 times, scored 100 runs 11 times, and reached 200 hits six times. Although he never paced the league in home runs, he topped the 30-level on six occasions, ending up with 475. In 1948 he missed a Triple Crown by a lone homer but led the NL in hitting with his career-high .376 as well as in slugging, hits, doubles, triples, runs, and RBIs; only two other players (Tip O'Neill in 1887 and Joe Medwick in 1937) have ever reached the top of as many significant offensive categories in the same year. If there was one flaw in Musial's game, it was his running: He never swiped more than nine bases in a season. In 1943, 1946, and 1948 he was awarded the league's MVP trophy.

Musial's charisma was aided by an odd batting stance that was all crouch and coil, giving him the appearance of a clamp gripping an invisible shelf. His popularity as much as his offensive prowess got him picked for 24 All-Star Games; even in 1957,

when Cincinnati fans stuffed the ballot boxes to elect Reds players to seven positions outside pitcher; even they conceded that first base belonged to Musial. His six All-Star Game homers are a high, and his eight extra-base hits and 40 total bases tie him with Willie Mays. The first player to appear in more than 1,000 games at two positions, he was so consistent at the plate that he finished with a career average higher than .323 for every month of the season. He also managed the odd feat of dividing his 3,630 lifetime hits evenly between 1,815 at home and 1,815 on the road.

In 1946 Musial became the prime target of Jorge Pasquel's attempts to lure American players to Mexico. Commissioner Happy Chandler asserted later that his refusal to abandon the Cardinals removed most of the threat from Pasquel's raids; at the very least, it enabled Chandler to outlaw the players who did go without fear of costing the major leagues a superstar. In 1960 St. Louis manager Solly Hemus provoked the wrath of St Louis when he announced that he intended benching the aging star to give more playing time to rookies; Musial himself helped smooth over the minicrisis by proposing he do most of his sitting on the road. In 1962 he was dragged into another controversy when franchise adviser Branch Rickey suggested that his .330 comeback that year at age 42 was the last hurrah and that he should retire. Musial allowed as how Rickey's advice was "embarrassing," and the uproar chilled the executive's relations with other St Louis front office people for good, but in fact it turned out to be an accurate prediction. He retired after a .255 performance the following year.

In 1967 Musial agreed to succeed Bob Howsam as Cardinals general manager, mainly at the urging of field manager and former roommate Red Schoendienst. He remained at the post for a single pennant-winning season, making him the only one-for-one general manager.

JIM MUTRIE

The holder of the second-highest won-lost percentage (.611) among managers with more than two years of service, Mutrie was the first to call the New York National League club the Giants, in an exuberant reference to the height of several players on his 1885 squad. While known in the clubhouse as a player's manager, he had another reputation in league councils as a double-dealer. His locker room popularity was the result of his genial backseat approach, sporting his trademark stovepipe hat, cheering his charges from the stands, and leaving the actual direction of field activity to a succession of field captains, most notably catcher Buck Ewing. He alienated American Association officials by leaking private information to the National League while managing the AA's New York Metropolitans franchise.

In 1884 Mutrie challenged the NL-flag-winning Providence Grays to a postseason series with his own first-place Metropolitans but lost all three games of the first officially sanctioned inter-league championship series. The following year he ended up in the NL himself after the AA fined and suspended him for his part in transferring third baseman Dude Esterbrook and pitcher Tim Keefe from the Metropolitans to their NL rivals in New York. The expulsion prompted John B. Day, who owned both franchises, to transfer the manager to his NL organization as well.

In reduced circumstances in the 1920s, Mutrie worked as a ticket taker at the Polo Grounds until Giants president Charles Stoneham found out who he was and pensioned him off generously.

N

JIM NABORS

A righthander with the 1916 Athletics, Nabors went 1–20 for the worst record by any pitcher with 20 decisions in a season. Indicative of the Connie Mack cellar dwellers, that made him merely third in staff losses. Nabors had five other decisions during his career—all losses.

HEATHER NABOZNY

Hired by the Tigers in 1999, Nabozny was the first woman to head a big league grounds crew.

FRANK NAVIN

Navin was an insurance company bookkeeper who gained control of the Tigers in record time and maintained it for more than three decades. He was a critical player in just about every major dispute that affected the American League in the early going, and functioned as league president for a period. Many of his conflicts stemmed from having Ty Cobb on his club and from having AL president Ban Johnson as an on-and-off ally.

Navin got involved with the Tigers in 1902, when his employer, Detroit insurance man and railroad contractor Samuel Angus, was awarded the franchise by Johnson in its second year of existence. At first it seemed like a brief involvement when Johnson sought to move the team to Pittsburgh for the larger Pennsylvania market, but that plan was ditched with the January 1903 peace agreement between the American and National leagues. With Angus preoccupied with other business ventures, Navin had the influential say in the hiring and firing of several early-century managers; he continued to have it after Angus

sold out to William Yawkey in 1904. When Yawkey revealed he didn't have enough money to buy star prospects, Navin formalized his own role by advancing the cash and taking over as club president. From that vantage point he felt strong enough to oppose Johnson's dictum against extroverted managers who would give the AL the NL's raucous image, hiring Old Oriole Hughie Jennings in 1907. Jennings immediately piloted the club to three straight pennants—the only ones Navin would enjoy for almost 25 years.

From the day Cobb joined the Tigers on August 30, 1905, he became Navin's chief antagonist—not least in bitter annual contract talks. Partly because of these set-tos, but also because of Cobb's frequent violence on and off the diamond, the executive was always open to a trade offer for his star, but could never finalize anything because of the apprehension of other owners about importing friction into their own clubhouses. One of Navin's worst crises with Cobb erupted in 1912, when Tigers players refused to take the field in a game against Philadelphia unless Johnson rescinded a suspension and fine levied on the outfielder for slugging a fan in New York. Terrified by the prospect of having to cough up a $1,000-a-day fine of his own for not fulfilling Detroit's schedule, Navin ordered Jennings to scour Philadelphia to find amateurs for the game, signed them to one-day pacts, and then watched as they were drubbed by the Athletics. The crisis ended only when Cobb himself appealed to teammates to end their protest.

Navin found his third compliant boardroom partner in 1919, when Yawkey died of a stroke and his heirs sold out to auto body builder Walter Briggs.

With Navin's franchise holdings up to 50 percent, he was confirmed as president by the new owner. Again, though, it initially appeared to be a short-term victory because of another attack threatening the survival of the Tigers. This time the trouble arose from Johnson's resistance to a Cubs-inspired proposal to name Kenesaw Landis as baseball's first commissioner. The Chicago initiative had the backing of the other seven NL clubs, plus the White Sox, Red Sox, and Yankees. When Navin came out in support of Johnson more vocally than other AL loyalists, the pro-Landis teams concocted a scheme for a single, 12-club National League—the incumbents in the senior circuit, their three AL allies, and a brand new Detroit franchise. Navin wasn't *that* loyal to Johnson: He quickly brokered a conference of all existing clubs and forced the AL president to read the writing on the wall, leading to Landis's election.

One of Navin's more unorthodox moves was naming Cobb manager in 1920. Despite the star's often virulent relations with teammates, his hunch was that the players respected Cobb's baseball ability enough to play for him, especially with his relative mellowing over the years. Navin was proved right to the extent that Cobb kept the pitching-short team over .500 in five of his six years at the helm and supervised a clubhouse no worse than several others around the league. When the explosion came, it had more to do with his own relations with Cobb. In October 1926 Navin announced that Cobb was stepping down as manager and also retiring as a player. The surprise move came in the wake of accusations by former Detroit pitcher Dutch Leonard that he, Cobb, Cleveland player-manager Tris Speaker, and Indians outfielder Joe Wood had fixed a September 1919 game. Although Landis stepped in to quash the charges with suspicious alacrity, Cobb had in the meantime accused Navin and Johnson of being behind the scandal in an attempt to break his multiyear contract with the club, and threatened to sue. Thanks to Landis, the suit was never filed, but the episode ended Cobb's association with the Tigers. It also put a practical end to Johnson's tenure as AL president. Stung by allegations that he had covered up the Leonard charges, Landis demanded a showdown with Johnson and AL owners, making it clear he would resign if he didn't receive full vindication. He did, and Johnson took off on a sabbatical from which he never truly returned; for several months Navin took over the league's day-to-day affairs.

Navin's last moments of glory were partly the result of a miscalculation by Babe Ruth. Avid for a box office name to manage the team in 1934, the owner offered the job to Ruth. But despite years of talking about wanting to be a manager and face to face with the only serious proposal he would ever receive to be one, the slugger asked Navin to hold off until he returned from a series of personal appearances he had scheduled in Hawaii. Deciding that Ruth's interest was too vague, Navin obtained catcher Mickey Cochrane from the Athletics for $100,000 and named him to the piloting post. Cochrane proceeded to lead the team to two consecutive pennants, the organization's first since 1909. A month after the Tigers won their only World Series during his reign, in 1935, Navin died of a heart attack.

RON NECCIAI

As a 19-year-old rookie on May 13, 1952, Necciai pitched the dream game, striking out 27 batters in a 7–0 no-hitter for Bristol of the Class D Appalachian League. Since one batter grounded out in the second inning, it took a catcher's error on the 26th strikeout to give the righthander the opportunity to record number 27. Promoted to parent Pittsburgh later in the year as a gate attraction for the last-place team, Necciai struck out 31 batters in 54 $\frac{2}{3}$ innings, racking up a record of 1–6, 7.08.

BOB NEIGHBORS

A shortstop for the 1939 Browns, Neighbors was the only major leaguer to be killed in action during the Korean War.

GRAIG NETTLES

While carving a niche for himself as a formidable power hitter and nimble third baseman defensively in 22 big league seasons (1967–88), Nettles became almost as renowned for his glib observations on playing for George Steinbrenner's Yankees. Asked once about the constant chaos around the team, Nettles declared: "When I was a little boy, I wanted to be a baseball player and join the circus; with the Yankees I've been able to do both." Noting on another occasion that the previous year's top American League reliever, Sparky Lyle, had been displaced in the New York bullpen by free agent pickup Goose

Gossage, Nettles allowed as how it was a case of "from Cy Young to Sayonara."

On the field, Nettles cracked at least 20 homers 11 times, pacing the AL in that category with 32 in 1976. While in the Bronx, the lefty swinger contributed to five Eastern Division titles, four pennants, and two world championships. His personal *bête noire* in pinstripes was slugger Reggie Jackson, with whom he swapped ugly punches during a World Series victory dinner and about whom he once said:"The best thing about being a Yankee is getting to watch Reggie play every day; of course, the worst thing about being a Yankee is getting to watch Reggie play every day."

For much of his career, Nettles was considered second only to Brooks Robinson as a defensive third baseman. His four dazzling fielding plays in the third game of the 1978 World Series against the Dodgers were eerily reminiscent of the glovework displayed by Robinson in the 1970 Series between the Orioles and Reds.

DON NEWCOMBE

Although the dominant pitcher on the Boys of Summer Dodgers in the 1950s and the only major leaguer to have swept Rookie of the Year, Most Valuable Player, and Cy Young awards, Newcombe could never overcome a reputation for not winning the big game. The righthander's troubles started in the opener of the 1949 World Series, when he yielded a ninth-inning home run to Tommy Henrich to lose to the Yankees, 1–0. After that, Newcombe was the loser to Dick Sisler's homer in the 10th inning of the final game of the 1950 season; the exhausted hurler who had to yield to Ralph Branca in the ninth inning of the final playoff game against the Giants in 1951; and the perennial batting practice target of the Yankees in World Series competition. His overall record in Series play was 0–4, with an 8.59 ERA. Often overlooked, though, was his clutch pitching in the stretch of the 1949 pennant race, when he even started both ends of a doubleheader in September to keep the Dodgers in contention. His 27 victories in 1956 has been reached by NL pitchers only twice since then—by Hall of Famers Sandy Koufax in 1966 and Steve Carlton in 1972.

Newcombe was also one of baseball's best hitting pitchers, ending his career with 15 home runs and a .271 average; on the slugging Brooklyn teams of the 1950s, he was the chief pinch-hitter for a couple of years. An admitted alcoholic for a substantial part of his playing days, he has worked for the Los Angeles Dodgers for some years as a counselor for players with drinking problems.

HAL NEWHOUSER (Hall of Fame, 1992)

Nobody was admitted to Cooperstown more begrudgingly than lefty Newhouser. Although his 207 career wins included four years of 20 victories and he is the only pitcher to have claimed back-to-back MVP trophies, he was belittled for years by critics who noted that he did most of his exceptional pitching during World War II, when major league talent was at a minimum. But in fact Newhouser also collected 82 wins between 1946 and 1949, when there was no such talent scarcity. Indicative of the franchise's priorities over the years, he is the only Detroit pitcher in the Hall of Fame.

BOBO NEWSOM

Newsom was either the best bad pitcher or the worst good one in the history of baseball; he was certainly the player who changed uniforms the most times, with several of his departures caused by his swagger and bombast. The righthander never ran into a fact, especially about his own abilities, that he couldn't exaggerate, or a lie he couldn't defend indignantly as a fact.

In a 20-year career between 1929 and 1953, Newsom won at least 20 games three times, but also lost 20 on three occasions; for the Browns in 1938, his first 20-win season, he set the big league mark for the highest ERA (5.08) of any 20-game winner. He ended his career with a 211–222 record, linking him to Jack Powell as the only two to win more than 200 games and lose more than they won. None of it prevented Newsom from regarding himself as the best pitcher in baseball and passing along his assessment to anyone willing to listen.

Although he didn't play for as many different teams as Mike Morgan, Newsom's round-trip adventures led him to change clubs a record 17 times. He never lasted with any organization more than two years in a row and was traded during a season an astounding eight times. He served a record five terms with the Senators; for lack of any other logical reason for his recurrent pursuit of somebody who seemed to save his most mediocre years for Washington, club owner Clark Griffith once asserted he never enjoyed pinochle so much as when he played with Newsom. The pitcher also did three stretches with the Browns and two each with the Dodgers and Athletics; his other homes (briefly) were with the Cubs, Red Sox, Tigers, Yankees, and Giants. He earned his nickname from his habit of calling all teammates Bobo—a practicality since he was never around long enough to learn their names.

Just between 1937 and 1944, Newsom changed teams nine times. Traded by the Senators to the Red Sox in mid-1937, he took to chasing Boston shortstop-manager Joe Cronin back to his position, complaining that player-managers were more of a nuisance than the bench variety because they had less distance to travel to annoy him; he was traded to St. Louis at the end of the year. Two years later he irritated Browns bench boss Fred Haney by warming up on his own in a contest against the Yankees and bringing the abuse of the crowd down on the pilot when he called down to the bullpen for someone other than the fan favorite Newsom; Haney, too, couldn't wait to get rid of him at the end of the year. When he complained loudly about the Tigers slashing his salary by two-thirds before the 1942 season as a wartime economy measure, Detroit peddled him back to Washington. Shipped by Griffith to Brooklyn in the middle of that season, Newsom managed to last the year with the Dodgers, but then got into another set-to with manager Leo Durocher the following year. The incident was triggered by Durocher's suspension of the pitcher for allegedly uncurling a spitter that the catcher couldn't grab, costing the team an important game. Newsom, at the time the biggest winner on the staff, denied that he had thrown a spitter, and was backed up by shortstop Arky Vaughan and other Dodgers teammates who threatened a walkout. President Branch Rickey had to step in to quell the budding revolt against Durocher—and, not surprisingly, decided a part of the remedy was packing Newsom off to the Browns.

The other side of the story is that Newsom often pitched well for some awful clubs—and did so with grit. In 1936, for example, Earl Averill smashed a line drive off his kneecap, but he finished the game before going on crutches for close to two months. On Opening Day in 1937, Newsom brashly traded autographs with Franklin D. Roosevelt (even though the president hadn't asked for his), then, once the game began, got knocked unconscious by a throw

from his own third baseman, Ossie Bluege. Once again, though, he finished the game, after a brief application of a cold towel. When he finally got to pitch for a winner, the 1940 Tigers, his opening game victory in the World Series against the Reds quickly lost its luster when his father, on hand for the game, died of a heart attack an hour later. Nevertheless, he went out and won the fourth game, as well, and pitched ably enough to take the seventh, but came up on the short end of a 2–1 score.

Newsom's observation on the owners he worked for was, characteristically, a malaprop: "Those maggots are nuts."

AL NICHOLS

Although he made only six appearances for the 1877 Louisville Grays, Nichols was one of four team members blacklisted for throwing games—a scandal that led to the collapse of the franchise. Purchased in July as a backup infielder, he served as a go-between with gamblers while outfielder George Hall made good on a couple of promised exhibition game losses. Nichols also suggested involving pitcher Jim Devlin in the conspiracy, but Hall apparently doublecrossed him and did separate business with Devlin. Suspected of foul play by manager Jack Chapman, Nichols left the club before the end of the season, making him even fairer game in a private investigation opened by the Grays. Former teammates like outfielder Orator Shaffer showed little hesitation testifying against him. Although ultimately banned along with Hall, Devlin, and shortstop Bill Craver, Nichols was the only one of the quartet to play professional ball again; he reappeared under an assumed name with the Brooklyn Franklins in 1884, and was also probably the "Williams" who played for Jersey City of the Eastern League in 1886.

KID NICHOLS (Hall of Fame, 1949)

Nichols was the best thing that happened to the Boston Beaneaters during the 1890 Players League war. Signed to bolster a depleted roster, the fastball specialist went on to what was probably baseball's greatest decade-long pitching performance, averaging almost 30 annual wins through the 1890s. He reached a career total of 361 victories without ever developing an off-speed pitch, led Boston to five pennants, and topped the NL in wins in three of his seven 30-victory seasons. So dominating was Nichols that opposition batters frequently resorted to bizarre tactics to break his concentration. On August 6, 1891, for instance, Cap Anson was awarded first base for jumping from the right to the left side of the plate, distracting the righthander in the middle of his windup. Since the rules of the day required the pitcher to deliver the ball no matter what, umpire John McQuaid sent Anson to first base on a free pass for Nichols's "refusal" to comply.

BILL NICHOLSON

Long before grandstands were resounding with "LOOOOUUUU" or "MOOOOKIE" for every appearance by a favorite player, Nicholson was setting off a stadium call of "SWISH" whenever he strode to the plate. Originally inspired by the hulking outfielder's classic strikeout form, it evolved into a shout of respect as Nicholson tore up wartime pitching as a member of the Cubs to lead the National League in home runs and RBIs in both 1943 and 1944. The only other player who accomplished that tandem in back-to-back years was Mike Schmidt, and he had the benefit of the strike-shortened 1981 season.

GEORGE NICOLAU

Nicolau was the arbitrator who ruled in the Players Association favor on the second and third collusion cases. In 1988 he found the owners guilty of conspiring against 79 players and awarded new-look free agency status to 12 others. In 1990 he similarly decided that a data bank set up by owners through which they could share information about offers to available players constituted a violation of the right to an unrestricted free market of 76 members of the 1987 free agent class. The players affected included such stellar names as Paul Molitor, Jack Morris, Jack Clark, and Dave Righetti. By the time these two cases, plus Collusion I (decided by Thomas Tuttle Roberts), were decided, the cost to big league owners topped $100 million.

PHIL NIEKRO (Hall of Fame, 1997)

The knuckleballer Niekro won 318 games over 24 years, and his 121 victories after the age of 40 are the high for grayheads, but he also holds a number of negative records. They include ties for the most consecutive seasons (four) leading a league in losses and for the most years (three) leading in runs allowed. More predictably, his knuckleball was responsible for all the significant NL records for career, game, and inning wild pitches. The righthander was also the last to win and lose 20 games in the same season (1978).

With the Braves from 1964, Niekro's close ties to Atlanta owner Ted Turner caused friction with manager Joe Torre in 1983, prompting a me-or-him ultimatum from the pilot. Niekro ended up the temporary loser by not being offered another contract and then wandering around the American League for several years. It was while with the Yankees in 1985 that he recorded his 300th win; to mark the occasion, he refrained from throwing a knuckler until his final two deliveries of the game. In line with a Turner promise that he would make his final mound appearance in a Braves uniform, Niekro went to the hill in Atlanta on September 23, 1987, but had to withdraw early after giving up six hits and six walks in three innings. His most noteworthy appointment since retirement came in December 1993, when he took over as manager-coordinator of the Colorado Silver Bullets, the first all-women's team to compete regularly against all-male minor league clubs.

Niekro's younger brother Joe, who also used a knuckleball more than other pitches, was one of the NL's most effective hurlers in the late 1970s and 1980s. The Niekros hold the records for both most wins (579) and most years of service in the big leagues (46) by two brothers. They also hold the mark for most combined losses (478).

BOB NIEMAN

Called up by the Browns in 1951, Nieman put his name in the record book immediately by becoming the first major leaguer to homer in his first two at bats. The righthand-hitting outfielder had as many as 20 home runs in only one of his 12 big league seasons. The only other player to circle the bases with his first two plate appearance was Keith McDonald of the 2000 Cardinals. While Nieman did it in the same game, catcher McDonald did it three days apart.

RICHARD NIXON

Nixon courted—and was courted by—baseball before, during, and after his years as President of the United States. In the 1960s he was approached by Robin Roberts and Jim Bunning to succeed Robert Cannon as attorney for the Players Association; the idea died when Marvin Miller refused to work with

him. While in the White House between 1969 and
1974, Nixon popularized the ritual of receiving world
championship teams; it was on one such occasion
that he spurred Oakland's Vida Blue into demanding
more money from Charlie Finley. Despite his Watergate scandal disgrace, Nixon's name remained on
the lips of major league owners whenever a league
presidency or the commissioner's job had to be filled,
in part because of his regular presence at Shea Stadium and in Gene Autry's box for Angels home games.
His most formal relationship to the game came in
1985, when he accepted an arbitration role in a
threatened strike by umpires; he averted the job action with support for a 40 percent pay raise with the
expansion of the League Championship Series from
a best-of-five to a best-of-seven formula. Nixon was
also known for a series of notes to players he perceived as struggling against adverse circumstances.
Among those receiving them were Luis Aparicio,
when the shortstop was enduring a lengthy slump in
the 1960s, and George Brett, when the third baseman was awaiting the verdict on his pine tar home
run in the 1980s.

HIDEO NOMO

Nomo's signing with the Dodgers for the 1995
season was the crack in the door for player movement from Japan to the United States. Although he
had been preceded by Masanori Murakami in the
1960s, the righthander was the first to skip the minors and go directly from Japanese baseball to the
major leagues and his taking of Rookie of the Year
honors galvanized the attention of scouts for more
Asian recruits. While subsequently outdone by Ichiro Suzuki, he was also the first to attract hordes of
Japanese sportswriters and photographers to his every mound appearance.

In his rookie year Nomo employed his Luis Tiant-
like swivel and hesitation at-the-hat delivery to win
13 games for Los Angeles; his 236 strikeouts were
good enough to lead the National League and the
first of three straight years in which he topped the
200-level. He won 16 the following year amid a
growing Nomomania at Dodger Stadium along the
lines of the Fernandomania 15 years before; among
other things, concessionaires began selling sushi. It
was also on September 17 of that year that he accomplished what many thought impossible—no-hit
the Rockies in the batter-friendly thin air of Coors

Field. In 1997, though, Nomo began showing signs
of a "wild in the strike zone" weakness: While never
reaching 100 walks and usually among the stingiest
in yielding hits, his ERA began to swell because of a
proclivity for grooving the wrong pitch at the wrong
time. When he was slow to rebound from an off-season elbow operation in 1998, the Dodgers got over
their Nomomania and dealt him to the Mets.

Between 1998 and 2000 Nomo drifted from New
York to Milwaukee to Detroit, only occasionally
flashing his old form. It didn't help that, even beyond
language problems, he had developed a reputation as
aloof with teammates and the media. But in 2001 he
made giant strides back with the Red Sox, once again
striking out 200 hitters (a league-best 220) and joining
a small handful of pitchers to throw no-hitters in both
leagues; in addition to the no-no against Baltimore on
April 4, he authored a one-hitter against Toronto during the season. When Boston wasn't quick to reward
him for his comeback season with a multiyear pact,
he returned to the Dodgers as a free agent.

BILLY NORTH

The only thing North did better than run was start
clubhouse fights. The center fielder for the brawling
Athletics of the 1970s, he was in one major confrontation after another with teammates because of
cracks about their abilities or their criticisms of his.
The most serious battle took place on June 5, 1974,
when North and Reggie Jackson went at it so vio-
lently that catcher Ray Fosse felt compelled to break
it up; what he got for his trouble was a crushed disc
in his neck that sidelined him for the year. North
was also among the most vocal Oakland players in
regular advice to the American League to take the
club away from Charlie Finley before the owner left
it in ruins. On the field, the switch-hitting speedster
led the league in steals in 1974 and 1976, and teamed
with Bert Campaneris for the most aggressive top of
the order of the period.

JACK NORWORTH

It was while riding in a train past the Polo Grounds
in 1908 that Norworth got the inspiration to write
"Take Me Out to the Ball Game," first sung by Nora
Bayes, the lyricist's wife. Neither Norworth nor Albert Van Tilzer, who supplied the music, attended a
major league game until decades after the song had
become the baseball anthem.

LOU NOVIKOFF

Novikoff came up to the Cubs in the early 1940s ballyhooed as another Babe Ruth, but managed only 15 home runs in four seasons. Aside from his troubles with National League pitching, he was undone by a phobia of Wrigley Field's outfield ivy. Despite a parade of doctors and psychologists brought in to reassure him that he had no particular vulnerability to the vine, Novikoff found it easier to chase after caroms off the wall than to plunge after any long shots while still in the air. When he refused to pay attention even to a frantic campaign by teammates to chew ivy to show him it was harmless, the outfielder was farmed out.

GERRY NUGENT

Nugent was an affable shoe salesman who married the personal secretary of ruinous Philadelphia owner William Baker, thereby putting himself in a position to take over the Phillies in 1933. To considerable surprise (and titters), Baker left most of his stock in the team not to his wife, but to May Mallon Nugent; Baker's widow did the same thing when she died a few years later. Gerry Nugent, who had quit the shoe business to work in the Philadelphia front office and who had risen to organization president amid all the chaos of the Baker reign, distinguished himself from his predecessor only in personality: Whereas Baker had been hard pressed to hide a cutthroat demeanor, Nugent managed to maintain his cordiality while justifying one astounding player sale after another. Among those he dealt away (claiming the alternative would have been moving the franchise out of Philadelphia) were Chuck Klein, Don Hurst, Dolf Camilli, Bucky Walters, Claude Passeau, Spud Davis, Kirby Higbe, and Dick Bartell, insuring that the club remained last or next to last for every year of his ownership. About the only positive news for the franchise in the period was the move out of dilapidated Baker Bowl (although even that decision carried an asterisk insofar as the Phillies had to accept being tenants of the Athletics in Shibe Park).

Nugent missed his last chance for glory in 1942 when, faced with an NL order to upgrade his operation or sell out, he considered a revolutionary proposal from Bill Veeck to break baseball's color line unilaterally and stock the team with Negro league stars. But then he and Veeck made the tactical error of telling Commissioner Kenesaw Landis about their idea, and the league took over the team before it could be accused of countenancing antisegregationist acts. It was under league auspices that the Phillies were sold to lumber magnate William Cox.

JOE NUXHALL

On June 10, 1944 Nuxhall took the mound for Cincinnati at the age of 15 years, 10 months, and 11 days, making him the youngest major leaguer since the 19th century. In two-thirds of an inning the southpaw yielded two hits and five bases on balls, retiring for the season with an ERA of 67.50. He returned to the Reds eight years later, remaining with them through the 1950s; his best year was 1955, when he won 17. After ending his 16-year career in 1966, he went into the Cincinnati broadcasting booth.

O

REBEL OAKES

Oakes was testimony to the informal blacklisting of players active in the Federal League. After five solid seasons with the Reds and Cardinals, the lefty-swinging outfielder moved to the FL Pittsburgh Rebels as a player-manager, in the process providing the club nickname from his own. Seeking to improve on a seventh-place finish in 1914, club owner Edward Gwinner encouraged Oakes to raid NL and AL teams with lavish money offers for defectors. Oakes did what he was asked, and paid for it after the 1915 season when, despite the dissolution of the Feds and the official reinstatement of most players who had jumped, he couldn't find a job.

PETE O'BRIEN

First baseman O'Brien signed with Seattle as a free agent for the 1990 season after turning down offers from the Tigers and Phillies because of stated fears the two clubs might be contenders. He remained at peace with the bottom-dwelling Mariners into 1993, when a sudden midseason spurt brought (short-lived) hopes of a West Division title. Around the same time O'Brien announced his intention of retiring.

DICK O'CONNELL

No general manager has ever had a more embattled run than O'Connell did for the Red Sox in the 1960s and 1970s, and that was only a prelude to the bizarre circumstances under which he returned to the post in the 1980s.

After serving as business manager for some years, O'Connell took over Boston's baseball operations in 1965. His first big move was to bring in Dick Wil- liams, who managed the club beyond all expectations to the Impossible Dream pennant of 1967. Mainly because of frictions involving owner Tom Yawkey and star outfielder Carl Yastrzemski, O'Connell had to get rid of Williams again in 1969, igniting several years of dim dugout leadership and the evolution of the team's identity as "25 players who took 25 cabs" after games. The general manager added to the oppressive atmosphere by evoking the Curse of the Bambino in dealing relief ace Sparky Lyle to the Yankees for bit player Danny Carter.

In 1976 O'Connell met his Waterloo. With the winds of free agency blowing around the franchise, he hemmed and hawed through the season about renegotiating the contracts of front liners Fred Lynn, Carlton Fisk, and Rick Burleson. But at the same time he announced that the Red Sox were ready to pay Charlie Finley $1 million each for Oakland reliever Rollie Fingers and outfielder Joe Rudi. Commissioner Bowie Kuhn ultimately scotched the deal with the A's, but its mere possibility strengthened the hands of the three Boston players, especially with the local media and protesting fans asking why the club had money for Fingers and Rudi, but not for three homegrown stars. Making matters even worse was scouting director Haywood Sullivan, who was so bent on getting O'Connell's job that he leaked the particulars of the negotiations with Lynn, Fisk, and Burleson, then, giving a new definition to tackiness, turned around and led the tsk-tsk chorus about their inflated salary demands. When later in the year O'Connell also became the first front office executive to offer a big contract to a free agent (reliever Bill Campbell), Sullivan closed the net by persuading owner Jean Yawkey that the general manager should be allowed to spend only what she approved personally. O'Connell didn't hang around too long after it was announced that Sullivan, Yawkey, and one-time club trainer Buddy LeRoux had formed a new owner partnership.

In 1983 O'Connell came back as part of LeRoux's administrative coup attempt against Sullivan and Yawkey. For two days O'Connell sat in the club's offices with the title of general manager—the same one Sullivan was brandishing. A Boston judge finally put an end to the farce by issuing a restraining order against LeRoux and O'Connell. O'Connell was long gone from the scene when the ownership conflict was worked out months later.

JIMMY O'CONNELL

An outfielder for the 1924 Giants, O'Connell starred in one of the era's big fixing scandals when he approached Philadelphia shortstop Heinie Sand near the end of the season and offered him $500 if he didn't bear down in a series against New York. Within 24 hours the naïve O'Connell was in Commissioner Kenesaw Landis's office, saying he had been put up to the bribery bid by Giants coach Cozy Dolan and star players Frankie Frisch, Ross Youngs, and George Kelly. While Frisch, Youngs, and Kelly adamantly denied the accusation, Dolan confined himself to saying he couldn't remember whether he had urged O'Connell to approach Sand. In a story that left more questions than produced answers, Landis banned the coach and the outfielder, but exonerated the three future Hall of Famers.

JACK O'CONNOR

O'Connor loathed Ty Cobb enough to get himself thrown out of the major leagues. Manager of the cellar-dwelling Browns in 1910, he ordered third baseman Red Corriden to play deep throughout a doubleheader on the final day of the season so that Cleveland's Nap Lajoie might dump enough bunt hits to beat Cobb for the batting title. In fact, Lajoie collected eight hits on the day, six of them bunts Corriden was unable to field. But when AL president Ban Johnson heard of the finagling, he threw O'Connor out of the league and sent St. Louis pitching coach Harry Howell packing with him for offering the official scorer a new suit to change an obvious error to a hit for Lajoie. Cobb was accredited with the batting title by less than

one point anyway—at least until 1980, when *Sporting News* researcher Paul MacFarlane offered evidence that the Tigers star had been given two hits too many and that the race had really been won by Lajoie. But Commissioner Bowie Kuhn was in no mood to revive memories of the doubleheader against the Browns, so ruled that the title would remain Cobb's.

PADDY O'CONNOR

A backup catcher of no particular distinction at the beginning of the 20th century, O'Connor was as responsible as anyone for Leo Durocher's long stay in the majors as a player and then a manager. While piloting a minor league club in Hartford in 1925, O'Connor suspected that Durocher was the thief who had been going through the pockets of his players for some weeks. To catch the shortstop, he planted a marked bill in a pair of pants, then followed Durocher after the game to a nearby hotel. As soon as Durocher handed a bill to a hotel restaurant waiter, O'Connor moved in and seized his evidence. But despite demands by most of the team that Durocher be denounced to the league (a move that would have certainly meant a lifetime ban from organized ball), O'Connor worked out a compromise under which the infielder would continue playing for the pennant-contending club until the end of the season and then be shown the door. No sooner had Hartford clinched the flag than O'Connor made good on his promise—by selling Durocher to the Yankees. With the sale price at stake, the thefts were not mentioned to New York and Durocher's big league career was launched.

HANK O'DAY

O'Day was never far from controversy as a pitcher, umpire, manager, or rules committee member. His single most notorious moment in any role came in September 1908 when, as an umpire, he called Giants first baseman Fred Merkle out for not touching second base after what appeared to be a game-winning hit in a game against the Cubs. That necessitated a replay of the game in what amounted to a playoff that enabled Chicago to win the pennant.

An umpire for most of the time between 1895 and 1925, O'Day represented the National League in the first World Series, in 1903. Before donning blue, he had had a seven-year (1884–90) pitching career during which he won 20 games in one season but lost that many three times. He managed for parts of two campaigns—for the Reds in 1912 and Cubs in 1914—and compiled an overall record of a game below .500.

The Merkle Boner aside, O'Day saved his most acrimonious moments for meetings of the league rules committee, on which he sat for years. His 1920 clash with sportswriter Fred Lieb over a possible modification in the scoring of sudden death home runs with men on base was indicative of his crustiness. Insisting that "you can't score runs after a game is over," and that the batter should be credited in such circumstances only with the number of bases required to score the winning run, he accused Lieb of trying to accumulate more home runs for his friend Babe Ruth. Lieb's counterargument, that a fair ball hit into the seats was a home run no matter the circumstances, carried a majority. But because the ruling was not made retroactive, Ruth wasn't awarded what would have been a 715th round-tripper for a ninth-inning blast with a man on first on July 8, 1918.

EMMETT O'DONNELL

Major General "Rosey" O'Donnell was elected baseball commissioner at a meeting of league owners on August 21, 1951. The appointment had to be voided, however, when President Harry Truman refused to release him from his duties as the commander of bomber forces in the Korean War. A subsequent vote endorsed Ford Frick as commissioner.

O'Donnell had won the owners' favor because his military background was considered a public relations coup in a period when congressmen were challenging baseball's reserve clause. The owners had initially sought General Douglas MacArthur as their chief spokesman, but he declined for reasons of age. So intent were they on drafting a military man that they subsequently considered giving the post to Erle Crocke, Jr., the head of the American Legion. Crocke put himself out of the running with one too many rant about how the State Department was controlled by communists and fellow travelers who didn't want to win in Korea.

LEFTY O'DOUL

O'Doul was a legend on the West Coast, but only an explosive short story in the East.

After trying to make it as a pitcher for the Yankees and Red Sox between 1919 and 1923, O'Doul returned to the Pacific Coast League where, partly thanks to a sore arm, he gained renown as a slugger.

Back with the Giants in his new role as a lefty swinging outfielder in 1928, he batted .319, but, considered too slow and old (he was 31) by manager John McGraw, he was traded to the Phillies. Within the comfortable confines of Baker Bowl, O'Doul proceeded to win the NL batting title in 1929 with a .398 mark; he also banged out 254 hits—the league record (tied by Bill Terry the following year). After a .383 campaign in the lively ball year of 1930, he was turned into one of Philadelphia owner William Baker's cash cows by being shipped to Brooklyn for negligible players and a conspicuous sum of money. With the Dodgers he won another batting crown in 1932, hitting .368. O'Doul's 11 years of major league service, which include his time as an AL pitcher, saw him bat .349 overall; not counting the mound years, his average was .352.

With the end of his big league career, O'Doul returned again to the Pacific Coast League, where he added to his West Coast reputation as the manager of the San Francisco Seals, the mentor of Joe DiMaggio, and the proprietor of a popular restaurant. Both before and after World War II, O'Doul was a key figure in the consolidation of baseball in Japan.

JOE OESCHGER

On May 1, 1920 Oeschger locked up with Brooklyn's Leon Cadore in the longest game in major league history—a 26-inning 1–1 tie. The Boston righthander went the distance, as did Cadore. Along the way Oeschger set another record in hurling 16 consecutive scoreless innings in a game. The contest lasted less than four hours and involved the use of only three baseballs.

BOB O'FARRELL

A 21-year catcher for the Cubs, Cardinals, Giants, and Reds from 1915 to 1935, O'Farrell provided the most unusual end to a World Series by throwing out Babe Ruth on an attempted steal in the ninth inning of the final 1926 game. Popular already with St. Louis fans for his gritty receiving, the play helped persuade owner Sam Breadon to name O'Farrell Cardinals manager in 1927 as a hedge against the outcry over the trading of player-pilot Rogers Hornsby. Although he guided the team to an even better record than it had compiled under Hornsby, O'Farrell was fired after only one season for failing to deliver another pennant.

CURLEY OGDEN

Ogden's career added up to merely 18–19 over five seasons, but he played a pivotal role in the most elaborate deception in World Series history. In the decisive seventh game of the 1924 Series against the Giants, Washington manager Bucky Harris unexpectedly picked the righthander as his starter. But when the third New York batter, lefty Bill Terry, came to the plate, Harris yanked Ogden for southpaw George Mogridge. Harris's ploy had been aimed at seeing whether John McGraw would replace Terry with the platooning righthand-hitting first baseman George Kelly. McGraw didn't bite, Terry remained in the game, and the Giants even had a 3–1 lead well into the contest, but Washington ended up pulling out the championship anyway.

SADAHARU OH

The greatest slugger of the Japanese leagues, Oh's 868 home runs over 22 seasons (1959–80) with the Yomiuri Giants is the most by a professional baseball player. The son of a Chinese father and a Japanese mother, he was signed by the Giants as a schoolboy pitching sensation before switching to first base. Unable for several years to hit a curve, the lefty batter took up samurai swordsmanship for balance and in 1962 developed his famous "flamingo stance," which resembled of Mel Ott's front-foot-in-the-air approach. This change in technique brought Oh 13 straight seasons of leading his league in homers, 13 RBI titles, two Triple Crowns, and nine MVP honors. Along the way the 18-time All-Star led the Giants to 11 championships. He set a Japanese record of 55 home runs in 1964, passed Hank Aaron with his 756th homer on September 3, 1977, and retired at the end of the 1980 season with a .301 average and a world-record 2,504 walks.

Oh's single-season home run record gained shadows in recent years because of the refusal of Japanese pitchers, especially those on teams being managed by him, to pitch to Americans Randy Bass and Tuffy Rhodes in their pursuit of the mark. Rhodes tied the Japanese slugger's 55 blasts in 2001.

BILL O'HARA

While only nine pinch-hitters have ever stolen two bases in the same inning, O'Hara managed to do it twice—on the consecutive days of September 1 and 2, 1909. Although he stole 31 bases altogether

for the Giants during the season, he barely lasted in the majors through the following year.

NOVELLA O'HARA

O'Hara was a fanatical San Francisco fan who tried to buy herself a pitcher from the team. The object of her affections was John Pregenzer, a righthander who made token appearances at Candlestick Park in 1963 and 1964. When she first heard that the Giants had purchased Pregenzer's contract from a low minor league for merely $100, O'Hara offered the club $110 for him. Rejected on that, she organized a fan club for the pitcher that swelled to a claimed 3,000 members, including Peace Corps Director Sargent Shriver. When plans for a John Pregenzer Day at Candlestick were aborted by his demotion to the minors, O'Hara got to organizing a Bring Back John Pregenzer Day. A San Francisco restaurateur who had counted on a guest appearance from the pitcher posted a sign in his window reading: "John Pregenzer was going to eat here."

STEVE OLIN

The bullpen stopper for the Indians in 1991 and 1992, Olin was killed in a grisly boating accident during spring training in 1993, sending the rebuilding club into a collective depression from which it didn't recover all year. Fellow reliever Tim Crews also died when a motorboat with the pitchers smacked into a pier, while veteran pitcher Bob Ojeda suffered severe physical injuries and psychological lacerations that effectively ended his career. The crash was the single most lethal accident in big league history.

TONY OLIVA

Nobody had a Hall of Fame career so clearly aborted by injuries as Oliva did. A lifetime .304 hitter with the Twins from 1962 to 1976, the lefty-swinging outfielder established a record by being the first AL rookie to win a batting title, in 1964, then cemented that feat by winning another the following season. Also in 1964, he entered the record books as the league's first rookie to get 200 hits, and he tied Hal Trosky's first-year mark of 374 total bases. No singles hitter, Oliva threw 32 home runs and a league-leading 43 doubles into the mix. It was the first of five years in which he led in hits and the first of four for setting the pace in doubles. On his way to a third batting championship in 1971, however, Oliva was beset by shoulder and leg injuries; before his career was up, he would have seven knee operations. It was principally because of Oliva that Minnesota owner Calvin Griffith cast the decisive vote backing Charlie Finley's proposal for a designated hitter in the AL.

DIOMEDES OLIVO

Next to Satchel Paige, Olivo was the oldest rookie in baseball history—and without racism as an extenuating circumstance. When he joined the Pirates bullpen in 1960, the righthander admitted only to being in his "early 40s." A few years later (apparently in his "middle to late 40s") he tossed a no-hitter in the International League, making him the oldest pitcher to fashion such a masterpiece on the higher rungs of organized baseball.

PETER O'MALLEY

O'Malley's buttoned-down ways with the Dodgers between the 1970s and the mid-1990s were more a change of style than substance from the way his father Walter had run the franchise before him. The main difference was that, partly because of the Wharton School of Business attitudes he brought to Los Angeles, the younger O'Malley never took for granted, let alone enjoyed, being the first among equals in the league boardroom. His biggest crisis occurred in 1987, after longtime Dodgers executive Al Campanis blithely told a national television audience that African Americans didn't have "the necessities" to hold important baseball jobs. After a stab at trying to quell the resultant uproar through a mere apology, O'Malley fired Campanis, then hired former basketball star Tommy Hawkins to a newly created public relations post to show the Dodgers weren't bigoted.

O'Malley ended his family's half-century control of the Dodgers in September 1997, when he sold the club and all its properties to the Rupert Murdoch-owned News Corporation for an announced $311 million. He motivated the move by saying he felt obligated to provide for the future of his children.

WALTER O'MALLEY

O'Malley reigned as baseball's General Motors for almost three decades: What was good for him was good for the rest of the National League (and sometimes the American League, too). As owner of the Dodgers, he brought the major leagues to California, made sure a succession of commissioners and league presidents didn't bring teams anywhere he didn't want them, and called most of management's signals in the bitter labor wars with players in the 1960s and 1970s. On the other hand, his long series of defeats in his dealings with the Players Association also underlined how he ultimately proved more successful in building up his own franchise as a flourishing megacorporation than in imposing his will on others to any long-term advantage.

A corporation lawyer with a Tammany Hall tinge, O'Malley bought into the Brooklyn version of the Dodgers in 1944, as a partner with Branch Rickey and John Smith of the Pfizer chemical company. For several years he remained largely in Rickey's shadow as the club president tussled with Leo Durocher, broke the color barrier with Jackie Robinson, and put together pennant-winning teams in 1947 and 1949. It was already clear that O'Malley had a distaste for the headlines Rickey appeared attached to. By October 1950 he had accumulated enough power in the organization to have the final say on whether Rickey should be given a new contract as the franchise's chief baseball man. Knowing that he was probably going to be turned down on a renewal, Rickey offered instead to sell his holdings; to make sure O'Malley paid heavily for the privilege of buying them, he worked out a scheme with real estate developer William Zeckendorf for the latter to present himself as a competitive bidder to jack up the selling price. Chalking it up to boardroom education, O'Malley persuaded the Smith estate to contribute to a substantial Rickey profit to get rid of the executive and head off Zeckendorf.

As owner and president, O'Malley brought in Buzzie Bavasi and Fresco Thompson to oversee what turned out to be the peak performances of The Boys of Summer Dodgers. During this period he also initiated a three-decade policy of acceding to only one-year contracts for managers; when Charlie Dressen objected to the policy after winning the pennant in 1953, he was fired and replaced by Walter Alston. Where O'Malley found it harder to get his way was in his demands for the city of New York to build Brooklyn a new ballpark, ideally in the downtown area near a Long Island Railway terminus. His cardinal arguments for the new facility were the limited seating capacity of Ebbets Field (32,111) and the lack of adequate parking for the white, middle-class

Long Island fans who were perceived as the organization's most reliable long-term customers. But even after he scheduled several Dodgers games in Jersey City in 1956 and 1957 as a sign of how serious his move threats were, City Hall refused to consider the downtown Brooklyn site for a park, and in fact wasn't even all that concrete in its commitment to a suggested alternative in Queens (where Shea Stadium is now located).

O'Malley's October 8, 1957 announcement that he was shifting the Dodgers from Brooklyn to Los Angeles formalized the most traumatic franchise move in big league history, and only partly because of the simultaneous transfer of the Giants to San Francisco. Unlike the Giants, the Dodgers had been making money; moreover, they had become so integral to Brooklyn that the community's subsequent economic and social decline was laid by many to the club's departure. The enduring bitterness of borough residents toward O'Malley has been captured best in the apocryphal story of the Brooklynites who privately listed their choices for the three most evil people of the 20th century and who, in comparing their picks, discovered that each had written down Hitler, Stalin, and O'Malley.

Although he had been studying a move to Los Angeles since Lou Perini had opened his eyes to the consequences of air travel for baseball by shuffling the Braves from Boston to Milwaukee in 1953, O'Malley actually completed all the practicalities for the transfer in months. To secure economic and political collateral, he bought Phil Wrigley's Wrigley Field in Los Angeles, traded minor league franchises with the Cubs owner, and then made the grand gesture of deeding his newly obtained stadium to the city. In return, the city ceded him the Chavez Ravine section of Los Angeles with its substantial fuel deposits, plus $4.7 million to help get construction under way on a new park. The sweetheart deal caused an uproar with City Hall's political opponents, but it was sanctioned by a referendum organized in June 1958—if by the unexpectedly small margin of 345,435 to 321,142. The generous city contribution aside, Dodger Stadium was the first privately financed major league park to be built since Yankee Stadium in 1923. The city's last direct contact with the project was in ousting the 1,800 Chicanos living at the Chavez Ravine site.

After four years in Los Angeles Memorial Coliseum, O'Malley moved the Dodgers into Dodger Sta-

dium in 1962. From its bright blue paint to its painfully polite personnel, the facility fulfilled its intention of being the Disneyland of baseball. If there was a downside to the new quarters, it was that the team had to share it for four seasons with the AL expansion Angels. O'Malley's consolation was an astronomical rent that infuriated Angels owner Gene Autry. Then again, Autry also partly owed O'Malley for coming into possession of his franchise in the first place, since it had been the Dodgers boss who had screamed most effectively before initial indications that the AL expansion club would be awarded to a consortium that included veteran showman Bill Veeck. Having no desire to compete with Veeck for the southern California market, O'Malley had used his influence to promote the Hollywood cowboy Autry as a worthier bidder.

For the most part, O'Malley left team personnel decisions up to Bavasi. One exception was in the coaching area, where the owner delighted in surrounding the taciturn Alston with such boisterous egotists as Durocher, Dressen, and Bobby Bragan—all in the name of what he termed "creative tension." He also personally demanded that Bavasi get rid of Maury Wills after the shortstop did not accompany he team on a 1966 tour of Japan, and was second to no owner in dispatching players who served as club representatives for the Players Association and in ignoring free agents.

In the 1960s O'Malley was a prime mover in the election of compliant big league administrators—a role he had played in the boosting of Ford Frick to the commissioner's office and that he continued with the likes of NL president Chub Feeney and commissioners William Eckert and Bowie Kuhn. O'Malley was not amused when former Brooklyn partner Rickey wielded the threat of a third major league to win NL expansion membership for the Mets and Astros in 1962, but regained some leverage by successfully advising New York's moneymen not to entrust their new team to the authoritarian Rickey. That detail taken care of, he offered the Mets the nostalgic gate attractions of Gil Hodges, Duke Snider, and other former Brooklyn Dodgers in the name of helping the league as a whole prosper. By his own timetable the senior circuit was not to have expanded again until the early 1970s, but he was forced into pressing for the addition of Montreal and San Diego in 1969 after the AL announced its intention of going to 12 teams and two divisions that season. His consolations were considerable: a substantial territorial payment for giving up the Dodgers top minor league team, in Montreal; first dibs in moving the AAA club into the New Mexico market for Albuquerque; and the seeding of a new major league rivalry with the Padres. It was also integral to the O'Malley persona that appearances be maintained as much as possible, so that, although it was Bavasi who went off to operate the new San Diego franchise, player transactions between the two southern California teams were nonexistent.

By 1970 O'Malley had turned most day-to-day Dodgers business over to his son Peter. From his new position as chairman of the board Walter proved especially conspicuous as the chief strategist for the owners in their dealings with the Players Association. At first that strategy was simple: Say no. But as a disciple of Tammany Democrats who understood the advantages of dealing with one labor voice, he eventually accepted the Association as a collective bargaining unit. After the 1972 season he demonstrated the cynical lengths of that attitude by jettisoning the only four Dodgers who had voted against empowering the union with a strike threat earlier in the year; according to O'Malley, it would have been nice if all 25 players had voted against the walkout, but since they hadn't, the four who had were potential sources of trouble in the clubhouse.

O'Malley wasn't nearly as subtle after the 1975 Messersmith-McNally decision effectively scrapped the reserve clause. After several court challenges proved futile, he tried to organize the owners in a blacklist plot against players seeking free agency; that scheme was aborted when Ted Turner signed Messersmith to an Atlanta contract. He was only briefly more successful in imposing a lockout on training camps in the spring of 1976; as soon as he saw that the tactic was only uniting players more, he called it off, merely shrugging when Kuhn went around claiming credit for the change of mind.

O'Malley died in 1979, less than a year after fulfilling a goal of attracting three million fans to the ballpark that had gained the nickname of the Taj O'Malley. He left a personal estate valued at $20 million to his children, a family trust estimated as equal to that, plus a controlling interest in the Dodgers that was put at some $240 million by the 1990s. Then there were the oil and gas deposits in the soil under Dodger Stadium. By any standard, O'Malley's move from Brooklyn amounted to the greatest business coup in baseball history. For some, it also consolidated his standing next to Hitler and Stalin.

MICKEY O'NEIL

A backup catcher for the 1926 Dodgers, O'Neil asked manager Wilbert Robinson to let him coach third base for an inning in an August game against Boston at Ebbets Field. He stood in the box as, a few minutes later, Babe Herman came to bat with the bases loaded and doubled off the right field wall. The blow sent Hank DeBerry home from third, but then chaos ensued. Dazzy Vance lumbered from second around third. Chick Fewster hustled from first to third. Herman himself tore all the way around to third—where he found Vance and Fewster waiting for him. The Braves promptly tagged out Fewster and Herman, and the latter went into the lore of the game for having "doubled into a double play." O'Neil didn't coach another inning until he was with Cleveland four years later.

BUCK O'NEILL

In 1962 the Cubs signed O'Neill as the first black coach in major league history. A longtime player and manager for the Kansas City Monarchs, O'Neill had signed originally with Chicago as a scout in 1956. He had earned points in the organization for urging the signing of Monarchs slugger Ernie Banks. As a scout, O'Neill also recommended the signing of a second Hall of Famer, Lou Brock.

TIP O'NEILL

O'Neill is the only player ever to lead a major league in batting average, doubles, triples, home runs, RBIs, and slugging in the same year. The outfielder had his landmark season in 1887 while leading the St. Louis Browns to the third of four consecutive American Association pennants. For decades his 1887 average was officially tabulated as .492, with walks regarded as hits in that season only. But even after the statistical fastidiousness of the 1960s corrected that aberration, his astonishing 225 hits (in 124 games) still produced a .435 mark. O'Neill's presence in the St. Louis lineup was the result of the first major front office blunder. As a rookie pitcher with the AA New York Metropolitans in 1883, he was slated to be transferred to the NL Giants the following year—a seemingly simple operation since John B. Day owned both clubs. But the owner and manager Jim Mutrie overlooked a rule prohibiting a club from signing a player until 10 days after his release from another organization, making O'Neill free to sign with the Browns.

JESSE OROSCO

The all-time leader in games pitched, Orosco concluded the 2001 season for the Dodgers with 1,131 appearances spread over 22 years. Although primarily identified with the Mets because of photos showing his euphoria after getting the last outs in both the 1986 playoffs against the Astros and the subsequent World Series against the Red Sox, the southpaw's nine-year stint in New York has long been eclipsed by 11 seasons in the American League, most notably with Baltimore between 1995 and 1999. By that time, he had also been moved from the role of closer to that of situational lefty; as of 1991, his innings pitched total has never equaled his number of appearances. Orosco's longevity has tended to cloud the fact that his best season (10 wins and 31 saves) traces back to 1984 and that only once again (in 1986) did he ever compile at least 20 saves. Apart from the Mets, Dodgers, and Orioles, he has also pitched for the Indians, Brewers, and Cardinals.

JIM O'ROURKE (Hall of Fame, 1945)

Known as Orator Jim for his verbosity and rhetorical flourishes, O'Rourke earned Cooperstown standing for his .313 average over 19 seasons. The right-hand-hitting outfielder got the first National League hit—a two-out single for Boston in the first inning of the league's inaugural game, on April 22, 1876. O'Rourke was a fervid supporter of the Players Brotherhood, and by the time the Brotherhood had evolved into the Players League in 1890 he had a long history of defiance of owners. In 1877, for example, he objected to a new rule requiring players to buy their own uniforms; when Boston owner Arthur Soden backed out of an agreement to exempt him from the charge, he refused to sign a new contract until fans chipped in to buy his flannels.

After his big league days O'Rourke became a successful lawyer and minor league official—and also developed memory loss about having been a supporter of the Brotherhood and the Players League. His final big league game was also his most famous.

When Giants manager John McGraw allowed him to catch the first game of a doubleheader on September 22, 1904, the 54-year-old not only became the oldest man ever to play a full game, but he also got a hit and scored a run in what turned out to be a pennant clincher.

PATSY O'ROURKE

O'Rourke showed little as a second baseman for the Cardinals in 1908, but he always showed up as a scout for the Phillies in the 1930s—and that was the trouble. As Philadelphia's one and only talent evaluator in the tawdry organization run by Gerry Nugent, O'Rourke had even this distinction diluted by the owner's refusal to spring for any train tickets that might have allowed him to see prospects. The upshot was that he did little but attend Phillies home games—a routine that became so predictable that manager Jimmie Wilson got into the habit of sardonically announcing to his bench during every game that he was going to make his "O'Rourke check."

JORGE ORTA

Orta collected 1,619 hits in a 16-year (1972–87) career with the White Sox, Royals, and others, but none was as important as a dribbler wide of first base in the ninth inning of the sixth game of the 1985 World Series between Kansas City and St. Louis. Although a toss from Cardinals first baseman Jack Clark to pitcher Todd Worrell appeared to be on time, umpire Don Denkinger called Orta safe, opening the gates to a comeback victory by the Royals that ultimately proved to be the turning point of the Series.

ROBERTO ORTIZ

The Cuban Ortiz was not particularly gifted offensively or defensively, but he kept his roster spot with the 1950 Senators as an interpreter for pitchers Connie Marrero and Sandy Consuegra.

MARTY O'TOOLE

Because spitballer O'Toole loaded up for his only pitch by slobbering over the ball with his tongue, Phillies first baseman Fred Luderus rubbed the game ball with liniment when Philadelphia faced the Pittsburgh righthander in a 1912 game. After three innings, the Pirates had to replace O'Toole on the mound.

PATSY O'TOOLE

O'Toole was the classic foghorn-voiced fan—and the only one who ever had his seat changed by the President of the United States. From his customary Tiger Stadium perch behind the Detroit dugout, he spent 25 years bellowing, "Boy, oh, boy, boy, oh, boy. Keep cool with O'Toole," punctuating the irritating refrain with hollers of "You're a bum!" to every visiting player and "You're a great guy!" to every member of the home team. In the third game of the 1933 World Series O'Toole started in with his usual cries while sitting a few rows behind Franklin D. Roosevelt. When the monotony got to Roosevelt, he had O'Toole removed to the other side of the infield.

MARY OTT

The Horse Lady of St. Louis, Ott turned her equine shrillness on Cardinals opponents for three decades. Capable not only of nuancing her braying to reflect just about every human emotion but also of downing prodigious amounts of beer, she once estimated that it took her about three innings to get a visiting pitcher to the showers when she put all her animal energy into the effort.

MEL OTT (Hall of Fame, 1951)

As brilliant a career as Ott had in 22 years (1926–47) in a New York uniform, he remains almost as noted today for being a common crossword puzzle answer and for being the subject of Leo Durocher's crack that "nice guys finish last." What Durocher actually said, in a conversation with broadcaster Red Barber prior to a 1946 game between the Giants and Dodgers, was: "Look over there. Do you know a nicer guy than Mel Ott? Or any of the other Giants? Why, they're the nicest guys in the world. And where are they? In last place!" The telescoped version of the quote about the then-Giants manager appeared the following day in the New York *Journal-American* in a Frank Graham story.

In sheer baseball terms the lefthand-hitting Ott had already carved a niche before replacing Bill Terry as manager in 1942. Only 16 when he made his debut in the Polo Grounds, the outfielder went on to become the first National Leaguer to pile up 500 home runs; his career total of 511 was accompanied by 1,860 RBIs and a .304 average. He paced the NL in homers six times, and between 1929 and 1942 failed to clout at least 25 only once. His RBI count was equally impressive—totaling at least 100 eight years in a row and nine overall. As prolific as he was as a slugger, Ott was equally popular with the fans, who might have just appreciated some relief after decades of the stern John McGraw and Terry. Helping Ott's popularity was an unorthodox batting stance that saw him elevate his front foot almost to the knee of the other leg when stepping into a pitch.

As a manager, Ott presided over mostly second-division clubs that knew how to do only what he did—hit the long ball. The 1947 team, for instance, set an NL record with 221 home runs, but finished only fourth. Although he tried to inject some fire into his managing style—levying fines liberally; blasting players publicly; even becoming, in 1946, the first pilot to be thrown out of both ends of a doubleheader—he lasted as long as he did only because of the sufferance of owner Horace Stoneham and his fan support. When he finally was replaced in the middle of the 1948 season, it was by Durocher.

MICKEY OWEN

Owen's reputation as a solid defensive catcher was marred forever by the passed ball in the ninth inning of the fourth game of the 1941 World Series that enabled Tommy Henrich to reach first base and sent the Yankees on the way to a comeback victory over the Dodgers. He himself always downplayed suggestions that Hugh Casey's two-strike pitch to Henrich was a spitter, saying that he ought to have caught it anyway.

After nine years with the Cardinals and Dodgers, Owen became one of the first recruits of the Pasquel brothers for the Mexican League in 1946, signing on as a playing manager for Vera Cruz. Within weeks, though, he thought better of it and took a $250 cab ride to El Paso to "escape." Then he had third thoughts amid a flurry of threatened lawsuits, going back to Vera Cruz. He ended up being fired at the end of the season, anyway. Readmitted to the big leagues in 1949, Owen wound up his career as a backup receiver for the Cubs and Red Sox.

RAY OYLER

Oyler's lack of hitting assumed almost legendary proportions in the 1960s. The ultimate gloveman, he demonstrated that pennant winners didn't need offense at shortstop in 1967, when he batted an hallucinating .135 in 111 games for Detroit. Manager

Mayo Smith knew to quit when he was ahead, however: In the World Series against the Cardinals, he opted to stick outfielder Mickey Stanley at short and make room for Al Kaline in the lineup rather than suffer through any more Oyler at bats. In 1969 the righty swinger was adopted by desperate Pilots fans for a Ray Oyler Fan Club; he responded to the Seattle welcome by batting .165. In six major league seasons he averaged .175, reaching the .200 mark (barely) only once.

DANNY OZARK

Ozark may have been the managing fraternity's most hapless winner. Despite steering the Phillies to three straight division titles (1976–78), he was seldom portrayed as anything but a dim bulb. The image was affixed to him for good in 1975, after the Pirates had defeated Philadelphia in a late September game to win the East Division title, and Ozark, standing only a few yards away from the raucous Pittsburgh clubhouse, told reporters that he would stick with his starting rotation "because we're not out of this thing yet." The manager's approximate command of clichés also fueled ridicule; among the more-often cited ones attributed to him are:

- "I have always had a wonderful repertoire with my players."
- "Even Napoleon had his Watergate."
- "I don't want to get into a Galphonse-Aston act."
- "I will not be cohorsed."

Even worse was when Ozark tried to be witty. Asked once why he never gave straight answers, he replied: "You'll have to ask these people who are always calling me a fascist—a guy who says one thing and means another."

P

JOHN PACIOREK

In a September 29, 1963 game against the Mets, Paciorek collected three hits and two walks in five plate appearances for Houston. Forced into premature retirement by a back ailment, the outfielder left baseball with the most hits by a player with a career 1.000 average.

ANDY PAFKO

In spite of a laudable 17-year career with the Cubs, Dodgers, and Braves, Pafko's most memorable moments on the field were the stuff of embarrassment and shock. On April 30, 1949, in the outfield for Chicago, he made what appeared to be a diving catch on a liner by St. Louis's Rocky Nelson to end a 3–2 contest. When umpire Al Barlick ruled instead that the ball had only been trapped, a furious Pafko kept after the arbiter, not realizing that Nelson was circling the bases for an inside-the-park home run and a Cardinals victory. Alluding to the famous Homer in the Gloamin' by Cubs catcher Gabby Hartnett in 1938, local wits tagged the Pafko brainlock the Homer in the Glove.

On October 3, 1951 the then-Brooklyn outfielder gained even more dubious fame by being photographed against the wall of the Polo Grounds looking up at Bobby Thomson's playoff-winning home run. Decades later, the image inspired a noted piece of fiction by novelist Don DeLillo.

JOE PAGE

The bullpen ace of the Yankees in the late 1940s, Page held the single-season record for most saves (27 in 1949) until the age of the relief specialist dawned in the 1960s. He also played a key role in the resignation of the most successful manager in baseball history.

A mediocre starter with a blazing fastball, unlimited potential, and a devil-may-care attitude when he came to New York in 1944, the southpaw engaged in a running battle with manager Joe McCarthy over his daytime indifference and evening carousing. Page shuttled between Newark and the Bronx for two years, and his lack of discipline finally got to McCarthy, who, already at odds with the franchise ownership over other matters, quit as dugout boss in May 1946 after a shouting match with the pitcher aboard an airplane.

Converted to a reliever by Bucky Harris the following year, Page led the AL in saves and relief victories in both 1947 and 1949. He took special pleasure in beating the Red Sox—first, because McCarthy took over Boston in 1948, second, because his uncommon success against Ted Williams reflected well on teammate Joe DiMaggio in the ongoing debate about who was the better player. In fact, the lefty's single most memorable appearance came on the penultimate day of the 1949 season, when he entered the game in the third inning, walked two batters with the bases loaded to give Boston a 4–0 lead, then pitched one-hit ball the rest of the way while New York came back to win, 5–4, on its way to the pennant.

Released in 1950 after tearing an arm muscle, Page tried a comeback in 1954 with the Pirates, but then quit for good. He ended up at 57–49, with 76 saves.

SATCHEL PAIGE (Hall of Fame, 1972)

As a pitcher, Paige was without peer; as a legend, only Babe Ruth was in his league.

Even without the tall tales that grew up around it, the righthander's career often reads like fiction. For one thing, Paige was even more of an itinerant than other Negro leaguers. In his first two years (1926–27) as a professional, with the Chattanooga Black Lookouts, he jumped the team twice, to play for the New Orleans Black Pelicans and the Baltimore Black Sox. He lasted only three seasons (1928–30) with the Birmingham Black Barons and only one (1931) with the Cleveland Cubs. After winning 63 games in 1932 and 1933 with the Pittsburgh Crawfords, he drifted off to pitch for a white semipro outfit in North Dakota, staying there through the 1935 season after the Negro National League banned him for his defection. Returning to the Crawfords in 1936, Paige was practically shanghaied to Santo Domingo, where he won a politically charged championship for dictator Rafael Trujillo's team in 1937. Sold by the Crawfords to the Newark Eagles in 1938, he refused even to negotiate with Eagles owner Effa Manley and took off for the Mexican League, where he developed the first sore arm of his career and suffered a permanent NNL ban.

Paige was signed next by the Kansas City Monarchs road team (rebaptized Satchel Paige's All-Stars), with whom he worked the kinks out of his arm before a promotion to the varsity squad. Even while helping the Monarchs to six American Negro League pennants between 1939 and 1948 and winning three games in a 1942 sweep of the Homestead Grays in the black World Series, he remained a pitcher-for-hire, rented out to semipro clubs a day at a time. He also did the customary winter league tours in Puerto Rico, Cuba, and California. Finally, between and after major league stints (in 1948–49, 1951–53, and 1965), he barnstormed virtually non-stop until 1967, when he wasn't on the roster of the Miami International League club (1956) and Portland's entry in the Pacific Coast League (1961).

The numbers Paige amassed in this 42-year career are staggering, even if necessarily approximate: Appearing in more than 2,500 games for about 250 teams, he racked up some 2,000 victories (100 of them no-hitters), earning upward to $40,000 a year, several times what all but the biggest stars in the white major leagues grossed in the period. He defeated squads of white big leaguers regularly, including four wins against Dizzy Dean in six 1934 contests. His single best game was probably one on a 1930 barnstorming tour in which he struck out 22 major leaguers.

As the oldest rookie in major league history, with the Indians in 1948, Paige proved to be more than one of Bill Veeck's stunts, contributing a 6–1 (2.48) record to a Cleveland pennant; he followed that up with a 4–7 (3.04) mark in 1949. Rehired by Veeck in 1951, he spent three seasons with the Browns, pitching creditably in relief and as a spot starter. He closed out his career with a single appearance for Kansas City in 1965, yielding only one hit in three innings as the oldest man ever to take a major league mound. In 1968 Ted Turner's Braves put him on the roster to qualify him for a major league pension. His overall record was 28–31 (3.29) with 32 saves.

Throughout his career Paige did nothing to discourage his elevation into the realm of folklore. From a vagueness about the year of his birth (probably 1906) and the inspiration for his nickname (probably involving suitcases he carried for tips as a child in his hometown of Mobile), he graduated to (possible) exaggerations of his pitching prowess. Whether (or how often) he summoned his outfielders to sit behind him on the mound while he struck out the side or fulfilled advertised promises to fan the first nine men he faced in a game is irrelevant; more to the point is that people believed he had, and paid for the possibility of seeing him do it again. Even in the majors at his advanced age, he was a significant drawing card: More than 200,000 paid to see his first three starts, in the process setting attendance records for night games in both Cleveland and Chicago. In St. Louis Paige and Veeck contrived to provide a rocking chair in the bullpen for the pitcher's use between appearances.

Paige had names for his various pitches. His fastball, for instance, was Long Tom (or, alternatively, the Bee Ball, Jump Ball, or Trouble Ball)—all the better for its mythical pedigree. Even his own fabulous accounts of his velocity were outdone by Negro leagues catcher Biz Mackey, who claimed that a particularly high-powered Paige fastball once disappeared on the way to the plate. Paige's most famous delivery, however, was the Hesitation Pitch, which he developed in the 1940s and offered after deliberately pausing as his forward foot hit the ground. The discontinuity in his motion was so disorienting to opposing batters that the American League banned the pitch after he introduced it in 1948.

As a barnstormer, Paige refused to play in towns where black teammates were barred from hotels and restaurants. He was also given to sardonic observations about how to keep young and to train. Among them were: "Go very light on the vices, such as carrying on in society. The social ramble ain't restful." "Avoid running at all times." "Don't look back. Something might be gaining on you."

Ultimately, Paige's ability, longevity, and showmanship gave the Negro leagues much of whatever visibility they had in the white world. Among those who called him the best pitcher they ever saw were Dean, Joe DiMaggio, and Charlie Gehringer. Fittingly, Paige was the first of the Negro leagues stars admitted to Cooperstown.

DAVE PALLONE

Scurrilous press reports put an end to Pallone's 10-year (1979–88) umpiring career in the National League—and to the opportunity for firing him for more valid reasons. A scab hired during the 1979 umpires strike, Pallone was retained after the settlement of the labor dispute despite constant hostility from colleagues, mockery from players, and routinely bad calls that marked him as one of the most incompetent men in blue. Mainly to save face for its own original hiring, the league kept him around through regular diamond explosions until 1988, when a protracted argument with Reds manager Pete Rose almost caused a riot at Riverfront Stadium. The clash prompted a 30-day suspension of Rose and league censures of Cincinnati broadcasters Joe Nuxhall and Marty Brennaman for their on-air attacks on the arbiter. The incident took on added resonance a short time later, when Pallone was falsely linked to an upstate New York investigation of sex crimes committed against teenage boys. By the time police spokesmen got around to refuting the media reports. Pallone had admitted he was gay. While the admission suggested deeper insinuations in the macho notions about baseball sustained by Nuxhall and Brennaman in their blasts, it also offered the league a more convenient excuse for terminating the umpire. Pallone went on to publish a book filled with coy hints about gay big leaguers in the closet.

JIM PALMER (Hall of Fame, 1990)

For the better part of his 19 seasons (between 1965 and 1984) with the Orioles, Palmer was the franchise pitcher; for almost as long, he was the bane of manager Earl Weaver's existence.

Palmer's career was almost derailed by arm miseries, a shoulder ailment, and back problems after going 15–10 in his first full season in 1966. He was regarded as such a high risk physically that Baltimore left him off its protected list for the 1969 expansion draft and neither Kansas City nor Seattle thought it prudent to test the decision. But after coming off the disabled list six weeks into the 1969 season, he no-hitted the Athletics and went on to pace AL hurlers in winning percentage (16–4, .800) for the first of two times. In 1970 the righthander posted the first of eight 20-win seasons, a total topped in the AL only by Walter Johnson and matched only by Lefty Grove; in three of those campaigns he led the league in wins, in two of them in ERA. His best efforts—in 1973 (22–9, 2.40), 1975 (23–11, 2.09), 1976 (22–13, 2.51)—brought Cy Young awards. Palmer was released in May 1984 after a battle with the Baltimore front office, which had hinted several times that he retire. In 1991, after having already been inducted into the Hall of Fame, he tried to make a comeback but failed to make the club in spring training.

Almost from the moment Weaver joined the Orioles in 1968, the pilot was at loggerheads with Palmer. At the root of their differences was the pitcher's aversion to the much-vaunted Orioles fundamentals that Weaver had had a hand in developing in the organization's farm system and Weaver's belief that Palmer's often-proclaimed ills were just in his head. Palmer's side of the running dialogue between the two—which sometimes seemed designed as entertainment—included sarcastic cracks about how long he would be sidelined ("You never know with psychosomatic injuries") and the intelligence level of most managers ("Most pitchers are too smart to manage"). Palmer's summary of the relationship ("I don't want to win my 300th game while he's still here; he'd take credit for it") proved moot. The manager left after the 1982 season and the hurler's record stood at 268–152 when he was cut less than two years later.

CHAN HO PARK

Park's status as the first Korean major leaguer has been rivaled by his penchant for yielding milestone home runs. On April 23, 1999 he became the first pitcher to surrender two grand slam homers in the same inning—both to St. Louis third baseman Fernando Tatis. In 2001, the Los Angeles righthander was on the hill when Barry Bonds surpassed Mark McGwire's single-season record of 70 home runs with his 71st, and again a couple of innings later when the Giants outfielder made it 72. In 2001 as well, Park delivered a gopher pitch to Cal Ripken in the All-Star Game, setting off (angrily denied) conjecture that he had grooved the serving for the Baltimore star's swan song.

Park's big league debut came in the ninth inning of an April 9, 1994 game against Atlanta. After surrendering two runs, he went back to the bench and watched as Kent Mercker of the Braves completed a no-hitter.

DAVE PARKER

Parker set the tone for his stormy 19-year (1973–91) major league career by wearing a Star of David "because my name is David and I'm a star." A lefty swinging outfielder who epitomized the Lumber Company Pirates of the 1970s, he won successive battle titles in 1977 and 1978, paced the NL in slugging average in 1975 and 1978, and collected the most hits in 1977, the most doubles in 1977 and 1985, and the most RBIs in 1985. The lifetime .290 hitter earned an MVP in 1978.

But for all his slugging feats, Parker was equally adept at stirring controversy—not always through his own doing. In the early 1980s, the fact that he was one of the game's first million-dollar players (in a contract covering five years) caused resentment in a city enmeshed in grave unemployment problems; the same Pirates fans who were amused by Willie Stargell's balloon proportions attacked Parker vehemently for his own expanded waistline and, in one notorious incident, showered him with batteries and other objects after he had made an error. Moving over to the Reds as a free agent in 1984, he rediscovered the clout he had lost after a couple of seasons of leg injuries, excess weight, and fan harassment, but also came into constant conflict with manager Pete Rose over his defensive nonchalance and elaborate styling whenever he belted a ball out of the park. The relationship was sufficiently fractious for Parker to be one of the few players who voiced delight when Rose was suspended for betting on games.

Parker's worst hours came when he was named

as a cocaine user in the Pittsburgh drug trials. His own admissions of involvement led the Pirates to file suit for the return of some of the salary he had made while snorting. A protracted legal battle over whether he had violated the "physical condition" clauses of his contract ended with an out-of-court settlement. Parker concluded his career by moving around as a designated hitter for the Athletics, Brewers, Angels, and Blue Jays.

JORGE PASQUEL

The millionaire president of the Mexican League, Pasquel and his four brothers staged a major raid on big league rosters in 1946 with offers of extravagant salaries for those willing to play south of the border. The first prominent player to bite was Browns shortstop Vern Stephens, who signed a two-year pact for $50,000. Otherwise, Pasquel largely zeroed in on the Cardinals and Giants, picking up pitchers Max Lanier, Sal Maglie, and Fred Martin, infielder Lou Klein, and outfielder Danny Gardella, among others. He also offered Stan Musial a five-year contract at $30,000 a year, but the St. Louis star declined. When Commissioner Happy Chandler announced that the jumpers would be banned from organized ball, they began to drift back to the United States. Their return trip hardly mattered since the importation of high-priced Yanqui talent had mainly been a bread-and-circus campaign tactic on behalf of Miguel Aleman's candidacy for the presidency of Mexico. With Aleman's election, Pasquel showed less interest in baseball amid all his other business and political affairs.

ROY PATTERSON

When rain washed out three of the four scheduled games on April 24, 1901, White Sox righthander Patterson became the winner of the American League's first game by beating Cleveland, 8–2.

GABE PAUL

Paul always knew when to leave. As the top front office official for the Reds, Astros, Indians (twice), and Yankees over more than three decades, he built winners when he worked for an owner with deep pockets, patched over problems (sometimes of his own making) when he didn't, and always moved on before a bad situation got worse. Promoted to Cincinnati general manager in 1952, Paul had already served in various administrative capacities since 1919 as the protégé of Warren Giles with both Rochester of the International League and the Reds. His most notable achievement as Cincinnati GM was putting the finishing touches on the second biggest Red Machine. His trades for outfielder Gus Bell, third baseman Ray Jablonski, and role players Smokey Burgess and George Crowe, along with the drafting of future Hall of Fame slugger Frank Robinson in 1953, completed the ensemble that tied the NL home run mark with 221 in 1956. He also put together the less spectacular but more successful team that won the 1961 NL pennant.

Paul quit the Reds in 1960 after quarrels with Powel Crosley over the owner's efforts to move the club to New York, and signed a three-year agreement to run the soon-to-be expansion Astros. But when Robert E. Smith and Judge Roy Hofheinz came in as new principal owners a few months later, he took one look at the erratic Texas millionaires and decided his future lay elsewhere. That turned out to be Cleveland.

Paul spent much of his first tour of duty with the Indians (1961–72) looking for a succession of buyers. With owner William Daley near bankruptcy and putting out feelers about moving the club to Seattle, Paul took advantage of the backlash to the threatened move and put together his own syndicate to acquire the team in 1963. But when he ended up suffering from the same cash shorts as Daley in 1966, he had little choice but to sell the franchise to frozen food magnate Vernon Stouffer. Then in 1972 Stouffer was out and sports entrepreneur Nick Mileti was in. Paul survived all the changes for no apparent reason other than to provide some organization continuity: In making more than 100 deals involving big league players, he could only give Cleveland a winning club twice in 13 years. The last of the deals raised some eyebrows when he shipped third baseman Graig Nettles to the Yankees for four uniforms in November 1972, then jumped off the sinking ship just before yet another sale of the club and followed Nettles to New York.

Paul's major burden in the Yankees front office was to mediate in the three sided lunacy prevailing among owner George Steinbrenner, manager Billy Martin, and slugger Reggie Jackson. But he was hardly inactive on the player personnel front. Aside from encouraging Steinbrenner to dig into his wallet to sign free agents Jackson and Catfish Hunter, he pulled off deals for Willie Randolph, Chris Chambliss, Lou Piniella, and Mickey Rivers. But just when Paul seemed to be on the verge of proving that he was the only one of Steinbrenner's "baseball people" with the savvy and authority to improve the club, he showed up as powerless to prevent an ill-considered June 1976 transaction that sent pitching prospects Tippy Martinez and Scott McGregor, along with catcher Rick Dempsey, to Baltimore in return for southpaw Ken Holtzman and four bodies. Two pennants and one world championship later, he had enough of the constant strife and, in December 1977, went back to Cleveland as a minority owner and president.

Paul's return began with a franchise bailout of owner Ted Bonda engineered by transportation tycoon Steve O'Neill; O'Neill insisted he would hang around only until Paul found another savior for the franchise. But when Paul wasn't queering sales he himself had arranged (in one case because he had second thoughts about the "aggressiveness" of the would-be buyers), he was desperately adding limited partners to the club stationery for quick infusions of cash. His approach to the team smacked of the same revolving door tactics of the past; in seven years he completed almost 70 trades, 15 in just 1978. Another favorite ploy was to get headlines for giving pitchers big raises (e.g. Rick Sutcliffe), then deal away the hurlers before the Indians actually had to pay them. When O'Neill died in 1983, his heirs clamored even more loudly for an angel to rescue them from their (unwanted) commitment to the club. Around this time bumper stickers began to appear in Cuyahoga County declaring: SAVE THE TRIBE, FIRE THE CHIEF.

Paul was unable to broker another successful sale. When protracted negotiations with Wall Street lawyer Dave LeFevre ended up in litigation, he sold his five percent share in the team to LeFevre and, in December 1954, retired. His Cleveland legacy after two stints totaling 19 years was a financial situation at least as bad as when he had first arrived and a single third-place finish (1968).

GENE PAULETTE

Paulette, not the Chicago players implicated in the Black Sox scandal, was the first player banned from baseball by Commissioner Kenesaw Landis. The first baseman's offense was his association with

St. Louis gambler Elmer Farrar, who had given him a loan that had never been repaid; the incriminating evidence was a letter from the player to the gambler offering to throw games in exchange for more money. Traded from the Cardinals to the Phillies in 1919 while the subject of rumors about his Farrar connection, Paulette escaped punishment initially by signing a statement that he had done nothing wrong. But then Landis got his hands on the incriminating letter and announced the ban, in March 1921 (five months before dealing similarly with the Eight Men Out).

JOAN PAYSON

The original owner of the Mets when the team joined the National League in 1962, Payson was more missed in her absence than particularly assertive in her presence. Right up to her death in 1975 she represented the franchise's genial face as the reverse side to devious board chairman M. Donald Grant and sour president George Weiss. The image was fastened to her from the club's inaugural season, when she dsclosed she would have preferred the nickname Meadowlarks to Mets. It also helped her negotiate potentially troublesome publicity when her racehorse investments were played down while the leagues piously rejected ownership bids in San Diego, Cleveland, and Chicago on the grounds that the candidates had racetrack interests. With Payson's death the Mets franchise lurched toward self-destruction under her widower Charles, their daughter Lorinda de Roulet, and Grant.

DICKEY PEARCE

In 22 years of professional play beginning with the Brooklyn Atlantics in 1856, Peace exercised considerable influence on the development of the game by originating the bunt and by popularizing the placement of the ninth man between second base and the third baseman. On June 29, 1876, as the shortstop for the St. Louis Brown Stockings, Pearce started the first major league triple play. In addition to the bunt (or "tricky hit," as it was called), he is also credited with patenting the fair-foul hit popular in the 19th century.

ROGER PECKINPAUGH

A 17-year (between 1910 and 1927) shortstop with the Indians, Yankees, Senators, and White Sox, Peckinpaugh derived most of his celebrity from his 10–10 mark as the manager of New York at the end of the 1914 season. Only 23 years old at the time, he went into the record books as baseball's youngest pilot. Peckinpaugh later served a couple of terms as manager of Cleveland.

As a player, Peckinpaugh endured the worst defensive World Series of all time, when his eight errors, including two in the eighth inning of the decisive seventh game, went a long way toward sealing Pittsburgh's 1925 victory over Washington. His play was so porous that Commissioner Kenesaw Landis put a detective on him for the stated purpose of having preemptive evidence that Peckinpaugh didn't make the errors as part of a gambling fix.

TERRY PENDLETON

Pendleton gave new definition to leadership during the 1993 season when he abruptly walked off the field into the clubhouse in the middle of an inning to protest teammate Marvin Freeman's refusal to deck opposition batters. According to Pendleton, Freeman was remiss for not retaliating for several Atlanta batters who had been hit or knocked away from the plate during the game. Although both the Braves and the National League did a lot of tsk-tsking about the third baseman's gesture, its main consequence was to consolidate his standing as the club's field and clubhouse leader.

Signed as a free agent by the Braves in 1991 after seven seasons with the Cardinals, Pendleton was the catalyst for Atlanta's becoming the first NL team to go from last to first in one year. The switch-hitter took MVP honors for the season for his league-best .319 average and 187 hits. Pendleton's biggest moment in a St. Louis uniform came in a late September 1987 game, when his ninth-inning homer off Mets reliever Roger McDowell stemmed a Cardinals collapse before the onrushing Mets and ultimately proved to be the turning point in a division win.

HERB PENNOCK (Hall of Fame, 1948)

Southpaw Pennock was the exception among the players picked up by the Yankees from the Red Sox in the early 1920s: Whereas Babe Ruth, Carl Mays, Joe Bush, Joe Dugan, and others were at the top of their game when dealt, Pennock was thought to be washed up at 29 after two losing seasons. Instead, the lefty went on to pace the AL in winning percentage in his first year in New York, record two 20-win seasons, and go 5–0 in four World Series. In 22 seasons (between 1912 and 1934) with the Red Sox, Yankees, and Athletics, he ended up with 241 victories.

After his playing days, Pennock directed the Red Sox farm system and served as Phillies general manager from 1944 to his death in 1948. He was credited with the major role in assembling the Philadelphia Whiz Kids club that won the 1950 NL pennant.

H. C. PENNYPACKER

Appointed president of the Athletics in 1888, Pennypacker presided over the most precipitous slide of any major league team. With a declared $30,000 profit in 1889, Philadelphia should have been able to survive the Players League rebellion the following season. Instead, on September 17, Pennypacker announced that the franchise was in the red to the tune of $17,000, forcing him to disband the organization and release all players. He blamed everything on the Players League. Only when the American Association took over the franchise did it come to light that Pennypacker and team secretary William Whitaker had swallowed the money by paying themselves exorbitant salaries.

JOE PEPITONE

As a 17-year-old out of Brooklyn, Pepitone gave a hint of things to come in blowing his $20,000 1958 signing bonus with the Yankees on a car and a boat. Arriving in the Bronx in 1962 as a backup first baseman to Bill Skowron, the lefthand-hitting rookie had to dissuade some admirers from his old neighborhood from separating Skowron from some of his bones to make room for the local boy in the starting lineup. He got the job on merit the following year.

Ordinarily a slick fielder and the winner of three Gold Gloves, Pepitone had his most memorable diamond moment in the seventh inning of the fourth game of the 1963 World Series, when he lost a throw by third baseman Clete Boyer in the crowd's white shirts, allowing Jim Gilliam of the Dodgers to advance to third, from where he scored the Series-winning run. His memorable moments off the field were usually as embarrassing. He took to frequenting after-hours spots armed with a bow and arrow. Dogged in his last years in New York by loan sharks and multiple ex-wives, he jumped the team three times before being traded to the Astros following the 1969 season. After bouncing around the NL for awhile, he moved on to the Yakult Swallows in Japan where

things only got worse. In fact, Pepitone became so much the Ugly American abroad (griping about prices and food, partying through the night, playing merely 14 games before quitting with a .163 average, skipping out on a $2,000 phone bill) that his name became a Japanese eponym for a player who goofs off. In 1989 he served two months of a six-month jail term on drug and gun charges. The Yankees hired him on a work release program.

PASCUAL PEREZ

One of the most flamboyant diamond figures of the 1980s, Perez was brought down by a drug problem and by a refusal of major league teams to accord him the repeated chances given to such other cocaine users as Steve Howe. A graduate of the Pirates farm system, the righthanded hurler first gained notoriety after being traded to Atlanta in 1982 and losing his way to Fulton County Stadium for a start because he kept driving past a highway exit. In 1984 doubts were raised about the driving story when he admitted to a drug problem. After a stint in rehab Perez returned to the National League with Montreal in 1987, establishing himself as a flake with such antics as trying to pick off runners by throwing to first base through his legs. His wafer-thin physique and dreadlocks made him a fan favorite at Olympic Stadium, but he chose (against most advice) to sign with the Yankees as a free agent in 1990. A combination of injuries and a drug relapse ended his big league career in 1991, the first of six seasons for the equally recidivist Howe in the New York bullpen.

TONY PEREZ (Hall of Fame, 2000)

Perez had his best playing years in Cincinnati, but he gained equal notoriety for his unexpected departures from the club. The first exit occurred after the 1976 season, when the first baseman-third baseman was traded to Montreal after 13 years of heavy RBI duty for the team that had developed into the Big Red Machine. The swap was denounced by such teammates as Pete Rose and Joe Morgan as lethal to Cincinnati's field leadership, and proved to be so when the Reds took a two-year vacation from postseason play. While with Cincinnati, the righthand-hitting Perez had put together six 100 RBI seasons, enjoying his best year in 1970 with 40 home runs, 129 RBIs, 107 runs scored, and a .317 average. After roaming around for another decade as a member of the Expos, Red Sox, Phillies, and (again) Reds, he retired with a 23-year (1964–86) sum of 379 home runs, 1,652 RBIs, and a .279 average.

Perez's second, uglier departure from Cincinnati came in 1993, when he had been on the job only a few weeks as manager. His abrupt ouster for Davey Johnson strongly suggested that the Latin star had been hired initially only to help blunt the fallout from revelations of owner Marge Shott's racist hiring policies and had been bounced as soon as the front office thought the worst of the controversy was over. Some Cincinnati players called for a strike over the firing, but satisfied themselves with just calling in their efforts for the remainder of the season. In 2001 Perez was asked to take over the Marlins dugout after John Boles left under circumstances as disturbing as his own had been in Cincinnati; again, he was treated as only a stop-gap solution.

LOU PERINI

Perini's transfer of the Braves from Boston to Milwaukee in 1953 signaled the start of the franchise moves that would both extend the major leagues geographically and wreak havoc with the minor leagues. The intrigues and procrastinations behind the uprooting of the Braves also underscored the lengths to which big league owners would go to get rid of unwanted members of their circle.

Perini and fellow construction industry millionaires Joseph Maney and Guido Rugo bought into the Braves in 1941 and needed only a couple of years to gain total control. Known as the Three Little Steamshovels, they undertook an ambitious spending program aimed at both raising the club to the heights of the National League and winning Bostonians away from the Red Sox. Their biggest setback came on Opening Day in 1946, when an estimated 5,000 fans had their clothing ruined by newly painted seats at Braves Field; for the rest of the year lawyers and accountants had to pore over more than 13,000 damage claims. Their biggest success was a 1948 pennant—the first by the team since the Miracle Braves of 1914. Then things started to go downhill.

Committed to a long-term contract with Billy Southworth, Perini backed the manager in a conflict with star infielders Alvin Dark and Eddie Stanky, trading them away in what proved to be the first of several ruinous deals. Within a couple of years the club was back to thinking of .500 as a lofty goal and

Bostonians were back to Fenway Park. Although he always denied it, Perini and his brothers kept their hands busy by buying out Maney and Rugo in preparation for a move to Milwaukee without internal interference. For awhile their intended transfer was embroiled in a controversy affecting both leagues, with both Bill Veeck of the Browns and Fred Saigh of the Cardinals also talking with Milwaukee interests about a franchise shift. Perini ultimately prevailed—first because he had territorial rights in the Wisconsin city through a minor league club, second because the other owners were determined to get rid of both Veeck and Saigh and blocked every move by the two St. Louis owners to go north.

Although the Braves received an ardent welcome in Milwaukee, Perini was never quite as popular. His first problem was his procrastination before finally making the move—interpreted by locals as a ploy for gaining an even better deal from the county than that offered through the free construction of County Stadium. He alienated other sectors by refusing to move his residence from Boston—increasing the image of a carpetbagger who could leave Milwaukee again at the first hint of a better offer. The owner didn't win any points, either, with his ban on bringing beer into the ballpark, forcing fans to buy their brew at inflated prices from concession stands. When the team began to slip toward the second division in the early 1960s, Russ Lynch of the Milwaukee *Journal* and other sportswriters warned that the scant potential for a lucrative television contract in the area would surely push Perini into pulling up stakes again. The sportswriters were halfright: A television package put on the table by Atlanta did lead to the club's defection after the 1965 season, but by that time Perini himself was no longer calling the shots for the franchise. Worn out by narrowing revenues and constant criticism, and dismayed that none of his children wanted to run a big league club, he sold out in 1962 to a Milwaukee-Chicago syndicate headed by Illinois insurance broker Bill Bartholomay.

The last word on Perini's ownership fell to Dodgers president Walter O'Malley, who acknowledged that the move from Boston to Milwaukee had opened his eyes to the real impact of air travel on major league baseball. Four years after Perini's transfer, O'Malley was shifting his club from Brooklyn to Los Angeles.

GAYLORD PERRY (Hall of Fame, 1991)

In his 22 years (1962–83) in the majors, Perry practically had two careers—as the pitcher who logged 314 victories and as the professional coquette who might or might not have been using a spitball. Long before he revealed his techniques for loading up his pitches, the righthander made it clear that the doubts he planted in the minds of opposition hitters and managers with his every delivery were as vital to his arsenal as the spitter itself.

The first hurler to win the Cy Young Award in both leagues (1972 Indians, 1978 Padres), Perry wore eight different uniforms during his travels, usually being shown the door upon some organization's conviction that he was finished. In fact, there was little reason to think he would ever get started, having compiled a record of only 24–30 by the time he was 28. His 239 wins from age 30 to his retirement at 45 put him behind only Cy Young and Warren Spahn for victores after 30. Along the way Perry had five 20-win seasons and eight years of at least 200 strikeouts. In spite of racking up 3,534 strikeouts, however, he never once led a league in the category. As a member of the Giants on September 17, 1968, he pitched his only no-hitter, a 1–0 blanking of the Cardinals. As a member of the Indians on July 3, 1973, he and his brother Jim Perry became the first siblings to start against one another in an American League game; Gaylord took the loss.

The only time Perry was actually caught doctoring the ball was on August 23, 1982, while with the Mariners. He was fined $250 and suspended for 10 days. He has credited his 1964 San Francisco teammate Bob Shaw with teaching him the pitch.

SCOTT PERRY

Although he led the American League in losses twice, Perry was good enough for Philadelphia owner-manager Connie Mack to risk war with the National League over him. After moving from the Browns to the Cubs to the Reds without distinction, the righthander became the property of the Class A Atlanta Crackers in the Southern Association, who sold his contract to the Braves in 1917. Refusing to report, he jumped to an outlaw league only to discover that Atlanta had resold him to the Athletics; this time he went and was given enough work to finish the 1918 season with 20 wins and a league-leading 19 losses.

When Boston president Percy Haughton protested what he considered the illegal reassignment of the pitcher, the case was referred to the National Commission. The Commission's ruling favored the Braves, but Mack secured an injunction preventing Perry from joining the NL team. The spectacle of dragging what they regarded as an intramural dispute into court infuriated NL owners, while league president John Tener went them one better by proposing that the World Series be cancelled. Faced with the prospect of losing World Series income, the NL owners decided Tener was more of a problem than Mack, and the league chief eventually resigned. In the end, Mack agreed to pay the Braves $2,500 in compensation for Perry's services.

JOHNNY PESKY

As with Bill Buckner, Pesky's solid career is doomed to remain overshadowed by a single World Series moment—in his case, a hesitation on a relay that enabled Enos Slaughter to score from first base and give St. Louis the 1946 world championship over Boston. As a shortstop in the 1940s, however, the lefty swinger broke from the gate with more hitting consistency than any other AL player at his position, racking up averages of .331, .335, and .324 in his first three seasons and leading the league with more than 200 hits each year. Although he would never again bat that high, he did have three other years over .300, closing out his 10-year career (between 1942 and 1954) with a .307 mark.

GARY PETERS

Southpaw Peters was the best the White Sox had on the mound for several years in the 1960s, especially in 1963, when he took Rookie of the Year honors, and in 1964, when his 20 wins paced the AL. In May 1968 he had another impact on the club after manager Eddie Stanky inserted him into the sixth slot in the lineup—the highest in the starting order a pitcher had batted in decades or, outside of stunts, has hit since. Stanky's move, in the name of shaking up a torpid offense, inflamed an already dissident clubhouse and just about ended his reign. For a pitcher, Peters was an above-average hitter, batting .222 in 14 seasons.

JOHNNY PETERS

A shortstop with Chicago in 1879, Peters was the first "player to be named later" when he was sent to

Providence after the season to complete a trade for catcher Lew Brown.

FRITZ PETERSON

Peterson announced baseball's most singular trade in 1973, when he told reporters that he and Yankees teammate Mike Kekich had decided to trade lives by moving in with each other's family. He eventually married Susan Kekich, but the relationship between Kekich and Marilyn Peterson didn't last. Both pitchers were later traded to the Indians, though in separate swaps. After retiring, Peterson took over as head of the Baseball Chapel.

FRED PFEFFER

The popular second baseman of Chicago's Stone Wall Infield (along with Cap Anson, Ned Williamson, and Tom Burns) in the 1880s, Pfeffer was later part of an abortive effort to form a new league. In 1894 he joined with Louisville pilot Billy Barnie, Pittsburgh manager Al Buckenberger, and some financial backers to establish a new American Association. The circuit died without playing one game, or even signing a single player, for several reasons, including a frontal assault by the National League. Unlike Barnie and Buckenberger, who capitulated almost immediately, Pfeffer refused to cooperate with NL inquiries into the initiative. What that got him was a suspension and exile to a coaching job at Princeton University. When he let it be known that he was still eager to play, however, 10,000 fans took up his cause and signed a petition saying they would boycott major league games if Pfeffer weren't reinstated. That emboldened Louisville president Fred Dresler to break ranks with the other owners and send him a contract. The league backed off, settling for a $500 fine that was raised by Pfeffer's friends.

Pfeffer has been credited with being the first middle infielder to cut off the catcher's throw to second and throw home again to thwart the front end of a planned double steal.

BABE PHELPS

Phelps did two things very well: hit and imagine illnesses. With regard to the former, he holds the record for the highest batting average (.367 in 1936) by a catcher with at least 300 at bats, had another part-time season (1935) batting .364, and broke the .300 mark two other times in his 12-year career. On the other hand, he became a progressively more serious neurasthenic, begging out of games regularly with the Dodgers in the late 1930s and early 1940s. One of his personal medical theories, which accounted for sharp mood swings, was that if his heart missed one or two beats, he was all right, but that if it missed four, he was about to suffer cardiac arrest. According to teammates, Phelps frequently showed up for games in a haggard state because he had spent the night sitting up listening to his heartbeat.

The catcher burned his bridges with the Dodgers in 1941, first by refusing to go to spring training in Havana because it required getting on a boat, then by jumping the team before a crucial series because he said he wasn't feeling well. He lived to the age of 84.

DAVE PHILLEY

A switch-hitting outfielder for several American League teams in the 1940s and 1950s, Philley came into his own near the end of his career as a premier pinch-hitter. With the Phillies in 1958 he banged out eight consecutive hits coming off the bench, then added a ninth straight in his first 1959 appearance for a major league record. With the Orioles in 1961 he set an AL pinch-hitting mark with 24 safeties. An overall .270 batter for 18 years, Philley averaged .299 as a pinch-hitter.

DEACON PHILLIPPE

A much underrated righthander at the dawn of the 20th century, Phillippe won the very first World Series game when he hurled Pittsburgh to a 7–3 triumph over Boston on October 1, 1903. It was the first of five appearances for him in the best-of-nine matchup; he also won the only other two games taken by the Pirates, while losing twice. With Louisville in 1899 and then with Pittsburgh for the next 12 seasons, Phillippe had six 20-win seasons, finishing up with 189 victories and a 2.59 ERA. When the Pirates set a major league record in June 1903 by hurling six consecutive shutouts, he contributed two of them. Phillippe's mere 363 walks in 2,607 innings give him the lowest ratio of walks per nine innings of any pitcher working from a mound distance of 60 feet, six inches.

E. LAWRENCE PHILLIPS

In 1902 Phillips introduced the concept of a regular public address announcer by walking around

Washington's American League Park and using a megaphone to relay lineups to fans. Wolfie Jacobs had clarified some rules decisions to fans by using a megaphone in Boston the year before.

RICHIE PHILLIPS

Phillips's suicidal strategy of getting umpires to resign en masse in 1999 as a means of gaining leverage in contract talks with the leagues reversed more than two decades of union gains for the arbiters. When the leagues accepted the resignations, the umpires were out of jobs, Phillips was out of his own as head of the Major League Umpires Association, and the leagues had leverage to dictate talks with a replacement union made up of anti-Phillips arbiters.

A Philadelphia lawyer, Phillips had been the union leader since the late 1970s. He scored his first coup in 1979, when he kept umpires on picket lines for the first seven weeks of the season while negotiating significant salary increases, annual no-cut contracts, per diem traveling money, and a midyear two-week vacation for members. On the other hand, he failed in attempts to pressure the leagues to fire eight scab umpires who donned blue during the strike, prompting many years of crew tensions between the strikers and non-strikers. Phillips also threatened to call walkouts in 1984 and 1985 over postseason working conditions, and again in 1991 over a new contract; eleventh-hour settlements were reached all three times, but in 1991 not before retired and minor league umpires had to be summoned to work Opening Day games.

As the profession's most authoritative spokesman for more than 20 years, Phillips had drawn much of the blame for the increasing arrogance and short tempers of his members on the field in the 1980s and 1990s. He had only fueled the accusations with a personality that brooked no argument. That proved to be a double-edged sword when he had little trouble gaining a majority vote for his resignation strategy.

MIKE PIAZZA

The best offensive catcher in baseball history, Piazza has had to spend his mid-career resisting pressures to switch to another position. While some have argued he was on borrowed physical time (33 entering the 2002 season) behind the plate, others have contended he has always been an inadequate receiver and would benefit both himself and his club by shifting to first base or the outfield. Both assertions are half-truths. Although there have been catchers whose offensive production dropped off as soon as they hit their 30s (most notably, Bill Dickey and Johnny Bench), there have been just as many who have not regressed dramatically (to name three: Gabby Hartnett, Ernie Lombardi, and Carlton Fisk). And while Piazza has been anything but an ace at throwing out opposition baserunners, usually ranking near the bottom of the NL in that category, he has continually caught staffs for both the Dodgers and Mets near the top of league standings in ERA and has never seen a bounced curve or a sliding runner he wasn't able to meet with whatever part of his body was required.

The rest of the story has been less controversial. A 62nd round selection in the 1988 draft, and that only because his father and Los Angeles manager Tommy Lasorda were friends, he took Rookie of the Year honors in 1993 for the first of eight seasons in which he clouted at least 30 home runs, the first of six in which he knocked in 100 runs, and the first of 10 (every year) in which he averaged .300. His 201 hits for the Dodgers in 1997 were the most ever by a catcher in a season. But just as the habitués of Dodger Stadium were assuming they had a backstop for life, the new Los Angeles ownership of Rupert Murdoch got into a spitting contest with Piazza over a new long-term contract and ended up dealing him to Florida in 1998 for five players, including sluggers Gary Sheffield and Bobby Bonilla. A few days later, the Marlins passed him on to the Mets in a deal for Preston Wilson and other prospects.

A weeks-long slump in his first year created a little rocky weather with Shea Stadium fans, but rather than use that as an excuse to go elsewhere as a free agent, Piazza insisted it energized him, and proceeded to sign an extended contract. Just as his often monstrous home runs and clutch hitting since then have established him as the best offensive player in Mets history, his off-field ease with the media and New York City in general have laid to rest initial impressions that the Norristown, Pennsylvania native's Dodgers years had turned him into a beach boy.

OLLIE PICKERING

When he stepped into the batter's box on April 24, 1901, Cleveland center fielder Pickering became the first American League hitter. He flied out to Chicago center fielder Dummy Hoy.

JOHN PICKETT

Pickett is the only big leaguer who ever needed teammates to testify he was qualified as a player to collect his pay. Cut by Baltimore in the middle of the 1892 season after three years in the majors, the second baseman sued for the balance of his salary. When the Orioles claimed he didn't have the requisite skills to play in the majors, Pickett dragged team members into court to swear that he had demonstrated ordinary diamond abilities, and won a judgment of $1,285.72. A career .252 batter, he never played in the big leagues again.

JACK PIERCE

A Brooklyn restaurateur, Pierce was the most fanatical of Ebbets Field fans. With a devotion bordering on idolatry, he attended almost every home game of the Dodgers in the late 1930s and most of the 1940s to cheer on his favorite, third base man Cookie Lavagetto. He didn't come empty-handed, either—toting along two big cartons of balloons, a helium tank, a giant banner, and two bottles of scotch. Ensconced in a third base box seat, he would belt down his scotch, scream out the name "COOKIE!," then puncture one of the inflated balloons for emphasis. When Lavagetto was drafted during World War II, Pierce turned his attention to Joe Medwick, but with less enthusiasm.

JIMMY PIERSALL

Piersall came as close as anybody to awakening baseball to the possibility its "colorful stars" might sometimes have just been deeply troubled men. Following a nervous breakdown while with the Red Sox in 1952, he described some of the emotional stresses he had been under in the best-selling book *Fear Strikes Out;* the autobiography, which laid heavy emphasis on a win-at-all-costs father, was later adapted for the screen, with Tony Perkins (ludicrously) portraying the outfielder. Once he had branded himself through the book, Piersall became a daily target for abuse from opponents and fans. Matters got so bad for him in 1961 during a return trip to Fenway Park as a member of the Indians that Massachusetts legislators were moved to introduce bills outlawing fan profanity at sports contests in the state.

Piersall did little to discourage the abuse; on the contrary, he enjoyed mocking the game's traditional symbols and promotional rituals, providing more fodder for pundits who treated his excesses as an extension of his breakdown. In Yankee Stadium he urinated on the Babe Ruth monument that then stood in a playing area of the outfield. In Comiskey Park he fired baseballs at Bill Veeck's scoreboard for the avowed purpose of shortcircuiting the fireworks that were set off whenever a Chicago player hit a home run. After being traded to the Mets in 1963, he celebrated his 100th home run by circling the bases backward.

As a White Sox broadcaster after his retirement, Piersall found himself in hot water constantly—with the league office, players, and umpires. On one occasion he almost cost the club a forfeited loss by giving the finger from the press box to umpire Joe Brinkman. After calling Veeck's wife "a colossal bore" during an interview, he almost came to blows with the owner's son. He *did* come to blows with a Chicago-area reporter who questioned his sanity and with a Red Sox official who questioned one of his boasts about the talent of the White Sox. Veeck, forever vacillating between Piersall's popularity with fans and his own loathing of him, instigated a referendum on whether he should be kept in the broadcasting booth, and was chagrined to get an overwhelming yes vote. In pregame comments on another evening, Piersall advised listeners to stay away from Comiskey Park because of inclement weather, provoking still another scene with Veeck. Another suspension came during the subsequent ownership of Jerry Reinsdorf and Eddie Einhorn, when Piersall told a television panel that all ballplayers thought of their wives as "horny broads who . . . wanted to get married and wanted a little money." It was for remarks like this that he had to give up a part-time coaching job with Chicago.

Lost amid all the controversies was a 17-year career (between 1950 and 1967) that, at least in the 1950s, established Piersall as one of the AL's peskiest leadoff men and most talented center fielders.

LIP PIKE

Pike was one of the first players acknowledged as a professional. While others had certainly been paid before 1866, Pike and two teammates on the ostensibly amateur Philadelphia Athletics were ordered that year to answer charges before the governing National Association of Base Ball Players that they had received as much as $20 for their services. Although the matter was dropped when nobody bothered to show up for the hearing, the incident ex-

Ralph Kiner (pg. 226) led the National League in home runs during each of his seven seasons with the Pirates. *Photo reprinted courtesy of the Pittsburgh Pirates.*

Bill Mazeroski (pg. 273) earned a Cooperstown plaque for being the greatest defensive second baseman of the 20th century. *Photo reprinted courtesy of the Pittsburgh Pirates.*

Willie McCovey (pg. 276) was the most popular player ever to wear the San Francisco Giants uniform. *Photo reprinted courtesy of the San Francisco Giants.*

John McGraw (pg. 278) dominated baseball—and not just on the field—for a third of a century. *Photo reprinted courtesy of the authors' private collection.*

Pete Rose (pg. 363) bangs out his record-setting 4,192nd hit. *Photo reprinted courtesy of the Cincinnati Reds.*

The legendary Babe Ruth (pg. 369), otherwise known as the Sultan of Swat. *Photo reprinted courtesy of the National Baseball Hall of Fame and Library, Cooperstown, N.Y.*

Tris Speaker (pg. 398) was second only to Ty Cobb as an American League hitter in the first decades of the 20th century. *Photo reprinted courtesy of the National Baseball Hall of Fame and Museum, Cooperstown, N.Y.*

George "Buck" Weaver (pg. 447) was banned as one of the Black Sox, although he was never proved to have been a part of the conspiracy to throw the 1919 World Series. *Photo reprinted courtesy of the National Baseball Hall of Fame and Museum, Cooperstown, N.Y.*

Called "Pops" by his teammates, Willie Stargell (pg. 401) was a menace to opposing pitchers for two decades. *Photo reprinted courtesy of the Pittsburgh Pirates.*

Honus Wagner (pg. 441) was the National League's equivalent of Ty Cobb—without the controversial personality. *Photo reprinted courtesy of the National Baseball Hall of Fame and Museum, Cooperstown, N.Y.*

In the past 60 years only 13 players have hit as high in one season as Ty Cobb (pg. 73) hit during his career. *Photo reprinted courtesy of the authors' private collection.*

posed the widespread practice of paying supposedly amateur players. The outfielder later became the first Jewish major leaguer (with the St. Louis Brown Stockings in 1876) and the first Jewish manager (with the Cincinnati Reds the following year).

BABE PINELLI

After playing a solid third base for the Reds in the 1920s, Pinelli switched to umpiring, remaining with the National League for 22 years (1935–56). His last game behind the plate was Don Larsen's perfect effort for the Yankees against the Dodgers in the 1956 World Series. Even decades later, Dale Mitchell, the Brooklyn pinch-hitter who took a half-hearted swing at Larsen's final delivery, insisted Pinelli had been wrong in ringing him up as a strikeout. According to Mitchell, Pinelli "should have retired before the game, not after it."

LOU PINIELLA

Called Sweet Lou for the smoothness of his right-handed swing rather than for his disposition, Piniella attracted attention as a player for his manic quest for a flawless cut and for his tantrums when he didn't achieve it. Because of his temper he had been considered a short-term managerial prospect, at best; in fact, he entered the 2002 season in his 16th year as a pilot, having won 1,226 games against only 1,066 losses (.535).

Following brief stints with the Orioles and Indians, Piniella arrived with the Royals in 1968, taking Rookie of the Year honors. But it was with the Yankees between 1974 and his retirement in 1984 that he drew the most attention. Although he topped .300 six times and batted .291 overall, his most vivid playing moment came when, playing right field in the 1978 playoff game against the Red Sox, he lost a ninth-inning drive by Boston's Jerry Remy in the sun but decoyed everyone into believing he would make a routine catch; baserunner Rick Burleson could advance only one base after the ball bounced, and was unable to score the tying run on a subsequent fly ball by Jim Rice.

Promising a calmer, sweeter Lou, Piniella succeeded Billy Martin as Yankees manager in 1986. The only discernible difference was that he stopped trashing bat racks and water coolers when he struck out in favor of tossing the rack's contents on the field when he disagreed with an umpire's call. His

rages became all the more frequent when he heard about his predecessor Martin's questioning his every move up in the broadcasting booth. Still, he was the only New York manager to survive two full seasons at the height of owner George Steinbrenner's caprices in the 1980s, before being kicked upstairs to the front office in 1987 to make room for Martin again. That change lasted only until the following season, when he was once again sent to the bench as dugout leader.

In 1990, in his first season as Reds manager, Piniella won a West Division title, beat the Pirates in the League Championship Series, and swept the startled A's in the World Series. When the club slipped to fifth the following year, he was rumored on his way out, but instead gained an even bigger say in player procurement. When the players he recommended turned out to be busts, he was shown the door—but not before getting into a clubhouse punch-up with Rob Dibble after the reliever voiced displeasure at having been removed from a game.

With the Mariners since 1993, Piniella has presided over the renaissance of a franchise on the verge of collapsing in the mid-1990s. At the same time, his piloting has continually come up as a triple more than a home run. In 1995 he guided a team that roared back to beat the Yankees with one out to go in the last inning of the Division Series, but Seattle was then defeated by Cleveland in the ALCS. In 1997 he won another division title, only to be knocked off by the Orioles in the opening round of the postseason. He proved an invaluable protector and mentor to superstars Ken Griffey, Jr. and Alex Rodriguez, but had to watch both of them leave the organization. In 2000 he saw another season end, this time against the Yankees, in the League Championship Series. Most painful of all, he managed the most successful club in AL history in 2001 with 116 wins, but again lost to the Yankees in the ALCS. Through it all Piniella has assured reporters that the setbacks have not driven him to the cigarettes and furies they once did—true except for those times when he reaches for a cigarette or a bat in the bat rack.

WALLY PIPP

Pipp was considerably more than the first baseman who made the mistake of saying he had a headache on June 2, 1925. Before leaving the field to Lou Gehrig's 2,130-consecutive game streak, he had been the first (and only) Yankee to lead the

American League in any important offensive category, setting the pace for homers in both 1916 and 1917. Pipp also led in triples in 1924.

EDDIE PLANK (Hall of Fame, 1946)

Plank was a deliberate southpaw who annoyed opponents and spectators with the slow pace of his games; he annoyed Connie Mack even more by jumping to the Federal League in 1915.

Coming off the Gettysburg College campus in 1901, Plank notched seven 20-win seasons for Philadelphia over the next 14 seasons, recording close to a quarter of the victories by a team that won six pennants and fell out of the first division only in two years in the period. But he was also a World Series Jonah: Although holding the opposition to a 1.32 ERA in seven Series appearances, he lost five games (against only two wins)—four of them when the Athletics were shut out. He also missed the entire 1910 postseason because of a sore arm.

Plank's desertion to the Feds was such a bitter pill for Mack that the owner-manager accelerated the dismantling of his powerhouse team as a result. After one more 20-win season for the St. Louis Terriers and the collapse of the Feds, he was assigned to the Browns. Traded to the Yankees two years later, he refused to report, retiring with 326 wins, the most by a lefthander until Warren Spahn.

JOHNNY PODRES

Possessor of the best changeup of his era and the hero of the 1955 World Series, Podres never won 20 games, reaching a career high of 18 for the 1961 Dodgers. Even when he led the NL in ERA (2.66) and shutouts (six) for Brooklyn in 1957, he managed a record of only 12–9. But as far as Ebbets Field denizens were concerned, the southpaw could just as well have retired after his seventh-game 2–0 victory over the Yankees in 1955, giving the Dodgers their only world championship in Brooklyn. There probably never would have been a seventh game if Podres hadn't also won the third game after the Yankees had won the first two contests. The two wins were all the more surprising in that Podres's record during the regular season was 9–10, with a very visible 3.95 ERA.

CAL POHLAD

A Minneapolis banker, Pohlad ended the 65-year ownership of the Washington Senators-Minnesota Twins by the Griffith family when he put together a group of buyers to purchase the franchise in 1984 for $44 million. One of the 100 wealthiest people in America, he then endeavored to put an end to the Twins themselves by exposing them to contraction after the 2001 season.

Although he endorsed the signing of expensive free agents immediately after taking over the team, helping the Twins to world championships in 1987 and 1991, Pohlad soon became conspicuous even among baseball's tightest owners for making little effort to improve the club. His main excuse was the refusal of Minnesota voters and the legislature to approve another tax financed-stadium despite various schemes involving lotteries and non-profit corporations and threats to sell the franchise to interests in the Tri-Cities of North Carolina. At the same time, he became a chief beneficiary of revenue sharing, so much so that by holding the team payroll under $25 million, he was actually turning a profit at the turn of the millennium. But with the prospect of a major league buyout providing several times even that profit, he showed no perceptible resistance to the idea of disbanding the Twins altogether through contraction. He was in the minority, with Minnesota Governor Jesse Ventura, members of the U.S. Congress, and fans raising roadblocks to the contraction plan during the 2001–2002 offseason.

ALEX POPOV

Popov's suit to acquire the ball Barry Bonds hit for his 73rd home run dramatized the capricious, if not lunatic, spirals of the memorabilia market The Giants fan filed the legal action against Patrick Hayashi, who claimed ownership of the ball after a scramble for it in the right field arcade of Pac Bell Park on October 14, 2001. Popov's contention was that he gloved the drive, then had it wrested away from him in what amounted to an assault by Hayashi and other spectators. Hayashi's rebuttal included testimony from former major league umpire Rich Garcia that anyone catching a ball without closing his glove around it couldn't claim possession. The ball was turned over to a San Francisco court pending a disposition of the rival claims.

At the root of the controversy were the mercurial values attached to objects of the game. Most experts agreed the Bonds ball would attract offers merely starting at $1 million—until, that was, it was devalued by somebody hitting 74 home runs in a season, by the market becoming glutted with supposedly significant home run balls, or by some other whim that major league baseballs weren't always what they were cracked up to be.

CUM POSEY

The guiding genius behind the Homestead Grays, Posey's club won nine straight Negro National League pennants from 1937 to 1945.

Joining the team as an outfielder in its second year of existence in 1911, Posey served as player (1912–29) booking agent (1912–16), manager (1917–37), and owner in a career that lasted until his death in 1946. Often raiding the organized leagues for star players, he kept his team independent until 1929, when he joined the American Negro League, but returned to independent status the following year. When Gus Greenlee's Pittsburgh Crawfords lured Josh Gibson, Oscar Charleston, and Judy Johnson away, he took on as a partner Pittsburgh racketeer Rufus "Sonnyman" Jackson, whose money enabled him to get back Gibson in 1937. That year Posey also moved half the Grays games to Washington to take advantage of Sunday ball and the capital's growing black population, playing in Pittsburgh when the Pirates were on the road and in Washington when the Senators were away. In 1933 he helped organize the first East-West Game, the Negro leagues All-Star Game. The contests became black baseball's biggest event, drawing as many as 50,000 fans.

PAM POSTEMA

Postema's 13 years as a minor league arbiter was the longest umpiring tenure by a woman in organized baseball; the circumstances of her dismissal aroused suspicions that sexist attitudes, not her ability to call balls and strikes, were the reason she never reached the big leagues. Released in December 1989 after seven years at the AAA level and several spring tryouts for the majors, she was given no specific reason why neither the National nor American league wanted her services, but there were numerous suggestions that the circuits didn't want to be bothered providing separate facilities for a woman umpire or dealing with inevitable conflicts arising from resentful, women-belong-in-the-kitchen players and managers. Postema brought suit against the major leagues and the Triple A alliance of minor leagues, settled out of court, and later wrote a book of her experiences entitled *You've Got to Have Balls to Make It in This League.*

NELSON POTTER

Although the spitball had been outlawed for almost a quarter-century, it was not until July 20, 1944 that anyone enforced the rule, with umpire Cal Hubbard tossing Potter out of a game for going to his mouth while on the mound for the Browns. The right-hander was later fined and suspended for 10 days.

JACK POWELL

Powell has the most wins of any pitcher with a losing record. His 245 victories for the (Cleveland) Spiders, Cardinals, Browns, and Yankees included four 20-win seasons; his 254 defeats were compiled by losing in double figures in every one of his 16 major league seasons (1897–1912) despite a lifetime ERA of 2.97.

JAKE POWELL

Powell threw one of the ugliest lights on baseball racism prior to the arrival of Jackie Robinson in the majors. Interviewed by Bob Elson in Chicago on a July 1938 pregame radio show, the Yankees outfielder boasted that he had spent his off-season as a Dayton, Ohio cop "cracking niggers over the head." Elson immediately cut off the interview, but Powell's remark ricocheted around the country for weeks. While black dailies from coast to coast demanded Powell be banned from both the big leagues and Ohio police work, the baseball establishment and the mainstream press sought to interpret the incident as nothing more than an attempt at "jocularity." Even when Commissioner Kenesaw Landis finally sensed the depth of anger in the black community and suspended Powell for 10 days, he insisted that the player had spoken "carelessly, not purposely." For his part, Yankees president Ed Barrow described the remark as a "thoughtless blunder," while also providing assurances that he had talked with "two of my colored servants and they seem to feel it was just an unfortunate mistake that cannot happen again."

Faced with calls by black groups to boycott the beer products of New York owner Jacob Ruppert, the club prevailed upon Powell to visit a newspaper in Harlem and issue an apology directly. Like most of the rest of the case, this, too, was ignored by a majority of white dailies; it was only when Powell returned to action at Griffith Stadium after his suspension and was welcomed by boos and bottles that more attention was paid, and then largely in the interests of denouncing the bottle throwers as being worse than the outfielder.

Powell had an 11-year career with the Yankees, Senators, and Phillies in the 1930s and 1940s, batting .271 overall. He started going downhill after fracturing his skull while chasing a fly ball in a 1940 game. In 1948 he was arrested in Washington for passing bad checks, and shortly afterward committed suicide in his cell.

VIC POWER

Power's flamboyant style of playing first base has usually been cited as why the Yankees, endeavoring to break their color line as quietly as possible, traded him to Kansas City in 1954. In fact, there is just as much evidence that the main problem New York had with him was that he was simply good enough to make the team—a concession the club wasn't about to make during the Bronx regime of George Weiss. Either way, the Power deal was the only one of dozens between the clubs in the 1950s that benefited the Athletics more than New York. As deft as he was flashy, the Puerto Rican native ended up collecting seven Gold Gloves and leading first basemen in fielding three times. No slouch with a bat, either, Power batted over .300 three times and concluded a 12-year run at .284. While with Cleveland on August 14, 1958, he stole home twice in a game—the only time that has been accomplished since Walter Gautreau did it for the Braves in 1927. For sure, he had the element of surprise working for him since he stole only one other base that season and never more than nine in a season.

MIKE POWERS

Powers sustained the first fatal injury on a major league diamond during the opening of Shibe Park on April 12, 1909. A backup receiver for four teams over 11 seasons, he was behind the plate for the inaugural only because he was Eddie Plank's personal catcher. In the seventh inning he crashed into a wall going after a foul. Though he remained in the game, he was rushed immediately afterward to emergency surgery for internal bleeding. Two weeks and two more operations later, Powers died of gangrene of the bowels.

AL PRATT

A former National Association pitcher, Pratt was tending bar in Pittsburgh in October 1881 when he overheard two customers from Cincinnati, Justus Thorner and O. P. Caylor, lamenting that no one had shown up for a meeting they had called to discuss the prospects for forming a new major league. The American Association was born after the pair acted on Pratt's suggestion they seek out a local sportsman, Denny McKnight. The bartender got his reward a year later when he was named manager of the new league's Pittsburgh entry.

TODD PRATT

Pratt has hit the only walkoff home run to end a Division Series. The backup Mets catcher clouted his drive off Arizona's Matt Mantei in the 10th inning of the fourth game of the 1999 NLDS. Pratt was in the game only because of an injury to regular New York receiver Mike Piazza

GERRY PRIDDY

Priddy became the focal point of clubhouse tensions on the 1947 Senators when he refused to sign a statement saying the team stood squarely behind manager Ossie Bluege. The declaration had been fashioned by Bluege himself amid press reports that the players were in full revolt against the pilot. Owner Clark Griffith immediately stepped in to quash the statement before it too became media fodder, then, after the season, traded Priddy to the Browns and fired Bluege. On his way to St. Louis, Priddy got in the last shot by predicting that he would have his best year there without the distractions of the Washington organization; in fact, his next two seasons were the best of his career, the second baseman topping .290 in both years.

CHARLES PRINCE

Boston blueblood and Harvard graduate Prince attempted to challenge the National League in Boston twice—first as backer of the Players League Reds in 1890, then as owner of an American Association franchise of the same name the following year. He failed both times despite pennant-winning seasons in the two leagues. The first venture flopped even though the Reds had recruited almost the entire roster of the NL Beaneaters; in the peace talks that followed the campaign, Prince growled about the

PL's readiness to fight on even while maneuvering to move on to an American Association franchise. His second foray was doomed as soon as he acceded to conditions by Beaneaters owner Arthur Soden that Prince charge the NL admission of 50 cents and not use Boston as part of the club name. Even with these handicaps Prince signed King Kelly in mid-season and looked as if he might make a go of it; but when the Hub City favorite switched over to So-den's team four games later, Prince, the Reds, and, as it turned out, the whole American Association were through. Prince quit as club president when his board of directors retaliated against Soden by lowering ticket prices to 25 cents, and had to sit on the sidelines as the AA unraveled behind empty demands to return Kelly.

LOU PROCTOR

Proctor was a Western Union telegraphist in Boston who inserted his name into the box score of a May 13, 1912 game between the Browns and Red Sox. Several publications, including *The Sporting News* and early editions of *The Baseball Encyclopedia,* recorded him as having gone hitless in a pinch-hitting appearance.

DOC PROTHRO

Prothro wasn't much of a third baseman in the 1920s, but he was even less than that as a manager. His record of 138–320 (.301), for the Phillies between 1939 and 1940, is the worst by a big league manager with at least two full seasons.

HUB PRUETT

Pruett was a mediocre southpaw who went 29–48 for the Browns and three National League teams between 1922 and 1932. On the other hand, he was a Hall of Famer when he faced Babe Ruth, striking out the New York slugger 13 times in 21 at bats.

KIRBY PUCKETT (Hall of Fame, 2001)

The most popular player ever to don a Minnesota uniform, Puckett was the offensive backbone and morale leader of the club's World Series wins in 1987 and 1991. By the same token, his forced retirement in 1995 at the age of 34 because of glaucoma accelerated the collapse of the franchise.

Although he quickly established his credentials as an offensive force in his rookie year of 1984, the fireplug-built outfielder also managed to get through 557 at bats without hitting a home run—a statistic that turned even more anomalous when he walloped 31 two years later. The righty swinger also won the AL batting crown in 1989 (.339), led the league in hits four times, compiled at least 200 hits five times, and paced the circuit in RBIs in 1994. In 1993 Twins fans came close to protest demonstrations when owner Carl Pohlad's rigid stance against signing free agents had Puckett only hours away from going to Boston; Pohlad caved in at the eleventh hour, signing his star to a lucrative contract.

Puckett's most visible moment nationally came in the 11th inning of the sixth game of the 1991 World Series, when his home run off Atlanta's Charlie Leibrandt kept the Twins alive for a seventh game, which they also won. He entered Cooperstown with a .318 mark for 12 seasons, topping .300 eight times.

ALBERT PUJOLS

No big league rookie ever had a more significant impact on his team than Pujols did on the 2001 Cardinals. His record-shattering offense (for a rookie) of 37 home runs, 47 doubles, 130 RBIs, a slugging average of .610, and a batting average of .329 was only part of his contribution to leading St. Louis into the playoffs. In addition, he played at least 39 games at four positions (first base, third base, left field, right field) and was called on to fill the offensive vacuum left by the immensely popular injured slugger Mark McGwire.

HARRY PULLIAM

The president of the National League from 1903 to 1909, Pulliam owed his position to Pittsburgh owner Barney Dreyfuss; he owed his tragic end in good part to John McGraw.

A minority partner with Dreyfuss in the Louisville Colonels in the 1890s, Pulliam moved to Pittsburgh as organization secretary when the Kentucky team was dissolved at the end of the decade. After season-long strife in 1900 between major stockholders Dreyfuss and William Kerr, Pulliam turned into a *casus belli* when Kerr tried to get him removed from his post. Knowing this was just an initial move aimed at pushing him out too, Dreyfuss countered ably enough to force Kerr to sell out and take over the Pirates completely. Three years later, Dreyfuss had gained enough influence in league councils to impose Pulliam as president of the circuit. In that role Pulliam endorsed his sponsor's call for the first World Series in 1903 and also made an enemy for life when he scolded McGraw for not being willing to field his Giants against the Red Sox in a 1904 Series.

In 1905 Pulliam made another big mistake when he gave in to a Dreyfuss demand that McGraw be fined and suspended; the Giants manager's sin had been to taunt the prim Pittsburgh owner about (nonexistent) gambling habits and debts in public before a game in the Polo Grounds. When McGraw refused to serve 15 days on the sidelines and pay an ordered $150, throwing in charges that Pulliam heard only his master's voice, other NL owners stepped in quickly before the affair threatened the league as a whole. The Solomonic verdict was that McGraw should abide by the suspension and fine, Dreyfuss should be censured for unbecoming behavior, and Pulliam should be congratulated for acquitting himself so responsibly. It all went for nought when McGraw continued to ignore the penalties, and Pulliam, trying to end his daily pillorying in the New York press, let the matter drop.

Worse followed in 1908 after the Merkle Boner debacle. When Pulliam ruled—belatedly—that the New York first baseman's failure to touch second on a hit had nullified an apparent Giants victory, McGraw exploded in further rage against the league official, leaving him barely enough room for still greater fury when the makeup game necessitated by the Merkle decision cost New York the pennant. Throughout the offseason New York sportswriters stirred up by McGraw lashed out at Pulliam unmercifully. The league president finally cracked, and had to take a six-month leave of absence for a nervous breakdown. It didn't help. Shortly after returning to his position, on July 28, 1909, Pulliam blew out his brains at the New York Athletic Club; he was 39. An official league communique attributed the suicide to the fact that Pulliam had been "broken in health from overwork in his long fight to maintain a high standard of baseball." The only team not represented at the funeral was the Giants. Informed of what had taken place, McGraw was quoted as commenting: "I didn't think a bullet to his head could hurt him."

Q

TOM QUALTERS

A righthander for the 1954 Phillies, Qualters spent the entire season on the team without getting into a single game. He was neither injured nor suspended, but a bonus baby who had to be carried on the major league roster for two years. Steve O'Neill and Terry Moore, who split managing duties during the year, shared a resentment at losing a pitching spot to the bonus rule, refusing to drop the hurler even into a laugher. The Phillies finished fourth, 22 games out of first.

JOE QUEST

A light-hitting second baseman for six teams in the 1870s and 1880s, Quest contributed the term "charley horse" to the baseball lexicon. He applied the label to a leg injury suffered by teammate George Gore when the outfielder pulled a muscle on a steal attempt in 1882. The day before Quest had been the only one of several Chicago players in attendance at a local racetrack who had refused to bet on a favorite named Charley; his doubts had been justified when Charley pulled up lame in the backstretch after leading the field by several lengths.

In 1907, two decades after leaving baseball, Quest was suspected of peculation while employed in the Chicago City Clerk's office by his old manager Cap Anson. His response to the accusation was to drop out of sight forever.

FRANK QUILICI

Qulici owed his managing job with the Twins between 1973 and 1975 to his ethnic background. Asked why the former infielder had been named to replace Bill Rigney as Twins skipper, owner Calvin Griffith said it was because the team "played better under Italian managers." The reference was to Cookie Lavagetto, Sam Mele, and Billy Martin. Minnesota's record under Qulici was three third-place and one fourth-place finish for an overall 280–287 (.494).

BOB QUINN

As an owner, general manager, or combination of the two, Quinn was baseball's all-time loser. Operating from the front offices of the Browns, Red Sox, Dodgers, and Braves almost continuously between 1917 and 1944, the executive presided over clubs that compiled a record of 1,726–2,357 (.423), not a single pennant in the mix. Only four of the teams broke .500, while nine of them couldn't even reach .400.

Quinn began his administrative career with the Browns, taking over as general manager under owner Phil Ball, who prided himself on not interfering in baseball decisions. Ball was so ecstatic over an unexpected second-place finish in 1922 that he handed around bonuses to his top aides; Quinn promptly used his money to buy into the Red Sox. Although initially welcomed in New England for taking over from Harry Frazee, the owner who had sold Babe Ruth and other stars to New York, he was soon operating a club even worse than that run by his predecessor. The ill-advised deals with the Yankees didn't stop, either; one of the worst was the peddling of future Hall of Famer Red Ruffing to the Bronx in 1930. Managers came and went so regularly that one of them, Horace McManus, got considerable mileage out of the crack that he had been offered the job while in church with Quinn and instantly had another reason to feel humbled.

Like Frazee, Quinn spent much of his time in Boston scrambling after cash. Some of his financial shorts stemmed from the 1926 death of his chief backer, Indiana glassworks millionaire Palmer Wilson. In the same year, a fire destroyed a substantial part of Fenway Park, necessitating costly rebuilding. With the 1929 stock market crash the usually hotheaded Quinn became even more so in having to rely still more heavily on creditors; at one time or another he threatened to sell every player on his roster and to close Fenway Park and move into Braves Field to save on overhead. Hardly a visionary in the best of times, his daily turmoils led him to ridicule an idea before its time in 1931: that the Red Sox become the first club to offer telecasts of their games. But even as he was laughing at the notion of undermining his already thin attendance with free television coverage, he was dipping into his own insurance policies to help meet the payroll. When Tom Yawkey appeared in 1933 with an offer to buy the club for little more than its accumulated $350,000 in debts, Quinn accepted.

As general manager of the Dodgers in 1934 and 1935, Quinn's main contributions were continuing the sideshow antics of the incompetent regime known as The Daffiness Boys, hiring Casey Stengel as manager, and blowing up a casual remark by Giants pilot Bill Terry into a declaration of battle between the teams. It was in fact out of personal irritation that his trading prowess was being questioned that Quinn made Terry's "Is Brooklyn still in the league?" a war cry that echoed across the East River until, on the final weekend of the 1934 season, the Dodgers knocked the Giants out of the pennant race.

After the 1935 season the National League asked Quinn to take over as the president of the Braves because of regulations prohibiting chief stockholder Charles Adams, a heavy investor in a racetrack, from holding the office. Quinn's first act with still another franchise reeling from financial problems was to poll Boston sportswriters for a new team nickname in an effort to end the New York Tammany Hall connotations of the Braves. After sorting through such proposals as the Basements and the Bankrupts, he decided on the Bees; he also changed the name of the team stadium from Braves Field to National League Park. Once these cosmetic alterations had been made, Quinn sent one humpty-dumpty club after another onto the field and, as in Brooklyn, brought in Stengel as a sideshow. There was also his usual series of players-for-cash deals—in this instance keeping the franchise so visibly afloat that a group of Boston businessmen backed Quinn in 1941, when he bought out Adams's 73 percent holding.

Quinn barely got through World War II with his second Boston franchise. By 1943, three of his backers (construction industry millionaires Lou Perini, Guido Rugo, and Joseph Maney) had bought up a controlling interest. Quinn remained as president until 1944, before being demoted to minor league director and being replaced as head of the organization by his son John Quinn. Before abdicating to Perini and his partners, he changed the name of the team back to the Braves and the name of the ballpark back to Braves Field.

JACK QUINN

Quinn lasted long enough as a pitcher (23 years between 1909 and 1933) to become the oldest hurler both to win a major league game and to finish a World Series contest, and the oldest player to hit a home run. A dispute over his contract was also instrumental in pushing American League president Ban Johnson from power. Quinn's best and worst years came for the Baltimore Terrapins of the Federal League, when he won 26 games in 1914 and then slipped to a league-leading 22 losses the following year. After the collapse of the Feds, the righthanded spitballer went to the Pacific Coast League, where he pitched for the Vernon club until World War I closed down the circuit in 1918. When the pitcher signed with the White Sox and Vernon simultaneously sold his contract to the Yankees, the two AL teams locked horns over which had the prior rights to his services. Even though Quinn appeared in six games for Chicago in late 1918, the National Commission ruled in favor of the Yankees, with Johnson supplying the critical vote against White Sox owner Charlie Comiskey. Comiskey became so irate—more at what he viewed as a betrayal by an old friend than over the loss of the hurler—that the two became implacable enemies, with the Chicago owner joining the swelling ranks of those plotting Johnson's overthrow.

Quinn went on to register 18 wins for New York in 1920 and another 18 for Philadelphia in 1928. On June 27, 1930, still with the Athletics at eight days shy of his 47th birthday, he hit the last of his eight career home runs; later in the season he pitched the final two innings of the third game of the World Series. He recorded his final victory, for the Dodgers, on August 14, 1932, at age 49, while leading the National League in saves for the second year in a row. Quinn retired with 247 victories.

R

CHARLIE RADBOURNE (Hall of Fame, 1939)

The winner of 309 games, Radbourne was a formidable hurler before 1884, having already led the National League in won-lost percentage in 1881, strikeouts in 1882, and wins in 1883. But in 1884 the Providence righthander known as Old Hoss for his durability had the single greatest season by a 19th-century pitcher when he won an all-time record 60 times while pacing the league in strikeouts and ERA.

Difficult when sober and impossible most of the time, Radbourne was suspended in mid-July after a tantrum over a balk call; upon his return he offered to pitch every day for the rest of the season after mound partner Charlie Sweeney had jumped to the Union Association. The underhander proceeded to complete his next 35 starts, winning 30 of them and turning a tight pennant race into a rout. After defeating the American Association's New York Metropolitans three straight in the postseason, he received his reward in the form of a blank contract that he filled in with only a modest raise. What emerged only later was that, during his Iron Man streak, he was also collecting Sweeney's salary.

FREDERICK RAH

Rah designed dandelion-colored baseballs with the idea that they would be safer for batters against white-shirt backgrounds. Larry MacPhail of the Dodgers secured league permission to use them in a 1938 game and in three more games in 1939, but then abandoned the experiment. Thirty years later Charlie Finley of the A's pressed for a similar switch to yellow balls, but without success.

TIM RAINES

Raines didn't rack up the most steals (808) in his 22-year career between 1979 and 2001, but his rate of success (.847) in scooting from one base to another was the highest in baseball history. As a Montreal rookie in 1981, the switch-hitting outfielder had even bigger numbers in his sights when the players strike forced him to the sidelines: He ended up with 71 steals in 88 games (a rookie record), the first of four consecutive seasons that he led the National League in stolen bases and the first of six straight in which he swiped at least 70. A lifetime .295 hitter, Raines also paced NL batters in hitting (.334) and on-base percentage (.415) in 1986.

The Rock, as he was called for his muscular physique, had to overcome cocaine problems early in his career—a background that cost him a free agent contract when the Padres announced in 1986 that they would not sign deals for longer than one year with anyone with a drug addiction past. He eventually moved to the American League, where he played with the White Sox, Yankees, and Athletics until he was diagnosed with lupus after the 1999 season. He sat out most of the 2000 season, then tried to work his way back to the major leagues by trying out for the U.S. Olympic team, but was cut from the squad. He nevertheless did come back in 2001—first returning to the Expos before injuries disabled him and then, toward the end of the year, going to the Orioles so, like Ken Griffey, he could say he had played on the same team with his son (Tim Raines, Jr.).

WILLARD RAMSDELL

Ramsdell didn't let team loyalty stand in the way of $50. As a member of the Cubs in 1952, the knuckleballer drew a walk off Carl Erskine in the fifth inning of what turned out to be the Brooklyn hurler's first no-hitter. In the ninth inning Ramsdell was informed that his walk entitled him to be the Chicago representative on a postgame show that paid $50—provided no other Cub reached base. The righthander openly cheered for Erskine to strike out teammate Eddie Miksis so he could collect the money. Miksis went down swinging.

TOAD RAMSEY

Ramsey was the first knuckleballer, a pitch he called a drop curve. Pitching for the Louisville Colonels of the American Association on June 23, 1887, Ramsey fanned 17 Cleveland batters. Although record books cite Roger Clemens and Kerry Wood for the single-game strikeout mark, Ramsey's achievement remains noteworthy because, under rules of the day, he had to get four strikes for a whiff.

RICHARD RAVITCH

Ravitch triggered the firing of Commissioner Fay Vincent in 1992 when he took over as the chief labor negotiator for major league owners. He accepted the position on the condition that he have a free hand in dealing with the Players Association, with no intrusions from anyone inspired by the traditionally nebulous "best interests of baseball." With Milwaukee owner Bud Selig moving in as the temporary commissioner, Ravitch labored for months to work out an agreement among owners for a revenue sharing scheme he deemed an indispensable prelude to opening negotiations with the players. He then became the owners' chief spokesman for the salary cap demands that were generally viewed as an attempt to break the players union and that precipitated the 1994 action that brought a premature end to the season.

DAVE RAYMOND

As the Phillie Phanatic, Raymond wore a Philadelphia home uniform longer than anyone but Mike Schmidt. For 16 years up to 1993 he cavorted around the field and in the stands of Veterans Stadium in the flouncy, big-bellied attire of a green ant-eater. His performance specialties were mocking umpires and visiting players, leading fans in ridiculous dances, and "swallowing" spectators with his oversized beak. Another constant of the mascot's act was to speed

over the artificial turf on a scooter, chasing groundskeepers and coaches away. Raymond's explanation for the effectiveness of his antics was that he had been raised by a hearing-impaired mother with whom he had to learn extravagantly physical communication skills. Since 1993, the Phanatic's act has been primarily in the hands of Tom Burgoyne.

AL REACH

One of the earliest paid players (with the Brooklyn Eckfords in the early 1860s), the British-born Reach built one of the great baseball fortunes, both as a team owner and sporting goods manufacturer. As part-owner and president of the Phillies from the team's inception in 1883 until 1902, he was responsible for the construction of Huntington Avenue Grounds, the first concrete stadium, which opened in 1887. Reach's partnership with Ben Shibe encompassed both a jointly held half-interest in the Phillies and full control of the sporting goods company that bore his name. Incorporated in the late 1870s, the firm sold out to rival Al Spalding in 1892, although the Philadelphia branch continued being run by the founder. This cozy relationship got even cozier when partner Shibe accepted the presidency of the upstart American League Athletics in 1901 and the contract to produce AL baseballs. The only one who seemed bothered by this conflict of interest was John Rogers, the holder of the other 50 percent of the Phillies. Rogers grew even more concerned after the A's began raiding the Phillies for such stars as Nap Lajoie, Elmer Flick, and Bill Duggleby. After two years of lawsuits and mutual recriminations, all three stockholders sold out to a group headed by broker Jimmy Potter. A.J. Reach and Co. continued manufacturing baseballs—for both leagues—until well into the 20th century (even though the NL balls carried a Spalding imprint). Similarly, Reach published the annual AL guides, while Spalding did the NL books.

RICK REED

Reed was the most experienced of the former major leaguers drafted as so-called replacement players by owners during the 1994–95 lockout. Denounced as a scab by teammates and other Players Association members when he returned to the majors with the Mets in 1997, the righthander had little choice but to let his pitching do his talking for him, gradually lowering clubhouse barriers thanks to his reincarnation as a control specialist who won in double figures for New York four years in a row. Prior to the lockout, Reed had pitched in 61 games for the Pirates, Royals, Rangers, and Reds. It was while with Cincinnati that he agreed to defy a Players Association ban on playing during the lockout, saying he needed the money for an operation for an ailing family member.

JIMMY REESE

Nobody in baseball wore a uniform longer than Reese, who died in 1994 at the age of 88 while still serving as a coach for the Angels. Once an outfielder for the Yankees and a Babe Ruth roommate, the New York native donned his first togs as a batboy for the Los Angeles Angels of the Pacific Coast League in 1917. The next 77 years encompassed three seasons with the Yankees and Browns (for a career average of .278); decades of minor league managing and coaching; and, from 1972 to his death, conditioning coach and fungo hitter for the AL Angels.

PEEWEE REESE (Hall of Fame, 1984)

Reese owed his 16 years (between 1940 and 1958) in a Dodgers uniform to the vanity of another Hall of Fame shortstop. Ready for promotion to the majors from the Boston farm system in 1939, he was kept where he was because Red Sox shortstop-manager Joe Cronin wouldn't admit that his best years were behind him. Purchased by Brooklyn, the righthand-hitting Reese took a finishing course from still another Cooperstown shortstop-manager, Leo Durocher, then went on to captain The Boys of Summer teams through the 1950s.

Reese was the classic playmaker—hitting behind the runner, bunting, and turning the double play with agility. In an era that didn't think too highly of stolen bases, he paced the NL in that category in 1952; he also topped the league in walks in 1947 and in runs scored in 1949. As much as in his physical skills, however, the solidly built infielder (his nickname came from his boyhood talent in shooting marbles, not from his size) was invaluable to Brooklyn for his leadership qualities—and never more so than when Jackie Robinson broke the color barrier in 1947. After acknowledging his own misgivings about playing with Robinson, the Kentuckian ended up turning the tide for his teammate's brutal orientation when,

taking the field at a game at Crosley Field, he paused at first base and, to a sudden silence from Cincinnati fans, put his arm around his teammate. A footnote to the relationship between the two was that in six of the 10 seasons they played together, Reese stole more bases than Robinson.

CHARLIE REILLY

An otherwise undistinguished third baseman for eight seasons, Reilly stroked the first big league pinch-hit—a single for the Phillies in the ninth inning on April 28, 1892.

JERRY REINSDORF

Reinsdorf had his moment as a Walter O'Malley-like First Among Equals with major league owners in the early 1990s, especially after leading the successful campaign to dump Commissioner Fay Vincent. The White Sox owner certainly felt invulnerable enough in his position after the September 1992 ouster of Vincent to assert that the time had come to "run the business for the owners, not the players or the umpires or the fans." If he hasn't developed any humility since then, his behind-the-scenes power has been scaled down somewhat by the entry of several media moguls into league boardrooms and by signs that Bud Selig, once deemed little more than a Reinsdorf stooge, has begun to savor his own sense of authority.

A real estate magnate, Reinsdorf and his partner Eddie Einhorn took on the Chicago franchise in 1981 after the AL had blocked previous owner Bill Veeck's attempts to sell to Edward DeBartolo. Reinsdorf's first move was to sign catcher Carlton Fisk, rendered a free agent by Boston's failure to send him a contract by a regulated deadline. It proved to be a pivotal pickup when Fisk went on to establish various franchise power records, but it would also ultimately serve as an example of the owner's crassness when it came to people he no longer wanted around.

Although the White Sox won a division title in 1983, Reinsdorf didn't have many other satisfactions for quite some time. For one thing, there was the mid-decade purchase of the Cubs by the Chicago *Tribune,* which meant that the city's main newspaper and its associated broadcasting network devoted about 20 words to the National League club for every one spent on the White Sox. In 1984 Reinsdorf irritated other owners by indirectly causing the demise of the free agent compensation pool by plucking Tom Seaver from the Mets; although New York itself assumed an ambiguous stance over the loss of the Hall of Fame pitcher, smaller market clubs had viewed the pool as a way of obtaining better prospects for departed free agents and cringed before the critical fallout over Seaver's loss to Shea Stadium. The owner also had to settle for a Pyrrhic victory when he appointed machine-gun-mouthed Ken Harrelson as general manager in 1985 in an attempt to beat the Cubs to the local sports headlines; he got the headlines, but they were mostly about such misguided Harrelson moves as switching the heavy-footed Fisk to the outfield and the ensuing protests by White Sox pitchers at losing one of the game's most astute receivers.

But more than anything, the Reinsdorf-Einhorn partnership was consumed in the 1980s by its demand that the city provide a new stadium for the team. While municipal and state legislators got bogged down in one argument after another, the pair grew less subtle about threats to leave Chicago for Florida. By the beginning of 1988 St. Petersburg had started construction on a $140 million domed facility with a capacity of 43,000. On June 27, only three days before the deadline that the Illinois legislature had for approving a new Comiskey Park, Florida officials disclosed that Reinsdorf had taken a 15-year lease on the dome and had already worked out an agreement for the fourth-best television package in baseball. With Illinois governor James Thompson pulling out all the stops to save the franchise for the state, the legislature put the finishing touches on the construction bill with literally only minutes to spare. The second Comiskey Park opened in 1991 directly across the street from the old facility, with Reinsdorf maintaining the air of somebody who wouldn't have been all that crushed to have to go to Florida.

His successful pressuring of the Illinois legislature together with an ambitious cable sports network launched a few years earlier to carry White Sox games put Reinsdorf at the center of financial strategy sessions in the early 1990s. He figured prominently in the selection of Richard Ravitch as the owners' chief negotiator and, after Vincent stubbed his toe with several teams, in replacing the commissioner on an interim basis with Selig—an interim that lasted six years. In recent years he has viewed a more humbling landscape: a Comiskey Park II that is as uninviting as any stadium in the majors, the newly created Devil Rays taking over the St. Petersburg dome, the need to make his peace with the *Tribune*'s WGN for televising White Sox games, and Selig spending more time with other power brokers.

Reinsdorf has also had his share of public relations gaffes. The most short-lived was an attempt to bring back Minnie Minoso in 1990 as a stunt so that the 1950s star, in his seventies, could claim to have played in six decades; even the White Sox players protested that gambit. In 1993 Reinsdorf climaxed years of uneasy relations with Fisk by first allowing him to appear in a game to establish the mark for most games by a catcher, then releasing him a few days later. Prior to spring training in 1994, with most attention on the prospects for Chicago to repeat its 1993 division title, he threw a publicity bombshell by announcing that retired basketball great Michael Jordan would be in camp for a tryout. Reinsdorf, who also owned Jordan's former (and future) Chicago Bulls, feigned surprise when even manager Gene Lamont voiced annoyance at the distraction, but clearly relished the ensuing media circus. In 1997, with the White Sox only two games behind Cleveland in the Central Division race, the owner announced his own team had no real chance and, to the dismay of Southsiders, ordered the July trading of two pitchers in the starting rotation and closer Roberto Hernandez to the Giants for prospects. All three hurlers were in the walk year of their contracts, and Reinsdorf hasn't added a major free agent since.

PETE REISER

Legal roadblocks kept Reiser from getting to the Dodgers until 1940; once in Brooklyn, he was overwhelmed by an incredible series of physical obstacles preventing him from fulfilling predictions as a superstar.

Signed by the Cardinals before his 16th birthday, Reiser was hidden through such subterfuges as listing him as a scout's chauffeur until he was of age. But when St. Louis boss Branch Rickey got caught shuffling players from one farm club to another, Reiser was among the "slaves from the St. Louis chain gang" freed by Commissioner Landis for illegal contract manipulations. The shortstop-turned-outfielder then signed as a free agent with the Dodgers, but he was kept in the low minors by general manager Larry MacPhail as part of a secret deal with Rickey that would deliver him back to the Cardinals after three years. It was only through the intervention of Brooklyn manager Leo Durocher and Bill Killefer, the pilot of the Dodgers farm team in Elmira, that he escaped becoming the player to be named later in the transaction that sent Joe Medwick from St. Louis to Ebbets Field.

In 1941 Reiser's .343 average made him the National League's youngest (22) batting titlist ever; the lefty swinger (he also tried switch-hitting later on in his career) paced the circuit in doubles, triples, runs scored, and slugging as well, despite two serious beanings. The following year he fractured his skull crashing into the center field wall in St. Louis on July 2; he still managed to pick up the ball and fire it back to the infield before being carried off the field on a stretcher for one of 11 times in his career. Two days later he was back as a pinch-hitter, driving in the winning run in an extra-inning contest—and passing out at first base and winding up back in the hospital. Three weeks after that he was back in the lineup. At .383 when he hit the wall in St. Louis, he slumped off to .310 for the season, but still managed to lead the NL in stolen bases.

After three years of World War II military service, Reiser broke an ankle sliding back to first on a pick-off throw two days before the end of the 1946 season. His second stolen base title held up, but without him the Dodgers ended up in a pennant playoff series they lost to the Cardinals. Early the next season, he had his second dramatic encounter with an outfield wall, this time in Ebbets Field, when he misjudged the distance to the fence because it had been brought in during the offseason. Paralyzed for 10 days and out of uniform for five weeks, he bumped into pitcher Clyde King during batting practice shortly after returning and revealed a previously undetected blood clot that required surgery and kept him sidelined for all but the final weeks of the season; when he did play, he averaged .309. In the World Series against the Yankees in 1947, he fractured an ankle still again but kept playing and set up the winning run in Bill Bevens's near-no-hitter when he was walked intentionally; pinch-runner Eddie Miksis replaced him on the bases and scored minutes later on Cookie Lavagetto's double.

The injuries—and the efforts to play despite them—finally caught up with Reiser in 1948, when he played in only 64 games. After four more seasons of bouncing around from the Braves to the Pirates to the Indians, he retired at the end of 1952 with a lifetime .295 average, leaving behind endless speculation about what he might have achieved if he had been able to avoid outfield walls.

JOE RELFORD

A 12-year-old black batboy for the Fitzgerald club of the Class D Georgia State League, Relford was the youngest person ever to play in a professional game. On July 19, 1952, with Fitzgerald losing to Statesboro, 13-0, manager Charlie Ridgeway responded to crowd taunts to "put in the batboy" by sending Relford up to hit in the eighth inning for Ray Nichting, a .330 batter at the time. The boy grounded out, then went out to play center field, where he made a running catch. Relford, Ridgway, and umpire Ed Kubrick were all fired for the stunt.

ED REULBACH

Reulbach spent the meat of his 13-year (1905–17) career pitching for Chicago in the shadow of Three Finger Brown, so he never quite achieved the distinction due him for two 20-win seasons, three straight years of leading the league in winning percentage, and an overall 182 wins with a 2.28 ERA. But the righthander was only too well known to the Dodgers because in 1908 he defeated them a record nine times. Two of the victories came on September 26, when Reulback became the only pitcher to hurl shutouts in both ends of a doubleheader.

ALLIE REYNOLDS

Reynolds's overall contribution to Yankees pennants in the 1940s and 1950s have been obscured by the fact that he is one of only three pitchers to twirl two no-hitters in the same season. A decent but hardly overpowering righthander with the Indians between 1942 and 1946, he reached the Bronx only after Joe DiMaggio persuaded owner Larry MacPhail that the hurler wasn't "gutless," incapable of winning the big game. Vindicating DiMaggio's endorsement of a swap for second baseman Joe Gordon, Reynolds led the American League in winning percentage in 1947, but was kept from a 20th win (and a big salary increase) by being pulled out of the rotation after notching his 19th victory with two weeks remaining in the season.

Reynolds's most impressive season was 1951, when he won 17 games (the two no-hitters among them), led the league in shutouts, and earned seven saves in 14 relief appearances. Neither no-hitter came easily. In the first, on July 12 against Cleveland, he fell delivering a pitch to Bobby Avila before striking out the second baseman for the final out; in the second, on September 28 against Boston, he had to watch as batterymate Yogi Berra dropped a Ted Williams foul pop, then retired the slugger for the final out on an almost identical play. The latter gem also clinched a pennant tie for the Yankees. Despite all this, general manager George Weiss tried to cut his salary because he had completed only 16 of his 26 starts. Weiss hadn't needed much encouragement for going after Reynolds because of the pitcher's activities on behalf of player pension demands.

DUSTY RHODES

Rhodes was a hard-drinking outfielder for the 1950s Giants who became almost as known for his all-night binges with owner Horace Stoneham and manager Leo Durocher as for the respectability he brought to pinch-hitting. Most of his on-field reputation stemmed from the single, pennant-winning year of 1954, when he came off the bench during the season to hit .333 and then devastated the Indians during a World Series sweep with a pinch-homer, two pinch-singles, and seven RBIs. Otherwise, the lefty-swinging Rhodes had a career pinch-hitting average of only .186 (40 for 215).

TUFFY RHODES

Rhodes is the only player to hit home runs in his first three at bats in a season. The lefty-swinging outfielder did it as a Cub on Opening Day in 1994; all three blasts came off Doc Gooden of the Mets. In 2001 Rhodes tied Sadaharu Oh's Japanese league mark of 55 home runs in a season.

KEVIN RHOMBERG

Rhomberg showed promise as a hitter with the Indians in the 1990s, but he ended up psyching himself out of a big league career. The most superstitious player in baseball history, he had a particular aversion to being touched last, and whenever anyone even grazed him, he insisted on touching that person back. When opponents got wind of the tic, they went out of their way to bump him, pat him on the shoulder, or just a bounce a ball at him and run

off with Rhomberg in pursuit. On one occasion a teammate tapped him with a ball, then fired the ball over an outfield fence; the outfielder immediately climbed the wall to get the ball so he could touch it back. Even fans eventually got into the act, sending him letters that said nothing more than "Ha, ha, you touched this letter last." Rhomberg's reaction was to answer each and every letter from his ill-wishers. Aside from his touching mania, the Cleveland prospect refused to make right turns, so that even when he was thrown out on a grounder, he made a counterclockwise turn rather than simply veer off toward a first base dugout.

JIM RICE

The left field successor to Hall of Famers Ted Williams and Carl Yastrzemski in Fenway Park, Rice posted Cooperstown-caliber numbers of his own for 12 of his 16 years (1974–89) with the Red Sox.

After a cup of coffee in 1974, Rice was edged out as Rookie of the Year in 1995 by teammate Fred Lynn despite a .309 average, 22 home runs, and 102 RBIs. The righthanded slugger went on to top .300 six more times, stroke 200 hits in four years, knock at least 20 home runs in 11 seasons, and run up 100 RBIs for eight campaigns. In the mix were three home run titles and two each in slugging and RBIs. Rice's 406 total bases in 1978—when he took MVP honors for pacing the AL in slugging, hits, homers, triples, and RBIs—was the highest total since Stan Musial's 429 in 1948. So potent was his bat that year that teams often deployed a fourth outfielder against him.

Rice never accepted criticism of his fielding, nor a demotion to designated hitting in 1988. Manager Joe Morgan offered an even dimmer view of his fading talents when he sent light-hitting shortstop Spike Owen up to hit for Rice in a 1989 game. The no-longer outfielder exploded, shoving Morgan in the dugout in full view of the team and reporters. An elbow injury kept him off the scene for most of the rest of the year, after which he was released altogether. Although Rice went out blasting Morgan and the Red Sox organization, he ended up coming back as a hitting coach in 1994. His final statistics include a .298 batting average and 382 home runs; the latter figure, as well as his totals in hits, total bases, and RBIs, ranks third in Boston history behind Williams and Yastrzemski.

SAM RICE (Hall of Fame, 1963)

Rice reported to the Senators in 1915 as a pitcher, tossed a complete-game victory, then was told to get an outfielder's glove. The lefty hitter's mistake had been to put on a show in batting practice, where he struck manager Clark Griffith as having more of a future as an everyday player. By the time he finished his 20-year career he had an overall average of .322, never dipping below .293 and slipping even that far only in his final season at the age of 44. Relishing the gaps of spacious Griffith Stadium, he strung together 10 straight seasons of at least 30 doubles and 10 triples; he also clubbed 200 hits six times. Even when he made an out it wasn't for lack of contact: In nearly 10,000 plate appearances, Rice struck out merely 275 times.

Rice proved comically solemn about the most controversial moment in his playing career. In the third game of the 1925 World Series against Pittsburgh, he chased an eighth-inning drive by Earl Smith into the stands, disappeared from view for long seconds, then reemerged holding the ball. When umpire Cy Rigler signaled a fair catch, Pirates owner Barney Dreyfuss jumped onto the field in protest, precipitating a heated argument. After the game (won by the Senators), Rice refused to go beyond saying "the umpire said I caught it." That would have ended the story except for the outfielder's periodically coy remarks over the years that he had left a letter about the catch that was to be opened only after his death. When the letter was finally opened in 1974, it offered only bathos: "At no time did I lose possession of the ball," it declared laconically.

J. R. RICHARD

Richard was a glaringly tragic example of white baseball's attitude toward black players. The National League's most dominating mound force in the late 1970s, the Houston fireballer turned in consecutive seasons of 20, 18, 18, and 18 wins, in the process becoming the circuit's first righthander to register 300 strikeouts (in 1978) and then doing it again the following year. In 1979 he also paced the league with his 2.71 ERA, and seemed on his way to bettering that in 1980 (10–4, 1.89) when he suddenly collapsed of a stroke. Only in the aftermath of the career-ending seizure did it emerge that he had confessed to feeling sluggish for some time but had been talked out of his concern by Astros officials. The episode

bred a nationwide debate about whether baseball people in general, and not just the Houston management, would have been more responsive to the hurler's sluggishness if it had not fit so neatly into stereotypes about "lazy blacks."

PAUL RICHARDS

Richards is usually recalled as the designer of the oversized catcher's mitt intended to spare Baltimore receivers from breaking every record for passed balls while Hoyt Wilhelm was on the mound. Less well remembered are his sometimes bizarre tactical moves as a manager and his successes as a general manager with expansion and transferred franchises.

A backup receiver with the Dodgers, Giants, and Athletics in the 1930s, Richards retired to manage in the minor leagues, but then returned as a catcher for the Tigers during and immediately after World War II. After another stint as a minor league pilot, he took over the White Sox in 1951. Although his teams won as many as 94 games (in 1954), he could never get them past Casey Stengel's Yankees or Al Lopez's Indians. In 1955 he took on the challenge of a dual role as field leader and general manager of the Orioles, only one year removed from their earlier existence as the St. Louis Browns. Given a $250,000 fund for player procurement by owner Clarence Miles, Richards spent $700,000 within two years—a spree that led one Baltimore official to observe that "Paul was the only man in baseball who had an unlimited budget and exceeded it." Most of the money went into signing young players, including five bonus babies who had to be carried on the major league roster. Having clogged his club with the inexperienced and the unproductive, Richards began bending the rules by putting players on the disabled list without cause and hiding new recruits under aliases. The results were, in the first instance, a commissioner's office ruling demanding doctor notes for DL cases and, in the second, hefty fines for the team and Richards personally.

Outflanked, Richards turned to trading, and with a vengeance. On November 18 and December 1, 1954, he completed the biggest trade in baseball history in two stages. The key players in the 18-man deal were pitchers Don Larsen and Bob Turley and shortstop Billy Hunter, who went to the Yankees for, among others, catcher Gus Triandos, outfielder Gene Woodling, and shortstop Willie Miranda. Richards's hectic quest for a radical turnaround for the franchise almost produced an even bigger swap: In 1956 he offered Kansas City general manager Parke Carroll a 25-for-25 trade of complete rosters, a transaction that fell through mainly because Carroll couldn't reach Athletics owner Arnold Johnson before the expiration of the June 15 trading deadline.

When the continuing mediocre play of the Orioles forced Richards to abandon one of his posts, he elected to stay in the dugout, where he displayed his penchant for esoteric tactics. He had already made it a practice, while with the White Sox, to move his starting pitcher to third base only long enough to permit a reliever to retire a special batter; on September 11, 1958 he went himself one better, listing three pitchers in the starting lineup (only to be foiled by a first inning rally that required him to pinch-hit for one of them). In 1960 he told leadoff hitter Jerry Adair to bat out of order in the hope he would run the count up to 3–0 and Richards could then rush the pitcher up to the plate to complete the walk before anyone noticed; he ended up outsmarting himself when Adair singled home two runs but had the at bat voided when Tigers manager Jimmy Dykes appealed to the umpire.

It was also in 1960 that Richards revealed the oversized mitt, 50 inches in circumference, for use in handling Wilhelm's knuckleball. The innovation followed performances in which two Baltimore catchers had each allowed three passed balls in an inning within a week. The "pancake mitt" was outlawed in 1964. Mind games and mitts aside, Richards's most notable achievement with Baltimore was in bringing the 1960 team—sparked by the Kiddie Korps rotation of Chuck Estrada, Milt Pappas, Jack Fisher, and Steve Barber—up to second place.

Attracted by Houston's new expansion franchise, Richards quit the Orioles before the end of the 1961 season. In the expansion draft he concentrated on younger players, leaving the more familiar names to the Mets, and stocked the rest of the organization with high school and junior college prospects. The strategy paid off when the Colt .45s finished eighth in 1962, ahead of not only New York but also Chicago. His biggest find for the club was Rusty Staub. Midseason in 1964, Richards replaced manager Harry Craft with Lum Harris, at the price of a warning from owner Roy Hofheinz that the new pilot had better produce when the team moved into the Astro-

dome in 1965. When the 1965 Astros won a game less than the 1964 Colt .45s, Hofheinz fired both Richards and Harris. Twenty years later Richards remained bitter enough about his ouster to reject a reporter's suggestion that Hofheinz was his own worst enemy by remarking "not while I'm alive he isn't."

Richards's next stop was Atlanta, where he produced a divisional title in 1969, in good part through the acquisitions of first baseman Orlando Cepeda and third baseman Clete Boyer. On the other hand, the Cepeda deal with the Cardinals turned sour when the slugger became injury-prone after only two productive seasons and Joe Torre, who had gone to St. Louis in the exchange, won an MVP award.

After leaving the Braves in 1973, Richards reappeared to manage the White Sox in 1976. His condition for coming out of retirement was that he not have to be part of any of owner Bill Veeck's promotional stunts, changing his mind only for a Bicentennial replication of the Spirit of '76 on Opening Day. When Chicago finished in sixth place, he retired for good.

BOBBY RICHARDSON

A slick-fielding second baseman for the Yankees for 12 seasons (1955–66), Richardson saved his most potent offense for the World Series. Among the career .266 hitter's records are most RBIs (12) in a seven-game series (1960) and ties for most runs (8 in 1960) and hits (13 in 1964) in seven-game championships. Richardson also holds the mark for most consecutive World Series games (30 between 1960 and 1964).

SPEC RICHARDSON

Richardson did such a bad job as head of Houston's baseball operations for a decade that the National League entrusted him with taking emergency administrative control of the Giants. While serving as a righthand man to Judge Roy Hofheinz between the mid-1960s and mid-1970s, Richardson saw to it that no Astro uttered anything in public that contradicted the All-American pretensions of the franchise or attempted to hold out for a significant raise. In the meantime he was making one disastrous trade after another—getting rid of the likes of Joe Morgan, Mike Cuellar, Rusty Staub, Jerry Grote, and Dave Giusti, while importing such sluggers as Lee May, Donn Clendenon, and Curt Blefary to the homer-unfriendly Astrodome. He was finally bounced as general manager in 1975.

After working a few months in the commissioner's office, Richardson was sent by the NL to San Francisco to try to make some order out of the administrative mess left by Horace Stoneham, the disenchanted Giants owner for whom even signing monthly checks had become a burden. Richardson stayed on for years even after Bob Lurie had bought the franchise from Stoneham, but spent most of his time sitting on his hands while managers Joe Altobelli and Dave Bristol warned futilely about the problems being created in the clubhouse by baseball's most fervid Born Again movement.

PETE RICHERT

Richert could never live up to his major league debut. Making his maiden appearance for the Dodgers in the second inning of an April 12, 1962 game, he struck out the first six batters he faced, including (because of a passed ball) four whiffs in the third inning. The southpaw spent 13 seasons (1962–74) with five clubs, reaching his peak for the Orioles in 1969 and 1970, when he saved a combined 25 games.

LEE RICHMOND

Despite a lifetime losing record (75–100), Richmond crammed several firsts into his six-year career. He was the first lefthanded curveballer, the first medical student to play major league baseball, the first to win 20 games with a basement club (the 1881 Worcester Brown Stockings), the victim of the first grand slam (surrendered to Troy's Roger Connor on September 9, 1881), and the first to throw a perfect game. Richmond's masterpiece—against Cleveland on June 12, 1880—came after he had stayed up all night at a Brown University party, played in an early-morning game between Brown and Yale, and skipped lunch to reach Worcester in time for his start. His effort was helped by a right field-to-first base putout in the fifth inning and interrupted by a seven-minute thunderstorm in the eighth inning.

FRANCIS RICHTER

As the founder and editor of the Philadelphia-based weekly *Sporting Life* between 1883 and 1917, Richter was as much participant in as commentator on the goings and comings of 19th-century franchises and leagues. He helped form the American Association in 1882; supported the Players League in 1890; tried to resuscitate the AA in 1895 and 1900; tried to create a major league National Association in 1900; promoted the Players Protective Association in the late 1890s; and encouraged the forces behind the Federal League in 1914. His so-called Millennium Plan, introduced in 1887, met with initial approval in all quarters. It called for all major league players to be dropped into a common pool annually and then doled out "impartially" among clubs as a means of equalizing competition; according to Richter, his scheme would end labor disputes and boardroom conflicts, bringing about "a thousand years of peace and harmony." Five years later, both sides welcomed Richter's services as a go-between in the amalgamation of the NL and AA. In 1907 NL owners thought sufficiently of him to offer him the league presidency, which he declined. Five years after Richter left *Sporting Life* in 1917, his successor Edgar Wolff transformed the once-powerful baseball weekly into a monthly dealing exclusively with bowling and billiards.

TEX RICKARD

Rickard was the malaprop field announcer at Ebbets Field in the 1940s and 1950s. On one occasion he told the crowd that "a small boy has been found lost." To a request by an umpire to have fans remove their jackets from an outfield railing, he relayed the message as: "Will the fans along the left field railing please take off their clothing." Dodgers players on the bench vied with one another to exploit Rickard's unfamiliarity with newly promoted prospects, leading him in two celebrated cases to identify pitchers on his loudspeaker as bandleaders Wayne King and Spike Jones.

BRANCH RICKEY (Hall of Fame, 1967)

Even without his two most significant contributions to baseball, the development of the farm system and the racial integration of clubhouses, Rickey would have probably ended up in Cooperstown. In more than half a century as player, instructor, manager, executive, owner, and league founder, there wasn't an aspect of the game he didn't influence, alter, or perfect. By turns pedantic, sanctimonious, and ruthless, he battled everyone from Kenesaw Landis to Walter O'Malley, provided career opportunities for everyone from Jackie Robinson to Larry MacPhail, and devised everything from spring training sliding pits to the Vero Beach camp that mushroomed into Dodgertown. All the while he never stopped padding his own pockets, raining Biblical adages on the people around him, and padding his pockets some more. Once likened to Mohandas Gandhi for being "a combination of your father and Tammany Hall," the teetotaling lawyer was baseball's ultimate Mahatma—hold the passive resistance.

Rickey's least impressive role was as a player. A lefty swinging catcher, he got into 117 games for the Browns and Yankees between 1905 and 1907—long enough for his .239 average and bad throwing arm to persuade him to pursue a law degree. Before leaving New York, however, he strapped on the tools for a June 28, 1907 game in which a record 13 runners stole on him. He was a much more respected presence at the University of Michigan, where he undertook the baseball coaching job after leaving the major leagues at 26. Aside from winning various championships for the school, he was acclaimed as an instructor, to the point that several big league managers dropped by to audit his sessions when they were in Michigan to play the Tigers. Of the numerous future major leaguers who passed through his hands at the university, the most accomplished was first baseman George Sisler. It was Rickey who, as a member of the Browns front office in 1914, talked Sisler into challenging an ambiguous contractual arrangement he had with the Pirates and who then signed the future Hall of Famer for St. Louis.

Rickey was drawn back to the Browns by Robert Hedges, the club's millionaire owner who offered him an open assignment as an administrative factotum for dealing with emergencies. The emergencies turned out to cover just about everything from scouting to managing, with Rickey doing most of the team's signing and dealing by 1914 and its piloting by the end of 1913. Although he couldn't get the club above fifth place, he continued to impress Hedges for his money smarts and his meticulous instructional programs. Rickey was equally impressed by Hedges, especially with the owner's ideas on developing a minor league farm system that would feed players to the parent club. It therefore came as a shock when Hedges, apprehensive about the outcome of the 1915 Federal League suit against the National and American leagues, decided to sell the Browns before being charged with being part of a monopoly. Rickey barely got along with Hedges's successor Phil Ball, particularly after the new owner bounced

him from the dugout and told him to concentrate on the franchise's administrative affairs. In 1917, with a new ownership in place with the Cardinals, Rickey asked out of his contract to accept an offer as president of the Browns city rivals. Although Ball initially took the position that he would never stand in the way of anyone who didn't want to work for him, he was talked into a harder stand by AL president Ban Johnson, winning a court injunction to block the move. But the maneuver quickly died when Johnson and the Browns were portrayed in the press as the heavies of the situation. Needing all the good publicity he could engender in his rivalry with the Cardinals, Ball let Rickey go, and created his chief nemesis for the next decade.

Rickey joined the Cardinals just long enough to establish himself as a ferocious contract negotiator with players, then went off to the military as a major in the same World War I chemical testing unit that recruited Sisler and Ty Cobb and where an explosion shortened the life of Christy Mathewson. When he returned to St. Louis after the war, he found the franchise in such disarray that he had to persuade his own parents to invest in it to help insure its survival; during one spring training, with no money available for regular washings, he kept the players in one uniform to keep the backup one ready for Opening Day. The crisis began to abate only in 1920, when car salesman Sam Breadon moved in as majority owner. Although Breadon also insisted on taking Rickey's title as organization president, the tradeoff was the acquisition of a business partner who was ready to spend to improve the team.

Even before Breadon had come along, Rickey had invested money in several minor league clubs. But it wasn't until the new owner gave him $25,000 from the sale of League Park (the Cardinals had moved into Sportsman's Park as Ball tenants) that he had the wherewithal to indulge his project of the farm system his old boss Hedges had claimed was a necessity for money-poor clubs. As he noted, even when St. Louis scouts were the first to discover raw talent, a minor league operator, college coach, or parent would waste little time in contacting the Giants, Cubs, or another affluent team to disclose Rickey's interest in the prospect and dicker for better terms. It was in the name of thwarting this tactic that Rickey persuaded Breadon to purchase an 18 percent interest in Houston of the Texas League, then even larger parts of an Arkansas team in the Western Association and the Syracuse franchise of the International League. The trickle soon became a flood: Before farm club foe Landis began intervening, Rickey and Breadon had deals with more than 30 teams around the country, even controlling two entire leagues (the Nebraska State League and the Arkansas-Missouri League).

As Rickey found out to his chagrin, however, even a substantial minority investment in a club wasn't always a guarantee of his minor league pipeline functioning smoothly. Following the 1921 season, he "called up" from Syracuse the very first product of his farming policy, first baseman Jim Bottomley, only to be held up to ransom demands by the owner of the New York state team. With the validity of his entire project at stake, he had to go to Syracuse to negotiate the purchase of the rest of the franchise to insure the delivery of Bottomley. From then on he was extra careful about not leaving financial or legal loopholes in his arrangements with minor league operators.

Next to his playing, Rickey was weakest at managing—according to his contemporaries, because of a tendency to intellectualize the simplest situations. He himself didn't share such evaluations of his dugout skills, and was incensed when Breadon emulated Ball in removing him from the field and confining him to front office duties; in fact, he was so angered by a 1925 managerial switch to Rogers Hornsby that he insisted on selling all his stock in the club. Nevertheless, he maintained his roles as vice-president and business manager, from that vantage point watching his farm system supply a steady flow of talent to Sportsman's Park, much of it of Hall of Fame caliber. Between 1926 and 1942, Rickey's farm chain scheme helped deliver four world championships, six pennants, and five second-place finishes. Aside from furnishing the St. Louis varsity, the minor league clubs provided trading material for desirable players elsewhere and allowed Rickey to indulge his pet philosophy of unloading a player at or just after his peak to get maximum value for him. The exchanges became only more frequent in the mid-1930s after Breadon agreed to give Rickey 10 percent of every cash transaction he worked out. This led to periods when the Cardinals obtained no players, but a lot of checks, for their players.

While never the best of friends, Rickey and Breadon worked off one another successfully for most of the 1920s and 1930s. Frictions were never far away, however. For his part, Rickey never completely disguised a snobbishness toward the relatively uneducated Breadon, and was never sure the owner was as God-fearing as God (and Rickey) would have liked. On the other hand, Breadon was never at ease with Rickey's religiosity (he had always observed the Sabbath even as manager, turning the club over to others for the day), especially when it seemed to leave room for a lot of shady dealings with minor league operators he preferred not to know too much about. The first major conflict between the pair erupted in 1938, when Landis decided to summarily release 74 organization farmhands because of contractual irregularities. Rickey wanted to fight back by breaking a pact with Landis prohibiting teams from ever contesting his decisions in court, but Breadon, more embarrassed by than innocent of any collusion in what became known as the Cedar Rapids Case, refused to go along; despite the lack of formal charges from Landis, the owner even declined to petition the commissioner's office to keep the minor leaguers.

The rip in the Rickey-Breadon relationship caused by the Cedar Rapids Case grew to a gaping hole over the next few years. The point of no return came in 1942, when Breadon announced that Hyde Park Beer had been signed as a sponsor for the club's games on radio. When Rickey objected that a brewery wasn't an appropriate sponsor for games heard by tens of thousands of children, Breadon gave vent to his skepticism about the convenient latitude of Rickey's moral principles. Soon after St. Louis defeated the Yankees in the 1942 World Series, the Mahatma tendered his resignation.

Only a few weeks later Rickey landed on his feet as president of the Dodgers. He took over from Larry MacPhail—a onetime law school classmate, the most prominent of a dozen protégés Rickey spent his career recommending for positions he didn't want, and already an on-again off-again antagonist who was destined to turn into even more of a snapping hound from hell within a few years. Mainly because of MacPhail's easy way with bar bills, Rickey received a cold shoulder from New York sportswriters—a relationship that so worsened in subsequent years that the executive admitted even giving up such pastimes as going to the track for fear that the newsmen would make capital on it within the context of their caricature of him as something of a holy roller. (Which was not to say that he couldn't manage the press when he needed to. In 1946, for example, he dared not recall Luis Olmo from Montreal for fear of local press reaction over the departure of the hot-hitting outfielder. He got around the problem by going to Montreal, sitting down with Royals beat writers, and soliciting their opinion on which minor leaguer was ready for Ebbets Field. When they all suggested Olmo, he kept disagreeing until they practically begged him to take the slugger back to Brooklyn with him.)

Aside from the press, Rickey's most immediate problem in Brooklyn was talking himself into retaining the services of Leo Durocher despite one excuse after another the fractious Dodgers manager gave him for being fired. In what was eventually explained by his belief that Durocher was the ideal pilot for running the first racially mixed club in the majors, Rickey abided a team revolt over some gratuitous Durocher fines and follow-up lies to the press; felonious assault charges against the manager and an Ebbets Field security guard stemming from the beating up of a grandstand heckler; regular flights by Durocher from spring training camp for evenings on the town; and daily intelligence about how players were losing money in card games to Durocher and his righthand man Charlie Dressen.

By the time World War II ended Rickey had two further incentives for going ahead with what was dubbed The Great Experiment. The first was the death of Landis, who, in addition to hating farm systems, had also systematically discouraged notions about allowing blacks into the major leagues. The second was his own financial investment in the Dodgers. In 1944 he joined with corporation lawyer Walter O'Malley and John Smith of the Pfizer chemical company in the first of several stock purchases that would give the trio 75 percent of the franchise within a couple of years. As Rickey laid it out to O'Malley and Smith, the fastest way of fielding a winning team for enriching their investments was to outflank the dominant Cardinals by signing up blacks as well as whites.

The Rickey plan began taking shape May 7, 1945, when he announced the organization of the Brown Dodgers as his entry in the planned Black United States Baseball League. The announcement elicited little reaction, despite his cryptic references at a press conference to black players who might someday play in the majors. About five months later he dropped the second veil by disclosing that Jack Roosevelt Robinson, the shortstop for a Negro league team in Kansas City, had signed to play with Brooklyn's farm club in Montreal, thereby knocking down the outer wall of organized baseball's racial barriers. Most of what followed seemed scripted too neatly even for Rickey. Robinson was the sensation of the International League. Rickey set up 1947 spring training quarters in Havana—a city far more physically suggestive of racial equality than any in the U.S. at the time. Several Dodgers saw what was coming and tried to organize a protest against playing with a black, but were stopped in their tracks by Durocher. Landis's successor, Happy Chandler, endorsed the move, so NL president Ford Frick also got into line and warned other clubs not to go through with their threats to boycott games against Brooklyn. Only a short time after Enos Slaughter had completed one of the most dramatic runs in baseball history to give the Cardinals a World Series victory, the Dodgers were the most talked about franchise in the country. Robinson, who shared with Rickey a college degree and an aversion to alcohol, turned the other cheek as promised against shouts, spittings, and spikings. The righthand-hitting first baseman was named Rookie of the Year and sparked the Dodgers to a pennant. As Rickey was fond of saying in other contexts, in a popular paraphrase of a thought expressed by Louis Pasteur, "luck (was) the residue of design."

The one unexpected development for the Brooklyn official in 1947 was that the Dodgers manager was his longtime assistant Burt Shotton rather than Durocher, who was suspended by Chandler before Opening Day for a series of incidents that added up to loose living, that brought moralistic censures from pulpits and editorial pages, and that were formulated by the commissioner's office as "actions detrimental to baseball." Rickey himself added to months of scandal-tinged headlines by accusing MacPhail, who had resurfaced as an owner of the Yankees, of being seen with the same kind of gamblers Chandler had disciplined Durocher for frequenting. What rankled him most of all, however, were strong indications that Durocher had been in secret talks with MacPhail for jumping to the Yankees. With Robinson's debut in the history books and the club under fire from religious groups for employing a morally dubious manager, Rickey had little compunction about pushing Durocher toward the Giants in 1948 and installing Shotton as his full-time pilot.

Rickey spent the rest of the decade putting into place the final pieces of the team that gained fame as The Boys of Summer. By 1950, however, his relations with O'Malley had soured to the point that he was pretty sure he wouldn't receive an extension on his contract as baseball operations chief. Resolved to beat O'Malley and the Smith estate to the punch, he first offered to sell his interest in the franchise to his partners, then set up real estate developer William Zeckendorf as a rival straw man for demanding a higher price. Zeckendorf ended up with $1 million for doing little more than nodding that he was thinking of buying into the club, while Rickey collected three times as much as O'Malley had initially offered him for his stock.

Just as he had wasted little time in moving from the Cardinals to the Dodgers, Rickey waited only a few weeks before going from Brooklyn to Pittsburgh. At first glance his six-year stay with the Pirates was a disaster, with the club taking up permanent residence in eighth place with talent barely up to high minor league standards. To make matters worse he made a personal crusade of downplaying the abilities of the franchise's only legitimate star, outfielder Ralph Kiner. On one level, Kiner irritated Rickey for his visibility in player contract causes, his regular appearance in gossip columns as an escort to Hollywood actresses, and his annual salary demands and denunciations of the executive as a miser and hypocrite; on another level, the slugger galled him for winning over Pittsburgh fans with the generally one-dimensional skills (power) Rickey had always preached against in dispensing opinions about the ideal player. Behind the crack that the Pirates could finish last without Kiner as easily as with him, he dealt the future Hall of Famer to the Cubs in June 1953 for six undistinguished players and $150,000.

What did not emerge clearly until Rickey had severed his ties with Pittsburgh after the 1955 season was that his philosophy of signing hundreds of cheaply paid prospects with the hope that at least a few of them would work out, had in fact given the franchise such future stars as Bill Mazeroski, Dick Groat, Bob Skinner, Vernon Law, and Frank Thomas. It was also Rickey who plucked Roberto Clemente out of the Brooklyn farm system.

After remaining on the Pittsburgh payroll as a consultant for a few years, the then-78-year-old Rickey was talked into becoming pointman for the would-be Continental League by New York attorney William Shea. Whether or not the league ever nurtured real hopes of setting up shop as a third major circuit, its main impact was to force the National League into expanding in 1962 with the addition of the Astros and the Mets. Despite his age, Rickey made it clear he wanted to head up the baseball operations for the New York team; his ambition was thwarted when both O'Malley, not forgetting the Zeckendorf strawman ploy, and franchise chairman M. Donald Grant warned Mets owner Joan Payson against Rickey's protean sense of power.

Rickey's fabled wiles were less than honed when he took on another consultancy for Cardinals owner Gussie Busch after the 1962 season. What he realized too late was that Busch had thrown him in with front office executives Dick Meyer and Bing Devine the way he might have thrown a fox into a hen house, with the fox defanged and declawed. Rickey fell into one political trap after another. When he wasn't embarrassing Stan Musial by suggesting the star retire, he was recommending an immediate overhaul of the 1964 club (even as it was beginning to stir into a pennant win). One of his last public acts in the baseball world was attending the 1964 pennant victory dinner, where he was snubbed by both players and executives. A few days later he was informed by Busch that his services were no longer required. On the other hand, still another of his protégés, Bob Howsam, took over the organization's baseball affairs.

CY RIGLER
A National League umpire for 29 years beginning in 1906, Rigler began the practice of using hand signals to indicate balls and strikes.

JIMMY RING
Ring's honesty brought Hal Chase to his first major accounting for suspicious play. On August 24, 1917, while both were with the Reds, the righthander was brought into a tie game in relief only to have the first baseman sidle up to him with the suggestion that there might be something in it for him if Cincinnati were to lose. Ring brushed off the approach, but lost the game anyway, and the following day he was thrown an envelope with $50 in it by Chase. The

pitcher went to Reds manager Christy Mathewson with the story, but there it died for more than a year. It wasn't until January 1919 that the National League got around to hearing a slew of charges against Chase for purported game throwing, including those leveled by Ring. Partly because the young pitcher had nothing to offer against a 14-year veteran but his own word, Chase was exonerated.

CAL RIPKEN, JR.

By the time he finally called it a career in 2001, Ripken had lingered as long as Monty Wooley's Man Who Came to Dinner and had sparked as many gala sendoffs as Frank Sinatra's retirement announcements. Shunted aside by all the last-act pomp, primarily generated by Major League Baseball and television, was a power-hitting and nimble-fielding résumé of 3,001 games—and questions about whether that was an example of more being less.

Ripken's boon and bane throughout his 21-year (1981–2001) career with the Orioles was The Streak. Even when he finally broke Lou Gehrig's venerable record of playing in 2,130 consecutive games on September 6, 1995, the righthand-hitting shortstop-third baseman continued to take the field day in and day out, almost as if afraid to tamper with destiny. Ultimately it came down to Ripken himself to let Baltimore management off the hook by volunteering to take a seat on the bench against the Yankees on September 20, 1998; at that point the consecutive game mark stood at 2,632. If the 1998 decision was the warrior opting for his own rest, it was his father Cal Ripken, Sr. who, as Orioles manager on September 14, 1987, chose to end the infielder's even more remarkable skein of having played 8,243 consecutive innings from June 5, 1982. As with the game mark, there was no urgent occasion for ending the streak when the decision was made—which was half the problem. Bolstered by media attention, the records had taken on a life of their own so that nothing seemed more urgent than their continuance. It was in that context that the ongoing debate for much of the 1990s was whether Ripken—and the Orioles as a whole—would have been better off if he had ended the distractions earlier.

Ripken's on-field performance provided conflicting answers. In 1982 he was named Rookie of the Year, in 1983 and 1991 the American League's MVP. But minus the two MVP years, he had only two other seasons when he knocked in 100 runs and none when he reached 200 hits; for the shortstop who accumulated the most career home runs at that position, he reached the 30-plateau only in 1991. Eight times he batted under the mid-.260s, 11 times he drove in fewer than 90 runs. Even as a member of the 3,000-hit club (3,184), his .276 average is the lowest. As with his appearance streaks, his most impressive offensive numbers were of the cumulative variety, not least his 431 home runs and 1,695 RBIs. If he had been a pitcher, he would have been Tommy John or Jim Kaat.

Where Ripken was slighted was in his fielding abilities. Aside from a couple of Gold Gloves and a one-time big league record of 95 straight errorless games, his ability to read batters more than compensated for his relatively narrow range. Only in his final seasons was he shifted from shortstop back to his original third base position. (At six feet, four inches, he also undercut objections to tall athletes manning shortstop.) On the other hand, nobody ever confused him with Maury Wills: Not only did he steal a mere 36 bases in his 21 seasons, but he was caught 39 times. He also went into retirement with the record for hitting into the most double plays (350).

Ripken broke the Gehrig streak just as Major League Baseball and television were looking for promotional tools for overcoming the sour taste left by the 1994–95 labor struggles. The lavish coverage of his 2,131st game was just the opening act of a years-long script in which he (and later Mark McGwire and Sammy Sosa) would be credited as a hero for reviving interest in the national pastime. Again like the streaks themselves, this view took on a life of its own with the help of Ripken's image as the ultimate cleancut American who had never wanted to do anything but play baseball (and who with his brother Billy in 1987 were the first siblings to be managed by their father). His farewell tour around AL parks in 2001 sparked one goodbye ceremony after another, while his final game at Camden Yards was turned into a light-and-sound show lacking only an Orson Welles narration for the sonorous reminder that Ripken's time had come.

SWEDE RISBERG

Risberg's offensive and defensive performance in 1919 World Series against Cincinnati did nothing to prevent him from being banned as one of the Chicago Black Sox. The shortstop managed only a single and a triple in 25 at bats (.080) while leading both teams in errors (four). In 1927 Risberg came to the fore of another scandal in charging before Commissioner Kenesaw Landis that the White Sox had won the 1917 pennant in significant part because Ty Cobb's Tigers had thrown two straight doubleheaders to his team. He was backed in his allegations by Chick Gandil, another of the Chicago Eight. But a Landis investigation prompted a parade of witnesses from the two teams to refute the charge. The defense offered was that, in common with a practice of the period, Chicago players had taken up an end-of-the-season collection for Detroit pitchers who had defeated the runnerup Red Sox in a key September series. Landis, who had developed blinders to events that had occurred before he agreed to become commissioner in November 1920, was only too happy to accept this version of events and reject the claims from Risberg and Gandil. He did, however, issue new regulations ending the "gift" practice between teams and threatening expulsion for players wagering on games in any form.

MARIANO RIVERA

Rivera's indispensability to the Joe Torre Yankees has been demonstrated as much by his setbacks as by his successes. The only two mistakes made by the righthanded reliever in postseason play between 1996 and 2001—against the Indians in 1997 and against the Diamondbacks in 2001—keyed the club's only two series losses out of 16 matchups. In between he rolled off a record-demolishing 23 consecutive saves.

Rivera assumed the closer role in the Bronx in 1997 after a brief assignment as a starter and an effective performance as John Wetteland's setup man on the 1996 world champions. Since then, he has racked up 210 saves, easily the most in the American League over that period and earning descriptions of him as "automatic." Just as amazing, he has missed no action in that time because of arm injuries despite his exclusive reliance on fastballs.

One of the best defensive pitchers in the game, Rivera all but doomed New York to its 2001 World Series loss to Arizona by throwing away a sacrifice in the ninth inning of the seventh game. The other chink in his record came in the eighth inning of the fourth game of the 1997 AL Division Series, when

he yielded a home run to Cleveland catcher Sandy Alomar that tied the score and set the Indians up for a ninth-inning victory.

EPPA RIXEY (Hall of Fame, 1963)

Rixey's career mark of 266–251 between 1912 and 1933 has made him one of the prime targets of critics of Cooperstown's standards. In fact, he was a classic hard-luck hurler for two generally bad teams who still managed the most victories by a National League southpaw until Warren Spahn came along. Even when Rixey led the league in losses with the Phillies in 1917, he did so with a 2.27 ERA. The previous year, when Philadelphia had finished second, he won 22 with a 1.85 ERA. Dealt to Cincinnati in 1921, in one of owner William Baker's habitual transactions for cash, the lefthander went on to post three more 20-win seasons, including an NL best 25 in 1922.

PHIL RIZZUTO (Hall of Fame, 1994)

Rizzuto's long wait to gain entry to the Hall of Fame, the heavy-handed campaign waged on his behalf by Yankees owner George Steinbrenner, and the actual circumstances of the election were almost enough to bury the merits of the case.

With New York (1941–42, 1946–56), the right-hand-hitting shortstop averaged .273. His career year in 1950 earned him MVP honors on the basis of personal highs in batting (.324), slugging (.439), doubles (36), runs (125), and walks (92). Practically reinventing the art of bunting, Scooter, as he was known, had his most vivid diamond moment when he squeezed Joe DiMaggio home on a high, inside pitch in the ninth inning of a September 17 contest against Cleveland; the run put New York in first place to stay. Defensively, he was the premier AL shortstop of his era, making up for a weak arm by playing shallow to exploit his extraordinary lateral flexibility.

Callously released on Old Timers Day in 1956, Rizzuto declined any public criticism of the move, winning points that he cashed in the following year by being assigned to the club's broadcasting booth. From then until his retirement in the late 1990s he won even more fame for his television persona than for his achievements on the field. His broadcasts featured an avalanche of birthday and anniversary greetings to friends, acquaintances, and people who had just shouted to him on the street; regular exclamations of "Holy Cow!" before even mildly unusual diamond activity; distracted rejoinders of "Huckleberry!" when corrected by his broadcast parts for one of his inevitable lapses of memory or diction; recountings of his numerous phobias (snakes, flying, spiders, lightning); on-air tastings of the canoli and other delicacies sent by fans; and references to his idiosyncratic method of scoring a game, including the invention of the WW code (for "Wasn't Watching").

Steinbrenner's public disparaging of the Veterans Committee every time it failed to put Rizzuto's name on a Cooperstown plaque went on for a decade; rather than being helpful, and worse than embarrassing, it appeared to stiffen the resistance of the electors. Only when teammate Yogi Berra, old friend Peewee Reese, and former broadcasting colleague Bill White joined the committee did Rizzuto get elected.

ROBIN ROBERTS (Hall of Fame, 1976)

Roberts was the Phillies pitching staff for most of the 1950s, demonstrating it not only by six straight 20-win seasons but also by hurling at least 300 innings an equal number of times. A hard thrower, he paid little attention to the record-breaking 505 home runs he yielded over his 19-year (1948–66) career, especially since the overwhelming majority of them were bases-empty shots when the game wasn't on the line. The righthander turned in his best effort in 1952, when he led the league with a 28–7 mark; he lost the MVP prize that year because of a Philadelphia writer who didn't like him and left his name off the ballot altogether. It was the first of four consecutive years he paced the NL in victories. His single biggest game was the finale of the 1950 season, when he went 10 innings to defeat the Dodgers, 4–1, on Dick Sisler's home run and gain his only entry to a World Series. The start was one of four he had in the pennant pressure of the last eight games of the year.

Always active in union causes, it was Roberts who introduced Marvin Miller to player representatives in 1966. He was also a key player voice in prohibiting Pete Rose from consideration for the Hall of Fame.

THOMAS TUTTLE ROBERTS

Roberts was the arbitrator who decided the first collusion case against free agents. In September 1978 he ruled that 139 players had been denied their right to an unfettered market after the 1985 season, granting second-look free agency to seven of them

(including Kirk Gibson and Carlton Fisk). The total damages collected by the injured parties eventually totaled more than $10 million.

BOB ROBERTSON

Robertson is the only National League player to hit three home runs in the League Championship Series. The Pittsburgh first baseman did it against the Giants in 1971 in the second game.

CHARLIE ROBERTSON

Robertson was the author of baseball's most unlikely perfect game. He twirled his masterpiece for the White Sox in his third big league start on April 30, 1922, against the Tigers. The performance was particularly startling in that the righthander never had a winning season in eight years, closing with a career record of 49–80 and an ERA of 4.44.

SHERRY ROBERTSON

Because he was Clark Griffith's nephew and Calvin Griffith's brother, Robertson wore a Washington uniform for 10 seasons between 1940 and 1952. Hyped during his minor league days as a hitting machine with speed, he ended up batting merely .230 and stealing only 32 bases. When the family finally persuaded him his playing days were over, Robertson took over as farm director of the Senators. In addition to his brother Calvin (whose original surname was also Robertson), his front office colleagues included his brother-in-law Joe Haynes as vice-president, his brother Jimmy as head of concessions, and his brother Billy as head of operations for Griffith Stadium. His sister Thelma, Haynes's wife, shared control of the club with Calvin.

BROOKS ROBINSON (Hall of Fame, 1983)

Robinson's defensive brilliance at third base was such that he ended his 23-year (1955–77) career with Baltimore as the first big leaguer to hold every lifetime fielding mark for a position, encompassing assists, putouts, double plays, and fielding average. Thrown into the mix were Gold Gloves every year from 1960 to 1975 and AL-leading numbers in fielding 11 times and in assists and putouts eight times. Although no secret in the 1960s, Robinson's fielding abilities didn't become a national assumption until the 1970 World Series against Cincinnati, when his snatches of balls hit by Tony Perez, Tommy Helms, and Johnny Bench marked the coming of age of third base defense.

Robinson's glovework overshadowed his offensive abilities. In 1964 he added a .317 average, 28 home runs, and a league-leading 118 RBIs to his defense for the MVP award. On five other occasions the righthanded hitter also had at least 20 home runs and three other times a minimum of 90 RBIs. His slowness, on the other hand, produced a mere 28 stolen bases and helped him to the league record for hitting into the most double plays until surpassed by Cal Ripken, Jr.

Robinson became so critical to the Orioles (he and Carl Yastrzemski share the record for length of service with one club) that teammates insisted he become player-representative in 1968 for their own protection. The union-busting franchise had traded away or released every previous representative since 1960.

FRANK ROBINSON (Hall of Fame, 1982)

Robinson developed such a reputation as a no-holds-barred hustler that his prodigious slugging sometimes seemed like an afterthought. He even trumped the attention focused on him as the first black manager in the majors by tagging a homer in his first at bat as a player-pilot.

Before free agency made it more common, Robinson stood almost alone in duplicating feats in the National and American leagues, not least winning MVP recognition in both circuits. He began his assault on the record book with Cincinnati in 1956, clouting 38 home runs to tie Wally Berger's NL rookie mark. In his first seven years with the Reds he dipped as low as 29 home runs only once, along the way picking up an MVP trophy for leading the club to a 1961 pennant with 37 homers, 124 RBIs, 117 runs, a batting average of .323, and a slugging average of .611. He was even better in 1962, batting .342, with 39 homers, 136 RBIs, 208 hits, and leading the league in doubles (51), runs (134), and slugging (.624). Before winding up his 21-year career, the righthand-hitting slugger would compile 586 home runs, 1,812 RBIs, and 1,829 runs to go with his .294 average and .537 slugging percentage.

Despite hitting another 33 home runs and registering triple figures again in both RBIs and runs scored in 1965, Robinson impressed Cincinnati president Bill DeWitt as "an old 30," so the executive traded him after the season to Baltimore in exchange for pitchers Milt Pappas and Jack Baldschun and outfielder Dick Simpson. Robinson made it one of the worst trades in baseball history when he won the Triple Crown for the Orioles with a .316 average, 49 home runs, and 122 RBIs; he also piled up AL-leading numbers in slugging (.637) and runs (122). Moreover, in leading Baltimore to a world championship, he put on display as never before his character as the ultimate team player, as likely to produce a run by taking out an infielder to thwart a double play as by reaching the seats. Later on, more than one manager admitted fining pitchers for throwing at the outfielder and making him even more aggressive. He added sprinkles to the cake by also taking MVP honors for the four-game sweep over the Dodgers in the World Series. Although he never again reached his 1966 numbers, Robinson was the heart of three more Baltimore pennant winners, in 1969, 1970, and 1971. He then became the centerpiece of other headline-making trades involving the Dodgers, Angels, and Indians, with his best twilight performance coming with California in 1973, when he reached 30 homers for the last time. Along the way he shattered all records for players jumping back and forth between the leagues: Among other things he was the first to hit 200 home runs in each circuit and the first to hit All-Star Game home runs for both sides.

Throughout his playing career Robinson never hid his ambition to manage; as he admitted subsequently, however, until his trade to Baltimore, he had never been especially eager to gain pioneering status as the first black pilot. Quite the contrary, the star described at the time by *The Sporting News* as a "Grade A Negro" even refused to join a Baltimore chapter of the NAACP unless he received assurances he wouldn't be called upon to make public appearances while active as a player. He began changing his attitude after coming up against the unwritten rules of Baltimore's segregated housing and finding little support from the team. Within a couple of years he became one of the game's most outspoken critics of such racist niceties as the league's systematic failure to penalize white pitchers who threw at black batters. By the time he was with the Angels in 1973, he was widely touted as the most likely candidate to break the managerial color ban—a forecast that did nothing for the nerves of incumbent California manager Bobby Winkles. Winkles turned so hostile to Robinson that he first demanded general manager

Harry Dalton trade him, then upped the ante by going to the Angels players and telling them he had made the demand. The tactic backfired when Dalton fired Winkles instead.

Still, Robinson never had a chance of breaking the color barrier with a team located in conservative Orange County. Rather, the opportunity came with Cleveland in 1975. To add drama to the occasion, Robinson, in the lineup as the team's designated hitter, walloped a home run in his first at bat in the first inning of Opening Day. He remained at the helm of the Indians for two-and-a-half years—a stint largely distinguished by his run-ins with Gaylord Perry, John Ellis, and other players because of both his sharp tongue and his penchant for expecting others to perform at the level he had. For the next few years he coached for the Angels and Orioles, exciting periodic reports he was about to take over the clubs. Instead, he again pulled off a twin-league feat by being named the NL's first black manager when he was given the job in San Francisco in 1981. He remained with the Giants three-and-a-half years, showing more restraint toward his players than he had displayed in Cleveland but also clashing regularly with general manager Tom Haller over the latter's timidity about pulling the trigger on deals.

In the wake of the furor caused by Al Campanis's racist observations on the abilities of blacks to hold down executive positions, Robinson was hired by Baltimore as a special presidential assistant in 1987. Against his declared wishes, he returned to the dugout at the beginning of the 1988 season while the club was wading its way through 21 straight losses from the starting gate. The one-time firebrand startled everyone with his philosophical patience as the wretched club endured 107 losses, then provoked a surprise of another kind when he turned the team around to finish within two games of the East Division title in 1989. He returned to the front office in 1991. His most recent assignment has provided still another surprise. Named as something of a disciplinary dean in the commissioner's office in 2000, Robinson has shown no patience with the brushback pitching tactics his contemporaries have been wont to boast about as normal on-field competition in their day. His itchy trigger finger for fines and suspensions (even in some highly dubious cases of deliberate mischief) has brought criticism from managers and players that Frank Robinson the administrator has forgotten all about Frank Robinson the player.

JACKIE ROBINSON (Hall of Fame, 1962)

Next to Babe Ruth, no single player has had as much impact on baseball as Robinson. Most obviously, he was Brooklyn president Branch Rickey's choice in 1945 for breaking the color barrier. But almost as striking, Robinson also introduced a daring style of play to the major leagues that made him as much of a direct antecedent to Pete Rose as to Willie Mays.

Rickey's selection of Robinson as the vehicle for challenging baseball's segregationist policies was controversial for more than racial reasons. For one thing, his professional career consisted of merely one season with the Kansas City Monarchs, where he had performed ably but not spectacularly. Second, he was already 26 years old. Third, although one of UCLA's greatest athletes, he had distinguished himself in football, basketball, and track more than in baseball. Fourth, he was a player still in search of a position, all scouting reports at the time agreeing he lacked the arm to be the shortstop he was for Kansas City. By Rickey's own testimony, Robinson emerged as the top candidate through a combination of raw athleticism, fierce competitiveness, superior intelligence, and mental toughness. It couldn't have hurt, either, that he was as much of a teetotaler as Rickey, that he was used to playing on integrated teams from his UCLA days, and even that he shared the birth date of Branch Rickey, Jr., the Brooklyn president's much-doted-upon son. Robinson was formally signed to a Dodgers contract on October 23, 1945, and assigned to the Montreal Royals farm club for the following season.

During his one year in Montreal and for his first few seasons in Ebbets Field, Robinson generally endured the racial taunts of fans, opponents, and even some teammates with a forbearance he had promised Rickey. His fiery play on the field won him Rookie of the Year honors in 1947 and an MVP trophy in 1949. His single finest performance came on September 30, 1951, when he made an acrobatic catch in the bottom of the ninth inning in Philadelphia to rescue Brooklyn from pennant elimination, then homered in the 13th inning to force a playoff against the Giants. Robinson's apparent off-field stoicism in the middle of such diamond dash gradually won over the baseball establishment and forged a model other black players were to be measured against for some time. On the other hand, any departure from his initial behavioral model quickly laid bare the sport's persisting racism, most often through front office or press criticism that the perceived mistakes of an individual black player were ruinous to his entire race. This patronizing attitude had a couple of long-term consequences: It effectively kept the big leagues out of the reach of some of the most flamboyant players in the Negro leagues (and of some who simply weren't married or part of a model family), and it imposed a higher standard of playing excellence for the black player than for his white counterpart. For years, even decades, to come, a black player's road from the minors to the parent club was to prove almost as rocky as the one that had led from the Negro leagues to a big league organization, and for similar reasons.

Once he had established himself in Brooklyn, however, not too much stymied Robinson. One important factor in his development as a major leaguer was that he was playing in a city already heated to passionate, frequently bitter levels by long-standing rivalries between the National League Dodgers and Giants and between both of them and the American League Yankees. Robinson's dynamic presence boiled the water over the rim of a pot that already contained the likes of Leo Durocher, Charlie Dressen, Larry MacPhail, and other volatile tempers in a continuous bubbling of controversies, scandals, and vows of vengeance against somebody or other. He excited Brooklyn not only by contributing his bat, glove, and speed to the confrontations with the Giants and Yankees, but also by embarrassing the opposition into the kinds of mental and physical errors that led them to beat themselves. Or, as Durocher once noted: "You want a guy that comes to play. But (Robinson) didn't just come to play. He came to beat you. He came to stuff the goddam bat right up your ass."

The results of Robinson's aggressiveness were not totally translatable into his career numbers. His lifetime .311 average, for example, ranked him only seventh among the second basemen in the Hall of Fame at the turn of the century. Due to his relatively brief stay (1947–56) in the majors, he compiled fewer hits than any of the others and topped only the mediocre-hitting Johnny Evers in most key categories. He never hit 20 home runs or 40 doubles in a season and knocked in 100 runs only once—the same number

of times he reached 30 stolen bases. What the statistics do not convey are what Rickey called Robinson's "thinking man's game." His speed, for instance, was deployed not primarily for stealing bases but for running the opposition into defensive mistakes. As a member of the power-laden Boys of Summer, his thefts tended to be surgical cuts in late-inning situations rather than mechanical charges from base to base. Then there were the prancings and shoutings to the opposition pitcher, causing balks, wild pitches, and wild throws to the first baseman; the threatening moves toward the next base to pull out of position both infielders and the outfielders backing them up; and the endlessly taunting, jockeying advances toward the next base on routine popups and singles in a dare to outfielders to take the chance of throwing behind him. These "tricky ball" maneuvers, a Negro league staple for years, flew in the face of white baseball's traditional wisdom about riling the adversary. As somebody who was already playing in a pressure cooker because of his race, Robinson pursued his antagonistic kind of game with the self-assurance that his determination was stronger than anyone else's and that, pressure pitted against pressure, he wouldn't be the first to crack.

But that was not all. If Robinson brought his Negro league education to the majors, he also brought along the instincts and talents from his extraordinary athletic days at UCLA. With the same indifference to retaliation that he displayed with his psychological taunting, he never hesitated to throw rolling blocks into opposition infielders or, in some cases, opposition pitchers who went after bunts he deliberately laid down along the first base line. Playing in the field, particularly at second or third base, he defied a runner to knock him down. For the sturdy, muscular Robinson baseball was very much a contact sport. It was not the least of Rickey's insights that he had foreseen this all-consuming kind of play as a spontaneous, productive outlet for the turmoils and frustrations Robinson had to endure privately; it was not the least of Robinson's strengths that there was very little of the gratuitous in his aggressiveness and that his on-field actions didn't precipitate any more physical brouhahas than did those of his white teammates.

By the mid-1950s, with other blacks established as stars, Robinson had begun to go public with his grievances about baseball's discriminating practices. This reawakened the old critics who had been opposed to integration from the start, as well as stirred earlier supporters into complaints that Robinson was an ingrate or that he was losing sight of the turn-the-other-cheek philosophy that had been crucial to his gaining a foothold in the majors. More indirectly, he drew reprimands from other black players who didn't want him rocking the boat. With his skills also on the wane, his outspokenness prompted frequent (and unfavorable) comparisons to Mays, Roy Campanella, and Ernie Banks, all of whom were embraced by the media as black stars embodying the "joy" of the game. In effect, Robinson's new and sometimes angry candor represented a second beachhead for black players, and one that once again left him as something of a lonely pioneer. It was to take many more years for black players to follow him down this road than had been needed to follow him into the big leagues.

Robinson's playing career came to an end with the 1956 season, when he opted to retire rather than accept a completed trade to the Giants. In 1987 the Rookie of the Year Award was redesignated the Jackie Robinson Award. The 50th anniversary of his debut in 1997 occasioned a great deal of self-congratulation by Major League Baseball, but no practical followup to Commissioner Bud Selig's promise to see to it that more blacks got meaningful front office positions. The most conspicuous consequence of all the speeches was the retirement of Robinson's number 42 for every franchise in both leagues.

WILBERT ROBINSON (Hall of Fame, 1945)

Robinson's career was one of the most picaresque in baseball history, providing him with signal moments as player, manager, coach, and franchise president; he even umpired a game in an emergency. Along the way he got involved in political intrigues affecting three leagues and, more fatefully, in the emotional highs and lows of John McGraw.

A catcher by trade, Robinson began his 17-year (1886–1902) career with the American Association Athletics, remaining with the team as a backup receiver until he was peddled to the league's Baltimore entry in 1890; it was there in 1891 that he became a teammate of McGraw. With the collapse of the AA at the end of that season, the Orioles moved into the National League and Robinson moved into the starting catching job with a good glove and an awakening bat. A lifetime .275 hitter, he had five

.300 seasons, including a career-high .353 in 1894; on June 12, 1894 he also became the first of two major leaguers (with Rennie Stennett) to get seven hits in a nine-inning game.

Aside from his defense and offense, Robinson served the club in two fundamental ways: first by personifying the Old Orioles way in such ploys as throwing his mask in the general direction of oncoming baserunners, and secondly by acquiring the raw material from which he would enchant generations of listeners with stories about the grittiness of his teammates. As much as anyone, Robinson was responsible for the exaggerated—if not false—image of the NL Orioles as macho cutthroats who were avid to play as long as they had at least one functioning limb; in fact, Robinson's own career was proof of the exaggeration. Between 1895 and 1898, while the Orioles were winning two pennants and finishing second the other two times, for example, he was sidelined with a variety of ailments, appearing behind the plate in only 267 games. He finally recanted all his years of puffery after watching the Yankees sweep the Cardinals in the 1928 World Series, telling columnist Dan Daniel that the Murderers Row New York team "would have beaten our brains out." (This immediately brought down the wrath of McGraw and other old Baltimore teammates.)

Because he was already 36, Robinson was not one of the Baltimore players shifted to Brooklyn in 1899 as part of an elaborate syndication scheme for common control of the two franchises. Instead, staying behind with manager-third baseman McGraw, he contributed enough Old Orioleism to field fights and other ruckuses to embarrass the syndicators by having fourth-place Baltimore outdraw pennant-winning Brooklyn on the road. That moral victory achieved, he and McGraw moved on to the Cardinals for the 1900 season, but making it clear from the start they intended to be a part of Baltimore's new American League franchise in 1901. They carried through on their intention, even becoming minority investors in the new team. That became signicant a year later when they used their stock as a lever in another labyrinthian scheme aimed at getting McGraw and some of Baltimore's top players to the Giants. The good soldier in all the finagling, Robinson stayed behind as McGraw's managerial successor to play out the Orioles schedule with a roster largely contributed by other AL organizations. When what was left of the Baltimore franchise was sold to New York's Frank Farrell and the Orioles were transformed into the Highlanders (later Yankees), he withdrew from baseball for some years to run a local meat concern. He had hardly started.

In 1911 Robinson was back in uniform for McGraw at the Polo Grounds, serving as the first full-time pitching coach. As in Baltimore and St. Louis, another part of the job was playing the good cop to McGraw's bad cop with umpires. According to Robinson, the routine was instinctive, with McGraw ranting and screaming as nastily as he could until he stepped in with patented, good-natured smiles, assuring the arbiter that "Mac just says things, he really likes you." The same roly-poly tactic was used on sportswriters, and most of them fell for it, making Robinson as popular as his manager with sports cartoonists. For his part, the more jaded Damon Runyon insisted on referring to him only and always as Your Uncle Wilbert.

Robinson's 22-year friendship with McGraw ended after the 1913 World Series, when the exasperated manager, looking for any fall guy at all for New York's loss to the Athletics, decided the main culprit had been his first base coach for sending the sore-legged Fred Snodgrass to second in a futile steal attempt in the final game. If Robinson was stunned by his abrupt firing, he got over it quickly enough when Brooklyn offered him its managing job for the 1914 season. It was the start of several things: an 18-year stay by Robinson as the Dodgers pilot, the popular designation of his team as the Robins, and a bitter rivalry with former friend McGraw.

In his third year at Ebbets Field Robinson steered the Dodgers to the NL pennant. The win was all the sweeter in being clinched in a late September game against the Giants; it came all the more suspiciously when several New York errors contributed to it, prompting a seething McGraw to stalk off the field before the end of the contest. Although McGraw seemed to get over it by the next day, runnerup Philadelphia demanded that NL president John Tener investigate whether the known sympathies of several New York players for Robinson had contributed to their errors. Tener dismissed the accusation, and it was about the last time the league's New York clubs would ever be charged with trying to help one another. In 1920 Robinson's squad won another pennant, and again the victory came under a cloud—this time from a headline-seeking Brooklyn district attorney who sought to make political hay with an investigation similar to the one under way against the 1919 Chicago White Sox. But claims that Dodgers players had been approached by gamblers to throw the World Series to the Indians also died a quick death.

Through the first half of the 1920s Robinson's chief nemesis was the miserly spending of owner Charlie Ebbets. Relations between them grew tenuous enough for Robinson to consider piloting the Yankees—a prospect that faded only when Jacob Ruppert decided against the advice of his partner Cap Huston and hired Miller Huggins instead. With the death of Ebbets in 1925, however, Robinson learned what a genuine enemy was when, to his announced surprise, the Ebbets heirs backed him as club president over half-owner Stephen McKeever. The resentful McKeever immediately declared war on the president-manager, creating so much organizational chaos that franchise executives were soon lumped together by the press as The Daffiness Boys.

Robinson's attempts at wearing two hats also cost him the benevolence of the sportswriting fraternity. The first rupture appeared when the Brooklyn *Eagle,* close to McKeever, criticized the selection of Robinson as president as confirmation that "the common sense of the common people is a common fallacy." Even sharper was a clash between Your Uncle Wilbert and the New York *Sun* after the paper had run a cartoon in 1926 mocking the high salaries of Brooklyn's unproductive stars, contrasting them with the pittances being earned by the team's only productive players. When Robinson called the paper to protest the publication of all the salaries, *Sun* sports editor Joe Vila doubled the poison not merely by reporting the call but also by ordering the paper never again to print either Robinson's name or the Robins designation for the club. It was from that point on that the *Sun* (and gradually other dailies) recognized the franchise more regularly as the Dodgers.

By 1930 the Robinson-McKeever feud had left the team in such disarray that other league owners insisted NL president John Heydler do something to restore order. Heydler's compromise solution was to have Robinson given a new two-year pact as manager but have him resign as president so a new board of directors could start with a fresh slate. The board included two McKeever votes, two from the Robinson-Ebbets faction, and the deadlock-breaking presence of Walter Carter, brother-in-law of U.S. Supreme Court chief justice Charles Evans Hughes. It proved to be the beginning of the end for Robinson. A year later, with the Dodgers still stumbling on the field and in the boardroom and with other owners still complaining that their trips to Ebbets Field were a waste of time because of the sparse attendance in a rundown facility, Carter used his tie-breaking vote to endorse Robinson's replacement by Max Carey.

With the help of former Yankees owner Huston, Robinson took over as manager and president of the Atlanta franchise in the Southern Association for a season, but then fell down a flight of stairs, sustaining serious injuries. While recovering from the accident, he died in a hospital of a heart attack at the age of 70.

FRANK ROBISON

Originally a Cleveland streetcar operator, Robison was an ardent promoter of syndicated ownership of big league clubs. Denied permission by the National League to sell the Cleveland Spiders to interests in Detroit and Toronto in the 1890s, he took the tack of purchasing the St. Louis Browns in 1899 and then cannibalizing the Spiders for his new team, moving among others future Hall of Famers Cy Young, Jesse Burkett, and Bobby Wallace. With Robison's brother Stanley nominally in charge, the shell that had been the Spiders suffered through the worst season in history—a 20–134 (.130) record that included 24 consecutive losses and no winning streak longer than two games. Initially dubbed the Leftovers, Discards, and Castoffs by the press, the club quickly enough turned into the Wanderers and Exiles when the Robisons began shifting home games to the road, permitting fans in Cleveland only six opportunities to see the team after July 1. At the end of the year, with the league cutting back from 12 to eight clubs, the brothers accepted $25,000 in mercy killing money to dissolve the franchise.

In St. Louis Robison became an ally of Andrew Freedman in the New York owner's 1900 syndication scheme. Even though that effort died of its own weight, he resurrected it to coincide with the reconciliation talks between the National and American leagues. Under the Robison plan there would have been one eight-team circuit organized as a holding company with eight wholly owned subsidiaries. "What people want is good baseball," he liked to tell reporters before his plan was voted down once and for all, "they don't care who owns the clubs."

Robison's most lasting contribution was his proposal to establish a purse for the first- and second-place teams in each league—a plan he sought to impose as part of an across-the-board 20 percent pay cut for players. Minus the salary slashing, the proposal eventually became the basis for the division of World Series monies among the top four clubs in each league.

JOHN ROCKER

For Rocker baseball has been less a game of inches than of feet in his mouth. In two years he has made himself *persona non grata* in two clubhouses, an embarrassment to baseball's always-fragile public relations, and a code word for idiocy in New York City. Entering the 2002 season, his once-promising career as a dominating closer for Atlanta was close to ruins.

Rocker started the ball rolling with a December 1999 interview published by *Sports Illustrated* in which he found nothing to like about the ethnic groups and gays in New York City, the trains that brought them to Shea Stadium, or the municipality that operated the trains; for good measure he shot some racial slurs in the direction of some Braves teammates and questioned Bobby Cox's wiles as a manager. Cox was about the only one who affected stoicism. After the customary I-was-misquoted reactions from Rocker and the he-doesn't-represent-baseball ritual from officialdom, Commissioner Bud Selig suspended the hurler for spring training and the first month of the 2000 season—a judgment later appealed down by the Players Association to a handful of regular season games. Apparently on the assumption that those holding Rocker's racist, homophobic views had to be on neurotic terms with a deeper and truer self, Selig also ordered him into psychological counseling.

However much they talked about his importance to their bullpen, Atlanta players made it clear that, a month or a few days, they could have done without the reliever's return altogether (and in fact went through the next 15 months being frazzled by questions about him). When the team reached New York City for its first visit in June, and after months of local uproar about the remarks in *Sports Illustrated,* Shea Stadium resembled a police convention. In the event, the only trouble came for the Mets when, after rushing in from the bullpen to a cascade of booing, Rocker locked up an Atlanta victory and then slowly, tauntingly, shambled off the field drinking in the hostile response. For the rest of the season he was a magnet for both boos and redneck approval around the league whenever he appeared.

After saving 38 games in 1999 and 24 in 2000, Rocker began the 2001 season with another fast string of saves, but also with much more of the wildness that had occasionally stymied his success. Then in quick succession he went out of his way to instigate a fight with the Blue Jays, got into a shouting match with a Yankees fan, made some obscene references to the New York media, and brushed off a Cox warning about such episodes. In June the Braves traded him to the Indians, acknowledging that locker room strains between the pitcher and his teammates had become intolerable. But once in Cleveland Rocker found a disgruntled Bob Wickman, who didn't appreciate losing his closing job to the new arrival. Wickman needn't have worried: After a handful of outings in which he once again showed little control, Rocker was reassigned as a setup man. His immediate reaction was to attack Wickman for the veteran's alleged complicity some years earlier in the systematic abuse of a Yankees clubhouse boy; a subsequent response was to get into a water-throwing incident with a fan at Safeco Field. At the end of the year the Indians announced a new contract for the free agent Wickman, leaving no one surprised when Rocker was dealt away again, this time to the Rangers.

ALEX RODRIGUEZ

If Texas had any argument about giving Rodriguez a multiyear pact valued at $252 million after the 2000 season, it was this: It was buying the services of the player it expected to be able to pool enough of the separate abilities of Honus Wagner, Ozzie Smith, and Ernie Banks to emerge as the best ever at his position. Similar hopes have not been nurtured for any other beneficiary of a nine-figure contract.

Even excluding his far superior defensive skills, Rodriguez had, by the end of the 2001 season, already begun to put distance between himself and the shortstop with whom he has been most often compared, the Hall of Famer slugger Banks. After six complete seasons, the Texas infielder had accumulated 241 home runs and 730 RBIs with a .311 aver-

age; Banks's numbers over a comparable period were 228 home runs, 661 RBIs, and a .295 average. Rodriguez's steals in the single season of 1998 (46) almost equaled the 50 collected by Banks over his entire 19-year career. Among sluggers from any position, only Harmon Killebrew (272) and Ralph Kiner (257) had belted more home runs after six full big league seasons. He summed up his double threat in 1998 with his original team of Seattle by becoming one of only three 40–40 players, tagging 42 home runs and stealing 46 bases. Under the pressure of his new contract and a shambles of a team around him, he more than matched that for Texas in 2001, when he led the league in home runs (52) and runs scored (133) while batting .318. Among his various achievements for the season were becoming the first infielder other than a first baseman to hit 50 balls out of the park and the first player at any position to collect 50 homers and 200 hits in the same season since Jimmie Foxx in 1932.

The size of Rodriguez's contract with the Rangers created a tsunami throughout baseball, and in the AL West in particular. Those not preoccupied with accusing his agent Scott Boras of being an extortionist directed their criticism at Texas owner Tom Hicks for once again destroying the game's salary structure (the assumption being that there had been one to destroy).

IVAN RODRIGUEZ

As the 2002 season began, Rodriguez was one Rodriguez too many for Texas, and for some of the same reasons his shortstop teammate had been given a $252 million contract. The catcher has been on track to being the best all-around at his position in big league history, making his scheduled free agent payday at the end of the season too much even for the lavishly spending Rangers.

Although always a good hitter, Rodriguez has attracted attention mostly for his defense, where his ability to block pitches, throw out runners, and lead staffs of so-so Texas pitchers to victorious seasons has left opposition managers dumbstruck. With a throwout percentage above 50 percent in several seasons, running has not been much of an option for adversaries since he took over as a regular in 1992. It has been almost as an afterthought that his offense has matured to being second only to Mike Piazza's among contemporary receivers, and even Piazza hasn't been up to his ability to steal bases. In 1999 he took MVP honors after batting .332 (the highest by an AL catcher since Bill Dickey in 1936), walloping 35 home runs (the league record for his position), driving home 113 runs, and stealing 25 bases.

BULLET JOE ROGAN (Hall of Fame, 1998)

If most Negro league stars labored in the shadow of the major leagues, Rogan performed in the shadow's shadow until he was past his 30th birthday, toiling for Army teams in the Philippines, Hawaii, and Arizona. Discovered by Casey Stengel in 1919, he joined the Kansas City Monarchs of the Negro National League the following year, going on to lead the league in wins in 1924 and 1925. He also paced his team in homers twice and consistently batted over .300 while seeing extra duty as an outfielder and a second baseman. In the first Negro World Series, against Hilldale in 1924, Rogan won twice, threw a complete-game loss, and relieved in a fourth contest; he also hit .325 appearing in all nine games. The following year he was 3–1 in the league playoff, but had to sit out the Series because of an injury. Rogan also managed the Monarchs between 1926 and 1938.

JOHN ROGERS

A Philadelphia lawyer and half-owner of the Phillies from 1883 to 1902, Rogers was also the author of the standard player contract of his time. After the National League lost significant court battles to the Players League over the services of John Montgomery Ward, Buck Ewing, and Bill Hallman, he considered eliminating the reserve clause from all future pacts to insure peace. Instead, he ended up tightening the clause so effectively that, after Nap Lajoie bolted from the Phillies to the Athletics, he won an injunction prohibiting the second baseman's appearance in a Philadelphia uniform anywhere in Pennsylvania. Rogers sold out his interests in the Phillies in 1903 when the conflicting involvements of his partners Al Reach and Ben Shibe in the two leagues strained relations among the three.

BILLY ROHR

Rohr came within one strike of being the only pitcher since the 19th century to hurl a no-hitter in his major league debut. Facing New York at Yankee Stadium on April 14, 1967, the Boston southpaw got all the way down to a full count in the ninth inning when Elston Howard ruined his masterpiece with a single. Although he held on for a 3–0 shutout, Rohr pitched only one more complete game and was out of the big leagues (with a 3–3 mark) after only two seasons.

PETE ROSE

Rose's obsession with numbers and money over his 24-year (1963–86) career were fitting for somebody nicknamed Charlie Hustle; what wasn't so expected was that baseball's most prolific hitter would be denied his place in the Hall of Fame by a commissioner who had built an intellectual altar to his diamond virtues.

Rose began his assault on the record books as the first piece of the Big Red Machine in 1963, when, as a second baseman for Cincinnati, he took NL Rookie of the Year honors for batting .273 and scoring 100 runs for the first of 10 times. A career .303 batter, his subsequent achievements included three hitting titles (1968, 1969, 1973); 15 years of averaging .300; leading the league in hits seven times and in doubles five times; and reaching the 200-hit plateau an unprecedented 10 times. The switch-hitting leadoff man's most productive year was 1973, when he took the MVP award for his .338 batting title, 36 doubles, and 115 runs. His most magnetic season was 1978, when he pursued Joe DiMaggio's 56-game hitting streak before national cameras, finally having to settle for tying Willie Keeler's NL mark of 44 games. In 1985 he sparked another media event by pursuing Ty Cobb's all-time hit record, finally surpassing the Detroit star with a single off San Diego's Eric Show for hit number 4,192 on September 11.

Rose closed out his career with 4,256 hits. He had an additional 45 safeties (and a .381 average) in League Championship Series for another record. He also retired with marks for the most games played (3,562) and most at bats (14,053), and a second-place finish for doubles (746). While hardly a power hitter, he did whack up to 16 home runs in a season, and drove three balls out of the park against the Mets in a Shea Stadium game in April 1978. While never especially fast (in 1975 he had 662 official at bats without one stolen base), his trademark belly flops were an incentive for a whole generation of players to eschew sliding feet first into bases. While not a brilliant defense player, his doggedness and intense work habits permitted managers to move him around over the years from second base to the outfield to third base to first base; he ended up being elected to All-Star teams at five different positions.

The immediate Rose persona was a pit bull as capable of dispatching close friend Ray Fosse to the disabled list for two months after a home plate collision in the 1970 All-Star Game, as he was accustomed to fielding his position and returning to the dugout at the end of every inning on the run. It was a quality some identified with a winning attitude and others with mania, but that became part of seven division titles, six pennants, and three world championships. The worst fallout from his rugged style occurred during the 1973 NLCS, when his hard slide into second base precipitated punches with Mets shortstop Bud Harrelson and then mass disorder in the Shea Stadium stands. Only when New York players begged fans to control themselves did Cincinnati lose a fleeting hope of winning the game by forfeit.

Off the field Rose could spit out at a moment's notice statistics covering not only every facet of his play but those pertaining to players with whom he was competing in some offensive category. The only numbers of equal importance to him were those relating to his salary—a source of friction more than once during his career. On the eve of the 1977 season, for instance, he complained bitterly that the Reds had given shortstop Dave Concepcion a five-year, $1 million contract, dropping leaden hints that he would leave the team as a free agent at the end of the year if he didn't get considerably more. That mini-crisis ended when general manager Bob Howsam was inundated with letters and calls demanding he work out a deal with the local hero. Two years later, however, the team braved hostile fan reaction by dropping out of the bidding fairly early for Rose's free agent services. For most of the offseason he was wined and dined by several NL teams—offered a racing stable by the Pirates, a national identification through Ted Turner's cable network by the Braves, and the chance to become the king of New York by the Mets. Rose dismissed the horses, decided he didn't need the exposure provided by Turner, and told the Mets he didn't "play for losers," coming down in favor of the Phillies. To get the infielder-outfielder, however, Philadelphia had to borrow heavily from a television station to meet a Rose contract demand that he be the highest paid player in any of the four pro-fessional sports (a primacy held then by David Thompson of the NBA Denver Nuggets).

Rose proved to be the sparkplug in Philadelphia's only world championship, in 1980. On the other hand, he was mortified when he was benched in favor of Tony Perez during the 1983 World Series against Baltimore. After starting the 1984 season with Montreal, he realized an often-stated ambition by being traded back to the Reds so he could take over his original club as a player-manager. As the dugout leader, he brought together all his field instincts and his encyclopedic knowledge of both players and the rule book to guide the team to four consecutive second-place finishes between 1985 and 1988. Against expectations that he would be an able motivator but a disaster in shaping a pitching staff, there were extended periods when just the opposite was the case. His worst moment on the field as manager came in 1988, when he engaged in so protracted an argument with umpire Dave Pallone that he was suspended 30 days for provoking a near-riot by Riverfront Stadium fans. But that turned out to be a mere prelude to the crisis that was to keep him out of the Hall of Fame.

In spring training in 1989 Commissioner Bart Giamatti confirmed reports that he was looking into the possibility that Rose had been betting on baseball games and that he was in debt to various bookmakers for an estimated $500,000. What followed was a circus: months of accumulating evidence about Rose's addiction to betting on sports events, independent investigations linking him to ambiguous figures around the country, and his own repeated denials that he had ever wagered on baseball. Eventually the media pressure became so great that he decided against leading the Reds up to Cooperstown for the annual induction exhibition game lest he divert attention from Johnny Bench, a former teammate elected to the Hall of Fame that year. Then, finally, with a suit challenging Giamatti's authority losing wind as it bounced from courtroom to courtroom, Rose announced on August 24 that he would abide by the commissioner's decision to ban him permanently from baseball.

Although a behind-doors accord between the sides made no mention of Rose's alleged betting on baseball (a significant concession since such an activity was criminally liable), Giamatti couldn't even get through his first subsequent press conference without reiterating his belief that the manager had indeed been wagering on games, including Cincinnati games. For his part, Rose continued issuing denials in this regard, also spurning suggestions for a long time that his monumental losses to bookmakers (estimated in the millions) indicated an addiction. His public image didn't improve when, barely a week after the ban deal, Giamatti died of a heart attack, prompting a lot of glib charges from columnists that the chain-smoking commissioner, who had once spoken of Rose as the perfect major leaguer, had been done in by his one-time hero. He lost still more of his following when, clearly desperate for money, he stepped up his appearances at card shows to sell his autograph at inflated prices and turned up regularly on home shopping networks to peddle the trophies and memorabilia that he had accumulated over the years.

In 1990 a federal court found Rose guilty of tax evasion and sentenced him to several months of imprisonment. On top of that, the committee charged with overseeing Hall of Fame election procedures made him ineligible for consideration as a member of Cooperstown. The decision—based on Hall of Fame regulations about the moral character of candidates—made little mention of the fact that the museum was already honoring racists like Cap Anson, assailants like Ty Cobb, drunkards like Rabbit Maranville and Grover Cleveland Alexander, and numerous others who should have come up as short of this criterion as Rose. Like Giamatti, the committee decided that what Charlie Hustle had achieved between the white lines had become irrelevant. The absurdity of the situation was driven home at the 2000 All-Star Game when, to the enormous discomfort of Commissioner Bud Selig, Rose had to be honored along with other members of the so-called All-Century Team elected by fans across the country.

AL ROSEN

Rosen squeezed a lot into what were essentially only seven big league seasons. As a rookie third baseman for Cleveland in 1950, he led the AL in home runs with 37, also reaching the century mark in RBIs, runs, and walks. It was the first of five straight seasons of 100 RBIs, including league-leading numbers in 1952 and 1953. In the latter year he also won his second home run title and came within one point of Mickey Vernon for a tainted batting title. There was sentiment in Cleveland for the righthand-hitting

slugger to protest the outcome because two members of the Senators had intentionally committed baserunning gaffes to spare Vernon another time at bat. Rosen declined to protest, even though he had collected his own three hits on the final day of the season after ignoring a patent invitation by Detroit infielders to lay down as many bunts as he wanted to claim a Triple Crown; one of the two outs he made that day came when he deprived himself of a fourth hit by running over first base without touching the bag.

In 1954, playing for the pennant-winning Indians all year with a broken finger, Rosen managed only 24 home runs, but batted .300 and drove in 102 runs. It was his last joyful season. Over his last two years he attracted boobirds whipped on by insinuations in the press that the only reason he was allowed to continue playing through a protracted slump was that he and co-owner Hank Greenberg were both Jews. The ugliness reached a climax in 1956, when Rosen was hooted for leaving a game with a broken nose. Manager Al Lopez was so disgusted by the grandstand reaction that he resigned after the season. Rosen went with him, having averaged 27 home runs and 102 RBIs for his seven full campaigns. He later became a front office executive for the Yankees, Astros, and Giants.

ROSEY ROSWELL

Longtime Pittsburgh announcer Roswell had the most distinctive home run call of any baseball broadcaster. Whenever a ball started toward the outfield seats, he would shout, "Open the window, Aunt Minnie, here she comes!", then key a sound effects recording of glass shattering.

ALLAN ROTH

In the same year that Branch Rickey brought Jackie Robinson to Brooklyn, 1947, he brought in Roth, baseball's first full-time statistician. A Montreal native, Roth got the job by detailing for the Dodgers boss such offensive categories as RBI opportunities and sacrifice successes. The only previous instance of a club compiling—even briefly—such statistics had been the Cubs in the 1930s.

Although Roth's data was less than appreciated by Dodgers managers Burt Shotton and Charlie Dressen, Walter Alston pored over the statistical information before every game.

ARNOLD ROTHSTEIN

Rothstein was the biggest money man behind the 1919 Black Sox scandal. Initially skeptical of an approach made by former boxing champion Abe Atell and ex-big leaguers Bill Burns and Billy Maharg, the New York racketeer subsequently collected enough information to persuade himself that Chicago players were indeed ready to throw the Series against Cincinnati. Papers found after his death indicate that he laid out $80,000 to facilitate the fix.

In 1920, feigning outraged virtue, Rothstein appeared before the grand jury in Chicago investigating the Series, claiming he had even lost money on the White Sox's unexpected loss. It was a convincing enough performance to keep him from being indicted with numerous players and gamblers from other parts of the country. Helping matters along was the mysterious disappearance from the state's attorney's office of several player confessions linking Rothstein to the fix. The confessions, swiped with the undoubted connivance of White Sox owner Charles Comiskey and his attorney Alfred Austrian, later showed up in the hands of a Comiskey lawyer in a case against Joe Jackson.

Rothstein was a long-time partner of both Giants owner Charles Stoneham and manager John McGraw in various business ventures, including bucket shops and pool halls. He was shot to death in November 1928 for welshing on losses at a poker game. There was never any estimate of his winnings on the 1919 Series.

EDD ROUSH (Hall of Fame, 1962)

Roush had some of the most curious—and curiously overlooked—numbers of early 20th century players. A lefthand-hitting outfielder who did his damage with a 46-ounce bat, he averaged .323 over 18 seasons (between 1913 and 1931) spent mostly with the Reds and Giants. In 1917 and 1919 he won the NL batting title; in 1918 he took league slugging honors; in 1924 he totaled the most triples. Most impressive of all, Roush had a 10-year streak of never hitting below .321—the highest minimum for so long by any NL player except Honus Wagner. His batting eye was so sharp that he struck out only 260 times in his career. On the other hand, Roush was the model case of a hitter surrounded by outs: Despite his lifetime batting average and on-base percentage of .369, he never once scored 100 runs or drove in 100.

Roush arrived in the NL with the Giants in 1916 as one of the players picked up by John McGraw from the disbanded Federal League. After only a few at bats at the Polo Grounds he was dealt to Cincinnati for Buck Herzog in the so-called Hall of Fame Trade; accompanying him to the Reds were fellow Cooperstown notables Christy Mathewson and Bill McKechnie. It was Roush who alerted Cincinnati officials to attempted bribes of Reds players prior to the 1919 World Series and who insisted to his dying day that some of his teammates had played as suspiciously as the White Sox during the tarred Series.

When Roush wasn't tagging NL pitchers, he was playing tag with Reds owner Garry Herrmann in annual contract negotiations; it was in fact a rare season that he didn't miss spring training in a holdout tactic. Despite his star outfielder's popularity with Reds fans, Herrmann finally had enough of the yearly tug-of-war in 1927, sending him back to the Giants. Reunited with McGraw, Roush continued his holdout pattern every year, actually sitting out the 1930 season altogether in protest against the contract offered to him. He was then bounced back to Cincinnati, where he finally called it quits.

DAVE ROWE

Outfielder Rowe was pressed into service as a pitcher by the Cleveland Forest Citys on July 24, 1882. He pitched a complete game, but yielded 29 hits, seven bases on balls—and a major league-record 35 runs. He established another mark of dubious achievement by playing for seven different teams in his seven major league seasons.

JACK ROWE

Shortstop Rowe, brother of Dave, played 75 games for the NL Buffalo Bisons in 1882, putting the ball in play in every one of his 308 official at bats. That is the record for plate appearances in a season without a strikeout.

BAMA ROWELL

Second baseman Rowell inspired novelist Bernard Malamud's climactic scene in *The Natural* when he smashed the Bulova clock atop the right field scoreboard in Ebbets Field as a member of the Braves on Memorial Day in 1946. The blow showered Brooklyn's Dixie Walker in glass. In the novel by the Brooklyn-born Malamud, the home run was hit by fictional hero Roy Hobbs and won a pennant for the New York Knights. In reality, Rowell had to wait 41 years even to collect the watch Bulova had promised anyone who hit the clock.

PANTS ROWLAND

As president of the Pacific Coast League in 1946, Rowland petitioned the big leagues for equal status to head off any future encroachments on his turf by transferred or expansion franchises. Turned down on that one, he later championed a vote to desert the National Association of Professional Baseball Leagues unless the player draft was abolished; he gathered enough backing to pressure the National and American leagues into granting to the PCL a promotion from Triple A status to a vaguely defined open classification that exempted it from the major league draft. The league existed in this limbo between the major and minor leagues until 1958, when the incursion of what Rowland called the "vultures" (the Dodgers and Giants) extended the major leagues to California and curtailed the PCL's ambitions once and for all.

As a major league manager in 1917, Rowland led the White Sox to a world championship.

MUDDY RUEL

Ruel scored the most important run in the 66-year history of the Washington Senators. A catcher who bounced around for 19 years between 1915 and 1934, he doubled to ignite a rally in the bottom of the 12th inning in the seventh game of the 1924 World Series against the Giants, eventually scoring when Earl McNeely hit an apparent double play ball that bounced over Freddie Lindstrom's head. Ruel whacked his double after New York catcher Hank Gowdy had tripped over his mask going after an easy pop foul. A lawyer when he wasn't crouching behind the plate, Ruel is credited with having coined the phrase "tools of ignorance" for a catcher's gear.

RED RUFFING (Hall of Fame, 1967)

Ruffing's trade from the Red Sox to the Yankees in May 1930 hardly looked like a steal at the time; as it turned out, the deal became the last of New York's raids in New England for future Hall of Famers.

In slightly more than six seasons for Boston Ruffing compiled a record of 39–96, leading the AL in losses twice and getting his ERA as low as 3.89 only once. After moving to the Bronx he became the staff ace through the 1930s, winning 20 games four years in a row (1936–39), leading the league in wins, winning percentage, strikeouts, and shutouts once each. He also racked up seven World Series wins. Originally a power-hitting outfielder, Ruffing turned to pitching after he lost four toes in a mining accident; he didn't lose his ability with a bat, though, averaging .269 with 36 home runs during his career. His 273 RBIs are the most by any pitcher.

VERN RUHLE

Ruhle was the protagonist of what should have been the only triple play in a League Championship Series. Pitching for the Astros in the fourth game of the 1980 Series against the Phillies, the righthander speared a soft liner and threw to first base to complete what appeared to be a double play. Philadelphia manager Dallas Green protested that the ball had been trapped, and during an ensuing argument Houston first baseman Art Howe realized that nobody had called time, so he grabbed the ball and stepped on second to catch another Phillies runner who had wandered away. To resolve the confusion umpire crew chief Doug Harvey consulted with NL president Chub Feeney who, ignoring the fact that Howe had been right about no time having been called, ruled a double play only and sent the Philadelphia runner back to second.

JACOB RUPPERT

Millionaire socialite and brewer Ruppert bought half-interest in the Yankees in January 1915 as a promotional stunt. His main objective was to rename the club the Knickerbockers after his brewery's best selling product. Although daily newspapers scotched that plan because the name was too long for headline writers, he would remain synonymous with Yankees ownership until George Steinbrenner came along.

Ruppert and his partner Cap Huston had tried separately to buy the Giants before being brought together on the Yankees deal by John McGraw, manager of the NL team. They spent money freely, most of it going to the Red Sox for established Boston players, but they differed over just about everything else except their loathing of American League president Ban Johnson. When they tangled with Johnson over the right to purchase suspended pitcher Carl

Mays from the Red Sox in 1919, they helped reshape the governance of baseball by breaking the executive's dictatorial control over the league and clearing the way to the election of Kenesaw Landis as commissioner.

The appointment of Miller Huggins as manager in 1918 triggered irreparable tensions in the Yankees boardroom, with the partners sniping at each other until Huston sold out in 1923. Ruppert's cable to the team at the time—declaring "I am now sole owner of the Yankees. Miller Huggins is my manager,"—should have served as a warning to Babe Ruth and other anti-Huggins players on the team, but it wasn't a particularly effective one. The only thing more predictable than clubhouse groaning about Huggins's iron-fisted methods was Ruppert's support of the pilot. After being slapped with a suspension and a $5,000 fine by Huggins in 1925, for instance, Ruth showed up at the owner's office with a him-or-me ultimatum, only to be chastened by another "Huggins is in absolute command" speech.

Ruppert's most lasting contribution to the franchise was the construction of Yankee Stadium in 1923. As early as 1919, he and Huston had approached Giants owner (and Yankees landlord) Charles Stoneham with a proposal that both teams abandon the Polo Grounds and build a new 100,000-seat facility. Instead, Stoneham, irritated that Ruth was making the Yankees more of a draw in the Giants park than the NL team, sent one signal after another that he wanted Ruppert out. Matters came to a head in 1922 when Johnson, with little to do since Landis's election except plot against his enemies, sought to buy the Yankees Polo Grounds lease with the intention of leaving them with nowhere to play in 1923. Stoneham didn't go that far, but he proved to be more effective in serving notice of another huge rent increase if the Yankees wanted to sign another annually renewable lease. It was at that point that Ruppert gave the green light for building to begin on the Bronx site he had purchased some time before. Yankee Stadium opened on April 18, 1923, with New York defeating Boston, 4–1, on the strength of a Ruth three-run home run.

Leaving front office matters up to general manager Ed Barrow and dugout affairs to Huggins and then Joe McCarthy, Ruppert presided over the first 10 Yankees pennants and seven world championships during his 24-year tenure. The honorary colonel died on January 13, 1939, at the age of 71. A bachelor, he bequeathed the baseball portion of his $100 million estate to two nieces and to Helen Winthrope Weyant, a chorus girl whose name had never surfaced publicly before.

AMOS RUSIE (Hall of Fame, 1977)

Known as The Hoosier Thunderbolt for his fastball, Rusie has often been credited with being responsible for the moving of the mound back from 50 to 60 feet, six inches in 1893. At the very least he was the hurler who, taking advantage of newly licensed overhand pitching, so dominated hitters that officialdom deemed it necessary to take steps to restore the balance between pitching and hitting.

Rusie spent eight of his 10 big league seasons between 1889 and 1901 with the Giants, arriving in and departing in wily deals engineered by John T. Brush. As a Giant he posted four consecutive 30-win seasons (1891–94) on his way to 246 career victories; he also led the NL in ERA twice and in strikeouts five times. Just as conspicuous were his five straight years (1890–94) of issuing the most walks, establishing along the way the modern single-season record of 218 free passes in the first year of the new pitching distance.

As contentious in salary negotiations as he was formidable on the hill, the righthanded Rusie was a frequent holdout, sitting out the entire 1896 season over a $200 fine and suing Giants owner Andrew Freedman for $5,000 in a case that wasn't resolved until other league owners chipped in for a $3,000 settlement lest the fractious issue of the reserve clause be raised in a courtroom.

Brush had Rusie going, coming—and going again. After his 1889 rookie season with Indianapolis, the hurler became part of a package put together by the executive (then the Hoosiers owner) to shore up the Giants in their war against the Players League; Brush's reward for essentially liquidating his franchise was a promissory note that soon became a part interest in the New York club. By 1900, now running Cincinnati, Brush reacquired Rusie from the Giants in exchange for Christy Mathewson. It was one of the worst trades in baseball history, but not for Brush: He already knew he was about to go back to the Giants as the franchise's majority partner, so he not only sent ahead the man who would win 373 games, but also cleared his horizon of somebody who had proven to be a constant thorn to ownership. With the Reds in 1901, Rusie lost his only decision.

BILL RUSSELL

Converted from the outfield, Russell ended up plugging the Dodgers hole at shortstop throughout the 1970s and well into the 1980s. He also ended up plugging his share of spectators behind first base with an arm that contributed to the league lead in errors twice and to at least 29 miscues in eight seasons. Although never directly involved in any of the drug scandals of the period, Russell became attached to the issue when the Dodgers offered him a 1985 contract that stipulated regular urine tests. Los Angeles had to cancel the clause under pressure from the Players Association that it violated player-owner understandings about dealing with drug addicts.

When he was fired in 1998 after about two years as Dodgers manager, Russell became the first franchise pilot to get the boot in the middle of the season since Billy Barnie in Brooklyn exactly 100 years before.

WILLIAM RUSSELL

In partnership with Boston publishers Louis and George Page, Russell, a New York attorney, bought the Braves in 1910; what ensued was 11 months of hell. Bickering constantly with the Pages over on-field and off-field decisions, he ceded to the strain, dying of a heart attack in November 1911. During his tenure the team was sometimes called the Rustlers.

BABE RUTH (Hall of Fame, 1936)

The best and most influential player of his time, Ruth scaled dizzying statistical heights, and did it with a flair that brought the adjective "Ruthian" into the language. His feats at the plate compelled changes in equipment, style, strategy, and salaries, altering the game forever in each of these areas. The circumstances around his departure from Boston for New York in 1920 shifted the destinies of both franchises, in the process seeding both one of the sport's great rivalries and one of its great myths. As undisciplined in his personal life as he was talented on a professional level, his Rabelaisian personality provided the final ingredients for a legend that transcended baseball.

Although it was his unexcelled hitting that eventually elevated him to stardom, Ruth began as a pitcher. Joining the Red Sox from the International League Baltimore Orioles late in the 1914 season, he quickly became the best southpaw in the American League, winning 65 times in his first three full years and leading the league in ERA in 1916. In the course of winning three World Series games (with no losses) in 1916 and 1918, he shaped an ERA of 0.87 around 29 scoreless innings in a row—a record that stood for 42 years. He later pitched five games for the Yankees, all victories, for a career record of 94–46.

Initially reluctant to alter Ruth's role, Boston manager Ed Barrow finally capitulated before the importunings of team captain Harry Hooper and others in 1918 to get the pitcher's already potent bat (a .325 average in 1917) in the lineup more often. Patterning his batting stance after that of White Sox star Joe Jackson, Ruth moved to the outfield (and, on occasion, first base) between starts, averaged .300, and hinted at what was to come by leading the AL in home runs (11), slugging (.555), and strikeouts (58) while compiling a mound record of 13–7 (2.22). Appearing as a position player regularly for the first time in 1919, the lefty swinger rose to .322, slugged .657 (leading the league for the second of seven consecutive times and of 13 seasons overall), paced the league in RBIs for the first of six times and in runs scored for the first of eight times, and established a major league record with his 29 homers. He also pitched frequently enough to win nine games while losing only five.

By then the Ruth persona was firmly established. On June 23, 1917, he was ejected for assaulting umpire Brick Owens, who had called a base on balls on opposing Washington's first batter (the ouster led to a 26-batter "perfect game" by reliever Ernie Shore). That July he jumped the team in a dispute over whether he should stay in the starting rotation, threatening to play in an industrial league rather than return to the Red Sox. Habitually disregarding training rules, he came close to a fist fight with Barrow in 1919. In both 1918 and 1919 he held out, successfully enough in the latter year to end up with a bigger contract than anybody except Ty Cobb.

On January 3, 1920 Boston owner Harry Frazee, trying to make up for losses in his Broadway theatrical productions, sold Ruth to the Yankees for $100,000 (double the highest previous amount paid for a player), plus a $300,000 loan secured by a mortgage on Fenway Park. The sale eventually gained the aura of a curse on the New England franchise that has lasted into the new century; more tangibly, it marked the beginning of both the Yankees dynasty and of baseball's live ball era.

Over the next 15 seasons with New York Ruth not only rewrote the baseball record book in a way that exhausted superlatives but also redefined the game itself. In 1920 he broke his own home run mark by clouting an eye-popping 54, eclipsed that with 59 in 1921, then slugged 60 in 1927 to create a threshold that would not be crossed until 1961 by Roger Maris. He topped the league in home runs a record 12 times, swatted 40 or more 11 times, and averaged more than 50 a year between 1926 and 1931. Seventy years later, despite juiced up balls and all the other factors behind accelerated home run rates, he had still left the park (714 times) more than anyone except Hank Aaron.

Even if Ruth didn't actually call his home run in the third game of the 1932 World Series against the Cubs (as contended by New York *World-Telegram* writer Joe Williams and maintained for six decades by teammate Joe Sewell), he would have had a reasonable shot at being right if he had; topped only by Mark McGwire, he reached the seats eight-and-a-half times per 100 at bats. His one-year slugging and walks numbers have also survived as AL standards (and were all of baseball's until Barry Bonds's 2001 season). So has his career walks total (passed only by Rickie Henderson, also in 2001). His career slugging mark of .690, however, stands unchallenged. Even his sometimes romantically observed strikeouts bear scrutiny: Unlike the free-swinging power hitters who followed him, he never whiffed 100 times in a season, always making enough contact to compile a .342 career average.

The Bambino's home run totals become even more impressive in context. When he reached the fences 29 times in 1919, the next highest total was Gavvy Cravath's NL high of 12, while the *team* high was the Yankees 45. When he popped 54 in 1920, the runnerup was George Sisler with 19; moreover, Ruth's personal total that year was higher than that of every big league club except the Phillies, and represented almost one of every nine homers hit. Earning the sobriquet of The Sultan of Swat, he broke Roger Connor's career mark of 138 round-trippers in 1921, reached 700 in 1934 (when only two other players had as many as 300), and could point to his final 714 as more than twice as many as the runnerup.

Ruth appeared in 10 World Series, seven of them for New York. In the 1923 and 1928 games he put together slugging averages of at least 1.000. In both 1926 and 1928 he had three-homer games. On the other hand, he suffered two of his most embarrassing

moments in Series play: getting thrown out trying to steal second by St. Louis catcher Bob O'Farrell for the final out of the 1926 Series and fanning on a quick pitch from Bill Sherdel of the Cardinals in 1928.

Ruth's prodigious slugging not only allowed him to tower over the game; it also changed the sport in substantive ways. The unprecedented one million fans who flocked to Yankees games in the Polo Grounds in 1920 suggested to owners that they were better off serving up offense and more offense. If the spitball had already been discouraged because of the Spanish flu epidemic after World War I, it and other doctored pitches soon found themselves on the permanently banned list so batters could have an easier time bringing people through turnstiles. The adoption of a livelier ball and the strategic abandonment of one-run-at-a-time baseball were translated into radical statistical leaps. The overall big league batting average of .250 in the teens, for example, jumped to almost .285 in 1921. The number of runs scored annually in the two leagues rose from fewer than 9,000 in the teens to almost 12,000 in the 1920s, up to more than 13,000 in 1930. In emulation of Ruth, hitters switched to longer, heavier, and thinner-handled bats.

If only by a trickle-down effect, Ruth also altered baseball's salary structure. It cost New York owners Jacob Ruppert and Cap Huston $41,000 to sign him for the 1920 and 1921 seasons. In 1922 he accepted a five-year contract calling for the then-unheard-of annual salary of $52,000 because, as he told reporters, "I always wanted to make a grand a week." The amount rose to $70,000 with a three-year pact in 1927, then to $80,000 with another three-year deal in 1930. (It was after signing the latter contract that he was reportedly told he was earning more than President Herbert Hoover and allegedly replied: "Why not? I had a better year than he did.") In addition, he made large amounts of money from endorsements, barnstorming, movies, and vaudeville shows. After Ruth's retirement in 1935, the highest salary in the game belonged to Lou Gehrig, who was making $30,000, but even that had been a previously fanciful plateau. Ruth's wages so helped jack up salaries across the board that teammate Waite Hoyt insisted decades later that every ballplayer and his family owed thanks for Ruth's existence.

Besides conquering new heights in power hitting and income, Ruth set standards for intransigence and intemperance. His problems with baseball authorities were at their worst in 1921 and 1925. No sooner had the 1921 World Series ended than he found himself in trouble with Commissioner Kenesaw Landis for flouting an old rule prohibiting Series participants from barnstorming. Although the trip was canceled because of poor attendance after only a few days, and Ruth accepted a $3,000-a-week offer to hit the vaudeville circuit, an incensed Landis suspended the slugger and teammate Bob Meusel for the first month of the 1922 season. Even before serving the sentence, Ruth ran afoul of the commissioner again. The distractions of training in New Orleans proved so compelling that even the usually compliant sportswriters of the day began filing stories about the team's, and especially Ruth's, partying. One dispatch, headlined "Yankees Training on Scotch," led Ruppert and Huston to hire a detective, who ingratiated himself with the players and persuaded Ruth and other Yankees to attend a party at a Joliet, Illinois brewery and to pose for a group picture. The incriminating evidence found its way to Landis, who invaded the New York clubhouse to issue admonitions about cavorting with bootleggers. After getting back into uniform, Ruth climbed into the stands on May 25 to go after a heckling fan and was fined $25, suspended for a game, and forced to give up his title as Yankees captain. On June 19 he drew another three-day suspension for protesting a call by umpire Bill Dinneen too strenuously, then had two days tacked on to the penalty when he went after the arbiter the next day.

Ruth's appetite for willing women, fast cars, and huge quantities of food and alcohol was protean. In 1920 outfielder Ping Bodie, nominally a roommate, observed that he mainly shared hotel accommodations with the star's suitcase. But on the way north from spring training before the 1925 season, the carousing exacted a price. Saying he felt ill, the 270-pound outfielder got off the team train in Asheville, North Carolina, and collapsed. Hustled back onto the train, he passed out again, this time cracking open his head. Reports of his death appeared as far away as London even as management was announcing that he was undergoing emergency abdominal surgery. Reporters and others around the team suspected that Ruth's ailment was the result not of the immediately rumored food and liquor, but of his third excess: women. Speculation about which combination of venereal diseases he had contracted reached

Ruthian proportions, but the postoperative scar he carried was undeniably abdominal.

Ruth's illness, which kept him out of the lineup until June 1, won him no sympathy from Miller Huggins. On the contrary, his unaltered habits during his recuperation and after returning to the lineup only increased the manager's irritation. Huggins continued to seethe when Ruth stayed out all night on a trip to Cleveland and even when he twice ignored signs from the bench—first bunting when he had been told to swing away, then swinging away when he had been told to sacrifice. The breaking point came on August 29, when Ruth showed up late for a game in St. Louis; acting with the prior approval of Ruppert and general manager Ed Barrow, Huggins slapped Ruth with a $5,000 fine, the largest in history up to that time, and suspended him indefinitely. The furious Ruth responded by laying the blame for the team's languishing in seventh place on Huggins and announced through the press that "either he quits or I quit." Returning to New York, he was confident his ultimatum would carry the day but was sorely disillusioned: In a closed-doors session with Ruppert, the owner underlined his support for Huggins. Whatever else was said to him, Ruth emerged from the meeting to apologize to the manager before the entire team, never again challenging Huggins's authority in public.

Thwarted by Ruppert in his desire to succeed Huggins, who died toward the end of the 1929 season, Ruth deeply resented the appointment of pitcher Bob Shawkey as the new manager; he was just as bitter in 1931 when Shawkey was jettisoned for Joe McCarthy. For his part, McCarthy bided his time, let Ruth pick his spots to play, and ignored his casual violations of the rules. Ruppert and Barrow had no such compunction: They cut the aging slugger's salary to $52,000 in 1933, then again to $35,000 the following year. Ruth himself forced the issue of his future when, following the 1934 campaign, he virtually demanded McCarthy be fired and he be given the manager's job. The brass rejected the demand, even after McCarthy had offered to resign; instead, Ruppert proposed that Ruth take the piloting job with the Yankees top farm club in Newark. When Ruth refused, the owner and Barrow felt free to orchestrate a deal that sent him to the Braves in a position the outfielder was led to believe would carry front office responsibilities and eventually control of the dugout, but that Ruppert knew was mere window dressing.

It took Ruth only a couple of weeks into the season to realize he was back in Boston only as a drawing card for the last-place Braves. On May 25, in a contest against the Pirates, he summoned up what was left of his hitting prowess and clouted three home runs and a single to drive in six runs. After striking out three times facing Cincinnati's Syl Johnson in a subsequent game and a final plate appearance against the Phillies, he retired on June 2.

In 1938 Ruth signed on as a coach with Brooklyn under circumstances similar to those of the Boston fiasco—this time being regarded as a drawing card even just for batting practice. The relationship with Brooklyn ended bitterly when, despite his own illusions about eventually succeeding Burleigh Grimes as the manager, he was ignored for Leo Durocher, a one-time roommate with the Yankees.

The Ruth legend transcended baseball: Japanese soldiers fighting in the Pacific during World War II, for instance, taunted their American enemies by shouting out "Fuck Babe Ruth!" Learned essays have been written about how he was the benign American alternative to the demagogic winds blowing around the globe in the 1920s; i.e., cheering on the Babe instead of Mussolini or Hitler. If the King Kellys and Hal Chases had been local icons for a few years, he and John L. Sullivan were seminal figures in creating national sports celebrities. And then, of course, there was also the mythic detail about his purported affection for children. In fact, Ruth did call on sick children in hospitals, the most noted episode being the speedy recovery of a suburban New Jersey boy named Jimmy Sylvester following such a visit. It was equally true—and equally typical—that a year later Ruth had no recollection of the event.

JIMMY RYAN

Ryan's clubhouse needling proved the undoing of two Chicago managers in the 1890s. With Cap Anson, the japes were calculated to undermine the longtime pilot's authority (and were eventually successful). But Anson's successor, Tom Burns, was an unintended victim. When the new manager appointed Ryan team captain for the 1898 season, players who had also come in for the outfielder's sarcasm objected to the move, warning that they would sit out the season opener at Louisville if Burns didn't give

the job to Bill Lange, instead. Burns ceded before the clubhouse pressure, thereby losing his authority over the club and insuring that he would last only a couple of seasons.

Ryan was also the first player ever given an intentional walk. In an 1896 contest the Giants, ahead at the time by four runs, walked him with the bases loaded to get at the next batter, the relatively weaker hitter George Decker. Decker struck out.

JOHNNY RYAN

Ordinarily an outfielder, Ryan took to the mound once for Louisville in 1876—long enough to establish himself as the original Wild Thing. In eight innings of relief work on July 22 he yielded 22 hits—and threw a never-topped 10 wild pitches.

NOLAN RYAN (Hall of Fame, 1999)

Starting with his unprecedented 27 years (1966, 1968–93) as an active major leaguer, Ryan tore up the record books with his career. Equally significant, until injuries plagued him over the last couple of seasons, his compilation marks were not merely the result of a pitcher hanging on with accommodating franchises, but reflected a craftsman still regarded well into his 40s as a staff anchor. The righthander attributed both his endurance and his performance to the training methods of the Mets farm system in the 1960s and to his own rigorous daily exercises, which left him few idle moments around a ballpark. Still another factor was Ryan's flexibility—evolving from a strict fastballer with only an approximate notion of the strike zone, to a fastballer with a masterly curve, to an occasional spitballer and headhunter whose reputation afforded him unusual protection from umpires. In the latter connection, White Sox third baseman Robin Ventura gained suddenly undammed vocal support from players around the league in 1993 when he charged Ryan on the mound after taking a pitch too close to the skull. Although most coverage of the ensuing melee centered on the 46-year-old's ability to use his fists, the incident also made it obvious that many hitters resented what they considered a separate set of umpiring rules for the hurler.

Ryan's numbers were endless. By the time he had taken off his Texas uniform for the last time after the 1993 season, he had squirreled away the records for most strikeouts (5,714), most no-hitters (seven), and most consecutive starts (595). Along with these peaks went such other marks as most walks yielded (2,795) and most grand slams surrendered (10). On a seasonal basis, he set the modern standard with 383 whiffs while pitching for the Angels in 1973—one of 11 seasons in which he led in that category. He also led in shutouts three times and earned run average twice. What might have been his most overpowering performance of all took place within an eight-day period in 1972, when he ripped off three wins for California by fanning 15 Rangers, 16 Red Sox, and 16 Athletics. Two years later he had his highest strikeout game against Boston, notching 19. His seven no-hitters broke down into four for the Angels (two in 1973 and one each in 1974 and 1975), one for the Astros (1981), and two for the Rangers (1990 and 1991).

Ryan critics, who grew thinner on the ground as he returned to the hill year after year, usually jumped on the fact that he won 20 games only twice (for California in 1973 and 1974), normally had a won-lost mark hovering near .500 (324–292 overall), and topped the league in walks eight times. Overlooked was the fact that he was almost always the ace on mediocre teams. He made his only World Series appearance as a young reliever with the 1969 Mets, and totaled only six games in League Championship Series. More striking, he never won a Cy Young Award.

Over his career the righthander was at the center of several notable front office and clubhouse incidents. His trade from New York to California for third baseman Jim Fregosi during the 1971–72 off-season is routinely cited as one of the worst in baseball history. In 1977 he came back to haunt the Mets a second time with reports that his higher salary with the Angels had become a bone of contention between Tom Seaver and the New York ownership; Seaver not only denounced the claim by *Daily News* columnist Dick Young, but, suspecting it had been inspired by the front office, demanded the trade that landed him in Cincinnati. While with the Angels, Ryan accused southpaw Frank Tanana of compromising his training by living it up so hectically between starts that the team couldn't adopt the four-man rotation that would make both of them more effective. Tanana's retort was that a four-man rotation had given him a sore arm and that the club was ruining its entire pitching staff to accommodate Ryan.

In 1981 Ryan became the first $1 million pitcher in signing a four-year contract with the Astros worth $4.5 million. In 1989 he signed a $2 million free agent deal with the Rangers. As with the earlier pact with Houston, the team more than made up for the outlay with the crowds drawn for every Ryan appearance to see if he would pitch another no-hitter, break a new strikeout record, or simply pass another of the milestones he had established.

S

FRED SAIGH

Saigh got into baseball by buying the Cardinals from Sam Breadon at the end of the 1947 season; he got out of it by going to prison. When he took over the club, the lawyer was partnered with Robert Hannegan, one-time U.S. Postmaster General and an intimate of Roosevelt Democrats. With Hannegan's death in 1948 Saigh moved quickly (and ruthlessly, in the opinion of many) to buy up the rest of the franchise from his widow. His most prominent act as owner-president-general manager was to lead the move for dumping Commissioner Happy Chandler after the 1950 season. His peeves against Chandler were that the commissioner had allowed racial integration and had denied a request for the Cardinals to play summer home games in the evening because of St. Louis's intense heat.

Two years after getting rid of Chandler, Saigh was charged with federal income tax evasion. Accepting the advice of his attorneys, he pleaded *nolo contendere* with the understanding that he would be given only a heavy fine and suspended sentence. But when sentencing came due, the judge who had agreed to the deal had been replaced by a hard-liner, who sentenced the owner to 15 months in jail. There was considerable thought that the bench switch was the work of politicians who had never forgiven Saigh for his reputed hustling of Hannegan's widow. Chandler loyalists then got in their innings by blocking Saigh's attempt to sell the Cardinals to a group in Milwaukee. Facing his imprisonment and needing money urgently to pay off his back taxes, he was ultimately forced to sell out to the Anheuser-Busch brewery for a lower price than that offered by the Milwaukee interests.

JOHNNY SAIN

As good as he was as a pitcher in the post-World War II years, Sain became equally controversial as a pitching coach between the late 1950s and mid-1980s. Although numerous hurlers credited him with turning around their careers, almost as many managers and general managers came to resent him for his autonomous hold over a succession of mound staffs, for his endorsement of four-man rotations and disparagement of the value of making pitchers run, for his reliably acerbic views of the organization he was working for, and for his occasional pointers on how players should approach contract negotiations. The result was a nomadic coaching career that included the (Kansas City) Athletics, Yankees, Twins, Tigers, White Sox, and two stops with the Braves. Through it all he tutored 17 pitchers into 20-win seasons for the first time in their careers.

The righthander Sain was the main reason for the Braves 1948 pennant—one of three straight 20-win years. There were, however, two asterisks to the noted evaluation of the 1948 squad's starting rotation as "Spahn, Sain, and pray for rain." For one thing, it was Sain, not the future Hall of Famer Warren Spahn, who fashioned Boston's key wins down the stretch; for another, manager Billy Southworth didn't bother with any prayers over the final three weeks, sending out his two aces just about every day between September 6 and September 27.

LENN SAKATA

Utility infielder Sakata occasioned one of the most bizarre innings in major league history. On August 24, 1983 he was pressed into service as a catcher for the Orioles in an extra-inning game against the Blue Jays when only 1 1/2 games separated the teams at the top of the East Division. Toronto's first batter in the 10th inning singled off reliever Tippy Martinez and, with no fear of Sakata's arm, took a huge lead off first base; he was promptly picked off by Martinez. The second batter did exactly the same thing, and was also picked off by the Baltimore southpaw. The third batter, figuring he must have at least had the odds on his side, followed suit—and was also caught napping by the reliever. Sakata later hit a home run to win the game, effectively ending Toronto's challenge for the division flag.

SLIM SALLEE

Taking a pitch wasn't in the cards against Sallee. In 1919 the Reds righthander set the mark for bat contact by walking only 20 and striking out merely 24 over 227 2/3 innings. He knew what he was doing, though, since he went 21–7 (2.09) in leading Cincinnati to a National League pennant and its fateful encounter with the White Sox in the World Series. What made the low walk and strikeout figures particularly striking was that, in pitching for the Cardinals earlier in his career, Sallee surrendered enough free passes to post one of the league's highest on-base-percentage-against ratios. An even greater problem over his 14-year (1908–21) career was the bottle, which kept him on the move between the Reds and the Giants. It was Sallee who acknowledged on the eve of the Black Sox Series that he too had been approached by gamblers sniffing around to see if Cincinnati was willing to throw the games.

JUAN SAMUEL

Samuel's defensive and contact limitations seemed secondary when he burst on the scene for the Phillies in the 1980s as the only player to reach double figures in each of his first four years in doubles, triples, home runs, and steals. But his four consecutive seasons of leading the league in strikeouts (including the rookie record of 168 in 1984) and leaden glove at both second base and in the outfield came to the fore after he was traded to the Mets in 1989. He was soon bouncing around from one team to another in the 1990s, rarely reaching double figures in any of the categories.

RYNE SANDBERG

When Sandberg retired for good in 1997, he did so with the highest fielding average (.989) and most home runs (277) by any second baseman in the game. Prior to Mark McGwire's withdrawal after the 2001 season, he had also held the mark for walking away from the biggest contract in major league history.

Acquired by the Cubs from the Phillies before the 1982 season, Sandberg was the People's Choice at Wrigley Field for most of the next decade. In 1984 he took National League MVP honors for pacing Chicago to an East Division title with a .314 average and the circuit's top numbers in triples and runs scored; in 1990 he led the league with his 40 home runs, the first second baseman to do it since Rogers Hornsby in the 1920s. His high fielding average wasn't because he played it safe, either, as attested to by the 10 Gold Gloves he picked up for his agility and range. For a record span of 123 games in 1989 and 1990 he didn't commit a single error.

After an injury-plagued 1993 and a slow start in 1994, Sandberg shocked Cubs fans by announcing his retirement in June, saying he had "lost his competitive edge"; at the time he still had $16 million due him on a long-term contract. Despite his own declared reasons for the move, intimates said the real trigger for the decision was the infielder's marital problems, and in fact a week later his wife filed for divorce. Sandberg stayed on the sidelines through the 1995 campaign, then announced he had missed the game, returning in 1996. Somewhat slower afoot at 37, he still made only six errors in 1,234 innings and clouted another 25 home runs. He retired for good after both his bat and glove began betraying him in 1997.

DEION SANDERS

Sanders went Bo Jackson one better by playing baseball, football, and the media *simultaneously,* but with more glitter than charm. Unlike Jackson, he also went through a few seasons in the late 1980s and early 1990s playing his baseball and football employers off against one another in a cash grab that still left him notably more petulant than those vying for his services as an outfielder or combination defensive back-punt receiver.

Already under contract to the NFL Falcons, Sanders made his first stab at baseball with the Yankees in 1989, and wasted little time rattling traditionalists.

In one game, after hitting his first big league home run, he stopped at home plate and deliberately bent over to lace up his shoes with his rear end pointed at the pitcher. In another contest he hit a lazy infield pop and immediately veered off toward the New York dugout—prompting White Sox catcher Carlton Fisk to give him an embarrassing tongue lashing in front of 20,000 fans. Although he claimed he had learned his lesson about hustling from Fisk, the Yankees cut him loose because of front office certainty he would ultimately choose football over baseball.

Instead, Sanders spent the next few years choosing both, and within the same Atlanta market. Egged on by the financial possibilities of replacing Jackson as the country's top two-sports star, he waged a series of contract battles with the Braves that made it impossible for the club to count on him once the football season began. In 1992 he enraged manager Bobby Cox by playing for the Falcons in the afternoon and then, trailed by CBS cameras, returning to suit up for the Braves for a night LCS game against the Pirates; although Cox had ample opportunity to make Sanders the first player ever to perform in two professional sports on the same day, he deliberately kept the outfielder on the bench. When announcer Tim McCarver denounced the publicity ploy on the air, Sanders responded by attacking him with ice water three times during Atlanta's clubhouse celebrations after defeating Pittsburgh. He was let off with a laughable fine by NL president Bill White.

By 1994 Sanders, known as Neon Deion for the ropes of gold jewelry habitually around his neck, seemed to have settled in as Atlanta's leadoff hitter, but in May the Braves suddenly traded him to Cincinnati for Roberto Kelly. The transaction followed complaints that he wasn't a team player, other Braves protesting especially about his absence from promotional events obligatory for the rest of the club. The lefty-swinging speedster spent a few years going back and forth between baseball and football, making his biggest mark with 56 stolen bases for the 1997 Reds. He then concentrated on the NFL for a few years, until, after retiring from football, he tried a brief (and unsuccessful) comeback with Cincinnati in 2001.

RON SANTO

Following the 1974 season, Santo became the first major leaguer to insist on the recently introduced Five-and-10 rights of major league players. Stand-

ing on his more than five years with the Cubs and 10 plus in the league, he forced Chicago to cancel a completed trade with the Angels and make another deal that moved him across town to the White Sox.

EDDIE SAWYER

Sawyer managed the Whiz Kid Phillies to the pennant in 1950, but gained as much attention for the way he walked away from the team in a second tenure at the end of the decade. After piloting the club to the cellar in 1959 and seeing little improvement in spring training the following year, he waited only until an Opening Day loss before announcing his resignation. "I'm 49," he told reporters, "and I want to live to be 50."

When he took over as Philadelphia's manager the first time in 1948, Sawyer brought along his practice of counting the pitches of his starters—the first known instance of what would become de rigueur for all clubs near the end of the century.

PAT SCANTLEBURY

When he joined Cincinnati in 1956, Scantlebury became the last player to reach the majors from the Negro leagues. Already 39, the lefthanded pitcher lost his only decision.

AL SCHACHT

Schacht dubbed himself The Clown Prince of Baseball for a pregame act of pantomime and anecdotes, but he was more like one of The Sunshine Boys. A pitcher who brought himself to the attention of Clark Griffith by sending the Senators owner clippings of his minor league victories with exhortations to "get this guy," signing himself "A fan," he eventually went 14–10 over three seasons with Washington. When he wasn't sitting around or coaching as one of the members of the Griffith inner circle, he and Nick Altrock were partners in on-field comedy routines like The Near-Sighted Pitcher before games. They did their act for more than 12 years—the last eight of them in resentful silence because of an Altrock anti-Semitic crack directed at Schacht.

In later years Max Patkin, a one-time minor league pitcher, also dubbed himself The Clown Prince of Baseball in a pregame act inspired by Schacht. Thanks to his appearances in movies and on television, Patkin became even more identified with the comedy form than Schacht or Altrock.

GERMANY SCHAEFFER

Because of a story that he once stole first base, Schaefer is usually credited with a rule specifying that runners will be out if they run the bases in reverse order. The trouble with the tale is that no one has been able to pin down exactly when the Tigers second baseman pulled off the bizarre theft. One version has him playing against the Indians in 1908, stealing second successfully as the front part of an intended double steal, but then having to go back to steal first because the Cleveland backstop didn't fall for the ruse to get a runner home from third. At that point, as the tale goes, he stole second again, this time drawing the throw and getting Detroit its run. Another version says it happened in 1911, when Schaefer was with the White Sox playing the Senators. According to this variant, the Senators catcher watched the infielder steal second, first, and then second again without ever being lured into going after him. The rule about not running the bases in reverse order was not introduced until 1920, a year after Schaefer's retirement.

RAY SCHALK (Hall of Fame, 1955)

Schalk's .253 batting average, the lowest by any Hall of Fame position player, has put him on many people's "Why him?" list; another way of looking at it is that Ozzie Smith wasn't the first Cooperstown resident elected for his defense. It also didn't hurt the receiver's credentials that, for awhile anyway, he was the most vociferous of the Chicago players condemning their Black Sox teammates.

When he retired in 1929 after 18 years in the majors (all except a handful of games for the White Sox), Schalk held a host of defensive records for catchers; his marks for the most seasons pacing backstops in putouts (9) and fielding average (8), as well as for double plays (226) and most 20th-century assists (1,811), are still in the record book. In addition, he is the only one to have called four no-hitters, including Charlie Robertson's perfect game in 1922.

The righty swinger did the best hitting of his career (.304) in the tainted 1919 World Series against the Reds, but spent most of the fall in a fury. He got thrown out of the fifth game for pushing umpire Cy Rigler, less incensed with Rigler than with pitcher Lefty Williams for ignoring his signs and with center fielder Happy Felsch for dropping a fly ball. (He later dragged Williams aside and worked him over with his fists.) That winter Schalk dropped some un-subtle hints in an interview that a number of Chicago players would not be back with the team in 1920. Proven wrong when Williams, Felsch, and most of the others returned, he put his name to an official complaint against the Black Sox as an injured party who had been defrauded by their collusion in the fix, and celebrated with Red Faber and Dickie Kerr when an indictment was handed down by a grand jury against the so-called Eight Men Out. On the other hand, he was much less forthcoming by the time the case was heard in court in 1921, leaving an impression that owner Charles Comiskey had asked him to be a good soldier in the crisis afflicting the franchise.

Schalk later managed the White Sox for a year-and-a-half. As a rookie pilot in 1927, he expected the team to contend, but the attempted suicide of center fielder Johnny Mostil, guilt-stricken over an affair with a teammate's wife, sank the club's chances. Years later, in 1949, the death of former Chicago infielder Bill Cissell after years of bumming around prompted Schalk to help organize Baseball Anonymous, a society for assisting needy ex-major leaguers.

JACK SCHAPPERT

Although he had only one big league season, Schappert used it to become the first headhunter. The righthander was so notorious about aiming at the skulls of batters that other American Association owners persuaded St. Louis's Chris Von der Ahe to drop him after the 1882 season. With Schappert in mind, the league soon afterward decided to award hitters first base when struck by a pitch.

MABEL SCHLOEN

Schloen turned a successful career as a catcher into an equally notable one as a stage performer. Nicknamed Lefty though she threw and batted righthanded, she played in the 1920s for the semipro East Rutherford (New Jersey) Cubs, for whom she once caught Walter Johnson for three innings in a Fenway Park exhibition contest. Schloen also put on the gear for several exhibitions organized by the Eastern League Providence Grays; while in a Providence uniform, she laid down the signs for another future Hall of Famer, Rube Marquard.

When Schloen wasn't crouching behind home plate, she was hitting the vaudeville circuit in such shows as *Follies* and *Powder Puff Frolics*. Her act included comedy skits about baseball—a particular she publicized to the hilt by showing up at local afternoon games before an evening performance. In 1926 she and Johnson also attempted to reenact Gabby Street's 1908 stunt of catching a ball dropped from atop the Washington Monument. Although Washington police stopped them, she milked the situation for weeks, gaining more publicity than she would have gotten if she had been allowed to go through with the lark.

ALLIE MAY SCHMIDT

A church worker in St. Louis, Schmidt was responsible for one of baseball's most distinctive emblems. While overseeing the decorations for a February 1921 social function to which St. Louis executive Branch Rickey had been invited, she was struck by the sight of two cardinals perched on a snowy limb outside the church hall and proceeded to create cardboard cutouts of the bird for each table. Although the St. Louis team had been called the Cardinals for some years, Rickey was so taken with the cutouts that he had the bird figures added to club uniforms the following season.

HENRY SCHMIDT

Righthander Schmidt broke in with a flourish when he posted 22 wins for the 1903 Dodgers. But confessing that he didn't like pitching in the East, the native Texan then retired, making him the only pitcher to win 20 games in his lone major league season.

MIKE SCHMIDT (Hall of Fame, 1995)

Not even his status as baseball's best all-around third baseman saved Schmidt from regular catcalls from Philadelphia fans during his 18-year (1972–89) career with the Phillies. But more philosophical than such earlier boobird targets as Del Ennis and Dick Allen, the righthanded slugger gradually won over the grandstands even when he was going bad. A poll conducted after his retirement named him as the greatest player in franchise history.

Schmidt had one of the slowest starts of any Hall of Famer when he batted only .196 and struck out 136 times in 1973, his first year as a regular. But the following year he won the first of eight NL home run titles and the first of five slugging percentage crowns. Among his other conspicuous numbers were belting at least 30 homers 13 times, driving in 100 runs nine times (and leading the league four times), and drawing more than 100 walks seven times (and leading the league four times). On April 17, 1976, against the Cubs in Wrigley Field, he joined the small handful of sluggers to whack four home runs in a game. Schmidt's biggest offensive weakness was the strikeout—leading the league in that category four times, including a glaring 180 whiffs in 1975. Defensively, he was one of the first third basemen to overcome the greater precariousness of artificial turf, winning 10 Gold Gloves, turning the most double plays six times, and registering the most assists on seven occasions. Overall, he clouted 548 home runs and drove in 1,595 runs while averaging .267. He collected MVP awards in 1980, 1981, and 1986.

Aside from his inaugural season, Schmidt's roughest moments usually came in the postseason. In going only 8-for-44 (.181) in the NLCS against Cincinnati in 1976 and against Los Angeles in 1977 and 1978, he was targeted by both fans and the media as the principal reason for Philadelphia's failure to win three pennants. He was equally ineffective in the 1980 NLCS against Houston, but then won MVP honors by going 8-for-21 (.381) against Kansas City for the Phillies only world championship. Against Baltimore in the 1983 World Series he gave his worst performance of all, managing merely one single in 20 at bats.

In the clubhouse Schmidt had more than one clash with his manager. In 1976 he objected to Danny Ozark's exclusion of the veteran Tony Taylor from the postseason roster; in 1980 he figured prominently in the charges by manager Dallas Green and general manager Paul Owens that some Phillies were more interested in personal statistics than team success; and in 1983 he blasted Owens for taking it upon himself to succeed the fired Pat Corrales and then depending too much on his coaches before making any move.

RED SCHOENDIENST (Hall of Fame, 1989)

Schoendienst was a solid second baseman for 19 seasons (1945–63) whose election to Cooperstown suggested to many that the Hall of Fame had a side door. Not only was the switch-hitting slap hitter overshadowed at his position in his heyday by Jackie Robinson, but he was bested in almost every offensive category by Nellie Fox, who had to wait long years before reaching Cooperstown. His overall numbers were really those of such a contemporary as Johnny Temple.

A lifetime .289 hitter, Schoendienst had his biggest impact in 1957, when a midseason trade from the Giants to the Braves allowed him to spark Milwaukee to a pennant with a league-leading 200 hits. His best personal performance was for his original team the Cardinals in 1953, when he batted .342 and narrowly missed winning the batting championship. Despite leading off for good-hitting teams most of his career, he scored 100 runs only twice and, after a rookie season in which he led the league with 26 stolen bases, only once again ever reached double figures in thefts.

Schoendienst has no rivals for the length of time spent in a St. Louis uniform. After playing for the Cardinals for all or parts of 15 seasons, he went to the coaching lines for the club in 1963 and 1964, took over as manager for another unprecedented 12 years in 1965, then returned in 1979 for another string of 15 years as coach or emergency manager. His closest associate for decades, starting with their years together as roommates, was Stan Musial, a power on the Cooperstown Veterans Committee that tapped the second baseman for a plaque.

MARGE SCHOTT

As chief operator of the Reds between 1984 and the late 1990s, Schott was a combination of George Steinbrenner, Uriah Heep, and a racist ignoramus. Her often brutal handling of front office employees, draconian budget cutting, and casual conversational references to "niggers" and "sneaky Jews" regularly discomfited other owners for publicizing illustrations of some of their own attitudes. They all breathed a sigh of relief when, thanks to some falsified records in her automobile dealerships, they were able to throw her out of the league boardroom once and for all in October 1998.

Although she had hardly been a secret in Cincinnati beforehand, Schott gave the country its first good look at her management style in 1990, when she refused to fly Eric Davis back from California after the outfielder had lacerated his kidney making a dive on artificial turf in the World Series. By the fall of 1992 there had been enough complaints about her discriminatory hiring practices that the league had to look into them. After months of dragging their feet, the other owners decided Schott might have been guilty of "racially and ethnically insensitive language" on numerous occasions, but they resisted calls for

forcing her to sell her interest in the Reds in favor of a $25,000 fine and a slap-on-the-wrist suspension that lasted little more than 10 months. Unchastened, Schott declared in May 1994 that she didn't want any of her players to wear earrings because "only fruits wear earrings." Even an early 1993 public relations gesture of hiring Tony Perez as manager for padding over past crudenesses to Latins could barely pretend to be meaningful: first, because Cincinnati simultaneously hired a host of former managers (Davey Johnson, Jack McKeon, Bobby Valentine) to look over the new pilot's shoulder; second, because Perez was fired only weeks into the season.

Over the next few years Schott stripped her general manager of his seat at Riverfront Stadium so she could sell it to the general public; insisted that players cavort with her pet dog Schottzie before games; cut back on training room and medical supplies to the point that the club physician quit; said she "felt cheated" when umpire John McSherry's on-field heart attack on Opening Day in 1996 forced postponement of the game; told an ESPN interviewer that same year that "Hitler was good at the beginning" but "went too far"; and resisted even minimal decorations for the exquisitely institutional Riverfront Stadium because they would have cost money. In the wake of the remarks about Hitler and other pearls about blacks and Jews NL owners felt compelled to move again, this time forcing her to surrender day-to-day control of the team until 1998. When she continued to interfere in the decisions of John Allen, installed as the chief operating officer of the franchise, she was even barred for awhile from the ballpark. With news of the hanky-panky at her GM dealerships the league had the *deus ex machina* it needed to compel Schott to sell out.

PAUL SCHREIBER

Nobody waited for a second cup of coffee longer than Schreiber. A righthander who appeared in 10 games for the 1922 and 1923 Dodgers, he made his next major league appearance with the Yankees an astonishing 22 years later, in 1945. After adding two games to his résumé, he retired for good without ever having won or lost.

CAREY SCHUELER

The daughter of White Sox general manager Ron, Schueler has been the only woman selected in baseball's amateur draft. A basketball and baseball star at Campolindo High School in Moraga, California, the southpaw pitcher was selected in the 43rd round by her father's club in 1993. She chose to play basketball at DePaul University instead.

JOHN SCHUERHOLZ

Successful as he has been as an engineer of Atlanta's domination of National League division races since the early 1990s, Schuerholz has owed more of it to an ability to throw big money at free agents than to any unique trading skills. Since taking over from Bobby Cox as the Braves general manager in 1991, his greatest coups have come in the signing of stars such as Terry Pendleton, Greg Maddux, Andres Galarraga, and Brian Jordan with Ted Turner's financing. On the other hand, his most significant pickups in the trade market through the 2001 season were two fire sale acquisitions—Fred McGriff from San Diego in 1993 and Denny Neagle from Pittsburgh in 1996. The overwhelming majority of his other trade imports (Reggie Sanders, Kenny Lofton, Bret Boone, Quilvio Veras, among the more prominent) labored through mediocre Atlanta seasons before being released or going elsewhere to revive their careers. At the same time, the Atlanta players dealt for these turnstile acquisitions have included Ryan Klesko, David Justice, and Jermaine Dye. Schuerholz didn't have much better luck at his former post as Kansas City general manager. Among those he swapped away there in exchange for little or nothing were future 20-game winners David Cone and Danny Jackson.

HERB SCORE

The Gil McDougald line drive that struck Score in the face on May 7, 1957 may have been one of the goriest moments on a major league field, but that didn't end the Cleveland southpaw's big league career; a less dramatic torn elbow tendon the next year did. After winning 16 games and leading the league in strikeouts with an AL rookie record of 245 in 1955, Score came back the following season to notch 20 wins and raise his strikeout count to 263. Then came the McDougald liner at Municipal Stadium that left him blind in one eye for hours and the sudden elbow pain in a game against Washington the next year. Over his last five years with the Indians and White Sox Score managed a record of only 17–26.

FRANK SCOTT

A traveling secretary for the Yankees in the late 1940s, Scott doubled as baseball's first player agent. Although he never got involved in team contract negotiations, he represented the game's biggest stars (Joe DiMaggio, Willie Mays, Yogi Berra, Hank Aaron, among them) in their off-field activities, paving the way for cash payments for personal appearances at card shows and other events.

MIKE SCOTT

Scott was pitching guru Roger Craig's prime pupil in learning the split-finger fastball; the pitch transformed him from a so-so righthander to the ace of Houston's pitching staff in the second half of the 1980s. On September 25, 1986 Scott clinched a West Division title for the Astros by no-hitting the Giants—the only time a no-hitter has decided a division or pennant race.

VIN SCULLY

Even longer than the O'Malley bloodline, sportscaster Scully has been the most prominent continuum for the Dodgers from Brooklyn to Los Angeles. A Red Barber protégé when he first occupied an Ebbets Field broadcasting booth in 1950, his mellifluous play-by-play on the radio has come in particularly handy before protests over the team's limited television coverage on the West Coast; a poll conducted in the early 1990s among Dodgers fans named him as the most valuable member of the franchise. Scully's one-time television work for network games didn't always gain as much enthusiasm; aside from a fairly patronizing tone toward clubs he didn't see on a regular basis, he lent himself too easily to the "theme" mania imposed on given games before they were actually played. His worst moment in this regard came in the 1986 World Series, when Mets and Red Sox fans took turns accusing him of being slanted against their team. In fact, Scully was preoccupied trying to shoehorn in the network's preestablished motif of the moment (an imminent New York loss, an imminent Boston loss, a comeback New York win) without especially alert concern for the contradictions unfolding in front of him. He only made matters worse by claiming, after decades of working for the O'Malleys and the Dodgers, that he has never had a personal interest in the outcome of a game.

TOM SEATS

Seats was a southpaw for the 1945 Dodgers who was able to make his starts only after being fed liquor by manager Leo Durocher. When the teetotaling Branch Rickey found out about Durocher's cure for the pitcher's nerves, he got rid of Seats despite the lefty's second-best-on-the-staff 10 victories.

TOM SEAVER (Hall of Fame, 1993)

The most popular pitcher ever to toe a slab in New York, Seaver still had an unusually stormy relationship with the team with which he was associated for most of his career as The Franchise. When he wasn't leaving the Mets in one of the most emotion-wracked trades in baseball history, he was leaving them because they hadn't protected him in suspicious circumstances against the compensation pool draft or not joining them in favor of broadcasting for the Yankees. Two of the righthander's most significant diamond moments—hurling his only no-hitter and notching his 300th win—took place when he was pitching for other teams.

Seaver's 20-year career began with Rookie of the Year honors for his 16 victories and 2.76 ERA for New York in 1967. He had reached Shea Stadium thanks to pure luck—via a special lottery overseen by the commissioner's office after an earlier signing by Atlanta was disallowed as a violation of amateur drafting rules; losing out to the Mets in the drawing were the Phillies and Indians. After his rookie season he won another 16 games in 1968. striking out 200 batters for the first of nine consecutive years. Then came the even bigger numbers. In 1969 he topped the NL with 25 wins—the first of five 20-win seasons and the first of three times that he won the Cy Young Award (the other years were 1973 and 1975). In 1970, 1971, and 1975 Seaver recorded the lowest ERA in the league, ending up with a career ratio of 2.86 to go with his 311 victories and 205 losses. He also paced NL hurlers three times in winning percentage and five times in strikeouts. His single most overpowering moment on the hill came on April 22, 1970, when he fanned the last 10 San Diego batters to come to bat in a 19-strikeout performance. He concluded his career with 3,640 strikeouts.

Aside from his major contribution to turning around the previously lowly Mets into a contender in the late 1960s, Seaver was a forceful clubhouse presence, at an early point in the 1969 championship campaign turning on teammates for celebrating the reaching of .500. The prize pupil of manager Gil Hodges, he was also extremely articulate with the media—a skill initially welcomed, but later turned against him by Dick Young and other stiff-necked sportswriters who didn't share his negative views of the war in Vietnam and positive appreciation of Marvin Miller's work for the Players Association. Another antagonist was professed admirer M. Donald Grant, the chairman of the board of the Mets who first sought to get rid of the pitcher after the 1975 Messersmith-McNally decision, fearing the franchise favorite would hold up the organization for millions to sign again. When word leaked of Grant's attempts to trade Seaver to the Dodgers for Don Sutton, an avalanche of protests persuaded the club to quickly negotiate another contract.

Similar tensions in 1977 had a different outcome. Annoyed the Mets had done nothing to sign outfielder Gary Matthews or other offensively gifted free agents, Seaver questioned Grant's commitment to putting a winning team on the field. That was a good enough opening for Young to jump in with almost daily attacks on the pitcher, culminating in a June column that attributed Seaver's criticisms to nothing more than his wife's envy that Nolan Ryan was making more money with the Angels. A devastated Seaver asked for a trade away from Grant and Young, and was accommodated by being sent to Cincinnati for pitcher Pat Zachry, infielder Doug Flynn, and outfielders Steve Henderson and Dan Norman. New York reaction to what became known as the Midnight Massacre (slugger Dave Kingman was traded away in another deal the same day) ran the gamut from rage to fury. While Seaver broke down in tears before television cameras, fans picketed Shea Stadium, others canceled season tickets, and cranks made so many menacing calls to Grant's office that he went around with a bodyguard for the rest of the year.

Seaver remained with the Reds until 1982, enjoying his best moment on June16, 1978 (a year and a day from the trade) when he hurled his only no-hitter, against the Cardinals. Prior to the 1983 season he was traded back to the Mets, precipitating a New York love-in when he went to the mound to oppose Philadelphia on Opening Day. He went through the rest of the year pitching well for a bad team, and was rumored to be the leading candidate for New

York manager in 1984. Instead, the assignment went to Davey Johnson, who in one of his first public statements stressed that he wanted to bring his young pitchers (Dwight Gooden, Ron Darling, Walt Terrell) with him from Tidewater in the International League to New York. It was in light of this stated aim that some subsequently interpreted an avowed Mets "mistake" in leaving Seaver off the protected 40-man roster and exposing him to a compensation pool draft by the White Sox. While the pitcher once again questioned the ways of the New York front office, general manager Frank Cashen lashed out at Chicago for being insensitive to the feelings of Mets fans and Johnson didn't say much of anything. Mainly because of the White Sox grab of Seaver, the compensation pool was eliminated a short time later.

Seaver's last big moment as a player in New York came on August 4, 1985, when, as a member of the White Sox, he secured his 300th win against the Yankees at Yankee Stadium. The following year, he was sold to the Red Sox for pennant insurance; although injuries kept him off the postseason roster, he was in the Boston dugout as the Mets came from behind to defeat the Red Sox in the 1986 World Series.

After retiring as a player, Seaver teamed up with Phil Rizzuto to do Yankees telecasts. Regular reports that he was about to rejoin the Mets as either a broadcaster or front office executive seemed to die merely in being reported. But in 1999, at least in part to offset some of the fallout over not resigning popular telecaster Tim McCarver, he was finally brought back to do Mets games. In 2001 Seaver was also a primary mover behind changes in Hall of Fame voting procedures that had previously been the province of the Veterans Committee.

PAT SEEREY

Of the 12 major leaguers who have hit four home runs in a game, the least likely has been Seerey, who did it for the White Sox against the Athletics on July 18, 1948. The overweight outfielder accomplished the feat little more than a month after Cleveland had despaired of his strikeout rate and fielding lapses and dealt him to Chicago. Seerey's shots came in the course of an 11-inning contest; only he and Mike Schmidt have needed overtime to join the four-homer club. Outside that day against Philadelphia the righthanded slugger did for Chicago what he had done for Cleveland—sandwiching the occasional long ball between strikeouts and errors. The following year he was out of the league, with his final numbers reading a .224 average, 86 home runs, and 485 strikeouts in less than 2,000 at bats.

PETER SEITZ

Seitz was the arbitrator who, on December 23, 1975, ruled that Los Angeles righthander Andy Messersmith and Montreal lefthander Dave McNally could not be tied to their teams by an automatic turnover of baseball's reserve clause. The verdict effectively authorized all players to become free agents a year after the expiration of the specific duration of their contracts. Seitz announced his decision after weeks of hinting to both Players Association chief Marvin Miller and owners' representative John Gaherin what his ruling would be, suggesting they seek a compromise before it was too late. Although both Miller and Gaherin indicated readiness to enter into compromise negotiations, the latter couldn't persuade owners of such a course. The key part of the Seitz declaration said: "The grievances of Messersmith and McNally are sustained. There is no contractual bond between these players and the Los Angeles and Montreal clubs, respectively. Absent such a contract, their clubs had no right or power, under the Basic Agreement, the uniform player contract, or the Major League Rules to reserve their services for their exclusive use for any period beyond the 're-newal year' in the contracts which these players had heretofore signed with their clubs."

FRANK SELEE (Hall of Fame, 1999)

The first long-term successful manager who had never played in the majors, Selee won five pennants for Boston in the 1890s, built the Cubs roster that won four pennants under successor Frank Chance between 1906 and 1910, and ended up with an impressive .598 winning percentage. Among his skills was repositioning players to take better advantage of their talents; e.g., moving Bobby Lowe from the outfield to second base and both Chance and Fred Tenney to first base from alternating in the outfield and behind the plate. Selee surrendered the helm at Chicago to Chance after discovering in 1905 that he was suffering from tuberculosis. He moved to the southwest for his health, but was soon managing minor league teams. He died in 1909.

BUD SELIG

Selig was known as Mr. Baseball in Milwaukee for 35 years, but his actions as both temporary and official commissioner have made him Mr. No Baseball for a lot of people in other parts of the country and Canada. As with his immediate predecessors, most of his impulses supposedly in the interests of the game have ended up in courtrooms before unsympathetic judges or in congressional hearing rooms with unconvinced politicians.

A successful automobile dealer, Selig's first big baseball adventure was as a charter member of the group that fought the flight of the Braves from Milwaukee in the mid-1960s; the team was forced to spend a lame duck year in the city before going to Atlanta. In 1968 he was prominent in convincing the White Sox to play 10 home games in Milwaukee, as well as in the boosterism that had those contests account for one-third of Chicago's total home attendance for the season. After being denied one of the American League expansion franchises in 1969, he headed a consortium of businessmen that bought the expansion Pilots for transfer from Seattle to Milwaukee for the 1970 season. Not only did the group overpay ($10.8 million) for the shambles of a club, but it had to wait until the very end of spring training before the failure of a lawsuit in Seattle confirmed that the Pilots would indeed be moving to Wisconsin as the Brewers.

As an owner, Selig's most dramatic act was the November 19, 1977 firing of manager Alex Grammas and general manager Jim Baumer in favor of George Bamberger and Harry Dalton, respectively; the arrival of what became known as The Dalton Gang ushered in the franchise's most successful seasons, including a pennant in 1982. Otherwise, the organization largely reflected Selig's penny-wise inclinations, rarely making even a pretense at going after costly free agents and assuming Brewers fans regarded this as more virtuous than a winning team The consequent colorlessness of the team year after year even prompted sarcasm in the U.S. Congress, when during testimony from Selig in December 2001, New York representative Anthony Weiner cracked that he was "particularly impressed with (Selig's) management of the Brewers because it's always a good weekend when the Brewers come to town."

In 1992 Selig was White Sox owner Jerry Reinsdorf's chief ally in dumping Commissioner Fay Vincent. Asked to fill in as interim commissioner, Selig played the part for 2,131 days—longer than the tenures of four formally elected commissioners. Only on July 9, 1998 did he drop the interim part of his title and accept the post officially (with a later extension, through 2006). This did and didn't make a difference. As temporary commissioner, Selig was seen for years as little more than a Reinsdorf mouthpiece. This was particularly so in 1994, when his public stance before the expiration of the collective bargaining agreement with players was to stress the importance of salary caps, this largely being code for breaking the players union; the resultant lockout forced interruption of the season and cancellation of the World Series, prompted eight months of futile negotiations, and led owners to attempt to organize squads of scabs known as "replacement players."

In recent years, and especially since taking over the commissioner's office formally, Selig has sought to make it clear that he is nobody's stooge but his own. Administratively, he has effectively eliminated the league offices for greater central control; one tangible result has been the end to the league separation of umpires. Financially, he has made Major League Baseball an all-inclusive income generator. Diplomatically, he has cracked down on owners and executives for speaking publicly about ongoing negotiations of any kind. But none of this has added up to another Kenesaw Landis. In the concrete his most prominent achievement has been to administer the revenue-sharing deal engineered by Richard Ravitch under which big market owners channel some of their surplus toward clubs at the bottom of the economic scale. But even this modest task has faced elimination with his most substantive idea—the contraction of two economically besieged franchises (Montreal and Minnesota) and an ownership musical chairs game for injecting new blood into two other withering organizations (Florida and Anaheim). That he has encountered little opposition from owners on the issue has been totally logical: the revenue-giving clubs would have fewer hands to fill, and the owners of the outgoing franchises would be bought out to greater profit than if they continued operating. It was partly in defense of his contraction plan that Selig made an embarrassing appearance before Congress in December 2001, winning little but hoots for claims that major league owners were a half-billion dollars in debt and that only five teams had been profitable in the 2001 season.

While serving as interim commissioner, Selig left the day-to-day operations of the Brewers to his daughter Wendy Selig-Prieb. His two-month suspension of Dwight Gooden in June 1994 for failing a drug test raised questions in some quarters about a potential conflict of interest if the player had been a Brewer or simply with a Milwaukee rival (the team had not yet moved to the National League). The Brewers have also been a beneficiary of the revenue sharing and, were the Twins to be eliminated through contraction, would undoubtedly gain fans from the north-central part of the country. Selig has denied that any such considerations have colored his thinking as commissioner. He maintained his denial even in the face of disclosures that he had borrowed $3 million from Minnesota owner Carl Pohlad in the mid-1990s without informing other owners, as required by ownership by-laws. Prieb took over the club altogether with her father's 1998 election.

JOE SEWELL (Hall of Fame, 1977)

No one struck out less than Sewell. In a 14-year (1920–33) career, the lefty-hitting infielder whiffed a mere 114 times in 7,132 at bats, including full-season totals of only three and four (three times) and another 109-game year when he fanned three times.

Sewell joined Cleveland in September 1920 after Ray Chapman was killed by Carl Mays's fastball and backup shortstop Harry Lunte was injured. He batted .300 nine times, had more than 40 doubles five times, and twice drove in at least 100 runs. His lifetime average for the Indians and Yankees was .312.

RIP SEWELL

A righthander for the Pirates in the World War II years, Sewell was a crowd pleaser for the blooper he dubbed his Eephus Ball. The name was the creation of outfielder Maurice Van Robays, who explained that "an eephus ain't nothin', and that's what that ball is." Sewell added the pitch to his arsenal after a December 1941 hunting accident forced him to deliver his pitches with a damaged toe held upward. The tantalizingly high arc to the slow pitch caused as much trouble for umpires as it provided entertainment for fans. It was only after Pittsburgh complained to the league office that umpires were automatically calling the pitch a ball that Bill Klem or-

dered Sewell to give him a special demonstration and, satisfying himself that it did indeed enter the strike zone, passed the word it should be judged like any other pitch. The Eephus Ball's most dramatic moment came in the 1946 All-Star Game, when Ted Williams became the only player ever to knock one out of the park. After leading the NL in losses in 1941, Sewell used his new pitch to win 17 in 1942, a pace-setting 21 in 1943, and another 21 in 1944.

Sewell's days in Pittsburgh weren't always so pleasant. In 1946 he was the team's chief spokesman against the unionizing efforts of Robert Murphy's American Baseball Guild. When the Murphy initiative failed, the pitcher was given a watch by Commissioner Happy Chandler for his pro-management stand—a ceremony that only increased existing tensions in the clubhouse between pro- and anti-union factions.

MARY SHANE

Shane was the first woman to do play-by-play on a regular basis. A Milwaukee sportswriter, she was given the microphone for an inning in 1976 by Harry Caray during a White Sox-Brewers game. When Chicago owner Bill Veeck heard her, he signed her to do the 1977 White Sox games. She was let go after the season.

BOBBY SHANTZ

Nothing else Shantz accomplished in his 16-year (1949–64) career—including an MVP season in 1954—was as spectacular as his nine consecutive no-hit innings in relief in his second big league appearance. With only two-thirds of an inning of experience under his belt, the Athletics lefthander took over from Carl Scheib in the fourth inning on May 6, 1949, set down the Tigers without a safety through the 12th inning, and recorded his first victory (despite yielding a run and two hits in the 13th inning). Shantz took MVP honors for fifth-place Philadelphia with a league-top 24 wins. As a member of the Yankees in 1957, he had the AL's lowest ERA (2.45).

BILL SHARMAN

Basketball Hall of Famer Sharman is the only player to be thrown out of a game without appearing in one. Called up by the Dodgers in September 1951, the future Boston Celtic was in the visitors' dugout at Braves Field on the 27th, when umpire Frank Dascoli cleared the bench in retaliation for the abuse Brooklyn had been heaping on him since missing a close play at the plate. Sharman went back to the minors without ever getting his name in a big league box score.

WILLIAM SHEA

Shea was a New York lawyer prominent in the organization of the Continental League after the 1957 departure of the Dodgers and Giants for California. A stalking horse for forcing an expansion of the National League, the circuit spawned the Astros and the Mets. New York named its stadium after Shea.

FRANK SHELLENBACK

Nobody suffered from the 1920 ban against spitballers more than Shellenback. Because he had been farmed out after two mediocre seasons with them, the White Sox forgot to include him on the list of practicing spitballers to be exempt from the regulation. Not able to use his best pitch, the righthander never made it back to the majors.

Shellenback had his consolations. For one thing, he won 315 games in the minor leagues over 20 years. While coaching for the Red Sox in the 1940s, he had on his staff Nelson Potter, later to be the first big league pitcher suspended for violating the 1920 rule. Shellenback was also a member of the Giants coaching staff in the 1950s, when Sal Maglie, Ruben Gomez, and others were accused of throwing spitters.

BERT SHEPARD

Shepard was a minor league pitcher who lost a leg when he was shot down over Germany in World War II. Hired by the Senators as a coach as a public relations gesture in 1945, he was activated for a laugher against the Red Sox on August 14. The lefthander yielded only one run in $5^{1}/_{3}$ innings, and maneuvered well enough on his wooden leg to come to bat three times. Shepard never appeared in another major league game.

BEN SHIBE

A partner of Al Reach in both a sporting goods business and the Philadelphia Phillies, Shibe effectively sacrificed the latter venture for the former in 1901 when he agreed to become half-owner and president of the American League Athletics, as well. His reason for double dipping in the Philadelphia market was a promise by AL president Ban Johnson

to give the Reach firm exclusive manufacturing rights to league balls. Although Reach and Shibe were compelled to sell their interest in the Phillies after the 1902 season, the industrial partnership continued until Shibe's death in 1922. The company profited greatly from Shibe's patents on the machines that wind the yarn in baseballs and that punch the stitching holes in their covers; he also designed the cork-and-rubber-centered ball that replaced the rubber-only core and that sent batting averages soaring in 1911. Shibe Park, the first concrete and steel stadium, was named for him in 1909.

BEN SHIELDS

Shields has more wins—four—than any other pitcher without a defeat. The southpaw's perfect record took 13 appearances over four seasons (1924–25 with the Yankees, 1930 with the Red Sox, and 1931 with the Phillies). His career ERA was a less-than-perfect 8.27.

BILL SHINDLE

In 1890 Shindle made 119 errors at shortstop for the Philadelphia Quakers of the Players League—the highest season total for any player at any position. In his other 12 big league years he was mainly a third baseman.

ART SHIRES

If Shires wasn't the most violent player in baseball history, it wasn't for lack of trying. His brief four-year (1928–30, 1932) career was bracketed by an attempted killing and a killing.

A cocky first baseman, Shires joined the White Sox at the end of the 1928 campaign, got four hits in his first game, and so impressed manager Lena Blackburne that he was appointed team captain for the following year. Blackburne had second thoughts in spring training when his ostensible field leader knocked him down for suggesting that bright red party hats were not appropriate attire for batting practice. On two other occasions during the 1929 season Shires used his fists to answer Blackburne threats, also belting Chicago traveling secretary Lou Barbour in a dispute over hotel accommodations. Despite his .312 batting average, he was suspended by the club, amassing fines of $3,000. To make up for the money he lost on baseball, Art the Great, as he liked to call himself, hooked up with boxing trainer

Jack Blackburn for several fights. He won his first bout against a construction worker, lost his second to professional football player George Trafton, won or lost a few more depending on the memory of the judges, but succeeded in making enough money to compensate for his White Sox fines. The show came to an end when he challenged Hack Wilson of the Cubs to a ring meeting; Commissioner Kenesaw Landis stepped in to issue a ban against big leaguers engaging in organized boxing.

With his fight money dried up, the disgruntled Shires demanded a $25,000 contract from Charlie Comiskey; after several accusations that the Chicago owner was a cheapskate, he settled for $7,000. Once his hitting fell off in 1930, Comiskey was only too pleased to unload him on the Senators. Shires the ballplayer had one big shot left in him: After telling Washington reporters he was playing in the city where "phony politicians think it's their job to cheat the country," he went out and got three hits to beat his former Chicago teammates. It made for his last big headlines on the sports pages.

But there were other pages in the newspaper. Even before joining Chicago in 1928, Shires had been in trouble for firing a ball at a black spectator prior to a Texas League game in Waco; although the man was severely injured, racism had a hand in making sure no charges were pressed. In 1948 Shires was arrested for murdering a longtime friend. Despite his own admission that "I had to rough him up a good deal because he grabbed a knife and started whittling on my legs," he was acquitted because of medical testimony saying the victim had actually died of natural causes brought on by preexisting conditions of pneumonia and cirrhosis of the liver.

ERNIE SHORE

Except for Lou Gehrig, no player was more associated with Babe Ruth than Shore. Teammates on the International League Orioles, they were both dealt to the Red Sox in 1914 for $8,000. Together they helped pitch Boston to pennants in 1915 and 1916, also fashioning masterly wins in the 1916 World Series. On June 13, 1917 their association was cemented for good when Ruth walked the first batter in a game against Washington, got ejected for protesting the fourth ball, and was replaced by Shore. In what amounted to the greatest relief appearance in history, Shore watched the Washington runner get thrown out on a steal attempt and then retired the next 26 batters. In December 1918 the pitchers became linked still again when Boston owner Harry Frazee, desperate for cash, traded Shore to the Yankees. The deal was the first in the decade-long New York stripping of Fenway Park's best talents; the most notorious of the exchanges occurred in January 1920, when Ruth followed Shore to New York.

BOB SHORT

Short was responsible for bringing American League baseball to Texas—and for leaving Washington without it, again. A Minnesota hotel entrepreneur and a one-time treasurer of the Democratic National Committee, he bought the second 20th-century version of the Senators in January 1969, then spent the next three years trying to hide his inept club by importing distracting gate attractions. Among his moves were hiring Ted Williams as manager, trading for the scandal-ridden former 30-game winner Denny McLain, and signing Curt Flood while the outfielder was still engaged in his legal challenge against baseball's reserve clause. All the while Short was also setting the stage for transferring the franchise to Texas: He defaulted on rent payments for Robert F. Kennedy Stadium on the grounds that he was out of money and he dared Commissioner Bowie Kuhn and other AL owners to come up with a buyer who could meet his asking price of $12 million. After several prospective purchasers were turned down for one reason or another, Kuhn and the league approved the moving of the franchise to Dallas-Fort Worth after the 1971 season.

In Texas Short distinguished himself mainly by insisting in 1973 that manager Whitey Herzog stick David Clyde, a raw 18-year-old just out of high school, into the starting rotation. On the positive side, Clyde's starts accounted for almost one-third of the club's 686,000 attendance on the year; negatively, the forced feeding proved to be too much for the southpaw, and he never won more than eight games in a season. The Clyde affair accelerated Herzog's departure for Billy Martin. "If my mother were managing the Rangers and I had the opportunity to hire Billy Martin," Short said in justifying the switch, "I'd fire my mother." Martin didn't have much time to bask in the flatery: A couple of months later Short sold out to a consortium headed by industrial parts manufacturer Brad Corbett.

BURT SHOTTON

A slap-hitting outfielder over 14 seasons (between 1909 and 1923), Shotton had stints with the Browns and Cardinals in St. Louis that forged his even longer career as Branch Rickey's righthand man. Even while still active, he managed the Cardinals on Sundays in Rickey's stead because of the latter's rigid observance of the Sabbath. It was on Rickey's endorsement that Shotton later piloted the Phillies (to preside over the worst team in franchise history) and snagged coaching jobs with the Reds and Indians. More dramatically, he was Rickey's choice to manage the Dodgers after Leo Durocher was suspended for the 1947 season—the year of Jackie Robinson's debut. When the Giants sought Shotton's services the following year, Rickey said no, letting them have Durocher instead. Although he remained at Brooklyn's helm through the 1950 season, Shotton was never particularly visible at Ebbets Field or on any other diamond: Because he declined to wear a uniform, he had to remain on the bench and, Connie Mack-style, send coaches out to change pitchers and wrangle with umpires. That also made it easier for some antagonistic arbiters (e.g., Jocko Conlan) to go after Robinson in his rookie year without fear of triggering a general rhubarb.

BUCK SHOWALTER

Because of a pious soft-spokenness that seemed like comic relief compared to an even more conspicuous control mania, Showalter was the delight of cartoonists in the 1990s. What got lost in the mockery were his accomplishments as a manager.

Taking over the Yankees in 1992 after the fabled champions had finished no higher than fourth for five years, Showalter guided them back into first place in the lockout-interrupted year of 1994 and into the postseason in 1995. When that wasn't enough for owner George Steinbrenner, Showalter was accused of not permitting his team to relax enough and shown the door for Joe Torre. Two full years before the expansion draft for admitting Arizona and Tampa Bay, he was hired by Jerry Colangelo to help put the Diamondbacks together. Showalter not only had a critical advisory voice on player priorities, but helped design Bank One Ballpark (especially with such touches as the traditional mound-to-plate cutout) and, reflecting his Bronx past, chose the pinstripes for the new club's uniforms.

After a predictably drab inaugural season in 1998, Showalter guided Arizona to 100 victories and the playoffs in 1999—the fastest an expansion club had reached the postseason. A playoff loss to the Mets, however, made Colangelo suddenly as anxious about his manager's aversion to fun as Steinbrenner had been, so Showalter (his windbreaker zippered to the top even at the height of summer) endured the 2000 campaign waiting for the second shoe to fall. Replaced by Diamondbacks broadcaster Bob Brenly after the season, he was again accused of having kept his clubhouse too tight. Remaining tightlipped about such charges, he signed on as a broadcaster for ESPN, and watched his successors Torre and Brenly tangle in the 2001 World Series.

WILLIAM SIANIS

Sianis was a Chicago bar owner who put a hex on the Cubs after Wrigley Field refused to admit him for the 1945 World Series in the company of his pet goat. Since then, the team has never gotten to the final round of the postseason. In 1994 one of the goat's descendants was flown from Milwaukee to the ballpark to break the spell of 10 consecutive Chicago home losses; the animal didn't work any magic that day, but the Cubs did win a couple of days later. Sianis's Billy Goat Tavern was the model for a series of comedy routines ("Cheezburger, Cheezburger") on television's *Saturday Night Live*.

AL SIMMONS (Hall of Fame, 1953)

Despite a foot-in-the-bucket batting stance Simmons was such a feared slugger that Connie Mack suggested that cloning him eight times would make for the perfect team. The righthand-hitting outfielder hit .334 over 20 seasons between 1924 and 1944, leading the American League with .381 in 1930 and .390 in 1931. He also led in hits twice (among six 200-hit seasons), RBIs once (among 12 100-RBI years), and runs once (among six times topping 100). In the power department he reached double numbers in home runs 13 times, including three seasons with more than 30. His most memorable diamond moment came in Philadelphia's 10-run seventh inning in Game Four of the 1929 World Series; with the Athletics trailing, 8–0, he homered to lead off the frame, then singled in the tying run as the team batted around in its record scoring fest.

Unloaded by Mack after the 1932 season, Simmons spent three productive campaigns with the White Sox before being sold to the Tigers, piloted by former teammate Mickey Cochrane. Cochrane figured Simmons was insurance for a third straight pennant, but when that didn't materialize (despite the outfielder's .327 and 112 RBIs), the two fell to regular quarreling. Simmons bounced around between the leagues until 1941, then retired. The World War II player shortage lured him back onto the field with the prospect of reaching 3,000 hits, but he ended up 73 hits short.

TED SIMMONS

Simmons came close to beating Andy Messersmith and Dave McNally to the punch in challenging the reserve clause. Emboldened by Curt Flood's suit against the automatic option in baseball contracts, the Cardinals catcher announced he intended to play the 1972 season without a pact, then declare free agency afterward. He held out until August 9, when he agreed to a two-year deal covering 1972 and 1973.

HARRY SINCLAIR

Oil millionaire Sinclair was the Federal League's last hurrah in 1915. Lured into taking over the pennant-winning but unprofitable Indianpolis franchise, he moved it to Newark for the avowed purpose of making the New Jersey city a gateway to the New York City market. It didn't happen, but the man once described as having the other half of the money in the world that John D. Rockefeller didn't have, made a show of it. First, he offered Giants manager John McGraw $100,000 to take over the Peppers. Then, after the season, he also took over the foundering Kansas City Packers for the announced intention of merging them with Newark for a New York club in 1916. He went so far as to apply to the city for permits to close off streets at the proposed construction site for a new $800,000 stadium and to unveil designs by architect C.B. Comstock for a double-decked grandstand with no obstructing posts. In a challenge to the owners of the Giants, Yankees, and Dodgers, he said he would "stand at the Battery and match any of them in pitching dollars into New York Harbor. We'll see who quits first."

It was all a giant bluff—and it worked. In the ensuing peace treaty Sinclair was offered a direct $100,000 buyout and the right to sell off Federal League play-

ers to the American and National leagues. As a result, he was one of the few backers of the Feds to emerge with a profit. Sinclair later became a central figure in the Teapot Dome Scandal, allegedly bribing Secretary of the Interior Albert Hall in 1922. While acquitted of conspiracy charges, Sinclair was found guilty of contempt of Congress and sentenced to three months in prison. His oil holdings were also a source of contention in the saber rattling between the United States and Mexico in the 1920s.

BILL SINGER

Singer had 20-win seasons for both the Dodgers and Angels, but had a greater impact on a team for which he never played. Before the 1977 season the righthander was traded by the Blue Jays to the Yankees for a New York pitching prospect. But when Toronto realized that Singer was on the cover of the expansion franchise's first media guide, it called off the deal so as not to give the impression of an organizational instability in its inaugural year. The New York prospect who should have gone to the Blue Jays was Ron Guidry. Singer had a 2–8 record for the year, then retired.

While with the Dodgers in 1969, Singer was the first pitcher formally credited with the new computation of a save. Saves compiled before that year were given retroactively.

DICK SISLER

A first baseman-outfielder who never hit more than 13 home runs in any of his eight major league seasons (1946–53), Sisler banged the most dramatic roundtripper in Philadelphia history in the 10th inning of the final game of 1950. The lefthanded swinger's three-run opposite field blast off Brooklyn ace Don Newcombe gave the Whiz Kid Phillies the pennant.

GEORGE SISLER (Hall of Fame, 1939)

Considered by many second only to Hal Chase as the greatest defensive first baseman of all time, the .340-hitting Sisler was no slouch with a bat, either. But none of his on-field exploits contained the intrigue and high drama of his circuitous route to the Browns, for whom he was the all-time franchise player.

Signing with Akron of the Ohio-Pennsylvania League when he was only 17, Sisler became the ostensible property of the Pirates when they purchased his contract in 1912. But in the meantime he elected to attend the University of Michigan, where he became the foremost college player of the period under coach Branch Rickey. As Sisler's graduation approached, Pittsburgh owner Barney Dreyfuss pressed his claim for the first baseman's services with the National Commission. But advised by Rickey, Sisler rejected the claim on the grounds that he had been underage when he had signed the Akron contract. The National Commission agreed, declaring him a free agent, and paving the way for him to sign in 1915 with the Browns—whose manager just happened to be Rickey.

With St. Louis in his freshman year Sisler pitched (4–4, 2.83) as well as played first base. Shifted to first full-time in 1916, the lefty swinger went on to a 15-year career in which he batted over .400 twice, set the big league mark for most hits in a season (257 in 1920), averaged an American League high of .420 in 1922, and led the circuit in batting twice, triples twice, and stolen bases four times. Defensively, his 1,529 career assists held up as the record until broken by Keith Hernandez some 60 years later. He was a master of the 3–6–3 double play, pulling off 13 of them in 1920.

Sisler's lifetime .340 average might have even been higher but for a sinusitis attack that infected his optic nerves and left him with double vision for more than a year. After being forced to sit out the 1923 season with the problem, he returned the following year to bat higher than .300 six more times (with the Senators and Braves, as well as with the Browns), but was never again the dominant force he had been.

SEYMOUR SIWOFF

Siwoff pioneered the use of computers in assembling sports statistics. General manager of the Elias Sports Bureau, his innovation in the 1960s made possible the breakdown of player statistics into every conceivable category: how batters performed against righthanders and lefthanders, in day and night contests, on grass and artificial turf, etc. The Elias bureau has been compiling numbers for the National and American leagues since 1916.

JOEL SKINNER

Catcher Skinner was the first player picked up (by the White Sox from the Pirates) in the short-lived compensation pool created in the early 1980s as a means of giving something back to clubs that had lost free agents. The scheme—which made vulnerable any club engaged in free agent signings—ended after a couple of years, partly because of the uproar caused when the same White Sox snatched New York favorite Tom Seaver away from the Mets.

ENOS SLAUGHTER (Hall of Fame, 1985)

Baseball's model hustler before Pete Rose, Slaughter batted an even .300 over 19 seasons (between 1938 and 1959) for the Cardinals, Yankees, and other teams. In one season or another he led the National League in RBIs (1946), hits (1942), doubles (1939), and triples (1942 and 1949). The lefty swinging right fielder also had a strong arm, coming up with a critical assist in the 1946 playoffs against the Dodgers when he nailed a runner at third in the ninth inning of a one-run game. In that year's World Series against the Red Sox, Slaughter entered major league lore in the eighth inning of the seventh game when, playing with a broken elbow and ignoring a stop sign from the third base coach, he scored from first on a Harry Walker double after shortstop Johnny Pesky hesitated on a relay throw to the plate; his slide across home, captured in a memorable photograph, gave the Cardinals the world championship. As a member of the Yankees in 1956, he provided another indelible picture when he was pulled away from a melee with White Sox players with his jersey ripped off his chest and his cap askew.

ROY SMALLEY, SR.

Smalley was such a notorious presence at shortstop for the Cubs in the 1950s that Wrigley Field fans updated the traditional Tinker-to-Evers-to-Chance refrain to "Miksis to Smalley to Addison Street." The infielder reached his nadir in 1950 with 51 errors and a .945 fielding average.

AL SMITH

Being a member of the 1959 pennant-winning White Sox was not all roses for Smith. Booed a good part of the year for shoddy defense and lackluster hitting, the left fielder became so depressed that Chicago owner Bill Veeck decided to buoy his spirits by staging Al Smith Night at Comiskey Park, allowing anybody named Smith free admission. Before thousands of fans sporting buttons that declared "I'm a Smith and I'm for Al," he dropped a late-inning fly ball that allowed Boston to defeat Chicago. In that season's World Series against the Dodgers his humiliation went national when he was photographed being drenched by beer from the stands as he watched after a Charlie Neal home run.

Smith, who batted a solid .272 over 12 years (1953–64), was the only player besides Early Wynn who represented the American League in the two World Series of the 1950s that didn't include the Yankees; he was also a member of the 1954 Indians.

ELMER SMITH

An outfielder for the 1920 Indians, Smith hit the first World Series grand slam home run. He did it in the first inning of the fifth game against Brooklyn's Burleigh Grimes.

HILTON SMITH (Hall of Fame, 2001)

Righthander Smith achieved most of his success while a member of the Kansas City Monarchs from 1936 to 1948, often replacing Satchel Paige after the more famous gate attraction had pitched only three innings. Smith won 20 games in each of his first 12 seasons with the Monarchs, including a 93–11 mark from 1939 to 1942, and added a win in both the 1942 and the 1946 Negro World Series. In 1937 he fashioned a perfect game against the Chicago American Giants. His lasting place in history was assured when he recommended Jackie Robinson, then just out of the Army, to Monarchs owner J. L. Wilkinson in the winter of 1945.

LEE SMITH

Smith is the all-time saves leader with 478. Bridging the eras when closers were and weren't expected to get more than three outs, he wore eight uniforms over 18 years (1980–97), almost always moving on when a front office decided that he had seen his best days. Although his biggest years were with the Cubs (leading the league in saves in 1983 and topping 30 saves four other years), the righthander also had five other seasons of at least 33 saves, including league-leading totals for St. Louis in 1991 and 1992 and for Baltimore in 1994. A hulking six feet, six inches, Smith was never averse to a little show business, shambling in from the bullpen like the bouncer called on to bang some heads together. Despite his size, he established a big league record by going 546 games, from 1982 to 1992, without making a single error.

LONNIE SMITH

Smith is the only player to appear in a World Series for four different teams. The righthand-hitting outfielder did it for the Phillies in 1980, the Cardinals in 1982, the Royals in 1985, and the Braves in 1991 and 1992. In playing for Atlanta in 1991 he made one of the biggest gaffes in postseason play, contributing mightily to Minnesota's world championship. In the eighth inning of the seventh game, in a scoreless tie, he led off with a single, but was then decoyed by Twins second baseman Chuck Knoblauch and shortstop Greg Gagne into breaking his stride around the bases on a subsequent double by Terry Pendleton. The hesitation made it impossible for Smith to get beyond third base, where he was ultimately stranded; Minnesota won the game and the World Series in the 10th inning, 1–0.

OZZIE SMITH (Hall of Fame, 2002)

Probably the greatest defensive shortstop of all time, Smith nevertheless had his most dramatic diamond moment with a bat—with a home run in the ninth inning of the fifth game of the 1985 National League Championship Series. The switch-hitter's blast off Dodgers closer Tom Niedenfuer came batting lefthanded for St. Louis even as the Busch Stadium scoreboard was pointing out he had never reached the seats from that side of the plate in his career. The home run set up a Cardinals pennant the next day.

Brought to the majors by the Padres in 1978, Smith established the seasonal record for shortstop assists (621) in 1980, and would ultimately retire with the career mark (8,375) in 1996. With San Diego and then St. Louis (as of 1982) he earned the sobriquet of The Wizard of Oz, winning 13 consecutive Gold Gloves. A skilled acrobat who did pregame flips on the field until advised by doctors to stop, he employed his tumbling abilities to good purpose—throwing on the run, diving right and left, bouncing to his feet and throwing in one seemingly seamless motion. His single most noted defensive play was on a bad-hop grounder up the middle by Bob Horner of the Braves: Diving to his left, Smith reached behind him, caught the ball barehanded after it took an erratic bounce, and threw to first in time.

A baserunning threat as well as a steadily improving slap hitter, Smith averaged more than 35 thefts in his first 16 seasons. With the Padres in 1980 he swiped 57 bases to join Gene Richards (61) and Jerry Mumphrey (54) as the only trio of teammates to pilfer more than 50 in a year. He ended up with 580 steals and 2,460 hits (.262).

While with San Diego in the late 1970s, Smith was so badly paid that he had to take out a newspaper ad looking for work as a gardener. With the Cardinals in the early 1990s he ran into so much front office reluctance about giving him a new multiyear contract that he became a *cause célèbre* in St. Louis, with fans finally pressuring general manager Dal Maxvill to come up with the pact.

REGGIE SMITH

For most of his 17 years (1966–82) on the field Smith was a solid slugger who established several switch-hitting records before the coming of Eddie Murray. Off the field the outfielder figured prominently in clubhouse frictions from Boston to Los Angeles.

While with the Red Sox, Smith was a leading critic of Marvin Miller's union tactics, joining with teammates Carl Yastrzemski and Butch Hobson in stressing their gratitude to owner Tom Yawkey; this led to more than one punchup in the team clubhouse, usually featuring pro-union spokesman Bill Lee. As a Dodger in the 1970s, he groused over the preferential treatment given regularly to Steve Garvey despite numbers at least the equivalent of the popular first baseman. When Don Sutton took up his cause, pointedly telling newsmen that Smith was the most valuable player on the team, the pitcher and Garvey ended up swapping punches.

Between the lines Smith clouted 30 home runs in 1971 and 1977; in the latter year he was one of four record-setting Dodgers to reach that plateau. On August 25, 1981 he was a principal in a bizarre fight when he screamed out from the bench for Pittsburgh righthander Pascual Perez to stop brushing back Los Angeles hitters. Perez charged off the hill after the inning, the two players led both teams into the passageway behind the Pirates dugout, and there began pushing and shoving one another while 16,000 fans at Three Rivers Stadium stared at an empty playing field. It took the umpires 10 minutes to get the teams back in their dugouts; since the fracas was considered "private," nobody was ejected.

TAL SMITH

Smith created a new baseball occupation in 1980 when he formed a company to handle arbitration hearings for big league front offices. For the clubs he was seen as an attractive alternative to having general managers disparage the qualities of their own players in order to save money on contracts. At its height of operations Tal Smith Enterprises was arguing the cases of more than half the teams in the majors, with a success rate of about 50 percent.

Smith went into his consulting work after building up the Houston team that won the West Division title in 1980. He was fired right after the LCS because owner John McMullen couldn't afford the attendance clause in his contract. For most of the rest of the decade he worked as something of an efficiency expert—among other things, appraising the value of the Red Sox for a 1984 buyout and keeping the Padres afloat administratively in 1989 while owner Joan Kroc looked for a buyer for the organization. Most recently, he has been back as president of the Astros, where he has found it easy to smooth the way for numerous trades with his son Randy Smith, the general manager of San Diego and then Detroit.

WENDELL SMITH

Smith played a pivotal role in most of the events that led to the integration of the major leagues in the 1940s. While covering the Kansas City Monarchs for a Pittsburgh daily in 1945, he arranged for Jackie Robinson and two other black players to have a tryout with the Red Sox. Although it was an empty exercise primarily aimed at defusing City Hall pressures on owner Tom Yawkey for desegregation, Smith immediately afterward tipped off Branch Rickey about Robinson. In 1947 Rickey hired Smith to accompany Robinson on the rookie's road trips.

In the late 1940s Smith became the first black sportswriter to have a byline in a major white newspaper (for the Chicago *Herald American*). In the 1960s he wrote an investigative series that effectively put an end to Jim Crow housing in spring training camps. In 1994 he was inducted into the writers' wing of the Hall of Fame.

DUKE SNIDER (Hall of Fame, 1980)

The most productive lefthanded power hitter in Dodgers history, Snider has nevertheless had to put up with muttering about his accomplishments. The first reservation has stemmed from the fact that he was the third best center fielder in New York in the 1950s, after Willie Mays of the Giants and Mickey

Mantle of the Yankees. Other criticism has arisen from his place in a lineup of otherwise righthanded batters in the Ebbets Field teams of the era, allowing him to elude the southpaw pitching that usually gave him fits. That said, Snider was baseball's most prolific home run hitter of the 1950s, clouting 326 round-trippers in the decade. Included in the total were five straight seasons of 40 or more and a league-leading 43 in 1956. He drove in 100 runs six times, with an NL high of 136 in 1955. He also scored 100 runs six times, including three straight league-leading totals. Although he struck out more than any other league batter three times, Snider was no all-or-nothing hitter. He paced the league in hits in 1950, averaged better than .300 seven times, and ended his career at .295 only because of his final desultory seasons. In both the 1952 and 1955 World Series, he hit four home runs. While not gifted with the speed of a Mays or Mantle and given to allowing hits to roll out to him, he was an exceptional defensive outfielder. His leaping catch of a Yogi Berra drive against the Yankee Stadium auxiliary scoreboard in the fifth game in 1952 ranks as one of the greatest World Series fielding plays.

Nobody was more affected than Snider by the Dodgers move from Brooklyn to Los Angeles after the 1957 season. Instead of Ebbets Field's friendly right field wall, he had to deal with the Yellowstone distances of the Coliseum, and he tailed off precipitously. After some time in a platoon role with the Dodgers, he was sold to the Mets in a gate-appeal move by the expansion New York franchise. He managed one more season of 14 home runs, but spent most of the year sitting next to Casey Stengel and listening to the pilot's nostalgic tales of the days the Dodgers and Yankees faced off regularly in the World Series. The outfielder ended his 18-year career in 1964 with a short stint with the Giants.

Snider's 1947 debut occurred in the same game in which Jackie Robinson broke the color line; while Robinson went hitless, he got a pinch-single. In 1956 he attracted attention for telling *Collier's* magazine that he played baseball for money. The declaration horrified baseball executives and sportswriters for, as one of them put it, "disillusioning young fans."

FRED SNODGRASS

Although he was in the National League for nine years, Snodgrass might as well have played only in the 1912 and 1913 World Series as far as baseball history is concerned. The Giants outfielder is most frequently remembered for dropping the Clyde Engle fly ball in the 10th inning of the final game of the 1912 Series that opened the way for the Red Sox to produce a comeback championship; in fact, he also did both better and worse than that. The better was a circus catch of a Harry Hooper line drive immediately after the error on the Engle fly; the worse was that Snodgrass had also misjudged a smash by Tris Speaker in the first game that led to another Boston victory.

Snodgrass's critical error in the final game—dubbed The $30,000 Muff (the difference between the winning and losing Series shares)—occasioned a strong display of support for the outfielder from manager John McGraw; to shut up Snodgrass critics, McGraw announced he was raising the besieged player's salary for 1913. But the manager wasn't feeling as generous a year later when Snodgrass was thrown out trying to steal at a critical juncture in the World Series against the Athletics. The aborted theft prompted a McGraw tirade against first base coach Wilbert Robinson for having sent the sore-legged Snodgrass, a rupture between the two old friends, and a move by Robinson across the river to manage the Dodgers for 18 years.

LOU SOCKALEXIS

A member of the Penobscot Native American Indian tribe, Sockalexis had woven a legend even before reaching the major leagues; in fact, his were the deeds in amateur Maine summer leagues in the early 1890s that inspired Gilbert Patten to write his Frank Merriwell stories under the pseudonym of Burt L. Standish. A hard drinker by the time he joined the Cleveland Spiders in 1897, Sockalexis silenced the war whoops that greeted him around the league by tearing apart National League pitching until, sporting a .338 average and little else, he injured his foot in a fall or a jump from a whorehouse window during a Fourth of July celebration. From then on, his drinking no longer under control, the phenom appeared sparingly.

In 1915, two years after Sockalexis's death, readers of the Cleveland *Press* memorialized him by choosing Indians in a poll to name the local big league club The name and attendant logos have survived ever since in spite of recurrent protests that they have fostered racial stereotyping.

ARTHUR SODEN

The leader of a troika that owned the National League's Boston franchise for three decades, Soden was the author of the first reserve rule blinding a player to a club in perpetuity, as well as a sufficient presence in league councils to be elected interim president in 1882. The reserve clause, introduced in 1879, failed to win enthusiastic approval from other owners, who initially applied it only to five players on each club. Belatedly realizing that the rule's net effect was the depression of salaries, the skeptical soon enough became converts and, within 10 years, joined in extending the restriction to virtually every player.

Reserving players suited Soden's pathological penny-pinching. Among his economies over the years were charging admission to players' wives, removing the press box to make room for more paying customers, and brownbagging his lunch every day of his tenure with the team. His frugality also surfaced in such club policies as ignoring requests to sign new players and issuing dividends so infrequently that small stockholders invariably got disgusted and sold out to him. But at least on one occasion he was generous with retroactive advice: After the folding of the Players League in 1890, Soden told PL organizer John Montgomery Ward that the rebels should have played without signing their contracts, since that would have forced NL owners either to accept a break in the chain of automatic contract renewals or to suffer public wrath by locking out the vast majority of major leaguers.

MOSES SOLOMON

A lefthand-hitting outfielder, Solomon was one of the New York Giants periodic attempts to find a Jewish player who would appeal to the city's vast Jewish population. Manager John McGraw also hoped that he would help offset the enormous popularity of Babe Ruth, and to that end encouraged sportswriters to refer to him as The Rabbi of Swat. Unfortunately for the Giants and McGraw, Solomon managed a mere eight plate appearances in 1923 before being demoted back down to the minors. Although he managed two singles and a double in his at bats, he was a catastrophe in the field, and never returned to the major leagues.

CHARLES SOMERS

Nobody was more vital than Somers to the creation and early survival of the American League. In addition to owning Cleveland, the coal magnate's open purse and belief in the aims of AL president Ban Johnson provided seed money for Philadelphia and St. Louis to start their franchises, supplied the capital for Chicago's Comiskey Park, and paid off Boston's bills for years. Somers's crucial role was so conspicuous that, though he had only a brief formal tie to the club, Boston carried the nickname of Somersets for a while. In a less grateful mood, some newsmen in Ohio noted the owner's coal mining background and the dissension of Cleveland players over their salaries to dub the team the Molly McGuires—making Somers the only one to inspire nicknames for two different clubs.

Aside from his liberal outlays of cash, Somers's most valuable contribution to the league's survival was his bluffing ability. Running into Frank Robison of the National League Cardinals on a train in December 1902, for instance, he euchred him into believing the AL had already secured a ballpark for its embryonic franchise in New York. Robison swallowed the tale and, deciding it was useless to fight the junior league, reported the news and his attitude at an NL meeting; his surrender was a major turning point in the NL's accepting the AL as an equal.

Over the first half of his reign as Cleveland owner (1901–15), Somers sought to remain in the background, taking only a vice-presidential title and leaving day-to-day organization affairs to president John Kilfoyle. Thanks to Somers's loans here, there, and everywhere, Kilfoyle didn't have a particularly hard time obtaining players in an emergency. When Connie Mack couldn't keep future Hall of Famers Nap Lajoie and Elmer Flick because of a Pennsylvania court order, for example, the A's chief sent them to Somers; some years later, the still-helpful Mack would send Joe Jackson. Only when Kilfoyle's health began to deteriorate in 1908 did Somers take on the presidency and, in a move with long-range consequences for the organization, bring in one-time college coach and Columbus *Dispatch* sports editor Ernest Barnard as his chief assistant. He eagerly accepted Barnard's recommendation for setting up a minor league chain by investing heavily in clubs in New Orleans, Toledo, Portland (Oregon), Westbury (Connecticut), and Ironton (Ohio). Nor was Somers above getting Red Sox owner John Taylor drunk and, between sips, prying away from him the game's most successful pitcher, Cy Young, in a one-sided deal.

Somers encountered his first big setback in 1910 when he rebuilt the League Park grandstand with nonunion labor and the American Federation of Labor issued a call for a boycott of all Cleveland games, at home and on the road. Only Johnson's intervention prevented the conflict from engulfing the whole league. The bottom began falling out altogether in 1914 with the rise of the Federal League and its threats to put a franchise in Cleveland. To head off such a move Somers shifted his Toledo minor league team to the city, so that local fans would have some kind of baseball without the Feds even when the Indians were on the road. What he mainly achieved was showing Clevelanders that Toledo was a better club in its league than Cleveland was in the AL, aggravating already serious attendance problems. Finding himself overextended by almost $2 million, Somers resorted to a fire sale of his players, including his two prizes from Philadelphia, Lajoie and Jackson. But it was all too little much too late, and creditors moved in to take away all of the owner's properties except the team in New Orleans. Acting as agent for the creditors, Johnson then arranged for the Indians to be sold to James Dunn, head of a Chicago-based railroad building company.

DEWEY SORIANO

Soriano was the chief operating officer of the 1969 expansion Seattle Pilots—and the chief reason why the franchise disappeared after only one season. As a minority partner to Cleveland-based William Daley, he persuaded American League officials that he could make the Pilots commercially viable by having minor league Sicks Stadium enlarged for a temporary playing site, by winning voter approval for a new domed stadium, and by heading off challenges from a displaced Pacific Coast League team by paying a $300,000 indemnity. In the event, he ended up fighting the city throughout the season about the pace of the stadium expansion work, to the point that Mayor Floyd Miller threatened to evict the club; the bond issue was not approved until after the Pilots had ceased to exist; and the indemnity to the PCL was not handed over until years more after that. And that was only the beginning.

Even as he was telling everyone that Sicks Stadium would house the team for two years at the most, Soriano inked a five-year agreement for use of the facility. Even though he acknowledged the Pilots were probably going to be inhabiting the AL cellar for a couple of years, he announced the highest ticket prices in either league. Even as he was talking about enlarging the team's spring training quarters in Tempe, Arizona lawyers were suing the franchise for not paying its first-year bills. It finally dawned on the AL that it had made a mistake. But still insisting they were committed to remaining in Seattle, the other owners of the league rejected a purchase offer from a group in Milwaukee, instead entertaining various proposals from a rogues gallery of entrepreneurs and would-be entrepreneurs based in the state of Washington. The common characteristic of the suitors was that not one of them turned out to have the funds he claimed; one didn't even have the money to cover a single day of payroll.

With Daley and Soriano refusing to invest another penny in the franchise, the league had to finance the Pilots spring training in 1970. That contribution won over those who had been opposed to accepting the Milwaukee offer. After another lawsuit probing Soriano's claims of being bankrupt, the AL approved the creation of the Milwaukee Brewers for the 1970 season. One major consequence of the fiasco was that it prompted serious enough lawsuit threats by the abandoned city of Seattle that the AL had to make a commitment to create the Mariners.

SAMMY SOSA

Although topped first by Mark McGwire (in 1998 and 1999) and then by Barry Bonds (in 2001), Sosa was baseball's most formidable power hitter at the turn of the millennium. Between 1998 and 2001, his total of 243 round-trippers included an unprecedented three 60-plus seasons, while his 597 RBIs left him trailing only Lou Gehrig and Babe Ruth for a four-year period. The outfielder's 160 RBIs in 2001 were 94 more than teammate runnerup Rickey Gutierrez—the most dominant power performance within a team in baseball history. It was practically as an afterthought that he forged such marks as most home runs in one month (20 in June 1998), most times in a season with multiple-homer games (11 in 1998), and most three-home run games in a year (three in 2001).

Sosa's 1998 breakout has dramatized a career that was already respectable in terms of traditional slugging baseball, but that ever since has underlined the dynamic importance of Latin fans to the sport. If he shared billing with McGwire in 1998 during their joint pursuit of Roger Maris's single-season home run record, both of them gaining praise for supposedly restoring baseball's popularity after the 1994 lockout, he has been far more of a one-man show since. By turns ebullient and humble, jaunty and pious to the edge of ham acting, seemingly unaffected by the daily necessity of spewing clichés about his performance *vis à vis* that of his Chicago team, he had only Pedro Martinez as an individual box office rival entering the new century—not least among Dominicans and other walkup-trade Latins normally excluded from baseball's long-term economic visions. In Chicago, where he routinely takes the field by dashing out to the right field stands with a salute to fans, Sosa has achieved the unthinkable by all but eclipsing Ernie Banks as "Mister Cub." Even his acquisition by the Cubs from the White Sox in March 1992 in exchange for George Bell implicitly mocked some of baseball's hoary expectations: Both sluggers grew up in San Pedro de Macoris, traditionally thought of as the breeding ground for defensively agile but offensively famished shortstops.

Sosa's diamond and box-office feats have not left him invulnerable to criticism. While named the NL MVP for leading the Cubs to a Wild Card berth in the 1998 playoffs, he has still toiled for a club whose whole has fallen far short of its part. Before the 2000 season, new manager Don Baylor shifted some of the blame for this on Sosa, insisting his outfielder struck out far too much, had to think of more than all-or-nothing home runs and lift his batting average from a typical .260 zone, and had to assert more team leadership. What followed were weeks of melodrama, right up to a probable trade of Sosa to the Yankees. When that crisis was finally overcome, the outfielder went on to bat .320 (in 2000) and .328 (in 2001) as seasoning for his home runs and RBIs, in the process becoming far more demonstrative about team affairs in the clubhouse. On the other hand, he maintained an average of 147 strikeouts over his explosive four-year period and the Cubs drew no closer to a World Series.

BILLY SOUTHWORTH

Southworth's passage from a 13-year (between 1913 and 1929) playing career to 13 years as a manager was like Dr. Jekyll's transformation into Mr. Hyde. A genial, outgoing outfielder who batted .297 overall and who made significant contributions to the

Cardinals world championship in 1926, he showed up as such a martinet when St. Louis made him the dugout boss three years later that owner Sam Breadon had to farm him back to the minors in midseason because of incessant player complaints. Although he mellowed somewhat in his later years, he also developed a severe drinking problem that took the luster off some of his best strategic efforts for the Cardinals and Braves in the 1940s.

As a player, Southworth arrived in St. Louis in 1926 after stints with the Indians, Pirates, Braves, and Giants. While he had no appreciable power, he averaged .300 six times on his journeying, led the National League in triples in 1919, and was a deft fielder. Some of his travels were the result of controversial trades. When the Pirates packed him off to the Braves in 1921, it was for the popular Rabbit Maranville—a fact Boston fans were slow to forget with their constant booing of the outfielder; when the Braves sent him to the Giants in 1924, it was so future Hall of Famer Dave Bancroft could pilot Boston and consolidate New York manager John McGraw's hold on the New England club.

After his first bitter taste of managing in 1929, Southworth ran several clubs in the minors until Bill Terry hired him as a coach for the Giants in 1933. Their relationship got no further than spring training, when they swapped punches in disagreement over the final roster. After an even longer period of running minor league teams, Southworth popped up in 1940 with the Cardinals again, mainly as Breadon's emergency solution to getting rid of Branch Rickey confidant Ray Blades as manager. A kinder and gentler Southworth—at least when he was sober—remained at the helm for the next six years, reeling in three pennants, two world championships, and two second-place finishes with teams that played above .600 every season. By the end of World War II, however, not even that shining record was enough to prevent Breadon from seeking to cut salaries across the board because of financial shorts, and Southworth took the opportunity to skip off to Boston.

With the Braves Southworth's drinking became even heavier and his authoritarian airs returned in full force, but owner Lou Perini turned a blind eye to both problems as the club ended decades of wretched play to climb the ladder to the top of the league. It was during Boston's pennant-winning year of 1948 that the pitching-short Southworth acknowledged that his starting rotation plan consisted of "Spahn, Sain, and pray for rain." Once they had their NL flag, Perini and his general manager Bob Quinn emulated Breadon in going after player salaries, but with the added twist of emphasizing that only Southworth was indispensable to the franchise. It was a tack that only heightened clubhouse agitation, and the manager worsened an already bad situation by issuing new spring training rules in 1949 that left the players with little to do but play games and then return to their rooms. Alvin Dark and Eddie Stanky, the double play combination that had been pivotal for the team's success in 1948, took it upon themselves to ask Southworth to ease up on his drinking, but instead of interpreting the duo's request in the light of their almost obsessive religious attitudes, let alone from human concern, he took it as final confirmation of press rumors that Stanky was jockeying for his job.

In August 1949 Southworth suffered what was officially described as a nervous breakdown, and asked to be relieved of his post for the remainder of the season. Totally unsympathetic, the players voted him only a half-share of their fourth-place World Series money. Despite the deteriorated morale of the club, Perini let the three years remaining on Southworth's contract determine his course of action: He traded away Dark and Stanky to the Giants for three one-dimensional sluggers and got rid of several other players fingered as rebels. Southworth came back in 1950 for another fourth-place finish, but in June 1951 told Perini his health was more important to him than guiding another also-ran club, and finally quit.

WARREN SPAHN (Hall of Fame, 1973)

Already 25 when he won his first game for the Braves in 1946, Spahn went on to post the most victories (363) by any lefthander in the history of the game. His biggest numbers included 13 20-win seasons, most career shutouts by a southpaw (63), and the NL leader in wins eight times, strikeouts four times, and ERA three times. He didn't get a no-hitter until he was 39, but then followed up his 1960 masterpiece against Philadelphia with a second one against San Francisco in 1961. Spahn also won four World Series games, carrying three of his starts into extra innings. An offensive threat as well, he was often used as a pinch-hitter, and ended up with 35 home runs over his 21-year career.

If there was one stain on Spahn's record, it was his inability to beat the Dodgers teams that dominated the NL in the late 1940s and 1950s; in 1952 and 1953, for instance, he went 0–7 against Brooklyn, after which he was generally kept away from the righthand-hitting Ebbets Field lineup. The hex even followed him to Los Angeles In a 1959 playoff game that ended up settling the pennant race, he came in from the bullpen against pinch-hitter Carl Furillo with the bases loaded, threw one pitch, and had only a circus catch from Hank Aaron to thank for a mere sacrifice fly instead of a grand slam. The Dodgers later won the game.

AL SPALDING (Hall of Fame, 1939)

Starting as a 17-year-old pitching phenom and ending up at the center of titanic struggles over the future of the National League, Spalding was the dominant figure in the development of 19th-century baseball. He has also been responsible more than anyone for the fiction that Abner Doubleday was the Thomas Edison of baseball.

While pitching for a Rockford (Illinois) club, Spalding gained attention nationally for the first time by handing the Washington Nationals their only loss in an 1867 tour of the Midwest. He went on to post 204 victories (against 53 losses) during five years of National Association play, including a 54–5 record for the Boston Red Stockings in 1875 when he had already committed himself to playing for Chicago the following year and even as Hub fans booed his every move. After his defection to William Hulbert's White Stockings triggered the creation of the National League, Spalding hurled the circuit's first shutout (a 4–0 blanking of Louisville on April 25, 1876), following it up with a repeat performance two days later, becoming the first pitcher to launch his big league career with back-to-back whitewashings. He ended up with a record of 47–12 while doubling as the manager for the pennant-winning team.

After an injury two years later forced his retirement, Spalding devoted his attention to building up a sporting goods company he had launched with his brother J. Walter and to purchasing stock in the Chicago club. When Hulbert died in 1882, he was in position to buy a majority interest in the franchise and take active control of its day-to-day operations. His 10-year regime was marked by a paternalism designed to keep player salaries down and their deportment standards up. Toward the former end he encouraged the formation of the League Alliance of NL-affiliated independent clubs and sold King Kelly for $10,000 when the fan favorite's salary demands reached levels he wasn't prepared to pay; in the interests of the latter, he hired private detectives to trail his players and insisted they take a no-alcohol pledge in force over the winter as well as during the season. Part of the money he saved on salaries went into a renovation of Lake Front Park that included the first private boxes; the boxes were furnished with armchairs for comfort, curtains for protection against the wind, and a personal suite area with a telephone.

Spalding was markedly selective in his attitude toward efforts to break the NL's monopoly on major league play. He agreed to have his club meet the Cincinnati Reds, winners of the first American Association pennant in 1882, in a postseason championship series even before a settlement had been reached with the rival league. Two years later, during the Union Association war, he incurred the anger of NL president A. G. Mills for surreptitiously backing a profitable effort by Samuel Morton, one of his employees, to funnel players to the Unions; he also rented Lake Front Park to the UA Browns for several games. Years later he all but welcomed the American League challenge to the NL. On the other hand, though, he regarded the Players League as evil incarnate. After an initial blunder in confiding to Players Brotherhood organizer John Montgomery Ward that he considered the demands for an end to player sales important enough to merit immediate attention, Spalding directed the NL's wartime strategy, suing defecting players, pumping money into faltering clubs, attempting to win ex-employee Kelly back into the league fold, and orchestrating a massive public relations campaign for discrediting the jumpers. He also called the signals on the final assault, getting PL financial backers to admit their heavy losses while keeping silent about the equal damage to the NL, excluding the players from settlement negotiations, and rearranging franchises and owners to suit the needs of the hour.

Perhaps Spalding's greatest genius was for publicizing the game—in the quasi-official *Spalding Guide* annual; through a 1907 commission that pulled Abner Doubleday from the obscurity of Civil War histories and put him at the center of a baseball creation myth; and through a 1911 autobiography. His most spectacular publicity endeavor was a six-month world tour in 1888–89 that brought baseball to 13 countries, on every continent except Antarctica.

The world tour would have probably included the South Pole, too, if there had been anyone there to purchase the uniforms, balls, bats, gloves, and other equipment the millionaire peddled through A.G. Spalding and Brothers. At bottom all his other undertakings (probably including his encouragement of the American Association, Union Association, and American League) were geared toward increasing the profits from the sporting goods company that eventually became an international monopoly with the gobbling up of such competitors as A.J. Reach and the Wright and Ditson firm.

Spalding's final appearance on baseball's center stage was also his least succesful. Retired since 1891, the sporting goods executive was called on in December 1901 to undo the damage caused by New York owner Andrew Freedman's syndication plan. The choice was a curious one in that Spalding himself had been the force behind the dissolution of the AA in 1891 and the creation of "one great league," and more recently had sounded out AL president Ban Johnson about a consolidation of the two leagues along lines not dissimilar to what Freedman was proposing. With the issue hinging on an election for league president, Brooklyn, Chicago, Philadelphia, and Pittsburgh (the four teams with nothing to gain from Freedman's scheme) supported Spalding for the NL's chief executive post through 25 ballots, while St. Louis, New York, Boston, and Cincinnati voted for incumbent Nick Young. The deadlock was broken—and Spalding elected, four votes to none—only after the pro-syndication faction had left the meeting room without clarifying all the balloting rules. What followed was *opéra bouffe,* with Spalding seizing league records from Young in the wee hours of the morning, announcing a quorum at the following day's meeting because a minor Giants official was standing in the doorway to the conference room, evicting Freedman from baseball, scurrying out of New York to avoid an injunction restraining him from serving in office, and finally resigning the following spring.

Spalding spent his last years in California, where he died in 1915.

THE SPANISH LADY

The Spanish Lady was the name given to the catastrophic flu epidemic that claimed between 25 and 30 million lives around the world between 1916 and 1918; in the United States the death toll was estimated at 500,000. The emergency sanitary regulations imposed to combat the disease provided a critical justification for banning the spitball. In the atmosphere of the period even apparently unrelated ailments, such as a diphtheria attack suffered by spitballer Ad Brennan, were ascribed to the handling of spittle-covered baseballs.

JOE SPARMA

Sparma's wildness prompted a refinement of one of the game's fundamental rules. Convinced his righthander was unable to issue an intentional walk without hitting the backstop, Montreal manager Gene Mauch assigned one of his infielders to a spot behind the catcher during a 1970 game while the base on balls was being doled out. The National League subsequently intervened to rule more specifically that only a catcher could be standing in foul territory with the delivery of a pitch.

TRIS SPEAKER (Hall of Fame, 1937)

For somebody who batted .345 and revolutionized outfield play during his 22-year (1907–28) career, Speaker came in for a lot of rejection. It started when an unimpressive trial with the Red Sox in 1907 caused owner John Taylor to laugh at his contract demands. Pittsburgh owner Barney Dreyfuss said he didn't want him because he smoked, and Giants manager John McGraw said he didn't need him because he already had too many outfielders. Speaker was taken back by Taylor only to help pay off some spring training expenses by leasing him to a minor league club in Arkansas. Rejections of a more dramatic kind awaited the lefthanded hitter after he had established himself as one of the great early 20th-century players.

Speaker batted over .300 18 times, including an AL-leading .386 in 1916 and three other years when he reached the .380 plateau. At one time or another he led his contemporaries in hits (twice), doubles (eight times), home runs (once), and slugging average (once). He had 200 hits four times, 50 doubles four times, scored 100 runs seven times, knocked in 100 twice, and stole at least 30 bases seven times.

His lifetime 792 doubles are the most in history, while his 3,514 hits rank him behind only Pete Rose, Ty Cobb, Hank Aaron, and Stan Musial. Defensively, Speaker was a pioneer "reader," moving to his left or right even as the pitch was being delivered to the plate—an ability that allowed him to play so shallow that he was able to pull off four unassisted double plays, take pickoff throws from the pitcher and catcher, throw batters out on balls hit up the middle, and even turn the pivot on a double play. The Gray Eagle, as he was dubbed, led AL outfielders in putouts seven times, in assists three times, in double plays five times, and in fielding average twice. His 448 career assists remain a benchmark for outfielders.

While with Boston, Speaker was a major force in the club's 1912 and 1915 world championships. In that same period he was also prominent in clubhouse tensions between Protestants and Catholics on the team; the rift particularly pitted Speaker and Joe Wood against Bill Carrigan and Heinie Wagner, and helped trigger two managerial switches and a franchise sale. Following the dissolution of the Federal League in 1915, Red Sox owner Joseph Lannin adopted a popular boardroom ploy of slashing player salaries to redress the inflated wages paid two years earlier to impede defections to the Feds; Speaker's refusal to accept a cut led to a tug-of-war up to Opening Day in 1916, when Lannin announced a deal sending the star to the Indians. The Yankees and other teams protested the transaction because of the suspected involvement of AL president Ban Johnson; the suspicion was that Johnson had pressured Lannin to swap Speaker to the president's friend, Cleveland owner James Dunn, to help the Ohio franchise at the turnstiles.

In Cleveland Speaker was a player-manager in all but title. Rarely did nominal Indians pilot Lee Fohl make a move in the lineup or with the starting rotation without consulting his center fielder; Fohl even made pitching changes during games on the basis of prearranged signals from Speaker in the outfield. The star also had a big say in player transactions, and wasted little time in acquiring some of his teammates from Boston; among them was clubhouse ally Wood. Although Cleveland showed a marked improvement after Speaker's arrival, the club's failure to go all the way to the top fueled trouble with Fohl. The breaking point came during an August 1919 game against the Red Sox, when Fohl either ignored or misinterpreted the signals from his center fielder and brought in reliever Fritz Coumbe to pitch to Babe Ruth. When Ruth homered, Speaker let everyone in the ballpark know how he felt about the manager's move. The humiliated Fohl resigned that very day, forcing Speaker to take over in title as well as function. With his managerial duties now weighing on him formally, Speaker slumped enough over the final weeks of the 1919 season to cost Cleveland the flag. He made up for it in 1920 by rebounding with a .388 average and gaining the first pennant for the franchise. The victory didn't come cheaply. For one thing, rumors throughout the year said that the same Chicago players who were being investigated for selling out the 1919 World Series were on the take again for assuring the Indians the pennant. For another, Speaker was devastated by the fatal August 16 beaning of shortstop Ray Chapman by Carl Mays. Amid the fix rumors, Chapman's death, and the lynch mob atmosphere when Mays and the Yankees came to Cleveland late in the season, Speaker admitted to having "lost some of the taste" for the pennant run. Neverthless, after winning the flag, the club also topped the Dodgers in the World Series.

Speaker stayed on as manager through the 1926 campaign, when he received his biggest rejection of all. At the end of the year the team announced he was stepping down as the pilot and retiring as a player because of charges by former Tigers pitcher Dutch Leonard that he had conspired with the hurler, Wood, and Ty Cobb to throw a 1919 game for assuring Detroit's third-place finish. The smoking gun in the charges were notes written by Wood and Cobb to Leonard alluding to bets placed on the game in question. Although the correspondence never mentioned Speaker by name, and he denied any involvement, he had to wait through weeks of executive intrigue while AL president Johnson and Commissioner Kenesaw Landis came to contradictory conclusions before he was semi-cleared. He ended up playing two final seasons for the Senators and Athletics.

J. G. TAYLOR SPINK

A character out of *The Front Page,* Spink inherited the fiscally shaky *Sporting News* in 1914; by his death in 1962 the weekly had become the Bible of Baseball. Variously abrasive and sensitive, contentious and sentimental, Spink stormed through the

baseball world for the better part of four decades, working the phones seven days a week at all hours to track down stories. A Ban Johnson ally against Kenesaw Landis, he helped the AL president in his pursuit of leads in the Black Sox scandal.

Spink's publication created its own Most Valuable Player Awards in 1929 after the two leagues abandoned similar honors, continuing the practice even after the Baseball Writers Association started its more widely recognized prizes in 1931. Similar *Sporting News* recognition followed for rookies (1946), pitchers (1948), and relievers (1960). His son C. C. Spink took over as publisher until the weekly was sold out of the family in 1977. *The Sporting News* has seldom found reasons to criticize owners in their battles with players on contractual matters.

KARL SPOONER

Spooner was the flashiest of flashes when he debuted for Brooklyn in the final week of the 1954 season with back-to-back shutouts of the Giants and Pirates, striking out 27 batters along the way. But in 1955 the southpaw hurt his arm, winning a mere eight games. His final big league appearance (he finished with a career mark of 10–6) came in the sixth game of that season's World Series against the Yankees, when he was knocked out in the first inning.

CHICK STAHL

Stahl's womanizing produced a grisly suicide. An outfielder for the Braves at the turn of the 20th century, he had little trouble attracting Baseball Annies when he emerged as one of the club's steadier bats. His popularity only increased when he jumped to the newly created Red Sox with Jimmy Collins in 1901 and helped to make the American League team an instant success. In 1906 Stahl succeeded Collins as Boston manager on an interim basis, then was offered a contract to return as the official pilot the following year. But during spring training he kept changing his mind about accepting the job, indicating some deep stress. Then, one evening, Collins returned to the room they shared to find Stahl dying of a lethal dose of carbolic acid. Stahl's last words as reported by Collins and another player—"Boys, I couldn't help it; it drove me to it."—remained enigmatic until 1986, when a Boston magazine reported that the outfielder had been overwhelmed by guilt for having married one woman in November 1906 even as he was discovering that he had impregnated another, who was demanding her own walk down the aisle. Moreover, according to the report, a third woman had taken shots at him on two different occasions for leaving her in the lurch.

GEORGE STALLINGS

Stallings was as schizophrenic a personality as baseball has ever seen. Polite to the point of courtliness away from the diamond, he bordered on the savage when he donned a uniform. Although mainly associated with the Miracle Braves of 1914, he had already disenchanted scores of players, umpires, and front office officials before ever reaching Boston. He also rivaled John McGraw as AL president Ban Johnson's greatest obsession.

After cups of coffee as a catcher with the Dodgers and Phillies in the 1890s, Stallings got his first managerial shot with Philadelphia in 1897. Only 28 and still trying to hang on as a receiver, he was a walking profanity who spent as much time imposing regulations and lashing into his players as he did trying to outwit the opposition. The result was a team revolt that led to his firing during the 1898 campaign. After a couple of seasons managing Detroit in the minor Western League, he found himself in perfect position when the club was elevated to major league status in the first year of the American League; it didn't hurt that he was also half-owner of the franchise. Stallings always claimed he was the first one to dub his club the Tigers after having them don the black-and-yellow striped socks of Princeton University (other sources attribute the nickname to Philip Reid, sports editor of the Detroit *Free Press*).

Stallings's stay in Detroit was even stormier than his experience in Philadelphia. While AL president Johnson anxiously tried to pass off his circuit as a decorous alternative to the brawling National League, Stallings drew fine upon fine for invective against opposition players and baiting of umpires; he interrupted this only to accuse his partner Jim Burns of financial irregularities and to open secret negotiations for shifting the Tigers to the NL. Faced with an ultimatum from Johnson, Stallings finally agreed to sell his interest in the team—an opening that the league executive used to get rid of Burns, as well. With this antagonism in place, Johnson tried unsuccessfully to dissuade the Yankees from hiring Stallings as their manager in 1909. By way of compensation

he turned a deaf ear to Stallings charges a year later that first baseman Hal Chase was trying to undermine him; instead, Johnson exploited hovering charges that Stallings had been stealing signs during New York home games to justify pressuring Yankees owner Frank Farrell to get rid of the pilot. The AL president tried not to look too happy when Farrell appointed Chase to take over the team. In departing from New York, Stallings blamed his firing equally on Chase and Johnson.

Moving over to Boston in 1913, Stallings inherited a team that had not risen above sixth for a decade. He did nothing to spoil that record in his first year, finishing in the cellar. Once again he was at daily odds with the few stars on the club, on more than one occasion to the point of blows; his version of leadership earned him the nickname of Bonehead—not because the players thought he was an imbecile, but because he thought they were and made a habit of summoning them with that perjorative. But at the same time a slightly older Stallings also showed that he was capable of being as patient with rookies as he was impatient with veterans, and the first-year players praised him then and afterward for building up their self-confidence. What he also brought to Boston was the sign stealing abilities that had been used as an excuse to get him out of New York. On the other hand, Stallings had so many superstitions about paper that adversaries regularly assigned bench players to sneak up behind the Boston dugout and shred newspapers to distract him from his strategizing. It worked so predictably that he had to take countermeasures and have security guards keep an eye on the people approaching his dugout.

Stallings began Boston's greatest season in 1914 by leading the team to a mere four wins in its first 22 games. In July the Braves couldn't even get past an amateur club of soap company employees in an exhibition. But in one of the most unlikely comebacks in baseball history the team ran roughshod over the National League in the second half, winning 52 of its final 66 games. The Miracle Braves then completed their startling season by sweeping the heavily favored Athletics in the World Series.

Stallings kept the team competitive for a couple of more years, but against a background of increasing chaos in the franchise's executive suite and of a parade of John McGraw-recommended owners who were never reluctant to pass along the club's most promising players to the Polo Grounds. More than once Stallings himself tried to acquire the franchise, but was always turned down, primarily because he was a distrusted outsider to the cozy New York-Boston entente. In 1920 he finally got tired of pleading for good players and took owner George Washington Grant (another McGraw inspiration) up on a challenge to quit if he didn't like the way the team was being run.

EDDIE STANKY

Stanky was never quite able to get out from under Branch Rickey's backhanded compliment that "he can't hit and can't field . . . all he can do is beat you." In fact, the second baseman could very much hit, as witness the .320, .285, and .300 seasons he had between 1948 and 1951 and the fact that neither his predecessors nor his successors on the Cubs, Giants, or Braves neared his offensive production. In addition, he led the National League in walks three times, on-base percentage twice, and runs scored another time.

But overriding these achievements was the image of The Brat—the no-holds barred scrapper who kicked balls away from infielders (most famously, the Yankees Phil Rizzuto in the 1951 World Series) and who never saw a diamond situation he couldn't worsen by starting a fight. If these qualities were essential to Stanky's play on three pennant-winning teams (the Dodgers in 1947, the Braves in 1948, and the Giants in 1951), and were openly encouraged by his mentor Leo Durocher, they were equally destructive during his subsequent managing career. As pilot of the Cardinals in the mid-1950s he became an embarrassment to upper management with his constant heckling of umpires and regular early trips to the showers; his players didn't think too highly of him, either, and, on his way to the Yankees in 1954, Enos Slaughter singled him out as the only person in St. Louis he wouldn't miss. With the White Sox in the 1960s he alienated most of Chicago by blaming his team's mediocre showing on the media, compromising his coaches by having them spy on players, insisting on martinet disciplinary rules, getting opposing teams up for their visits to Comiskey Park by ridiculing their managers and personnel, and publicly scorning his own front office.

In June 1977 the Rangers hired Stanky to replace Frank Lucchesi, but after sitting in the dugout for a single game (a victory), he returned to his home in Alabama with the announcement that he wasn't up to dealing with modern players.

WILLIE STARGELL (Hall of Fame, 1988)

Stargell was Reggie Jackson without the 24-hour-a-day preening. Dubbed Pops in his later years for his expansive manner and expanded waistline, the lefty-swinging outfielder-first baseman rolled up a Reggie-like 475 home runs in his 21-year (1962–82) career with the Pirates and, like his American League counterpart, established his own circuit's strikeout record with 1,936. Along the way Stargell paced the NL in home runs twice and in RBIs, doubles, and slugging average once each. Six times he belted at least 30 home runs—some of them titanic blasts. Of the 18 balls hit out of Forbes Field in 61 years, for instance, seven came off his bat.

Although already 38, Stargell was at his best in Pittsburgh's world championship year of 1979. After walloping 32 homers in the regular season to win the MVP award with Keith Hernandez, he completed the hat trick by also taking MVP honors for both the NLCS against Cincinnati and the World Series against Baltimore. Aside from the five home runs and 13 RBIs he contributed to the two postseason series, he was singled out for being the soul of the We Are Family Pirates—a role he played to the hilt by conferring gold stars on teammates who had distinguished themselves in games and who proudly sported their prizes on their helmets throughout the year.

RUSTY STAUB

Staub was one of the few players who didn't make his time with the Expos sound like exile in Siberia; as a result, *Le Grande Orange,* as fans came to call him for his carrot hair, has been the most popular player to wear a Montreal uniform. As nobody's fool during his 23-year (1963–85) career, on the other hand, he wasn't always popular with front offices. In 1968, for instance, he raised the hackles of his Houston employers by demanding that teams suspend spring training games in the wake of the assassination of Martin Luther King; though the Astros biggest offensive threat at the time, he was packed off to the Expos at the end of the year. Other times he irked the Mets with long-term contract demands (and was traded to the Tigers) and the Tigers by sitting out spring training over a contract impasse (and was dealt back to the Expos).

A lefty-hitting first baseman-outfielder, Staub is the only big leaguer to have collected at least 500 hits for four different teams (Astros, Expos, Mets, and Tigers) and the only one apart from Ty Cobb to hit a home run before he was 20 and after he was 40. In his waning years, during a second stint with the Mets, he became a potent pinch-hitter, at one point in 1983 tying Dave Philley's record of eight straight pinch-hits in a season.

TURKEY STEARNS (Hall of Fame, 2000)

Noted as much for his unorthodox batting stance as for his ability to bat both cleanup and leadoff, Stearns won seven home run titles in one Negro league or another while maintaining an average of about .350. A lefty-hitting center fielder, he might not have been as fast as Cool Papa Bell, but he was regarded as a better defensive player. He played on Negro National League pennant winners with the American Giants (1933) and the Kansas City Monarchs (1940–41). Stearns stood at the plate with his right foot in the bucket, his heel dug in and his toes pointed upward. His daughter claimed his nickname was inspired by his flapping his elbows when he ran, but Stearns himself said it came from a pot belly he had as a child.

GEORGE STEINBRENNER

There have been three principal reasons why Steinbrenner seems to have adopted a lower profile in recent years—four Yankees world championships and five World Series appearances between 1996 and 2001; successful front office personnel moves that he had opposed; and the previously manic level of the psychodrama that he had reduced the franchise to in the 1980s and first part of the 1990s. By comparison, his firing of a couple of coaches and scouts in the immediate wake of New York's loss to Arizona in the 2001 World Series was a mere burp.

Operator of the Cleveland-quartered American Ship Building Company, Steinbrenner arrived in the Bronx in April 1973 after heading a consortium that paid a bargain $10 million to CBS for the Yankees; his first memorable declaration was that "we plan absentee ownership. I'll stick to building ships." For awhile he kept his word, in part because he was busy defending himself against an indictment for illegal contributions to President Richard Nixon's 1972 reelection campaign. Finally pleading guilty in Au-

gust 1974, Steinbrenner was fined $15,000 by the courts and suspended from club operations for two years by Commissioner Bowie Kuhn. The suspension was just shy of a formality, however, since the owner was forever sending taped messages into the clubhouse and certainly signing off on such major player moves as the 1975 acquisition of free agent Catfish Hunter. Kuhn officially reinstated him in March 1976, five months prematurely—and soon after the Yankees had switched sides to cast the deciding vote in awarding the commissioner a second term.

If Hunter had been a unique contractual case, the free agents who hit the market in 1976 after the Messersmith-McNally decision represented Steinbrenner's first opportunity to throw money here, there, and everywhere for attracting names to Yankee Stadium. His signing of Cincinnati southpaw Don Gullett also set a pattern of recruiting high-priced pitchers who would develop physical or psychological diabilities that restricted their usefulness in New York. Among those who paraded in and out after Gullett to no great gain up to the early 1990s were Andy Messersmith, Luis Tiant, Rudy May, Rick Reuschel, Doyle Alexander, Bob Shirley, John Montefusco, Ed Whitson, Britt Burns, Steve Trout, Andy Hawkins, Rich Dotson, and Tim Leary.

The acquisition of Gullett was eclipsed, however, by the signing of future Hall of Famer Reggie Jackson, a move that made manager Billy Martin fume for his exclusion from the front office decision to bring in the outfielder. Throughout the 1977 season tensions simmered among the owner, the manager, and the slugger, with club president Gabe Paul barely keeping the lid on. But when Paul went back to Cleveland in 1978, Steinbrenner stepped up the pace of his phone calls to Martin to tell him what he was doing wrong (mainly not batting Jackson cleanup). The team's slow start and the open resentment between Martin and Jackson also had the owner increasing the frequency of his trips to New York, ostensibly to set matters right but usually only making them worse. It was in this context that third baseman Graig Nettles summed up the feeling in the Yankees clubhouse as: "The more we lose, the more he'll fly in, and the more he flies in, the better chance that there'll be a plane crash."

What followed was Steinbrenner-directed comic opera: the firing of Martin in the wake of the manager's description of Jackson as a "born liar" and of

Steinbrenner as a "convicted" one (i.e., the campaign contributions); the hiring of Bob Lemon as a managerial successor; and the announcement to a stunned Old Timers Day crowd that Martin would be back in the dugout in 1980, with Lemon moving up to the front office. In the meantime, the team launched a stretch run that ended with Bucky Dent's three-run home run off the Red Sox to win the AL East title, then went on to a world championship. Steinbrenner brought Martin back in 1979, a year earlier than announced, for a season of haranguing reminders about remaining on good behavior, then dismissed him a second time for getting into a fist fight with a marshmallow salesman.

Dick Howser followed Martin into the manager's office in 1980 and right out again after winning 103 games but being swept by Kansas City in the ALCS. Over the next 11 years there were 14 managerial changes, with Martin returning three additional times. Coaches were even more expendable in the Steinbrenner universe; in 1982 alone there were three hitting coaches and five pitching tutors. The front office picture was no clearer: In rapid succession into the 1990s, Cedric Tallis, Gene Michael, Bill Bergesch, Murray Cook, Clyde King, Woody Woodward, Lou Piniella, Syd Thrift, and Michael again were formally responsible for baseball operations.

Unsurprisingly, the roster changed with head-spinning regularity. For half the 1978 season, for example, Steinbrenner saddled the club with Jim Spencer, Jay Johnstone, and Gary Thomasson, lefty-swinging outfielder-first basemen-designated hitter clones; as if that were not sufficient folly, Spencer's contract carried a provision, inserted at the owner's insistence, that the player would start every game in which the Yankees faced a righthanded pitcher. The confusion was so rampant that in 1991 general manager George Bradley kept offering second baseman Steve Sax a contract extension that would make him untradeable for a couple of years, while at the same time vice-president Pete Peterson was trying to peddle the infielder.

Young players suffered the most in the turmoil, finding no room for error and having even their manhood questioned by Steinbrenner if they gave up a home run or contributed in any other way to a New York defeat; among the more conspicuous victims were Jim Beattie, Ken Clay, and Bobby Meacham. Always a bully, The Boss, as he was not adverse to

being called, regularly called front office staffers a few minutes after 5:00 P.M. to make sure they were still at their desks. Failing to understand what spring training was about, he would become hysterical over exhibition losses to the Mets, insisting that his regular lineup play most of the game so he would have a leg up in the battle for New York's back page sports headlines. Regularly congratulating himself for having restored the "Yankee tradition," he would nonetheless publicly apologize for team losses, most notably after losing to the Dodgers in the 1981 World Series. On the other hand, he didn't apologize for a claimed run-in with two Dodgers fans in an elevator in Los Angeles; on the contrary, he displayed his bruised knuckles as a badge of honor, even though there was conjecture that the victim of the punches had been an elevator wall.

Steinbrenner didn't confine his outbursts to employees and phantoms. In January 1983 he called White Sox owners Jerry Reinsdorf and Eddie Einhorn "the Abbott and Costello of baseball" for criticizing the big money he had given to free agent outfielder Steve Kemp; Kuhn fined him $5,000 for the crack. In spring training of the same year he accused umpire Lee Weyer of being under instructions from NL president Chub Feeney to call all close plays in exhibition games for the senior circuit team; the fine for this was $50,000. Outbursts a few months later against AL president Lee MacPhail for reversing the umpires' decision in the Pine Tar Incident and awarding a home run to George Brett brought a $250,000 fine and $50,000 in legal fees. In 1987 he finally won one—a court case triggered by the umpires union over an accusation that arbiter Dallas Parks was "incompetent." In 1989 he took on his own fans, ordering Yankee Stadium security guards to confiscate signs saying "George Must Go!" Only a legal action filed by the American Civil Liberties Union prevented a recurrence. It was in the same period, however, that he dispensed with Yankee Stadium's ushers and left the park's seating sections exclusively in the hands of a private security agency; the union-busting move made for regular scenes of fans stumbling around in the grandstands looking for their seats.

In fact, Steinbrenner did go—for awhile, at least. In 1990 Commissioner Fay Vincent came up with evidence that the owner had paid professional gambler Howard Spira $40,000 to dig up dirt on outfielder Dave Winfield, then engaged in a feud with the

Yankees executive. Vincent was about to announce a two-year suspension when Steinbrenner stepped forward with an offer to remove himself indefinitely from club affairs, provided the actual word "suspension" wasn't used in the official decree. The Yankee Stadium announcement of the arrangement caused a standing ovation. But other owners weren't so sanguine. Steinbrenner had been a key voice on any number of league matters, and none of the people left behind for watching the store had his authority or smarts in those areas. Because of this other AL owners pressured Vincent for a specific date for his return, and in one of his final pronouncements in office the commissioner ruled that the owner could return to full control of his team in March 1993.

As irritating as it might have been for other owners, Steinbrenner's enforced absence proved to be a godsend for general manager Michael. Despite ongoing frictions about who was responsible for what in the front office, Michael and others who answered to Steinbrenner's condescending description of "my baseball people" suddenly had relative freedom for picking up the pieces and putting them together again, starting with the dangerously drained farm system. Their time on the job even intimidated the returning Steinbrenner from following up demands that young players such as Bernie Williams be traded off for veterans. By the time Joe Torre arrived on the scene in 1996, the franchise was ready with Derek Jeter, Mariano Rivera, and other key elements of the club that would sweep through the American League for the second half of the decade. His most overt act of old-style vindictiveness didn't come until 2001, when, increasingly annoyed by the praise heaped on Torre and general manager Brian Cashman for the club's success, he let both of them play out their contracts through the World Series amid reminders that nobody was indispensable; both were resigned during the winter.

If Steinbrenner seemed abnormally content with garden variety bullying upon his return, it was also because he was preoccupied by the imminent bankruptcy of American Ship Building. Only later did it emerge that he had been borrowing heavily against more than $500 million in long-term contracts with the Madison Square Garden cable network (MSG) and WABC radio—initially to try to salvage his shipbuilding interests, then to increase his already considerable personal profits. He also began stepping

up his threats to end "Yankee tradition" altogether by moving the club out of the Bronx, and in this he had a willing accomplice in Mayor Rudolph Giuliani, who never stopped talking about the Garden of Paradise to be had if tax payers would endorse a $1 billion bond for the construction of a new park on the West Side of Manhattan. Even when Steinbrenner and Giuliani retreated to the backup hope for a new stadium next to the existing facility, the idea was a non-starter, not least because the mayor was simultaneously promising another new stadium (and another taxpayer hit) to the Mets. The issue all but died altogether after the September 11, 2001 attacks on the World Trade Center suggested the city had more urgent ways to spend money than to provide Steinbrenner with more luxury boxes. By way of compensation, he announced the organization of his own cable television network (YES) for carrying the games of the Yankees and their New Jersey Nets basketball and New Jersey Devils hockey partners.

BILL STEMMEYER

Stemmeyer established an unapproachable record for wildness in 1896, when he uncorked 64 wild pitches in only 41 games. The Braves righthander still managed to post 22 victories.

CASEY STENGEL (Hall of Fame, 1966)

The earliest public perception of Stengel as a clownish buffoon gave way to that of a gifted raconteur whose Stengelese made more sense than was immediately apparent; this, in turn, yielded to one of a venerable old man wisecracking his way through otherwise exasperating seasons with a wretched expansion club. What was often lost in all these characterizations was the shrewdness that made Stengel a millionaire from oil and banking investments and the guile of the only manager to win five successive world championships or even five straight pennants. They also missed a mean streak that surfaced more and more frequently with age.

Stengel arrived in the major leagues as a lefthand-hitting outfielder with the Dodgers in 1912. Before he was through as a player 14 seasons later he would wear the uniform of five National League teams, put up a lifetime .284 average, and gain a well-deserved reputation as a zany. Like protégé Billy Martin decades later, he did his best work in World Series play, batting .393 in three Series. In the 1923 postseason, in a losing cause for the Giants against the Yankees, he batted .417; won the first game with a ninth-inning inside-the-park home run; and clubbed another home run in the third game to provide the margin for a 1–0 victory. His emerging persona was evident in such antics as carrying a flashlight onto the field to persuade an unpersuaded umpire that it was too dark to continue a game and doffing his cap to release a bird to the delight of the crowd. More important, he became a devoted acolyte of Giants manager John McGraw.

Referring to their time together with the Braves and Mets around the glorious Yankees years, Warren Spahn summed up Stengel's managerial career by saying he played for him "both before and after he was a genius." In fact, he hadn't been much of a genius running the Dodgers before the Braves, either. On the other hand, he did show flashes of brilliance before the Yankees by winning minor league pennants in Toledo, Milwaukee, and Oakland. He also demonstrated early on the cunning (typically disguised as tomfoolery in the retelling) that would mark his later years when, as outfielder-manager-president of the Eastern League Worcester club in 1925, he got out from under all three jobs by releasing himself from the first, firing himself from the second, and resigning from the third to take over McGraw-owned Toledo for the following season.

After two years as a Dodgers coach, Stengel took over as dugout boss in 1934. His first big league piloting job lasted three years, and had its moments. In 1934 the club took two late-season games from the Giants that cost them the pennant, satisfying general manager Bob Quinn's vow that the Dodgers would get back at New York manager Bill Terry for his spring training sarcasm about whether Brooklyn was still in the league. Stengel also brought the daffiness of the front office down to the field in ways calculated to charm newsmen and help fans avert their eyes from the team's second-division finishes; his diversions included protesting the continuation of a game in inclement weather by coaching at third base under an umbrella and staging races between his players so he could win a few dollars from reporters. The daffiness occasionally took on a life of its own, such as when center fielder Frenchy Bordagaray once gave priority to chasing after his cap rather than a fly ball and when the perennially hungover right fielder Hack Wilson, assuming it was a line drive, ran after a ball

fired in anger by pitcher Boom Boom Beck for being removed from a game.

Six years (1938–43) at the helm of the Braves was more of the same. That period ended when Stengel, responding to a question about a spring training play, let go with a classic rush of Stengelese at an unamused Lou Perini, who was about to take over as Boston's principal owner. Others had the laugh when, just before the opening game of the 1943 season, the manager was run over by a taxi and missed the first two months of the campaign with a broken leg, prompting columnist Dave Egan to nominate the cabbie as the man who had done the most for Boston baseball that year.

When Stengel succeeded Bucky Harris as Yankees manager in 1949, kind observers regarded the move as a crowd-pleasing sideshow for once again keeping fans distracted while a rebuilding effort went on; the unkind, who weren't used to the New Yorkers conceding any season in the name of rebuilding, thought the appointment disastrous. In fact, general manager George Weiss had spent considerable time convincing owners Del Webb and Dan Topping to accept his choice. Stengel vindicated Weiss by turning in his finest managerial effort, winning the pennant over Boston by one game on the final day of the campaign. All year he had to juggle lineups to compensate for 71 injuries, platooning at practically every position. He also made uncannily successful decisions, often going against orthodoxy. One of his biggest moves in this sense came in the eighth inning of the next-to-last game of the season when he allowed the righthand-swinging Johnny Lindell to bat against Boston righthander Joe Dobson in spite of the fact that he had been platooning Lindell with the lefty Gene Woodling all season; Lindell homered to break a 4–4 tie.

After beating the Dodgers for his first world championship, Stengel decided he had the leverage to start moving out some of the old guard that had broken down on him during the season. The acerbic, even authoritarian traits that he had kept under check in 1949 emerged clearly in 1950, straining his relations with team veterans, and especially with Joe DiMaggio. Although he went out of his way to declare the fabled center fielder the best player he had ever managed, he also seemed to look for ways to put him in his place. At one time or another Stengel had Topping persuade the star to try playing first base (an experiment that lasted one game); dropped him from fourth to fifth in the lineup without telling him beforehand; and sent an embarrassed Cliff Mapes out to replace him in the outfield in the middle of an inning. In the last instance DiMaggio waved his would-be substitute back to the bench disdainfully, then took himself out of the game at the end of the inning. By the end of the season DiMaggio was barely acknowledging Stengel's presence.

It was with younger players that Stengel shone. Martin and Whitey Ford arrived in 1950. In 1951 the organization ran the first of its pre-spring training instructional camps, producing Mickey Mantle, Gil McDougald, and Tom Morgan. Even though he was to become the jewel in Stengel's crown, Mantle had to endure constant barbs from the manager for the perceived disparity between his potential and his productivity. Even years later Stengel mused about what might have happened to Mantle if he had left him at his original shortstop position instead of making him DiMaggio's successor in center field, insisting he would have been greater than Honus Wagner.

Through 1960 Stengel won 10 pennants (tying him with McGraw for the most ever) and seven World Series (matching Joe McCarthy), using his standard approach of riding his players when they were doing well and heaping praise on them during rough stretches. He also evolved into The Old Perfesser, holding forth into all hours in bars around the AL with what he called "my writers." His Stengelese— a jabberwocky of rambling, doubletalk, gibberish, non sequiturs, and catchphrases—left his audiences amused, bewildered, and sometimes slightly better informed. Those subjected to his monologues needed a dictionary for knowing that a "butcher boy" meant a chopped ground ball in sacrifice situations, a "whiskey slick" a carouser, and "the Youth of America" the current crop of rookies. The U.S. Senate Subcommittee on Monopoly and Antitrust had no such help when Stengel delivered a vintage dose of his private language in a July 1958 hearing on baseball's exemption from federal antitrust regulations; all the panel understood was that, never one to challenge baseball's suits to any extreme, he was against lifting the exemption.

As he grew older, however, Stengel became increasingly impatient with his "Youth of America." For several years Webb and Topping were anxious to replace him before some other club snatched Ralph

Houk away from the New York affiliate in Denver. Their opportunity came after the team's 1960 World Series loss to Pittsburgh, when Stengel was criticized heavily for getting only two starts out of his ace Ford and for getting Ralph Terry up in the bullpen four times before finally calling him in to serve up Bill Mazeroski's decisive home run in the final game. Two days after the Series Stengel officially "retired," while putting up no pretense that it had been his idea. "I'll never make the mistake of being 70 again," he complained.

Two years later Weiss, in his new role as president of the embryonic Mets, hired Stengel to manage the expansion team, making him the only one to wear the uniforms of all four 20th-century New York clubs. Stengel's task was less to direct the sorry collection of veterans that compiled one of the worst records in the history of baseball than to promote his Amazin' Mets as better entertainment than the Bronx club he had just left. For nearly four years hardly a day went by without the sports pages reporting some bizarre or bizarrely stated observation from him on the miserable state of his squad. The brilliance of his public relations performance endeared the incompetent Mets to The New Breed fans, who relished the incompetence almost as much as its promotion. "Can't anybody here play this game?" became as much of a trademark Stengel line as "You could look it up." He ended up wisecracking his way through three 10th-place finishes and part of another.

But when he wasn't winning public relations points for the Mets, Stengel was snoozing on the bench or castigating his players. Told that southpaw Ken McKenzie was probably the lowest paid member of the Yale graduating class, he retorted: "But he has the highest ERA." Catcher Chris Cannizzaro was jettisoned with: "He's a great catch, that Canzoneri (sic). He's the only defensive catcher who can't catch." The ever-hyper Jimmy Piersall he described as "great but you gotta play him in a cage." Catcher Greg Goossen entered all of baseball's quotation books when his manager, asked about his big league potential, said "he's only 20 and with a good chance in 10 years of being 30." Everybody laughed except the players.

In 1965 a broken wrist forced the 74-year-old manager to turn the club over to coach Wes Westrum temporarily. Then in late July, after a banquet the night before an Old Timers Game, another fall fractured his hip. Everybody but the Mets players were sorry about the announcement of his retirement. Stengel lived for more than a decade after returning to his California home in Glendale. The inscription on his tombstone is one of his most quoted lines: "There comes a time in every man's life, and I've had plenty of them."

RENNIE STENNETT

Stennett was the only 20th-century player to bang out seven hits in a nine-inning game. The Pirates second baseman collected four singles, two doubles, and a triple against the Cubs on September 16, 1975. Pittsburgh's 22–0 win was also the most one-sided shutout in baseball history. The only other player to get seven hits in a regulation contest was Wilbert Robinson, in the 19th century.

GENE STEPHENS

Stephens was known throughout his eight years with the Red Sox as a defensive caddy for Ted Williams. But on June 18, 1953, in the course of a 17-run seventh inning, the outfielder also became the only 20th-century player to get three hits in an inning.

VERN STEPHENS

Stephens was a slugging shortstop who proved the power of contrition. While with the Browns the righty hitter signed a five-year, $175,000 contract to play for the Mexican League in 1946. After only two games south of the border, however, his father and St. Louis scout Jack Fournier drove to Mexico to get him and whisk him back. He avoided the suspension imposed on the other Mexican League jumpers when Commissioner Happy Chandler ruled that, since he hadn't signed a 1946 contract with the Browns before taking off, he hadn't broken any regulations; in fact, he had at the very least violated the supposedly sacrosanct reserve clause.

Stephens played 15 big league seasons (1941–55), mostly with the Browns and Red Sox, leading the AL in homers once and RBIs three times.

RIGGS STEPHENSON

Stephenson's .336 lifetime average is the highest among 20th-century players eligible for the Hall of Fame but without a plaque there. A second baseman with the Indians from 1921 to 1925 and an outfielder with the Cubs between 1926 and 1934, he batted over .300 in 12 of his 14 big league seasons. In 1929

the righthanded hitter combined with Hack Wilson and Kiki Cuyler as the century's only outfield with three 100 RBI producers.

LESLIE STERLING

Sterling became the first woman public address announcer in the American League when she succeeded the deceased Sherm Feller in Fenway Park in 1994.

HARRY STEVENS

Stevens was a paid informer for Cincinnati who cost the franchise a manager and baseball's greatest player in 1914. Protesting an order that Stevens would be accompanying his club on road trips to report on player antics, manager Joe Tinker refused to sign a contract with the Reds and was sold to the Dodgers. Then, during the season, Reds boss Garry Herrmann decided to get more for his money than his spy's bland reports, so he dispatched Stevens to Baltimore to make a recommendation on two players owed to Cincinnati by the minor league Orioles. Lacking any experience as a scout, Stevens endorsed the acquisition of outfielder George Twombly and shortstop Claude Derrick—but urged the club not to bother with pitchers Ernie Shore and Babe Ruth.

HARRY M. STEVENS

Dissatisfied with the scorecard he had purchased for an American Association Columbus Colts game in the 1880s, the English-born Stevens won a contract to design and hawk an improved version, reputedly originating the pitch "You can't tell the players without a scorecard" in the process. After expanding to other cities and branching out into food and drink, he won an exclusive concession contract at the Polo Grounds in 1893 and, using his new city connections, was soon operating in Madison Square as well. By 1911 he was so wealthy that he was able to lend the Giants the money to rebuild the Polo Grounds grandstand after a fire. His innovations include the hot dog (at the Polo Grounds in 1901) and serving drinks with a straw (so thirsty patrons didn't have to tilt back their heads, possibly missing a vital play while sipping his soda or beer). Stevens's multimillion-dollar business eventually included the concessions at racetracks and hotels as well as sports arenas and stadiums.

DAVE STEWART

Stewart's field reputation as the quintessential late bloomer has been rivaled since his retirement by those of a masterly pitching coach and the typically blocked African American in baseball's front offices. After wandering around from the Dodgers to the Rangers to the Phillies as a long reliever from 1978 to 1986, he set down in Oakland, where manager Tony LaRussa and pitching coach Dave Duncan decided he was better suited as a starter. The result was four consecutive 20-victory seasons. With the A's and then later with the Blue Jays, the righthander also racked up a record 10 wins between the League Championship Series and the World Series.

After retiring in 1995, Stewart worked in administrative capacities in Oakland and San Diego. When the Padres needed a pitching coach in 1998, he went back down to the field to tutor the staff that would bring a surprising NL pennant to southern California by cutting an entire run off its ERA from 1997. Still more interested in front office responsibilities (and leaving behind a staff whose ERA would bounce back up one full run), Stewart moved over to Toronto in 1999 as an assistant to the general manager, never disguising his ambition to one day have full charge of some franchise's baseball operations. But after a couple of years of ceremonious interviews and rhetorical assurances from Commissioner Bud Selig that more room would be made for minorities in major league front offices, he was again passed over in the fall of 2001 in Toronto's search for a new general manager. Blasting the hypocrisy of the interview process, he again returned to the dugout as the Brewers pitching coach for 2002.

ERNEST STEWART

An umpire during the 1941–45 war years, Stewart discovered the hard way that league offices were reluctant to cede authority to the commissioner's office. When the recently elected Happy Chandler indicated his willingness to discuss the grievances of umpires, Stewart took that as an endorsement of his plans to form a union of arbiters. American League President Will Harridge moved quickly: first firing Stewart, then reminding Chandler that he, not the commissioner, had jurisdiction over umpires. Chandler made no attempt to overrule Harridge and reinstate Stewart.

SAMMY STEWART

Based on what he actually did for the Orioles in 1981, Stewart won the American League ERA title. But under a rule stipulating that the number of innings pitched be rounded off to the nearest complete inning, the righthander lost the honor to Oakland's Steve McCatty. In September 1978 Stewart set a new standard by striking out seven consecutive batters in his major league debut.

DAVE STIEB

Toronto's best pitcher for most of the 1980s, Stieb played tag with no-hitters for three years. In back-to-back games in September 1988 the righthander retired two batters in the ninth inning before yielding his first hit. On August 4, 1989 he went one better (or worse) by throwing a perfect game until his 27th hitter, Roberto Kelly of the Yankees, slashed a double. In that same season he threw two other one-hitters. Stieb finally ended the frustration on September 2, 1990, when he no-hit the Indians. That game also finished his mound dominance; shortly afterward he was injured and, after 10 years of double-number wins, never again had more than four victories in a season.

TONI STONE

Stone was the first woman to play in the Negro leagues. With a background as a high school softball player, the 22-year-old second baseman hit .243 in 50 games for the Indianapolis Clowns of the Negro American League in 1953. She was generally regarded as a publicity stunt to attract fans after the best black players had been skimmed off by the majors. Traded to the Kansas City Monarchs in 1954, Stone was replaced on the Indianapolis roster by 19-year-old Connie Morgan, the second woman Negro leaguer.

CHARLES STONEHAM

Stoneham's 17-year (1919–35) ownership of the Giants was a daredevil act over actual and threatened indictments and lawsuits. His survival owed mainly to Tammany Hall connections and to adversaries as legally dubious as he was.

When he purchased the club from Harry Hempstead and the John T. Brush estate in January 1919 for $1 million, Stoneham had already seen courtrooms on corporate fraud charges. Although New York's buddy-boy press depicted him as a Wall St. broker, he was in fact the proprietor of a string of bucket shops for off-market speculation; one of his partners in the bucket shop venture was Arnold Rothstein, the gambler who shortly afterward became implicated in the Black Sox scandal. On the other hand, Stoneham was also a close associate of Governor Alfred E. Smith and most of the powers-that-be in the state's Democratic Party. It also helped that he had cultivated local hero John McGraw for years and gave the manager a piece of the club and a vice-presidency title.

Through most of the 1920s Stoneham was content to endorse the McGraw inspirations that brought the Giants four pennants and produced a succession of future Hall of Famers at the Polo Grounds. His most nervous moments came in 1924, when several of his players were accused of trying to bribe Philadelphia shortstop Heinie Sand to throw a game, and in 1927, when newly acquired Rogers Hornsby was sued by the Kentucky Gambling Commission for some $70,000 in unpaid wagering debts. Both episodes reminded too many people of his own gambling connections, prompting reports of some imminent investigation of the franchise by Commissioner Kenesaw Landis. As it turned out, Stoneham contracted a much bigger headache from minority stockholder and city magistrate Francis X. McQuade.

Between 1928 and 1933 Stoneham and McQuade took turns at legal suits over the owner's charges that the since-fired club treasurer had sought to "destroy" the Giants, among other ways by trying to draw McGraw into a plot to find new ownership for the organization. McQuade retaliated by offering evidence that Stoneham had been using franchise money for years to finance his other ventures, not least his periodically investigated bucket shops. But those charges would have been more compelling if Stoneham hadn't been able to counter with proof of his own that McQuade had used his position as treasurer to "borrow" money for his private purposes. With the various trials entertaining everybody in the city except McQuade and the owner's business and political associates, an appeals court finally took the high road by ruling that, whatever had ensued during McQuade's stint as treasurer, it was secondary to the fact that his simultaneous standing as a city magistrate precluded such activities as being an officer of a baseball club. The ruling followed the emergence of McQuade's (but not Stoneham's) name in the unrelated Seabury Commission's 1931–32 probe of corruption in the Tammany Hall administration of Mayor Jimmy Walker.

Stoneham died in 1935, leaving the Giants to his son Horace.

HORACE STONEHAM

Like Boston's Tom Yawkey, Stoneham kept a Mr. Nice Guy reputation in his 40-year (1936–75) reign as an owner; unlike Yawkey, he was still on his feet when he was overwhelmed by the changes brought by free agency.

When he took over the Giants from his father, Stoneham was known mainly as a hard drinker who liked to talk baseball into the wee hours with his favorite players and others he regarded as part of the franchise family. The only thing that changed over the years was that he became as knowledgeable as he was garrulous, largely thanks to his all-night sessions in the late 1940s and 1950s with manager Leo Durocher. What he didn't realize until after the fact was that Durocher, who himself kept away from alcohol, used the gab and drinking fests to find out who Stoneham's favorite players were and then played them into the ground if he didn't share the owner's opinion. Among the players disposed of this way were sluggers Sid Gordon and Willard Marshall.

In the mid-1950s Stoneham began warning New York and the National League he would be forced to move to another city if he didn't get a new stadium. Unlike the similar warnings coming from Brooklyn's Walter O'Malley, Stoneham's had some basis in economic reality because of a sharp attendance decline at the Polo Grounds and the third serving the franchise was receiving from local broadcasting rights after the Dodgers and Yankees. The fact that the Polo Grounds was in Harlem did not help attract the carriage trade, especially after a spectator was killed in 1956 by a sniper firing into the park from a rooftop across the street. By the opening of the 1957 season the question wasn't whether Stoneham would move, but where he would. For some weeks the likely destination seemed to be Minneapolis, site of the club's chief farm team. But then in May the league gave its formal approval for the Dodgers to move to Los Angeles and the Giants to San Francisco if they were unable to conclude local deals. With O'Malley turning on the pressure (the league had made it a condition that one club could move only if both did), Stoneham went before the franchise board of directors on August 19, 1957, and got an 8–1 vote in favor of moving to California.

Stoneham took some time to get used to San Francisco. He was particularly irritable about suggestions the club change its nickname to the Seals, asserting that "it's one thing to move a team, another to erase a glorious past." He was also as appalled as Willie Mays that Bay Area fans didn't take to the Polo Grounds star for quite a number of years, preferring Orlando Cepeda and then Willie McCovey because they had no tie to New York. What he never got used to was Candlestick Park—or to the fact that he had been given a tour of the land for the facility in the early afternoon, a couple of hours before the arrival of the daily winds that made it the worst outdoor stadium in the major leagues. Although the park was little more than an obstacle during the club's successive winning seasons in the 1960s, it became a decisive reason for fans to stay home when the play on the field turned mediocre in the early 1970s, to the point that attendance figures began dipping below those registered in the final Polo Grounds years.

By 1972 Stoneham was talking about selling out. It ended up taking more than four years, but not for lack of trying. Prospective buyers came and went amid demands by Mayor George Moscone that any deal contain a commitment to keep the club in San Francisco, the threatened alternative being a lawsuit. Stoneham paid lip service to the commitment, then in 1975 announced his intention of selling out to a Canadian beer company with the undisguised aim of moving the Giants to Toronto. This didn't bother the league too much; it was mainly interested in getting rid of Stoneham. The franchise's finances had in fact become so chaotic under his steady drinking and sporadic attention that the league had been forced to delegate Spec Richardson as a special representative to make sure checks were issued on time. But once again Mayor Moscone stepped in to thwart the deal. It was only then that real estate developer Bob Lurie concluded an agreement to buy the team with a commitment for keeping it in the city. As for Stoneham, he confessed to being relieved at getting out of "a world of agents and boardroom accountants where there's no more personal touch."

CARL STOTZ

Together with Bert and George Bebble, Stotz started the Little League in 1939 in Williamsport, Penn-

sylvania. Then consisting of only a handful of local teams, it has since grown to include some three million participants, mostly in the United States but to one degree or another in more than 100 other countries as well.

The Little League has had its critics. The very comprehensiveness of its organization has aroused fears that the preteens in its program have simply not been allowed to be children. Its steady commercialization through television also helped pressure a 2001 scandal in which the pitcher for the winning team from the Bronx was subsequently revealed as having used a doctored birth certificate for making him eligible.

GEORGE STOVALL

A competent first baseman from 1904 to 1915, Stovall was in the forefront of a threat by Cleveland players to strike unless they were allowed to attend the funeral of teammate Addie Joss in April 1911. After conferring with team executives, American League president Ban Johnson thought better of his original order to the players to fulfill a game commitment instead of attending the rites. Stovall had several other disputes with management that didn't turn out so well. In 1907 he was suspended for heaving a chair at Indians manager Nap Lajoie. In 1913 he was fired as Browns manager for spitting at umpire Charlie Ferguson and told to forget about playing first base for the rest of the year, as well. Despite reassurances from owner Robert Hedges that the player portion of his contract would be honored, Stovall showed up at the ballpark every day just to make sure he wasn't being conned out of his money. When he asked for his outright release, Hedges refused, and the war of nerves continued through the end of the season. Although he was indeed paid as promised, the first baseman became the first big leaguer to jump to the Federal League, asserting that "no white man ought to submit to be bartered like a broken-down plow horse."

HARRY STOVEY

Though ignored by Hall of Fame electors, Stovey was the game's first great slugger. Among other things he was the first player to break into double figures for home runs (14 with the American Association Athletics in 1883) and he led all major leaguers in the category during the 1880s (with 89). Also gifted with speed, Stovey was the first to wear sliding pads, an innovation he came up with to protect a bad leg.

A righthand-hitting first baseman-outfielder, Stovey played for 14 years (1880–93). His best seasons were with the AA, but he also contributed to the league's demise, at least indirectly. When the Players League folded after the 1890 campaign, Stovey, who had jumped to that circuit's Boston Reds, should have been returned to the Athletics, his 1889 club. But Philadelphia made the mistake of leaving him off its protected list, assuming that he would remain with the Reds, who were about to be absorbed into the AA. Taking advantage of the player's technical free agent status, the National League Boston Bean-eaters signed him, precipitating still another inter-league war and one that the American Association was ill equipped to fight.

For the better part of a century record books credited Stovey with a .404 average in 1884, but the actual mark was .326. The discrepancy was probably caused by chicanery on the part of an official scorer in Philadelphia who sought to give the local player the batting crown over New York's Dave Orr. Stovey was born Harry Stowe, but played under a pseudonym to spare his mother the shame of seeing the family name in the sports pages.

MONTY STRATTON

Stratton's back-to-back 15-win seasons in 1937 and 1938 with a darting fastball he called The Gander seemed to mark the start of a brilliant pitching career for the White Sox. But in November 1938 the righthander accidentally shot himself on a hunting foray, leading to the loss of a leg. Stratton's tenacity got him back to the mound at a minor league level for a few games, but it was more of a psychological than physical victory. He was the subject of a popular 1949 film with James Stewart.

DARRYL STRAWBERRY

Strawberry's mountainous personal miseries have made his days as a Mets slugger seem like part of another century more than in calendar terms. The right fielder once boomed as a prime prospect for the Hall of Fame has been measured for years mainly by his recurrent bouts with colon cancer, his relapses into drug addiction, and the grave depressions resulting from both.

Called up by New York in 1983, Strawberry sprang out of the gate faster than any previous power hitter, smashing at least 26 home runs a year in his first nine seasons. Along the way the lefty swinger captured Rookie of the Year honors (1983), led the National League in home runs and slugging (1988), and reached the 200-home run plateau at the young age of 27. The only thing longer than some of his drives was his tongue—especially in his annual predictions that he intended carrying the team with a "monster season"; his attacks on teammates; and his endless declarations of higher levels of awareness for having overcome alcoholism, a bad marriage, an irreligious life, bad companions, and then, to close the circle, an obsession with the religious life. In between were on-field episodes when hangovers made him less than quick after fly balls and off-field incidents involving wife-beating and gun-carrying charges.

Feeling rejected by Mets general manager Frank Cashen, Strawberry signed as a free agent with the Dodgers in 1991. After one passable season, he sat on the disabled list for most of the next two years with a herniated disc that ultimately required surgery. In 1994, shortly after another of his spring training pronouncements about the monster season to come, he was admitted to a rehab clinic with a relapse into drink and drugs. Within weeks the Dodgers bought out his contract—a solution Strawberry accepted because he was also having problems with the IRS and needed cash immediately. In June, after undergoing rehabilitation, he signed with the Giants. He had a bad year at the plate, and a worse one afterward when he was indicted on federal income tax evasion charges arising from a wide-ranging investigation of fees paid to players for signing autographs at memorabilia shows. A number of other active and retired players, including Hall of Famers Duke Snider and Willie McCovey, also ended up in the net, and Strawberry went along with the general script in paying a heavy fine.

Strawberry's final baseball chapters centered around the Yankees—and around owner George Steinbrenner's heavily publicized tough love attitude toward getting the outfielder back on his feet. After serving a suspension for the drug violation at the beginning of the 1995 campaign, Strawberry worked out on his own until Steinbrenner picked him up for New York's stretch run. His contributions were modest, and not enough to prevent the Yankees from releasing him at the end of the year, but he played well enough for the St. Paul Saints of the independent Northern League to earn another invitation to Yankee Stadium in July 1996. His 11 home runs over the last part of the season included three in one game against the White Sox on August 8. Just when he appeared to be on the road back, a knee injury sidelined him for all but a handful of at bats in 1997. Even this setback promised to be only a minor hurdle when he attacked 1998 with his biggest power display (24 home runs) since the Dodgers in 1991, but then came the first diagnosis of the colon cancer. His battle with the disease won him back much of the sympathy he had lost through his drug and alcohol misadventures, at least until he was arrested in Florida in the offseason on charges of drug use and solicitation. There was one more return to the Yankees toward the end of 1999, but also further episodes of drugs and flights from rehab centers, as well as a return of the cancer. In the course of one court appearance, Strawberry told the judge he just wanted to die.

GABBY STREET

Street caught for eight years (1904–12, 1931) and managed the Cardinals and Browns for another six, but he is primarily remembered for catching a ball thrown to him from the top of the Washington Monument. The stunt was arranged in August 1908 by Pres Gibson, a theater critic intent on proving his friend Street was the finest defensive receiver in the league. Gibson took 13 balls to the top of the 555-foot-high monument and, with a crowd in attendance, dropped them one at a time down to the waiting Street. Because of high winds the first 12 balls either caromed off the side of the obelisk or fell completely beyond the catcher's reach. On the very last drop, however, the backstop made a successful grab.

Whether or not the demonstration proved Gibson's case about Street's fielding skills, it certainly wasn't offense that kept him in the big leagues: He had a career average of only .208. Taking over the Cardinals in 1930, Street became one of the few managers to win pennants in his first two years on the job.

CUB STRICKER

A light-hitting second baseman for several clubs in the 19th century, Stricker had his best day at the plate on July 29, 1883, when he went four-for-four while playing for the American Association Phila-

delphia Athletics against Louisville's ace Guy Hecker. It also turned out to be his worst day on the basepaths because Hecker picked him off first a record three times.

CURTIS STRONG

Strong was a Philadelphia caterer whose drug trafficking trial in Pittsburgh in 1985 shed glaring light on the pervasive use of drugs by major league players. Among those testifying during the proceedings (all under grants of immunity) were Keith Hernandez, Dave Parker, Lonnie Smith, and Jeffrey Leonard. All admitted having bought one kind of drug or another from Strong or one of his confederates, with Hernandez raising the most hackles in baseball circles by estimating that up to 40 percent of major league players had tried cocaine at least once.

Trial testimony revealed that Strong and other pushers had enjoyed almost total access to the clubhouse and team flights of the Pirates over a six-year period beginning with the team's championship 1979 season. At one point, a law enforcement witness disclosed, the FBI had even wired the team mascot, the Pirate Parrot, to gain evidence against the dealers and the players. Chuck Tanner, the manager throughout the period indicated by the witnesses, denied ever noticing anything untoward. When he did not return to the club in 1986, the most benign interpretation was that Tanner had lost touch with his players.

DICK STUART

In an era of such brilliant first basemen as Gil Hodges, Vic Power, and Bill White, Stuart gained equal fame as Dr. Strangeglove for his fielding ineptitude. Nevertheless, he also managed to lead the American League in both putouts and assists in 1963—an anomaly he was usually the first to asterisk by noting that he had also committed the most errors at his position. A classic all-or-nothing slugger who played for six teams between 1958 and 1969, Stuart was the first to hit 30 home runs and drive in 100 runs in a season in both leagues. When he signed with the Angels in 1969, he also became the first player to return to the majors after playing in Japan.

MOOSE STUBING

As a coach for the 1988 Angels, Stubing replaced fired manager Cookie Rojas for the final eight games of the season, losing them all. That tied him with

George Creamer of the 1884 Pittsburgh Alleghenys as baseball's most unsuccessful pilot.

JIMMY ST. VRAIN

A lefthanded pitcher but righthanded batter for the 1902 Cubs, St. Vrain was so useless at the plate that manager Frank Selee suggested during a game that he try batting lefthanded. From this unfamiliar position he did indeed make contact, hitting a grounder to Pittsburgh shortstop Honus Wagner and ran as fast as he could—to third base.

CLYDE SUKEFORTH

A backup catcher in the 1920s and 1930s, Sukeforth acted as Branch Rickey's middleman in the secret maneuvers to break the color ban with Jackie Robinson. Never told explicitly what was in the offing, Sukeforth was sent to Chicago to scout Robinson for an all-black team, the Brown Bombers, Rickey had been touting as a new venture. Finding Robinson sidelined with a sore arm, he brought him back to New York, fretting the whole time that he hadn't seen him play.

Sukeforth declined a couple of opportunities to manage the Dodgers in the 1940s, preferring to stay in the background as a coach or troubleshooter. But he was thrust into unhappy prominence during the 1951 playoffs against the Giants when, asked by Charlie Dressen who was ready to come in to face Bobby Thomson, he reported from the bullpen that Carl Erskine had just bounced a curve and Ralph Branca looked sharp. After Thomson reached the seats against Branca, Rickey's successor Walter O'Malley fired Sukeforth.

BILL SULLIVAN

As promotions director of the Boston Braves in 1946, Sullivan devised the first team yearbook. *The Braves' Sketch Book,* as it was called, sold an estimated 22,000 copies.

DAVE SULLIVAN

Objections to Sullivan's umpiring by St. Louis Browns manager Charlie Comiskey resulted in the only forfeited game in postseason championship play. In the sixth inning of the second game of the 1885 series played between National League and American Association titlists, the umpire hesitated in calling a fair ball on a slow roller by Chicago's Ned Williamson. The hit put the White Stockings ahead, 5–4, but Comiskey, already having had a long day with Sullivan, ordered his team off the field, saying he preferred a forfeit to a theft by an NL partisan. Both teams subsequently agreed to disregard the forfeit, but when the series ended in a three-three standoff with one tie, Chicago manager Cap Anson pulled it back out of the hat to declare his club the world champion. Sullivan never officiated in another big league game after the series.

TED SULLIVAN

An energetic promoter of 19th-century baseball, Sullivan earned his niche in the game's history when he had Charlie Comiskey experiment with playing wide of the first base bag and with stretching for throws from other infielders. After coming up with these innovations as the founder and manager of the Dubuque Rabbits in 1878, Sullivan formed the minor Northwestern League to give his club more structured competition. His major league career included managerial assignments with the American Association St. Louis Browns in 1883, when the club went 53–26 before his repeated clashes with owner Chris Von der Ahe forced him to depart. He also guided the Union Association St. Louis Maroons to victory in their first 20 contests in 1884 before moving on again to take over the Kansas City Unions.

While organizing one profitable minor league team after another, the tireless Sullivan championed Ladies Day promotions, night games, the importation of English football, and the exportation (to England) of baseball. The weekly *Sporting Life* once tagged him a "queer genius" for his outrageous suggestion that pitchers should be omitted from batting orders. In later life he published two books on the game, *Humorous Stories of the Ball Field* (1903) and *History of World's Tour* (1914), along with several plays with baseball plots. Sullivan has also been often cited as the first to dub baseball enthusiasts "fans." He claimed it was his personal abbreviation for what his one-time boss Von der Ahe called "fanatics."

ED SUMMERS

The most accomplished of the old-fashioned knuckleball pitchers who used the top joints of their fingers rather than their fingertips to flick the ball, Summers established an American League rookie record by posting 24 wins for the Tigers in 1908. He also won 19 the following year, but was out of the league within three years because of injuries. The more common fingertip knuckler was not used to any great extent until Ed Romell joined the Athletics in 1920.

BILLY SUNDAY

A speedster, mostly with the Cubs, from 1883 to 1890, Sunday is reported to have once stolen second, third, and home on consecutive pitches to win a game. Despite such real or imagined heroics, he is most often remembered as a fiery Prohibitionist orator. Converted in 1887, the outfielder retired after the 1890 season to devote himself exclusively to evangelism. Usually opening his temperance lectures by executing a perfect hook slide onto the stage, he roused audiences with emotional descriptions of how he would punch, kick, and bite the plague of demon rum until he was "old and fistless and footless and toothless," and even then would go on to "gum it to death until it goes home to perdition and I go home to glory." Another of his obsessions in his various crusades was the violation of the Sabbath with the playing of baseball games.

JIM SUNDBERG

Sundberg was a key figure in the disheveling of the Rangers franchise in the late 1970s and early 1980s. It was when the defensively brilliant catcher was offered a six-year contract by Brad Corbett that other Texas stockholders united to force the erratic owner to sell the team. A couple of years later Sundberg exercised his contractual rights by refusing a trade to Los Angeles that would have brought the Rangers pitchers Orel Hershiser, Dave Stewart, and Burt Hooten. Texas eventually traded the receiver to Milwaukee for the .182-hitting Ned Yost.

RICK SUTCLIFFE

Sutcliffe is the only pitcher to win a Cy Young Award for a team he joined with the season already under way. On June 13, 1984 the righthander was dealt by the Indians to the Cubs for outfielders Joe Carter and Mel Hall. Sutcliffe went on to fashion a 16–1 record for Chicago in its East Division win.

BRUCE SUTTER

Sutter's arbitration win prior to the 1980 season alerted major league owners that they had more to worry about than free agency. With the Cubs for merely four seasons when his case was heard, the relief ace's award of $700,000—double the team's offer—effectively recognized diamond stardom regardless of tenure.

The decision brought the ire of other owners down on Chicago for not reaching an agreement with the righthander before arbitration—an irritation that gradually became academic with higher awards. Forkball specialist Sutter found himself in his advantageous position after leading the National League in saves in 1979. He managed to do that four more times during his 12-year career, including 1982, when his bullpen work was vital to a Cardinals world championship.

DON SUTTON (Hall of Fame, 1998)

Sutton's career was more whole than parts. In 23 seasons (1966–88) with the Dodgers and four other teams, the righthander won 20 games only once, paced National League hurlers in ERA and shutouts only once each, never led in any other category, never pitched a no-hitter, and never won a Cy Young Award. On the other hand, he won 324 games and retired in fifth place in strikeouts (3,574). His ability to elude the disabled list his entire career also left him high on several all-time durability lists, as well as contributed to his having the most wins (233) by any Dodgers pitcher, in either Brooklyn or Los Angeles.

An accomplished scuffballer, Sutton was thrown out of a game against the Cardinals on June 14, 1978 after umpire Doug Harvey collected several similarly doctored balls. Sutton threatened both Harvey and the league with a lawsuit for endangering his ability to earn a living—an imaginative reaction that persuaded the league to be satisfied with a warning without a fine or a suspension.

EZRA SUTTON

Sutton made the first big league error when he threw wildly past first base after fielding a grounder in the National League's inaugural game on April 22, 1876. After one season with Philadelphia, the third baseman moved on to Boston and to a reputation over the next decade as the best gloveman at his position in the circuit.

LARRY SUTTON

Although his baseball background had consisted of little more than umpiring for a few years in a minor league in New Jersey, Sutton was responsible for the signing of just about every top player on the Dodgers in the years immediately before and after World War I. Having persuaded Brooklyn owner Charles Ebbets that he knew talent when he saw it and that he had the freedom to roam around the country for a salary that was close to a tip, Sutton dug out of the minors such stars as Casey Stengel, Jake Daubert, Otto Miller, and Jeff Pfeffer. Even more impressive, he signed future Hall of Famer Zach Wheat and urged Ebbets to make trades for two other eventual Cooperstown residents—pitchers Dazzy Vance and Burleigh Grimes.

ICHIRO SUZUKI

When Mets manager Bobby Valentine heard Seattle had signed Japanese outfielder Suzuki in the 2000–2001 offseason, he congratulated the Mariners for getting what he called "one of the five best players in the world." A year later, many who had sneered at Valentine's claim were ready to pare the field down from five.

In his sensational debut for Seattle, the lefty-swinging Ichiro (as he prefers to be called) joined Fred Lynn (in 1975) as the only players to win both the league MVP and Rookie of the Year honors in a debut season. He also went two better than Lynn by leading the American League in batting (.350) and steals (56)—the first player of any seniority to set the pace in those two categories in the same year since Jackie Robinson did it for the Dodgers in 1949. In addition, he batted .445 with runners in scoring position, slugged .457, compiled 316 total bases, and managed an unprecedented (for a rookie) 242 hits; it was the most hits by a major leaguer since Bill Terry's 254 in 1930. The American League batting crown followed seven straight titles for the Orix Blue Wave in Japan.

Ichiro's contributions to Seattle's record 116 wins in 2001 didn't stop with offense. His ability to track down flies, whirl, and fire back to the infield in one motion had Yankees manager Joe Torre (among others) praising him as the best outfielder in baseball in decades. None of this hurt the Seattle franchise, where anything Ichiro was supplied to souvenir and food stands and quickly gobbled up. The outfielder's rapid adaptability to American baseball not only laid to rest the canard that only Japanese pitchers could make the transition across the Pacific, but raised some serious doubts about Japan's ability to keep its stars in the face of expected big contract offers from the major leagues.

CHARLIE SWEENEY

Sweeney was helping to pitch Providence to a National League pennant in July 1884, when he got drunk during an exhibition game, staggered out of the park, and failed to show up for practice the following morning. Sent to the mound for the afternoon game anyway, the righthander sulked his way through seven innings, refusing to acknowledge manager Frank Bancroft's first order to turn the ball over to somebody else, then storming off the field after a second, more insistent command. He fumed right into the arms of Union Association angel Henry V. Lucas, signing a contract with that circuit's St. Louis Maroons that made him the highest paid pitcher in baseball. The question is still open whether the truculent nature of Sweeney's defection was the result of an alcoholic pique or a premeditated sham to cover an intentional contract jumping.

What there is no question about, on the other hand, is that Sweeney is the only pitcher to play a cardinal winning role on two pennant teams in the same season. While his first-half 17–8 mark gave Providence a significant boost to its flag, his 24 wins for St. Louis in the second half made the difference for the Maroons, as well.

LES SWEETLAND

Sweetland's 1930 ERA of 7.71 is the highest for any pitcher in a season with enough qualifying innings. It wasn't all the fault of the Year of the Hitter, either, because in five big league seasons for the Phillies and Reds the southpaw never got his ERA below 5.04.

STUART SYMINGTON

Of all the U.S. senators who have threatened to lift baseball's exemption from anti-trust statutes, Missouri Democrat Symington got the quickest action. Outraged at the American League's decision in 1967 to allow Charlie Finley to move the Athletics from Kansas City to Oakland, he rejected generic promises from league president Joe Cronin that another club would eventually move into the city, demanding a specific calendar. With most of the AL owners already on their way home from the meeting that had approved the franchise shift, a panicked

Cronin managed to assemble a bare quorum for an extra session, where it was decided that Kansas City would have a new team by 1969. The second thoughts had a ricochet effect in the National League, where equally vague plans for some kind of expansion in the 1970s had to be scrapped in favor of admitting San Diego and Montreal in 1969. Symington denounced Finley on the Senate floor as "one of the most disreputable characters ever to enter the American sports scene," going to the ludicrous extreme of comparing the impact of the Athletics boss on Kansas City to that of the atomic bomb on Nagasaki.

T

WILLIAM HOWARD TAFT

Taft became the first president of the United States to throw out the ceremonial first pitch on Opening Day, when the long-time baseball fan tossed a ball to Walter Johnson before a Senators-Athletics game on April 14, 1910. Vice President James Sherman, also in attendance, was knocked unconscious during the game when a foul ball off the bat of Philadelphia's Frank Baker struck him in the head.

EDWARD TALCOTT

A principal backer of the Players League New York Giants in 1890, Talcott made a mistake in meeting with National League representative Al Spalding after the season to discuss mutual problems, then compounded his error by revealing the extent of the PL's financial losses. Keeping the NL's equally desperate situation to himself, Spalding used the information to negotiate a PL surrender.

FRANK TANANA

Tanana had more major league starts (616) than any other pitcher who never had a 20-win season. In 21 years (1973–93) with six clubs he won 240 and lost 236, with a personal high of 19 victories for the Angels in 1976. Before signing with the Mets in 1993, the lefthander had also been the only player to complete 20 seasons without once ever going to bat.

CHUCK TANNER

Tanner's genial persona over 18 consecutive years (1970–87) of managing didn't hide his obtuse handling of various crises under his command—some of his own making. With the White Sox between 1970 and 1975 his problem was the players he alienated by making it clear they were secondary to slugger Dick Allen. With the Athletics in 1976 he lost clubhouse authority by not protesting against the season-long attempts by owner Charlie Finley to sell off imminent free agents even as the team was contending for the West Division title. As pilot of the We Are Family Pirates in the late 1970s and early 1980s he never noticed (by his own claim) the drug dealers who not only invaded the locker room regularly but also rode on team flights. With the Braves in 1985 and 1986 his main concern was public relations assistant Robin Monsky, whom he insisted be axed for not saying "more positive" things about the cellar-dwelling team in her press releases.

Tanner was one of the rare managers swapped for an active player, when Finley sent him to Pittsburgh after the 1976 season for catcher Manny Sanguillen.

RANDY TATE

A righthanded pitcher for the 1975 Mets, Tate went to bat 41 times without a hit, making him statistically the worst lifetime hitter in baseball history.

FERNANDO TATIS

Tatis is the only major leaguer to have hit two grand slams in an inning. The then-Cardinals third baseman did it on April 23, 1999—both four-run blows coming off Los Angeles righthander Chan Ho Park. His eight RBIs for the inning are also a record.

The only other National Leaguer to hit two grand slams in the same game is pitcher Tony Cloninger, who did it for the Braves against the Giants on July

3, 1966. Several American League sluggers have accomplished the feat.

BILLY TAYLOR

Taylor's pitching career exemplifies the effects of expansion. When the Union Association set up as a third league in 1884 and the American Association went from eight to 12 teams in the same year, hundreds of new, undeveloped players were suddenly able to call themselves major leaguers. With the UA's St. Louis franchise over the first half of the season Taylor went 25–4; skipping over to the AA's Philadelphia entry in the middle of the campaign, he won another 18 games while losing 12. In none of his other six major league years did the righthander win more than four times.

DUMMY TAYLOR

Deaf-mute Taylor spent almost his entire nine-year (1900–08) career with the Giants, where he taught manager John McGraw the fundamentals of signing. Both of them were once kicked out of a game by an umpire who knew enough signing of his own to understand that what the pitcher and pilot were flashing between the hill and the dugout had less to do with what pitch to throw than with their opinion of the arbiter. The righthander Taylor ended up with a mark of 116–106, including 21 victories in 1904.

HARRY TAYLOR

A first baseman for three teams in the 1890s, Taylor became the attorney for the Players Protective Association in 1900 just as the American League's raids on the National League were about to give players some leverage in their dealings with owners. Turning up the heat under a pot of player resentment, Taylor offered the NL owners several proposals: reciprocity in the 10-day advance notice required for letting go of a player; club responsibility for medical fees incurred by injured players; player consent for any sale, trade, or demotion to the minors; and creation of an impartial arbitration panel for settling disputes. When the owners rejected the demands out of hand, a majority of NL players agreed not to sign contracts for the 1901 season. But then, with Taylor called away to take care of other legal business in his native Buffalo, the owners called another meeting in New York with union president Chief Zimmer, getting him (and later Taylor) to sign off on

mere cosmetic changes in relations between the two sides. The accord aborted the budding union's power. Taylor later went on to serve as president of the minor Eastern League.

JACK TAYLOR

Of all baseball records, Taylor's mark of 188 consecutive complete games is the most unassailable. What was less so was his reputation for honesty once he took the mound.

From June 20, 1901, when he was with the Cubs, through August 9, 1906, when he was with the Cardinals, Taylor was never removed for a relief pitcher. In addition to the 188 complete efforts during that stretch, the righthander also finished another 15 games from the bullpen, for a total of 1,727 innings without seeing a teammate coming in behind him. Because he was on mediocre teams Taylor's overall record for 10 seasons (1898–1907) was only 152–139 (2.65 ERA).

In 1904 Taylor came under fire for comments about accepting money to lose during the previous year's postseason Chicago city championship series against the White Sox. After denying the charges and being exonerated by the National Commission, he was immediately confronted by other allegations that he had thrown a regular season game while with St. Louis that year. Admitting only to heavy drinking the night before the game, he was slapped with a $300 fine for what was essentially a "hangover defense." When Taylor refused even to pay the fine, a suspiciously consenting Cardinals manager Kid Nichols suggested the club make good on the penalty to put an end to talk about the incident. Before he was through, Taylor would be accused of another dump during a postseason city series in St. Louis between the Cardinals and Browns. Again then, the main reaction of officials was to scamper to sweep everything under the rug.

JOHN TAYLOR

Taylor was a particularly pathetic example of a millionaire operating a team as a toy. The son of Boston *Globe* publisher Charles Henry Taylor, he was given the Red Sox by his father in 1904 mostly to show that he could do more than live it up at night and sleep late in the morning. He took the mandate seriously enough to go marching into the clubhouse to lecture the players whenever they lost. When pilot Jimmy Collins barred him from the locker room, he stationed himself in a corridor out to the field to get in his remarks anyway. On two occasions AL president Ban Johnson, who had brokered the sale of the club to the Taylors, was called in to dissuade Collins not to resign over the interference. A third try failed, and Collins was succeeded by a parade of managers who either resigned for the same reason or were fired for talking back to Taylor.

Another source of grievance for Boston's many pilots was Taylor's insistence on completing deals. His transactions included swapping future batting king George Stone to the Browns for a washed up Jesse Burkett, unloading Collins on the Athletics for .239-hitting Jack Knight, and sending future National League home run leader Gavvy Cravath to the White Sox. The biggest storm of all blew in Boston after he got tipsy drinking with Cleveland owner Charles Somers and agreed to send Cy Young to the Indians. Johnson finally persuaded the elder Taylor to sell effective command of the franchise to Jimmy McAleer and Bob McRoy in December 1911.

KENT TEKULVE

The underhanding Tekulve holds the record for most pitching appearances (1,050) without making a start. As the bullpen ace for the Pirates in the late 1970s and 1980s, the righthander led the National League in games three times and, both in 1978 and 1979, racked up 31 saves. In the 1979 World Series against Baltimore Tekulve saved three of Pittsburgh's four victories.

WILLIAM TEMPLE

The president of the Pittsburgh franchise in the 1890s, sportsman Temple donated the two-and-a-half-foot Temple Cup awarded to the winner of a postseason championship series between the expanded National League's two top finishers. The initial idea was that the trophy would become the permanent property of the first club to win three series, but neither players nor fans took the games very seriously, and they were discontinued after four years. Even Temple conceded the futility of his intentions in 1897, when Boston and Baltimore players filled the cup with wine and passed it around a post-series banquet like a communal goblet. The teams winning the cup were the New York Giants in 1894, the Cleveland Spiders in 1895, and the Baltimore Orioles in 1896 and 1897.

GARRY TEMPLETON

In 1979 Templeton became the first switch-hitter to get 100 hits from both sides of the plate in a season. For the Cardinals shortstop it proved to be the last big act in a 16-year (1976–91) career that saw him decline from leading the league in hits once and in triples for three consecutive years to hitting the trail as a journeyman. His most trouble-riven season was 1981, when, exasperated by heckling for what was perceived as lackadaisical play, he gave Busch Stadium fans the finger, prompting manager Whitey Herzog to pull him down the steps of the dugout and shove him onto the bench. Templeton was subsequently admitted to a hospital for depression, but that didn't save him from being shipped to San Diego after the season in exchange for Ozzie Smith—an exchange that proved vital to St. Louis's winning teams for the next decade. Templeton also raised establishment hackles in once refusing to go to an All-Star Game as a backup selection, declaring: "If I ain't startin', I ain't departin'."

GENE TENACE

As a member of the 1972 Athletics, Tenace had one of the biggest World Series ever. After homering in his first two at bats of the opening game, he went on to add two more four-baggers and compile nine RBIs in Oakland's world championship effort over Cincinnati. In the ALCS before the Series the right-hand-hitting backstop went hitless in his first 16 at bats, but then singled home the pennant-winning run in his last at bat against the Tigers. An otherwise modest hitter over his 15-year (1969–83) career, Tenace had a special aversion to putting the ball in play: Aside from registering at least 90 strikeouts seven years in a row, he walked 100 times in six seasons, leading each league in that category (the 1974 Athletics and 1977 Padres).

JOHN TENER

Tener was the first former player to become president of a major league. As a righthanded pitcher for three years (1888–90) in Chicago and Pittsburgh, he gained his greatest prominence as secretary of the Players Brotherhood. A subsequent political career led him to the U.S. Congress and then, in 1912, to the governor's mansion in Pennsylvania. Over the last two years of his term he took on the added responsibility of serving as National League president.

With two exceptions Tener's reign was pretty predictable. He issued the customary fines against John McGraw's antics and warned the public of the dangers posed to the baseball fabric by both the Federal League and the Players Fraternity. What he wasn't ready for were World War I and the Scott Perry case. The war came to color Tener's relations with the other two members of the ruling National Commission when chairman Garry Herrmann and AL president Ban Johnson resorted to any and every ploy to keep players exempted from the military draft and keep games going on the field; Tener was appalled by the implication big league players were more important than other draftable Americans and deserved special consideration. He was equally disturbed when Johnson and Connie Mack of the Athletics decided to go to court to press Philadelphia's rights to minor league pitcher Perry despite a National Commission verdict that the hurler belonged to the NL Braves. But when NL owners refused to back his call to cancel the 1918 World Series to show Johnson how seriously they regarded the Perry matter, Tener had little choice but to resign his post.

FRED TENNEY

The slickest fielding first baseman between the reigns of Charlie Comiskey in the 1890s and Hal Chase in the 1900s, Tenney was probably the first to execute the 3-6-3 double play; certainly, no witnesses to a June 14, 1897 game between Boston and Cincinnati recalled having seen it before. After anchoring the infield for Boston pennant winners in 1897 and 1898, the lefty swinger also managed the team—in 1905 under a contract that induced him to chase foul balls into the stands for a bonus, then in 1907 as a minority stockholder in the franchise who took the ball-recovery habit to the hysterical extreme of patting down umpire Bill Klem behind the accusation that the arbiter was stealing balls.

When senior partners George and John Dovey fired him as manager after the 1907 season, Tenney's demand for a 25 percent profit on his share of the club triggered an unexpected trade to the Giants. But even in New York he refused to sell his Boston equity for less than what he thought fair, ignoring NL president Harry Pulliam's protests that it wasn't appropriate for a player to be on one team and have interests in another. He finally settled for much more than the Doveys had offered him originally.

In his first season in New York Tenney affected the outcome of one of baseball's most legendary games when he took a day off because of a backache; manager John McGraw replaced him with Fred Merkle, who nine innings later would make his infamous boner.

JERRY TERRELL

Terrell was the lone dissenter in the Players Association's 967–1 vote authorizing the 1980 spring training strike. The Kansas City infielder pointed to religious convictions as his reason for breaking ranks with fellow players.

BILL TERRY (Hall of Fame, 1954)

The last National League player to reach .400 (.401 in 1930), Terry was that rare RBI producer not especially noted for home runs. Even with the friendly right field porch of the Polo Grounds in front of him for his entire 14-year (1923–36) career, the lefty-swinging first baseman managed 20 homers only three times but still used the gaps to drive across 100 runs six seasons in a row. He also scored 100 runs seven times and had at least 200 hits in six different seasons, in 1930 tying Lefty O'Doul's league mark of 254. Terry closed out with a lifetime average of .341.

Like his successor Mel Ott, Terry took on the added task of managing New York in his later playing years; unlike Ott, his prickly personality never gained him public relations points. Just being named McGraw's successor in 1932 brought him frictions with coach Dave Bancroft and third baseman Freddie Lindstrom, both of whom had coveted the job. His own first appointment of Billy Southworth as coach ended badly when the two of them got into a fistfight in spring training in 1933. But despite all the turmoil he reanimated the sagging franchise with a World Series win in 1933 and pennants in 1936 and 1937.

Terry attained a special place in Giants-Dodgers rivalry lore during the 1934 winter meetings thanks to an off-the-cuff remark made to Roscoe McGowan of *The New York Times*. After discussing the deals made by other NL clubs at the busy gathering and noting that the Dodgers hadn't completed any trades, he mused aloud if "Brooklyn is still in the league." Dodgers officials used it as a rallying cry for their misbegotten team, making it sound as though Terry had been referring to the team's playing abilities.

Brooklyn was beside itself when, on the final weekend of the year, it defeated the Giants twice to let the Cardinals snatch the pennant.

Because he considered himself "a Giant first and last," Terry turned down several lucrative offers to jump to other clubs as a dual manager-general manager. Even when he stepped aside for Ott after the 1941 season, he stayed in the organization for a few years as a minor league director, and later in the 1950s sought unsuccessfully to buy the club to keep it in New York. His loyalty to the Giants was never too far from his practical sense, however; in fact, nobody more than Terry liked to talk about how he played primarily for money and regarded the game as just another business. Baseball writers, who liked neither his pragmatism nor his fractious personality in general, did not vote him into the Hall of Fame until 1954, his 15th year of eligibility.

ERNEST THAYER

First published under a pseudonym in the San Francisco *Examiner* on June 3, 1888, Thayer's "Casey at the Bat" became a sensation a year later when matinee idol DeWolf Hopper recited it for the first of some 10,000 times in his stage career. Hopper gave his reading as an encore to a New York performance of the play *Prince Methusalem* attended by members of the New York Giants and Chicago White Stockings.

Over the years there have been as many claimants to the authorship of the poem as there have been to being "mighty Casey" himself. Among those demanding the writing credit was George D'Vys, who maintained he had taken the name of Casey's team from his own Mudville Nine of Somerville, Massachusetts, that he had been inspired by seeing King Kelly strike out with the bases loaded in an August 1886 game, and that he had submitted the work to *Sporting Times*. But the issue of the *Times* that carried a garbled version of "Casey" was in fact dated later than the *Examiner* version and specifically credits the San Francisco paper as its source.

The first to proclaim himself the prototype for the failed hero was O. Robinson Casey, the president of the Syracuse Society for the Prevention of Cruelty to Animals. His claim that he struck out in similar circumstances while playing for Detroit against Minneapolis in 1885, however, was patently spurious since Minneapolis had no major league team

that year and Casey himself had never played for Detroit or any other big league club. Pitcher Dan Casey and his outfielder brother Dennis also tried to pick up a few drinks at one time or another saying the poem was about them. Thayer himself insisted until his death in 1940 that the filler for which he had been paid five dollars by the *Examiner* had no basis in fact.

BOBBY THIGPEN

Righthander Thigpen set the season record for saves in 1990 when, pitching for the White Sox, he closed out 57 victories.

HARRY THOBE

Thobe was a retired bricklayer from Oxford, Ohio who served as an unofficial mascot for the Reds in the late 1930s and 1940s. He showed up regularly at Crosley Field wearing a white suit with red trouser stripes, one shoe matching the suit and the other the stripes. He also sported a straw hat with a red band and carried an umbrella of the same colors. Well into his 70s, Strobe would dance a jig through an entire game to spur on the home team.

BILL THOMAS

Between 1926 and 1952 righthander Thomas won 383 games—the most by any pitcher in minor league history. He never wore a big league uniform.

DANNY THOMAS

Thomas spent parts of 1976 and 1977 with the Brewers before his fanatical religious devotion cost him a career. The outfielder belonged to the World Wide Church of God, which prohibited any form of labor between sundown Friday and sundown Saturday. Unwilling to hold on to a six-day-a-week player, even one who had been a first round draft pick with power and speed, Milwaukee sent him back to the minors to stay. Three years later Thomas committed suicide in an Alabama jail cell while awaiting trial on a rape charge.

LUCILLE THOMAS

Thomas's acquisition of the Wichita franchise in the Western League in 1930 made her the first woman to buy a professional ballclub. The owner of a chain of movie theaters and drug stores, she promptly moved the team from Kansas to Tulsa, Oklahoma.

ROY THOMAS

A speedy center fielder for the Phillies at the dawn of the 20th century, Thomas's skill at intentionally hitting foul balls (22 in a row on one occasion) prompted the National League to declare, in 1901, that the first two fouls were to be registered as strikes; the American League adopted the same standard in 1903. Despite the ruling Thomas managed to lead the NL in walks seven times.

HANK THOMPSON

Thompson was the only black player to break the color ban on two teams. In 1947 he made his debut with the St. Louis Browns shortly after Larry Doby had become the first black in the American League. In 1949 he broke the whites-only policy of the New York Giants.

SAM THOMPSON (Hall of Fame, 1974)

Thompson was the first National Leaguer to bang out 200 hits in a season (235 in 1887). In a 15-year (1885–98, 1906) career with two Detroit teams in both the National and American leagues and the Phillies, the lefty-swinging outfielder paced the league in home runs twice and in RBIs three times, drove in 100 runs eight times, and topped .300 eight times. His career-high average of .415 in 1894 still left him only third in that year's batting race.

BOBBY THOMSON

Thomson's three-run home run off Brooklyn's Ralph Branca in the ninth inning of the third game of the 1951 National League playoffs has been the most dramatic hit in baseball history. The one-strike clout climaxed a miracle drive by the Giants to the pennant after dropping behind the Dodgers by as much as 13 1/2 games in August. The home run cast into the shadows Thomson's otherwise solid career as New York's chief clutch hitter in the late 1940s and early 1950s; among other things, his earlier home run in the first game of the 1951 playoffs had also helped defeat Branca.

If indirectly, Thomson triggered the launching of the careers of the NL's two greatest outfielders. In 1951 he was moved from center field to third base to make room for Willie Mays in the lineup, and in 1954, as a member of the Braves, he tore up an ankle in spring training, forcing Milwaukee to keep Hank Aaron on the club.

JUSTUS THORNER

Thorner headed three clubs in the same city in three different major leagues: the National League Cincinnati Reds in 1880, the American Association Reds in 1882, and the Union Association Outlaw Reds in 1884. In 1882 he devised a scheme to play the NL champion Chicago White Stockings in the first interleague championship series despite an AA ban on such contests. Releasing all his players on October 1, two weeks before the end of their contracts, Thorner arranged for a local Cincinnati entrepreneur to sign them to barnstorming pacts for games against Chicago. AA president Denny McKnight shortcircuited the gambit with a fine and threats of expulsion for the Reds, but not before the two clubs had traded shutouts.

JIM THORPE

The first American to win the Olympic decathlon (in 1912), Thorpe had a modest baseball career for the Giants, Reds, and Braves between 1913 and 1919. A righthanded outfielder, he batted .252 with only 29 stolen bases. Thorpe was initially signed by John McGraw as a batting practice gate attraction. His most conspicuous moment on a diamond came on May 2, 1917, when he drove in the winning run for the Reds against Hippo Vaughn in the 10th inning after the Chicago southpaw had matched Cincinnati's Fred Toney in baseball's only double no-hit game. Because he had played professionally in the minor leagues in 1909, Thorpe was forced to return his Olympic medals.

MARV THRONEBERRY

Symbol of the ineptitude of the expansion Mets in the 1960s, Throneberry owed his derisive moniker of Marvelous Marv to a sincere outburst by owner Joan Payson, who exclaimed after a game-winning homer by the first baseman: "Wasn't that marvelous of Marv!" Throneberry made the sarcasm inevitable with such feats as once legging out a triple and being called out for having failed to touch second; when manager Casey Stengel began to protest the call, he was told not to bother because his player hadn't touched first, either. Stengel himself added to the legend at a clubhouse birthday party when he cracked to Throneberry that the team hadn't gotten him a cake because "you would have probably dropped it."

The marketing of the Throneberry image was so intense it obscured the fact that he played only 130 games for the Mets over a season and a fraction. More ironic, he actually had a better fielding average than other New York infielders in that period. Like Joe Garagiola, Bob Uecker, and others, Throneberry later tried to cash in on his playing infamy by doing commercials, but he also admitted to never being at ease with a reputation that contradicted one-time hopes as a Yankees prospect of being the next Mickey Mantle.

JAMES THURBER

Thurber's short story "You Could Look It Up," which appeared in *The Saturday Evening Post* in 1941, concerned a baseball team so desperate it hires a midget as a pinch-hitter. The tale inspired both Bill Veeck's stunt with Eddie Gaedel and Casey Stengel's signature tag line.

ALLAN W. THURMAN

Nobody had to put up with a more embarrassing sobriquet than Thurman, who was known for awhile as The White-Winged Angel of Peace. He earned the tag in October 1890 when, as a minority stockholder in the Columbus Solons, he put forth a proposal to combine the warring National League, the Players League, and his own American Association into two leagues. When this became the basis for the settlement among the three circuits, Thurman was given the AA presidency, one of the three seats on a ruling National Board, and his angel wings. They lasted only for a few months: When he cast the deciding vote endorsing the piracy of Lou Bierbauer and Harry Stovey by the NL from the AA, he was recalled by owners of his circuit. The AA then went back to war against the NL, eventually being absorbed out of existence.

LUIS TIANT

Tiant drew attention for one of the most unorthodox deliveries in big league history, but he also won 20 games four times and was the glue of the Boston teams of the 1970s. A portly righthander, he dazzled opponents over his 19-year (1964–82) career by swiveling practically all the way around to center field before unleashing pitches at one of numerous possible release points. The motion was so disorienting that American League umpires had to reach a special agreement for not calling the hurler regularly for balking.

The Cuban-born Tiant arrived in the majors with Cleveland, where he had great years (1968, when he recorded the league's lowest ERA in 49 years) and bad years (1969, when he lost 20). After a season with the Twins and time in the minors he was fished back up by the Red Sox, for whom he won 20 in 1973, 1974, and 1976. He also starred in the 1975 World Series against Cincinnati, hurling two complete-game victories and pitching into the seventh inning of a third contest before tiring. The gregarious, cigar-wielding Tiant was the very opposite of the "25 players, 25 cabs" reputation affixed to the Boston clubs of the period, most teammates agreeing he provided a necessary buffer among clubhouse factions. It was in this context that, informed that the pitcher had signed a free agent contract with the Yankees in 1979, Carl Yastrzemski moaned that "they have cut out our heart and soul." New York owner George Steinbrenner also acknowledged that one of the reasons he had gone after Tiant was for its impact on Boston morale.

Tiant closed out his career at 229–172 (3.30 ERA).

MIKE TIERNAN

An outfielder for the Giants, Tiernan once hit a home run that brought fans in two stadiums to their feet. The incident occurred on May 12, 1890, when he hit a shot that cleared the center field fence of the Polo Grounds and landed in the outfield of adjoining Brotherhood Park, where a Players League game was under way. Spectators in both parks applauded as Tiernan rounded the bases. The clout ended a 13-inning scoreless duel between Kid Nichols and Amos Rusie.

JOE TINKER (Hall of Fame, 1946)

Unlike his double play partner Johnny Evers, Tinker at least led the National League in twin killings once, also pacing shortstops in fielding average four times and in assists twice. On the other hand, he committed more than 60 errors in three seasons.

In contrast to the hectoring Evers, Tinker was relatively silent in his first 11 years with the Cubs at the beginning of the 20th century; there was nothing even relative about it toward Evers, after Tinker decided his double play partner had offended him in a 1905 mixup over a cab, refusing to talk to him for

33 years. At the plate the shortstop wasn't especially loud, either, hitting .262 over 15 seasons (1902–16).

In 1913 Tinker underwent a change. For openers, he objected so strenuously to the appointment of Evers as Chicago manager that he demanded a trade. He was sent to Cincinnati, where, as player-manager, he made it clear from the start that he wasn't used to associating with losers. When owner Garry Herrmann turned down a couple of his trade suggestions, he went to the press with charges that the franchise was more interested in saving money than fielding a winner. That gained him backing from fans but little else. Informed before the 1914 season that the organization had decided to send a spy on road trips to report on player activities, Tinker refused to sign a new contract. Herrmann retaliated by replacing him as manager with Buck Herzog and selling him to the Dodgers. Rather than report to Brooklyn, he jumped to the Federal League's newly formed club in Chicago as player-manager. As the field boss of the FL Whales, he assembled a team entertaining enough to outdraw the Cubs in both 1914 and 1915; in the latter year, his club won the closest pennant race in major league history, Chicago nosing out St. Louis by a single percentage point on the final day of the season.

With the folding of the Feds after the 1915 campaign, Whales owner Charles Weeghman, who had purchased the Cubs, brought Tinker back to manage the club with which he had started his career. It proved to be an unhappy experience, and Tinker was fired after a single season.

JIM TOBIN

As a member of the Braves on May 13, 1942, Tobin became the only pitcher in the modern era to hit three home runs in a game. In nine years (1937–45) with Pittsburgh, Boston, and Detroit, he had less success on the mound, going 105–112.

BOBBY TOLAN

Tolan came closer than anyone else to threatening the reserve clause before Andy Messersmith and Dave McNally finally undid the rule in 1975. Refusing to sign his 1974 contract with the Padres, the outfielder filed two grievances in October of that year, one seeking free agency for himself and the other insisting on a clarification of the one-year-at-a-time right of a club to renew player contracts perpetually and on its own terms. Even though he later signed a retroactive, two-year pact with San Diego in December, the second grievance remained in place until it was voluntarily withdrawn by Players Association negotiator Marvin Miller. Miller's move was calculated to take the heat off arbitrator Peter Seitz, who had recently decided the Catfish Hunter case in the pitcher's favor, and to encourage owners to bargain an end to the offending contract clause.

Tolan, who began his career with the Cardinals in 1965, was the original center fielder for the Big Red Machine and the National League's leading base stealer in 1970. He was never the same after a 1971 injury kept him on the disabled list all year.

FRED TONEY

On May 2, 1917 Toney pitched a 10-inning no-hitter for the Reds, besting Cubs southpaw Hippo Vaughn, who didn't allow a hit until the final frame. The double no-hitter ended with a single by Cincinnati's Larry Kopf, who eventually moved around to third and scored the decisive run on a scratch single by Jim Thorpe.

Righthander Toney won 139 games in a 12-year (1911–23) career with four teams. Off the field he had a bad war—first being prosecuted for criminal draft evasion during World War I, then, after being acquitted of those charges, being imprisoned for several months on conviction of Mann Act violations. The second felony, involving a woman he had been living with for some time, arose from the vindictiveness of a prosecutor chagrined by the draft evasion acquittal.

GEORGE EARL TOOLSON

Toolson was a pitcher in the Yankees farm system who refused to accept a demotion from Newark to Binghamton, suing the organization on the grounds that the reserve clause was a monopolistic practice preventing him from advancing himself in his chosen profession. Linked with similar suits brought by Dodgers farmhand Walter Kowalski and minor league operator Jack Corbett, the action reached the U.S. Supreme Court in November 1953. By a 7–2 majority the High Court found in favor of organized baseball, upholding the 1922 precedent that exempted the sport from federal antitrust statutes. The Court's reasoning wasn't that baseball was not "commerce," the 1922 rationale for the exemption, but that the remedy for the problem had to be legislative (even though Congress had chosen not to act in the 31 years since the original decision).

DAN TOPPING

Topping was half of the partnership that owned the Yankees in the period of their greatest successes and that sowed the seeds of their worst failures. Starting off as a quarter-owner while Larry MacPhail ran the franchise from 1945 to 1947, the multimillionaire and the equally wealthy Del Webb bought MacPhail out following a nervous breakdown by their senior partner. While Topping held the title of president until 1966, he almost always deferred to the judgement of his front office people in player personnel matters. This hands-off policy extended to tacit support of general manager George Weiss's refusal to put black players in a Yankees uniform until 1955, even though he employed African Americans on the Brooklyn Dodgers football team that he also owned.

Topping was more active in the selection of managers. A great admirer of Joe DiMaggio, he had to talk the outfielder out of retiring twice because of clashes with Casey Stengel, offered him the piloting job in 1949, and again tried to bring him back as a coach (and eventual successor to Stengel) after his 1951 retirement. The forced retirement of both Stengel and Weiss after the 1960 World Series was Topping's doing, as were the hirings of Ralph Houk and Roy Hamey, respectively, to replace them. More damaging was his scheme to install Yogi Berra as dugout leader in 1964, kicking Houk upstairs to succeed Hamey. If bad publicity overwhelmed whatever good reasons there had been to oust Stengel and Weiss, bad chemistry sabotaged the Berra-Houk changes. But there was much worse. As early as 1962 Topping and Webb decided to sell out—and to stop spending money on the franchise until they found a buyer. Even as the team continued to win pennants in the early 1960s, its stars increasingly broke down with injuries and the once-heralded farm system ran out of Mantles and Fords. By 1963 New York's four highest minor league clubs were finishing last in their leagues.

When talks to sell to the Lehman Brothers stock brokerage house fell apart over a tax ruling, Topping turned to CBS, which purchased 80 percent of the club for $11.2 million in 1964. This set off boardroom fears around both leagues that the media conglomerate would interfere with baseball's lucrative television agreements and that the wrath of Congress or the Justice Department would threaten the sport's exemption from anti-trust laws. The other owners approved the sale only with assurances from Topping and Webb that they would continue to run the team for another five years. The promise of gradual departure was written on water: In February 1965 Webb sold his remaining 10 percent to CBS, while Topping held out only until September 1966.

JOE TORRE

The storied Miller Huggins, Joe McCarthy, and Casey Stengel notwithstanding, Torre has been the most successful manager in the history of the Yankees. Not only have Torre's teams at the turn of the millennium had to negotiate playoff tiers for championships that his three Hall of Fame predecessors didn't, but he has bettered them in either the winning percentage or number of postseason victories. Against Torre's 56–22 (.718) record for October, for instance, Stengel's 10 pennants produced a 37–26 (.588) record in the World Series, while Huggins converted his six flags into an 18–15 (.545) World Series count. If McCarthy's eight pennants and mark of 29–9 (.763) are superior to Torre's winning percentage, they were built out of seven series wins and one loss; the Yankees of the late 20th and early 21st centuries played 16 postseason series, losing only to Cleveland in 1997 and Arizona in 2001. Between the two defeats Torre's Yankees ripped off 11 series in a row.

Before the Yankees, Torre had managed the three teams on which he had accumulated all-star numbers as a catcher, third baseman, and first baseman in the 1960s and 1970s—the Braves, Cardinals, and Mets. Those experiences gave him another nod over Stengel: the dugout boss who had managed the most wins (845), defeats (1,003), and games (1,848) before capturing a pennant. In the same vein, he had accumulated the most days in uniform as player or manager (4,272) before reaching the World Series. Torre's best season as a player was 1971, when he took MVP honors in St. Louis for topping the National League in hits (230), RBIs (137), and batting (.363).

SALOMON TORRES

Few rookies have broken into the big leagues as inauspiciously as Torres did for the Giants in 1993. Called up in September to fill a hole in the starting rotation, the righthander suffered four losses in the club's last 18 games. They were the only defeats in that span for San Francisco, which lost the division title on the final day of the season to Atlanta.

DAVID TRACY

The Browns were so bad in the post-World War II years that owner Bill DeWitt hired the hypnotist Tracy to instill some self-confidence in the players. On June 6, 1950, immediately after his arrival, the Browns were savaged by the Red Sox, 20–4. On June 7 Boston won 29–4. On June 8 Tracy was sent packing.

ALOYSIUS TRAVERS

Travers was a 19-year-old Philadelphia seminarian who was drafted by the Tigers on May 18, 1912 to pitch a major league game against the Athletics because visiting Detroit players had walked off on strike to protest the suspension of Ty Cobb. With Detroit coaches and other amateurs from Philadelphia behind him, Travers hurled all nine innings of a 24–2 Athletics whipping. His penance done, he then went back to concentrating on the priesthood.

CECIL TRAVIS

World War II affected Travis's career more than any other major league regular's. Prior to Pearl Harbor the Senators third baseman-shortstop averaged .327 over nine seasons; in 1941, when Ted Williams hit .406 and Joe DiMaggio batted safely in 56 consecutive games, the lefty swinger topped both of them and everyone else with 218 hits. But after freezing his feet at the Battle of the Bulge, Travis was all but through when he returned to Washington after the war. For all that, though, he still ended up with a career average of .314 and is undoubtedly the best player never to have received a single vote for the Hall of Fame.

PIE TRAYNOR (Hall of Fame, 1948)

Traynor spent more than 55 years with the Pirates as a player, manager, and broadcaster. A shortstop when he joined the club in 1920, he was moved to third base because of the acquisition of Rabbit Maranville, going on to become the first player elected to the Hall of Fame from that position in the normal writers' balloting. Although he led the league only once in an offensive category (a tie for triples in 1923), Traynor ended up with a .320 average for 17 big league seasons. A 100-RBI man seven times, he set the record for power thrift in 1928 by batting across 124 with only three home runs. Defensively, he led the NL in assists three times, double plays four times, and putouts seven times. Traynor's career effectively ended after breaking his arm in 1934, but during a subsequent five-and-a-year stint as Pittsburgh manager he sometimes stuck himself in as the first baseman or a pinch-hitter. He did radio work for the team for 33 years. His nickname derived from a childhood habit of asking for pie when a priest wanted to reward him for recovering balls hit by a parish team.

GUS TRIANDOS

Statistics citing the 1950s Baltimore catcher as the slowest man in baseball history lie; he was even slower than that. According to the record, Triandos's theft of merely one base in 1,206 games stands as the all-time low for players with 1,000 appearances. But even that swipe, in a late season 1958 game against the Yankees, was an uncontested steal of second in the final minutes of a New York pounding of the Orioles; it wasn't until some years later that "defensive indifference" was scored for such situations.

Triandos was the first catcher to call no-hitters in both leagues—for Baltimore's Hoyt Wilhelm against the Yankees in 1958 and for Philadelphia's Jim Bunning (a perfect game) against the Mets in 1964.

HAL TROSKY

Trosky was headed for a Hall of Fame career before being sidetracked by one of the game's most notorious managers and by his own headaches. After six straight 100-RBI seasons, the righthand-hitting first baseman emerged as one of the leaders in a 1940 player revolt against Cleveland pilot Ossie Vitt. The uprising capped years of Vitt's public mocking of the team and other incidents that inspired some players to start fistfights in the hope that the manager would try to break them up. When the Cleveland press got wind of the trouble, it began referring to the team as the Crybaby Indians—a label gleefully picked up in grandstands around the league. For their part, Trosky and his teammates sought to outmaneuver Vitt even on the field by designing their own codes for steals, bunts, and other plays in defiance of the pilot's tactics. Although Vitt was fired after the 1940 season, the tensions did nothing for Trosky's chronic migraine condition, and he had to retire after the following year.

DIZZY TROUT

After 14 solid seasons (1939–52) that included two 20-win years for the Tigers, Trout made the mistake of looking good at an old timers game five years after his retirement. Persuaded by the Orioles that he still had something, he made two appearances for them as a reliever in 1957, failing to get out of an inning both times and finally calling it quits for good with a season ERA of 81.00. The righthander's finest year was 1944, when he won 27 games and led the league in ERA and shutouts. In 1945 he gave Detroit an indispensable boost to the flag by notching four wins over the last 11 days of the campaign.

DASHER TROY

Troy's contract jumping from the Detroit Wolverines to the Philadelphia Athletics and back again in 1882 occasioned the first war between the National League and the American Association. Until the infielder's double defection, the two circuits had merely watched each other warily, waiting for each other to make the first aggressive move. Troy defended his desertion of the Athletics by claiming that he hadn't known the team intended playing on Sundays. In retaliation, the AA immediately opened its doors to players blacklisted by the NL.

VIRGIL TRUCKS

Trucks was as much of a no-hitter specialist who ever toed a mound. After hurling at least one in every minor league he played for, the righthander completed two of them for the Tigers in 1952. What made that doubly remarkable was that he managed only three other victories while losing 19; the other wins included a one-hitter and a two-hitter. Trucks spent 11 of his 17 seasons between 1941 and 1958 with Detroit, but had his only 20-win year in 1953 while dividing time between the Browns and White Sox.

TOMMY TUCKER

Tucker's .372 for the American Association Orioles in 1889 is the highest season average ever for a switch-hitter. But the first baseman was known less for his hitting than for a combativeness that incensed both opponents and umpires and usually ended with punches thrown. His most memorable encounter came after he spiked John McGraw on May 15, 1894; the brawl that followed so engaged fans that they didn't notice a burgeoning fire until it was too late to stop

the destruction of Boston's South End Grounds. Two months later, on July 17, Tucker's antics in the third base coaching box failed to persuade the umpire that the game ought to have been called for rain; they did, however, sufficiently impress the Philadelphia fans sitting behind him to make them jump out of the stands to beat him up, breaking his cheekbone.

TED TURNER

Turner's nemesis has been success. The pioneer of cable television in baseball, his intuition of the 1970s had become so much of an assumption by the new millennium that his less imaginative archrival Rupert Murdoch was practically dominating the sport through it. The money he threw at high-priced free agents for the Braves contributed to 10 straight division titles between 1991 and 2001—and almost as many embarrassments in the postseason. Most recently, his merger with the Time-Warner conglomerate has made him wealthy beyond measure—and reduced him to just one voice on a board not as dedicated to spending to keep Atlanta at the top of the National League heap.

Turner bought the Braves in January 1976 with the announced goal of making them "America's Team" through his cable TBS coverage. Although he never quite succeeded at that in other than on-air time, his very articulation of the aim underscored the thinking of a new generation of major league entrepreneurs for whom specific metropolitan geographics and market numbers were only casually compatible. His first move after the purchase was to sign free agent Andy Messersmith even as Walter O'Malley was organizing other owners to blackball the pitcher and any other player who sought to declare free agency in the wake of the 1975 decision by arbitrator Peter Seitz. His second move was to skirt the owners' lockout of spring training camps in 1976 with a technicality by inviting minor leaguers down to Florida on schedule. On the other hand, Turner went along with other owners on a contractual perogative permitting clubs to slash by 20 percent the salary of any player who announced his intention of playing out his option year. In the first blush of his ownership he also played to the grandstand with such stunts as leaping out onto the field to welcome Braves at home plate after a home run and joining the ground crew in sweeping the infield in the fifth inning.

In 1977 Turner decided that the best way to distract

attention from a wretched club was to manage it himself. That stunt lasted a single game (a 16th consecutive loss) before NL president Chub Feeney dug out an old regulation barring managers from owning stock in the club that employed them. Turner turned the team back to regular manager Dave Bristol, then moved on to the courtroom where he was battling a fine and suspension levied on him by Commissioner Bowie Kuhn for allegedly tampering with free agent outfielder Gary Matthews. The highlight of the action was a threat by the Braves owner to give Kuhn's attorney "a knuckle sandwich" for his crossexamination techniques; otherwise, the suspension was upheld, and he put baseball behind him for a year, concentrating instead on taking the America's Cup.

In the late 1970s and early 1980s Turner was often attacked by other owners for his lavish contract offers to free agents who were something less than all-stars. In 1979, for instance, he agreed to pay reliever Al Hrabosky $170,000 annually for 30 years; Hrabosky ended up with seven saves over three seasons. In 1980 he signed up Claudell Washington for five years at almost $1 million a year; to that point in his career the outfielder had never hit more than 13 home runs in a season and had batted .300 only once. In his five-and-a-half years with Atlanta Washington proved to be a solid but unspectacular performer, most noted for inspiring grandstand placards declaring WASHINGTON SLEPT HERE. Even the rash signings were forgotten when the club won the West Division title under Joe Torre in 1982, but between its loss to the Cardinals in the NLCS and 1991 Atlanta was not a bright sight on the field. Turner himself adopted a lower profile for most of the rest of the decade, regaining sports headlines mainly in connection with pitcher Phil Niekro—first in having to deny that Niekro had been working for him as a spy in Torre's clubhouse, then in allowing the knuckleballer to walk away in 1983 as an embittered free agent after 20 years in a Braves uniform, and then in bringing him back for a final mound appearance in 1987.

With Atlanta's revival in the 1990s under Bobby Cox, Turner once again began throwing money at free agents, only this time it was usually good money after good money. Along with his then-wife Jane Fonda, he also became a familiar presence at postseason games joining in on the so-called Tomahawk Chop in the face of calls by Native Americans to eliminate what they regarded as a reinforcement of racial stereotyping. If Turner was bothered that all his money and rekindled enthusiasm produced merely one world championship (in 1995), he was even more irritated by his frustrated endeavors to buy CBS or some other media giant to make him as much of a force on broadcasting channels as he was on cable. It was with the ambition of realizing that dream that he agreed in 1995 to the merger with Time-Warner, not realizing until too late that it was Time-Warner's executives who would emerge as chief spokesmen for the amalgamated company.

TUCK TURNER

As the fourth outfielder for the 1894 Phillies, Turner got into enough games for his .418 average to qualify for the batting crown. But the switch-hitter had two problems: Hugh Duffy's league-leading .440 and the three regulars ahead of him—Ed Delahanty, Billy Hamilton, and Sam Thompson—who hit a combined .407 on the season. Tucker's .418 is the highest average not to win a batting title.

WILLIAM MARCY TWEED

From 1860 to 1871 the notorious Boss Tweed, head of New York's Tammany Hall and champion grafter, was president of the Mutual Club of New York. For the better part of its existence the team was theoretically amateur, although Tweed provided players with no-show patronage jobs in the coroner's office or the street department that cost taxpayers about $30,000 a year.

JIM TYNG

A pitcher and catcher for the Harvard University team, Tyng's mishaps behind home plate persuaded him to wear the first catcher's mask, designed by teammate Fred Thayer. He tried it out for the first time in a game against the Live Oaks of Lynn on April 11, 1877. In 1879, while pursuing his law career, Tyng was persuaded by Boston manager Harry Wright to pitch three late-season games for the Red Stockings; his two losses gave the pennant to the Providence Grays. He went back to the National League to pitch another inning in 1888 for the Phillies, again at Wright's request, but only after having his contract stipulate that he was the attorney and director of athletics for Huntington Street Grounds, Philadelphia's park. Tyng didn't want the social stigma of being viewed as a professional ballplayer.

U

PETER UEBERROTH

Money come, money go was the motif of Ueberroth's four-and-a-half year term as commissioner between October 1984 and April 1989. Adopting a decidedly CEO approach to his job, he played a prominent role in negotiating lucrative television contracts with CBS and ESPN, as well as in persuading companies to pay substantial fees in order to be called "official sponsors" of Major League Baseball. The underbelly of the deals was that the contract with CBS stopped the traditional season-long Game of the Week while creating unrealistic criteria for TV revenues and the sponsorship associations overwhelmed the game with plugs for everything from the call to the bullpen for a relief pitcher to the simple reading of a lineup.

Where individual franchises were concerned, Ueberroth pressured the Cubs into installing lights at Wrigley Field and blocked a couple of sale moves by Texas owner Eddie Chiles until the franchise could be peddled to George W. Bush. It was also during Ueberroth's reign that major league clubs stepped up their plaints about losing money, to the point where only the New York teams and the Dodgers seemed to be profitable. At the height of this public relations ploy against player salary demands he suggested to the owners the collusion tactic against free agents that ended up costing several of them millions, as well as star players.

Ueberroth, who was elected commissioner shortly after heading the 1984 Los Angeles Olympic Organization Committee, was even less successful when it came to nonfinancial matters. After a lot of tough talk about dealing with baseball's drug problems, he had little legal choice but to accept a significantly watered down rehabilitation-discipline program advanced by the Players Association. Still emptier were his periodic pronouncements to pressure owners into ending discriminatory practices against minorities for managing and front office jobs.

BOB UECKER

Uecker made a second career as a broadcaster by ridiculing his first one as a catcher. A .200 hitter in six seasons (1962–67) with the Braves, Cardinals, and Phillies, he has primarily aimed his humor at his anemic offensive output, his inability to handle Phil Niekro's knuckleballs, and Philadelphia fans. In addition to his platform as a long-time Brewers broadcaster, he has written the best-selling *Catcher in the Wry,* starred in the television sitcom "Mr. Belvedere," and played somebody close to the original in several films, most notably in *Major League* where his broadcasting call of "Just a little bit outside" for a madly wild pitch gained catchphrase currency.

Among the more popular Ueckerisms have been:

"Instead of having the word 'powerized' on my bats, they said 'For display only.'"

"When I went to bat with three men on and two out in the ninth, I looked over in the other team's dugout, and they were in street clothes."

"The way to catch a knuckleball is to wait until the ball stops rolling and then pick it up."

"I made a major contribution to the Cardinals

pennant drive—I came down with hepatitis. The trainer injected me with it."

"Philly fans are so mean that one Easter Sunday when the players staged an Easter egg hunt for their kids, the fans booed the kids who didn't find any eggs."

"The cops picked me up on the street and fined me $500 for being drunk and $100 for being with the Phillies."

"The average age in Sun City, Arizona is deceased."

GEORGE UHLE

Uhle was among the earliest practitioners of the slider, naming it for its motion. The righthander used the pitch to lead the American League in victories twice while with the Indians (1923 and 1926), overall winning 200 games for four clubs between 1919 and 1936. Uhle's 52 hits in 1923 (for a .361 average) are the season record for a pitcher. He is also the only big league hurler to catch, donning a mask and chest protector for Cleveland in a 1921 game.

V

BOBBY VALENTINE

Valentine has had the fewest losing seasons (two) of active managers with at least 10 years of running a club. It is a record of success often eclipsed by his abrasive attitude toward those who suggest they know as much baseball as he does, by a genuine dislike for him by other managers around both leagues, and by his highly publicized run-ins with star players. Making him even more vulnerable to criticism has been his failure to reach the top with a world championship team. In some respects he is the rich man's Gene Mauch.

Once considered a golden prospect by the Dodgers, Valentine's playing career was all but ended by a broken leg in 1973 and a separated shoulder the following season, both injuries occurring when he was with the Angels. After hanging on as a utilityman for several teams until 1979, he put in time as a minor league instructor for the Padres and Mets and then as a New York coach before taking over the Rangers in 1985. Although he turned around a previously bad club and picked up manager-of-the-year accolades for himself in the process, his penchant for implying that he had written the rule book raised the hackles of some of his counterparts around the league, notably Bobby Cox and Tony LaRussa. By the time he was bounced in 1992 (by George W. Bush, then the owner of Texas) he was well on his way to having managed the most games (1,704) without getting into the postseason since the start of divisional play in 1969.

After a stint in the Mets minor league system, Valentine became the first American hired to manage in Japan, leading the Chiba Lotte Marines to a franchise-mark season in 1995. The connections he forged there (and his at least basic command of the language) soon helped make the Mets the biggest raider of Japanese talent, signing Takashi Kashiwada, Masato Yoshii, Tsuyoshi Shinjo, and Satoru Komiyama directly, as well as picking up Hideo Nomo from the Dodgers. In 1996 he was back at the helm of the New York farm club at Norfolk, from where he was promoted in late August to replace Dallas Green at Shea Stadium.

Putting an end to six straight losing seasons, Valentine revived the franchise with help from such pivotal acquisitions as Mike Piazza and Al Leiter, but also with an ability to reanimate dormant careers (e.g., pitcher Rick Reed). On the other hand, the faltering of the club down the stretch in 1998 and a near-repeat stumble in 1999 reawoke criticisms that he overmanaged in pressure situations. The criticism did not abate despite a club recovery to win a wild card postseason appearance in 1999 (the end of his personal futility record) and the pennant in 2000. All the time he kept the back pages of the New York tabloids going with an offer to resign in June 1999 after his chief coaches were fired; with a trading of insults with catcher Todd Hundley over the latter's all-night carousing habits; with separate clashes with outfielders Lance Johnson, Bobby Bonilla, Rickey Henderson, and Darryl Hamilton; with a return to the bench in a daffy Groucho Marx mask after being kicked out of a game; with sybilline charges while talking to a business school class that he had "five losers" on his team; and with his cool relations with general manager Steve Phillips. For good measure he also declared on one occasion that he was ready to go on television to match his grasp of the game against other so-called geniuses—a presumed reference to Cox and LaRussa, who had preceded him over to the National League and who had routinely managed games against the Valentine-led Mets as though each one were the seventh game of the World Series.

Valentine's egomaniacal image took a big hit after the September 11, 2001 attack on the World Trade Center for his tireless relief work, on both personal and organizational levels.

FERNANDO VALENZUELA

Few debuts have matched that of Valenzuela. After yielding no earned runs in 17 $\frac{2}{3}$ innings of relief for the Dodgers in 1980, the southpaw won his first eight games in 1981, five of them shutouts; tied the big league rookie mark of eight shutouts despite working in the strike-shortened season; became the first NL rookie to be tops in strikeouts; and (another first) took both Rookie of the Year and Cy Young honors. The Mexican screwballer's success combined with an unathletic physique and an unorthodox delivery in which he glanced skyward before releasing the ball to create Fernandomania, the name given to the excitement generated by his every start on both sides of the U.S.-Mexico border. While millions of Mexican radio listeners and TV viewers tuned into Los Angeles's Spanish-language networks, millions more coast-to-coast viewers took in his appearances on network television and Dodger Stadium filled to capacity for 11 of his starts. Thanks in large part to Valenzuela, the team drew 2.3 million fans despite losing 25 home dates to the strike. In Mexico his popularity spawned a comic strip.

Over his first few years Valenzuela was the most effective Dodgers lefthander since Sandy Koufax. In 1986 he established a record of going 44 $\frac{1}{3}$ innings from the start of a season without yielding an earned run, then went on to lead the league with 21 wins. But a shoulder injury in 1988 started his career downward, and for the next six years—with the Angels, Orioles, and Phillies, as well as back in the Mexican an League—he was signed more as a gate attraction than as a reliable starter.

CLARENCE VAN BUSKIRK

Van Buskirk was the architect who designed Ebbets Field, which opened on April 5, 1913 for an exhibition game between the Dodgers and Yankees.

Despite the legendary status the park would gain, it was only when Van Buskirk saw the thousands of fans descending on its single rotunda entrance that he realized he had built a firetrap. Under orders from Brooklyn owner Charlie Ebbets other access points were quickly carved into street walls before the opening of the regular season a few days later.

DAZZY VANCE (Hall of Fame, 1955)

Vance is the most unlikely player in the Hall of Fame. Already 31 before he won his first game, for Brooklyn in 1922, the righthander had spent the previous decade moving from one minor league club to another, failing miserably in trials with the Pirates and Yankees, and then coming up with a series of arm ailments that jeopardized even his travels in the boondocks. When Dodgers scout Larry Sutton recommended he be acquired after a winning season for a minor league team in New Orleans, owner Charlie Ebbets agreed only because it was a way of obtaining catcher Hank DeBerry. The odds against the fastball specialist becoming a premier pitcher of the 1920s didn't get any shorter playing for Brooklyn, a less-than-mediocre club that had merely one unexpected second-place finish to show for his tenure.

But despite all these obstacles Vance won 20 games three times, led the league in ERA three times, and struck out more batters than anyone else seven years in a row. In 1924 he captured pitching's Triple Crown by leading the league in wins (28), strikeouts, and ERA. He also contributed involuntarily to the rule book when a ploy of fraying his pitching sleeve to distract batters was outlawed.

JOHNNY VANDER MEER

Vander Meer had two extraordinary boosts to a Hall of Fame career but was unable to take advantage of them. The more noted one was his never-equaled back-to-back no-hitters against the Braves on June 11, 1938 and against the Dodgers four days later. Less well known is that the Cincinnati southpaw was second to no National League pitcher in overpowering the puny lineups put together during World War II; before he himself was drafted, he led the league in strikeouts three straight years. But for all that he also had to deal with his own team's modest offense, never winning more than 18 games and concluding his career under .500 (119–121).

Vander Meer's second no-hitter was also the first

night game in Brooklyn's Ebbets Field. While the contest itself was never at issue (Cincinnati led 6–0), he had to negotiate the perils of Pauline in the ninth inning after walking the bases loaded. Following a visit to the mound by Reds manager Bill McKechnie that aroused the boos of 38,748 fans, the lefthander concluded matters by getting Ernie Koy to tap into a forceout at home and Leo Durocher to hit a soft outfield fly. He didn't surrender a hit until the fourth inning of his next game, when Boston's Debs Garms connected safely.

JOHN VANDER WAL
Vander Wal's 28 hits off the bench for the 1995 Rockies is the mark for most pinch-hits in a season. The previous mark of 25 had been held by José Morales of the 1976 Expos.

ARKY VAUGHAN (Hall of Fame, 1985)
Vaughan's election to Cooperstown remedied his long standing as the most underrated shortstop in National League history. Mainly because he led the league in errors with Pittsburgh in 1932 and 1933, he was perceived even by some backers as a one-dimensional, offensive infielder. But in fact many of his errors were from ambition, and his range was wide enough to lead the league in both putouts and assists three times despite such slick-fielding contemporaries as Leo Durocher, Billy Jurges, Dick Bartell, and Eddie Miller. What was never in question, on the other hand, was the righthander's hitting, starting with the fact that he averaged .300 in every one of his (10) seasons with Pittsburgh—something not even Honus Wagner or Paul Waner could say. Usually at or near the top of yearly leaders in doubles, triples, and runs scored, Vaughan hit a career-high .385 in 1935—not only a franchise record, but a plateau not topped in the league until lockout-shortened 1994. Although he reached double figures in home runs only twice, he was the first to leave the park twice in an All-Star Game (in 1941).

Vaughan was generally regarded as low-key, but he left both the Pirates and Dodgers after fights with his manager. In Pittsburgh in 1941 he got into months of wrangling with Frankie Frisch over playing time, precipitating one of Pittsburgh's worst trades when he was sent to Brooklyn for four dim lights. With the Dodgers he sparked a revolt against manager Durocher after the pilot had talked out of both sides

of his mouth over a suspension of pitcher Bobo Newsom; in Vaughan's eyes the incident demonstrated that Durocher was capable of lying about any player. It took Branch Rickey to restore something like peace, but the shortstop announced at the end of the 1943 season that he was quitting at the age of 31 because he just couldn't stand Durocher. Rickey took him at his word because when Durocher was suspended for the year in 1947, the executive called Vaughan back, and he replied with a .325 contribution to the Brooklyn pennant. Jackie Robinson also credited the Arkansas native with giving him moral support through the worst days of racial baiting by other teams. Vaughan's career mark of .318 is second only to Wagner's .328 among shortstops.

BILL VEECK, JR.
Even Veeck conceded that, whatever else he accomplished, he would end up best remembered as the man who sent a midget up to bat. In fact, Eddie Gaedel's single plate appearance, while the most famous of Veeck's stunts, was dwarfed by countless significant contributions to the game, especially in financial areas. In ownership stints with the Indians, Browns, and White Sox (twice), he also gained the distinction of being the last person to purchase a franchise without a fortune independent of baseball.

Veeck's start in baseball—as a stockboy and vendor—came about thanks to his father's being president of the Cubs in the 1920s. After William Veeck died in 1933, his son went to work in the Chicago front office, working up from ticket sales to organization treasurer; in the latter capacity he was responsible for planting the ivy that still adorns the walls of Wrigley Field. Veeck's first independent venture, in partnership with Charlie Grimm, was as owner of the American Association Milwaukee Brewers, which turned out to be a proving ground for his promotional genius. Giveaways of everything from six live squab to a 200-pound block of ice kept fans laughing—and coming. His most lasting contribution as a minor league boss was the institution of a rule prohibiting adjustable fences—passed the day after he unveiled a gadget for raising the height of the Milwaukee park's fence during the visiting team's turn at bat and lowering it again when the Brewers came to bat. Not so incidentally, he brought around a moribund franchise to three pennants in five years, then sold it in 1945 for a profit of $275,000.

In 1943, while still in Milwaukee, Veeck secured sufficient backing to purchase the Phillies from a bankrupt Gerry Nugent. His intention was to revitalize the club with Negro league stars, making the franchise instantly competitive, not to mention revolutionary. But then he and Nugent made the mistake of informing Commissioner Kenesaw Landis of their plan, and within days the National League took over the Philadelphia franchise and made sure it was sold to William Cox. In 1945 he also made a bid on the Yankees, but lost out to the Larry MacPhail-Dan Topping-Del Webb triumvirate.

When The Sport Shirt, as he came to be called for his favorite attire, finally did purchase a big league club—Cleveland in June 1946—he was, at 42, one of the youngest men ever to do so. He did it with a creative piece of financing called a debenture-common stock group that involved investors putting up money partly to buy stock and partly as a loan, then getting remunerated through nontaxable repayments of their loans rather than through taxable dividends. Toward the end of the 1947 season he broke ground of another kind when he made Larry Doby the first black player in the American League.

Veeck almost undid all his good work in 1948 by trying to trade popular shortstop-manager Lou Boudreau to the Browns. As soon as the Cleveland press got wind of the possible deal, Boudreau supporters organized protest demonstrations and circulated petitions demanding that Veeck be the one to leave town. The stunned Veeck ran all over Cleveland, going from bar to restaurant to bar, to concede as personally as he could that he had made a mistake while simultaneously denying the trade had been consummated or even that it had been his idea to begin with. Skepticism remained in the air until he signed Boudreau to a two-year extension in his dual role. The playing manager rewarded the vote of confidence (on the part of Clevelanders if not of his employer) by winning the franchise's first pennant and World Series since 1920. A key contributor to the club's success was Negro leagues star Satchel Paige, who became the oldest rookie in history when Veeck signed him; a non-contributor was Joe Earley, for whom Veeck organized a night at Cleveland Stadium after the fan had protested that the owner seemed to honor everybody but "the average Joe." Good Old Joe Earley Night, held on September 28, drew an estimated 60,000 fans.

The highlight of the rest of Veeck's stay in Cleveland was a ceremonial burial of the 1948 championship flag as soon as it became clear the club wouldn't be able to overtake the Yankees and Red Sox for a repeat in 1949. Soon afterward, in desperate need of money to settle a divorce suit from his wife, he sold out to insurance executive Ellis Ryan and his executive suite protégé Hank Greenberg.

Less than two years later Veeck reemerged as owner of the Browns, boasting from the start that he intended driving the Cardinals out of the city they shared. Woefully underfinanced, he managed mostly to irritate Cardinals owner Fred Saigh—first by hiring any number of former employees of St. Louis's National League team, then by decorating Sportsman's Park (owned by the Browns but used by both clubs) with Brownie memorabilia. The Gaedel stunt took place on August 19, 1951, and, never one to let an absurdity rest, Veeck was still arguing with AL president Will Harridge about the inclusion of the midget's appearance in baseball's official records when, five days later, he staged Grandstand Managers Day. The promotion this time was for publicity director Bob Fischel to walk up and down the field with cards proposing such moves as stealing or changing the pitcher; in response, Veeck, former Athletics manager Connie Mack, and 4,000 fans flashed placards given out at the gate—the green side for Yes, the red side for No. While regular pilot Zack Taylor sat in a rocking chair puffing on a pipe on the sidelines, the fans called an excellent game; the Browns won, 5–3, to end a four-game losing streak.

Veeck's undoing in St. Louis began after the 1952 season, when he proposed that AL teams share local radio and television revenue with visiting clubs. Voted down 7–1, he refused to sign releases to allow broadcasts of games in which St. Louis was the visiting team. The other owners retaliated by changing the schedule to eliminate lucrative Friday night games (such as with the Yankees) in Missouri. While contemplating a suit over this collusion, Veeck learned that Saigh, who had been indicted for federal tax evasion, had sold the Cardinals to the Anheuser-Busch breweries. Daunted by the resources of his new NL rival, he decided to move his own franchise. Assured by other owners that his proposed relocation to Baltimore was a done deal, he nevertheless found himself on the short end of a 6–2 vote at the winter meetings. Petitioning again after a disastrous lame duck season in 1953, he was informed only too definitively that the transfer of the Browns to Baltimore would be approved only if he stepped aside.

After abortive attempts to buy the Athletics in 1954 and the Tigers in 1957 (as well as the Ringling Brothers Circus and a Cleveland NBA franchise), Veeck popped up again in 1959 at the head of a group willing to get between Chuck Comiskey and his sister Dorothy Rigney, who owned both the White Sox and the record for interfamilial lawsuits. Veeck's syndicate purchased Rigney's 54 percent of the club and inherited Comiskey's animosity and the endless litigation through which he expressed it. But Comiskey was only a sideshow to the Go-Go White Sox pennant and to more of the familiar Veeck antics, one of them involving Gaedel's helicoptering onto the field for a conversation with Chicago infielders Nellie Fox and Luis Aparicio.

In 1960, however, Veeck began suffering anew from a leg that had been injured during World War II and that had already been amputated to the knee. Told the rest of the limb had to come off and that he had stretched blood vessels in his head that required complete rest, Veeck stayed around only long enough to install baseball's first exploding scoreboard and to put player names on the backs of uniforms. He then sold out to Arthur Allyn, Jr., son of one of his perennial partners.

A decade-and-a-half later, in December 1975, following a thwarted attempt to buy the Orioles, Veeck repurchased Chicago from Allyn's bankrupt brother John. Nobody in the AL's executive chambers was thrilled by his return, but the only alternative at the time seemed to be a far more wrenching transfer of the White Sox to Seattle and a move by the equally abhorred Charlie Finley from Oakland to Chicago. Veeck wasted little time pouring salt in the league's wounds by setting up shop in the lobby of the hotel where winter meetings were being conducted and completing four trades within full view of spectators. Two weeks later, however, arbitrator Peter Seitz introduced the age of free agency by coming down on the side of the players in the Messersmith-McNally case. Veeck's career as an owner—and the possibility of anyone else without extensive outside money becoming one—were effectively over. Ironically, Veeck himself had always regarded the reserve clause as stupid at best and illegal at worst; he had even testified on behalf of Curt Flood's effort to overturn the rule in 1972.

Still, the once-again White Sox owner hung on for five seasons. In that time his best gimmick was a Bicentennial-inspired "Spirit of '76" parade for the Opening Day ceremonies at Comiskey Park in 1976, featuring himself as the peg-legged fifer ("If you've got the guy with the wooden leg, you've got the casting beat"). His best idea was a "rent-a-player" scheme for taking over the stars of other clubs in their option years. His best season was 1977, when leased sluggers Richie Zisk and Oscar Gamble powered the team to 90 victories and third place. His best sentimental gesture came in 1976, when he reactivated 54-year-old Minnie Minoso, who picked up his last big league hit in eight at bats and who could say he had played in four different decades. The worst sentimental gesture was bringing Minoso back again in 1980 for two futile at bats so the one-time outfielder could say that he had played in five decades. His longest surviving idea was having announcer Harry Caray sing "Take Me Out to the Ball Game" during the seventh-inning stretch—a custom the broadcaster later took with him to Wrigley Field. His most copied idea was having players take curtain calls after hitting home runs. His least copied idea was having the team play in short pants for a year. The worst idea of his career was Disco Demolition Night on June 12, 1979, when a local disc jockey's stunt of blowing up disco records between games of a doubleheader resulted in thousands of fans jumping out of the stands, policemen trying futilely to restore order, firefighters abandoning efforts to put out the blazes caused by exploding platters, and umpires declaring the second game a forfeit win for the visiting Tigers. Veeck finally gave up and sold the club to Jerry Reinsdorf and Eddie Einhorn in January 1981.

Veeck, who died in 1986, recorded many of his adventures in the best-selling *Veeck As in Wreck.*

WILLIAM VEECK

A sportswriter given to criticizing the club, Veeck took over baseball operations for the Cubs in 1918 on a challenge from owner William Wrigley to do a better job. In his first two years he became embroiled in a couple of game-fixing scandals that took the flavor out of a Chicago pennant win in his debut season.

Veeck's baptism of fire came in January 1919, when he released Lee Magee for admitting that he had thrown games with the Reds the year before. He managed to get Cincinnati owner Garry Herrmann and Brooklyn boss Charlie Ebbets to give him $2,500 each for having passed along damaged goods when Herrmann sold the second baseman to Ebbets and then Ebbets traded him to Chicago. The episode became public only months later when Magee (unsuccessfully) sued the Cubs for the salary owed him on a two-year contract.

Tipped off in August 1919 that some Cubs players were involved in a fix in an upcoming game against the last-place Phillies, Veeck ordered manager Fred Mitchell to pull scheduled starter Claude Hendrix in favor of Grover Cleveland Alexander while he investigated quietly. Both efforts failed when Chicago lost anyway and the press got hold of the story. Veeck then made things worse by asking the Baseball Writers Association to help him look into the affair—a request interpreted as getting Chicago dailies to keep quiet about the skullduggery. Resultant stories in the *Tribune* and other papers kicked up such a fuss that State's Attorney MacClay Hoyne was forced to initiate the grand jury investigation that soon turned its attention to the larger Black Sox scandal. Over the next couple of years, while the Chicago Eight continued at the center of off-field news, Veeck quietly dropped several Cubs players, including Hendrix and Fred Merkle, thought to have been compromised.

Veeck continued to run the franchise until his death in 1933, also winning the NL pennant in 1929 and 1932.

ROBIN VENTURA

Ventura put his mark on the grand slam home run in 1999. On May 20, in a doubleheader against the Brewers, the Mets third baseman became the first big leaguer to leave the park with the bases loaded in both ends of a twinbill. On October 17, in the 15th inning of an excruciating NLCS fifth game against the Braves, he ended matters with another grand slam —only to have his winning hit reduced to a single when ecstatic teammates jumped him, preventing him from circling the bases.

MICKEY VERNON

Vernon's second of two batting titles, for the 1953 Senators, gave new definition to the team game. With the lefty-swinging first baseman and Cleveland's Al Rosen separated by less than a point on the final day of the season, the word reached the Wash-

ington bench that Rosen had picked up three hits in five at bats against the Tigers in his quest for a Triple Crown. Quick arithmetic showed that Vernon's two hits in four at bats against the Athletics would be enough for the title, but that he couldn't afford another hitless plate appearance. To make sure that Vernon didn't get into the batter's box again in the ninth inning, catcher Mickey Grasso doubled but was then conveniently picked off and outfielder Kite Thomas singled only to be tagged out strolling around the first base bag.

Vernon batted .286 in a 20-year career between 1939 and 1960 for the Senators and several other clubs; he also won the batting title in 1946. In 1961 he was named the first manager of the expansion Washington club.

ZOILO VERSALLES

Playing shortstop for the Twins in 1965, Versalles led the league in strikeouts and errors—and was named American League MVP. It helped that he was regarded as the heart of pennant-winning Minnesota for also setting the pace for runs scored, doubles, triples, plate appearances, and defensive double plays. Indicative of his importance (or of the scarcity of other candidates), he took the honor with more than 100 votes more than the runnerup, teammate Tony Oliva.

JOE VILA

The sports editor of the New York *Sun,* Vila was more responsible than anybody else for popularizing Brooklyn's team as the Dodgers. While the nickname Trolley Dodgers had been used on occasion for years, it had never gained official status and had, since Wilbert Robinson's hiring as manager in 1914, been eclipsed by the more casual Robins. But when Robinson and Vila got into a dispute in 1926 over a *Sun* article that had printed the salaries of Brooklyn players, the editor ordered his staff never to use Robinson's name or the nickname Robins in any story. In solidarity with the *Sun,* a couple of other city papers also began using Dodgers regularly until, with the departure of Robinson in 1931, it became the accepted nickname.

FAY VINCENT

Vincent sat down in the commissioner's chair because of the sudden death of Bart Giamatti in September 1989; when he got up again two years later, the office itself was all but dead. In between he became proficient at employing liberal arguments for making authoritarian points.

Vincent had been a corporate lawyer and executive for Columbia Pictures and Coca-Cola before signing on as old friend Giamatti's deputy commissioner in April 1989. In his first year as Giamatti's successor he spent a good part of his time on the investigation and subsequent suspension of George Steinbrenner for paying gambler Howard Spira to dig up dirt on Yankees star Dave Winfield. Even after the New York owner volunteered to step aside indefinitely as managing partner of the club, Vincent had to wade through lawsuits filed by limited partners in the franchise seeking first to reinstate him, then demanding that Leonard Kleinman, also implicated in the Spira nastiness, be allowed to succeed him. The Steinbrenner case didn't go away until Vincent announced a reinstatement in June 1992, effective the following March.

In the meantime Vincent irritated club owners by intervening in the 32-day spring training lockout that delayed the start of the 1990 season for a week. Joining the discussions in February, he had little impact on the eventual solution other than to restart talks with players after they had been stalled, but a majority of owners resented his assumption that labor relations fell within his province. His handling of pitcher Steve Howe's seventh known involvement with drugs brought more criticism. Vincent started the ball rolling in June 1992 by suspending the Yankees hurler indefinitely. When the Players Association filed a grievance over the penalty and hearing officer George Nicolau suggested the commissioner define the length of the suspension, he responded by expelling Howe permanently. With Howe accepting a three-year probation sentence as his punishment from a criminal court, Nicolau overruled the permanent banishment. This sent Vincent into a fury that his authority was being challenged, so he summoned New York manager Buck Showalter, general manager Gene Michael, and vice-president Jack Lawn to his office to warn them of their own precarious positions if they didn't support baseball's drug policies at the Howe grievance hearing. The Players Association immediately filed an unfair labor-practices suit against the commissioner's office.

Vincent hadn't needed more enemies. On top of the hackles he had raised by intervening in the 1990 lockout, he had also alienated clubs by going before a U.S. Senate subcommittee to attack the influence of cable superstations and by insisting on realigning the National League according to greater geographical logic. The latter rearrangement would have moved the Braves and Reds to the East Division and shifted the Cubs and Cardinals to the West. Ten of the 12 NL teams saw nothing wrong with that, but the Cubs had nothing to gain by such a shift except a later starting time for most of their road games, a consequent smaller audience on their WGN superstation, and lower profits for the Chicago *Tribune,* which owned both the club and the station. When Vincent imposed the plan over Chicago's dissenting vote, the Cubs took the issue to court and won.

Encouraged by his threats against the Yankees officials and by the absence of any support from the Players Association, an ownership faction banded around Jerry Reinsdorf of the White Sox and Bud Selig of the Brewers blasted Vincent for overstepping the bounds of his office and demanded his resignation. His answer on August 20 was that "I will not resign—ever." But two weeks later he was handed a no-confidence vote by a 2–1 margin, and two weeks after that announced that he was stepping down "in the best interests of baseball." His successor was Selig, who held on to the post on a temporary basis for six years and with the clear understanding that serious matters such as negotiating with the players were not to be entrusted to a commissioner.

For the duration of his term Vincent was given to populist pronouncements that made him sound like the owners' chief critic; at the same time, he anguished publicly over such ills as drug taking. When push came to shove, however, his remedies smacked of the same disregard for due process that he claimed to be surprised by in his dealings with the owners.

OSSIE VITT

Vitt piloted the so-called Crybaby Indians who blew the 1940 pennant because they were more preoccupied with outwitting him than the Tigers. Although statistically one of the franchise's most successful managers, the one-time infielder brought most of the trouble on himself by criticizing his players to the front office and the press but rarely to their own faces. Another frequent tactic was jeering at players from the dugout after they had committed an error or surrendered a big hit. By the middle of the 1940 season Vitt's relations with the players had degenerated to the point that they were marching regularly into general manager Cy Slapnicka's office demanding either a trade or a new dugout boss; outfielder Jeff Heath acknowledged starting fights on the bench and in the clubhouse in the hope that Vitt would try to break them up.

Mainly because of Vitt's close ties to a couple of Cleveland newsmen, the clubhouse dissatisfaction was portrayed in the press as nothing more than whining—a perception that prompted the Crybaby Indians tag. Fans around the American League took to pelting the players with everything from jars of baby food to baby bottle nipples. Through it all such team leaders as first baseman Hal Trosky, pitcher Mel Harder, and catcher Frankie Pytlak began running parallel games through a private set of signs when they disagreed with Vitt's tactical calls. They didn't help the totally demoralized club from finishing a game behind Detroit. Vitt was fired at the end of the year.

BILL VOISELLE

Voiselle gained more attention during his nine-year (1942–50) career for his uniform number than for his pitching A native of Ninety-Six, South Carolina, that was also the number on his back when he won 21 games for the 1944 Giants and led the league in strikeouts. Although he never again won 20, the righthanded Voiselle contributed 13 victories to the pennant-winning Braves in 1948; as much as anybody, he was the "rain" in the season's popular cry of "Spahn, Sain, and pray for rain."

WILLIAM VOLTZ

In 1885 Philadelphia sportswriter Voltz tried to form the first benevolent protective association that would establish a fund for sick and needy players. The idea died because most players viewed him as an outsider who couldn't be trusted with their contributions to the fund.

CHRIS VON DER AHE

Von der Ahe built a dynasty in one league and destroyed it in another. If his initial interest in baseball was just to sell beer, he grasped decades before the Anheuser-Busch family that winning teams attracted more potential drinkers.

Between 1885 and 1888 Von der Ahe's St. Louis Browns won four consecutive American Association pennants. But he was not only a winner, he was a winner with flair. For starters, there were his personal style and appearance—checked slacks, spats, and diamond stickpins; ever-present greyhounds he called Schnauzer and Snoozer; references to himself in his comic book German accent as Der Poss President; and a bulbous nose turned scarlet from his incessant samplings of his own wares. For another, there was his abysmal ignorance of even the grosser points of the game. (On one occasion he told a group of visitors that his Sportsman's Park had the biggest diamond in the world; informed by his manager Charlie Comiskey that all diamonds were the same size, he amended his boast to saying it had the biggest infield.) Then there was his lavish spending. His personal indulgences included a sequence of very expensive and very public mistresses and a life-size statue of himself that was eventually put atop his grave; among his business expenses were private trains and first-class accommodations for his victorious teams.

But with the beneficences came equally lavish abuse: fines for routine errors, demands that his players live in rooming houses he owned and drink only in his establishments, insistence that they be willing to play exhibition games on offdays (he once laced into the club for refusing to play the black Cuban Giants, accusing it of spite against him rather than "honest prejudice"). Moreover, when the club performed below his standards, he turned vindictive, such as when it lost a postseason championship series to Detroit in 1887 and he not only withheld the losers' shares due the players, but sold off important parts of his roster to make up for the money he had expected to pocket winning the series. If there was no open revolt against him, it was only because of the critical mediating of manager Comiskey.

Other owners disliked him as much as most of his players did, with Brooklyn's Charles Byrne hardly alone in viewing him a buffoon. Even those who might have had plenty to gain by being friendly to his wealth couldn't quite bring themselves to having to deal with him on a regular basis; in 1890, for example, John Montgomery Ward turned down his bid to line up the Browns within the Players League.

Von der Ahe's little dynasty began unraveling in the early 1890s, after being forced to move with the

Browns into an enlarged National League because of the demise of the American Association. With Comiskey taking both his managerial skills and diplomatic talents off to Cincinnati, the club plummeted to the depths of the league, making even civility toward the owner a rarity. In an attempt to compensate for his wretched club, Von der Ahe surrounded it with what he called the Coney Island of the West—carousels, carnival rides, band contests, and boxing matches preceding and following a game as the total Sportsman's Park Experience. As fanciful as it sounded, it was a better idea than the crazed pace with which he started to hire and fire managers; between 1895 and 1897 alone he changed pilots 12 times, taking on the job himself for parts of each of the three seasons.

The end came in 1898. Sportsman's Park burned down, his wife sued him for divorce, his son took him to court over a property matter, and he himself ended up in a Pittsburgh jail after Pirates owner William Nimick had him kidnapped by private detectives and shanghaied to Pennsylvania over a seven-year-old debt. Destroyed financially, Von der Ahe couldn't even sell his team because a Missouri court had appointed a receiver to dispose of it. He died of cirrhosis of the liver in 1913. At his funeral Comiskey called him "the grandest figure baseball has ever known."

W

RUBE WADDELL (Hall of Fame, 1946)

Waddell's "colorful" career is a conspicuous example of the casual treatment baseball historians have given to players with grave emotional disturbances. The American League's premier lefthanded pitcher at the start of the 20th century was in fact a walking psychological problem tempered by mild retardation and alcoholism.

When he was in peak form mentally, there were few better than Waddell. Between 1902 and 1905 he racked up four consecutive 20-win years for Connie Mack's Athletics. He was even better whiffing opposition batters, leading the AL in that category every season between 1902 and 1907; his 349 strikeouts in 1904 stood as the big league mark for more than 60 years. Armed with a fastball compared by contemporaries to Walter Johnson's, he delighted crowds at exhibition games by waving his defense behind him off the field and then proceeding to fan irate batters. Only later would some decide that this macho posturing was part of the bigger problem they preferred to ignore while it was in front of their eyes.

At least in the beginning, Waddell's erratic behavior had a childlike tinge. He held up the start of games to shoot marbles. He was easily distracted by pets and toys. He was even more easily sidetracked by fishing, taking off for a favorite hole for days at a time without telling anyone. Most of all, he loved to follow after fire engines and firefighters, on several occasions missing games while watching a blaze being extinguished.

Together with some on-field tantrums, this off-field zaniness kept Waddell on the move from one team to another in the National League and the minor Western League for some years. Only Mack, who had already managed him for part of the WL season in Milwaukee in 1900, seemed unfazed by the hurler's behavior, though he also took the precaution of doling out Waddell's salary in tiny portions so too much of it wouldn't end up in a saloon. Their relations only began to sour in 1905, when Waddell missed his one and only opportunity to pitch in a World Series by injuring his shoulder during a playful train station tussle with teammate Andy Coakley. (The so-called Straw Hat Injury would be dug up later on by some for the implausible charge that Waddell had hurt himself deliberately as part of a fix on behalf of the Giants.) Never again the same pitcher after the accident, the lefthander became increasingly unstable, even violent—so much so that several teammates told Mack after the 1907 season they wouldn't be showing up in spring training the following year if he didn't trade away Waddell. A deal was quickly concluded with the Browns. Although Waddell came back to win 19 for St. Louis in 1908, it was his last hurrah. He was out of the big leagues in less than two years and, despite his dominating performances at the start of the decade, his overall record ended up at only 193–143.

DICK WAGNER

Wagner might not have been the most unpopular general manager to sit in a National League front office, but he was a finalist. Taking over from Bob Howsam in Cincinnati after the 1978 season, his first move was to fire Sparky Anderson as manager of the Big Red Machine and his second was to let Pete Rose go off and sign a free agent contract with the Phillies. Among the fans protesting was Cincinnati mayor Gerald Springer, who suggested Wagner had "gone bananas." Although he justified the moves by claiming that the Reds had grown complacent under Anderson and that Rose had overpriced himself, and found a degree of vindication in 1979 when John McNamara piloted the club to a division title, it soon enough became obvious that the executive's brief from the franchise was to dismantle the Big Red Machine for budgetary reasons. In short order he traded Ken Griffey and George Foster and showed little interest in resigning Joe Morgan and Dave Collins. When fan and media protest grew even louder, owners William and James Williams defiantly backed their general manager by giving him a new five-year contract. That gesture only further depressed attendance at Riverfront Stadium and prompted then-minority partner Marge Schott to crack that "if they want to fill the ballpark, they should have an I Don't Like Dick Wagner Night." In the event, Wagner lasted only midway through his new pact before the Williams brothers got rid of him for not turning his cheaply assembled club into winners.

In September 1985 Wagner resurfaced as general manager of Houston, and was in place when the team put together by his predecessor Al Rosen won the 1986 West Division title. But a year later he was forced to step down when manager Hal Lanier persuaded the Astros ownership he couldn't work with the executive.

HONUS WAGNER (Hall of Fame, 1936)

One of the Five Immortals elected to Cooperstown in the inaugural year of balloting, Wagner had his lack of flair to blame for later-day surprise that many had considered him superior to Ty Cobb. He inspired about as many extravagant stories in his 21-year (1897–1917) career with Louisville and Pittsburgh as Cobb did in one month.

Of all the numbers next to Wagner's name the most astonishing may be the .299 he batted for Louisville in 1898—the only time in his first 17 years that he didn't hit .300. His career average of .328 encompassed an NL record eight batting titles (tied by Tony Gwynn), 3,420 hits, 643 doubles, 252 triples, 101 home runs, 723 stolen bases, 1,739 runs, and 1,733 RBIs. Despite bowlegs that inspired one writer to describe him as "a hoop rolling down the baselines," he led the league in steals five times, attaining a high of

61 in 1907; on three occasions he stole his way around the bases from first to home in the same inning. Defensively, he spent several seasons shifting from first to third to the outfield before settling in as a shortstop in 1903. It was the weakest part of his game: Even allowing for the lower defensive standards of the period and his NL-leading double play turns in five seasons, his minimum 49 errors in his first eight years at the position were hardly the stuff of fielding brilliance. On the other hand, his defense offered his most colorful field trait—a proclivity for scooping up a shovelful of dirt and polluting the air around him every time he grabbed a grounder and threw to first.

The righthand-hitting Wagner moved from Louisville to Pittsburgh as part of the mass transfer of Colonels players following the folding of the Kentucky franchise after the 1899 season. Because of his aversion to tobacco he was a favorite of the abstemious Barney Dreyfuss, and the club owner never needed encouragement to contrast the character of his shortstop to that of rowdier stars. (Wagner's dislike of tobacco also triggered his objections to a baseball card with his image issued in 1910 by Piedmont cigarettes; the card was removed from circulation, ultimately making it so rare that it was being sold and resold for more than $1 million by the end of the century.) More than once Wagner stepped into the breach to manage the Pirates after a firing, but when he was officially offered the post in 1917, he lasted merely four defeats in five games before bowing out again. His decision produced strains in his relationship with Dreyfuss that the owner took to his grave.

Wagner left the Pirates after the 1917 season, going on to coach at Carnegie Tech and to open a sporting goods store with Pie Traynor. But the Depression left him destitute—a fact he did his best to hide from Dreyfuss. Only when sportswriter Fred Lieb revealed the extent of the former star's plight did Bill Benswanger, a Dreyfuss son-in-law who had taken over the franchise with the old man's death, ask him to come back to the Pirates as a coach. Wagner stayed with the club for 20 years, always sidestepping attempts to have him take over as manager.

J. EARL WAGNER

Wagner and his brother George set the standard for robber baron ownership. Wholesale butchers by trade, they entered baseball by rescuing the Players League Philadelphia Quakers in July 1890, then trading that franchise for an American Association entry from the same city. Their most noteworthy moment in the AA was contributing to its demise by neglecting to include on their reserve list Harry Stovey and Lou Bierbauer, whom Boston and Pittsburgh, respectively, then pirated to trigger a war with the National League. Taking a $56,000 buyout from the NL after the AA's collapse, they invested $16,000 of that money in the Washington Senators in an expanded 12-team NL. In Washington they hit their stride—selling any quality player who could bring them their price; transferring home games away from disgusted Washington fans to other cities for the larger crowds available there; and, in 1885, detaching manager Gus Schmelz from the team to run what they called The Texas Show, a clone of the Buffalo Bill Wild West Show they also owned. The Wagners showed little resistance when the NL, cutting back to eight teams again in 1900, offered them $46,500 to go away. Their total take over 10 years was an estimated $230,000; their only winning seasons were the first two in Philadelphia.

EDDIE WAITKUS

Phillies first baseman Waitkus was the inspiration for the episode in Bernard Malamud's novel *The Natural* in which Roy Hobbs is shot by a woman he invites to his hotel room. Waitkus was cut down by Ruth Ann Steinhagen while on a road trip to Chicago in 1949. Steinhagen subsequently told police she had loved the first baseman from afar and had been determined nobody else would have him. Waitkus recovered from a serious chest wound and ended up playing 11 big league seasons.

CHARLIE WAITT

The first player to wear a glove on the field, Waitt appeared in 83 big league games. Ordinarily an outfielder, he donned a tight-fitting, fingerless glove while at first base for the National Association St. Louis Brown Stockings in 1875.

DICK WAKEFIELD

Wakefield became the first bonus baby when he signed with Detroit in 1941 for $52,000 and an automobile. For awhile the Tigers seemed to have struck gold with the outfielder, especially when he came close to winning the batting title in 1943 and then used an extended leave from the Navy in 1944 to provide crucial slugging help in the team's pennant battle with the Browns. Never one to hide his bat under a bushel, Wakefield was discharged from the Navy in time for the 1946 season and a $1,000 challenge to Ted Williams about which of them would win the batting crown. Commissioner Happy Chandler immediately summoned both outfielders to tell them he didn't like such talk. It proved academic when neither won the title: Williams lost despite an average of .342, while Wakefield's mere .268 started his slide toward parttime status on several clubs.

DIXIE WALKER

Known as The Peepul's Cherce, Walker was the most popular of the pre-Boys of Summer Dodgers in Ebbets Field. Part of the lefty-swinging outfielder's appeal lay in his troubled route to Brooklyn, another part in his club-leading offense. His tenure with the team ended sourly, however, when he asked to be traded rather than have to play with Jackie Robinson.

Walker came up originally with the Yankees in 1931. Although praised regularly for his hitting by manager Joe McCarthy, he was used sparingly until dealt to the White Sox in 1936. After batting .308 for Chicago, he took his bat to the Tigers and seemed to be settling in as one of the AL's reliable .300 hitters when an arm injury and subsequent operation jeopardized his entire career. In 1939 Larry MacPhail picked him up cheaply, calculating that even his defensive shortcomings would be minimized by Ebbets Field's short right field wall. MacPhail got much more than he bargained for. In seven of eight full seasons with the Dodgers Walker batted over .300, including a league-leading .357 in 1944. In 1945 he paced the league with his 124 RBIs. The lifetime .306 hitter also recovered sufficient arm strength to deter baserunners by leading in outfield assists one year.

Walker's off-field performances were not as smooth. In 1941 he tussled publicly with both MacPhail and manager Leo Durocher over their announced intention of opening the season with the aging Paul Waner in right field. When 5,000 Dodgers fans signed a petition protesting the move, MacPhail threatened to fire Durocher if he gave in to the pressure. The issue became academic when Waner quickly showed his age, and Walker's .311 helped the club to a pennant. In 1942 the outfielder ridiculed a midseason warning from MacPhail that the Dodgers were about to blow a big lead over St. Louis, offering to bet $500 on another Brooklyn pennant. There seemed little doubt that MacPhail, galled by Walker's arrogance, would unload him when the Cardinals did indeed win the pennant; but at the last minute it was the executive himself who left, for wartime military service. In 1943 Walker sided with Arky Vaughan in a clubouse revolt against Durocher's managing style. The incensed pilot promised the Peepul would have to find another Cherce after the season was over, but that didn't happen, either.

It was only with Branch Rickey's signing of Robinson in 1946 that Walker's days as a Dodger began being numbered seriously. Because of his Georgian roots, he was a frequent target of reporters bent on underscoring the folly of Rickey's move. He kept his peace through most of 1946, content to note that Robinson in Montreal was not Robinson in Brooklyn, but then read the writing on the wall when Rickey disclosed that the Dodgers would be training together with their top farm club in Havana in 1947. Walker then circulated a petition among teammates aimed at thwarting Robinson's imminent promotion—an initiative that was first squelched by Durocher, then by Rickey. When Walker demanded a trade, Rickey said he would think about it. He continued to think about it while both Walker and Robinson played major roles in a 1947 pennant. Only after the season was the outfielder dealt to Pittsburgh. The press played into Rickey's hands by assuming the swap was purely a consequence of Walker's racist views; in fact, it also had a great deal to do with the fact that the outfielder had seen his best days. He stayed with the Pirates for two years before retiring. In the meantime the players acquired for him—pitcher Preacher Roe and third baseman Billy Cox—were providing further foundation for The Boys of Summer.

FLEET WALKER

Walker's presence on the 1884 American Association Toledo Blue Stockings defied the unwritten rule barring black players from major league baseball. A better-than-average catcher, he had joined Toledo the year before when the club had been part of the minor Northwestern League. It was when the team had still been a minor league franchise that Cap Anson had refused to allow his Chicago White Stockings to take the field against a black man, that Toledo manager Charlie Morton had warned there

would be no game without Walker (even though he had been scheduled for a day off because of a sore hand), and that Anson had finally decided that his racist principles weren't as important as the anticipated gate from the exhibition game. In 1881 Walker, then playing for an independent Cleveland club, had been kept out of a game in Lousiville when future big leaguers Fred Pfeffer and John Reccius had refused to play against him.

Life in the AA was more of the same. Among Walker's teammates the worst attitude belonged to mound ace Tony Mullane. When he wasn't deliberately bouncing balls in the dirt, Mullane was ignoring his receiver's signs; the two finally reached a tacit agreement to dispense with signs altogether. Without recanting his racism, Mullane later called his batterymate "the best catcher I ever worked with." Fans in Louisville were particularly abusive, on one occasion attacking Walker in the street after a game. A potentially uglier incident, a threatened mob assault in Richmond, was averted only because Walker was released, ostensibly because of injuries, before the Blue Stockings arrived in the Virginia capital. In 42 games for the 1884 club he had averaged .263. There would not be another recognized black player in the majors until Jackie Robinson in 1947.

His big league career over, Walker played in the minors for five more seasons, most notably when he teamed with southpaw George Stovey to form the first all-black battery in organized ball for the International League's Newark Little Giants in 1887. It was also in Newark, on July 19 of that year, that Anson again refused to play in an exhibition contest if there were blacks on the field; unlike the confrontation with Toledo four years earlier, this one ended with the benching of Walker and Stovey. On the very same day the International League voted not to admit any more black players, in effect becoming the first circuit to formalize segregation policies.

In 1908 Walker published *Our Home Colony,* a booklet offering his analysis of race relations in America. One of his conclusions was that blacks could never achieve justice in a country so tainted with racism (even though he himself had been acquitted by an all-white Syracuse jury in 1891 for the lethal stabbing of a white man who had attacked him). According to Walker, the only solution was a complete "separation of the races by Emigration of the Negro from America" to Africa.

HARRY WALKER

Dixie Walker's younger brother is the only National League player to win a National League batting crown after being traded in midseason; he averaged .363 for the Cardinals and Phillies in 1947. He and Dixie are also the only brothers to take batting titles.

The lefthand-hitting Walker started his 11-year career with St. Louis in 1940, but his lack of power bred organization critics. Still, it was in a Cardinals uniform that he had his biggest hit—the eighth-inning double in the seventh game of the 1946 World Series on which Enos Slaughter caught Johnny Pesky napping for the winning run. He built most of his 1947 hitting title while with Philadelphia, also leading the NL in triples. He retired with a .296 average.

Walker had three stints as a manager—with the Cardinals in 1955, with the Pirates between 1965 and 1967, and with the Astros from 1968 to 1972. None of his clubs got higher than third. On the other hand, he became a renowned batting coach, especially when working with the kind of slap hitter he had been; his most prominent pupil was Matty Alou, who won a batting title after off-season sessions with him. His windy monologues on hitting were also one of two running irritants among the players he managed; the other was his Neanderthal racial views.

Walker was called The Hat because of his repeated tugs at the bill of his cap as he got ready to hit.

RUBE WALKER

Walker popularized the five-man rotation while serving as pitching coach for the Mets in the late 1960s. Although the concept suited New York's starter-rich pitching staff, it has come under increasing criticism in recent years for both encouraging the use of mediocre fifth starters and for pampering arms to the point of making them more vulnerable to injury. One of the chief critics of Walker's philosophy was Nolan Ryan, a principal reason why the Mets went from a four-man to a five-man rotation in the first place.

WELDAY WALKER

Outfielder Walker was the second black to appear in the major leagues when he joined his brother Fleet on the American Association Toledo Blue Stockings for a handful of games in 1884. He had four hits in 18 at bats. In 1888 Walker lodged a protest with the Ohio State League for having formally banned African

Americans. "There should," he declared, "be some broader cause—lack of ability, behavior, and intelligence—to bar a player, rather than his color."

MURRAY WALL

In 1959 Wall pitched for a team to which he didn't belong. Swapped to the Senators by the Red Sox for Dick Hyde, he took the mound for Washington for an inning, after which he was told the deal had been canceled because of Hyde's sore arm.

BOBBY WALLACE (Hall of Fame, 1953)

The strongest hints of Wallace's abilities come from his longevity and from the fact that he was once the highest paid player in the major leagues; certainly, the statistical record doesn't indicate his Hall of Fame credentials. While batting .268 in 25 seasons (1894–1918) for the Cleveland Spiders and two St. Louis organizations, he had as many bad defensive numbers as good ones.

Wallace began as a righthanded pitcher for the Spiders, compiling a record of 24–22 over three seasons. Moved to third base in 1897, he posted career highs with a .335 average and 112 RBIs. A shortstop for the rest of his career, he had a second 100-RBI year in 1899 for the Cardinals and another .300 season for the club in 1901. With the AL Browns as of 1902, he never hit higher than .285. It was the Browns that valued his defensive skills so highly that they lured him away from the Cardinals with a $32,000, five-year, no-trade contract, making him the highest salaried player at the beginning of the 20th century.

Wallace was the first AL shortstop elected to the Hall of Fame and among the handful who got there through the first vote of the Veterans Committee in 1953. His most idiosyncratic claim to fame while a player was that he interrupted his career between June 1915 and August 1916 to serve as an American League umpire.

DICK WALSH

Walsh was baseball's most despised general manager. Moving into the Angels front office after the 1968 season with an extraordinary seven-year contract, he soon earned the nickname of The Smiling Python for actions that were variously described as paranoid, dictatorial, and hypocritical; a greater consensus, including the vote of Angels owner Gene

Autry, formed around the opinion that he was also a liar.

Among Walsh's moves with the team were threatening to tell a pitcher's wife about an adulterous affair unless he signed a proffered contract; refusing to allow star shortstop Jim Fregosi to undergo a needed foot operation because he didn't want the expense of having to get another infielder; and lying that Boston hadn't informed him of outfielder Tony Conigliaro's delicate physical and psychological condition before concluding a trade with the Angels. Walsh was so hated by most of his players that he was advised to stay off the field during batting practice after line drives started to find him with astonishing regularity; he also had to quit the clubhouse after a couple of incidents, avoiding one beating only when the team batboy escorted him to safety. Autry unloaded him before even the midpoint of the seven-year contract.

ED WALSH (Hall of Fame, 1946)

Walsh was a great pitcher, but an even greater technical advisor. On the hill the cocky righthander won 195 games with the White Sox between 1904 and 1916, in the process establishing the career-record ERA of 1.82. In 1908 he enjoyed what was undoubtedly the best year by any post-19th century pitcher—setting another perduring mark of 464 innings pitched while leading the American League in wins (40), shutouts (11), starts (49), complete games (42), saves (six), and strikeouts (269). His 1.42 ERA represented the third time in five straight seasons that he permitted fewer than 1.88 runs per nine innings; his 40 wins were also the last time that level was reached in the major leagues.

Walsh's Herculean efforts were necessary since the team behind him didn't come by its name of The Hitless Wonders by accident. In 1910, for instance, when he led the league in losses (20), Chicago batted .211; as for Walsh, he suffered his defeats despite an ERA of 1.27. After his brilliant 1908 season, he was given a modest raise by owner Charlie Comiskey but decided it wasn't enough and sat out the first month of 1909 in protest. Shortly after rejoining the club, Comiskey asked him to accompany architect Zachary Taylor Davis on a tour of the site where the owner was building his new stadium. It was thanks to Walsh's suggestions that Comiskey Park opened in 1910 with foul lines stretching 363 feet; the stadium proved to be a pitcher's paradise for the next 80 years.

Walsh was thought to have been the model for the overbearing narrator in Ring Lardner's "You Know Me, Al."

BILL WAMBSGANSS

In the fifth game of the 1920 World Series against the Dodgers, Cleveland second baseman Wambsganss snared Clarence Mitchell's line drive and turned it into the only unassisted triple play pulled off in postseason competition.

LLOYD WANER (Hall of Fame, 1967)

Although overshadowed by his older brother Paul, Waner was a pesky leadoff man for most of his 18 years (between 1927 and 1945) with the Pirates and other teams. His career mark of .316 included 11 .300 seasons, four of at least 200 hits, and three of 100 runs scored. In the Pittsburgh tradition of Bible hitters ("Thou shalt not pass"), he nevertheless struck out as much as 20 times only twice, and in several years kept his whiffs in single-digit numbers. Little Poison, as he was dubbed, combined with his brother for the highest batting average by siblings by far.

PAUL WANER (Hall of Fame, 1952)

Like Honus Wagner and Arky Vaughan, Waner didn't know what less than a .300 average was while wearing a Pittsburgh uniform. Arriving in the big leagues in 1926, the lefty-hitting outfielder didn't drop below that mark until his 13th season, and this despite being a notorious drinker who had to do 15 minutes of backflips for overcoming hangovers before games. Big Poison, as the press labeled him, won the NL batting title three times with averages that rose as high as .380; he ended his 20-year career with 3,152 hits and a .333 average. Waner reached the 200-hit level eight times, pacing the league in doubles and triples twice each and in RBIs once. Batting ahead of potent RBI men, he scored 100 runs nine times. Picked up by the Dodgers as a gate attraction during World War II when he was pushing 40, he had little left, but still hit .311. The Braves and Yankees gave him similar shots before he finally called it a career.

ARCH WARD

The sports editor of the Chicago *Tribune,* Ward pressed successfully for the playing of the first All-

Star Game, in 1933. He lobbied for the contest as part of the city's Century of Progress Exhibition. A formula devised by Ward and big league teams provided for all the all-stars to be chosen by both fans and the managers of the opposing squads, John McGraw and Connie Mack. The selection method has gone back and forth over the years: exclusive managerial choices (1935–46); fan selection of position player starters (1947–57); players, managers, and coaches doing all the picking (1958–69); and fans again choosing the position player starters, with the rest of the teams left up to the pilots (1970 to the present). In recent years league offices, with an eye toward television ratings, have put in more than their two cents worth about backup players.

The inaugural game, played at Comiskey Park on July 6, 1933, was won by the American League, 4–2. The starting pitchers were Lefty Gomez of the Yankees and Bill Hallahan of the Cardinals. Hallahan surrendered the key blow in the game—a two-run home run by the 38-year-old Babe Ruth in the third inning.

JOHN MONTGOMERY WARD (Hall of Fame, 1964)

In each of his three baseball careers as a player, union organizer, and lawyer-executive, the less conspicuous Ward was, the more successful he was.

As a player, he is most remembered as an outfielder-shortstop, primarily with the Giants in the 1880s and early 1890s; in fact, his performance as a position player (a lifetime .278 average and a paucity of league-leading achievements) was inferior to his pitching elsewhere. Before being curbed by a sore arm, he was Providence's regular hurler, contributing to an 1879 pennant with league-leading totals in wins (47) and strikeouts (239). That was sandwiched between his league-best ERA for the Grays in 1878 and a 39-win season in 1880, when he also hurled more shutouts than anyone else. His lifetime ERA of 2.10 ranks fourth, behind only Ed Walsh, Addie Joss, and Mordecai Brown. Among his 164 wins (with 103 losses) was the second perfect game, against Buffalo on June 17, 1880.

As both the president of the Players Brotherhood, which he helped put together in 1885, and the driving force behind the Players League in 1890, Ward fought on the wrong issues and with the wrong allies, consequently losing the war. From the begin-

ning he constricted his cause by saying salaries were excessive, contracts inviolable, blacklists not without merit, and the reserve clause a necessary evil to protect owners from themselves; refusing an offer of affiliation with the Knights of Labor didn't help, either. Although there was no end of discussion about salary ceilings and the reserve clause, there was little movement in the faceoffs between the players and management until, with Ward out of the country on Al Spalding's 1888–89 world tour, the National League passed Indianapolis owner John T. Brush's Classification Plan; the scheme solidified the salary scale but based it on elusive player behavior standards instead of performance, edging an already tense situation to critical mass. The explosion came with the sale of Deacon White and Jack Rowe to Pittsburgh. While comparing the player sales to slavery and the reserve rule to the Fugitive Slave Laws, Ward, who had vetoed his own sale to Washington in 1889, talked his cohorts out of striking and into forming a new league.

An artistic success but financial disaster, the Players League ultimately failed for three reasons: First, the rebels overestimated the meaning of their victories in lawsuits brought by the owners; second, they overrated the drawing power of the vast majority of quality players recruited from the established leagues; third and most important, they failed to realize that their financial backers had more in common with the NL owners than with the PL players. The bond between the monied interests on both sides emerged clearly at postseason meetings that Ward himself initiated; the resultant settlement shut out the players.

Ward spent the two seasons after the PL collapse as player-manager for Brooklyn. Traded to the Giants for the same double role in 1893, he ended up owning stock in both clubs as part of a unique deal in which Brooklyn's compensation was a share of New York's gate receipts. Retiring after the 1894 season, Ward, who had earned a law degree, won acclaim for his representation of Amos Rusie and the New York *Sun* in separate cases against Giants owner Andrew Freedman. Less successful were his forays into baseball's executive suites. In 1910 he got nowhere with a candidacy to become president of the NL. In 1912 he lasted little more than half the season as president of the Braves—hampered on one side by old guard owners who wouldn't deal with him because of his challenges to them as a player and an attorney, on the other by Boston owner James Gaffney, who couldn't understand why his club wasn't improving right away. In 1914 he accepted the role of business manager of the Federal League's Brooklyn Tip-Tops before realizing that, all their rhetoric notwithstanding, the powers behind the upstart circuit were more interested in worming their way into the National and American leagues than in offering a genuine third alternative.

The long memory of the baseball establishment kept Ward out of Cooperstown until almost four decades after his death. His plaque carries no reference to the Players League.

LON WARNEKE

Warneke is the only man ever to play and umpire in both a World Series and an All-Star Game. As a righthander for the Cubs and Cardinals between 1930 and 1945, he won 193 games, with three 20-win seasons. He reached the World Series with Chicago in 1932 and 1935, and was also a three-time All-Star. As a National League umpire, he saw service in the 1954 Series and the 1952 All-Star contest.

HERB WASHINGTON

Washington was Oakland owner Charlie Finley's experiment in designated running. With the Athletics in 1974, he didn't appear in a single game as a hitter or fielder, being used exclusively as a pinch-runner. The experiment proved to be less than a success when the former indoor track star managed only 29 steals in 45 tries, a below-average 64 percent. Washington was released early in 1975 after swiping two of his first three bases.

BOB WATSON

Watson was the first black given the title of general manager when he was put in charge of Houston's baseball operations after the 1993 season. A couple of years later he took on the same duties with the Yankees. Like all front office executives working in the Bronx under George Steinbrenner, Watson was exposed to a daily dose of harassments over matters big and niggling, and announced his resignation in 1998 with a confession that he was "burned out." He also left the impression that he didn't think he had received enough credit for the New York championships in 1996 and 1998.

As a 19-year (1966–84) first baseman-outfielder,

Watson averaged .295, including seven seasons of .300 or better and two with 100 RBIs. Until John Olerud matched him in 2001 he had been the only player to hit for the cycle in both leagues, having done it for the 1977 Astros and 1979 Red Sox. On May 4, 1975, Watson also became part of baseball promotional history by scoring the 1,000,000th run in the major leagues. The righthanded slugger generally tried to dodge batting practice after a ball off his bat seriously injured a woman fan.

BUCK WEAVER

Weaver didn't even have the consolation of some spending money before he was outlawed by Commissioner Kenesaw Landis for his part in the 1919 Black Sox scandal. Unlike the other players affected by the ban, he was never accused of being a participant in the conspiracy, only of knowing about it and not reporting it. Landis maintained his hard-line approach in the face of several reinstatement petitions from Weaver, deeming as irrelevant even the third baseman's .324 average against Cincinnati in the tainted Series. After his blacklisting Weaver sued Chicago owner Charlie Comiskey for the balance of his money on a three-year contract. The case dragged on in court until 1924, when Comiskey settled privately.

Before his association with the Black Sox the switch-hitting Weaver had been among baseball's premier third basemen. He enjoyed his best season in 1920, batting .331 while waiting for the other shoe to drop in the investigation into the 1919 Series. In 1917 Weaver duked it out with gamblers in Fenway Park when they jumped out of the stands onto the field to protect their bets against what was obviously going to be a Boston win over Chicago.

EARL WEAVER (Hall of Fame, 1996)

As manager of Baltimore's top farm team in Rochester, Weaver wrote the organization's instruction book stressing good pitching, good defense, and the three-run home run as the keys to victory; promoted to the parent club, he used the book to dominate the American League East for more than a decade.

Between 1968 and 1982 Weaver's Orioles finished fourth twice (once in the split season of 1981), third once, second seven times (once in 1981), and first on six occasions; the division wins led to four pennants and two world titles. True to his manual, the main ingredients for success over the period were 22

20-game winners, a nonpareil defense built around shortstop Mark Belanger, center fielder Paul Blair, and third baseman Brooks Robinson, and a long-ball offense centered on Frank Robinson and Boog Powell. Weaver abhorred bunting, claiming its place was "at the bottom of a long-forgotten closet." A firm believer in the odds, he pioneered the use of index cards detailing personal matchups between pitchers and hitters; this allowed him to platoon to extraordinary effect, most prominently with left fielders John Lowenstein and Gary Roenicke between 1979 and 1982.

An accomplished umpire baiter, Weaver used a trademark backward-turned cap to facilitate face-to-face confrontations with arbiters who had displeased him. If the tactic saved him from violating the rule against personal contact with an umpire, it didn't prevent him from being ejected 91 times (including both ends of one doubleheader) and suspended six times in his final seven years. An infamous chain smoker, he was thrown out of one 1969 game against the Twins even before it began for puffing away in the dugout; the next day he brought the lineup card out with a candy cigarette in his mouth, daring the umpires to make something of it. His most noted clash with umpires came in September 1977, when he refused to let his team take the field in Toronto until the grounds crew removed what he considered a dangerous tarpaulin from the Blue Jays bullpen; the tarp stayed where it was and the Orioles forfeited the game.

On his own team Weaver had running feuds with catcher Rick Dempsey and pitcher Jim Palmer. He once compared the Hall of Fame hurler's imaginary ailments to the Chinese calendar: "The Chinese tell time by the Year of the Horse or the Year of the Dragon. I tell time by the Year of the Back and the Year of the Elbow. This year's the Year of the Ulnar Nerve."

Mainly as a favor to the organization, Weaver came out of retirement for another managerial stint in Baltimore in mid-1985, but showed little enthusiasm for the task, lasting only a season-and-a-half.

DEL WEBB

Webb never allowed owning the Yankees get in the way of his chief priority—his construction business. And he never worried too much, either, about how his ties to the Mob and the gaming industry might complicate his standing in baseball.

Originally a minority member of a triumvirate that purchased the Yankees in 1945 from Jacob Ruppert's estate, Webb and Dan Topping each took on half-ownership when their third partner, Larry MacPhail, had a nervous breakdown in 1947. But it was no cut-and-dried succession. Three months earlier mobster Bugsy Siegel had been gunned down in his girl friend's apartment, and Webb, whose construction firm was building the Flamingo Hotel in Las Vegas for Siegel, had bought into the project to protect his investment. Not liking that development, Commissioner Happy Chandler ordered the builder to divest himself of his holdings in either the Flamingo or the Yankees. Webb's response was to join with Cardinals owner Fred Saigh in leading a successful campaign to oust Chandler. Ford Frick, the new commissioner, adopted a more accommodating stance that the Yankees executive should cash in his Las Vegas chips as soon as possible but without making a financial sacrifice.

Webb generally left the Yankees to Topping—except when his ownership of the team could help his construction business. In 1951 he persuaded Horace Stoneham of the Giants to switch spring training sites between St. Petersburg and Phoenix mainly so he could show off his prize possession to his Arizona friends and increase his business profile in the region. With much of his business centered around southern California, he constantly hyped the prospects for a major league franchise in Los Angeles. In 1954, when the Browns were on the verge of leaving St. Louis for Baltimore, he blocked the move, pushing through a resolution committing the franchise to Los Angeles, instead. It took league owners another 24 hours to realize that this last-minute change of plans would expose them to a massive lawsuit from Baltimore and to talk Webb into being satisfied with a paper promise to establish a franchise in California in the near future. But not even Los Angeles was more important to him than his business. A year after the Baltimore mess, when the Athletics were ready to move out of Philadelphia, he worked both sides of the street—telling everyone in California he was doing everything possible to bring the club there, while simultaneously doing what he could to get the team to Kansas City, where he had the inside track on a contract to enlarge the minor league stadium to be used by the A's. Kansas City won.

In 1962 Webb declined an offer to buy out Topping, saying he couldn't give the Yankees his full attention; instead, the partners decided to sell out altogether and to spend as little as possible in the meantime. By the time they found their buyer in CBS in 1964, their refusal to spend on the franchise had doomed it to a decade of inept teams.

Webb sought to make a comeback in the early 1970s by purchasing the White Sox. The deal never got off the ground because he refused to sell his holdings in several Las Vegas casinos—a precondition imposed by Commissioner Bowie Kuhn. As an outsider this time, he didn't have the clout to dispose of Kuhn as he had Chandler.

EARL WEBB

Webb established the record for doubles in a season (67) with the 1931 Red Sox. In none of his other six major league years did the outfielder hit half as many.

CHARLES WEEGHMAN

Weeghman, who had made a fortune running a chain of lunch counters, took over the Chicago Federal League franchise in 1914 with assurances that his $26,000 investment would be the full extent of his commitment. Before he was through, he and his partner William Walker would have to lay out $412,000 to keep the Whales afloat. The largest chunk of their money went to build Weeghman Park on the city's North Side.

Weeghman emerged from the Federal war as one of the victors, when he was permitted to purchase the Cubs for $500,000. By 1918, however, he had surrendered most of his stock for loans from chewing gum magnate William Wrigley, who then took over the franchise. In 1926 Wrigley renamed the park Weeghman had brought over from the Federal League as Wrigley Field.

Weeghman was the first owner to allow fans to keep the balls hit into stands. He introduced the practice in 1916, his first year as Cubs owner.

AL WEIS

A lifetime .219 hitter, Weis was the improbable offensive hero of the 1969 Miracle Mets World Series victory over the Orioles. The second baseman drove in the winning run in the ninth inning of the second game with a single, then tied the final game with a seventh-inning home run that positioned New York to win in the eighth. Weis ended up batting .455 for the five games. The switch-hitter had merely seven regular season home runs in a 10-year (1962–71) career with the White Sox and Mets.

GEORGE WEISS (Hall of Fame, 1971)

There never was anybody in baseball better at winning pennants or at making money from them than Weiss; there wasn't anyone who seemed to enjoy it less, either.

In 1920, at the age of 24, Weiss sold his family store to purchase the New Haven franchise in the Eastern League. He first attracted the attention of Yankees general manager Ed Barrow when he withheld the New York club's share of gate receipts for an exhibition game because Babe Ruth, the main drawing card for the game, had skipped making the trip to Connecticut. An infuriated Barrow appealed the matter to Commissioner Kenesaw Landis, but Landis sided with Weiss.

After working as general manager for the International League Baltimore Orioles from 1929 to 1931, Weiss was hired by Barrow to build a farm system as a less expensive alternative to buying players. He succeeded so brilliantly that, during his 16 years at the job, New York had to pay cash for only five minor leaguers, two of whom were Joe DiMaggio and Tommy Henrich. The acquisition of DiMaggio, from the San Francisco Seals of the Pacific Coast League, was also noteworthy in that Barrow didn't want the outfielder because of his injured knee and Weiss didn't hesitate to go over his superior's head to owner Jacob Ruppert to make the deal. But whatever his ambitions, Weiss had to wait until 1947 and the new majority ownership of Dan Topping and Del Webb to take the general manager's title for himself. By then the Yankees had the most productive farm system in baseball and the man behind it had developed a well-deserved reputation as a drill sergeant. So obsessive was he about every detail that on one occasion he went out of his way to upbraid Frank Lane, operator of the franchise affiliate in Kansas City, for failing to wash the windows on a telephone booth in the lobby of the team offices.

Weiss's first significant move as general manager was to bring in Casey Stengel as manager in 1949. The odd couple pair of the excruciatingly formal executive and the exhaustingly effusive pilot had been friends since Weiss's Eastern League days. As a tandem, they forged the club that brought 10 pennants and seven world championships to the Bronx between 1949 and 1960. But at the same time that the Yankees were riding roughshod over the American League, Weiss was doing pretty much the same thing to the players who were making the pennants possible. His brutally cold-blooded attitude to the business of baseball calcified the image of the 1950s Yankees as a corporate machine. His aloofness led him to negotiate directly only with top stars, leaving the handling of other contracts to assistant Roy Hamey. Weiss's salary battles, especially with pitchers Allie Reynolds and Vic Raschi, were acrimonious, and because of profit-sharing incentives instituted by Topping and Webb, he was not above subterfuge in holding down pay levels. When Phil Rizzuto demanded $50,000 after winning the AL MVP in 1951, Weiss offered $35,000. At a meeting to settle the difference the general manager acceded to the demand, but, claiming his secretary was not available to type up a revision from his initial offer, persuaded the shortstop to sign the contract he had and accept the other $15,000 immediately in a check. The following year negotiations between the two started from the $35,000 figure on the signed document.

Weiss didn't abide troublemakers, real or perceived. Billy Martin, regarded as a bad influence on stars Mickey Mantle and Whitey Ford, was traded away off after a May 1957 fracas at New York's Copacabana night club even though he had nothing to do with the punches thrown between a customer and outfielder Hank Bauer. When the time came to release a player, Weiss usually conveyed the news by telegram. Rizzuto received his walking papers on Old Timers Day in 1956 after the executive insisted on taking him through the entire roster name by name, ostensibly soliciting his advice on how to make room for the reacquired Enos Slaughter.

In addition to what the Yankees farm system provided, Weiss also had the advantage of being able to offer Stengel players recruited from the Kansas City Athletics, which practically functioned as another New York affiliate in the late 1950s and early 1960s; among those brought to the Bronx from Missouri were Ryne Duren, Roger Maris, and Clete Boyer. On the other hand, his narrow ideas about what constituted a "Yankee type" deterred him from signing Herb Score and Frank Lary. The worst blot on his record, however, was his unwillingness to sign black players. Although he said the proper things in public about how the franchise was looking for a black player who also happened to be that "Yankee type," he needed only a couple of drinks to admit the truth—his belief, as he asserted once, that "boxholders from Westchester don't want that sort of crowd. They would be offended to have to sit with niggers." It was an attitude that prompted the trade of flashy first baseman Vic Power to the Athletics in December 1954—behind the whispered excuse that he was a quick-tempered hot dog (and, rumor had it, fond of white women), but essentially because he was good enough to make the team. When Elston Howard forced his way onto the club in 1954 by winning the International League's MVP trophy, the Yankees made no effort whatsoever to compel segregated facilities in the South and elsewhere to accept the catcher. Seven years after Jackie Robinson had broken the color line, Weiss told Howard that he wouldn't be needed for an exhibition game in Birmingham, Alabama because of a state law forbidding blacks from competing with whites on the same field.

Weiss was forced out of his post in November 1960 when Topping and Webb decided the franchise needed younger blood; he left less noisily, but no less bitterly, than Stengel, who had suffered a similar fate a few weeks earlier. Resurfacing as the president of the expansion Mets two years later, he once again hired Stengel, mainly as a clownish cover for the aged, bad team he was about to put on the diamond. When the New Breed fans responded more enthusiastically than he could have imagined, he was at a total loss. His compulsion about winning had nothing in common with the ironic banners unfurled by Mets fans to cheer on their antiheroes; or, as he put it once, "These noisy people with their bedsheets—where do they come from? Why don't they keep quiet?" True to form, however, when he retired in 1966, the essential ingredients of the Miracle 1969 pennant—Tom Seaver, Jerry Koosman, Nolan Ryan, among them—were to be found in the Mets farm system; equally true to form, only one of them—Cleon Jones—was black.

CURT WELCH

Welch's so-called $15,000 Slide to win the 1886 "World Series" for the American Association St. Louis Browns in the 10th inning of the sixth game was all embellishment, and in more ways than one.

The play itself developed from a pitchout by Chicago hurler John Clarkson that, according to different accounts from the day, either sailed completely over catcher King Kelly's head or glanced off his glove for a passed ball; either way, Welch could have scored standing up. Under an agreement reached between the clubs the winning team got to keep all the gate receipts—not the fabled $15,000, but slightly less than $13,000. But perhaps the biggest embellishment of all was the whole series, since subsequent evidence pointed strongly to the possibility that the heavily favored White Stockings had thrown the games in order to clean up significantly more than $13,000 or $15,000 from gamblers.

MICKEY WELCH (Hall of Fame, 1973)

Welch was the co-ace (with Tim Keefe) of the Giants in the 1880s—and the team's poet laureate. On the mound the righthander won 307 games between 1880 and 1892 for Troy and then New York, including nine seasons of at least 20 victories and four with 30 or more. Although never a power pitcher, Welch established a major league mark by fanning the first nine batters he faced on August 28, 1884.

As a poet, Smiling Mickey (as he was called) had but one subject—beer. His most popular effort, which he set to music, also hinted that suds weren't the only painkiller available to players in his day: "Pure Elixir or malt and hops/Beats all the drugs and all the drops."

WILLIE WELLS (Hall of Fame, 1997)

The successor to John Henry Lloyd as the Negro leagues' greatest shortstop, Wells starred in both the United States and Mexico from the 1920s to 1940s, earning the nickname *El Diablo* below the border for his defensive prowess. In eight seasons (1924–31) with the St. Louis Stars, he won two batting titles (with averages of .368 in 1929 and .404 in 1930) and contributed to three pennants (1928, 1930, and 1931). When the Stars folded along with the old Negro National League after the 1931 season, he caught on with the Detroit Wolves and Homestead Grays for a year each before landing with the Chicago American Giants.

With the Newark Eagles in 1936, Wells pioneered the use of a batting helmet; after being knocked unconscious by a fastball, he modified a construction worker's hardhat and played the next day's game against the orders of his doctor. With Newark he never averaged below .346 between 1936 and 1939, then he took his bat to Mexico for a similar offensive consistency. During World War II he crossed Abe and Effa Manley, the owners of the Eagles, by going back and forth between Newark and Mexico, and they retaliated by trying (futilely) to get his draft exemption revoked.

Wells continued playing after Jackie Robinson integrated major league ball, but with the black leagues faltering he drifted from team to team before finally calling it quits in 1954.

TOM WERNER

Werner has been the perfect expression of big league ownership in the Bud Selig era. From San Diego to Boston he has cut a trail marked by show business vulgarities, alienated fans, and boardroom maneuverings involving astronomical dollars.

A television producer, Werner purchased the Padres in April 1990 for an estimated $90 million. He made his first big impression when he asked Roseanne, star of one of his sitcoms, to do "The Star-Spangled Banner" before a home game. When her painfully screechy rendition was booed by fans, she returned the compliment by grabbing at her crotch and making similar gestures toward the grandstand. Baseball officialdom professed itself scandalized by that episode, but was more silent in 1993 when Werner broke up a pennant-contending club with the justification that he couldn't afford the high arbitration salaries that were imminent for such stars as Fred McGriff and Gary Sheffield. The fire sale was viewed in some quarters as a ploy, at least tacitly approved by Selig and other owners, to highlight the allegedly precarious economic situation of smaller-market franchises prior to player contract negotiations the following year. After months of being besieged by lawsuits from infuriated season-ticket holders, Werner sold out to John Moores in December 1994.

Whether or not his dismantling of the Padres had been in collusion with Selig, Werner had enough clout with the commissioner to emerge as the favorite for buying the Red Sox even before bids were officially tendered in the fall of 2001. His preferred status became all the more evident after Boston rejected even initially higher offers to wait for Werner and partner John Henry to sweeten their bid. They did, forking out an unprecedented $660 million for the team, Fenway Park, and the regional New England Sports Network. In addition to the commodities trader Henry, Werner's partners in the venture included former U.S. Senator George Mitchell and the New York Times Company, parent of both *The New York Times* and the Boston *Globe*. In the aftermath of the deal, Massachusetts Attorney General Thomas Reilly confessed that he couldn't do much with his instinct to open an investigation into the manipulated sales process. "When you see how they operate," Reilly said of the principals involved in the deal, "it's not a pretty sight."

ZACH WHEAT (Hall of Fame, 1959)

The National League's most dangerous lefthanded hitter for most of his 19-year (1909–27) career, Wheat would have had even bigger numbers than his .317 average if the lively ball had come along a little earlier. Having already won a batting title in 1918 and reached the .300 level seven times before 1920, he then really laid it on, going three straight seasons (1923–25) of .375, .375, and .359. Apart from providing most of Brooklyn's offense for almost two decades, Wheat was also the franchise's most popular player, with teammates as much as with fans. This became acutely evident after the 1915 season, when he led a player revolt against attempts by Charlie Ebbets to slash salaries because of the dissipated threat of the rival Federal League; by the same token, when he was talked into accepting a contract, the revolt died.

Wheat's up-and-down relations with manager Wilbert Robinson eventually led to his release after the 1926 season. Initially, Robinson was so convinced of the outfielder's smarts that he turned the day-to-day managing over to him while he sat in the stands for what he termed "a cooler appraisal" of NL clubs. But when Brooklyn began stumbling, Robinson returned to the dugout, drawing Wheat's annoyance for what he regarded as a vote of no confidence.

HARRY WHEELER

Wheeler is the only player to appear for five major league teams in one season. The outfielder's 1884 odyssey encompassed five games for the St. Louis Browns (American Association), 14 for the Kansas City Unions (Union Association), 20 for the Chicago Browns (Union Association), 17 for the Pittsburgh Stogies (Union Association), and 17 for the Balti-more Monumentals (Union Association). His combined average was .242. Wheeler never played in a major league game after 1884.

PETE WHISENANT

A vagabond outfielder who played with seven clubs in eight seasons in the 1950s and 1960s, Whisenant is the only player to appear in a box score for a team that had already traded him. Sent up as a pinch-hitter for the Indians in the second game of a doubleheader at 6:35 P.M. on May 15, 1960, he was just as quickly removed as part of a lefty-righty pitching switch engineered by White Sox manager Al Lopez. When Chicago went on to lose the game, Lopez protested that Whisenant had been ineligible because, prior to the twinbill, Cleveland had issued an embargoed announcement for 6:00 P.M. revealing that he had been traded to Washington. According to Lopez, even though Whisenant hadn't seen a single pitch, his mere insertion into the contest had affected the outcome in necessitating a change of pitchers. American League president Joe Cronin denied the protest on the grounds that, notwithstanding the specific hour of the embargoed announcement, Cleveland and Washington had essentially intended the trade to become effective after the Indians-White Sox doubleheader.

BILL WHITE

White's three distinct careers in baseball made him about as nimble a personality as the sport has seen. As a player, he was a slick-fielding first baseman bridging the defensive eras of Gil Hodges and Keith Hernandez and an alley hitter who reached .300 four times. His most impressive feat at the plate came on July 17–18, 1961, when he collected 14 hits in back-to-back doubleheaders. Off the field in his playing days, his protests in 1960 at the exclusion of the Cardinals black players from social functions at the club's Florida spring training site mushroomed into a nationwide protest against Anheuser-Busch products and demands that the state desegregate its hotels and restaurants or face the loss of big league teams.

Upon retirement, White went into the broadcasting booth, most notably serving as a combination goader and straight man for Phil Rizzuto's antic observations on Yankees telecasts. His style included a lot of pregnant silences and monosyllabic sarcasm that suggested someone who wanted to say much more than his prudence dictated. The same qualities came to the fore when, in 1989, he was selected as president of the National League, making him the highest ranking black in the game's history. While given to the same macho views about umpires trying to hog the limelight and pitchers being too intimidated to throw inside that he had grunted during his broadcasts, there was little practical followup to his attitude in setting league policy, in part because of countermanding attitudes by Commissioner Fay Vincent. He also took a hit in 1992 for unilaterally delaying the sale of the Giants to a Florida consortium so a San Francisco group could find the money to buy the franchise (and for a lower price). More than once he let newsmen know that he wasn't enamored of his office and was only staying on because of the chaos created by the forced resignation of Vincent. He even submitted a formal resignation on March 31, 1993 but agreed to stay on until a suitable replacement was found.

White's breaking point came in January 1994, when club owners passed resolutions he clearly considered inimical to the game; among them were a decision to diminish further the already dubious powers of the league presidents, approval of rotating advertising signs behind home plate, and a stiffening of positions prior to negotiating with players on a new contract. In making way for Leonard Coleman in March 1994, he made no effort to disguise his disgust.

CHARLEY WHITE

The projected owner of a New York franchise in the stillborn United States League before World War I, White planned to build his stadium atop Grand Central Station. As he described it to the press, the ballpark would be domed by the station's roof, extending west from Lexington Avenue to Madison Avenue and north from 44th Street to 50th Street. One of its chief virtues, he noted, would be its accessibility to travelers arriving at the station below. In the 1990s Mayor Rudolph Giuliani offered a similar rationale for building a new Yankee Stadium near Penn Station.

CHARLIE WHITE

Both White and teammate Hank Aaron homered in their debut games for the Braves on April 23, 1954. But while Aaron went on to clout 754 more

for the career record, catcher White never again left the park in his two-year stint with Milwaukee.

DEACON WHITE

When White moved from one team to another, franchises and even leagues collapsed behind him. Together with pitcher Al Spalding, first baseman Cal McVey, and second baseman Ross Barnes, the catcher-third baseman jumped in 1876 from the National Association's dominating team in Boston to the Chicago White Stockings; the move by The Big Four effectively ended the National Association and established the National League. Nine years later White was part of another Big Four (with first baseman Dan Brouthers, second baseman Hardy Richardson, and shortstop Jack Rowe) in a Buffalo sale to Detroit. When NL president Nick Young voided the deal, the quartet refused to return to the financially faltering Bisons, preferring to sit out the final weeks of the 1885 season. A crisis was averted only because Buffalo folded its franchise, allowing the second Big Four to go on to Detroit where they led the way to a pennant in 1887.

In 1889 White got into still another transaction hassle when he was sold by Detroit to Pittsburgh after he had already made a commitment to manage Buffalo in the International League. He refused to report to Pittsburgh until the team gave him a bonus and a raise, and even then only after John Montgomery Ward of the Players Brotherhood had asked him to honor his contract and not spoil the union's more dramatic plans for a breakaway league. White's complaint against the reserve clause—"No man can sell my carcass unless I get at least half!"—expressed a key rallying point for the 1890 Players League.

White paired with pitcher-brother Will as the first sibling battery, with Cincinnati in 1878. The receiver also pioneered in several other areas. Playing for the Cleveland Forest Citys on May 4, 1871, he was the first batter—and collected the first base hit, a double—in a professional league (National Association) game; he also hit into the first double play in the contest. In addition, he was credited (along with Nat Hicks) with being the first catcher to move up directly behind the batter, in 1875; with developing the quick pitch while working with Spalding; and, with Detroit manager Jim O'Rourke, with designing the first primitive chest protector, in the early 1880s. White got his nickname from being a Sunday school superintendent.

SOL WHITE

An infielder with several minor league clubs and numerous black ones in the late 19th century, White slipped under color barriers to play on integrated teams as late as 1895. With sportswriter H. Walter Schlichter he then organized the Philadelphia Giants, a club so formidable in the early 20th century that he couldn't find a taker for a proposed 1905 Black World Series against his 134–21 squad. In 1906, after a 108–31 season, he challenged the winners of the Cubs-White Sox World Series to a duel, but never received a reply. White's most enduring legacy to baseball was the publication in 1907 of *Sol White's Official Baseball Guide,* the primary information source on early black baseball. A patchwork of fact, legend, playing tips, and verse, it included the prediction that the major leagues would soon be integrated. At least White lived long enough (until 1955) to see the prediction come true.

WILL WHITE

White's 75 complete games and 680 innings for the National League Cincinnati Reds in 1879 rank with baseball's most unbreakable records. The brother of catcher Deacon White, the righthander was also the first hurler to reach 200 victories, achieving it with the American Association franchise in Cincinnati in 1884. His career mark for 10 seasons was 229–166 (2.28).

White is an answer-and-a-half to two trivia questions: the first player wearing glasses on the field (in 1877 with Boston) and the first sibling battery (in 1878 with Deacon in Cincinnati).

WILLIAM WARREN WHITE

As Union Association secretary in 1884, White was the first to publicly invoke "the best interests of baseball" when he committed the new league to that elusive standard in a letter to the New York *Clipper.* The phrase has been baseball's only acknowledged commandment ever since.

EARL WHITEHILL

Whitehill is the only pitcher to win 200 games with a 4.00 ERA. In 17 seasons (1923–39) mostly with the Tigers and Senators, the southpaw went 218–185, while yielding 4.36 runs per nine innings.

MARK WHITEN

On September 7, 1993 Whiten had the greatest offensive day in baseball history. In a doubleheader against Cincinnati, the Cardinals outfielder tied three of the game's most conspicuous power records—hitting four homers in one game, driving in 12 runs in one game, and driving in 13 runs in a twinbill. The three records he reached had been held by different players.

ROBERT WHITLOW

Whitlow was an Air Force colonel who was brought in as "athletic director" of the Cubs in the early 1960s as part of owner Phil Wrigley's College of Coaches managerial experiment. As conceived by Wrigley, Whitlow's standing in the franchise was to have been second only to his own, with even general manager John Holland having to report to him. For his part, the colonel was supposed to have infused the organization with radical reforms borrowed in part from the military and in part from university administrative structures.

Wrigley's notion lasted only as long as it took Bob Kennedy to assert himself as the first coach of coaches and to order Whitlow to stay clear of his players. In announcing the military man's departure, Wrigley lamented that his ideas had been "too far ahead of their time." But aside from installing an auxiliary fence in the center field bleachers, nobody in Chicago could put a finger on what exactly Whitlow's ideas had been.

ALAN WIGGINS

Wiggins was the first major leaguer known to have died from AIDS. He succumbed in 1991 after having his once-promising career destroyed by repeated drug problems.

HOYT WILHELM (Hall of Fame, 1985)

Wilhelm was the first reliever elected to the Hall of Fame, as well as its most traveled inductee, appearing with nine teams in 21 years (1952–72) before finally retiring a week shy of his 49th birthday. Despite the recognition he won from Cooperstown voters, the knuckleballer never once led the league in saves. On the other hand, he holds the record for most relief wins (123), is the only rookie ever to lead a league in ERA (2.43 with the 1952 Giants), and picked up a second ERA title with the Orioles in 1959.

Already 29 when he joined the Giants, Wilhelm was to discover that he didn't bring out the patience in his employers—in part because of his age and in part because his knuckleball terrorized his catchers (and collaborated in most of the passed ball records now standing). His most noted escape from premature retirement came in 1958, when Baltimore manager Paul Richards gave him one final chance to stick with the club after a string of disastrous relief outings; the righthander responded by starting and no-hitting the Yankees. It was also Richards who designed a special pancake catcher's mitt for the Orioles receivers who had been griping about having to catch Wilhelm.

In addition to the Orioles, and between the Giants at the start and the Dodgers at the finish, Wilhelm pitched for the Cardinals, Indians, White Sox, Angels, Braves, and Cubs. In his first at bat for the Giants in 1952 he hit a home run; 21 years later he was still looking for his second one.

J. L. WILKINSON

A white businessman who owned the Kansas City Monarchs from the club's founding in 1920 to 1947, Wilkinson made history by resurrecting Satchel Paige's career after the Hall of Famer's arm went dead and by launching Jackie Robinson's professional career.

Wilkinson's Monarchs were a power in both the first Negro National League, winning four pennants (1923–25, 1929), and the Negro American League, adding six more flags (1937, 1939–42, 1946). In between the demise of the first NNL in 1930 and the inception of the NAL in 1937, the Monarchs barnstormed throughout North America. In 1930 he was the first club owner to sponsor night baseball on a regular basis; unlike the minor league Des Moines Demons and a semi-pro team in Independence, Kansas, which began using lights the same year, Wilkinson's were portable. The lights and their 250-horsepower motor were the reason the Monarchs survived the Depression.

It was during the barnstorming years that Paige called Wilkinson asking for a tryout. The owner assigned him to the Monarchs B team, which hit the smaller towns while the main club played in bigger cities. Paige's arm came around, and he became the club's biggest draw. Robinson, just out of the Army, joined the team in 1945 on the suggestion of pitcher Hilton Smith; he became the first of a record 27 players to move from the Monarchs to the major leagues.

BILLY WILLIAMS (Hall of Fame, 1987)

Williams woke up Wrigley Field from the left side of the plate as Ernie Banks did from the right side, if with slightly less power and slightly more consistency; the difference was that he finally got away from the Cubs in his waning years to play in the postseason. The outfielder had the first of his 13 straight seasons of 20 or more home runs in 1961, reaching a career high of 42 in 1972. Williams was no hit-or-miss proposition, though, winning the batting title in 1972, attaining the .300 level five times, compiling 200 hits in three seasons, banging out at least 30 doubles seven times, and winding up with a career average of .290. He also scored 100 runs five times and drove in 100 in three years.

From 1963 to 1970 Williams was the National League's Iron Man, appearing in 1,117 consecutive games. Although he shared Banks's plight of never being on a pennant winner during his 16 years with the Cubs, he managed to get into an LCS as a designated hitter for the Athletics in 1975. That was the good part; the bad part was that he went hitless in eight plate appearances.

CY WILLIAMS

One of the most productive sluggers in the early 20th century, Williams was the victim of the first Williams Shift. While his dead pull hitting was ideal for his home park at Philadelphia's Baker Bowl, it also encouraged opposing managers to bunch defenders on the right side—a tactic adopted many years later by Indians pilot Lou Boudreau against Ted Williams.

In a 19-year (1912–30) career with the Cubs and Phillies, Williams hit .292 and reached the seats 251 times; his highs were .345 in 1926 and 41 home runs in 1923. He was such a standout defensive center fielder that his flankers in left and right usually saw little reason to move after anything not hit directly at them. The situation became so glaring that local sportswriters once decided that the club's slogan for the 1920s should have been "GET IT, CY, GET IT!"

DIB WILLIAMS

A second baseman for the 1935 Red Sox, Williams developed a mental block against being able to score from third on a grounder or fly ball. The problem became so acute that Boston manager Joe

Cronin had to send in a pinch-runner for him whenever he considered his run important. Williams was gone at the end of the year.

DICK WILLIAMS

Williams shares with Jimmy Dykes the post-19th-century record for piloting the most teams (six). Unlike perennial also-ran Dykes, he reached the World Series four times with three of them, along the way also winning points as one of the most fractious personalities in the history of the game.

Williams got his first managerial shot with the Red Sox in 1967, turning it to gold with the Impossible Dream pennant. When Boston failed to repeat in 1968, his martinet tendencies surfaced, imposing so many petty rules and fines that Tom Yawkey took the advice of his favorite player Carl Yastrzemski to find another manager. Williams resurfaced with the Athletics in 1971, turning his instinctive distance from the players into an asset by ignoring their contempt for him and their relentless goadings of one another over inferior performances; rarely did he attempt to intervene in the clubhouse punchups that became Oakland's regular fare in the period, concluding it would be opposing teams that would pay the heaviest price ultimately. He was also good at mind games on the field. In the third game of the 1972 World Series against Cincinnati, for example, his gesticulations toward first base and on-deck hitter Tony Perez so fooled batter Johnny Bench that an intentional walk was coming that relief ace Rollie Fingers was able to slip a third strike past the Reds catcher. Just as he had crossed swords with Yastrzemski in Boston, Williams had some of his worst troubles in Oakland with franchise star Reggie Jackson. But when Jackson complained to owner Charlie Finley during the 1973 season that the manager and his coaches had become dictators, Finley did the opposite of Yawkey by extending the contracts of the entire brain trust.

The contract extension aside, Williams despised Finley as much as his players did, and the existence of a common enemy was another factor in blunting clubhouse hostilities toward him. The three-way Mutual Lack of Admiration Society came apart at the seams during the 1973 World Series against the Mets, when Finley tried to put second baseman Mike Andrews on the disabled list after making a couple of crucial errors. Although the ploy was thwarted by

Commissioner Bowie Kuhn, the incident prompted Williams to call a clubhouse meeting and announce his intention of resigning as soon as the World Series was over. He made good on the threat after another Oakland world championship, attracting immediate attention from the Yankees. But holding the ace of another year on Williams's contract, Finley demanded various New York regulars in exchange for his erstwhile manager. The Yankees said no, then signed Williams anyway, precipitating months of courtroom squabbles. Finley's piece of paper, signed in the wake of the Jackson complaint, won, and Williams had to sit at home for a year.

A stint with the Angels from midseason 1974 to midseason 1976 was equally troubled. With the California front office constantly shifting gears on him as it had with his predecessors, Williams started taking out his frustrations on the team. When he wasn't shouting at the players on the field or in the dugout, he was ignoring their simplest requests, making each and every one of them feel responsible for his broken promise before the 1975 campaign that he would never pilot a last place club. Early in 1976 he chilled relations with just about everybody in the organization by naming second baseman Jerry Remy and pitchers Nolan Ryan and Frank Tanana as "the only major leaguers" on the team. Shortly afterward he tried to get owner Gene Autry to dump general manager Harry Dalton in favor of Angels broadcaster Don Drysdale. The last act before getting his walking papers was a dugout clash with slugger Bill Melton.

Popping up in the National League with the Expos in 1977, Williams followed the usual script—raising the club to the status of serious contender, but so alienating his players that he had to be replaced by Jim Fanning just before reaching the playoffs in 1981. With San Diego in 1982 he began a four-year tenure that included a Padres pennant in 1984. But after a disappointing 1985 season he clashed with general manager Jack McKeon over the firing of longtime confidant and coach Ozzie Virgil. Owner Joan Kroc stepped in to order the rehiring of Virgil, but Williams and McKeon continued sniping at each other in the offseason, particularly on the issue of whether coach Harry Dunlop was a front office spy. On the very day that pitchers and catchers reported to spring training in 1986, the club announced that it had bought out the rest of Williams's contract.

Next to his days with the Angels, Williams spent

his most miserable years in a dugout with the Mariners between 1986 and 1988. By his second year he was telling newsmen that he had lost his taste for managing bad teams like Seattle; in June 1988 he was telling anyone who would listen that he intended retiring at the end of the season. When staff ace Mark Langston approached him to ask if he didn't think he was hurting the club with his despondent, lame duck airs, Williams called him "gutless." Immediately after that the front office told him to stay home for the rest of the year.

In recent years Williams has become one of George Steinbrenner's unofficial advisors on the Yankees. His overall managing record for 21 seasons was 1,571–1,451 (.520). As a utility outfielder-infielder for the Dodgers, Orioles, and others between 1951 and 1964, he batted .260.

ELISA GREEN WILLIAMS

Williams was an official scorer for the Cubs who remained anonymous for many years. The wife of the team treasurer, she was offered the job in 1882 by owner Al Spalding, who was suspicious of some of the statistics submitted to his annual guide. Her identity was kept secret—even from her own family—so as not to expose her to pressure from players.

GEORGE H. WILLIAMS

In October 1891 restaurateur Williams was granted a Chicago franchise in the American Association as part of the circuit's renewed warfare with the National League. Paying no attention to the fact that the addition of his club would make for an awkward nine-team league, Williams raised $50,000 and set about signing such star players as Amos Rusie and Fred Pfeffer at impressive salaries. Unwilling to compete against such extravagance, NL owners absorbed four AA franchises and bought out the others. Williams accepted $14,000 for his trouble, and his nameless club disappeared without ever playing a game.

KEN WILLIAMS

Williams was the founder of the 30–30 club. A .319 career hitter, he had the best of his 14 big league seasons with the Browns, averaging between .324 and .357 from 1921 to 1925. His 30–30 season of 1922 (39 home runs, 37 steals) was not matched until Willie Mays did it in 1956.

LEFTY WILLIAMS

Williams's dire performance in the 1919 World Series made him one of the least sympathetic of the Chicago players outlawed because of the Black Sox scandal. After posting 23 wins during the regular season, the southpaw lost all three of his starts to Cincinnati. Prior to the concluding game, in which he yielded four runs to the Reds in the first inning, he and his wife were threatened by gamblers wanting to make sure he didn't go back on the fix conspiracy. Williams won another 22 games in 1920 before being suspended.

MITCH WILLIAMS

Williams earned his nickname of Wild Thing: His 544 walks in 691 innings is baseball's worst control ratio for any pitcher with an appreciable number of hill appearances. On the other hand, the southpaw had more than 30 saves three times, including a career-high 43 for the pennant-winning Phillies in 1993. But it was also Williams who surrendered Joe Carter's three-run home run in the ninth inning of the sixth game that year to give Toronto a world championship. So bitter were Philadelphia fans about the gopher ball that the pitcher was traded to Houston shortly after the season. Williams didn't mind playing off the Wild Thing character portrayed by Charlie Sheen in the 1989 movie *Major League*. After retiring, he did several commercials playing up his reputation.

TED WILLIAMS (Hall of Fame, 1966)

Williams had only Babe Ruth as a peer for hitting with power and consistency. In 19 seasons with Boston between 1939 and 1960 he assaulted every offensive record standing; like the greatest entertainers, he also left fans hungry for more with the endless speculation about what else he might have accomplished if he hadn't lost three years to World War II and most of two others to the Korean War. His trophy case might have also been a little fuller if he hadn't put off writers with tantrums that, while mild by subsequent standards, were recalled when MVP votes had to be tallied.

The Red Sox got wind of Williams only after the Yankees and Cardinals had lost interest in him as a high school prospect because of his demand for a $1,000 bonus upon signing. The Boston front office was also opposed to the bonus, but was persuaded to fork it over by assistant general manager Billy Evans. Williams's brashness became evident at a 1938 spring training trial when, after being informed that he was being sent to the minors, he told the veterans in the clubhouse that he would be back to make more money than they had ever dreamed of making. Once back with the parent team, he compiled numbers verging on the eerie. A career .344 hitter with a slugging average of .634, the lanky lefthanded hitter dubbed The Splendid Splinter captured six batting titles, including one in 1941 when his .406 marked the last time anyone got to the .400 plateau. He led the American League in home runs four times, RBIs four times, runs scored six times, doubles twice, walks eight times, and slugging average eight times. For all his long-ball hitting he struck out as many as 50 times only twice—in his first two years in the league. His discrimination at the plate fueled stories—and fables—about his extraordinary eyesight.

In 1941, while Joe DiMaggio was hypnotizing the country with a .408 average during his 56-game hitting streak, Williams was batting .412 over the same period. In 1957 he set the record for most consecutive times on base by putting together four home runs, two singles, nine walks, and one hit-by-pitch in 16 successive at bats. In 1958 he became the oldest player (40 years, 28 days) to win a batting title. With the numbers went the drama. With his average at .3995 and eligible to be rounded off to .400 on the final day of the 1941 season, the outfielder insisted that he play both ends of a doubleheader so as not to be accused of "backing in" to his achievement; he collected six hits and gained six points. In the 1941 All-Star Game he hit a home run with two outs in the ninth inning to give the AL the win. In the 1946 All-Star Game he ran up on Rip Sewell's Eephus Ball and deposited it over the wall. In his final career at bat in 1960 he tagged his 29th home run of the season, providing a dreamy climax to John Updike's noted essay on his farewell.

Williams's arrogance kept him on the outs with the Boston press, which was never reluctant to point out he was no Gold Glove in left field. He only made things worse by once completing a tour of the bases on a home run, then spitting up at the press box. Struck out in a key situation in another game, he brought on weeks of bad coverage by firing his bat at the screen behind home plate. On a third occasion he returned to left field after failing in the clutch

and punted his glove against the wall. Although he took MVP honors in 1946 and 1949, he was denied the prize in 1941, when he reached the .400 mark, and in 1942 and 1947, when he won the Triple Crown each time. In 1947 one vindictive Boston writer left his name off the ballot altogether, and DiMaggio ended up edging him out by a single point.

Williams and DiMaggio were also co-stars of the Greatest Trade Never Made. The most popular account of the would-be exchange said it was the Yankees who approached the Red Sox shortly after World War II, proposing the swap so DiMaggio could take advantage of the Green Monster in Fenway Park and Williams could cavort with Yankee Stadium's short right field porch; the deal was said to have died because Boston owner Tom Yawkey, wary of DiMaggio's foot problems, demanded New York add Yogi Berra to the transaction. If Williams had any reason to envy DiMaggio, it was for the Yankees outfielder's regular appearances in the postseason; he himself got into a single World Series, in 1946 against St. Louis, managing only one RBI and five singles in seven games. On the other hand, he has cited his 2,019 walks (the equivalent of four entire seasons of plate appearances) as his "proudest record."

Despite his often truculent manner as a player, Williams turned out to be both a successful batting coach and a surprisingly effective manager. Even in the 1990s he was receiving praise from players like Tony Gwynn and Steve Finley for helping them polish their swings. As manager of the expansion Senators in 1969, he weakened the argument that great players make bad pilots by steering the team to its only .500 showing before moving to Texas. Part of his success was due to his unexpectedly deft handling of the pitching staff, but that didn't change an opinion about pitchers he had first uttered in joining Boston in the 1930s. According to Williams, pitchers were simply "stupid."

SMOKEY JOE WILLIAMS (Hall of Fame, 1999)

A half-Indian righthander with a fastball to rival Walter Johnson's, Williams pitched as long as Satchel Paige and always claimed, not altogether accurately, that nobody ever pitched at a more advanced age than he did.

Williams's most productive years were with the New York Lincoln Giants (1911–23), for whom he didn't lose a game in his first five seasons, and the Homestead Grays (1925–32), for whom he was the mound ace for one of the greatest black teams of all times. The Chicago *Defender* credited him with a 41–3 record against all kinds of competition in 1941. He regularly averaged more than a strikeout per inning. His greatest performance was a 27-strikeout 12-inning one-hitter against the Kansas City Monarchs in 1930, when he was in his mid-40s (but not his mid-50s, as he liked to claim).

The bedrock of the Williams legend is his recorded 30 outings against major league teams in which he came out victorious 22 times. Among those encounters were two shutouts over the National League champion Giants in 1912; a 9–2 win over Grover Alexander and the Phillies in 1913; a shutout of the Highlanders and a 16-strikeout win over an all-star team, both in 1913; a 10-inning, 20-strikeout no-hitter (but a 1–0 loss) against the pennant-winning Giants of 1917; and victories over all-star squads with Hall of Famers Rube Marquard (twice), Chief Bender, Johnson (a 1–0 affair), and Waite Hoyt. So dominant was he against major league teams that even the notorious racist Ty Cobb called him a "sure 20-game winner" in the big leagues.

In 1950 Williams, who had remained in New York after he retired, was given a day at the Polo Grounds. Perhaps more satisfying to him, the following year he beat out Paige 20 to 19 as best Negro leagues pitcher in a poll of former players and sportswriters conducted by the Pittsburgh *Courier*.

NED WILLIAMSON

Called the "best all-around ballplayer the country ever saw" by his long-time manager Cap Anson, Williamson held the single-season record for home runs before Babe Ruth. Exploiting an 1883 renovation that reduced the dimensions of Chicago's Lake Front Park to 196 feet down the right field line and to 180 to the left field foul pole, the third baseman set an NL record of 49 doubles, many of them into the near seats. The following year the groundrules were revised so that 25 of Williamson's drives into the two areas were counted as home runs. Together with two long balls on the road, that gave him the major league high of 27 until 1919. He never again reached double figures in home runs.

VIC WILLIS (Hall of Fame, 1995)

Willis got a Veterans Committee pass into Cooperstown after waiting most of the century for elec-

tors to forget his 29 losses for the 1905 Braves is the all-time defeat mark. Together with 25 losses the year before, the righthander also holds the record for combined defeats over two seasons. But Willis had his points, including eight 20-win seasons for Boston and Pittsburgh between 1898 and 1910 and a never-bettered post–19th-century 45 complete games for the 1902 Braves. His career record was 249–205, with a 2.63 ERA.

MAURY WILLS

Wills restored the stolen base as a potent offensive weapon while with the Dodgers in the 1960s, paving the way for the even greater speed stardom of Lou Brock and Rickey Henderson. Although players from Ross Youngs to Jackie Robinson had demonstrated the power of speed in the interim, the switch-hitting shortstop's 50 thefts in 1960 represented the first time a National League played had attained that level since Max Carey in 1923. It was also his first of six straight years of leading the league in steals. His biggest season of all was 1962, when he took an MVP trophy for galvanizing the Dodgers offense with a record-razing 104 stolen bases.

Wills's prime years with the Dodgers ended abruptly after the 1966 season, when Walter O'Malley ordered him traded for failing to accompany the team on a trip to Japan. After some time with Pittsburgh and Montreal he returned to Los Angeles, closing out a 14-year (1959–72) career with 586 steals and a .281 average. He later had a brief and stormy stint as manager of the Mariners. Deeply dependent on drugs, he was given to sending out conflicting or no signals at all to the third base coach, leaving the bench in the middle of games, or muttering to himself about the play of charges sitting only a few feet away. The final straw for his May 1981 firing came when he showed up late for that season's spring training because, 15 years after infuriating O'Malley, he decided to keep a commitment in Japan.

WALT WILMOT

Nobody holds more obscure records than Wilmot, an outfielder for the Cubs in the 1890s. On September 30, 1890 he was called out twice in the same game for being hit by a batted ball. On August 21, 1891 he became the first player to be walked six times in a game. And over two games on August 6 and 7, 1894 he pulled off eight stolen bases.

CRAIG WILSON

Wilson's seven home runs off the bench for the 2001 Pirates tied Dave Hansen's record for most pinch-homers in a season. The Pittsburgh catcher accomplished it in 43 tries, while Hansen had needed 55 swings for the 2000 Dodgers. The previous record of six pinch-homers, by the Dodgers Johnny Frederick, had stood since 1932. Frederick had done it in only 29 at bats.

HACK WILSON (Hall of Fame, 1979)

Wilson is one of the best arguments for electing Roger Maris to the Hall of Fame. Although a prodigious slugger with the Cubs between 1926 and 1930 and the holder of the record for most RBIs in a season (191), he racked up his biggest numbers in 1930—a season in which the exceptionally lively ball had the entire National League batting over .300. Moreover, while he topped Maris in batting consistency, the righthand-hitting outfielder clouted 31 fewer home runs (275–244) over an identical 12 years of major league service, and was nowhere near as talented as the 1960s star in fielding, throwing, and running. One thing they do have in common is Mark McGwire, whose 70 home runs in 1998 not only surpassed Maris's season standard but also obliterated Wilson's National League mark of 56 (also dating from 1930).

Originally the property of the Giants, Wilson was sent down to the American Association Toledo Mud Hens in 1925, but a front office mixup left his name off the club's reserve list. This made him eligible for the postseason draft, and Chicago took him over the protests of John McGraw. From the start of his career Wilson was dogged by a drinking problem; eventually it reduced him to an overweight figure of ridicule as he sought to battle through hangovers while winding down his career with miserable Brooklyn and Philadelphia teams.

JIMMIE WILSON

A top defensive catcher for most of his 18-year (1923–40) career, Wilson attracted more notoriety after ostensibly retiring as a player. As a coach with the 1940 Reds, he was pressed into service in the final days of the season because of an injury to regular Ernie Lombardi and the suicide of backup Willard Hershberger. In the ensuing World Series against the Tigers the 40-year-old Wilson not only threw out the

only runner who tried to steal on him, but also swiped a base of his own while batting .353.

Wilson had fewer glorious moments while managing the Cubs in the World War II years, spending most of his time feuding with general manager Jim Gallagher and refusing to cooperate with beat writers to the point of keeping his starting lineup secret until it was on the field. His less than sweet personality also manifested itself in his habit of removing both ends of a battery if the Chicago pitcher and catcher didn't obey his sign to knock down an opposition hitter. The ploy became obvious enough for other National League teams to protest (futilely) to the league whenever Wilson called time to bring in a new pitcher and receiver.

MOOKIE WILSON

A Shea Stadium favorite for his wild runs around the bases, the equally wild-swinging Wilson astonished even his fans in the sixth game of the 1986 World Series by fouling off one two-out two-strike pitch after another in a 10th-inning duel against Boston's Bob Stanley. The switch-hitting outfielder's tenacity finally paid off with a wild pitch that enabled New York to tie the Red Sox and with the grounder between the legs of Bill Buckner that pointed the Mets toward a world championship.

When Wilson and Lee Mazzilli were dealt to the Blue Jays in August 1988, their positive impact on Toronto led local writers to dub them Mazzookie; Wilson's influence on the division-winning club was considered so pivotal that he made the cover of the Canadian weekly *MacLean's*. The black Wilson's nickname—usually heard only in German-speaking countries—came from his grandmother, who once worked for a German.

OWEN WILSON

Wilson used the spacious alleys of Forbes Field to fashion the mark for most triples in a season (36), in 1912. It was one of 16 times that a Pirate finished with the most triples in a season during the existence of Forbes Field (1909–70).

HOOKS WILTSE

Nobody blew a perfect game more painfully than Wiltse. On the mound for the Giants against the Phillies on July 4, 1908, the southpaw hit the 27th man he faced; more embarrassing, the batter was opposing pitcher George McQuillan. Wiltse retired the next hitter, then won an extended no-hitter when New York scored the only run of the game in the 10th inning.

DAVE WINFIELD (Hall of Fame, 2001)

As both player and Hall of Fame inductee Winfield's ability to get big bucks brought him controversy. The embroilments, usually about what he and the Yankees owed each other, led to a suspension of George Steinbrenner in one case and changes in Cooperstown's induction procedures in another.

An all-star athlete at the University of Minnesota, Winfield chose to sign with the Padres in 1973 after having received other offers from the Minnesota Vikings of the National Football League, the Atlanta Hawks of the National Basketball Association, and the Utah Stars of the American Basketball Association. It was the start of a 22-year career in which the righthand-hitting outfielder accumulated 3,110 hits, 465 home runs, 1,833 RBIs, and seven Gold Gloves. Winfield, Hank Aaron, and Willie Mays are the only players to have amassed 3,000 hits, 400 home runs, and 200 stolen bases. But oddly, his 118 RBIs in 1979 for San Diego represented the only time he led the league in any offensive category; outside of Cal Ripken, Jr. his .283 average is also the lowest for retired members of the 3,000 hit club.

Following eight seasons with the Padres, Winfield agreed to a 10-year free agent contract with the Yankees in 1981. Although the pact stirred comment initially for its length and the $1.4 million annually guaranteed to the slugger, two other provisions—a cost-of-living escalator clause and an obligation by Steinbrenner to pay $300,000 a year to a youth program foundation of Winfield's—turned out to be far more significant. Realizing too late that the cost-of-living stipulation would end up costing him a small fortune, Steinbrenner turned nasty, most famously disparaging Winfield as "Mr. May" for hitting early in the season but (unlike "Mr. October" Reggie Jackson) then freezing up in the postseason, getting merely one hit in 22 at bats against the Dodgers in the World Series. Relations between the pair didn't improve much for the next several years, then they turned outright hostile: By the end of the 1980s Winfield was suing for reneged payments to his foundation and Steinbrenner was talking about a need to investigate "irregularities" in the charity. Unfortunate-

ly for him, he chose to do his investigating with small-time gambler and extortionist Howard Spira, who seemed to tailor his information according to how much was being paid for it. Once Commissioner Fay Vincent grasped the bizarre facts, he suspended Steinbrenner *sine die*. No evidence of mismanagement of the foundation surfaced.

But Winfield had other problems. Because of a herniated disk and some related spine problems he was forced to sit out the 1989 season. The Yankees were happy to see him again the following spring only to be able to trade him. When Winfield vetoed a swap to the Angels for pitcher Mike Witt, it signaled another storm of hearings and negotiations involving Winfield, the two teams, the Players Association, and Vincent. By the time it was all sorted out in May, Winfield had a heady extension on his contract, the Angels had an outfielder, and Steinbrenner had another fine ($250,000) to pay for being so eager to get rid of Mr. May that he was found guilty of tampering to get him out to California.

Winfield had a couple of solid years for the Angels, and an even more solid one for the pennant-winning Blue Jays in 1992. His important leadership role with Toronto included being the oldest player in baseball history to drive in 100 runs and clouting a two-run double in the 11th inning of the final World Series game with the Braves to provide the margin for a world championship. He hung on with the Twins and Indians until 1995. Between his retirement and his election to Cooperstown, the outfielder evaded questions about the cap he wanted to be depicted with on his Hall of Fame plaque. When he announced that he was choosing a San Diego hat, despite having played longer and more productively in New York, the impression was that he had simply not forgotten his bitter quarrels with Steinbrenner. But when it then also emerged that he had been hired as a consultant for the Padres at $1 million, enough questions were raised for the Hall of Fame to announce that it, not the inducted player, would decide on team affiliations in the future.

ERASTUS WINMAN

When impresario Winman bought the New York Metropolitans from John B. Day in December 1885, he intended adding the team to a cluster of attractions (Buffalo Bill's Wild West Show, among them) he was offering on Staten Island. The promoter also counted on the Mets to increase the traffic on his Staten Island ferry from Manhattan and to trigger profits from another proposed transportation deal with the Baltimore & Ohio Railroad. The American Association turned thumbs down on the sale, though, out of suspicion that Day had sold the team to Winman mainly to isolate the Mets on Staten Island so he could have Manhattan exclusively for his other property, the National League Giants. Winman won a court battle to keep the club, but lost so much money in two years that he had to sell out to Brooklyn's Charles Byrne at the end of the 1887 season.

TOM WINSETT

Outfielder Winsett was a model example of Branch Rickey's ability to fob off mediocre players on unsuspecting teams. As St. Louis general manager in the mid-1930s, Rickey boasted to one and all that Winsett was "a coming Babe Ruth." In December 1936 the Dodgers bit, sending the Cardinals Frenchy Bordagaray, Dutch Leonard, and Jimmy Jordan for the supposed superstar. After Winsett had retired seven years later with a .237 average and a grand total of eight home runs, Rickey defended his ballyhooing by declaring: "Woe unto the pitcher who throws the ball where the Winsett bat is functioning. But throwing it almost anywhere else in the general area of home plate is safe."

SAM WISE

Wise was the prize the first time major league baseball resorted to litigation to settle an intramural squabble. After a single game with the National League's Detroit Wolverines in 1881, the infielder signed an 1882 contract with Cincinnati of the new American Association, only to turn around and jump back to the NL, this time with the Boston Red Stockings. With AA backing Cincinnati sought—but was denied—an injunction from a Massachusetts court to prevent Wise from appearing for Boston. He remained with the Red Stockings for seven seasons, during which he became the first player to strike out more than 100 times in a season (104 in 1884).

WILLIAM ABBOTT WITMAN

A wealthy contractor with investments in coal and sand, Witman was a glutton for punishment when it came to trying to establish a third league. His first effort, the United States League, got off the ground

in 1912 with the barest touch of major league blood (alcoholic pitcher Bugs Raymond and aging slugger Socks Seybold). While the circuit boasted six cities with existing American or National league teams, it also included Richmond and Reading (Witman's hometown). Notwithstanding the entrepreneur's claim that the league had "enough money to pay salaries for the entire season even if not a single fan comes into our grounds," it was precisely because of sparse attendance that the venture fell apart. By June 1 he was filing for bankruptcy.

Six months later Witman was back to announce a second edition of the United States League, only this time, when the season opened in May 1913, there was not even a Bugs Raymond for establishing pedigree. Within days of Opening Day two clubs were unable to meet even the $75 guarantee to visiting teams, and everything collapsed again. For *The Sporting News* this made for "the quickest and most ridiculous failure in the long history of baseball."

WHITEY WITT

Victim of one of the ugliest incidents to occur on a big league field, Witt exacted an appropriate revenge. During a late September 1922 game at Sportsman's Park the Yankees center fielder was knocked unconscious by a bottle thrown from the stands and had to be carried into the clubhouse. The Browns offered a reward for the identification of the culprit and American League president Ban Johnson hurried to St. Louis to investigate, but the only result was a ludicrous tale that the bottle had been tossed by a small boy and had landed on the outfield grass, where Witt had stepped on it, sending it spinning upward to conk him on the head. Witt had the last word, however, when he returned for the third game of the series and singled in the game-winning run. The Yankees ended up winning the pennant by one game over St. Louis.

CHICKEN WOLF

The only player on a roster for all 10 years of the American Association's major league status, Wolf also holds the dubious distinction of being the lowest paid player in history. In his rookie season of 1882 the outfielder was paid a paltry $9 a week by Louisville—ridiculous even by the standards of the time. Wolf won the league batting title for Louisville in 1890.

KERRY WOOD

On May 6, 1998 Wood established the National League mark for strikeouts in a nine-inning game by whiffing 20 Astros. It was the Cubs righthander's third big league appearance and his only complete game on the way to Rookie of the Year honors. On May 8, 2001 Arizona's Randy Johnson tied the record by fanning 20 Reds.

DICK WOODSON

Woodson was the first player to benefit from binding arbitration, when he was awarded a $20,000 raise from Minnesota in 1974. Twins owner Calvin Griffith angrily told newsmen that he would make up for the setback by selling Woodson, then, to avoid a fine, lied that he had ever made such a statement. Shortly afterward he did indeed peddle the southpaw to the Yankees.

AL WORTHINGTON

Few players have been as rigid about their religious beliefs as Worthington, a reliever in the 1950s and 1960s. Early in the 1960 season the righthander, then on the White Sox, announced his retirement because of his moral objections to owner Bill Veeck's use of the scoreboard to steal signs. He stayed out of baseball for three years while studying for the ministry, then returned in 1963 with the Reds. In 1968, as a member of the Twins, his 18 saves were the high for the American League.

GEORGE WRIGHT (Hall of Fame, 1937)

While primarily remembered as the younger brother of Harry, Wright was the star of the teams on which they played and, then as a manager, the most successful pilot in baseball history. After two years (1869–70) as the highest paid member of the fabled Cincinnati Red Stockings, Wright moved to Boston in the National Association, where he batted .350 and was the league's best defensive shortstop between 1871 and 1875. When the National League came into existence in 1876, he remained in Boston with the Red Stockings, slipping with the bat but continuing to excel defensively; his .900-plus fielding average for seven major league seasons, a rarity for the pre-glove era, sparked his brother's pennant-winning clubs in 1877 and 1878.

In 1879 Wright left Boston for Providence and, separated from his brother for the first time in a dec-

ade, piloted the Grays to a pennant, bringing them in five games ahead of Harry's Red Stockings. Retiring from the dugout at the end of the season made him the only manager in baseball history to win a flag in his one try at calling the shots. For a few years Wright concentrated on running the sporting goods firm Wright and Ditson. When he reemerged in 1884 as the president of the Union Association Boston Reds, it was as part of a deal in which the UA agreed to use his company's wares. The collapse of the circuit after one year sent him back to Wright and Ditson full time.

With the incentive of opening markets for his company, Wright was an early force for popularizing golf, ice hockey, and tennis in the United States. (His son Beals was an early tennis star.) When the National League began issuing ballpark passes to former lions of the game, he received pass #1.

HARRY WRIGHT (Hall of Fame, 1953)

The English-born Wright became the first professional manager when he assembled and piloted the Cincinnati Red Stockings of 1869–70; his hallmark over 23 years of subsequent managing in the National Association and National League was an incessant emphasis on fundamentals.

An accomplished cricketeer before switching to baseball, Wright was a competent outfielder and alternate pitcher with the Knickerbocker Club of New York, as of 1858; on the mound he was the first successful junkballer. As a manager, he was the first to win four successive pennants (with the NA Boston Red Stockings, from 1872 to 1875); added two more with the NL Boston Red Stockings in 1877 and 1878; led the first baseball tour to England, in 1874; and was the first to employ coaching signs. By 1877 he had shown himself to be such an accomplished heckler that the NL contemplated barring managers from the bench just to get him off the field. His stress on team play evolved into an insistence on morning practice sessions, an exercise regimen, and pregame batting and fielding practice. After the Red Stockings and a couple of years of running the Providence Grays, he spent a final decade (1884–93) in Philadelphia, producing profits with mediocre teams.

Wright was an early advisor to William Hulbert in the organization of the National League. He was the new entity's secretary at founding meetings in 1875.

TAFFY WRIGHT

Wright had the highest batting average in the American League in 1938, but was denied the hitting title despite qualifying under the rules of the day. Appearing in the required 100 games for the Senators, the lefty-swinging outfielder averaged .350 for his rookie year, but because 39 of his 263 at bats were as a pinch-hitter, the crown was awarded instead to Jimmie Foxx, who batted .349. There had been no explicit rule saying players had to start the necessary 100 games.

PHIL WRIGLEY

Wrigley's association with the glories of day baseball at Wrigley Field during his 43-year (1934–77) ownership of the Cubs was the romantic version of the story. Not only was he ready to install lights in the Chicago park in the early 1940s but, nostalgia buffs notwithstanding, several of his other organizational moves anticipated by decades the development of the major leagues into a corporate flowchart interrupted every so often by a single to right.

The deaths of his father William and organization president William Veeck left Wrigley in charge of the Cubs before he was ready for the job. His first solution was to surround himself with yes-men from his chewing gum company, and they in turn were backed up by such timid souls as club president Boots Weber and scouting director Pants Rowland. The result was that Wrigley's own doubts (about purchasing minor league prospect Joe DiMaggio, for instance) and enthusiasms (about obtaining modest outfielder Tuck Stainback, for example) ended up being decisions that nobody dared contradict. On the other hand, he didn't need fawners when it came to product research. Using the same techniques that had made Juicy Fruit and Doublemint popular, he brought in a battery of statisticians in the mid-1930s to break down every possible game situation involving pitchers and hitters, all in the interest of getting a better idea of individual productivity. Other specialists began filming Cubs players for closer looks at their mechanics. It was also Wrigley who, at about the same time, ordered his field announcers and broadcasters never to refer to the home park without qualifying it as "beautiful Wrigley Field" and who then set about to make the claim true; in particular, he approved Bill Veeck, Jr.'s proposal to cover the outfield walls with ivy and engineer Otis Shepard's suggestion for a hand-operated scoreboard.

Although depicted for a long time as baseball's chief foe of artificial lighting, Wrigley thought long and hard about bringing night games to Chicago in the 1930s. By 1941 he had so convinced himself that night ball was the future that he had light towers shipped to Wrigley Field for use the following season. But with the bombing of Pearl Harbor in December he changed his mind, mainly in apprehension that the government would eliminate baseball altogether during World War II; the light towers ended up being donated to the Great Lakes Naval Air Station for the war effort, and afternoon games remained the rule at Wrigley Field for another four decades.

Wrigley was far more opposed to minor league chains than he was to games under dark, and to a somewhat bizarre degree. In spite of owning the Los Angeles Angels of the Pacific Coast League, for instance, he did so personally, not as an extension of his Cubs holdings. Similarly, the American Association Milwaukee Brewers depended on his subsidies to survive, but were equally free to make the best deals that came along without having to go through the Chicago franchise. It was only with the arrival of Jim Gallagher as general manager in the 1940s that Wrigley was talked out of his aversion to a farm system; through working agreements or outright ownerships he was soon financing a chain of some 20 clubs.

In another financial hedge against the major leagues being shut down during World War II, Wrigley bankrolled the All-American Girls Professional Baseball League in 1943. The league, which remained in operation until 1954, had teams in Illinois, Indiana, Wisconsin, and Michigan, with such names as the Fort Wayne Daisies and Kalamazoo Lassies. Among the managers were Hall of Famers Jimmie Foxx and Max Carey.

As far as the Cubs were concerned, Wrigley spent the 1940s and 1950s hiring and firing managers and general managers who were alike only in their failure to lift the team much above seventh or eighth place. That the team still made money was due in part to home run hitters (Bill Nicholson, Hank Sauer, Ernie Banks) who kept fans interested until bad pitching blew it all away. Then, in December 1960, the owner announced he had become convinced that managers needed to be rotated as frequently as pitchers, so to that end was putting the Cubs under a constantly moving octet that became popularly known as the College of Coaches. The experiment officially lasted until Leo Durocher took over as manager in 1966, but in practice it ended as soon as Bob Kennedy emerged as the first coach of coaches in 1963.

The Durocher years (1966–72) proved far more wearying to Wrigley than the College of Coaches period—partly because of the manager's constant battles with his players, partly because of a politically motivated scheme in Chicago to embarrass a Durocher brother-in-law by suggesting the pilot was involved with city racketeers. On both issues Wrigley stood behind Durocher, at one point taking out a full-page ad in Chicago papers to declare that the "Dump Durocher Clique" was wasting its time. Durocher took it upon himself to step down in 1972, but remained close enough to the franchise that Wrigley asked him to come back as manager in 1975. When Durocher replied that he would consider returning only as a general manager with Maury Wills as the manager, Wrigley said no.

Over the final years of his life Wrigley showed increasing crustiness. When he wasn't blasting his players as "clowns," he was warning about the dire effects of free agency or instituting money-saving measures that sometimes sounded as though they were in response to some discovered front office swindling. Shortly before he died in April 1977 at the age of 82, he insisted that the Wrigley family would never permit lights to be installed at Wrigley Field. He proved sincere insofar as it wasn't until his son William had sold the franchise to the Chicago *Tribune* conglomerate that, on August 8, 1988, the first night game was played in the park.

WILLIAM WRIGLEY

Aside from putting his name on what became baseball's most venerable ballpark, Wrigley helped shape the sport's administrative structure and beat Larry MacPhail to the intuition that broadcasting could be more of an incentive than an impediment to attendance. The chewing gum king was also responsible for the involvement of the Veeck family in major league boardrooms.

Originally a junior partner in the Charles Weeghman consortium that bought into the Cubs in 1916, Wrigley needed only five years to gain majority control of the franchise through a series of stock-for-loan arrangements. Even before then, however, he was the first to plump for the election of Federal Judge Kenesaw Landis as commissioner. His proposal of Landis followed a call by fellow Cubs stockholder A. D. Lasker for a special commission of Three Wise Men to clean up the sport's chaotic administration and identification with gambling scandals; although hostile in principle to an outsider coming in, Wrigley couldn't forget the involvement of many members of his own team in various fix charges and regarded the jurist, a highly visible Cubs fan, the kind of compromise he could live with.

Within his own organization Wrigley's most important hire was that of sportswriter William Veeck as vice-president for baseball affairs; he brought in the father of Bill Veeck, Jr. as a put-up-or-shut-up challenge after months of seething at the writer's criticisms of the franchise. Although the club played respectably through most of the 1920s, it was also a period of frequent managerial changes until Joe McCarthy assumed command in 1926. Wrigley held his fire against Veeck mainly because, win or lose, the team drew well; in 1927, with help from Hack Wilson's slugging and Rabbit Maranville's clowning, the Cubs became the first NL team to go over the million mark in attendance (1,163,347). In Wrigley's view another factor in the turnout was his decision to allow as many as five radio stations in the Chicago area to carry games. Statistical breakdowns showed he had a point, insofar as roughly similar clubs studied over seven-year periods with and without air coverage indicated a 119 percent attendance rise when fans had their interest whetted by play-by-play. It would be another decade, however, before MacPhail would make the same point more dramatically, and with more lasting impact, with Cincinnati.

Wrigley lived to see only one Cubs pennant—in 1929. When the team blew the World Series to the Athletics, he reprimanded McCarthy for some tactical moves, and got such a testy reply that he soon afterward fired the manager for Rogers Hornsby. He died in January 1932, just before the club returned to the World Series.

BUTCH WYNEGAR

Wynegar made two mistakes in his 13-year (1976–88) career—first playing for the wrong owner, then playing for the wrong team. After hitting a puny .229 for the Twins in 1978, the switch-hitting catcher was blasted by a drunken Calvin Griffith for having spent too much of his spring training time that year chasing his new wife around the bedroom.

According to Griffith, Wynegar would have been better off picking up women for one-night stands because "love comes pretty cheap these days for ballplayers, and they should take advantage of it." In 1986, while with the Yankees, Wynegar deserted the team for what was later diagnosed as a breakdown caused by the pressures of playing in New York for George Steinbrenner. Even as some teammates were sniping at him for being a quitter, he was being put on medication for severe depression. The receiver finally escaped to the Angels in 1987, but was already finished as a front-line player.

EARLY WYNN (Hall of Fame, 1972)

Wynn's prolonged quest for his 300th win in 1963 served as a pathetic ending to a 23-year (between 1939 and 1963) career in which he racked up five 20-win seasons, paced the American League in wins and strikeouts twice apiece and in ERA once, and established the record (later tied by Brooks Robinson and Carl Yastrzemski) for most seasons in the junior circuit. Wynn labored through much of the 1940s as one of the few bright spots on perennially losing Washington, not enjoying his first 20-victory season until he was with Cleveland in 1951. He was a key element of pennant wins by the Indians in 1954 and then by the White Sox in 1959, taking Cy Young honors for his 22 wins with Chicago. But 42 years old in 1962, the righthander was released by the White Sox, one victory short of 300. He remained unsigned until the following June, when he finally talked Cleveland into taking him back for a shot at a win that had become an obsession. His initial outings were unsuccessful, and he didn't pitch much better against Kansas City on July 13, but thanks to a big lead he was able to get through five innings and leave it up to long reliever Jerry Walker to snag number 300 for him.

Wynn's tough demeanor spawned numerous responses to the question of whether he would brush back his son, mother, or grandmother: "It would depend on how well he was hitting," or "Only if she was digging in," or "If she crowds the plate." After retiring, he was active in organizations for assisting needy ex-major leaguers.

Y

ABE YAGER

The sports editor of the Brooklyn *Eagle,* Yager took it upon himself to avert a threatened strike by Dodgers players against Charlie Ebbets in 1916. The conflict had developed over the owner's move to slash salaries for the season. Knowing that star outfielder Zach Wheat was a leader of the agitation, Yager sent him a telegram in Ebbets's name, voicing regret for the crisis and inviting the future Hall of Famer to the club's Arkansas spring training site to talk over differences. Wheat fell for the ruse and, alone with Ebbets, gave in to his blandishments and agreed to a new contract. The revolt died immediately afterward. Yager always denied sending the cable with Ebbets's knowledge, claiming he was motivated only by a need for daily coverage of the Dodgers to help sell his paper. It was also Yager who first reported Willie Keeler's hitting formula as "hit 'em where they ain't."

HIROSHI YAMAUCHI

The president of Nintendo, Yamauchi was targeted by baseball yahoos in 1992 for offering to buy the Seattle Mariners and keep them in the Northwest. Other owners and Commissioner Fay Vincent immediately began fretting about the perils of a foreign ownership—not only failing to mention the Canadian and European interests behind the Blue Jays and Expos, but also giving the back of their hand to Seattle fans since the most likely alternative to Yamauchi's proposal was relocating the team to Florida. The transparent anti-Japanese attitude forced a bizarre compromise under which Yamauchi put up 60 percent of the $125 million to purchase the club, but held only 49 percent of the stock and could have no hand in operating the franchise. Local businessman John Ellis, representing one percent of the capital investment, took over as chief executive officer.

CARL YASTRZEMSKI (Hall of Fame, 1989)

Yastrzemski managed to be the thinking man's player without being a particularly thoughtful player. Identified throughout his 23-year (1961–83) career with Boston as one of the game's best players under pressure, he also drew fire regularly for shortsighted tantrums and remarks that left teammates in the lurch, not least during labor-management wars in the 1970s. More than one contemporary described him as "an all-star from the neck down."

Yaz, as he was known, was the rare case of one Hall of Famer directly succeeding another, taking over Ted Williams's left field slot in 1961. In the years that followed at Fenway Park he led the American League at least once in every significant category except triples and steals. The lefty swinger's best season was 1967, when he took the Triple Crown, with 44 home runs, 121 RBIs, and a .326 average, while also pacing AL batters with 189 hits, 112 runs, and a .622 slugging percentage; he was an easy MVP choice for the year. Yastrzemski also won batting titles in 1963 and 1968 and topped the slugging category in both 1965 and 1970. He consolidated his reputation for timely hitting down the stretch of Boston's successful 1967 pennant drive by batting .444 with 26 RBIs over the last 19 games; his home run against chief rival Minnesota on the next to last day of the season proved to be decisive for the flag.

Yastrzemski's 3,419 career hits still left him within that small (but, recently, widening) circle of players who have reached the 3,000-hit mark without averaging .300 (.285); he was also the first in that club never to have gotten 200 hits in a season. His league-leading .301 in 1968 was also the lowest ever for a batting titlist. On the other hand, he retired trailing only Pete Rose for most games in a career (3,308).

As Boston owner Tom Yawkey's fair-haired boy, Yaz had more room than his teammates for dealing with managers. His biggest mistake in this area was taking on Dick Williams in 1969 after the pilot had accused him of not running out a ground ball. Although other Red Sox players had been bridling for some time against the martinet ways of Williams, Yastrzemski's involvement of Yawkey in the squabble and the subsequent firing of the manager turned Fenway Park against the outfielder, perceived as a pampered superstar responsible for getting rid of the franchise's most successful dugout boss in decades. In 1972 he alienated many teammates by defending Yawkey during the players strike, insisting that the militant Players Association was in danger of driving away "generous" owners such as the Red Sox boss; in turn, he was accused of elitism and worse by players in Boston and elsewhere aware of his special relationship with Yawkey. In 1975 his nemesis was manager Darrell Johnson, who forbade him to leave the team for a one-day business trip after Boston had wrapped up the AL East Division title; he went anyway, defying Johnson to make an issue of it. Johnson didn't.

In his last years Yastrzemski willy-nilly became the symbol of a team on which the regulars stayed away from the bench players and, in the words of shortstop Frank Duffy, "25 players took 25 cabs" after games. For all his reputation as a clutch hitter, he also had to retire without a world championship ring and with the knowledge that he had made the last out in the 1967 World Series, the 1975 World Series, and the 1978 special playoff against the Yankees.

TOM YAWKEY (Hall of Fame, 1980)

Rarely photographed when he wasn't smiling or hugging his favorite players Ted Williams and Carl Yastrzemski, Yawkey had an image of the most benevolent of owners. The image held up against more than one ugly fray, but failed to extend to the Red Sox organization over which he presided for more than four decades (1933–76). In just about every-

thing from racial integration to arbitration, Boston brought up the rear under his ownership.

The nephew of one-time Detroit owner William Yawkey and the heir to a fortune built up in the lumber trade, Yawkey purchased Boston from Bob Quinn for little more than the $350,000 in debts the outgoing owner had accumulated. Announcing his resolve to end years of second-division finishes by the club, he hired Eddie Collins as manager and went on a buying and trading spree that imported such future Hall of Famers as Joe Cronin, Lefty Grove, Jimmie Foxx, Rick Ferrell, and Heinie Manush. Of equal symbolic value, he opened his purse to the Yankees to acquire hurler George Pipgras and third baseman Billy Werber. Although Pipgras was near the end of his career, nobody in New England missed the significance of the Red Sox being the ones to pay the Yankees for players after 15 years of watching New York strip Boston of its best players for quick cash.

Yawkey's deals made the team a respectable entertainment and then a contender, but it wasn't until 1946 that it got into a World Series. But even then, as would be the case again in 1967 and 1975, he could not claim the world championship that he had targeted from the start as his objective. On the other hand, thanks to the improved talent on the field and a $750,000 renovation of Fenway Park, the Red Sox won back the city from the Braves, outdrawing the National League club regularly until the latter's move to Milwaukee in the early 1950s.

In the 1940s Yawkey managed to pass the buck to Collins and then to Cronin whenever asked about the organization's failure to follow the Dodgers and Indians in integrating the team racially. The franchise remained lily-white until 1959, making it the last club to bring down color barriers. Instead, Yawkey continued his publicity romance with Williams and then Yastrzemski, pointing them out as adopted sons who would never lack for anything while he was alive. He never wavered from this stance, even when the outfielders got into brouhahas with the press, managers, or teammates, a couple of times to the point of creating a bitterly fractured clubhouse.

The labor struggles of the 1970s caught him unawares. Conceding that he had been stunned by the new militancy of the players and the failed impact of the owners lockout in 1973, he began talking about selling the franchise. Although he backed off whenever he was approached by an interested buyer, he projected a constant uncertainty that was soon felt throughout the organization. It reached a critical stage in 1976, when general manager Dick O'Connell got into stubborn contract renewal talks with team stars Carlton Fisk, Fred Lynn, and Rick Burleson while simultaneously announcing that the team was ready to give Oakland's Charlie Finley $2 million for relief ace Rollie Fingers and outfielder Joe Rudi. The deal with the A's was killed by Commissioner Bowie Kuhn, but not until after Minnesota owner Calvin Griffith accused Yawkey of doing more to destroy baseball's salary structure than George Steinbrenner and Ted Turner. A month later Yawkey died in a Boston hospital. Media loyalists, responsive to the benevolence image to the last, accused Fisk, Lynn, and Burleson, as well as their agent Jerry Kapstein, of killing the old man by not being satisfied with his generosity.

WALLY YONAMINE

An Hawaiian-born Nisei, Yonamine was the first American elected to the Japanese Hall of Fame. Known as the Jackie Robinson of Japan, he was a slash-hitting outfielder who initially scandalized Asian spectators with rolling blocks into infielders and other aggressive tactics. In the United States he played only in the low minor leagues for a few years. Before joining the Yomiyuri Giants in 1951, Yonamine had played briefly for the NFL San Francisco 49ers.

RUDY YORK

Detroit got lucky twice in retaining the services of York, one of the American League's top sluggers in the late 1930s and 1940s. The first time was when his name was omitted from the long list of players Commissioner Kenesaw Landis released as free agents from the organization in 1940 because of paper scams aimed at holding them in the Tigers minor league chain; despite blatant manipulations in his case as well, Landis allowed York to stay with Detroit because he had already reached the parent club. The second time was during World War II, when the right-handed slugger was one of baseball's few stars to escape the military draft. A first baseman converted from catching because of defensive liabilities, York banged at least 30 home runs four times and drove in 100 runs in six seasons; in 1943 he led the league in both categories, as well as in slugging percentage.

ANTHONY YOUNG

Young set the major league record for mound futility by losing 27 consecutive games for the Mets between May 6, 1992 and July 24, 1993. The right-hander finally broke the streak with a relief win, but still went 1–16 in 1993.

CY YOUNG (Hall of Fame, 1937)

Young's tireless arm over 22 major league seasons (1890–1911) allowed him to set the career marks for wins (511) *and* losses (315). Although the righthander was overshadowed at one point or another by Amos Rusie, Kid Nichols, and Christy Mathewson, no one has come close to his 16 years with at least 320 innings pitched or such other lifetime records as most innings (7,356) and most complete games (749). Not to say he was just an arm that posted innings: In five seasons for the National League's Cleveland Spiders and American League's Boston Red Sox he won 30 games or more and in 10 others at least 20. His most overpowering performance was pitching 23 consecutive hitless innings over four games for the Red Sox in 1904; the streak included the AL's first perfect game, over the Athletics on May 5. He had three no-hitters altogether. Young finally called it quits at the age of 44 in 1911, not because his arm had given out but because he had gained so much weight that opposing batters were starting to bunt their way on against him at will. Baseball's top pitching award was named after him in 1956.

DICK YOUNG

For both good and bad, Young was one of the most influential reporters ever to cover baseball. As a beat writer for New York's *Daily News* in the late 1940s, he was one of the first to realize that radio had usurped much of the straight play-by-play reportorial function of newspapers, concentrating instead on personal, behind-the-scenes angles through clubhouse interviews. He was also conspicuous in defending the arrival of Jackie Robinson in Brooklyn, often coming into conflict with some of the furrier heads in the press box and on his own paper. A few years later, however, the same Young was among the more transparently chagrined when Robinson had enough of turning the other cheek and began getting into field brawls and speaking up about baseball's racist establishment; he began accenting the virtues of

Dodgers catcher Roy Campanella, viewed (in contrast to Robinson) as a genial black who avoided "making trouble."

Although he cracked wise and often about the arrogance of what he called the Lords of Baseball, Young moved relentlessly toward a pro-owner stance on most issues affecting the sport in the 1960s and 1970s. He also occasioned considerable griping from other writers for what was seen as uncomfortably close relationships with Mets manager Gil Hodges and organization chairman M. Donald Grant. The ties enabled the *News* to gain exclusive photographs of Hodges after the manager's heart attack in 1968—coverage denounced by rivals as a franchise public relations ploy aimed at assuring readers the pilot would be back on the job. With Hodges's death in 1973, Young's long-swelling rancor toward some Mets players, particularly ace pitcher Tom Seaver for salary demands and expressed skepticism about the war in Vietnam, exploded in regular tirades. Given the fact that his son-in-law worked in the Mets front office, the newsman was seen, even by colleagues on his own paper, as using the *News* to convey the franchise's party line.

Matters came to a head in July 1977 when Seaver, worn out by Young's innuendos and suspecting they had been inspired by Grant, demanded a trade off the team. The pitcher's breaking point had been a Young column suggesting that Seaver's wife was jealous that Nolan Ryan had received more money from the Angels than her husband had been offered by New York. When Seaver was traded to Cincinnati, on June 15, 1977, New York fans and other sportswriters blamed Young as much as Grant. For his part, the newsman brushed aside the charges, continuing to write increasingly sour pieces on the erosion of what he called "My America."

DON YOUNG

Young was everybody's scapegoat when the Cubs blew the East Division title to the Mets in 1969. A good-glove no-hit center fielder who had never played a full big league season, he was pressed into daily service mainly because manager Leo Durocher wasn't ready to admit he had been wrong about insisting on trading away the more experienced Adolfo Phillips. When Young began sagging under the pressure down the stretch, even the normally team-spirited Ron Santo lashed out at him, losing some of his own credibility

in the process. After the season Durocher was suddenly the first to admit the outfielder had been in over his head. Young never played in the majors again.

IRV YOUNG

There have been only two big league staffs with four 20-game losers, and Young was the ace of both rotations. In 1905 Vic Willis, Chick Fraser, and Kaiser Wilhelm joined the southpaw in suffering at least 20 defeats for the Braves; in 1906 he repeated the trick for Boston with Gus Dorner, Jeff Pfeffer, and Viva Lindaman. His ERA for the two seasons was 2.90 and 2.91. Young lost more than 20 in 1907, as well, but that time had no company.

NICK YOUNG

The fifth president of the National League (from 1885 to 1902), Young was either permanently out of the loop or a well-paid decoy. When he said black, the reality was almost sure to be white. During the dismantling of the Union Association in 1885, for instance, he repeatedly defended the blacklist drawn up against players who had jumped to the circuit from the National League and the American Association, while owners were dickering to reinstate them. In 1889 he refused to meet with the Players Brotherhood, tabbing it "a secret society," even as Al Spalding was sitting down with Brotherhood organizer John Montgomery Ward. In 1890, during the Players League war, he voiced outrage at the possibility that the NL would reward jumpers by offering them more money to jump back, even as Spalding (one example of many) was offering $10,000 to King Kelly to change his mind again. In 1891, after the American Association had followed the Players League into extinction, he assured players they had no reason to fear slashed salaries just because the NL had no more rivals—this while the owners were holding one meeting after another about the best way to cut payrolls.

Some attributed Young's near-perfect inaccuracy to distractions from his other job as a clerk in the U.S. Treasury Department in Washington. But in fact even after he left the government he showed little improvement in confronting crises. He was overmatched by obstreperous Giants owner Andrew Freedman and his 1900 syndication plan, by the ambitious Ban Johnson and his major league plans for the American League in 1901, and by the wily Spalding and a 1902 coup aimed directly at Young's own office. Finally let go in favor of a troika of owners, Young returned to the position of league secretary-treasurer he had held before becoming president.

JOEL YOUNGBLOOD

On August 4, 1982 Youngblood became the only major leaguer to play for one team in one city in the afternoon and for another in a second city in the evening. Even better, he got a hit for the Mets in Chicago and, after being traded to the Expos, arrived in Philadelphia in time to get another hit for Montreal.

ROSS YOUNGS (Hall of Fame, 1972)

Next to Christy Mathewson, Youngs was Giants manager John McGraw's favorite player. A slight speedster, he was the chief table-setter for New York for his 10-year (1917–26) career, batting over .300 nine times. Although the lefthanded-swinging outfielder never stole more than 24 bases in a year, his daring running gained him the nickname Pep among teammates, and McGraw was never reluctant about pointing out that he sparked more rallies than the more well-known Hall of Famers on the club. The one year in which Youngs failed to reach .300, 1925, was when he was feeling the initial effects of Bright's disease, the kidney ailment that killed him at the age of 30. In 1926 McGraw insisted a male nurse accompany him on road trips, with the team footing the bills. Although growing progressively weaker, Youngs still managed to bat .306 and steal 21 bases. His death the next year sent McGraw into a funk he never truly recovered from.

ROBIN YOUNT (Hall of Fame, 1999)

Yount was the franchise player for most of his 20 seasons (1974–93) with the Brewers, achieving that status despite an early career decision to quit baseball for professional golf. Because of his lifetime loyalty to Milwaukee's usually humdrum teams, he walked into Cooperstown with a profile not all that much higher than some of the early 20th century selections made by the Veterans Committee.

Yount's only significant mark over his first six seasons was in leading the American League in errors by a shortstop (44 in his sophomore year). Along with his uninspired hitting, his defensive woes persuaded him to switch to golf in 1977—a decision that lasted through spring training into May. Once back in uniform, he was still a singles hitter with an unrealiable arm until offseason Nautilus workouts bulked him up. The big payoff came in 1982, when he took MVP honors for leading the Brewers into the World Series with 29 home runs, 114 RBIs, an average of .331, and league-leading marks in doubles (46), slugging (.578), and infield assists (489). Although he never again reached any of those figures, he attained the .300 plateau five more times.

A shoulder operation after the 1984 season necessitated a years-old notion about moving Yount from shortstop to center field. When he won a second MVP trophy in 1989, he became only the third player after Hank Greenberg and Stan Musial to cop the honor at two different positions; moreover, Greenberg and Musial did it from the relatively less taxing positions of first base and the corner outfield. When the Brewers hesitated about resigning Yount after his second MVP year, even letting him test the market, Milwaukee fans and the press put up such a protest that the team had second thoughts and inked him to a five-year deal. He didn't have much left, though, providing little excitement except for becoming the first Brewer to collect 3,000 hits (3,142).

Z

ZIP ZABEL

On June 17, 1915 Zabel was called in from the Cubs bullpen in the first inning of a game against the Dodgers because of an injury to starter Bert Humphries. The righthander ended up pitching $18\frac{1}{3}$ innings, allowing only two unearned runs, before being credited with a 4–3 victory. Zabel's stint is the longest ever by a relief pitcher.

JACK ZELLER

Detroit general manager Zeller cost his team the loss of more players than any other executive in baseball history. He achieved the distinction on January 14, 1940, when Commissioner Kenesaw Landis released 91 Tigers farmhands as free agents because Zeller and Cecil Coombs, business manager of a minor league club in Fort Worth, had been conniving for years with fake contracts and other hustles to keep the players under franchise control even though they weren't needed by the parent team. In addition, Landis ordered the Tigers to cough up indemnities to another 15 minor leaguers who had been treated unfairly in the club's farm system.

There were two surprising consequences to the Landis order. First, of all the players released, only outfielder Roy Cullenbine had an appreciable career elsewhere. Second, not only wasn't Zeller fired, but he stayed at his post until he himself resigned in 1945. Some attributed his odd survival to the possibility that he had been largely a front man for Detroit owner Walter Briggs. Zeller had been hired originally as Tigers farm director in 1926 to clean up another franchise scandal involving scouts who had been recommending only prospects who had slipped them a few dollars.

CHIEF ZIMMER

The best defensive catcher of his day, Zimmer served as the first president of the Players Protective Association, an early 20th-century effort to unionize ballplayers. In a 20-year career (between 1884 and 1903) with seven clubs, he left his biggest mark on the game while with Cleveland in the mid-1880s by abandoning the traditional practice of receivers to move several paces behind the batter if there were no runners on base, instead playing directly behind the plate on every pitch.

Zimmer was elected head of the players group in January 1900 in good part because he hadn't joined the Players League a decade before and was thus not viewed as threatening to owners. Tactically, he walked a narrow line between militants and conciliators, refusing help from the American Federation of Labor but also hiring Harry Taylor, a former player and union hardliner, as organization attorney. National League owners broke with precedent and agreed to negotiate with the players association, mainly to blunt massive defections to the new American League. Zimmer won a round by getting the owners to discuss previously untouchable questions by promising to consider the expulsion of any player who jumped his contract. It proved to be a hollow victory when the AL attracted large numbers of National Leaguers anyway, costing the union its leverage with the senior circuit.

DON ZIMMER

Zimmer's 50-plus years as player, coach, and manager have been filled with conflict, comedy, and near-tragedy. As a shortstop in the Brooklyn farm

system in 1951, he was beaned so badly that he remained unconscious for two weeks and had to be
fitted with a cranial plate. With the varsity Dodgers
he never lived up to billing as Peewee Reese's successor, but proved to be a valuable bit player in the
club's 1955 World Series win when he was removed
for defense late in the seventh game, enabling Sandy
Amoros to be inserted in left field just in time to
snag the Yogi Berra liner that was the turning point
of the finale. Wandering from team to team, Zimmer
was the first of the Mets innumerable third basemen
in 1962, but failed to get a hit for the franchise until
he had been to bat more than 30 times; after finally
breaking through with a couple of singles, he was
dealt to Cincinnati behind a Casey Stengel crack that
"we wanted to trade him while he was hot."

As of 1971 Zimmer began moving around between managing and coaching positions, making
stopovers in one capacity or another for eight different teams, a few of them more than once. His first
managerial experience, with the 1972 Padres, was
relatively uneventful, but the same couldn't be said
when he took over the Red Sox in 1976. Replacing
the unpopular Darrell Johnson after a pennant-winning season, he squandered much of his goodwill
with Boston players by showing little talent for running a pitching staff. Since the Red Sox hurlers included the outspoken Bill Lee and Ferguson Jenkins, the result was almost daily quotes from the clubhouse on how the team was going down the drain.
Zimmer's special nemesis was a clique of players
(prominently, Lee, Jenkins, and outfielder Bernie
Carbo) who called themselves the Loyal Order of
the Buffalo Heads because, according to its members, the buffalo was the dumbest animal on earth,
as was anybody who played for Zimmer and the
Red Sox. Lee also contributed the zoological view
that the manager resembled a "designated gerbil." It
was a crack that Zimmer never lived down in Boston and, with the help of continuing tensions and the
Bucky Dent home run that defeated the Red Sox in
the 1978 playoffs, he had become the most unpopular figure in New England sports by the end of the
decade. He was finally replaced near the end of the
1980 season.

Following another humdrum tour as manager
of the Rangers, Zimmer had a rebirth of sorts when
he took over the Cubs in 1988. The following year
he guided Chicago to a division title, in the process

becoming something of an attraction himself for
his increasingly pudgy, pop-eyed appearance, volcanic explosions against umpires, and game tactics
that ran the gamut from the highly imaginative to
the bizarre (e.g., hit-and-run plays with the bases
loaded and less than two out). Then, early in 1991,
he was discharged for little apparent reason; after
a couple of weeks of official silence, the commissioner's office issued a cryptic statement saying that
an investigation into Zimmer's noted racetrack betting had "produced insufficient evidence of any
wrongdoing."

When Joe Torre took over the Yankees in 1996,
he insisted on Zimmer as his bench coach; owner
George Steinbrenner agreed, despite having already
fired him as a coach on two separate occasions. When
Torre missed the opening weeks of the 1999 season
recuperating from prostate surgery, Zimmer took
over the club, going 21–15.

HEINIE ZIMMERMAN

Zimmerman's spottled playing career has gotten
even worse since he retired and died. Blackballed
after the 1919 season for his involvement in game
fixes, the third baseman was identified for decades
as the only Triple Crown winner without a Hall of
Fame plaque. But that was before researchers took
another look at his banner 1912 season for the Cubs
and concluded that, while his .372 average and 14
homers remained the National League's best, his
originally documented 103 RBIs had been miscal-
culated and that he actually finished third in that category (with 99 RBIs) behind both Honus Wagner
and Bill Sweeney. The same researchers confirmed
his NL RBI wins in 1916 and 1917.

A 13-year (1907–19) veteran, Zimmerman left
baseball in a blaze of charges that he had conspired
to throw Giants games against the Cubs and Cardinals in his final season; his own retort was to suggest
manager John McGraw hadn't been above hanky-
panky, either. The infielder was otherwise best known
for chasing Eddie Collins across home plate in the
final game of the 1917 World Series with the White
Sox; although sometimes referred to as the winning
run resulting from a botched rundown, it was in fact
only Chicago's first tally in an eventual 4–2 victory
and not a rundown since neither catcher Bill Rari-
den nor first baseman Walter Holke were anywhere
to be found near home plate.

RICHIE ZISK

Zisk was the emblem of White Sox owner Bill Veeck's rent-a-player solution to free agency in the late 1970s. Knowing ahead of time that he would never be able to meet the outfielder's contract demands after the season, Veeck obtained him in his walk year in 1977 from the Pirates for a couple of pitchers. The good news was that Zisk responded with 30 home runs and 101 RBIs. The inevitable news was that he signed with Texas for the 1978 season. The bad news was that the pitchers surrendered to Pittsburgh for the righthanded slugger were future relief aces Goose Gossage and Terry Forster.

GEORGE ZOETERMAN

When the White Sox drafted Zoeterman out of prep school in 1947, they set into motion a series of events culminating in the team's suspension from the American League, the only time since the 19th century such a sanction has been imposed. Because the contract violated the spirit, if not the letter, of a ban against signing high schoolers, it was voided almost immediately despite a hair-splitting defense offered by Chicago general manager Leslie O'Connor. O'Connor, who had helped formulate the stricture while serving as an assistant to Commissioner Kenesaw Landis, had argued that his own handiwork failed to explicitly cover students in private schools not part of the National Federation of State Athletic Associations. O'Connor's sophistry so irritated Commissioner Happy Chandler that, after voiding the drafting of Zoeterman, he fined the White Sox $500. When O'Connor refused to pay, Chandler declared the team suspended from the league, leaving a seven-club circuit from October 25 to November 4. The crisis ended only when White Sox owner Lou Comiskey overruled O'Connor and agreed to pay the fine.